A Patriot's History
of the United States

A Patriot's History
of the United States

FROM COLUMBUS'S GREAT DISCOVERY

TO THE WAR ON TERROR

Larry Schweikart and Michael Allen

SENTINEL

SENTINEL
Published by the Penguin Group
Penguin Group (USA) Inc., 375 Hudson Street,
New York, New York 10014, U.S.A.
Penguin Books Canada Ltd, 10 Alcorn Avenue,
Toronto, Ontario, Canada M4V 3B2
Penguin Books Ltd, 80 Strand,
London WC2R 0RL, England
Penguin Books Australia Ltd, 250 Camberwell Road, Camberwell,
Victoria 3124, Australia
Penguin Books India (P) Ltd, 11 Community Centre, Panchsheel Park,
New Delhi – 110 017, India
Penguin Group (NZ), Cnr Airborne and Rosedale Roads, Albany,
Auckland 1310, New Zealand
Penguin Books (South Africa) (Pty) Ltd, 24 Sturdee Avenue,
Rosebank, Johannesburg 2196, South Africa

Penguin Books Ltd, Registered Offices:
80 Strand, London WC2R 0RL, England

First published in 2004 by Sentinel,
a member of Penguin Group (USA) Inc.

10   9   8   7   6   5   4   3   2   1

CIP DATA AVAILABLE.

ISBN 1-59523-001-7

This book is printed on acid-free paper. ∞

Printed in the United States of America
Set in Fairfield LH Light
Designed by Daniel Lagin

To Dee and Adam

—Larry Schweikart

For my mom

—Michael Allen

ACKNOWLEDGMENTS

Larry Schweikart would like to thank Jesse McIntyre and Aaron Sorrentino for their contribution to charts and graphs; and Julia Cupples, Brian Rogan, Andrew Gough, and Danielle Elam for research. Cynthia King performed heroic typing work on crash schedules. The University of Dayton, particularly Dean Paul Morman, supported this work through a number of grants.

Michael Allen would like to thank Bill Richardson, Director of Interdisciplinary Arts and Sciences at the University of Washington, Tacoma, for his friendship and collegial support for over a decade.

We would both like to thank Mark Smith, David Beito, Brad Birzer, Robert Loewenberg, Jeff Hanichen, David Horowitz, Jonathan Bean, Constantine Guzman, Burton Folsom Jr., Julius Amin, and Michael Etchison for comments on the manuscript. Ed Knappman and the staff at New England Publishing Associates believed in this book from the beginning and have our undying gratitude. Our special thanks to Bernadette Malone, whose efforts made this possible; to Megan Casey for her sharp eye; and to David Freddoso for his ruthless, but much needed, pen.

CONTENTS

INTRODUCTION

I s America's past a tale of racism, sexism, and bigotry? Is it the story of the conquest and rape of a continent? Is U.S. history the story of white slave owners who perverted the electoral process for their own interests? Did America start with Columbus's killing all the Indians, leap to Jim Crow laws and Rockefeller crushing the workers, then finally save itself with Franklin Roosevelt's New Deal? The answers, of course, are no, no, no, and NO.

One might never know this, however, by looking at almost any mainstream U.S. history textbook. Having taught American history in one form or another for close to sixty years between us, we are aware that, unfortunately, many students are berated with tales of the Founders as self-interested politicians and slaveholders, of the icons of American industry as robber-baron oppressors, and of every American foreign policy initiative as imperialistic and insensitive. At least Howard Zinn's *A People's History of the United States* honestly represents its Marxist biases in the title!

What is most amazing and refreshing is that the past usually speaks for itself. The evidence is there for telling the great story of the American past honestly—with flaws, absolutely; with shortcomings, most definitely. But we think that an honest evaluation of the history of the United States must begin and end with the recognition that, compared to any other nation, America's past is a bright and shining light. America was, and is, the city on the hill, the fountain of hope, the beacon of liberty. We utterly reject "My country right or wrong"—what scholar wouldn't? But in the last thirty years, academics have taken an equally destructive approach: "My country, always wrong!" We reject that too.

Instead, we remain convinced that if the story of America's past is told fairly, the result cannot be anything but a deepened patriotism, a sense of awe at the obstacles overcome, the passion invested, the blood and tears spilled, and the nation that was built. An honest review of America's past would note, among other observations, that the same Founders who owned slaves instituted numerous ways—political and intellectual—to ensure that slavery could not survive; that the concern over not just property rights, but all rights, so infused American life that laws often followed the practices of the common folk, rather than dictated to them; that even when the United States used her military power for dubious reasons, the ultimate result was to liberate people and bring a higher standard of living than before; that time and again America's leaders have willingly shared power with those who had none, whether they were citizens of territories, former slaves, or disenfranchised women. And we could go on.

The reason so many academics miss the real history of America is that they assume that ideas don't matter and that there is no such thing as virtue. They could not be more wrong. When John D. Rockefeller said, "The common man must have kerosene and he must have it *cheap*," Rockefeller was already a wealthy man with no more to gain. When Grover Cleveland vetoed an insignificant seed corn bill, he knew it would hurt him politically, and that he would only win condemnation from the press and the people—but the Constitution did not permit it, and he refused.

Consider the scene more than two hundred years ago when President John Adams—just voted out of office by the hated Republicans of Thomas Jefferson—mounted a carriage and left Washington even before the inauguration. There was no armed struggle. Not a musket ball was fired, nor a political opponent hanged. No Federalists marched with guns or knives in the streets. There was no guillotine. And just four years before that, in 1796, Adams had taken part in an equally momentous event when he won a razor-thin close election over Jefferson and, because of Senate rules, had to count his own contested ballots. When he came to the contested Georgia ballot, the great Massachusetts revolutionary, the "Duke of Braintree," stopped counting. He sat down for a moment to allow Jefferson or his associates to make a challenge, and when he did not, Adams finished the tally, becoming president. Jefferson told confidants that he thought the ballots were indeed in dispute, but he would not wreck the country over a few pieces of paper. As Adams took the oath of office, he thought he heard Washington say, "I am fairly out and you are fairly in! See which of us will be the happiest!"[1] So much for protecting his own interests! Washington stepped down freely and enthusiastically, not at bayonet point. He walked away from power, as nearly each and every American president has done since.

These giants knew that their actions of character mattered far more to the nation they were creating than mere temporary political positions. The ideas they fought for together in 1776 and debated in 1787 were paramount. And that is what American history is truly about—ideas. Ideas such as "All men are created equal"; the United States is the "last, best hope" of earth; and America "is great, because it is good."

Honor counted to founding patriots like Adams, Jefferson, Washington, and then later, Lincoln and Teddy Roosevelt. Character counted. Property was also important; no denying that, because with property came liberty. But virtue came first. Even J. P. Morgan, the epitome of the so-called robber baron, insisted that "the first thing is character . . . before money or anything else. Money cannot buy it."

It is not surprising, then, that so many left-wing historians miss the boat (and miss it, and miss it, *and miss it* to the point where they need a ferry schedule). They fail to understand what every colonial settler and every western pioneer understood: character was tied to liberty, and liberty to property. All three were needed for success, but character was the prerequisite because it put the law behind property agreements, and it set responsibility right next to liberty. And the surest way to ensure the presence of good character was to keep God at the center of one's life, community, and ultimately, nation. "Separation of church and state" meant freedom *to* worship, not freedom *from* worship. It went back to that link between liberty and responsibility, and no one could be taken seriously who was not responsible to God. "Where the Spirit of the Lord is, there is liberty." They believed those words.

As colonies became independent and as the nation grew, these ideas permeated the fabric of the founding documents. Despite pits of corruption that have pockmarked federal and state politics—some of them quite deep—and despite abuses of civil rights that were shocking, to say the least, the concept was deeply imbedded that only a virtuous nation could achieve the lofty goals set by the Founders. Over the long haul, the Republic required virtuous leaders to prosper.

Yet virtue and character alone were not enough. It took competence, skill, and talent to build a nation. That's where property came in: with secure property rights, people from all over the globe flocked to America's shores. With secure property rights, anyone could become successful, from an immigrant Jew like Lionel Cohen and his famous Lionel toy trains to an Austrian bodybuilder-turned-millionaire actor and governor like Arnold Schwarzenegger. Carnegie arrived penniless; Ford's company went broke; and Lee Iacocca had to eat crow on national TV for his company's mistakes. Secure property rights not only made it possible for them all to succeed but, more important, established a climate of competition that rewarded skill, talent, and risk taking.

Political skill was essential too. From 1850 to 1860 the United States was nearly rent in half by inept leaders, whereas an integrity vacuum nearly destroyed American foreign policy and shattered the economy in the decades of the 1960s and early 1970s. Moral, even pious, men have taken the nation to the brink of collapse because they lacked skill, and some of the most skilled politicians in the world—Henry Clay, Richard Nixon, Bill Clinton—left legacies of frustration and corruption because their abilities were never wedded to character.

Throughout much of the twentieth century, there was a subtle and, at times, obvious campaign to separate virtue from talent, to divide character from success. The latest in this line of attack is the emphasis on diversity—that somehow merely having different skin shades or national origins makes America special. But it was not the color of the skin of people who came here that made them special, it was the content of their character. America remains a beacon of liberty, not merely because its institutions have generally remained strong, its citizens free, and its attitudes tolerant, but because it, among most of the developed world, still cries out as a nation, "Character counts." Personal liberties in America are genuine because of the character of honest judges and attorneys who, for the most part, still make up the judiciary, and because of the personal integrity of large numbers of local, state, and national lawmakers.

No society is free from corruption. The difference is that in America, corruption is viewed as the exception, not the rule. And when light is shown on it, corruption is viciously attacked. Freedom still attracts people to the fountain of hope that is America, but freedom alone is not enough. Without responsibility and virtue, freedom becomes a soggy anarchy, an incomplete licentiousness. This is what has made Americans different: their fusion of freedom and integrity endows Americans with their sense of right, often when no other nation in the world shares their perception.

Yet that is as telling about other nations as it is our own; perhaps it is that as Americans, we alone remain committed to both the individual and the greater good, to personal freedoms and to public virtue, to human achievement and respect for the Almighty. Slavery was abolished because of the dual commitment to liberty and virtue—neither capable of standing without the other. Some crusades in the name of integrity have proven disastrous, including Prohibition. The most recent serious threats to both liberty and public virtue (abuse of the latter damages both) have come in the form of the modern environmental and consumer safety movements. Attempts to sue gun makers, paint manufacturers, tobacco companies, and even Microsoft "for the public good" have made distressingly steady advances, encroaching on Americans' freedoms to eat fast foods, smoke, or modify their automobiles, not to mention start businesses or invest in existing firms without fear of retribution.

The Founders—each and every one of them—would have been horrified at such intrusions on liberty, regardless of the virtue of the cause, not because they were elite white men, but because such actions in the name of the public good were simply wrong. It all goes back to character: the best way to ensure virtuous institutions (whether government, business, schools, or churches) was to populate them with people of virtue. Europe forgot this in the nineteenth century, or by World War I at the latest. Despite rigorous and punitive face-saving traditions in the Middle East or Asia, these twin principles of liberty and virtue have never been adopted. Only in America, where one was *permitted* to do almost anything, but *expected* to do the best thing, did these principles germinate.

To a great extent, that is why, on March 4, 1801, John Adams would have thought of nothing other than to turn the White House over to his hated foe, without fanfare, self-pity, or complaint, and return to his everyday life away from politics. That is why, on the few occasions where very thin electoral margins produced no clear winner in the presidential race (such as 1824, 1876, 1888, 1960, and 2000), the losers (after some legal maneuvering, recounting of votes, and occasional whining) nevertheless stepped aside and congratulated the winner of a different party. Adams may have set a precedent, but in truth he would do nothing else. After all, he was a man of character.

A Patriot's History
of the United States

CHAPTER ONE

The City on the Hill, 1492–1707

The Age of European Discovery

God, glory, and gold—not necessarily in that order—took post-Renaissance Europeans to parts of the globe they had never before seen. The opportunity to gain materially while bringing the Gospel to non-Christians offered powerful incentives to explorers from Portugal, Spain, England, and France to embark on dangerous voyages of discovery in the 1400s. Certainly they were not the first to sail to the Western Hemisphere: Norse sailors reached the coasts of Iceland in 874 and Greenland a century later, and legends recorded Leif Erickson's establishment of a colony in Vinland, somewhere on the northern Canadian coast.[1] Whatever the fate of Vinland, its historical impact was minimal, and significant voyages of discovery did not occur for more than five hundred years, when trade with the Orient beckoned.

Marco Polo and other travelers to Cathay (China) had brought exaggerated tales of wealth in the East and returned with unusual spices, dyes, rugs, silks, and other goods. But this was a difficult, long journey. Land routes crossed dangerous territories, including imposing mountains and vast deserts of modern-day Afghanistan, northern India, Iran, and Iraq, and required expensive and well-protected caravans to reach Europe from Asia. Merchants encountered bandits who threatened transportation lanes, kings and potentates who demanded tribute, and bloodthirsty killers who pillaged for pleasure. Trade routes from Bombay and Goa reached Europe via Persia or Arabia, crossing the Ottoman Empire with its internal taxes. Cargo had to be unloaded at seaports, then reloaded at Alexandria or Antioch for water transport across the Mediterranean, or continued on land before crossing the Dardanelles Strait into modern-day Bulgaria to the Danube River. European demand for such goods seemed endless, enticing merchants and their investors to engage in a relentless search for lower costs brought by safer and cheaper routes. Gradually, Europeans concluded that more direct water routes to the Far East must exist.

The search for Cathay's treasure coincided with three factors that made long ocean voyages possible. First, sailing and shipbuilding technology had advanced rapidly after the ninth century, thanks in part to the Arabs' development of the astrolabe, a device with a pivoted limb that established the sun's altitude above the horizon. By the late tenth century, astrolabe technology had made its way to Spain.[2] Farther north, Vikings pioneered new methods of hull construction, among them the use of overlapping planks for internal support that enabled vessels to withstand violent ocean storms. Sailors of the Hanseatic League states on the Baltic coast experimented with larger ship designs that incorporated sternpost rudders for better control. Yet improved ships alone were not enough: explorers needed the accurate maps generated by Italian seamen and sparked by the new inquisitive impulse of the Renaissance. Thus a wide range of technologies coalesced to encourage long-range voyages of discovery.

Political changes, a second factor giving birth to the age of discovery, resulted from the efforts of several ambitious European monarchs to consolidate their possessions into larger, cohesive dynastic states. This unification of lands, which increased the taxable base within the kingdoms, greatly increased the funding available to expeditions and provided better military protection (in the form of warships) at no cost to investors. By the time a combined Venetian-Spanish fleet defeated a much larger Ottoman force at Lepanto in 1571, the vessels of Christian nations could essentially sail with impunity anywhere in the Mediterranean. Then, in control of the Mediterranean, Europeans could consider voyages of much longer duration (and cost) than they ever had in the past. A new generation of explorers found that monarchs could support even more expensive undertakings that integrated the monarch's interests with the merchants'.[3]

Third, the Protestant Reformation of 1517 fostered a fierce and bloody competition for power and territory between Catholic and Protestant nations that reinforced national concerns. England competed for land with Spain, not merely for economic and political reasons, but because the English feared the possibility that Spain might catholicize numbers of non-Christians in new lands, whereas Catholics trembled at the thought of subjecting natives to Protestant heresies. Therefore, even when economic or political gains for discovery and colonization may have been marginal, monarchs had strong religious incentives to open their royal treasuries to support such missions.

Time Line

1492–1504: Columbus's four voyages

1519–21: Cortés conquers Mexico

1585–87: Roanoke Island (Carolinas) colony fails

1607: Jamestown, Virginia, founded

1619: First Africans arrive in Virginia

1619: Virginia House of Burgesses formed

1620: Pilgrims found Plymouth, Massachusetts

1630: Puritan migration to Massachusetts

1634: Calverts found Maryland
1635–36: Pequot Indian War (Massachusetts)
1638: Anne Hutchinson convicted of heresy
1639: Fundamental Orders of Connecticut
1642–48: English Civil War
1650: First Navigation Act (mercantilism)
1664: English conquer New Netherlands (New York)
1675–76: King Philip's (Metacomet's) War (Massachusetts)
1676: Bacon's Rebellion (Virginia)
1682: Pennsylvania settled
1688–89: English Glorious Revolution and Bill of Rights
1691: Massachusetts becomes royal colony
1692: Salem witch hunts

Portugal and Spain: The Explorers

Ironically, one of the smallest of the new monarchical states, Portugal, became the first to subsidize extensive exploration in the fifteenth century. The most famous of the Portuguese explorers, Prince Henry, dubbed the Navigator, was the brother of King Edward of Portugal. Henry (1394–1460) had earned a reputation as a tenacious fighter in North Africa against the Moors, and he hoped to roll back the Muslim invaders and reclaim from them trade routes and territory.

A true Renaissance man, Henry immersed himself in mapmaking and exploration from a coastal center he established at Sagres, on the southern point of Portugal. There he trained navigators and mapmakers, dispatched ships to probe the African coast, and evaluated the reports of sailors who returned from the Azores.[4] Portuguese captains made contact with Arabs and Africans in coastal areas and established trading centers, from which they brought ivory and gold to Portugal, then transported slaves to a variety of Mediterranean estates. This early slave trade was conducted through Arab middlemen or African traders who carried out slaving expeditions in the interior and exchanged captive men, women, and children for fish, wine, or salt on the coast.

Henry saw these relatively small trading outposts as only the first step in developing reliable water routes to the East. Daring sailors trained at Henry's school soon pushed farther southward, finally rounding the Cape of Storms in 1486, when Bartholomeu Dias was blown off course by fantastic winds. King John II eventually changed the name of the cape to the Cape of Good Hope, reflecting the promise of a new route to India offered by Dias's discovery. That promise became reality in 1498, after Vasco de Gama sailed to Calicut, India. An abrupt decline in Portuguese fortunes led to her eclipse by the larger Spain, reducing the resources available for investment in exploration and limiting Portuguese voyages to the Indian Ocean to an occasional "boatload of convicts."[5] Moreover, the prize for which Portuguese explorers had risked so much now seemed small in comparison to that discovered by their rivals the Spanish under the bold seamanship of Christopher Columbus, a man the king of Portugal had once refused to fund.

Columbus departed from Spain in August 1492, laying in a course due west and ultimately in a direct line to Japan, although he never mentioned Cathay prior to 1493.[6] A native of Genoa, Columbus embodied the best of the new generation of navigators: resilient, courageous, and confident. To be sure, Columbus wanted glory, and a motivation born of desperation fueled his vision. At the same time, Columbus was "earnestly desirous of taking Christianity to heathen lands."[7] He did not, as is popularly believed, originate the idea that the earth is round. As early as 1480, for example, he read works proclaiming the sphericity of the planet. But knowing intellectually that the earth is round and demonstrating it physically are two different things.

Columbus's fleet consisted of only three vessels, the *Niña,* the *Pinta,* and the *Santa María,* and a crew of ninety men. Leaving port in August 1492, the expedition eventually passed the point where the sailors expected to find Japan, generating no small degree of anxiety, whereupon Columbus used every managerial skill he possessed to maintain discipline and encourage hope. The voyage had stretched to ten weeks when the crew bordered on mutiny, and only the captain's reassurance and exhortations persuaded the sailors to continue a few more days. Finally, on October 11, 1492, they started to see signs of land: pieces of wood loaded with barnacles, green bulrushes, and other vegetation.[8] A lookout spotted land, and on October 12, 1492, the courageous band waded ashore on Watling Island in the Bahamas, where his men begged his pardon for doubting him.[9]

Columbus continued to Cuba, which he called Hispaniola. At the time he thought he had reached the Far East, and referred to the dark-skinned people he found in Hispaniola as Indians. He found these Indians "very well formed, with handsome bodies and good faces," and hoped to convert them "to our Holy Faith by love rather than by force" by giving them red caps and glass beads "and many other things of small value."[10] Dispatching emissaries into the interior to contact the Great Khan, Columbus's scouts returned with no reports of the spices, jewels, silks, or other evidence of Cathay; nor did the khan send his regards. Nevertheless, Columbus returned to Spain confident he had found an ocean passage to the Orient.[11]

Reality gradually forced Columbus to a new conclusion: he had not reached India or China, and after a second voyage in 1493—still convinced he was in the Pacific Ocean—Columbus admitted he had stumbled on a new land mass, perhaps even a new continent of astounding natural resources and wealth. In February 1493, he wrote his Spanish patrons that Hispaniola and other islands like it were "fertile to a limitless degree," possessing mountains covered by "trees of a thousand kinds and tall, so that they seem to touch the sky."[12] He confidently promised gold, cotton, spices—as much as Their Highnesses should command—in return for only minimal continued support. Meanwhile, he continued to probe the *Mundus Novus* south and west. After returning to Spain yet again, Columbus made two more voyages to the New World in 1498 and 1502.

Whether Columbus had found parts of the Far East or an entirely new land was irrelevant to most Europeans at the time. Political distractions abounded in

Europe. Spain had barely evicted the Muslims after the long *Reconquista,* and England's Wars of the Roses had scarcely ended. News of Columbus's discoveries excited only a few merchants, explorers, and dreamers. Still, the prospect of finding a waterway to Asia infatuated sailors; and in 1501 a Florentine passenger on a Portuguese voyage, Amerigo Vespucci, wrote letters to his friends in which he described the New World. His self-promoting dispatches circulated sooner than Columbus's own written accounts, and as a result the term "America" soon was attached by geographers to the continents in the Western Hemisphere that should by right have been named Columbia. But if Columbus did not receive the honor of having the New World named for him, and if he acquired only temporary wealth and fame in Spain (receiving from the Crown the title Admiral of the Ocean Sea), his place in history was never in doubt. Historian Samuel Eliot Morison, a worthy seaman in his own right who reenacted the Columbian voyages in 1939 and 1940, described Columbus as "the sign and symbol [of the] new age of hope, glory and accomplishment."[13]

Once Columbus blazed the trail, other Spanish explorers had less trouble obtaining financial backing for expeditions. Vasco Núñez de Balboa (1513) crossed the Isthmus of Panama to the Pacific Ocean (as he named it). Ferdinand Magellan (1519–22) circumnavigated the globe, lending his name to the Strait of Magellan. Other expeditions explored the interior of the newly discovered lands. Juan Ponce de León, traversing an area along Florida's coast, attempted unsuccessfully to plant a colony there. Pánfilo de Narváez's subsequent expedition to conquer Tampa Bay proved even more disastrous. Narváez himself drowned, and natives killed members of his expedition until only four of them reached a Spanish settlement in Mexico.

Spaniards traversed modern-day Mexico, probing interior areas under Hernando Cortés, who in 1518 led a force of 1,000 soldiers to Tenochtitlán, the site of present-day Mexico City. Cortés encountered powerful Indians called Aztecs, led by their emperor Montezuma. The Aztecs had established a brutal regime that oppressed other natives of the region, capturing large numbers of them for ritual sacrifices in which Aztec priests cut out the beating hearts of living victims. Such barbarity enabled the Spanish to easily enlist other tribes, especially the Tlaxcalans, in their efforts to defeat the Aztecs.

Tenochtitlán sat on an island in the middle of a lake, connected to the outlying areas by three huge causeways. It was a monstrously large city (for the time) of at least 200,000, rigidly divided into nobles and commoner groups.[14] Aztec culture created impressive pyramid-shaped temple structures, but Aztec science lacked the simple wheel and the wide range of pulleys and gears that it enabled. But it was sacrifice, not science, that defined Aztec society, whose pyramids, after all, were execution sites. A four-day sacrifice in 1487 by the Aztec king Ahuitzotl involved the butchery of 80,400 prisoners by shifts of priests working four at a time at convex killing tables who kicked lifeless, heartless bodies down the side of the pyramid temple. This worked out to a "killing rate of fourteen victims a minute over the ninety-six-hour bloodbath."[15] In addition to the abominable sacrifice system, crime and street carnage were commonplace. More intriguing to the Spanish than the buildings, or even the sacrifices, however, were the legends of gold, silver, and other riches Tenochtitlán contained, protected by the powerful Aztec army.

Cortés first attempted a direct assault on the city and fell back with heavy losses, narrowly escaping extermination. Desperate Spanish fought their way out on *Noche Triste* (the Sad Night), when hundreds of them fell on the causeway. Cortés's men piled human bodies—Aztec and European alike—in heaps to block Aztec pursuers, then staggered back to Vera Cruz. In 1521 Cortés returned with a new Spanish army, supported by more than 75,000 Indian allies.[16] This time, he found a weakened enemy who had been ravaged by smallpox, or as the Aztecs called it, "the great leprosy." Starvation killed those Aztecs whom the disease did not: "They died in heaps, like bedbugs," wrote one historian.[17] Even so, neither disease nor starvation accounted for the Spaniards' stunning victory over the vastly larger Aztec forces, which can be credited to the Spanish use of European-style disciplined shock combat and the employment of modern firepower. Severing the causeways, stationing huge units to guard each, Cortés assaulted the city walls from thirteen brigantines the Spaniards had hauled overland, sealing off the city. These brigantines proved "far more ingeniously engineered for fighting on the Aztecs' native waters than any boat constructed in Mexico during the entire history of its civilization."[18] When it came to the final battle, it was not the brigantines, but Cortés's use of cannons, muskets, harquebuses, crossbows, and pikes in deadly discipline, firing in order, and standing en masse against a murderous mass of Aztecs who fought as individuals rather than a cohesive force that proved decisive.

Spanish technology, including the wheel-related ratchet gears on muskets, constituted only one element of European military superiority. They fought as other European land armies fought, in formation, with their officers open to new ideas based on practicality, not theology. Where no Aztec would dare approach the godlike Montezuma with a military strategy, Cortés debated tactics with his lieutenants routinely, and the European way of war endowed each Castilian soldier with a sense of individual rights, civic duty, and personal freedom nonexistent in the Aztec kingdom. Moreover, the Europeans sought to kill their enemy and force his permanent surrender, not forge an arrangement for a steady supply of sacrifice victims. Thus Cortés captured the Aztec capital in 1521 at a cost of more than 100,000 Aztec dead, many from disease resulting from Cortés's cutting the city's water supply.[19] But not all diseases came from the Old World to the New, and syphilis appears to have been retransmitted back from Brazil to Portugal.[20]

If Europeans resembled other cultures in their attitude toward conquest, they differed substantially in their practice and effectiveness. The Spanish, especially, proved adept at defeating native peoples for three reasons. First, they were mobile. Horses and ships endowed the Spanish with vast advantages in mobility over the natives. Second, the burgeoning economic power of Europe enabled quantum leaps over Middle Eastern, Asian, and Mesoamerican cultures. This economic wealth made possible the shipping and equipping of large, trained, well-armed forces. Nonmilitary technological advances such as the iron-tipped plow, the windmill, and the waterwheel all had spread through Europe and allowed monarchs to employ fewer resources in the farming sector and more in science, engineering, writing, and the military. A natural outgrowth of this economic wealth was improved military technology, including guns, which made any single Spanish soldier the equal of several poorly armed natives, offsetting the latter's numerical advantage. But these two factors were magnified by a third element— the glue that held it all together—which was a western way of combat that emphasized group cohesion of free citizens. Like the ancient Greeks and Romans, Cortés's Castilians fought from a long tradition of tactical adaptation based on individual freedom, civic rights, and a "preference for shock battle of heavy infantry" that "grew out of consensual government, equality among the middling classes," and other distinctly Western traits that gave numerically inferior European armies a decisive edge.[21] That made it possible for tiny expeditions such as Ponce de León's, with only 200 men and 50 horses, or Narváez's, with a force of 600, including cooks, colonists, and women, to overcome native Mexican armies outnumbering them two, three, and even ten times at any particular time.

More to the point, no native culture could have conceived of maintaining expeditions of thousands of men in the field for months at a time. Virtually all of the natives lived off the land and took slaves back to their home, as opposed to colonizing new territory with their own settlers. Indeed, only the European industrial engine could have provided the material wherewithal to maintain such armies, and only the European political constructs of liberty, property rights, and nationalism kept men in combat for abstract political causes. European combat style produced yet another advantage in that firearms showed no favoritism on the battlefield. Spanish gunfire destroyed the hierarchy of the enemy, including the aristocratic dominant political class. Aztec chiefs and Moor sultans alike were completely vulnerable to massed firepower, yet without the legal framework of republicanism and civic virtue like Europe's to replace its leadership cadre, a native army could be decapitated at the head with one volley, whereas the Spanish forces could see lieutenants fall and seamlessly replace them with sergeants.

Did Columbus Kill Most of the Indians?

The five-hundred-year anniversary of Columbus's discovery was marked by unusual and strident controversy. Rising up to challenge the intrepid voyager's courage and vision— as well as the establishment of European civilization in the New World—was a crescendo of damnation, which posited that the Genoese navigator was a mass murderer akin to Adolf Hitler. Even the establishment of European outposts was, according to the revisionist critique, a regrettable development. Although this division of interpretations no doubt confused and dampened many a Columbian festival in 1992, it also elicited a most intriguing historical debate: did the esteemed Admiral of the Ocean Sea kill almost all the Indians? A number of recent scholarly studies have dispelled or at least substantially modified many of the numbers generated by the anti-

Columbus groups, although other new research has actually increased them. Why the sharp inconsistencies? One recent scholar, examining the major assessments of numbers, points to at least *nine* different measurement methods, including the time-worn favorite, guesstimates.

1. Pre-Columbian native population numbers are much smaller than critics have maintained. For example, one author claims "Approximately 56 million people died as a result of European exploration in the New World." For that to have occurred, however, one must start with early estimates for the population of the Western Hemisphere at nearly 100 million. Recent research suggests that that number is vastly inflated, and that the most reliable figure is nearer 53 million, and even that estimate falls with each new publication. Since 1976 alone, experts have lowered their estimates by 4 million. Some scholars have even seen those figures as wildly inflated, and several studies put the native population of North America alone within a range of 8.5 million (the highest) to a low estimate of 1.8 million. If the latter number is true, it means that the "holocaust" or "depopulation" that occurred was one fiftieth of the original estimates, or 800,000 Indians who died from disease and firearms. Although that number is a universe away from the estimates of 50 to 60 million deaths that some researchers have trumpeted, it still represented a destruction of half the native population.

   Even then, the guesstimates involve such things as accounting for the effects of epidemics—which other researchers, using the same data, dispute ever occurred—or expanding the sample area to all of North and Central America. However, estimating the number of people alive in a region five hundred years ago has proven difficult, and recently several researchers have called into question most early estimates. For example, one method many scholars have used to arrive at population numbers—extrapolating from early explorers' estimates of populations they could count—has been challenged by archaeological studies of the Amazon basin, where dense settlements were once thought to exist. Work in the area by Betty Meggers concludes that the early explorers' estimates were exaggerated and that no evidence of large populations in that region exists. N. D. Cook's demographic research on the Inca in Peru showed that the population could have been as high as 15 million or as low as 4 million, suggesting that the measurement mechanisms have a "plus or minus reliability factor" of 400 percent! Such "minor" exaggerations as the tendencies of some explorers to overestimate their opponents' numbers, which, when factored throughout numerous villages, then into entire populations, had led to overestimates of millions.

2. Native populations had epidemics long before Europeans arrived. A recent study of more than 12,500 skeletons from sixty-five sites found that native health was on a "downward trajectory long before Columbus arrived." Some suggest that Indians may have had a nonvenereal form of syphilis, and almost all agree that a variety of infections were widespread. Tuberculosis existed in Central and North America long before the Spanish appeared, as did herpes, polio, tick-borne fevers, giardiasis, and amebic dysentery. One admittedly controversial study by Henry Dobyns in *Current Anthropology* in 1966 later fleshed out over the years into his book, argued that extensive epidemics swept North America before Europeans arrived. As one authority summed up the research, "Though the Old World was to contribute to its diseases, the New World certainly was not the Garden of Eden some have depicted." As one might expect, others challenged Dobyns and the "early epidemic" school, but the point remains that experts are divided. Many now discount the notion that huge epidemics swept through Central and North America; smallpox, in particular, did not seem to spread as a pandemic.

3. There is little evidence available for estimating the numbers of people lost in warfare prior to the Europeans because in general natives did not keep written records. Later, when whites could document oral histories during the Indian wars on the western frontier, they found that different tribes exaggerated their accounts of battles in totally different ways, depending on tribal custom. Some, who preferred to emphasize bravery over brains, inflated casualty numbers. Others, viewing large body counts as a sign of weakness, de-emphasized their losses. What is certain is that vast numbers of natives were killed by other natives, and that only technological backwardness—the absence of guns, for example—prevented the numbers of natives killed by other natives from growing even higher.

4. Large areas of Mexico and the Southwest were depopulated more than a hundred years before the arrival of Columbus. According to a recent source, "The majority of Southwesternists . . . believe that many areas of the Greater Southwest were abandoned or largely depopulated over a century before Columbus's fateful discovery, as a result of climatic shifts, warfare, resource mismanagement, and other causes." Indeed, a new generation of scholars puts more credence in early Spanish explorers' observations of widespread ruins and decaying "great houses" that they contended had been abandoned for years.

5. European scholars have long appreciated the dynamic of small-state diplomacy, such as was involved in the Italian or German small states in the nineteenth century. What has been missing from the discussions about native populations has been a recognition that in many ways the tribes resembled the small states in Europe: they concerned themselves more with traditional enemies (other tribes) than with new ones (whites).

Sources: The best single review of all the literature on Indian population numbers is John D. Daniels's "The Indian Population of North America in 1492," *William and Mary Quarterly,* April 1999, pp. 298–320. Among those who cite higher numbers are David Meltzer, "How Columbus Sickened the New World," *The New Scientist,* October 10, 1992, 38–41; Francis L. Black, "Why Did They Die?" *Science,* December 11, 1992, 139–140; and Alfred W. Crosby Jr., *Ecological Imperialism: The Biological Expansion of Europe, 900–1900* (New York: Cambridge University Press, 1986). Lower estimates come from the Smithsonian's Douglas Ubelaker, "North American Indian Population Size, A.D. 1500–1985," *American Journal of Physical Anthropology,* 77 (1988), 289–294; and William H. MacLeish, *The Day Before America* (Boston: Houghton Mifflin, 1994). Henry F. Dobyns, *American Historical Demography* (Bloomington, Indiana : Indiana University Press, 1976), calculated a number somewhat in the middle, or about 40 million, then subsequently revisited the argument, with William R. Swagerty, in *Their Number Become Thinned: Native American Population Dynamics in Eastern North America,* Native American Historic Demography Series (Knoxville, Tennessee: University of Tennessee Press, 1983). But, as Nobelist David Cook's study of Incaic Peru reveals, weaknesses in the data remain; see *Demographic Collapse: Indian Peru, 1520–1660* (Cambridge: Cambridge University Press, 1981). Betty Meggers's "Prehistoric Population Density in the Amazon Basin" (in John W. Verano and Douglas H. Ubelaker, *Disease and Demography in the Americas* [Washington, D.C.: Smithsonian Institution Press, 1992], 197–206), offers a lower-bound 3 million estimate for Amazonia (far lower than the higher-bound 10 million estimates). An excellent historiography of the debate appears in Daniel T. Reff, *Disease, Depopulation, and Culture Change in Northwestern New Spain, 1518–1764* (Salt Lake City, Utah: University of Utah Press, 1991). He argues for a reconsideration of disease as the primary source of depopulation (instead of European cruelty or slavery), but does not support inflated numbers. A recent synthesis of several studies can be found in Michael R. Haines and Richard H. Steckel, *A Population History of North America* (Cambridge: Cambridge University Press, 2000). Also see Richard H. Steckel and Jerome C. Rose, eds., *The Backbone of History: Health and Nutrition in the Western Hemisphere* (Cambridge: Cambridge University Press, 2002). The quotation referring to this study is from John Wilford, "Don't Blame Columbus for All the Indians' Ills," *New York Times,* October 29, 2002.

Technology and disease certainly played prominent roles in the conquest of Spanish America. But the oppressive nature of the Aztecs played no small role in their overthrow, and in both Peru and Mexico, "The structure of the Indian societies facilitated the Spanish conquest at ridiculously low cost."[22] In addition, Montezuma's ruling hierarchical, strongly centralized structure, in which subjects devoted themselves and their labor to the needs of the state, made it easy for the Spanish to adapt the system to their own control. Once the Spanish had eliminated Aztec leadership, they replaced it with themselves at the top. The "common people" exchanged one group of despots for another, of a different skin color.

By the time the Aztecs fell, the news that silver existed in large quantities in Mexico had reached Spain, attracting still other conquistadores. Hernando de Soto explored Florida (1539–1541), succeeding where Juan Ponce de León had failed, and ultimately crossed the Mississippi River, dying there in 1542. Meanwhile, marching northward from Mexico, Francisco Vásquez de Coronado pursued other Indian legends of riches in the Seven Cities of Cibola. Supposedly, gold and silver existed in abundance there, but Coronado's 270-man expedition found none of the fabled cities, and in 1541 he returned to Spain, having mapped much of the American Southwest. By the 1570s enough was known about Mexico and the Southwest to attract settlers, and some two hundred Spanish settlements existed, containing in all more than 160,000 Europeans.

Traveling with every expedition were priests and friars, and the first permanent building erected by Spaniards was often a church. Conquistadores genuinely believed that converting the heathen ranked near—or even above—the acquisition of riches. Even as the Dominican friar and Bishop of Chiapas, Bartolomé de Las Casas, sharply criticized his countrymen in his writings for making "bloody, unjust, and cruel wars" against the Indians—the so-called Black Legend—a second army of mercy, Spanish missionaries, labored selflessly under harsh conditions to bring the Gospel to the Indians. In some cases, as with the Pueblo Indians, large numbers of Indians converted to Christianity, albeit a mixture of traditional Catholic teachings and their own religious practices, which, of course, the Roman Church deplored. Attempts to suppress such distortions led to uprisings such as the 1680 Pueblo revolt that killed twenty-one priests and hundreds of Spanish colonists, although even the rebellious Pueblos eventually rejoined the Spanish as allies.[23]

Explorers had to receive from the king a license that entitled the grantee to large estates and a percentage of returns from the expedition. From the estates, explorers carved out ranches that provided an agricultural base and encouraged other settlers to immigrate. Then, after the colonists had founded a mission, the Spanish government established formal forts (presidios). The most prominent of the presidios dotted the California coast, with the largest at San Diego. Royal governors and local bureaucrats maintained the empire in Mexico and the Southwest with considerable autonomy from Spain. Distance alone made it difficult for the Crown to control activities in the New World.

A new culture accompanied the Spanish occupation. With intermarriage between Europeans and Indians, a large mestizo population (today, referred to as Mexican or Hispanic people) resulted. It generally adopted Spanish culture and values.

The Pirates of the Caribbean

Despite frantic activity and considerable promise, Spanish colonies grew slowly. Southwestern and Mexican Spanish settlements had a population of about 160,000 by the 1570s, when the territory under the control of the king included Caribbean islands, Mexico, the southwestern part of today's United States, large portions of the South American land mass, and an Indian population of more than 5 million. Yet when compared to the later rapid growth of the English colonies, the stagnation of Spain's outposts requires examination. Why did the Spanish colonies grow so slowly? One explanation involves the extensive influence in the Caribbean and on the high seas of pirates who spread terror among potential settlers and passengers. A less visible and much more costly effect on colonization resulted from the expense of outfitting ships to defend themselves, or constructing a navy of sufficient strength to patrol the sea-lanes. Pirates not only attacked ships en route, but they also brazenly invaded coastal areas, capturing entire cities. The famous English pirate Henry Morgan took Portobelo, the leading Spanish port on the American Atlantic coast in 1668, and Panama City fell to his marauders in 1670–71.[24] Sir Francis Drake, the Master Thief of the unknown world, as the Spaniards called him, "became the terror of their ports and crews" and he and other "sea dogs" often acted as unofficial agents of the English Crown.[25]

Other discouraging reports dampened Spanish excitement for settling in the New World. In 1591, twenty-nine of seventy-five ships in a single convoy went down trying to return to Spain from Cuba; in 1600 a sixty-ship fleet from Cádiz to Mexico encountered two separate storms that sank seventeen ships and took down more than a thousand people; and in 1656 two galleons collided in the Bahamas, killing all but fifty-six of the seven hundred passengers. Such gloomy news combined with reports of piracy to cause more than a few potential Spanish settlers to reconsider their plans to relocate in Mexico.[26]

Another factor that retarded Spain's success in the New World was its rigid adherence to mercantilism, an economic theory that had started to dominate Europe. Mercantilism held that wealth was fixed (because it consisted of gold and silver), and that for one nation to get richer, another must get poorer.

Spain thoroughly embraced the aspects of mercantilism that emphasized acquiring gold and silver. Spanish mines in the New World eventually turned out untold amounts of riches. Francisco Pizarro transported 13,000 pounds of gold and 26,000 pounds of silver in just his first shipment home. Total bullion shipped from Mexico and Peru between 1500 and 1650 exceeded 180 tons. Yet Spain did not view the New World as land to be developed, and rather than using the wealth as a base from which to create a thriving commercial sector, Spain allowed its gold to sit in royal vaults, unemployed in the formation of new capital.[27]

Spanish attitudes weighed heavily upon the settlers of New Spain, who quickly were outpaced by the more commercially oriented English outposts.[28] Put another way, Spain remained wedded to the simplest form of mercantilism, whereas the English and Dutch advanced in the direction of a freer and more lucrative system in which business was less subordinated to the needs of the state. Since the state lacked the information possessed by the collective buyers and sellers in the marketplace, governments inevitably were at a disadvantage in measuring supply and demand. England thus began to shoot ahead of Spain and Portugal, whose entrepreneurs found themselves increasingly enmeshed in the snares of bureaucratic mercantilism.

France in the New World

France, the last of the major colonizing powers, abandoned mercantilism more quickly than the Spanish, but not as rapidly as the English. Although not eager to colonize North America, France feared leaving the New World to its European rivals. Following early expeditions along the coast of Newfoundland, the first serious voyages by a French captain into North America were conducted under Jacques Cartier in 1534. Searching for the fabled Northwest Passage, a northerly water route to the Pacific, he sailed up the St. Lawrence, reaching the present site of Montreal. It was another seventy years, however, before the French established a permanent settlement there.[29]

Samuel de Champlain, a pious cartographer considered one of the greatest inland explorers of all time, searched for a series of lakes that would link the Atlantic and Pacific, and in 1608 established a fort on a rocky point called Quebec (from the Algonquin word "kebec," or "where the river narrows"). Roughly twenty years later, France chartered the Company of New France, a trading firm designed to populate French holdings in North America. Compared to English colonial efforts, however, New France was a disappointment, in no small part because one of the most enthusiastic French groups settled in the southeastern part of the United States, not Canada, placing them in direct contact with the powerful Spanish. The French government, starting a trend that continued to the time of the Puritans, answered requests by religious dissidents to plant a colony in the southernmost reaches of North America. Many dissenters born of the Protestant Reformation sought religious freedom from Catholic governments. These included French Protestants known as Huguenots. Violent anti-Protestant prejudices in France served as a powerful inducement for the Huguenots to emigrate.

Huguenots managed to land a handful of volunteers in Port Royal Sound (present-day South Carolina) in 1562, but the colony failed. Two years later, another expedition successfully settled at Fort Caroline in Florida, which came under attack from the Spanish, who slaughtered the unprepared inhabitants, ending French challenges to Spanish power in the southern parts of North America. From that point on, France concentrated its efforts on the northern reaches of North America—Canada—where Catholicism, not Protestantism, played a significant role in French Canadian expansion alongside the economics of the fur trade.

French colonization trailed that of the English for several reasons. Quebec was much colder than most of the English colonial sites, making it a much less attractive destination for emigrants. Also, the conditions of French peasants in the 1600s were better than that of their English counterparts, so they were less interested in leaving their mother country. Finally, the French government, concerned with maintaining a large base of domestic military recruits, did not encourage migration to New France. As a result, by 1700, English colonists in North America outnumbered French settlers six to one. Despite controlling the St. Lawrence and Mississippi rivers, New France, deprived by its inland character of many of the advantages available to the coastal English settlements, saw only a "meagre trickle" to the region.[30] As few as twenty-seven thousand French came to Canada in 150 years, and two-thirds of those departed without leaving descendants there.[31]

Even so, New France had substantial economic appeal. Explorers had not found gold or silver, but northern expeditions discovered riches of another sort: furs. Vast Canadian forests offered an abundance of highly valued deer, elk, rabbit, and beaver skins and pelts, harvested by an indigenous population eager to trade. Trapping required deep penetration into forests controlled by Indians, and the French found that they could obtain furs far more easily through barter than they could by deploying their own army of trappers with soldiers to protect them. Thus, French traders ventured deep into the interior of Canada to exchange knives, blankets, cups, and, when necessary, guns with the Indians for pelts. At the end of a trading journey, the *coureurs de bois* (runners of the woods) returned to Montreal, where they sold the furs to merchants who shipped them back to Europe. That strategy demanded that France limit the number of its colonists and discourage settlement, particularly in Indian territories. France attempted to deal with natives as friends and trading partners, but quickly realized that the Indians harbored as much enmity for each other as they did for the Europeans. If not careful, France could find itself on the wrong end of an alliance, so where possible, the French government restrained colonial intrusions into Indian land, with the exception of missionaries, such as Jacques Marquette (1673) and René de La Salle (1681).[32]

The English Presence

Despite the voyages of John Cabot, English explorers trailed in the wake of the Portuguese, Spanish, and French. England, at the beginning of the sixteenth century "was backward in commerce, industry, and wealth, and therefore did not rank as one of the great European nations."[33] When Queen Elizabeth took the throne in 1558, the situation changed: the nation developed a large navy with competent—often skilled—sailors. Moreover, profits from piracy and privateering provided strong incentives to bold seamen, especially "sea dogs" like John Hawkins and Francis Drake, to join in plundering the Spanish sea-lanes.

By that time, the English reading public had become fascinated with the writings of Humphrey Gilbert, especially *A Discourse to Prove a Passage by the North-West to Cathaia and the East Indies* (1576), which closed with a challenge to Englishmen to discover that water route.

In 1578, Elizabeth granted him rights to plant an English colony in America, but he died in an attempt to colonize Newfoundland. Walter Raleigh, Gilbert's half brother, inherited the grant and sent vessels to explore the coast of North America before determining where to locate a settlement. That expedition reached North Carolina in the summer of 1584. After spending two months traversing the land, commenting on its vegetation and natural beauty, the explorers returned to England with glowing reports. Raleigh supported a second expedition in 1585, at which time one hundred settlers landed at Roanoke on the Carolina coast. When the transports had sailed for England, leaving the colony alone, it nearly starved, and only the fortunate arrival of Drake, fresh from new raiding, provided it with supplies. Raleigh, undeterred by the near disaster, planned another settlement for Roanoke, by which time Richard Hakluyt's *Discourse on Western Planting* (1584) further ginned up enthusiasm for settling in the region.[34]

Settlers received stock in Raleigh's company, which attracted 133 men and 17 women who set sail on three ships. They reached Roanoke Island in 1587, and a child born on that island, Virginia Dare, technically became the first European born in America. As with the previous English expedition, the ships, under the command of the governor, John White, returned to England for more supplies, only to arrive under the impending threat of a Spanish invasion of England—a failed invasion that would result in the spectacular defeat of the Spanish Armada in 1588, leaving England as the predominant sea power in the world. Delays prohibited the supply ships from returning to Roanoke until 1591, when John White found the Roanoke houses standing, but no settlers. A mysterious clue—the word CROATOAN carved on a tree—remains the only evidence of their fate. Croatoan Indians lived somewhat nearby, but they were considered friendly, and neither White nor generations of historians have solved the puzzle of the Lost Colony of Roanoke. Whatever the fate of the Roanoke settlers, the result for England was that by 1600 there still were no permanent English colonies in America.

Foundations for English Success in the New World: A Hypothesis

England had laid the foundation for successful North American settlements well before the first permanent colony was planted at Jamestown in 1607. Although it seemed insignificant in comparison to the large empire already established by the Spanish, Virginia and subsequent English colonies in Massachusetts would eclipse the settlement of the Iberian nations and France. Why?

It is conceivable that English colonies prospered simply by luck, but the dominance of Europe in general and England in particular—a tiny island with few natural resources—suggests that specific factors can be identified as the reasons for the rise of an English-Atlantic civilization: the appearance of new business practices, a culture of technological inquisitiveness, and a climate receptive to political and economic risk taking.

One of the most obvious areas in which England surpassed other nations was in its business practices. English merchants had eclipsed their Spanish and French rivals in preparing for successful colonization through adoption of the joint-stock company as a form of business. One of the earliest of these joint-stock companies, the Company of the Staple, was founded in 1356 to secure control over the English wool trade from Italian competitors. By the 1500s, the Moscovy Company (1555), the Levant Company (1592), and the East India Company (1600) fused the exploration of distant regions with the pursuit of profit. Joint-stock companies had two important advantages over other businesses. One advantage was that the company did not dissolve with the death of the primary owner (and thus was permanent). Second, it featured limited liability, in which a stockholder could lose only what he invested, in contrast to previous business forms that held owners liable for all of a company's debts. Those two features made investing in an exciting venture in the New World attractive, especially when coupled with the exaggerated claims of the returning explorers. Equally important, however, the joint-stock feature allowed a rising group of middle-class merchants to support overseas ventures on an ever-expanding basis.

In an even more significant development, a climate receptive to risk taking and innovation, which had flourished throughout the West, reached its most advanced state in England. It is crucial to realize that key inventions or technologies appeared in non-Western countries first; yet they were seldom, if ever, employed in such a way as to change society dramatically until the Western societies applied them. The stirrup, for example, was known as early as A.D. 400–500 in the Middle East, but it took until 730, when Charles Martel's mounted knights adopted cavalry charges that combat changed on a permanent basis.[35] Indeed, something other than invention was at work. As sociologist Jack Goldstone put it, "The West did not overtake the East merely by becoming more efficient at making bridles and stirrups, but by developing steam engines . . . [and] by taking unknown risks on novelty."[36] Stability of the state, the rule of law, and a willingness to accept new or foreign ideas, rather than ruthlessly suppress them, proved vital to entrepreneurship, invention, technical creativity, and innovation. In societies dominated by the state, scientists risked their lives if they arrived at unacceptable answers.

Still another factor, little appreciated at the time, worked in favor of English ascendancy: labor scarcity ensured a greater respect for new immigrants, whatever their origins, than had existed in Europe. With the demand for labor came property rights, and with such property rights came political rights unheard of in Europe.

Indeed, the English respect for property rights soon eclipsed other factors accounting for England's New World dominance. Born out of the fierce struggles by English landowners to protect their estates from seizure by the state, by the 1600s, property rights had become so firmly established as a basis for English economic activities that its rules permeated even the lowest classes in society. English colonists found land so abundant that anyone could own it. When combined with freedom from royal retribution in science and technological fields, the right to retain the fruit of one's labor—even intellectual property—gave England a substantial advantage in the colonization process over rivals that had more than a century's head start.[37] These advantages would be further enhanced by a growing religious toleration brought about by religious dissenters from the Church of England called Puritans.[38]

The Colonial South

In 1606, James I granted a charter to the Virginia Company for land in the New World, authorizing two subsidiary companies: the London Company, based in Bristol, and the Plymouth Company, founded by Plymouth stockholders. A group of "certain Knights, Gentlemen, Merchants, and other Adventurers" made up the London Company, which was a joint-stock company in the same vein as the Company of the Staple and the Levant Company. The grant to the London Company, reaching from modern-day North Carolina to New York, received the name Virginia in honor of Queen Elizabeth (the "Virgin Queen"), whereas the Plymouth Company's grant encompassed New England. More than 600 individuals and fifty commercial firms invested in the Virginia Company, illustrating the fund-raising advantages available to a corporation. The London Company organized its expedition first, sending three ships out in 1607 with 144 boys and men to establish a trading colony designed to extract wealth for shipment back to England.

Seeking to "propagate the Christian religion" in the Chesapeake and to produce a profit for the investors, the London Company owned the land and appointed the governor. Colonists were considered "employees." However, as with Raleigh's employees, the colonists enjoyed, as the king proclaimed, "all Liberties, Franchises, and Immunities . . . as if they had been abiding and born, within this our Realm of England."[39] Most colonists lacked any concept of what awaited them: the company adopted a military model based on the Irish campaigns, and the migrants included few farmers or men skilled in construction trades. After a four-month voyage, in April 1607, twenty-six-year-old Captain John Smith piloted ships fifty miles up the James River, well removed from eyesight of passing Spanish vessels. It was a site remarkable for its defensive position, but it sat on a malarial swamp surrounded by thick forests that would prove difficult to clear. Tiny triangle-shaped James Forte, as Jamestown was called, featured firing parapets at each corner and contained fewer than two dozen buildings. Whereas defending the fort might have appeared possible, stocking the fort with provisions proved more difficult: not many of the colonists wanted to work, and none found gold. Some discovered pitch, tar, lumber, and iron for export, but many of the emigrants were gentleman adventurers who disdained physical labor as had their Spanish counterparts to the Southwest. Smith implored the London Company to send "30 carpenters, husbandmen, gardeners, fishermen, blacksmiths, masons and diggers up of trees . . . [instead of] a thousand of such as we have."[40] Local Indians, such as the Monacan and Chickahominy, traded with the colonists, but the English could neither hire Indian laborers nor did Indian males express any interest in agriculture themselves. Reaping what they had (not) sown, the settlers of James Forte starved, with fewer than one third of the 120 colonists surviving a year. So few remained that the living, Smith noted, were scarcely able to bury the dead.

Disease also decimated the colony. Jamestown settlers were leveled by New World diseases for which they had no resistance. Malaria, in particular, proved a dreaded killer, and malnutrition lowered the immunity of the colonists. The brackish water at that point of the James River also fostered mosquitoes and parasites. Virginia was hardly a "disease-free paradise" before the arrival of the Jamestown English.[41] New microbes transported by the Europeans generated a much higher level of infection than previously experienced by the Indians; then, in a vicious circle, warring Indian tribes spread the diseases among one another when they attacked enemy tribes and carried off infected prisoners.

Thanks to the efforts of Smith, who as council president simply assumed control in 1608, the colony was saved. Smith imposed military discipline and order and issued the famous biblical edict, "He who will not work will not eat." He stabilized the colony, and in the second winter, less than 15 percent of the population died, compared to the more than 60 percent who died just a year earlier. Smith also organized raids on Indian villages. These brought immediate returns of food and animals, but fostered long-term retribution from the natives, who harassed the colonists when they ventured outside their walls. But Smith was not anti-Indian per se, and even proposed a plan of placing white males in Indian villages to intermarry—hardly the suggestion of a racist. Subsequent settlers developed schools to educate Indians, including William and Mary. Smith ran the colony like an army unit until 1609, when confident of its survival, the colonists tired of his tyrannical methods and deposed him.

At that point he returned to England, whereupon the London Company (by then calling itself the Virginia Company) obtained a new charter from the king, and it sought to raise capital in England by selling stock and by offering additional stock to anyone willing to migrate to Virginia. The company provided free passage to Jamestown for indentures, or servants willing to work for the Virginia Company for seven years. A new fleet of nine ships containing six hundred men and some women left England in 1609. One of the ships sank in a hurricane, and another ran aground in Bermuda, where it remained until May 1610.

The other vessels arrived at Jamestown only to experience the "starving time" in the winter of 1609–10. English colonists, barricaded within James Forte, ate dogs, cats, rats, toadstools, and horse hides—ultimately eating from the corpses of the dead. When the remnants of the fleet that had been stuck in Bermuda finally reached Virginia in the late spring of 1610, all the colonists boarded for a return to England. At the mouth of the James River, however, the ships encountered an English vessel bringing supplies. The settlers returned to James Forte, and shortly thereafter a new influx of settlers revived the colony.[42]

Like Smith, subsequent governors, including the first official governor, Lord De La Warr, attempted to operate the colony on a socialist model: settlers worked in forced-labor gangs; shirkers were flogged and some even hanged. Still, negative incentives only went so far because ultimately the communal storehouse would sustain anyone in danger of starving, regardless of individual work effort. Administrators realized that personal incentives would succeed where force would not, and they permitted private ownership of land. The application of private enterprise, combined with the introduction of tobacco farming, helped Jamestown survive and prosper—an experience later replicated in Georgia.

During the early critical years, Indians were too divided to coordinate their attacks against the English. The powerful Chief Powhatan, who led a confederation of more than twenty tribes, enlisted the support of the Jamestown settlers—who he assumed were there for the express purpose of stealing Indian land—to defeat other enemy Indian tribes. Both sides played balance-of-power politics. Thomas Dale, the deputy governor, proved resourceful in keeping the Indians off balance, at one point kidnapping Powhatan's daughter, Pocahontas (Matoaka), and holding her captive at Jamestown. There she met and eventually married planter John Rolfe, in 1614. Their marriage made permanent the uneasy truce that existed between Powhatan and Jamestown. Rolfe and Pocahontas returned to England, where the Indian princess, as a convert to Christianity, proved a popular dinner guest. She epitomized the view that Indians could be evangelized and "Europeanized."[43]

Tobacco, Slaves, and Representative Government

Rolfe already had made another significant contribution to the success of the colony by curing tobacco in 1612. Characterized by King James I as a "vile and stinking . . . custom," smoking tobacco had been promoted in England by Raleigh and had experienced widespread popularity. Columbus had reported Cuban natives rolling tobacco leaves, lighting them on fire, and sticking them in a nostril. By Rolfe's time the English had refined the custom by using a pipe or by smoking the tobacco directly with the mouth. England already imported more than £200,000 worth of tobacco per year from Spanish colonies, which had a monopoly on nicotine until Rolfe's discovery. Tobacco was not the only substance to emerge from Virginia that would later be considered a vice—George Thorpe perfected a mash of Indian corn that provided a foundation for hard liquor—but tobacco had the greatest potential for profitable production.

Substantial change in the production of tobacco only occurred, however, after the Virginia Company allowed individual settlers to own land. In 1617, any freeman who migrated to Virginia could obtain a grant of one hundred acres of land. Grants were increased for most colonists through the headright policy, under which every head of a household could receive fifty acres for himself and an additional fifty acres for every adult family member or servant who came to America with him. The combination of available land and the growing popularity of tobacco in England resulted in a string of plantations stretching to Failing Creek, well up the James River and as far west as Dale's Gift on Cape Charles. Virtually all of the plantations had riverfronts, allowing ships' captains to dock directly at the plantation, and their influence extended as far as the lands of the Piedmont Indians, who traded with the planters.[44]

Tobacco cultivation encouraged expansion. The crop demanded large areas of farmland, and the methods of cultivation depleted the soil quickly. Growers steadily moved to interior areas of Virginia, opening still more settlements and requiring additional forts. But the recurring problem in Virginia was obtaining labor, which headright could not provide—quite the contrary, it encouraged new free farms. Instead, the colony placed new emphasis on indentures, including "20 and odd Negroes" brought to Virginia by a Dutch ship in 1619.

The status of the first blacks in the New World remains somewhat mysterious, and any thesis about the change in black status generates sharp controversy. Historian Edmund Morgan, in *American Slavery, American Freedom,* contended that the first blacks had the same legal status as white indentured servants.[45] Other recent research confirms that the lines blurred between indentures of all colors and slaves, and that establishing clear definitions of exactly who was likely to become a slave proved difficult.[46] At least some white colonists apparently did not distinguish blacks from other servants in their minds, and some early black indentured servants were released at the end of their indentures. Rather than viewing Africa as a source of unlimited labor, English colonists preferred European indentured servants well into the 1670s, even when they came from the ranks of criminals from English jails. But by the 1660s, the southern colonists had slowly altered their attitudes toward Africans. Increasingly, the southerners viewed them as permanent servants, and in 1664 some southern colonies declared slavery hereditary, as it had been in ancient Athens and still was throughout the Muslim world.[47]

Perhaps the greatest irony surrounding the introduction of black servants was the timing—if the 1619 date is accurate. That year, the first elected legislative assembly convened at Jamestown. Members consisted of the governor and his council and representatives (or burgesses) from each of the eleven plantations. The assembly gradually split into an upper house, the governor and council, and the lower house, made up of the burgesses. This meant that the early forms of slavery and democracy in America were "twin-born at Jamestown, and in their infancy . . . were rocked in the Cradle of the Republic."[48]

Each of the colonists already had the rights of Englishmen, but the scarcity of labor forced the Virginia Company to grant new equal political rights within the colony to new migrants in the form of the privileges that land conferred. In that way, land and liberty became intertwined in the minds and attitudes of the Virginia founders. Virginia's founders may have believed in "natural law" concepts, but it was the cold reality of the endless labor shortages that put teeth in the colony's political rights. Still, the early colonial government was relatively inefficient and inept in carrying out its primary mission of turning a profit. London Company stockholders failed to resupply the colony adequately, and had instead placed their hope in sending ever-growing numbers of settlers to Jamestown. Adding to the colony's miseries, the new arrivals soon encroached on Indian lands, eliciting hostile reaction. Powhatan's death in 1618 resulted in leadership of the Chesapeake tribes falling to his brother, Opechancanough, who conceived a shrewd plan to destroy the English. Feigning friendship, the Indians encouraged a false sense of security among the careless colonists. Then, in 1622, Opechancanough's followers launched simultaneous attacks on the settlements surrounding Jamestown, killing more than three hundred settlers. The English retaliated by destroying Indian cornfields, a response that kept the Indians in check until 1644. Though blind, Opechancanough remained the chief and, still wanting vengeance, ordered a new wave of attacks that killed another three hundred English in two days. Again the settlers retaliated. They captured Opechancanough, shot him, and forced the Indians from the region between the York and James rivers.[49]

By that time, the Virginia Company had attracted considerable attention in England, none of it good. The king appointed a committee to look into the company's affairs and its perceived mismanagement, reflecting the fact that English investors—by then experiencing the fruits of commercial success at home—expected even more substantial returns from their successful operations abroad than they had received. Opechancanough's raids seemed to reinforce the assessment that the London directors could not make prudent decisions about the colony's safety, and in 1624 the Court of King's Bench annulled the Virginia Company's charter and the king assumed control of the colony as a royal province.

Virginians became embroiled in English politics, particularly the struggle between the Cavaliers (supporters of the king) and the Puritans. In 1649 the Puritans executed Charles I, whose forces had surrendered three years earlier. When Charles was executed, Governor William Berkeley and the Assembly supported Charles II as the rightful ruler of England (earning for Virginia the nickname Old Dominion). Parliament, however, was in control in England, and dispatched warships to bring the rebellious pro-Charles Virginians in line. After flirting with resistance, Berkeley and his Cavalier supporters ultimately yielded to the Puritan English Parliamentarians. Then Parliament began to ignore the colony, allowing Virginia to assume a great deal of self-government.

The new king, Charles II, the son of the executed Charles I, rewarded Berkeley and the Virginia Cavaliers for their loyalty. Berkeley was reappointed governor in 1660, but when he returned to his position, he was out of touch with the people and the assembly, which had grown more irascible, and was more intolerant than ever of religious minorities, including Quakers. At the same time, the colony's population had risen to forty thousand, producing tensions with the governor that erupted in 1676 with the influx of settlers into territories reserved for the Indians. All that was needed for the underrepresented backcountry counties to rise against Berkeley and the tidewater gentry was a leader.

Bacon's Rebellion

Nathaniel Bacon Jr., an eloquent and educated resident in Charles City County, had only lived in Virginia fourteen months before he was named to the governor's council. A hero among commoners, Bacon nonetheless was an aristocrat who simmered over his lack of access to the governor's inner circle. His large farm in the west stood on the front line of frontier defense, and naturally Bacon favored an aggressive strategy against the Indians. But he was not alone. Many western Virginians, noting signs of unrest among the tribes, petitioned Berkeley for military protection. Bacon went further, offering to organize and lead his own expedition against the Indians. In June 1676 he demanded a commission "against the heathen," saying, "God damme my blood, I came for a commission, and a commission I will have before I goe!"[50] Governor Berkeley, convinced that the colonists had exaggerated the threat, refused to send troops and rejected Bacon's suggestion to form an independent unit.

Meanwhile, small raids by both Indians and whites started to escalate into larger attacks. In 1676, Bacon, despite his lack of official approval, led a march to track hostiles. Instead, he encountered and killed friendly Indians, which threatened to drag the entire region into war. From a sense of betrayal, he then turned his 500 men on the government at Jamestown. Berkeley maneuvered to stave off a coup by Bacon when he appointed him general, in charge of the Indian campaign. Satisfied, Bacon departed, whereupon Berkeley rescinded his support and attempted to raise an army loyal to himself. Bacon returned, and finding the ragtag militia, scattered Berkeley's hastily organized force, whereupon Bacon burned most of the buildings at Jamestown.

No sooner had Bacon conquered Jamestown than he contracted a virus and died. Leaderless, Bacon's troops lacked the ability to resist Berkeley and his forces, who, bolstered by the arrival of 1,100 British troops, regained control of the colony. Berkeley promptly hanged 23 of the rebels and confiscated the property of others—actions that violated English property law and resulted in the governor's being summoned back to England to explain his behavior. Reprimanded by King Charles, Berkeley died before he could return to the colony.[51]

The Maryland Experiment

Although Virginia was a Protestant (Anglican) colony—and it must be stated again that the London Company did not have a religious agenda per se—a second Chesapeake colony was planted in 1634 when George Calvert received a grant from James I. Calvert, who enjoyed strong personal support from the king

despite his conversion to Catholicism in 1625, already had mounted an unsuccessful mission to plant a colony in Newfoundland. After returning from the
aborted Newfoundland venture, Calvert worked to obtain a charter for the northern part of Chesapeake Bay. Shortly after he died, the Crown issued a charter in
1632, to Cecilius Calvert, George's son, naming George Calvert Lord Baltimore.
The grant, named in honor of Charles I's sister, Queen Mary, gave Baltimore a
vast expanse of land stretching from the Potomac River to the Atlantic Ocean.

Calvert's grant gave him full proprietary control over the land, freeing him
from many of the constraints that had limited the Virginia Company. As proprietor,
Calvert acted *rex in abstentia* (as the king in his absence), and as long as the proprietor acted in accordance with the laws of England, he spoke with the authority
of the Crown. Calvert never visited his colony, though, governing the province
through his brother, Leonard, who held the office of governor until 1647. Like Virginia, Maryland had an assembly (created in 1635) elected by all freeholders.

In March 1634 approximately three hundred passengers arrived at one of
the eastern tributaries of the Potomac and established the village of St. Mary's.
Located on a high cliff, St. Mary's had a good natural harbor, fresh water, and
abundant vegetation. Father Andrew White, a priest who accompanied the
settlers, observed of the region that "we cannot set down a foot without but tread
on strawberries, raspberries, fallen mulberry vines, acorns, walnuts, [and] sas-
safras."[52] The Maryland colony was planned better than Jamestown. It possessed
a large proportion of laborers—and fewer adventurers, country gentlemen, and
gold seekers—and the settlers planted corn as soon as they had cleared the fields.

Calvert, while not unaware of the monetary returns of a well-run colony, had
another motive for creating a settlement in the New World. Catholics had faced
severe persecution in England, and so Lord Baltimore expected that a large number of Catholics would welcome an opportunity to immigrate to Maryland, when
he enacted the Toleration Act of 1649, which permitted any Christian faith to be
practiced in the colony.[53] The Act provided that "no person . . . professing to believe in Jesus Christ, shall from henceforth be in any ways troubled, molested, or
discountenanced."[54] Yet the English Catholics simply did not respond the way
Calvert hoped. Thus, he had to welcome Protestant immigrants at the outset.
Once the news of religious toleration spread, other religious immigrants came
from Virginia, including a group of persecuted Puritans who established Annapolis. The Puritans proved a thorn in Baltimore's side, however, especially after the
English Civil War put the Puritans in control there and they suspended the Toleration Act. After a brief period in which the Calvert family was deprived of all
rights to govern, Lord Baltimore was supported, ironically, by the Puritan Lord
Protector of England, Oliver Cromwell, and he was reinstated as governor in
1657. Religious conflict had not disappeared, however; an early wave of Jesuits
worked to convert all of the colonies, antagonizing the Protestant majority. Thus,
in many ways, the attempt to permit religious toleration resulted in conflict and,
frequently, bloodshed.

Nor did the immigration of Protestants into Maryland allay the nagging labor shortage. In 1640, Maryland established its own headright system, and still the demands for labor exceeded the supply. As in Virginia, Maryland planters solved the shortage through the use of indentured servants and, at the end of the 1600s, African slaves. Maryland enacted a law "concerning Negroes and Other Slaves" in 1664, which not only perpetuated the slave status of those already in bondage, but expanded slave status to "whosoever freeborn woman shall intermarry with any slave."[55] Maryland, therefore, with its large estates and black slaves, looked very much like Virginia.

The Carolinas: Charles Town vs. Cracker Culture

Carolina, England's final seventeenth-century mainland slave society was established in 1663, when Charles II chartered the colony to eight wealthy proprietors. Their land grant encompassed the territories known today as North and South Carolina. Although Charles's aim was to create a strategic buffer zone between Spanish Florida and Virginia, Carolina's proprietors instead sought agricultural riches. Charles Town, now Charleston, South Carolina, founded in 1670, was populated largely by English Barbados planters and their slaves. Soon they turned portions of the sweltering Carolina seacoast into productive rice plantations; then, over the next century, indigo, a vegetable dye, became the planters' second most important cash crop thanks to the subsidies available in the mercantilist system.

From its outset, Carolina society was triracial: blacks eventually constituted a majority of Carolinians, followed by a mix of Indians and Europeans. White Carolinians allied with Cherokee Indians to soundly defeat the rival Yamasees and Creeks and pushed them westward. Planters failed in their attempts to enslave defeated Indians, turning instead to black slaves to cultivate the hot, humid rice fields. A 1712 South Carolina statute made slavery essentially permanent: "All negroes, mulattoes, mustizoes, or Indians, which at any time heretofore have been sold . . . and their children, are hereby made and declared slaves."[56] Slave life in the Carolinas differed from Virginia because the rice plantation system initially depended almost exclusively on an all-male workforce. Life in the rice and indigo fields was incredibly harsh, resembling the conditions in Barbados. The crops demanded full-time attention at harvest, requiring exhausting physical labor in the Carolina sun.

Yet colonial slave revolts (like the 1739 Stono revolt, which sent shock waves through the planter community) were exceptions because language barriers among the slaves, close and brutal supervision, a climate of repression, and a culture of subservience all combined to keep rebellions infrequent. The perceived threat of slave rebellions, nevertheless, hung over the southern coastal areas of Carolina, where slaves often outnumbered whites nine to one. Many planters literally removed themselves from the site of possible revolts by fleeing to the port cities in the summer. Charles Town soon became an island where planter families spent the "hot season" free from the plantations, swamps, and malaria of the lowlands. By mid-eighteenth century, Charles Town, with a population of eight thousand and major commercial connections, a lively social calendar of balls and cotillions, and even a paid symphony orchestra, was the leading city of the South.

Northern Carolinians differed socially, politically, economically, and culturally from their neighbors to the south. In 1729 disputes forced a split into two separate colonies. The northern part of the colonies was geographically and economically more isolated, and it developed more slowly than South Carolina. In the northeastern lowlands and Piedmont, North Carolina's economy turned immediately to tobacco, while a new ethnic and cultural wave trekked south from Pennsylvania into North Carolina via Virginia's Great Valley. German and Celtic (Scots-Irish) farmers added flavor to the Anglo and African stew of Carolina society. Germans who arrived were pious Quaker and Moravian farmers in search of opportunities to farm and market wood, leather, and iron handicrafts, whereas Celts (or Crackers, as they came to be known) were the wild and woolly frontiersmen who had fast worn out their welcome in the "civilized" areas of Pennsylvania and Virginia. Crackers answered their detractors by moving on, deeper and deeper into the forests of the Appalachian foothills and, eventually, the trans-Appalachian West. Such a jambalaya of humankind immediately made for political strife as eastern and western North Carolinians squared off time and again in disputes that often boiled down to planter-versus-small-farmer rivalries.

Life of the Common Colonials

By the mid-1700s, it was clear across the American colonies that the settlers had become increasingly less English. Travelers described Americans as coarse-looking country folk. Most colonials wore their hair long. Women and girls kept their hair covered with hats, hoods, and kerchiefs while men and boys tied their hair into queues until wigs came into vogue in the port cities. Colonials made their own clothes from linen (flax) and wool; every home had a spinning wheel and a loom, and women sewed and knitted constantly, since cotton cloth would not be readily available until the nineteenth century. Plentiful dyes like indigo, birch bark, and pokeberries made colorful shirts, pants, dresses, socks, and caps.

Americans grew their own food and ate a great deal of corn—roasted, boiled, and cooked into cornmeal bread and pancakes. Hearty vegetables like squash and beans joined apples, jam, and syrup on the dinner table. Men and boys hunted and fished; rabbit, squirrel, bear, and deer (venison) were common entrees. Pig raising became important, but beef cows (and milk) were scarce until the eighteenth century and beyond. Given the poor quality of water, many colonials drank cider, beer, and corn whiskey—even the children! As cities sprang up, the lack of convenient watering holes led owners to "water" their cattle with the runoff of breweries, yielding a disgusting variant of milk known as swill milk, which propagated childhood illnesses.

Even without swill milk, infant mortality was high, and any sickness usually meant suffering and, often, death. Colonials relied on folk medicine and Indian cures, including herbs, teas, honey, bark, and roots, supplemented with store-bought medicines. Doctors were few and far between. The American colonies had no medical school until the eve of the American Revolution, and veterinarians usually doubled as the town doctor, or vice versa. Into the vacuum of this absence of professional doctors stepped folk healers and midwives, "bone crackers" and bleeders. Going to a physician was usually the absolute last resort, since without anesthesia, any serious procedures would involve excruciating pain and extensive recovery. Women, especially, suffered during childbirth, and infants often had such high mortality rates that babies were not named until age two. Instead, mothers and fathers referred to the child as "the little visitor" or even "it." Despite the reality of this difficult life, it is worth noting that by 1774 American colonists already had attained a standard of living that far surpassed that found in most of the civilized parts of the modern world.

Far more than today, though, politics—and not the family—absorbed the attention of colonial men. Virtually anyone who either paid taxes or owned a minimum of property could vote for representation in both the upper and lower houses of the legislature, although in some colonies (Pennsylvania and New York) there was a higher property qualification required for the upper house than for the lower house. When it came to holding office, most districts required a candidate to have at least one hundred pounds in wealth or one hundred acres, but several colonies had no requirements for holding office. Put another way, American colonials took politics seriously and believed that virtually everyone could participate. Two colonies stand out as examples of the trends in North American politics by the late 1700s—Virginia and Maryland.

The growth and maturation of the societies in Virginia and Maryland established five important trends that would be repeated throughout much of America's colonial era. First, the sheer distance between the ruler and the governed—between the king and the colonies—made possible an extraordinary amount of independence among the Americans. In the case of Bacon's Rebellion, for example, the Virginia rebels acted on the principle that it is "easier to ask forgiveness than to seek permission," and were confident that the Crown would approve of their actions. Turmoil in England made communication even more difficult, and the instability in the English government—the temporary victory of Cromwell's Puritans, followed by the restoration of the Stuarts—merely made the colonial governments more self-reliant than ever.

Second, while the colonists gained a measure of independence through distance, they also gained political confidence and status through the acquisition of land. For immigrants who came from a nation where the scarcity of land marked those who owned it as gentlemen and placed them among the political elites, the abundance of soil in Virginia and Maryland made them the equals of the owners of manorial estates in England. It steadily but subtly became every citizen's job to ensure the protection of property rights for all citizens, undercutting from the outset the widespread and entrenched class system that characterized Europe.

Although not universal—Virginia had a powerful "cousinocracy"—nothing of the rigid French or English aristocracies constrained most Americans. To be sure, Virginia possessed a more pronounced social strata than Maryland (and certainly Massachusetts). Yet compared to Europe, there was more equality and less class distinction in America, even in the South.

Third, the precedent of rebellion against a government that did not carry out the most basic mandates—protecting life, property, and a certain degree of religious freedom (at least from the Church of England)—was established and supported by large numbers, if not the vast majority, of colonists. That view was tempered by the assumption that, again, such rebellion would not be necessary against an informed government. This explains, in part, Thomas Jefferson's inclusion in the Declaration of Independence the references to the fact that the colonists had petitioned not only the king, but Parliament as well, to no avail.

Fourth, a measure of religious toleration developed, although it was neither as broad as is often claimed nor did it originate in the charity of church leaders. Although Virginia Anglicans and Maryland Catholics built the skeleton of state-supported churches, labor problems forced each colony to abandon sectarian purity at an early stage to attract immigrants. Underlying presuppositions about religious freedom were narrowly focused on Christians and, in most colonies, usually Protestants. Had the colonists ever anticipated that Jews, Muslims, Buddhists, Hindus, or members of other non-Christian groups would constitute even a small minority in their region, even the most fiercely independent Protestants would have agreed to the establishment of a state church, as Massachusetts did from 1630 to 1830.

America's vast size contributed to a tendency toward "Live and let live" when it came to religion.[57] Dissidents always could move to uninhabited areas: certainly none of the denominations were open to evangelizing from their counterparts. Rather, the colonists embraced toleration, even if narrowly defined, because it affected a relatively cohesive group of Christian sects. Where differences that were potentially deeply divisive did exist, the separation caused by distance prevented one group from posing a threat to others.

Finally, the experiences in Virginia and Maryland foreshadowed events elsewhere when it came to interaction with the Indians. The survival of a poorly armed, ineptly organized colony in Jamestown surrounded by hostile natives requires more of an explanation than "white greed" provides. Just as Europeans practiced balance-of-power politics, so too the Indians found that the presence of several potential enemies on many sides required that they treat the whites as friends when necessary to balance the power of other Indians. To the Doeg Indians, for example, the English were no more of a threat than the Susquehannock. Likewise, English settlers had as much to fear from the French as they did the natives. Characterizing the struggle as one of whites versus Indians does not reflect the balance-of-power politics that every group in the New World struggled to maintain among its enemies.[58]

New England's Pilgrims and Puritans

Whereas gold provided the motivation for the colonization of Virginia, the settlers who traveled to Plymouth came for much different reasons.[59] The Puritans had witnessed a division in their ranks based on their approach to the Anglican Church. One group believed that not only should they remain in England, but that they also had a moral duty to purify the church from the inside. Others, however, had given up on Anglicanism. Labeled Separatists, they favored removing themselves from England entirely, and they defied the orders of the king by leaving for European Protestant nations. Their disobedience to royal decrees and British law often earned the Separatists persecution and even death.

In 1608 a group of 125 Separatists from Scrooby, in Nottinghamshire, slipped out of England for Holland. Among the most respected leaders of these "Pilgrims," as they later came to be known, was a sixteen-year-old boy named William Bradford. In Holland they faced no religious persecution, but as foreigners they found little work, and worse, Puritan children were exposed to the "great licentiousness" of Dutch youth. When few other English Separatists joined them, the prospects for establishing a strong Puritan community in Holland seemed remote. After receiving assurances from the king that they could exercise their religious views freely, they opened negotiations with one of the proprietors of the Virginia Company, Sir Edwin Sandys, about obtaining a grant in Virginia. Sandys cared little for Puritanism, but he needed colonists in the New World. Certainly the Pilgrims already had displayed courage and resourcefulness. He therefore allowed them a tract near the mouth of the Hudson River, which was located on the northernmost boundary of the Virginia grant. To raise capital, the Pilgrims employed the joint-stock company structure, which brought several non-Separatists into the original band of settlers. Sailing on the *Mayflower*, 35 of the original Pilgrims and 65 other colonists left the English harbor of Plymouth in September 1620, bound for the Hudson River. Blown off course, the Pilgrims reached the New World in November, some five hundred miles north of their intended location. They dropped anchor at Cape Cod Bay, at an area called Plymouth by John Smith.

Arriving at the wrong place, the colonists remained aboard their vessel while they considered their situation. They were not in Virginia, and had no charter to Plymouth. Any settlement could be perceived in England as defiance of the Crown. Bradford and the forty other adult men thus devised a document, before they even went ashore, to emphasize their allegiance to King James, to renounce any intention to create an independent republic, and to establish a civil government. It stated clearly that their purpose in sailing to Virginia was not for the purposes of rebellion but "for the glory of God, and advancement of the Christian faith, and honor of our king and country. . . ."[60] And while the Mayflower Compact provided for laws and the administration of the colony, it constituted more than a mere civil code. It pledged each of them "solemnly and mutually in the presence of God and one another" to "covenant and combine ourselves under a civil Body Politick" under "just and equal laws . . . [for the] furtherance of" the glory of God. To the Pilgrims, a just and equal society had to be grounded in religious faith. Developing along a parallel path to the concepts of government emerging in Virginia, the Mayflower Compact underscored the idea that government came from the governed—under God—and that the law treated all equally. But it also extended into civil affairs the concept of a church contact (or covenant), reinforcing the close connection between the role of the church and the state. Finally, it started to lay a foundation for future action against both the king of England and, eighty years after that, slavery by establishing basic principles in the contract. This constituted a critical development in an Anglo-European culture that increasingly emphasized written rights.

As one of the first acts of their new democracy, the colonists selected Bradford as governor. Then, having taken care of administrative matters, in late December 1620, the Pilgrims climbed out of their boats at Plymouth and settled at cleared land that may have been an Indian village years earlier. They had arrived too late in the year to plant, and like their countrymen farther south, the Pilgrims suffered during their first winter, with half the colony perishing. They survived with assistance from the local Indians, especially one named Squanto— "a spetiall instrument sent from God," as Bradford called him.[61] For all this they gave thanks to God, establishing what would become a national tradition.

The Pilgrims, despite their fame in the traditional Thanksgiving celebration and their Mayflower Compact, never achieved the material success of the Virginia colonists or their Massachusetts successors at Massachusetts Bay. Indeed, the Plymouth colony's population stagnated. Since the Separatists' religious views continued to meet a poor reception in England, no new infusions of people or ideas came from the Old World. Having settled in a relatively poor region, and lacking the excellent natural harbor of Boston, the Pilgrims never developed the fishing or trading business of their counterparts. But the Pilgrims rightly hold a place of high esteem in America history, largely because unlike the Virginia settlers, the Separatists braved the dangers and uncertainties of the voyage and settlement in the New World solely in the name of their Christian faith.

Other Puritans, though certainly not all of them Separatists, saw opportunities to establish their own settlements. They had particular incentives to do so after the ascension to the throne of England of Charles I in 1625. He was determined to restore Catholicism and eradicate religious dissidents. By that time, the Puritans had emerged as a powerful merchant group in English society, with their economic power translating into seats in Parliament. Charles reacted by dissolving Parliament in 1629. Meanwhile, a group of Dorchester businessmen had provided the perfect vehicle for the Puritans to undertake an experiment in the New World.

In 1623 the Dorchester group established a small fishing post at Cape Ann, near present-day Gloucester, Massachusetts. After the colony proved a dismal economic failure, the few settlers who had lived at Cape Ann moved inland to Salem, and a new patent, granted in 1628, provided incentives for a new group of emigrants, including John Endicott, to settle in Salem. Ultimately, the New England Company, as it was called, obtained a royal charter in 1629. Stockholders in the company elected a General Court, which chose the governor and his eighteen assistants. Those prominent in founding the company saw the Salem and Cape Ann areas as opportunities for establishing Christian missions.

The 1629 charter did not require the company's headquarters to be in London, as the Virginia Company's had. Several Puritans, including John Winthrop, expressed their willingness to move to the trading colony if they could also move the colony's administration to Massachusetts. Stockholders unwilling to move to the New World resigned, and the Puritans gained control of the company, whereupon they chose John Winthrop as the governor.[62] Called the Moses of the great Puritan exodus, Winthrop was Cambridge educated and, because he was an attorney, relatively wealthy. He was also deeply committed to the Puritan variant of Christianity. Winthrop suffered from the Puritan dilemma, in that he knew that all things came from God, and therefore had to be good. Therefore all things were made for man to enjoy, except that man could not enjoy things too much lest he risk putting material things above God. In short, Puritans had to be "in the world but not of it."

Puritans, far from wearing drab clothes and avoiding pleasure, enjoyed all things. Winthrop himself loved pipe smoking and shooting. Moreover, Puritan ministers "were the leaders in every field of intellectual advance in New England."[63] Their moral codes in many ways were not far from modern standards.[64]

A substantial number of settlers joined Winthrop, with eleven ships leaving for Massachusetts that year. When the Puritans finally arrived, Winthrop delivered a sermon before the colonists disembarked. It resounded with many of the sentiments of the Plymouth Pilgrims: "Wee must Consider that wee shall be as a City upon a Hill, the eyes of all people are upon us." Winthrop wanted the Puritans to see themselves as examples and, somewhat typical of his day, made dire predictions of their fate if they failed to live up to God's standard.

The Massachusetts Bay colony benefited from changes in the religious situation in England, where a new policy of forcing Puritans to comply with Anglican ceremonies was in effect. Many Puritans decided to leave England rather than tolerate such persecution, and they emigrated to Massachusetts in what was called the Great Migration, pulled by reports of "a store of blessings."[65] This constant arrival of new groups of relatively prosperous colonists kept the colony well funded and its labor force full (unlike the southern colonies). By 1640, the population of Massachusetts Bay and its inland settlements numbered more than ten thousand.

Puritan migrants brought with them an antipathy and distrust of the Stuart monarchy (and governmental power in general) that would have great impact in both the long and short term. Government in the colony, as elsewhere in most of English America, assumed a democratic bent. Originally, the General Court, created as Massachusetts Bay's first governing body, was limited to freemen, but after 1629, when only the Puritan stockholders remained, that meant Puritan male church members. Clergymen were not allowed to hold public office, but through the voting of the church members, the clergy gained exceptional influence. A Puritan hierarchy ran the administrative posts, and although non-Puritan immigrant freemen obtained property and other rights, only the church members received voting privileges. In 1632, however, the increasing pressure of additional settlers forced changes in the minority-run General Court. The right to elect the governor and deputy governor was expanded to all freemen, turning the governor and his assistants into a colonial parliament.[66]

Political tensions in Massachusetts reflected the close interrelationship Puritans felt between civil and religious life. Rigorous tests existed for admission to a Puritan church congregation: individuals had to show evidence of a changed life, relate in an interview process their conversion experience, and display knowledge of scripture. On the surface, this appeared to place extraordinary power in the hands of the authorities, giving them (if one was a believer) the final word on who was, and was not, saved. But in reality, church bodies proved extremely lenient in accepting members. After all, who could deny another's face-to-face meeting with the Almighty? Local records showed a wide range of opinions on the answer.[67] One solution, the "Halfway Covenant," allowed third-generation Puritan children to be baptized if their parents were baptized.[68]

Before long, of course, many insincere or more worldly colonists had gained membership, and with the expansion of church membership, the right to participate in the polity soon spread, and by 1640 almost all families could count one adult male church member (and therefore a voter) in their number. The very fact that so many people came, however tangentially, under the rubric of local—but not centralized—church authority reinforced civic behavior with a Christian moral code, although increasingly the laity tended to be more spiritually conservative than the clergy.[69]

Local autonomy of churches was maintained through the congregational system of organization. Each church constituted the ultimate authority in scriptural doctrine. That occasionally led to unorthodox or even heretical positions developing, but usually the doctrinal agreement between Puritans on big issues was so widespread that few serious problems arose. When troublemakers did appear, as when Roger Williams arrived in Massachusetts in 1631, or when Anne Hutchinson challenged the hierarchy in 1636, Winthrop and the General Court usually dispatched them in short order.[70] Moreover, the very toleration often (though certainly not universally) exhibited by the Puritans served to reinforce and confirm "the colonists in their belief that New England was a place apart, a bastion of consistency."[71]

There were limits to toleration, of course. In 1692, when several young Salem girls displayed physical "fits" and complained of being hexed by witches, Salem village was thrown into an uproar. A special court convened to try the witches. Although the girls initially accused only one as a witch (Tituba, a black slave woman), the accusations and charges multiplied, with 150 Salemites eventually standing accused. Finally, religious and secular leaders expressed objections, and the trials ceased as quickly as they had begun. Historians have subsequently ascribed the hysteria of the Salem witch trials to sexism, religious rigidity, and even the fungus of a local plant, but few have admitted that to the Puritans of Massachusetts, the devil and witchcraft were quite real, and physical manifestations of evil spirits were viewed as commonplace occurrences.

The Pequot War and the American Militia System

The Puritan's religious views did not exempt them from conflict with the Indians, particularly the Pequot Indians of coastal New England. Puritan/Pequot interactions followed a cyclical pattern that would typify the next 250 years of Indian-white relations, in the process giving birth to the American militia system, a form of warfare quite unlike that found in Europe.

Initial contacts led to cross-acculturation and exchange, but struggles over land ensued, ending in extermination, extirpation, or assimilation of the Indians. Sparked by the murder of a trader, the Pequot War commenced in July of 1636. In the assault on the Pequot fort on the Mystic River in 1637, troops from Connecticut and Massachusetts, along with Mohican and Narragansett Indian allies, attacked and destroyed a stronghold surrounded by a wooden palisade, killing some four hundred Pequots in what was, to that time, one of the most stunning victories of English settlers over Indians ever witnessed.

One important result of the Pequot War was the Indians' realization that, in the future, they would have to unify to fight the Englishmen. This would ultimately culminate in the 1675–76 war led by Metacomet—known in New England history as King Philip's War—which resulted in a staggering defeat for northeastern coastal tribes. A far-reaching result of these conflicts was the creation of the New England militia system.

The Puritan—indeed, English—distrust of the mighty Stuart kings manifested itself in a fear of standing armies. Under the colonial militia system, much of the population armed itself and prepared to fight on short notice. All men aged sixteen to sixty served without pay in village militia companies; they brought their own weapons and supplies and met irregularly to train and drill. One advantage of the militia companies was that some of their members were crack shots: as an eighteenth-century American later wrote a British friend,

> In this country . . . the great quantities of game, the many lands, and the great privileges of killing make the Americans the best marksmen in the world, and thousands support their families by the same, particularly the riflemen on the frontiers. . . . In marching through the woods one thousand of these riflemen would cut to pieces ten thousand of your best troops.[72]

But the American militia system also had many disadvantages. Insubordination was the inevitable result of trying to turn individualistic Americans into obedient soldiers. Militiamen did not want to fight anywhere but home. Some deserted in the middle of a campaign because of spring plowing or because their time was up. But the most serious shortcoming of the militia system was that it gave Americans a misguided impression that they did not need a large, well-trained standing army.

The American soldier was an amateur, an irregular combatant who despised the professional military. Even 140 years after the Pequot War, the Continental Congress still was suspicious that a professional military, "however necessary it may be, is always dangerous to the liberties of the people. . . . Standing armies in time of peace are inconsistent with the principles of republican government."[73]

Where muskets and powder could handle—or, at least, suppress—most of the difficulties with Indians, there were other, more complex issues raised by a rogue minister and an independent-minded woman. Taken together, the threats posed by Roger Williams and Anne Hutchinson may have presented as serious a menace to Massachusetts as the Pequots and other tribes put together.

Roger Williams and the Limits of Religious Toleration

The first serious challenge to the unity of state and religion in Massachusetts came from a Puritan dissident named Roger Williams. A man Bradford described as "godly and zealous," Williams had moved to Salem, where he served as minister after 1635. Gradually he became more vocal in his opinion that church and state needed to be completely separated. Forced religion, he argued, "Stinks in God's nostrils." Williams had other unusual views, but his most dangerous notion was his interpretation of determining who was saved and thus worthy of taking communion with others who were sanctified. Williams demanded ever-increasing evidence of a person's salvation before taking communion with him—eventually to the point where he distrusted the salvation of his own wife. At that point, Williams completed the circle: no one, he argued, could determine who was saved and who was damned.

Because church membership was so finely intertwined with political rights, this created thorny problems. Williams argued that since no one could determine salvation, all had to be treated (for civil purposes) as if they were children of God, ignoring New Testament teaching on subjecting repeat offenders who were nevertheless thought to be believers to disfellowship, so as not to destroy the church body with the individual's unrepentant sin. Such a position struck at the authority of Winthrop, the General Court, and the entire basis of citizenship in Massachusetts, and the magistrates in Boston could not tolerate Williams's open rebellion for long. Other congregations started to exert economic pressure on Salem, alienating Williams from his own church. After weakening Williams sufficiently, the General Court gave him six weeks to depart the colony. Winthrop urged him to "steer my course to Narragansett Bay and the Indians."[74]

Unable to stay, and encouraged to leave, in 1636 Williams founded Providence, Rhode Island, which the orthodox Puritans derisively called "Rogues Island" or "the sewer of New England."[75] After eight years, he obtained a charter from England establishing Rhode Island as a colony. Church and state were separated there and all religions—at least all Christian religions—tolerated. Williams's influence on religious toleration was nevertheless minimal, and his halo, "ill fitting." Only a year after Williams relocated, another prominent dissident moved to Rhode Island. Anne Hutchinson, a mother of fifteen, arrived in Boston in 1631 with her husband, William ("a man of mild temper and weak parts, wholly guided by his wife," deplored Winthrop). A follower of John Cotton, a local minister, Hutchinson gained influence as a Bible teacher, and she held prayer groups in her home. She embraced a potentially heretical religious position known as antinomianism, which held that there was no relationship between works and faith, and thus the saved had no obligation to follow church laws—only the moral judgment of the individual counted. Naturally, the colonial authorities saw in Hutchinson a threat to their authority, but in the broader picture she potentially opened the door to all sorts of civil mischief. In 1636, therefore, the General Court tried her for defaming the clergy—though not, as it might have, for a charge of heresy, which carried a penalty of death at the stake. A bright and clever woman, Hutchinson sparred with Winthrop and others until she all but confessed to hearing voices. The court evicted her from Massachusetts, and in 1637 she and some seventy-five supporters moved to Rhode Island. In 1643, Indians killed Hutchinson and most of her family.

The types of heresies introduced by both Williams and Hutchinson constituted particularly destructive doctrinal variants, including a thoroughgoing selfishness and rejection of doctrinal control by church hierarchies. Nevertheless, the experience of Hutchinson reaffirmed Rhode Island's reputation as a colony of religious toleration. Confirming the reality of that toleration, a royal charter in 1663 stated, "No person . . . shall be in any wise molested, punished, disquieted, or called in question, for any differences in opinion in matters of religion [but that all] may from time to time, and at all times hereafter, freely and fully have and enjoy his and their judgments and consciences, in matters of religious concernments." Rhode Island therefore led the way in establishing toleration as a principle, creating a type of "religious competition."[76] Quakers and Baptists were accepted. This was no small matter. In Massachusetts, religious deviants were expelled; and if they persisted upon returning, they faced flogging, having their tongues bored with hot irons, or even execution, as happened to four Quakers who were repeat violators. Yet the Puritans "made good everything Winthrop demanded."[77] They could have dominated the early state completely, but nevertheless gradually and voluntarily permitted the structures of government to be changed to the extent that they no longer controlled it.

Rhode Island, meanwhile, remained an island of religious refugees in a Puritan sea, as new Puritan settlers moved into the Connecticut River Valley in the 1630s, attracted by the region's rich soil. Thomas Hooker, a Cambridge minister, headed a group of families who moved to an area some hundred miles southwest of Boston on the Connecticut River, establishing the town of Hartford in 1635; in 1636 a colony called New Haven was established on the coast across from Long Island as a new beacon of religious purity. In the Fundamental Articles of New

Haven (1639), the New Haven community forged a closer state-church relation-ship than existed in Massachusetts, including tax support for ministers. In 1662 the English government issued a royal charter to the colony of Connecticut that incorporated New Haven, Hartford, Windsor, New London, and Middletown.

The Council for New England, meanwhile, had granted charters to still other lands north of Massachusetts: Sir Ferdinando Gorges and John Mason received territory that comprised Maine and New Hampshire in 1629, although settlements had appeared throughout the region during the decade. Gorges acquired the Maine section, enlarged by a grant in 1639, and after battling claims from Massachusetts, Maine was declared a proprietary colony from 1677 to 1691, when it was joined to Massachusetts until admitted to the Union in 1820 as a state. Mason had taken the southern section (New Hampshire), which in 1679 became a royal province, with the governor and council appointed by the king and an assembly elected by the freemen.

Unique Middle Colonies: New York, New Jersey, and Quaker Pennsylvania

Sitting between Virginia, Maryland, and the Carolinas to the south and New England to the north was an assortment of colonies later known as the middle colonies. Over time, the grants that extended from Rhode Island to Maryland assumed a character that certainly was not Puritan, but did not share the slave-based economic systems of the South.

Part of the explanation for the differences in the region came from the early Dutch influence in the area of New Amsterdam. Following the explorations of Henry Hudson in 1609, the West India Company—already prominent in the West Indies—moved up the Hudson Valley and established Fort Orange in 1624 on the site of present-day Albany. Traveling to the mouth of the Hudson, the Dutch settled at a site called New Amsterdam, where the director of the company, Peter Minuit, consummated his legendary trade with the Indians, giving them blankets and other goods worth less than a hundred dollars in return for Manhattan.

The Dutch faced a problem much like that confronting the French: populating the land. To that end, the company's charter authorized the grant of large acreages to anyone who would bring fifty settlers with him. Few large estates appeared, however. Governor Minuit lost his post in 1631, then returned to the Delaware River region with a group of Swedish settlers to found New Sweden. Despite the relatively powerful navy, the Dutch colonies lacked the steady flow of immigrants necessary to ensure effective defense against the other Europeans who soon reached their borders. The English offered the first, and last, threat to New Amsterdam.

Located between the northern and southern English colonies, the Dutch territory provided a haven to pirates and smugglers. King Charles II sought to eliminate the problem by granting to his brother, the Duke of York (later James II), all of the land between Maryland and Connecticut. A fleet dispatched in 1664 took

New Amsterdam easily when the Dutch governor, Peter Stuyvesant, failed to mobilize the population of only fifteen hundred. The surrender generously permitted the Dutch to remain in the colony, but they were no match for the more numerous English, who renamed the city New York. James empowered a governor and council to administer the colony, and New York prospered. Despite a population mix that included Swedes, Dutch, Indians, English, Germans, French, and African slaves, New York enjoyed relative peace.

The Duke of York dispensed with some of his holdings between the Hudson and Delaware Rivers, called New Jersey, giving the land to Sir George Carteret and John (Lord) Berkeley. New Jersey offered an attractive residence for oppressed, unorthodox Puritans because the colony established religious freedom, and land rights were made available as well. In 1674 the proprietors sold New Jersey to representatives of an even more unorthodox Christian group, the Society of Friends, called Quakers. Known for their social habits of refusing to tip their hats to landed gentlemen and for their nonviolence, the Quakers' theology evolved from the teachings of George Fox. Their name came from the shaking and contortions they displayed while in the throes of religious inspiration. Highly democratic in their church government, Quakers literally spoke in church as the Spirit moved them.

William Penn, a wealthy landlord and son of an admiral, had joined the faith, putting him at odds with his father and jeopardizing his inheritance. But upon his father's death, Penn inherited family lands in both England and Ireland, as well as a debt from King Charles II, which the monarch paid in a grant of territory located between New York and Maryland. Penn became proprietor and intended for the colony to make money. He advertised for settlers to migrate to Pennsylvania using multilingual newspaper ads that rival some of the slickest modern Madison Avenue productions. Penn also wanted to create a "holy experiment" in Pennsylvania, and during a visit to America in 1682 designed a spacious city for his colony called Philadelphia (brotherly love). Based on experience with the London fire of 1666, and the subsequent plan to rebuild the city, Penn laid out Philadelphia in squares with generous dimensions. An excellent organizer, Penn negotiated with the Indians, whom he treated with respect. His strategy of inviting all settlers brought talent and skills to the colony, and his treatment of the Indians averted any major conflict with them.

Penn retained complete power through his proprietorship, but in 1701, pressure, especially from the southern parts of the colony, persuaded him to agree to the Charter of Liberties. The charter provided for a representative assembly that limited the authority of the proprietor; permitted the lower areas to establish their own colony (which they did in 1703, when Delaware was formed); and ensured religious freedom.

Penn never profited from his proprietorship, and he served time in a debtors' prison in England before his death in 1718. Still, his vision and managerial skill in creating Pennsylvania earned him high praise from a prominent historian of American business, J.R.T. Hughes, who observed that Penn rejected expedient considerations in favor of principle at every turn. His ideals, more than his business sense, reflected his "straightforward belief in man's goodness, and in his abilities to know and understand the good, the true and beautiful." Over the years, Pennsylvania's Quakers would lead the charge in freeing slaves, establishing antislavery societies even in the South.

The Glorious Revolution in England and America, 1688–89

The epic story of the seventeenth-century founding and development of colonial America ended on a crucial note, with American reaction to England's Glorious Revolution. The story of abuses of power by Stuart kings was well known to Americans. Massachusetts Puritans, after all, had fled the regime of Charles I, leaving brethren in England to wage the English Civil War. The return of a chastened Charles II from French exile in 1660 did not settle the conflict between Parliament and the king.

When James II ascended to the throne in 1685, he decided to single-handedly reorganize colonial administration. First, he violated constitutionalism and sanctity of contract by recalling the charters of all of the New England and Middle colonies—Massachusetts Bay, Pennsylvania, New York, and New Jersey—and the compact colonies Plymouth, Rhode Island, and Connecticut. In 1686 he created the so-called Dominion of New England, a centralized political state that his appointee, Governor Edmund Andros, was to rule from Boston, its capital city. James's plan for a Dominion of New England was a disaster from the start. Upon arrival, Andros dismissed the colonial legislatures, forbade town meetings, and announced he was taking personal command of the village militias. In reality, he did no such thing, never leaving the city limits of Boston.

In the meantime, the countryside erupted in a series of revolts called the colonial rebellions. In Maryland's famed Protestant Revolt, discontented Protestants protested what they viewed as a Catholic oligarchy, and in New York, anti-Catholic sentiments figured in a revolt against the dominion of New England led by Jacob Leisler. Leisler's Rebellion installed its namesake in the governorship for one year, in 1689. Soon, however, English officials arrived to restore their rule and hanged Leisler and his son-in-law, drawing-and-quartering them as the law of treason required. But Andros's government was on its last leg. Upon hearing of the English Whigs' victory over James II, colonials arrested him and put him on a ship bound for the mother country.

James II's plans for restoring an all-powerful monarchy dissolved between 1685 and 1688. A fervent opposition had arisen among those calling themselves Whigs, a derogatory term meaning "outlaw" that James's foes embraced with pride. There began a second English civil war of the seventeenth century—between Whigs and Tories—but this time there was little bloodshed. James was exiled while Parliament made arrangements with his Protestant daughter, Mary, and her husband, William, of the Dutch house of Orange, to take the crown. William and Mary ascended the throne of England in 1689, but only after agreeing to a contract, the Declaration of Rights. In this historic document, William and

Mary confirmed that the monarch was not supreme but shared authority with the English legislature and the courts. Moreover, they acknowledged the House of Commons as the source of all revenue bills (the power of the purse) and agreed to acknowledge the rights to free speech and petition. Included were provisions requiring due process of law and forbidding excessive bail and cruel and unusual punishment. Finally, the Declaration of Rights upheld the right of English Protestants to keep and bear arms, and forbade "standing armies in time of peace" unless by permission of Parliament.

The resemblance of this Declaration and Bill of Rights to the eighteenth-century American Declaration of Independence, Articles of Confederation, Constitution, and Bill of Rights is striking, and one could argue that the Americans were more radicalized by the Glorious Revolution than the English. In England, the Glorious Revolution was seen as an ending; in America, the hatred and distrust sown by the Stuart kings was reaped by subsequent monarchs, no matter how "constitutional" their regimes. Radical Whig ideas contained in the Glorious Revolution—the pronounced hatred of centralized political, religious, economic, and military authority—germinated in America long after they had subsided in England.

By 1700, then, three major themes characterized the history of the early English colonies. First, religion played a crucial role in not only the search for liberty, but also in the institutions designed to ensure its continuation. From the Mayflower Compact to the Charter of Liberties, colonists saw a close connection between religious freedom and personal liberty. This fostered a multiplicity of denominations, which, at a time when people literally killed over small differences in the interpretation of scripture, "made it necessary to seek a basis for political unity" outside the realm of religion.[78]

A second factor, economic freedom—particularly that associated with land ownership—and the high value placed on labor throughout the American colonies formed the basis of a widespread agreement about the need to preserve private property rights. The early colonists came to the conclusion that the Indians' view of land never could be harmonized with their own, and they understood that one view or the other had to prevail.[79] They saw no inherent contradiction in taking land from people who did not accept European-style contracts while they continued to highly value their own property rights.

Finally, the English colonies developed political institutions similar to those in England, but with an increased awareness of the need for individuals to have protection from their governments. As that understanding of political rights percolated up through the colonial governments, the colonies themselves started to generate their own aura of independent policy-making processes. Distance from England ensured that, barring significant British efforts to keep the colonies under the royal thumb, the colonies would construct their own self-reliant governments. And it was exactly that evolution that led them to independence.

CHAPTER TWO

Colonial Adolescence, 1707–63

The Inability to Remain European

England's American colonies represented only a small part of the British Empire by the late 1700s, but their vast potential for land and agricultural wealth seemed limitless. Threats still remained, especially from the French in Canada and Indians on the frontier, but few colonists saw England herself as posing any threat at the beginning of the century. Repeatedly, English colonists stated their allegiance to the Crown and their affirmation of their own rights as English subjects. Even when conflicts arose between colonists and their colonial governors, Americans appealed to the king to enforce those rights against their colonial administrators—not depose them.

Between 1707 (when England, Scotland, and Wales formed the United Kingdom) and 1763, however, changes occurred within the empire itself that forced an overhaul of imperial regulations. The new policies convinced the thirteen American colonies that England did not see them as citizens, but as subjects—in the worst sense of the word. By attempting to foster dependence among British colonists throughout the world on each other and, ultimately, on the mother country, England only managed to pit America against other parts of the empire. At the same time, despite their disparate backgrounds and histories, the American colonies started to share a common set of understandings about liberty and their position in the empire. On every side, then, the colonies that eventually made up the United States began to develop internal unity and an independent attitude.

Time Line

1707: England, Wales, and Scotland unite into the United Kingdom (Great Britain)

1702–13: Queen Anne's War

1714–27: George I's reign

1727–60: George II's reign
  1733: Georgia founded
1734–41: First Great Awakening
  1735: John Peter Zenger Trial
1744–48: King George's War
  1754: Albany Congress
1754–63: French and Indian War
  1760: George III accedes to throne
  1763: Proclamation of 1763

Shaping "Americanness"

In *Democracy in America,* the brilliant French observer Alexis de Tocqueville predicted that a highly refined culture was unlikely to evolve in America, largely because of its "lowly" colonial origins. The "intermingling of classes and constant rising and sinking" of individuals in an egalitarian society, Tocqueville wrote, had a detrimental effect on the arts: painting, literature, music, theater, and education. In place of high or refined mores, Tocqueville concluded, Americans had built a democratic culture that was highly accessible but ultimately lacking in the brilliance that characterized European art forms.[1]

Certainly, some colonial Americans tried to emulate Europe, particularly when it came to creating institutions of higher learning. Harvard College, founded in 1636, was followed by William and Mary (1693), Yale (1701), Princeton (1746), the College of Philadelphia (University of Pennsylvania) (1740), and—between 1764 and 1769—King's College (Columbia), Brown, Queen's College (Rutgers), and Dartmouth. Yet from the beginning, these schools differed sharply from their European progenitors in that they were founded by a variety of Protestant sects, not a state church, and though tied to religious denominations, they were nevertheless relatively secular. Harvard, for example, was founded to train clergy, and yet by the end of the colonial era only a quarter of its graduates became ministers; the rest pursued careers in business, law, medicine, politics, and teaching. A few schools, such as the College of New Jersey (later Princeton), led by the Reverend John Witherspoon, bucked the trend: Witherspoon transformed Princeton into a campus much more oriented toward religious and moral philosophy, all the while charging it with a powerful revolutionary fervor.[2]

Witherspoon's Princeton was swimming against the tide, however. Not only were most curricula becoming more secular, but they were also more down to earth and "applied." Colonial colleges slighted the dead languages Latin and Greek by introducing French and German; modern historical studies complemented and sometimes replaced ancient history. The proliferation of colleges (nine in America) meant access for more middle-class youths (such as John Adams, a Massachusetts farm boy who studied at Harvard). To complete this democratization process, appointed boards of trustees, not the faculty or the church, governed American universities.

Early American science also reflected the struggles faced by those who sought a more pragmatic knowledge. For example, John Winthrop Jr., the son of the Massachusetts founder, struggled in vain to conduct pure research and bring his scientific career to the attention of the European intellectual community. As the first American member of the Royal Society of London, Winthrop wrote countless letters abroad and even sent specimens of rattlesnakes and other indigenous American flora and fauna, which received barely a passing glance from European scientists. More successful was Benjamin Franklin, the American scientist who applied his research in meteorology and electricity to invent the lightning rod, as well as bifocals and the Franklin Stove. Americans wanted the kind of science that would heat their homes and improve their eyesight, not explain the origins of life in the universe.

Colonial art, architecture, drama, and music also reflected American practicality and democracy spawned in a frontier environment. Artists found their only market for paintings in portraiture and, later, patriot art. Talented painters like John Singleton Copley and Benjamin West made their living painting the likenesses of colonial merchants, planters, and their families; eventually both sailed for Europe to pursue purer artistic endeavors. American architecture never soared to magnificence, though a few public buildings, colleges, churches, and private homes reflected an aesthetic influenced by classical motifs and Georgian styles. Drama, too, struggled. Puritan Massachusetts prohibited theater shows (the "Devil's Workshop"), whereas thespians in Philadelphia, Williamsburg, and Charleston performed amateurish productions of Shakespeare and contemporary English dramas. Not until Royall Tyler tapped the patriot theme (and the comic potential of the Yankee archetype) in his 1789 production of *The Contrast* would American playwrights finally discover their niche, somewhere between high and low art.

In eighteenth century Charleston, Boston, and Philadelphia, the upper classes could occasionally hear Bach and Mozart performed by professional orchestras. Most musical endeavor, however, was applied to religion, where church hymns were sung a cappella and, occasionally, to the accompaniment of a church organ. Americans customized and syncopated hymns, greatly aggravating pious English churchmen. Reflecting the most predominant musical influence in colonial America, the folk idiom of Anglo, Celtic, and African emigrants, American music already had coalesced into a base upon which new genres of church and secular music—gospel, field songs, and white folk ballads—would ultimately emerge.

Colonial literature likewise focused on religion or otherwise addressed the needs of common folk. This pattern was set with Bradford's *Of Plymouth Plantation,* which related the exciting story of the Pilgrims with an eye to the all-powerful role of God in shaping their destiny. Anne Bradstreet, an accomplished seventeenth-century colonial poet who continued to be popular after her death, also conveyed religious themes and emphasized divine inspiration of human events. Although literacy was widespread, Americans read mainly the Bible, political tracts, and how-to books on farming, mechanics, and moral improvement—

not Greek philosophers or the campaigns of Caesar. Benjamin Franklin's *Autobiography* is a classic example of the American penchant for pragmatic literature that continues to this day. Franklin wrote his *Autobiography* during the pre-Revolutionary era, though it was not published until the nineteenth century. Several generations of American schoolchildren grew up on these tales of his youthful adventures and early career, culminating with his gaining fame as a Pennsylvania printer, writer, scientist, diplomat, and patriot politician. Franklin's "13 Virtues"—Honesty, Thrift, Devotion, Faithfulness, Trust, Courtesy, Cleanliness, Temperance, Work, Humility, and so on—constituted a list of personal traits aspired to by virtually every Puritan, Quaker, or Catholic in the colonies.[3]

Franklin's saga thereby became the first major work in a literary genre that would define Americanism—the rags-to-riches story and the self-improvement guide rolled into one. Franklin's other great contribution to American folk literature, *Poor Richard's Almanac,* provided an affordable complement to the *Autobiography. Poor Richard* was a simply written magazine featuring weather forecasts, crop advice, predictions and premonitions, witticisms, and folksy advice on how to succeed and live virtuously.[4]

Common Life in the Early Eighteenth Century

Life in colonial America was as coarse as the physical environment in which it flourished, so much so that English visitors expressed shock at the extent to which emigrants had been transformed in the new world. Many Americans lived in one-room farmhouses, heated only by a Franklin stove, with clothes hung on wall pegs and few furnishings. "Father's chair" was often the only genuine chair in a home, with children relegated to rough benches or to rugs thrown on the wooden floors.

This rugged lifestyle was routinely misunderstood by visitors as "Indianization," yet in most cases, the process was subtle. Trappers had already adopted moccasins, buckskins, and furs, and adapted Indian methods of hauling hides or goods over rough terrain with the travois, a triangular-shaped and easily constructed sled pulled by a single horse. Indians, likewise, adopted white tools, firearms, alcohol, and even accepted English religion, making the acculturation process entirely reciprocal. Non-Indians incorporated Indian words (especially proper names) into American English and adopted aspects of Indian material culture. They smoked tobacco, grew and ate squash and beans, dried venison into jerky, boiled lobsters and served them up with wild rice or potatoes on the side. British-Americans cleared heavily forested land by girdling trees, then slashing and burning the dead timber—practices picked up from the Indians, despite the myth of the ecologically friendly natives.[5] Whites copied Indians in traveling via snowshoes, bullboat, and dugout canoe. And colonial Americans learned quickly—through harsh experience—how to fight like the Indians.[6]

Even while Indianizing their language, British colonists also adopted French, Spanish, German, Dutch, and African words from areas where those languages were spoken, creating still new regional accents that evolved in

New England and the southern tidewater. Environment also influenced accents, producing the flat, unmelodic, understated, and functional midland American drawl that Europeans found incomprehensible. Americans prided themselves on innovative spellings, stripping the excess baggage off English words, exchanging "color" for "colour," "labor" for "labour," or otherwise respelled words in harder American syllables, as in "theater" for "theatre." This new brand of English was so different that around the time of the American Revolution, a young New Englander named Noah Webster began work on a dictionary of American English, which he completed in 1830.

Only a small number of colonial Americans went on to college (often in Great Britain), but increasing numbers studied at public and private elementary schools, raising the most literate population on earth. Americans' literacy was widespread, but it was not deep or profound. Most folks read a little and not much more. In response, a new form of publishing arose to meet the demands of this vast, but minimally literate, populace: the newspaper. Early newspapers came in the form of broadsides, usually distributed and posted in the lobby of an inn or saloon where one of the more literate colonials would proceed to read a story aloud for the dining or drinking clientele. Others would chime in with editorial comments during the reading, making for a truly democratic and interactive forum.[7] Colonial newspapers contained a certain amount of local information about fires, public drunkenness, arrests, and political events, more closely resembling today's *National Enquirer* than the *New York Times*.

Americans' fascination with light or practical reading meant that hardback books, treatises, and the classics—the mainstay of European booksellers—were replaced by cheaply bound tracts, pamphlets, almanacs, and magazines. Those Americans interested in political affairs displayed a hearty appetite for plainly written radical Whig political tracts that emphasized the legislative authority over that of an executive, and that touted the participation of free landholders in government. And, of course, the Bible was found in nearly every cottage.

Democratization extended to the professions of law and medicine—subsequently, some would argue, deprofessionalizing them. Unlike British lawyers, who were formally trained in English courts and then compartmentalized into numerous specialties, American barristers learned on the job and engaged in general legal practices. The average American attorney served a brief, informal apprenticeship; bought three or four good law books (enough to fill two saddlebags, it was said); and then, literally, hung out his shingle. If he lacked legal skills and acumen, the free market would soon seal his demise.[8]

Unless schooled in Europe, colonial physicians and midwives learned on the job, with limited supervision. Once on their own they knew no specialization; surgery, pharmacy, midwifery, dentistry, spinal adjustment, folk medicine, and quackery were all characteristic of democratized professional medical practitioners flourishing in a free market.[9] In each case, the professions reflected the American insistence that their tools—law, medicine, literature—emphasize application over theory.

Religion's First Great Awakening

A free market of ideas benefited American colonists in religion too. Affairs of the spirit in the English colonies, where religion was varied, unregulated, and enthusiastic, differed from those of the mother country, with its formality and stiffness. Sects multiplied, split apart into new divisions, and multiplied some more, due in part to the Protestant/Puritan emphasis on individual Bible reading and in part because of the congregational nature of the churches. Although Virginia, South Carolina, Connecticut, and Massachusetts retained official churches in varying degrees, the decentralization of religious denominations made them impossible to control. American Baptist ministers, for example, required no formal training in theology, much less a formal degree in divinity, to preach the Gospel. Instead, they were "called" to the pulpit, as were many new Methodists, radical Presbyterians, and other enthusiastic men of God. Both the presbytery system, which constituted a top-down hierarchical structure, and the Baptists' congregational organization of churches (a bottom-up arrangement) met different needs of saint and sinner alike, all the while rejecting Anglican hierarchical control.[10] American preachers displayed a thorough anti-intellectual bent in which sermons replaced written lectures with a down-home, oratorical religious style. Itinerant preachers roamed New England, western Pennsylvania, and the Piedmont and Appalachian frontiers, spreading the Word.[11]

A major source of what Americans today call old-time religion originated in the First Great Awakening work of clergymen Jonathan Edwards and George Whitefield. At first glance, Edwards seems an unlikely candidate for delivering fire and brimstone sermons. Born in Connecticut in 1703, the third-generation Puritan was a brilliant, deep-thinking philosopher and theologian. After his 1720 graduation from Yale, he coupled a rational defense of biblical doctrine with a profoundly mystical teaching style that his Presbyterian parishioners found compelling. Edwards and others inspired unprecedented religious fervor in Massachusetts in 1735.

When English Methodist George Whitefield—as much a showman as preacher—arrived on American shores in 1741, American ministers had already seeded the ground for the religious revival known as the First Great Awakening. Essentially, this movement was characterized by tremendous religious growth and enthusiasm, the first such upsurge since the original Puritan migration a hundred years earlier. As the waves of the awakening spanned America's eastern shore, church attendance soared and ministers like Edwards and Whitefield hosted open air camp meetings to exhort true believers to accept the Lord and avoid the flames of hell. Throughout the Connecticut River Valley thousands flocked to the glow of this New Light Christianity, as it was called, camping out in the open air and enjoying the fellowship of their fellow devotees.

George Whitefield's dramatic preaching both frightened and inspired his audiences. Literally acting out biblical stories on stage, playing each of the major parts himself, Whitefield voiced the word of God to sinners. His impersonation of Satan and descriptions of the horrors of hell terrified audiences and evidently gave them much to think about. Edwards called this tactic "salutary terror." His most famous sermon, "Sinners in the Hands of an Angry God" (1741), remains a fire-and-brimstone classic in which he warned sinners that "God holds you over the pit of hell, much as one holds a spider, or some loathsome insect."[12] The climax of any Whitefield/Edwards sermon was salvation. Parishioners came forward in tears and humility, confessing their sins and swearing to begin life anew as saved Christians. Thus, out of the old Calvinist tradition of saving grace, came a more modern, public, and theatrical American outpouring of religious emotion that remains common today, which elicited no small degree of condemnation from traditionalists.[13]

By the late 1740s, the Great Awakening began to fade. Even Jonathan Edwards fell into disfavor and withdrew as a recluse to a small congregation of pioneers and Indians in western Massachusetts. Yet the First Great Awakening left an indelible legacy by further diffusing and decentralizing church authority. It fathered new Protestant sects—Baptist, Methodist, and New Light Presbyterian movements—and enhanced the role of the independent itinerant preachers. Like American doctors and lawyers, the clergy grew less intellectual and more pragmatic. Saving souls was more important to them than preaching doctrine, and a college education in theology became optional if not irrelevant or even, later, an impediment to sound doctrine. All of this fit perfectly into the large antiauthoritarian pattern in colonial America, giving the First Great Awakening a political as a well as social impact.

Finally, the First Great Awakening foreshadowed another religious movement—a movement that would, during the first half of the nineteenth century, echo and supersede the first crusade's fervency. The Second Great Awakening that followed gave birth to abolitionism as the true believers of the Second Great Awakening added slavery to their list of man's sins and, in fact, moved it to the top of the list.

Slavery's American Origins and Evolution

As Edmund Morgan has shown, African American slavery evolved slowly in the seventeenth-century American South.[14] White Virginians and Carolinians did not come to America with the intention of owning slaves, yet that was precisely what they did: between 1619 and 1707 slavery slowly became entrenched. Opportunities in the economically diverse Northeast proved much more attractive to immigrants than the staple-crop agriculture of Virginia and the Carolinas, making for permanent labor shortages in the South. Increasingly, it became more difficult to persuade white indentured servants or Indian workers to harvest the labor-intensive tobacco and rice crops. This was hard physical labor best performed in gang systems under the supervision of an overseer. No free whites would do it, and Southerners discovered that the few Indians they put to work soon vanished into the forest. Southern tobacco planters soon looked elsewhere for a more servile work force.

Yet why did tobacco and rice planters specifically turn to African slaves? In retrospect, one must conclude that Africans were more vulnerable to enslavement than white indentured servants and Indians. The African Gold Coast was open to exploitation by European sea powers and already had a flourishing slave trade with the Muslims. This trade was far more extensive than previously thought, and involved far more Europeans than earlier scholars had acknowledged.[15] Thanks to this existing trade in human flesh, there were already ample precedents of black slavery in the British West Indies. More important, those African slaves shipped to North America truly became captives. They did not (initially) speak English, Spanish, French, or Indian language and could not communicate effectively outside their plantations. Even before they were shipped across the Atlantic, traders mixed slaves by tribe and language with others with whom they shared nothing in common except skin color, isolating them further. The first generation of slave captives thus became extremely demoralized, and rebellion became infrequent, despite the paranoia over slave revolts that constantly gripped plantation whites.

How could these English colonists, so steeped in the Enlightenment principles of liberty and constitutionalism, enslave other human beings? The answer is harsh and simple: British colonists convinced themselves that Africans were not really human beings—that they were *property*—and thus legitimate subjects for enslavement within the framework of English liberty. Into English folk belief was interwoven fear of the color black, associating blackness with witchcraft and evil, while so-called scientists in Europe argued that blacks were an inferior species of humans. English ministers abused the Bible, misinterpreting stories of Cain and Abel and Noah's son Ham, to argue for separate creation and an alleged God-imposed inferiority on blacks as the "curse of Ham."[16] When combined with perceived economic necessity, English racism and rationalization for enslavement of African people became entrenched.[17]

Slavery's institutionalization began in Virginia in 1619 when a small group of black slaves arrived. The term "slave" did not appear in Virginia law for fifty years, and there is evidence that even the earliest Africans brought over against their will were viewed as indentures. Free blacks, such as "Antonio the negro," were identified in public records as early as 1621, and of the three hundred Africans recorded as living in the South through 1640, many gained freedom through expiration of indenture contracts. Some free blacks soon became landholders, planters, and even slaveholders themselves. But at some point in the mid-seventeenth century, the process whereby all blacks were presumed to be slaves took root, and this transformation is still not well understood. Attempts by scholars such as Peter Kolchin to isolate race begs the question of why whites permitted *any* blacks to be free, whereas Edmund Morgan's explanation of slavery stemming from efforts by poor whites to create another class under them is also unpersuasive.[18] However it occurred, by 1676, widespread legalized slavery appeared in Maryland, Virginia, and the Carolinas, and within thirty years, slavery was an established economic institution throughout the southern and, to a much smaller degree, northern American colonies.[19]

English, Dutch, and New England merchant seamen traded in human flesh. West African intertribal warfare produced abundant prisoners of war to fuel this trade. Prisoners found themselves branded and boarded onto vessels of the Royal African Company and other slavers. On the ships, slaves were shackled together and packed tight in the hold—eating, sleeping, vomiting, and defecating while chained in place. The arduous voyage of three weeks to three months was characterized by a 16 percent mortality rate and, occasionally, involved suicides and mutinies. Finally, at trip's end, the slavers delivered their prisoners on the shores of America.

Every American colony's legislators enacted laws called black codes to govern what some would later call America's Peculiar Institution. These codes defined African Americans as chattels personal—moveable personal property—not as human beings, and as such slaves could not testify against whites in court, nor could they be killed for a capital crime (they were too valuable). Black codes forbade slave literacy, gun or dog ownership, travel (excepting special travel permits), gatherings numbering more than six slaves, and sex between black males and white women (miscegenation). However, as the development of a large mulatto population attests, white men were obviously free to have sex with—or, more often, rape—black women. All of the above laws were open to broad interpretation and variation, especially in northern colonies. This fact did not alter the overall authoritarian structure of the peculiar institution.[20]

The vast majority of slaves in the New World worked in either Virginia tobacco fields or South Carolina rice plantations. Rice plantations constituted the worst possible fate, for Carolina lowlands proved to be a hot, humid, and horrible work environment, replete with swarms of insects and innumerable species of worms. Huge all-male Carolina work forces died at extraordinary rates. Conditions were so bad that a few Carolina slaves revolted against their masters in the Cato Conspiracy (1739), which saw seventy-five slaves kill thirty whites before fleeing to Spanish Florida; white militiamen soon killed forty-four of the revolutionaries. A year later, whites hanged another fifty blacks for supposedly planning insurrection in the infamous Charleston Plot.

Slave revolts and runaways proved exceptions to the rule. Most black slaves endured their fate in stoic and heroic fashion by creating a lifestyle that sustained them and their will to endure slavery. In the slave quarters, blacks returned from the fields each day to their families, church and religion, and a unique folk culture, with music, dance, medicine, folktales, and other traditional lore. Blacks combined African customs with Anglo- and Celtic-American traits to create a unique African American folk culture. Although this culture did not thoroughly emerge until the nineteenth century, it started to take shape in the decades before the American Revolution. African American traditions, music, and a profound belief in Christianity helped the slaves endure and sustained their hopes for "a better day a comin'."

Although the institution of slavery thoroughly insinuated itself into southern life and culture in the 1600s, it took the invention of the cotton gin in the 1790s to fully entrench the peculiar institution. Tobacco and rice, important as they were, paled in comparison to the impact of cotton agriculture on the phenomenal growth of slavery, but the tortured political and religious rationales for slavery had matured well before then, making its entrenchment a certainty in the South.[21]

A few statistics clarify these generalizations. By the mid-1700s, Americans imported approximately seven thousand slaves from Africa and the Caribbean annually. Some 40 percent of Virginians and 66 percent of all South Carolinians in 1835 were black. Of these, probably 95 percent were slaves. By 1763, between 15 and 20 percent of all Americans were African Americans, free and slave—a larger per capita black population than in modern-day America. Yet 90 percent of all these African Americans resided south of the Pennsylvania line. Northern slavery, always small because of the absence of a staple crop, was shriveling, its death accelerated by northern reformers who passed manumission acts beginning late in the 1700s, and by the formation in 1775 of the world's first abolitionist group, the Quaker Anti-Slavery Society—by Pennsylvania Quakers. Other Northerners routinely freed their slaves or allowed them to buy their own freedom, so that by 1830 there were only three thousand slaves left in all of the North, compared to more than two million in the South.[22] When individual initiative did not suffice, Northerners employed the law. The Northwest Ordinance of 1787 would forbid slavery above the Ohio River, and the Constitution would allow abolition of the slave trade by 1807.[23]

Some Northerners envisioned, and prayed for, an end to American slavery, as did a small number of Southerners. George Washington would free all of his slaves following his death; Jefferson and Madison would not. They privately decried slavery as a "necessary evil"—something their fathers and they had come to depend upon, but not something they were proud of or aimed to perpetuate.[24] Jefferson's commitment to ending slavery may be more suspect than Washington's or, certainly, Franklin's. But virtually all of these men believed that slavery would some day end, and often they delayed confronting it in hopes that it would just go away. Until the invention of the cotton gin, their hope was not necessarily a futile one. After the advent of the Cotton Kingdom, however, increasingly fewer Southerners criticized slavery, and the pervading philosophy about it slowly shifted from its presence as a necessary evil to a belief that slavery was a positive good.

Georgia: The Last Colony

Unlike the Puritans, who wanted to create a "city on a hill," or the Virginia Company, which sought profit, the founders of Georgia acted out of concern for Spanish power in the southern area of America. Although Queen Anne's War ended in 1713, Spain still represented a significant threat to the Carolinas. General James Oglethorpe, a military hero, also had a philanthropic bent. He had headed an investigation of prisons and expressed special concern for debtors, who by English law could be incarcerated for their obligations. If he could open a settlement south of the Carolinas, he could offer a new start to poor English and settle a region that could stand as a buffer to Spanish power.

In 1732, Oglethorpe received a grant from King George II for land between the Savannah and Altamaha rivers. Oglethorpe and his trustees deliberately limited the size of the landholdings to encourage density and, thus, better defense. Debtors and prisoners were released on the condition that they emigrate to Georgia; they helped found the first fortified town on the Savannah River in 1733. The trustees, though, had planned well by encouraging artisans, tradesmen, farmers, and other skilled workers from England and Scotland to emigrate. In addition, they welcomed all religious refugees—to the point of allowing a small group of Jews to locate in Georgia—except Catholics, fearing they might ally with the Spanish.

Within a decade, Britain's fears of Spanish aggression proved well founded. The European War of the Austrian Succession (1740–48) spawned conflict in the Western Hemisphere when Spain and France allied with Indian tribes to attack the British. During the 1739–42 War of Jenkins's Ear, General Oglethorpe led Georgians and South Carolinians into Spanish Florida to thwart a Spanish invasion. They enjoyed mixed success but failed to wrest Saint Augustine from Spain. Despite limited military success, Oglethorpe soon found that his colonists wanted to limit his power. Former convicts actively opposed his ban of rum (sobriety, they believed, would not expedite their rehabilitation!). Planters chafed at his prohibition of slavery. In 1750, Georgians repealed the ban on slavery, importing nearly ten thousand Africans by 1770. One year before its original charter expired, Oglethorpe's group surrendered control and Georgia became a Royal colony.

With the stabilization of Georgia as the thirteenth American colony, the final American adjustment to empire was complete. Britain's colonies spanned the entire Atlantic seaboard, and the system appeared relatively sound. At the same time, on paper, the mercantile apparatus of the 1600s seemed to function satisfactorily. The king and Parliament handed down laws to the secretary of state who, with the Board of Trade, issued orders for commerce and governance of the New World. Britain deployed a small network of royal governors, officials, and trade and customs officers who were directed to carry out these laws.

Ultimately, it would be up to these officials to prevent the American Revolution—a challenge well beyond them. The most common thread that connected the British colonies was their governmental structure: eleven colonies had an appointed council and elected assembly (with the franchise, or voting rights, bestowed on adult white male property owners); ten colonies had a governor selected by the king, in the case of a royal colony, or by the directors of the joint-stock company. The legislators' right to vote on taxes, the governor's salary, and all other revenue measures—the coveted power of the purse—constituted a central part of the rights of Englishmen the colonists enjoyed. Thus, citizens took even relatively minor local levies as serious business. As they grew more prosperous, wealth permeated through the greater part of the body politic, making inevitable the ascendancy of the legislative bodies over the executives. Despite resistance from the governors, virtually all the American colonies in 1770 had seen the elected legislative bodies supersede the governors' offices, wresting almost all important decision-making power from the king's proxies.[25]

American Whigs clung to (and radicalized) a distrust of power that Puritans had displayed in the English Civil War and Glorious Revolution. Colonists distrusted appointed governors and held them at bay with the economic power of the lower house of the legislature and its budgetary/appropriation powers. If a governor proved uncooperative, the legislature might hold back his salary to foster compromise. Separated from the mother country by three thousand miles and beholden to the legislatures for their pay, most governors learned how to deal with the provincials on their own terms. But colonial governments were not balanced governments in any sense. Elected representatives commanded disproportionate power, as the colonists and English Whigs desired. At the same time, a separation of powers was clearly visible, if imperfectly weighted in favor of the legislature.

Benign Neglect

Continued clashes between colonial legislators and governors picked by the Crown only heralded a larger dissatisfaction among Americans with their position in the empire. Three factors fueled their growing discomfort with English rule. First, there was the tenuous nature of imperial holdings themselves: overseas possessions required constant protection and defense against foreign threats, especially those posed by the French. Not only did Britain have to maintain a large, well-equipped navy capable of extending English power to all areas of the globe, but colonial settlements also needed troops to defend against natives and encroachments from other nations' colonies. A nation as small as England could not hope to protect its possessions with English soldiers alone: it needed conscripts or volunteers from the colonies themselves. Even so, the cost of supporting such far-flung operations, even in peacetime, was substantial. In wartime, the expense of maintaining armies overseas soared still further. Attempts to spread that expense to the colonists themselves without extending to them representation in England soon bred animosity in the North American colonies.

A second factor, already evident in Bacon's Rebellion, involved a growing difference between Americans and Englishmen caused by the separation of the English colonists from the motherland in both distance and time. In the case of America, absence did not make the heart grow fonder. Instead, the colonists started to see themselves differently—not as Americans, to be sure, but as Virginians, Georgians, and so on.[26]

The final source of unrest originated in the flawed nature of mercantilism itself. Mercantilist doctrine demanded that the individual subordinate his economic activity to the interests of the state. Such an attitude may have been practicable in Rome or in Charlemagne's empire; but the ideas of the Enlightenment soon gave Americans the intellectual basis for insisting that individuals could pursue wealth for themselves, and give the state only its fair share. It did not help the English that mercantilism was based on a conceptual framework that saw wealth as fixed and limited, meaning that for the government to get more wealth, individuals had to receive less of the fruit of their own labor.[27]

After the Glorious Revolution, the English government failed to develop a cohesive or coherent policy for administering the colonies, even though by 1754 there were eight colonies under the authority of royal governors. The British utilized a series of laws collectively called the Navigation Acts (originated in 1651 as a restriction against trading with the Dutch), which placed regulations on goods manufactured or grown within the empire. Various acts provided subsidies for sugar, molasses, cotton, or other agricultural items, but only if they were grown in an approved colony. The British West Indies, for example, were to produce sugar, and any other colony attempting to grow sugar cane faced penalties or taxes. Britain hoped to foster interdependence among the colonies with such policies, forcing New England to get its sugar from the British West Indies, cotton from India, and so on. Above all, the Navigation Acts were intended to make all the colonies dependent on England for manufactured goods and English currency, and thus they prohibited or inhibited production of iron ore or the printing of money.[28] As the governor of New York revealed in a letter to the Board of Trade, all governors were commanded to "discourage all Manufactures, and to give accurate accounts [of manufacturing] with a view to their suppression."[29]

Having the state pick winners and losers in the fields of enterprise proved disastrous, and not merely because it antagonized the Americans. The Board of Trade, desperate to boost shipbuilding, paid subsidies for products such as pitch, tar, rosin, hemp, and other seafaring-related products to reduce Britain's reliance on Europe. As production in the colonies rose, prices for shipbuilding basics fell, encouraging fishing and shipping industries that none of the other colonies had. Not only did a government-controlled economy fail to keep the colonials pacified, but it also unwittingly gave them the very means they eventually needed to wage an effective war against the mother country.

Americans especially came to despise regulations that threatened the further development of America's thriving merchant trade in the port cities: Boston, New York, Philadelphia, Baltimore, and Charleston. Those urban centers had sprouted a sturdy population of aspiring merchants, self-employed artisans, and laborers, perhaps one in ten of whom were criminals, leading William Byrd II to instruct an English friend in 1751, "Keep all your felons at home."[30] In the country and on the frontier, farmers and planters exported surplus produce. Traders at the top favored the regulations because they allowed them to freeze out aspiring competitors, but producers and consumers disliked the laws, and they were swiftly becoming the majority.

But even by clinging to the outmoded mercantilist structure, entrepreneurs in places like Philadelphia found that nothing could stem the advance of more energetic people with better products or ideas. In Philadelphia, "Opportunity, enterprise, and adversity reinforced each other. A young business man could borrow money and move into trade, challenging the commercial position of older, more established merchants. His opportunity was . . . their adversity."[31] The rich got richer, but so too did the poor and a large middle class. All Americans except slaves were energized by the emergent global economy. In this new economy, raw materials from the American frontier—furs, fish, naval stores, tobacco, lumber, livestock, grain—moved to American port cities and then east and south across the Atlantic in sailing ships.[32] In return, manufactured goods and slaves flowed to America over the same routes. Americans prospered from this booming economy, witnessing unprecedented growth to the extent that on the eve of the Revolution, colonists had per capita annual incomes of $720 in 1991 dollars, putting these people of two hundred years ago "on a par with the privately held wealth of citizens in modern-day Mexico or Turkey."[33]

The conflict lay in the fact that, in direct violation of British mercantile policy, Americans traded with both French and Spanish colonies. Large quantities of wine and salt came from Spain's Madeira Islands, and molasses, gold coin, and slaves came from the French Caribbean colonies of Guadeloupe and Martinique. Great Britain was engaged in war against France and Spain throughout the eighteenth century, making this illicit trade, quite literally, treasonous. Yet that trade grew, despite its illegality and renewed British efforts to put teeth in the Navigation Acts.

Enforcement of British trade policies should have fallen to the Board of Trade, but in practice, two administrative bodies—the king's Privy Council and the admiralty courts—carried out actual administration of the laws. Admiralty courts almost exclusively dealt with the most common violation, smuggling by sea. But like any crime statistics, the records of the courts reflect only those caught and prosecuted, and they fail to measure the effort put into enforcement itself. Smuggling made heroes out of otherwise obnoxious pirates, turning bloodthirsty cutthroats into brave entrepreneurs. Moreover, the American colonies, in terms of their size, population, and economic contribution to the empire, represented a relatively minor part of it, meaning that prior to 1750 most acts were designed with the larger and more important possessions in mind. A critical, yet little-noticed, difference existed between America and the other colonies, however. Whereas in India, for example, British-born officials and troops constituted a tiny minority that dominated a huge native population, in America British-born subjects or their descendants accounted for the vast majority of the nonslave, non-Indian population.

Another factor working against a successful economic royal policy was the poor quality of royal officials and royal governors. Assignment in America was viewed as a less desirable post than, say, the British West Indies, Madras (India), or even Nova Scotia. These colonies were more "British," with amenities and a lifestyle stemming from a stronger military presence and locations on major trade routes.

Colonial governorships offered havens for corrupt officials and royal cronies, such as New York governor Lord Cornbury, a cousin of Queen Anne, who was a dishonest transvestite who warranted "the universal contempt of the people."[34] Sir Danvers Osborn, the most mentally fragile of the colonial governors, hanged himself after one week in America.[35]

When governors and other officials of the empire, such as tax collectors and naval officers, administered the laws, they did so with considerable laxity, waiving or reducing duties in cases of friendship or outright bribery (which was widespread because of the low pay of the administrators). For the most part, the administrators approached the Navigation Acts with a policy of salutary or benign neglect, postponing any serious harms contained in the taxes until the laws were enforced in the future. This process of benign neglect may well have continued indefinitely had a critical event not forced a change in the enforcement of the laws: the last of the colonial wars, the French and Indian War.

Franco-British Warfare, 1689–1748

Tensions between England, France, and Spain led to several European conflicts with American theaters. In America, King William's War (1689–97), Queen Anne's War (1701–13), the War of Jenkins's Ear (1739–42), King George's War (1744–48), and the French and Indian War (1756–63) served as provincial mirrors of European rivalry. The first two conflicts saw fierce fighting in both the southern and northern colonies, from the Caribbean to Canada. In the South, Spain allied with France to fight British sailors and soldiers over the contested lands lying between the Carolinas and Florida (Georgia was not yet a colony). The northern theater of King William's and Queen Anne's wars saw naval and land forces clash throughout the Atlantic maritime region—the modern-day Canadian provinces of Quebec, New Brunswick, and Nova Scotia, and the American states of New York and Maine. The St. Lawrence River Valley outpost of Quebec and the Atlantic coastal towns of Louisbourg, Falmouth, and Port Royal became coveted prizes in both of these colonial wars.

Queen Anne's War resulted in the 1713 Treaty of Utrecht, with France ceding Nova Scotia and Newfoundland to England. This, and the War of Jenkins's Ear, almost seamlessly merged with King George's War (known in Europe as the War of the Austrian Succession, 1740–48).[36] In the American theater, Britain, again pitted against the French, focused on the north, especially the important French naval base at Louisbourg. Located on Cape Breton Island, just north of Nova Scotia, Louisbourg guarded the entrance to the all-important St. Lawrence River. In a daring and uncharacteristic move, American colonials grabbed the military initiative themselves. Massachusetts governor William Shirley raised money and troops to launch a 1745 attack led by Maine colonel William Pepperell. On June 17, 1745, Pepperrell and his 4,000 troops successfully captured Louisbourg, the "Gibraltar of the New World."

Despite the glorious Louisbourg victory, King George's War dragged on inconclusively for two and a half more years. Savage guerrilla warfare stretched from Spanish Florida/Georgia to Vermont, western Massachusetts, and the frontiers of New York and Maine. The 1748 Treaty of Aix-la-Chappelle was more of a truce than a true conclusion to the war, and it greatly disappointed the American colonists by returning Louisbourg and other French territories (though not Nova Scotia) to France.

Inadvertently, King George's War created what would soon become a unique American subculture—the Louisiana Cajuns. Before the end of the war, Governor William Shirley pointed to the dangers posed by French nationals residing in British (formerly French) Nova Scotia. Shirley feared that these Acadians, who still bore the name of their old province in France, would remain loyal to France and would thus constitute an "enemy within" the British colonies. Even after King George's War came to a close, fear of the Acadians remained strong. In 1755, at the start of the French and Indian War, Nova Scotia's governor, Colonel Charles Lawrence, expelled six thousand Acadians to the lower thirteen American colonies. This Acadian diaspora saw some of the exiles return to France and the French Caribbean, whereas others trickled back to Nova Scotia. However, sixteen hundred Acadians trekked to Louisiana between 1765 and 1785. Although the Gulf Coast climate and geography proved a drastic change, they sought the familiarity and protection of Franco-American culture. Today these French Cajuns (a slurred version of "Acadian") still reside in or near the marshes and Louisiana bayous where they fled more than 250 years ago, retaining a speech pattern as impenetrable as it was in the 1700s.

Returned to its 1713 boundaries after King George's War, Britain's fifteen-hundred-mile-long American territory was thin, often extending no farther than a hundred miles inland. Huge chunks of unsettled open territory divided the colonial towns, and genuine differences in regional culture split the American colonies further. Still, for all their internal disagreements, the British colonies had distinct advantages over the French in any American conflict. France's unwillingness to encourage colonial settlement weakened its military designs in the New World. England could transport troops from home, and her colonies could also draw upon local militias, which meant that despite the fact that the population of New France had doubled since 1660, the population of the British colonies, 1.5 million, greatly exceeded that of the 60,000 French in North America. Moreover, the British, taking advantage of a navy much superior to France's, could command seacoasts, trading ports, and major rivers.

The latter advantage proved particularly acute when considering that the French hitched their fate to the success of fur trading operations. Important port cities like New Orleans (founded 1718), Biloxi, and Mobile in the South and Detroit, Montreal, and Quebec in the North rivaled Boston, Philadelphia, and other Atlantic urban areas, but they were vulnerable to surgical attacks by the British navy, even to the extent that the inland waterways (especially the St. Lawrence River) became primary targets. France's trading strategy of sparse settlement and an emphasis on fur trading left her only one significant asset: her good relations with the Indians.

Advantages provided by alliances with Indians, however, could not overcome the vulnerabilities created by making fur trading the cornerstone of the French economic and colonial policy. The wars with England exposed these weaknesses, wherein the small French population and nonexistent industrial base proved incapable of raising, equipping, and supporting large militias in North America. Even with their Indian allies, the French found themselves outnumbered and, more important, outproduced in every geopolitical conflict with England. Worse, the French had tied themselves to allies who did not embrace the Western way of war, rendering them even less effective than other traditional European armies.

Meanwhile, the Indians, who realized that the English settlers were arriving like locusts, were pushed toward the French, although each tribe had to weave its own tapestry of diplomatic alliances carefully and shrewdly. Indeed, northeastern Indians, unlike those in most other regions, shared a common threat: the Iroquois Confederacy, made up of the Mohawks, Senecas, Cayugas, Onondagas, Oneidas, and Tuscaroras. Fresh from a total victory over the Hurons, the Iroquois established themselves as a force in the region. For a time, they managed to maintain neutrality between the British and the French, all the while realizing that they must eventually choose a side.

Initially, the Iroquois favored the British by allowing English traders into their territories, a practice that convinced the French that British colonists soon would follow in greater numbers. French troops therefore moved into the Ohio Valley in the late 1740s, building forts as a buffer against further English expansion, determined to demonstrate control over the trans-Appalachian frontier lands by occupation—something the British had never done systematically. From 1749 to 1754, France continued this construction program, establishing outposts at strategic points that guarded the approaches to Canada, producing a situation where British settlers and speculators were almost certain to bump up against them.

The French and Indian War

France's eviction from North America began in 1753, when Virginia governor Robert Dinwiddie dispatched an expedition against Fort Duquesne in western Pennsylvania. At the head of the militia was a young patrician landowner and surveyor, George Washington.[37] Meeting early success, Washington reached the Ohio Valley, where he defeated a tiny force of Canadians, then constructed Fort Necessity near the French outpost. In 1754 a French counterattack captured Fort Necessity and forced a bloodless surrender by Washington—hardly an auspicious start for the American Revolution's "indispensable man." Still, the encounter showed something of Washington's mettle: he wrote that he "heard the bullets whistle and . . . there is something charming in the sound."[38] Of more immediate concern to Washington and his fellow Virginians, however, was the fact that the episode signaled the American origins of the French and Indian War, called the Seven Years' War in Europe.

Leaders of the thirteen colonies, virtually all of whom faced a threat from either the French or the Indians, decided in 1754 that they had to unify to meet the enemy. The English government agreed, and it instructed them to negotiate a treaty with the Iroquois. Representatives from all the New England colonies, as well as Pennsylvania, Maryland, and New York met in Albany in 1754 and quickly concluded an agreement with the five northern tribes. Some delegates used the gathering for more than concluding a nonaggression pact with the natives, however. Benjamin Franklin, a representative from Pennsylvania, proposed a plan of union that would create a federal council composed of delegates from all the colonies. Under Franklin's Albany Plan, the council would have the power to treat with the Indians, levy taxes, and raise armies. Delegates approved the plan, but the colonial assemblies rejected the concept, fearing that it would infringe on the independence of the individual colonies.

Meanwhile, Washington's capitulation at Fort Necessity proved only the first British disaster of the war. A year later, General Edward Braddock led a second expedition of 2,500 men against Fort Duquesne. After failing to capture the fort, Braddock retreated in column formation through the thick forests, where French and Indian forces ambushed his troops and slaughtered them. Braddock was killed in the battle, and the apparent British incompetence in forest warfare encouraged the Indians to step up their activities on behalf of the French. Only the Iroquois refused to ally with France. However, the threat from other tribes on the frontier grew so substantial that many English settlers removed themselves eastward of the Allegheny Mountains.

The northern theater of the French and Indian War proved the most critical. There, in 1756, France appointed the Marquis de Montcalm as the commander of the Canadian forces. A capable military leader, Montcalm assessed the situation as less than favorable for France, but he nevertheless launched effective preemptive strikes to stabilize the approaches to Canada. Within one year, he had captured the British forts Oswego and William Henry.[39]

Montcalm also built Fort Ticonderoga, a new post on Lake Champlain. At the beginning of 1757, the entry points to French territory remained secure. Britain's new secretary of state, William Pitt, responded to French successes by forging a policy of total war that would simultaneously quell Britain's enemies in India, Africa, the West Indies, America, and on the high seas. Pitt's bold plan carried a high price tag: in America he mustered a 50,000-man army, counting colonial militia, and appointed two young generals—Jeffrey Amherst and James Wolfe—to attack the French forts. Those forces captured Louisbourg and Fort Frontenac (and thereby Lake Ontario) by 1758, and avenged Braddock by retaking Fort Duquesne. The following year Pitt believed he was ready for a master stroke. He ordered General James Wolfe to deliver France the "knockout punch" at Quebec City on the St. Lawrence River. The sickly General Wolfe, though only thirty-two years old, possessed a fierce martial spirit. He used the availability of a British naval superiority of two hundred ships to land a 10,000-man force at the foot of the steep cliffs of Quebec City.

After seven weeks of unsuccessful maneuvering, Wolfe located unguarded paths leading up to the bluffs and on the evening of September 12, 1759, marched 4,500 men up to the Plains of Abraham. There, Wolfe controlled the supply routes to Quebec, and his presence constituted a threat to the entire French colony. Had Montcalm waited inside the city's walls, he might have been relieved, but he lacked confidence in the French navy (with good reason), and embarked on a hurried, ill-conceived attack outside the fort. In the ensuing fifteen-minute battle, Montcalm was wounded (he died a day later) and Wolfe killed.[40] By the end of September thirteenth, however, the British held the field, and four days later they marched into Quebec. A year later Montreal itself fell.[41]

Peace might have been imminent had Spain not entered into the war in 1762. This was too late for Spain to affect the war's outcome, but allowed sufficient time for her to fully embarrass herself. Soon Britain relieved Spain of Gibralter, Cuba (later traded back to Spain for western Florida), and the Philippines (also later restored to Spain). The war ended in 1763 with the Treaty of Paris, in which France gave England her colonies in India—then considered the most important booty of war. As a reward for loyalty and alliance, France had earlier awarded Spain the Louisiana Territory, which Spain held until giving it back to Napoleon and France in 1802.

The long-term significance of the treaty involved the transfer of Canada and all French possessions east of the Mississippi (and north of Florida and Louisiana) to England. Great Britain now possessed nearly the entirety of eastern North America—an empire unimaginable a few decades earlier.

Enter King George III

In 1760 a young, inexperienced, and not particularly bright George III ascended to the throne as king of Great Britain and presided over the glorious conclusion to the French and Indian War. The first of the Hanoverian monarchs to speak English (instead of low German) as his primary language, the good-looking George III fathered fifteen children and developed a reputation as a solid family man. His domesticity earned him the nickname among the people of the Farmer, and what he lacked in intellect he made up for with hard work.

Britain's empire had changed significantly, though, since the time of George's ancestor King William, who had fought the first of the five colonial wars seventy years earlier. During the eighteenth century, George's American colonial subjects had grown more distinct from their English brethren than even those independent Americans of the time of Queen Anne's War. Whether in economics, material culture, dress, language, educational institutions, professions, religions, law, and governmental institutions, the colonials had become further radicalized and Americanized in the New World.[42]

George III neither admired nor approved of this independent spirit. But the conclusion of the French and Indian War brought him problems as well as opportunities, and he needed America's full cooperation to meet the new financial demands on his government. William Pitt's brilliant policies had achieved victory, but at a high price: Britain left the war saddled with a huge debt—£137 million, with £5 million in annual interest payments. At home, a new group of British politicians quite naturally opposed higher taxes following on the heels of their severe wartime privation.[43]

This was bad timing indeed, for now Britain possessed vast and costly territories stretching from southern Asia to Canada. The latter territory alone demanded a substantial military force to police the native Indian frontier and watch over sullen Frenchmen who now found themselves unwilling Britons. Pontiac's Rebellion, a violent and widespread 1763 Ottawa Indian uprising, served as a grim reminder that the situation on the Canadian-American frontier urgently demanded a British standing army. But who would pay the bill?

Only the most myopic observer would argue that Americans had not benefited greatly from British sacrifice in the colonial wars and now, thought the royal ministers, the Americans ought to pay their share of the costs of Britain's (and their own) glory. According to Americanized governmental beliefs, however, if the colonists were to bear new taxes and responsibilities, they had to have a *say* in their creation. The radical new view of law and politics could produce no other solution, and Americans' belief in the power of the purse led quite naturally to their opposition to taxation without representation. These were challenges to George III's authority that the king could not allow.

CHAPTER THREE

Colonies No More, 1763–83

Farmers and Firebrands

The changes brought by the French and Indian War were momentous, certainly in the sheer size and unique character of the territory involved. (Historian Francis Parkman maintained that the fall of Quebec began the history of the United States.) British acquisition of the new territories carried a substantial cost for almost every party involved. England amassed huge debts, concluding, in the process, that the colonists had not paid their fair share. France likewise emerged from the war with horrific liabilities: half the French annual budget went to pay interest on the wartime debt, not to mention the loss of vast territories. Some Indian tribes lost lands, or were destroyed. Only the American colonists really came out of the seven years of combat as winners, yet few saw the situation in that light.

Those Indians who allied with the French lost substantially; only the Iroquois, who supported the British in form but not substance, emerged from the war as well as they had entered it.[1] Immediately after the war, pressures increased on the tribes in the Appalachian region as settlers and traders appeared in ever-increasing numbers. An alliance of tribes under the Ottawa chief Pontiac mounted a stiff resistance, enticing the Iroquois to abandon the British and join the new confederacy.[2] Fearing a full-blown uprising, England established a policy prohibiting new settlers and trading charters beyond a line drawn through the Appalachians, known as the Proclamation Line of 1763. There was more behind the creation of the line than concern about the settlers' safety, however. Traders who held charters before the war contended they possessed monopoly powers over trade in their region by virtue of those charters. They sought protection from new competitors, who challenged the existing legal status of the charters themselves.[3]

Such concerns did not interest the Indians, who saw no immediate benefit from the establishment of the line. Whites continued to pour across the boundary in defiance of the edict, and in May 1763, Pontiac directed a large-scale infiltration and attack of numerous forts across the northern frontier, capturing all but Detroit and Fort Pitt. English forces regrouped under General Jeffrey Amherst, defeating Pontiac and breaking the back of the Indian confederacy. Subsequent treaties pushed the Indians farther west, demonstrating both the Indians' growing realization that they could not resist the English on the one hand or believe their promises on the other.

Paradoxically, though, the beneficence of the English saved the Indians from total extermination, which in earlier eras (as with the Mongol or Assyrian empires) or under other circumstances (as in the aftermath of King Philip's War) would have been complete. As early as 1763, a pattern took shape in which the British (and later, the Americans) sought a middle ground of Indian relations in which the tribes could be preserved as independent entities, yet sufficiently segregated outside white culture or society. Such an approach was neither practical nor desirable in a modernizing society, and ultimately the strategy produced a pathetic condition of servitude that ensnared the Indians on reservations, rather than forced an early commitment to assimilation.

Time Line

1763: Proclamation of 1763
1765: Stamp Act and Protest
1770: Boston Massacre
1773: Tea Act and Boston Tea Party
1774: Intolerable Acts; First Continental Congress
1775: Battles of Lexington and Concord; Washington appointed commander in chief
1776: Paine's *Common Sense;* Declaration of Independence
1777: Articles of Confederation; Battle of Saratoga
1778: French Alliance
1781: Articles of Confederation ratified; Cornwallis surrenders at Yorktown
1783: Treaty of Paris

Land, Regulation, and Revolution

By establishing the Proclamation line, the British not only disturbed aspiring traders and disappointed the besieged Indians, but also alienated many of the new settlers in the west. After all, many had come to the New World on the promise of available land, and suddenly they found it occupied by what they considered a primitive and barbarous people.[4] Some settlers simply broke the law, moving beyond the line. Others, including George Washington, an established frontiersman and military officer who thought westward expansion a foregone conclusion, groused privately. Still others increasingly used the political process to try to influence government, with some mild success. The Paxton Boys movement of 1763 in Pennsylvania and the 1771 Regulator movement in North Carolina both reflected the pressures on residents in the western areas to defend themselves despite high taxes they paid to the colonial government, much of which were supposed to support defense. Westerners came to view taxes not as inherently unfair, but as oppressive burdens when incorrectly used.

Westward expansion only promised to aggravate matters: in 1774, Lord Dunmore of Virginia defeated Indians in the Kanawha River Valley, opening the trails of Kentucky to settlement. The white-Indian encounter, traditionally described as Europeans "stealing" land from Native Americans, was in reality a much more complex exchange. Most—but certainly not all—Indian tribes rejected the European view of property rights, wherein land could become privatized. Rather, most Indians viewed people as incapable of owning the land, creating a strong incentive for tribal leaders to trade something they could not possess for goods that they could obtain. Chiefs often were as guilty as greedy whites in thinking they had pulled a fast one on their negotiating partners, and more than a few Indians were stunned to find the land actually being closed off in the aftermath of a treaty. Both sides operated out of misunderstandings and misperceptions.[5] Under such different world views, conflict was inevitable, and could have proved far bloodier than it ultimately was if not for the temperance provided by Christianity and English concepts of humanity, even for "barbarian" enemies.

Tribes such as the Cherokee, realizing they could not stem the tide of English colonists, sold their lands between the Kentucky and Cumberland rivers to the Transylvania Company, which sent an expedition under Daniel Boone to explore the region. Boone, a natural woodsman of exceptional courage and self-reliance, proved ideal for the job. Clearing roads (despite occasional Indian attacks), Boone's party pressed on, establishing a fort called Boonesborough in 1775. Threats from the natives did not abate, however, reinforcing westerners' claims that taxes sent to English colonial governments for defense simply were wasted.[6]

Had westerners constituted the only group unhappy with British government, it is unlikely any revolutionary movement would have appeared, much less survived. Another more important group was needed to make a revolution—merchants, elites, and intellectuals in the major cities or the gentlemen farmers from Virginia and the Carolinas. Those segments of society had the means, money, and education to give discontent a structure and to translate emotions into a cohesive set of grievances. They dominated the colonial assemblies, and included James Otis, Samuel Adams, and Patrick Henry—men of extraordinary oratorical skills who made up the shock troops of the revolutionary movement.[7]

Changes in the enforcement and direction of the Navigation Acts pushed the eastern merchants and large landowners into an alliance with the westerners. Prior to 1763, American merchant interests had accepted regulation by the mercantilist system as a reasonable way to gain market advantage for American products within the British Empire. American tobacco, for example, had a monopoly within the English markets, and Britain paid bounties (subsidies) to American shipbuilders, a policy that resulted in one third of all British vessels engaged in Atlantic trade in 1775 being constructed in North American (mostly New England) shipyards. Although in theory Americans were prohibited from manufacturing finished goods, a number of American ironworks, blast furnaces, and other iron suppliers competed in the world market, providing one seventh of the world's iron supplies, and flirted with the production of finished items.[8]

Added to those advantages, American colonists who engaged in trade did so with the absolute confidence that the Royal Navy secured the seas.[9] England's eight hundred ships and 70,000 sailors provided as much safety from piracy as could be expected, and the powerful overall trading position of Britain created or expanded markets that under other conditions would be denied the American colonies. As was often the case, however, the privileges that were withheld and not those granted aroused the most passion. Colonists already had weakened imperial authority in their challenge to the Writs of Assistance during the French and Indian War. Designed to empower customs officials with additional search-and-seizure authority to counteract smuggling under the Molasses Act of 1733, the writs allowed an agent of the Crown to enter a house or board a ship to search for taxable, or smuggled, goods. Violations of the sanctity of English homes were disliked but tolerated until 1760, when the opportunity presented itself to contest the issue of any new writs. Led by James Otis, the counsel for the Boston merchants' association, the writs were assailed as "against the Constitution" and void. Even after the writs themselves became dormant, colonial orators used them as a basis in English law to lay the groundwork for independence.

Only two years after Otis disputed the writs in Massachusetts, Virginia lawyer Patrick Henry won a stunning victory against the established Anglican Church and, in essence, managed to annul an act of the Privy Council related to tobacco taxes in Virginia. Henry and Otis, therefore, emerged as firebrands who successfully undercut the authority of the Crown in America.[10] Other voices were equally important: Benjamin Franklin, the sage of Philadelphia, had already argued that he saw "in the system of customs now being exacted in American by Act of Parliament, the seeds sown of a total disunion of the two countries."[11]

Mercantilism Reborn

The British government contributed to heightened tensions through arrogance and ineptness. George III, who had ascended to the throne in 1760 at the age of twenty-two, was the first of the German-born monarchs who could be considered truly English, although he remained elector of Hanover. Prone to periodic bouts of insanity that grew worse over time (ending his life as a prisoner inside the palace), George, at the time of the Revolution, was later viewed by Winston Churchill as "one of the most conscientious sovereigns who ever sat up on the English throne."[12] But he possessed a Teutonic view of authority and exercised his power dogmatically at the very time that the American situation demanded flexibility. "It is with the utmost astonishment," he wrote, "that I find any of my subjects capable of encouraging the rebellious disposition . . . in some of my colonies in America."[13] Historians have thus described him as "too opinionated, ignorant, and narrow-minded for the requirements of statesmanship," and as stubborn and "fundamentally ill-suited" for the role he played.[14]

Worse, the prime minister to the king, George Grenville (who replaced William Pitt), was determined to bring the colonies in tow by enforcing the Navigation Acts so long ignored. Grenville's land policies produced disaster. He reversed most of the laws and programs of his predecessor, Pitt, who had started to view land and its productivity as a central component of wealth.

To that end, Pitt had ignored many of the provisions of the Navigation Acts in hopes of uniting the colonies with England in spirit. He gave the authority to recruit troops to the colonial assemblies and promised to reimburse American merchants and farmers for wartime supplies taken by the military, winning himself popular acclaim in the colonies. Grenville, on the other hand, never met a tax he didn't like, and in rigid input-output analysis concluded (probably with some accuracy) that the colonists were undertaxed and lightly burdened with the costs of their own defense. One of his first test cases, the Sugar Act of 1764, revived the strictures of the Molasses Act against which the Boston merchants had chafed, although it lowered actual rates. This characterized Grenville's strategy—to offer a carrot of lower rates while brandishing the stick of tighter enforcement.[15] The plan revealed another flaw of the British colonial process, namely allowing incompetents to staff the various administrative posts so that the colonials had *decades* of nonenforcement as their measuring rod. (Franklin compared these posts to the modern equivalent of minimum wage jobs.)[16]

Despite lower rates, opposition arose over the new enforcement mechanisms, including the referral of all smuggling cases to admiralty courts that had judges instead of juries, which normally handled such cases. Any colonial smuggler knew that the outcome of such a trial was less often in his favor, and complaints arose that the likelihood of real prosecution and conviction was higher under the new law. A second law, the Currency Act of 1764, prohibited the colonies from issuing paper money. When combined with the taxes of the Sugar Act, colonists anticipated that the Currency Act would drain the already scarce metallic money (specie, or gold and silver coins) from America, rendering merchants helpless to counteract inflation that always followed higher taxes.[17]

By 1764, then, colonists drew a direct correlation between paying taxes and governing, and between government intervention in the economy and inflation. A few early taxes had existed on land, but land ownership conferred voting status. Other than that, only a handful of other direct taxes were levied, especially in light of the small size and limited power of government. "The more revenue governments had, the more mischief they could create," was the prevailing colonial view. In sharp contrast to land taxes, Grenville's new duties were in no way associated with rights, and all subjects—landowners or otherwise—now had to pay.[18]

There is truth to the British claim that the colonists had received the benefits of government on the cheap for decades, a development that provides a cautionary tale for contemporary Americans. This concealment of the actual costs of government fostered the natural inclination to think that the services were free. Unfortunately, any attempt to withdraw or reduce the benefit is then fought tooth and nail because it is viewed as a right. In the case of the American colonists, they correctly identified their rights to protection from attack and to a fair system of courts and laws, but they had avoided paying for the benefits for so long that by the 1770s they viewed any imposition of taxes as oppression.

Dissatisfaction with the Navigation Acts themselves only reflected the deeper changes in economic thought being developed at exactly that time by Scottish professor Adam Smith, who had formulated his *Theory of Moral Sentiments* in 1754. Arguing that men naturally had a self-interest based on information that only they could know—likes, dislikes, personal foibles—Smith had laid the groundwork for his more famous book, *Wealth of Nations,* which would appear concurrent with the Declaration of Independence. Smith reformulated economics around individual rights rather than the state's needs. His concepts fit with Thomas Jefferson's like a hand in a glove; indeed, it would be Alexander Hamilton and some of the Federalists who later would clash repeatedly with Smith's individual-oriented economic principles. While *Wealth of Nations* in no way influenced the writings of Adams or others in 1776, the ideas of personal economic liberty had already seeped into the American psyche, almost as if Adams and Jefferson had read Smith extensively.[19]

Thus, at the very time that the British started to enforce a creaky, antiquated system that had started its drift into obsolescence, Americans—particularly seaboard merchants—started to flex their entrepreneurial muscles in Smith's new free-market concepts. Equally important, Americans had started to link economic rights and political rights in the most profound ways. At accelerating rates the colonists used the terms "slavery" and "enslavement" in relation to British government policies.[20] If the king could assault citizen's liberties when it came to trade, how long before he issued edicts on political speech, and even religion?

The Stamp Act of 1765

Parliament, meanwhile, continued to shift the fiscal burdens from overtaxed landowners in England to the American colonists with the awareness that the former voted and the latter did not. Attempting to extract a fraction of the cost of troops sent to defend the colonies, Grenville—who, as historian Paul Johnson notes, "had a gift for doing the wrong thing"—pushed through a stamp tax, which was innocuous in its direct effects but momentous in its symbolism.[21] The act placed a tax on virtually every paper transaction. Marriage certificates, ships' papers, legal documents, newspapers, even playing cards and dice were to be stamped and therefore taxed. Worse, the act raised the terrifying threat that if paper documents were subject to government taxation and control, how long before Puritan, Baptist, Quaker, and Methodist religious tracts or even Bibles came under the oversight of the state? To assume as much was not unrealistic, and certainly Sam Adams argued that this was the logical end-point: "The Stamp-Act itself was contrived with a design only to inure the people to the habit of contemplating themselves as slaves of men; and the transition from thence to a subjection to Satan, is mighty easy."[22] Although most colonists were alarmed at the precedent set by the Stamp Act, the fact that newspapers were taxed ensured that the publishing organs of the colonies universally would be aligned against England on the issue.[23]

Hostility to the new act ran far deeper than its narrow impact on newspapers, however. An often overlooked component of the policies involved the potential for ever-expanding hordes of administrators and duty collectors in the colonies. Had the pecuniary burdens been completely inconsequential, the colonists still would have protested the insidious, invasive presence of an army of royal bureaucrats and customs officials. Several organizations were formed for the specific purpose of harassing stamp agents, many under the name Sons of Liberty. They engaged in violence and intimidation of English officials, destroying the stamps and burning the Boston house of the lieutenant governor, Thomas Hutchinson. Sympathetic colonial juries then refused to convict members of the Sons of Liberty, demonstrating that the colonists saw the economic effects as nil, but the political ramifications as substantial.[24]

Parliament failed to appreciate the firestorm the new policies were causing. Edmund Burke observed of the House of Commons, "Far from any thing inflammatory, I never heard a more languid debate in this House."[25] In the colonies, however, reaction was immediate and dramatic. Virginia again led the way in resistance, focused in the House of Burgesses with Patrick Henry as the chief spokesman for instant response. He offered five resolutions against the Stamp Act that constituted a radical position. Many strongly disagreed with his views, and a Williamsburg law student named Thomas Jefferson, who witnessed the debates, termed them "most bloody."[26] Nevertheless, the delegates did not disagree with Henry's assessment of the legality of the act, only his methods in responding to them, which many thought could have been more conciliatory. Henry achieved immortality with the provocative tone of his resolutions, reportedly stating: "If this be treason, make the most of it."

Leaders from Massachusetts, led by James Otis, agreed. They suggested that an intercolonial congress be held at City Hall, in New York, a meeting known as the Stamp Act Congress (1765). Delegates drafted a bill of rights and issued a statement of grievances, reiterating the principle of no taxation without representation. Confronted with unified, outraged opposition, Parliament backed down. A new government under the Marquis of Rockingham repealed the Stamp Act in 1766, in no small degree because of internal dissatisfaction with the program in England, where manufacturers had started to lose sales. But other groups in England, particularly landholders who again faced increased tax burdens themselves, denounced the repeal as appeasement. In retreat, Parliament issued a Declaratory Act, maintaining that it had the authority to pass new taxes any time it so chose, but both sides knew Britain had blinked.

A "Massacre" in Boston

After Rockingham was dismissed under pressure from English landlords, the king recalled ailing William Pitt from his peerage to form a new government. Pitt's coalition government included disparate and uncooperative groups and, after 1767, actual power over England's mercantilist policies devolved upon Charles Townshend, the chancellor of the Exchequer. Under new duties enacted by Parliament, the words changed but the song remained the same: small taxes on glass, lead, tea or other products but significant shifts of authority to Parliament. This was Parliament's shopworn tactic: exchange small initial duties for gigantic new powers that could be used later oppressively.

Townshend persuaded Parliament to suspend the New York Assembly for its refusal to provide necessary supplies under the Mutiny Act (also called the Quartering Act) of 1765. He hoped to isolate New York (even though Massachusetts' Assembly similarly had refused to vote funds for supplies), realizing that the presence of the army headquarters in New York City made it imperative that the English government maintain control of the situation there. Once again, the colonists did not object to the principle of supporting troops or even quartering them, but instead challenged the authority of Parliament to mandate such support. A series of written arguments by Charles C. Pinckney and Edward Rutledge (both of South Carolina), Daniel Dulany of Maryland, and John Dickinson of Pennsylvania provided a comprehensive critique of the new acts based on English law and traditions. Dickinson's "Letters from a Farmer in Pennsylvania" reached wide audiences and influenced groups outside the seaboard elites. British officials were stunned to find that, rather than abandoning New York, other colonies expressed their support for their sister colony.

No more important ally of New York could exist than Massachusetts, where Sam Adams and a group of vocal followers organized resistance in the Massachusetts Assembly. Letters went out from the assembly to other colonies urging them to resist the new taxes and to boycott British goods until the measures were lifted. The missive might have died, except for further meddling by the British secretary of state, who warned that Parliament would dissolve any colonial assemblies that endorsed the position of the Massachusetts Assembly. All of the colonies promptly supported the Massachusetts letter, even Pennsylvania, which had refused to support the earlier correspondence.

Whereas New York had borne the brunt of England's initial policies, Boston rapidly became the center of revolutionary ferment and British repercussions. Britain transferred four regiments of troops from Halifax to Boston, stationing them directly within the city in a defiant symbol of occupation. Bostonians reacted angrily to the presence of "redcoats" and "lobsterbacks," whereas the soldiers treated citizens rudely and competed with them for off-hour work. Tensions heightened until on March 5, 1770, a street fight erupted between a mob of seventy or so workers at a shipyard and a handful of British sentries. Snowballs gave way to gunfire from the surrounded and terrified soldiers, leaving five colonists dead and six wounded. American polemicists, especially Sam Adams, lost no time in labeling this the Boston Massacre. Local juries thought otherwise, finding the soldiers guilty of relatively minor offenses, not murder, thanks in part to the skillful legal defense of John Adams.

If Britain had had her way, the issue would have died a quiet death. Unfortunately for Parliament, the other Adams—John's distant cousin Sam—played a crucial role in fanning the fires of independence. He had found his calling as a writer after failing in private business and holding a string of lackluster jobs in government. Adams enlisted other gifted writers, who published under pen names, to produce a series of broadsides like those produced by Dickinson and the premassacre pamphleteers. But Adams was the critical voice disturbing the lull that Britain sought, publishing more than forty articles in a two-year period after the massacre. He established the Lockean basis for the rights demanded by Americans, and did so in a clear and concise style that appealed to less-educated citizens. In November 1772 at a town meeting in Boston, Adams successfully pressed for the creation of a "committee of correspondence" to link writers in different colonies. These actions demonstrated the growing power of the presses churning out a torrent of tracts and editorials critical of England's rule. The British were helpless to stop these publishers. Certainly court actions were no longer effective.[27]

Following the example of Massachusetts, Virginia's House of Burgesses, led by Jefferson, Henry, and Richard Henry Lee, forged resolutions that provided for the appointment of permanent committees of correspondence in every colony (referred to by one governor as "blackhearted fellows whom one would not wish to meet in the dark"). Committees constituted an "unelected but nevertheless representative body" of those with grievances against the British Empire.[28] Josiah Quincy and Tom Paine joined this Revolutionary vanguard, steadfastly and fearlessly demanding that England grant the colonists the "rights of Englishmen." Adams always remained on the cutting edge, however, and was among the first advocating outright separation from the mother country. Tied to each other by the committees of correspondence, colonies further cemented their unity, attitudes, and common interests or, put another way, became increasingly American.

By 1775 a wide spectrum of clubs, organizations, and merchants' groups supported the committees of correspondence. Among them the Sons of Liberty, the Sons of Neptune, the Philadelphia Patriotic Society, and others provided the organizational framework necessary for revolution; the forty-two American newspapers—and a flood of pamphlets and letters—gave voice to the Revolution. Churches echoed the messages of liberty, reinforcing the goal of "ting[eng] the minds of the people and impregnat[ing] them with the sentiments of liberty."[29] News such as the colonists' burning in 1772 of the *Gaspee*, a British schooner that ran aground in Rhode Island during an ill-fated mission to enforce revenue laws, circulated quickly throughout the colonies even before the correspondence committees were fully in place, lending further evidence to the growing public perception that the imperial system was oppressive. Thus, the colonial dissatisfaction incorporated the yeoman farmer and the land speculator, the intellectual and the merchant, the parson and the politician—all well organized and impressively led.

Boston emerged as the focal hub of discontent, and the brewing rebellion had able leaders in the Adamses and a dedicated coppersmith named Paul Revere. Lacking the education of John Adams or the rhetorical skill of Sam, Revere brought his own considerable talents to the table of resistance. A man plugged in to the Boston social networks as were few other men, Revere was known by virtually all. One study found that besides the Sons of Liberty, there were six other main revolutionary groups in Boston. Of the 255 leading males in Boston society, only two were in as many as five of these groups—Joseph Warren and Paul Revere.[30] Revere percolated the Revolutionary brew, keeping all parties informed and laying down a vital structure of associations that he would literally call upon at a moment's notice in 1775. Only through his dedicated planning was an effective resistance later possible.

Boston's Tea Party
Under such circumstances, all that was needed to ignite the Revolutionary explosion was a spark, which the British conveniently provided with the passage of the Tea Act in 1773. Tea played a crucial role in the life of typical America colonists. The water in North America remained undrinkable in many locations—far more polluted with disease and bacteria than modern drinking water—thus tea, which was boiled, made up the staple nonalcoholic drink. The East India Company had managed to run itself into near bankruptcy despite a monopoly status within the empire. Its tea sent to America had to go through England first, where it was lightly taxed. But smugglers dealing directly with Dutch suppliers shipped directly to the colonies and provided the same tea at much lower prices. The Tea Act withdrew all duties on tea reexported to America, although it left in place an earlier light tax from the Townshend Act.

Britain naturally anticipated that colonists would rejoice at the lower aboveboard prices, despite the imposition of a small tax. In fact, not only did average colonists benefit from drinking the cheap smuggled tea, but a number of merchant politicians, including John Hancock of Massachusetts, also regularly smuggled tea and stood to be wiped out by enforcement of the new act. Even those merchants who legitimately dealt in tea faced financial ruin under the monopoly privileges of the East India Company. Large public meetings produced a strategy toward the tea, which involved not only boycotting the product but also preventing the tea from even being unloaded in America.

Three ships carrying substantial amounts of tea reached Boston Harbor in December 1773, whereupon a crowd of more than seven thousand (led by Sam Adams) greeted them. Members of the crowd—the Sons of Liberty dressed as Mohawk Indians—boarded the vessels and threw 342 chests of tea overboard while the local authorities condoned the action. The British admiral in charge of the Boston Harbor squadron watched the entire affair from his flagship deck.

In Delaware, nine days later, a similar event occurred when another seven hundred chests of tea sank to the bottom of the sea, although without a Sam Adams to propagandize the event, no one remembers the Delaware Tea Party. New Yorkers forced cargo to remain on its ships in their port. When some tea was finally unloaded in Charleston, it couldn't be sold for three years. Throughout, only a few eminent colonists, including Ben Franklin and John Adams, condemned the boardings, and for the most part Americans supported the "Mohawks." But even John Adams agreed that if a people rise up, they should do something "to be remembered, something notable and striking."[31]

"Notable and striking," the "tea party" was. Britain, of course, could not permit such outright criminality. The king singled out Boston as the chief culprit in the uprising, passing in 1774 the Intolerable or Coercive Acts that had several major components. First, Britain closed Boston Harbor until someone paid for the tea destroyed there. Second, the charter of Massachusetts was annulled, and the governor's council was to be appointed by the king, signaling to the citizens a revocation of their rights as Englishmen. Third, a new Quartering Act was passed, requiring homeowners and innkeepers to board soldiers at only a fraction of the real cost of boarding them. Fourth, British soldiers and officials accused of committing crimes were to be returned to England for trial. Fifth, the Quebec Act transferred lands between the Ohio and Mississippi rivers to the province of Quebec and guaranteed religious freedom to Catholics. New Englanders not only viewed the Quebec Act as theft of lands intended for American colonial settlement, they also feared the presence of more Catholics on the frontier. John Adams, for one, was terrified of the potential for a recatholicization of America. Antipapism was endemic in New England, where political propagandists fulminated against this new encroachment of the Roman "Antichrist."

Southerners had their own reasons for supporting independence. Tidewater planters found themselves under an increasing debt burden, made worse by British taxes and unfair competition from monopolies.[32] Lord Dunmore's antislavery initiatives frightened the Virginia planters as much as the Catholic priests terrified New Englanders. At a time when slavery continued to exert mounting tensions on Whig-American notions of liberty and property, the fact that the Southerners could unite with their brethren farther north had to concern England.

Equally as fascinating as the alliance between the slave colonies and the nonslaveholding colonies was the willingness of men of the cloth to join hardened frontiersmen in taking up arms against England. John Witherspoon, a New Jersey cleric who supported the resistance, warned that "there is not a single instance in history in which civil liberty was lost, and religious liberty preserved entire."[33] Virginia parson Peter Muhlenberg delivered a sermon, then grabbed his rifle.[34]

Massachusetts attorney and New Jersey minister; Virginia farmer and Pennsylvania sage; South Carolina slaveholder and New York politician all found themselves increasingly aligned against the English monarch. Whatever differences they had, their similarities surpassed them. Significantly, the colonists' complaints encompassed all oppression: "Colonists didn't confine their thoughts about [oppression] simply to *British* power; they generalized the lesson in terms of human nature and politics at large."[35] Something even bigger than resistance to the king of England knitted together the American colonists in a fabric of freedom. On the eve of the Revolution, they were far more united—for a wide variety of motivations—than the British authorities ever suspected. Each region had its own reason for associating with the others to force a peaceful conclusion to the crisis when the Intolerable Acts upped the ante for all the players.

If British authorities truly hoped to isolate Boston, they realized quickly how badly they had misjudged the situation. The king, having originally urged that the tea duty be repealed, reluctantly concluded that the "colonists must either triumph or submit," confirming Woodrow Wilson's estimate that George III "had too small a mind to rule an empire."[36] Intending to force compliance, Britain dispatched General Thomas Gage and four regiments of redcoats to Massachusetts. Gage was a tragic figure. He proved unrelenting in his enforcement methods, generating still more colonial opposition, yet he operated within a code of "decency, moderation, liberty, and the rule of law."[37] This sense of fairness and commitment to the law posed a disturbing dilemma for his objective of crushing the rebellion.

The first united resistance by the colonies occurred in September 1774, when delegates to a Continental Congress convened in Philadelphia in response to calls from both Massachusetts and Virginia. Delegates from every colony except Georgia arrived, displaying the widespread sympathy in the colonies for the position of Boston. Present were both Adamses from Massachusetts and Patrick Henry, Richard Henry Lee, and the "indispensable man," George Washington, representing Virginia. Congress received a series of resolves from Suffolk County, Massachusetts, carried to the meeting by Paul Revere. These Suffolk Resolves declared loyalty to the king, but scorned the "hand which would ransack our pockets" and the "dagger to our bosoms." When Congress endorsed the Suffolk Resolves, Lord Dartmouth, British secretary of state, warned, "The [American] people are generally ripe for the execution of any plan the Congress advises, should it be war itself." King George put it much more succinctly, stating, "The die is cast."

No act of the Congress was more symbolic of how far the colonies had come toward independence than the Galloway Plan of union. Offered by Joseph Galloway of Pennsylvania, the plan proposed the establishment of a federal union for the colonies in America, headed by a president general (appointed by the king) and advised by a grand council, whose representatives would be chosen by the colonial assemblies. Presented roughly three weeks after the Suffolk Resolves, the Galloway Plan was rejected only after a long debate, with the final vote taken only in the absence of many of the advocates. Still, it showed that the colonies already had started to consider their own semiautonomous government.

Revolutionary Ideas

In October 1774, the First Continental Congress adopted a Declaration of Rights and Grievances, twelve resolutions stating the rights of the colonists in the empire. Among the resolutions was a statement of the rights of Americans to "life, liberty, and property . . . secured by the principles of the British Constitution, the unchanging laws of nature, and [the] colonial charters." Where had the colonists gotten such concepts?

Three major Enlightenment thinkers deeply affected the concepts of liberty and government held by the majority of the American Revolutionary leaders. Certainly, all writers had not read the same European authors, and certainly all were affected by different ideas to different degrees, often depending on the relationship any given writer placed on the role of God in human affairs. Nevertheless, the overall molding of America's Revolution in the ideological sense can be traced to the theories of Thomas Hobbes, John Locke, and the Baron Charles de Montesquieu.

Hobbes, an English writer of the mid-1600s, was a supporter of the monarchy. In *The Leviathan* (1661), Hobbes described an ancient, even prehistoric, "state of nature" in which man was "at warre with every other man," and life was "solitary, poor, nasty, brutish, and short."[38] To escape such circumstances, man created the "civil state," or government, in which people gave up all other rights to receive protection from the monarch. As long as government delivered its subjects from the "fear of violent death," it could place on them any other burden or infringe on any other "rights." From Hobbes, therefore, the Revolutionary writers took the concept of "right to life" that infused virtually all the subsequent writings.

Another Englishman, John Locke, writing under much different circumstances, agreed with Hobbes that a state of nature once existed, but differed totally as to its character. Locke's state of nature was beautiful and virtually sinless, but somehow man had fallen out of that state, and to protect his rights entered into a social compact, or a civil government. It is significant that both Hobbes and Locke departed substantially from the classical Greek and Roman thinkers, including Aristotle, who held that government was a natural condition of humans. Both Hobbes and Locke saw government as artificial—created by man, rather than natural to man. Locke, writing in his "Second Treatise on Government," described the most desirable government as one that protected human "life, liberty, and estate"; therefore, government should be limited: it should only be strong enough to protect these three inalienable rights. From Locke, then, the Revolutionary writers took the phrase "right to liberty," as well as to property.[39] Hobbes and Locke, therefore, had laid the groundwork for the Declaration of Rights and Grievances and, later, the Declaration of Independence, which contained such principles as limitations on the rights of the government and rule by consent of the governed.

All that remained was to determine how best to guarantee those rights, an issue considered by a French aristocrat, Charles de Montesquieu. In *The Spirit of the Laws*, drawing largely on his admiration for the British constitutional system, Montesquieu suggested dividing the authority of the government among various branches with different functions, providing a blueprint for the future government of the United States.[40]

While some of the crème de la crème in American political circles read or studied Locke or Hobbes, most Virginia and Massachusetts lawyers were common attorneys, dealing with property and personal rights in society, not in abstract theory. Still, ideas do seep through. Thanks to the American love of newspapers, pamphlets, oral debate, and informal political discussion, by 1775, many of the Revolutionaries, whether they realized it or not, sounded like John Locke and his disciples.

Locke and his fellow Whigs who overthrew James II had spawned a second generation of propagandists in the 1700s. Considered extremists and "coffee house radicals" in post-Glorious Revolution England, Whig writers John Trenchard, Lord Bolingbroke, and Thomas Gordon warned of the tyrannical potential of the Hanoverian Kings—George I and George II. Influential Americans read and circulated these "radical Whig" writings. A quantified study of colonial libraries, for example, shows that a high number of Whig pamphlets and newspaper essays had made their way onto American bookshelves. Moreover, the Whig ideas proliferated beyond their original form, in hundreds of colonial pamphlets, editorials, essays, letters, and oral traditions and informal political discussions.[41]

It goes without saying, of course, that most of these men were steeped in the traditions and teachings of Christianity—almost half the signers of the Declaration of Independence had some form of seminary training or degree. John Adams, certainly and somewhat derogatorily viewed by his contemporaries as the most pious of the early Revolutionaries, claimed that the Revolution "connected, in one indissoluble bond, the principles of civil government with the principles of Christianity."[42] John's cousin Sam cited passage of the Declaration as the day that the colonists "restored the Sovereign to Whom alone men ought to be obedient."[43] John Witherspoon's influence before and after the adoption of the Declaration was obvious, but other well-known patriots such as John Hancock did not hesitate to echo the reliance on God. In short, any reading of the American Revolution from a purely secular viewpoint ignores a fundamentally Christian component of the Revolutionary ideology.

One can understand how scholars could be misled on the importance of religion in daily life and political thought. Data on religious adherence suggests that on the eve of the Revolution perhaps no more than 20 percent of the American colonial population was "churched."[44] That certainly did not mean they were not God-fearing or religious. It did reflect, however, a dominance of the three major denominations—Congregationalist, Presbyterian, and Episcopal—that suddenly found themselves challenged by rapidly rising new groups, the Baptists and Methodists. Competition from the new denominations proved so intense that clergy in Connecticut appealed to the assembly for protection against the intrusions of itinerant ministers. But self-preservation also induced church authorities to lie about the presence of other denominations, claiming that "places abounding in Baptists or Methodists were unchurched."[45] In short, while church membership rolls may have indicated low levels of religiosity, a thriving competition for the "religious market" had appeared, and contrary to the claims of many that the late 1700s constituted an ebb in American Christianity, God was alive and well—and fairly popular!

Lexington, Concord, and War

Escalating the potential for conflict still further, the people of Massachusetts established a revolutionary government and raised an army of soldiers known as minutemen (able to fight on a minute's notice). While *all* able-bodied males from sixteen to sixty, including Congregational ministers, came out for muster and drill, each militia company selected and paid additional money to a subgroup—20 to 25 percent of its number—to "hold themselves in readiness at a minute's warning, complete with arms and ammunition; that is to say a good and sufficient firelock, bayonet, thirty rounds of powder and ball, pouch and knapsack."[46] About this they were resolute: citizens in Lexington taxed themselves a substantial amount "for the purpose of mounting the cannon, ammunition, and for carriage and harness for burying the dead."[47] It is noteworthy that the colonists had already levied money for burying the dead, revealing that they approached the coming conflict with stark realism.

The nearly universal ownership and use of firearms as a fact bears repetition here to address a recent stream of scholarship that purports to show that Americans did not widely possess or use firearms.[48] Some critics of the so-called gun culture have attempted to show through probate records that few guns were listed among household belongings bequeathed to heirs; thus, guns were not numerous, nor hunting and gun ownership widespread. But in fact, guns were *so prevalent* that citizens did not need to list them specifically. On the eve of the Revolution, Massachusetts citizens were well armed, and not only with small weapons but, collectively, with artillery.[49]

General Thomas Gage, the commander of the British garrison in Boston, faced two equally unpleasant alternatives. He could follow the advice of younger officers, such as Major John Pitcairn, to confront the minutemen immediately, before their numbers grew. Or he could take a more conservative approach by awaiting reinforcements, while recognizing that the enemy itself would be reinforced and better equipped with each passing day.

Gage finally moved when he learned that the minutemen had a large store of munitions at Concord, a small village eighteen miles from Boston. He issued orders to arrest the political firebrands and rhetoricians Samuel Adams and John Hancock, who were reported in the Lexington area, and to secure the cannons from the colonists. Gage therefore sought to kill two birds with one stone when, on the night of April 18, 1775, he sent 1,000 soldiers from Boston to march up the road via Lexington to Concord. If he could surprise the colonials and could capture Adams, Hancock, and the supplies quietly, the situation might be defused. But the patriots learned of British intentions and signaled the British route with lanterns from the Old North Church, whereupon two riders, Paul Revere and William Dawes left Boston by different routes to rouse the minutemen. Calling, "To Arms! To Arms!" Revere and Dawes's daring mission successfully alerted the patriots at Lexington, at no small cost to Revere, who fell from his horse after warning Hancock and Adams and was captured at one point, but then escaped.[50] Dawes did not have the good fortune to appear in Longfellow's famous poem, "The Midnight Ride of Paul Revere," and his contributions are less appreciated; but his mission was more narrowly defined. Once alerted, the minutemen drew up in skirmish lines on the Lexington town common when the British appeared. One of the British commanders shouted, "Disperse, you dam'd rebels! Damn you, disperse!"[51] Both sides presented their arms; the "shot heard 'round the world" rang out—although historians still debate who fired first—and the British achieved their first victory of the war. Eight minutemen had been killed and ten wounded when the patriots yielded the field. Major Pitcairn's force continued to Concord, where it destroyed the supplies and started to return to Boston.[52]

By that time, minutemen in the surrounding countryside had turned out, attacking the British in skirmishing positions along the road. Pitcairn sent for reinforcements, but he knew that his troops had to fight their way back to Boston on their own. A hail of colonial musket balls fell on the British, who deployed in battle formation, only to see their enemy fade into the trees and hills. Something of a myth arose that the American minuteman were sharpshooters, weaned on years of hunting. To the contrary, of the more than five thousand shots fired at the redcoats that day, fewer than three hundred hit their targets, leaving the British with just over 270 casualties.

Nevertheless, the perception by the British and colonists alike quickly spread that the most powerful army in the world had been routed by patriots lacking artillery, cavalry, or even a general. At the Centennial Celebration at Concord on April 19, 1875, Ralph Waldo Emerson described the skirmish as a "thunderbolt," which "falls on an inch of ground, but the light of it fills the horizon."[53] News crackled like electricity throughout the American colonies, sparking patriotic fervor unseen up to that time. Thousands of armed American colonists traveled to Boston, where they surrounded Gage and pinned him in the town. Franklin worked under no illusions that the war would be quick. To an English acquaintance, he wrote, "You will have heard before this reaches you of the Commencement of a Civil War; the End of it perhaps neither myself, nor you, who are much younger, may live to see."[54]

For the third time in less than a century, the opponents of these American militiamen had grossly underestimated them. Though slow to act, these New Englanders became "the most implacable of foes," as David Fischer observed. "Their many enemies who lived by a warrior-ethic always underestimated them, as a long parade of Indian braves, French aristocrats, British Regulars, Southern planters, German fascists, Japanese militarists, Marxist ideologues, and Arab adventurers have invariably discovered to their heavy cost."[55]

Resolutions endorsing war came from all quarters, with the most outspoken coming from North Carolina. They coincided with the meeting of the Second Continental Congress in Philadelphia beginning on May 10, 1775. All the colonies sent representatives, most of whom had no sanction from the colonial governors, leaving their selection to the more radical elements in the colonies. Accordingly, men such as John Adams attended the convention with the intent of declaring independence from England. Some conservatives, such as John Dickinson of Pennsylvania, struggled to avoid a complete break with the mother country, but ultimately the sentiments for independence had grown too strong. As the great American historian George Bancroft observed, "A new principle, far mightier than the church and state of the Middle Ages, was forcing itself into power. . . . It was the office of America to substitute for hereditary privilege the natural equality of man; for the irresponsible authority of a sovereign, a dependent government emanating from a concord of opinion."[56] Congress assumed authority over the ragtag army that opposed Gage, and appointed George Washington as the commander in chief. Washington accepted reluctantly, telling his wife, Martha, "I have used every endeavor in power to avoid [the command], not only from my unwillingness to part with you . . . but from a consciousness of its being a trust too great for my capacity."[57] Nor did Washington have the same intense desire for separation from England that burned within Samuel Adams or Patrick Henry: his officers still toasted the health of King George as late as January 1776.

The "Indispensable Man"

Washington earned respect in many quarters because he seldom beat his own drum. His modesty and self-deprecation were refreshing and commendable, and certainly he had real reasons for doubting his qualifications to lead the colonial forces (his defeat at Fort Necessity, for example). But in virtually all respects, Washington was the perfect selection for the job—the "indispensable man" of the Revolution, as biographer James Flexner called him. Towering by colonial standards at six feet four inches, Washington physically dominated a scene, with his stature enhanced by his background as a wealthy plantation owner of more than modest means and his reputation as the greatest horseman in Virginia. Capable of extracting immense loyalty, especially from most of his officers (though there were exceptions), Washington also inspired his soldiers with exceptional self-control, personal honor, and high morals. While appearing stiff or distant to strangers, Washington reserved his emotions for his intimate friends, comrades in arms, and his wife.

For such a popular general, however, Washington held his troops in low regard. He demanded clear distinctions in rank among his officers, and did not tolerate sloth or disobedience. Any soldier who went AWOL (absent without leave) faced one hundred to three hundred lashes, whereas a soldier deserting a post in combat was subject to the death penalty. He referred to Yankee recruits as "dirty and nasty people," and derided the "dirty mercenary spirit" of his men.[58] On occasion, Washington placed sharpshooters behind his army as a disincentive to break ranks. Despite his skill, Washington never won a single open-field battle with the British, suffering heartbreaking defeats on more than one occasion.

Nevertheless, in the face of such losses, of constant shortages of supplies and money, and of less than unified support from the colonists themselves, Washington kept his army together—ignoring some of the undisciplined antics of Daniel Morgan's Virginians and the Pennsylvania riflemen—and skillfully avoided any single crushing military debacle that would have doomed the Revolution. What he lacked in tactics, he made up for in strategy, realizing that with each passing day the British positions became more untenable. Other colonial leaders were more intellectually astute, perhaps; and certainly many others exhibited flashier oratorical skills. But more than any other individual of the day, Washington combined a sound mind with practical soldier's skills; a faith in the future melded with an impeccable character; and the ability to wield power effectively without aspiring to gain from it personally (he accepted no pay while commander in chief, although he kept track of expenses owed him). In all likelihood, no other single person possessed these essential qualities needed to hold the Revolutionary armies together.

He personified a spirit among militia and regular soldiers alike, that Americans possessed superior fighting capabilities to the British military. They "pressed their claim to native courage extravagantly because they went to war reluctantly."[59] Americans sincerely believed they had an innate courage that would offset British advantages in discipline: "Gunpowder and Lead shall be our Text and Sermon both," exclaimed one colonial churchgoer.[60] Led by Washington's example, the interrelationship between the freeman and the soldier strengthened as the war went on.

"Give Me Liberty, or Give Me Death!"

Washington shuddered upon assuming command of the 30,000 troops surrounding Boston on July 3, 1775. He found fewer than fifty cannons and an ill-equipped "mixed multitude of people" comprising militia from New Hampshire, Connecticut, Rhode Island, and Massachusetts. (Franklin actually suggested arming the military with bows and arrows!)[61] Although Washington theoretically commanded a total force of 300,000 scattered throughout the American colonies, in fact, he had a tiny actual combat force. Even the so-called regulars lacked discipline and equipment, despite bounties offered to attract soldiers and contributions from patriots to bolster the stores. Some willingly fought for what they saw as a righteous cause or for what they took as a threat to their homes and families, but others complained that they were "fed with promises" or clothed "with filthy rags."[62] Scarce materials drove up costs for the army and detracted from an efficient collection and distribution of goods, a malady that plagued the colonial armies until the end of the war. Prices paid for goods and labor in industry always exceeded those that the Continental Congress could offer—and beyond its ability to raise in taxation—making it especially difficult to obtain troops. Nevertheless, the regular units provided the only stable body under Washington's command during the conflict—even as they came and went routinely because of the expiration of enlistment terms.

Against the ragtag force mustered by the colonies, Great Britain pitted a military machine that had recently defeated the French and Spanish armies, supplied and transported by the largest, best-trained, and most lavishly supplied navy on earth. Britain also benefited from numerous established forts and outposts; a colonial population that in part remained loyal; and the absence of immediate European rivals who could drain time, attention, or resources from the war in America. In addition, the British had an able war commander in the person of General William Howe and several experienced officers, such as Major General John Burgoyne and Lord Cornwallis.

Nevertheless, English forces faced a number of serious, if unapparent, obstacles when it came to conducting campaigns in America. First and foremost, the British had to operate almost exclusively in hostile territory. That had not encumbered them during the French and Indian War, so, many officers reasoned, it would not present a problem in this conflict. But in the French and Indian War, the British had the support of most of the local population; whereas now, English movements were usually reported by patriots to American forces, and militias could harass them at will on the march.

Second, command of the sea made little difference in the outcome of battles in interior areas. Worse, the vast barrier posed by the Atlantic made resupply and reinforcement by sea precarious, costly, and uncertain. Communications also hampered the British: submitting a question to the high command in England might entail a three-month turnaround time, contingent upon good weather.

Third, no single port city offered a strategic center from which British forces could deploy. At one time the British had six armies in the colonies, yet they never managed to bring their forces together in a single, overwhelming campaign. They had to conduct operations through a wide expanse of territory, along a number of fronts involving seasonal changes from snow in New Hampshire to torrid heat in the Carolinas, all the while searching for rebels who disappeared into mountains, forests, or local towns.

Fourth, British officers, though capable in European-style war, never adapted to fighting a frontier rebellion against another western-style army that had already adapted to the new battlefield. Competent leaders such as Howe made critical mistakes, while less talented officers like Burgoyne bungled completely. At the same time, Washington slowly developed aggressive officers like Nathaniel Greene, Ethan Allen, and (before his traitorous actions) Benedict Arnold.

Fifth, England hoped that the Iroquois would join them as allies, and that, conversely, the colonists would be deprived of any assistance from the European powers. Both hopes were dashed. The Iroquois Confederacy declared neutrality in 1776, and many other tribes agreed to neutrality soon thereafter as a result of efforts by Washington's able emissaries to the Indians. A few tribes fought for the British, particularly the Seneca and Cayuga, but two of the Iroquois Confederacy tribes actively supported the Americans and the Onondaga divided their loyalties. As for keeping the European nations out, the British succeeded in officially isolating America only for a short time before scores of European freedom fighters poured into the colonies. Casimir Pulaski, of Poland, and the Marquis de Lafayette, of France, made exemplary contributions; Thaddeus Kosciusko, another Pole, organized the defenses of Saratoga and West Point; and Baron von Steuben, a Prussian captain, drilled the troops at Valley Forge, receiving an informal promotion from Benjamin Franklin to general.

Von Steuben's presence underscored a reality that England had overlooked in the conflict—namely, that this would not be a battle against common natives who happened to be well armed. Quite the contrary, it would pit Europeans against their own. British success in overcoming native forces had been achieved by discipline, drill, and most of all the willingness of essentially free men to submit to military structures and utilize European close-order, mass-fire techniques.[63] In America, however, the British armies encountered Continentals who fought with the same discipline and drill as they did, and who were as immersed in the same rights-of-Englishmen ideology that the British soldiers themselves had grown up with.

It is thus a mistake to view Lexington and Concord, with their pitiable shot-to-kill ratio, as constituting the style of the war. Rather, Saratoga and Cowpens reflected the essence of massed formations and shock combat, with the victor usually enjoying the better ground or generalship. Worth noting also is the fact that Washington's first genuine victory came over mercenary troops at Trenton, not over English redcoats, though that too would come. Even that instance underscored the superiority of free soldiers over indentured troops of any kind.

Sixth, Great Britain's commanders in the field each operated independently, and each from a distance of several thousand miles from their true command center, Whitehall. No British officer in the American colonies had authority over the entire effort, and ministerial interventions often reflected not only the woefully outdated appraisals of the situation—because of the delay in reporting intelligence—but also the internal politics that afflicted the British army until well after the Crimean War.

Finally, of course, France decisively entered the fray in 1778, sensing that, in fact, the young nation might actually survive, and offering the French a means to weaken Britain by slicing away the North American colonies from her control, and providing sweet revenge for France's humiliating defeat in the Seven Years' War. The French fleet under Admiral Françoise Joseph de Grasse lured away the Royal Navy, which secured Cornwallis's flanks at Yorktown, winning at Sandy Hook one of the few great French naval victories over England. Without the protection of the navy's guns, Yorktown fell. There is little question that the weight of the French forces tipped the balance in favor of the Americans, but even had France stood aside, the British proved incapable of pinning down Washington's army, and despite several victories had not broken the will of the colonists.

Opening Campaigns

Immediately before Washington took command, the first significant battle of the conflict occurred at Breed's Hill. Patriot forces under General Israel Putnam and Colonel William Prescott had occupied the bluffs by mistake, intending instead to occupy Bunker Hill. The position overlooked the port of Boston, permitting the rebels to challenge ships entering or leaving the port and even allowing the Americans to shell the city itself if they so desired. William Howe led a force of British troops in successive assaults up the hill. Although the redcoats eventually took Breed's Hill when the Americans ran out of ammunition, the cost proportionately to the British was enormous. Almost half the British troops were either killed or wounded, and an exceptional number of officers died (12 percent of all British officers killed during the entire war). England occupied the heights and held Boston, but even that success proved transitory.

By March 1776, Henry Knox had arrived from Fort Ticonderoga in New York, where, along with Ethan Allen and Benedict Arnold, the patriots had captured the British outpost. Knox and his men then used sleds to drag captured cannons to Dorchester Heights overlooking Boston. The British, suddenly threatened by having their supply line cut, evacuated on St. Patrick's Day, taking a thousand Tories, or Loyalists, with them to Halifax, Nova Scotia. Only two weeks before, in North Carolina, patriot forces had defeated a body of Tories, and in June a British assault on Charleston was repulsed by 600 militiamen protected by a palmetto-wood fort.

Early in 1776 the Americans took the offensive. Benedict Arnold led a valiant march on Quebec, making the first of many misguided attempts to take Canada. Americans consistently misjudged Canadian allegiance, thinking that exposure to American "liberators" would provoke the same revolutionary response in Canada as in the lower thirteen colonies. Instead, Arnold's force battled the harsh Canadian winter and smallpox, living on "boiled candles and roasted moccasins." Arriving at the city with only 600 men, Arnold's small army was repulsed in its first attack on the city. After receiving reinforcements, a second American attack failed miserably, leaving three hundred colonists prisoner. Arnold took a musket ball in the leg, while American Colonel Aaron Burr carried Montgomery's slain body from the city. Even in defeat, Arnold staged a stubborn retreat that prevented British units under General Guy Carleton from linking up with General Howe in New York. Unfortunately, although Washington appreciated Arnold's valor, few others did. Arnold's theater commanders considered him a spendthrift, and even held him under arrest for a short time, leading the hero of many of America's early battles to become bitter and vengeful to the point of his eventual treason.

Gradually, even the laissez-faire American armies came to appreciate the value of discipline, drill, and long-term commitment, bolstered by changing enlistment terms and larger cash bonuses for signing up. It marked a slow but critical replacement of Revolutionary zeal with proven military practices, and an appreciation for the necessity of a trained army in time of war.[64]

While the northern campaign unfolded, British reinforcements arrived in Halifax, enabling Howe to launch a strike against New York City with more than 30,000 British and German troops. His forces landed on Staten Island on July second, the day Congress declared independence. Supported by his brother, Admiral Lord Howe, General Howe drove out Washington's ill-fed and poorly equipped army, captured Long Island, and again threatened Washington's main force. Confronted with a military disaster, Washington withdrew his men across the East River and into Manhattan. Howe missed an opportunity to capture the remainder of Washington's troops, but he had control of New York. Loyalists flocked to the city, which became a haven for Tories throughout the war.

Washington had no alternative but to withdraw through New Jersey and across the Delaware River, in the process collecting or destroying all small vessels to prevent the British from following easily. At that point the entire Revolution might have collapsed under a less capable leader: he had only 3,000 men left of his army of 18,000, and the patriot forces desperately needed a victory. In the turning point of the war, Washington not only rallied his forces but staged a bold counterattack, recrossing the Delaware on Christmas night, 1776, against a British army (made up of Hessian mercenaries) at Trenton. "The difficulty of passing the River in a very severe Night, and their march thro' a violent Storm of Snow and Hail, did not in the least abate [the troops'] Ardour. But when they came to the Charge, each seemed to vie with the other in pressing forward," Washington wrote.[65] At a cost of only three casualties, the patriots netted 1,000 Hessian prisoners. Washington could have chalked up a victory, held his ground, and otherwise rested on his laurels, but he pressed on to Princeton, where he defeated another British force, January 2–3, 1777. Washington, who normally was reserved in his comments about his troops, proudly informed Congress that the "Officers and Men who were engaged in the Enterprize behaved with great firmness, poise, advance and bravery and such as did them the highest honour."[66] Despite the fact that large British armies remained in the field, in two daring battles Washington regained all the momentum lost in New York and sent a shocking message to the befuddled British that, indeed, they were in a war after all.

Common Sense and the Declaration of Independence

As Washington's ragtag army tied up British forces, feelings for independence grew more intense. The movement awaited only a spokesman who could galvanize public opinion around resistance against the king. How unlikely, then, was the figure that emerged! Thomas Paine had come to America just over a year before he wrote *Common Sense*, arriving as a failure in almost everything he attempted in life. He wrecked his first marriage, and his second wife paid him to leave. He destroyed two businesses (one as a tobacconist and one as a corset maker) and flopped as a tax collector. But Paine had fire in his blood and defiance in his pen. In January 1776 he wrote his fifty-page political tract, *Common Sense*, which began with one of the most memorable lines in history: "These are the times that try men's souls. The summer soldier and the sunshine patriot will, in this crisis, shrink from the service of his country."[67] But eager readers did not shrink from buying the book, which quickly sold more than a hundred thousand copies. (Eventually, Paine sold close to a half-million copies prior to 1800, and he could have been a wealthy man—if he hadn't donated every cent he earned to the Revolution!) *Common Sense* provided the prelude to Jefferson's Declaration of Independence that appeared in July 1776. Paine argued that the time for loyalty to the king had ended. "The blood of the slain, the weeping voice of nature cries, 'Tis Time to Part,' " Paine wrote.

He thus tapped into widespread public sentiment, evidenced by the petitions urging independence that poured into the Continental Congress. Many colonial delegations received instructions from home to support independence by May 1776. On May fifteenth, Virginia resolved in its convention to create a Declaration of Rights, a constitution, a federation, and foreign alliances, and in June it established a republican government, for all intents and purposes declaring its independence from England. Patrick Henry became governor. Virginia led the way, and when the state congressional delegations were sent to vote on independence, only Virginia's instructions were not conditional: the Commonwealth had already thrown down the gauntlet.[68]

In June, Virginia delegate Richard Henry Lee introduced a resolution that "these United Colonies are, and of right ought to be, free and independent States." The statement so impressed John Adams that he wrote, "This day the Congress has passed the most important resolution . . . ever taken in America."[69] As the momentum toward separation with England grew, Congress appointed a committee to draft a statement announcing independence. Members included Adams, Franklin, Roger Sherman, Robert Livingston, and the chairman, Thomas Jefferson, to whom the privilege of writing the final draft fell. Jefferson wrote so eloquently and succinctly that Adams and Franklin made only a few alterations, including Franklin's "self-evident" phrase. Most of the changes had to do with adding references to God.

Even so, the final document remains a testament to the skill of Jefferson in capturing the essence of American ideals. "We hold these truths to be self-evident," he wrote, that "all men are created equal; that they are endowed by their creator with certain unalienable rights; that among these are life, liberty, and the pursuit of happiness."[70] It is worth noting that Jefferson recognized that humans were "created" by a Supreme Being, and that all rights existed only in that context. Further reiterating Locke, he wrote that "to secure these rights, governments are instituted among men, deriving their just powers from the consent of the governed; that, whenever any form of government becomes destructive of these ends, it is the right of the people to alter or abolish it, and to institute new government." Government was natural, not artificial, so that when one government disappeared, the citizenry needed to establish another. But it should be kept in mind that these "self-evident" rights constituted "an escalating sequence of connected assertions" that ended in revolution, appealing not only to God, but to English history and law.[71]

This distanced Jefferson from the writings of Hobbes, and even though he borrowed heavily from Locke, he had further backed away from the notion that the civil state was artificial. On the other hand, Jefferson, by arguing that men "instituted" governments, borrowed entirely from the Enlightenment proposition that government was a human creation in the first place. In short, the Declaration clearly illustrated the dual strains of Western thought that had emerged as predominant by the 1700s: a continuing reverence for the primacy of God in human affairs, and yet an increasing attraction to the notion that earthly systems depended on human intellect and action, even when all aspects of that philosophy were not fully embraced.

Jefferson's original draft, however, contained "censures on the English people" that some in Congress found excessive, and revisions, despite John Adams's frequent defenses of Jefferson's words, excised those sentences. The most offensive was Jefferson's traditional Virginia account of American slavery's being the fault of England. But any criticism of slavery—no matter whose fault—also indicted the slave colonies, and was not tolerated.[72] After a bitter debate over these phrases, and other editing that changed about half of the draft, Congress adopted the final Declaration on July 4, 1776, after adopting a somewhat less refined version on July second. Two weeks later Congress voted to have the statement engrossed on parchment and signed by the members, who either appeared in person on August second or later affixed their names (Hancock's being the largest since he, reportedly, wanted the king to be able to read it without his spectacles). Each one of the fifty-six signers knew that the act of signing the Declaration made them traitors to the Crown, and therefore the line in which the delegates "mutually pledge to each other our Lives, our Fortunes, and our sacred Honor" literally exposed these heroes to execution. By the end of the war, almost every one had lost his property; many had lost wives and families to British guns or prisons; and several died penniless, having given all to the Revolution.

North to Saratoga

Following his stunning surprise attack at Trenton and his subsequent victory at Princeton, Washington experienced more defeats at Brandywine Creek and Germantown. In the second battle, the Americans nearly won and only the timely arrival of reinforcements gave the British a victory. Washington again had to retreat, this time to winter quarters at Valley Forge, near Philadelphia.

What ensued was one of the darkest times for Washington and his army: while the British enjoyed warmth and food in one of America's richest cities, the Continentals suffered through a miserable winter, decimated by illness and starvation, eating soup made of "burnt leaves and dirt." Washington deluged Congress with letters and appeals. "Soap, Vinegar, and other Articles allowed by

Congress we see none," he wrote. Few men had more than a shirt, and some "none at all, and a number of Men confined to Hospitals for want of shoes."[73] Gradually, the army obtained supplies and equipment, and in the Spartan environment Washington fashioned a disciplined fighting force. Washington proved the glue that held the entire operation together. Consistent and unwavering, he maintained confidence in front of the men, all the while pouring a steady stream of requests for support to the Congress, which was not so much unreceptive as helpless: its only real source of income was the confiscation of Tory properties, which hardly provided the kind of funds demanded by armies in the field. The printing of paper money—continentals—had proven a disaster, and American commanders in the field had taken to issuing IOUs in return for food, animals, and other supplies. Yet in that frozen Pennsylvania hell, Washington hammered the Americans into a tough fighting force while the British grew lazy and comfortable, especially in New York and Philadelphia. Franklin quipped that Howe did not take Philadelphia so much as Philadelphia had taken Howe. The policy of occupying and garrisoning "strategic hamlets" proved no more successful in the 1770s than it did just under two hundred years later when the American army tried a similar strategy in Vietnam, and with much the same effect on the morale of the occupiers.

Washington's was not the only American army engaging the British. General John "Gentleman Johnny" Burgoyne launched an invasion of the Mohawk Valley, where he was to be supported by a second British column coming from Oswego under Barry St. Leger. A third British force under Howe was to join them by moving up the Hudson. The plan came apart rapidly in that Howe never moved north, and St. Leger retreated in the face of Benedict Arnold and Nicholas Herkimer's forces. Further, the Indian allies of the British abandoned them, leaving Burgoyne in a single column with extended supply lines deep in enemy territory. Having forgotten the fate of Varus's Roman legions in the Teutoburg Forest centuries earlier, Burgoyne's wagons bore the general's fine china, best dress clothes, four-poster bed, and his mistress—with all her personal belongings. (His column's entourage included four hundred "women camp-followers," some wives; some paid servants; most, prostitutes.) Whatever their intangible contributions to morale, they slowed Burgoyne's army to a crawl.

Burgoyne's scavenging units ran into the famed Green Mountain Boys, commanded by Ethan Allen, who killed or captured all the British detachments. When news of the victory reached New England towns, militia flooded into General Horatio Gates's command. He had 12,000 militia and 5,000 regulars facing Burgoyne's 6,000 troops with their extended supply lines. Burgoyne sensed he had to break the colonial armies before he was surrounded or his overtaxed transport system collapsed, prompting him to launch two attacks at Freeman's Farm near Saratoga in September and October. The patriots decisively won the second encounter, leaving Burgoyne to ponder escape or surrender. Still placing his faith in reinforcements that, unbeknownst to him, would not arrive, Burgoyne partied in Saratoga, drinking and cavorting with his mistress. On October seventeenth, when it at last dawned on him that no relief was coming, and with his army hungry, stranded, and surrounded, Burgoyne surrendered his entire force as the band played "Yankee Doodle." In this age of civility in warfare, the defeated British troops merely turned in their arms and marched to Boston, where they boarded transports for England, promising only that they would not take up arms against Americans again.

Trust the French

When spring arrived, the victory at Saratoga, and the thousands of arms it brought to Washington's forces, gave Americans a new resolve. The ramifications of Saratoga stretched far beyond the battlefields of North America, all the way to Europe, where the colonists had courted France as a potential ally since the outbreak of hostilities. France sensibly stayed out of the conflict until the patriots proved they had a chance of surviving. After Saratoga, however, Louis XVI agreed to discreetly support the American Revolution with munitions and money. A number of factors accounted for the willingness of France to risk involvement. First, the wounds of the Seven Years' War still ached, and France wanted revenge. Second, if America won independence without the help of European allies, French (and Spanish) territories in North America might be considered fair game for takeover by the new republic. Finally, any policy that weakened English power abroad was viewed favorably at Versailles. Thus, France furnished funds to the colonists through a front business called Rodrigue Hortalez and Company. It is estimated that until 1780 the colonial army received 90 percent of its powder from the French enterprise.

Even before official help arrived from Louis's court, numbers of individual Frenchmen had volunteered for service in the Continental Army, many seeking merely to advance mercenary careers abroad. Some came strictly for glory, including the extremely talented Louis Berthier, later to gain fame as Napoleon's chief of staff. More than a few sincerely wished to see America succeed for idealistic reasons, including Lafayette, the young nobleman who in 1777 presented himself to Washington, who accorded him a nomination for major general. But the colonies needed far more than laundered money and a handful of adventurers: they needed the French navy to assist in transporting the Continental Army—giving it the mobility the British enjoyed—and they could benefit from the addition of French troops as well.

To that end, the Continental Congress dispatched Silas Deane in early 1776 as its agent to Paris, and several months later Arthur Lee and Benjamin Franklin joined him. Franklin emerged as the premier representative in France, not just because Congress recalled Deane in 1777, but because the droll Franklin was received as a celebrity by the Parisians. Varying his dress from Quaker simplicity to frontier buckskins, the clever Pennsylvanian effortlessly quoted Voltaire or Newton, yet he appealed to common footmen and chambermaids. Most important to the struggle to enlist French aid, however, Franklin adroitly utilized British conciliation proposals to convince France that America might attain independence without her. In February 1778 France signed commercial and political treaties with the Continental Congress, agreeing that neither side would make a separate peace without the other.

Spain joined the war in April 1779 as an ally of France for the purpose of regaining Gibraltar, Minorca, Jamaica, and Florida. By 1780, France and Spain had put more than 120 warships into action in the American theater and, combined with the heroic, harassing escapades of John Paul Jones, menaced British shipping lanes, besieged Gibraltar, threatened Jamaica, and captured Mobile and Pensacola. French ships commanded by Admiral Jean-Baptiste d'Estaing even mounted an unsuccessful attack on Newport, Rhode Island, before retreating to the West Indies.

British abuses at sea already had alienated Holland, which in 1780 joined Denmark, Sweden, Portugal, and Russia in the League of Armed Neutrality, whose members agreed their ships would fire on approaching British vessels at sea rather than submit to boarding. In an amazing display of diplomatic ineptitude, Britain had managed to unite all the major navies of the world against its quest to blockade a group of colonies that lacked a navy of their own! Not only did that place all of England's supply and transport strategies in America at risk, but it internationalized the war in such a way as to make England seem a bully and a villain. Perhaps most important of all, the aid and support arrived at the very time that Washington's army had dwindled to extremely low levels.

Southern Invasion, Northern Betrayal

Despite the failures at Trenton, Princeton, and Saratoga, the British still fielded five substantial armies in North America. British generals also concluded, however, that their focus on the northern colonies had been misplaced, and that their true base of loyalist support lay in the South. Georgia and the Carolinas contained significant numbers of Tories, allowing the British forces to operate in somewhat friendly territory. In 1778 the southern offensive began when the British landed near Savannah.

In the meantime, Washington suffered a blow of a personal nature. Benedict Arnold, one of his most capable subordinates and an officer who had been responsible for victories at Ticonderoga, Quebec, and, in part, Saratoga, chafed under the apparent lack of recognition for his efforts. In 1778–79 he commanded the garrison in Philadelphia, where he married Peggy Shippen, a wealthy Tory who encouraged his spending and speculation. In 1779 a committee charged him with misuse of official funds and ordered Washington to discipline Arnold. Instead, Washington, still loyal to his officer, praised Arnold's military record.

Although he received no official reprimand, Arnold had amassed huge personal debts, to the point of bankruptcy. Arnold played on Washington's trust to obtain a command at the strategic fort West Point, on the Hudson, whereupon he intrigued to turn West Point over to British general Henry Clinton. Arnold used a courier, British major John André, and nearly succeeded in surrendering the fort. André—wearing civilian clothes that made him in technical terms a spy—stumbled into the hands of patriots, who seized the satchel of papers he carried. Arnold managed to escape to England, but André was tried and executed for his treason (and later interred as an English national hero at Westminster Abbey). Britain appointed Arnold a brigadier general and gave him command of small forces in Virginia; and he retired to England in 1781, where he ended his life bankrupt and unhappy, his name in America equated with treason. As colonial historian O. H. Chitwood observed, if Arnold "could have remained true to his first love for a year longer his name would probably now have a place next to that of Washington in the list of Revolutionary heroes."[74]

Events in the South soon required Washington's full attention. The British invasion force at Savannah turned northward in 1779, and the following year two British columns advanced into the Carolinas, embattled constantly by guerrilla fighters Thomas Sumter, Andrew Pickens, and the famed "Swamp Fox," Francis Marion. Lord Cornwallis managed to forge ahead, engaging and crushing a patriot army at Camden, but this only brought the capable Nathaniel Greene to command over the inept Horatio Gates. Greene embraced Washington's view that avoiding defeat was as important as winning battles, becoming a master at what Russell Weigley calls "partisem war," conducting a retreat designed to lure Cornwallis deep into the Carolina interior.[75]

At Cowpens (January 1781), colonial troops under Daniel Morgan met Sir Banastre Tarleton near the Broad River, dealing the British a "severe" and "unexpected" blow, according to Cornwallis. A few months later Cornwallis again closed with the Greene's forces, this time at Guilford Courthouse, and again Greene retreated rather than lose his army. Once more he sucked Cornwallis farther into the American interior. After obtaining reinforcements and supplies, Cornwallis pressed northward after Greene into Virginia, where he expected to join up with larger contingents of British forces coming down from the northern seaboard.

Washington then saw his opportunity to mass his forces with Greene's and take on Cornwallis one on one. Fielding 5,000 troops reinforced by another 5,000 French, Washington quickly marched southward from New York, joining with French Admiral Joseph de Grasse in a coordinated strike against Cornwallis in Virginia.

By that time, Washington's men had not been paid for months, a situation soon remedied by Robert Morris, the "financier of the Revolution." News arrived that the *Resolve* had docked in Boston with two million livres from France, and the coins were hauled to Philadelphia, where the Continental troops received their pay. Alongside the formal, professional-looking French troops, Washington's men looked like a rabble. But having survived the winter camps and evaded the larger British armies, they had gained confidence. It was hardly the same force that Washington had led in retreat two years earlier. Now, Washington's and Rochambeau's forces arrived in the Chesapeake Bay region, where they met a second French column led by Lafayette, and together the Franco-American forces outnumbered the British by 7,000 men.

Cornwallis, having placed his confidence in the usually reliable Royal Navy, was distressed to learn that de Grasse had defeated a British fleet in early September, depriving the general of reinforcements. (It was the only major victory in the history of the French navy.) Although not cut off from escape entirely, Cornwallis—then fortified at Yorktown—depended on rescue by a British fleet that had met its match on Chesapeake Bay. Over the course of three weeks, the doomed British army held out against Henry Knox's artillery siege and Washington's encroaching trenches, which brought the Continentals and French steadily closer. Ultimately, large British redoubts had to be taken with a direct attack, and Washington ordered nighttime bayonet charges to surprise the defenders. Alexander Hamilton captured one of the redoubts, which fell on the night of October 10, 1781, and the outcome was assured. Nine days later Cornwallis surrendered. As his men stacked their arms, they "muttered or wept or cursed," and the band played "The World Turned Upside Down."[76] Nevertheless, in October of 1781, Britain fielded four other armies in North America, but further resistance was futile, especially with the French involved. Washington had proven himself capable not only of commanding troops in the field but also of controlling a difficult international alliance. The colonists had shown themselves—in large part thanks to Robert Morris—clever enough to shuffle money in order to survive. Tory sentiment in America had not provided the support England hoped, and efforts to keep the rebels isolated from the Dutch and Spanish also had collapsed. As early as 1775, British Adjutant General John Harvey recognized that English armies could not conquer America, and he likened it to driving a hammer into a bin of corn, with the probable outcome that the hammer would disappear. Although they controlled Boston, New York, Newport, Philadelphia, and Charleston, the British never subdued the countryside, where nine out of their fourteen well-equipped forces were entirely captured or destroyed. In the nine Continental victories, British losses totaled more than 20,000 men—not serious by subsequent Napoleonic standards, but decisive compared to the total British commitment in North America of 50,000 troops.

Although Washington never equaled the great military tacticians of Europe, he specialized in innovative uses of riflemen and skirmishers, and skillfully maneuvered large bodies of men in several night operations, then a daunting command challenge. By surviving blow after blow, Washington (and Greene as well) conquered. (In 1781, Greene even quipped, "Don't you think that we bear beating very well, and that . . . the more we are beat, the better we grow?")[77]

The Treaty of Paris, 1783

In April 1782, John Adams, John Jay, and Benjamin Franklin opened negotiations with British envoy Richard Oswald.[78] Oswald knew Franklin and was sympathetic to American positions. By November, the negotiations were over, but without the French, who still wanted to obtain territorial concessions for themselves and the Spanish. Although the allies originally agreed to negotiate together, by 1783, French foreign minister Vergennes was concerned America might obtain too much western territory in a settlement, and thus become too powerful. America ignored the French, and on November 30, 1792, representatives from England and America signed the Treaty of Paris, ending the War of Independence.

The treaty also established the boundaries of the new nation: to the south, Spain held Florida and New Orleans; the western boundary was the Mississippi River; and the northern boundary remained what it had been *ante bellum* under the Quebec Act. Americans had the rights to fish off Newfoundland and in the Gulf of St. Lawrence, and vessels from England and America could navigate the Mississippi River freely. France, having played a critical role in the victory, came away from the conflict with only a few islands in the West Indies and a terrific debt, which played no small part in its own revolution in 1789. Spain never recovered Gibraltar, but did acquire the Floridas, and continued to lay a claim to the Louisiana Territory until 1802. Compensation for losses by the Tories was a sticking point because technically the individual states, and not the Continental Congress, had confiscated their properties. Nevertheless, the commissioners ultimately agreed to recommend that Congress encourage the states to recompense Loyalists for their losses. In sum, what Washington gained on the field, Jay and Franklin more than held at the peace table.[79]

One final ugly issue raised its head in the negotiations. American negotiators insisted that the treaty provide for compensation to the owners of slaves who had fled behind British lines. It again raised the specter, shunted away at the Continental Congress's debate over the Declaration, that the rights of Englishmen—or, in this case, of Americans—still included the right to own slaves. It was a dark footnote to an otherwise impressive diplomatic victory won by the American emissaries at the peace negotiations.[80]

CHAPTER FOUR

A Nation of Law, 1776–89

Inventing America

Gary Wills aptly described the early Revolutionaries' efforts at making new governments as "inventing America."[1] Jefferson's Declaration literally wiped the slate clean, providing the new nation's leaders with tremendous opportunities to experiment in the creation of the Republic. Yet these opportunities were fraught with dangers and uncertainties; the Revolutionary Whigs might fail, just as the Roundheads had failed in the English Civil War, and just as the Jacobins in France would soon fail in their own revolution.

Instead, these "founding brothers" succeeded. The story of how they invented America is crucial in understanding the government that has served the United States for more than two hundred years, and, more broadly, the growth of republican institutions in Western civilization. John Adams knew the opportunities and perils posed by the separation from England and the formation of a new government, noting that he and his contemporaries had been "thrown into existence at a period when the greatest philosophers and lawgivers of antiquity would have wished to live. A period when a coincidence of circumstances . . . has afforded to the thirteen Colonies . . . an opportunity of beginning government anew from the foundation."[2] Contrary to popular belief, America's federal Constitution was not an immediate and inevitable result of the spirit of 1776. Indeed, briefly, in March 1783, some question existed about whether an army mutiny over pay might not result either in a military coup or Washington relenting to pressures to "take the crown," as one colonel urged him to do. Instead, Washington met with the ringleaders, and while putting on his eyeglasses, shattered their hostility by explaining that he had "not only grown gray but almost blind in service to my country."[3] Their resistance melted, as did the neonatal movement to make him king—though the regal bearing stayed draped over him until the end. As late as 1790, Franklin observed of Washington's walking stick, "If it were a sceptre, he would have merited it."[4] More than anyone, Washington knew that he had helped found a republic and for that reason, if no other, his presence at the Constitutional Convention was important, if not necessary.

Washington's actions aside, the story of the drafting and ratification of the federal Constitution was not one of "chaos and Patriots to the rescue," with wise Federalists saving the nation from anarchy and disarray under the Articles of Confederation. Rather, a complex story emerges—one that contained the origins of political parties in the United States and the adoption of the legal basis of republican government.

Time Line

1776: Declaration of Independence; states adopt new constitutions
1777: Articles of Confederation (Congress adopts, but states do not finish ratifying until 1781); Articles of Confederation ratified; Congress establishes Bank of North America
1783: Treaty of Paris; Newburgh Conspiracy
1784: Ordinance of 1784
1785: Land Ordinance of 1785
1786: Jay-Gardoqui Treaty rejected; Virginia Religious Freedom Act; Shays' Rebellion; Indian Ordinance of 1786; Annapolis Convention
1787: Constitutional Convention; Northwest Ordinance; the *Federalist Papers*
1788: Constitution ratified by all states except Rhode Island and North Carolina
1789: New government forms

Highways and Wolves

Having declared the American colonies independent of Great Britain, the patriot Whigs immediately set about the task of creating new governments as sovereign states. The task was huge and the possibilities were unprecedented; and one sentiment seemed unanimous: *no* kings! Americans, Jefferson observed, "shed monarchy" like an old suit of clothes. But what kind of government would the Whigs create? No nation in existence at the time had elected leaders; there were no precedents. On the other hand, Americans had considerable experience governing themselves, and they possessed a vast arsenal of ideas about the proper forms and nature of government.[5] Governing a nation, however, was different. Adams worried that "the lawgivers of antiquity . . . legislated for single cities [but] who can legislate for 20 or 50 states, each of which is greater than Greece or Rome at those times?"[6] His concerns, while not inconsequential, ignored the reality that the "lawgivers of antiquity" did not have a shared understanding of Enlightenment precepts—a rich tapestry interwoven with the beliefs of radical English Whigs. Adams also missed a fundamental demographic fact of the infant United States, namely that it was young. By 1790 half the nation's population of four million was under sixteen years of age, meaning a homogenous revolutionary generation started with the same Whig/Enlightenment principles and, to some degree, matured in their thinking along similar lines. Probably the most important value they shared was a commitment to the principle that constitutions should take the form of succinct, written documents. They rejected the ethereal English "constitution," with its diffuse precedent-based rulings, unwritten common law bases, and patchwork of historic charters spanning five hundred years of English history. About constitutions, Americans insisted on getting it down on paper, a trait that would characterize virtually all of their legal processes, even to a fault.

Second, the designers of the post-Revolutionary governments were localists and provincials. They wanted government small and close to home. Just as they opposed royal rule from a distance of fifteen hundred miles, so too they distrusted suggestions to form a centralized North American state. Aside from fighting the British, they had few needs from a grand governmental establishment—perhaps commercial treaties and common weights and measures, but even those came under scrutiny. One Briton sarcastically wrote that Americans were primarily concerned with "the regulation of highways and the destruction of wolves."[7]

In eighteenth-century terms, these Whigs espoused egalitarianism and democracy: the struggling gods of monarchy, divine right, absolutism, and the rest of the feudal golems were utterly rejected. But one should take care to temper terms like "democracy" and "republicanism" in the understanding of the day. American Revolutionaries did not envision citizenship for Indians, women, and blacks, even in their most radical egalitarian fantasies. Yet despite their narrow definition of polity, these transplanted Englishmen lived in what was undoubtedly the most radically democratic society on the face of the earth. Land was abundant and cheap, and because they tied the right to vote to property ownership, more Americans became voters every year and, with the age demographic noted earlier, a mass of politically active men obtained the franchise at nearly the same time.

It is difficult to quantify data in the period before the first federal census, but most historians agree that 50 to 75 percent of the white, male Revolutionary population obtained the right to vote, leading Tory governor Thomas Hutchinson to write disparagingly that in America, the franchise was granted to "anything with the appearance of a man."[8] All did not share such a low view of the yeomen, though, especially Jefferson, who thought that if a farmer and a professor were confronted with the same problem, the "former will decide it often better than the latter, because he had not been led astray by artificial rules."[9] Surprisingly to some, Adams (initially) agreed: "The mob, the herd and the rabble, as the Great always delight to call them," were as entitled to political rights as nobles or kings: the "best judges," as editorialist Cato called the public.[10]

Implicit in the emerging vision of government was the separation-of-power doctrine borrowed from Montesquieu—the division of authority between executive, judicial, and legislative branches of government. This did not equate with a belief in the balance of powers, which became more popular after the Revolutionary War, especially among the Federalists. Rather, most Whigs argued that governmental branches should indeed be separate, but that one—the legislative—should retain most power. Given the colonists' recent experience with King George and his royal governors, such a view is easy to understand. The legislature's power of the purse entitled it, they held, to a paramount position in the government.

Whig political thinkers of the day also adopted what we today call civil libertarianism, or the organized articulation of the Whig fear of abusive power and the people's need to sustain a militia and to keep and bear firearms. "Due process," a term derived from the Whigs' advocacy of jury trial; the right to file petitions of habeas corpus; opposition to cruel and unusual punishment—all flowed from this concern for government's capacity for abuse. Other libertarian beliefs revolved around freedom of speech, petition, assembly, and religion, and freedom of the press. Except for religious practice, all of these freedoms dealt explicitly with *political* issues. "Free speech" meant the right to address publicly the shortcomings of government, the right to assembly related to groups massing to demonstrate against the state, and so on. By the twenty-first century, legislators would become so concerned about the impact of money in financing political advertisements that they would attempt to regulate it. But the founders' intentions were clear: the right to speak out against government (including financing of pamphlets, broadsides, or other forms of "advertising") was the single most important right they addressed, aside from possession of firearms. Other widely held beliefs included Locke's declaration of a right to attain and keep property, which Americans radicalized even further by insisting on minimal taxation. All of it, of course, had to be written down.

Those who invented America did not forget their recent difficulties communicating with Parliament and George III, a point that led them to require that legislators directly represent their constituents. This translated into smaller legislative districts, short terms, and close contact with the constituents. It also meant, however, that since the legislatures would have the most power, the Whig constitution makers would bridle them even more through frequent (annual) elections, recall, and impeachment. Concerns about character, when legislators and their constituents knew each other personally and met frequently, could be addressed firsthand.

Thus, the Revolutionary Whigs came to the task of creating a government with an array of strong principles grounded in localism, egalitarianism, and libertarianism expressed through written constitutions, and constrained by separation of power, legislative dominance, and direct representation. Constraint, constraint, constraint—that was the overriding obsession of the Founders. Whigs recognized that while government was necessary to protect life, liberty, and property, the people who comprised the government inevitably tried to accumulate and abuse power unless properly checked by fundamental law. Sam Adams assessed it when he wrote, "Jealousy is the best security of publick Liberty."[11]

Such priorities also underscored another important point, that despite enthusiastically accepting the end product of the Lockean view of rights, American political theorists had rejected the underlying assumptions of both Hobbes and Locke that government was artificial. Jefferson said so himself in the Declaration, insisting that even when people abolished a tyrannical government, they had to replace it with a just and benign one. At its very origins, therefore, the American idea had certain tensions between civil rights that emanated from a worldview and the basis of the worldview itself.

In part, the direction of the young Republic took the turns that it did precisely because the hands at the tiller were those of Revolutionary liberals who shared the basic Whig assumptions, and their dominance, in turn, had in part arisen from the departure of more conservative, pro-monarchy voices that found remaining in the new nation untenable. The flight of the Loyalists to Canada and England played no small role in guaranteeing one type of consensus at the deliberating bodies that produced the subsequent state and federal constitutions.

Chaos and Patriots to the Rescue?

The standard fare for most twentieth-century high school and college texts expressed the view that the Articles of Confederation period constituted a "critical period" during which America experienced a precarious brush with anarchy. Modern big-government liberals look upon the era with disgust. Genuine problems plagued the young nation. The economy plummeted and crowds rioted, with Shays' Rebellion (1786) epitomizing the new nation's problems stemming from the Articles. This "preconstitution" that governed the nation from 1783–87 proved ill suited to organizing the country, leaving the Confederation Congress corrupt, bankrupt, and inept—a body that bungled domestic affairs and drifted into weakness against foreign powers. Then, according to this story, a band of heroes galloped to the rescue. Washington, Hamilton, Jay, Franklin, and others called the 1787 Philadelphia Convention and wrote the Constitution, lifting the endangered nation out of its morass and providing a sensible governing framework. These Founders saved America from ruin and established a system of government that endured to the present day.[12] Unfortunately, little of this interpretation is accurate. Historian Merrill Jensen, especially, spent much of his career debunking what he called the "Myth of the Confederation Era."[13]

Like all good stories, the "Chaos and Patriots to the Rescue" interpretation of John Fiske contains several elements of truth. Certainly, Confederation governmental institutions did not provide all the answers to the new nation's most pressing problems. And some of the story, no doubt, was driven by the partisan political viewpoint of the early historians, who tended to glorify the role of the Founders. The 1780s, in fact, witnessed a division of the early Whigs into factions that strongly disagreed over the course that the new nation should follow. Nationalists (later called Federalists) cried "anarchy," while others (later known as Anti-Federalists or Jeffersonian Republicans) pointed to the successes of the Confederation government and noted that, among its other accomplishments, it had waged a war against—and defeated—Great Britain, the greatest military power on earth. So which historical view is correct? Although historians continue to debate the successes of the Articles of Confederation, matters become clearer if it is approached as the document it was, the first Constitution.

Even dating the Articles, though, is difficult. Although not legally adopted until 1781, Congress in fact functioned within the framework of the Articles from the time of its drafting in 1777. To make matters more complex, the First and Second Continental Congresses of 1774–76 operated under a system exactly like the one proposed in 1777; therefore, realistically, the United States was governed under the Articles of Confederation from the time of the Declaration of Independence until Washington was inaugurated as the first president of the United States under the federal Constitution in March 1788.[14]

While the Continental Congress developed a structure for running the colonies' affairs during the early part of the Revolution, it remained informal until three weeks prior to the Declaration of Independence, at which time the states sought to formalize the arrangements through a government that would fight the war while simultaneously leaving to the individual states most of their powers and prerogatives. On June 12, 1776, Congress appointed a committee with one representative from each state to draft such a constitution. Headed by the "Pennsylvania Farmer," John Dickinson, the committee one month later presented a draft of the Articles of Confederation (given its name by another committee member, Benjamin Franklin).

Objections to the new plan surfaced quickly, and immediately drifted into territory that many delegates had avoided, the issue of slavery. The heavily populated areas protested the fact that each state had an equal vote in the Congress (akin to today's United States Senate), but the more lightly populated southern colonies had different concerns involving the counting of slaves for representation in a body determined by population (such as today's House of Representatives). Perhaps more important at the time, however, the states disagreed over what is often referred to as public domain. Several of the thirteen states possessed sea-to-sea charters and claimed lands within the parallels stretching from the Atlantic to the Pacific Oceans. These "landed" states (Virginia, the Carolinas, Georgia, and others) were opposed by "landless" states (Maryland, Delaware, and New Jersey), which insisted that the landed states relinquish all their claims west of the Appalachian crest to the Confederation as a whole. Ultimately, the parties agreed to postpone the discussion until the ratification of the Articles of Confederation in 1781, but it raised the question of charters and grants in a broad sense. Was a charter from the king an inviolable contract? If so, did England's grip on the colonies remain, even after independence? If not, were all pre-Independence contracts null and void? And if such contracts were void, what did that say about property rights—that they only existed after the new nation was born?

Congress, meanwhile, continued to operate under the terms of the unratified Articles throughout the 1776–78 period, becoming one of the most successful Revolutionary legislatures in the history of Western civilization. In retrospect, the

Articles created a remarkably weak central government, precisely because that was what the radical Whigs wanted. Not surprisingly, the Whigs who had battled royal governors and a king for seven years did not leap to place power in a new chief executive in 1777, and the same logic applied to the courts, which Whigs assumed functioned best at the state, not national, level. There was provision in the Articles for congressional litigation of interstate disputes, but it proved ineffective.

That left only the legislative branch of government at the national level, which was exactly how the Whigs wanted it. Their definition of federalism differed significantly from the one taught in a modern political science class. Federalism meant a system of parallel governments—state, local, and national—each with its specified powers, but sovereignty ultimately rested in the states and, by implication, the people themselves. Whigs saw this as completely different from "nationalism," which divided power among the same three levels (state, local, and national) but with the national government retaining the ultimate authority. This latter model appeared after the federal Constitution of 1787, but a decade earlier, anyone who called himself a Federalist embraced the decentralized Confederation model, not that of a sovereign centralized state. In this way, the Articles preceded or, more appropriately, instigated, a raucous debate over the federalism of the American Revolution.

After independence, delegates to the Congress changed the name of that body from Continental Congress to Confederation Congress. The number of delegates each state sent had varied throughout the war, from two to seven per state, although each state retained one vote, cast according to a majority of its congressmen. This aspect of the Confederation seemed to lend credibility to the argument that the nation was merely an affiliation of *states,* not a unified American *people.* But other sections appeared to operate on different assumptions. A seven-state majority could pass most laws, but only a nine-state vote could declare war and ratify treaties, clauses that challenged the contention that the states were sovereign. After all, if states were sovereign, how could even a vote of twelve of them, let alone nine, commit all to a war? The schizophrenic nature of some of these provisions came to a head in the amendment clause, where thirteen votes—unanimous agreement—were needed to amend the Articles themselves. Given the nature of Revolutionary state politics, this stipulation rendered certain provisions of the Articles, for all intents and purposes, invulnerable to the amendment process.

Congressmen wrote all the national laws then executed them through a series of congressional committees, including foreign affairs, war, finance, post office, and so on. Congress possessed limited fundamental powers. Only Congress could conduct diplomacy, make treaties, and declare war; it could coin and borrow money, deliver mail through a national post office, and set a uniform standard of weights and measures. As part of its diplomatic charge, Congress dealt with the Indian tribes, negotiated treaties with them, and created a national Indian policy. And, when a national domain came into being in 1781, Congress had exclusive charge to legislate policies for land sales and territorial government (as it turned out, one of its most important powers).

These powers put Congress on a sound footing, but in true Whig fashion, the Articles of Confederation saved many important prerogatives for the states and the people. For example, Congress could only requisition money and soldiers from the states, thus leaving true taxation and military power at the local level. This taxation provision meant that Congress could not regulate commerce through import and export duties. So the Confederation Congress was a true Whig government—which had its economic and military arm tied behind its back. As Article 2 of the Articles of Confederation stated clearly (and the Tenth Amendment to the Constitution would later reiterate), "Each State retains its sovereignty, freedom, and independence, and every power, jurisdiction, and right, which is not by this Confederation expressly delegated to the United States, in Congress assembled."

The New State Constitutions

Meanwhile, the states had simultaneously developed their own constitutions, claiming state sovereignty over the national Congress in many matters. During the years immediately following the Declaration of Independence, eleven of the thirteen states drafted and ratified new constitutions. In nearly all cases, radicals squared off against moderates, with the radicals carrying the day. State constitution making is a complex subject, with variations spanning the thirteen new American states. Yet certain patterns emerged: all of the constitution makers acknowledged the almost sacred nature of writing constitutions and sharply differentiated that process from that of merely passing legislation. Moreover, most of the new constitutions showed marked radical Whig tendencies, including written bills of rights, and institutionalized broad suffrage for white males. They fostered republicanism through direct representation, and provided for separation of power between executive, legislative, and judicial branches, but not "balance" of power. Indeed, the thirteen state governments, with notable exceptions, severely limited the executive and judicial branches of government. The result was that there were smaller state versions of the national model: strong, legislative government with important but less powerful judicial and executive components.[15]

Once again, the drafters all accepted the premise that their constitutions should appear in concise written form. They also agreed that a crucial difference between constitutional law and mere statute law existed. Constitutional law stood as close to natural law (God's law) as mere mortals could possibly place it. In this the drafters inherently sided with classical thinkers like Aristotle over modernists like Thomas Hobbes: the former all held that government was natural, even to the point of being a spiritual exercise, whereas the latter held that the state was artificial. Thus, Jefferson, one of the most vocal advocates of small government, wrote in the Declaration that after altering or abolishing government, it is the "right" of the people to "institute new Government." By siding with the classical thinkers, Americans avoided some of the assumptions that weakened

European constitutions where the "artificiality" model dominated (think of post–World War II France, with its twenty-four governments in twelve years). Consequently, the natural basis of constitutional law made it *fundamental* law, which positioned it much higher than statute law. Thus, constitutions must, whenever possible, be drafted and ratified by special bodies—constitutional conventions—not merely state legislatures, and ultimately nine of the eleven new constitutions were drafted and appeared in this manner.

The state constitutions emerged during the most radical years of Revolutionary political thought, and most of them reflect that radicalism, a point most noticeable in the constitutions' tendencies to hedge and restrain their executives. After 1776, for example, governors could no longer introduce legislation, convene or adjourn assemblies, command state militia, pardon criminals, or veto bills. Pennsylvania axed the governorship from its constitution, allowing the legislature to serve in executive capacity. The judiciary suffered similar checks on its powers. Legislators and voters selected judges to serve set terms in office, or even on the basis of "good behavior." Judges' salaries were fixed by the legislatures, which also retained the right to impeach or recall magistrates, and no judge had the prerogative for judicial review or determining constitutionality. Like the executive, the judiciary in most states remained a creature of the legislature.

Nearly all of the new constitutions expanded suffrage, republicanism, and the civil liberties of the constituents. Eight constitutions contained bills of rights, delineating the terms of freedom of speech and religion, citizen protections from the military, the right to keep and bear arms, and components of due process. Taxpayers saw their enfranchisement expanded to the extent that Rhode Island granted universal white male suffrage. Representation was proportional; state capitals moved westward to better serve growing frontier constituents; legislators stood for annual election, and voters kept them in check through term limits and recall. Three states eliminated their upper legislative house, but in all other cases the lower house retained more power than the upper, controlling each state's economic and military policies as well as important judicial and executive powers. Pennsylvania and Massachusetts represented two opposite extremes of state constitution making. Pennsylvania eliminated the governorship and the upper house of the legislature. "We . . . never shall have a hereditary aristocracy," wrote one Pennsylvania Whig in opposition to a state senate.

God and the Americans

Few issues have been more mischaracterized than religion, and the government's attitude toward religion, in the early Republic. Modern Americans readily cite the "separation of church and state," a phrase that does not appear in the Constitution, yet is a concept that has become a guiding force in the disestablishment of religion in America. Most settlers had come to America with the quest for religious freedom constituting an important, if not *the* most important, goal of their journey. Maryland was a Catholic state; Pennsylvania, a Quaker state; Massachusetts, a Puritan state; and so on. But when Thomas Jefferson penned Virginia's

Statute for Religious Freedom (enacted 1786), the state's relationship to religion seemed to change. Or did it?

Jefferson wrote the Virginia sabbath law, as well as ordinances sanctioning public days of prayer and fasting and even incorporated some of the Levitical code into the state's marriage laws. In 1784, however, controversy arose over the incorporation of the Protestant Episcopal Church, with Baptists and Presbyterians complaining that the act unfairly bound church and state. The matter, along with some related issues, came before several courts, which by 1804 had led the legislature to refuse petitions for incorporation by churches or other religious bodies.

By that time, the American religious experience had developed several characteristics that separated it from any of the European churches. Americans de-emphasized the clergy. Not only did states such as Virginia refuse to fund the salaries of ministers, but the Calvinist/Puritan tradition that each man read, and interpret, the Bible for himself meant that the clergy's authority had already diminished. Second, Americans were at once both evangelically active and liturgically lax. What mattered was salvation and "right" living, not the form or structure of the religion. Ceremonies and practices differed wildly, even within denominations. And finally, as with America's new government itself, the nation's religion made central the personal salvation experience. All of this had the effect of separating American churches from their European ancestors, but also of fostering sects and divisions within American Christianity itself.

Above all, of course, America was a Christian nation. Jews, nonbelievers, and the few Muslims or adherents to other religions who might make it to the shores of North America in the late 1700s were treated not so much with tolerance as with indifference. People knew that Jews, Muslims, Buddhists, or others were a minority and, they thought, were going to remain a minority. So in the legal context, the debates never included non-Christian groups in the deliberations. At the same time, this generic Christian faith, wherein everyone agreed to disagree, served as a unifying element by breaking down parish boundaries and, in the process, destroying other political and geographic boundaries. The Great Awakening had galvanized American Christianity, pushing it even further into evangelism, and it served as a springboard to the Revolution itself, fueling the political fire with religious fervor and imbuing in the Founders a sense of rightness of cause. To some extent, then, "the essential difference between the American Revolution and the French Revolution is that the American Revolution . . . was a religious event, whereas the French Revolution was an anti-religious event."[16] John Adams said as much when he observed that the "Revolution was in the mind and hearts of the people; and change in their religious sentiments of their duties and obligations."[17]

Consequently, America, while attaching itself to no specific variant of Christianity, operated on an understanding that the nation would adopt an unofficial, generic Christianity that fit hand in glove with republicanism. Alexis de Tocqueville, whose perceptive *Democracy in America* (1835) provided a virtual road map for the future direction of the young nation, observed that in the United States the spirit of religion and the spirit of freedom "were intimately united, and that they reigned in common over the same country."[18] Americans, he added, viewed religion as "indispensable to the maintenance of the republican institutions," because it facilitated free institutions.[19] Certain fundamentals seemed unanimously agreed upon: posting of the Ten Commandments in public places was appropriate; prayers in virtually all official and public functions were expected; America was particularly blessed because of her trust in God; and even when individuals in civic life did not ascribe to a specific faith, they were expected to *act* like "good Christians" and conduct themselves as would a believer. Politicians like Washington walked a fine line between maintaining the secularist form and yet supplying the necessary spiritual substance. In part, this explains why so many of the early writings and speeches of the Founders were both timeless and uplifting. Their message of spiritual virtue, cloaked in republican processes of civic duty, reflected a sense of providential mission for the young country.

With no state boundaries to confine them, religious doctrines found themselves in a competition every bit as sharp as Adam Smith's "invisible hand" of the market. Most communities put up a church as one of their first civic acts, and traveling preachers traversed the backwoods and frontiers even where no churches existed. Ministers such as Lyman Beecher (1775–1863) characterized this new breed of traveling evangelist. Beecher, a New Haven Presbyterian who later assumed the presidency of the Cincinnati Theological Seminary, gained fame for his essay against dueling after Hamilton's death in 1803. Well before that, however, he pioneered American religious voluntarism. Like other westward-looking Americans, Beecher accepted the notion that the nation's destiny resided in the west—precisely where the frontier spread people out so much that a revival was the only way to reach them. Beecher's revivals took place in settings that enjoyed great popularity among evangelists—the camp meetings. At these gatherings, occasionally in the open air or in a barn, the traveling preachers spread the Gospel, occasionally emphasizing the emotional by urging the participants to engage in frenzied shouting, jerking, or falling, presumably under the influence of the Holy Spirit.

With each new congregation that the itinerant ministers formed, new doctrines and sects appeared. Regional differences in established churches produced reasoned differences, but also encouraged rampant sectarianism. Each new division weakened the consensus about what constituted accepted doctrines of Christianity, to the point that in popular references America ceased being a "godly" nation and became a "good" nation that could not agree on the specifics of goodness. In education, especially, the divisions threatened to undermine the Christian basis of the young country. Other dangerous splits in doctrine developed over the proper relationship with Indians. Eleazar Wheelock (1711–79), for example, a Congregationalist and a key influence in the Awakening movement, founded a school for Indians that became Dartmouth College in 1769. To the extent that Indians were offered education, it had to occur in segregated schools like Wheelock's, though he was not the first religious leader to establish a school. Religious groups of all denominations and doctrines accounted for the majority of quality education, especially at the higher levels. Brown University, in Rhode Island (1764), was established by the Baptists; Princeton, in New Jersey, by the Revivalist Presbyterians (1746), which later became a theological institute (1812); Yale, in New Haven, Connecticut, by the Congregationalists (1701); William and Mary, in Virginia, by the Anglicans (1693); and Georgetown College in Washington, D. C. (then Maryland), by the Jesuit father John Carroll (1789); and so on.

Frequently, however, rather than reinforcing existing orthodoxy, colleges soon produced heretics—or, at least, liberals who shared few of their founders' doctrinal views. At Harvard University, founded to enforce Puritanism in 1636 by the Reverend John Harvard, its original motto, *Veritas, Christo et Ecclesiae* (Truth, Christ and the Church), and its logo of two books facing open and one facing downward to represent the hidden knowledge of God, were ditched when the school slipped into the hands of liberal groups in 1707. The new motto, simply *Veritas,* and its symbol of all three books facing up aptly illustrated the dominance of a Unitarian elite that dominated the school, including such notables as John Quincy Adams and Henry Wadsworth Longfellow. By focusing on a rationalistic Enlightenment approach to salvation in which virtually all men were saved—not to mention the presumption that all knowledge could be known—the Unitarians (who denied the Trinity, hence the term "Unitarian," from unity, or one) had opposed the Great Awakening of the 1740s. Henry Ware, at Harvard, and later William Ellery Channing, whose 1819 sermon, "Unitarian Christianity" established the basis for the sect, challenged the Congregational and Puritan precepts from 1805–25. At that point, the American Unitarian Association was formed, but much earlier it had exerted such a powerful influence in Boston that in 1785 King's Chapel removed all references to the Trinity in the prayer books.[20]

Unitarians were not alone in their unorthodox views. Many sects strained at the limits of what was tolerable even under the broadest definitions of Christianity. Yet they still maintained, for the most part, a consensus on what constituted morality and ethics. Consequently, a subtle yet profound shift occurred in which the religious in America avoided theological issues and instead sought to inculcate a set of moral assumptions under which even Jews and other non-Christians could fit.

This appeared in its most visible form in education. Jefferson's concern over state funding of a particular religion centered on the use of tax money for clerical salaries. Eventually, though, the pressure to eliminate any sectarian doctrines from public schools was bound to lead to clashes with state governments over which concepts were denominational and which were generically Christian. Church-state separation also spilled over into debates about the applicability of charters and incorporation laws for churches. Charters always contained elements of favoritism (which was one reason banks were steeped in controversy), but in seeking to avoid granting a charter to any particular church, the state denied religious organizations the same rights accorded hospitals and railroads. Even in Virginia, where "separation of church and state" began, the reluctance to issue religious charters endowed churches with special characteristics that were not applied to other corporations. Trying to keep religion and politics apart, Virginia lawmakers unintentionally "wrapped religion and politics, church and state ever more closely together."[21]

The good news was that anyone who was dissatisfied with a state's religion could move west. That dynamic would later propel the Methodists to Oregon and the Mormons to Utah. Meanwhile, the call of the frontier was irrepressible for reasons entirely unrelated to heaven and completely oriented toward Mammon. And every year more adventurers and traders headed west, beyond the endless mountains.

Beyond the Endless Mountains

The end of the American Revolution marked the beginning of a great migration to the West across the Appalachian Mountains. The migrants followed four major routes. Pennsylvania Germans and Scots-Irish moved south, down the Great Valley of the Appalachians, to settle in western Virginia and North Carolina. The Wilderness Road, blazed by Daniel Boone in 1775, led some of them into Kentucky and the Bluegrass region via the Cumberland Gap. One traveler described this route as the "longest, blackest, hardest road" in America. Carolinians traversed the mountains by horseback and wagon train until they found the Tennessee River, following its winding route to the Ohio River, then ascending the Cumberland south to the Nashville region. But the most common river route—and the most popular route to the West—was the Ohio. Migrants made the arduous journey over Forbes Road through the Alleghenies to Pittsburgh. There they built or bought a flatboat, purchased a copy of Zadok Cramer's river guide, *The Western Navigator*, and launched their crafts and their fortunes into *le belle rivière*. If the weather and navigation depth was good, and fortune smiled upon them, the trip from Pittsburgh to Louisville took seven to ten days.[22]

During the decade following the Revolution, tens of thousands of pioneers moved southwest of the Ohio River. Harrodsburgh, Boonesborough, Louisville, and Lexington, in Kentucky, were joined by the Wautauga and Nashville settlements in the northeastern and central portions of what is now the state of Tennessee. Pioneers like Daniel Boone played an irreplaceable role in cutting the trails, establishing relations with Native Americans (or defeating them, if it came to a fight), and setting up early forts from which towns and commercial centers could emerge. Daniel Boone (1734–1820) had traveled from Pennsylvania, where his family bucked local Quakers by marrying its daughters outside the Society of Friends, through Virginia, North Carolina, then finally to explore Kentucky. Crossing the famed Cumberland Gap in 1769, Boone's first expedition into the raw frontier resulted in his party's being robbed of all its furs. Boone returned a few years later to establish the settlement that bears his name. When the Revolutionary War reopened hostilities in Kentucky, Boone was captured by Shawnee Indians and remained a prisoner for months, then had to endure a humiliating court-martial for the episode. Nevertheless, few individuals did more to open the early West to British and American settlement than Daniel Boone.[23]

Daniel Boone, Civilizer or Misanthrope?

As Revolutionary-era Americans began to move beyond the "endless mountains" into the frontier of the Ohio and Mississippi valleys, they followed the trails blazed by Daniel Boone. Stories of Daniel Boone's exploits as a hunter, pathfinder, Indian fighter, war hero, and community builder, loom large in the myth of the American West. Many of these stories are true. It is interesting to note, however, that the stories of Daniel Boone often portray him in two completely different ways—either as a wild, uncivilized frontiersman or as a leader of the vanguard aiming to tame and civilize that wild frontier. Was Daniel Boone running away from civilization, or was he bringing it with him? Was he a misanthrope or a civilizer, or both?

Born in Pennsylvania in 1734, Daniel Boone became a hunter at twelve years of age, soon staying away from home years at a time on long hunts. He worked his way down the eastern slope of the Appalachians before plunging into the unexplored regions westward. From 1767–69, he blazed the Wilderness Trail through the Cumberland Gap to the Kentucky Bluegrass region, where, in 1775, he established Boonesborough, an outpost for his family and friends to settle the new West. He was subsequently captured and adopted by Shawnee Indians in 1778, fought Indian and Briton alike in the Revolutionary War, and was elected sheriff in 1782 and, later, to the legislature of the new state of Kentucky. During this time Boone also worked as a land company scout and land speculator. Drawn into protracted court battles over disputed land claims, Boone went bankrupt in 1798 and then moved his large family to the uninhabited expanses west of the Mississippi River. He died near St. Charles Missouri in 1820, having spent an eventful eight decades on the American frontier.

During the course of Daniel Boone's life, stories of his exploits spread far and wide, and he became America's first frontier folk hero. Thousands claimed to know the exact spot where Boone carved on a tree, HERE D. BOONE CILL'D A BAR (bear). Americans have told Boone's stories for more than two hundred years, and his legend has appeared in formal artistic works ranging from James Fenimore Cooper's novel The Last of the Mohicans (1827), and painter George Caleb Bingham's rendering Daniel Boone (1851) to twentieth-century movies and television shows, the most famous being Fess Parker's near-decade-long 1960s television role as Boone.

It is important to note the symbolic contrasts in the roles Daniel Boone takes on in the various famous stories about him. On the one hand, he is portrayed as a loner and a misanthrope who longs to escape society and live for years utterly alone in the wilderness. On the other hand, there is the Daniel Boone who was a husband and father, founder of Boonesborough, successful politician, and real estate developer. This Daniel Boone, another biographer wrote, was an "empire builder" and "philanthropist" known for his "devotion to social progress."

Daniel Boone was above all else, an archetypal American. He loved the wilderness and the freedom that came with frontier individualism. Like all Americans, he simultaneously believed in progress and the advance of capitalism and republican political institutions. While he may have sometimes wished that America would always remain a sparsely inhabited wilderness, he knew that America could not and should not stand still.

Sources: Theodore Roosevelt, *The Winning of the West*, 6 vols. (New York: G. P. Putnam's Sons, 1889); John Mack Faragher, *Daniel Boone: The Life and Legend of an American Pioneer* (New York: Henry Holt, 1992).

North of the Ohio, a slower pace of settlement took place because of strong Indian resistance. Even there, the white presence grew. Marietta, Ohio, became the first permanent American settlement in the region, but soon was joined by Chillicothe, Fort Wayne, and Detroit. Census figures in 1790 showed the non-Indian population at 73,000 Kentuckians and 35,000 Tennesseans, while the Old Northwest (Ohio, Indiana, Illinois, Michigan, and Wisconsin) boasted 5,000, with numbers rising daily. Counting the pre-1790 residents, the combined American population in all areas between the Appalachian crest and the Mississippi River numbered an impressive 250,000. As one traveler later observed:

> Old America seems to be breaking up, and moving westward. We are seldom out of sight, as we travel on this grand track towards the Ohio, of family groups, behind and before us. . . . Add to these numerous stages loaded to the utmost, and the innumerable travelers on horseback, on foot, and in light wagons, and you have before you a scene of bustle and business extending over three hundred miles, which is truly wonderful.[24]

On the eastern seaboard, the Confederation Congress watched the Great Migration with interest and concern. Nearly everyone agreed that Congress would have to create a national domain, devise a method for surveying and selling public lands, formulate an Indian policy, and engage in diplomatic negotiations with the British and Spanish in the Old Northwest and Southwest. Most important, Congress had to devise some form of territorial government plan to establish the rule of law in the trans-Appalachian West. Nearly everyone agreed these measures were necessary, but that was about all they agreed to.

Western lands commanded much of Congress's attention because of the lingering problem of national domain.[25] The Articles remained unratified because some of the landed states still refused to surrender their sea-to-sea claims to the central government, and Maryland refused to ratify the document until they did. This logjam cleared in 1781, when Virginia finally ceded her western claims to Congress. Maryland immediately ratified the Articles, officially making the document, at long last, the first Constitution of the United States. Although one state, Georgia, continued to claim its western lands, the remaining states chose to ignore the problem.

Congress immediately set to work on territorial policy, creating legal precedents that the nation follows to this day. Legislators saw the ramifications of their actions with remarkably clear eyes. They dealt with a huge question: if Congress, like the British Parliament before it, established colonies in the West, would they be subservient to the new American mother country or independent? Although the British model was not illogical, Congress rejected it, making the United States the first nation to allow for gradual democratization of its colonial empire.[26]

As chair of Congress's territorial government committee, Thomas Jefferson played a major role in the drafting of the Ordinance of 1784. Jefferson proposed to divide the trans-Appalachian West into sixteen new states, all of which would eventually enter the Union on an equal footing with the thirteen original states. Ever the scientist, Jefferson arranged his new states on a neat grid of latitudinal and longitudinal boundaries and gave them fanciful—classical, patriotic, and Indian—names: Cherroneseus, Metropotamia, Saratoga, Assenisipia, and Sylvania. He directed that the Appalachian Mountains should forever divide the slave from the free states, institutionalizing "free soil" on the western frontier. Although this radical idea did not pass in 1784, it combined with territorial self-governance and equality and became the foundation of the Northwest Ordinance of 1787.

Jefferson also applied his social liberalism and scientific method to a land policy component of the Ordinance of 1784. He called for use of a grid system in the survey of public lands. Moreover, Jefferson aimed to use the national domain to immediately place free or, at least, cheap land in the hands of actual settlers, not the national government. His and David Howell's land policy proposal reflected their agrarianism and acknowledgment of widespread de facto "preemption" (squatter's rights) on the American frontier that was later codified into law. As economist Hernando DeSoto has argued in *The Mystery of Capital*, the American "preemption" process gave common people a means to get a legal title to land, which was an early basis for capital formation. This kind of liberal—and legal—land policy is not present in 90 percent of the world even to this day.[27]

By 1785, however, Jefferson had left Congress, and nationalists were looking to public lands sales as a source for much-needed revenue. A Congressional committee chaired by nationalist Massachusetts delegate Rufus King began to revise Jefferson's proposal. Borrowing the basic policies of northeastern colonial expansion, Congress overlaid the New England township system on the national map. Surveyors were to plot the West into thousands of townships, each containing thirty-six 640–acre sections. Setting aside one section of each township for local school funding, Congress aimed to auction off townships at a rate of two dollars per acre, with no credit offered. Legislators hoped to raise quick revenue in this fashion because only entrepreneurs could afford the minimum purchase, but the system broke down as squatters, speculators, and other wily frontiersmen avoided the provisions and snapped up land faster than the government could survey it. Despite these limitations, the 1785 law set the stage for American land policy, charting a path toward cheap land (scientifically surveyed, with valid title) that would culminate in the Homestead Act of 1862. To this day, an airplane journey over the neatly surveyed, square-cornered townships of the American West proves the legacy of the Confederation Congress's Land Ordinance of 1785.[28]

Moving to Indian policy in 1786, Congress set precedents that remain in place, the most important of which was the recognition of Indian "right of soil," a right that could be removed only through military conquest or bona fide purchase. No one pretended that this policy intended that the laws would favor the Indians, and certainly Congress had no pro-Indian faction at the time. Rather, nationalist leaders wanted an orderly and, if possible, peaceful settlement of the West, which could only be accomplished if the lands obtained by Indians came with unimpeachable title deeds.

Congress then appointed Indian commissioners to sign treaties with the Iroquois, Ohio Valley, and southeastern "civilized" tribes. Treaty sessions soon followed at Fort Stanwix, Hopewell, and other sites. Obviously, these agreements did not "solve the Indian problem" nor did they produce universal peaceful relations between the races. On the other hand, the Indian Ordinance of 1786 did formalize the legal basis of land dealings between whites and Indians. Most important, it established the two fundamental principles of American Indian policy: the sovereignty of the national government (versus the states) in orchestrating Native American affairs, and the right of soil, which also necessitated written contractual agreements. To reiterate the points made in earlier chapters, the concept that land could be divided and privately owned was foreign to some, though not all, tribes, making the latter principle extremely important if only for claims against the government that might arise generations later.[29]

Congress returned to the territorial government question in a 1787 revision of Jefferson's Ordinance of 1784. Again, Rufus King, Nathan Dane, and the nationalists led the effort to stabilize westward expansion. The nationalist imprint in the Ordinances of 1786 and 1787 showed a marked difference from the point of view of agrarian Whigs like Jefferson and David Howell. Dane and King acknowledged the inevitability of westward expansion, but they preferred that it be slow, peaceful, and regulated by the government. Although not all their ideas were feasible, they nevertheless composed the basis of the American territorial system. Even in twenty-first-century America, when a territory becomes part of the American empire and, in some cases, seeks statehood (for example, Alaska, Hawaii, and perhaps someday Puerto Rico or the Virgin Islands), that territory's governmental evolution is charted under the terms remarkably similar to those established by the Northwest Ordinance. Only a few states—Texas, an independent republic that never went through territorial status; West Virginia, which was admitted directly to the Union during the Civil War; and Hawaii, which was annexed—did not come into the Union in this process.

The Northwest Ordinance established a territorial government north of the Ohio River under a governor (former Continental Army general and staunch Federalist Arthur St. Clair was soon appointed) and judges whom the president chose with legislative approval. Upon reaching a population of five thousand, the landholding white male citizens could elect a legislature and a nonvoting congressional representative. Congress wrote a bill of rights into the Ordinance and stipulated, à la Jefferson's 1784 proposal, that no slavery or involuntary servitude would be permitted north of the Ohio River.

Yet the slavery issue was not clear-cut, and residents themselves disagreed over the relevant clause, Article VI. William Henry Harrison, Indiana's first territorial governor, mustered a territorial convention in Vincennes in 1802 for the purpose of suspending Article VI for ten years.[30] Petitioners in Illinois also sought to "amend" the clause. It is easy to miss the enormity of the efforts to undercut the slavery prohibition in the Northwest, which became the basis for the popular sovereignty arguments of the 1850s and, indeed, for the infamous *Dred Scott* ruling of 1857. In a nutshell, the proslavery forces argued that the U.S. Congress had no authority over slaves in, say, Indiana—only the citizens of Indiana did. In that context, the Northwest Ordinance of 1787 put the issue of slavery on the front burner. More than that, it spoke directly to the divisive issue of state sovereignty, which, fortunately, the people of the Northwest Territory and the Congress decided in favor of the federal authority.[31]

The Ordinance produced other remarkable insights for the preservation of democracy in newly acquired areas. For example, it provided that between three and five new states could be organized from the region, thereby avoiding having either a giant super state or dozens of small states that would dominate the Congress. When any potential state achieved a population of sixty thousand, its citizens were to draft a constitution and apply to Congress for admission into the federal union. During the ensuing decades, Ohio, Indiana, Illinois, Michigan, and Wisconsin entered the Union under these terms. The territorial system did not always run smoothly, but it endured. The Southwest Ordinance of 1789 instituted a similar law for the Old Southwest, and Kentucky (1791) and Tennessee (1786) preceded Ohio into the Union.

But the central difference remained that Ohio, unlike the southern states, abolished slavery, and thus the Northwest Ordinance joined the Missouri Compromise of 1820 and the Compromise of 1850 as the first of the great watersheds in the raging debate over North American slavery. Little appreciated at the time was the moral tone and the inexorability forced on the nation by the ordinance. If slavery was wrong in the territories, was it not wrong everywhere? The relentless logic drove the South to adopt its states' rights position after the drafting of the Constitution, but the direction was already in place. If slavery was morally right—as Southerners argued—it could not be prohibited in the territories, nor could it be prohibited anywhere else. Thus, from 1787 onward (though few recognized it at the time) the South was committed to the expansion of slavery, not merely its perpetuation where it existed at the time; and this was a *moral* imperative, not a political one.[32]

Popular notions that the Articles of Confederation Congress was a bankrupt do-nothing body that sat by helplessly as the nation slid into turmoil are thus clearly refuted by Congress's creation of America's first western policies legislating land sales, interaction with Indians, and territorial governments. Quite the contrary, Congress under the Articles was a legislature that compared favorably to other revolutionary machinery, such as England's Long Parliament, the French radicals' Reign of Terror, the Latin American republics of the early 1800s, and more recently, the "legislatures" of the Russian, Chinese, Cuban, and Vietnamese communists.[33]

Unlike those bodies, several of which slid into anarchy, the Confederation Congress boasted a strong record. After waging a successful war against Britain, and negotiating the Treaty of Paris, it produced a series of domestic acts that can only be viewed positively. The Congress also benefited from an economy rebuilding from wartime stresses, for which the Congress could claim little credit. Overall, though, the record of the Articles of Confederation Congress must be reevaluated upward, and perhaps significantly so.

Two Streams of Liberty

Well before the Revolutionary War ended, strong differences of opinion existed among the Whig patriots. While the majority favored the radical state constitutions, the Articles of Confederation, and legislative dominance, a minority viewpoint arose.[34] Detractors of radical constitutionalism voiced a more moderate view, calling for increased governmental authority and more balance between the executive, judicial, and legislative branches at both the state and national levels. During this time, the radicals called themselves Federalists because the Articles of Confederation created the weak federal union they desired. Moderates labeled themselves nationalists, denoting their commitment to a stronger national state. These labels were temporary, and by 1787, the nationalists would be calling themselves Federalists and, in high irony, labeling their Federalist opponents Anti-Federalists.[35]

The nationalist faction included Robert Morris, Benjamin Franklin, John Adams, Henry Knox, Rufus King, and their leader, Alexander Hamilton. These men found much wanting at both the state and national levels of government. They wanted to broaden the taxation and commercial regulatory powers of the Confederation Congress, while simultaneously curtailing what they perceived as too much democracy at the state level. "America must clip the wings of a mad democracy," wrote Henry Knox. John Adams, retreating from his 1776 radicalism, concurred: "There never was a democracy that did not commit suicide."[36] "The people!" Hamilton snorted. "The people is a great beast."[37]

Yet it should not be assumed that this antidemocratic language was monarchical or anti-Revolutionary in nature, because Hamilton himself would also refer to "the majesty of the multitude." Rather, the nationalist criticism reflected a belief in republicanism as a compromise before the tyranny of a monarch and what James Madison feared to be a potential "tyranny of the majority." It was a philosophical stance dating back to Aristotle's distinction between a polis (good government by the many) and a democracy (abusive government of the many). Nationalists concluded that the Spirit of '76 had become too extreme.

At the state level, nationalists attacked the actions of all-powerful legislatures produced by expanded suffrage. They were also disturbed when seven states issued inflated currency and enacted legislation that required creditors to accept these notes (leading to scenes in which debtors literally chased fleeing creditors, attempting to "pay" them in spurious money). Additional "debtors' laws" granted extensions to farmers who would have otherwise lost their property through default during the postwar recession. Reaction to the state-generated inflation is explainable in part by the composition of the nationalists, many of whom were themselves creditors in one way or another. But an underlying concern for contractual agreements also influenced the nationalists, who saw state meddling in favor of debtors as a potentially debilitating violation of property rights.[38]

When it came to government under the Articles, nationalists aimed their sharpest jabs at the unstable leadership caused by term limits and annual elections. A role existed for a strong executive and permanent judiciary, they contended, especially when it came to commercial issues. The Confederation's economic policy, like those of the states, had stifled the nation's enterprise, a point they hoped to rectify through taxation of international commerce through import tariffs. Significantly, the new nationalists largely espoused the views of Adam Smith, who, although making the case for less government interference in the economy, also propounded a viable—but limited—role for government in maintaining a navy and army capable of protecting trade lanes and national borders.

Weaknesses in the Articles also appeared on the diplomatic front, where America was being bullied despite its newly independent status. The British refused to evacuate their posts in the Old Northwest, claiming the region would fall into anarchy under the United States.[39] Farther south, the Spanish flexed their muscles in the lower Mississippi Valley, closing the port of New Orleans to the booming American flatboat and keelboat trade. Congress sent nationalist John Jay to negotiate a settlement with Spain's Don Diego de Gardoqui. Far from intimidating the Spaniards, Jay offered to suspend American navigation of the Mississippi for twenty-five years in return for a trade agreement favorable to his northeastern constituents! Western antinationalists were furious, but had to admit that without an army or navy, the Confederation Congress was powerless to coerce belligerent foreign powers. Nevertheless, Congress could not swallow the Jay-Gardoqui Treaty, and scrapped it.[40]

Mike Fink, King of the River

The complicated issues of politics in the 1780s were paralleled by related, real-life dramas far removed from the scenes of government. For example, shortly after John Jay negotiated with Spain's Don Diego de Gardoqui over American trading rights on the inland rivers, Big Mike Fink was pioneering the burgeoning river traffic of the Ohio and

Mississippi rivers. Fink gained such a mighty reputation during America's surge west of the Appalachians that he was dubbed King of the River.

Back in the days before steam power, the produce of the American frontier—pork, flour, corn, animal skins, and whiskey—was shipped up and down the Ohio and Mississippi rivers on thousands of flatboats and keelboats. Flatboats were crude flat-bottomed craft that could travel only downstream; keelboats were sleeker sixty-foot craft that could be poled upstream by the Herculean efforts of their crewmen. Early rivermen lived hard lives, enduring the hazards of ice, fog, snags, sandbars, waterfalls, and even Indian attacks as they plied their trade in the early West. Upon sale of their cargoes in Natchez or New Orleans, most rivermen walked back to their Ohio Valley homes via the Natchez Trace, braving the elements and attacks from outlaws.

Mike Fink so captured the public imagination that oral legends of his exploits spread far and wide and ultimately found their way into print in newspapers and almanacs. According to these stories, Fink was "half horse, half alligator" and could "outrun, out-hop, out-jump, throw down, drag out, and lick any man in the country!" In some tales, Fink outfoxed wily farmers and businessmen, cheating them out of money and whiskey. He could ride dangerous bulls, one of which, he said, "drug me over every briar and stump in the field." The most famous and oft-repeated Mike Fink story is one in which he, à la William Tell, shoots a "whiskey cup" off a friend's head.

These are good yarns, and some of them were no doubt true. But who was the real Mike Fink? Born near Pittsburgh, Pennsylvania (at the headwaters of the Ohio River), around 1770, Fink grew into a fine woodsman, rifleman, and frontier scout. He took up boating around 1785 and rose in the trade. He mastered the difficult business of keelboating—poling, rowing, sailing, and cordelling (pulling via a rope winch) keelboats upstream for hundreds of miles against the strong currents of the western rivers. Fink plied the Ohio and Mississippi during the very time frontier Americans angrily disputed Spanish control of America's downriver trade.

By the early 1800s, Fink owned and captained two boats headquartered at Wheeling, West Virginia. Working his way west, Fink's career paralleled that of American expansion into the Mississippi Valley, while at the same time reflecting the coarse and violent nature of the American frontier. One of the few documented accounts of the historic Mike Fink is an early nineteenth-century St. Louis newspaper story of his shooting the heel off a black man's foot.

Responding to an advertisement in the March 22, 1822, St. Louis *Missouri Republican*, which called for "one hundred young men to ascend the Missouri River to its source" and establish a fur trading outpost in the Montana country, Fink was hired to navigate one of the company's keelboats up the Missouri, working alongside the legendary mountain man Jedediah Smith.

An 1823 feud between Fink and two fellow trappers flared into violence that led to Fink's murder. Thus ended the actual life of the King of the River. But mythical Mike Fink had only begun to live. He soon became a folk hero whose name was uttered in the same breath with Daniel Boone, Andrew Jackson, and Davy Crockett. Celebrated in folklore and literature, Mike Fink's legend was assured when he made it into a 1956 Walt Disney movie.

Source: Michael Allen, *Western Rivermen, 1763–1861: Ohio and Mississippi Boatmen and the Myth of the Alligator Horse* (Baton Rouge: Louisiana State University Press, 1990), pp. 6–14, 137–39.

Nationalists held mixed motives in their aggressive critique of government under the Articles of Confederation. Honest champions of stronger government, they advanced many valid political, economic, military, and diplomatic ideas. Their opponents, perhaps correctly, called them reactionaries who sought to enrich their own merchant class. True, critics of the Articles of Confederation represented the commercial and cosmopolitan strata of the new nation. It just so happened that for the most part, the long-range interests of the young United States coincided with their own.

Throughout the early 1780s, nationalists unsuccessfully attempted to amend the Articles. Congress's treasury chief, Robert Morris, twice proposed a 5 percent impost tax (a tariff), but Rhode Island's solo resistance defeated the measure. Next he offered a plan for a privately owned "national" bank to manage fiscal matters and, again, twelve states concurred, but not Rhode Island. Matters came to a boil in September 1786, when delegates from the five states bordering the Chesapeake Bay convened in Annapolis, Maryland, ostensibly to discuss shared commercial problems. The nationalists among the Annapolis Convention delegates proceeded to plant the seed of a peaceful counterrevolution against the Confederation Congress.[41] Delegates unilaterally called for a new meeting of representatives of all thirteen states to occur in Philadelphia in the spring of 1787. Although these nationalists no doubt fully intended to replace the existing structure, they worded their summons to Philadelphia in less threatening tones, claiming only to seek agreements on commercial issues and to propose changes that "may require a correspondent adjustment of other parts of the federal system." The broadest interpretation of this language points only to amending the Articles of Confederation, although Hamilton and his allies had no such aim. They intended nothing less than replacing the Articles with a new federal Constitution. In that light, Rufus King captured the attitudes of many of these former Revolutionaries when he wrote of the delegate selection, "For God's sake be careful who are the men."[42]

The fly in the ointment when it came to making changes to the Articles was the clause requiring unanimous consent among the states to ratify any alterations, which made any plan to change them without such consent illegal. Consequently, the Constitutional Convention and the federal Constitution it produced, technically, were illegal. Yet this was a revolutionary age—only ten years earlier, these same Founders had "illegally" replaced one form of government with another. It is not incongruous, then, that these same patriots would seek to do so again, and, to their credit, they planned for this change to be nonviolent.[43]

Still, the nationalists' call to Philadelphia might have failed but for one event that followed on the heels of the Annapolis Convention. Shays' Rebellion, a tax revolt in Massachusetts, provided the catalyst that convinced important leaders to attend the Philadelphia meeting. Unlike other states, Massachusetts had not passed debtors' laws, and thousands of farmers faced loss of their lands to unpaid creditors. Daniel Shays, a Pelham, Massachusetts, farmer and a retired captain in the Continental Army, organized farmers to resist the foreclosures, and under his leadership armed bands closed the courts of western Massachusetts, ostensibly to protect their property. Creditors, however, saw their own property rights in jeopardy.

By January 1787, Shays' rebels were on the run. A lone battle in the rebellion occurred at Springfield, in which Massachusetts militia, under Continental general Benjamin Lincoln, attacked the Shaysites and dispersed them. After the smoke cleared, four men lay dead and Shays had fled the state. Lincoln's troops arrested some of the rebels, fourteen of whom were tried and sentenced to death. But the government hardly wanted the blood of these farmers on its hands, so it worked out a compromise in which the governor commuted the men's sentences and freed them. Shays' Rebellion, however, quickly transcended the military and legal technicalities of the case, becoming a cause célèbre among nationalists, who pointed to the uprising as a prime example of the Articles' weak governance. Only a stronger government, they argued, could prevent the anarchy of the Shaysites from infecting America's body politic.[44]

Armed with a new battle cry, nationalists prepared to march to Philadelphia and conduct their own revolution. Although the general public had not yet discovered the aims of this "revolutionary" movement, Hamilton, Morris, Adams, Madison, Washington, and their fellow nationalists had formulated a distinct program. They aimed to replace the Articles with a new government that would (1) suborn state sovereignty to that of a national government; (2) replace legislative dominance with a more balanced legislative-executive-judicial model; and (3) end the equality of states in Congressional decision making with a system of proportional representation. Most important, they planned to keep their deliberations secret, else, as Francis Hopkinson noted, "No sooner will the chicken be hatch'd than every one will be for plucking a feather."[45] Under strict secrecy, and with clear and noble goals, the American Revolution truly entered its second phase.[46]

A Republic, If You Can Keep It

Like the swing of a pendulum, momentum began to move in favor of the nationalists' vision. Even the suspicious Confederation Congress issued a belated February authorization for the Philadelphia convention, stipulating its "sole and express purpose" was "revising the articles of Confederation," not replacing them.[47] State legislatures appointed delegates, and twelve of the thirteen sent representatives (Rhode Island, again, was the exception, leading one legislator to refer to it as an "unruly member . . . a reproach and a byeword." By May fourteenth, most of the fifty-five delegates (of whom thirty-nine stayed the summer to draft and ratify the completed Constitution) had arrived at the meeting. Their names were so impressive that Jefferson, reading the list from Paris, called the Convention "an assembly of demi-gods."[48]

Nearly all of the delegates were nationalists. A few who opposed the principles of nationalism—most notably Melancton Smith, Luther Martin, and

Abraham Yates—refused to sign the final document, eventually becoming Anti-Federalists.[49] Some opponents, such as Patrick Henry, Sam Adams, and Richard Henry Lee (all key instigators of the American Revolution) had refused to attend in the first place. "I smell a rat," Henry fumed when informed of the convention. But he would have served himself and the nation if he had gone to personally investigate the odor!

Other delegates who did attend were relatively young (averaging forty-two years of age) in comparison to the older Whigs who had fomented the Revolution nearly twenty years earlier. Aside from Washington, Franklin arrived with the most prominent reputation. His famous and familiar face, with his innovative bifocals and partially bald head, made him the best-known American in the world. He had become America's public philosopher, a trusted soul whose witticisms matched his insight. While in Philadelphia, Franklin, often posing as the voice of reason, brought a distinct agenda. He had only recently been named president of the Philadelphia Abolition Society, and in April 1787 he intended to introduce a proposal calling for a condemnation of slavery in the final document. Only through the persuasions of other northern delegates was he convinced to withdraw it.

Franklin stood out from the other delegates in areas other than age as well. Nearly a third of the delegates had held commissions in the Continental Army, and most came from the upper tier of American society—planters, lawyers, merchants, and members of the professional class. They were, above all, achievers, and men well familiar with overcoming obstacles in order to attain success. Contrary to the critiques of historians such as Charles Beard and Howard Zinn, who saw only a monolithic "class" of men manipulating the convention, the fact that most of the delegates had been successful in enterprise was to their credit. (Does any society truly want nonachievers, chronic failures, malcontents, and perennial pessimists drafting the rules by which all should live?) Each had blemishes, and even the leaders—Hamilton, Franklin, Madison, Morris, James Wilson, Washington (who presided)—possessed flaws, some of them almost insurmountable. But a rampant lust for power was not among them. As British historian Paul Johnson noted, "These were serious, sensible, undoctrinaire men, gathered together in a pragmatic spirit to do something practical, and looking back on a thousand years of political traditions, inherited from England, which had always stressed compromise and give-and-take."[50]

Sharp differences existed between factions within the convention, not only from the handful of antinationalists, who threatened to disrupt any program that seemed odious, but also from the natural tensions between farmers and merchants, between slaveholders and free-soil advocates, and between Northerners and Southerners. A final source of contention, though, arose between states with larger populations, such as Virginia, and those with smaller populations, such as New Jersey.[51]

Another split emerged, this one between Madison and Hamilton, over the occupations of those who would govern, Hamilton advocating a distinction between what he called the "private interests" (whether of individual members, states, or localities) and the "public interest" (which included the continuation of republican ideals). It boiled down to a simple question, Were men governed by altruistic motives or base self-interest? Washington thought the latter. It was unrealistic, he contended, to expect ordinary people to be influenced by "any other principles but those of interest."[52] Hamilton agreed, arguing that lawyers comprised the only class with no immediate economic stake in matters. Offering a suggestion that tends to make modern Americans shudder, Hamilton said that while the state legislatures should rightly be dominated by merchants, planters, and farmers, the national legislature should be populated by lawyers! For all his insight—French minister Talleyrand called him the greatest of the "choice and master spirits of the age"—Hamilton failed to foresee that by the middle of the twentieth century, through tort litigation, lawyers would come to have an immediate and extremely lucrative "interest" in certain types of legislation, and that every law passed by the national Congress would require a geometrical increase in the numbers of attorneys needed to decipher (and attempt to evade) it.

The ultimate irony is that no matter which group triumphed on the other compromise issues, it was the inexorable demand generated by the need to write laws and the concomitant legalisms that gradually pushed the farmers and merchants out of the halls of the legislatures and pulled the lawyers in. Only toward the end of the twentieth century, when it was almost too late, did Americans start to appreciate the dangers posed by a bar that had virtually unlimited access to the lawmaking apparatus.

The division over proportional representation versus state representation formed the basis for two rival plans of government, the so-called Virginia Plan and the New Jersey Plan. Madison, Washington, and Edmund Randolph had drafted the Virginia Plan, an extreme nationalist program that aimed to scrap the Articles and create a powerful republican government in its place. Their proposal called for an end to state sovereignty and the creation of a viable national state comprised of three equal branches. A president would serve alongside federal judges (with lifetime terms) and a bicameral legislature, in which the lower house would be elected proportionately and the upper house would be selected from a list of nominees sent from the state legislatures on the basis of equal representation for the states. According to their plan, the lower house would give the highly populated states more representation. Finally, the Virginia Plan proposed a veto power over state laws so that, as John Jay said, the states would lose sovereignty and be viewed "in the same light in which counties stand to the state of which they are parts . . . merely as districts."[53]

Even the nationalist-dominated Philadelphia convention opposed such sweeping change. In June, opponents rallied around William Paterson's New Jersey plan, calling for a beefed-up confederation type of central government. Small states agreed that the national government needed muscle, most especially the powers to tax internally and externally.[54] They also proposed three, but much less powerful, branches of government. Congress was to appoint a supreme court and plural executive committee, creating the semblance of a three-branch system. Its most important feature, though, lay in what the New Jersey plan rejected: proportional representation. Instead, Paterson proposed a unicameral Congress, with equal representation for each state, with all the powers of the Confederation Congress.

Delegates began to debate the disparate plans, but all realized the Virginia Plan would triumph as long as its adherents were willing to compromise over the proportional representation feature and the national veto of state laws. Several compromises ensued, the most important of which, the Connecticut Compromise, (or Great Compromise), concerned proportional representation. Divisions between large and small state factions dissolved as each gained one legislative body tailored to its liking. The House of Representatives, in which members would be elected directly by the people, would be based on population determined by a federal census. It represented "the people" in the broadest sense, and terms of the members were kept at a brief two years, requiring representatives to face the voters more often than any other elected group. On the other hand, the Senate would represent the interests of the states, with senators chosen by state legislatures for six-year terms, one third of whom would come up for election every two years. Clearly, the structure of the compromise not only addressed the concerns of each side, but it spoke to another overarching concern—that change be difficult and slow. No matter what burning issue consumed Americans, at any given time only one third of the Senate would be up for reappointment by the state legislature, providing a brake on emotion-driven legislation. Their wisdom in this matter has been magnified over time. Issues that one moment seemed momentous faded from popular interest in years or even months. Slow the process down, the Founders would say, and many problems will just disappear without laws.

There was another touch of genius to the numerous staggered terms and differing sets of requirements. As the French observer Alexis de Tocqueville later pointed out, "When elections recur only at long intervals, the state is exposed to violent agitation every time they take place. Parties then exert themselves to the utmost . . . to gain a price which is so rarely within their reach; and as the evil is almost irremediable for the candidates who fail, everything is to be feared from their disappointed ambition."[55] For a House seat, the loser of a contest could try again in two years, and after the Seventeenth Amendment to the Constitution, at least one of a state's Senate seats could be contested every four years. No matter how bad the election, and how massive the defeat, those out of power knew that political winds changed, and with the single-member district system, a person only had to win by one vote to win the seat. Thus the system encouraged a fundamental political patience that proved so successful that the Democrats, in the late 1800s, would go sixty-two years—from Lincoln to Franklin Roosevelt—and elect only three Democratic presidents (one of them, Grover Cleveland, twice), while the Republicans, in the late twentieth century, went forty years without a majority in the House of Representatives. In each case, the party out of power never came close to desperation or violence. Indeed, the opposite occurred, in which unceasing campaigning led to a new quest for office beginning the day after an election.

If arguments over how to count representatives seemed at the top of the delegates' agenda, the disagreements often only masked an even more important, but unspoken, difference over slavery between the members from the northern and the southern sections. Virginia, Georgia, and the Carolinas had sufficient population at the time to block antislavery legislation under the new proposed House of Representatives structure, but already ominous trends seemed to put the South on the path to permanent minority status. First, the precedents being set that same summer in the Northwest Ordinance suggested that slavery would never cross the Ohio River. More important, the competition posed by slave labor to free labor, combined with the large plantations guaranteed by primogeniture, made it a surety that immigration to southern states would consistently fall behind that of the North. Fewer immigrants meant fewer representatives. So the House was in jeopardy in the foreseeable future. To ensure a continued strong presence in the House, southern delegates proposed to count slaves for the purposes of representation—a suggestion that outraged antislavery New Englanders, who wanted only to count slaves toward national taxes levied on the states by the new government. (Indians would not count for either representation or taxation.)

On June 11, 1787, Pennsylvanian James Wilson who personally opposed slavery, introduced a compromise in which, for purposes of establishing apportionment and for taxation, a slave would be counted as three fifths of a free inhabitant.[56] (The taxation aspect of the compromise was never invoked: the new secretary of the treasury, Alexander Hamilton, had a different plan in place, so it became a moot element of the compromise, essentially giving the South an inflated count in the House at no cost). At any rate, Wilson's phrase referred obliquely to "free inhabitants" and all other persons not comprehended in the foregoing description, and therefore "slavery" does not appear in the founding document.[57]

Putting aside the disturbing designation of a human as only three fifths of the value of another, the South gained a substantial advantage through the agreement. Based on the percentage of voting power by the five major slave states—Georgia, Maryland, Virginia, and the two Carolinas—the differential appeared as follows: (1) under the one-state-one-vote proposal, 38 percent; (2) counting all inhabitants (except Indians), 50 percent; (3) counting only free inhabitants, 41 percent; and (4) using the eventual three-fifths compromise numbers, 47 percent.[58] This amounted to no less than a tacit agreement to permanently lock a slave block into near-majority status, "perpetually protecting an institution the Fathers liked to call temporary."[59]

Delegates to the Constitutional Convention thus arrived at the point at which they all knew they would come. Americans had twice before skirted the issue of slavery or avoided dealing with it. In 1619, when black slaves were first unloaded off ships, colonists had the opportunity and responsibility to insist on their emancipation, immediately and unconditionally, yet they did not. Then again, in 1776, when Jefferson drafted the Declaration of Independence and included the indictment of Great Britain's imposition of slavery on the colonies, pressure from South Carolina and other southern states forced him to strike it from the final version. Now, in 1787, the young Republic had a third opportunity (perhaps its last without bloodshed) to deal with slavery. Its delegates did not.

Several examples can be cited to suggest that many of the delegates thought slavery was already headed for extinction. In 1776 the Continental Congress had reiterated a prohibition in the nonimportation agreement against the importation of African slaves, despite repealing the rest. During the war, various proposals were submitted to the Congress to offer freedom after the conflict to slaves who fought for the Revolution. Southern colonies blocked these. After the war, several northern states, including New Hampshire (1779), Pennsylvania (1780), Massachusetts (1783), Rhode Island (1784), and Connecticut (1784) all expressly forbade slavery in their constitutions, adopted immediate or gradual emancipation plans, or had courts declare slavery unconstitutional.[60] Most encouraging to antislave forces, however, in 1782 Virginia passed a law allowing slave owners discretion on freeing their slaves.

Jefferson's own *Notes on the State of Virginia* imagined a time after 1800 when all slaves would be free, and Madison labeled proslavery arguments in 1790 "shamefully indecent," calling slavery a "deep-rooted abuse."[61] Founders such as Hamilton, who helped start the New York Manumission Society, and Franklin, whose last major public debate involved a satirical lambasting of slavery, had established their antislavery credentials. Perhaps the most radical (and surprising) was Washington, who, alone among the southern Founders, projected an America that included both Indians and freed slaves as citizens in a condition of relative equality. He even established funds to support the children of his (wife's) slaves after her death and, in his last will and testament, freed his own slaves.[62]

The compromise over slavery did not come without a fight. Gouverneur Morris, one of the most outspoken critics of slavery at the convention, attacked Wilson's fractional formula and asked of the slaves counted under the three-fifths rule, "Are they admitted as Citizens? Then why are they not admitted on an equality with White Citizens? Are they admitted as property? Then why is not other property admitted to the computation?"[63] Massachusetts' Elbridge Gerry, later made famous for gerrymandering, the creative shaping of legislative districts for political gain, echoed this line of thinking, sarcastically asking why New Englanders would not be allowed to count their cattle if Georgians could count their slaves.[64]

Morris and others (including Jefferson) recognized that slavery promised to inject itself into every aspect of American life. Consider "comity," the principle that one state accept the privileges and immunities of other states to encourage free travel and commerce between them. Article IV required states to give "full faith and credit" to laws and judicial decisions of other states. Fugitives from justice were to be returned for trial to the state of the crime, for example. Almost immediately, conflicts arose when slaves escaped to northern states, which then refused to oblige southern requests for their return. Northern free blacks working in the merchant marine found themselves unable to disembark from their ships in southern ports for fear of enslavement, regardless of their legal status. Seven southern coastal states actually imprisoned free black sailors upon their arrival in port.[65] At the time, however, the likelihood that the southerners would cause the convention to collapse meant that the delegates had to adopt the three-fifths provision and deal with the consequences later. Realistically, it was the best they could do, although it would take seventy-eight years, a civil war, and three constitutional amendments to reverse the three-fifths compromise.[66]

Modern historians have leaped to criticize the convention's decision, and one could certainly apply the colloquial definition of a compromise as: doing less than what you know is right. Historian Joseph Ellis noted that "the distinguishing feature of the [Constitution] when it came to slavery was its evasiveness."[67] But let's be blunt: to have pressed the slavery issue in 1776 would have killed the Revolution, and to have pressed it in 1787 would have aborted the nation. When the ink dried on the final drafts, the participants had managed to agree on most of the important issues, and where they still disagreed, they had kept those divisions from distracting them from the task at hand. More important, the final document indeed represented all: "In 560 roll-calls, no state was always on the losing side, and each at times was part of the winning coalition."[68] The framers were highly focused only on Republic building, acting on the assumption that the Union was the highest good, and that ultimately all problems, including slavery, would be resolved if they could only keep the country together long enough.

From the outset, the proceedings had perched perilously on the verge of collapse, making the final document indeed a miracle. When the convention ended, a woman buttonholed Franklin and asked what kind of government the nation had. "A Republic, madam," Franklin replied, "if you can keep it."

Federalism Redefined

The completed constitution represented a marked transformation in the American system of federalism. Defined in the early state constitutions, "federalism" meant a belief in separate governments—state, local, national, with state sovereignty—but the 1787 document turned the system upside down. Article VI is an uncompromising statement that the laws of Congress are "the supreme law of the land." Nevertheless, the purpose of this power—the preservation of liberty—remained evident throughout the document.

This achievement required the delegates to endow the national government with a grant of specific, crucial "enumerated powers," including the authority to tax internally and externally (via excises and tariffs), regulate foreign and interstate commerce, enforce contracts and property rights, raise armies in time of peace and war, make treaties, and make all laws "necessary and proper" to carry out these enumerated powers. Conversely, the states could no longer levy tariff and customs duties, coin and print money, or impair contracts (via debtors' laws). These changes had crucial, far-reaching consequences.

Under the three-branched federal government, which boasted the checks and balances for which the Federalists are rightly famous, Article II created a first-ever American national executive, the president of the United States. Elected indirectly by an electoral college (a shield against direct democracy and the domination of large population centers), the president was to serve a four-year term with the option of perpetual reelection. He had authority to appoint all executive officials and federal judges, with the approval of the Senate. Most important, the president was to be the major architect of American foreign policy, serving as the civilian commander in chief of the military forces and generally designing and executing foreign policy with the advice and consent of the Senate. Perhaps the most significant power given the president was the executive's ability to veto congressional laws, subject to an override vote by Congress of two thirds of the members, "checking" an otherwise mighty chief executive.

In retrospect, despite concern raised at numerous points in America's history about an "imperial" presidency or a chief executive's wielding "dictator's powers," the Founders cleverly avoided the bloody instability that characterized many European nations like France, and the complete powerlessness that afflicted other foreign executives in places like the 1920s German Weimar Republic, site of the ill-considered splitting of executive authority. And if American presidents have aggrandized their power, it is largely because Congress, the courts, and most of all, the people, have willingly tolerated unconstitutional acquisitiveness. Ironically, this has occurred largely because of the very success and integrity of the process: Americans tend to think, despite frequent rhetoric to the contrary, that their leaders are *not* "crooks," nor do they view them as power mad. The expansion of presidential power has, then, relied on the reality that, over time, the large majority of chief executives have done their job with a degree of humility, recognizing that the people remain sovereign in the end.

Article III outlined a first-ever national judiciary. Federal judges would have the jurisdiction over all federal and interstate legal disputes. They would serve lifetime terms on condition of good behavior, and federal district courts would hear cases that could be appealed to federal circuit courts and, ultimately, to the Supreme Court of the United States. It is important to note that the Constitution in no way granted the federal courts the power of judicial review, or an ultimate interpretive power over constitutional issues. Modern federal courts possess this huge power thanks to a long series of precedents beginning with the 1803 case of *Marbury v. Madison.* If the Founders intended courts to possess this ultimate constitutional authority, they did not say so in the Constitution. Moreover, the federal courts' authority was simultaneously checked by Congress's prerogative to impeach federal judges (and the president) for "high crimes and misdemeanors," and a score of federal judges have been impeached and removed for offenses such as perjury as recently as the 1980s.

Article I, the most complex section of the Constitution, outlined the legislative branch of government. Congressmen would serve in the House of Representatives at a number proportional to their states' census figures, with the three-fifths clause intact. Representatives were to be elected directly by the people to two-year terms and, unlike the Confederation legislators, would have the option of perpetual reelection. The House members' chief authority, the power of the purse, descended from English and colonial precedent that tax and revenue measures had to emanate from the House of Representatives.

The United States Senate is the second legislative component. Each state legislature elected two senators to serve six-year terms with the option of perpetual reelection. Older than congressmen, senators ruled on bills passed by the House. Most important, the Senate had the approval power over all presidential appointees, and also had ratification power over treaties. Both houses of Congress had to agree to declare war, and both were involved in removal of a president should the need arise: if a federal judge or the president committed high crimes and misdemeanors, articles of impeachment were to be voted out of the House, with the subsequent trial in the Senate, where senators served as jurors.

Surveying the Constitution, it is apparent that the nationalistic proponents of the Virginia Plan carried the day. No branch of the federal government had ultimate veto power over state legislation, as ardent nationalists advocated, and the Connecticut Compromise guaranteed a degree of state equality and power in the Senate. Yet the new Constitution marked a radical departure from the old Confederation model, and ultimately the nationalists gained a veto of sorts through the extraconstitutional practice of judicial review. Opponents of centralized governmental authority were awed by the proposed document, and many doubted that the public would ratify and institute such a powerful central government so soon after overthrowing a monarch.

The ratification stipulations enumerated in the final article thus carried great importance. How would the proposed governmental plan be debated and voted upon? Had the delegates followed the letter of the law, they would have been forced to submit the new Constitution to the Confederation Congress in vain hope of the unanimous approval necessary to legally change the government. Of course, the nationalists had no intention of obeying such a law. The Constitution instead contained its own new rules, calling each state to convene a special convention to debate and ratify or defeat the proposed governmental plan. If nine states (not thirteen) ratified, the Constitution stipulated a new government would form.[69]

Having thus erected their grand plan to reshape American republicanism, the nationalists returned to their home states to labor on behalf of its ratification. They did so well aware that the majority of Americans were highly suspicious of the term "nationalism." Politically aware citizens thought of themselves as Whigs who backed the kind of federalism represented by the Confederation and the New Jersey Plan. In modern parlance, then, an image makeover was due. Nationalists shrewdly began, in direct contradiction to historical and constitutional precedent, to refer to themselves and their philosophy as federalism, not nationalism. Naturally, their Federalist opponents were aghast to hear their political enemies using the name Federalists for their own purposes and, worse, to hear the original federalism now redefined by the new Federalists as Anti-Federalism! Two rival political factions had formed and the debate was on, but one already had perceived that control of the language is everything in politics.[70]

Revolutionary and Early National Political Factions and Parties, 1781–1815

1776–1787	Federalists	vs. Nationalists
1787–1793	Anti-Federalists	vs. Federalists
1793–1815	Jeffersonian Republicans	vs. Federalists

The Ratification Debate

The call for special ratifying conventions perfectly met the new Federalists' practical needs and ideological standards, for they suspected they would lose a popular vote, a vote in the Confederation Congress, or a vote of the state legislatures. Their only hope lay in a new venue where they had a level playing field and could use their powers of persuasion and growing command of the language of politics to build momentum. Their pragmatism dovetailed nicely with ideological precedents that turned the tables on the radicals, who had always argued that constitutional law was *fundamental* law and should be approved by specially selected governmental bodies, not common state legislatures. Nearly all of the new state constitutions were ratified by special conventions, which added to the leverage of precedent. Combining the ideological precedents with a rhetorical call for the sovereignty of the people, Federalist orators masterfully crafted a best-case scenario for their cause. They portrayed the special ratifying conventions as the best means of voicing the direct will of the people, and did this while studiously avoiding both a direct democratic vote and circumventing established elected bodies that stood against them. Their strategy was nothing less than a political tour de force.[71]

Each state proceeded to select delegates in different ways. In four states, voters directly elected delegates, whereas in the remainder (except Rhode Island), delegates served by a vote of state legislators or executive appointment. Only Rhode Island held a direct voter referendum on the Constitution. The Federalists knew that by moving quickly they could frame the ratification process, and they won controlling majorities in five of the thirteen states. Each of those states ratified the document within a few weeks. Using this initial support as a base, the

Federalists continued to wage a propaganda campaign calling for sovereignty of the people over the state legislatures and outflanking the less articulate Anti-Federalist majority.

Much printer's ink has been spilled by historians arguing about the relative merits of the positions held by the Federalists and the Anti-Federalists. Prior to the twentieth century, the Federalists held an elevated position in the minds of most Americans who were conscious of history. But in 1913, Charles Beard's *Economic Interpretation of the Constitution* delivered a broadside accelerated by economic principles of class struggle.[72] Beard argued that the Federalists, acting on their own self-interest as planters and businessmen, greedily plotted to ensure their own economic supremacy. Using voting records of the delegates, and examining their backgrounds, Beard concluded there was little concern for the public interest by these founders. In 1958, Forrest McDonald dismantled Beard's economic determinism, only to be countered by Robert McGuire and Robert Ohsfelt's voting-model analysis.[73]

It goes without saying that Beard is correct to identify the Anti-Federalists as farmers and middle-class workingmen, but this definition bridges a wide range of the population in 1787, including subsistence farmers in western Pennsylvania and upstate New York alongside elite southern planters who led the movement. Patrick Henry, Richard Henry Lee, William Grayson, and James Monroe, firm Anti-Federalist leaders, were as wealthy as any in the Federalist camp, and were joined by Sam Adams (a chronic bankrupt), Melancton Smith, Luther Martin, and New York's George Clinton. Thomas Jefferson, arguably the best known Anti-Federalist of all, did not join the movement until the early 1790s and, at any rate, was out of the country from 1787–88.

And yet, Beard's definitions and the complaints by Howard Zinn and his disciples wrongly assume that people were (and are) incapable of acting outside of self-interest. Had not the great Washington argued as much? Yet Washington had to look no further than his own life to realize the error of his position: he was on track to gain a general officer's commission in the British army, replete with additional land grants for dutiful service to His Majesty. Instead, Washington threw it away to lead a ragtag army of malcontents into the snow of Valley Forge and the icy waters of the Delaware. Self-interest indeed! What self-interest caused Francis Lewis, a signer of the Declaration, to lose his properties and see his wife taken prisoner by the British? How does self-interest account for the fate of Judge Richard Stockton, a delegate from New Jersey to the Continental Congress, who spent time in British jails and whose family had to live off charity—all because he dared sign the Declaration? On the other hand, Patrick Henry, Richard Henry Lee, and others all stood to gain handsomely from the growing value of slave labor in the new Constitution—the one they opposed! In sum, no matter how Beard and his successors torture the statistics, they cannot make the Constitutional Convention scream "class struggle."[74] The debate was genuine; it was about important ideas, and men took positions not for what they gained financially but for what they saw as the truth.

After a slow start, the Anti-Federalists rallied and launched an attack on the proposed Constitution. Employing arguments that sounded strikingly Whiggish, Anti-Federalists spoke of the Federalists in the same language with which they had condemned the British monarchy in the previous decade. They described the Constitution as a document secretly produced by lawyers and a hated "aristocratic monied interest" that aimed to rob Americans of their hard-won liberties. Echoing Montesquieu and other Enlightenment thinkers, they insisted government should remain close to home, and that the nation would be too large to govern from a "federal town." Richard Henry Lee captured the emotion of the Constitution's opponents, calling the document "dangerously oligarchic" and the work of a "silent, powerful and ever active conspiracy of those who govern."[75] Patrick Henry warned Americans to "Guard with jealous attention the public liberty. Suspect everyone who approaches that jewel."[76] James Monroe, the future president, worried that the document would lead to a monarchical government.

Anti-Federalists expressed shock at the extent of the taxation and warfare powers. One delegate asked, "After we have given them all our money, established them in a federal town, given them the power of coining money and raising a standing *army* to establish their arbitrary government; what resources [will] the people have left?"[77] Anti-Federalists furiously attacked the Federalists' three-tiered system, arguing that the proposed constitutional districts did not allow for direct representation, that congressmen should be elected annually, and that the proposed Senate was undemocratic. They saw the same aristocratic tendency in the proposed federal judiciary, with its life terms. And, of course, because Whigs feared executive authority, Anti-Federalists were appalled at the specter of an indirectly elected president serving unlimited terms and commanding a standing army. Cato, one of the most widely read Anti-Federalists, predicted such a system would degenerate into arbitrary conscription of troops for the army.

However, the Anti-Federalists' most telling criticism, and the one for which American civilization will forever remain in their debt, was their plea for a bill of rights. Federalists, who believed the state constitutions adequately protected civil liberties, were stunned by this libertarian critique of their work. Jefferson, who had studiously avoided the debate, wrote from France that "a bill of rights is what a people are entitled to against every government on earth, general or particular, and what no just government should refuse or rest on inference."[78] To grant such sweeping powers without simultaneously protecting life, liberty, and property seemed like madness. Political rhetoric aside, Anti-Federalists were amazed at what they saw as a direct assault on the principles of the Revolution. One Anti-Federalist, writing as Centinel, spoke for all his brethren when he expressed "astonishment" that "after so recent a triumph over British despots . . . a set of men amongst ourselves should have the effrontery to attempt the destruction of our liberties."[79]

Obviously, the Anti-Federalists opposed many things, but what were they for? By 1787–88 most of them supported a Confederation government revised along the lines of the New Jersey Plan. They maintained that no crisis actually existed—that the nation was fine and that a few adjustments to the Articles would cure whatever maladies existed. But the Anti-Federalists waited too long to agree to any amendment of the Articles, and they lost their opportunity. Even some of their leading spokesmen, such as Patrick Henry, unwittingly undercut the sovereign-state position when he wrote, "The question turns . . . on that poor little thing—the expression, *We, the People* instead of the United States of America."[80] With that statement, Henry reinforced Jefferson's own assertion in the Declaration that the people of the colonies—and not the colonies themselves—separated from England. By invoking "the people" as opposed to the "states," Henry also stated a position not far from that of Lincoln in 1861, when he argued that disunion was no more possible than cutting a building in half and thinking it would still keep out the rain. The Federalists saw their opening and brilliantly sidestepped the question of state-versus-federal sovereignty by arguing that the Constitution made the *people* sovereign, not the state or the federal government.

Far from being the traitors or aristocrats alleged by their opponents, the Federalists showed that they too had inherited the ideology of the Revolution, but only that they took from it different political lessons. Through a series of eighty-five *Federalist Papers* (written as newspaper articles by Hamilton, Madison, and Jay under the pseudonym Publius), they demonstrated the depth and sophistication of their political philosophy.[81] Hamilton, ever the republican centralist, saw the Constitution as a way to foster a vigorous centralized republic (not a democracy) that would simultaneously promote order and economic liberty in the Lockean tradition.

Madison emerged as the most significant of the three *Federalist Papers* authors in one respect: he correctly analyzed the necessity of political parties ("factions," as he called them) and understood their role. An extensive republic, especially one as large as the United States would become, inevitably would divide society into a "greater variety of interests, of pursuits, of passions, which check each other." Factions, then, should be encouraged. They provided the competition that tested and refined ideas. More important, they demanded that people inform themselves and take a side, rather than sliding listlessly into murky situations they did not choose to understand out of laziness.

Modern Americans are assaulted by misguided calls for "bipartisanship," a code word for one side ceding its ideas to the party favored by the media. In fact, however, Madison detested compromise that involved abandoning principles, and in any event, thought that the Republic was best served when factions presented extreme differences to the voters, rather than shading their positions toward the middle. The modern moderate voters—so highly praised in the media—would have been anathema to Madison, who wanted people to take sides as a means of creating checks and balances.

His emphasis on factions had another highly practical purpose that, again, reflected on his fundamental distrust of human nature; namely, factions splintered power among groups so that no group dominated others. Like Hamilton then, and later Tocqueville and Thoreau, Madison dreaded the "tyranny of the majority," and feared that mobs could just as easily destroy personal rights as could any monarch. Madison demanded an intellectual contest of ideas, and recognized that the Constitution's separation of powers only represented one layer of protections against despotism. The vigorous competition of political parties constituted a much more important safeguard.[82]

Hamilton shared Madison's dark view of human nature, but where Madison stressed personal liberties, Hamilton thought more in terms of the national interest and the dangers posed by the Articles. Portrayed as more radical than Madison—one author referred to Hamilton as the Rousseau of the Right—the New Yorker has often been viewed as a voice for elitism. In fact, Hamilton sought the alliance of government with elites because they needed to be enlisted in the service of the government on behalf of the people, a course they would not take if left to their own devices. To accomplish that, he intended to use the Treasury of the new republic, and its financial/debt structure, to encourage the wealthy to align themselves with the interests of the nation.[83]

Only the wealthy could play that role: middle-class merchants, farmers, or artisans were too transient and, at any rate, did not have enough surplus to invest in the nation. Permanent stability required near-perpetual investment, which in turn required structuring property laws so that the wealthy would not hesitate to place their resources at the disposal of the government. Hamilton also argued that the new government would thrive once the "power of the sword" (a standing army) was established, opening the door for his detractors to label him both a militarist and a monarchist, whereas in reality he was a pragmatist.

Taken together, the ideas of Madison and Hamilton further divided power, and when laid atop the already decentralized and balanced branches, added still more safeguards to the system of multiple levels of voting restrictions, staggered elections, and an informed populace—all of which provided a near-impenetrable shield of republican democracy. Laminating this shield, and hardening it still further, was the added security of religious conviction and righteousness that would not only keep elected and appointed officials in line on a personal level, but would infuse the voting public with a morality regarding all issues. At least, this was the plan, as devised by the Federalist Founders.

State after state cast votes, and the Federalists advanced to a dramatic victory. Five states—Delaware, Pennsylvania, New Jersey, Georgia, and Connecticut—ratified the Constitution within three months of first viewing the document. Anti-Federalists claimed the voters had not been given enough time to debate and assess the proposal, but the Federalists brushed away their objections and the Constitution sailed through. The process slowed in Massachusetts, New York, North Carolina, New Hampshire, and Virginia. In those states, Anti-Federalist majorities attacked the documents, but the Federalists answered them point by point.

As the spring and summer of 1788 wore on, the Anti-Federalist cause gradually lost support. In some states, tacit and written agreements between the factions traded Anti-Federalist support for a written bill of rights. New Hampshire's

June twenty-first ratification technically made the Constitution official, although no one was comfortable treating it as such until New York and Virginia had weighed in. Washington helped swing Virginia, stating flatly that "there is no alternative between the adoption of [the Constitution] and anarchy," and "it or disunion is before us to choose from."[84] Virginia, thanks to Washington's efforts, ratified on June twenty-fifth, and New York followed a month later. Despite North Carolina's and Rhode Island's opposition, the Constitution became the "law of the land."[85] The Constitution was "a Trojan horse of radical social and economic transformation," placing once and for all the principles espoused by Jefferson in the Declaration into a formal code whose intent was usually, though not always, obvious.[86]

The Anti-Federalist Legacy

Given the benefit of hindsight, it is remarkable that the Anti-Federalists fared as well as they did. They lost the battle, but not the war. In 1787–88, the Anti-Federalists lacked the economic resources, organizational skill, and political vision to win a national struggle. Nor did they have the media of the day: of one hundred Revolutionary newspapers, eighty-eight were solidly in the Federalist camp. This proved advantageous when Virginians read false Federalist newspaper reports that New York had ratified on the eve of their own state's narrow vote! Moreover, Franklin, Jay, Hamilton, John Marshall, and General Washington himself—the cream of Revolutionary society—all backed the Constitution and worked for its ratification. On the other hand, the Anti-Federalists were lesser-known men who were either aged or less politically active at the time (for example, Sam Adams, George Mason, and Patrick Henry) or young and just getting started in their political careers (James Monroe and John Randolph).

And, ironically, the Anti-Federalists' love of localism and states' rights sealed their fate. This first national political election demanded a *national* campaign organization and strategy—the kind that typifies our own two-party system in the present day. Anti-Federalists, though, tended to cling to local allegiances; they were fearful of outsiders and ill equipped to compete on a national stage. To their credit, when they lost, they grudgingly joined the victors in governing the new nation.[87] Yet the Anti-Federalists' radicalism did not disappear after 1788. Instead, they shifted their field of battle to a strategy of retaining local sovereignty through a philosophy constitutional historians call strict construction. This was an application of the narrowest possible interpretation of the Constitution, and the Anti-Federalists were aided in arriving at strict construction through their greatest legacy, the Bill of Rights.

Following ratification, leaders of both factions agreed to draft amendments to the Constitution.[88] Madison took charge of the project that started him on the path on which he soon transformed from a Federalist to an Anti-Federalist leader. Strong precedents existed for a bill of rights. The English Magna Charta, Petition of Right, and Bill of Rights enumerated, in various ways, protections against standing armies and confiscation of property, and guaranteed a number of legal rights that jointly are referred to as due process. These precedents had taken form in most of the Revolutionary state constitutions, most famously Virginia's Declaration of Rights, penned by George Mason. Madison studied all of these documents carefully and conferred with Anti-Federalist leaders. He then forged twelve proposed constitutional amendments, which Congress sent to the states in 1789. The states ratified ten of them by 1791.

The First Amendment combined several rights—speech, press, petition, assembly, and religion—into one fundamental law guaranteeing freedom of expression. While obliquely related to religious speech, the clear intent was to protect political speech. This, after all, was what concerned the Anti-Federalists about the power of a national government—that it would suppress dissenting views. The amendment strongly implied, however, that even those incapable of oral speech were protected when they financially supported positions through advertising, political tracts, and broadsides. Or, put simply, money equals speech.

However, the Founders hardly ignored religion, nor did they embrace separation of church and state, a buzz phrase that never appears in the Constitution or the Bill of Rights. Madison had long been a champion of religious liberty. He attended the College of New Jersey (later Princeton), where he studied under the Reverend John Witherspoon. In May 1776, when Virginia lawmakers wrote the state's new constitution, Madison changed George Mason's phrase that "all men should enjoy the fullest toleration" of religion to "all men are entitled to the full and free *exercise* of religion" [emphasis ours].

Madison thus rejected the notion that the exercise of faith originated with government, while at the same time indicating that he expected a continual and ongoing practice of religious worship. He resisted attempts to insert the name Jesus Christ into the Virginia Bill for Religious Liberty, not because he was an unbeliever, but because he argued that "better proof of reverence for that holy name would be not to profane it by making it a topic of legislative discussion." Late in his life Madison wrote, "Belief in a God All Powerful wise and good, is so essential to the moral order of the World and the happiness of man, that arguments to enforce it cannot be drawn from too many sources." Even at the time, though, he considered the widespread agreement within the Constitutional Convention "a miracle" and wrote, "It is impossible for the man of pious reflection not to perceive in [the convention] a finger of that Almighty hand."[89]

Religious, and especially Christian, influences in the Constitution and the Bill of Rights were so predominant that as late as the mid-twentieth century, the chairman of the Sesquicentennial Commission on the Constitution answered negatively when asked if an atheist could become president: "I maintain that the spirit of the Constitution forbids it. The Constitution prescribes and oath of affirmation . . . [that] in its essence is a covenant with the people which the President pledges himself to keep with the help of Almighty God."[90] Modern interpretations of the Constitution that prohibit displays of crosses in the name of religious freedom would rightly have been shouted down by the Founders, who intended no such separation.

The Second Amendment addressed Whig fears of a professional standing army by guaranteeing the right of citizens to arm themselves and join militias. Over the years, the militia preface has become thoroughly (and often, deliberately) misinterpreted to imply that the framers intended citizens to be armed only in the context of an army under the authority of the state. In fact, militias were the exact opposite of a state-controlled army: the state militias taken together were expected to serve as a counterweight to the federal army, and the further implication was that citizens were to be as well armed as the government itself![91] The Third Amendment buttressed the right of civilians against the government military by forbidding the quartering (housing) of professional troops in private homes.

Amendments Four through Eight promised due process via reasonable bail, speedy trials (by a jury of peers if requested), and habeas corpus petitions. They forbade self-incrimination and arbitrary search and seizure, and proclaimed, once again, the fundamental nature of property rights. The Ninth Amendment, which has lain dormant for two hundred years, states that there might be *other* rights not listed in the amendments that are, nevertheless, guaranteed by the Constitution. But the most controversial amendment, the Tenth, echoes the second article of the Articles of Confederation in declaring that the states and people retain all rights and powers not expressly granted to the national government by the Constitution. It, too, has been relatively ignored.

These ten clear statements were intended by the framers as absolute limitations on the power of government, not on the rights of individuals. In retrospect, they more accurately should be known as the Bill of Limitations on government to avoid the perception that the rights were granted by government in the first place.[92]

Two streams of liberty flowed from 1776. First, the Federalists synthesized Whig opposition to centralized military, economic, political, and religious authority into a program built upon separation of power, checks and balances, and staggered terms of office, which simultaneously preserved many state and local prerogatives. Second, the Anti-Federalists completed the process with the Bill of Rights, which further reinforced laws that protected states, localities, and individuals from central government coercion. Both these streams flowed through an American Christianity that emphasized duty, civic morality, skeptical questioning of temporal authority, and economic success. In addition, both streams were fed by Enlightenment can-do doctrines tempered by the realization that men were fallible, leading to an emphasis on competition, political parties, and the marketplace of ideas.

But it was a close-run thing. As Adams recalled, "All the great critical questions about men and measures from 1774 to 1778" were "decided by the vote of a single state, and that vote was often decided by a single individual."[93] It was by no means inevitable. Nevertheless, the fountain of hope had turned to a river of liberty, nourishing the new nation as it grew and prospered.

CHAPTER FIVE

Small Republic, Big Shoulders, 1789–1815

George Washington's famed 1796 Farewell Address contains one plea that, in retrospect, seems remarkably futile: the president expressed frustration over the ongoing political strife and the rise of permanent political parties. It was an odd statement, considering that if anyone created parties (or factions, as James Madison had termed them), it was Washington, along with his brilliant aide Alexander Hamilton, through his domestic program and foreign policy. They had assistance from the *Federalist Papers* coauthor Madison, who relished divisions among political groups as a means to balance power. Washington's warnings reflected his sorrow over the bitter debates that characterized politics throughout his two administrations, more so because the debates had made enemies of former colleagues Hamilton, Madison, Jefferson, and Adams. By 1796 most of those men could not stand each other: only Jefferson and Madison still got along, and Washington, before his death, ceased corresponding with his fellow Virginian, Jefferson. Other Founders chose sides among these powerhouses.

Washington thought good men could disagree without the venom of politics overriding all other interests. He hoped that a band of American Revolutionaries could achieve consensus over what their Revolution was all about. In fact, Washington might well have voiced as much pride as regret over the unfolding events of the 1790s because he and his generation shaped an American political party system that endures, in recognizable form, to this day, and because the emergence of those factions, of which he so strongly disapproved, in large part guaranteed the success and moderation of that system.

From 1789 to 1815, clashes between Federalists and Anti-Federalists translated into a continuing and often venomous debate over the new nation's domestic and foreign policies. Political parties first appeared in this era, characterized by organized congressional leadership, party newspapers whose editorials established party platforms and attacked the opposition, and the nomination of partisan national presidential candidates. Washington's cabinet itself contained the seeds of this partisanship. Secretary of State Jefferson rallied the old Anti-Federalists under the banner of limited government and a new Jeffersonian Republican Party. Meanwhile, Secretary of the Treasury Hamilton, chief author of the *Federalist Papers* with Madison (who himself would make the transition to Republican), set the agenda for the Federalists. Both sides battled over Hamilton's economic plan—his reports on debt, banking, and manufactures—while Madison, often the voice of conciliation and compromise, quietly supported the Federalist position. They simultaneously fought over whether American foreign policy would favor France or Britain in the European struggle for power. In every case the debates came down to a single issue: given that the people retained all powers but those most necessary to the functioning of the Republic, what powers did the government absolutely need? Thus, from the moment the ink dried on the Constitution, an important development had taken place in American government whereby the debate increasingly focused on the size of government rather than its virtue.

Time Line

1789: Washington elected; new government forms; Congress meets; French Revolution begins

1790: Hamilton issues the *Report on Public Credit*

1791: First Bank of United States (BUS) established

1793: Washington begins second term; Proclamation of Neutrality; cotton gin patented

1794: Whiskey Rebellion; Battle of Fallen Timbers

1795: Jay's Treaty; Pinckney's Treaty

1796: Washington's Farewell Address; John Adams elected president

1798: X,Y,Z Affair; Quasi War with France; Alien and Sedition Acts; Virginia and Kentucky Resolutions

1800: Washington, D. C., becomes national capital

1801: Congress narrowly selects Jefferson president; Adams appoints John Marshall and "midnight judges"

1802: Congress recalls most "midnight judges"

1803: *Marbury v. Madison;* Louisiana Purchase; Lewis and Clark expedition

1804: Aaron Burr kills Alexander Hamilton; Jefferson reelected

1805: British seize American ships

1807: Embargo Act; Burr acquitted of treason

1808: African slave trade ends; James Madison elected president

1809: Congress boycotts British and French trade

1810: *Fletcher v. Peck*

1811: Battle of Tippecanoe; BUS charter expires; first steamboat on Ohio and Mississippi rivers

1812: United States and Britain engage in War of 1812; Madison reelected

1813: Battles of Lake Erie and Thames

1814: British burn Washington, D. C. ; Battle of Lake
Champlain/Plattsburgh; Hartford Convention;
Treaty of Ghent ends war
1815: Battle of New Orleans

Following the ratification of the Constitution, the Federalists continued their momentum under Washington, and they deserve credit for implementing a sound program during the general's two terms. Washington's exit in 1796 constituted no small event: although the election of his vice president, the famed Revolutionary organizer and diplomat John Adams, essentially maintained Federalist power, a popular and respected leader had stepped down voluntarily. Relinquishing the "crown" under such circumstances was unheard of in Europe, much less in the rest of the world, where monarchs clung to their thrones even if it required the assassination of family members. It is not an overstatement to say that Adams's election in 1796 was one of the most significant points in the evolution of the Republic, and although not on the momentous scale of the complete upheaval four years later, it nevertheless marked a bloodless change in leadership seldom seen in human history.

When the Federalist dynasty evaporated in the span of Adams's administration, and the Jeffersonian Republicans took over the ship of state in 1800, this, too, contained elements of continuity as well as the obvious components of change. For one thing, Jefferson propagated the "Virginia dynasty," which began with Washington, then Jefferson, followed later by Madison and, still later, James Monroe. Never in the nation's history would it again be dominated by so many from one state in such a brief span of time (although Texas, in the late twentieth century, has come close, electing three presidents in thirty-five years).

Movers and Shakers

In New York City in March of 1789, George Washington and John Adams took the oaths of office to become the first president and vice president of the United States of America.[1] Both had stood unopposed in the country's first presidential election five months earlier, and Washington bungled his words, appearing more "agitated and embarrassed . . . than he ever was by the leveled Cannon or pointed musket."[2] If ceremony threw the general off, neither the responsibility nor the power of the position unnerved him. After all, few knew what the office of the presidency was—indeed, it would have been little without a man such as Washington moving its levers—and someone who had commanded an army that defeated the British was unlikely to be reluctant to exercise power. Washington, as always, disliked public speaking, and although he delivered his addresses to Congress in person, he found pomp and circumstance distasteful. He was, after all, a farmer and a soldier.

Washington knew, however, that in this grand new experiment, the president was in a sense more powerful than any king. A political priest, he governed by virtue of the power of the people, making him in a sense beyond reproach.

Certainly Washington had his critics—his enemies pummeled him mercilessly. Philip Freneu's *National Journal* attacked Washington so viciously that the general referred to the editor as "that rascal"—damning words from Washington![3] Radical Tom Paine went even further. In a letter to the *Aurora,* Payne "celebrated Washington's [ultimate] departure, actually prayed for his imminent death," and contemptuously concluded that the world would have to decide "whether you are an apostate or an impostor, whether you have abandoned good principles or whether you ever had any."[4] Washington endured it with class. Paine's reputation, already questionable, never recovered from his ill-chosen words regarding "the man who unites all hearts."[5]

If Washington was "the American Zeus, Moses, and Cincinnatus all rolled into one," he was not without faults.[6] His rather nebulous personal religion left him exposed and isolated. Many of his biographers trumpeted Washington's faith, and a famous painting captures the colonial general praying in a snowy wood, but if Washington had any personal belief in Jesus Christ, he kept it well hidden. Like Franklin, Washington tended toward Deism, a general belief in a detached and impersonal God who plays no role in human affairs. At any rate, Washington approached his new duties with a sense that although he appealed frequently to the Almighty for help, he was going it alone, and for better or worse, the new government rested on his large shoulders.[7]

The president's personality has proven elusive to every generation of American historians, none more so than modern writers who, unsatisfied with what people wrote or said, seek to reach the emotions of the popular figures. At this, Washington would have scoffed. The son of a prosperous Virginia planter, Washington married well and rose to high economic, military, and political power, becoming undisputed leader of the American Revolution. Yet the qualities that brought him this power and respect—self-control, solid intellect, hard work, tenacity, and respectability—also shielded the life of the inner man. No one, not even his wife and closest family, really knew the intensely private George Washington.

Washington was, reportedly, unhappy at home. Economics had weighed heavily in his choice of a wife—supposedly, he deeply loved another woman—and his relationship with his own mother was strained. His goal of becoming a British army officer, a task for which he was particularly well suited, evaporated with the Revolution. Although he assumed the duties of commander in chief, it was a position the Virginian reluctantly took out of love of country rather than for personal fulfillment. Solace in religion or the church also evaded him, although he fully accepted man's sinful nature and his own shortcomings. Stiff and cold, the general nevertheless wept at the farewell to his officers. Never flamboyant and often boring, Washington eludes modern writers dazzled by the cult of celebrity. Once, on a bet, a colleague approached Washington warmly and greeted him by patting him firmly on his back; the individual won his bet, but for the rest of his life shivered at the memory of the look of reproach on Washington's face!

A top-down centralist and consolidator by the nature of his military experiences, much like another general/president, Dwight D. Eisenhower some two hundred years later, Washington compromised and negotiated when it seemed the right strategy.[8] As a result, it is not surprising that he thoroughly endorsed, and spent the next eight years implementing, the centralist economic and military policies of his most important aide, Alexander Hamilton. To ignore Washington's great vision and innovations in government, however, or dismiss them as Hamilton's, would shortchange him. He virtually invented out of whole cloth the extraconstitutional notion of a cabinet. At every step he carefully weighed not only the needs of the moment, but also the precedents he set for all future leaders of the nation. For a man to refuse a crown from his adoring nation may have been good sense in light of the fate of Louis XVI a few years later; to refuse a third term marked exceptional character.

That character also revealed itself in those with whom he kept counsel—his associates and political appointees, most of whom had great virtues but also suffered from fatal flaws. Vice President John Adams, for example, possessed the genius, personal morality, and expertise to elevate him to the presidency. But he antagonized people, often needlessly, and lacked the political savvy and social skills necessary to retain the office. Short and stocky (his enemies disparagingly called Adams His Rotundity), Adams rose from a humble Massachusetts farming family to attend Harvard College and help lead the American Revolution.[9] A brilliant attorney, patriot organizer, and Revolutionary diplomat, Adams exuded all the doctrinal religion missing in Washington, to the point of being pious to a fault. Other men at the Continental Congress simply could not stand him, and many a good measure failed only because Adams supported it. (His unpopularity at the Continental Congress required that a declaration of independence be introduced by someone else, even though he was the idea's chief supporter.) On the other hand, Adams brought a sense of the sacred to government that Washington lacked, placing before the nation an unwavering moral compass that refused compromise. By setting such an unbending personal standard, he embarrassed lesser men who wanted to sin, and sin greatly, without consequence.

Predictably, Adams failed in the arena of elective politics. His moderate Revolutionary views and distrust of direct democracy combined with his ability to make others despise him ensured his lack of a political base. Thanks to his own failings and Republican propaganda, the public wrongly came to perceive Adams as an elitist and monarchist (and in Adams's terminology the phrase executive and monarch were almost interchangeable). But to portray him as antithetical to Revolutionary principles is unwarranted and bizarre. Where Washington subtly maneuvered, Adams stubbornly charged. He had much—perhaps too much—in common with Alexander Hamilton, almost guaranteeing the two would be at odds sooner or later. Ultimately, Adams's great legacy, including his Revolutionary-era record, his dealings with foreign powers, and his judicial appointments, overshadowed perhaps an even greater mark he made on America: establishing the presidency as a moral, as well as a political, position.[10]

The third of these Founder giants, James Madison, arguably the most brilliant thinker of the Revolutionary generation, soon put his talents to work against his fellow Federalists Washington and Hamilton. A Virginian and Princeton graduate, Madison stood five feet four inches tall and reportedly spoke in a near whisper. He compensated for a lack of physical presence with keen intelligence, hard work, and a genius for partisan political activity. Madison's weapons of choice were the pen and the party caucus, the latter of which he shares much credit for inventing. Into his endeavors he poured the fervent ideology of a Whig who believed that strands from both the national and state governments could be woven into a fabric of freedom.

Throughout the course of his intellectual development, Madison veered back and forth between the poles of national versus state government authority. By the early 1790s, he leaned toward the latter because his old protégé Hamilton had drifted too far toward the former. Always alert to the blessings of competition in any endeavor, Madison embraced the concept of factions and divided government. As the first Speaker of the House of Representatives, James Madison began to formulate the agenda of the party of Jefferson and in so doing became heir apparent to his Virginia ally.[11]

Creating the Cabinet

One of Washington's most important contributions to American constitutionalism involved his immediate creation of a presidential cabinet. Although the Constitution is silent on the subject, Washington used executive prerogative to create a board of advisers, then instructed them to administer the varied economic, diplomatic, and military duties of the executive branch and report directly back to him. He did so instantly and with surprisingly little controversy. He perceived that these appointees should be specialists, yet the positions also could reward loyalists who had worked for the success of the party. As appointees, needing only the approval of the Senate, Washington bypassed the gridlock of congressional selection systems.

Soon after his election and establishment of the cabinet, Washington realized that staffing the government would be a permanent source of irritation, writing, "I anticipated in a heart filled with distress, the ten thousand embarrassments, perplexities, and troubles to which I must again be exposed . . . none greater [than those caused] by applications for appointments."[12] Little could the Virginian have dreamed that federal job seeking would only grow worse, and that eighty years later Abraham Lincoln would have lines of job seekers stacked up outside his office while he was in the middle of running a war.

The importance of the cabinet to evolving party politics was, of course, that Washington's inner circle hosted the two powerhouses of 1790s politics Hamilton and Jefferson. Secretary of State Jefferson is ever present in the history of American Revolutionary culture and politics.[13] A tall, slender, redheaded Virginian, Jefferson was the son of a modest Virginia planter. Young Jefferson, a student at William and Mary College, developed a voracious appetite for learning and culture in myriad forms. In his *Notes on the State of Virginia,* for example, he wrote ably about Mound Builder culture, Native American languages, meteorology, biology, geology, and, of course, history and political science.[14] He spoke French fluently, learned architecture from books (and went on to design and build his own elaborate Monticello home), and practiced his violin for at least an hour each day. Everything he touched reflected his wide and extraordinary tastes. For example, military expeditions that he ordered to explore the Louisiana Territory received their instructions for scientific endeavors from the-then president Jefferson; and he worked with his nemesis Hamilton to devise one of the most commonsense coinage systems in the world (based on tens and hundreds), an approach that Jefferson naturally tried to apply to the land distribution system.[15] Widowed in the 1780s, Jefferson promised his wife on her deathbed he would never remarry; he later apparently pursued a decades-long love affair with one of his slaves, Sally Hemmings, with a historical debate still raging over whether this union resulted in the birth of at least one son.[16]

Jefferson's political career soared. After authoring the Declaration of Independence, he followed Patrick Henry as Virginia's wartime governor, although in that capacity he was merely adequate. Unlike Washington or Hamiliton, Jefferson never served in the Continental Army and never saw combat. After the war, as American ambassador to France, he developed a pronounced taste for French food, wine, and radical French politics. Back home in the 1790s, he claimed to detest partisan politics at the very time he was embracing some of its most subtle and important forms—the anonymous political editorial, the private dinner party, and personal lobbying. Anyone who knew Jefferson said he possessed a certain kind of magic—a charisma. Love of good company and conversation provided him great joy and, simultaneously, a lethal weapon to use against his political foes.

Fueling Jefferson's political endeavors was a set of radical Whig beliefs that had not changed much since he penned the Declaration of Independence in 1776. That famed document's denunciation of centralized economic, military, judicial, and executive governmental authority combined with a hatred of state religion to spotlight his classic radical Whig ideas. Although it is debatable whether Jefferson in fact penned the celebrated words, "Government is best which governs least," there is no doubt that he believed and acted on them in virtually all areas except slavery. On all other issues, though, Jefferson remained consistently oriented toward small government, and he may well have flirted with the principles behind the words later penned by Henry David Thoreau: "That government is best which governs not at all."

Just as Jefferson did not unthinkingly favor small and weak government, as has been portrayed, neither did his antithesis, the secretary of the treasury Alexander Hamilton, endorse a Leviathan state, as his opponents have asserted. Hamilton was Washington's brilliant aide-de-camp during the war and the nation's most noted nationalist economic thinker. His origins were humble. Born out of wedlock in the British West Indies, he was saved from a life of obscurity when a wealthy friend recognized his talents and sent him to study in New York City at King's College (now Columbia University).[17] Possessing a talent for writing about economics, law, and radical politics, he rose in patriot ranks to stand as General Washington's chief military, and later, political, adviser. He personally commanded one of the assaults on the redoubts at Yorktown. In the early 1780s, Hamilton became a disciple of Robert Morris's program to grant the Confederation national taxing and banking powers. A moderate Whig, Hamilton was neither a mercantilist nor a follower of the free-market ideas of Adam Smith, but was a fusion of the two—and so suspicious of government that he thought the only way to ensure it did not spin out of control was to tie it to the wealthy.[18]

Like Adams, Hamilton was not a popular man. His illegitimate birth and humble origins always loomed in his personal and professional background, building within him a combative edge to his demeanor early in life. Hamilton's foreign birth prohibited him from becoming president, sentencing him to be forever a power behind the throne. As treasury secretary, Hamilton hit the ground running, proposing a bold economic program based on a permanent national debt, internal and external taxation, a national bank, and federal subsidies to manufacturers. Whether agreeing or not with his solutions, few could doubt that his reports constituted masterful assessments of the nation's economic condition. Naturally, Jefferson and Madison opposed Hamilton's views, setting the stage for the dramatic political debate that came to characterize the Washington administration.[19]

Hamilton's Three Reports

Congress spent the first two years of Washington's administration launching the federal ship and attending to numerous problems inherent in a new government. James Madison's first order of business had been to draft a bill of rights, move it through both houses of Congress, and send it on to the states, which had ratified all of the first ten amendments by 1791. Another weighty matter involved the creation of the federal judiciary. Congress's Judiciary Act of 1789 created thirteen federal district courts (one for each state of the union), three circuit courts of appeal, and a supreme court manned by six justices. John Jay became the first chief justice of the Supreme Court; he and each of his five colleagues rode the circuit several weeks of the year, providing the system with geographic balance. The remarkable feature of the plan was the latitude Congress enjoyed in setting the number of federal justices, courts, and the varied details of the operations of the federal court system.

Those issues, while of great importance, nevertheless took a backseat to the overriding economic issues that had, after all, sparked the creation of the new Republic in the first place. Few people in American history have been so perfectly suited to an administrative post as Alexander Hamilton was to the position of Treasury secretary. His plans took the form of three reports delivered to Congress in 1790–91 that laid the problems before the lawmakers and forced them to give legal weight to his fiscal inclinations.[20]

His first paper, the "Report on Public Credit" (January 1790), tackled the n____
tion's debt problem. At the end of the Revolution, the national government owe____
more than $70 million to bondholders. On top of that, some (not all) states owed____
monies amounting, collectively, to an additional $25 million. A third layer of____
$7 million existed on top of that from various IOUs issued by Washington and
other generals on behalf of the Continental Congress. American speculators held
75 percent of this combined $102 million debt; most of them had paid approxi-
mately fifteen cents on the dollar for national and state bonds at a time when
many doubted their worth. Hamilton's problem was how to pay off the bondholders and simultaneously refinance the nation's many upcoming expenses in order
to establish a sound fiscal policy and a good credit rating. It was an ironic situation in that "the United States, which sprang from the stock of England, whose
credit rating was the model for all the world, had to pull itself out of the pit of
bankruptcy."[21]

Hamilton called his proposal "assumption." First, the national government
would assume all of the remaining state debts—regardless of the inequities between states—and combine them with the national debt and any legally valid
IOUs to individuals. Then the federal government would pay off that debt at face
value (one hundred cents on the dollar), a point that caused an immediate firestorm among those who complained that the debts should be paid to the original
holders of the instruments. Of course, there was no proving who had originally
held anything, and the idea flew in the face of Anglo-American tradition that possession is nine tenths of the law. Originally, Hamilton intended to tax the states to
fund the payments—hence the source of the confusing "three-fifths" compromise for taxation—but this never occurred because of the success of Hamilton's
other proposals. Equally controversial, however, was the plan Hamilton submitted for paying the debts. He wanted the federal government to issue new bonds
to borrow more money at better terms, creating a permanent national debt to
help finance the government's operations. Hamilton's aims were clear. He wanted
to establish confidence in and good credit for the new government among creditors at home and abroad, and thus ally creditors with the new government, ensuring its success.[22] As he noted, "The only plan that can preserve the currency is
one that will make it the *immediate* interest of the moneyed men to cooperate
with the government."[23] "A national debt," he wrote in a sentence that thoroughly
shocked old Whigs, "*if not excessive,* is a national blessing" [emphasis ours].[24] The
secretary had no intention that the nation, having broken the shackles of English
oppression, should succumb to a form of debt peonage, but he fully understood
that monetary growth fueled investment and economic expansion. In that sense,
he departed from the mercantilists and joined arms with Adam Smith.

Contrary to traditional portrayals, Hamilton and Jefferson shared much
ground on these issues. Jefferson, in an oft-cited letter of September 1789, had
stated that "the earth belongs . . . to the living," or, in other words, those alive at
any given time should not be saddled with debts and obligations of earlier generations.[25] Defining a generation as nineteen years, Jefferson sought to restrain the

.n following the destructive French model and creating a debt so
. would collapse. Yet Hamilton's plan called for a Jeffersonian struc-
,n a sinking fund that would require the legislature to always pay off
,efore legally being allowed to issue new bonds. Or, in modern terms, it
American Express form of credit, whereby the balance had to be paid, not
.he interest on the debt, which he also feared. So whereas Jefferson wanted
put a generational time limit on the nation's debts, Hamilton preferred a functional limit, but it was a distinction without a difference.

Both also boiled the debt issue down to the political dangers it presented, but
here they came to radically different conclusions. Where Jefferson hated the notion of tying the wealthy to government because he thought it put the bankers in
power, Hamilton embraced it for the same reason. If the nation owed financiers a
great deal of money, *they* were in the weaker position, not the government.

Hamilton's desire to rally creditors and bankers to support the new federal
government was also apparent in his second paper, a "Report on a National Bank"
(December 1790). This plan voiced Hamilton's desire for a national fiscal agency,
a Bank of the United States modeled after the Bank of England. This Bank of the
United States (BUS) would safeguard all federal tax and land-sales revenues,
transact government financial affairs, meet the government payroll, and issue and
circulate currency, thereby regulating smaller banks. To Hamilton, all these missions were subordinated to the bank's role as a steady source of credit to the national government. It did not disturb Hamilton, though, that with 80 percent of
its stock held by private investors, the BUS would provide its owners with access
to public funds for their private speculative ventures. It is essential to understand
that, contrary to practices today, insider trading and insider investing were among
the primary purposes of starting a bank.[26] Virtually everyone understood that in
order to marshal a community's—or a nation's—finances around important projects, the primary owners of banks had to have legitimate access to those large
pools of capital. Hamilton's bank plan thus aimed to bring sound fiscal practices
and a strong currency to the government through an alliance lucrative to private
bankers and the investor class at large.

At this point, it is worthwhile to reiterate that contrary to the popular image,
Hamilton had no illusions about the dangers inherent in big government. He
rightly understood that over the long term, prices did not lie. Monetary values reflect real value in short order. While the will of the people might swing wildly,
depending on emotions, news coverage, propaganda, or other factors, markets
generally are constrained by reality, and he wanted to let that reality enforce its
discipline on American finances.[27] It worked: when Hamilton's plan took effect
in 1791, U.S. debt per capita, in real dollars, stood at $197, but within twenty
years it had plummeted to $49.[28]

A third report, the "Report on Manufactures" (December 1791), proved significant mainly as a portent of things to come: Congress rejected this ambitious
neomercantilist plan. Hamilton, keenly aware of the significance of the burgeoning Industrial Revolution, sought a departure from the market disciplines he had

invoked in his earlier reports. Without question, Hamilton was one of the few Americans who fully understood the impact of capitalists' rapidly accelerating use of technology, capital, labor, raw materials, transportation, and global markets to create wealth. In this, the stodgy Adams wholeheartedly agreed, noting, "Property must be secured, or liberty cannot exist."[29] Hamilton, however, went beyond merely protecting private property. He called on America to immediately accelerate its own industrial revolution, creating a modern nationally regulated economic system. For all of his foresight, Hamilton's serious flaw was looking backward to mercantilism to accomplish these ends. He advocated protective tariffs and federal bounties (subsidies) to incubate industry. Neither of the British finance ministers, Townshend or Pitt, would have criticized such policies. In a style anticipating Henry Clay, Abraham Lincoln, and Franklin D. Roosevelt, Hamilton wrote, "The public purse must supply the deficiency of private resources."[30]

Anti-Federalists, and even some Federalists, reacted to Hamilton's three reports with utter amazement. In some specifics, the white papers recommended the creation of a system they deemed suspiciously similar to the mercantilism Americans had just overthrown, with the latter report sparking Madison's immediate and crucial defection to the Anti-Federalist cause. Southerners, westerners, agrarians, and small-government men everywhere rallied to challenge the secretary. Madison represented Virginia, which had already paid off its debts. Why, asked congressmen from the solvent states, should they subsidize the lax fiscal policies of the indebted states? Moreover, why should they reward bondholders—stockjobbers, as some farmers called them—who had bought cheap during the nation's crisis and now demanded payment at par? Further, Madison argued, the Constitution in no way authorized funding, assumption, and a permanent national debt.

A compromise temporarily settled this dispute over a permanent national debt. At a dinner party sponsored by Jefferson, and with Madison in attendance, Hamilton surrendered on the location of the national capital—at least this party concluded those behind-the-scenes negotiations, which had been conducted for months. By agreeing to move the capital to Philadelphia and, ultimately, to the Virginia-Maryland border in a separate District of Columbia, Hamilton gained the support of southerners anxious to see the seat of government located in their neck of the woods. Philadelphia relented, in part, because Pennsylvania congressmen thought that once they had the capital—even for a while—it would never move. An attempt to move the location of government, said one representative in an ill-fated prophecy, "will be generally viewed . . . as a mere political maneuver [with no more credibility than] inserting Mississippi, Detroit, or Winniprocket Pond."[31] Significantly, in the winter of 1791, Jefferson publicly joined Madison in opposing the BUS. Planters and farming folk were known for their antibanking prejudices (one southerner wrote that he deemed entering a bank as disgraceful as entering a "house of ill repute"); they decried what they perceived as bankers' feeding at the public trough. Moreover, they argued forcefully that the

Constitution was silent on the issue, precluding a BUS. Hamilton countered that the BUS was "necessary and proper" (Article I, Section 8) to carry out the enumerated powers of taxation, coining of money, and commercial regulation. Hamilton's argument of implied powers—that if the end (taxation, and so forth) is constitutional, then the means of achieving that end is too—would become extremely important in years to come. Jefferson countered that "necessary and proper" included only powers indispensable to carrying out enumerated duties, but on this count he met defeat. Despite southern opposition, both houses of Congress voted to create a BUS and chartered it for twenty years. It would fall to James Madison's (and, later, Andrew Jackson's) administration to renew the ongoing battle over the BUS.

Feuding Patriots

By the end of 1791, America had harvested a bumper crop from the seeds of partisan political dispute. Adding to southern opposition to Hamilton's program, a strong protesting voice arose from frontiersmen in western Pennsylvania, upstate New York, and the new frontier settlements of the Ohio Valley. In these places frontiersmen rallied around the cause of Jefferson, forging a southern/western alliance that would affect national politics for more than a generation.

Westerners were outraged by Hamilton's initial fiscal policies and, later, by his "whiskey tax," a measure aimed to subsidize debt assumption by taxing western corn products at 25 percent.[32] In this case, again, Hamilton stood on weak economic ground. He primarily urged Washington to enforce the tax to demonstrate the federal government's ultimate taxation authority. It constituted a flexing of federal muscle that was unnecessary and immature. By levying these excise taxes on one of the most untaxed and unregulated groups in America—frontier farmers—Hamilton sparked a firestorm of opposition.

Most economic life in the West revolved around corn; corn whiskey even served as a medium of exchange in the cash-short territories. Many farmers lacked cash at all, using whiskey as their currency. Protesting the tax, furious westerners resorted to violence, just like the Shaysites before them. Riots erupted in the Pittsburgh region, Kentucky, the Carolina backcountry, and even Maryland. Led by David Bradford and James Marshall, these self-styled "whiskey rebels" terrorized tax collectors, closed down courts, and threatened to invade Pittsburgh. When President Washington offered amnesty for surrender, the rebels rejected the offer.

The Whiskey Rebellion marked a critical juncture for the new Federalist government. Unless it was crushed, Washington believed, "We can bid adieu to all government in this country except mob and club government." He added, "If the laws are to be trampled upon with impunity, then there is an end put, with one stroke, to republican government."[33] In August, Washington sent Hamilton to lead a 13,000–man army (larger than the Continental Army) to crush the rebels. With this show of force the rebel cause instantly evaporated; Bradford, Marshall, and others bid a hasty retreat by flatboat down the Ohio River. Although courts convicted two whiskey rebels of treason, Washington magnanimously pardoned them both in July of 1795.

Washington and Hamilton took pride in their decisive action; the Federalists had proven the ability of the new government to enforce the law. In the process, however, they handed the Republicans a political victory. Many Revolutionary-era Americans were alarmed at the sight of an American standing army moving against a ragged band of Pennsylvania farmers—fellow Americans, no less! Rightly or wrongly, the Republicans saw an uncanny resemblance between the Whiskey Rebellion and the patriots' stamp and tea tax revolts of the Revolutionary era.[34]

Federalists rightly feared new frontier states would bolster Jefferson's support in Congress, and they opposed the statehood of these new territories. A compromise exchanged statehood for Kentucky with that of Vermont in 1791, but Tennessee proved to be an entirely different matter. In 1796, Federalists vainly threw roadblocks in front of the statehood drive, arguing that Tennessee's census and constitution were problematic, and that statehood was "just one more twig in the electioneering cabal of Mr. Jefferson."[35] Despite this arch-Federalist opposition, Tennessee entered the Union in time to cast its 1796 electoral votes for Jefferson and send a young Jeffersonian, Andrew Jackson, to Congress.

Meanwhile, by the start of Washington's second term in office, the Hamilton-Jefferson feud had spun out of control, well past the point of resolution. Worse, their political differences only exacerbated an obvious personality conflict between these two young lions. Washington's cabinet meetings lost civility as the men settled into a pattern of continued verbal sparring and political oneupsmanship. When not debating in person, they maneuvered in congressional caucuses and cloakrooms or sniped by letter to acquaintances before finally ceasing speaking to each other altogether, resorting to firing anonymous newspaper editorials.

Jefferson initially clung to the hope that the president's evenhandedness would ultimately manifest itself in public policy. Employing his considerable skills of persuasion to lobby the president, Jefferson urged Washington to break from Hamilton or to at least blend some of Madison's and his own ideas into the Federalist policy mix. Continually thwarted on the domestic front, Jefferson might have endured had he not been so often overruled in his own area of expertise, foreign affairs. Over the course of Washington's first term, the secretary of state saw his foreign policy aims slowly erode under Hamilton's assaults, and it was in the area of foreign policy where the disagreements reached their most vindictive stage.

Beyond the Oceans

Although America was an independent nation under the terms of the Treaty of Paris of 1783, that independence was fraught with ironies and contradictions. In the family of nations, America was a kitten among tigers. European powers with strong armies and navies still ruled the oceans and much of North and South America, despite American independence. In addition, fading, but still dangerous, forces such as those of the Ottoman Empire and the Barbary States were constantly a concern on the high seas. But an alliance with France threatened to embroil the young nation in continental warfare almost immediately with the French Revolution of 1789.

What course would American foreign policy follow? Would Americans form alliances with their democratic brethren in France, or honor their English roots? Would they be able to trade with both nations? Was neutrality an option? These were the questions the secretary of state faced, yet his proposed solutions ran counter to those of his archenemy Hamilton and his Federalist allies. Under this cloud the members of the administration attempted to shape a foreign policy. Their first foreign policy initiative was to re-create the military establishment Congress had disbanded following the Revolutionary War.[36] Federalist proponents of the Constitution had called for a viable army and navy to back up national foreign policy decrees; the ratification of the Constitution brought this "power of the sword" once again to American government.

Led by the secretary of war, Henry Knox, Washington's artillery chief during the Revolution, Federalists reconstituted the Continental Army, renaming it the United States Army. Knox recruited 5,000 troops and commissioned an officer corps comprised mainly of Revolutionary War veterans and Federalist stalwarts. Then Congress turned its attention to the navy, which, since the Revolution, had been a small collection of privateers. Congress appropriated monies for construction and manning of six frigates capable of long-range operations.[37] Following Revolutionary precedent, small companies of U.S. Marines accompanied each navy command unit. Congress did not create a separate Department of the Navy until 1798, when Federalists would realize their aim of a 10,000–man combined American military force.

As is often the case, events did not wait on policy makers to fully prepare. The Ohio Valley frontier had erupted into warfare after a flood of immigrants crossed the Appalachians, infringing on Indian lands. Miami, Shawnee, Delaware, and other tribes witnessed hordes of American pioneers streaming into their ancestral domain. Indian warfare escalated into attacks on rivermen; one boatman reported that "the Indians were very troublesome on the river, having fired upon several boats" and killing and wounding the boat crews.[38] The U.S. government had to respond. General Arthur St. Clair, Federalist governor of the Northwest Territory, led an army into the fray, but met initial defeat. Newly recommissioned U.S. Army general Mad Anthony Wayne fared better, marching a large column into Indian territory in 1794 to win an important victory at the Battle of Fallen Timbers. Arrayed against a broad alliance of Indian tribes (Shawnee, Ottawa, Chippewa, Potawatomi), as well as Canadians, British, some French, and even a handful of renegade Americans, Wayne's larger force pushed the 2,000 Indians through the forest and pinned them against a British fort, which refused to open its gates.[39] "Mad" Anthony preferred to let the Indians escape and deal with the chiefs, who, having their influence shattered, signed the Treaty of Greenville (1795). Although these events temporarily marked the defeat of the upper Ohio Valley tribes, violence plagued the lower Ohio and Mississippi valleys for another fifteen years.[40]

This warfare revived concerns that Britons and Spaniards aided and encouraged Indian uprisings. These accusations highlighted another western foreign policy problem—the hostile British and Spanish presence in, respectively, the Old Northwest and Southwest. Spain laid claim south of Natchez and west of the Mississippi by virtue of a French grant and the 1763 Treaty of Paris. Americans desperately wanted to sail goods down the river to New Orleans, but the Spaniards rightly saw this trade as the proverbial foot in the door, and resisted it. Both sides found a temporary solution in Pinckney's Treaty, also called the Treaty of San Lorenzo (1795), which granted American traders a three-year privilege of deposit (the ability to unload, store, and transship produce) in Spanish New Orleans.[41]

English presence in the Ohio Valley presented an even more severe problem. In addition to being a violation of the 1783 Treaty of Paris, British ties to Indian tribes made every act by hostiles on the frontier seem suspiciously connected to British interests. Washington's solution to these challenges, however, requires us to take a detour through events in France.

The French Revolution and Neutrality

The French Revolution of 1789 precipitated a huge crisis in American foreign policy. It was a paradoxical development, for on the surface Americans should have been pleased that their own Revolution had spawned a similar republican movement across the Atlantic, just as European intellectuals pointed with pride to America's war for independence as validation of Enlightenment concepts. Many Americans, most notably Jefferson and his Anti-Federalist supporters, as well as the rabble-rouser Tom Paine, enthusiastically supported France's ouster of the corrupt regime of Louis XVI. French republican leaders echoed Jefferson's words in the Declaration when they called for *liberté, égalité, fraternité* and issued their own Declaration of the Rights of Man and the Citizen. Unfortunately, France's revolutionary dreams went largely unfulfilled, in part because of important differences in the presumption of power and the state in their revolutionary declarations. The tyranny of King Louis was soon replaced by the equally oppressive dictatorship of the mob and Robespierre. Blood ran in the streets of Paris and heads literally rolled, beginning with Louis' own in 1793. A new wave of violence and warfare swept across Europe, pitting France against every monarchy on the continent, exactly as John Adams had predicted in a letter to his wife.[42]

Federalist leaders wisely saw that the fledgling United States could ill afford to become entangled in Europe's power struggle.[43] There were plenty of problems at home, and certainly neither the army nor the navy could stand toe to toe with European forces on neutral ground for any length of time. With Britain and France at war, however, America had to choose. Washington did so when—in opposition to Jefferson's advice and the Constitution's stipulation that the president must seek the advice and consent of the Senate—he unilaterally issued the

Proclamation of Neutrality in April of 1793. The United States, declared the president, was neutral and would not aid or hurt either Britain or France.[44]

What constituted "neutrality" when three quarters of American exports went to Britain, and 90 percent of American imports emanated from Britain or her colonies? The British aggressively thwarted French-bound American commerce, and neither American traders nor the U.S. Navy resisted. Throughout the 1790s and early 1800s, British naval vessels routinely halted, boarded, and inspected American ships, sometimes seizing cargo in direct violation of property rights, free trade, and "freedom of the seas." To add insult to injury, Britain began a policy of impressment, in which American sailors on a boarded vessel could be forced into British service as virtual slaves under the dubious claim that the sailors had deserted the British navy. By her actions, Britain shredded concepts of "right to life and liberty" that had rested at the center of the Declaration. France rightly questioned and furiously denounced the neutrality of a nation that bowed so easily to Great Britain. The French found enthusiastic supporters in Madison and Jefferson, who conspired to undercut the president. At the height of debate over Washington's Proclamation of Neutrality, Jefferson wrote Madison a heated note attacking Hamilton and imploring, "For God's sake, my dear sir, take up your pen, select his most striking heresies, and cut him to pieces in the face of the public."[45] Adams was equally horrified at the changes he noticed in Jefferson. "I am really astonished," he wrote to Abigail, "at the blind spirit of party which has seized on the whole soul of this Jefferson."[46] Worse, Washington had already ceased to listen to the foreign policy advice of his own secretary of state, leaving Jefferson no choice but to resign. On January 31, 1794, he officially left his post, returned home to Monticello, and plotted his political revenge.

Washington, meanwhile, had come under a relentless barrage of vitriol. More than two hundred years later the temptation is to think that the Father of our country was loved by all. Yet then, as now, no one was safe from criticism, least of all the president. The *Aurora*, for example, led the pack of wolves after Washington: "If ever a nation was debauched by a man, the American nation has been debauched by Washington."[47] In a line destined to go down as one of the stupidest statements ever made, the paper warned, "Let his conduct, then, be an example to future ages."[48] (The author did not mean that Washington's conduct would be a good example!) Adams, for one, favored retaliation: the Federalists must let "nothing pass unanswered; reasoning must be answered by reasoning; wit by wit; humor by humor; satire by satire; burlesque by burlesque and even buffoonery by buffoonery."[49]

The opportunity for "buffoonery" reached epic proportions when, in 1793, the new French Revolutionary government sent Edmund Genet to represent it in America. Jefferson, at the time still in his post, and his ally Madison were initially delighted. Edmund Charles Genet, who could speak fluently seven languages, enjoyed a reputation as a true believer in the French radicalism that American radicals saw as a welcome extension of their own Revolutionary experi-

ment. "War with all kings and peace with all peoples," as the French revolutionary saying went, might have originated with Genet. Jefferson and his followers
welcomed Citizen Genet, as he was called, with open arms.

They soon regretted their enthusiasm. The obnoxious little man had scarcely
set his shoes on American soil before he launched into an attack on the Federalists. Ignoring the standard protocol for diplomats serving in foreign lands, he immediately waded into domestic politics. He helped to organize pro-French
Jacobin clubs and "democratick" societies to spur the Jeffersonians' support of
France. He actually tried to engage in military campaigns—organizing armed expeditions against France's Spanish and English enemies in Florida, Louisiana,
and Canada. Perhaps worst of all, Genet, while ambassador, hired privateers to
attack America-bound British shipping in the Atlantic Ocean.

Needless to say, Federalists like Washington, Hamilton, and Adams were
aghast at Citizen Genet's audacity and lack of professionalism. The last straw
came when Genet threatened to go, in essence, over Washington's head to the
public via the press. Genet literally gave Jefferson one of his famous migraine
headaches, so the secretary was unavailable when Washington sought Genet's
head or, at least, his credentials. To make matters worse, broadside publisher
Philip Freneau, of the Anti-Federalist and anti-Washington *National Gazette*, infuriated Washington with an editorial called "The Funeral of George Washington." By then, even Jefferson and Madison were humiliated by their arrogant
French ally, retreating into an embarrassed silence. Jefferson described Genet as
"hotheaded, all imagination, no judgment, passionate, disrespectful, and even indecent towards the President."[50] Genet lost his job, but when his own party in
France was swept out—and more than a few Jacobin heads swept off—Genet
begged Washington for mercy. Given another chance, Genet settled in New York
State, married into the respected Schuyler family, and spent the rest of his days
basking in the receding light of perhaps the most infamous foreign diplomat of
the early national era.[51] Genet's end, however, did not solve Washington's ongoing
foreign policy tensions with France and England. Rather, the path that began in
Paris now turned toward London as a new traveler, John Jay, came to the fore.

Jay's Treaty

Unable to stabilize volatile French diplomacy, Washington heightened tension by
sending New Yorker and Chief Justice of the Supreme Court John Jay to negotiate a long overdue treaty with the British. American conflicts with Britain were
numerous: finalization of the disputed Maine-Canadian boundary; British evacuation of the Northwest posts (which they occupied in direct violation of the 1783
Treaty of Paris); overdue compensation to American slave owners (those whose
slaves Britain had liberated during the war); and, most important, British acknowledgment of freedom of the seas—the right of American ships to trade with
the French West Indies and continental Europe without fear of seizure and
impressment.

Jay received sharp criticism for his handling of the negotiations. The stalwart Federalist was an Anglophile inclined to let the British have their way. In Jay's defense, however, he was in no position to talk tough to Great Britain in 1794. America completely lacked the military and economic clout necessary to challenge Britain so soon after the improbable military victory in the Revolution. More important, the United States needed what Britain could offer—trade—and lots of it.

Nevertheless, Jay's negotiations were marked by a tone of appeasement that enraged pro-French Jeffersonians. His treaty, signed in November of 1794, yielded to the British position by dropping compensation for American slavers, and agreed to the British definition of neutrality at sea, namely the shipment of naval stores and provisions to enemy ports. Maine's boundary dispute was turned over to a commission, and the U.S. government agreed to absorb all losses arising from debts to British merchants. In return for these concessions, Britain agreed to evacuate the Northwest posts by 1796, in essence opening the fur trade in the region. As for the French West Indies, the British begrudgingly agreed to allow small American ships (seventy tons or less) to do business with the French, whereas both England and the United States granted most-favored-nation trading status to each other, providing both nations with the most lucrative trading partner possible.[52]

Although John Jay believed he had gained the best deal possible, his Jeffersonian opponents cried treason. Southerners hated his concessions on slavery, whereas some northerners disliked the trade clauses. One editor wrote, "I believe that the treaty formed by Jay and the British king is the offspring of a vile aristocratic few . . . who are enemies to the equality of men, friends to no government but that whose funds they can convert to their private employment."[53] Jay was not unaware of such vitriol, observing in 1794 that he could travel from New York to Boston by the light of his own burning effigies (a line repeated by several politicians at later dates).[54] New Yorkers threatened impeachment, and Jay's colleague Alexander Hamilton was stoned by angry mobs. "To what state of degradation are we reduced," a Jeffersonian newspaperman exclaimed, "that we *court* a nation more perfidious than Savages—more sanguinary than Tigers—barbarous as Cannibals—and prostituted even to a proverb!"[55]

Over Jeffersonian opposition, the Senate ratified Jay's Treaty in June of 1795. Aware it antagonized some of his former friends and allies, Washington let the bill sit on his desk before finally signing it in August, convinced this was the proper course for an honorable man to follow. Jay's success allowed Washington to deploy Pinckney to Spain to secure the Mississippi navigation rights. Taken together, Jay's and Pinckney's treaties opened the West for expansion. Lost in the international diplomacy was a remarkable reality: what some saw as a sign of weakness in the political system in fact emerged as its strength, proving Madison right. Foreign policy honed each side's positions, and the partisanship resulted in clearly defined opposing views.

Republicans Versus Federalists

These fierce disputes created a political enmity Washington and others sought to avoid—two vibrant, disputing political parties instead of consensus.[56] Although Republicans and Federalists of the 1790s may appear old-fashioned in comparison to modern politicians, they performed the same vital functions that characterize members of all modern political parties. They nominated candidates, conducted election campaigns, wrote platforms, pamphlets, and newspaper editorials, organized partisan activity within the executive and legislative branches of government, dispensed patronage, and even conducted social events like parties, barbecues, fish fries, and so on.

Unfortunately, some have overgeneralized about the parties, characterizing them as rich versus poor men's parties, big government versus small government parties, or even proslavery and antislavery parties. The truth is much more complex. The Federalists and the Republicans were closely related to their 1787–89 Federalist and Anti-Federalist predecessors. For the most part, Republicans were more rural and agricultural than their Federalist opponents. Whereas an Alexander Hamilton would always be suspicious of the masses and their passions, to the Republicans, "Honest majorities, unmolested by priests, quacks, and selfish deceivers, necessarily would make good decisions."[57] This did not mean that all Republicans were poor yeomen farmers, because much of their leadership (for example, Jefferson, Madison, and Monroe) consisted of affluent southern planters; at the same time affluent merchants and entrepreneurs led a Federalist following of poorer, aspiring middle-class tradesmen. Because the northeastern part of the United States was more populous and enjoyed a more diverse economy than the agricultural South and West, this rural/urban dichotomy tended to manifest itself into a southern/western versus northeastern party alignment. Characterizing the first party system as one of agrarian versus cosmopolitan interests would not be wholly inaccurate.

Ideologically, Republicans clung to the Anti-Federalists' radical Whig embrace of small, democratic, decentralized government. They accepted the Constitution, but they read and interpreted it closely (strict constructionism), with special attention to the first ten amendments. In this spirit they retained their suspicion of direct taxation and standing armies; in foreign policy they were naturally drawn to the radical French Revolutionaries. Federalists, on the other hand, continued their drift toward a policy of expansive, vigorous national government—certainly not a monarchy or coercive state, but a government that nevertheless could tax, fight, regulate commerce, and provide Hamilton's revered "general welfare" for all Americans. Federalists wanted a viable army and a foreign policy that courted New England's foremost trading partner, Great Britain.

Members of both parties strongly believed in republican government and the division of power; both aimed to use the Constitution to govern fairly and avoid a return to authoritarianism; and both ultimately rejected violence as a legitimate means of achieving their political goals. While both groups feared tyranny, only the Federalists thought it likely to come from the masses as easily as from a monarch, with Adams arguing that "unbridled majorities are as tyrannical and cruel as unlimited despots."[58]

One supremely important issue was missing from the list: slavery. It would be hard to claim that the Federalists were antislave, especially with slaveholders such as Washington at the helm. On the other hand, it would seem to be equally difficult to paint the small-government Republicans as proslave. Yet that is exactly the direction in which each party, respectively, was headed. Because of their view of general welfare and equality for all, but even more so because of their northern origins, the Federalists laid the framework for ultimately insisting that all men are created equal, and that included *anyone* defined as a man. Under other circumstances, few Republicans would have denied this, or even attempted to defend the proslavery position. Their defense of states' rights, however, pushed them inevitably into the proslavery corner.

How to Recognize a 1790s Republican or Federalist*

	REPUBLICANS	FEDERALISTS
Leaders:	Jefferson, Madison, Monroe, Gallatin, Clinton, Burr	Washington, Adams, Hamilton, Morris, Pickering, King, Knox
Origins:	Anti-Federalist faction of Revolutionary Whigs	Federalist faction of Revolutionary Whigs
Regional Demographic Base:	South, West, and Middle States	New England and Middle States
Local Demographic Base:	Rural (farms, plantations, and villages)	Urban (cities, villages, and river valleys)
Economic Base:	Farmers, planters, artisans, and workingmen	Merchants, financiers, tradesmen, and some exporting farmers
Class:	Lower and middling classes led by planter elite	Upper and middling classes
Ideology:	Radical Whig	Moderate Whig
	Localists	More centralist
	Agrarians	Commercial
	Promilitia	Professional military
	Less taxation, balanced budget	Taxation and deficit
	Egalitarian	More elitist enlightened paternalists

	Strict construction (of Constitution)	Broad constructionist
	Pro-French	Pro-British
	Expansionists	Reluctant expansionists
Future incarnations:	Whig Party and Modern Republican Party (GOP)	Democratic Party

---

*These are generalizations only; there are exceptions, which nonetheless prove the rules.

Sometime in the early 1790s, Madison employed his political savvy in offi-cially creating the Jeffersonian Republican Party. He began his organization in Congress, gathering and marshaling representatives in opposition to Hamilton's reports and Jay's Treaty. To counter the Hamiltonian bias of John Fenno's influen-tial *Gazette of the United States*, Madison, in 1791, encouraged Freneau to pub-lish a rival Republican newspaper, the *National Gazette*. Madison himself wrote anonymous *National Gazette* editorials lambasting Hamilton's three reports and Washington's foreign policy. He simultaneously cultivated national support, en-couraged grassroots Republican political clubs, and awaited an opportunity to thwart the Federalists' electoral dominance. When Jefferson resigned as secretary of state in protest in 1793, the stage was set for the first national electoral show-down between Republicans and Federalists.

It is true these were not parties in the modern sense of the word.[59] They lacked ward/precinct/district organizations; since voting was still the privilege of a few, they did not rely on "getting out the vote." The few existing party papers were not comparable in influence to those of the Jacksonian age twenty years later. Most important, these parties still relied on ideology—the person's philosophy or worldview—to produce votes; whereas the Second American Party System, founded by Martin Van Buren and William Crawford in the 1820s, was built on a much more crass principle, patronage. Still, these organs did galvanize those holding the franchise into one of two major groups, and to that extent they gener-ated excitement during elections.

Democracy's First Test

Whereas Hamilton crafted the major Federalist victories of the 1790s, Vice Presi-dent John Adams dutifully defended them. After Washington, unwilling to serve a third term, finally announced his retirement in 1796, Adams became his party's de facto standard-bearer against Jefferson in the nation's first contested presiden-tial election. At an early point, then, the nation came to this key crossroads: could the people transfer power, without bloodshed, from one group to another group holding views diametrically opposed to the first group?

Federalists enjoyed a distinct advantage, thanks to Washington's popularity and the lateness of his retirement announcement (the Republicans did not dare announce opposition until it was certain the venerated Washington would not run). Yet Jefferson's popularity equaled that of the tempestuous Adams, and the two joined in a lively race, debating the same issues that raged in Congress—Jay's Treaty, the BUS, national debt, and taxation, especially the whiskey tax.

Adams's worst enemy turned out to be a former ally, Hamilton, whom the vice president referred to as "a Creole bastard," and whom Abigail Adams termed Cassius, out to assassinate her Caesar.[60] Hamilton distrusted Adams, whom he considered too moderate, and schemed to use the electoral college to elect Federalist vice presidential candidate Thomas Pinckney to the presidency. Similar machinations would reemerge in 1800, when Hamilton and Aaron Burr both tried to manipulate the electoral college for their Machiavellian ends. Under the system in place at the time, the electors voted separately for president and vice president, leaving open the possibility that there could be a president of one party and a vice president of another. (Bundling the two together did not occur until later.) The Founders had anticipated that each state would vote for its own favorite son with one vote, and for the next best candidate with the other elector. Adams won with 71 electoral votes to Jefferson's 68; Pinckney gathered 59, and Aaron Burr, Jefferson's vice presidential running mate, finished last with 30. Yet it was a divided and bitter victory. Georgia's ballot had irregularities that put Adams, in his capacity as presider over the Senate, which counted the votes, in a pickle. If he acknowledged the irregularities, the election could be thrown open because no candidate would have a majority. Adams took the unusual step of sitting down when Georgia's ballot was handed to him, thereby giving the Jeffersonians an opportunity to protest the ballot. Jefferson, aware of the incongruities, instructed his followers to say nothing. After a moment, Adams affirmed the Georgia ballot and thereby assumed the presidency. This Constitutional confusion (which would soon be corrected by the Twelfth Amendment) made Adams's rival Jefferson his reluctant vice president. Adams seemed not to mind this arrangement, thinking that at least "there, if he could do no good, he could do no harm."[61] But the arrangement was badly flawed, ensuring constant sniping at the administration from within and a reluctance to pass legislation because of the anticipation that a new election would bring Jefferson into power. Indeed, Jefferson and Madison immediately began to look to the election of 1800.

Two months earlier, President Washington had delivered his famed Farewell Address. Physically and mentally wearied by decades of service, and literally sickened by the political bickering that characterized his last term in office, Washington decided to step down. He was also motivated by a desire to set a precedent of serving only two terms, a move that evinced the strong fear of authoritarianism shared by all Whig Revolutionaries, Federalist and Republican alike. The Constitution placed no limit on the number of terms a chief executive could serve, but Washington set such a limit on himself, and every president adhered to the 1796 precedent until 1940. Franklin Delano Roosevelt's reversal (via third and fourth terms), even if coming as it did during national crises, so concerned the nation that the Twenty-second Amendment (1951) was added to the Constitution, making Washington's practice a fundamental law.

Appropriately, Washington's farewell speech was written to a great extent by Hamilton, although the president read and edited several drafts. The address called for nationalism, neutrality, and nonpartisanship; Republicans no doubt pondered over the sincerity of Washington's and Hamilton's last two points. Certainly, nationalism was a Federalist hallmark, and Washington reiterated his deep belief in the need for union versus the potential dangers of regionalism, states' rights, and "geographical distinction." In foreign policy, the chief executive reemphasized the goals of his Proclamation of Neutrality—to offer friendship and commerce with all nations, but to "steer clear" of "political connection . . . and permanent alliances with any portion of the foreign world."

Much has been made of Washington's warning not to become involved in European affairs—this, after having just cemented new international trade agreements with Spain and Great Britain! Washington knew better than to think the United States could isolate itself permanently. He stated, "Twenty years peace with such an increase of population and resources as we have a right to expect; added to our remote situation from the jarring powers, will in all probability enable us in a *just cause to bid defiance to any power on earth*" [emphasis ours].[62] His concern that the young nation would be drawn into strictly Continental squabbles, especially those between Britain and France, reflected not an unwillingness to engage in the international use of power, but an admission of the weakness of American might. In North America, for example, Washington himself had virtually instigated the French and Indian War, so he certainly was under no illusions about the necessity for military force, nor did he discount the ability of the Europeans to affect America with their policies. Rather, the intent was to have the United States lay low and *where prudent* refrain from foreign interventions. Note that Washington gave the United States twenty years to gain international maturity, a time frame ending with the the War of 1812.[63] Further, America's insulation by the oceans kept these goals at the core of American foreign policy for the next century, until transportation and communication finally rendered them obsolete. But would Washington, a man willing to fight for liberty, have stood by and allowed an Adolf Hitler to invade and destroy England, or Japanese aggressors to rape Nanking? His phrase, "in a just cause," suggests not.

Finally, and incongruously, Washington cautioned against political partisanship. This phrase, penned by Hamilton, at best was a call to better behavior on all sides and at worst was simply a throwaway phrase for public consumption. Washington apparently did not see Hamilton's scheming and political maneuvering as partisan endeavor, and therefore saw no irony in the pronouncement.

Concluding with an appeal to the sacred, as he frequently did, Washington stated that "Religion and Morality are indispensable supports."[64] It would be hopeless, he implored, to think that men could have "security for property, for reputation, for life if the sense of *religious obligation* desert the oaths" of officeholders [emphasis ours]. In such arenas as the Supreme Court, where oaths provided enforcement of those protections, Washington somberly noted, mere morality alone could not survive without "religious principle." His speech was the quintessential embodiment of a phrase often ridiculed more than two hundred years later, "Character counts." Washington's warning to the nation, though, was that effective government required more than a chief executive of high moral fiber—the entire nation had to build the country on the backs of its citizens' behavior. Having delivered this important speech, the general quietly finished out his term and returned to his beloved Virginia, attending one last emotional ceremony inaugurating his vice president, John Adams, after he had won the election of 1796.

The Father of Our Country would not live to see the new century, but his legacy to American posterity was never exceeded, and rarely matched. Historian John Carroll listed no fewer than ten achievements of Washington's two administrations, including developing a policy for the disposition of public lands, establishing credit at home and abroad, removing the British troops from the Northwest, and several others.[65] Another historian concluded, "By agreeing to serve not one, but two terms of office, Washington gave the new nation what above all else it needed: time."[66] It might also be said that Washington loaned the young republic some of his own character, modeling virtuous behavior of a president for all who followed.

Quasi War

Despite the succession of a member of Washington's own party and administration, the election of 1796 elevated to power a man much different in temperament and personality than the great general he replaced. John Adams was both ably suited for, and considerably handicapped in, the fulfillment of his presidential duties. The sixty-two-year-old president-elect still possessed a keen intellect, pious devotion, and selfless patriotism, but age had made him more irascible than ever. His enemies pounced on his weaknesses. The *Aurora* referred to him as "old, Guerelous [sic], bald, blind, and crippled," to which Abigail quipped that only she was capable of making such an assessment about her husband![67] Adams, however, excelled in foreign policy matters, which was fortunate at a time when the nation had been thrust into the imbroglio of Anglo-French rivalry. With no help from Republican opponents or Federalist extremists within his own party, Adams rose above factionalism and averted war. In the process he paid a huge political price for his professionalism.

For at least a decade the British had bullied Americans on the high seas and at the treaty table; in 1797 the French decided it was their turn. Angered by Federalist Anglophilia and the subservience evidenced in Jay's Treaty, France, too, began to seize and confiscate American shipping to the tune of three hundred vessels. French aggression shocked and silenced Republicans. Among the Federalists, the response was surprisingly divided. Predictably, Hamiltonians and other arch-Federalists, who had bent over backward to avoid war with Britain, now pounded the drums of war against France. A popular toast of the day to Adams was, "May he, like Samson, slay thousands of Frenchmen with the jawbone of a Jefferson."[68] Adams himself and the moderates, however, followed the president's lead and tried to negotiate a peace. They were stymied initially by unscrupulous Frenchmen.

To negotiate with the French foreign minister Charles Talleyrand—a master of personal survival skills who had avoided the guillotine under the Jacobins, later survived the irrationalities of *l'empereur* Napoléon, and later still had returned to represent the restored Bourbon monarchy—Adams sent Charles Cotesworth Pinckney (Thomas's brother), John Marshall, and Elbridge Gerry to Paris. Upon arrival, however, the Americans were not officially allowed to present their credentials to the foreign minister—an immense snub. At an unofficial meeting with three French agents—referred to anonymously by the American press as Agents X, Y, and Z—the Americans learned that the French agents expected a bribe before they would be granted an audience with French officials. Pinckney, Marshall, and Gerry refused such a profane act, and immediately returned home. Newspapers later reported that Pinckney had proclaimed to Agents X, Y, and Z that Americans would gladly spend "millions for defense, but not one cent for tribute." It's more probable he uttered the less quotable, "It is no, not a sixpence," but regardless, the French got the message. The negotiations abruptly ended, and the arch-Federalists had their issue.[69]

Before long, the infamous X, Y, Z Affair produced a war fever and temporarily solidified the Federalists' power base. After recovering somewhat from their initial shock, Republicans asked why Americans should declare war on France for aggression identical to that which Great Britain had perpetrated with impunity for nearly a decade. Adams stood between the two groups of extremists, urging more negotiations while simultaneously mustering thousands of soldiers and sailors in case shooting started. He had benefited from the authorization by Congress, two years earlier, of six frigates, three of which were rated at forty-four guns, although only the *United States* and the *Constellation* actually carried that number.[70] These vessels, which Adams referred to as "floating batteries and wooden walls," entered service just as tensions on the oceans peaked. In February 1799, open fighting between American and French ships erupted on the high seas, precipitating an undeclared war, dubbed by historians thereafter as the Quasi War.

Adams already had his hands full with peacemaking initiatives without the interference of George Logan, a Pennsylvania Quaker who traveled to Paris on his own funds to secure the release of some American seamen. Logan may have been well intentioned, but by inserting himself into international negotiations, he endangered all Americans, not the least of which were some of those he sought to help.[71] His actions spawned the Logan Act of 1799, which remains in effect to the present, forbidding private citizens from negotiating with foreign governments in the name of the United States.

Meanwhile, buoyed by a 1798 electoral sweep, the so-called arch-Federalists in Congress continued to call for war against France. Pointing to alleged treason at home, they passed a set of extreme laws—the Alien and Sedition Acts—that would prove their political undoing. A Naturalization Act, aimed at French and Irish immigrants, increased from four to fourteen the number of years required for American citizenship. The fact that these immigrants were nearly all Catholics and Republicans no doubt weighed heavily in deciding their fate. A new Alien Act gave the president the power to deport some of these "dangerous Aliens," while the Sedition Act allowed the Federalists to escalate their offensive against American Francophiles by abridging First Amendment speech rights. The Sedition Acts forbade conduct or language leading to rebellion, and although the wording remained rather vague, Federalist judges evidently understood it. Under the act, they arrested, tried, convicted, and jailed or fined twenty-five people, mostly Republican newspaper editors, including Matthew Lyon, a jailed Republican congressman who won his reelection while still behind bars.

Application of modern-day values, not to mention civil liberties laws, would make the Alien and Sedition Acts seem outrageous infringements on personal liberties. In context, the sedition clauses originated in the libel and slander laws of the day. Personal honor was a value most Americans held quite dear, and malicious slurs often resulted in duels. The president of the United States, subjected to vile criticism, had no means of redress to defamatory comments. It would be almost a half century before courts routinely held that a much higher bar governed the protection of public figures' reputations or character from attacks that, to an ordinary citizen, might be considered libelous or slanderous.

Newspapers rushed to Adams's defense, with the *Guardian* of New Brunswick declaring "Sedition by all the laws of God and man, is, and ever has been criminal." Common law tradition in England long had a history of restricting criticism of the government, but with the French Revolution threatening to spread the Reign of Terror across all of Europe, public criticism took on the aura of fomenting rebellion—or, at least, that was what most of the Federalists thought, provoking their ham-handed response. Adams, above all, should have known better.

Suffering from one of his few moral lapses, Adams later denied responsibility for these arguably unconstitutional laws, yet in 1798 he neither vetoed nor protested them. Republicans countered with threats to disobey federal laws, known as the Virginia and Kentucky Resolutions. Authored in 1798 and 1799 by Madison and Jefferson, respectively, the resolutions revived the Anti-Federalist spirit with a call for state sovereignty, and comprised a philosophical bridge between the Articles of Confederation (and Tenth Amendment) and John C. Calhoun's 1832 Doctrine of Nullification. Madison and Jefferson argued from a "compact" theory of government. States, they claimed, remained sovereign to the national government by virtue of the fact that it was the states, not the people, who formed the Union. Under this interpretation the states had the duty to "judge the constitutionality of federal acts and protect their citizens from unconstitutional and coercive federal laws."[72] Such a Lockean argument once thrilled true Revolutionaries, but now the Declaration (through inference) and the Constitution (through express statement) repudiated these doctrines. If one follows the Jeffersonians' logic of deriving all government from "first things," however, one must go not to the Constitution, per se, but to its roots, the Declaration, wherein it was the people of the colonies who declared independence; and the preamble to the Constitution—which, admittedly is not law itself but the intention for establishing the law—still begins, "We the People of the United States of America . . ." In either case, the states never were the activating or motivating body, rather simply the administering body. No other state supported Madison or Jefferson's resolutions, which, if they had stood, would have led to an endless string of secessions—first, states from the Union, then, counties from states, then townsips from cities.

Adams's Mettle and the Election of 1800

In one of his greatest triumphs, John Adams finally rose above this partisan rancor. Over the violent objections of Hamilton and his supporters, he dispatched William Vans Murray to negotiate with Talleyrand. The ensuing French capitulation brought an agreement to leave American shipping alone. With long-term consequences unsure, the short-term results left the Quasi War in abeyance and peace with France ensued. Adams showed his mettle and resolved the crisis. As his reward, one month later, he was voted out of office.

Much of the anger stemmed from higher tax burdens, some of which the Federalists had enacted for the large frigates. A new tax, though, the Direct Tax of 1798, penalized property ownership, triggering yet another tax revolt, Fries's Rebellion, wherein soldiers sent into Philadelphia to enforce the tax encountered not bullets but irate housewives who doused the troops with pails of hot water. Fries was arrested, convicted of treason, and sentenced to be executed, but he found the Federalists to be far more merciful than their portrayal in the Jeffersonian papers. Adams pardoned Fries, and although the tax protest shriveled, so did Federalist support in Pennsylvania.[73] It bears noting, however, that in the twenty-nine years since the conclusion of the Revolutionary War, Americans had already risen in revolt *three* times, and on each occasion over taxation.

By 1800, the president had spent much of his time in the new "city" of Washington. Hardly a city at all, the District of Columbia was but a clump of dirty buildings, arranged around "unpaved, muddy cesspools in winter, waiting for summer to transform them into mosquito-infested swamps."[74] Adams disliked Washington—he had not liked Philadelphia much better—and managed to get back to Quincy, Massachusetts, to his beloved Abigail whenever possible. Never possessed of a sunny disposition, Adams drifted into deep pessimism about the new nation. Although he ran against Jefferson again in 1800, this time the Virginian (a "shadow man," Adams called him, for his ability to strike without leaving his fingerprints on any weapon) bested him. Anger and bitterness characterized the two men's relationship by that point. Of Jefferson, Adams wrote, "He has talents I know, and integrity, I believe; but his mind is now poisoned with passion, prejudice, and faction."[75] Political warfare had soured Adams even more since he had become president. Hamilton, whom Adams called the "bastard brat of a Scotch pedlar," vexed him from behind and Jefferson, from in front. Besieged from both ends of the political spectrum—the Jeffersonian Republicans blamed him for the Alien and Sedition Acts, while Hamilton's arch-Federalists withdrew their support because of his peace with France—Adams was left with few friends. When the electoral college met, Jefferson and his vice presidential candidate Aaron Burr tied with 73 electoral votes each; Adams trailed in third place with 65.

Then, as in 1796, wily politicians tried to alter the choice of the people and the rule of law. Jefferson and Burr had tied in the electoral college because the Constitution did not anticipate parties or tickets and gave each elector two votes, one each for president and vice president. A tie threw the election to the lame-duck Federalist House of Representatives, which now had the Constitutional prerogative to choose between the two Republicans. To make matters worse, the Federalists expected from Burr, but never received, a polite statement declining the presidency if it were to be offered to him. Burr had other ideas, hoping some deadlock would result in his election, in spite of failing to win the electoral college and all of his prior agreements with the Republican leadership.

House Federalists, with Hamilton as their de facto leader, licked their chops at the prospect of denying Jefferson the presidency. Yet the unscrupulous and unpredictable Burr was just not tolerable. Hamilton was forced to see the truth: his archenemy Jefferson was the lesser of two evils. By siding with the Virginian, Hamilton furthered American democracy while simultaneously (and literally) signing his own death warrant: Colonel Burr would soon take vengeance against Hamilton over letters the secretary had written supposedly impugning Burr's honor.

Meanwhile, the lame-duck president frantically spent his last hours ensuring that the Jeffersonians did not destroy what he and Washington had spent twelve years constructing. The Republicans had decisively won both the legislative and executive branches of government in November, leaving Adams only one hope for slowing down their agenda: judicial appointments. His unreasonable fear and hatred of the Jeffersonians led him to take a step that, although constitutional, nevertheless directly defied the will of the voters. In February 1801, Adams sent a new Judiciary Act to the lame-duck Congress, and it passed, creating approximately five dozen new federal judgeships at all levels, from federal circuit and district courts to justices of the peace. Adams then proceeded to commission ardent Federalists to each of these lifetime posts—a process so time consuming that the president was busy signing commissions into the midnight hours of his last day in office. These "midnight judges," as the Republicans soon dubbed them, were not Adams's only judiciary legacy to Jefferson. In the final weeks of his tenure, Adams also nominated, and the lame-duck Senate approved, John Marshall as chief justice of the United States Supreme Court.[76]

Marshall's appointment was, Adams later wrote, "a gift to the people of the United States" that was "the proudest of my life."[77] Throughout a brilliant career that spanned the entirety of the American Revolutionary era, Adams left America many great gifts. In Marshall, Adams bequeathed to the United States a chief justice fully committed to capitalism, and willing to amend pristine property rights to the cause of rapid development. Unlike Jefferson and fellow Virginian John Taylor, who weighed in as one of the leading economic thinkers of the day, Marshall perceived that true wealth came from ideas put into action, not vaults of gold or acres of land.[78] Whereas the Jeffersonians, Taylor, and other later thinkers such as William Gouge would pin the economic hopes of the country on agriculture and metallic money, Marshall understood that the world had moved past that. Without realizing it, Adams's last-minute appointment of Marshall ensured the defeat of the Jeffersonian ideal over the long run, but on the morning of Jefferson's inauguration, America's first involuntary one-term president (his son John Quincy would be the second) scarcely felt victorious. Adams departed Washington, D.C., at sunrise, several hours before his rival's inauguration. Adams was criticized for lack of generosity toward Jefferson, but his abrupt departure, faithful to the Constitution, echoed like a thunderclap throughout the world. Here was the clear heir to Washington, narrowly beaten in a legitimate election, not only turning the levers of power over to a hated foe, but entrusting the entire machinery of government to an enemy faction—all without so much as a single bayonet raised or a lawsuit threatened. That event could be described as the most important election in the history of the world. With one colossal exception in 1860, the fact is that with this selfless act of obedience to the law, John Adams ensured that the principle of a peaceful and legal transfer of power in the United States would never even be questioned, let alone seriously challenged.

Growing America

Adams handed over to Jefferson a thriving, energetic Republic that was changing before his very eyes. A large majority of Americans remained farmers, yet increasingly cities expanded and gained more influence over the national culture at a rate that terrified Jefferson. Baltimore, Savannah, Boston, Philadelphia, and Charleston all remained central locations for trade, shipping, and intellectual life, but new population centers such as Cincinnati, Mobile, Richmond, Detroit, Fort Wayne, Chicago, Louisville, and Nashville surfaced as regional hubs. New York gradually emerged as a more dominant city than even Boston or Philadelphia. A manumission society there worked to end slavery, and had won passage of the Gradual Manumission Act of 1799. Above all, New York symbolized the transformation in city government that occurred in most urban areas in the early 1800s. Government, instead of an institution that relied on property holdings of a few as its source of power, evolved into a "public body financed largely by taxation and devoting its energies to distinctly public concerns."[79]

A city like New York, despite its advances and refinements, still suffered from problems that would jolt modern Americans. An oppressive stench coming from the thousands of horses, cattle, dogs, cats, and other animals that walked the streets pervaded the atmosphere. (By 1850, one estimate put the number of horses alone in New York City at one hundred thousand, defecating at a rate of eighteen pounds a day and urinating some twenty gallons per day, each!) If living creatures did not suffice to stink up the city, the dead ones did: city officials had to cope with hundreds of carcasses per week, hiring out the collection of these dead animals to entrepreneurs.

Combined with the garbage that littered the streets, the animal excrement and road kill made for a powerful odor. And human bodies mysteriously turned up too. By midcentury, the New York City coroner's office, always underfunded, was paying a bounty to anyone collecting bodies from the Hudson River. Hand-to-hand combat broke out on more than one occasion between the aquatic pseudoambulance drivers who both claimed the same floating cadaver and, of course, its reward.

Most important, though, the urban dwellers already had started to accept that the city owed them certain services, and had gradually developed an un-healthy dependence on city hall for a variety of services and favors. Such dependence spawned a small devil of corruption that the political spoils system would later loose fully grown. City officials, like state officials, also started to wield their authority to grant charters for political and personal ends. Hospitals, schools, road companies, and banks all had to "prove" their value to the community before the local authorities would grant them a charter. No small amount of graft crept into the system, quietly undermining Smithian concepts that the community was served when *individuals* pursued profit.

One fact is certain: in 1800, Americans were prolific. Population increases continued at a rate of 25 percent per decade and the constitutionally mandated 1800 census counted 5,308,473 Americans, double the 1775 number.[80] Foreign immigrants accounted for some of that population increase, but an incredibly high birthrate, a result of economic abundance and a relatively healthier lifestyle, explained most of the growth. Ethnically, Americans were largely of Anglo, Celtic (Scots and Scots-Irish), and African descent, with a healthy smattering of French, Swedes, Dutch, and Germans thrown in. And of these 5.33 million Americans, 24 of 25 lived on farms or in country villages.

At least 50 percent of all Americans were female, and although their legal status was unenviable, it had improved considerably from that of European women. Most accepted the idea that a woman's sphere of endeavor was dedi-cated to the house, church, and the rearing of children, a belief prevailing among American men and women alike. Women possessed no constitutional political role. Economically, widows and single women (*feme sole*) could legally hold prop-erty, but they surrendered those rights with marriage (*feme covert*). Trust funds and prenuptial agreements (an American invention) helped some middle-class families circumvent these restrictions. A few women conducted business via power of attorney and other American contractual innovations, and a handful en-gaged in cottage industry. None of the professions—law, medicine (midwifery excepted), ministry, or of course the army—were open to females, although, in the case of medicine, this had less to do with sexism than it did the physical necessity of controlling large male patients while operating without anesthetic. Women could not attend public schools (some attended private schools or were tutored at home), and no colleges accepted women students.

Divorce was extremely difficult to obtain. Courts limited the grounds for separation, and in some states only a decree from the state legislature could effect a marital split. Despite the presentist critique by some modern feminists, the laws in the early Republic were designed as much to protect women from the unreliability and volatility of their husbands as to keep them under male control. Legislatures, for example, tailored divorce laws to ensure that husbands honored their economic duties to wives, even after childbearing age.

In stark contrast to women stood the status of African Americans. Their lot was most unenviable. Nearly one million African Americans lived in the young United States (17 percent), a number proportionately larger than today. Evolving slowly from colonial days, black slavery was by 1800 fully entrenched. Opponents of slavery saw the institution thrive after the 1794 invention of the cotton gin and the solidification of state black codes defining slaves as chattels personal—moveable personal property.

No law, or set of laws, however, embedded slavery in the South as deeply as did a single invention. Eli Whitney, a Yankee teacher who had gone south as a tutor, had conceived his cotton gin while watching a cat swipe at a rooster and gather a paw full of feathers. He cobbled together a machine with two rollers, one of fine teeth that sifted the cotton seeds out, another with brushes, that swept off the residual cotton fibers. Prior to Whitney's invention, it took a slave an hour to process a single pound of cotton by hand; afterward, a slave could process six to ten times as much.[81] In the decade of the 1790s, cotton production increased from 3,000 bales a year to 73,000; 1810 saw the production soar to 178,000 bales, all of which made slaves more indispensable than ever.[82]

Somehow, most African American men and women survived the ordeal of slavery. The reason for their heroic survival lies in their communities and family lives, and in their religion. The slaves built true sub-rosa societies with marriage, children, surrogate family members, and a viable folk culture—music, art, medicine, and religion. All of this they kept below the radar screen of white masters who, if they had known of these activities, would have suppressed them. A few slaves escaped to freedom, and some engaged in sabotage and even insurrections like Gabriel's Uprising in 1800 Virginia. But for the most part, black survival came through small, day-to-day acts of courage and determination, fueled by an enthusiastic black Christian church and Old Testamaent tales of the Hebrews' escape from Egyptian slavery.

Between the huge social gulf of master and slave stood a vast populace of "crackers," the plain white folk of the southern and western frontier.[83] Usually associated with humble Celtic-American farmers, cracker culture affected (and continues to affect) all aspects of American life. Like many derogatory terms, cracker was ultimately embraced by those at whom it was aimed. Celtic-American frontiersmen crossed the Appalachian Mountains, and their coarse, unique folk culture arose in the Ohio and Mississippi valleys. As they carved out farms from the forest, crackers planted a few acres of corn and small vegetable gardens. Cattle, sheep, and the ubiquitous hogs ("wind splitters" the crackers called them) were left to their own devices in a sort of laissez-faire grazing system. Men hunted and fished, and the women worked the farms, kept house, and bore and raised children. They ate mainly meat and corn—pork, beef, hominy, johnnycake, pone, and corn mush. Water was bad and life was hard; the men drank corn whiskey.

Their diet, combined with the hardships of frontier lifestyle, led to much sickness—fevers, chills, malaria, dysentery, rheumatism, and just plain exhaustion. Worms, insects, and parasites of every description wiggled, dug, or burrowed their way into pioneer skin, infecting it with the seven-year itch, a generic term covering scabies and crabs as well as body lice, which almost everyone suffered from. Worse, hookworm, tapeworm, and other creatures fed off the flesh, intestines, and blood of frontier Americans. Crackers seemed particularly susceptible to these maladies. Foreign travelers were shocked at the appearance of the "pale and deathly looking people" of bluish-white complexion.

Despite such hardships, the crackers were content with their hard lives because they knew that land ownership meant freedom and improvement. Armed with an evangelical Christian perspective, crackers endured their present hardships with the confidence that their lives had improved, and would continue to get better. Historian George Dangerfield captured the essence of cracker ambitions when he wrote of their migration: "[T]he flow of human beings beyond the Alleghenies was perhaps the last time in all history when mankind discovered that one of its deepest needs—the need to own—could be satisfied by the simple process of walking towards it. Harsh as the journey was . . . the movement could not help but be a hopeful one."[84]

"We Are All Republicans, We Are All Federalists"

The election of 1800 marked the second peaceful transfer of power (the first was 1788) in the brief history of the new nation. Perhaps it was the magnanimity of this moment that led Jefferson, in his 1801 inaugural address, to state, "We are all Republicans, we are all Federalists." Reading the entire text of the speech two hundred years later, however, it appears that most of the audience members must have been Republicans.

Far from the Revolution of 1800 that some historians have labeled the election, Jefferson and his followers did not return the nation to the radical Whig precepts of Anti-Federalism and the Articles of Confederation era, although they did swing the political pendulum in that direction. Jefferson's two terms in office, from 1801 to 1809, did, however, mark a radical departure from the 1789–1800 Federalist policies that preceded them.

By the time he became president—the first to function from Washington, D.C.—Jefferson already had lived a remarkable life. Drafter of the Declaration, lawyer, member of the Virginia House of Burgesses, governor of Virginia, minister to France, secretary of state, the Sage of Monticello (as he would later be called) had blessed the nation richly. His personal life, however, never seemed to reflect the tremendous success he had in public. When his wife died in 1782, it left him melancholy, and whereas he still had daughters upon whom to lavish affection, he reimmersed himself in public life thereafter. His minimal religious faith offered little solace. Monticello, the mansion he built with his own hands, offered little pleasure and produced an endless stream of debts. He founded the University of Virginia and reformed the curriculum of William and Mary, introducing medicine and anatomy courses. A slaveholder who freed only a handful of his chattel, Jefferson is said to have fathered children with his slave Sally Hemings. But modern DNA testing has proven only the strong probability that one of the Hemingses, Eston, was fathered by one of some twenty-four Jefferson males in Virginia at the time, including at least seven whom documentary evidence suggests were at Monticello at the time. This left only a handful of candidates, most noticeably Thomas's brother Randolph Jefferson. But archival evidence putting him at Monticello on the key dates does not entirely support naming him as Eston's father—but it cannot rule him out either.[85]

The public, political Jefferson was more consistent. His first inaugural address set the tone for the Jefferson that most Americans would recognize. He called for a return to Revolutionary principles: strict construction of the Constitution, state power ("the surest bulwark against antirepublican tendencies"), economy in government, payment of the national debt, "encouragement of agriculture, with commerce as its hand maiden," and, in an obvious reference to the reviled Alien and Sedition Acts, "Freedom of religion, press, and person." These were not empty phrases to Thomas Jefferson, who waited his whole life to implement these ideals, and he proceeded to build his administration upon them.

Albert Gallatin, Jefferson's secretary of the treasury, was point man in the immediate assault on Alexander Hamilton's economic policy and the hated three reports. Gallatin, a French immigrant to Pennsylvania, an Anti-Federalist, and an early target of Federalist critics of so-called alien radicals, had led the attack on speculators and stockjobbers. A solid advocate of hard money, balanced budgets, and payment of the national debt, Gallatin was one of the most informed critics of Hamilton's system.

With a Republican Congress passing enabling legislation, Gallatin abolished internal taxation and built a Treasury Department funded solely by customs duties and land sales. The Federalists' annual $5 million budgets were slashed in half, and the Treasury began to pay off the national debt (by 1810, $40 million of the $82 million debt had been paid, despite Jefferson's extravagant purchase of the Louisiana Territory).

Lest one credit the Jeffersonians with genius or administrative magic, this success was to a large degree Hamilton's legacy. He had stabilized the money supply by insisting that the debt holders would, in fact, be repaid. The blessings of the Federalist years, including soaring commerce that could support the customs base (Jay's and Pinckney's treaties at work), the stable frontiers and safe oceans, the pacification of the Indians, and the state of peace (the result of Washington and Adams's commitment to neutrality), all provided the undergirding that allowed revenues to flow in while expenses were kept relatively low. Land, already abundant, would become even more so after Jefferson's acquisition of Louisiana, and this, too, gave the Republicans the freedom to pursue budget cutting, as the revenues of land sales were enormous, giving the Land Office plenty of work for decades.[86] More broadly, though, the nation had already adopted critical business practices and philosophies that placed it in the middle of the capitalist revolution, including sanctity of contracts, competition, and adoption of the corporate form for business. This foundation of law and good sense guaranteed relative prosperity for a number of years.

Jefferson wanted to benefit his natural constituency, the farmers, just as Hamilton had befriended the bankers. He did not believe in any direct subsidies for farmers, but he tasked Gallatin to help the agrarian interests in other ways, specifically in reducing transportation costs.[87] Congress "experimented after 1802 with financing western roads from the proceeds of federal land sales, and Congress in 1806 ordered Jefferson to build a national road to Ohio."[88] Even Jefferson inquired as to whether Congress could do anything else to "advance the general good" within "the pale" of its "constitutional powers."[89] But in 1806, Jefferson became even more aggressive with internal improvements, recognizing a federal role in the "improvement of the country."[90] It is significant that Jefferson, like Henry Clay and John C. Calhoun after him, saw this physical uniting of the nation as a means to defuse the slavery issue. Calhoun, of South Carolina—a leading advocate of slavery—would argue in 1817 that the Congress was under the "most imperious obligation to counteract every tendency to disunion" and to "bind the republic together with a perfect system of roads and canals."[91]

In an extensive report to Congress, finally delivered in 1808, Gallatin outlined a massive plan for the government to remove obstacles to trade.[92] Proposing that Congress fund a ten-year, $20 million project in which the federal government would construct roads and canals itself, or provide loans for private corporations to do so, Gallatin detailed $16 million in specific programs. He wanted a canal to connect the Atlantic Coast and the Great Lakes, and he included more than $3 million for local improvements.[93] Jefferson endorsed the guts of the plan, having reservations only about the possible need for a constitutional amendment to ensure its legality. But for the small-government Republicans, it constituted a breathtaking project, amounting to five times all of the other total government outlays under Jefferson.[94] The project showed the selectivity of Jefferson's predisposition to small government. He concluded in 1807 that "embracing every local interest, and superior to every local consideration [was] competent to the selection of such national objects" and only the "national legislature" could make the final determination on such grand proposals.[95] (Madison did not dissent at the time, but a decade later, as president, he vetoed the Bonus Bill, which called for an internal improvement amendment.)[96]

However Jefferson and Gallatin justified their plan, it remained the exception to the Republicans' small-government/budget-cutting character, not the norm. While Gallatin labored over his report—most of which would eventually be funded through private and state efforts, not the federal government—Jefferson worked to roll back other federal spending. The radical $2.4 million reduction of the national budget (one can barely imagine the impact of a 50 percent budget cut today!) sent shock waves through even the small bureaucracy. Gallatin dismissed all excise tax collectors and ordered every federal agency and cabinet office to cut staff and expenses. (Only a few years later, James Madison conducted the business of the secretary of state with a staff of three secretaries.) Then half of the remaining federal employees were replaced with Jeffersonian Republican employees. The Federalist bureaucracy, in which a mere six of six hundred federal employees were Republicans, was thus revolutionized.

The Department of War was the next target for the budget slashers. Jefferson and his followers had never been friendly to the military establishment, and they cut the navy nearly out of existence, eliminating deep-sea vessels and maintaining only a coastal gunboat fleet, virtually all of which were sunk in the War of 1812. With the Northwest Indian wars concluded, the Republicans chopped the army's budget in half; troop strength shrank from 6,500 to 3,350 men in uniform. To further eliminate what they saw as an overly Federalist officer corps, the Jeffersonians launched a radical experiment—a military academy to train a new "republican" officer class, thus producing a supreme irony, in that the United States Military Academy at West Point became a great legacy of one of America's most antimilitary presidents.

Finally, Jefferson sought to change the alleged undemocratic tone of the Federalist years through simplicity, accessibility, and lack of protocol. The president literally led the way himself, riding horseback to his March 1801 inauguration, instead of riding in a carriage like Washington or Adams. He replaced the White House's rectangular dinner table with a round one at which all guests would, symbolically at least, enjoy equal status. Widower Jefferson ran a much less formal household than his predecessors, hosting his own dinner parties and even personally doing some of the serving and pouring of wine. The informality distressed the new British ambassador to the United States when, upon paying his first visit to the White House, his knock upon the door was not answered by house servants, but rather by the president of the United States, dressed in house robe and slippers.

Judiciary Waterloo for Minimalist Government

While the Federalists in Congress and the bureaucracy ran before this flood of Jeffersonian democrats, one branch of government defiantly stood its ground. The lifetime appointees to the judiciary branch—the United States federal courts and the Supreme Court—remained staunchly Federalist. Jefferson thus faced a choice. He could let the judges alone and wait for age and attrition to ultimately create a Republican judiciary, or he could adopt a more aggressive policy. He chose the latter course, with mixed results.

Much of Jefferson's vendetta against Federalist judges came from bitterness over John Adams's last two years in office. Federalist judges had unfairly convicted and sentenced Republican editors under the Sedition Act. Adams and the lame-duck Congress added insult to injury by passing a new Judiciary Act and appointing a whopping sixty new Federalist judges (including Chief Justice John Marshall) during Adams's last sixty days in office. Jefferson now sought to legally balance the federal courts.

The Virginian might have adopted an even more incendiary policy, because his most extreme advisers advocated repealing all prior judiciary acts, clearing the courts of all Federalist judges, and appointing all Republicans to take their place. Instead, the administration wisely chose to remove only the midnight judges and a select few sitting judges. With the Amendatory Act, the new Republican Congress repealed Adams's 1801 Judiciary Act, and eliminated thirty of Adams's forty-seven new justices of the peace (including a fellow named William Marbury) and three federal appeals court judgeships. Attempts to impeach several Federalist judges, including Supreme Court justice Samuel Chase, met with mixed results. Chase engaged in arguably unprofessional conduct in several of the Sedition Act cases, but the attempt to remove him proved so partisan and unprofessional that Republican moderates joined the minority Federalists to acquit Chase.

Congressional Republicans won a skirmish with the Amendatory Act, but the Federalists, under Supreme Court chief justice John Marshall, ultimately won the war. This victory came thanks to a subtle and complex decision in a case known as *Marbury v. Madison* (1803), and stemmed from the appointment of William Marbury as a midnight judge. Adams had commissionied Marbury as a justice of the peace, but Marbury never received the commission, and when he inquired about it, he was told by the secretary of state's office that it had vanished. Marbury then sued the secretary of state James Madison in a brief he filed before the United States Supreme Court itself.

Chief Justice Marshall wrote an 1803 opinion in *Marbury* that brilliantly avoided conflict with Jefferson while simultaneously setting a precedent for judicial review—the prerogative of the Supreme Court, not the executive or legislative branches—to decide the constitutionality of federal laws. There is nothing in the U.S. Constitution that grants the Supreme Court this great power, and the fact that we accept it today as a given has grown from the precedent of John Marshall's landmark decision. Marshall sacrificed his fellow Federalist Marbury for the greater cause of a strong centralized judiciary. He and fellow justices ruled the Supreme Court could not order Marbury commissioned because they lacked jurisdiction in the case, then shrewdly continued to make a ruling anyway. The Supreme Court lacked jurisdiction, Marshall ruled, because a 1789 federal law granting such jurisdiction was *unconstitutional;* the case should have originated in a lower court. While the ruling is abstruse, its aim and result were not. The Supreme Court, said Marshall, was the final arbiter of the constitutionality of federal law. In *Fletcher v. Peck* (1811), Marshall's court would claim the same national authority over state law. Chief Justice Marshall thus paved the first segment of a long road toward nationalism through judicial review. In the Aaron Burr treason trial (1807), when the chief justice personally issued a subpoena to President Jefferson, it sent a powerful message to all future presidents that no person is above the law.

Equally as important as judicial review, however, Marshall's Court consistently ruled in favor of capitalism, free enterprise, and open markets. Confirming the sanctity of private contracts, in February 1819 the Supreme Court, in *Dartmouth College v. Woodward*, ruled that a corporate charter (for Dartmouth College) was indeed a contract that could not be violated at will by the state legislature. This supported a similar ruling in *Sturges v. Crowninshield*: contracts are contracts, and are not subject to arbitrary revision after the fact. Some of the Marshall Court's rulings expanded federal power, no doubt. But at the same time, they unleashed market forces to race ahead of regulation. For example, five years after *Dartmouth*, the Supreme Court held that only the federal government could limit interstate commerce. The case, *Gibbons v. Ogden*, involved efforts by the famous Cornelius Vanderbilt, who ran a cheap water-taxi service from New York to New Jersey for a steamboat operator named Thomas Gibbons. Their service competed against a New York firm that claimed a monopoly on the Hudson River. The commodore boldly carried passengers in defiance of the claim, even offering to transport them on his People's Line for nothing if they agreed to eat two dollars' worth of food on the trip. Flying a flag reading NEW JERSEY MUST BE FREE, Vanderbilt demonstrated his proconsumer, low-price projects over the next thirty years and, in the process, won the case.[97]

Lower courts took the lead from Marshall's rulings. For thirty years American courts would favor developmental rights over pure or pristine property rights. This was especially explicit in the so-called mill acts, wherein state courts affirmed the primacy of privately constructed mills that required the owners to dam up rivers, thus eroding or destroying some of the property of farmers having land adjacent to the same river. Emphasizing the public good brought by the individual building the mill, the courts tended to side with the person developing property as opposed to one keeping it intact.[98] Legal historian James Willard Hurst has labeled this propensity toward development "release of energy," a term that aptly captures the courts' collective goal: to unleash American entrepreneurs to serve greater numbers of people. As policy it pleased neither the hard-core antistatists, who complained that it (rightly) put government authority on the side of some property owners as opposed to others, nor militant socialists, who hated all private property anyway and called for heavy taxation as a way to spur development.[99]

A final pair of Marshall-like rulings came from Roger B. Taney, a Marylander named chief justice when Marshall died in 1835. Having established the sanctity of contracts, the primacy of development, and the authority of the federal government over interstate trade, the Court turned to issues of competition. In *Charles River Bridge v. Warren Bridge*, the Charles River Bridge Company claimed its charter implicitly gave it a monopoly over bridge traffic, and thus sued Warren Bridge Company which sought to erect a competing crossing. Although many of the early colonial charters indeed had implied a monopoly power, the Court took a giant step away from those notions by ruling that monopoly powers did not exist unless they were expressly stated and delegated in the charter. This opened the floodgates of competition, for no company could hide behind its state-originated charters any longer. Then, in 1839, in *Bank of Augusta v. Earle*, a debtor from Alabama, seeking to avoid repaying his debts to the Bank of Augusta in Georgia, claimed that the bank had no jurisdiction in Alabama. Appreciating the implications for stifling all interstate trade with a ruling against the bank, the Court held that corporations could conduct business under laws of comity, or mutual good faith, across state lines unless explicitly prohibited by the legislatures of the states involved.[100] Again the Court opened the floodgates of competition by forcing companies to compete across state boundaries, not just within them. Taken together, these cases "established the framework that allowed entrepreneurs in America to flourish."[101]

"We Rush Like a Comet into Infinite Space!"

Prior to the American Revolution, few white men had seen what lay beyond the "endless mountains."[102] By 1800, the Great Migration had begun in earnest, and American settlers poured into and settled the trans-Appalachian West. Jefferson aimed to assist frontier immigrants by securing a free-trade route down the entirety of the Mississippi River to the Gulf of Mexico, requiring the United States of America to purchase the port of New Orleans. Jefferson's motives appeared solely economic, yet they were also based on strategic concerns and an overriding agrarian philosophy that sought new outlets for America's frontier farmers. At the time, Jefferson sought to secure only the port of New Orleans itself. American purchase of all of the Louisiana Territory came as a surprise to nearly everyone involved.

Spain, ever fearful of the American advance, had returned the Louisiana Territory to France in the secret Treaty of San Ildefonso (1800), then later made public. Napoléon Bonaparte, on his rise to become France's post-Revolutionary emperor, promised the Spanish he would not sell Louisiana. He then immediately proceeded to do exactly that, convinced, after a revolution in Haiti, that he could not defend French possessions in the New World. The British, ever anxious to weaken France, made the information of the 1801 treaty available to the envoy to England, Rufus King, who hastily passed the news on to Jefferson.

America's minister to France, Robert Livingston, was quickly authorized to negotiate for the right of deposit of American goods in New Orleans. Livingston got nowhere, at which point Jefferson dispatched his Virginia friend, James Monroe, to Paris to assist in the negotiations.

Monroe arrived in Paris to parlay, whereupon he was astounded to hear Napoleon's minister, Talleyrand, ask, "What will you give for the whole?" By "the whole," Talleyrand offered not just New Orleans, but all of the remaining Louisiana Territory—that area draining the Mississippi River from the Rocky Mountains to the Mississippi—for $15 million, a sum that included $3 million in debts American citizens owed the French.[103] The actual price tag of Louisiana was a stunningly low $11.2 million, or less than one-tenth the cost of today's Louisiana Superdome in New Orleans!

The Jefferson administration, which prided itself on fiscal prudence and strict adherence to the Constitution, now found itself in the awkward position of arguing that Hamiltonian means somehow justified Jeffersonian ends. Livingston and Monroe never had authority to purchase Louisiana, nor to spend 50 percent more than authorized, no matter what the bargain. In the dollars of the day, the expense of Louisiana was enormous, and nothing in the Constitution specifically empowered the federal government to purchase a territory beyond its boundaries, much less grant American citizenship to tens of thousands of French nationals who resided within that territory. After a little hand-wringing and inconsequential talk of constitutional amendments, however, the administration cast aside its fiscal and constitutional scruples. Minority Federalists erupted over the hypocrisy of this stance, and one cried in protest over spending "fifteen million dollars for bogs, mountains, and Indians! Fifteen million dollars for uninhabited wasteland and refuge for criminals!"[104]

The Federalists no doubt appreciated the fact that this new land would also become a cradle for numerous Jeffersonian Republican senators and congressmen representing a number of new agricultural states. Jefferson typically framed the argument in more philosophical terms: Louisiana would become an "empire of liberty" populated by farmers who just happened to vote for his party. In the end, the majority Republicans prevailed and, of thirty-two U.S. senators, only six Arch-Federalists voted against the Louisiana Purchase. In a telling example of the self-destructive nature of old Federalism, Fisher Ames wrote gloomily, "Now by adding this unmeasured world beyond [the Mississippi] we rush like a comet into infinite space. In our wild career we may jostle some other world out of its orbit, but we shall, in any event, quench the light of our own."[105]

Even before receiving senatorial approval for the Louisiana Purchase, Jefferson secretly ordered a military expedition to explore, map, and report on the new territory and its borders.[106] The president chose his personal aide, U.S. Army captain Meriwether Lewis, to lead the force, making sure that the captain was sufficiently attuned to the scientific inquiries that had captivated Jefferson his entire life.

Lewis, a combat veteran and woodsman who possessed considerable intellect, went to Philadelphia for a crash course in scientific method and biology under Charles Wilson Peale prior to departure. For his coleader, Lewis chose William Clark, an affable, redheaded soldier (and much younger brother of Revolutionary hero George Rogers Clark). The two spent the winter of 1803–04 encamped on the Mississippi at Wood River, directly across from French St. Louis. Official word of the Louisiana Purchase arrived, and in May of 1804, Lewis and Clark led their fifty-man Corps of Discovery across the Mississippi and up the Missouri River, bound for the unknown lands of the North American Great Plains.[107]

Lewis and Clark aimed to follow the Missouri River to its headwaters in present-day western Montana. While encamped near modern-day Bismarck, North Dakota, during the winter of 1804–5, they met and hired a pregnant Indian woman, Sacajawea, and her husband, Toussaint Charbonneau, to act as their translators and guides. After an arduous upriver journey, the corps arrived in the summer of 1805 at the Missouri's headwaters, ending serious discussion of an all-water Northwest Passage route to Asia. Then the expedition crossed the Rocky Mountains, leaving the western bounds of the Louisiana Purchase. Near the western base of the Rockies, Sacajawea secured horses for the explorers, and they rode onto the Columbia Plateau in the late fall. Sailing down the Snake and Columbia rivers, Lewis and Clark arrived at the Pacific Ocean on November seventh, and promptly carved BY LAND FROM THE U. STATES IN 1804 & 1805 on a tree. They wintered on the Oregon coast, then returned east, arriving to a hero's welcome in St. Louis, Missouri, in September 1806.

Lewis and Clark's great journey has become legendary, and a reading of the Lewis and Clark extensive journals today reveals not only Jefferson's strategic and economic motives, but other, more idealistic, motives as well. President Jefferson sent Lewis and Clark west in search of scientific data to further man's knowledge and, at the same time, to explore what he dreamed would become an expanded agrarian American Republic.

Other American adventurers headed west to explore the new Louisiana Territory. In 1806, U.S. Army captain Zebulon Pike led an official expedition up the Arkansas River to what is now Colorado, then attempted, but failed, to climb Pike's Peak.[108] Like Lewis and Clark's, Pike's expedition set out with keenly defined instructions for what the government sought to find, making it truly an exploration as opposed to a discovery expedition. Uncle Sam expected political, diplomatic, economic, and scientific fruits from its expenditures, and Congress routinely shared this information with the public in a series of some sixty reports. However, the most fascinating probe of the West in these early years came not from an official U.S. expedition, but from an illegal and treasonous foray into the West by none other than former vice president Aaron Burr.

The Cataline of America

John Adams, no friend of Burr's, once wrote of him, "Ambition of military fame and ambition of conquest over female virtue were the duplicate ruling powers of his life."[109] A direct descendant of theologian Jonathan Edwards, Burr's early military and political career seemed promising. As a patriot colonel, he heroically, though unsuccessfully, stormed the British garrison at Quebec; afterward he practiced law, espoused Anti-Federalism, and was elected a Republican senator from New York State. A relentless schemer, Burr entertained notions of getting New England to secede; when that went nowhere, he moved on to more elaborate and fantastic designs. As has been noted, he attempted to stab his running mate, Jefferson, in the back in 1800, ending his career in Washington, D.C., as soon as it began. He ran for the governorship of New York in 1804 while still serving as vice president. Thwarted in this attempt by his old rival Alexander Hamilton, Burr and Hamilton exchanged heated letters. Neither would back down, and a duel ensued, at Weehawken, New Jersey, where dueling was still legal.

Dueling was common in Burr's day. Some of America's most respected early leaders were duelists—indeed, in some parts of the South and West, dueling had become an essential component of political résumés. Andrew Jackson, Henry Clay, John Randolph, Jefferson Davis, Sam Houston, Thomas Hart Benton, and a score of other national leaders fought duels during the first half of the nineteenth century. Hamilton had slandered Burr on numerous occasions, once calling him the Cataline of America, in reference to the treacherous schemer who nearly brought down the Roman Republic.[110]

At Weehawken Heights in New Jersey in the late Autumn of 1804, the two scaled a narrow ledge more than 150 feet above the water. They prepared to duel in formal, time-honored tradition, pacing off steps, then turning to face one another. Two shots were fired, though historians know little else. Letters published later revealed that Hamilton had said he intended to throw away his shot. No one knows exactly what Hamilton had on his mind, though it appeared to one of the seconds that Hamilton fired first and that his shot went high and wide, just as he had planned. Whether Burr, as some suspect, was jolted into firing quickly, or whether he maliciously took his time, one thing is certain: only Colonel Burr left the field alive.

After winning his duel—and losing what little reputation, he had left—Burr continued his machinations without pause. He wandered west; in 1806, along with a hundred armed followers, Burr sailed in gunboats down the Ohio and Mississippi to Natchez, Mississippi, where he was arrested and marched to Richmond, Virginia, to stand trial for treason. Versions of Burr's plans vary wildly, and he evidently told all of his confidants whatever they wanted to hear so long as they would lend him money.[111] In court Burr claimed he was only moving to Louisiana to start a farm and perhaps begin political life anew. Others suspect he had formed a western U.S. secession movement. Jefferson learned of it from Burr's coconspirator, U.S. Army general James Wilkinson. The president charged Burr with planning not only secession, but a unilateral war against Spain with the aim of bringing Spanish Texas under his own leadership.

The administration tried mightily to convict Burr of treason, but the former vice president had outsmarted everyone. The federal circuit court, presided over by the chief justice John Marshall, was quick to spotlight the weakness of the administration's case, setting huge legal precedents in the process. When President Jefferson claimed executive privilege in refusing to supply the court with original documents as evidence, Marshall insisted on a compromise. As for treason, the court ruled that since the government could not prove that Burr had levied war against the United States, he was not guilty. Freed, Burr returned to New York City, where he practiced law, courted rich widows, and schemed and dreamed to no avail for three decades. He never again crossed the Hudson to visit New Jersey, where there was a murder warrant for him. Having extinguished his own career, as well as that of one of America's brightest lights, Aaron Burr departed into infamy.

America's First Preemptive War

Throughout the 1790s, Republicans had leveled a number of highly critical attacks at Federalist foreign policy makers. Now, at last, the party of Jefferson was free to mold its own foreign policy. Jefferson dealt with some of North Africa's Barbary pirates, sea-going Muslim outlaws from Morocco, Tunis, Algiers, and Tripoli who regularly plundered 1790s American Mediterranean shipping. Washington and Adams had paid some small bribes at first—the trade was not sufficient to warrant a military expedition—and it could be rationalized as the way of doing business in that part of the world. But when the pasha of Tripoli chopped down the flagpole at the U.S. consulate there, it was a direct affront and an act of war. In 1801, Jefferson slowed down his mothballing of the naval fleet and sent ships to blockade the port. Operating only under a set of joint resolutions, not a declaration of war, Jefferson nevertheless informed all the Barbary States that the United States was at war with them. He sought to get an international coalition to help, but no European states wanted to alter the status quo. So, in 1804, Lieutenant Stephen Decatur went ashore with eight U.S. Marines; set fire to a captured frigate, the *Philadelphia*; and through an expedition across the desert led by William Eaton and Greek mercenaries, organized locals who detested the pasha. The American desert army also threatened the pirates' lucrative slave trade, and the presence of the powerful British fleet not far away put even more teeth into this threat. This stick, combined with a carrot of a small ransom for the *Philadelphia*'s crew, sufficed to force the pirates down, and after releasing the crew, they recognized American freedom to sail the high seas uninterrupted.[112] By dispatching even such a small body of men so far to secure American national interests, Jefferson put the world on notice that the United States intended to be a force— if only a minor one—in world affairs. It was a remarkably brazen display of preemptive war by a president usually held up as a model of limited government, and it achieved its results. The United States squashed the threat of the Barbary pirates—alone. Yet these foreign policy successes only served as a prelude to a recurrence of America's major diplomatic headache—continuing Anglo-French warfare during the rise of Napoleonic Europe. As before, American foreign policy became bogged down in this European morass; like his Federalist predecessors, Jefferson floundered in the high seas of European diplomacy.

Between John Adams's conclusion of the Quasi War in 1799 and renewed attacks on neutral American commerce in 1806, New England traders had carried on a brisk trade with both France and Britain, earning an estimated $60 million annually. But Britain objected to a particularly lucrative aspect of this trade—Caribbean goods shipped to America in French vessels and then reshipped to France in neutral American vessels. Britain aimed to crush these "broken voyages" through the Orders in Council (1806 and 1807), prohibiting American trade with France and enforced by a British blockade. When Americans tried to run the blockade, the Royal Navy seized their ships and impressed (drafted) American sailors to serve His Majesty. Britain justified this kidnapping by insisting that all of the impressed sailors—ultimately numbering 10,000—were in fact British deserters. Americans once again found themselves treated like colonial subjects in a mercantile system, forced yet again to demand fundamental neutral rights and freedom of the seas. As tempers flared, the U.S. administration aimed its fury at Great Britain, whose strong navy represented a greater threat to American shipping than France's. Jefferson's old prejudices now resurfaced with dangerous consequences: failing to construct large warships as the Federalists had, Jefferson's navy consisted of some two hundred, single-gun gunboats incapable of anything other than intercepting ill-armed pirates or the most basic coastal defense.

Jefferson avoided war for many reasons, not the least of which was that he had spent much of his administration dismantling the federal army and navy and now was in no position at all to fight on land or sea. Congress sought to accommodate his policies with the 1806 Nonimportation Act. Britain, however, was unfazed by the boycotts and continued to attack and seize shipping. An 1807 clash on the open oceans between the American ship *Chesapeake* and Britain's *Leopard* resulted in four Americans dead, eighteen wounded, and four impressed. "Never since the battle of Lexington," wrote Jefferson, "have I seen the country in such a state of exasperation."[113]

In order to avoid the war that should have naturally followed the *Chesapeake-Leopard* duel, Jefferson combined nonexportation with nonimportation in the Embargo Act of December 1807. This law prohibited Americans from trading with any foreign countries until France and Britain buckled under to national and international pressure and recognized America's free-trade rights. But the results of the Embargo Act were disastrous. Neither Britain nor France acquiesced and in blatant violation of federal law, New Englanders continued to trade with Britain, smuggling products along the rugged New England coast and through the ports of Nova Scotia and New Brunswick. When Jefferson left office in 1809, the main results of his well-intentioned foreign policy were economic downturn, a temporarily revived Federalist opposition, and a perception by both France and England that the United States was weak and lacking in conviction.

Exit the Sage of Monticello

Former president Jefferson at last returned to his beloved Monticello in 1809. Appropriately, Monticello faced west, anticipating the future, not replaying the past. Jefferson's record had, in fact, replayed some past mistakes too often. Republicans had undoubtedly reshaped the federal government in a democratic and leaner form. The Louisiana Purchase and the Lewis and Clark Expedition were nothing less than magnificent triumphs. But the (technically illegal) Louisiana Purchase had added more to the public domain than Washington or Adams had, requiring, even in minimalist Jeffersonian terms, a bigger army, navy, and federal bureaucracy to protect and govern it. The judiciary contests and foreign policy exercises, except for the decisive preemptive war against the pirates, had not advanced the nation's interests. In losing the judiciary battles to Marshall, Jefferson's obsolete agrarian Republic was scraped away to make room for a capitalist engine of wealth creation. Moreover, his years in office had done nothing to relieve his personal debts, rebuild his deteriorated friendship with Adams, or constrain the size of government. In some ways, the nation he helped found had, like an unruly teenager, grown beyond his ability to manage it in the way he had envisioned. His successor, fellow Founder James Madison, in many ways proved a far better father for the child.

Quids and War Hawks

The career of James Madison symbolized the breadth of early American republicanism. Beginning in 1787 as a Federalist advocate of a strengthened national state, Madison jumped ship in the 1790s to form a Republican opposition party demanding a return to decentralized, agrarian, frugal, and peaceful government. It was in this philosophical mood that Madison inherited Jefferson's mantle of succession in 1809, but he also inherited the foreign policy and war fever he had helped create as Jefferson's secretary of state. The War of 1812 naturally swung the American political pendulum back to the more vigorous nationalist beliefs of early Federalism, returning Madison's philosophical journey to a point near, though not exactly coinciding with, his 1787 Federalist beginnings.

As the Republicans amassed a huge national following during the 1800–1808 period, their Federalist opponents began to wither. This important political development was much more complex than it appears on the surface. To begin with, the Federalist party died a slow death that was not absolutely apparent until around 1815. Throughout Madison's two terms in office, he faced stiff Federalist opposition and even saw a brief revival of Federalism at the ballot box. At the same time, whatever ideological purity the Republicans may have possessed in the 1790s became diluted as more and more Americans (including former Federalists) flocked to their banner.

That this specter of creeping Federalist nationalism was seen as a genuine threat to Republican ideological purity is evident in the clandestine efforts of James Monroe to wrest the 1808 Republican presidential nomination from his colleague Madison. Monroe, an old Anti-Federalist who had served the Jeffersonians well as a congressman and diplomat, led a group of radical, disaffected southern Republicans known as the Quids, an old English term for opposition leaders. Quids John Randolph, John Taylor, and Randolph Macon feared the Revolution of 1800 had been sidetracked by a loss of vigilance. They complained there was too much governmental debt and bureaucracy, and the Federalist judiciary had too free a reign. Quids aimed to reverse this turn to centralization by nominating the radical Monroe to succeed Jefferson. But they met defeat in the Madison-dominated Republican congressional caucus.

That November, Madison and his running mate George Clinton (the aged New York Anti-Federalist) faced off against Federalists Charles Cotesworth Pinckney and Rufus King. Madison won handily—122 electoral votes to 47—yet the Federalists had actually bettered their 1804 numbers; furthermore, they gained twenty-four new congressmen (a 34 percent increase) in the process. They fared even better in 1812, with antiwar sentiment fueling support for Federalist De Witt Clinton, who garnered 89 electoral votes to Madison's 128. This temporary Federalist resurgence was partially due to the administration's mistakes (especially the embargo), but much credit goes to the Young Federalists, a second generation of moderates who infused a more down-to-earth style into the formerly stuffy Federalist political demeanor.

Many Young Federalists, however, bolted the party altogether and joined the opposition. A prime example was John Quincy Adams, who resigned as Massachusetts' Federalist senator and joined the party of his father's archenemies. Adams's defection to Republicanism may seem incredible, yet on reflection it shows considerable political savvy. Adams had already recognized that the Federalist Party was dying and he wisely saw there was room for moderate nationalist viewpoints in an expanded Republican Party. Most important, however, young Adams astutely perceived that his only hope for a meaningful national political career (and the presidency) lay within the political party of Jefferson, Madison, and Monroe.

During his first term in office, Madison attempted to carry forward the domestic aims of the Revolution of 1800. Gallatin, the chief formulator of Republican fiscal policy, stayed on as secretary of the treasury, and he and the president continued the Republicans' policy of balanced budgets and paying off the national debt, pruning administrative and military expenditures to balance the ledgers. Republicans continued to replace retiring Federalist judges, though the new ideological breadth of the Republican Party, combined with Marshall's dominance of the Supreme Court, tempered the impact of these appointments. Meanwhile, the diplomatic crisis continued, ultimately rendering many of the administration's domestic policies unattainable.

Madison assumed office at a time when diplomatic upheaval and impending warfare made foreign policy the primary focus of his administration. The former secretary of state certainly possessed the credentials to launch a forceful foreign policy, yet through his political party's own efforts, he lacked an army and navy to back that policy up. This fact would ultimately bring the administration to the brink of disaster.

Because of strong domestic opposition to Jefferson's embargo, Madison immediately called for its repeal. He replaced it with the Nonintercourse Act (1809), which forbade trade only with France and Britain (the embargo had forbidden all foreign trade) and promised to reopen trade with whichever party first recognized America's neutral rights. This policy, a smuggler's dream, failed utterly; it was replaced by Macon's Bill No. 2 (1810), which reopened trade with both France and Britain, but again promised exclusive trade with whichever power recognized America's right to trade. The French eagerly agreed, and with their weak navy, they had nothing to lose. But the British naturally resumed seizing American ships bound for France, at which point the administration was stymied. Peaceable coercion had failed. War with Britain seemed America's only honorable alternative.

Pushing Madison and the nation toward war was a group of newly elected congressmen, many from the West, most notably Henry Clay of Kentucky. Known as the War Hawks, the group included Peter Porter of New York, Langdon Cheves and John C. Calhoun of South Carolina, Felix Grundy of Tennessee, and Clay's Kentucky colleague, Richard M. Johnson. They elected Clay Speaker; then, using his control of the committee system, they named their own supporters to the Foreign Relations and Naval Committees. Although some of the maritime issues only touched their constituencies indirectly, the War Hawks saw Britain (and her ally Spain) as posing a danger in Florida and the Northwest, in both cases involving incitement of Indians. In 1811, General William Henry Harrison won the Battle of Tippecanoe against British-aided Shawnee warriors in Indiana, launching a renewed Indian war in the Old Northwest. At the same time, frontier warfare fueled expansionist desires to invade Canada, and perhaps Spanish Florida as well. Southern and western farmers openly coveted the rich North American agricultural lands held by Britain and Spain.

Madison's war message of June 1, 1812, concentrated almost exclusively on maritime rights, noting "evidence of hostile inflexibility" on the part of the British. This put the Federalists, whose New England ships were the ones being attacked, in the ironic position of having to vote against that declaration, in part because of their pro-British sentiments and in part because they just opposed "anything Republican."[114] The War Hawks, equally paradoxically, did not suffer directly from impressment, but they represented deep-seated resentment and anger shared by many Americans. They fumed that a supposedly free and independent American republic still suffered under the yoke of British military and buckled under her trade policies.

On June 4 and June 18, 1812, Congress voted for war, with the House splitting 79 to 49 and the Senate 19 to 13. This divided vote did not bode well for a united, successful war effort. Nor could the nation expect to successfully fight with its most advanced and industrialized section ambivalent about the conflict. Yet strong Federalist opposition (and a weak military) did not seem to dampen Republican enthusiasm for a war they now termed the "Second War of American Independence."

"Half Horse and Half Alligator" in the War of 1812

Americans' recollections of the War of 1812 provide an excellent example of selective memory. Today, those Americans who know anything about it at all remember the War of 1812 for Andrew Jackson's famed Battle of New Orleans (1815), one of the most spectacular victories in the history of the American military, and more generally, that we won. What most Americans do not know, or tend to forget, is that the Battle of New Orleans was fought two weeks *after* the war ended. Slow communications delayed news of the peace treaty, and neither British nor American troops in Louisiana learned of the war's end until after the famed battle.

The United States squared off against a nation that possessed the greatest navy on earth and would soon achieve land superiority as well. The British could count on 8,000 Anglo-Canadian and Indian allies to bolster their strength. Americans enjoyed many of the same military advantages held during the Revolution—a defensive stance and Britain's embroilment in global warfare with France. As in the Revolution, however, the Yankees had few regular troops and sailors to press those advantages. Meanwhile, the U.S. Navy possessed a competent officer corps, but few ships and gunboats for them to command—or, to use the British assessment of American naval capabilities, "a few fir-built frigates, manned by a handful of bastards and outlaws."[115]

Events seemed ominous indeed when General William Hull marched his 1,600 regular U.S. Army troops and militia supplement into Canada via Detroit in July of 1812, only to surrender to Anglo-Canadian troops without firing a shot! (Hull became a scapegoat and was court-martialed for cowardice but pardoned by President Madison.) A second Canadian land invasion (in December 1813) fared only a little better, resulting in stalemate, followed by General Jacob Brown's July 1814 campaign on the Niagara Peninsula, again ending in a stalemate. Three Canadian campaigns, three embarrassments. The long-held American dream of adding Canada to the United States by military conquest ended once and for all during the War of 1812.

On the high seas, the United States fared somewhat better. American privateers carried on the Revolutionary strategy of looting British shipping, but with little tactical impact. The U.S. Navy, with minimal forces, somehow won 80 percent of its initial sea battles. Although the strategic impact was insignificant, these actions yielded the most famous lines in American seafaring. Captain James Lawrence in 1807, for example, his ship the *Chesapeake* defeated by the *Leopard* and her veteran crew lying mortally wounded, shouted, "Don't give up the ship. Fight her till she sinks."[116] The war also produced the most notable one-on-one naval confrontation in the annals of the U.S. Navy when the *Constitution* engaged the British *Guerriere*. Marines boarded the British ship, and after blasting away her rigging, forced her to surrender. After the battle, the resiliency of the *Constitution*'s hull left her with the nickname, Old Ironsides. It was a single engagement, but the London *Times* noted its galling significance: "Never before in the history of the world did an English frigate strike to an American."[117]

Much of the war at sea did not go as well. Jefferson's gunboats, thoroughly outclassed by British frigates, retreated to guard duty of ports. This constituted a demoralizing admission that Jefferson's policies had failed, and was confirmed by a congressional vote in 1813 to fund six new frigates, essentially doubling the U.S. fleet in a single stroke![118] There were also famous naval battles on inland waters. On Lake Erie in 1813, Captain Oliver Hazard Perry built a fleet from scratch, deployed it on the lake, and defeated the British in an impressive victory at Put-in-Bay. Not to be outclassed by Captain Lawrence, Perry declared afterward, "We have met the enemy and they are ours."[119] Those few victories gave Americans hope that after the second full year of war, the tide was turning.

After the British defeated Napoleon at Leipzig in October 1813, they turned their attention to the North American war. Fortified by battle-hardened veterans of the European theater, England launched an ambitious three-pronged offensive in 1814 aimed at the Chesapeake Bay (and Washington, D.C.), Lake Champlain, and New Orleans. They planned to split America into thirds, crippling resistance once and for all.

Initially their plan worked well. On August 24, 1814, 7,000 American militiamen turned tail, allowing the British army to raid Washington, D.C., and burn government buildings, sending President Madison and his wife running to the countryside, literally yanking valuables off the White House walls as they ran to save them from the invaders. The British had not intended to burn the White House, preferring to ransom it, but when they could find no one to parlay with, they torched everything. This infamous loss of the nation's capital, albeit temporary, ranks alongside Pearl Harbor and the surrender of Corregidor as low points in American military history, and the destruction of the White House marked the most traumatic foreign assault on mainland American soil until the terrorist attacks of September 11, 2001. As the British withdrew, they unsuccessfully bombarded Baltimore's Fort McHenry, inspiring patriot Francis Scott Key to compose "The Star-Spangled Banner."

Farther north, at Plattsburgh, New York, Sir George Prevosts's 10,000–man army met defeat at the hands of an American force one-tenth its size at the Battle of Chippewa. There American regulars relieved the militia—with stunning results. At a distance of seventy yards, the British and American infantry blasted at each other until the British broke, and the Americans, clad in the gray cadet uniforms of the United States Military Academy, chased them off the field. The British commander, shocked that he had not come up against militia, blurted, "Those are Regulars, by God."

On nearby Lake Champlain, a concurrent naval battle brought a spectacular American victory. Captain Thomas Macdonough, the thirty-year-old American commander, rallied his sailors, reminding them, "Impressed seamen call on every man to do his duty!" Although knocked unconscious by a soaring decapitated sailor's head, Macdonough delivered so much firepower that he sent Prevost and the British running.

Despite these morale builders, there was more potential trouble in store. By late fall of 1814, a 3,000–man British army under General Edward Packenham was en route, via ocean vessel, to attack New Orleans. More than two years of warfare on land and sea had produced no clear victor.

Combat and stalemate had, however, inspired new opposition from New England's Federalists. When war commenced, Federalists thwarted it in many ways, some bordering on treason. A planned invasion of Canada through lower Maine proved impossible because the Massachusetts and Connecticut militias refused to assist. Meanwhile, New Englanders maintained personal lines of communication with Britons, providing aid and comfort and thereby reducing the bargaining powers of American negotiators at Ghent. And they appeared to be rewarded at the polls with solid 1812 electoral gains in the presidential campaign and large 1814 victories for Federalists in Massachusetts, Connecticut, Delaware, and Maryland.

Their dissent came to a head with the Hartford Convention of December 1814, which marked the height of Federalists' intransigence and the last installment in their dark descent. Federalist delegates from Massachusetts, Connecticut, Vermont, and Rhode Island gathered in Hartford, Connecticut; discussed and debated administration foreign policy and other issues; and concluded by issuing a call for a separate peace between New England and Britain and constitutional amendments limiting the power of southern and western states. (This was the second time New Englanders had danced around the issue of secession, having hatched a plot in 1804 to leave the Union if Jefferson was reelected.)

Across the ocean at Ghent, in Belgium, British and American negotiators, including Henry Clay, John Quincy Adams, and Albert Gallatin, parlayed well into the Christmas season. The days wore on, and Adams complained to his diary that the gregarious Clay kept him awake all night drinking and gambling with their British colleagues. At last, both sets of negotiators conceded they possessed no military advantage. Britain's European victory over Napoléon, meanwhile, opened up a series of prospects and obligations they needed to immediately pursue. At long last, both nations agreed it was time to compromise and end the War of 1812.

On Christmas Eve the deal was struck. Americans withdrew their two major demands—that Britain stop impressing American seaman and officially acknowledge neutrals' trade rights and freedom of the seas. Both sides knew that Britain's European victory meant England would now honor those neutral rights de facto if not de jure. Other territorial disputes over fishing waters and the American-Canadian boundary near Maine were referred to commissions (where they languished for decades). The Treaty of Ghent thus signified that, officially at least, the war had changed nothing, and the terms of peace were such that conditions were now the same as they had been prior to the war—*status quo ante bellum.*

Madison must have been apprehensive about presenting such a peace without victory for the approval of the U.S. Senate. Fortunately for Madison's party, news of the Ghent Treaty arrived in Washington, D.C., at exactly the same time as news of an untimely, yet nevertheless glorious, American military victory. On January 8, 1814, Andrew Jackson's odd coalition of American troops had pounded General Packenham's British regulars and won the famed Battle of New Orleans.

Jackson's victory was mythologized, once again with a David and Goliath twist in which outnumbered American sharpshooters defeated the disciplined redcoats.

The fact was that Jackson's men were seasoned combat veterans of the Creek Indian theater of the War of 1812 and the Battle of Horseshoe Bend (1814). Now, at New Orleans, they were joined by a polyglot collection of local French (Creole and Cajun), Spanish, and free black troops, with a few Caribbean pirates under Jean Laffite thrown in for good measure. The nub of the army remained hard-core Jackson veterans, except for key Creole militia artillery units. Together they manned the breastworks of Chalmette (near New Orleans) and awaited Packenham's force of 2,600.

Jackson had all the advantages. His men were dug in on both sides of the Mississippi protected by a thick breastwork, and the British had to either endure murderous enfilade fire or simultaneously attack both positions—always a tricky proposition. Most important, Jackson had plenty of artillery and had chosen the perfect ground—a dense swamp forest on his left, the canal on his right, and a huge expanse of open field over which the redcoats would have to cross. Merely getting to the battlefield had proven a disaster for the British because their troops had had to row through the lakes and marshes, and each British guardsman carried an eight-pound cannonball in his knapsack. When several of those boats tipped over, the soldiers sank like the lead they carried.[120]

Under the cover of a dawn fog, the British drew up for a bold frontal assault on the American position. Then, suddenly, the same fog that had concealed their formation on the field lifted, revealing them to Jackson's guns. Sharp-shooting militiamen, using Kentucky long rifles—accurate at hundreds of yards—took their toll, but the British ranks were broken by the Louisiana artillerymen. Packenham himself was shot several times and died on the field, alongside more than 2,000 British regulars, dramatically contrasting the 21 Americans killed. Adding insult to injury (or death in this case), the deceased Packenham suffered the indignity of having his body stuffed into a cask of rum for preservation en route to England.

Jackson emerged a hero, Madison pardoned pirate Jean Laffite as thanks for his contributions, and the Federalists looked like fools for their untimely opposition. It was a bloody affair, but not, as many historians suggest, a useless one—a "needless encounter in a needless war," the refrain goes. One conclusion was inescapable after the war: the Americans were rapidly becoming the equals of any power in Europe.

A Nation Whose Spirit Was Everywhere

"Notwithstanding a thousand blunders," John Adams wrote candidly (and jubilantly) to Jefferson in 1814, President James Madison had "acquired more glory and established more Union than all his three predecessors, Washington, Adams, Jefferson, put together."[121] Perhaps Adams meant to rub salt in Jefferson's wounds, but by any measure, the changes for America over a period of just a few months were, indeed, stunning.

America's execution of the war had extracted a begrudging respect from Britain. In the future, Britain and all of Europe would resort to negotiation, not war, in disputing America; they had learned to fear and respect this new member in the family of nations. Americans' subsequent reference to the War of 1812 as the Second War for Independence was well founded.

On the home front, the war produced important military and political changes, especially in the Ohio Valley, where the hostile Indian tribes were utterly defeated. But so too were the Creek of Alabama, Mississippi, and Florida. The War of 1812 set the stage for the first Seminole War (1818), Black Hawk's War (1832), and the federal Indian Removal that would, in a mere twenty-five years, exile most remaining Cherokee, Choctaw, Creek, Seminole, and Chickasaw Indians to the Indian Territory in Oklahoma. In a sense, the War of 1812 was not so much a victory over England as over the Indians, smashing the power forever of all tribes east of the Mississippi.

Politically, the Federalist Party died, its last stalwarts slinking into the Republican opposition and forming a viable new National Republican caucus. They learned to practice the democratic politics the Jeffersonians had perfected—mingle with the crowds (and buy rounds of liquor), host campaign barbecues and fish fries, shake hands, and, perhaps, even kiss a few babies. In this way these nationalists were able to continue to expound Hamilton's program of tariffs, banks, and subsidized industrialism, but do so in a new democratic rhetoric that appealed to the common man, soon seen in the programs championed by Henry Clay.[122] Within the Republican Party, National Republicans continued to battle Old Republicans over the legacy of the American Revolution. Within a generation, these National Republicans would form the Whig Party. Jefferson's ideologically pure Old ("democratic") Republicans died, yielding to a newer, more aggressive political machine under the Jacksonians.

Tragically, the increasingly southern bent of the Old Republicans meant that the radical individualism, decentralism, and states' rights tenets of Jeffersonianism would, under the southern Democrats, be perverted. Jefferson's libertarian ideals—the ideals of the American Revolution—would, incongruously, be used to defend the enslavement of four million human beings.

CHAPTER SIX

The First Era of Big Central Government, 1815–36

Watershed Years

Northeastern Americans awoke one morning in 1816 to find a twenty-inch snowfall throughout their region, with some flakes reported as being two inches across. This might not seem unusual except that it was June sixth, and snow continued throughout July and August in what one diarist called "the most gloomy and extraordinary weather ever seen."[1] Little did he know that on the other side of the world, the eruption of Mount Tambora in Java had shot clouds of dust into the stratosphere, creating a temporary global cooling that left Kansas farmers to deal with a rash of ruined crops and a disorienting haze to match the economic malaise gripping the nation. Within just twenty years, the United States would suffer another depression blamed on the financial repercussions of Andrew Jackson's war on the Bank of the United States. Journalists of the day and generations of historians since—until well into the 1960s—agreed that government policies had brought on the recession. In fact, the root cause was outside our borders, in the case of the Panic of 1837, in Mexico, where the silver mines dried up.

In each case Americans experienced the effects at home of relatively normal and natural events (a volcano and the depletion of a silver vein) that had their origins abroad. And in each case, despite the desire of many citizens to quietly live isolated within the nation's 1815 boundaries, the explosion of Mount Tambora and the silver depletion of Mexican mines revealed how integrated the young United States already was with the natural, financial, and political life of the entire world.

Having stood toe to toe with Britain for the second time in forty years, in the War of 1812, the young Republic had indeed attained a new position in world affairs and in international influence. Although hardly a dominant national state capable of forcing the Europeans to rethink most of their balance-of-power principles, the United States nevertheless had proven its mettle through a victory over the Barbary pirates, careful diplomacy with Napoleon's France, and a faltering but eventually successful war with England.

At home the nation entered its most important era since the early constitutional period. James Madison, successor to Jefferson, and John Adams's own son, John Quincy Adams, both referred to themselves as republicans. Consensus blended former foes into a single-party rule that yielded the Era of Good Feelings, a term first used by a Boston newspaper in 1817.

In a natural two-party system, such unanimity is not healthy and, at any rate, it began to mask a more substantial transformation occurring beneath the tranquil surface of uniparty politics. Change occurred at almost every level. States individually started to reduce, or waive entirely, property requirements to vote. New utopian movements and religious revivals sprang up to fill Americans with a new spiritual purpose. The issue of slavery, which so many of the Founders hoped would simply go away, thrust itself into daily life with an even greater malignant presence. How the generation who came to power during the Age of Jackson, as it is called, dealt with these issues has forever affected all Americans: to this day, we still maintain (and often struggle with reforming) the two-party political system Jacksonians established to defuse the explosive slavery issue. We also continue to have daily events explained by—and shaped by—a free journalistic elite that was born during the Jacksonian era. And modern Americans frequently revert to class demagoguery that characterized debates about the economic issues of the day, especially the second Bank of the United States.

Time Line

1815: Treaty of Ghent ends War of 1812

1816: James Monroe elected president

1818: Andrew Jackson seizes Florida from Spain and the Seminoles

1819: Adams-Onis Treaty

1819: *McCulloch v. Maryland*

1819–22: Missouri Compromises

1823: Monroe Doctrine; American Fur Company establishes Fort Union on Missouri River

1824: John Quincy Adams defeats Jackson in controversial election

1828: Tariff of Abominations; Jackson defeats Adams

1831: William Lloyd Garrison publishes first issue of *The Liberator*

1832: Nullification Crisis; *Worster v. Georgia*

1836: Texas Independence; Martin Van Buren elected president

1837: Panic of 1837

The Second Bank of the United States

Contrary to the notion that war is good for business, the War of 1812 disrupted markets, threw the infant banking system into confusion, and interrupted a steady pattern of growth. Trade was restored to Britain and Canada quickly and, after Waterloo, markets to France opened as well. But the debts incurred by the war made hash of the Jeffersonians' strict fiscal policies, sending the national debt from $45 million in 1812 to $127 million in 1815, despite the imposition of new taxes.[2] Since the nation borrowed most of that money, through short-term notes from private banks, and since Congress had refused to recharter the Bank of the United States in 1811, both the number of banks and the amount of money they issued soared. Banking practices of the day differed so sharply from modern commercial banking that it bears briefly examining the basics of finance as practiced in the early 1800s. First, at the time, *any* state-chartered bank could print money (notes) as long as the notes were backed by gold or silver specie in its vault. During the War of 1812, most state-chartered banks outside New England suspended specie payments, even though they continued to operate and print notes without the discipline of gold backing.

Second, state legislatures used the chartering process to exert some measure of discipline on the banks (a number of private banks operated outside the charter process, but they did not print notes). Nevertheless, it was the market, through the specie reserve system, that really regulated the banks' inclination to print excessive numbers of notes. Most banks in normal times tended to keep a reserve of 5 to 20 percent specie in their vaults to deal with runs or panics. Pressures of war, however, had allowed the banks to suspend and then continue to print notes, generating inflation.

Rather than wait for the private banking system to sort things out—and with some support from the financiers themselves, who wanted a solution sooner rather than later—in 1816 Congress chartered a new national bank, the second Bank of the United States (BUS). Like its predecessor, the second BUS had several advantages over state-chartered private banks, most notably its authority to open branches in any state it chose. Its $35 million capitalization dwarfed that of any state-chartered private bank, but more important, its designation as the depository of federal funds gave the BUS a deposit base several times greater than its next largest competitor. "Special privilege" became an oft-repeated criticism of the BUS, especially the uncertain nature of who, exactly, enjoyed that special privilege. More than a few Americans of a conspiratorial bent suspected that foreigners, especially British investors, secretly controlled the bank. Combined with the bank's substantial influence and pervasive presence throughout the nation, special privilege made the BUS an easy target for politicians, who immediately took aim at the institution when any serious economic dislocation occurred.

It should be restated that the BUS carried strong overtones of Hamilton's Federalists, whose program, while dormant, was quietly transforming into the American system of the National Republicans (soon-to-be Whigs). Immediately after the War of 1812, the Federalist political identification with the BUS faded somewhat, even though important backers, such as Stephen Girard and Albert Gallatin, remained prominent. More important were the economic fluctuations the bank dealt with as it attempted to rein in the inflation that had followed the Treaty of Ghent. Calling in many of its outstanding loans, the BUS contracted the money supply, producing lower prices. That was both good news and bad news. Obviously, consumers with money thrived as prices for finished goods fell. At the level of the common man, in a still largely agrarian republic, falling farm prices and a widespread difficulty in obtaining new loans for agriculture or business caused no small degree of economic dislocation. Cotton prices crashed in January 1819, falling by half when British buyers started to import Indian cotton. Land prices followed. Although the BUS had only limited influence in all this, its size made it a predictable target. BUS president William Jones shouldered the blame for this panic, as depressions were called at the time. Bank directors replaced Jones with South Carolinian Langdon Cheves. To the directors' horror, Cheves continued Jones's policy of credit contraction, which left the bank with substantial lands taken as mortgage foreclosures, and added to complaints that the BUS existed for a privileged elite.

By that time, the depression had spread to the industrial sector. Philadelphia mills that employed more than 2,300 in 1816 retained only 149 in 1819, and John Quincy Adams warned that the collapse posed a "crisis which will shake the Union to its center."[3] Cheves was not intimidated, however, by the necessity to purge the once-inflated bank paper or dump worthless land. Despite recriminations from Congress and complaints from monetary experts like William Gouge, who moaned that "the Bank was saved but the people were ruined," Cheves kept the BUS open while continuing a tight money policy.[4] The economy revived before long, though its recovery was linked more to the influx of Mexican silver than to any central bank policies undertaken by Cheves. The episode convinced many Americans, however, that the bank wielded inordinate powers—for good or evil.

Marshall and Markets

In the meantime, the BUS was at the center of one of the more important cases in American law, *McCulloch v. Maryland.* The state of Maryland sought to levy a tax on the Baltimore branch of the BUS, which the cashier of the bank, James McCulloch, refused to pay, forcing a test of federal power. Two constitutional issues came before the Court. First, did states have the power to tax federal institutions within their borders? Second, since the BUS was not explicitly mentioned in the Constitution, was it even legal in the first place? Chief Justice Marshall, famous for his perception that "the power to tax involves the power to destroy," led a unanimous Court in upholding the 1790s decision that no state could tax federal property. Marshall's ruling was a reasonable and critical position on the primacy of the national government in a federal system.

When it came to the legality of the BUS, Marshall turned to Article I, Section 8, of the Constitution, which Hamilton had used to justify the first BUS: Congress has the power "to make all laws which shall be necessary and proper for carrying into execution the foregoing powers." Referred to as the "necessary and proper" clause, Section 8 essentially allowed Congress to do anything that either the United States Supreme Court by a ruling or the people through an amendment to the Constitution itself did not prohibit. In future generations that would include such questionable initiatives as Social Security, welfare, funding for the arts and humanities, establishing scientific and medical agencies, and creating the Departments of Energy, Education, and Commerce. Still, the essential power always rested with the people—regardless of Court decisions—because, as the old maxim goes, "The people generally get what they want." If the public ever grew fearful or dissatisfied with any governmental agency, the voters could abolish it quickly through either the ballot box or an amendment process. Marshall well knew that every undertaking of the federal government could not be subject to specific constitutional scrutiny, a point reflected by his ruling in favor of the constitutionality of the BUS.[5] Marshall then turned the states' rights arguments against the states themselves in 1821 with *Cohens v. Virginia*, wherein the Supreme Court, citing New Hampshire courts' proclivity for judicial review of that state's legislature, affirmed that the United States Supreme Court had judicial review authority over the states' courts as well.

McCulloch came the same year as the *Dartmouth College* decision and coincided with another ruling, *Sturgis v. Crowninshield*, in which Marshall's Court upheld the Constitution's provisions on contracts. That Marshall sided with greater centralized federal power is undeniable, but the conditions were such that in these cases the struggles were largely between private property and contract rights against government authority of any type. In that sense, Marshall stood with private property. In the *Dartmouth College* case, the state of New Hampshire had attempted to void the charter of Dartmouth College, which had been founded in 1769 by King George III, to make it a public school. Dartmouth employed the renowned orator and statesman Daniel Webster—and Dartmouth alumnus—to argue its case. Marshall's Court ruled unanimously that a contract was a contract, regardless of the circumstances of its origination (save duress) and that New Hampshire was legally bound to observe the charter. The Marshall Court's unanimous decision reinforced the 1810 *Fletcher v. Peck* ruling in which the Court upheld a state legislature's grant of land as a valid contract, even though a subsequent legislature repealed it.

Taken with *Peck,* the *Dartmouth* decision established without question the primacy of law and contractual arrangements in a free society. Later supplemented by other decisions that maintained a competitive marketplace, such as *Gibbons v. Ogden* (1824) and *Charles River Bridge v. Warren Bridge* (1837, under Chief Justice Roger Taney), the Supreme Court continually reaffirmed the importance of property rights in a free society. At first glance, *Gibbons v. Ogden* related only to federal authority over waterways, but in fact the Court in broad terms established that, barring federal prohibitions, interstate trade was open to all competitors. And in the *Charles River Bridge* case, the Court again upheld the principle of competition, stating that the charter did not imply a monopoly, and that a monopoly could exist only if expressly granted by a state.

Thus, as the Marshall era came to a close, the Supreme Court had chipped away at some state powers, but Marshall himself enthusiastically admitted that when it came to the federal government, "the powers of the government are limited, and . . . its limits are not to be transcended." To those who complained about Marshall's aggrandizement of power at the federal level, the chief justice in clear Hamiltonian tones stated guidelines: "Let the end be legitimate, let it be within the scope of the Constitution, and all means, which are appropriate, which are plainly adapted to that end, which are not prohibited, but consist with the *letter and spirit of the Constitution,* are constitutional" [emphasis ours].[6] It is equally true, though, that Marshall—later aided and abetted by Taney— enhanced the broader and more important mechanisms of the free market over state government, and in the process solidified the critical premise of "sanctity of contract."[7] Without John Marshall, whom John Taylor, one of his severest critics, denigrated as part of a "subtle corps of miners and sappers [working] to under- mine the foundations of our confederated fabric," that fabric would have unrav- eled in a frenzy of property rights abridgments at the state level.[8]

The Virginia Dynasty, Continued

In December 1816, James Monroe of Virginia perpetuated the dominance of Virginians in the office of the presidency, defeating the Federalist, Rufus King of New York, in a landslide (183 to 34 votes in the electoral college). Virginia's con- tinued grip on the nation's highest office had in fact been ensured earlier when Monroe bested William H. Crawford of Georgia in a narrow vote for the Republi- can nomination. That meant that of America's first five presidents, all had come from Virginia except Adams. Following the Burr fiasco, the Twelfth Amendment to the Constitution eliminated the possibility that a president and vice president could come from different parties, meaning that the Republicans' choice for vice president, Daniel D. Tompkins of New York, helped initiate a common practice of adding sectional balance to a ticket.

Monroe (born 1758) had attended William and Mary College before leaving to serve in the Continental Army under Washington. He saw action at many of the Revolution's famous battles, including White Plains, Trenton (where he was wounded), Germantown, Brandywine, and Monmouth, attaining the rank of colonel. A deliberate, even slow, thinker, Monroe gathered ideas and advice from associates and subordinates before proceeding, a trait that kept him from a field command in the Revolution. He therefore resigned his commission to study the law under Jefferson and then won a seat in the Virginia House of Delegates (1782), the Continental Congress (1783–86), and the Virginia state convention (1788). Working under Jefferson led to a friendship between the two, and drew Monroe somewhat naturally into the Sage's antifederal views. Consequently, he was not a delegate at the Constitutional Convention, yet when Virginia needed a U.S. senator in 1790, Monroe won the seat. Senator Monroe proved an able lieu- tenant to Secretary of State Jefferson and clashed repeatedly with Alexander Hamilton and President Washington himself.

A natural successor to Jefferson as the minister to France (1794), Monroe failed to assuage French concerns over the pro-British treaty negotiated by John Jay, and thus was recalled after two years, although he returned as an envoy extraordinaire in 1802. During the gap in his years abroad, Monroe became governor of Virginia. He joined Robert Livingston during the negotiations over Louisiana, then made ministerial journeys to England and Spain. None of these overtures accomplished their intended purposes, indeed failing miserably to placate the French over Jay's Treaty, settle the boundary dispute with Spain, or obtain a commercial treaty with England. In the case of the British negotiations conducted with special envoy William Pinkney, Monroe was convinced he had obtained reasonable terms easing trade restrictions. Jefferson, however, dismissed the effort as unworthy of submission to the Senate—an act by Monroe's mentor that stung him deeply. Whether a better diplomat might have succeeded, of course, is speculation. By the time Monroe had become Madison's secretary of state in 1811, he had as much experience as any living American with diplomatic issues and much experience at failing at such undertakings. It is ironic, then, that Monroe is best remembered for a foreign policy success, the Monroe Doctrine.

Lacking the fiery oratorical skills of his fellow Virginian Patrick Henry, the unceasing questioning mind of Jefferson, or the wit and intellect of Franklin, Monroe nonetheless possessed important qualities. He had a reputation for the highest integrity (Jefferson once said that if Monroe's soul was turned inside out there would not be a spot on it), and at the same time the man refused to bear a grudge. It was this genial personality and willingness to work with others that inspired him to take a goodwill tour of the Northeast in 1816, initiating the Era of Good Feelings. Old-fashioned in his dress (he was the last president to wear his hair in a queue), Monroe in many ways was a throwback to the pre-Revolutionary period. Above all, he valued productivity and practicality, which accounted for his policies and his toleration—even embrace—of those who held sharply different views but with whom he thought compromise possible. Unlike either Ronald Reagan or Dwight Eisenhower—two twentieth-century advocates of limited or small government—Monroe favored a weak executive, seeing the power as emanating from the people through the legislature.

Monroe's past failures at diplomacy notwithstanding, he quickly secured an arrangement with Great Britain limiting warships on the Great Lakes.[9] This he followed by an equally rapid settlement of the U.S.–Canadian boundary dispute. Then came Andrew Jackson's campaigns against Indian incursions in Florida, which led to the Adams-Onis Treaty in 1819, all of which gave Monroe the international capital to issue the famous doctrine that bore his name.

It also helped that Monroe's own sense of security led him to name some of the most powerful and politically contentious men in the nation to his cabinet: John C. Calhoun of South Carolina as secretary of war; his rival William H. Crawford as secretary of the treasury; and John Quincy Adams as secretary of state. Only a man unintimidated by powerful personalities would tolerate such characters, let alone enlist them. Ultimately, they jointly failed to live up to their potential, although individually Adams and Calhoun achieved reputations apart from the Monroe administration. Inside the cabinet they bickered, eventually turning the atmosphere poisonous.

Monroe acceded to a legislative program of internal improvements—a name given to federally funded harbor and river clearing efforts, road building, and otherwise upgrading infrastructure, to use the twenty-first-century buzzword. Although he disapproved of government activism, he thought it proper to facilitate a climate of cooperation that funded construction of coastal forts, which fell perfectly within the constitutional mandates of national defense. In other areas, however, Monroe's strict constructionist side would not approve, without a constitutional amendment, appropriations for internal improvements that did not relate directly to national defense, maintaining that the Constitution had not given the government the authority to spend money for such programs.

In the short term, minor government-funded construction programs paled beside the phenomenal economic explosion about to envelop the country. Despite the lingering economic dislocations of the War of 1812, already one could sense a restless, growing, entrepreneurial nation replete with its share of vigor, vice, and virtue. This stirring occurred largely outside of Monroe's influence, although he certainly kept the government out of the way of growth. During the Madison-Monroe years, the United States gained ground on the British in key industries, so much so that by 1840 the Industrial Revolution that had started in England had not only reached American shores, but had accelerated so fast that Yankee shippers, iron merchants, publishers, and textile manufacturers either equaled or exceeded their John Bull competitors in nearly all categories.

The Restless Spirit

From the outset, America had been a nation of entrepreneurs, a country populated by restless souls. No sooner had settlers arrived along the port cities, than they spread inland, and after they had constructed the first inland forts, trappers and explorers pressed farther into the forests and mountains. The restless spirit and the dynamic entrepreneurship fed off each other, the former producing a constant itch to improve and invent, the latter demanding better ways of meeting people's needs, of organizing better systems of distribution and supply, and of adding to the yearning for still more, and improved, products.

In a society where most people still worked the land, this incessant activity worked itself out in the relationship with the land—cutting, clearing, building, irrigating, herding, hunting, lighting (and fighting) fires, and populating. Unlike Europeans, however, Americans benefited from a constantly expanding supply of property they could possess and occupy. Unlike Europeans, Americans often never saw themselves as permanently fixed to a location. Alexis de Tocqueville, the observant French visitor, remarked,

An American will build a house in which to pass his old age and sell it before the roof is on. . . . He will plant a garden and rent it just as the trees are coming into bearing; he will clear a field and leave others to reap the harvest; he will take up a profession and leave it, settle in one place and soon go off elsewhere with his changing desires. If his private business allows him a moment's relaxation, he will plunge at once into the whirlpool of politics.[10]

To some degree, money (or the lack of it) dictated constant churning. The same desire to experience material abundance drove men and women to perpetually invent and design, innovate and imagine. The motivations for moving, though, were as diverse as the country itself. For every Daniel Boone or Davy Crockett who constantly relocated out of land fever, there was a Gail Borden, a New York farm boy who wound up in Galveston, Texas, where he invented the terrapin wagon, a completely amphibious vehicle, before returning to New York to invent his famous condensed-milk process.[11] In the same vein, Vermonter John Deere, who moved his farm-implement business steadily westward, developing the finest farm implements in the world, epitomized the restless frontier spirit observed by Tocqueville.

This restless generation produced a group of entrepreneurs unparalleled in American history, including Andrew Carnegie (born 1835), J. P. Morgan (1837), John D. Rockefeller (1839), and Levi Strauss (1829). Most came from lower- to middle-class backgrounds: Carnegie arrived in America virtually penniless, and Strauss worked his way up with a small mercantile store. They typified what a Cincinnati newspaper stated of this generation: "There is not one who does not desire, even confidently expect, to become rich."[12]

Yet the lure of the land had its own dark side, turning otherwise honorable men into scalawags and forgers. Jim Bowie, who would die at the Alamo with Davy Crockett in 1836, surpassed everyone with his ingenuity in developing fraudulent land grants. (One writer noted that whereas Bowie was "hardly alone in forging grants . . . he worked on an almost industrial scale compared to others.")[13] Through a labyrinth of forged documents, Bowie managed to make himself one of the largest landowners in Louisiana—garnering a total holding of 45,700 acres. An official smelled the rat, but Bowie managed to extract all the suspicious documents before they landed him in jail.

Land attracted small farmers to Indiana, then Illinois, then on to Minnesota and Wisconsin. Assuming that the minimal amount of land for self-sufficiency was forty to fifty acres, it took only a few generations before a father would not bequeath to his son enough land to make a living, forcing countless American young men and their families westward. Southern legal traditions, with vestigial primogeniture, or the custom of bequeathing the entire estate to the eldest son, resulted in fewer landowners—and a smaller population—but much larger estates. Men like Bowie thus dealt not only in land, but also in slaves needed to run the plantations. Whether it was the Yazoo in Mississippi or the forested sections of Michigan, land hunger drew Americans steadily westward.

Abundant land—and scarce labor—meant that even in agriculture, farmer-businessmen substituted new technology for labor with every opportunity. Handmade hoes, shovels, rakes, and the like, soon gave way to James Wood's metal plow, whose interchangeable parts made for easy repair. This, and other designs, were mass-produced by entrepreneurs like Charles Lane of Chicago, so that by the 1830s metal plows were commonplace. Pittsburgh had "two factories . . . making 34,000 metal plows a year even in the 1830s," and by 1845, Massachusetts had seventy-three plow-manufacturing firms turning out more than 60,000 farm implements a year.[14] No more important, but certainly more celebrated, the famous McCormick reaper, perfected by Cyrus McCormick, opened up the vast prairies to "agribusiness." McCormick began on the East Coast, but relocated to Chicago to be closer to the land boom. After fashioning his first reaper in 1834, he pumped up production until his factory churned out 4,000 reapers annually. In an 1855 exposition in Paris, McCormick stunned Europeans by harvesting an acre of oats in twenty-one minutes, or one third of the time taken by Continental machines.[15]

If land provided the allure for most of those who moved to the Mississippi and beyond, a growing, but important, substrata of mechanics, artisans, inventors, salesmen, and merchants soon followed, adapting their businesses to the new frontier demands.

No one captured the restless, inventive spirit better than Eli Whitney. After working on his father's farm in Connecticut, Whitney enrolled in and graduated from Yale. There he met Phineas Miller, who managed some South Carolina properties for Catherine Greene, and Miller invited the young Whitney to take a position as a tutor to the Greene children on a plantation. His cotton gin—in retrospect a remarkably simple device—shook the world, causing an explosion in textile production.

In 1810, 119 pounds of cotton per day could be cleaned, and by 1860 that number had risen to 759 per day.[16] Mrs. Greene soon came to say of Whitney, "He can make anything." Indeed he could. Whitney soon tried his hand at musket production, using a largely unskilled workforce. What emerged was the American system of manufacturing, which served as the basis for a powerful system.[17]

Advances in mass production, steam power, and management techniques coalesced in the textile mills founded in New England by Samuel Slater, a British emigrant. Slater built a small mill in Rhode Island with the support of Moses Brown, a Providence candle manufacturer, first using water wheels, then replacing water with steam power. Within twenty years, Slater and his close circle of associates had 9,500 spindles and controlled nearly half of all American spinning mills—Brown even wrote to his children that the mill founders had "cotton mill fever."[18] Francis Cabot Lowell exceeded even Slater's achievements in texile production, employing young girls who lived on site. Lowell further advanced the organizational gains made by Whitney and Slater.[19]

Gains in manufacturing resulted in part from widespread application of steam power. Steam revolutionized transportation, with Robert Fulton's *Clermont* demonstrating steam propulsion on water in 1807.

Within a decade, Cornelius Vanderbilt began using steam technology to cut costs in the New York–New Jersey ferry traffic, and steam power started to find its way to inland waterways. Entrepreneurs had already started to shift the focus of water travel in the interior from natural rivers to man-made canals. The period from 1817 to 1844 has been referred to as the canal era, in which some 4,000 miles of canals were constructed at a cost of $200 million. States collaborated with private interests in many of these projects, usually by guaranteeing state bond issues in case of default. But some of the earliest, and best, were built by private businesses, such as the Middlesex Canal in Massachusetts and the Santee and Cooper Canal in South Carolina. The most famous, the Erie Canal, linked the Hudson River and Lake Erie and opened up the upstate New York markets to the coast. Unlike some of the other early privately financed canals, the Erie was built at state expense over an eight-year period, and its completion was so anticipated that the state collected an advance $1 million in tolls before the canal was even opened.[20] It was a massive engineering feat: the canal was 40 feet wide, 4 feet deep, and 363 miles long—all bordered by towpaths to allow draft animals to pull barges and flatboats; 86 locks were used to raise and lower boats 565 feet. When the Erie opened in 1825, it earned 8 percent on its $9 million from the 3,000 boats traversing the canal. After the board of commissioners approved enlarging the canal in 1850, it reached its peak tonnage in 1880.[21]

Steam power soon replaced animal power on all the nation's waterways. Well before steam power was common, however, canals had driven down the costs of shipping from twenty cents per ton mile to a tenth of that amount, and even a "noted financial failure like the Ohio Canal yielded a respectable 10 percent social rate of return."[22] Steam vessels on the Great Lakes, where ships occasionally exceeded 1,000 tons, and in the case of the *City of Buffalo,* displaced a whopping 2,200 tons, also played an important role. By midcentury, "The tonnage on the Mississippi River and on the Great Lakes exceeded that of all shipping from New York City by over 200 percent."[23] The canal era provided the first model of state government support of large-scale enterprise (through bond guarantees), often with disastrous results. In the Panic of 1837, many states were pushed to the brink of bankruptcy by their canal-bond obligations.

Steam also reduced shipping costs for oceanic travel, where, again, Cornelius Vanderbilt emerged as a key player. Facing a competitor who received sizable federal mail subsidies, Vanderbilt nevertheless drove down his own transatlantic costs to the point where he consistently outperformed his government-supported opponent.[24]

Having won on the Hudson, then on the Atlantic, Vanderbilt next struck on the Pacific Coast, breaking into the subsidized packet-steamer trade. Vanderbilt's competition received $500,000 in federal subsidies and charged a staggering

$600 per passenger ticket for a New York to California trip, via Panama, where the passengers had to disembark and travel overland to board another vessel. After constructing his own route through Nicaragua, rather than Panama, Vanderbilt chopped passenger prices to $400 and offered to carry the mail free! Within a year, thanks to the presence of Vanderbilt, fares dropped to $150, then $100. As occurred in the Hudson competition, the commodore's competitors finally bought his routes, but even then they found they could never return to the high ticket prices they had charged before he drove costs down. When Vanderbilt left the packet-steamer business, a ticket cost just half what could be fleeced from passengers in the pre-Vanderbilt era.[25]

Steam technology also provided the basis for another booming American industry when Phillip Thomas led a group of Baltimore businessmen to found the Baltimore and Ohio (B&O) Railroad in 1828. Two years later, the South Carolina Canal and Railroad Company began a steam locomotive train service westward from Charleston, with its locomotive *Best Friend of Charleston* being the first constructed for sale in the United States. The king of American locomotive building was Matthias Baldwin, who made his first locomotive in 1832 and founded the Baldwin Engine and Locomotive works. His firm turned out more than fifteen hundred locomotives during his lifetime, including many for export.

Within a few years, contemporaries were referring to railroad building as a fever, a frenzy, and a mania. There were enormous positive social consequences of better transportation. By linking Orange County, New York, the leading dairy county, to New York City, the railroad contributed to the reduction of milk-borne diseases like cholera by supplying fresh milk.[26]

By 1840 most states had railroads, although the Atlantic seaboard states had more than 60 percent of total rail mileage. Like the canals, many railroads received state backing. Some were constructed by individual entrepreneurs. But the high capital demands of the railroads, combined with the public's desire to link up every burg by rail, led to states taking a growing role in the financing of American railroads.[27] Railroads' size and scope of operations required huge amounts of capital compared to textile mills or iron works. This dynamic forced them to adopt a new structure in which the multiple stockholder owners selected a professional manager to run the firm. By the 1840s, banks and railroads were inexorably linked, not only through the generation of capital, but also through the new layer of professional managers (many of them put in place by the banks that owned the majority stock positions). As transportation improved, communications networks also proliferated. Banks could evaluate the quality of private bank note issues through *Dillistin's Bank Note Reporter*, which was widely circulated. The Cincinnati-based Bradstreet Company provided similar evaluation of businesses themselves. Investor knowledge benefited from the expansion of the U.S. Post Office, which had over 18,000 branches by 1850—one for every 1,300 people. Congress had a direct stake in the Post Office in that congressional apportionment was based on population, and since constituents clamored for new routes, there was a built-in bias in favor of expanding the postal network. Most routes did not even bear more than 1 percent of their cost, but that was irrelevant, given the political gains they represented. In addition to their value in apportionment, the postal branches offered legislators a free election tool. Congressmen shipped speeches and other election materials to constituents free, thanks to the franking privileges. Partisan concerns also linked post office branches and the party-controlled newspapers by reducing the cost of distribution through the mails. From 1800 to 1840, the number of newspapers transmitted through the mails rose from 2 million to almost 140 million at far cheaper rates than other printed matter. Postal historian Richard John estimated that if the newspapers had paid the same rate as other mails, the transmission costs would have been 700 times higher.[28]

The new party system, by 1840, had thus compromised the independence of the mails and a large part of the print media, with no small consequences. Among other defects, the subsidies created incentives to read newspapers rather than books. This democratization of the news produced a population of people who thought they knew a great deal about current events, but who lacked the theoretical grounding in history, philosophy, or politics to properly ground their opinions. As the number of U.S. Post Office branches increased, the Post Office itself came to wield considerable clout, and the position of postmaster became a political plum. The postmaster general alone controlled more than 8,700 jobs, more than three fourths of the federal civilian workforce—larger even than the army. Patronage explained the ability of companies receiving federal subsidies to repel challenges from the private sector, allowing the subsidized postal companies to defeat several private expresses in the 1830s. The remarkable thing about the competition to the subsidized mails was not that it lasted so long (and did not resurface until Fred Smith founded Federal Express in 1971), but that it even appeared in the first place.

Setting the Table for Growth

At the end of the War of 1812 America emerged in a strong military and diplomatic position. The end of the Franco-British struggle not only quickened an alliance between the two European powerhouses, but also, inevitably, drew the United States into their orbit (and, a century later, them into ours). American involvement in two world wars fought primarily in Europe and a third cold war was based on the premise that the three nations shared fundamental assumptions about human rights and civic responsibilities that tied them together more closely than any other sets of allies in the world. Getting to that point, however, would not have been possible without consistently solid diplomacy and sensible restraint at critical times, as in the case of Florida, which remained an important pocket of foreign occupation in the map of the United States east of the Mississippi. In 1818, Spain held onto Florida by a slender thread, for the once mighty Spanish empire was in complete disarray. Spain's economic woes and corrupt imperial bureaucracy encouraged revolutionaries in Argentina, Columbia, and Mexico to follow the American example and overthrow their European masters. Within five years Spain lost nearly half of its holdings in the western hemisphere.

From the point of view of the United States, Florida was ripe for the plucking. President Monroe and his secretary of state John Quincy Adams understandably wanted to avoid overtly seizing Florida from Spain, a nation with which they were at peace. Adams opened negotiations with the Spanish minister Luis de Onis. Before they could arrive at a settlement, General Andrew Jackson seized Florida for the United States. But Jackson followed a route to Pensacola that is more complex and troublesome for historians to trace today than it was for Jackson and his men to march through it in 1818.

Jackson's capture of Florida began when Monroe sent him south to attack Seminole Indians, allies of the reviled Creeks he had defeated at Horseshoe Bend in 1814. Some Seminole used northern Florida's panhandle region as a base to raid American planters and harbor escaped slaves. Alabamians and Georgians demanded government action. On December 26, 1817, the secretary of war John C. Calhoun ordered Jackson to "adopt the necessary measures" to neutralize the Seminoles, but did not specify whether he was to cross the international boundary in his pursuit. In a letter to Monroe, Jackson wrote that he would gladly defeat the Seminoles *and* capture Spanish Florida if it was "signified to me through any channel . . . that the possession of the Floridas would be desirable to the United States." Jackson later claimed he received the go-ahead, a point the administration staunchly denied.[29] The general went so far as to promise that he would "ensure you Cuba in a few days" if Monroe would supply him with a frigate, an offer the president wisely refused. (Later, when questioned about his unwillingness to rein in the expansionist Jackson, Monroe pleaded ill health.)

Whoever was telling the truth, it mattered little to the Indians and Spaniards who soon felt the wrath of the hero of New Orleans. Between April first and May twenty-eighth, Andrew Jackson's military accomplishments were nothing short of spectacular (indeed, some deemed them outrageous). He invaded Florida and defeated the Seminole raiders, capturing their chiefs along with two English citizens, Alexander Arbuthnot and Robert Ambrister, who had the great misfortune of being with the Indians at the time. Convinced the Englishmen were responsible for fomenting Indian attacks, Jackson court-martialed and hanged both men. By mid-May, he had moved on Fort Pensacola, which surrendered to him on May 28, 1818, making Florida part of the United States by right of conquest, despite the illegality of Jackson's invasion—all carried out without exposure to journalists. Although Monroe and Adams later disclaimed Jackson's actions, they did not punish him, nor did they return the huge prize of his warfare—nor did Congress censure him for usurping its constitutional war power. Jackson was able to wildly supercede his authority largely because of the absence of an omnipresent media, but the United States gained substantially from the general's actions.

Illegal as Jackson's exploits were, the fact was that Spain could not patrol its own borders. The Seminole posed a "clear and present danger," and the campaign was not unlike that launched by General John Pershing in 1916, with the approval of Woodrow Wilson and Congress, to invade Mexico for the purpose of capturing the bandit Pancho Villa. Jackson set the stage for Adams to formalize the victory in a momentous diplomatic agreement. The Adams-Onis Treaty of 1819 settled the Florida question and also addressed three other matters crucial to America's westward advance across the continent. First, the United States paid Spain $5 million and gained all of Florida, which was formally conveyed in July 1821. In addition, Adams agreed that Spanish Texas was not part of the Louisiana Purchase as some American expansionists had erroneously claimed. (Negotiators had formalized the hazy 1803 Louisiana Purchase boundary line all the way to the Canadian border.) Finally, Spain relinquished all claims to the Pacific Northwest—leaving the Indians, Russians, and British with the United States as the remaining claimants.

From Santa Fe to the Montana Country

In 1820, Monroe dispatched an army expedition to map and explore the Adams-Onis treaty line. Major Stephen H. Long keelboated up the Missouri and Platte rivers in search of (but never finding) the mouth of the Red River and a pass through the Rocky Mountains. Labeling the central Great Plains a "Great American Desert," Long helped to perpetuate a fear of crossing, much less settling, what is now the American heartland. He also helped to foster a belief that this remote and bleak land was so worthless that it was suitable only for a permanent Indian frontier—a home for relocated eastern Indian tribes.

Concurrent with Long's expedition, however, a trade route opened that would ultimately encourage Americanization of the Great Plains. Following the Mexican Revolution of 1820, the Santa Fe Trail opened, bringing American traders to the once forbidden lands of New Mexico. Santa Fe, in the mountains of northernmost Mexico, was closer to St. Louis than it was to Mexico City, a fact that Missouri merchants were quick to act upon. Santa Fe traders brought steamboat cargoes of goods from St. Louis up the Missouri to Independence (founded officially in 1827). There they outfitted huge two-ton Conestoga wagons (hitched to teams of ten to twelve oxen), gathered supplies, and listened to the latest reports from other travelers. They headed out with the green grass of May and, lacking federal troop escorts, traveled together in wagon trains to fend off Kiowa and Comanche Indians. The teamsters carried American cloth, cutlery, and hardware and returned with much coveted Mexican silver, fur, and mules.[30]

The Santa Fe trade lasted until 1844, the eve of the Mexican-American War, providing teamsters practice that perfected Plains wagoneering techniques, and their constant presence in the West chipped away at the great American desert myth. Moreoever, they established the Missouri River towns that would soon serve the Oregon Trail immigrant wagon trains.

At the same time, Rocky Mountain fur traders—the "Mountain Men"— headed up the Missouri to Montana, Wyoming, and Colorado country. British and

American fur companies, such as the Northwest, American, and Hudson's Bay companies, had operated posts on the Pacific Northwest coast since the 1790s, but in the 1820s, Americans sought the rich beaver trade of the inland mountains. St. Louis, at the mouth of the Missouri, served again as a major entrepôt for early entrepreneurs like Manuel Lisa and William H. Ashley. Ashley's Rocky Mountain Fur Company sent an exploratory company of adventurers up the Missouri to the mouth of the Yellowstone River in 1822–23, founding Fort William Henry near today's Montana–North Dakota boundary. This expedition included Big Mike Fink, Jedediah Smith, and other independent trappers who would form the cadre of famous mountain men during the 1820s and 1830s.

But by the 1840s, the individual trappers were gone, victims of corporate buyouts and their own failure to conserve natural resources. They had, for example, overhunted the once plentiful beaver of the northern (and southern) Rockies. Significantly, mountain men explored and mapped the Rockies and their western slopes, paving the way for Oregon Trail migrants and California Forty-niners to follow.

Beyond the Monroe Doctrine

Expansion into the great American desert exposed an empire in disarray— Spain—and revealed a power vacuum that existed throughout North and South America. The weak new Mexican and Latin American republics provided an inviting target for European colonialism. It was entirely possible that a new European power—Russia, Prussia, France, or Britain—would rush in and claim the old Spanish colonies for themselves. America naturally wanted no new European colony standing in its path west.

In 1822, France received tacit permission from other European powers to restore a monarchy in Spain, where republican forces had created a constitutional government. To say the least, these developments were hardly in keeping with American democratic ideals. Monroe certainly could do little, and said even less given the reality of the situation. However, a somewhat different twist to the Europeans' suppression of republican government occurred in the wake of the French invasion of Spain. Both Monroe and John C. Calhoun, the secretary of war, expressed concerns that France might seek to extend its power to Spain's former colonies in the New World, using debts owed by the Latin American republics as an excuse to either invade or overthrow South American democracies.

Britain would not tolerate such intrusions, if for no other reason than traditional balance-of-power politics: England could not allow even "friendly" former enemies to establish geostrategic enclaves in the New World. To circumvent European attempts to recolonize parts of the Western Hemisphere, British foreign minister George Canning inquired if the United States would like to pursue a joint course of resistance to any European involvement in Latin America.

Certainly an arrangement of this type was in America's interests: Britain wanted a free-trade zone for British ships in the Western Hemisphere, as did the United States. But Adams, who planned to run for president in 1824, knew better than to identify himself as an "ally" of England, reviving the old charges of Adams's Anglophilia. Instead, he urged Monroe to issue an independent declaration of foreign policy.

The resulting Monroe Doctrine, presented as a part of the message to Congress in 1823, formed the basis of American isolationist foreign policy for nearly a century, and it forms the basis for America's relationship with Latin America to this day. Basically, the doctrine instructed Europe to stay out of political and military affairs in the Western Hemisphere and, in return, the United States would stay out of European political and military affairs. In addition, Monroe promised not to interfere in the existing European colonies in South America. Monroe's audacity outraged the Europeans. Baron de Tuyll, the Russian minister to the United States, wrote that the doctrine "enunciates views and pretensions so exaggerated, and establishes principles so contrary to the rights of the European powers that it merits only the most profound contempt."[31] Prince Metternich, the chancellor of Austria, snorted that the United States had "cast blame and scorn on the institutions of Europe," while *L'Etoile* in Paris asked, "By what right then would the two Americas today be under immediate sway [of the United States]?"[32] Monroe, *L'Etoile* pointed out, "is not a sovereign." Not all Europeans reacted negatively: "Today for the first time," the Paris-based *Constitutionnel* wrote on January 2, 1824, "the new continent says to the old, 'I am no longer land for occupation; here men are masters of the soil which they occupy, and the equals of the people from whom they came. . . .' The new continent is right."[33]

While no one referred to the statement as the Monroe Doctrine until 1852, it quickly achieved notoriety. In pragmatic terms, however, it depended almost entirely on the Royal Navy.

Although the Monroe Doctrine supported the newly independent Latin American republics in Argentina, Columbia, and Mexico against Europeans, many Americans hoped to do some colonizing of their own. Indeed, it is no coincidence that the Monroe Doctrine paralleled the Adams-Onis Treaty, Long's expedition, the opening of the Santa Fe Trail, and the Rocky Mountain fur trade. America had its eyes set west—on the weak Mexican republic and its northernmost provinces—Texas, New Mexico, and California. Nevertheless, when James Monroe left office in 1824, he handed to his successor a nation with no foreign wars or entanglements, an economy booming with enterprise, and a political system ostensibly purged of partisan politics, at least for a brief time. What Monroe ignored completely was the lengthening shadow of slavery that continued to stretch its hand across the Republic, and which, under Monroe's administration, was revived as a contentious sectional issue with the Missouri Compromise.

The Fire Bell in the Night
Opening Missouri to statehood brought on yet another—but up to that point, the most important—of many clashes over slavery that ended in secession and war. Proponents of slavery had started to develop the first "overtly distinct southern constitutional thought" that crafted a logical, but constitutionally flawed, defense

of individual states' rights to protect slavery.[34] Once again, it was Jefferson who influenced both the advance of liberty and the expansion of slavery simultaneously, for it was in the southern regions of the Louisiana Purchase territory—Oklahoma, Arkansas, Kansas, and Missouri—that slavery's future lay.

Difficulties over the admission of Missouri began in late 1819, when Missouri applied to Congress for statehood. At the time, there were eleven slave states (Virginia, the Carolinas, Georgia, Delaware, Maryland, Kentucky, Tennessee, Alabama, Mississippi, and Louisiana) and eleven free states (New York, New Jersey, Connecticut, Rhode Island, Massachusetts, Vermont, New Hampshire, Pennsylvania, Ohio, Indiana, and Illinois). Population differences produced a disparity in House seats, where, even with the three-fifths ratio working in favor of the South, slave states only counted 81 votes to 105 held by free states. Moreover, free-state population had already started to grow substantially faster than that of the slave states. Missouri's statehood threatened to shift the balance of power in the Senate in the short term, but in the long term it would likely set a precedent for the entire Louisiana Purchase territory.

Anticipating that eventuality, and that since Louisiana had already become a state in 1803, the South would try to further open Louisiana Purchase lands to slavery, Congressman James Tallmadge of New York introduced an amendment to the statehood legislation that would have prevented further introduction of slaves into Missouri. A firestorm erupted. Senator Rufus King of New York claimed the Constitution empowered Congress to prohibit slavery in Missouri and to make prohibition a prerequisite for admission to the Union. As a quick reference, his could be labeled the congressional authority view, which was quickly countered by Senator William Pinkney of Maryland, who articulated what might be called the compact view, wherein he asserted that the United States was a collection of equal sovereignties and Congress lacked the constitutional authority over those sovereignties.

Indeed, the Constitution said nothing about territories, much less slavery in the territories, and left it to statute law to provide guidance. That was the case with the Northwest Ordinance. But since the Louisiana Purchase was not a part of the United States in 1787, the Northwest Ordinance made no provision for slavery west of the Mississippi, necessitating some new measure. No sooner had the opposing positions been laid out than the territory of Maine petitioned Congress for its admission to the Union as well, allowing for not only sectional balance, but also providing a resolution combining the Maine and Missouri applications. A further compromise prohibited slavery north of the 36-degree, 30-minute line. There were also more insidious clauses that prohibited free black migration in the territory and guaranteed that masters could take their slaves into free states, which reaffirmed the state definitions of citizenship in the latter case and denied certain citizenship protections to free blacks in the former.[35] Packaging the entire group of bills together, so that the Senate and House would have to vote on the entirety of the measure, preventing antislave northerners from peeling off distasteful sections, was the brainchild of Henry Clay of Kentucky. More than any other person, Clay directed the passage of the compromise, and staked his claim to the title later given him, the Great Compromiser. Some, perhaps including Clay, thought that with passage of the Missouri Compromise, the question of slavery had been effectively dealt with. Others, however, including Martin Van Buren of New York, concluded just the opposite: it set in motion a dynamic that he was convinced would end only in disunion or war. Van Buren consequently devised a solution to this eventuality. His brilliant, but flawed, plan rested on certain assumptions that we must examine.

Southern prospects for perpetuating slavery depended on maintaining a grip on the levers of power at the federal level. But the South had already lost the House of Representatives. Southerners could count on the votes of enough border states to ensure that no abolition bill could be passed, but little else. Power in the Senate, meanwhile, had started to shift, and with each new state receiving two senators, it would only take a few more states from the northern section of the Louisiana Purchase to tilt the balance forever against the South in the upper chamber. That meant forcing a balance in the admission of all new states. Finally, the South had to hold on to the presidency. This did not seem difficult, for it seemed highly likely that the South could continue to ensure the election of presidents who would support the legality (if not the morality) of slavery. But the courts troubled slave owners, especially when it came to retrieving runaways, which was nearly impossible. The best strategy for controlling the courts was to control the appointment of the judges, through a proslavery president and Senate.

Still, the ability of the nonslave states to outvote the South and its border allies would only grow. Anyone politically astute could foresee a time in the not-distant future when not only would both houses of Congress have northern/antislave majorities, but the South would also lack the electoral clout to guarantee a proslavery president. On top of these troublesome realities lay moral traps that the territories represented. Bluntly, if slavery was evil in the territories, was it not equally evil in the Carolinas? And if it was morally acceptable for Mississippi, why not Minnesota?

These issues combined with the election of 1824 to lead to the creation of the modern two-party system and the founding of the Democratic Party. The father of the modern Democratic Party, without question, was Martin Van Buren, who had come from the Bucktail faction of the Republican Party. As the son of a tavern owner from Kinderhook, New York, Van Buren resented the aristocratic landowning families and found enough other like-minded politicians to control the New York State Constitutional Convention in 1821, enacting universal manhood suffrage. On a small scale, suffrage reflected the strategy Van Buren intended to see throughout the nation—an uprising against the privileged classes and a radical democratization of the political process. He learned to employ newspapers as no other political figure had, linking journalists' success to the fortunes of the party. Above all, Van Buren perceived the necessity of discipline and organization, which he viewed as beneficial to the masses he sought to organize.

With his allies in the printing businesses, Van Buren's party covered the state with handbills, posters, editorials, and even ballots.

Van Buren's plan also took into account the liberalization of voting require-ments in the states. By 1820 most states had abandoned property requirements for voting, greatly increasing the electorate, and, contrary to expectations, voter participation fell.[36] In fact, when property restrictions were in place, voter partici-pation was the highest in American history—more than 70 percent participation in Mississippi (1823) and Missouri (1820); more than 80 percent in Delaware (1804) and New Hampshire (1814); and an incredible 97 percent of those eligi-ble voting in 1819.[37]

The key to getting out the vote in the new, larger but less vested electorate was a hotly contested election, especially where parties were most evenly bal-anced. There occurred the "highest voter turnout [with] spectacular increases in Maine, New Hampshire, the Middle States, Kentucky, and Ohio."[38] Or, put an-other way, good old-fashioned "partisanship," of the type Madison had extolled, energized the electorate.

Van Buren absorbed the impact of these changes. He relished confrontation. Known as the Little Magician or the Red Fox of Kinderhook, Van Buren orga-nized a group of party leaders in New York, referred to as the Albany Regency, to direct a national campaign.[39] Whereas some scholars make it appear that Van Bu-ren only formed the new party in reaction to what he saw as John Quincy Adams's outright theft of the 1824 election, he had in fact already put the ma-chinery in motion for much different reasons. For one thing, he disliked what to-day would be called a new tone in Washington—Monroe's willingness to appoint former Federalists to government positions, or a practice called the Monroe heresy.[40] The New Yorker wanted conflict—and wanted it hot—as a means to ex-clude the hated Federalists from power. The election of 1824 at best provided a stimulant for the core ideas for future action already formed in Van Buren's brain.

Thus he saw the Missouri Compromise as a threat and, at the same time, an opportunity. Intuitively, Van Buren recognized that the immorality of slavery, and the South's intransigence on it, would lead to secession and possibly a war. His solution was to somehow prevent the issue from even being discussed in the po-litical context, an objective he sought to attain through the creation of a new po-litical party dedicated to no other principle than holding power.

When the Jefferonians killed off the Federalist Party, they lost their identity: "As the party of the whole nation [the Republican Party] ceased to be responsive to any particular elements in its constituency, it ceased to be responsive to the South."[41]

As he would later outline in an 1827 letter to Virginian Thomas Ritchie, Van Buren argued that "political combinations between the inhabitants of the differ-ent states are unavoidable & the most natural & beneficial to the country is that between the planters of the South and the plain Republicans of the North."[42] This alliance, soon called the Richmond-Albany axis, joined the free-soil Van Buren with the old Richmond Junto, which included Ritchie, editor of the *Enquirer*, and other southern leaders, including William Crawford of Georgia. Without a national party system, he contended, "the clamour against the Southern Influence and African Slavery" would increase.[43] But on the other hand, if Van Buren successfully managed to align with southern interests, how could his party avoid the charge of being proslavery in campaigns? The answer, he concluded, rested in excluding slavery from the national debate in entirety. If, through party success and discipline, he could impose a type of moratorium on all discussion of slavery issues, the South, and the nation, would be safe. Thus appeared the Jacksonian Democratic Party, or simply, the Democrats. Van Buren's vision for maintaining national unity evolved from the notion that money corrupts—a point that Andrew Jackson himself would make repeatedly, and which Jefferson endorsed—and therefore the "majority was strongest where it was purest, least subject to the corrupting power of money," which was the South.[44] Ironically, it was exactly the "corrupting power of money" that Van Buren intended to harness in order to enforce discipline. The growing size of the federal government, especially in some departments like the Post Office, provided an ever-larger pool of government jobs with which to reward supporters. At the state level, too, governments were growing. Van Buren realized that when federal, state, local, and party jobs were combined, they provided a significant source of compensation for the most loyal party leaders. Certainly not everyone would receive a government—or party—job. But a hierarchy was established from precinct to ward to district to state to the national level through which effective partisans were promoted; then, when they had attained a statewide level of success, they were converted into federal or state employees.

This structure relied on an American tradition, the spoils system, in which the winner of the election replaced all the government bureaucrats with his own supporters; hence, To the victor belong the spoils. It was also called patronage. However one defined it, the bottom line was jobs and money. Van Buren hitched his star to a practice that at its root viewed men as base and without principle. If people could be silenced on the issue of slavery by a promise of a job, what kind of integrity did they have? Yet that was precisely Van Buren's strategy—to buy off votes (in a roundabout way) with jobs for the noble purpose of saving the nation from a civil war.

In turn, the spoils system inordinately relied on a fiercely partisan (and often nasty) press to churn out reasons to vote for the appropriate candidate and to besmirch the record and integrity of the opponent. All the papers were wholly owned subsidiaries of the political parties, and usually carried the party name in the masthead, for example, Arkansas *Democrat*. Such partisan papers had existed in the age of the Federalists, who benefited from Noah Webster's *The Minerva*, and Jefferson's counterpart, Freneau's *National Gazette*. But they were much smaller operations, and certainly not coordinated in a nationwide network of propaganda as Van Buren envisioned. Under the new partisan press, all pretense of objective news vanished. One editor wrote that he saw it as irresponsible to be objective, and any paper which pretended to be fair simply was not doing its job. Readers understood that the papers did not pretend to be unbiased, and therefore they took what they found with an appropriate amount of skepticism.

There was another dynamic at work in the machinery that Van Buren set up, one that he likely had not thought through, especially given his free-soil predilections. Preserving a slave South free from northern interference not only demanded politicians who would (in exchange for patronage) loyally submit to a party gag order, but also required the party elect as president a man who would not use the power of the federal government to infringe on slavery. The successful candidate, for all practical purposes, had to be a "Northern man of Southern principles," or "Southerners who were predominantly Westerners in the public eye."[45] As long as the territorial issues were managed, and as long as the White House remained in "safe" hands with a sympathetic northerner, or a westerner with sufficient southern dispositions, the South could rest easy.

Unwittingly, though, Van Buren and other early founders of the new Democratic Party had already sown the seeds of disaster for their cause. Keeping the issue of slavery bottled up demanded that the federal government stay out of southern affairs. That, in turn, required a relatively small and unobtrusive Congress, a pliant bureaucracy, and a docile chief executive. These requirements fell by the wayside almost immediately, if not inevitably. Certainly the man that Van Buren ultimately helped put in the White House, Andrew Jackson, was anything but docile. But even if Jackson had not been the aggressive president he was, Van Buren's spoils system put in place a doomsday device that guaranteed that the new Jacksonian Democrats would have to deal with the slavery issues sooner rather than later.

With each new federal patronage job added, the bureaucracy, and the power of Washington, grew proportionately. Competition was sure to come from a rival party, which would *also* promise jobs. To get elected, politicians increasingly had to promise more jobs than their opponents, proportionately expanding the scope and power of the federal government. The last thing Van Buren and the Democrats wanted was a large, powerful central government that could fall into the hands of an antislave party, but the process they created to stifle debate on slavery ensured just that. By the 1850s, all it would take to set off a crisis was the election of the wrong man—a northerner of northern principles, someone like Abraham Lincoln.

Other changes accelerated the trend toward mass national parties. Conventions had already come into vogue for securing passage of favored bills—to marshal the support of "the people" and "the common man." Conventions "satisfied the great political touchstone of Jacksonian democracy—popular sovereignty."[46] Reflecting the democratic impulses that swept the nation, the nominating convention helped bury King Caucus. It was the election of 1824, however, that killed the king.

Corrupt Bargains?

A precedent of some degree had been set in American politics from the beginning when, aside from Vice President Adams, the strongest contender to succeed a president was the secretary of state. Jefferson, Washington's secretary of state, followed Adams; Madison, who was Jefferson's secretary of state, followed Jefferson; Monroe, Madison's secretary of state, followed Madison; and John Quincy Adams, Monroe's secretary of state, now intended to keep the string intact. Advantages accompanied the position: it had notoriety and, when the man holding the job was competent, a certain publicity for leadership traits whenever important treaties were negotiated. It was one of the few jobs that offered foreign policy experience outside of the presidency itself. Nevertheless, Adams's personal limitations made the election of 1824 the most closely and bitterly fought in the life of the young Republic.

John Quincy Adams, the former president's son, had benefited from his family name, but it also saddled him with the unpleasant association of his father's Anglophilia, the general aroma of distrust that had hung over the first Adams administration, and, above all, the perception of favoritism and special privilege that had become aspersions in the new age of the common man. Adams suffered from chronic depression (he had two brothers and a son die of alcoholism), whereas his self-righteousness reminded far too many of his father's piousness. Unafraid of hard work, Adams disdained "politiking" and refused to play the spoils system. Like Clay, he was an avowed nationalist whose concepts for internal unity harkened back to—indeed, far surpassed—the old Federalist programs. But in 1808, to remain politically viable, Adams abandoned the Federalists and became a Republican.

To some extent, Adams was overqualified to be president. Even the slanted Jackson biographer Robert Remini agreed that "unquestionably, Adams was the best qualified" for the job, unless, he added, "political astuteness" counted.[47] Having served as the U.S. minister to Russia and having helped draft the Treaty of Ghent, Adams had excellent foreign policy skills. Intelligent, well educated, and fiercely antislave (he later defended the *Amistad* rebels), Adams nevertheless (like his father) elicited little personal loyalty and generated only the smallest spark of political excitement. Worse, he seemed unable (or unwilling) to address his faults. "I am a man of reserved, cold, austere and forbidding manners," he wrote, and indeed, he was called by his political adversaries "a gloomy misanthrope"—character defects that he admitted he lacked the "pliability" to reform.[48]

Another equally flawed contender, Henry Clay of Kentucky, had a stellar career as Speaker of the House and a reputation as a miracle worker when it came to compromises. If anyone could make the lion lie down with the lamb, wasn't it Henry Clay? He had revolutionized the Speaker's position, turning it into a partisan office empowered by constitutional authority that had simply lain dormant since the founding.[49] Clay had beaten the drums for war in 1812, then extended the olive branch at Ghent in 1815. A ladies' man, he walked with an aura of power, magnified by a gift of oratory few could match, which, when combined with his near-Napoleonic hypnotism, simultaneously drew people to him and repulsed them. John Calhoun, who opposed the Kentuckian in nearly everything, admitted, "I don't like Clay . . . but, by God, I love him."[50] The Kentuckian could just as easily explode in fury or weep in sympathy; he could dance (well), and he could duel, and he could attract the support of polar opposites such as Davy Crockett and John Quincy Adams.

Possessing so much, Clay lacked much as well. His ideology hung together as a garment of fine, but incompatible, cloths. Having done as much as anyone to keep the nation from a civil war, Henry Clay in modern terminology was a moderate, afraid to offend either side too deeply. Like Webster and Jackson, he stood for union, but what was that? Did "Union" mean "compact"? Did it mean "confederation"? Did it mean "all men are created equal"? Clay supposedly opposed slavery in principle and wanted it banned—yet like the Sage of Monticello, he and his wife never freed their own slaves.

Ever the conciliator, Clay sought a middle ground on the peculiar institution, searching for some process to make the unavoidable disappear without conflict. He thought slavery was not a competitive economic structure in the long run, and thus all that was needed was a national market to ensure slavery's demise—all the while turning profits off slavery. Such inconsistencies led him to construct a political platform along with other nationalists like Adams, John Calhoun, and Daniel Webster that envisioned binding the nation together in a web of commerce, whereupon slavery would disappear peacefully.

Clay's American system (not to be confused with Eli Whitney's manufacturing process of the same name) involved three fundamental objectives: (1) tie the country together with a system of internal improvements, including roads, harbor clearances, river improvements, and later, railroads all built with federal help; (2) support the Bank of the United States, which had branches throughout the nation and provided a uniform money; and (3) maintain a system of protective tariffs for southern sugar, northeastern textiles, and iron. What was conspicuous by its absence was abolition of slavery. Without appreciating the political similarities of the American system, Clay had advanced a program that conceptually mirrored Van Buren's plans for political dominance. The American system offered, in gussied-up terms, payoffs to constituent groups, who in return would ignore the subject standing in front of them all.

Thus, between Adams and Clay, the former had the will but not the skill to do anything about slavery, whereas the latter had the skill but not the will. That opened the door for yet another candidate, William Crawford of Georgia. Originally, Van Buren had his eye on Crawford as the natural leader of his fledgling Democratic Party. Unlike Adams and Clay, however, Crawford stood for slavery, veiled in the principles of 1798, as he called them, and strict construction of the Constitution. Lacking any positive message, Crawford naturally appealed to a minority, building a base only in Virginia and Georgia, but he appealed to Van Buren because of his willingness to submit government control to party discipline. Van

Buren therefore swung the caucus behind the Georgian. Instead of providing a boost to Crawford, the endorsement of him sparked a revolt on the grounds that Van Buren was engaging in king making. Van Buren should have seen this democratic tide coming, as he had accounted for it in almost everything else he did, but he learned his lesson after the election. Crawford's candidacy also suffered mightily in 1823 when the giant man was hit by a stroke and left nearly paralyzed, and although he won some electoral votes in the election of 1824, he no longer was an attractive candidate for national office.

None of the three major candidates—Adams, Clay, or Crawford—in fact, could claim to be "of the people." All were viewed as elites, which left room for one final entry into the presidential sweepstakes, Andrew Jackson of Tennessee. Beginning with the Tennessee legislature, then followed by Pennsylvania, Jackson was endorsed at a mass meeting. Sensing his opportunity, Jackson ensured southern support by encouraging John C. Calhoun to run for vice president. Jackson appeared to have the election secure, having mastered the techniques Van Buren espoused, such as avoiding commitment on key issues, and above all avoiding the slavery issue.

When the ballots came in to the electoral college, no one had a majority, so the decision fell to the House of Representatives. There, only the three receiving the highest electoral count could be considered, and that eliminated Clay, who had won only 37 electoral votes. The contest now came down to Jackson with 99, Adams with 84, and Crawford with 41. Clay, the Speaker of the House, found himself in the position of kingmaker because his 37 electoral votes could tip the balance. And Clay detested Jackson: "I cannot believe that killing 2,500 Englishmen at New Orleans qualifies for the . . . duties of the First Magistracy," he opined.[51]

Clay should have known better. Washington before him had ridden similar credentials to the presidency. Nevertheless, between Crawford's physical condition and Clay's view of the "hero of New Orleans," he reluctantly threw his support to Adams. He had genuine agreements with Adams on the American system as well, whereas Crawford and Jackson opposed it. Whatever his thinking, Clay's decision represented a hideously short-sighted action.

Jackson had won the popular vote by a large margin over Adams, had beaten Adams and Clay put together, and had the most electoral votes. No evidence has ever surfaced that Clay and Adams had made a corrupt bargain, but none was needed in the minds of the Jacksonians, who viewed Clay's support of Adams as acquired purely through bribery. Nor was anyone surprised when Adams named Clay secretary of state in the new administration. Jackson exploded, "The Judas of the West has closed the contract and will receive the thirty pieces of silver, but his end will be the same."[52] It mattered little that Clay, in fact, had impeccable credentials for the position. Rather, the Great Compromiser muddied the waters by offering numerous, often conflicting, explanations for his conduct. Meanwhile, Calhoun, who saw his own chances at the presidency vanish in an Adams-Clay coalition, threw in completely with the Jacksonians; and overnight, Adams created an instant opposition built on the single objective of destroying his administration.[53]

Adams's Stillborn Administration

At every turn, Adams found himself one step behind Jackson and the Van Buren machine. Lacking an affinity for the masses—even though he spent countless hours receiving ordinary citizens daily, dutifully recording their meetings in his diary—Adams seemed incapable of cultivating any public goodwill. In his first message to Congress, Adams laid out an astounding array of plans, including exploration of the far West, the funding of a naval academy and a national astronomical observatory, and the institution of a uniform set of metric weights and measures. Then, in one of the most famous faux pas of any elected official, Adams lectured Congress that the members were not to be "palsied by the will of our constituents."[54] Bad luck and poor timing characterized the hapless Adams administration, which soon sought to pass a new tariff bill to raise revenue for the government, a purpose that seldom excited voters. When the Tariff of 1824 finally navigated its way through Congress, it featured higher duties on cotton, iron, salt, coffee, molasses, sugar, and virtually all foreign manufactured goods. Legislators enthusiastically voted for duties on some products to obtain higher prices for those made by their own constituents, hardly noticing that if all prices went up, what came into one hand went out of the other. Calhoun saw an opportunity to twist the legislation even further, giving the Jacksonians a political victory. A bill was introduced with outrageously high duties on raw materials, which the Machiavellian Calhoun felt certain would result in the northeastern states voting it down along with the agricultural states. As legislation sometimes does, the bill advanced, bit by bit, largely out of the public eye. What finally emerged threatened to blow apart the Union.

The stunned Calhoun saw Van Buren's northerners support it on the grounds that it protected his woolen manufacturing voters, whereas Daniel Webster of Massachusetts, one of those Calhoun thought would be painted into a corner, backed the tariff on the principle that he supported all protective tariffs, even one that high. Thus, to Calhoun's amazement and the dismay of southern and western interests, the bill actually passed in May 1828, leaving Calhoun to attack his own bill! He penned (anonymously) the "South Carolina Exposition and Protest," and quickly the tariff was dubbed the Tariff of Abominations.

As the next election approached, on the one side stood Jackson, who, despite his military record seemed a coarse man of little character. At the other extreme stood the equally unattractive Adams, who thought that *only* character counted. Jackson and his followers believed in "rotation in office," whereby virtually any individual could be plugged into any government job. The Whigs, on the other hand, emphasized character and social standing.[55] To Adams, and other later Whigs, simply stacking men of reputation in offices amounted to good government. Common experience at the end of Adams's term suggested that some men of character lacked sense, and some men of sense seemed to lack character.

Therefore, sometime after Jefferson, the fine balance that demanded both effectiveness *and* honor among elected officials had taken a holiday.

The Rise of the Common Man

Hailed by many historians as the first true democratic election in American history, the contest of 1828 was nearly a foregone conclusion owing to the charges of the "corrupt bargain" and the inept political traits of the incumbent Adams. The four years of the Adams administration actually benefited Van Buren's political machine, giving him the necessary time to line up the papers, place the proper loyalists in position, and obtain funding. By 1828, all the pieces were in place. Adams's supporters could only point to Jackson's "convicted adulteress" of a wife (the legal status of her earlier divorce had been successfully challenged) and his hanging of the British spies in Florida, going so far as to print up handbills with two caskets on them, known fittingly as the coffin handbills. Modern Americans disgusted by supposedly negative campaigning have little appreciation for the intense vitriol of early American politics, which makes twenty-first-century squabbles tame by comparison.

Jackson and his vice president, John Calhoun, coasted into office, winning 178 electoral votes to Adams's 83, in the process claiming all the country except the Northeast, Delaware, and Maryland. Old Hickory, as he was now called, racked up almost 150,000 more popular votes than Adams. Jackson quickly proved more of an autocrat than either of the Adamses, but on the surface his embrace of rotation in office and the flagrant use of the spoils system to bring in multitudes of people previously out of power seemed democratic in the extreme. More than 10,000 celebrants and job seekers descended on Washington like locusts, completely emptying the saloons of all liquor in a matter of days. Washington had no place to put them, even when gouging them to the tune of twenty dollars per week for hotel rooms. Webster, appalled at the rabble, said, "They really seem to think the country has been rescued from some general disaster," while Clay succinctly identified their true objective: "Give us bread, give us Treasury pap, give us our reward."[56] The real shock still awaited Washingtonians. After an inaugural speech that no one could hear, Jackson bowed deeply to the crowd before mounting his white horse to ride to the presidential mansion, followed by the enormous horde that entered the White House with him! Even those sympathetic to Jackson reacted with scorn to "King Mob," and with good reason: The throng jumped on chairs with muddy boots, tore curtains and clothes, smashed china, and in general raised hell. To lure them out, White House valets dragged liquor stocks onto the front lawn, then slammed the doors shut. But Jackson had already left his adoring fans, having escaped out a back window to have a steak dinner at a fancy eatery.

The entire shabby event betrayed Jackson's inability to control his supporters, on the one hand, and his lack of class and inherent hypocrisy on the other. He had no intention of hanging out with his people, but rather foisted them off on helpless government employees. Jackson ran the country in the same spirit.

Having hoisted high the banner of equality, in which any man was as good as another, and dispersed patronage as none before, Old Hickory relied on an entirely different group—elite, select, and skilled—to actually govern the United States. His kitchen cabinet consisted of newspaper editor Francis Preston Blair, scion of a wealthy and influential family; Amos Kendall, his speechwriter as well as editor; the ubiquitous Van Buren; and attorney Roger B. Taney. These individuals had official positions as well. Kendall received a Treasury auditorship, and Taney would be rewarded with a Supreme Court nomination.

Perhaps, if the Peggy Eaton affair had not occurred, Jackson might have governed in a more traditional manner, but the imbroglio of scandal never seemed far from him. Out of loyalty, he selected as secretary of war an old friend, John Eaton, who had recently married a pretty twenty-nine-year-old widow named Peggy. She came with a reputation. In the parlance of the day, other cabinet wives called Peggy a whore, and claimed she had "slept with 'at least' twenty men, quite apart from Eaton."[57] Her first husband, an alcoholic sailor, committed suicide after learning of her extramarital shenanigans with Eaton. To the matrons of Washington, most of whom were older and much less attractive, Peggy Eaton posed the worst kind of threat, challenging their propriety, their mores, and their sexuality. They shunned her: Mrs. Calhoun refused even to travel to Washington so as to avoid having to meet Peggy. Adams gleefully noted that the Eaton affair divided the administration into moral factions headed by Calhoun and Van Buren, a widower, who hosted the only parties to which the Eatons were invited—a group Adams called the "party of the frail sisterhood."

Jackson saw much of his departed Rachel in Peggy Eaton (Rachel had died in 1828), and the president demanded that the cabinet members bring their wives in line and invite Peggy to dinner parties, or face dismissal. But Jackson could not even escape "Eaton malaria" at church, where the local Presbyterian minister, J. M. Campbell, obliquely lectured the president on morality. A worse critic from the pulpit, the Reverend Ezra Stile Ely of Philadelphia, was, along with Campbell, summoned to an unusual cabinet meeting in September 1829, where Jackson grilled them on their information about Peggy. Jackson likely regretted the move when Ely brought up new vicious charges against the Eatons, and he uttered "By the God eternal" at pointed intervals. "She is chaste as a virgin," Jackson exclaimed.

The affair ended when Peggy Eaton withdrew from Washington social life, but Calhoun paid a price as well by alienating the president, who fell completely under the spell of Van Buren. When William Eaton died twenty-seven years later, Peggy Eaton inherited a small fortune, married an Italian dance teacher, then was left penniless when he absconded with her inheritance. Meanwhile, she had indirectly convinced Jackson to rely almost exclusively on his kitchen cabinet for policy decisions. With high irony, the "man of the people" retreated to the confidence of a select, secret few whose deliberations and advice remained well outside of the sight of the public.

Historians such as Arthur Schlesinger Jr. and others have tried to portray the triumph of Jackson as a watershed in democratic processes. That view held sway until so-called social historians, like Lee Benson and Edward Pessen, using quantitative methodology, exposed such claims as fantasy.[58] Thus, unable any longer to portray Jackson as a hero of the common man, modern liberal historians somewhat predictably have revised the old mythology of Jacksonian democracy, now explained and qualified in terms of "a white man's democracy that rested on the subjugation of slaves, women," and Indians.[59]

Andrew Jackson, Indian Fighter

For several generations, Europeans had encroached on Indian lands and, through a process of treaties and outright confiscation through war, steadily acquired more land to the west. Several alternative policies had been attempted by the United States government in its dealings with the Indians. One emphasized the "nationhood" of the tribe, and sought to conduct foreign policy with Indian tribes the way the United States would deal with a European power. Another, more frequent, process involved exchanging treaty promises and goods for Indian land in an attempt to keep the races separate. But the continuous flow of settlers, first into the Ohio and Mohawk valleys, then into the backwoods of the Carolinas, Kentucky, Georgia, and Alabama, caused the treaties to be broken, usually by whites, almost as soon as the signatures were affixed.

Andrew Jackson had a typically western attitude toward Indians, respecting their fighting ability while nonetheless viewing them as savages who possessed no inherent rights.[60] Old Hickory's campaigns in the Creek and Seminole wars made clear his willingness to use force to move Indians from their territories. When Jackson was elected, he announced a "just, humane, liberal policy" that would remove the Indians west of the Mississippi River, a proposal that itself merely copied previous suggestions by John C. Calhoun, James Monroe, and others.

Jackson's removal bill floundered, however, barely passing the House. National Republicans fought it on the grounds that "legislative government . . . was the very essence of republicanism; whereas Jackson represented executive government, which ultimately led to despotism."[61] Put another way, Indian removal exemplified the myth of the Jacksonian Democrats as the party of small government. No doubt the Jacksonians wanted their opponents' power and influence shrunk, but that never seemed to translate into actual reductions in Jackson's autonomy.

In 1825 a group of Creek Indians agreed to a treaty to turn over land to the state of Georgia, but a tribal council quickly repudiated the deal as unrepresentative of all the Creek. One problem lay in the fact that whites often did not know *which* chiefs, indeed, spoke for the nation; therefore, whichever one best fit the settlers' plan was the one representatives tended to accept as "legitimate." Before the end of the year troops from Georgia had forced the Creek out.

A more formidable obstacle, the Cherokee, held significant land in Tennessee, Georgia, Mississippi, and Alabama. The Cherokee had a written constitution, representative government, newspapers, and in all ways epitomized the civilization many whites claimed they wanted the tribes to achieve. Land hunger, again, drove the state of Georgia to try to evict the tribe, which implored Jackson for help. This time Jackson claimed that states were sovereign over the people within their borders and refused to intervene on their behalf. Yet his supporters then drafted a thoroughly interventionist removal bill, called by Jackson's most sympathetic biographer "harsh, arrogant, and racist," passed in 1830, with the final version encapsulating Jackson's basic assumptions about the Indians.[62] The bill discounted the notion that Indians had any rights whatsoever—certainly not treaty rights—and stated that the government not only had that authority, but the duty, to relocate Indians whenever it pleased. In fact, the Removal Bill did not authorize unilateral abrogation of the treaties, or forced relocation—Jackson personally exceeded congressional authority to displace the natives.[63] Jackson's supporters repeatedly promised any relocation would be "free and voluntary," and to enforce the removal, the president had to ride roughshod over Congress.

Faced with such realities, some Cherokee accepted the state of Georgia's offer of $68 million and 32 million acres of land west of the Mississippi for 100 million acres of Georgia land. Others, however, with the help of two New England missionaries (who deliberately violated Georgia law to bring the case to trial), filed appeals in the federal court system. In 1831, *The Cherokee Nation v. Georgia* reached the United States Supreme Court, wherein the Cherokee claimed their status as a sovereign nation subject to similar treatment under treaty as foreign states. The Supreme Court, led by Chief Justice Marshall, rejected the Cherokee definition of "sovereign nation" based on the fact that they resided entirely within the borders of the United States. However, he and the Court strongly implied that they would hear a challenge to Georgia's law on other grounds, particularly the state's violation of federal treaty powers under the Constitution.

The subsequent case, *Worcester v. Georgia* (1832), resulted in a different ruling: Marshall's Court stated that Georgia could not violate Cherokee land rights because those rights were protected under the jurisdiction of the federal government. Jackson muttered, "John Marshall has made his decision, now let him enforce it," and proceeded to ignore the Supreme Court's ruling. Ultimately, the Cherokee learned that having the highest court in the land, and even Congress, on their side meant little to a president who disregarded the rule of law and the sovereignty of the states when it suited him.[64]

In 1838, General Winfield Scott arrived with an army and demanded that the "emigration must be commenced in haste, but . . . without disorder," and he implored the Cherokee not to resist.[65] Cherokee chief John Ross continued to appeal to Washington right up to the moment he left camp: "Have we done any wrong? We are not charged with any. We have a Country which others covet. This is the offense we have ever yet been charged with."[66] Ross's entreaties fell on deaf ears. Scott pushed more than twelve thousand Cherokee along the Trail of Tears toward Oklahoma, which was designated Indian Territory—a journey in which three thousand Indians died of starvation or disease along the way. Visitors, who came in contact with the traveling Cherokee, learned that "the Indians . . . buried fourteen or fifteen at every stopping place. . . ."[67] Nevertheless, the bureaucracy—and Jackson—was satisfied. The Commissioner on Indian Affairs in his 1839 report astonishingly called the episode "a striking example of the liberality of the Government," claiming that "good feeling has been preserved, and we have quietly and gently transported eighteen thousand *friends* to the west bank of the Mississippi" [emphasis ours].[68] From the Indians' perspective, the obvious maxim With friends like these . . . no doubt came to mind, but from another perspective the Cherokee, despite the horrendous cost they paid then and in the Civil War, when the tribe, like the nation, had warriors fighting on both sides, ultimately triumphed. They survived and prospered, commemorating their Trail of Tears and their refusal to be victims.[69]

Other Indian tribes relocated or were crushed. When Jackson attempted to remove Chief Black Hawk and the Sauk and Fox Indians in Illinois, Black Hawk resisted. The Illinois militia pursued the Indians into Wisconsin Territory, where at Bad Axe they utterly destroyed the warriors and slaughtered women and children as well. The Seminole in Florida also staged a campaign of resistance that took nearly a decade to quell, and ended only when Osceola, the Seminole chief, was treacherously captured under the auspices of a white flag in 1837. It would be several decades before eastern whites began to reassess their treatment of the Indians with any remorse or taint of conscience.[70]

Internal Improvements and Tariff Wars

If John Quincy Adams wished upon Jackson a thorn in the flesh, he certainly did so with the tariff bill, which continued to irritate throughout the transition between administrations. By the time the smoke cleared in the war over the so-called Tariff of Abominations, it had made hypocrites out of the tariff's major opponent, John C. Calhoun, and Andrew Jackson, who found himself maneuvered into enforcing it.

In part, the tariff issue was the flip side of the internal improvements coin. Since Jefferson's day there had been calls for using the power and wealth of the federal government to improve transportation networks throughout the Union. In particular, advocates of federal assistance emphasized two key areas: road building and river and harbor improvements. In the case of road building, which was substantially done by private companies, Congress had authorized a national highway in 1806, from Cumberland, Maryland, westward. Construction actually did not start until 1811, and the road reached Wheeling, Virginia, in 1818. Work was fitful after that, with Congress voting funds on some occasions, and failing to do so on others. By 1850 the road stretched to Illinois, and it constituted a formidable example of highway construction compared to many other American roads. Paved with stone and gravel, it represented a major leap over "corduroy roads," made of logs laid side by side, or flat plank roads. More typical of road construction efforts was the Lancaster Turnpike, connecting Philadelphia to Lancaster, and completed in 1794 at a cost of a half million dollars. Like other private roads, it charged a fee for use, which tollhouse dodgers carefully avoided by finding novel entrances onto the highway past the tollhouse. Hence, roads such as this gained the nickname "shunpikes" for the short detours people found around toll-houses. The private road companies never solved this "free rider" problem. While the Pennsylvania road proved profitable for a time, most private roads went bankrupt, but not before constructing some ten thousand miles of highways.[71]

Instead, road builders increasingly went to the state, then the federal government for help. Jefferson's own treasury secretary, Albert Gallatin, had proposed a massive system of federally funded canals and roads in 1808, and while the issue lay dormant during the War of 1812, internal improvements again came to the fore in Monroe's administration. National Republicans argued for these projects on the ground that they (obviously, to them) were needed, but also, in a more ethereal sense, that such systems would tie the nation together and further dampen the hostilities over slavery.

When Jackson swept into office, he did so ostensibly as an advocate of states' rights. Thus his veto of the Maysville Road Bill of 1830 seemed to fit the myth of Jackson the small-government president. However, the Maysville Road in Kentucky would have benefited Jackson's hated rival, Henry Clay, and it lay entirely within the state of Kentucky. Other projects, however—run by Democrats—fared much better. Jackson "approved large appropriations for river- and harbor-improvement bills and similar pork-barrel legislation sponsored by worthy Democrats, in return for local election support."[72] In short, Jackson's purported reluctance to expand the power of the federal government only applied when his political opponents took the hit.

Battles over internal improvements irritated Jackson's foes, but the tariff bill positively galvanized them. Faced with the tariff, Vice President Calhoun continued his metamorphosis from a big-government war hawk into a proponent of states' rights and limited federal power. Jackson, meanwhile, following Van Buren's campaign prescription, had claimed to oppose the tariff as an example of excessive federal power. However distasteful, Jackson had to enforce collection of the tariff, realizing that many of his party's constituents had benefited from it. For four years antitariff forces demanded revision of the 1828 Tariff of Abominations. Calhoun had written his "South Carolina Exposition and Protest" to curb a growing secessionist impulse in the South by offering a new concept, the doctrine of nullification.[73]

The notion seemed entirely Lockean in its heritage, and Calhoun seemed to echo Madison's "interposition" arguments raised against the Alien and Sedition Acts. At its core, though, Calhoun's claims were both constitutionally and historically wrong. He contended that the unjust creation of federal powers violated the states' rights provisions of the Constitution. This was an Anti-Federalist theme that he had further fleshed out to incorporate the compact theory of union, in which the United States was a collection of states joined to each other only by common consent or compact, rather than a nation of people who happened to be residents of particular states. Claiming sovereign power for the state, Calhoun maintained that citizens of a state could hold special conventions to nullify and invalidate any national law, unless the federal government could obtain a constitutional amendment to remove all doubt about the validity of the law. Of course, there was no guarantee that even proper amendments would have satisfied Calhoun, and without doubt, no constitutional amendment on slavery would have been accepted as legitimate.

Many saw the tariff debate itself as a referendum of sorts on slavery. Nathan Appleton, a textile manufacturer in Massachusetts, noted that southerners' hostility to the tariff arose from the "fear and apprehension of the South that the General Government may one day interfere with the right of property in slaves. This is the bond which unites the South in a solid phalanx."[74] Adoption of the infamous gag rule a few years later would reinforce Appleton's assessment that whatever differences the sections had over the tariff and internal improvements on their own merits, the disagreement ultimately came down to slavery, which, despite the efforts of the new Democratic Party to exclude it from debate, increasingly wormed its way into almost all legislation.

Amid the tariff controversy, for example, slavery also insinuated itself into the Webster-Hayne debate over public lands. Originating in a resolution by Senator Samuel Foot of Connecticut, which would have restricted land sales in the West, it evoked the ire of westerners and southerners who saw it as an attempt to throttle settlement and indirectly provide a cheap work force for eastern manufacturers. Senator Thomas Hart Benton of Missouri, a staunch Jackson man who denounced the bill, found an ally in Robert Y. Hayne of South Carolina. Hayne contended that the bill placed undue hardships on one section in favor of another, which was the essence of the dissatisfaction with the tariff as well. During the Adams administration, Benton had proposed a reduction on the price of western lands from seventy-five to fifty cents per acre, and then, if no one purchased western land at that price, he advocated giving the land away. Westerners applauded Benton's plan, but manufacturers thought it another tactic to lure factory workers to the West.

Land and tariffs were inextricably intertwined in that they provided the two chief sources of federal revenue. If land revenues declined, opponents of the tariff would have to acknowledge its necessity as a revenue source. National Republicans, on the other hand, wanted to keep land prices *and* tariff rates high, but through a process of "distribution," turn the excess monies back to the states for them to use for internal improvement.[75]

Closing western lands also threatened the slave South, whose own soil had started to play out. Already, the "black belt" of slaves, which in 1820 had been concentrated in Virginia and the Carolinas, had shifted slowly to the southeast, into Georgia, Alabama, and Mississippi. If the North wished to permanently subjugate the South as a section (which many southerners, such as Calhoun, feared), the dual-pronged policy of shutting down western land sales and enacting a high tariff would achieve that objective in due time. This was the case made by Senator Hayne in 1830, when he spoke on the Senate floor against Foot's bill, quickly moving from the issue of land to nullification.

Hayne outlined a broad conspiracy by the North against westerners and southerners. His defense of nullification merely involved a reiteration of Calhoun's compact theories presented in his "Exposition," conjuring up images of sectional tyranny and dangers posed by propertied classes. The eloquent Black Dan Webster challenged Hayne, raising the specter of civil war if sectional interests were allowed to grow and fester. Although he saved his most charged rhetoric for last, Webster envisioned a point where two sections, one backward and feudal, one advanced and free, stood apart from each other. He warned that the people, not state legislatures, comprised the Union or, as he said, the Union was "a creature of the people."[76] To allow states to nullify specific federal laws would turn the Constitution into a "rope of sand," Webster observed—hence the existence of the Supreme Court to weigh the constitutionality of laws. Liberty and the Union were not antithetical, noted Webster, they were "forever, one and inseparable."[77] The Foot resolution went down to defeat.

Jackson, who sat in the audience during the Webster-Hayne debate, again abandoned the states' rights-small government view in favor of the federal government. At a Jefferson Day Dinner, attended by Calhoun, Jackson, and Van Buren, Jackson offered a toast directed at Calhoun, stating, "Our Union. It must be preserved."[78] Calhoun offered an ineffectual retort in his toast—"The Union, next to our liberty most dear!"—but the president had made his point, and it widened the rift between the two men.

An odd coalition to reduce tariff rates arose in the meantime between Jackson and the newly elected congressman from Massachusetts, John Quincy Adams, who had become the only president in American history to lose an election and return to office as a congressman. The revised Adams-sponsored tariff bill cut duties and eliminated the worst elements of the 1828 tariff, but increased duties on iron and cloth. South Carolina's antitariff forces were not appeased by the revisions nor intimidated by Jackson's rhetoric. In 1832 the legislature, in a special session, established a state convention to adopt an ordinance of nullification that nullified both the 1828 and the 1832 tariff bills. South Carolina's convention further authorized the legislature to refuse to collect federal customs duties at South Carolina ports after February 1, 1833, and, should federal troops be sent to collect those duties, to secede from the Union. Calhoun resigned the vice presidency and joined the nullification movement that advanced his theories, and soon ran for the U.S. Senate.

Jackson now faced a dilemma. He could not permit South Carolina to bandy about such language. Nullification, he rightly noted, was "incompatible with the existence of the Union." More pointedly, he added, "be not deceived by names. Disunion by armed force is treason."[79] The modern reader should pause to consider that Jackson specifically was charging John C. Calhoun with treason—an accurate application, in this case, but still remarkable in its forthrightness and clarity, not to mention courage, which Old Hickory never lacked. Jackson then applied a carrot-and-stick approach, beginning with the stick: he requested that Congress pass the Force Act in January 1833, which allowed him to send military forces to collect the duties. It constituted something of a bluff, since the executive already had such powers. In reality, both he and South Carolinians knew that federal troops would constitute no less than an occupation force. The use of federal troops in the South threatened to bring on the civil war that Jefferson, Van Buren, and others had feared. Yet Jackson wanted to prove his willingness to fight over the issue, which in his mind remained "Union." He dispatched General Winfield Scott and additional troops to Charleston, making plain his intention to collect the customs duties. At the same time, Jackson had no interest in the central issue, and the underlying cause of the dissatisfaction with the tariff, slavery, nor did he intend to allow the tariff to spin out of control. While acting bellicose in public, Jackson worked behind the scenes to persuade South Carolina to back down. Here, Jackson received support from his other political adversary, Henry Clay, who worked with Calhoun to draft a compromise tariff with greatly reduced duties beginning in 1833 and thereafter until 1842. Upon signing the bill, Jackson gloated, "The modified Tariff has killed the ultras, both tarifites, and the nullifiers," although he also praised the "united influence" of Calhoun, Clay, and Webster.[80] Then Congress passed both the tariff reduction and the Force Bill together, brandishing both threat and reward in plain sight. After the Tariff of 1833 passed, Clay won accolades, again as the Great Compromiser; Calhoun had earned Jackson's scorn as a sectionalist agitator, but Jackson, although he had temporarily preserved the Union, had merely skirted the real issue once again by pushing slavery off to be dealt with by another generation.

Far from revealing a visionary leader, the episode exposed Jackson as supremely patriotic but shallow. In his election defeat to Adams, then his clash with Calhoun, he personalized party, sectional, and ideological conflicts, boiling them down into political bare-knuckle fighting. He stood for Union, that much was assured. But to what end? For what purpose? Jackson's next challenge, the "war" with the Bank of the United States, would again degenerate into a mano a mano struggle with a private individual, and leave principle adrift on the shore.

Jackson's "War" on the BUS

Having deflated the Nationalist Republicans' programs on internal improvements and tariffs, there remained only one plank of their platform to be dismantled, the second Bank of the United States. Again, a great mythology arose over Jackson and his attitude toward the BUS. Traditional interpretations have held that the small-government-oriented Jackson saw the BUS as a creature in the grip of "monied elites" who favored business interests over the "common man." A "hard money" man, so the story goes, Jackson sought to eliminate all paper money and put the country on a gold standard. Having a government-sponsored central bank, he supposedly thought, was both unconstitutional and undesirable. At least that was the generally accepted story for almost a century among American historians.[81]

Nicholas Biddle had run the bank expertly for several years, having replaced Langdon Cheves as president in 1823. A Philadelphian, Biddle had served as a secretary to the U.S. minister to France, edited papers and helped prepare the documents detailing the Lewis and Clark Expedition's history, and briefly served in the Pennsylvania state senate. Biddle's worldliness and savoir faire immediately branded him as one of the noxious elites Jackson fretted about. But he intuitively knew banking and finance, even if he had little practical experience. He appreciated the BUS's advantages over state-chartered banks and used them, yet all the while cultivating good relationships with the local commercial banks.

What made Biddle dangerous, though, was not his capabilities as a bank president, but his political powers of patronage in a large institution with branches in many states—all with the power to lend. Only the Post Office and the military services, among all the federal agencies, could match Biddle's base of spoils. Biddle also indirectly controlled the votes of thousands through favorable loans, generous terms, and easy access to cash. Whether Biddle actually engaged in politics in such manner is irrelevant: his mere capability threatened a man like Jackson, who saw eastern cabals behind every closed door. Thus, the "bank war" was never about the BUS's abuse of its central banking powers or its supposed offenses against state banks (which overwhelmingly supported rechartering of the BUS in 1832). Rather, to Jackson, the bank constituted a political threat that must be dealt with.

Jackson sided with the hard-money faction, as governor of Tennessee having strongly resisted both the chartering of state banks and placement of a BUS branch in his state. But that was in the early 1820s, on the heels of the panic. His views moderated somewhat, especially when it came to the idea of a central bank. Jackson's hatred of a central bank is exaggerated.[82] Like Thomas Hart Benton, William Gouge, and Thomas Ritchie of the *Richmond Enquirer*, Democrats and Jackson supporters had reputations as hard-money men. Jackson himself once heaped scorn on the paper money he called rags emitted from banks. Still, a decade's worth of prosperity had an impact on Jackson's views, for by 1829, when he started to consider eliminating the BUS, he had asked his confidant Amos Kendall to draft a substitute plan for a national bank.[83] Few historians deal with this proposal: Jackson's best biographer, Robert Remini, dedicates approximately one page to it, but he misses the critical implications. Other noted writers all but ignore the draft message.[84] The president did not intend to eliminate central banking entirely, but to replace one central bank with another in a continuation of the spoils system. Why was the current BUS corrupt? Because, in Jackson's view, it was in the hands of the wrong people. As governor, he had not hesitated to write letters of recommendation to staff the Nashville branch of the BUS, using the same arguments—that the "right" people would purge the system of corruption. The existing BUS was corrupt, in Jackson's view, only partly because it was a bank; what was more important was its heritage as the bank of the panic, the bank of the elites.

Given the intensity to which pro-Jacksonian authors cling to the antibank Andrew Jackson, let the reader judge. According to his close associate James Hamilton, Jackson had in mind a national money: his proposed bank would "afford [a] uniform circulating medium" and he promised to support any bank that would "answer the purposes of a safe depository of the public treasure and furnish the means of its ready transmission." He was even more specific, according to Hamilton, because the 1829 plan would establish a new "national bank chartered upon the principles of the checks and balances of our federal government, with a branch in each state, and capital apportioned agreeably to representation. . . . A *national* bank, entirely *national* Bank, of deposit is all we ought to have."[85]

Was the same man who had proposed a "national" bank with interstate branches capable of furnishing the "ready transmission" of national treasure also eager to eliminate state banks? It seems unlikely, given his supposed affinity for the rights of states to exercise their sovereignty. Nothing in the U.S. Constitution prohibited a bank (or any other business, for that matter) from issuing and circulating notes. However, based on Jackson's willingness to crush state sovereignty in the Indian Removal and his repudiation of South Carolina's nullification, it is clear that to Andrew Jackson the concept of states' rights meant what Andrew Jackson said it meant. More disturbing, perhaps, and more indicative of his true goals, was a series of measures introduced by the Democrats to limit the country to a hard-money currency. Again, historians concentrated on the hard-money aspect of the bills while missing the broader strategy, which involved a massive transfer of state power to the federal government.[86] Jackson's forces in Congress began their assault seeking to eliminate small bills, or change notes, which in and of themselves testified to the shocking shortage of small coin needed for change. Prohibition of small notes constituted the first step in the elimination of all paper money to these zealots, and would have moved the control of the money supply from market forces to a federal, central bank such as Jackson proposed.[87]

Whatever his final intentions, Jackson needed to eliminate the BUS as both an institutional rival to whatever he had planned and as a source of political patronage for his foes. Between 1829, when he had asked Kendall to draft his own plan, and 1833, Jackson and his allies attempted to work out a compromise on the existing BUS recharter effort. They outlined four major areas where the bank could alter its charter without damaging the institution.[88] In fact, thanks to the advice of Clay and Webster, Biddle was assured that the BUS had enough support in Congress that a recharter would sail through without the compromises. Probank forces introduced legislation in 1832 to charter the BUS four years ahead of its 1836 expiration, no doubt hoping to coordinate the effort with the presidential campaign of Henry Clay, who had already been nominated as the choice of the National Republicans to run against Jackson. The gauntlet had been thrown.

Many bank supporters thought Jackson would not risk his presidential run by opposing such a popular institution, but Old Hickory saw it as an opportunity to once again tout his independence. In May 1832, typically personalizing the conflict, Jackson told Van Buren, "The Bank is trying to kill me. But I will kill it."[89] When the BUS recharter passed in Congress, Jackson responded with a July veto. In his eight-year term, Jackson issued more vetoes than all previous presidents put together, but the bank veto, in particular, represented a monumental shift in power toward the executive. Other presidential vetoes had involved questions surrounding the constitutionality of specific legislation, with the president serving as a circuit breaker between Congress and the Supreme Court. No longer. In a message written by Roger B. Taney of Maryland, Jackson invoked thin claims that the bank was "*un*necessary" and "*im*proper." Of course, Marshall's Court had already settled that issue a decade earlier. Jackson's main line of attack was to call the bank evil and announce that he intended to destroy it. Clay misjudged the appeal of Jackson's rhetoric, though, and printed thousands of copies of the veto message, which he circulated, thinking it would produce a popular backlash. Instead, it enhanced Jackson's image as a commoner standing against the monied elites who seemingly backed the Kentuckian. Jackson crushed Clay, taking just over 56 percent of the popular vote and 219 electoral votes to Clay's 49, but voter turnout dropped, especially in light of some earlier state elections.[90]

Upon winning, Jackson withdrew all federal deposits from the BUS, removing its main advantage over all private competitors. Without deposits, a bank has nothing to lend. Jackson then placed the deposits in several banks whose officials had supported Jackson, and while not all were Democrats, most were. These "pet banks" further revealed the hypocrisy of Jackson's antibank stance: he opposed banks, as long as they were not working for his party. Jackson's disdain for the law finally met with resistance. His own secretary of the treasury, Louis McLane, who had supported Jackson in his "war," now realized the dangerous constitutional waters in which the administration sailed. When Jackson instructed him to carry out the transfer of the deposits, McLane refused, and Jackson sacked him. The president then named William J. Duane to the post (which required senatorial approval by custom, though not according to the Constitution). Jackson ignored congressional consent, then instructed Duane to remove the deposits. Duane, too, viewed the act as unconstitutional and refused. Out went Duane, replaced by Jackson loyalist Roger B. Taney, who complied with Old Hickory's wishes, although Jackson had finally persuaded Congress to pass the Deposit Act of 1836, giving the actions a cloak of legitimacy. As a reward, Taney later was appointed chief justice of the United States. All in all, the entire bank war was a stunning display of abuse of power by the chief executive and demonstrated a willingness by the president to flout the Constitution and convention in order to get his way. At the same time, it reaffirmed the adage that the American people usually get what they deserve, and occasionally allow those who govern to bend, twist, or even trample certain constitutional principles to attain a goal.

What occurred next was misunderstood for more than a century. Biddle called in loans, hoping to turn up the heat on Jackson by making him appear the enemy of the nation's economy. A financial panic set in, followed by rapid inflation that many observers then and for some time to come laid at the feet of the bank war. Without the BUS to restrain the printing of bank notes, so the theory went, private banks churned out currency to fill the void left by Biddle's bank. A new type of institution, the "wildcat" bank, also made its first appearance. Wildcat banks were in fact "free banks," organized by state general incorporation statutes to relieve the burden on the state legislatures from having to pass special chartering ordinances to allow banks to open. In modern times, virtually no businesses need special legislation from government to operate, but the free bank and general incorporation laws had only just appeared in the 1830s. Supposedly, the wildcat banks printed up far more money than they had specie in vault, but established branches "where a wildcat wouldn't go" made it nearly impossible to redeem the notes. Or, in other words, the banks printed unbacked currency. Again, the theory held that without the BUS to control them, banks issued money willy-nilly, causing a massive inflation.

Much of this inflation, it was thought, moved westward to purchase land, driving up land prices. By the end of Jackson's second term, rising land prices had become, in his view, a crisis, and he moved to stem the tide by passing the Specie Circular of 1836, which required that all public land purchases be with gold or silver. Attributing the rising prices to speculation, Jackson naturally was pleased when the boom abruptly halted.

Economist Peter Temin found that for more than a century this consistent explanation of what happened after Jackson killed the BUS remained universally accepted.[91] The tale had no internal conflicts, and the technology did not exist to disprove it. But after the availability of computing tools, economists like Temin could analyze vast quantities of data on gold and silver movements, and they came to a startlingly different conclusion about Jackson's war—it meant little. What happened was that large supplies of Mexican silver had come into the country in the late 1820s over the newly opened Santa Fe Trail, causing the inflation (increasing prices), and this silver flowed into the trade network, financing porcelain and tea exchanges with China and ending up in England after the Chinese bought British goods. The British, in turn, lent it back to American entrepreneurs. But in the early 1830s, with the Texas revolt, the Mexican silver dried up, and so did the flow of silver around the world that finally found its way into English vaults. With the silver reserve disappearing, the Bank of England raised interest rates, which spun the U.S. economy into a depression. Temin proved that the BUS did not have the size or scope of operations to affect the American economy that historians had previously thought. No matter how petty and ill conceived Jackson's attack on the bank was, he must be absolved of actually causing much direct harm to industrial growth—although new research suggests that his redistribution of the surplus probably contributed to the damage in financial markets.[92] On the other hand, whatever benefits his supporters thought they gained by killing "the monster" were imagined.

Jackson and Goliath

By the end of his second term, Old Hickory suffered constantly from his lifetime of wounds and disease. Often governing from bed, the Hero of New Orleans had become a gaunt, skeletal man whose sunken cheeks and white hair gave him the appearance of a scarecrow in a trench coat. Weak and frail as he may have been, when he left office, Andrew Jackson had more totally consolidated power in the executive branch than any previous president, unwittingly ensuring that the thing Van Buren most dreaded—a powerful presidency, possibly subject to sectional pressures—would come to pass. His adept use of the spoils system only created a large-scale government bureaucracy that further diminished states' rights, over-riding state prerogative with federal might.

Jackson's tenure marked a sharp upward spike in real expenditures by the U.S. government, shooting up from about $26 million when Old Hickory took office to more than $50 million by the time Van Buren assumed the presidency.[93] In addition, real per capita U.S. government expenditures also rose suddenly under Jackson, and although they fell dramatically at the beginning of Van Buren's term, by 1840 they had remained about 50 percent higher when Van Buren left office than under Adams. The levels of spending remained remarkably small—about $3 per person by the federal government from 1800 to 1850. If optimistic claims about personal income growth during the era are accurate, it is possible that, in fact, government spending as a percent of real per capita income may have fallen. But it is also undeniable that the number of U.S. government employees rose at a markedly faster rate from 1830 to 1840, then accelerated further after 1840, although per capita government employment grew only slightly from 1830 to 1850. The best case that can be made by those claiming that the Jacksonian era was one of small government is that relative to the population, government only doubled in size; but in actual terms, government grew by a factor of five between the Madison and Harrison administrations. In short, citing the Jackson/Van Buren administrations as examples of small government is at best misleading and at worst completely wrong.

More important, no matter what had happened immediately, the Jacksonians had planted the seeds of vast expansions of federal patronage and influence. Jackson's Democrats had prefigured the New Deal and the Great Society in viewing the federal government—and the executive branch especially—as the most desirable locus of national power.

CHAPTER SEVEN

Red Foxes and Bear Flags, 1836–48

The End of Jackson, but not Jacksonianism

When Andrew Jackson polished off the BUS, he piously announced: "I have obtained a glorious triumph . . . and put to death that mammoth of corruption."[1] It was an ironic and odd statement from a man whose party had now institutionalized spoils and, some would say, a certain level of corruption that inevitably accompanied patronage. By that time, Jackson's opponents recognized as much, labeling him 'King Andrew I,' without much apparent effect on his popularity. Judging Jackson's clout, though, especially in light of the Panic of 1837, is problematic. His protégé was unceremoniously tossed out of office after one term, becoming the third one-term president in the short history of the Republic.

Old Hickory, of course, had named his vice president, Martin Van Buren, as his successor. In a sense, Van Buren had rigged the system to ensure his election when he crafted the Democratic Party structure years earlier, using Jackson as the pitch man to get the party off the ground. Van Buren was full of contradictions. He stood for liberty and later moved to the Free Soil Party. Yet before his departure, his Democratic Party structure required the quelling of discussions of slavery. He sided with free enterprise, except when it involved the freedom to start and operate banks, and he had voted for tariffs in the past. Associated with small government, he supported public funding of the early national road. Ultimately, the Red Fox of Kinderhook, as Van Buren was also known, led a third antislavery party, but it marked a deathbed conversion of sorts, since he had ensured the dominance of a proslavery party in national politics.

Squaring off against Van Buren and the Democrats was the new opposition party, the Whigs, who drew their name from the English and American Revolutionary opponents to the Tories. These Whigs were hardly the laissez-faire, limited-government firebrands who had brought about the Revolution: they supported a high protective tariff, a new national bank, and federal subsidies for internal improvements. Some Whigs were abolitionists; some advocated temperance; and many came from Protestant evangelical backgrounds, such as Presbyterians, Baptists, and Congregationalists.

Mostly, however, the men who composed the Whig Party were united only by their hatred of Jackson. The three leading Whigs—Clay, Calhoun, and Webster—could not agree on the most pressing issue of the day, slavery. Webster hated it, attacking the peculiar institution at every opportunity, although he also embraced compromises that, he thought, might put slavery on the road to extinction. Calhoun, on the other end of the spectrum, defended slavery with the most radical arguments.[2] Clay adopted a firm position: he was both for it and against it. One other thing they had in common was a shared view that the best men should rule—the notion that educated, landed elites were best suited to govern by virtue of their character. In the age of the common man, such views were doomed.

Clay emerged as the chief spokesman for the new party. He was clearly the most recognizable, had a sterling reputation as an influence in both the House and Senate, had drafted the famous Missouri Compromise, and represented the West or, at least, sections of the West. Clay argued that each part of his American system supported the other and that all sections benefited by pulling the nation together rather than tearing it apart. Internal improvements aided southerners and westerners in getting their crops to markets, including markets abroad. The tariff protected infant manufacturing industries, so that the workingmen, too, had their share of the pie. And the bank held it all together by providing a uniform currency and plenty of credit to both agriculture and industry.[3]

All of this seemed plausible, and might have been sufficient in other eras. In the 1830s, however, it seemed unrealistic at best to ignore the looming sectional divisions over slavery, none of which would be solved by Clay's somewhat superficial proposals. Indeed, northerners argued, the presence of a bank would only perpetuate slavery by lending to plantation owners, whereas southerners countered that the tariff only benefited the industrialists and abolitionists. Most agreed on internal improvements, but disagreed over where the government should involve itself, and to what degree. Naturally, the sections split over the locus of the proposed largesse.

Swimming upstream against an increasingly egalitarian sentiment, the Whigs were throwbacks to the Federalists. While they still commanded the votes of significant sections of the country (and, on occasion, a majority), their music simply was out of tune with the democratic rhythms of the mid-1800s. This emphasis on expanding the franchise and broadening educational opportunities—all spearheaded by a polyglot of reform and utopian movements—characterized Jacksonian culture in the age of the common man.

Time Line

1836: Martin Van Buren elected president; Alamo overrun by Santa Anna's forces; Battle of San Jacinto makes Texas an independent Republic

1837: Panic of 1837

1840: William Henry Harrison elected president; Harrison dies; John Tyler assumes presidency

1841: *Amistad* decision: Supreme Court frees African slave mutineers

1844: James K. Polk pledges to annex both Texas and Oregon Territory; Polk elected president

1845: Texas annexation

1846–47: Mexican-American War

1848: Treaty of Guadalupe Hidalgo ends Mexican War; annexation of Oregon Territory and Southwest (California, New Mexico, Nevada, and Utah); Zachary Taylor elected president

1849: Gold discovered in California

Buckskins and Bible Thumpers

The Jacksonian period ranks as one of the great periods of American social reform and cultural change. America's Hudson River school of artists emerged, as did distinct and talented regional northeastern and southwestern writers. There were transformations of attitudes about social relationships, health, prisons, education, and the status of women and African American slaves. Advocates of communalism, vegetarianism, temperance, prison reform, public schools, feminism, and abolition grew into a substantial Jacksonian reform movement.[4]

Religious revivals washed over America in six great waves, ranging from the Puritan migration and Great Awakening of the seventeenth and eighteenth centuries to the new millennialism of the late twentieth century. In between came the Age of Jackson's monumental Great Revival, known to scholars as the Second Great Awakening. Throughout the 1815–1860 period, religious enthusiasm characterized American culture, from the churches of New England, to the camp meetings on western frontiers, to the black slave churches of the Old South.[5]

Why did this era foster religious fundamentalism? The emergent Industrial Revolution caused huge changes in the lives of Americans, an upheaval that, in part, explains the urgency with which they sought spiritual sustenance. Industry, urbanization, and rapid social shifts combined with the impending crisis over slavery to foment a quest for salvation and perfection. Hundreds of thousands of Americans found answers to their profound spiritual questions in Protestant Christianity. They adopted a democratic brand of religion open to all, featuring a diverse number of Protestant sects. Great Revival Christianity was also enthusiastic: worshippers sang and shouted to the heavens above. Together, believers sought perfection here on earth.

"Perfectionism," or a belief that any sinner could be saved by Christ and, upon salvation, should pursue good works to ensure that saving grace, shifted the focus from the Puritan emphasis on the afterlife to the possibility of a sin-free world in this life. A few perfectionists were millenarians who believed that Christ's second coming was imminent. The Millerites (named for their leader, William Miller), America's most famous millenarians, actually donned white robes and climbed atop barn and house roofs in 1843 to meet Christ as he joined them on earth. He did not appear as the Millerites had prophesied—a nonevent they referred to as the Great Disappointment.[6] Thousands left the faith, although a young woman named Ellen G. (Harmon) White (herself converted at a Methodist camp meeting and a protégé of Miller's), a virtual American Joan of Arc, picked up the standard. She had several visions, and despite her sex and youth became a de facto leader of a group that, by 1860, had chosen the name Seventh-Day Adventists, referring to the impending advent of Christ. The church's membership rolls swelled. Espousing a healthy lifestyle and avoidance of certain foods and meat, Adventists produced the cereal empire of John and Will Kellogg and influenced the career of another cereal giant, Charles W. Post.[7]

Mary Baker Eddy (1821–1910), who made her most important mark in American religious history slightly after the Jacksonian era, nevertheless rode the Second Great Awakening revivalist quest, adding to the health-food orientation of Ellen White the more radical doctrine of faith healing. Healed of great pain in her youth, Eddy founded the First Church of Christ Scientist (today known as Christian Scientists), in which spiritual healing depended heavily on mind over matter. Like others, she founded a college and an influential newspaper, *The Christian Science Monitor*.[8]

These new millennial groups differed from the traditional churches not only in their perfectionist doctrine, but also in their religious practice. In sharp contrast to the prim and proper Puritans, many of the new sects exhibited an emotionalism characterized by falling, jerking, laughing, and crying. And it worked. Where old-line churches like the Presbyterians scoffed at the enthusiasm of the camp meetings (which had started as early as 1801 at Cane Ridge, in Kentucky), they could not match the attractiveness and energy of the evangelists. The Methodists, whose songs John Wesley had adapted from English pub tunes, grew rapidly to become the largest church in the United States by 1844. Like the Baptists, the Methodists believed in revivals, in which the evangelical fires would be fanned periodically by hellfire-and-brimstone preachers who crossed the countryside. While the sects posed doctrinal challenges for the established denominations, no one could deny that they nevertheless added to a climate of religious excitement, leading to the establishment of theological colleges in nearly every state.[9]

Most perfectionists believed that Christ's coming would be preceded by the millennium (Revelations 20:1–3), a thousand-year period on earth of perfection—peace, prosperity, and Christian morality. The Second Great Awakening was a time when perfectionists commenced this millennium of peace on earth. Perfectionists preached that although man was sinful, he did not have to be. Individuals possessed the power to save themselves and join together to create a perfect world order. "To the universal reformation of the world," evangelist Charles Grandison Finney exhorted, "they stand committed."[10]

The Second Great Awakening was thus a radical extension of the religious enthusiasm of the Puritan migration and the First Great Awakening. Down-to-earth Jacksonian preachers and laymen fanned out to convert tens of thousands of sinners and lead them to salvation. Baptists and Methodists, sects less than a century old, figured prominently, but so too did Presbyterians, Congregationalists, and Mormons. The Erie Canal route of upstate New York, a scene of tumultuous economic and social change, became such a hotbed of religious fervor that it was dubbed the "Burned-Over District" because of the waves of religious fire that regularly passed through. Here a new figure strode onto the scene: Charles Grandison Finney, a law student who simply woke up one morning to a realization that he needed the Lord. When he appeared before the bench that day, Finney was asked if he was ready to try the case. He responded, "I have a retainer from the Lord Jesus Christ to plead his cause, I cannot plead yours."[11] Abandoning the passive Puritan view of salvation—one either was or was not saved—Finney initiated an activist, evangelical ministry that introduced many new practices that shocked the prim and pious churchgoers of the day. Among Finney's new measures, as he called them, were allowing women to pray in mixed-sex meetings, camp services that ran for several days in a row, the use of colloquial language by the preachers, and praying for people by name. In 1827 the Presbyterians called a convention to investigate Finney's methods, but they adjourned without taking any action against the new measures, and Finney's revivals continued. The tall, athletic, spellbinding Presbyterian minister, whose popularity equaled that of Old Hickory himself, called on all Americans to "Stand up! Stand up for Jesus!"[12]

A much more radical sect appeared in Palmyra, New York, when Joseph Smith claimed that he had been visited by the angel Moroni. The angel showed him golden tablets, which he was allowed to translate through two mystical seer stones that broke the language code, dictating what was called the Book of Mormon (1830). Smith's remarkable book related the history of the migration of an ancient tribe of Israel to the New World and the Indian tribes prior to the arrival of Europeans as well as the New World appearance of Christ. Smith quickly built a loyal following, and the group took the name Church of Jesus Christ of Latter-day Saints, generally known as the Mormons. The members moved to Ohio, where they became entangled in a bank collapse, then to Missouri, where they were ensnared in the slavery debate, taking the antislavery side. Eventually settling in Nauvoo, Illinois—the largest town in the state—the Mormons posed a threat to the political structure by their policy of voting as a block. When the Whig Party in Illinois introduced a new charter, the Mormons supported it, and in 1844 Smith ran for the U.S. presidency as an independent on an abolition platform.[13] At the same time, Smith had (according to revelation) laid down as church doctrine the practice of polygamy. Clashes with local anti-Mormon groups led to Smith's arrest and then assassination while he was in a Carthage, Illinois, jail in 1844, so the Mormons prepared to move yet again, this time to the far West.[14]

Mormonism flourished on the frontiers of Ohio, Missouri, and Illinois, but so did other churches. Itinerant Baptist and Methodist preachers answered the "call" to scour the Ohio and Mississippi valleys in search of sinners, and most found their share. Westerners flocked to camp meetings, staying for as long as a week to hear preachers atop tree stumps deliver round-the-clock sermons. In 1832, English-woman Frances Trollope witnessed a rural Indiana revival and recorded this word picture of the scene:

> The perspiration ran in streams from the face of the preacher [as the camp meeting] became a scene of Babel; more than twenty men and women were crying out at the highest pitch of their voices and trying apparently to be heard above the others. Every minute the excitement increased; some wrung their hands and called out for mercy; some tore their hair. . . . It was a scene of horrible agony and despair; and when it was at its height, one of the preachers came in, and raising his voice high above the tumult, [e]ntreated the Lord to receive into his fold those who had repented. . . . Groans, ejaculations, broken sobs, frantic motions, and convulsions succeeded; some fell on their backs with a slow motion and crying out—"Glory, glory, glory!!"[15]

The religious fervor of the Second Great Awakening had not yet subsided even by 1857–58, the eve of the Civil War. That year city folk thronged to reach out to God. Philadelphians and New Yorkers witnessed a remarkable spectacle as thousands of clerks and businessmen gathered daily for prayer meetings in their cities' streets. These meetings were purely lay events; no clergy were present. Observers witnessed the remarkable sight of wealthy stockbrokers and messenger boys kneeling and praying side by side.

With such a wide variety of religious experiences in America, toleration was more than ever demanded. Schools certainly had to avoid specific denominational positions, so they emphasized elements of Christianity that almost all believers could agree upon, such as the Resurrection, love, faith, and hope. That in turn led to a revitalization of the Ten Commandments as easily agreed-upon spiritual principles. This doctrinal latitude of toleration, which applied to most Christians with different interpretations of scripture, did not extend to Catholics, who did not engage in the same level of evangelization as the revivalist sects, yet competed just as effectively in more traditional church-building and missionary activity among the Indians (where the Jesuits enjoyed much more success than Protestants).[16]

The "Isms"

Perfectionists sought not only to revise the traditional understandings of sin and redemption, but also to reorder worldly social and economic systems. Communalism—systems of government for virtually autonomous local communities—emerged in "hundreds of utopian societies that dotted the landscape of American reform."[17] Jacksonian communalism did not in any way resemble modern socialist states with their machines of autocratic centralized economic control. Early American communalism was voluntary and local and represented the most radical antebellum reform ideas. The most successful of the communes were rooted in religious fundamentalism. Like Hopedale communalist Adin Ballou, religious utopians believed man was ruled by "the law of God, written on his heart, without the aid of external bonds."[18]

Communalism in America began with the 1732 emigration of German Lutheran pietists, under Conrad Bissell, to Ephrata, Pennsylvania. Later, in 1805, George Rapp founded Harmony, in western Pennsylvania, moving to the Wabash River (in Indiana Territory) in 1815. Englishwoman Ann Lee brought her Shaker sect to upstate New York in 1774, where it grew and spread after her death. Like the radical Lutherans, Shakers experimented with property-sharing, vegetarianism, and sexual abstinence (their church membership thus grew only through conversion and adoption). They claimed private property was sinful and that sex was "an animal passion of the lower orders." Shakers also took the radical position that God was both male and female. Frugal and humble, Shakers practiced wildly enthusiastic religious dances (from which the term Shaker is derived, as was the earlier Quaker) and spoke to God in tongues.[19] Perhaps more significant, many of the new religious sects actually "had very ancient origins but it was only in the free air and vast spaces of America that they blossomed."[20]

The Transcendentalists, a famous group of Massachusetts reformers, left an important legacy in the field of American literature, but their attempts at communalism proved fairly disastrous. Transcendentalists were Congregationalists run wild. Unorthodox Christians, they espoused, in varying degrees, God in nature (Deism), deep meditation, individualism and nonconformity, perpetual inspiration, ecstasy, and a transcendence of reality to reach communion with God. Among the transcendentalists stand some of early America's greatest intellectuals and writers: Ralph Waldo Emerson, Henry David Thoreau, Margaret Fuller, Bronson Alcott, and others. To achieve their high goals, transcendentalists founded two utopias. Bronson Alcott's and Charles Lane's 1843 Fruitlands was a socialistic, agrarian colony whose members proved so inept at farming that they endured for less than a year.[21] George Ripley's Brook Farm and other communes likewise either buckled under the sacrifices or substantially modified their programs, leading Nathaniel Hawthorne to parody them in *The Blithedale Romance* (1852).[22]

The failure of one group seemed to have no impact on the appearance of others, at least in the short run. John Humphrey Noyes—an eccentric among eccentric reformers—founded one of the most famous American communes at Oneida, New York. Originally a millenarian, Noyes coined the term perfectionist in advocating what he called Bible Communism, which forbade private property, and instigated polygamous marriages. All the members, Noyes declared, "recognize the right of religious inspiration to shape identity and dictate the form of family life."[23]

Noyes demonstrated the great danger of all the utopian thinkers, whose search for freedom led them ultimately to reject any social arrangements, traditions, church doctrine, or even familial relationships as expressions of power.

Marriage, they held, constituted just another form of oppression, even slavery—a point upon which Karl Marx and Friedrich Engels would completely agree. Their oft-quoted ideals of liberty masked darker repudiation of the very order envisioned by the Founders, not to mention most Christian thinkers. Still other utopians abandoned social activism and turned to philosophy, most notably Ralph Waldo Emerson (1803–82) and his fellow Transcendentalists.[24] Fittingly, Emerson described himself as a "transparent eyeball."[25]

Scottish and French socialists Robert Dale Owen and Charles Fourier attracted American converts, but their experiments also failed miserably. Owen sought to eradicate individualism through education in New Harmony, Indiana, which he bought from the Rappites in 1825.[26] Yet despite Owen's doctrinal desires, individualism went untamed among the eight hundred unruly Owenites, whose children ran amok and who eagerly performed "head work" (thinking) but disdained "hand work" (physical labor of any sort). Predictably, New Harmony soon ran out of food. Promising to destroy the "Three Headed Hydra: God, marriage, property," Owen himself was nearly destroyed. He poured good money after bad into the colony, losing a fortune calculated in modern terms to have been in the hundreds of millions of dollars. Likewise, twenty-eight separate attempts to establish Fourierist "phalanxes" (Fouriers' utopian organizational scheme) from Massachusetts to Iowa from 1841 to 1858 also failed.[27] Members were expected to live on eighty cents a week, a sum below even what contemporary Benedictine and Franciscan monks survived on.

Most of these utopians advocated greatly expanded rights (some would say, roles) for women. White women had gained property rights within marriage in several Ohio and Mississippi Valley states. Divorce became slightly more prevalent as legal grounds increased, and a woman was awarded custody of children for the first time ever in the precedent-setting New York State court case *Mercein v. People* (1842). At the same time, the emerging industrial revolution brought young women work in New England's numerous new textile and manufacturing industries. Jacksonian education reforms and the growth of public schools opened up a new white-collar profession for females—teaching. Steadily, the woman's sphere overlapped the men's sphere in economic endeavor. As demand for teachers grew, women began to attend institutions of higher education; Oberlin, the radical abolitionist college presided over by Charles Grandison Finney, produced America's first female college graduate. And during the Civil War, nursing joined teaching as a profession open to educated women.

Women also became involved in social activism through the temperance movement. As wives and mothers, females sometimes bore the brunt of the alcoholism of husbands and male family members. The American Society for the Promotion of Temperance was one of many women's organizations educating the public on the evil of "strong drink" and seeking its eradication. The Washington Society, an antebellum equivalent of Alcoholics Anonymous, was formed to assist problem drinkers. A single overarching theme emerged, however—solving personal problems through political means. Women helped pass the Maine

Law (1851), which forbade alcohol throughout the entire state. Enforcement proved difficult, yet as society saw the implications of widespread drunkenness, thousands of Americans (including a young Whig named Abraham Lincoln) joined the campaign against "Demon Rum." By 1850 the movement had slashed alcohol consumption by three fourths.

All of these causes combined to lead women, inevitably, toward feminism, a religio-socio-political philosophy born at the end of the Age of Jackson. Sarah and Angelina Grimké, Lucy Stone, Frances Wright, Elizabeth Cady Stanton, Lucretia Mott, and others led a small, fiery band of Jacksonian feminists. These women gathered together in Seneca Falls, New York, in 1848, where they issued a proclamation—a Declaration of Sentiments—touching on nearly all of the issues (abortion is the notable exception) of today's feminists. They decried the lack of education, economic opportunities (especially in medicine, law, and the pulpit), legal rights, marital power, and, most important, the "elective franchise" (the right to vote). "The history of mankind is a history of repeated injuries and usurpations on the part of man towards woman," they declared, "having in direct object the establishment of an absolute tyranny over her."[28]

Abolitionism—the radical belief in the immediate prohibition of slavery—reached fever pitch during the Age of Jackson. It is important to distinguish at the outset the difference between abolitionists and those who merely opposed slavery: abolitionists wanted to abolish *all* American slavery *immediately* without compensation. Antislavery politicians (like some Whigs and Free-Soilers, and after 1854, Republicans) wanted only to keep slavery out of the western territories, while permitting it to continue in the South.

Quakers initially brought English abolitionist views to America, where they enjoyed limited popularity in the northern colonies. Revolutionary ideals naturally sparked antislavery sentiment, especially in Philadelphia and Boston. After the Revolution, the American Colonization Society was formed to advocate freeing and colonizing slaves (sending them back to Liberia in Africa). But the rise of the cotton kingdom fueled even more radical views. On January 1, 1831, a Massachusetts evangelical named William Lloyd Garrison published the first issue of *The Liberator*, calling the slave "a Man and a brother" and calling for his "immediate emancipation." The New England Anti-Slavery Society and the American Anti-Slavery Society formed soon thereafter. Garrison, joined by Lewis Tappan, Elijah P. Lovejoy, and Sarah and Angelina Grimké, gained a growing audience for the abolitionist cause. The Grimké sisters were themselves former slaveholders, but when they inherited their father's South Carolina plantation, they freed its black workers, moved north, and joined the Quaker church. They created a minor sensation as two of the nation's first female lecturers touring the northern states, vehemently speaking out against the evils of slavery.[29]

Former slaves also proved to be powerful abolitionist activists. Frederick Douglass, Sojourner Truth, Solomon Northrup, Harriet Tubman, and others brought their own shocking life experiences to the lecture stages and the printed pages of the abolitionist movement. Douglass, the son of a white slave master whom he had never even met, escaped Maryland slavery and headed north as a young man. In his autobiography, *My Bondage and My Freedom,* Douglass spoke eloquently of the hardships he had endured, how his slave mother had taught him to read, and how he rose from obscurity to become North America's leading Negro spokesman. His story served as a lightning rod for antislavery forces. At the same time, Harriet Tubman devoted much of her effort to helping the Underground Railroad carry escaped slaves to freedom in the North. Tubman put her own life on the line during a score of secret trips south, risking recapture and even death.[30]

The abolitionists succeeded in putting great pressure on the major political parties and beginning the long process by which their radical ideas became mainstream ideas in a democracy. Abolitionists succeeded at provoking an immediate and violent reaction among southern slaveholders. Georgians offered a five-thousand-dollar reward to anyone who would kidnap Garrison and bring him south. Abolitionist Arthur Tappan boasted a fifty-thousand-dollar price on his head. In North and South alike, proslavery mobs attacked abolitionists' homes and offices, burning their printing presses, and threatening (and delivering) bodily harm. Anti-abolitionist violence culminated in the 1837 mob murder of Illinois abolitionist Elijah P. Lovejoy.

American Renaissance

Education and the arts also experienced great change, to the point that some have described Jacksonian high culture as an American "renaissance" and a "flowering" of the arts.[31] Although such language is exaggerated, it is true that America saw its second generation of native intellectuals, writers, and artists achieve bona fide success and recognition during the antebellum years. Jacksonian writers and artists came into their own, but they did so in a uniquely American way.

American educators continued to pursue aims of accessibility and practicality. New England public schools provided near-universal co-ed elementary education, thanks to the efforts of Massachusetts state school superintendent Horace Mann and a troop of spirited educational reformers. Public school teachers, many of them women, taught a pragmatic curriculum stressing the three R's (reading, 'riting, and 'rithmetic). Noah Webster's "blue-backed speller" textbook saw extensive, and nearly universal, use as teachers adopted Webster's methodology of civics, patriotism, and secular but moralistic teachings.

New "booster colleges" appeared to supplement the elite schools and were derided because their founders often were not educators—they were promoters and entrepreneurs aiming to "boost" the image of new frontier towns to prospective investors. Illinois College and Transylvania College appeared west of the Appalachians and eventually became respected institutions. Ohio alone boasted nearly three dozen degree-granting institutions during the Age of Jackson. And although Ohio's Oberlin College produced excellent scholars (and scores of abolitionist radicals), many booster colleges failed to meet the high standards of, for example, Great Britain's degree-granting colleges—Oxford, Cambridge, and Edinburgh.

The arts flourished along with academics in this renaissance. Beginning in the 1820s and 1830s, northern painters Thomas Cole, George Innes, and others painted evocative scenes of New York's Hudson River Valley. Nature painting drew wide praise, and a market developed for their landscape art that spread to all regions. Missouri's George Caleb Bingham, for example, earned acclaim for painting scenes of the Mississippi and Missouri river valleys, fur trappers, local elections, and his famed *Jolly Flatboatmen*. Landscape and genre painters adopted America's unique frontier folkways as the basis for a democratic national art that all Americans—not just the educated and refined—could enjoy.

James Fenimore Cooper did for literature what the Hudson River school did for painting. A native of an elite upstate New York family, Cooper wandered from his socioeconomic roots to create his literary art. After a childhood spent on the edge of the vanishing New York frontier, Cooper dropped out of Yale College to become a merchant seaman and, ultimately, a novelist. In *The Pioneers* (1823) and *The Last of the Mohicans* (1826), he masterfully created what we now recognize as the first Western-genre novel. During two decades, Cooper wrote a five-book series featuring his hero Hawkeye (whose name changed in each book as his age advanced), who fought Indians and wily Frenchmen and battled the wild elements of nature. Hawkeye, a wild and woolly frontiersman, helped to advance the cause of American civilization by assisting army officers, settlers, townspeople, and, of course, damsels in distress. In classic American style, however, Hawkeye also constantly sought to escape the very civilization he had assisted. At the end of every tale he had moved farther into the wilderness until at last, in *The Prairie* (1827), he died—an old man, on the Great Plains, with the civilization he had both nurtured and feared close at his heels.

It is no accident that during this time of industrial revolution and social and political upheaval, America produced a literature that looked back longingly at a vanished (and, often, imagined) agrarian utopia. Henry David Thoreau's *Walden, or Life in the Woods* (1854) is perhaps the most famous example of American writers' penchant for nature writing. Thoreau spent nearly two years in the woods at Walden Pond (near Concord, Massachusetts) and organized his evocative *Walden* narrative around the four seasons of the year. His message was for his readers to shun civilization and urban progress, but unlike Hawkeye, Henry David Thoreau traveled to town periodically for fresh supplies! After his two-year stint in the "wilderness" of Walden Pond, Thoreau returned to his home in Concord and civilization only to land in the town jail for tax evasion. He wrote of this experience (and his opposition to slavery and the Mexican-American War) in his famed essay "On the Duty of Civil Disobedience" (1849).

Although Thoreau's fellow Massachusetts author Nathaniel Hawthorne was not a nature writer, he addressed crucial Jacksonian issues of democracy, individual freedom, religion, feminism, and economic power in his elegantly written novels *The Scarlet Letter* (1850) and *House of the Seven Gables* (1852). Later, Herman Melville provided a dark and powerful view of nature in the form of the great white whale of *Moby Dick* (1851). Indeed, some experts point to Melville's and Hawthorne's artful prose to refute Alexis de Tocqueville's criticism of the quality of American literature. They note their literary skill and that of their fellow northeasterners—Henry Wadsworth Longfellow, Ralph Waldo Emerson, Harriet Beecher Stowe, Emily Dickinson, and the transcendentalist authors as evidence of an accomplished Jacksonian literati. Yet another school of writers, active at the same time as the New Englanders, actually proves Tocqueville partially correct. The southwestern school of newspaper humorists was not as well known as the northeastern, yet it ultimately produced one of the most famous (and most American) of all American writers, Mark Twain. The southwestern writers were newspapermen residing in the Old Southwest—the emergent frontier towns along the banks of the Ohio and Mississippi rivers. In Louisville, St. Louis, Natchez, Baton Rouge, Cincinnati, and New Orleans newspapermen like James Hall, Morgan Neville, and Thomas Bangs Thorpe wrote short prose pieces for newspapers, magazines, and almanacs throughout the Jacksonian era.[32]

A new, entirely American frontier folk hero emerged through the exploits of Daniel Boone and Davy Crockett, although contemporaries thought Boone "lacked the stuff of a human talisman."[33] Instead, Crockett captured the imagination of the public with his stories of shooting, fighting, and gambling—all of which he repeated endlessly while running for public office. Crockett liked a frequent pull on the whiskey bottle—phlegm cutter and antifogmatic, he called it—and he bought rounds for the crowd when campaigning for Congress. Crockett named his rifle Old Betsy, and he was indeed a master hunter. But he embellished everything: in one story he claimed to have killed 105 bears in one season and told of how he could kill a racoon without a bullet by simply "grinning it" out of a tree![34] Not one to miss an opportunity to enhance his legend (or his wallet), Crockett wrote, with some editorial help, an autobiography, *Life and Adventures of Colonel David Crockett of West Tennessee.* It became an instant best seller, and far from leaving the author looking like a hick, Crockett's book revealed the country congressman for what he really was, a genuine American character, not a clown.[35]

Nearly all of the southwestern tales, like the Western genre they helped to spawn, featured heroes in conflicts that placed them in between nature and civilization. Like Hawkeye, the southwestern folk hero always found himself assisting American civilization by fighting Indians and foreign enemies and, above all, constantly moving west. Crockett's life generated still more romantic revisions after his fabled immigration to Texas, where he died a martyr for American expansion at the Alamo in 1836.[36]

Had Crockett lived long enough to make the acquaintance of a young author named Samuel Clemens from Missouri, the two surely would have hit it off, although the Tennessean's life may have surpassed even Mark Twain's ability to exaggerate. In his job as a typesetter and cub reporter for Missouri and Iowa newspapers, Sam Clemens learned well his lessons from the southwestern writers. One day Clemens—under the nom de plume Mark Twain—would create his own wonderful version of the Western. Speaking the language of the real American heartland, Twain's unlikely hero Huckleberry Finn and his friend the escaped slave Jim would try to flee civilization and slavery on a raft headed down the mighty Mississippi. Like Twain, Cooper, Thoreau, the Hudson River school, and scores of Jacksonian artists, Huck and Jim sought solace in nature—they aimed to "light out for the Territories" and avoid being "sivilized"!

Such antipathy for "sivilization" marked the last years of Andrew Jackson's tenure. When he stepped down, America was already headed west on a new path toward expansion, growth, and conflict. Perhaps symbolically, westerner Jackson handed over the reins to a New Yorker, Martin Van Buren, at a time when the nation's cities had emerged as centers for industry, religion, reform, and "politicking."

The Little Magician Takes the Stage

Martin Van Buren ran, in 1836, against a hodgepodge of Whig candidates, including William Henry Harrison (Old Tippecanoe), Daniel Webster, and North Carolinian W. P. Mangum. None proved a serious opponent, although it appeared that there might be a repeat of 1824, with so many candidates that the election would be thrown into the House. The Little Magician avoided that alternative by polling more of the popular vote than all the other four candidates put together and smashing them all combined in the electoral college, 170 to 124. (Harrison received the most of the opposing votes—73.) Notably, the combined positions of those who preferred to eliminate slavery, constitutionally or otherwise, accounted for more than half the electoral vote in the presidential election.[37]

Andrew Jackson exited the presidency just as a number of his policies came home to roost. His frenzied attacks on the BUS had not done any specific damage, but had contributed to the general erosion of confidence in the national economy. His lowbrow approach to the White House and diatribes against speculators who damaged "public virtue" in fact diminished the dignity and tarnished the class of the presidency. The vetoes and arbitrary backhanding of states' rights ate away at important principles of federalism.

Thus, no sooner did Van Buren step on the stage than it collapsed. The Panic of 1837 set in just as Van Buren took the oath of office. Wheat and cotton prices had already fallen, knocking the props out from under the agricultural sector and sending lenders scurrying to foreclose on farmers. Once banks repossessed the farms, however, they could do little with them in a stalled market, forcing land prices down even further. In the industrial sector, where rising interest rates had their most severe effects, some 30 percent of the workforce was unemployed and still others suffered from falling wages. A New York City journalist claimed there were two hundred thousand people "in utter and hopeless distress," depending entirely on charity for relief.[38] Even the shell of the old BUS, still operating in Philadelphia, failed.

Van Buren railed against the ever-convenient speculators and jobbers. Some sagacious individuals promised the president that the economy would rebound, and that land prices, especially, would return. But Van Buren, contrary to the claims that he embraced the concept of a small federal government, hastily convened a special session of Congress to stop the distribution of the surplus. It was static economic thinking: the federal government needed more money, so the additional funds were kept in Washington rather than sent back to the states, where they might in fact have spurred a more rapid recovery. He also advocated a new Independent Treasury, in which the government of the United States would hold its deposits—little more than a national vault.

The Independent Treasury became the pole star of the Van Buren presidency, but was hardly the kind of thing that excited voters. Whigs wanted another national bank, and lost again as Van Buren's Treasury bill passed in 1840. Meanwhile, without the BUS, the American banking system relied on private, state-chartered banks to issue money.

The panic exposed a serious weakness in the system that could be laid at the feet of the Democrats. A number of states had created state banks that were specifically formed for the purpose of providing loans to the members of the dominant party, particularly in Arkansas and Alabama.[39] In other states, the legislatures had provided state government guarantees to the bond sales of private banks. Either way, these state governments made a dramatic and unprecedented intrusion into the private sector, and the legislatures expected to tax the banks' profits (instead of levying direct taxes on the people). Packing the management of these banks ensured that they provided loans to the members of the ruling party. These perverted state/bank relationships had two things in common: (1) they occurred almost exclusively in states where the legislatures were controlled by the Jacksonians; and (2) they resulted in disaster when the market was subjugated to the demands of politicians. Arkansas and Alabama saw their state banks rapidly go bankrupt; in Wisconsin, Mississippi, and the Territory of Florida, the banks collapsed completely. Stung by their failed forays into finance, Democrats in some of these states (Arkansas, Wisconsin, then later, Texas) banned banks altogether.

And so even as the national economy revived by itself, as many knew it would, Arkansas, Mississippi, Michigan, Wisconsin, Missouri, and the Territory of Florida all teetered on bankruptcy; witnessed all of their banks close; or owed phenomenal debts because of defaulted bonds. Lacking any banks to speak of, Missouri—the center of the fur trade—often relied on fur money—hides and pelts that circulated as cash.

Van Buren rightly warned that "All communities are apt to look to government for too much . . . especially at periods of sudden embarrassment or distress." He urged a "system founded on private interest, enterprise, and competition, *without the aid of legislative grants or regulations by law* [emphasis added]."[40] This might have been laudable, except that Van Buren's party had been directly responsible for the "aid of legislative grants or regulations by law" that had produced, or at the very least contributed to, the "embarrassment and distress" that the government was called upon to relieve.

Those seeking to portray Van Buren as a free-market politician who brought the panic to a quick end have to explain why voters were so eager to give him the boot in 1840. It was no accident that Van Buren spent four years dodging the most important issue of the day, slavery; but then, was that not the purpose of the Democratic Party—to circumvent all discussions of the Peculiar Institution?

Tippecanoe and Tyler Too

By 1840, Van Buren had sufficiently alienated so many of the swing voters who had given him a decided edge in 1836 that he could no longer count on their votes. The economy, although showing signs of recovery, still plagued him. His opponent, William Henry Harrison, had run almost from the moment of his defeat four years earlier. Old Tippecanoe came from a distinguished political family. His father had signed the Declaration of Independence (and later his grandson would win the presidency in his own right). An officer at the Battle of the Thames (1813), then at Tippecanoe, both of which helped shatter the grip of the Indians in the Old Northwest, Harrison already had political experience as governor of Indiana. Like Calhoun and other disaffected Jacksonians, Harrison had once stood with the Democrats, and shared their states' rights sentiments. Also like Calhoun, he thought the federal government well within its constitutional rights to improve harbors, build roads, and otherwise fund internal improvements. Although he favored a national bank, Harrison did not make the BUS his main issue. Indeed, many of his critics complained that they did not know what Harrison stood for.

Harrison's inscrutability stemmed largely from his middle-of-the-road position on slavery, especially his view that whatever solution was enacted, it had to emanate from the states. He did urge the use of the federal surplus to purchase, and free, slaves. In 1833 he wrote that "we might look forward to a day . . . when a North American sun would not look down upon a slave."[41] Despite Van Buren's nebulous position, Calhoun had no doubts that "the soundest friends of slavery . . . were in the Democratic party"; moreover, had either Harrison's or Van Buren's hostility to slavery been apparent, it would have been impossible for a Liberty Party to appear in 1840.[42] Unlike Van Buren, it should be noted, Calhoun did not wish to avoid discussion of slavery, but, quite the opposite, he relished confronting it head on to demand concessions from the North. "[C]arry the war to the non-slave holding states," he urged in 1837.[43]

Van Buren had the recession working against him. Old Tippecanoe started his campaign at age sixty-eight, and it appeared that age would, in fact, prove detrimental to his aspirations when, seeking the Whig nomination, rival Henry Clay's supporters suggested Harrison retire to his log cabin and enjoy his hard cider. Harrison turned the tables on his opponents by adopting his "Log Cabin and Hard Cider Campaign." It appealed to the masses, as did the slogan "Tippecanoe and Tyler Too," referring to his Virginia vice presidential candidate, John C. Tyler. Harrison could also count on almost 200,000 votes of the men who had served under him at one time or another, and who knew him as "the General."

When the totals came in, Harrison and Tyler carried nineteen states to Van Buren's seven and crushed him in the electoral college, 234 to 60. (Ironically, Virginia voted for Van Buren and not her two native sons.) Harrison had improved his popular vote totals by almost 2 million from 1836. Paradoxically, it was the first true modern campaign in the two-party system that Van Buren had created. Vote totals rose from 1.2 million in 1828, when Van Buren first inaugurated the party machinery, to double that in 1840; and from 1836 to 1840, the popular vote skyrocketed up by 60 percent, the "greatest proportional jump between two consecutive elections in American history."[44]

Old Tippecanoe would not live long to enjoy his victory. Arriving in Washington in February 9, 1841, during a mild snowstorm, Harrison delivered the March inaugural in a brisk, cold wind. The new president then settled in to deal with an army of job seekers—a gift from the Van Buren party system. On Clay's advice, Harrison gave Webster his choice of the Treasury or State Department—Black Dan chose to be secretary of state—but otherwise the president-elect kept his distance from Clay. With the Whig victory, the Kentuckian had taunted the Democrats with their defeat and "descriptions of him at this time invariably contain the words 'imperious,' 'arrogant,' 'domineering.' "[45] Whether he could manipulate Harrison is doubtful, but before Clay had the opportunity to try, Harrison caught a cold that turned into pneumonia. On March 27, 1841, a doctor was summoned to the deteriorating president's bedside, and Harrison died on April third. Daniel Webster sent his son to recall Vice President Tyler from Williamsburg, arriving to join the mourners at the Episcopal Church. America's shortest presidency had lasted one month, and Old Tippecanoe became the first chief executive to die in office.

Upon Harrison's death, Democrats fidgeted, terrified that Clay would seize power and make Tyler his "pliant tool."[46] Instead, they found former Democrat John Tyler quite his own man. Although he was elected to Congress as a Jeffersonian Republican, he broke with Jackson in 1832 over the BUS veto. But he also voted against the Missouri Compromise bill, arguing that all the Louisiana Territory should be open to slavery.

At age fifty-one, Tyler was the youngest American president to that point—ironically following the oldest. He had not actively sought the vice presidency, and he owed few political debts. There was a brief stew about Article II, Section 1, Paragraph 6, in which the Constitution said that if the president died or could not discharge the duties of his office, "the same shall devolve on the Vice President." But the same what? Powers? Title? Was a special election necessary? A weaker, or less confident (certainly less stubborn), man would have vacillated, and many constitutional historians suspect that the Founders intended for the vice president to remain just that, until a new election made him president in his own right.[47] Instead, the Virginian boldly assumed that the office and duties were his, and he took control. In a little-noticed act, Tyler cemented the foundation of the Republic for future times of chaos and instability.

A classic ticket balancer with few genuine Whig sentiments, Tyler nevertheless immediately antagonized many of the extreme states' rights advocates from his own state and other parts of the Deep South by retaining nationalistic "Black Dan" Webster as his secretary of state.[48] This, too, set a precedent of a succeeding president accepting as his own the cabinet of the person who had headed the ticket in the general election.

A number of problems greeted the new president, most notably the depression still lingering from Van Buren's term. It had left the nation with a deficit of more than $11 million, which caused some in the May 1841 special session of Congress to press for additional tariffs. Tyler resisted. He did side with the Whigs on the distribution of monies from the sales of public lands and, in true Whig fashion, denounced the Independent Treasury as an unsatisfactory means of dealing with economic distress. Most stunning, this Virginian called for a new effort to suppress the slave trade.

Clay, meanwhile, thinking that a Whig occupant of the White House equated with victory for his American system, immediately pushed for a new BUS. When a Whig bill for a new national bank came out of Congress in August 1841, however, Tyler vetoed it, as well as a second modified bill. Far from opposing a national bank, Tyler disliked some of the specific provisions regarding local lending by national bank branches, and he might have yielded to negotiations had not Clay, full of venom at the first veto, taken to the Senate floor to heap scorn on the president. Rumors swirled that the Whigs planned to spring a trap on Tyler by inserting phrases he would object to, then threatening to encourage his cabinet to resign if he dared veto the second bill. For the second time in ten years, the national bank had become the centerpiece in a political struggle largely removed from the specifics of the bill.

By that time, the Whigs felt betrayed. Although doubtless that some of the dissatisfaction originated with the Clay faction, their protests were an astounding response by members of one party to their own president. It did not end with the bank bill either.

Whigs and Tyler clashed again over the reduction in tariff rates. By that time, the tariffs existed almost exclusively for generating federal revenue. Any beneficial effects for American industries—if any ever existed at all—had disappeared by 1830, but the tariff still held great appeal for those industries that could keep prices high because of protection and, more important, to the politicians who had money to dole out to their constituents. It was that money, in the early 1840s, that was in danger of disappearing if the scheduled rate reductions already enacted drove the rates down from 33 percent to 20 percent. Consequently, two bills came out of the Whig Congress in 1842 to delay the reductions, and, again, true to his earlier Democratic heritage, Tyler vetoed them both. With his shrinking constituencies about to abandon him, even to the point of suggesting impeachment, Tyler conceded on a third bill that delayed some tariff reductions, but at the same time ended plans to distribute federal revenues to the states. Tyler not only managed to make himself unpopular, but by forcing concessions, he also eliminated the few bones that the Whigs had hoped to throw to southern interests. In response, the South abandoned the Whigs in the midterm elections, giving the House back to the Democrats. Tyler's bullheadedness in vetoing the bank bill sparked a rebellion in which his entire cabinet resigned.

The resulting gridlock proved problematic for American foreign policy. Tyler had navigated one rocky strait when Daniel Webster, prior to his resignation as secretary of state, negotiated a treaty with the British in 1842 called the Webster-Ashburton Treaty. It settled the disputed Maine boundary with Canada, producing an agreement that gave 50 percent of the territory in question to the United States. He also literally dodged a bullet in early 1844, when, with Webster's replacement, Abel Upshur, and Senator Thomas Hart Benton, the president visited a new warship, the *Princeton,* with its massive new gun, the "peacemaker." Tyler was below decks during the ceremony when, during a demonstration, the gun misfired, and the explosion killed Upshur, Tyler's servant, and several others.

Following Upshur's death, Tyler named John C. Calhoun as the secretary of state. This placed a strong advocate of the expansion of slavery in the highest diplomatic position in the government. It placed even greater emphasis on the events occurring on the southern border, where, following Mexican independence in 1821, large numbers of Americans had arrived. They soon led a new revolutionary movement in the northern province known as Texas.

Empire of Liberty or Manifest Destiny?

Manifest destiny, often ascribed to the so-called Age of Jackson (1828–48), began much earlier, when the first Europeans landed on the sixteenth- and seventeenth-century colonial frontier. Later, eighteenth-century Americans fanned out into the trans-Appalachian West after the American Revolution, exploring and settling the Ohio and Mississippi valleys. It was from this perspective, then, that Jacksonian Americans began to see and fulfill what they believed to be their destiny—to occupy all North American lands east and west of the Mississippi and Missouri river valleys. Thomas Jefferson had expounded upon a similar concept much earlier, referring to an Empire of Liberty that would stretch across Indian lands into the Mississippi Valley. Jefferson, as has been noted, even planned for new territories and states with grandiose-sounding names: Saratoga, Vandalia, Metropotamia, and so on. The Sage of Monticello always envisioned a nation with steadily expanding borders, comprised of new farms and citizen-farmers, bringing under its wings natives who could be civilized and acculturated to the Empire of Liberty.

During the 1830s and 1840s the embers of Jefferson's Empire of Liberty sparked into a new flame called manifest destiny. It swept over a nation of Americans whose eyes looked westward. The term itself came from an 1840s Democratic newspaper editorial supporting the Mexican-American War, in which the writer condemned individuals and nations who were "hampering our [America's] power, limiting our greatness, and checking the fulfillment of our manifest destiny to overspread the continent allotted by Providence for the free development of our yearly multiplying millions."[49] Ralph Waldo Emerson's speech the "Young American" extolled the virtues of expansion, and John L. O'Sullivan agreed: "Yes, more, more, more!"[50]

Given that most of the expansionist talk revolved around Texas and points south, the popularization of manifest destiny by the press, to a certain extent, validated the abolitionists' claim that a "slave power" conspiracy existed at the highest reaches of power. A majority of newspapers owed their existence to the Democratic Party, which in turn loyally supported the slave owners' agenda, if unwittingly. Even the Whig papers, such as Horace Greeley's *Daily Tribune*, which was antislavery, indirectly encouraged a western exodus. Then, as today, contemporaries frequently fretted about overpopulation: President James K. Polk, in his inaugural address in 1845, warned that the nation in the next decade would grow from 3 to 20 million and obliquely noted that immigrants were pouring onto our shores.[51]

There were other, more common, economic motives interwoven into this anxiety, because the Panic of 1837 created a class of impoverished individuals eager to seek new opportunities in the West. Yet many of these individuals were white Missourians, not slaveholders, who headed for the Pacific Northwest, where they aimed to escape the South's slave-based cotton economy and the slave masters who controlled it. Complex economic motives constituted only one voice in the choir calling for manifest destiny. Religion played an enormous factor in the westward surge as Great Awakening enthusiasm prompted a desire to expunge Spanish Catholicism, spread Protestantism, and convert the Indians.

Other than California, if any one area captured the imagination of American vagabonds and settlers, it was Texas. Before Mexican independence, Texas had failed to attract settlers from Spain and subsequently proved difficult to secure against Indian raids. Since few Mexicans would settle in Texas, the Spanish government sought to entice American colonists through generous land grants. Moses Austin had negotiated for the original grant, but it was his son, Stephen F. Austin, who planted the settlement in 1822 after Mexico won independence from Spain. By 1831, eight thousand Texan-American farmers and their thousand slaves worked the cotton fields of the Brazos and Colorado river valleys (near modern-day Houston). Although the Mexican government originally welcomed these settlers in hopes they would make the colony prosperous, the relationship soured. Settlers accepted certain conditions when they arrived, including converting to Catholicism, conducting all official business in Spanish, and refraining from settling within sixty miles of the American border. These constraints, the Mexican government thought, would ensure that Texas became integrated into Mexico. However, few Protestant (or atheist) Texans converted to

Catholicism; virtually no one spoke Spanish, even in official exchanges; and many of the new settlers owned slaves. The Republic of Mexico had eliminated slavery in the rest of the country, but had ignored the arrival of Americans slave-holders in Texas. With the Mexican Colonization Act of 1830, however, the government of Mexico prohibited further American settlement and banned slavery in the northern provinces, specifically aiming the ordinance at Texas. These disputes all led to the 1830 formation of a Texan-American independence movement, which claimed its rights under the Mexican Constitution of 1824.

When Texans challenged Mexican authority, General Antonio Lopez de Santa Anna marched north from Mexico City in 1836. His massive column, which he quickly divided, numbered some 6,000 troops, some of whom he dispatched under General José de Urrea to mop up small pockets of resistance. The Texans responded with a March 1, 1836, Declaration of Independence founding the Republic of Texas. Sam Houston, an 1832 emigrant from Tennessee, was elected president of the Lone Star Republic, and subsequently the general of the Texan army, which prepared to fight Santa Anna's column.

Even before the declaration of Texan independence, Santa Anna had had to deal with a small resistance in San Antonio at the Alamo, an adobe mission-turned-fort. Opposing Santa Anna's 4,000-man army was the famed 187-man Texan garrison led by Colonel William B. Travis and including the already famous Jim Bowie and David Crockett. "Let's make their victory worse than a defeat," Travis implored his doomed men, who sold their lives dearly. It took Santa Anna more than a week to bring up his long column, and his cannons pummeled the Alamo the entire time. Once arrayed, the whole Mexican army attacked early in the morning on March sixth, following a long silence that sent many of the lookouts and pickets to sleep. Mexicans were at—or even over—the walls before the first alarms were raised. The Texans, having spent much of their ammunition, died fighting hand to hand. Crockett, one of the last survivors found amid a stack of Mexican bodies, was shot by a firing squad the following morning. "Remember the Alamo" became the battle cry of Houston's freedom fighters.

The generalissimo had won costly victories, whereas the Texans staged a re-treat that, at times, bordered on a rout. Only Houston's firm hand—Washington-like, in some respects—kept any semblance of order. Unknown to him, Santa Anna had sustained substantial losses taking an insignificant fort: some estimate that his assault on the Alamo left 500 dead outside the walls, reducing his force from one fourth to one third after accounting for the wounded and the pack trains needed to deal with them. If he won the Alamo, he soon lost the war. Pursuing Houston, Santa Anna continued to divide his weary and wounded force. Houston, convinced he had lured the enemy on long enough, staged a counterattack on April 21, 1836, at San Jacinto, near Galveston Bay. Ordering his men to, "Hold your fire! God damn you, hold your fire!" he approached the larger Mexican force in the open, struggling to push two cannons called the Twin Sisters up a ridge overlooking the Mexican positions. Given the nature of Houston's advance, Santa Anna apparently did not think the Texans would charge. He could not help but see their movements: the Texans had to unlimber their cannons and form up in battle lines, all within sight of Santa Anna's scouts, Mexican pickets who did not sound the alarm. Houston's troops charged and routed Santa Anna, who was seen "running about in the utmost excitement, wringing his hands and unable to give an order."[52] When the Texans screamed out the phrases, "Remember the Alamo, Remember Goliad," the Mexican forces broke and ran. Santa Anna escaped temporarily, disguised as a servant. His capture was important in order to have the president's signature on a treaty acknowledging Texan independence, and the general was apprehended before long, with 730 of his troops. Texan casualties totaled 9 killed, whereas the Mexicans lost 630. In return for his freedom, and that of his troops, Santa Anna agreed to cede all of Texas to the new republic, but repudiated the agreement as soon as he was released. He returned to Mexico City and plotted revenge. Meanwhile, the government of the Texas Republic officially requested to join the United States of America.[53]

The request by Texas brought to the surface the very tensions over slavery that Van Buren had sought to repress and avoid. In the House of Representatives, John Quincy Adams, who had returned to Washington after being elected as a Massachusetts congressman (he and Andrew Johnson, a senator, were the only former presidents ever to do so) filibustered the bill for three weeks. Van Buren opposed annexation, the Senate rejected a ratification treaty, and Texas remained an independent republic sandwiched between Mexico and America.

Mr. Polk's War

When, in 1842, the president of the Republic of Texas, Sam Houston, again invited the United States to annex his "nation," the secretary of state at the time, Daniel Webster, immediately suppressed the request. Webster, an antislavery New Englander, wanted no part in helping the South gain a large new slave state and, at a minimum, two Democratic senators. In 1844, however, with Calhoun shifting over from the Department of War to head the State Department, a new treaty of annexation was negotiated between Texas and the United States with an important wrinkle: the southern boundary was the Rio Grande. This border had been rejected by the Mexican Congress in favor of the Nueces River farther north.

Northern-based Whigs, of course, stood mostly against incorporating Texas into the Union, and thus to win their support, the Whig candidate, Henry Clay, whose name was synonymous with sectional compromise, could not come out in favor of an annexation program that might divide the nation. Both Clay and Van Buren, therefore, "issued statements to the effect that they would agree to annexation only if Mexico agreed."[54] In an amazing turn of events, the leaders of each major party, who personally opposed the expansion of slavery, adopted positions that kept them from addressing slavery as an issue. The system Van Buren designed had worked to perfection.

Yet there was a catch: at least half the nation wanted Texas annexed, and the impetus for annexation was the November 1844 election of Tennessean James K.

Polk. With both Van Buren and Clay unpopular in large parts of nonslaveholding states, and with Van Buren having to fight off a challenge within the Democratic Party from Lewis Cass of Michigan, a northerner who supported annexation, a deadlock ensued that opened the door for another annexationist nominee, a dark horse candidate congressman—Polk. The son of a surveyor, James Knox Polk was a lawyer, Tennessee governor, former Speaker of the House, and a southern expansionist who not only supported annexation, but even labeled it reannexation, claiming that Texas had been a part of the Louisiana Purchase. Defeated for reelection as Tennessee governor in 1843, he turned his attention to the national stage. Polk maneuvered his way to the Democratic nomination after nine ballots, to his own surprise.

Facing Clay in the general election, Polk turned Clay's conservatism against him. The Kentuckian said he had "no personal objection to the annexation of Texas," but he did not openly advocate it.[55] Polk, on the other hand, ran for president on the shrewd platform of annexing *both* Texas and Oregon. Clay's vacillation angered many ardent Free-Soilers, who found a purer candidate in James G. Birney and the fledgling Liberty Party. Birney siphoned off 62,300 votes, certainly almost all at the Whigs' expense, or enough to deprive Clay of the popular vote victory. Since Clay lost the electoral vote 170 to 105—with Polk taking such northern states as Michigan, New York, Illinois, Indiana, and Pennsylvania—it is likely that the Liberty Party cost Clay the election. New York alone, where Birney took 6,000 votes from Clay to hand the state to Polk, would have provided the Kentuckian his margin of victory. By any account, the election was a referendum on annexing Texas and Oregon, which Polk had cleverly packaged together. Linking the Oregon Territory took the sting out of adding a new slave state. The election accelerated the trend in which a handful of states had started to gain enough electoral clout that they could, under the right circumstances, elect a president without the slightest support or participation from the South.

Calling himself Young Hickory, Polk found that his predecessor had made much of the expansionist campaign rhetoric unnecessary. Viewing the results of the election as a mandate to annex Texas, in his last months in office Tyler gained a joint annexation resolution (and arguably a blatant violation of the Constitution) from Congress. This circumvented the need for a two-thirds Senate vote to acquire Texas by a treaty, and the resolution passed. Tyler signed the resolution in March 1845, a month before Polk took office, and Texas was offered the option of coming into the Union as one state or later subdividing into as many as five. On December 29, 1845, a unified Texas joined the Union as a slave state, a move John Quincy Adams called "the heaviest calamity that ever befell myself or my country."[56] Mexico immediately broke off diplomatic relations with the United States—a sure prelude to war in that era—prompting Polk to tell the American consul in California, Thomas Larkin, that if a revolt broke out among the *Californios* against the Mexican government, he should support it.

All along, Mexico suspected the United States of being behind an 1837 revolution in New Mexico. Then there remained the continuing issue of whether the

Nueces River, and not the Rio Grande, was the actual boundary. Despite his belligerent posturing, Polk sent Louisianan James Slidell as a special envoy to Mexico in January 1846 with instructions to try to purchase New Mexico and California with an offer so low that it implied war would follow if the Mexicans did not accept it. Anticipating the failure of Slidell's mission, Polk also ordered troops into Louisiana and alerted Larkin that the U.S. Navy would capture California ports in the event of war. Slidell's proposal outraged Mexico, and he returned home empty-handed. Satisfied that he had done everything possible to avoid war, Polk sent General Zachary Taylor, "Old Rough-and-Ready," with a large force, ordering them to encamp in Texas with their cannons pointed directly across the Rio Grande. Polk wanted a war, but he needed the Mexicans to start it. They obliged. General Mariano Arista's troops skirmished with Polk's men in May, at which point Polk could disingenuously write Congress asking for a war declaration while being technically correct: "Not withstanding our efforts to avoid it, war exists by the act of Mexico herself."[57] He did not mention that in December he had also sent John C. Frémont with a column west and dispatched the Pacific Fleet to California, ostensibly "in case" hostilities commenced, but in reality to have troops in place to take advantage of a war.

Northern Whigs naturally balked, noting that despite promises about acquiring Oregon, Polk's aggression was aimed in a decided southwesterly direction. A Whig congressman from Illinois, Abraham Lincoln, openly challenged the administration's policy, demanding to know the exact location—the "spot"—on which American blood had been shed, and sixty-seven Whigs voted against providing funds for the war. Lincoln's "spot resolutions" failed to derail the war effort, but gained the gangly Whig political attention for the future. For the most part, Whigs did their duty, including Generals Taylor and Winfield "Old Fuss and Feathers" Scott. The Democratic South, of course, joined the war effort with enthusiasm—Tennessee was dubbed the Volunteer State because its enlistments skyrocketed—and the Mexican War commenced.

Some observers, such as Horace Greeley, in the New York *Tribune*, predicted that the United States "can easily defeat the armies of Mexico, slaughter them by the thousands, and pursue them perhaps to their capital."[58] But Mexico wanted the war as well, and both Mexican military strategists and European observers expressed a near universal opinion that Mexican troops would triumphantly march into Washington, D.C., in as little as six weeks! Critics of American foreign policy, including many modern Mexican and Chicano nationalists, point to the vast territory Mexico lost in the war, and even Mexican historians of the day blamed the war on "the spirit of aggrandizement of the United States . . . availing itself of its power to conquer us."[59] Yet few have considered exactly what a victorious Mexican government would have demanded in concessions from the United States. Certainly Texas would have been restored to Mexico. The fact is, Mexico lusted for land as much as the gringos did and fully expected to win.

Polk made clear in his diary the importance of holding "military possession of California at the time peace was made," and he intended to acquire California,

New Mexico, and "perhaps some others of the Northern Provinces of Mexico" whenever the war ended.[60] Congress called for 50,000 volunteers and appropriated $10 million. Taking part in the operation were several outstanding junior officers, including Ulysses Grant, George McClellan, Robert E. Lee, Albert Sidney Johnston, Braxton Bragg, Stonewall Jackson, George Pickett, James Longstreet, and William Tecumseh Sherman.

At Palo Alto, in early May, the Americans engaged Arista's forces, decimating 1,000 Mexican lancers who attempted a foolish cavalry charge against the U.S. squares. It was a brief, but bloody draw in which Taylor lost 9 men to the Mexicans' 250, but he was unable to follow up because of nightfall. At his council of war, Taylor asked for advice. An artillery captain blurted out, "We whipped 'em today and we can whip 'em tomorrow." Indeed, on May ninth, the Americans won another lopsided battle at Resaca de la Palma.[61]

While the military was winning early victories in the field, Polk engaged in a clever plan to bring the exiled dictator who had massacred the defenders of the Alamo and Goliad back from exile in Cuba. On August 4, 1846, Polk negotiated a deal to not only bring Santa Anna back, but to pay him $2 million—ostensibly a bribe as an advance payment on the cession of California. The former dictator convinced Polk that if the United States could restore him to power, he would agree to a treaty favorable to the United States.

Two separate developments ended all hopes of a quick peace. First, Pennsylvania congressman David Wilmot attached a proviso to the $2 million payment that slavery be prohibited from any lands taken in the war. Wilmot, a freshman Democrat from Pennsylvania, further eroded the moratorium on slavery debate, which had been introduced in December 1835 to stymie all legislative discussion of slavery. Under the rule all antislavery petitions and resolutions had to be referred to a select committee, whose standing orders were to report back that Congress had no power to interfere with slavery.[62] This, in essence, tabled all petitions that in any way mentioned slavery, and it became a standing rule of the House in 1840. But the gag rule backfired. "This rule manufactures abolitionists and abolitionism," one Southerner wrote, comparing the rule to religious freedom: "It is much easier to make the mass of the people understand that a given prayer cannot be granted than that they have no right to pray at all."[63] (Ironically, the gag rule *had applied* to prayer in Congress too.) After it fell into disuse in 1845, Speakers of the House kept the slavery discussion under wraps by only recognizing speakers who had the Democratic Party's trust. The chair recognized Wilmot largely because he had proven his loyalty to Polk by voting with the administration on the tariff reduction when every other Democrat had crossed party lines to vote against it.[64] But Wilmot hammered the president with his opening statements before invoking the language of the Northwest Ordinance to prohibit slavery from any newly acquired territories.

Although the Wilmot Proviso never passed, a second obstacle to a quick treaty with Santa Anna was the Mexican president himself, who probably never had any intention of abiding by his secret agreement. No sooner had he walked ashore, slipped through the American blockade by a British steamer given a right-of-way by U.S. gunboats, than he had announced that he would fight "until death, to the defense of the liberty and independence of the republic."[65] Consequently, a Pennsylvania congressman and a former dictator unwittingly collaborated to extend the war neither of them wanted, ensuring in the process that the United States would gain territory neither of them wanted it to have.

Meanwhile, in the field, the army struggled to maintain discipline among the hordes of volunteers arriving. New recruits "came in a steamboat flood down the Mississippi, out onto the Gulf and across to Port Isabel and thence up the Rio Grande to Matamoros of Taylor's advanced base . . . [When the "12-monthers" came into camp in August 1846], they murdered; they raped, robbed and rioted."[66] Mexican priests in the area called the undisciplined troops "vandals" from hell and a Texas colonel considered them "worse than Russian Cossacks."[67] Each unit of volunteers sported its own dress: the Kentucky volunteers had three-cornered hats and full beards, whereas other groups had "uniforms" of every conceivable color and style. Once they entered Mexico, they were given another name, "gringos," for the song they sang, "Green Grow the Lilacs." With difficulty Taylor finally formed this riffraff into an army, and by September he had about 6,000 troops who could fight. He marched on Monterrey, defended by 7,000 Mexicans and 40 cannons—a formidable objective.

Even at this early stage, it became clear that the United States would prevail, and in the process occupy large areas of territory previously held by Mexico. At Monterrey, in September 1846, Taylor defeated a force of slightly superior size to his own. The final rush was led by Jefferson Davis and his Mississippi volunteers. On the cusp of a major victory, Taylor halted and accepted an eight-week armistice, even allowing the Mexicans to withdraw their army. He did so more out of necessity than charity, since his depleted force desperately needed 5,000 reinforcements, which arrived the following January. American troops then resumed their advance.

Attack was the American modus operandi during the war. Despite taking the offensive, the United States time and again suffered only minor losses, even when assaulting Mexicans dug in behind defenses. And *every* unit of Taylor's army attacked—light dragoons, skirmishers, heavy infantry. The success of the Americans impressed experienced commanders (such as Henry Halleck, who later wrote about the offensives in his book, *Elements of Military Art and Science*), who shook their heads in wonder at the Yanks' aggressiveness.[68]

Meanwhile, Taylor now had a reputation as a true hero. Suddenly it dawned on Polk that he had created a viable political opponent for any Democratic candidate in 1848, and he now scrambled to swing the military glory to someone besides Old Rough-and-Ready. Ordering Taylor to halt, Polk instructed General Winfield Scott, the only other man truly qualified to command an entire army, to take a new expedition of 10,000 to Vera Cruz. Polk ironically found himself relying on two Whig generals, "whom he hated more than the Mexicans."[69] Scott had no intention of commanding a disastrous invasion, telling his confidants that he intended to lose no more than 100 men in the nation's first amphibious operation: "for every one over that number I shall regard myself as a murderer."[70] In fact, he did better, losing only 67 to a fortified city that had refused to surrender.

Other offensives against Mexican outposts in the southwest and in California occurred simultaneous to the main Mexican invasion. Brigadier General Stephen Watts Kearny marched from Leavenworth, Kansas, to Santa Fe, which he found unoccupied by enemy forces, then set out for California. Reinforced by an expedition under Commodore Robert Stockton and by the Mormon battalion out of Utah, Kearny's united command captured San Diego, then swept on to Los Angeles. By that time, the Mexicans had surrendered—not to Stockton or Kearny, but to another American force under John C. Frémont. The Pathfinder, as Frémont was known, had received orders from Polk to advance to California on a "scientific" expedition in December 1845, along with the Slidell Pacific Fleet orders. Thus, from the outset, Polk had ensured that sufficient American force would rendezvous in California to "persuade" the local pro-American *Californios* to rise up. What ensued was the the Bear Flag Revolt (hence the bear on the flag of the state of California), and Polk's ambition of gaining California became a reality.

In Mexico, in August, Scott renewed his advance inland toward Mexico City over the rugged mountains and against stiff resistance. Scott had no intention of slogging through the marshes that protected the eastern flank of Mexico City, but instead planned to attack by way of Chapultepec in the west. As he reached the outskirts of Chapultepec, he found the fortress defended by 900 soldiers and 100 young cadets at the military college. In a pitched battle where American marines assaulted positions defended by "los niños"—students from the elite military school—and fighting hand to hand, saber to saber, Scott's forces opened the road to Mexico City. On September 14, 1847, in the first-ever U.S. occupation of an enemy capital, American marines guarded the National Palace, "the Halls of Montezuma," against vandals and thieves. Santa Anna was deposed and scurried out of the country yet again, but 1,721 American soldiers had died in action and another 11,155 of disease.

Occupying both California and Texas, plus the southwestern part of North America, and following Scott's capture of Mexico City, the United States was in a position to negotiate from strength. Polk instructed Nicholas Trist, a staunch Whig, to negotiate a settlement. Polk thought Trist, a clerk, would be pliant. Instead, Trist aggressively negotiated. Whigs and some Democrats cast a wary eye at occupied Mexico herself. The last thing antislavery forces wanted was a large chunk of Mexico annexed under the auspices of victory, then converted into slave territory. They recoiled when the editor of the New York *Sun* suggested that "if the Mexican people with one voice ask to come into the Union our boundary . . . may extend much further than the Rio Grande."[71] Poet Walt Whitman agreed that Mexico "won't need much coaxing to join the United States."[72]

Such talk was pure fantasy from the perspective of majorities in both the United States and Mexico. White Americans had no intention of allowing in vast numbers of brown-skinned Mexicans, whereas Mexico, which may have detested Santa Anna, had no love for the gringos.

Trist and Mexican representatives convened their discussions in January 1848 at the town of Guadalupe Hidalgo, and a month later the two sides signed the Treaty of Guadalupe Hidalgo. It provided for a payment of $15 million to Mexico, and the United States gained California, the disputed Texas border to the Rio Grande, and a vast expanse of territory, including present-day Arizona, New Mexico, Utah, and Nevada. Trist ignored Polk's revised instructions to press for acquisition of part of northern Mexico proper.

Polk was furious and recalled Trist, who then ignored the letter recalling him, reasoning that Polk wrote it without full knowledge of the situation. Trist refused to support Polk's designs on Mexico City; and Scott, another Whig on-site, concurred with Trist's position, thus constricting potential slave territory above the Rio Grande. Polk had to conclude the matter, leaving him no choice but to send the treaty to Congress, where it produced as many critics as proponents. But its opponents, who had sufficient votes to defeat it from opposite sides of the slavery argument, could never unite to defeat it, and the Senate approved the treaty on March 10, 1848. As David Potter aptly put it, "By the acts of a dismissed emissary, a disappointed president, and a divided Senate, the United States acquired California and the Southwest."[73]

Victorious American troops withdrew from Mexico in July 1848. Polk's successful annexation of the North American Southwest constituted only half his strategy to maintain a balance in the Union and fulfill his 1844 campaign promise. He also had to obtain a favorable settlement of the Oregon question. This eventually culminated in the Packenham-Buchanan Treaty. A conflict arose over American claims to Oregon territory up to Fort Simpson, on the 54-degree 40-minute parallel that encompassed the Fraser River. Britain, however, insisted on a Columbia River boundary—and badly wanted Puget Sound. Polk offered a compromise demarcation line at the forty-ninth parallel, just below Fort Victoria on Vancouver Island—which still gave Americans claim to most of the Oregon Territory—but the British minister Richard Packenham rejected Polk's proposal out of hand. Americans aggressively invoked the phrase "Fifty-four forty or fight," and the British, quickly reassessing the situation, negotiated with James Buchanan, secretary of state, agreeing to Polk's compromise line. The Senate approved the final treaty on June 15, 1846.

Taken together, Mexico and Oregon formed bookends, a pair of the most spectacular foreign policy achievements in American history. Moreover, by "settling" for Oregon well below the 54-degree line, Polk checked John Quincy

Adams and the Whigs' dreams of a larger free-soil Pacific Northwest. In four short years Polk filled out the present boundaries of the continental United States (leaving only a small southern slice of Arizona in 1853), literally enlarging the nation from "sea to shining sea."

At the same time, his policies doomed any chance he had at reelection, even should he have chosen to renege on his campaign promise to serve only one term. Polk's policies had left him a divided party. Free-soilers had found it impossible to support the Texas annexation, and now a reduced Oregon angered northern Democrats as a betrayal, signaling the first serious rift between the northern and southern wings of the party. This breach opened wider over the tariff, where Polk's Treasury secretary, Robert J. Walker, pressed for reductions in rates. Northerners again saw a double cross.

When Polk returned to Tennessee, where he died a few months later, he had guided the United States through the high tide of manifest destiny. Unintentionally, he had also helped inflict serious wounds on the Democratic Party's uneasy sectional alliances, and, as he feared, had raised a popular general, Zachary Taylor, to the status of political opponent. The newly opened lands called out once again to restless Americans, who poured in.

Westward Again

Beneath the simmering political cauldron of pro- and antislavery strife, pioneers continued to surge west. Explorers and trappers were soon joined in the 1830s by a relatively new group, religious missionaries. Second Great Awakening enthusiasm propelled Methodists, led by the Reverend Jason Lee, to Oregon in 1832 to establish a mission to the Chinook Indians.[74] Elijah White, then Marcus Whitman and his pregnant wife, Narcissa, followed later, bringing along some thousand migrants (and measles) to the region. White and Lee soon squabbled over methods; eventually the Methodist board concluded that it could not Christianize the Indians and dried up the funding for the Methodist missions. The Whitmans were even more unfortunate. After measles spread among the Cayuse Indians, they blamed the missionaries and murdered the Whitmans at their Walla Walla mission. Such brutality failed to stem the missionary zeal toward the new western territories, however, and a number of Jesuit priests, most notably Father Pierre De Smet, established six successful missions in the northern Rocky Mountains of Montana, Idaho, and Washington.

Pioneer farmer immigrants followed the missionaries into Oregon, where the population rose from fifty to more than six thousand whites between 1839 and 1846. They traveled the Oregon Trail from Independence, Missouri, along the southern bank of the Platte River, across Wyoming and southern Idaho, and finally to Fort Vancouver via the Columbia River. Oregon Trail pioneers encountered hardships including rainstorms, snow and ice, treacherous rivers, steep mountain passes, and wild animals. Another group of immigrants, the Mormons, trekked their way to Utah along the northern bank of the Platte River under the leadership of Brigham Young. They arrived at the Great Salt Lake just as the

Mexican War broke out; tens of thousands of their brethren joined them during the following decades. The Mormon Trail, as it was called, attracted many California-bound settlers and, very soon, gold miners.

Discovery of gold at Sutter's Mill near Sacramento in 1848 brought hordes of miners, prospectors, and speculators, virtually all of them men, and many attracted to the seamier side of the social order. Any number of famous Americans spent time in the California gold camps, including Mark Twain and Henry Dana, both of whom wrote notable essays on their experiences. But for every Twain or Dana who made it to California, and left, and for every prospector who actually discovered gold, there were perhaps a hundred who went away broke, many of whom had abandoned their families and farms to seek the precious metal. Even after the gold played out, there was no stopping the population increase as some discovered the natural beauty and freedom offered by the West and stayed. San Francisco swelled from a thousand souls in 1856 to fifty thousand by decade's end, whereas in parts of Arizona and Colorado gold booms (and discoveries of other metals) could produce an overnight metropolis and just as quickly, a ghost town.

The Pacific Coast was largely sealed off from the rest of the country by the Great Plains and Rocky Mountains. Travel to California was best done by boat from ports along the Atlantic to Panama, then overland, then on another boat up the coast. Crossing overland directly from Missouri was a dangerous and expensive proposition.

St. Joseph, Missouri, the jumping-off point for overland travel, provided plenty of reputable stables and outfitters, but it was also home to dens of thieves and speculators who preyed on unsuspecting pioneers. Thousands of travelers poured into St. Joseph, then on across the overland trail to Oregon on a two-thousand-mile trek that could take six months. Up to 5,000 per year followed the trail in the mid-1840s, of which some 2,700 continued on to California. By 1850, after the discovery of gold, more than 55,000 pioneers crossed the desert in a year. Perhaps another thousand traders frequented the Santa Fe Trail. Many Forty-niners preferred the water route. San Francisco, the supply depot for Sacramento, overnight became a thriving city. In seven years—from 1849 to 1856—the city's population filled with merchants, artisans, shopkeepers, bankers, lawyers, saloon owners, and traders. Access to the Pacific Ocean facilitated trade from around the world, giving the town an international and multiethnic character. Saloons and gambling dens dotted the cityscape, enabling gangs and brigands to disrupt peaceful commerce.

With the addition and slow settlement of California, the Pacific Northwest, and the relatively unexplored American Southwest, Americans east of the Mississippi again turned their attention inward. After all, the objective of stretching the United States from sea to shining sea had been met. Only the most radical and unrealistic expansionists desired annexation of Mexico, so further movement southward was blocked. In the 1850s there would be talk of acquiring Cuba, but the concept of manifest destiny had crested. Moreover, the elephant in the room could no longer be ignored. In the years that followed, from 1848 until 1860, slavery dominated almost every aspect of American politics in one form or another.

CHAPTER EIGHT

The House Dividing, 1848–60

The Falling Veil

A chilling wire service report from Harper's Ferry, Virginia, reached major U.S. cities on October 18, 1859:

> Harper's Ferry: 6 a.m.—Preparations are making to storm the Armory. . . . Three rioters are lying dead in the street, and three more lying dead in the river. . . . Another rioter named Lewis Leary, has just died, and confessed to the particulars of the plot which he says was concocted by Brown. . . . The rioters have just sent out a flag of truce. If they are not protected by the soldiers . . . every one captured will be hung.[1]

The "rioters" consisted of seventeen whites and five blacks (some former slaves) who intended to capture the federal armory in the city, use the arms contained therein to seize the town, and then wait for the "army" of radical abolitionists and rebel slaves that John Brown, the leader, believed would materialize. Brown, a Kansas abolitionist guerrilla fighter who had worked in the Underground Railroad, thought that the slave South would collapse if he conquered Virginia.

Virginia militiamen hastily grabbed guns and ammunition and began assembling. Farther away, other towns, including Charlestown, Martinsburg, and Shepherdstown, awakened to warnings from their church bells, with citizens mobilizing quickly to quell a rumored slave rebellion. The telegraph alerted Washington, Baltimore, and New York, whose morning newspapers reported partial information. Many accounts referred to a "Negro Insurrection" or slave revolt. Hoping to avoid a full-scale rampage by the militias, as well as intending to suppress Brown's insurrection quickly, the president, James Buchanan, ordered U.S. Marines under the command of Colonel Robert E. Lee and his lieutenant, J.E.B. Stuart, to Harper's Ferry. They arrived on October seventeenth, by which time Brown, who had hoped he could avoid violence for at least a few days to allow his forces to grow, was forced to act without any reinforcements. Lee's troops surrounded Brown's motley band, then broke into the engine house at the train station near the armory where the conspirators had holed up. In the ensuing gun battle, the soldiers killed ten, including two of Brown's sons, and soldiers bayoneted Brown several times. He lived to stand trial, but his conviction was a foregone conclusion, and on December 2, 1859, John Brown was hanged in Charlestown, Virginia.

Brown's raid triggered a wave of paranoia in the South, which lived in utter terror of slave rebellions, even though few had ever occurred and none succeeded. It also provoked Northern abolitionist sympathizers to try to differentiate the man from the cause. "A squad of fanatics whose zeal is wonderfully disproportioned to their senses," was how the Chicago *Press and Tribune* referred to Brown.[2] "His are the errors of a fanatic, not the crimes of a felon," argued editor Horace Greeley in his New York *Tribune*. "There are fit and unfit modes of combating a great evil."[3]

Few doubted Brown was delusional at some level, especially since his plan involved arming slaves with several thousand pikes. Historian C. Vann Woodward warned historians looking at Brown "not to blink, as many of his biographers have done," on the question of Brown's looniness. Woodward pointed to Brown's history of insanity and his family tree, which was all but planted in the insane asylum arboretum: three aunts, two uncles, his only sister, her daughter, and six first cousins were all intermittently insane, periodically admitted to lunatic asylums or permanently confined.[4] However, the fact that he suffered from delusions did not mean that Brown did not have a plan with logic and order to it, nor did it mean that he did not understand the objective for which he fought.[5]

Such distinctions proved insufficient for those seeking a genuine martyr, however. Ralph Waldo Emerson celebrated Brown's execution, calling him a "new saint, a thousand times more justified when it is to save [slaves from] the auction-block."[6]

Others, such as abolitionist Wendell Phillips, blamed Virginia, which he called "a pirate ship," and he labeled the Commonwealth "a chronic insurrection."[7] "Who makes the Abolitionist?" asked Emerson. "The Slaveholder." Yet Emerson's and Phillips's logic absolved both the abolitionist lawbreakers and Jayhawkers (Kansas border ruffians), and their rationale gave license to cutthroats like William Quantrill and the James Gang just a few years later. Worse, it mocked the Constitution, elevating Emerson, Phillips, Brown, and whoever else disagreed with any part of it, above the law.

One statesman, in particular—one might say, alone—realized that the abolition of slavery had to come, and could *only* come, through the law. Anything less destroyed the very document that ensured the freedom that the slave craved and that the citizen enjoyed. Abraham Lincoln owed his political career and his presidential success to the concept that the Constitution had to remain above emotion, free from the often heartbreaking injustices of the moment, if it was to be the source of redress. By 1861, when few of his neighbors in the North would have fully understood that principle, and when virtually all of his countrymen in the South would have rejected it on a variety of grounds, both sides nevertheless soon arrived at the point where they had to test the validity of Lincoln's assertion that the nation could not remain a "house divided."

Time Line

1848: Zachary Taylor elected president

1850: Compromise of 1850; California admitted as a free state; Fugitive Slave Law passed; Taylor dies in office; Millard Fillmore becomes president

1852: Harriet Beecher Stowe publishes *Uncle Tom's Cabin*; Franklin Pierce elected president

1853: Gadsden Purchase

1854: Kansas-Nebraska Act; formation of Anti-Nebraska Party (later called Republican Party)

1856: James Buchanan elected president; John C. Fremont, Republican, comes within three states of carrying election with only northern votes.

1857: Panic of 1857; *Dred Scott* decision

1858: Senatorial election in Illinois pits Stephen Douglas against Abraham Lincoln; Lincoln-Douglas debates; Douglas issues Freeport Doctrine

1859: John Brown's raid at Harper's Ferry, Virginia

1860: Abraham Lincoln, Republican, elected president without a single Southern electoral vote; South Carolina secedes

An Arsenic Empire?

Having added Texas, California, and the Southwest to the national map, and finalized the boundaries with England over Oregon, the nation in 1850 looked much the way it does in 2004. Within twenty years, Alaska and the Gadsden Purchase would complete all continental territorial expansion, with other additions to the Union (Hawaii, Guam, Puerto Rico) coming from the Caribbean or the Pacific. "Polk's war" interrupted—only temporarily—the rapid growth of American industry and business after the Panic of 1837 had receded.

The United States stood behind only Russia, China, and Australia as the largest nation in the world, whereas its economic power dwarfed those states. By European concepts of space and distance, America's size was truly astonishing: it was as far from San Francisco to Boston as it was from Madrid to Moscow; Texas alone was bigger than France, and the Arizona Territory was larger than all of Great Britain. The population, too, was growing; science, invention, and the arts were thriving; and a competitive balance had again reappeared in politics.

Throughout her entire history, however, the United States had repeatedly put off dealing with the issue of slavery—first through constitutional compromise, then through appeals to bipartisan good will, then through a political party system that sought to squelch discussion through spoils, then finally through compromises, all combined with threats and warnings about disunion. By the 1850s, however, the structure built by the Founders revealed dangerous cracks in the framework. Emerson warned that acquisition of the Mexican cession territories, with its potential for sectional conflict, would be akin to taking arsenic. How much longer could the nation ignore slavery? And how much longer would the perpetual-motion machine of growing government power, spawned by Van Buren, spin before abolitionist voices were thrust to the fore? The answer to both questions was, not long.

The Dark, Nether Side

Opponents of capitalism—especially those who disparaged northern factories and big cities—began their attacks in earnest for the first time in American history. Certainly there was much to lament about the cities. Crime was rampant: New York City had as high a homicide rate in 1860 per one hundred thousand people as it did in the year 2000 (based on the FBI's uniform crime reports). After falling in the 1830s, homicides in New York nearly tripled, to fifteen per one hundred thousand by 1860.

By far the worst sections of New York's dark, nether side, as reformers of the day called it, included Hell's Kitchen, which by the late 1850s had started to replace the Bowery as the most dangerous and notorious section of the city.[8] Hell's Kitchen received its name from policemen, one of whom complained that the place was worse than hell itself, to which the other replied, "Hell's a mild climate. This is Hell's Kitchen, no less." According to one writer, the Bowery, Hell's Kitchen, and other rough sections of town, such as Rag Picker's Row, Mulligan Alley, Satan's Circus, and Cockroach Row consisted of

> . . . streets . . . ill paved, broken by carts and omnibuses into ruts and perilous gullies, obstructed by boxes and sign boards, impassable by reason of thronging vehicles, and filled with filth and garbage, which was left where it had been thrown to rot and send out its pestiferous fumes, breeding fever and cholera. [The writer] found hacks, carts, and omnibuses choking the thoroughfares, their Jehu drivers dashing through the crowd furiously, reckless of life; women and children were knocked down and trampled on . . . hackmen overcharged and were insolent to their passengers; baggage-smashers haunted the docks . . . rowdyism seemed to rule the city; it was at risk of your life that you walked the streets late at night; the club, the knife, the slung-shot, the revolver were in constant activity. . . .[9]

Like other cities, New York had seen rapid population increases, leaping from 123,000 in 1820 to 515,000 in 1850, mostly because of immigrants, people

Charles Loring Brace called "the Dangerous Classes."[10] Immigrants provided political clout, leapfrogging New York past Boston, Philadelphia, and Baltimore in size, but they also presented a growing problem, especially when it came to housing. The tenement population, which had reached half a million, included 18,000 who lived in cellars in addition to 15,000 beggars and 30,000 unsupervised children (apparently orphans). When the state legislature investigated the tenements, it concluded that cattle lived better than some New Yorkers.

Prostitution and begging were omnipresent, even in the presence of policemen, who "lounged about, gaped, gossiped, drank, and smoked, inactively useless upon street corners."[11] Some women used babies as props, renting them and then entering saloons, inducing them to cry by pinching them in order to solicit alms.[12]

Gangs were also seen everywhere in the slums, sporting names such as the Dead Rabbits, the Gorillas, the East Side Dramatic and Pleasure Club, and the Limburger Roarers. Politicians like Boss Tweed employed the gangs on election day—paid in cash and alcohol—to disrupt the polling places of the opponent, intimidating and, if necessary, beating up anyone with an intention of voting there. No wonder the English writer Rudyard Kipling, who visited New York, thought its streets were "first cousins to a Zanzibar foreshore or kin to the approaches of a Zulu kraal," a "shiftless outcome of squalid barbarism and reckless extravagance."[13]

Cast into this fetid urban setting were masses of immigrants. The United States moved past the 50,000-per-year immigrant level in 1832, but by 1840 nearly fifteen times that many people would arrive from Ireland alone. Overall immigration soared from 20,000 in 1820 to 2.2 million in 1850, with Wisconsin, New York, California, and the Minnesota Territory receiving the most newcomers. In those states and Minnesota, immigrants made up 20 percent or more of the total population. But Ohio, Louisiana, Illinois, Missouri, Iowa, Michigan, and Pennsylvania were not far behind, since immigrants made up between 10 to 20 percent of their populations.[14]

Steam-powered sailing vessels made the transatlantic crossing faster and easier, and the United States had generally open borders. Still, immigrants had to *want* to come to America. After all, both Canada and Mexico were approximately the same distance from Europe, yet they attracted only a handful of immigrants by comparison.

Lured by jobs, land, and low taxes, a small standing army (with no conscription), a relatively tiny government, complete absence of mandatory state church tithes, no state press censorship, and no czarist or emperor's secret police, Europeans thronged to American shores. As early as 1818, John Doyle, an Irish immigrant to Philadelphia who had found work as a printer and a map seller, wrote home, "I am doing astonishingly well, thanks be to God, and was able on the 16th of this month to make a deposit of 100 dollars in the Bank of the United States. . . . [Here] a man is allowed to thrive and flourish without having a penny taken out of his pocket by government; no visits from tax gatherers, constables, or soldiers."[15]

Following the potato famine in Ireland in the 1840s, when one third of the total population of Ireland disappeared, new waves of poor Irish arrived in Boston and New York City, with an estimated 20 percent of those who set sail dying en route.[16] From 1841 to 1850, 780,000 Irish arrived on American shores, and unlike other immigrants, they arrived as families, not as single males. Then, from 1851 to 1860, another 914,000 immigrated. Eventually, there were more Irish in America than in Ireland, and more Irish in New York than in Dublin.[17] Fresh from decades of political repression by the British, the Irish congregated in big coastal cities and, seeing the opportunity to belong to part of the power structure, they, more than any other immigrant group, moved into the police and fire departments. An 1869 list of New York City's Irish and German officeholders (the only two immigrant groups even mentioned!) revealed the stunning dominance of the Irish:

	GERMANS	IRISH
Mayor's office	2	11
Aldermen	2	34
Street department	0	87
Comptroller	2	126
Sheriff	1	23
Police captains	0	32[18]

Hibernian primacy in New York City administration was so overwhelming that even in the wake of the 9/11 terrorist attack in New York City a century and a half later, the names of the slain firefighters and police were overwhelmingly Irish.

With the exception of some who moved south—especially the Presbyterian Scots-Irish—new immigrants from the Emerald Isle remained urban and northern. Some already saw this as a problem. An editorial in 1855 from *The Citizen*, an Irish American newspaper, noted: "Westward Ho! The great mistake that emigrants, particularly Irish emigrants, make, on arriving in this country, is, that they remain in New York, and other Atlantic cities, till they are ruined, instead of proceeding at once to the Western country, where a virgin soil, teeming with plenty, invites them to its bosom."[19]

It was true that land was virtually free on the frontier, even if basic tools were not. Steven Thernstrom found that if immigrants simply left New England, their chances for economic success dramatically improved, especially as they moved into the ranks of skilled laborers.[20] More than the Dutch or Germans, the Irish suffered tremendous discrimination. The work of a deranged Protestant girl, Maria Monk, *Awful Disclosures of the Hotel Dieu in Montreal* (1836), circulated in the United States and fomented anti-Catholic bias that touched off the "no-popery" crusade that afflicted the predominantly Catholic Irish.[21] Monk's surreal work related incredibly fantastic tales of her "life" in a convent in Montreal, where she claimed to have observed tunnels leading to the burial grounds for the babies produced by the illicit relations between priests and nuns, as well as allegations of seductions in confessionals. The Church launched a number of convent inspections that completely disproved these nonsensical claims, but the book had its effect. Protestant mobs in Philadelphia, reacting to the bishop's request for tax money to fund parochial schools, stormed the Irish sector of town and set off dynamite in Catholic churches.

More than other older immigrant groups, the Irish gravitated to the Democratic Party in overwhelming numbers, partly because of the antielite appeal of the Democrats (which was largely imaginary). Politically, the Irish advanced steadily by using the Democratic Party machinery to elect Irishmen as the mayors of Boston in the 1880s. But there was an underside to this American dream because the Irish "brought to America a settled tradition of regarding the formal government as illegitimate, and the informal one as bearing the true impress of popular sovereignty."[22] Political corruption was ignored: "Stealing an election was rascally, not to be approved, but neither quite to be abhorred."[23] That translated into widespread graft, bribery, and vote fraud, which was made all the easier by party politics that simply required that the parties "get out the vote," not "get out the *legal* vote." These traits, and Irish willingness to vote as a block for the Democrats, made them targets for the Know-Nothing Party and other nativist groups.[24]

The experiences of Germans, the other main immigrant group, differed sharply from the Irish. First recruited to come to Pennsylvania by William Penn, Germans came to the United States in a wave (951,000) in the 1850s following the failure of the 1848 democratic revolutions in Germany. Early Germans in Philadelphia were Mennonites, but other religious Germans followed, including Amish and Calvinists, originating the popular (but wrong) name, Pennsylvania Dutch, which was a mispronunciation of *Deutsch*. Germans often brought more skills than the Irish, especially in the steel, mechanical, musical instrument trades (including Rudolf Wurlitzer and, later, Henry Steinway), and brewing (with brewers such as Schlitz, Pabst, and Budweiser).[25] But they also had more experience in land ownership, and had no shortage of good ideas, including the Kentucky long rifle and the Conestoga wagon. John Augustus Roebling invented the wire cable for the suspension bridge to Brooklyn; John Bausch and Henry Lomb pioneered eyeglass lens manufacturing; and Henry Heinz built a powerful food company from the ground up.

Above all, the Germans were farmers, with their farming communities spreading throughout the Appalachian valley. Berlins and Frankforts frequently appear on the map of mid-American towns. For many of them, America did not offer escape so much as opportunity to improve. Unlike the Irish, Germans immediately moved to open land, heading for the German-like northern tier of the Midwest and populating some of the rapidly growing cities there, such as

Cincinnati (which in 1860 had 161,000 people—nearly half of them foreign born), Milwaukee, St. Louis, and even as far southwest as Texas.[26]

One should take care not to emphasize the urban ethnic component of discord in American life too much. For every bar fight in Boston, there was at least one (if not ten) in saloons on the frontier. In Alabama, for example, the local editor of the Cahaba paper editorialized in 1856 that "guns and pistols . . . [were] fired in and from the alley ways and streets of the town" so frequently that it was "hardly safe to go from house to house."[27] A knife fight on the floor of the Arkansas House led to the gutting of one state representative over the relatively innocuous issue of putting out a bounty on wolf pelts, and a few years later, in 1847, one set of bank directors at the Farmers and Merchants Bank in Nashville engaged in a gun battle with other directors outside the courtroom.[28] Many of these clashes were family feuds. Most lacked an ethnic component.

One ethnic group that has suffered great persecution in modern times came to America virtually unnoticed. The first Jews had come to New Amsterdam in 1654, establishing the first North American synagogue a half century later. Over time, a thriving community emerged in what became New York (which, by 1914, had become home to half of all European Jews living in the United States). By 1850 there were perhaps thirty thousand Jews in the United States, but within the next thirty years the number would grow to more than half a million.[29] After the boom in textiles in the early 1800s, the Jews emerged as the dominant force in New York's needle trade, owning all but 17 of the 241 clothing firms in New York City in 1885.[30]

The largest influx of Jews took place long after the Civil War when Russian Jews sought sanctuary from czarist persecutions. Nevertheless, Jews achieved distinctions during the Civil War on both the Union and Confederate sides. Best known, probably, was Judah P. Benjamin, a Louisiana Whig who was the first Jew elected to the U.S. Senate and who served as the Confederacy's secretary of war. But five Jews won the Medal of Honor for the Union; Edward Rosewater, Lincoln's telegrapher, was Jewish; and the Cardozo family of New York produced important legal minds both before and after the conflict, including a state supreme court justice (Jacob) and a United States Supreme Court justice (Benjamin), who followed Louis Brandeis, yet another Jew, onto the Supreme Court.

All the immigrant groups found niches, and all succeeded—admittedly at different rates. All except one, that is. African Americans, most of whom came to the colonies as slaves, could point to small communities of "free men of color" in the north, and list numerous achievements. Yet their accomplishments only served to contrast their freedom with the bondage of millions of blacks in the same nation, in some cases only miles away.

Slavery, Still

Thirty years after the Missouri Compromise threatened to unravel the Union, the issue of slavery persevered as strongly as ever. Historians have remained puzzled by several anomalies regarding slavery. For example, even though by the 1850s there were higher profits in manufacturing in the South than in plantation farming, few planters gave up their gang-based labor systems to open factories.

Several facts about slavery must thus be acknowledged at the outset: (1) although slavery was profitable, profits and property rights alone did not explain its perpetuation; (2) the same free market that allowed Africans to be bought and sold at the same time exerted powerful pressures to liberate them; and (3) Southerners needed the force of government to maintain and expand slavery, and without it, a combination of the market and slave revolts would have ultimately ended the institution. In sum, slavery embodied the worst aspects of unfettered capitalism wedded to uninhibited government power, all turning on the egregiously flawed definition of a human as "property."

Although the vast majority of Southern blacks were slaves prior to 1860, there were, nonetheless, a significant number of free African Americans living in what would become the Confederacy. As many as 262,000 free blacks lived in the South, with the ratio higher in the upper South than in the lower. In Virginia, for example, census returns counted more than 58,000 free blacks out of a total black population of 548,000, and the number of free blacks had actually increased by about 3,700 in the decade prior to the Civil War.[31] A large majority of those free African Americans lived in Alexandria, Fredericksburg, Norfolk, Lynchburg, and Petersburg. Virginia debated expelling all free blacks in 1832, but the measure, which was tied to a bill for gradual, compensated emancipation, failed. Free blacks could stay, but for how long?

It goes without saying that most blacks in the American South were slaves. Before the international slave trade was banned in 1808, approximately 661,000 slaves were brought into the United States, or about 7 percent of all Africans transported across the Atlantic.[32] America did not receive, by any stretch of the imagination, even a small portion of slaves shipped from Africa: Cuba topped the list with 787,000. By 1860 the South had a slave population of 3.84 million, a figure that represented 60 percent of all the "agricultural wealth" in Alabama, Georgia, Louisiana, Mississippi, and South Carolina.

Other indicators reveal how critical a position slavery held in the overall wealth of the South. Wealth estimates by the U.S. government based on the 1860 census showed that slaves accounted for $3 *billion* in (mostly Southern) wealth, an amount exceeding the investments in railroads and manufacturing combined! To an extent—but only to an extent—the approaching conflict was one over the definition of property rights.[33] It might therefore be said that whenever the historical record says "states' rights" in the context of sectional debates, the phrase "rights to own slaves" should more correctly be inserted.[34] When Alabama's Franklin W. Bowdon wrote about the property rights in slaves, "If any of these rights can be invaded, there is no security for the remainder," Northerners instinctively knew that the inverse was true: if one group of people could be condemned to slavery for their race, another could suffer the same fate for their religious convictions, or their political affiliations.[35]

This aspect of slavery gnawed at the many nonslaveholders who composed the South's majority. Of all the Southerners who did own slaves, about 12 percent held most of the slaves, whereas some 36 percent of Southern farms in the most fertile valley regions had no slave labor at all; overall nearly half the farms in the cotton belt were slaveless.[36] Indeed, in some regions free farmers dominated the politics, particularly eastern Tennessee, western Virginia, northwestern Mississippi, and parts of Missouri. Even the small farmers who owned slaves steadily moved away from the large cash-crop practice of growing cotton, entering small-scale manufacturing by 1860. If one had little land, it made no sense economically to hold slaves. A field hand in the 1850s could cost $1,200, although prices fell with age and remaining productive years.

The stability and permanence of the system, however, arose from the large plantations, where a division of labor and assignment of slave gangs under the whip could overcome any inefficiencies associated with unfree labor. Robert Fogel and Stanley Engerman, in their famous *Time on the Cross* (1974), found that farms with slaves "were 29 percent more productive than those without slaves," and, more important, that the gains increased as farm size increased.[37] What is surprising is that the profitability of slavery was doubted for as long as it was, but that was largely because of the biased comments of contemporaries like antislavery activist Frank Blair, who wrote that "no one from a slave state could pass through 'the splendid farms of Sangamon and Morgan, without permitting an envious sigh to escape him at the evident superiority of free labor.' "[38] Nathaniel Banks argued in the 1850s before audiences in Boston and New York that slavery was "the foe of all industrial progress and the highest material prosperity."[39] It was true that deep pockets of poverty existed in the South, and that as a region it lagged behind United States per capita value-added average in 1860 by a substantial seven dollars, falling behind even the undeveloped Midwest.[40]

Adding to the unprofitability myth was a generation of Southern historians that included Ulrich Bonnell Phillips and Charles Sydnor, who could not reconcile the immorality of slavery with the obvious returns in the market system; they used flawed methodologies to conclude plantations had to be losing money.[41] A final argument that slavery was unprofitable came from the "backwardness" of the South (that is, its rural and nonindustrial character) that seemed to confirm that slavery caused the relative lack of industry compared to that in the North.[42]

Conditions among slaves differed dramatically. Frederick Douglass pointed out that "a city slave is almost a free citizen" who enjoyed "privileges altogether unknown to the whip-driven slave on the plantation."[43] A slave undertaker in Savannah hired other slaves, and made "payments" to his master at $250 a year. Artisans, mechanics, domestic servants, millers, ranchers, and other occupations were open to slaves. Simon Gray, a Mississippi slave, became a lumber raft captain whose crew included whites.[44] Gray also invested in real estate, speculated in raw timber, and owned several houses. Half of the workforce at the Richmond Tredegar Iron Works was comprised of slaves.

Even the most "benign" slavery, however, was always immoral and oppressive. Every female slave knew that ultimately if her master chose to make sexual advances, she had no authority to refuse. The system legitimized rape, even though benign masters never touched their female slaves. Every field hand was subject to the lash; some knew it more often than others. Much slavery in the South was cruel and violent even by the standards of the defenders. Runaways, if caught, were mutilated or executed, sometimes tortured by being boiled in cauldrons; and slaves for any reason—usually "insubordination"—were whipped. Free-market advocates argue that it made no sense to destroy a "fifteen-hundred-dollar investment," but such contentions assume that the slave owners always acted as rational capitalists instead of (occasionally) racists involved in reinforcement of social power structures.

Often the two intermingled—the capitalist mentality and the racial oppression—to the point that the system made no sense when viewed solely in the context of either the market or race relations. For example, Fogel and Engerman's antiseptic economic conclusion that slaves were whipped an "average" of 0.7 times per year is put into perspective by pictures of slaves whose backs were scarred beyond recognition by the whip. Fogel and Engerman's data were reconstructed from a single slave owner's diary and are very questionable. Other evidence is that beatings were so frequent that they occurred more than once a week, and that fear of the lash permeated the plantations.[45] Some states had laws against killing a slave, though the punishments were relatively minor compared to the act. But such laws wilted in light of the slaves' actual testimony:

> It's too bad to belong to folks dat own you soul an' body; dat can tie you up to a tree, wid yo' face to de tree an' you' arms fastened tight aroun' it; who take a long curlin' whip an' cut de blood ever' lick. Folks a mile away could hear dem awful whippings. Dey was a terrible part of livin'.[46]

Plantation slave diets were rich in calories, but it is doubtful the provisions kept pace with the field labor, since data show that slaves born between 1790 and 1800 tended to be shorter than the free white population.[47] In other respects, though, Fogel and Engerman were right: while many historians have overemphasized the breakup of families under slavery—a point hammered home by Harriet Beecher Stowe's fictional *Uncle Tom's Cabin*—fewer slaves were separated from their mates than is often portrayed in television or the movies. As the result of narratives from living former slaves, collected during the New Deal by the Federal Writers Project, it has been determined that two thirds had lived in nuclear families.[48] If, however, one third of all slave families were destroyed by force in the form of sales on the auction block, that statistic alone reiterates the oppressive and inhumane nature of the institution. Nevertheless, the old saw that crime doesn't pay does not always apply, as was the case with slavery.

Several economic historians have placed the returns on slavery at about 8.5 percent, leaving no doubt that it was not only profitable in the short term, but viable in the long run because of the constantly increasing value of slaves as a scarce resource.[49] It would be equally mistaken, however, to assume that slave-based plantation agriculture was so profitable as to funnel the South into slavery in an almost deterministic manner. Quite the contrary, studies of Southern manufacturing have revealed that returns in fledgling Southern industries often exceeded 22 percent and in some instances reached as high as 45 percent—yet even those profits were not sufficient to pry the plantation owners' hands off their slaves.[50]

So what to make of a discrepancy of 45 percent returns in manufacturing compared with 8 percent in plantation agriculture? Why would Southerners pass up such gains in the industrial sector? Economic culture explains some of the reluctance. Few Southerners knew or understood the industrial system. More important, however, there were psychic gains associated with slave-based agriculture—dominance and control—that one could never find in industry. Gains on the plantations may have been lower, but they undergirded an entire way of life and the privileged position of the upper tiers of Southern society. The short answer to our question, then, is that it was about more than money. In the end, the persistence of slavery in the face of high nonagricultural returns testifies to aspects of its noneconomic character.

Ultimately slavery could exist only through the power of the state. It survived "because political forces prevented the typical decay and destruction of slavery experienced elsewhere."[51] Laws forcing free whites to join posses for runaway slaves, censoring mails, and forbidding slaves to own property all emanated from government, not the market. Slaveholders passed statutes prohibiting the manumission of slaves throughout the South, banned the practice of slaves's purchasing their own freedom, and used the criminal justice system to put teeth in the slave codes. States enforced laws against educating slaves and prohibiting slaves from testifying in court.[52] Those laws existed atop still other statutes that restricted the movement of even free blacks within the South or the disembarking of free black merchant sailors in Southern ports.[53] In total, slaveholders benefited from monumental reductions in the cost of slavery by, as economists would say, externalizing the costs to nonslaveowners. Moreover, the system insulated itself from market pressures, for there was *no true free market* as long as slavery was permitted anywhere; thus there could be no market discipline. Capitalism's emancipating powers could work only where the government served as a neutral referee instead of a hired gun working for the slave owner.

In contrast to Latin American countries and Mexico, which had institutionalized self-purchase, the American South moved in the opposite direction. It all made for a system in which, with each passing year, despite the advantages enjoyed by urban servant-slaves and mechanics, slaves were increasingly less likely to win their freedom and be treated as people. Combined with the growing perversion of Christian doctrines in the South that maintained that blacks were permanent slaves, it was inevitable that the South would grow more repressive, both toward blacks and whites.

Lincoln hoped that the "natural limits" of slavery would prove its undoing— that cotton production would peter out and slavery would become untenable.[54] In this Lincoln was in error. New uses for slave labor could always be found, and several studies have identified growing slave employment in cities and industry.[55] Lincoln also failed to anticipate that slavery could easily be adapted to mining and other large-scale agriculture, and he did not appreciate the significance of the Southern churches' scriptural revisionism as it applied to blacks. In the long run, only the market, or a war with the North, could have saved the South from its trajectory. When slaveholders foisted the costs of the peculiar institution onto the Southern citizenry through the government, no market correction was possible. Ultimately, Southern slave owners rejected both morality and the market, then went about trying to justify themselves.

Defending the Indefensible

Driven by the Declaration's inexorable logic that "all men are created equal," pressure rose for defenders of the slave system to explain their continued participation in the peculiar institution. John C. Calhoun, in 1838, noted that the defense of slavery had changed:

> This agitation [from abolitionists] has produced one happy effect; it has compelled us . . . to look into the nature and character of this great institution, and to correct many false impressions. . . . Many . . . once believed that [slavery] was a moral and political evil; that folly and delusion are gone; *we now see it in its true light . . . as the most safe and stable basis for free institutions in the world* [emphasis ours].[56]

Calhoun espoused the labor theory of value—the backbone of Marxist economic thinking—and in this he was joined by George Fitzhugh, Virginia's leading proslavery intellectual and proponent of socialism. Fitzhugh exposed slavery as the nonmarket, anticapitalist construct that it was by arguing that not only should all blacks be slaves, but so should most whites. "We are all cannibals," Fitzhugh intoned, "Cannibals all!" *Slaves Without Masters*, the subtitle of his book *Cannibals All!* (1854), offered a shockingly accurate exposé of the reality of socialism—or slavery, for to Fitzhugh they were one and the same.[57]

Slavery in the South, according to Fitzhugh, scarcely differed from factory labor in the North, where the mills of Massachusetts placed their workers in a captivity as sure as the fields of Alabama. Yet African slaves, Fitzhugh maintained, probably lived better than free white workers in the North because they were liberated from decision making. A few slaves even bought into Fitzhugh's nonsense: Harrison Berry, an Atlanta slave, published a pamphlet called *Slavery and Abolitionism, as Viewed by a Georgia Slave*, in which he warned slaves contemplating escape to the North that "subordination of the poor colored man [there], is greater than that of the slave South."[58] And, he added, "a Southern farm is the beau ideal of Communism; it is a joint concern, in which the slave consumes more than the master . . . and is far happier, because although the concern may fail, he is always sure of support."[59]

Where Fitzhugh's argument differed from that of Berry and others was in advocating slavery for whites: "Liberty is an evil which government is intended to correct," he maintained in *Sociology for the South*.[60] Like many of his Northern utopian counterparts, Fitzhugh viewed every "relationship" as a form of bondage or oppression. Marriage, parenting, and property ownership of any kind merely constituted different forms of slavery. Here, strange as it may seem, Fitzhugh had come full circle to the radical abolitionists of the North. Stephen Pearl Andrews, William Lloyd Garrison, and, earlier, Robert Owen had all contended that marriage constituted an unequal, oppressive relationship.[61] Radical communitarian abolitionists, of course, endeavored to minimize or ignore these similarities to the South's greatest intellectual defender of slavery.[62] But the distinctions between Owen's subjection to the tyranny of the commune and Fitzhugh's "blessings" of "liberation" through the lash nearly touched, if they did not overlap, in theory.

Equally ironic was the way in which Fitzhugh stood the North's free-labor argument on its head. Lincoln and other Northerners maintained that laborers must be free to contract with anyone for their work. Free labor meant the freedom to negotiate with any employer. Fitzhugh, however, arguing that all contract labor was essentially unfree, called factory work slave labor. In an astounding inversion, he then maintained that since slaves were free from all decisions, they truly were the free laborers. Thus, northern wage labor (in his view) was slave labor, whereas actual slave labor was free labor!

Aside from Fitzhugh's more exotic defenses of slavery, religion and the law offered the two best protections available to Southerners to perpetuate human bondage. Both the Protestant churches and the Roman Catholic Church (which had a relatively minor influence in the South, except for Missouri and Louisiana) permitted or enthusiastically embraced slavery as a means to convert "heathen" Africans, and in 1822 the South Carolina Baptist Association published the first defenses of slavery that saw it as a "positive good" by biblical standards. By the mid-1800s, many Protestant leaders had come to see slavery as the only hope of salvation for Africans, thus creating the "ultimate rationalization."[63] Dr. Samuel A. Cartwright of New Orleans reflected this view when he wrote in 1852 that it was impossible to "Christianize the negro without the intervention of slavery."[64]

Such a defense of slavery presented a massive dilemma, not only to the church, but also to all practicing Christians and, indeed, all Southerners: if slavery was for the purpose of Christianizing the heathen, why were there so few efforts made to evangelize blacks and, more important, to encourage them to read the Bible? Still more important, why were slaves who converted not *automatically* freed on the grounds that having become "new creatures" in Christ, they were now equals? To say the least, these were uncomfortable questions that most clergy and lay alike in Dixie avoided entirely.

Ironically, many of the antislavery societies got their start in the South, where the first three periodicals to challenge slavery appeared, although all three soon moved to free states or Maryland.[65]

Not surprisingly, after the Nat Turner rebellion in August 1831, which left fifty-seven whites brutally murdered, many Southern churches abandoned their view that slavery was a necessary evil and accepted the desirability of slavery as a means of social control. Turner's was not the first active resistance to slavery. Colonial precedents included the Charleston Plot, and in 1807 two shiploads of slaves starved themselves to death rather than submit to the auction block. In 1822 a South Carolina court condemned Denmark Vesey to the gallows for, it claimed, leading an uprising. Vesey, a slave who had won a lottery and purchased his freedom with the winnings, established an African Methodist Church in Charleston, which had three thousand members. Although it was taken as gospel for more than a century that Vesey actually led a rebellion, historian Michael Johnson, obtaining the original court records, has recently cast doubt on whether any slave revolt occurred at all. Johnson argues that the court, using testimony from a few slaves obtained through torture or coercion, framed Vesey and many others. Ultimately, he and thirty-five "conspirators" were hanged, but the "rebellion" may well have been a creation of the court's.[66]

In addition to the Vesey and Nat Turner uprisings, slave runaways were becoming more common, as demonstrated by the thousands who escaped and thousands more who were hunted down and maimed or killed. Nat Turner, however, threw a different scare into Southerners because he claimed as the inspiration for his actions the prompting of the Holy Spirit.[67] A "sign appearing in the heavens," he told Thomas Gray, would indicate the proper time to "fight against the Serpent."[68] The episode brought Virginia to a turning point—emancipation or complete repression—and it chose the latter. All meetings of free blacks or mulattoes were prohibited, even "under the pretense or pretext of attending a religious meeting."[69] Anne Arundel County, Maryland, enacted a resolution requiring vigilante committees to visit the houses of every free black "regularly" for "prompt correction of misconduct," or in other words, to intimidate them into staying indoors.[70] The message of the Vesey/Turner rebellions was also clear to whites: blacks had to be kept from Christianity, and Christianity from blacks, unless a new variant of Christianity could be concocted that explained black slavery in terms of the "curse of Ham" or some other misreading of scripture.

If religion constituted one pillar of proslavery enforcement, the law constituted another. Historian David Grimsted, examining riots in the antebellum period, found that by 1835 the civic disturbances had taken on a distinctly racial flavor. Nearly half of the riots in 1835 were slave or racially related, but those in the South uniquely had overtones of mob violence supported, or at the very least, tolerated, by the legal authorities.[71] Censorship of mails and newspapers from the North, forced conscription of free Southern whites into slave patrols, and infringements on free speech all gradually laid the groundwork for the South to become a police state; meanwhile, controversies over free speech and the right of assembly gave the abolitionists the issue with which they ultimately went mainstream: the problem of white rights affected by the culture and practice of slave mastery.[72]

By addressing white rights to free speech, instead of black rights, abolitionists sanitized their views, which in many cases lay so outside the accepted norms that to fully publicize them would risk ridicule and dismissal. This had the effect of putting them on the right side of history. The free-love and communitarian movements' association with antislavery was unfortunate and served to discredit many of the genuine Christian reformers who had stood in the vanguard of the abolition movement.[73]

No person provided a better target for Southern polemicists than William Lloyd Garrison. A meddler in the truest sense of the word, Garrison badgered his colleagues who smoked, drank, or indulged in any other habit of which he did not approve. Abandoned by his father at age three, Garrison had spent his early life in extreme poverty. Forced to sell molasses on the street and deliver wood, Garrison was steeped in insecurity. He received little education until he apprenticed with a printer, before striking out on his own. That venture failed. Undeterred, Garrison edited the *National Philanthropist*, a "paper devoted to the suppression of intemperance and its Kindred vices."[74] Provided a soapbox, Garrison proceeded to attack gambling, lotteries, sabbath violations, and war. Garrison suddenly saw himself as a celebrity, telling others his name would be "known to the world."

In his paper *Genius of Universal Emancipation*, Garrison criticized a merchant involved in the slave trade who had Garrison thrown into prison for libel. That fed his martyr complex even more. Once released, Garrison joined another abolitionist paper, *The Liberator*, where he expressed his hatred of slavery, and of the society that permitted it—even under the Constitution—in a cascade of violent language, calling Southern congressmen "thieves" and "robbers."[75]

Abolitionism brought Garrison into contact with other reformers, including Susan B. Anthony, the Grimké sisters, Frederick Douglass, and Elizabeth Cady Stanton. Each had an agenda, to be sure, but all agreed on abolition as a starting point. Garrison and Douglass eventually split over whether the Constitution should be used as a tool to eliminate slavery: Douglass answered in the affirmative, Garrison, having burned a copy of the Constitution, obviously answered in the negative.

The Political Pendulum

From 1848 to 1860, the South rode a roller-coaster of euphoria followed by depression. Several times solid guarantees for the continued protection of slavery appeared to be within the grasp of Southerners, only to be suddenly snatched away by new and even more foreboding signs of Northern abolitionist sentiment. This pendulum began with the election of Zachary Taylor, continued with the California statehood question, accelerated its swing with the admission of Kansas, and finally spun out of control with the *Dred Scott* decision and its repercussions.

The first swing of the pendulum came with the election of 1848. Van Buren's assumptions that only a "northern man of southern principles" could hold the nation together as president continued to direct the Democratic Party, which nominated Lewis Cass of Michigan. Cass originated a concept later made famous by Illinois Senator Stephen Douglas, popular sovereignty. As Cass and Douglas understood it, only the people of a territory, during the process by which they developed their state constitution, could prohibit slavery. Congress, whether in its function as administrator of the territories or in its national legislative function, had no role in legislating slavery. It was a convenient out, in that Cass and Douglas could claim they were personally opposed to slavery without ever having to undertake action against it, thus protecting them from Southern criticism over any new free-soil states that emerged from the process. In reality, popular sovereignty ensured exactly what transpired in Kansas: that both pro- and antislavery forces would seek to rig the state constitutional convention through infusions of (often temporary) immigrants. Once the deed was done, and a proslavery constitution in place, the recent arrivals could leave if they chose, but slavery would remain.

Whigs, too, realized that the proslavery vote was strong, and the free-soil vote not strong enough, to run strictly on slavery or related economic issues. They needed a candidate who would not antagonize the South, and many prominent Whigs fell in behind Zachary "Old Rough-and-Ready" Taylor, the Mexican War general. Taylor, however, was a Louisiana slaveholder who offended free-soil Whigs, who distrusted him. Taylor's ownership of slaves cost him within the party: except for "his negroes and cotton bales," one congressman wrote, he would have won the nomination without opposition.[76] Opposing Taylor was Henry Clay, ready for yet a fifth run at the presidency. But when Clay delivered an important address in Lexington, Kentucky, disavowing any acquisition of new (slave) territories in the Mexican War, he lost Southern support. His April 1844 Raleigh letter, in which he opposed annexation of Texas, did him irreparable damage.

Privately, Taylor was less Whiggish than he let on. He told intimates that the idea of a national bank "is dead & will not be revived in my time" and promised to raise tariffs only for revenue.[77] But Taylor benefited from a reviving economy, which made the election almost entirely about personality, where he had the reputation and the edge. A third party, the new Free Soil Party, siphoned off both Democrats and Whigs who opposed slavery. The Free-Soilers nominated Martin Van Buren, demonstrating the futility of Van Buren's earlier efforts to exclude slavery from the national politcal debate. Van Buren's forces drew in abolitionists, Liberty Party refugees, and "conscience Whigs" who opposed slavery under the slogan, "Free Soil, Free Speech, Free Labor, and Free Men."

Free-Soilers made a strong showing at the polls, raking in more than 10 percent of the vote, but did not change the outcome. Taylor won by an electoral vote margin of 163 to 137 and by a 5 percent margin in the popular vote. Virtually all of the Free-Soil ballots would have gone to the Whigs, who, despite Taylor's slave ownership, were viewed as the antislavery party. It is probable that Ohio would have gone to Taylor if not for the Free-Soilers.

The new president was nevertheless something of an odd duck. He had never voted in an American election. He relished his no-party affiliation. Most Americans learned what they knew of him through newspaper accounts of his remarkable military victories. Indeed, in a sense Taylor was the first outsider ever to run for the presidency. Jackson, although different from the elites who had dominated the White House, nevertheless willingly employed party machinery for his victory. Taylor, however, stressed his antiparty, almost renegade image much the way the Populist candidates of the 1880s and independents like H. Ross Perot did in the 1990s. The outsider appeal proved powerful because it gave people a sense that they could "vote for the man," largely on reputation or personality, without hashing out all the tough decisions demanded by a party platform. A Taylor supporter in Massachusetts claimed that enthusiasm for Taylor "springs from spontaneous combustion and will sweep all before it."[78] To assuage the concerns of Northern Whigs, Taylor accepted Millard Fillmore of Buffalo as his vice president.

In policy, Taylor surprised both parties. Although he sympathized with the South's need to protect slavery, he wanted to keep it out of California and New Mexico. He announced that in due course California, Utah, and New Mexico would apply for statehood directly, without going through the territorial stage. Under the circumstances, the states themselves, not Congress, would determine whether they allowed slaves. Taylor hoped to finesse the Southerners, reasoning that since they had already stated that they expected these territories to be free soil, there would be no need for the Wilmot Proviso. Nevertheless, he included a strong warning against the kind of disunion talk that had circulated in the South. When an October 1849 convention laid plans for a meeting of delegates from all the slaveholding states in Nashville the following year, attendees issued statements favoring disunion by leaders such as Congressman Robert Toombs of Georgia. Increasingly, such sentiments were invoked, and astute politicians of both sections took notice.

California presented an opportunity for Henry Clay to regain the initiative he had lost in the nominating process. He started machinery in motion to bring California into the Union—a plan that constituted nothing less than a final masterful stroke at compromise by the aging Kentuckian. Clay introduced legislation to combine the eight major points of contention over slavery in the new territories into four legislative headings. Then, his oratorical skills undiminished, Clay took the national stage one last time.

His first resolution called for California's admission as a free state; second, the status of the Utah and New Mexico territories was to be determined by popular sovereignty. Third, he proposed to fix the boundary of Texas where it then stood, leaving New Mexico intact. This provision also committed the federal government to assuming the debts of Texas, which was guaranteed to garner some support in the Lone Star State. Fourth, he sought to eliminate the slave trade in the District of Columbia and, finally, he offered a fugitive slave law that promised to deliver escaped slaves from one state to another.

Debate over Clay's compromise bill brought John Calhoun from his sickbed (although Senator James Mason of Virginia read Calhoun's speech), followed by stirring oratory from Daniel Webster. Both agreed that disunion was unthinkable. To the surprise of many, neither attacked the resolutions. Quite the contrary, Webster promised not to include Wilmot as a "taunt or a reproach," thereby extending the olive branch to the South. The debates culminated with Taylor supporter William H. Seward's famous "higher law" remark, that "there is a higher law than the Constitution," meaning that if the Constitution permitted slavery, Seward felt morally justified in ignoring it in favor of a higher moral principle.[79] Meanwhile, Clay thought that, tactically, he had guaranteed passage of the bill by tying the disparate parts together in a single package.

While Clay and his allies worked to defuse the sectional crisis, Taylor became ill and died on the Fourth of July. Millard Fillmore assumed the presidency amidst a rapidly unraveling controversy over the Texas-New Mexico border. At the end of July, Clay's compromise measures were carved away from the omnibus bill and were defeated individually. Only Utah's territorial status passed. California statehood, the Texas boundary, the fugitive slave law, all went down to stunning defeat. The strain proved so great on the seventy-three-year-old Clay that he left for Kentucky to recuperate. Jefferson Davis of Mississippi and Seward, archenemies of the compromise from opposite ends of the spectrum, celebrated openly. Their victory dance, however, did not last long.

Another rising force in American politics had stood patiently outside these contentious debates: Stephen A. Douglas of Illinois. Born in Vermont, Douglas studied law before moving to Ohio in 1833. There he contracted typhoid fever, recovered, and moved on to Illinois. A natural politician, Douglas had supported continuing the 36-degree 30-minute line and backed Polk on the Mexican War. In 1848 his new wife inherited more than one hundred slaves, which tarnished his image in Illinois; he nevertheless was elected senator by the Illinois legislature in 1846, after which he chaired the important committee on territories. From that position, Douglas could advance popular sovereignty in the territories.

When it came to the Compromise of 1850, Douglas saw the key to passage as exactly the opposite of Clay's strategy, namely, bringing up the various resolutions again independently and attempting to forge coalitions on each separately. Moreover, Fillmore announced his full support of the compromise and, after accepting the resignation of the Taylor cabinet, named Webster as his secretary of state.[80] Meanwhile, Douglas maneuvered the Texas boundary measure through Congress. One explosive issue was settled, and Douglas quickly followed with individual bills that admitted California, established New Mexico as a territory, and provided a fugitive slave law. Utah's territorial bill also passed. The final vote on the Fugitive Slave Law saw many Northerners abstaining, allowing the South to obtain federal enforcement. Douglas's strategy was brilliant—and doomed. Lawmakers drank all night after its passage and woke up with terrible hangovers and a sense of dread.

Moreover, whether it was truly a compromise is in doubt: few Southerners voted for any Northern provision, and few Northerners ever voted for any of the pro-Southern resolutions. All the "compromise" came from a group of Ohio Valley representatives who voted for both measures, on opposing sides of the issue. The very states that would become the bloody battlegrounds if war broke out— Maryland, Tennessee, Missouri, Kentucky—provided the entire compromise element. For the North and South, however, the compromise was an agreement to maneuver for still stronger positions, with the North betting on congressional representation as its advantage and the South wagering on federal guarantees on runaway slaves.

Fillmore called the compromise "final and irrevocable," not noticing that secessionists had nearly won control of four lower Southern state governments.[81] By supporting the compromise, Fillmore also ensured that the antislavery wing of the Whig party would block his nomination in 1852 in favor of Winfield Scott. (Scott's enemies referred to him as Old Fuss and Feathers while his supporters called him by the more affectionate Old Chippewa or Old Chapultepec, after his military victories.) A Virginian, Scott hoped to reprise the "Whig southerner" success of Taylor four years earlier. The Democrats, meanwhile, closed ranks around their candidate, Franklin Pierce of New Hampshire. Neither side took seriously the virulent secessionist talk bubbling forth from the lower South.

The Pendulum Swings North

Most man-made laws have unintended consequences. Such is human nature that even the wisest of legislators can seldom foresee every response to the acts of congresses, parliaments, and dumas. Few times, however, have legislators so misjudged the ramifications from their labor than with the Fugitive Slave Law.

The law contained several provisions that Southerners saw as reasonable and necessary, but which were guaranteed to turn ambivalent Northerners into fullfledged abolitionists. Runaway slaves were denied any right to jury trial, including in the jurisdiction to which they had escaped. Special commissions, and not regular civil courts, handled the runaways' cases. Commissioners received ten dollars for every runaway delivered to claimants, but only five dollars for cases in which the accused was set free, and the law empowered federal marshals to summon any free citizen to assist in the enforcement of the act. Not only did these provisions expose free blacks to outright capture under fraudulent circumstances, but now it also made free whites in the North accessories to their enslavement. When it came to the personal morality of Northerners, purchasing cotton made by slaves was one thing; actually helping to shackle and send a human back to the cotton fields was entirely different. The issue turned the tables on states' rights proponents by making fugitive slaves now a federal responsibility.

The law had the effect of both personalizing slavery to Northerners and inflaming their sense of righteous indignation about being dragged into the entire process. And it did not take long until the law was applied ex post facto to slaves who had run away in the past. In 1851, for example, an Indiana black named Mitchum was abducted from his home under the auspices of the act and delivered to a claimant who alleged Mitchum had escaped from him nineteen years earlier.[82] The trials were stacked against blacks: the closer one got to the South, the less likely commissioners were to take the word of Negroes over whites, and any black could be identified as a runaway. Northerners responded, not with cooperation, but violence. The arrest of a Detroit black man produced a mass meeting that required military force to disperse; a Pennsylvania mob of free blacks killed a slave owner attempting to corral a fugitive; and in Syracuse and Milwaukee crowds broke into public buildings to rescue alleged fugitives.

Politicians and editors fed the fire, declaring that the law embodied every evil that the radical abolitionists had warned about. Webster described the law as "indescribably base and wicked"; Theodore Parker called it "a hateful statute of kidnappers"; and Emerson termed it "a filthy law."[83] Whig papers urged citizens to "trample the law in the dust," and the city council of Chicago adopted resolutions declaring Northern representatives who supported it "traitors" like "Benedict Arnold and Judas Iscariot."[84] Even moderates, such as Edward Everett, recommended that Northerners disobey the law by refusing to enforce it. Throughout Ohio, town meetings branded any Northern officials who helped enforce the laws as "an enemy of the human race."[85]

Even had this angry resistance not appeared, there remained many practical problems with the law. Enforcement was expensive; Boston spent five thousand dollars to apprehend and return one slave, and after that it never enforced the law again. Part of the expense came from the unflagging efforts of the Underground Railroad, a system of friendly shelters aiding slaves' escape attempts. Begun sometime around 1842, the railroad involved (it was claimed) some three thousand operators who assisted more than fifty thousand fugitives out of slavery in the decade before the Civil War. One must be skeptical about the numbers ascribed to the Underground Railroad because it was in the interest of both sides— obviously for different reasons—to inflate the influence of the network.[86] Census data, for example, does not support the large numbers of escaped slaves in the North, and there is reason to think that much of the undocumented "success" of the Underground Railroad was fueled by a desire of radicals after the fact to have associated themselves with such a heroic undertaking.

Far more important than citizen revolts or daring liberation of slaves in Northern jails was the publication, beginning in 1851, of a serial work of fiction in the Washington-based *National Era*. Harriet Beecher Stowe, the author, and the daughter of abolitionist preacher Henry Ward Beecher, saw her serial take hold of the popular imagination like nothing else in American literary history. Compiled and published as *Uncle Tom's Cabin* in 1852, the best seller sold 300,000 copies in only a few months, eventually selling more than 3 million in America and 3.5 million more abroad.[87] Stowe never visited a plantation, and probably only glimpsed slaves in passing near Kentucky or Maryland, and her portrayal of slavery was designed to paint it in the harshest light. *Uncle Tom's Cabin* dramatized the plight of a slave, Uncle Tom, and his family, who worked for benign but financially troubled Arthur Shelby. Shelby had to put the slaves up for sale, leading to the escape of the slave maid, Eliza, who with her son, ultimately crossed the half-frozen Ohio River as the bloodhounds chased her. Uncle Tom, one of the lead characters, was "sold down the river" to a hard life in the fields, and was beaten to death by the evil slave driver, Simon Legree. Even in death, Tom, in Christ-like fashion, forgives Legree and his overseers.

The novel had every effect for which Stowe hoped, and probably more. As historian David Potter aptly put it, "Men who had remained unmoved by real fugitives wept for Tom under the lash and cheered for Eliza with the bloodhounds on her track."[88] Or as Jeffrey Hummel put the equation, "For every four votes that [Franklin] Pierce received from free states in 1852, one copy of *Uncle Tom's Cabin* was sold."[89]

Uncle Tom's Cabin quickly made it to the theater, which gave it an even wider audience, and by the time the war came, Abraham Lincoln greeted Stowe with the famous line, "So you're the little woman who wrote the book that made this great war."[90] Compared to whatever tremors the initial resistance to the Fugitive Slave Law produced, Stowe's book generated a seismic shock. The South, reveling in its apparent moral victory less than two years earlier, found the pendulum swinging against it again, with the new momentum coming from developments beyond American shores.

Franklin Pierce and Foreign Intrigue

Millard Fillmore's brief presidency hobbled to its conclusion as the Democrats gained massively in the off-term elections of 1850. Ohio's antislavery Whig Ben Wade, reminiscing about John Tyler's virtual defection from Whig policies and then Fillmore's inability to implement the Whig agenda, exclaimed, "God save us from Whig Vice Presidents."[91] Democrats sensed their old power returning. Holding two thirds of the House, they hoped to recapture the White House in 1852, which would be critical to the appointment of federal judges. They hewed to the maxim of finding a northern man of southern principles, specifically Franklin Pierce, a Vermont lawyer and ardent expansionist.[92]

Having attained the rank of brigadier general in the Mexican War, Pierce could not be successfully flanked by another Whig soldier, such as the eventual nominee, Winfield Scott. His friendship with his fellow Bowdoin alumnus, writer Nathaniel Hawthorne, paid dividends when Hawthorne agreed to ink Pierce's campaign biography. Hawthorne, of course, omitted any mention of Pierce's drinking problem, producing a thoroughly romanticized and unrealistic book.[93]

Pierce hardly needed Hawthorne's assistance to defeat Scott, whose antislavery stance was too abrasive. Winning a commanding 254 electoral votes to Scott's 42, with a 300,000-vote popular victory, Pierce dominated the Southern balloting. Free-Soiler John Hale had tallied only half of Van Buren's total four years earlier, but still the direction of the popular vote continued to work against the

Democrats. Soon a majority of Americans would be voting for other opposition parties. The 1852 election essentially finished the Whigs, who had become little more than me-too Democrats on the central issue of the day.

Pierce inherited a swirling plot (some of it scarcely concealed) to acquire Cuba for further slavery expansion. Mississippi's Senator Jefferson Davis brazenly announced, "Cuba must be ours."[94] Albert Brown, the other Mississippi senator, went further, urging the acquisition of Central American states: "Yes, I want these Countries for the spread of slavery. I would spread the blessings of slavery, like a religion of our Divine Master," and publicly even declared that he would extend slavery into the North, though adding, "I would not force it on them."[95] Brown's words terrified Northerners, suggesting the "slave power" had no intention of ceasing its expansion, even into free states.[96]

Pierce appointed Davis secretary of war and made Caleb Cushing, a Massachusetts manifest destiny man, attorney general. Far from distancing himself from expansionist fervor, Pierce fell in behind it. Davis, seeking a Southern transcontinental railroad route that would benefit the cotton South, sought to acquire a strip of land in northwest Mexico along what is modern-day Arizona. The forty-five thousand square miles ostensibly lay in territory governed by popular sovereignty, but the South was willing to trade a small strip of land that potentially could be free soil for Davis's railroad. Senator James Gadsden, a Democrat from South Carolina, persuaded Mexican president Santa Anna, back in office yet again, to sell the acreage for $10 million. Santa Anna had already spent nearly all the reparations given Mexico in the Treaty of Guadalupe Hidalgo five years earlier—much of it on fancy uniforms for his military—and now needed more money to outfit his army. As a result, the Gadsden Purchase became law in 1853.

Meanwhile, American ministers to a conference in Belgium nearly provoked an international incident over Cuba in 1854. For some time, American adventurers had been slipping onto the island, plaguing the Spanish. Overtures to Spain by the U.S. government to purchase Cuba for $130 million were rejected, but Spain's ability to control the island remained questionable. During a meeting of ministers from England, France, Spain, and the United States in Ostend, Belgium, warnings were heard that a slave revolt might soon occur in Cuba, leading American ministers to draft a confidential memorandum suggesting that if the island became too destabilized, the United States should simply take Cuba from Spain. Word of this Ostend Manifesto reached the public, forcing Pierce to repudiate it. He also cracked down on plans by rogue politicians like former Mississippi governor John A. Quitman to finance and plan the insertion of American soldiers of fortune into Cuba. (Quitman had been inspired by Tennessean William Walker's failed 1855 takeover of Nicaragua.)[97] Taken together, Pierce's actions dealt the coup de grâce to manifest destiny, and later expansionists would not even use the term.

Southern Triumph in Kansas

Despite smarting from the stiff resistance engendered by *Uncle Tom's Cabin*, Southerners in 1854 could claim victory. Despite several near riots over the Fugitive Slave Act, it remained the law of the land, and Stowe's book could not change that. Meanwhile, the South was about to receive a major windfall. An innocuous proposal to build a transcontinental railroad commanded little sectional interest. In fact, it promised to open vast new territory to slavery and accelerate the momentum toward war.

Since the 1840s, dreamers imagined railroads that would connect California with states east of the Mississippi. Asa Whitney, a New York merchant who produced one of the first of the transcontinental plans in 1844, argued for a privately constructed railroad whose expenses were offset by grants of public lands.[98] By 1852 the idea had attracted Stephen Douglas, the Illinois Democrat senator with presidential aspirations, who rightly saw that the transcontinental would make Chicago the trade hub of the entire middle United States. With little controversy the congressional delegations from Iowa, Missouri, and Illinois introduced a bill to organize a Nebraska Territory, the northern part of the old Louisiana Purchase, and, once again, illegally erase Indian claims to lands there.[99]

Suddenly, the South woke up. Since the Northwest Ordinance and Missouri Compromise, the understanding was that for every free state added to the Union, there would be a new slave state. Now a proposal was on the table that would soon add at least one new free state, with no sectional balance (the state would be free because the proposed Nebraska territory lay north of the Missouri Compromise 36-degree 30-minute line). In order to appease (and court) his concerned Southern Democrat brethren, Douglas therefore recrafted the Nebraska bill. The new law, the infamous Kansas-Nebraska Act of 1854, assuaged the South by revoking the thirty-three-year-old 36/30 Missouri Compromise line and replacing its restriction of slavery with popular sovereignty—a vote on slavery by the people of the territory. In one stroke of the pen, Douglas abolished a thirty-year covenant and opened the entire Lousiana Purchase to slavery![100]

Although the idea seems outrageous today—and was inflammatory at the time—from Stephen Douglas's narrow viewpoint it seemed like an astute political move. Douglas reasoned that, when all was said and done, the Great Plains territories would undoubtedly vote for free soil (cotton won't grow in Nebraska). In the meantime, however, Douglas would have given the South a fresh chance at the Louisiana Territory, keeping it on his side for the upcoming presidential election. The Kansas-Nebraska Act, Douglas naively believed, would win him more political friends than enemies and gain his home state a Chicago railroad empire in the process.

Douglas sooned learned he was horribly mistaken about the Kansas-Nebraska Act. After its passage, a contagion swept the country every bit as strong as the one sparked by *Uncle Tom's Cabin*. Free-Soilers, now including many Northern Democrats, arose in furious protest. The Democrats shattered over Kansas-Nebraska.

Meanwhile, the stunned Douglas, who had raised the whole territorial tar baby as a means to obtain a railroad and the presidency, succeeded only in fracturing his own party and starting a national crisis.[101]

The pendulum appeared to have swung the South's way again with the potential for new slave states in the territory of Louisiana Purchase, sans the Missouri Compromise line. Instead, the South soon found itself with yet another hollow victory. The ink had scarcely dried on the Kansas-Nebraska Act than Northern Democrats sustained massive defeats. Of ninety-one free-state House seats held by the Democrats in 1852, only twenty-five were still in the party's hands at the end of the elections, and none of the last sixty-six seats were ever recovered before the war.

Before the appointed Kansas territorial governor arrived, various self-defense associations and vigilante groups had sprung up in Missouri—and as far away as New York—in a strategy by both sides to pack Kansas with voters who would advance the agenda of the group sponsoring them. The Massachusetts Emigrant Aid Society, and others like it, was established to fund "settlers" (armed with new Sharp repeating rifles) as they moved to Kansas. Families soon followed the men into the territory, a prospect that hardly diminished suspicions of proslavery Kansans. Images of armies of hirelings and riffraff, recruited from all over the North to "preach abolitionism, and dig underground Rail-roads," consumed the Southern imagination.[102] The Kansas-Nebraska Act allowed virtually any "resident" to vote, meaning that whichever side could insert enough voters would control the state constitutional convention. Thousands of proslavery men, known as Border Ruffians or "pukes" (because of their affinity for hard liquor and its aftereffects) crossed the border from Missouri. The were led by one of the state's senators, David Atchison, who vowed to "kill every God-damned abolitionist in the district." And they elected a proslavery majority to the convention.[103] Most real settlers, in fact, were largely indifferent to slavery, and were more concerned with establishing legal title to their lands.

Missouri had a particularly acute interest in seeing that Kansas did not become a free-soil state. Starting about a hundred miles above St. Louis, a massive belt of slavery stretched across the state, producing a strip in which 15 percent of the population or more was made up of slaves lying along more than three-fourths of the border with Kansas. If Kansas became a free-soil state, it would create a free zone *below* a slave belt for the first time in American history.[104]

The proslavery legislature, meeting at Lecompton, enacted draconian laws, including making it a felony to even question publicly the right to have slaves. Unwilling to accept what they saw as a fraudulent constitutional convention, free-soil forces held their own convention at Topeka in the fall of 1855, and they went so far as to prematurely name their own senators! Now the tragic absurdity of the "house divided" surely became apparent to even the most dedicated moderates, for not only was the nation split in two, but Kansas, the first test of Douglas's popular sovereignty, divided into two bitterly hostile and irreconcilable camps with two constitutional conventions, two capitals, and two sets of senators! Proslavery and free-soil forces took up arms, each viewing the government, constitution, and laws of the other as illegitimate and deceitfully gained. And if there were not already enough guns in Kansas, the Reverend Henry Ward Beecher's congregation supplied rifles in boxes marked "Bibles," gaining the so-briquet Beecher's Bibles. Beecher's followers were not alone: men and arms flowed into Kansas from North and South. Bloodshed could not be avoided; it began in the fall of 1855.

A great deal of mythology, perpetuated by pamphleteers from both sides, created ominous-sounding phrases to describe actions that, in other times, might constitute little more than disturbing the peace. For example, there was the "sack of Lawrence," where in 1856 proslavery forces overturned some printing presses and fired a few cannon balls—ineffectively—at the Free States Hotel in Lawrence. Soon, however, enough, real violence ensued. Bleeding Kansas became the locus of gun battles, often involving out-of-state mercenaries, while local law enforcement officials—even when they honestly attempted to maintain order—stood by helplessly, lacking sufficient numbers to make arrests or keep the peace.

Half a continent away, another episode of violence occurred, but in a wholly different—and unexpected—context. The day before the "sack" occurred, Senator Charles Sumner delivered a major vitriolic speech entitled "The Crime Against Kansas." His attacks ranged far beyond the issues of slavery and Kansas, vilifying both Stephen Douglas and Senator Andrew Butler of South Carolina in highly personal and caustic terms. Employing strong sexual imagery, Sumner referred to the "rape" of "virgin territory," a "depraved longing" for new slave territory, "the harlot, slavery," which was the "mistress" of Senator Butler. No one stepped up to defend Douglas, and, given his recent reception among the southern Democrats, he probably did not expect any champions. Butler, on the other hand, was an old man with a speech impediment, and the attacks were unfair and downright mean.

Congressman Preston Brooks, a relative of Butler's and a fellow South Carolinian, thought the line of honor had been crossed. Since Sumner would not consent to a duel, Brooks determined to teach him a lesson. Marching up to the senator's seat, Brooks spoke harshly to Sumner, then proceeded to use his large cane to bash the senator repeatedly, eventually breaking the cane over Sumner's head. The attack left Sumner with such psychological damage that he could not function for two years, and according to Northern pamphleteers, Brooks had nearly killed the senator. The South labeled Brooks a hero, and "Brooks canes" suddenly came into vogue. The city of Charleston presented him with a new walking stick inscribed HIT HIM AGAIN! Northerners, on the other hand, kept Sumner's seat vacant, but the real symbolism was all too well understood. If a powerful white man could be caned on the Senate floor, what chance did a field slave have against more cruel beatings? It reinforced the abolitionists' claim that in a society that tolerated slavery anywhere, no free person's rights were safe, regardless of color.

Meanwhile, back in Kansas, violence escalated further when John Brown, a member of a free-soil volunteer group in Kansas, led seven others (including four of his sons) on a vigilante-style assassination of proslavery men. Using their broadswords, Brown's avengers hunted along Pottawatomie Creek, killing and mutilating five men and boys in what was termed the Pottawatomie massacre.

Northern propagandists, who were usually more adept than their Southern colleagues, quickly gained the high ground, going so far as to argue that Brown had not actually killed anyone. One paper claimed the murders had been the work of Comanches.[105] Taken together, the sack of Lawrence, the caning of Senator Butler, and the Pottawatomie massacre revealed the growing power of the press to inflame, distort, and propagandize for ideological purposes. It was a final irony that the institution of the partisan press, which the Jacksonians had invented to ensure their elections by gagging debate on slavery, now played a pivotal role in accelerating the coming conflict.

The Demise of the Whigs

Whatever remained of the southern Whigs withered away after the Kansas-Nebraska Act. The Whigs had always been a party tied to the American system but unwilling to take a stand on the major moral issue of the day, and that was its downfall. Yet in failing to address slavery, how did the Whigs significantly differ from the Democrats? Major differences over the tariff, a national bank, and land sales did not separate the two parties as much as has been assumed in the past. Those issues, although important on one level, were completely irrelevant on the higher plane where the national debate now moved.

As the Democrats grew stronger in the South, the Whigs, rather than growing stronger in the North, slipped quietly into history. Scott's 1852 campaign had shown some signs of a northern dominance by polling larger majorities in some northern states than Taylor had in 1848. Yet the Whigs disintegrated. Two new parties dismembered them. One, the American Party, arose out of negative reaction to an influx of Irish and German Catholic immigrants. The American Party tapped into the anti-immigrant perceptions that still burned within large segments of the country. Based largely in local lodges, where secrecy was the byword, the party became known as the Know-Nothings for the members' reply when asked about their organization, "I know nothing." A strong anti-Masonic element also infused the Know-Nothings.

Know-Nothings shocked the Democrats by scoring important successes in the 1854 elections, sweeping virtually every office in Massachusetts with 63 percent of the vote. Know-Nothings also harvested numerous votes in New York, and for a moment appeared to be the wave of the future. Fillmore himself decided in 1854 to infiltrate the Know-Nothings, deeming the Whigs hopeless.

Like the Whigs, however, the Know-Nothings were stillborn. They failed to see that slavery constituted a far greater threat to their constituents than did foreign "conspiracies." The fatal weakness of the Know-Nothing Party was that it alienated the very immigrants who were staunchly opposed to slavery, and thus, rather than creating a new alliance, fragmented already collapsing Whig coalitions. When their national convention met, the Know-Nothings split along sectional lines, and that was that. Abraham Lincoln perceived that a fundamental difference in principle existed between antislavery and nativism, between the new Republican Party and the Know-Nothings, asking "How can anyone who abhors the oppression of negroes be in favor of degrading classes of white people?" He warned, "When the Know-Nothings get control, [the Declaration] will read, 'All men are created equal, except Negroes and foreigners and Catholics.' "[106]

A second party, however, picking up the old Liberty Party and Free-Soil banners, sought to unite people of all stripes who opposed slavery under a single standard. Originally called the Anti-Nebraska Party, the new Republican Party bore in like a laser on the issue of slavery in the territories. Horace Greeley said that the Kansas-Nebraska Act created more free-soilers and abolitionists in two months than Garrison had in twenty years, and the new party's rapid growth far outstripped earlier variants like the Liberty Party. Foremost among the new leaders was Salmon P. Chase of Ohio, a former Liberty Party man who won the gubernatorial election as a Republican in Ohio in 1855. Along with William H. Seward, Chase provided the intellectual foundation of the new party.

Republicans recognized that every other issue in some way touched on slavery, and rather than ignore it or straddle it—as both the Democrats and Whigs had done—they would attack it head on, elevating it to the top of their masthead. Although they adopted mainstays of the Whig Party, including support for internal improvements, tariffs, and a national bank, the Republicans recast these in light of the expansion of slavery into the territories. Railroads and internal improvements? That Whig issue now took on an unmistakable free-soil tinge, for if railroads were built, what crops would they bring to market—slave cotton, or free wheat? Tariffs? If Southerners paid more for their goods, were they not already profiting from an inhumane system? And should not Northern industry, which supported free labor, enjoy an advantage? Perhaps the national bank had no strong sectional overtones, but no matter. Slavery dominated almost every debate. Southerners had even raised the issue of reopening the slave trade.

At their convention in 1856, the Republicans ignored William H. Seward, who had toiled for the free-soil cause for years, in favor of John C. Frémont, the Mexican War personality who had attempted to foment a revolt in California. Frémont had married Thomas Hart Benton's daughter, who helped hone his image as an explorer/adventurer and allied him with free-soil Democrats through Benton's progeny (Benton himself was a slave owner who never supported his son-in-law's candidacy, foreshadowing the types of universal family divisions that would occur after Fort Sumter). Beyond that, Frémont condemned the "twin relics of barbarism," slavery and polygamy—a reference to the Mormon practice of multiple wives in Utah Territory. Slavery and the territories were again linked to immoral practices, with no small amount of emphasis on illicit sex in the rhetoric.[107] Frémont also had no ties to the Know-Nothings, making him, for all intents and purposes, "pure." He also offered voters moral clarity.

Southerners quickly recognized the dangers Frémont's candidacy posed.

"The election of Fremont," Robert Toombs wrote in July 1856, "would be the end of the Union."[108] The eventual Democratic candidate, James Buchanan of Pennsylvania, chimed in: "Should Fremont be elected . . . the outlawry proclaimed by the Black Republican convention at Philadelphia against [the South] will be ratified by the people of the North." In such an eventuality, "the consequences will be immediate & inevitable."[109]

Buchanan—a five-term congressman and then senator who also served as minister to Russia and Great Britain, and was Polk's secretary of state—possessed impressive political credentials. His frequent absences abroad also somewhat insulated him from the domestic turmoil. Still, he had helped draft the Ostend Manifesto, and he hardly sought to distance himself from slavery. Like Douglas, Buchanan continued to see slavery as a sectional issue subject to political compromise rather than, as the Republicans saw it, a moral issue over which compromise was impossible. Then there was Fillmore, whose own Whig Party had rejected him. Instead, he had moved into the American Party—the Know-Nothings—and hoped to win just enough electoral votes to throw the election into the House.

In the ensuing three-way contest, Buchanan battled Fillmore for Southern votes and contended with Frémont for the Northern vote. When the smoke cleared, the Pennsylvanian had won an ominous victory. He had beaten Fillmore badly in the South, enough to offset Frémont's shocking near sweep of the North, becoming the first president to win an election without carrying a preponderance of free states. Buchanan had just 45 percent of the popular vote to Frémont's 33 percent. Frémont took all but five of the free states. Republicans immediately did the math: in the next election, if the Republican candidate just held the states Frémont carried and added Pennsylvania and either Illinois or Indiana, he would win. By itself, the Republican Party totaled 500,000 votes less than the Democrats, but if the American Party's vote went Republican, the total would exceed the Democrats by 300,000.

Buchanan, the last president born in the eighteenth century and the only man who never married to hold the presidency, came from a modest but not poor background. Brief service in the War of 1812 exposed him to the military; then he made a fortune in the law, no easy feat in those days. His one love affair, with the daughter of a wealthy Pennsylvania ironworks owner, was sabotaged by local rumormongers who spread class envy. The incident left his lover heartbroken, and she died a few days after ending the engagement, possibly by suicide. For several years Buchanan orbited outside the Jackson circles, managing to work his way back into the president's graces during Jackson's Pennsylvania campaigns, eventually becoming the minister to Russia. As a senator, he allowed antislavery petitions to be read before his committee, running contrary to the Democratic practice.

His first run at the presidency, in 1852, pitted him against Douglas, and the two split the party vote and handed the nomination to Pierce. After that, Buchanan had little use for the Little Giant, as Douglas was known, or so he thought. In 1856, Buchanan found that he needed Douglas—or at least needed him out of the way—so he persuaded the Illinois senator to support him that year, for which Buchanan would reciprocate in 1860 by supporting Douglas.

After the inauguration Buchanan surrounded himself with Southerners, including Howell Cobb, James Slidell, and his vice president, John Breckinridge. A strict constitutionalist in the sense that he thought slavery outside the authority of Congress or the president, he ran on the issue of retaining the Union. Yet his Southern supporters had voted for him almost exclusively on the issue of slavery, understanding that he would not act to interfere with slavery in any way. Buffeted by *Uncle Tom's Cabin* and the rise of the "Black Republican" Party, the South saw Buchanan's election as a minor victory. Soon the Supreme Court handed the South a major triumph—one that seemed to forever settle the issue of slavery in the territories. Yet once again, the South would find its victory pyrrhic.

Dred Scott's Judicial Earthquake

America had barely absorbed Buchanan's inaugural when two days later the Supreme Court of the United States, on March 6, 1857, set off a judicial earthquake. Buchanan had been made aware of the forthcoming decision, which he supported, and he included references to it in his inaugural address. The *Dred Scott* decision easily became one of the two or three most controversial high court cases in American history.

Dred Scott, the slave to a U.S. Army surgeon named John Emerson, moved with his master to Rock Island, Illinois, in 1834. Scott remained with Emerson for two years on the army base, even though Illinois, under the Northwest Ordinance of 1787, prohibited slavery. In 1836, Emerson was assigned to Fort Snelling (in modern-day Minnesota), which was part of the Wisconsin Territory above the Missouri Compromise line, again taking Scott with him. At the time of Emerson's death in 1843, the estate, including Scott and his wife, Harriet, went to Emerson's daughter. Meanwhile, members of the family who had owned Scott previously, and who had by then befriended Scott, brought a suit on his behalf in St. Louis County (where he then resided), claiming his freedom.

Scott's suit argued that his residence in both Illinois and the Wisconsin Territory, where slavery was prohibited (one by state law, one by both the Missouri Compromise and the principle of the Northwest Ordinance) made him free. A Missouri jury agreed in 1850. Emerson appealed to the Missouri Supreme Court, which in 1852 reversed the lower court ruling, arguing that the lower court had abused the principle of comity, by which one state agreed to observe the laws of another. The Constitution guaranteed that the citizen of one state had equal protection in all states, hence the rub: if Scott was a citizen by virtue of being free in one state, federal law favored him; but if he was property, federal law favored the Emersons. Refusing to rule on the constitutional status of slaves as either property or people, the Missouri court focused only on the comity issue.

Meanwhile, Mrs. Emerson remarried and moved to Massachusetts, where her husband, Calvin Chaffee, later would win election to Congress as an anti-slavery Know-Nothing. Emerson left Scott in St. Louis, still the property of her brother, John Sanford, who himself had moved to New York. Scott, then having considerable freedom, initiated a new suit in his own name in 1853, bearing the now-famous name, *Scott v. Sandford* (with Sanford misspelled in the official document). A circuit court ruled against Scott once again, and his lawyers appealed to the United States Supreme Court. When the Court heard the case in 1856, it had to rule on whether Scott could even bring the suit (as a slave); the second point involved whether Scott's residence in a free state or in a free federal territory made him free. In theory, the Court had the option to duck the larger issues altogether merely by saying that Scott was a slave, and as such had no authority to even bring a suit. However, the circuit court had already ruled that Scott could sue, and Scott, not Emerson, had appealed on different grounds.

If ever a Court was overcome by hubris, it was the Supreme Court of Roger B. Taney, the chief justice from Maryland who sided with his fellow Southerners' views of slavery. Far from dodging the monumental constitutional issues, Taney's nine justices all rendered separate opinions whose combined effect produced an antislavery backlash that dwarfed that associated with the Fugitive Slave Law. As far as the Court was concerned, the case began as a routine ruling—that the laws of Missouri were properly applied and thus the Court had no jurisdiction in the matter—and it might have washed through the pages of history like the tiniest piece of lint. Sometime in February 1857, however, the justices had a change of heart, brought about when they decided to write individual opinions. As it turned out, the five Southern justices wanted to overturn the Missouri Compromise, which they thought unconstitutional. In less than three weeks, the Court had shifted from treating the *Dred Scott* case as a routine matter of state autonomy to an earth-shattering restatement of the constitutionality of slavery.

Taney's decision included the position that freedmen were citizens of one state but not the United States. Nor could emancipated slaves or their progeny be free in all states because a citizen had to be born a citizen, and no slaves were. He also dismissed (despite considerable precedence at the state level) any citizenship rights that states offered blacks. In other words, even if free, Taney said Scott could not bring the suit. Moving to free soil did not free Scott either, as slaveholders could take their property into territories, and any act of Congress regarding slaves would be an impairment of property rights guaranteed in the Fifth Amendment. Scott's presence in Wisconsin Territory did not emancipate him either because, in Taney's view, the Missouri Compromise, as well as the Northwest Ordinance, was unconstitutional in that it violated the Fifth Amendment; and, therefore, provisions of statute law over the territories were of no legal import. Forced by the weight of his own logic to admit that if a state so desired, it could grant citizenship to blacks, Taney still maintained that did not make them citizens of all states. Taney considered African Americans "as a subordinate and inferior class of beings [who] had no rights which the white man was bound to respect."[110] Other members of the Court agreed that Scott was not a citizen, and after years of begging by Congress to settle the territorial citizenship question, the Court had indeed acted.

Doubtless Southerners, and perhaps Taney himself, expected intense condemnation of the ruling. In that, Taney was not disappointed: the Northern press referred to the "jesuitical decision" as a "willful perversion" and an "atrocious crime." But no one foresaw the economic disaster the Court had perpetrated as, once again, the law of unintended consequences took effect.

Until the Kansas-Nebraska Act, the politics of slavery had little to do with the expansion of the railroads. However, in the immediate aftermath of the *Dred Scott* ruling, the nation's railroad bonds, or at least a specific group of railroad bonds, tumbled badly. The Supreme Court ruling triggered the Panic of 1857, but for generations historians have overlooked the key relationship between the *Dred Scott* case and the economic crisis, instead pinning the blame on changes in the international wheat market and economic dislocations stemming from the Crimean War.[111] Had all railroad securities collapsed, such an argument might ring true, except that only *certain* railroad bonds plunged—those roads primarily running east and west.[112]

Business hates uncertainty and, above all, dislikes wars, which tend to upset markets and kill consumers. Prior to the *Dred Scott* case, railroad builders pushed westward confident that either proslavery or free-soil ideas would triumph. Whichever dominated, markets would be stable because of certainty. What the Court's ruling did was to completely destabilize the markets. Suddenly the prospect appeared of a Bleeding Kansas writ large, with the possibility of John Brown raids occurring in every new territory as it was opened. Investors easily saw this, and the bonds for the east-west roads collapsed. As they fell, the collateral they represented for large banks in New York, Boston, and Philadelphia sank too. Banks immediately found themselves in an exposed and weakened condition. A panic spread throughout the Northern banking community.

The South, however, because of its relatively light investment in railroads, suffered only minor losses in the bond markets. Southern state banking systems, far more than their Northern counterparts, had adopted branch banking, making the transmission of information easier and insulating them from the panic.

The South learned the wrong lessons from the financial upheaval. Thinking that King Cotton had protected Dixie from international market fluctuations (which had almost nothing to do with the recession), Southern leaders proclaimed that their slave-based economy had not only caught up with the North but had also surpassed it. Who needed industry when you had King Cotton?

A few voices challenged this view, appealing to nonslave-holding Southerners to reclaim their region. Hinton Rowan Helper, a North Carolina nonslaveholder, made a cogent and powerful argument that slavery crippled the South in his book *The Impending Crisis of the South* (1857). Helper touched a raw nerve as painful as that of slave insurrections. He spoke to poor whites, who had not benefited at all from slavery, a ploy that threatened to turn white against white. Southern polemicists immediately denounced Helper as an incendiary and produced entire books disputing his statistics.

Most of the fire eaters in the South dismissed Helper, insisting that the peculiar institution had proved its superiority to factories and furnaces. The few advocates of a modern manufacturing economy now found themselves drowned out by the mantra "Cotton is King." Others, such as Jefferson Davis, deluded themselves into thinking that Southern economic backwardness was entirely attributable to the North, an antebellum version of modern third-world complaints. "You free-soil agitators," Davis said, "are not interested in slavery . . . not at all. . . . You want . . . to promote the industry of the North-East states, at the expense of the people of the South and their industry."[113] This conspiracy view was echoed by Thomas Kettell in *Southern Wealth and Northern Profits* (1860).

Another conspiracy view that increasingly took hold in the North was that a "slave-power conspiracy" had fixed the *Dred Scott* case with Buchanan's blessing. No doubt the president had improperly indicated to Taney that he wished a broad ruling in the case. Yet historians reject any assertions that Taney and Buchanan had rigged the outcome, although Taney had informed the president of the details of his pending decision. Lincoln probably doubted any real conspiracy existed, but as a Republican politician, he made hay out of the perception. Likening Douglas, Pierce, Taney, and Buchanan to four home builders who brought to the work site "framed timbers," whose pieces just happened to fit together perfectly, Lincoln said, "In such a case we find it impossible not to believe that Stephen and Franklin and Roger and James all understood one another from the beginning. . . ."[114]

By the midterm elections of 1858, then, both sides had evolved convenient conspiracy explanations for the worsening sectional crisis. The slave power controlled the presidency and the courts, rigged elections, prohibited open debate, and stacked the Kansas constitutional application according to abolitionists. As Southerners saw it, radical abolitionists and Black Republicans now dominated Congress, used immigration to pack the territories, and connived to use popular sovereignty as a code phrase for free-soil and abolitionism. Attempting to legislate from the bench, Taney's Court had only made matters worse by bringing the entire judiciary system under the suspicion of the conspiracy theorists.

Simmering Kansas Boils Over

The turmoil in Kansas reached new proportions. When the June 1857 Kansas election took place, only 2,200 out of 9,000 registered voters showed up to vote on the most controversial and well-known legislation of the decade, so there could be no denying that the free-soil forces sat out the process. Fraud was rampant: in one county no election was held at all, and in another only 30 out of 1,060 people voted. In Johnson County, Kansas governor Robert J. Walker found that 1,500 "voters" were names directly copied from a Cincinnati directory.[115] Free-soilers warned that the proslavery forces controlled the counting and that their own ballots would be discarded or ignored. As a result, Free-Soilers intended to boycott the election. An outcome ensuring dominance by the proslavery forces was thus ensured.

Meanwhile, Buchanan had sent Walker, a Mississippi Democrat and Polk cabinet official, to serve as the territorial governor of Kansas. Walker announced his intention to see that the "majority of the people of Kansas . . . fairly and freely decided [the slavery] question for themselves by a direct vote on the adoption of the [state] Constitution, excluding all fraud or violence."[116] By appointing Walker, Buchanan hoped to accomplish two goals in one fell swoop—ending the Kansas controversy and making the state another Democratic stronghold to offset Oregon and Minnesota, whose admission to the Union was imminent (and became official in 1859). On the day Walker departed for Lecompton, Kansas, however, the Democratic house newspaper fully endorsed the Lecompton Constitution. Walker arrived too late to shape the Kansas constitutional convention of the radical proslavery delegates.

Douglas, his fidelity to popular sovereignty as strong as ever, condemned the Lecompton Constitution and urged a free and fair vote. His appeals came as a shock to Democrats and a blessing to Republicans, who internally discussed the possibility of making him their presidential candidate in 1860. Perceived as Buchanan's man in the Senate, Douglas and Buchanan engaged in a fierce argument in December 1857, which culminated in Buchanan's reminding the senator he would be "crushed" if he "differed from the administration" the way Andrew Jackson had excommunicated rebel Democrats in his day. Douglas, sensing the final rift had arrived, curtly told Buchanan, "General Jackson is dead."[117]

Buchanan knew he faced a dilemma.[118] He had supported the territorial process in Kansas as legitimate and had defended the Lecompton Constitution. To suddenly repudiate it would destroy his Southern base: the large majority of his electoral vote. If he read the Southern newspapers, he knew he was already in trouble there. The Charleston *Mercury* had suggested that Buchanan and Walker go to hell together, and other publications were even less generous. An even more ominous editorial appeared in the New Orleans *Picayune*, warning that the states of Alabama, Mississippi, South Carolina and "perhaps others" would hold secession conventions if Congress did not approve the Lecompton Constitution.[119] No matter how the advocates of the Lecompton Constitution framed it, however, it still came down to a relative handful of proslavery delegates determining that Kansas could have a constitution with slavery, no matter what "choice" the voters on the referendum made. When the free-soil population boycotted the vote, Lecompton was the constitution.

The Kansas Territorial Legislature, on the other hand, was already dominated by the free-soil forces. It wasted no time calling for another referendum on Lecompton, and that election, without the fraud, produced a decisive vote against the proslavery constitution. Now Kansas had popular sovereignty speaking against slavery from Topeka and the proslavery forces legitimizing it from Lecompton.

Buchanan sank further into the quicksand in which he had placed himself. Committed to the Lecompton Constitution, yet anxious to avoid deepening the rift, he worked strenuously for the free-state congressmen to accept the Lecompton Constitution. When the Senate and House deadlocked, Democrat William English of Indiana offered a settlement. As part of the original constitution proposal, Kansas was to receive 23 million acres of federal land, but the antislavery forces had whittled that down to 4 million. English sought to attach the reduced land grant to a free constitution, or bribe the Kansans with the 23 million for accepting Lecompton. There was a stick along with this carrot: if Kansas did not accept the proposal, it would have to wait until its population reached ninety thousand to apply for statehood again.

Kansas voters shocked Buchanan and the South by rejecting the English bill's land grant by a seven-to-one margin and accepting as punishment territorial status until 1861. It was a crushing defeat for the slavery forces. When the Kansas episode ended, the South could look back at a decade and a half of political maneuvers, compromises, threats, intrigue, and bribes with the sobering knowledge that it had not added a single inch of new slave territory to its core of states and in the process had alienated millions of Americans who previously were ambivalent about slavery, literally creating thousands of abolitionists. Southern attempts to spread slavery killed the Whig Party, divided and weakened the Democrats, and sparked the rise of the Republicans, whose major objective was a halt to the spread of slavery in the territories. The only thing the South had not yet done was to create a demon that would unite the slave states in one final, futile act. After 1858 the South had its demon.

A New Hope

For those who contend they want certain institutions—schools, government, and so on—free of values or value neutral, the journey of Illinois Senator Stephen Douglas in the 1850s is instructive. Douglas emerged as the South's hero. His role in the Compromise of 1850 convinced many Southerners that he had what it took to be president, truly a "Northern man of Southern principles." But "the Judge" (as Lincoln often called him) had his own principles, neither purely Southern nor Northern. Rather, in 1858, Douglas stood where he had in 1850: for popular sovereignty. In claiming that he was not "personally in favor" of slavery—that it ought to be up to the people of a state to decide—Douglas held the ultimate value-neutral position. In fact such a position *has its own value,* just as Abraham Lincoln would show. Not to call evil, evil, is to call it good.

Douglas's stance derived from a Madisonian notion that local self-government best resolved difficult issues and epitomized democracy. He supported the free-soil majority in Kansas against the Lecompton proslavery forces, and in the wake of the Supreme Court's *Dred Scott* decision, he attacked the bench's abuse of power and infringement on popular sovereignty.[120] Yet consistency did not impress Southern slave owners if it came at the expense of slavery, for which there could be no middle ground. Seeking the presidency, though, also positioned Douglas to regain control of the Democratic Party for the North and to wrest it from the slave power.

Whatever Douglas's aspirations for higher office or party dominance, he first had to retain his Illinois senate seat in the election of 1858. Illinois Republicans realized that Douglas's popular sovereignty position might appear antislavery to Northern ears, and wisely concluded they had to run a candidate who could differentiate Douglas's value-free approach to slavery from their own. In that sense, Lincoln was the perfect antithesis to Douglas.

The details of Abraham Lincoln's life are, or at least used to be, well known to American schoolchildren. Born on February 12, 1809, in a Kentucky log cabin, Lincoln's family was poor, even by the standards of the day. His father, Thomas, took the family to Indiana, and shortly thereafter Lincoln's mother died. By that time he had learned to read and continued to educate himself, reading *Robinson Crusoe, Decline and Fall of the Roman Empire,* Franklin's *Autobiography,* and law books when he could get them. He memorized the Illinois Statutes. One apocryphal story had it that Lincoln read while plowing, allowing the mules or oxen to do the work and turning the page at the end of each row. Lincoln took reading seriously, making mental notes of the literary style, syncopation, and rhythm. Though often portrayed as a Deist, Lincoln read the Bible as studiously as he had the classics. His speeches resound with scriptural metaphors and biblical phrases, rightly applied, revealing he fully understood the context.

Put to work early by his father, Lincoln labored with his hands on a variety of jobs, including working on flatboats that took him down the Mississippi in 1828. The family moved again, to Illinois in 1830, where the young man worked as a mill manager near Springfield. Tall (six feet four inches) and lanky (he later belonged to a group of Whig legislators over six feet tall—the "long nine"), Lincoln had great stamina and surprising strength, and just as he had learned from literature, he applied his work experiences to his political reasoning. As a young man, he had impressed others with his character, sincerity, and humor, despite a recurring bout of what he called the hypos, or hypochondria. Some suspect he was a manic depressive; he once wrote an essay on suicide and quipped that when he was alone, his depression overcame him so badly that "I never dare carry a penknife."[121]

Elected captain of a volunteer company in the Black Hawk War (where his only wound came from mosquitoes), Lincoln elicited a natural respect from those around him. While teaching himself the law, he opened a small store that failed when a partner took off with all the cash and left Lincoln stuck with more than a thousand dollars in obligations. He made good on them all, working odd jobs, including his famous rail splitting. He was the town postmaster and then, in 1834, was elected to the state assembly, where he rose to prominence in the Whig Party.

Lincoln obtained his law license in 1836, whereupon he handled a number of bank cases, as well as work for railroads, insurance companies, and a gas-light business. Developing a solid practice, he (and the firm) benefited greatly from a partnership with William Herndon, who later became his biographer. The scope and variety of cases handled by this self-taught attorney was impressive; delving into admiralty law, corporate law, constitutional law, and criminal law, Lincoln practiced before every type of court in Illinois.

He also worked at politics as an active Whig, casting his first political vote for Clay. "My politics can be briefly stated," he said in the 1830s: "I am in favor of the internal improvement system, and a high protective tariff."[122] Winning a seat in Congress in 1847, his entire campaign expenditure was seventy-five cents for a single barrel of cider. Lincoln soon lost support with his "Spot Resolution," but he campaigned for Taylor in 1848. He hoped to receive a patronage position as commissioner of the General Land Office, and when he did not, Lincoln retired to his private law practice, convinced his political career was over.

If Lincoln doubted himself, his wife, Mary Todd, never did. She announced to her friends, "Mr. Lincoln is to be president of the United States some day. If I had not thought so, I would not have married him, for you can see he is not pretty."[123] Indeed, Abraham Lincoln was hardly easy on the eye, all angles and sharp edges. Yet observers—some of whom barely knew him—frequently remarked on his commanding presence. Despite a high, almost screechy voice, Lincoln's words carried tremendous weight because they were always well considered before uttered. It is one of the ironies of American history that, had Lincoln lived in the age of television, his personal appearance and speech would have doomed him in politics.

Lincoln was homely, but Mary Todd was downright sour looking, which perhaps contributed to his having left her, literally, standing at the altar one time. Lincoln claimed an illness; his partner Willie Herndon believed that he did not love Mary, but had made a promise and had to keep it. Herndon, however, is hardly a credible witness. He strongly disliked Mary—and the feeling was mutual—and it was Herndon who fabricated the myth of Ann Rutledge as Lincoln's only true love.[124] What we do know is that when Lincoln finally did wed Mary, in 1842, he called it a "profound wonder." Mary wrote in the loftiest terms of her mate, who exceeded her expectations as "lover—husband—father, all!"[125] She prodded her husband's ambitions, and not so gently. "Mr. Douglas," she said, "is a very little, little giant compared to my tall Kentuckian, and intellectually my husband towers above Douglas as he does physically."[126] To the disorganized, even chaotic Lincoln, Mary brought order and direction. She also gave him four sons, only one of whom lived to maturity. Robert, the first son (known as the Prince of Rails), lived until 1926; Eddie died in 1850; Willie died in 1862; and Tad died in 1871 at age eighteen. The deaths of Eddie and Willie fed Lincoln's depression; yet, interestingly, he framed the losses in religious terms. God "called him home," he said of Willie. Mary saw things differently, having lived in constant terror of tragedy. When Robert accidentally swallowed lime, she became hysterical, screaming, "Bobby will die! Bobby will die!"[127] She usually took out her phobias in massive shopping sprees, returning goods that did not suit her, followed by periods of obsessive miserliness. If spending money did not roust her from the doldrums, Mary lapsed into real (or feigned) migraine headaches. Lincoln dutifully cared for his "Molly" and even finally helped her recover from the migraines.

Perhaps no aspect of Abraham Lincoln's character is less understood than his religion. Like many young men, he was a skeptic early in life. He viewed the "good old maxims of the Bible" as little different from the *Farmer's Almanac*, admitting in the 1830s, "I've never been to church yet, nor probably shall not [sic] be soon."[128] An oft-misunderstood phrase Lincoln uttered—purportedly that he was a Deist—was, in fact, "Because I belonged to no church, [I] was suspected of being a deist," an absurdity he put on the same plane as having "talked about fighting a duel."[129] Quite the contrary, to dispute an 1846 handbill that he was "an open scoffer at Christianity," Lincoln produced his own handbill in which he admitted, "I am not a member of any Christian Church . . . but I have never denied the truth of the Scriptures."[130] Some Lincoln biographers dismiss this as campaign propaganda, but Lincoln's religious journey accelerated the closer he got to greatness (or, perhaps, impelled him to it).

A profound change in Lincoln's faith occurred from 1858 to 1863. Mary had brought home a Bible, which Lincoln read, and after the death of Eddie at age four, he attended a Presbyterian church intermittently, paying rent for a pew for his wife. He never joined the church, but by 1851 was already preaching, in letters, to his own father: "Remember to call upon, and confide in, our great, and good, and merciful Maker. . . . He will not forget the dying man, who puts his trust in Him."[131] After 1860 Lincoln himself told associates of a "change," a "true religious experience," a "change of heart." Toward what? Lincoln prayed every day and read his Bible regularly. He followed Micah 6:8 to a tee, ". . . to do justly, and to love mercy, and to walk humbly with thy God." When a lifelong friend, Joshua Speed, commented that he remained skeptical of matters of faith, Lincoln said, "You are wrong, Speed; take all of this book [the Bible] upon reason you can, and the balance on faith, and you will live and die a happier and better man."[132]

What kept Lincoln from formal church association was what he viewed as overly long and complicated confessions of faith, or what might be called denominationalism. "When any church will inscribe over its altar the Saviour's condensed statement of law and gospel, 'Thou shalt love the Lord thy God with all thy heart and with all thy soul and with all they mind, and love thy neighbor as thyself,' that church I will join with all my heart."[133] In fact, he thought it beneficial that numerous denominations and sects existed, telling a friend, "The more sects . . . the better. They are all getting somebody [into heaven] that others would not."[134] To Lincoln, an important separation of politics and religion existed during the campaign: "I will not discuss the character and religion of Jesus Christ on the stump! That is no place for it."[135] It was Gettysburg, however, where Lincoln was born again. His own pastor, Phineas Gurley, noted the change after Gettysburg: With "tears in his eyes," Gurley wrote, Lincoln "now believed his heart was changed and that he loved the Saviour, and, if he was not deceived in himself, it was his intention soon to make a profession of religion."[136] Did he actually make such a profession? An Illinois clergyman asked Lincoln before his death, "Do you love Jesus?" to which Lincoln gave a straight answer:

> When I left Springfield I asked the people to pray for me. I was not a Christian. When I buried my son, the severest trial of my life, I was not a Christian. But when I went to Gettysburg and saw the graves of thousands of our soldiers, I then and there consecrated myself to Christ. Yes, I love Jesus.[137]

During the war Lincoln saw God's hand in numerous events, although in 1862 he wrote, "The will of God prevails. In great contests, each party claims to act in accordance with the will of God. Both *may* be, and one *must* be wrong. God can not be *for*, or *against*, the same thing at the same time."[138] Significantly, at Gettysburg, he again referred to God's own purposes, noting that the nation was "dedicated to the proposition" that "all men are created equal." Would God validate that proposition? It remained, in Lincoln's spirit, to be determined.[139] He puzzled why God allowed the war to continue, which reflected his fatalistic side that discounted human will in perpetuating evil. Lincoln called numerous days of national prayer—an unusual step for a supposed unbeliever. The evidence that Lincoln was a spiritual, even devout, man, and toward the end of his life a committed Christian, is abundant.

That spiritual journey paralleled another road traveled by Lincoln. His path to political prominence, although perhaps cut in his early Whig partisan battles, was hewed and sanded by his famous contest with Stephen Douglas in 1858 for the Illinois Senate seat. Together the two men made almost two hundred speeches between July and November. The most famous, however, came at seven joint debates from August to October in each of the remaining seven congressional districts where the two had not yet spoken.

In sharp contrast to the content-free televised debates of the twentieth century, where candidates hope to merely avoid a fatal gaffe, political debates of the nineteenth century were festive affairs involving bands, food, and plenty of whiskey. Farmers, merchants, laborers, and families came from miles away to listen to the candidates. It was, after all, a form of entertainment: the men would challenge each other, perhaps even insult each other, but usually in a good-natured way that left them shaking hands at the end of the day. Or, as David Morris Potter put it, "The values which united them as Americans were more important than those which divided them as candidates."[140] By agreeing to disagree, Lincoln and Douglas reflected a nineteenth-century view of tolerance that had no connection to the twentieth-century understanding of indifference to values—quite the contrary, the men had strong convictions that, they agreed, could only be solved by the voters.

To prepare for his debates with Douglas, Lincoln honed his already sharp logic to a fine point. Challenging notions that slavery was "good" for the blacks, Lincoln proposed sarcastically that the beneficial institution should therefore be extended to whites as well. Then, at the state convention at Springfield, Lincoln gave what is generally agreed as one of the greatest political speeches in American history:

> We are now far into the fifth year since a policy was initiated with the avowed object and confident promise of putting an end to slavery agitation. . . . That agitation has not ceased but has constantly augmented. In my opinion, it will not cease until a crisis has been reached and passed. "A house divided against itself cannot stand." I believe this government cannot endure permanently half slave and half free. I do not expect the Union to be dissolved—I do not expect the house to fall—but I do expect that it will cease to be divided.[141]

He continued to argue that the opponents of slavery would stop its spread, or that the proponents would make it lawful in all states.

Sufficiently determined to make slavery the issue, Lincoln engaged Douglas in the pivotal debates, where he boxed in the Little Giant over the issue of popular sovereignty on the one hand and the *Dred Scott* decision on the other. Douglas claimed to support both. How was that possible, Lincoln asked, if the Supreme Court said that neither the people nor Congress could exclude slavery, yet Douglas hailed popular sovereignty as letting the people choose? Again, contrary to mythology, Lincoln had not raised an issue Douglas had never considered. As early as 1857, Douglas, noting the paradox, produced an answer: "These regulations . . . must necessarily depend entirely upon the will and wishes of the people of the territory, as they can only be prescribed by the local legislatures."[142] What was novel was that Lincoln pounded the question in the debates, forcing Douglas to elaborate further than he already had: "Slavery cannot exist a day in the midst of an unfriendly people with unfriendly laws."[143]

Without realizing it—and even before this view was immortalized as the Freeport Doctrine—Douglas had stepped into a viper's pit, for he had raised the central fact that slavery was not a cultural or economic institution, but that it was a power relationship. In its most crystal form, slavery was political oppression. Yet the question was asked, and answered, at the debate at Freeport, where Lincoln maneuvered Douglas into a categorical statement: "It matters not what way the Supreme Court may . . . decide as to the abstract question of whether slavery may or may not go into a Territory. . . . The people have the lawful means to introduce it or exclude it as they please."[144]

To fire eaters in the South, Douglas had just given the people of the territories a legitimate rationale for breaking the national law. He had cut the legs out from under the *Dred Scott* decision, and all but preached rebellion to nonslave owners in the South. Lincoln's aim, however, was not to shatter Douglas's Southern support, as it had no bearing whatsoever on the Senate race at hand. Rather, he had shifted the argument to a different philosophical plane, that of the morality of slavery. Douglas had gone on record as saying that it did not matter if slavery was right or wrong, or even if the Constitution (as interpreted by the Supreme Court) was right or wrong.

In short, the contest pitted republicanism against democracy in the purest sense of the definition, for Douglas advocated a majoritarian dictatorship in which those with the most votes won, regardless of right or wrong. Lincoln, on the other hand, defended a democratic republic, in which majority rule was proscribed within the rule of law.[145] Douglas's defenders have argued that he advocated only local sovereignty, and he thought local majorities "would be less prone to arbitrary action, executed without regard for local interests."[146] America's federal system did emphasize local control, but never at the expense of "these truths," which the American Revolutionaries held as "self-evident."

"The real issue," Lincoln said at the last debate, "is the sentiment on the part of one class that looks upon the institution of slavery *as a wrong*. . . . The Republican Party," he said, "look[s] upon it as being a moral, social and political wrong . . . and one of the methods of treating it as a wrong is to *make provision that it shall grow no larger*. . . . That is the real issue."[147] A "moral, a social, and a political wrong," he called slavery at Quincy in the October debate.[148] Lincoln went further, declaring that the black man was "entitled to all the natural rights enumerated in the Declaration of Independence, the right to life, liberty, and the pursuit of happiness. . . . In the right to eat the bread, without leave of anybody else, which his own hand earns, *he is my equal and the equal of Judge Douglas, and the equal of every living man*."[149]

What made Lincoln stand out and gain credibility with the voters was that he embraced the moral and logical designation of slavery as an inherent evil, while distancing himself from the oddball notions of utopian perfectionists like the Grimké sisters or wild-eyed anti-Constitutionalists like William Lloyd Garrison. He achieved this by refocusing the nation on slavery's assault on the concept of law in the Republic.

Lincoln had already touched on this critical point of respect for the law in his famous 1838 Lyceum Address, in which he attacked both abolitionist rioters and proslavery supporters. After predicting that America could never be conquered by a foreign power, Lincoln warned that the danger was from mob law. His remedy for such a threat was simple: "Let every American, every lover of liberty . . . swear by the blood of the Revolution never to violate the least particular laws of the country, and never to tolerate their violation by others."[150] Then came the immortal phrase,

> Let reverence for the laws be breathed by every American mother to the lisping babe that prattles on her lap; let it be taught in schools, in

seminaries, and in colleges; let it be written in primers, spelling-books, and in almanacs; let it be preached from the pulpit, proclaimed in the legislative halls, and enforced in courts of justice. And, in short, let it become the political religion of the nation.[151]

It was inevitable that he would soon see the South as a threat to the foundations of the Republic through its blatant disregard for the law he held so precious.

Left-wing historians have attempted to portray Lincoln as a racist because he did not immediately embrace full voting and civil rights for blacks. He had once said, in response to a typical "Black Republican" comment from Stephen Douglas, that just because he did not want a black woman for a slave did not mean he wanted one for a wife. Such comments require consideration of not only their time, but their setting—a political campaign. Applying twenty-first-century values to earlier times, a historical flaw known as presentism, makes understanding the context of the day even more difficult.

On racial issues, Lincoln led; he didn't follow. With the exception of a few of the mid-nineteenth-century radicals who, it must be remembered, used anti-slavery as a means to destroy all social and family relationships of oppression—Lincoln marched far ahead of most of his fellow men when it came to race relations. By the end of the war, despite hostile opposition from his own advisers, he had insisted on paying black soldiers as much as white soldiers. Black editor Frederick Douglass, who had supported a "pure" abolitionist candidate in the early part of the 1860 election, eventually campaigned for Lincoln, and did so again in 1864. They met twice, and Douglass, although never fully satisfied, realized that Lincoln was a friend of his cause. Attending Lincoln's second inaugural, Douglass was banned from the evening gala. When Lincoln heard about it, he issued orders to admit the editor and greeted him warmly: "Here comes my friend Douglass," he said proudly.

By the 1850s, slavery had managed to corrupt almost everything it touched, ultimately even giving Abraham Lincoln pause—but only for a brief few years. He was, to his eternal credit, one politician who refused to shirk his duty and to call evil, evil. Virtually alone, Lincoln refused to hide behind obscure phrases, as Madison had, or to take high-minded public positions, as had Jefferson, while personally engaging in the sin.

Lincoln continually placed before the public a moral choice that it had to make. Although he spoke on tariffs, temperance, railroads, banks, and many other issues, Lincoln perceived that slavery alone produced a giant contradiction that transcended all sectional issues: that it put at risk *both* liberty and equality for all races, not just equality as is often presumed. He perceived politically that the time soon approached when a Northern man of Northern principles would be elected president, and through his appointment power could name federal judges to positions in the South where they would rule in favor of runaway slaves, uphold slaves' rights to bring suits or to marry, and otherwise undermine the awful institution.

Lincoln, again nearly alone, understood that the central threat to the Republic posed by slavery lay in its corruption of the law. It is to that aspect of the impending crisis that we now turn.

The Crisis of Law and Order

Questions such as those posed by Lincoln in the debates, or similar thoughts, weighed heavily on the minds of an increasing number of Americans, North and South. In the short term, Douglas and the Buchanan Democrats in Illinois received enough votes to elect forty-six Democratic legislators, while the Republicans elected forty-one. Douglas retained his seat. In an ominous sign for the Democrats, though, the Republicans won the popular vote.

Looking back from a vantage point of more than 140 years, it is easy to see that Douglas's victory was costly and that Lincoln's defeat merely set the stage for his presidential race in 1860. At the time, however, the biggest losers appeared to be James Buchanan, whose support of Lecompton had been picked clean by Douglas's Freeport Doctrine, and Abraham Lincoln, who now had gone ten years without holding an elected office. But the points made by Lincoln, and his repeated emphasis on slavery as a moral evil on the one hand, and the law as a moral good on the other, soon took hold of a growing share of public opinion. Equally important, Douglas had been forced into undercutting *Dred Scott*—had swung the pendulum back away from the South yet again. This swing, destroying as it did the guts of the Supreme Court's ruling, took on a more ominous tone with John Brown's Harper's Ferry raid in October 1859.

John Brown illustrated exactly what Lincoln meant about respect for the laws, and the likelihood that violence would destroy the nation if Congress or the courts could not put slavery on a course to extinction. Lincoln, who had returned to his legal work before the Urbana circuit court, despised Brown's vigilantism.[152] Mob riots in St. Louis had inspired his Lyceum Address, and although Lincoln thought Brown courageous and thoughtful, he also thought him a criminal. Brown's raid, Lincoln observed, represented a continuing breakdown in law and order spawned by the degrading of the law in the hands of the slave states. More disorder followed, but of a different type.

When the Thirty-fifth Congress met in December, only three days after Brown had dangled at the end of a rope, it split as sharply as the rest of the nation. The Capitol Building in which the legislators gathered, had nearly assumed its modern form after major construction and remodeling between 1851 and 1858. The physical edifice grew in strength and grandeur at the same time that the invisible organs and blood that gave it life—the political parties—seemed to crumble more each day. Democrats held the Senate, but in the House the Republicans had 109 votes and the Democrats 101. To confuse matters even more, more than 10 percent of the Democrats refused to support any proslavery Southerner. Then there were the 27 proslavery Whigs who could have held the balance, but wishing not to be cut out of any committees, treaded carefully. When the election for Speaker of the House took place, it became clear how far down the path of disunion the nation had wandered.

It took 119 votes to elect a Speaker, but once the procedures started, it became obvious that the Southern legislators did not want to elect a Speaker at all, but to shut down the federal government. Acrimony characterized floor speeches, and Senator James Hammond quipped that "the only persons who do not have a revolver and a knife are those who have two revolvers."[153] Republicans wanted John Sherman of Ohio, whereas the fragmented Democrats continued to self-destruct, splitting over John McClernand of Illinois and Thomas Bocock of Virginia. Ultimately, Sherman withdrew in favor of a man who had recently converted from the Whig Party to the Republican, William Pennington of New Jersey, widely viewed as a weak, if not incompetent, Speaker. He won just enough votes for election, thanks to a few Southerners who supported him because of his strong stand in favor of the Fugitive Slave Law eight years earlier. It would not be long until Congress either shut down entirely or operated with utterly maladroit, ineffectual, and politically disabled men at the top.

At the very moment when, to save slavery, the South should have mended fences with discordant Northern Democrats, many Southerners searched frantically for a litmus test that would force a vote on some aspect of slavery. This mandatory allegiance marked the final inversion of Van Buren's grand scheme to keep slavery out of the national debate by creating a political party: now some in the Democratic Party combed legislative options as a means to bring some aspect of slavery—*any aspect*—up for a vote in order to legitimize it once and for all. Their quest led them to argue for reopening the African slave trade.[154] Leading Southern thinkers analyzed the moral problem of a ban on the slave trade. "If it was right to buy slaves in Virginia and carry them to New Orleans, why is it not right to buy them in Africa and carry them here?" asked William Yancey.[155] Lincoln might have reversed the question: if it is wrong to enslave free people in Africa and bring them to Virginia, why is it acceptable to keep slaves in either Virginia or New Orleans?

In fact, 90 percent of Southerners, according to Hammond's estimate, disapproved of reopening the slave trade. Reasoning that slaves already here were content, and that the blacks in Africa were "cannibals," according to one writer, provided a suitable psychological salve that prevented Southerners from dealing with the contradictions of their views.

Debates over reopening the slave trade intensified after the case of the *Wanderer*, a 114-foot vessel launched in 1857 from Long Island that had docked in Savannah, where it was purchased (through a secret deal in New York) by Southern cotton trader Charles A. L. Lamar. The new owner made suspicious changes to the ship's structure before sailing to Southern ports. From Charleston, the *Wanderer* headed for Africa, where the captain purchased six hundred slaves and again turned back to the South, specifically, a spot near Jekyll Island, Georgia. By that time, only about three hundred of the slaves had survived the voyage and disease, and when rumors of the arrivals of new slaves circulated, a Savannah federal marshal started an investigation. Eventually, the ship was seized, and Lamar indicted and tried. During the court proceedings, it became clear how thick the cloud of obfuscation and deceit was in Southern courts when it came to legal actions against slavery. Judges stalled, no one went to trial, and even the grand jurors who had found the indictments in the first place publicly recanted. And in the ultimate display of the corruption of the legal system in the South, Lamar was the only bidder on the appropriated *Wanderer* when it was put up for auction, announcing that the episode had given him good experience in the slave trade that he would apply in the future.[156]

Federal officials realized from the case of the *Wanderer* and a few other similar cases that no Southern court would ever enforce any federal antislavery laws, and that no law of the land would carry any weight in the South if it in any way diminished slaveholding. Lamar had lost most of his investment—more than two thirds of the slaves died either en route or after arrival—but the precedent of renewing the slave trade was significant. It was in this context that the Civil War began. Two sections of the nation, one committed to the perpetual continuation of slavery, one committed to its eventual extinction, could debate, compromise, legislate, and judge, but ultimately they disagreed over an issue that had such moral weight that one view or the other had to triumph. Their inability to find an amicable solution gives lie to modern notions that all serious differences can yield to better communication and diplomacy. But, of course, Lincoln had predicted exactly this result.

CHAPTER NINE

The Crisis of the Union, 1860–65

Lurching Toward War

Despite a remarkable, and often unimaginable, growth spurt in the first half of the nineteenth century, and despite advances in communication and transportation—all given as solutions to war and conflict—the nation nevertheless lumbered almost inexorably toward a final definitive split. No amount of prosperity, and no level of communication could address, ameliorate, or cover up the problem of slavery and the Republicans' response to it. No impassioned appeals, no impeccable logic, and no patriotic invocations of union could overcome the fact that, by 1860, more than half of all Americans thought slavery morally wrong, and a large plurality thought it so destructive that it had to be ended at any cost. Nor could sound reasoning or invocations of divine scripture dissuade the South from the conviction that the election of any Republican meant an instant attack on the institution of slavery.

What made war irrepressible and impending in the minds of many was that the political structure developed with the Second American Party system relied on the continuation of two key factors that were neither desirable nor possible to sustain. One was a small federal government content to leave the states to their own devices. On some matters, this was laudable, not to mention constitutional. On others, however, it permitted the South to maintain and perpetuate slavery. Any shift in power between the federal government and the states, therefore, specifically threatened the Southern slaveholders more than any other group, for it was their constitutional right to property that stood in conflict with the constitutional right of due process for all Americans, not to mention the Declaration's promise that all men are created equal. The other factor, closely tied to the first, was that the South, tossed amid the tempest and lacking electoral power, found itself lashed to the presidential mast requiring a Northern man of Southern principles. That mast snapped in November 1860, and with it, the nation was drawn into a maelstrom.

Time Line

1860: Lincoln elected president; South Carolina secedes
1861: Lower South secedes and founds the Confederacy; Lincoln and
Davis inaugurated; Fort Sumter surrenders to the Confederacy;
Upper South secedes from the Union; Battle of Bull Run
1862: Battles of Shiloh and Antietam; preliminary Emancipation
Proclamation.
1863: Emancipation Proclamation; battles of Vicksburg and Gettysburg
1864: Fall of Atlanta and Sherman's March to the Sea; Lincoln reelected
1865: Lee surrenders to Grant at Appomattox; Lincoln assassinated;
Johnson assumes presidency

America's Pivotal Election: 1860

The electoral college, and not a majority of voters, elected the president. For the
South, based on the experience of 1848 and the near election of John Frémont in
1856, it was a good thing. Since 1840 the numbers had been running against
slavery. The choice of electors for the electoral college was made by a general
election, in which each state received electors equal to the number of its congressional and senatorial delegations combined. Generally speaking, states gave
their electoral total to whichever candidate won the general election in its state,
even if only by a plurality (a concept called winner-take-all). As has been seen
several times, this form of election meant that a candidate could win the popular
vote nationally and still lose the electoral college, or, because of third parties, win
a narrow plurality in the popular vote, yet carry a large majority in the electoral
college.

By 1860 two critical changes had occurred in this process. First, the two major parties, the Democrats and Republicans, held national conventions to nominate their candidates. Because of the absence of primaries (which are common
today), the conventions truly did select the candidate, often brokering a winner
from among several competing groups. After state legislatures ceased choosing
the individual electors, the impetus of this system virtually guaranteed that presidential contests would be two-party affairs, since a vote for a third-party candidate as a protest was a wasted vote and, from the perspective of the protester,
ensured that the least desirable of the candidates won. When several parties
competed, as in 1856, the race still broke down into separate two-candidate
races—Buchanan versus Frémont in the North, and Buchanan versus Fillmore in
the South.

Second, Van Buren's party structure downplayed, and even ignored, ideology
and instead attempted to enforce party discipline through the spoils system. That
worked as long as the party leaders selected the candidates, conducted most of
the campaigning, and did everything except mark the ballot for the voters. After
thirty years, however, party discipline had crumbled almost entirely *because of*
ideology, specifically the parties' different views of slavery. The Republicans, with

their antislavery positions, took advantage of that and reveled in their sectional appeal. But the Democrats, given the smaller voting population in the South, still needed Northern votes to win. They could not afford to alienate either proslavery or free-soil advocates. In short, any proslavery nominee the Democrats put forward would not receive many (if any) Northern votes, but any Democratic free-soil candidate would be shunned in the South.

With this dynamic in mind, the Democrats met in April 1860 in Charleston, South Carolina. It was hot outside the meeting rooms, and hotter inside, given the friction of the pro- and antislavery delegates stuffed into the inadequately sized halls. Charleston, which would soon be ground zero for the insurrection, was no place for conciliators. And, sensibly, the delegates agreed to adjourn and meet six weeks later in Baltimore.

Stephen Douglas should have controlled the convention. He had a majority of the votes, but the party's rules required a two-thirds majority to nominate. Southern delegates arrived in Baltimore with the intention of demanding that Congress pass a national slave code legitimizing slavery and overtly making Northerners partners in crime. Ominously, just before the convention opened, delegates from seven states announced that they would walk out if Douglas received the nomination. Northern Democrats needing a wake-up call to the intentions of the South had only to listen to the speech of William L. Yancey of Alabama, who berated Northerners for accepting the view that slavery was evil.[1] On the surface, disagreements appeared to center on the territories and the protection of slavery there. Southerners wanted a clear statement that the federal government would protect property rights in slaves, whereas the Douglas wing wanted a loose interpretation allowing the courts and Congress authority over the territories. A vote on the majority report declaring a federal obligation to protect slavery failed, whereupon some Southern delegates, true to their word, walked out. After Douglas's forces attempted to have new pro-Douglas delegations formed that would give him the nomination, other Southern delegations, from Virginia, North Carolina, and Tennessee, also departed. Remaining delegates finally handed Douglas the nomination, leaving him with a hollow victory in the knowledge that the South would hold its own convention and find a candidate, John Breckinridge of Kentucky, to run against him, further diluting his vote.

Where did sensible, moderate Southerners go? Many of them gravitated to the comatose Whigs, who suddenly stirred. Seeing an opportunity to revive nationally as a middle way, the Whigs reorganized under the banner of the Union Party. But when it came to actually nominating a person, the choices were bleak, and the candidates universally old: Winfield Scott, seventy-four; Sam Houston, sixty-seven; and John J. Crittenden, seventy-four. The Constitutional Union Party finally nominated sixty-four-year-old John Bell, a Tennessee slaveholder who had voted against the Kansas-Nebraska Act.

The Republicans, beaming with optimism, met in Chicago at a hall called the Wigwam. They needed only to hold what Frémont had won in 1856, and gain Pennsylvania and one other Northern state from among Illinois, Indiana, and New

Jersey. William H. Seward, former governor of New York and one of that state's U.S. senators, was their front-runner. Already famous in antislavery circles for his fiery "higher law" and "irrepressible conflict" speeches, Seward surprised the delegates with a Senate address calling for moderation and peaceful coexistence. Seward's unexpected move toward the middle opened the door for Abraham Lincoln to stake out the more radical position.

Yet the Republicans retreated from their inflammatory language of 1856. There was no reference to the "twin relics of barbarism," slavery and polygamy, which had characterized Frémont's campaign in 1856. The delegates denounced the Harper's Ferry raid, but the most frequently used word at the Republican convention, "solemn," contrasted sharply with the Charleston convention's repeated use of "crisis."[2] Despite his recent moderation, Seward still had the "irrepressible conflict" baggage tied around him, and doubts lingered as to whether he could carry any of the key states that Fremont had lost four years earlier. Lincoln, on the other hand, was from Illinois, although he went to the convention the darkest of dark horses. His name was not even listed in a booklet providing brief biographies of the major candidates for the nomination. He gained the party's nod largely because of some brilliant backstage maneuvering by his managers and the growing realization by the delegates that he, not Seward, was likely to carry the battleground states.

When Abraham Lincoln emerged with the Republican nomination, he entered an unusual four-way race against Douglas (Northern Democrat), Bell (Constitutional Union) and Breckinridge (Southern Democrat). Of the four, only Lincoln stood squarely against slavery, and only Lincoln favored the tariff (which may have swung the election in Pennsylvania) and the Homestead Act (which certainly helped carry parts of the Midwest).[3] As in 1856, the race broke down into sectional contests, pitting Lincoln against Douglas in the North, and Bell against Breckinridge in the South. Lincoln's task was the most difficult of the four, in that he had to win ouright, lacking the necessary support in the House of Representatives.

The unusual alignments meant that "the United States was holding two elections simultaneously on November 6, 1860," one between Lincoln and Douglas, and a second between Breckinridge and Bell. On election day, Douglas learned from the telegraph that he had been crushed in New York and Pennsylvania. More sobering was the editorial in the Atlanta *Confederacy* predicting Lincoln's inauguration would result in the Potomac's being "crimsoned in human gore," sweeping "the last vestige of liberty" from the American continent.[4] When the votes were counted, Lincoln had carried all the Northern states except New Jersey (where he split the electoral vote with Douglas) as well as Oregon and California, for a total of 160 electoral votes. Douglas, despite winning nearly 30 percent of the popular vote, took only Missouri and part of New Jersey; this was a stunning disappointment, even though he had known the Southern vote would abandon him. Breckinridge carried the Deep South and Maryland. Only Virginia, Tennessee, and Kentucky went to Bell, whose 39 electoral votes exceeded those of Douglas. The popular vote could be interpreted many ways. Lincoln received more than 1.86 million votes (almost 40 percent), followed by Douglas with 1.38 million. Lincoln did not receive a single recorded vote in ten slave states, but won every free state except New Jersey.

If one adds Lincoln's and Douglas's popular vote totals together, applying the South's faulty logic that Douglas was a free-soiler, almost 69 percent voted against slavery. And even if one generously (and inaccurately) lumps together the votes for Bell and Breckinridge, the best case that the South could make was that it had the support of no more than 31 percent of the voters. The handwriting was on the wall: slavery in America was on the road to extinction. The key was that Lincoln did not need the South. When this realization dawned on Southerners, it was a shocking comeuppance, for since the founding of the nation, a Southern slaveholder had held the office of president for forty-nine out of seventy-two years, or better than two thirds of the time. Twenty-four of the thirty-six Speakers of the House and twenty-five of the thirty-six presidents pro tem of the Senate had been Southerners. Twenty of thirty-five Supreme Court justices had come from slave states, giving them a majority on the court at all times.[5]

After the election, Lincoln found his greatest ally in preserving the Union in his defeated foe, Stephen Douglas. The Illinois senator threw the full force of his statesmanship behind the cause of the Union. His, and Lincoln's, efforts were for naught, since the South marched headlong toward secession. Southern states recognized that it would only be a matter of months until a "black Republican" would have control over patronage, customs officials in Southern states, and federal contracts. A black Republican attorney general would supervise federal marshals in Mississippi and Louisiana, while Republican postmasters would have authority over the mails that streamed into Alabama and Georgia—"black Republicans" with purposes "hostile to slavery," the South Carolina secession convention noted.

The Last Uneasy Months of Union

Democrat president James Buchanan presided over a nation rapidly unraveling, leading him to welcome emergency measures that would avoid a war. Lincoln agreed to a proposed constitutional amendment that would prohibit interference with slavery in states where it existed. Congress now attempted to do in a month what it had been unable to do in more than forty years: find a compromise to the problem of slavery.

In mid-December, Kentuckian John J. Crittenden, a respected Senate leader, submitted an omnibus set of proposals, which were supported by the Committee of Thirteen—politicians who could have averted war had they so chosen, including Jefferson Davis, Seward, Douglas, and from the House a rising star, Charles Francis Adams.

Crittenden's resolutions proposed four compromise measures. First, they would restore the Missouri Compromise line; second, prohibit the abolition of slaveholding on federal property in the South; third, establish compensation for owners of runaways; and last, repeal "personal liberty" laws in the North. More important, the compromise would insert the word "slavery" in the Constitution, and then repackage the guarantees with a constitutional guarantee that would make the provisions inviolate to future change.

By that time, the North held the decision for war in its hands. Given that the South was bent on violating the Constitution no matter what, Northerners glumly realized that only one of three options remained: war, compromise, or allowing the Deep South to leave. Since no compromise would satisfy the South, Northerners soberly assessed the benefits of allowing the slaveholding states to depart. The money markets already had plunged because of the turmoil, adding to the national anxiety. Northerners desperately wanted to avoid disunion, and had the Crittenden proposals been put to a national plebiscite, it is probable they would have passed, according to Horace Greeley, although the secessionists would have ignored them as well.[6]

But in Congress the measures died. Republicans never cast a single vote for the provisions and, more important, the South could not accede to any of the conditions. Now, truly, the issue was on the table: would slavery survive without the support of the people? Would a majority of Southerners long support the slaveholding elites if federal law opened up its mails and harbors? Answers came shortly, when a new government formed in the South.

The Confederate States of America

No sooner had the telegraphs stopped clattering with the 1860 electoral counts than Robert Barnwell Rhett, William Yancey, T. R. Cobb, and other Southern fire eaters led a movement to call the state governments of the Deep South into session. South Carolina, Alabama, and Mississippi met first, the legislators in Columbia, South Carolina, ablaze with secessionist rhetoric. American flags were ripped down, replaced by new South Carolina "secesh" flags of a red star on a white background. The Palmetto State's incendiary voices hardly surpassed those in Alabama, where the secession proposal had early widespread support.

Virginian Edmund Ruffin, one of the hottest fire eaters, had outlined a League of United Southerners in 1858, and the commercial conventions in 1858 advanced the notion still further. On November 10, 1860, the South Carolina legislature announced a convention to occur a month later. If necessary, South Carolina was ready to act unilaterally. Florida, Alabama, and Georgia announced similar conventions. Every step of the way, South Carolina took the lead, issuing an "Address to the People of South Carolina" that called the Constitution of the United States a failed "experiment." Rhett proposed a conference in Montgomery with other Southern states to form a government separate from the United States, and South Carolina officially seceded on December 20, 1860.

Stephen Douglas lambasted the movement as "an enormous conspiracy . . . formed by the leaders of the secession movement twelve months ago." Fire eaters, he said, manipulated the election in order to "have caused a man to be elected by a sectional vote," thereby proving that the Union was as divided as they claimed.[7] However, evidence paints a more complex picture. Aside from South Carolina and Texas, the vote on secession was quite close. In Mississippi, for example, the secessionists defeated the "cooperationists" by fewer than 5,000 votes.[8] January's secession conventions in other states produced even smaller prosecession margins. Secession carried in Georgia by 3,500 ballots and in Louisiana by 1,200. Nowhere in the South did the vote on secession approximate the numbers who had gone to the polls for the presidential election. Only 70 percent of the November total turned out in Alabama, 75 percent in Louisiana, and only 60 percent in Mississippi—making the prosecession vote even less of a mandate. Nevertheless, Douglas's conspiracy interpretation did not account for the fact that the secession forces won the elections, no matter how narrowly and no matter how light the vote, underscoring the old adage that all that is necessary for evil to triumph is for good men to do nothing, or in the case of an election, stay home. More important, the winner-take-all system led to a unanimous agreement by the states of the lower South to send delegates to a February convention in Montgomery. As an Alabamian put it, "We are no longer one people. A paper parchment is all that holds us together, and the sooner that bond is severed the better it will be for both parties."[9]

In fact, secession had been railroaded through even more forcefully than the final state convention votes suggested. There was no popular referendum anywhere in the South. Conventions, made up of delegates selected by the legislatures, elected 854 men, 157 of whom voted against secession. Put in the starkest terms, "some 697 men, mostly wealthy, decided the destiny of 9 million people, mostly poor," and one third enslaved.[10] The circumstances of secession thus lend some credence to the position that when war finally came, many Southerners fought out of duty to their state and indeed many saw themselves as upholding constitutional principles. Few believed they were fighting to protect or perpetuate slavery per se. Given the conception of "citizenship" at the time—in the North and South—wherein rights originated in the *state,* not the federal government, most Southerners normally would have sided with their state government in a fracas against the national government.

On February 7, 1861, the Montgomery delegates adopted a new constitution for the Confederate States of America, and two days later elected Jefferson Davis of Mississippi as the CSA's first president. Davis looked much like Lincoln, and had he worn a beard, from certain angles they would have been indistinguishable. Like Lincoln, he had served in the Black Hawk War, then saw combat at both Monterrey and Buena Vista under Zachary Taylor. Like Lincoln, Davis knew heartache: he had married Taylor's daughter, who died of malaria. Davis differed from his Northern counterpart in many ways though. He lived on a small estate given to him by his brother, but he never achieved the wealthy planter lifestyle of other Confederate spokesmen. His view of slavery was based on how he, personally, treated his slaves, which was well. Thus, the abominations perpetrated by other masters seemed pure fantasy to Davis, who did not travel extensively. Debates over issues became assaults on his personal honor, leading him to give short shrift to the advice of moderates.

An advocate of industrialism and manufacturing, Davis shared with other Southern commercial messengers a blind spot for the dampening effects of slavery on investment and entrepreneurship. Quite simply, most entrepreneurs steered clear of a slave system that stifled free speech, oppressed one third of its consumers, and co-opted the personal liberty of free men to enforce slavery. Although Davis once criticized the "brainless intemperance" of those who wanted disunion, his own secessionist utterances bordered on hysterical, earning him from the New York *Herald* the nickname Mephistophiles of the South.[11] When secession came, he had an office in mind—general in chief of the new army. He scarcely dreamed he would be president.

The new Confederate constitution over which Jefferson Davis presided prohibited tariffs, subsidies to businesses, and most taxation, and required that all appropriations bills be passed by a two-thirds majority. This seemed on the surface quite Jeffersonian. Other provisions were not so Jeffersonian. The CSA constitution granted de facto subsidies to slave owners through externalized costs, passed off on all nonslaveholders the enforcement expenses of slavery, such as paying posses and court costs. And the constitution ensured that censorship would only get worse. Although there was a provision for a supreme court, the Confederate congress never established one, and the court system that existed tended to support the centralized power of the Confederate government rather than restrict it.[12] Certainly there was no check on the Congress or the president from compliant courts.[13] As would become clear during the war, the absence of such checks in the Confederate constitution gave Davis virtually unlimited power, including a line-item veto. The document reflected, in many ways, a Southern abstraction of what differentiated the sections of the Union.

Southern ideals of what secession entailed sprang from three main sources. First, during the past decade Southerners had come to hate free-soil concepts, finding them deeply offensive not only to the cotton economy to which they were committed but to the system of white superiority ingrained in the culture of the South. Second, a residual notion of states' rights from the days of the Anti-Federalists, nurtured by such thinkers as George Mason and John Calhoun, had gained popularity in the 1850s. The sovereignty of the states over the Union had a mixed and contradictory record of support by leading Southerners, including Jefferson and Jackson. Under the Confederacy, the principle of states' rights emerged unfettered and triumphant. The third was the widespread view of the propagandists of the South that "Cotton Is King!" and that a Southern republic would not only be freer, but economically superior to the North.

Demonizing Northerners followed in short order. New Englanders were "meddlers, jailbirds, outlaws, and disturbers of the peace."[14] (There had to be some irony involved in the labeling of former Puritans as jailbirds and outlaws by a region that prided itself on its frontier violence and, in the case of Georgia, had

had felons as its first settlers!) Outright lies about Lincoln's intentions occurred with regularity in order to put the citizens of the new "republic" in the proper frame of mind.

Indeed, Lincoln's promise not to touch slavery where it already existed only irritated the fire eaters more, exposing as it did their ultimate fear: that without expansion, the South would only become darker. Being unable to transport slaves into the territories, as Senator Robert Johnson of Arkansas pointed out, would increase the population inequities, because of the "natural multiplication of colored people," until blacks became equal in numbers to whites, then exceeded them. At that point, a race war would ensue.[15] Despite thirty years of philosophizing, denials, obfuscation, scriptural revision, and constitutional sophistries, it all came down to this: the South was terrified of large numbers of blacks, slave or free. It is not an exaggeration to say that the Civil War was about slavery and, in the long run, *only* about slavery.

If anyone doubted the relative importance of slavery versus states' rights in the Confederacy, the new constitution made matters plain: "Our new Government is founded . . . upon the great truth that the negro is not the equal of the white man. That slavery—subordination to the superior race, is his natural and normal condition."[16] CSA Vice President Alexander H. Stephens of Georgia called slavery "the proper status of the negro in our form of civilization."[17] In contradiction to libertarian references to "states' rights and liberty" made by many modern neo-Confederates, the Rebel leadership made clear its view that not only were blacks not people, but that ultimately all blacks—including then-free Negroes—should be enslaved. In his response to the Emancipation Proclamation, Jefferson Davis stated, "On and after Febrary 22, 1863, all free negroes within the limits of the Southern Confederacy shall be placed on slave status, and be deemed to be chattels, they and their issue forever."[18] Not only blacks "within the limits" of the Confederacy, but "all negroes who shall be taken in any of the States in which *slavery does not now exist,* in the progress of our arms, shall be adjudged to . . . occupy the slave status . . . [and] all free negroes shall, *ipso facto,* be reduced to the condition of helotism, so that . . . the white and black races may be ultimately placed on a permanent basis. [italics added]"[19] That basis, Davis said after the war started, was as "an inferior race, peaceful and contented laborers in their sphere."[20]

Fort Sumter

By the time Lincoln had actually taken the reins of the United States government in March 1861, the Deep South had seceded. Although Virginia, North Carolina, Tennessee, Arkansas, and others still remained in the Union, their membership was tenuous. From November 1860 until March 1861, James Buchanan still hoped to avoid a crisis. But his own cabinet was divided, and far from appearing diplomatic, Buchanan seemed paralyzed. He privately spoke of a constitutional convention that might save the Union, hoping that anything that stalled for time might defuse the situation.

He was right in one thing: the crisis clock was ticking. Secessionists immediately used state troops to grab federal post offices, customs houses, arsenals, and even the New Orleans mint, which netted the CSA half a million dollars in gold and silver. Federal officials resigned or switched sides. Only a few forts, including Fort Moultrie and Fort Sumter, both in Charleston, possessed sufficient troops to dissuade an immediate seizure by the Confederates, but their supplies were limited. Buchanan sent the unarmed *Star of the West* to reprovision Fort Sumter, only to have South Carolina's shore batteries chase it off. Thus, even before the firing on Fort Sumter itself, the war was on, and whatever effectiveness "little Buchanan" (as Teddy Roosevelt later called him) might have had had evaporated. The leading Republican in his cabinet, Lewis Cass, resigned in disgust, and Northerners of all political stripes insisted on retaliation. Ignoring calls from his own generals to reinforce the Charleston forts, Buchanan hesitated. His subordinate, Major Robert Anderson, did not.

At Fort Sumter, Anderson and seventy Union soldiers faced South Carolina's forces. Fort Moultrie, on Sullivan's Island, and Fort Johnson, on James Island, straddled Sumter on each side, which sat in the middle of Charleston harbor. Fort Johnson was already in Southern hands, but Moultrie held out. Because Anderson could not defend both Moultrie and Sumter, he was forced to relocate his troops to Fort Sumter, transferring them on the night of December twenty-sixth. This bought Buchanan time, for he thought keeping the remaining states in the Union held the keys to success. After February first, no other Southern state had bolted, indicating to Buchanan that compromise remained a possibility.

Upon assuming office, Lincoln wasted no time assessing the situation. After receiving mixed advice from his new cabinet, the president opted to resupply the post—as he put it, to "hold and occupy" all federal property. He had actually at first thought to "reclaim" federal territory in Confederate hands, but at the urging of a friend struck the clause from his inaugural address. He further made clear to the Rebels that he would only resupply Anderson, not bring in additional forces. Nevertheless, the inaugural declared that both universal law and the Constitution made "the Union of these States perpetual." No state could simply leave; the articles of secession were null and void. He did hold out the olive branch one last time, offering to take under advisement federal appointees unacceptable to the South. Lincoln did not mince words when it came to any hostilities that might arise: "You can have no conflict without being yourselves the aggressors." "We are not enemies," he reminded them, but "friends. . . . The mystic chords of memory, stretching from every battlefield, and patriot grave, to every living heart and hearthstone, all over this broad land, will yet swell the chorus of the Union, when again touched, as surely they will be, by the better angels of our nature."[21]

Lincoln's cabinet opposed reprovisioning Sumter. Most of their opinions could be dismissed, but not those of William Seward, the secretary of state. Still smarting from the Republican convention, Seward connived almost immediately to undercut Lincoln and perhaps obtain by stealth what he could not gain by ballot. He struck at a time in late March 1861, when Lincoln was absorbed by war and suffering from powerful migraine headaches, leading to unusual eruptions of temper in the generally mild-mannered president.

At that point of weakness, Seward moved, presenting Lincoln with a memorandum audaciously recommending that he, Seward, take over, and, more absurdly, that the Union provoke a war with Spain and France. Not only did the secretary criticize the new president for an absence of policy direction, but suggested that as soon as Lincoln surrendered power, Seward would use the war he drummed up with the Europeans as a pretext to dispatch agents to Canada, Mexico, and Central America to "rouse a vigorous continental spirit of independence" against the Confederacy. The president ignored this impertinence and quietly reminded Seward that he had spelled out his policies in the inaugural address and that Seward himself had supported the reprovisioning of Fort Sumter. Then, he made a mental note to keep a sharp eye on his scheming secretary of state.

By April sixth, Lincoln had concluded that the government must make an effort to hold Sumter. He dispatched a messenger to the governor of South Carolina informing him that Sumter would be reprovisioned with food and supplies only. Four days later, General P.G.T. Beauregard got orders from Montgomery instructing him to demand that federal troops abandon the fort. On April twelfth, Edmund Ruffin, the South Carolina fire eater who had done as much to bring about the war as anyone, had the honor of firing the first shot of the Civil War. In the ensuing brief artillery exchange in which Beauregard outgunned Anderson, his former West Point superior, four to one, no one was killed. A day later, Anderson surrendered, leading Jefferson Davis to quip optimistically, "There has been no blood spilled more precious than that of a mule."[22]

Soon thereafter, the upper South joined the Confederacy, as did the Indian Territory tribes, including some of the Cherokee, Choctaw, Chickasaw, Creek, and Seminole. Lincoln expected as much. He knew, however, that victory resided not in the state houses of Richmond or Little Rock, but in Missouri, Maryland, Kentucky, and western Virginia. Each of these border states or regions had slaves, but also held strong pro-Union views. Kentucky's critical position as a jumping-off point for a possible invasion of Ohio by Confederates and as a perfect staging ground for a Union invasion of Tennessee was so important that Lincoln once remarked, "I'd like to have God on my side, but I've got to have Kentucky."

With long-standing commercial and political ties to the North, Kentucky nevertheless remained a hotbed of proslavery sentiment. Governor Beriah Magoffin initially refused calls for troops from both Lincoln and Davis and declared neutrality. But Yankee forces under Grant ensured Kentucky's allegiance to the Union, although Kentucky Confederates simultaneously organized their own countergovernment. Militias of the Kentucky State Guard (Union) and Kentucky Home Guard (Confederate) squared off in warfare that quite literally pitted brother against brother.

Maryland was equally important because a Confederate Maryland would leave Washington, D.C., surrounded by enemies. Lincoln prevented Maryland's proslavery forces (approximately one third of the populace) from joining the Confederacy by sending in the army. The mere sight of Union troops marching through Maryland to garrison Washington had its effect. Although New York regiments expected trouble—the governor of New York warned that the First Zouaves would go through Baltimore "like a dose of salts"—in fact, a wide belt of secure pro-Union territory was carved twenty miles across Maryland.[23] Rioting and looting in Baltimore were met by a suspension of habeas corpus laws (allowing military governors to keep troublemakers incarcerated indefinitely), and by the arrest of Maryland fire eaters, including nineteen state legislators. When General Benjamin "Beast" Butler marched 1,000 men to seize arms readied for the Confederates and to occupy Federal Hill overlooking Baltimore during a thunderstorm, Maryland's opportunity for secession vanished.

One of those firebrands arrested under the suspension of habeus corpus, John Merryman, challenged his arrest. His case went to the U.S. Supreme Court Chief Justice (and Marylander Democrat) Roger Taney, who sat as a circuit judge. Taney, seeing his opportunity to derail the Union's agenda, declared Lincoln's actions unconstitutional. Imitating Jackson in 1832, Lincoln simply ignored the chief justice.

In western Virginia, the story was different. Large pockets of Union support existed throughout the southern Appalachian mountains. In Morgantown, the grievances that the westerners in Virginia felt toward Richmond exceeded those suffered by the Tidewater planters who were against the Union. A certain degree of reality also set in: Wheeling was susceptible immediately to a bombardment from Ohio, and forces could converge from Pittsburgh and Cincinnati to crush any rebellion there. Wisely, then, on June 19, 1861, western Unionists voted in a special convention declaring theirs the only legitimate government of Virginia, and the following May, West Virginia became a new Union state. "Let us save Virginia, and then save the Union," proclaimed the delegates to the West Virginia statehood convention, and then, as if to underscore that it was the "restored" government of Virginia, the new state adopted the seal of the Commonwealth of Virginia with the phrase "Liberty and Union" added.[24]

West Virginia's defection to the Union buffered Ohio and western Pennsylvania from invasion the same way that keeping Kentucky's geographical location protected Ohio. In a few politically masterful strokes, Lincoln had succeeded in retaining the border states he needed.[25] The North had secured the upper Chesapeake, the entire western section of Virginia; more important, it held strategic inroads into Virginia through the Shenandoah Valley, into Mississippi and Louisiana through Kentucky and Missouri, and into Georgia through the exposed position of the Confederates in Tennessee.[26] Moreover, the populations of the border states, though divided, still favored the Union, and "three times as many white Missourians would fight for the Union as for the Confederacy, twice as many Marylanders, and half again as many Kentuckians."[27]

Missouri's divided populace bred some of the most violent strife in the border regions. Missourians had literally been at war since 1856 on the Kansas border, and Confederates enjoyed strong support in the vast rural portions of the state. In St. Louis, however, thousands of German American immigrants stood true to the Union. Samuel Langhorne Clemens (aka Mark Twain), who served a brief stint in a Missouri Confederate militia unit, remembered that in 1861 "our state was invaded by Union forces," whereupon the secessionist governor, Caleb Jackson, "issued his proclamation to help repel the invader."[28] In fact, Missouri remained a hotbed of real and pseudorebel resistance, with more than a few outlaw gangs pretending to be Confederates in order to plunder and pillage. William Quantrill's raiders (including the infamous Frank and Jesse James) and other criminals used the Rebel cause as a smokescreen to commit crimes. They crisscrossed the Missouri-Kansas borders, capturing the town of Independence, Missouri, in August 1862, and only then were they sworn into the Confederate Army. Quantrill's terror campaign came to a peak a year later with the pillage of Lawrence, Kansas, where his cutthroats killed more than 150 men. Unionist Jayhawkers, scarcely less criminal, organized to counter these Confederate raiders.

John C. Frémont, "the Pathfinder" of Mexican War fame, commanded the Union's Western Department. Responding to the Missouri violence, he imposed martial law in August 1861, invoking the death penalty against any captured guerrillas. Frémont further decreed arbitrarily that any slaves captured from rebel forces were emancipated, providing the prosecession forces in the border states all the ammunition necessary to push them into the Confederacy. This went too far for Lincoln, who countermanded Frémont's emancipation edict, while letting martial law stand.

The Combatants Square Off

One of the major questions about the American Civil War period is, "Why did it take the North four long and hard years to finally defeat the South?" On the surface, the Yankees seemed to possess most of the advantages: a huge population, a standing army and navy, the vast bulk of American industrial might, and a large and effective transportation system. They also had the powerful causes of union and free soil to inspire and propel their soldiers. Yet the North faced a grim and determined foe, whose lack of men and war matériel was balanced somewhat by an abundance of military leadership and combat expertise. Moreover, the war scenario gave an advantage to the defense, not the offense.

The conflict sharply illustrated the predictable results when the Western way of war met its exact duplicate on the field of battle, with each side armed with long-range cannons, new rifles, and even newer breech-loading and repeating weapons.

Over the course of four years, more than 618,000 men would die—more than the combined military losses of the Revolution, the War of 1812, the Mexican War, the Spanish-American War, Korea, and the twentieth century's two world wars combined. Gettysburg alone, in three bloody days, saw 50,000 killed, wounded, or missing. Sharpsburg—or Antietam—itself produced more casualties than the Revolution, the War of 1812, and the Mexican War put together. Worse, these were Americans fighting Americans. Stories of brother fighting brother abound. Mary Lincoln's three brothers all died fighting for the Confederacy, while Varina Davis (Jefferson Davis's second wife) had relatives in blue. John Crittenden's sons each held the rank of colonel, but in opposing armies. David Farragut, the hero of Mobile Bay, had lived in Virginia, and Lincoln himself was born in Kentucky, a slave state. Robert E. Lee had a nephew commanding a Union squadron on the James River. Union general George McClellan preferred letting the South go; Sam Houston, the governor of Texas, wanted the South to stay in the Union. As young boys, future presidents Theodore Roosevelt (New York) and Woodrow Wilson (Georgia) prayed for divine blessings, but Roosevelt prayed for the North and Wilson for the South.[29]

The forces of the Union seemed insurmountable. Northerners boasted a population of more than 20 million, while the white population of the South, that is, those who were eligible to bear arms, numbered under 6 million. Slaves were used in labor situations to supplement the Confederate Army in building bridges, digging trenches, and driving wagons, but the slaves often constituted, at best, a potentially hostile force that had to be guarded, further diminishing active front-line troops. In all, the Union put 2.1 million men into the field: 46,000 draftees, 118,000 paid substitutes, and the rest volunteers in the regular army or militia. Rebel forces totaled 800,000, of which almost one fourth were either draftees or substitutes. It is an irony, then, that today's neo-Confederates and libertarians who berate the Union as oppressing the rights of free men ignore the fact that the Confederacy forced more free whites under arms than the North.[30] Union forces deserted in higher absolute numbers (200,000 to just more than half that number of Confederates), but as a proportion of the total wartime force, the Rebels saw almost 12.5 percent of their army desert, compared to less than 10 percent of the Union forces.

Nevertheless, it would not take long before the Yankees realized the mettle of their opponent. The valor and tenacity of the Rebels, winning battle after battle with smaller forces and holding off the North for four years, is a testament to both their commitment to the Confederate cause (as they saw it) and, more important, to their nurturing as Americans, themselves steeped in the Western way of war. If only in the war's duration, the élan and skill of the Confederate soldiers is noteworthy.

The commercial differences between the Union and Confederacy were even more striking. Much has been made of the railroad mileage, although depending on how one measured the tracks laid in the territories and the border states, some of the Northern advantage disappears. The North had as many as twenty thousand miles of track, whereas the South had perhaps ten thousand. But even if these numbers had been roughly equal, they would have been misleading. Southern roads tended to run east and west, which was an advantage as long as the Mississippi remained open and Texas's cattle and horses could be brought in through Louisiana. But after New Orleans fell and Vicksburg was all but surrounded, all livestock the western Confederacy could supply were undeliverable. More important, Northern railroads often ran north-south, making for rapid delivery to the front lines of cannonballs, food, and clothing. Some Southern states actually built tracks that only connected to rivers, with no connection to other railroads, and Alabama had laid a shortcut railroad that connected two Tennessee River points.

Dominance by the North over the South in other areas was even more pronounced: 32 to 1 in firearms production, 14 to 1 in merchant shipping, 3 to 1 in farm acreage, 412 to 1 in wheat, and 2 to 1 in corn. Cotton might have been king, but Southerners soon found that their monarch did not make for good eating. And the North controlled 94 percent of manufactured cotton cloth and 90 percent of America's boot and shoe manufacturing. Pig-iron manufacturing was almost entirely Northern, with all but a few of the nation's 286 furnaces residing in the Union. Those facilities churned out iron for 239 arms manufacturers, again overwhelmingly located north of the Mason-Dixon Line. One county in Connecticut, which was home to nine firearms factories, manufactured guns worth ten times the value of all firearms in the entire South in 1860. The South had one cannon foundry, at the Tredegar Iron Works in Richmond. From Cyrus McCormick's reaper factory in Chicago to the Patterson, New Jersey, locomotive works, Northern manufacturing was poised to bury the South. In its navy alone, the North had an almost insurmountable advantage, and Lincoln perceived this, announcing an immediate blockade of the South by sea. The blockade underscored Lincoln's definition of the war as an insurrection and rebellion. Had the South had a navy, its seagoing commerce with England and France might have been substantial enough to legitimate its claims of being a nation. Winners set the rules, and the winner at sea was the Union Navy.

Yet even with these advantages, the Union still faced a daunting task. All the South had to do to succeed was to survive. The Confederates did not have to invade the North, and every year that passed brought the reality of an independent Confederate nation ever closer. The American Revolution had taught that all an army of resistance need do is avoid destruction. And more in 1861 than in 1776, the technology favored the defender. Combinations of earthworks with repeating or breech-loading rifles, long-range cannons, and mass transportation with railroads and steam vessels meant that defenders could resist many times their number, and receive timely reinforcements or perform critical withdrawals.

Moreover, the United States had only a small professional army by European standards, and after 1861, that army was reduced by about half as Southerners resigned to fight for the CSA. As a result, both sides relied heavily on militia troops. Militia units, as was learned in the Revolution and the War of 1812, had important strengths and failings. Village militia units, comprised of all men of the ages fifteen through fifty, mustered once a year, trained and drilled irregularly, and provided their own weapons. But militias lacked the critical discipline, professionalism, and experience that regular soldiers possessed, leading Samuel Clemens to refer to his militia company as a "cattle herd," in which an argument broke out between a corporal and sergeant—neither of whom knew who outranked the other![31] To overcome these weaknesses, state militias were retained intact as units, ensuring that Ohioans, Mainers, and New Yorkers fought together. This enhanced unit cohesion and loyalty, but also produced tragic results when the order of battle hurled the manhood of entire towns into enemy guns. As a result, some towns saw an entire generation disappear in four years of war.

The militia/regular army volunteer units became "largely a personal thing" in which "anyone who wished could advertise to . . . 'raise a company' . . . and invite 'all willing to join to come on a certain morning to some saloon, hotel, or public hall.' "[32] Units that emerged predictably had flashy names and even glitzier uniforms, including the Buena Vista Guards, the New York Fire Zouaves, the Polish Legion, the St. Patrick's Brigade, the Garibaldi Guards, and (again predictably) the Lincoln Guards.[33] Some, such as the Wisconsin Black Hats, also known as the Iron Brigade, were famous for their headgear, while New York Zouave units copied the French army's baggy red trousers. Some of the extremely decorative uniforms soon gave way to more practical battlefield gear, but the enthusiasm did not dim. The 6th Massachusetts, a regiment of 850 men, marched to Washington only forty-eight hours after Lincoln's call for volunteers, and between the time the president issued the call for 75,000 volunteers in April, and the time Congress convened in July, the Northern army had swollen by more than 215,000 over its pre-Sumter troop levels.

Indeed, Massachusetts outdid herself. A state of 1.25 million people marched six regiments (or roughly 72,000 men) to war by July, and promised eleven more, a total far exceeding the state's proportional commitment. Yet this enthusiasm itself came with a cost. Instead of too few men, the Union's greatest problem at the outset of the conflict was too many. Secretary of War Cameron complained he was "receiving troops faster than [the government] can provide for them."[34] When the first weary soldiers marched into Washington to defend the Capitol, all that awaited them was salted red herring, soda crackers, and coffee made in rusty cauldrons. Those who marched to the front were more fortunate than others crammed into coastal vessels and steamed down from New England port cities. Regardless of their mode of transportation, most of the young men who donned the uniform of either the North or South had never been more than twenty miles from home, nor had they ever ridden a steamboat. Many had never seen a large city.

Command in the Union Army was ravaged by the departure of a large number of the U.S. Army's officer corps, both active and retired, who left for the Confederate cause. Indeed, from 1776 to 1861 (and even to the present), Southerners filled the ranks of America's professional fighting forces in disproportionate numbers in relation to their population. Southern soldiers outnumbered Northerners significantly in the Mexican-American War, and West Point graduated a higher rate of Southern second lieutenants than Northern. Southern officers, such as Thomas J. "Stonewall" Jackson, Braxton Bragg, Albert Sidney Johnston, Joseph E. Johnston, and Robert E. Lee reneged on their oath to protect the United States from enemies "foreign and domestic" to fight in gray. In all, 313 U.S. Army officers resigned to join the Confederacy, whereas 767 regular army officers stayed to form the new Union cadre. Lee was especially reluctant, having been offered the position of commander in chief of the Union Army by Lincoln. Yet he could not persuade himself to raise his hand against Virginia, and reluctantly joined the Confederates. A more touching departure occurred with the resignation of Joseph E. Johnston of Virginia, who met Secretary of War Cameron in April 1861. He wept as he said, "I must go. Though I am resigning my position, I trust I may never draw my sword against the old flag."[35]

More than manpower and brains left the Union cause. Confederates stormed armories and arsenals. They captured the valuable Norfolk docks and shipyards, taking nine warships into custody at the Gosport Navy Yard. Although the *New York* and *Pennsylvania* went up in flames, the Confederates salvaged a third vessel, the *Merrimac*. Had the Union commander of the navy yard given the order, the steam-powered *Merrimac* could have escaped entirely, but he buckled to the pressure of the Rebels, providing the hull for what would become one of the world's first two ironclads. In the larger context, however, these losses were minimal, and paled beside the substantial advantages that the North possessed.

For example, supplementing the militias and regular army enlistments, in 1862, the Union allowed free blacks to join segregated infantry units. Thousands enlisted, at first receiving only $7 per month as compared to $13 allowed for a white private. Two years later, with Lincoln's support, Congress passed the Enrollment Act, authorizing equal pay for black soldiers. Even for white regulars, however, a military career was not exactly lucrative. Prior to the war, a general made less than $3,500 a year (compared to a senator's $5,000), whereas a captain received $768 annually.[36] Only the engineering corps seemed exempt from the low pay, attracting many of the best officers, including Robert E. Lee, who directed port improvements along the Mississippi River.

Like the North, the South hoped to avoid a draft, but reality set in. The Confederate congress enacted a Conscription Act in 1862, even before the Union, establishing the first military draft in American history. All able-bodied males eighteen to thirty-five had to serve for three years, although wartime demands soon expanded the ages from seventeen to fifty. Exemptions were granted postal employees, CSA officials, railroad workers, religious ministry, and those employed in manufacturing plants. Draftees could also hire substitutes, of which there were 70,000 in the South (compared with 118,000 in the North). Given the higher rates of Northern regular enlistments, however, it is apparent that Southerners purchased their way out of combat, or avoided going to war, at a higher overall rate than their counterparts in blue. Conscription, to many Southerners, violated the principles they seemed to be fighting for, leading to criticisms that the Confederate draft itself constituted an act of despotism.

Attack and Die?

There were powerful cultural forces at work that shaped each side's views of everything from what to eat to how to fight.[37] Historians Grady McWhiney and Perry Jamieson have proposed the famous Celtic Thesis to explain Confederate tactics.[38] Northerners tended to be more Anglo-Saxon and Teutonic, Southerners more Celtic. This had tremendous implications for the way in which each side fought, with the South consumed by "self-assertion and manly pride."[39]

In their controversial book, *Attack and Die,* McWhiney and Jamieson claimed that the Celtic herding and agrarian culture that dominated the South propagated a military culture based on attack and, especially, full frontal charges. Jefferson Davis, the Confederate president, urged his troops to go on the offensive and to "plant our banners on the banks of the Ohio."[40] (Historian Bernard De Voto quipped that Davis had just enough success in war in Mexico to ensure the South's defeat.)[41] Union colonel Benjamin Buell observed "an insane desire on the part of the Southern people, & some of the Generals to assume the offensive."[42] The Confederate/Celtic code of officer loyalty demanded they lead their men into battle. Such tactics devastated the Confederate command structure: 55 percent of the South's generals were killed or wounded in battle, and many had already been shot or wounded before they received their mortal wound. More telling, Confederate casualty rates (men wounded and killed to the number of soldiers in action) were consistently higher than the Union's in almost every major battle, regardless of the size of forces engaged, generals in command, or outcome of the engagement. Only at Fredericksburg, with Burnside's suicidal charges against Marye's Heights, did Union casualty rates exceed those of the supposedly better-led rebels.

Lee, for all his purported military genius, suffered 20 percent in casualties while inflicting only 15 percent on his enemy; whereas Grant suffered 18 percent in casualties but inflicted 30 percent on his foes. Overall, Lee only inflicted 13,000 more casualties on the federals than he absorbed—a ratio completely incompatible with a smaller population seeking to defeat a larger one. Grant, on the other hand, inflicted 12 percent more casualties on enemy commanders he encountered. Confederates attacked in eight of the first twelve big battles of the Civil War, losing a staggering 97,000 men—20,000 more than the Union forces lost. In only one major engagement, where the highest casualties occurred, Sharpsburg, did the Confederates substantially fight on the defensive. At Gettysburg, the worst of the Rebels' open-field charges, Lee lost more than 30 percent of his entire command, with the majority of the losses coming in Pickett's ill-fated charge.

Some of the propensity for taking the offensive must be blamed on the necessity for Confederate diplomatic breakthroughs. Until Gettysburg, the Confederacy pinned its dim hopes on Britain's or France's entering the fight on its side. But Europeans were unsure whether the Confederacy's defensive strategy was of its own choosing or was forced on it by Northern might. Thus, taking the war to the North figured prominently in the efforts to convince Britain and France that the CSA was legitimate.[43] Yet this strategy proved to be flawed.

The North, on the other hand, seriously misjudged the commitment and skill of its foe, but at least, from the outset, appreciated the nature of its initial military objectives and its economic advantages. Nevertheless, neither Lincoln nor his generals fully understood how difficult the task would be in 1861. Ultimately, however, the difference between North and South came down to Lincoln's being "a great war president [whereas] Jefferson Davis was a mediocre one."[44] Where Davis had graduated from West Point and fought in the Mexican War, Lincoln did not know how to write a military order. But he learned: "By the power of his mind, [he] became a fine strategist," according to T. Harry Williams and "was a better natural strategist than were most of the trained soldiers."[45] He immediately perceived that the Union had to use its manpower and economic advantage, and it had to take the offensive. Still, Lincoln had much to absorb, some of it from Union General in Chief Winfield Scott. Old Fuss and Feathers of Mexican War fame—by then seventy-four years old and notorious for falling asleep at councils of war—engineered the initial strategy for the Union Army, the Anaconda Plan.

Designed to take advantage of the Union's naval power, Scott envisioned U.S. naval vessels blockading the ports on the Atlantic and Gulf coasts and the lower Mississippi River. Gradually, using gunboats and ground forces, the North would sever the western Confederacy from the eastern Confederacy by controlling the Mississippi. This would have the twofold effect of starving the Confederates and denying them additional men and horses on the one hand, and preventing aid from overseas from reaching the Rebels on the other. Lincoln's advisers initially put far too much faith in the Anaconda Plan, hoping that it could strangle the enemy without the need for crushing all Rebel resistance. But the strategy of blockades and dividing the Confederacy in two along the Mississippi would prove vital when later combined with other strategic aims.

The blockade did have an effect. As early as July 1861, Jefferson Davis told James Chestnut in Richmond, "We begin to cry out for more ammunition and already the blockade is beginning to shut it all out."[46] But any fantasy that the North would simply cruise down the Mississippi River unopposed soon faded as the western Union commanders noted the Confederate troop buildups and fortifications along the river systems in Tennessee and Mississippi.

Once again, though, the Confederacy played to the Union's strength, this time through its shortsighted diplomatic decision to embargo the sale of cotton to Europe. Rebel leaders mistakenly believed that a cotton-starved Britain or France might enter the war in a few months, echoing the old cotton-is-king mantra of the 1850s. In reality, the cotton embargo proved disastrous. The British easily shifted to new sources of cotton, especially India and Egypt, so as a consequence the strategy simultaneously deprived the Confederacy of income from the *only* significant product that could have brought in funds, while coalescing the planter elites around protecting their cotton investment. Planters kept their slave work-forces growing cotton, when they could have been repairing railroads, building forts, or otherwise doing tasks that kept white soldiers from combat.[47]

Both the Anaconda Plan and cotton diplomacy clouded the real military pic-ture. In 1861 few thinkers in either army clearly saw that only a comprehensive, two-front war in the west and Virginia would produce victory. Neither side ever approached the "total war" level of mobilization and destruction later seen in World War I, but the North gradually adopted what historian James MacPherson called hard war.[48] "Hard war" meant two (and later, more) simultaneous fronts and the destruction of cities without, if possible, the slaughter of the inhabitants. It meant constant assault. It meant mobilizing public opinion. Most of all, it meant attacking the economic and commercial pillar of slavery that propped up the Confederacy. Lincoln only came to this understanding after a year of bloody battlefield setbacks.

At the outset, Lincoln had no intention of making emancipation the war aim, nor is it likely he could have persuaded his troops to fight to free blacks. North-erners went to war because the South had broken the law in the most fundamen-tal way. After "teachin' Johnny Reb a lesson" the war would be over. When it dragged on, a combination of other motivations set in, including retribution, a perceived threat to the Constitution, and later, emancipation. Southern soldiers, on the other hand, fought because they saw federal troops invading their home states. "Why are you fighting in this war?" Union troops asked a captured soldier. "Because you're down here," he replied.[49]

Bull Run and Union Failure

FORWARD TO RICHMOND blared a front-page headline from the New York *Tribune* in June 1861.[50] Already impatient with the Anaconda Plan, Northern voices called for a speedy victory to capture the new Confederate capital of Richmond and end the conflict. Lincoln unwisely agreed to an immediate assault, realizing that every day the Confederacy remained independent it gained in legitimacy. He told the commanding General Irwin McDowell, who headed the Army of the Po-tomac, "You are green, it is true, but they are green also; you are all green alike."[51] McDowell developed a sound plan, marching 36,000 men out of Washington and into northern Virginia on July 16, 1861. There, Confederate General Pierre Beauregard, fresh from his triumph at Fort Sumter, met him with a smaller force of 20,000 near a railroad crossing at Manassas, on the south bank of the river called Bull Run.

Another rebel force of 12,000, under Joe Johnston, operated in the Shenan-doah Valley; the aged Union general Robert Patterson was instructed to keep Johnston from reinforcing Beauregard. Benefiting from the scouting of J.E.B. Stuart's cavalry and from reliable spy reports, Johnston slipped away from Patter-son and headed for Manassas. Thus, McDowell would find not one, but two Rebel armies when he finally arrived at Bull Run on Sunday, July twenty-first.

Expecting an entertaining victory, hundreds of Washington civilians, including congressmen and tourists, arrived at the battlefield with picnic baskets in horse-drawn carriages. What they saw, instead, was one of the worst routs of the Civil War. General Johnston arrived and, aided by General Thomas "Stonewall" Jackson, drove the Yankees from the field. Federal forces fell back across the river, where they encountered the gawking civilians, now scrambling to pick up their lunches and climb into their carriages ahead of the retreating army. One congressman, who had come out as a spectator, reported

> There was never anything like it . . . for causeless, sheer, absolute, absurd cowardice, or rather panic, on this miserable earth. . . . Off they went, one and all; off down the highway, over across fields, towards the woods, anywhere they could escape. . . . To enable them better to run, they threw away their blankets, knapsacks, canteens, and finally muskets, cartridge-boxes, and everything else.[52]

An orderly retreat soon turned into a footrace back to Washington. A reporter for the London *Times,* W. H. Russell, who accompanied the reserves, had just started forward when terrified soldiers shot past him in the opposite direction. "What does this mean?" he asked a fleeing officer, who replied, "Why, it means that we are pretty badly whipped."[53] The road back to the capital was strewn with muskets, backpacks, caps, and blankets as men, tripping and stumbling, grabbing wagons or caissons, dashed for safety.

In the first of many missed opportunities on both sides, however, Johnston failed to pursue the Union Army into Washington and possibly end the war. While the South had a stunning victory, it also had six hundred deaths (matched by the federal casualties), making it the most costly battle fought on American soil since 1815. Within months, each army would long for the day when it marked its casualty figures in the hundreds instead of the thousands. Despite the North's shocking defeat, Bull Run proved indecisive, producing "no serious military disadvantage for the North, nor gain, except in terms of pride . . . for the South."[54] The South did find a new hero—Stonewall Jackson—whose nickname derived from the moment in the battle when a South Carolina general pointed to him, saying, "There is Jackson, standing like a stone wall."[55] Aside from that, the Rebel army was a mess. Johnston lamented it was "more disorganized by victory than that of the United States by defeat."[56] The South learned few lessons from the clash, but did comprehend the tremendous advantage railroads provided. Had the Confederacy carefully assessed the situation, it would have avoided any battlefield situation that did not provide close interior lines of support. The South also decided it had to change uniforms: the U.S. Army wore blue, as did many Southern units that had just recently resigned from the Union, leading entire units to come under friendly fire at Bull Run. The Confederates soon adopted the gray uniforms of the Virginia Military Institute.

Meanwhile, as Lincoln and his advisers soberly assessed the situation, the setback actually stimulated their war preparations. Some Lincoln critics assail him for not calling up a larger army sooner, whereas others castigate him for being overly aggressive. In fact, prior to the first musket balls' flying, Lincoln hoped to demonstrate his goodwill to the South by not mobilizing for an invasion. Bull Run obviously dashed such hopes, and Lincoln reconsidered the military situation. The Union quickly fortified Washington, D.C., with a string of defenses. "Troops, troops, tents, the frequent thunder of guns practising, lines of heavy baggage wagons . . . all indications of an immense army," noted one observer.[57] Another, using his spyglass to take detailed notes, recorded 34 regiments (more than 80,000 men) encamped, and on another day saw 150 army wagons on Pennsylvania Avenue alone.[58]

A massive manpower buildup was only one sign, though, of the Union's resolve. In July 1861, Congress passed the Crittenden-Johnson Resolutions, declaring support for a war "to defend and maintain the supremacy of the Constitution, and to preserve the Union with all the dignity, equality, and rights of the several states unimpaired."[59] Sponsored by Crittenden and Tennessee Democrat Andrew Johnson, the resolutions provided a broad-based warning from Northerners and border-state politicians of both parties that, if not addressed and punished, secession would lead to a collapse of law and order everywhere. Between the lines, the resolutions warned Lincoln that the war could not appear to be a campaign against slavery itself.

Theoretically, this put Lincoln in a bind, though one of his own making. He had held at the outset that the Confederacy represented a rebellion by a handful of individuals, and that the Southern states had never legally left the Union. That meant these states could be restored with constitutional protections intact, including slavery, if or when the Southern states returned. Congress, however, had already provided Lincoln a means of leveraging the war toward abolition at some future point. In May 1861, Union General Benjamin "Beast" Butler, having conquered Fortress Monroe, Virginia, announced his intention to retain slaves as "contrabands" of war, including any fugitive slaves who escaped behind his lines. Three months later, the Congress—with the Democrats in almost unanimous opposition—passed the First Confiscation Act, which provided for the seizure of property the Rebels used to support their resistance, including all slaves who fought with the Confederate Army or who worked directly for it.

Confiscation hurt Lincoln's efforts to keep Maryland, Kentucky, and Missouri in the Union. Not long after Congress acted, General John Fremont in Missouri issued orders to confiscate any Rebel slaves there, implying that the act amounted to a declaration of emancipation. Fremont's impetuous interpretation prompted a quick response from the president, who instructed Fremont to bring his orders in line with the letter of the Confiscation Act. This edict probably kept Kentucky in the Union.

Meanwhile, Lincoln responded to the Bull Run debacle by shaking up the command structure, replacing McDowell with General George B. McClellan, who then was elevated to the position of general in chief of the army after Scott's retirement in November 1861. McClellan, who likened himself to Napoléon, was an organizational genius whose training of the Union Army no doubt played a critical role in preparing it for the long war. Intelligent and energetic, occasionally arrogant, McClellan did indeed share some traits with Napoléon. But he completely lacked Napoléon's acute sense of timing—where the enemies' weaknesses were, where to strike, and when. Not wishing to risk his popularity with the men, McClellan was reluctant to sacrifice them when the need arose. Worse, he viewed his own abilities as far superior to those of Lincoln, a man he viewed as possessing "inferior antecedents and abilities."[60] A Douglas Democrat, politics were never far from George McClellan's mind, although, ironically, no general did more to educate Lincoln in the academic elements of strategy and tactics. Lincoln's wisdom in perceiving the overarching picture in 1862 and 1863 owed much to the Union's Napoléon.

McClellan's weaknesses were not apparent in mid-1861, when, even before his first big battle, he was touted as a future president. But he lacked aggressiveness, a trait fostered by his perfectionist nature. The general constantly complained he lacked adequate troops (often asserting that he needed an unreasonable ten-to-one advantage before he could attack), supplies, and artillery, where, in contrast, Napoléon had fought while outnumbered on numerous occasions, using the overconfidence of the enemy to defeat him. Secretary of War Edwin Stanton disparagingly said of McClellan, "We have ten generals there, every one afraid to fight. . . . If McClellan had a million men, he would swear the enemy had two million, and then he would sit down . . . and yell for three."[61]

McClellan did have two traits that made him too popular to replace easily. He fed his army well and displayed it on parade whenever possible. McClellan obtained good rations and established new examination boards that produced better quality officers, raising his reputation among the line soldiers. His frequent parades and displays of discipline instilled a public affection that would only dissipate after his first major loss. Lincoln bore a considerable degree of responsibility, however, for the McClellan monster: the president's unaffected manner of speaking, his penchant for storytelling to make a point, and above all his lack of social refinement led McClellan to misjudge him. The general wrote that Lincoln was "not a man of very strong character . . . certainly in no sense a gentleman."[62] Lincoln's deference finally reached its end. Unhappy with McClellan's dithering, in January 1862, Lincoln issued the "President's General War Order No. 1," instructing McClellan to move forward by February. As he had throughout most of the previous few months, McClellan outnumbered his Rebel opponents by about three-to-one. Yet he still advanced cautiously in what has been labeled the Virginia Peninsula Campaign of 1862. Rather than approach Richmond directly, McClellan advanced obliquely with an army of 112,000 along the peninsula between the York and James rivers where the Union Navy could provide cover. As McClellan neared Richmond, things fell apart. First, Lincoln unwisely reduced McClellan's command by withholding Irwin McDowell's entire corps in a reorganization of the army, placing McDowell south of Washington to protect the capital. Second, McClellan wasted valuable time (a month) capturing Yorktown.

Begging Lincoln for McDowell's men, who finally headed south toward Fredericksburg, McClellan reluctantly moved on Richmond.

By that time, Lee had become the commander of the Army of Northern Virginia and McClellan's main foe. Lee's second in command, Stonewall Jackson, set the table for Union failure through a series of bold raids on Yankee positions all over the Shenandoah Valley. Jackson's high theater struck terror in the hearts of Washingtonians, who were convinced he was going to invade at any moment, despite the fact that Jackson had only 16,000 men facing more than 45,000 Union troops. He succeeded in distracting McClellan long enough that the opportunity to drive into Richmond vanished. Instead, the Union and Confederate armies fought a series of moving battles throughout June and July of 1862, including the Battles of Seven Pines, Mechanicsville, Gaines's Mill, Frayser's Farm, and others. At Malvern Hill, McClellan finally emerged with a victory, though he still had not taken Richmond. Murmurings in Washington had it that he could have walked into the Confederate capital, but the last straw (for now, at least) for Lincoln came with a letter McClellan wrote on July seventh in which the general strayed far from military issues and dispensed political advice well above his pay grade.

At that point, a rising group of Republicans, known as the Radicals, emerged. Some of the Radicals had been abolitionists before the war, and they tended to view the conflict as not only about emancipation, but also about cleansing from the body politic the disloyal and treasonous plantation elites of the Democratic Party they saw as having brought on the war. Among the most prominent Radicals were Charles Sumner of Massachusetts, Thaddeus Stevens of Pennsylvania, Joshua Giddings of Ohio, and Union general Carl Schurz, all of whom wanted to severely punish the South as a region and the Democrats as a party for bringing on the war. When the Radicals heard of McClellan's insubordination (not to mention, in their eyes, incompetence), they pressured Lincoln to remove him, and he acceded to their demands, replacing America's Bonaparte with General John Pope. Demoted as supreme commander, McClellan remained in charge of the Army of the Potomac.

John Pope was a braggart who told Congress that if he had been in charge from the beginning, his forces would already be marching through New Orleans. Pope was soon humiliated more than McClellan. Despite victories over Pope, Lee had lost proportionately more staggering numbers of men. At the Seven Days' Battles (Mechanicsville, Malvern Hill), for example, the South lost 5,700 men (13 percent of the force committed) and at Second Manassas it lost more than 9,000 men (more than 18 percent of the troops engaged). For the time being, however, Union congressmen's anger at the outcome concealed from them the raw arithmetic of combat.

Water War
While conflict on land raged in the East, good news for the Union came from the war at sea. In September 1861, navy flotillas had captured the forts at Cape

Hatteras, North Carolina, establishing a tiny beachhead in the South. Two months later, the U.S. Navy seized the South Carolina Sea Islands and Port Royal. The relatively easy conquest reflected both the North's superiority at sea and, at the same time, the magnitude of the task that still remained. Jefferson Davis admitted as much. "At the inception of hostilities," he pointed out, "we had no commercial marine, while their merchant vessels covered the ocean. We were without a navy, while they had powerful fleets."[63] Nevertheless, the Union had to cover more than three thousand miles if one measured in a straight line rather than calculated the space of every inlet and bay. Policing the entire coastline was impossible, but grabbing key ports was not.

The blockade also posed the danger that an aggressive Union captain would fire on a foreign ship or board a neutral vessel. At all costs, Lincoln needed to keep Britain and France out of the conflict. In May, Britain announced strict neutrality, allowing for the Confederates to fight for their independence, but also acknowledging the legality of the Union blockade. Thus the British could simultaneously recognize the Confederate and Union war aims as legitimate. Reality dictated that John Bull might, therefore, fall on the Union side, since British ships would not cross the blockade line. In November 1861, however, when Jefferson Davis dispatched John Slidell and James Mason as permanent envoys to Britain and France aboard a British ship, the *Trent*, U.S. Navy Captain Charles Wilkes, aboard the USS *San Jacinto*, stopped the *Trent* by firing shots across her bow. Boarding the vessel, Union sailors removed Mason and Slidell and transported them to New York City, from where they were declared prisoners of war and remanded to Fort Warren in Boston. British outrage not only produced a stern letter from the foreign minister, but was also followed by deployment of 11,000 redcoats to Canada and vessels to the western Atlantic. Wilkes's unauthorized (and unwise) act threatened to do what the Rebels themselves had been unable to accomplish, namely, to bring in Britain as a Confederate ally. Seward, perhaps, relished the developments, having failed to provoke his multinational war of unification, but Lincoln was not amused. Scarcely a month after they were abducted, the two diplomats were released on Christmas Day, 1861. Britain considered this an acceptable apology, and the matter ended.[64]

All that remained of the naval war was a last-gasp Confederate attempt to leapfrog the North with technology. Had the roles been reversed, the North, with its industrial and technical superiority under pressure, might have successfully found a solution to a blockade. But for the already deficient Confederacy (despite its superlative naval secretary, Stephen R. Mallory), the gap between the two combatants became obvious when the Rebels launched their "blockade breaker," the CSS *Virginia*. Better known as the *Merrimac*, the vessel was the Union steam frigate the Confederacy had confiscated when it took the Norfolk navy yard. Outfitted with four inches of iron siding, the ship was impressive compared to wooden vessels, yet hardly a technological marvel. (Britain had launched an ironclad—*Warrior*—in 1859.) The *Virginia*'s ten guns fired from holes cut in the iron siding, which could be closed off by hand. A single gun covered the bow and stern. Most of the superstructure was above water, including the smokestack, lifeboat, and the entire gun deck. In March 1862, the *Virginia* sortied out under the command of Captain Franklin Buchanan to engage Union blockading vessels at Hampton Roads. The astonished Yankee sailors watched as their cannonballs bounced harmlessly off the sides of the monster, which quickly sank the *Cumberland* and then the *Congress*, two of the navy's best frigates. The Union itself had already had contracts for several variants of its own ironclads, known by the name of the lead vessel, the *Monitor*, whose design was the brainchild of a brilliant Swedish designer, John Ericsson. It surpassed the *Virginia* in almost every category. At 172 feet long, its hull barely sat above the waterline, leading to its description as "a crackerbox on a raft." It boasted a revolving turret capable of withstanding ten-inch shot at close range and brandished its own two eleven-inch Dahlgren smoothbore cannons; it also had some fifty of Ericsson's inventions aboard, including the first flushing toilets on a naval vessel. Upon the *Monitor*'s arrival at Hampton Roads, it was charged with protecting the larger *Minnesota*. On March 9, 1862, the *Virginia* sallied forth, and "Ericsson's pigmy" engaged it.[65] Blasting away at each other for hours, neither could gain an advantage, but the *Monitor* could position herself where the *Virginia* could not bring a single gun to bear. Still, neither could seriously damage the other, and the two ships withdrew, each for a different reason (the *Monitor*'s captain had been blinded by a shell, and the *Virginia*'s second in command, having replaced the wounded Buchanan, realized he could not outmaneuver or outshoot the *Monitor* with his current vessel). The *Virginia*'s draft was so deep that it continually ran aground, and efforts to lighten the ship so that it could better maneuver only exposed its hull. Subsequently, the *Virginia* was run ashore and burned when its commander feared that other ships like the *Monitor* were about to capture her. Later, in December 1862, the USS *Monitor* sank in a gale off Cape Hatteras, but many of her sisters joined the federal navy in inland waterways and along the coasts.

Confederate navy secretary Mallory, meanwhile, had funded other ironclads, and thirty-seven had been completed or were under construction by the war's end. He also approved an experiment using a mine ram in an underwater vessel called the CSS *Hunley*, an unfortunate vessel that suffered several fatalities during its sea trials. Although not the world's first submarine, the hand-cranked boat was the first to actually sink an enemy ship, the *Housatonic*—and itself—in February 1864. Yet these efforts smacked of desperation. The Confederacy had neither the resources nor a sufficient critical mass of scientific and technical brainpower or institutions to attempt to leapfrog the North in technology.

War in the West

While coastal combat determined the future of the blockade and control of the eastern port cities, and while the ground campaign in Virginia dragged on through a combination of McClellan's obsessive caution and Confederate defensive strategy, action shifted to the Mississippi River region. Offensives in the West, where Confederates controlled Forts Donelson and Henry on the Tennessee and Cumberland rivers, held the key to securing avenues into Tennessee and northern Alabama. Implementing the Anaconda Plan down the Mississippi, then, depended on wresting those important outposts from the rebels.

General Ulysses Simpson Grant, an engineer from West Point who had fought in the Mexican War, emerged as the central figure in the West. This was surprising, given that only a year earlier he had failed in a series of professions, struggled with alcohol, and wallowed in debt. Grant took his Mexican War experience, where he compiled a solid understanding of logistics as well as strategy, and applied his moral outrage over slavery to it. His father-in-law owned slaves, and James Longstreet (Lee's second in command at Gettysburg) was his wife's cousin and an army buddy. But Grant's own father had abolitionist tendencies, and he himself soon came to view slavery as a clear evil. When the Civil War came, Grant saw it not only as an opportunity for personal resurrection, but also as the chastisement he thought the slave South had earned. He was commissioned a colonel in the Illinois volunteers, and worked his way up to brigadier general in short order.

Grant did not take long to make his mark on the Confederates. Swinging down from Cairo, Illinois, in a great semicircle, he captured Paducah, Kentucky; then, supported by a river flotilla of gunboats, he moved on the two Confederate river-mouth forts that guarded the entrance to the western part of the Confederacy. On February 6, 1862, Grant's joint land-and-river force took Fort Henry on the Tennessee River, and Fort Donelson, the guardian of the Cumberland River, fell a few days later. When the fort's commander asked for terms, Grant responded grimly, "Unconditional and immediate surrender."[66] Given the army's penchant for nicknames, it was perhaps unavoidable that he soon became known as Unconditional Surrender Grant. Donelson's capitulation genuinely reflected Grant's approach to war. "Find out where your enemy is," he said, then "get at him as soon as you can, and strike him as hard as you can, and keep moving on."[67] Grant's success laid open both Nashville and Memphis.

Northern journalists, inordinately demoralized by Bull Run, swung unrealistically in the opposite direction after Grant's successes. The Chicago *Tribune* declared, "Chicago reeled mad with joy," and the New York *Times* predicted that "the monster is already clutched and in his death struggle."[68] Little did they know that the South was about to launch a major counterattack at a small church named Shiloh near Pittsburg Landing on the Tennessee River. Confederate General Albert Sidney Johnston knew by then (if he had not beforehand) the difficulty of the task confronting him. He clung to a perimeter line almost three hundred miles long, largely bordered by rivers, fighting an opponent who commanded the waterways, while he lacked sufficient railroads to counter the rapid concentration of forces by the Union at vulnerable points along the rivers. Now the South's reliance on river transportation, as opposed to railways, had come back to haunt the war effort.

Rather than dig in, Johnston (typically) attacked. Grant's troops were spread out while the general was planning the next part of his offensive. He had no defensive works, nor did he have any real lines of communication or supply. His headquarters was nine miles away, on the other side of the Tennessee River. Although the troops at Shiloh and Pittsburg Landing were the most raw of recruits, they had the good fortune of being commanded by the able William Tecumseh Sherman. Early on the morning of April 6, 1862, Confederate forces quietly marched through the fog, nearly into the Yankee camp until warnings sounded and musket fire erupted. For the next six hours, the armies slammed into each other at hurricane force, with shocking casualties. In the Peach Orchard, both sides were blinded by a blossom snowstorm created by the din of rifle and cannon shot. By all accounts, the midday hours at Shiloh were the bloodiest of the war, with more Union and Rebel bodies falling per minute than in any other clash. Albert Sidney Johnston himself became a casualty, hit below and behind the knee by a musket ball. Aides could not locate the wound, which was hidden by his high riding boots, and the unconscious Johnston died in their arms. Fighting at Shiloh ended on the first day with a Confederate advantage, but not a decisive victory. The Yanks found themselves literally backed up to the banks of the Tennessee River. General Lew Wallace, later famous for writing *Ben-Hur*, finally arrived after confusing orders that had him futilely marching across the Tennessee countryside; General Don Carlos Buell arrived after steaming up the Tennessee River with 25,000 men. Grant himself had come up from the rear ranks, and on the second day, with the reinforcements in place, the counterattack drove the Rebels from the field and forced Johnston's successor, P.G.T. Beauregard, to withdraw south to Corinth, Mississippi. It was a joyless victory, given the carnage. Grant recalled that he could "walk across the clearing in any direction stepping on dead bodies without a foot touching the ground."[69]

Tennessee was opened in 1862. Meanhile, Beauregard could not hope to hold Corinth against the combined forces of Pope, Grant, and Buell and therefore conducted a secret withdrawal that opened up northern Mississippi. Just two months earlier, in April 1862, Commander David Farragut captured New Orleans, and Memphis, too, had fallen. Now only Vicksburg stood between the Union and complete control of the Mississippi. Vicksburg not only dominated the river, but it also linked the South to the western Confederacy by rail. There, the blockade had been more porous, allowing food and horses to resupply Rebel armies in the East.

The story in the West seemed grimly monotonous: the Confederates would mount an offensive (despite their supposedly defensive strategy), suffer proportionately greater losses, retreat, then escape as the Union commander dawdled. Union general William Rosecrans attacked Mufreesboro, Tennessee, in December 1862. Again the Confederates had to leave the field despite achieving a draw. Slowly but surely, the Confederates, who took one step forward and two back, yielded ground. They were about to give up the plum of the West: Vicksburg.

From May to June, in 1862, the Union failed to capture Vicksburg, which sat on a high bluff commanding a hairpin curve in the Mississippi River. Vicksburg's geography held the key to the city's nearly invulnerable position. The Mississippi River flowed to the city at a 45-degree downward-sloping angle before abruptly turning due north, then sharply angled due south again. Vicksburg sat on the eastern (Mississippi) side of the hairpin, while directly north of the hairpin lay the Chickasaw Bayou, wedged between the Mississippi River and the Yazoo River. This swamp was all but impenetrable for an army, as Sherman found out, calling the approach "hopeless."[70] A main road and rail line connected Vicksburg with Jackson, Mississippi.

Throughout the remainder of 1862, Grant's army tried a number of novel approaches to defeat this geography, including diverting the river itself by constructing a canal and breaking a levee to create a channel from the Yazoo. Nothing worked. Using Memphis as a base, however, Grant now decided to take Vicksburg by preventing the two Rebel armies facing him (one under Joe Johnston, and one in Vicksburg under John Pemberton) from uniting.

Grant discarded traditional tactics and trudged southward along the Louisiana side of the river, through difficult bayous and lakes, to a point well below Vicksburg where he could recross into Mississippi. To do so, he needed the Union Navy, under Admiral David Porter, to make a critical run from above Vicksburg, past the powerful guns in the city, to the junction below, from where it could ferry Grant's forces across. Porter sent dozens of supply boats past the city on the night of April 22, 1863. The Confederates had poured turpentine over bales of hay and set them afire to illuminate the river in order to bombard the passing vessels. Although most federal ships sustained damage, all but one survived the run. Grant's army now crossed into Mississippi from below Vicksburg, inserting itself between Pemberton and Johnston. After he captured and torched Jackson, Mississippi, and blocked the railroad line, Vicksburg was totally isolated.

Then, from late May until July, the Union Army bombarded and closed the noose around the city from the east. Civilians living in Vicksburg, under constant fire, had run out of normal food. When Grant sealed off the city, the residents took to caves and bombproof shelters. They ate soup boiled from mule and horse ears and tails before finally consuming the remaining parts of the beasts. When the horses and mules were gone, they ate rats. Sickness and disease swept the inhabitants as well as the soldiers. At last, on the Fourth of July, 1863, Pemberton, unable to link up with Johnston outside the city, surrendered Vicksburg and its force of 30,000 starving soldiers, as well as 170 cannons, just one day after the crushing defeat of Lee's army at Gettysburg. Grant said, "The fate of the Confederacy was sealed when Vicksburg fell."[71]

Lincoln had, at last, found what he needed to defeat the Confederacy. With eerie prescience, Lincoln told his advisers just before news arrived from Vicksburg that if the general took the city, "Grant is my man, and I am his for the rest of the war."[72]

Growing Government(s)

No accusation against Abraham Lincoln has more merit than that he presided over the most rapid expansion of federal power in American history. Most of the expansion can be justified by wartime demands, but too much was little more than political pork barreling and fulfillment of campaign promises.

Shortly after the call had gone out for troops, the government possessed no proven method of raising large sums of money quickly. Lincoln's secretary of the treasury, Salmon P. Chase, proved to be the right man in the right office at the right time. Chase came from a New Hampshire family, where he learned politics from his state representative father. As a young man, Chase had also worked with his father at running a tavern and a glass factory, and when both failed, he was shipped off to an Ohio relative. After studying for the bar in Ohio, Chase practiced on behalf of the Cincinnati branch of the Bank of the United States, achieving some degree of financial success. Aloof, plodding, and occasionally without tact, Chase had been drawn to the antislavery cause following rioting in Cincinnati against a local abolitionist paper run by James G. Birney. Politically, Chase moved from the Whig Party to the Liberty Party, then adopted the label free Democrat.[73]

He had won a Senate seat as a Democrat from Ohio, but continued to push the free-soil cause before running for governor in Ohio under a fusion Republican ticket in 1855. Winning the governor's seat, Chase and the legislature attempted to expand the state's free banking laws, providing a harbinger of his financial expertise as treasury secretary. Like Seward, he was disappointed to lose the Republican presidential nomination in 1860, and even though he was offered another U.S. Senate seat by the Ohio legislature, he never took it. Instead, he reluctantly accepted Lincoln's offer of the Treasury post.

Chase confronted a daunting task. In 1850 the federal government's budget averaged 2 percent of gross national product (GNP) but by the end of the Civil War, it had soared to more than 15 percent. Merely *running* the Treasury in such circumstances constituted a challenge: the number of clerks in the department increased from 383 in 1861 to more than 2,000 in 1864. To fill the necessary positions, Chase unwisely appointed many party hacks who often could be relied upon for little else but their partisan loyalty.

Raising the necessary funds to run the war demanded that Chase not only develop systems for generating lots of revenue, but also for bringing it into the Treasury fairly quickly. At the same time, he did not want to sacrifice long-term stability for short-term gains. Copying Alexander Hamilton, Chase examined a menu of options to serve both short- and long-term needs. Taxes, for example, had to be passed by Congress, then collected, meaning that it would be 1862 or later before tax revenues provided much help to the cause. So while Chase immediately asked Congress for a new direct tax on incomes over $300, he simultaneously requested new tariffs and expanded land sales that would generate quicker revenues. Even when the taxes came in, at the end of 1863, the $2 million they produced was inadequate to the Union's needs, which by the end of

1861 ran $2 million *per day.* Meanwhile, in addition to other shorter-term bond issues, Congress authorized Chase to raise $250 million through sales of twenty-year bonds paying 7 percent interest.

Banks hesitated to buy bonds if they had to pay for them in gold, and in December 1861 the Northern banks suspended specie payments on all notes. (The Confederacy's banks had gone off the gold standard almost immediately after Fort Sumter.) Concerned that soldiers would go unpaid, Chase advanced a paper money concept to Congress that would allow the Treasury to issue $100 million in notes that would circulate as "lawful money, and a legal tender of all debts, public and private."[74] Enacted as the Legal Tender Act of February 1862, the proposal authorized the issue of more than Chase requested—$450 million of the new green-colored bills, called greenbacks.

The temporary money gave the nation a wartime circulating medium and also enabled the government to pay its bills. Congress also authorized Chase to borrow an additional $500 million. Nevertheless, the "five-twenty" bonds (redeemable after five years, maturing to full value after twenty-five, and paying 6 percent interest) did not sell as fast as Chase hoped. He relied on a personal friend, Philadelphia banker Jay Cooke, to sell the bonds through a special (though not exclusive) contract. Cooke received a nice commission, but more important, he held a virtual monopoly on the bond sales. In the hands of other men, that might have been a problem, but not with the motivated Cooke, who placed ads in newspapers and aggressively targeted the middle class as well as traditional silk-tie investors. Conceiving the first true "war bond," Cooke appealed to Northerners' patriotism, and oversubscribed every issue. He sold $400 million worth by the end of 1863 alone, netting himself $1 million in commissions and making him the Civil War equivalent of Robert Morris.[75]

Meanwhile, Chase came up with yet another menu option to accelerate the revenue stream. Using as a model the free-banking laws popular in the North prior to the war—wherein banks would purchase bonds that they would keep on deposit with the secretary of state as security against overissue of notes—in his December 1861 report to Congress, Chase argued for a national banking system in which the banks would receive their charters after purchasing government bonds. Congress passed the National Banking Act of February 1863, which provided for $300 million in national banknotes to be issued by the new network of national banks (who would, in turn, themselves purchase bonds as their "entry permit" into the business). Nevertheless, the law offered no incentive for people to hold national banknotes over private banknotes. By December 1863, fewer than 150 national banks operated, and only in 1864 did Congress fix the loophole by placing a 10 percent tax on money issued by state banks.

Of all the Civil War legislation—aside, obviously, from emancipation—this act had the most far-reaching consequences, most of them bad. Although Congress increased the number of national banks in operation (1,650 by December 1865), the destruction of the competitive-money/private-note issue system led to a string of financial upheavals, occurring like clockwork every twenty years until

1913. Competition in money had not only given the United States the most rapidly growing economy in the world, but it had also produced numerous innovations at the state level, the most important of which, branch banking, was *prohibited* for national banks. Thus, not only did the National Bank and Currency Acts establish a government monopoly over money, but they also excluded the most efficient and stable form of banking yet to emerge (although that mistake would be partially corrected in the 1920s). Critics of Lincoln's big-government policies are on firm ground when they assail the banking policy of the Civil War.

In contrast, however, the North's financial strategy far surpassed that of the Confederacy under its Treasury secretary, Christopher G. Memminger, a South Carolina lawyer. Memminger, like Chase, at one time was a hard-money man, and like Chase he also acceded to wartime requirements of quick revenues. He embraced taxation, borrowing, and fiat money. Although the Confederate Constitution forbade tariffs, the CSA's congress almost immediately imposed a range of duties, and with no supreme court to overrule it, the acts stuck. And in sharp contrast to the U.S. Constitution's prohibition against export tariffs, the CSA also imposed export taxes.[76] By 1863 the Confederacy had adopted a wide range of taxes, including direct income taxes and taxes on gold. Possessing a smaller and less industrial economy on which to draw, the South found it more difficult to borrow money through bond issues, raising one third of its wartime revenue needs through borrowing, compared to two thirds in the North.[77] Worse, when the Confederate congress authorized a second $100 million loan in August 1861, planters were allowed to pay for it in cotton, not gold. The Confederacy, thanks to its short-sighted embargo, was already drowning in cotton, and now more of it stacked up as "patriotic" planters subscribed to bonds with more of the worthless fiber. A small foreign loan of $14.5 million in France negotiated by Emile Erlanger brought in only $8.5 million.[78]

Thus Memminger copied Chase, far surpassing him in the introduction of fiat money when the Confederate congress began issuing Confederate notes in 1861. Starting slowly with only $1 million, wartime necessity soon drove the CSA to issue more than $1 *billion* in Confederate paper money, or more than double the number of greenbacks issued to a much larger population in the North. Before long, Confederate money attained a reputation for worthlessness previously seen only in the Revolutionary-era continentals and not seen again until the Weimar Republic's disastrous hyperinflation in the 1920s.[79] A Confederate dollar worth eighty-two cents in gold or silver in 1862 had plummeted to only $.017 in 1865.

Memminger never dreamed in 1862 that within a few years the Confederacy's needs for goods and services would become so desperate that the government would resort to outright confiscation—theft of private property. Already, however, the warning signs had appeared, heralding a type of war socialism. While the North skimmed off the top of private enterprise, the South, lacking an entrepreneurial base to match, was forced to put the ownership and control of war production in the hands of government. The Confederacy reached levels of government involvement unmatched until the totalitarian states of the twentieth century: seven eighths of all freight moved on the Virginia Central Railroad was for the government's account; government work done in Augusta, Georgia, by the main private company, the Augusta Textile Factory, accounted for 92 percent of its total; and the Confederate government created its own powder works, the second largest in the world.[80] By the end of the war, all pretense to a free market—which Southern plantation slavery never was—had disappeared as President Jefferson Davis confiscated all railroads, steam vessels, telegraph lines, and other operations, impressing their employees for government or military work. Swarms of Confederate officials soon resembled King George's agents that Jefferson had warned about in the Declaration. As one North Carolinian recalled, government officials were "thick as locusts in Egypt," and he "could not walk without being elbowed off the street by them."[81] Government bureaucrats not only confiscated food and other items, "paying" with the worthless money, but also forced both white and black workers onto construction projects for the Confederacy.[82] The Confederacy died of big government."[83]

By 1863 the Confederacy was employing seventy thousand civilian bureaucrats as the government itself ran ordinance bureaus, mills, clothing manufacturing, cotton gins, meat packing plants, salt storage sheds, distilleries, vegetable packing facilities, all the while forcing the industrialization of a rural region and literally sucking out its sustenance. Alabama produced four times as much iron in 1864 as *any* state had prior to the war; yet by 1864, Confederate soldiers were starving in the field. Stories of rebels bartering with Yankees, exchanging shoes or even powder for food, were not uncommon by the end of the war. Across the board—in everything from the treatment of (white) human rights, to freedom of speech and the press, to market freedoms—scholar Richard Bensel found that the North had a less centralized government and was a much more open society than the South. Six specific comparisons of private property rights between North and South, including control of railroads, destruction of property, and confiscation, showed the Confederacy to be far more government centered and less market oriented. Analyzing dozens of specific laws and points of comparisons, with possibly the suspension of habeas corpus the main exception, Bensel concluded that the North's commitment to liberty in all areas ensured its victory.[84]

The Proclamation

The Seven Days' Battles had provided an opportunity for McClellan to crush Lee, but once again, the Union forces let the Rebels off the hook. Lee's strategy, however, was deeply affected by the near defeat. Increasingly, lacking foreign support, the South perceived that it needed to deliver a knockout punch. Lee decided to invade Maryland. Misled into thinking the Marylanders would support the Confederate Army, Lee announced he was coming to liberate a "sister state." Swinging far to the west, away from Washington, the Rebel army entered Maryland at, fittingly, Leesburg on September 5, 1862. Dispatching Jackson with

25,000 men to seize Harper's Ferry, Lee divided his force in the face of superior odds.

McClellan, meanwhile, had by default regained overall command of the army in the East. Given the low quality of other commanders, he was Lincoln's only real choice. His men loved him. He was plodding, but he had inflicted terrible damage on the Rebel army. At the Seven Days' Battles, for example, despite failing to capture Richmond, McClellan had licked Lee's best forces. At that point, a jewel fell into McClellan's hands. A Union soldier picked up three cigars off a fallen Rebel officer, and found them wrapped in the actual orders Lee had given his company commanders. All the battle plans McClellan needed—the disposition of the Rebel army, its size, everything—had just dropped into his lap. He even enthusiastically announced to his staff, "Here is a paper with which if I cannot whip 'Bobbie Lee' I will be willing to go home."[85] Then McClellan proceeded to move cautiously.

Unaware McClellan had intercepted his battle orders, Lee nevertheless realized that he had badly divided his forces and that Union armies were converging on him like bats to fruit. He planned to stake out a defensive position at Sharpsburg, Maryland, along Antietam Creek. There the Potomac River protected his left and rear, but if the Union overran his position, it also would have him in a killing box. On September fifteenth, McClellan's advance forces located the Confederates and should have attacked immediately; instead, despite outnumbering the Rebels 87,000 to 35,000, McClellan hesitated. Finally, two days later, the battle commenced. While all the fighting exceeded human description in its savagery and desperation, the worst of the carnage occurred when Union forces attacked across open ground against Confederates dug in behind a sunken road. It was a premonition of Gettysburg, but the Yankees soon quit and outflanked the road to the south, peppering the Southern ranks with fire from the front and two sides. On September eighteenth, after two bloody days, the Confederates withdrew, and, incredibly, McClellan did not pursue them.[86]

Lee could technically claim victory since McClellan had not driven him out, but neither side could take much heart in the combined numbing losses of 24,000 men killed or wounded. It was the single bloodiest day in American history—September 11, 2001, notwithstanding. Although the numbers of men littering the battlefield in blue and gray uniforms were almost evenly divided, the Confederates again absorbed a disproportionate amount of punishment, losing well over 22 percent of their entire force. Yet McClellan inexplicably missed an opportunity to pursue Lee and use his superiority to end the war. An aggressive follow-up attack might have finished Lee off then and there, and McClellan's failure cemented his dismissal. Yet Lee's withdrawl under federal guns gave Lincoln the window of opportunity he needed to inform his cabinet of one of the most important proposals in American history.

For several years Frederick Douglass, the former slave who used his newspaper as a clarion for abolitionist columns, had edged Lincoln toward the abolitionist camp. He expressed his frustration that Lincoln had not embraced abolition as the central war aim in 1861, and continued to lament the president's unwillingness throughout 1862. After the Emancipation Proclamation, however, Douglass observed of Lincoln, "From the genuine abolition view, Mr. Lincoln seemed tardy, cold, dull, and indifferent, but measuring him by the sentiment of his country—a sentiment he was bound as a statesman to consult—he was swift, zealous, radical, and determined." Lincoln had inched further toward emancipation since July 1862, when he had met with a group of border-state representatives in the White House with another proposal for gradual compensated emancipation in the border states. "The war has doomed slavery," he told them, and if they rejected compensation at that time, they would not get a penny when it disappeared.[87] He received a chilly reception. Why should they—loyal Unionists—free their slaves when there was a chance that the Rebels might still come back into the Union and keep theirs? Lincoln could not disagree with their reasoning. That meeting impressed upon him that "if abolition was to come, it must commence in the Rebel South, and then be expanded into the loyal border states."[88]

Truly, it was a "Damascus Road" experience for the president. The following day, in a carriage ride with William Seward and Navy Secretary Gideon Welles, Lincoln stunned the two cabinet officials by stating that given the resistance and persistence of the Confederates, it was a necessity and a duty to liberate the slaves. Before the flabbergasted secretaries could respond, they saw a different Lincoln—one who in an "urgent voice" informed them that the time had passed when the two sections could reach an amicable agreement. He intended to rip out the "heart of the rebellion," destroy the institution that had torn the nation asunder, and end the charade that the South could reject the Constitution that created the Union on the one hand and invoke it to protect slavery on the other.[89]

Lincoln had firmed up in his own mind the issue that had nagged at him for years. The war was not about union, after all, because the Union as a constitutional entity was itself the result of something else. He put it best at Gettysburg when he said that it was "dedicated to the proposition that all men are created equal." A union not dedicated to that proposition was no union at all; thus, he seemed to realize, for years he had placed the cart ahead of the horse. For the United States as a union of states to have any moral force at all, it first had to stand for the proposition of equality before the law. The Rebels' actions were despicable not only because they rent that legal fabric embodied in the Constitution, but also because they rejected the underlying proposition of the Declaration.

So it is critical that an understanding of emancipation begin with Lincoln's perception that it first and foremost was a moral and legal issue, not a military or political one. However, Lincoln also understood the plexiform nature of emancipation as it involved the war effort: militarily, it would threaten the South's massive slave support system that took the place of civilian or noncombatant military personnel behind the lines; diplomatically, it struck at the heart of Rebel efforts to gain British and French support; and economically, it threatened to throw what was left of the Confederate financial system into chaos, depending as it did on slave valuations as assets used by planters to secure loans. The more Lincoln looked at emancipation, the more he liked it.

Congress had moved toward emancipation with its second confiscation act, which stated that if the rebellion did not cease in sixty days, the executive would be empowered to confiscate all property of anyone who participated in, aided, or abetted the rebellion. Lincoln thought such half measures impractical. Therefore, he determined to brush slavery away in a giant stroke, taking the burden upon himself. On July 22, 1862, he read the preliminary Emancipation Proclamation to his cabinet, making the abolition of slavery an objective of the Union war effort come January 1, 1863.

Despite the presence of many solid free-soilers and antislavery politicians in the cabinet, the response was tepid at best. Chase ruminated about the financial impact, possibly destabilizing the fragile banking structure. Secretary of War Stanton and Postmaster General Montgomery Blair, though supportive, nevertheless expressed grave reservations. They argued that the nation "was not ready" for such a step, whereas Seward feared that the Europeans would see the proclamation as a sign of weakness—"our last shriek on the retreat."[90] For it to appear legitimate, they argued, emancipation must wait until the Union had a victory in the eastern theater. Grant's piecemeal deconstruction of Rebel forces in the West was deadly efficient, but it did not constitute a good old "whippin" of "Bobby Lee."

Lincoln found those arguments persuasive. He appreciated that emancipation would produce some violent responses in the North as well as the South. There would be race riots, for example. So Lincoln used the remainder of the summer of 1862 to soften up the opposition by touting colonization again—a subject that he trotted out more as a deflector shield than a serious option. In August 1862, he met with several black leaders in Washington, informing them of a new colonization plan in Central America. "You and we are different races," he noted, and whites had inflicted great wrong on blacks. Oppression would only continue in freedom, he predicted, and he urged the leaders to consider colonization. Some supported it, but Frederick Douglass called Lincoln a hypocrite, full of "pride of race and blood."[91] Lincoln, of course, was neither—he was a practical politician who realized that the highest ideals had already demanded phenomenal sacrifices and that even in emancipation, the job would just be beginning.

Douglass's sincerely felt condemnations aside, Lincoln *had* moved steadily but inexorably toward emancipation and racial equality. A famous open letter in the *Tribune* to Horace Greeley, who, like Douglass, thought Lincoln too timid, contained the lines, "My paramount objective in this struggle is to save the Union, and is not either to save or destroy slavery. If I could save the Union without freeing any slave I would do it, and if I could save it by freeing all the slaves I would do it."[92] Missed in the debate about Lincoln's opinion on race is the fact that he had taken in this *Tribune* letter another concrete step toward emancipation by claiming in public the authority to free the slaves—something neither he nor any other president had ever advanced. As with a play-fake in football, Lincoln allowed his own views of race to mesmerize proponents and opponents of abolition, absorbing both the attention and the punishment, while his *actions* moved unflinchingly toward freedom.

Then came the news from McClellan at Antietam. It was an incomplete victory, but a victory nonetheless. Lincoln had the moment he had waited for, and called his cabinet together on September 22, 1862, to read them the proclamation. For the border states, he would urge Congress to pass compensated emancipation; for freed slaves who so desired, he would press for colonization. But for the states still in rebellion as of January 1, 1863, the president on his own authority would free "thence forward and forever" all slaves, and the military forces of the United States would protect their liberty. After entertaining criticisms— including the possibility of a mass slave uprising in the South—Lincoln went ahead to publish the decree the following day.[93]

Much has been made of the fact that not a single slave was freed by the proclamation itself. After all, those states still in rebellion were not under federal control, and thus no slaves were freed in the South. Since the proclamation said nothing about the border states, except that Lincoln would urge Congress to act there as well, no slaves were actually free there either. Thus, the famous charge that "where he *could* free the slaves, Lincoln would not, and where he *would* free the slaves, he could not," has a measure of truth to it. Nevertheless, word filtered South through a slave grapevine like wildfire, although slaves attempted to hide the fact that they had heard about the proclamation. Southern whites had suspicions that blacks had kept up with news of the war. A Louisiana planter complained that his slaves "know more about politics than most of the white men. They know everything that happens."[94]

Odd as it may seem, changing the status of slaves constituted only one of three critical goals of the proclamation. The second objective, and the one most easily achieved, involved perceptions. Lincoln needed to turn—in the eyes of Europe, particularly England and France—a set of brave Confederate revolutionaries into international pariahs. By shifting the war aims from restoring the Union (which evoked neither excitement nor sympathy abroad) to emancipation, Lincoln tapped into a strong current of Western thought. Both England and France had abolished slavery in their empires in the decades before the Civil War on strictly moral grounds. They could hardly retreat on that position now. As long as Jefferson Davis's diplomats could maintain the pretense that the war was a struggle for independence on the grounds of constitutional rights—not much different than the rights of Englishmen—then they could still hope for foreign support. Once Lincoln ripped away the facade of constitutionality and exposed the rebellion for what it was, an attempt by some to legitimate their enslavement of others, neither Britain nor France could any longer consider offering aid.

Lincoln's third objective, little commented upon because of its abstruse effects, was in fact to yank out the underpinnings from the entire Southern slave/plantation structure. In the twinkling of an eye, Lincoln (in theory, at least) had transformed millions of dollars worth of physical assets—no different from wagons, cattle, or lumber—into *people*. For the purposes of banking, the impact could not have been more staggering. Slaves (property) showed up on Southern bank books as assets along with the plantation land backing enormous planters' debts, and now, in an instant, they had (again, in theory) suddenly disappeared as mysteriously as the Roanoke colony! Slaves backed millions of dollars in planta- tion assets, not just in their physical persons, but also in the value that they imposed on the land. Without the slaves, much of the plantation land was worth- less, and the entire Southern banking structure—at one time as solid as a rock— turned to mush.

A fourth notion regarding the Emancipation Proclamation, however, must be addressed. Left-wing revisionists have argued that Lincoln freed the slaves mainly because he needed the black troops to feed his war machine—that only with the addition of African American soldiers could the North have won. This wrongheaded view not only deliberately and obviously trivializes Lincoln's genu- ine sentiments about emancipation, but also cynically and mistakenly discounts the efforts of white troops. It would soon be white Mainers and New Yorkers, not black troops, who would smash Lee at Gettysburg; and although black troops fought at Port Hudson and in the Vicksburg campaign, the bulk of the action was carried by white units from Indiana and Illinois and Ohio. Predominantly North- ern white troops would, a year after that, force the surrender of Atlanta and Co- lumbia and Mobile. But until the 1960s, historians had too long ignored or diminished the contributions of the 179,000 African American soldiers (plus 18,000 sailors), most of whom fought in American uniforms for the first time ever. At Fort Wagner, black troops bravely but vainly stormed beachfront Confed- erate citadels before being repulsed, with black and white alike leaving thousands of casualties in the sand. Their courageous efforts late in the war—especially (at their own prodding) at Cold Harbor—undoubtedly contributed to the Union vic- tory in important ways. But it is just as wrongheaded to overstate their signifi- cance out of political correctness. By late 1864, the doom of the Confederacy was sealed, no matter what color Grant's forces were.[95]

Some states, such as Massachusetts, had urged the creation of black regi- ments since 1861, but Lincoln resisted, fearing a white backlash. (Massachusetts would eventually put nearly 4,000 black soldiers in the field, fourth only to the much larger states of Pennsylvania, Ohio, and New York.) A change had oc- curred, though, in the thinking of Lincoln about the use of newly freed slaves between the preliminary Emancipation Proclamation and the January proclama- tion, which was demonstrated by the fact that the latter announced the intention of admitting freedmen into military service.[96] Certainly the dwindling recruit- ment numbers produced an attitude shift of its own in the North. Whites who previously had opposed arming blacks warmed to the idea of black soldiers in Union ranks.

Large-scale black recruitment began in 1863. One sticking point was their unequal pay, mandated by the Militia Act of 1862, of $10 per month, minus $3 for clothing, rather than $13 per month, plus clothing, given to white recruits. Governor John Andrew of Massachusetts offered state money to offset the pay differential to the 54th and 55th Massachusetts regiments, but the black troops refused. Equality had to be acknowledged from Washington. Congress finally equalized black and white pay in June 1864.

By that time, blacks had entered the Union Army in large numbers, yet often (though not exclusively) found themselves on guard duty or in physical labor battalions, not combat. Lobbying the War Department, blacks finally saw action at Fort Wagner, South Carolina (July 1863), and Port Hudson, Louisiana (May–July 1863). It was not until 1865, outside Richmond, however, that Grant used large numbers of blacks routinely alongside whites. While the grueling reduction of the Richmond defenses was bloody, the war had been decided months earlier, at Gettysburg, Vicksburg, and Atlanta.[97]

Thus, the fact that blacks soldiers did not by themselves tip the balance to the Union makes the Emancipation Proclamation all the more critical and, in context, brilliant. Even if the Confederacy somehow managed to string together several victories so as to make its military position sound, the financial chaos and instability caused by Lincoln's lone declaration would have been difficult to counteract.

Hard War, Unresolved War

Lincoln could call Antietam a victory, but the Army of Northern Virginia remained as deadly as ever. As if to underscore that fact, in October, Lee sent Jeb Stuart's cavalry on a raid of Chambersburg, Pennsylvania. Riding around McClellan, Stuart terrified Northerners and again embarrassed Lincoln, who replaced the general for the last time. In McClellan's stead came the new commander of the Army of the Potomac, Ambrose Burnside, an honest and modest man who was an effective subordinate, but not the war chieftain Lincoln needed. Indeed, Burnside had twice refused earlier offers of command because he doubted his own ability.[98]

At the same time as he replaced McClellan in the East, Lincoln removed General Don Carlos Buell in the West, also for lack of aggressiveness. After a series of disastrous appointments and counterappointments, Lincoln sent William S. Rosecrans to take command of the Army of the Cumberland. Fortunately, the musical chairs of commanders from the Ohio region had little impact on Grant and his vise around Vicksburg. Whatever the Union Army accomplished in the West seemed unimpressive to Washington politicians and war critics, if for no other reason than the press and the politicians were in Washington, not Cincinnati. Thus, Burnside's new offensive would be closely watched. The new general drafted a plan to march to Fredericksburg, and from there to Richmond. Neither Lincoln nor his commander in chief, Henry Halleck, liked it, since both perceived that Burnside would have to move faster than any other Union commander (save Grant) had moved before. In mid-November 1862, Burnside's forces arrived at Fredericksburg. The Confederates had plenty of time to entrench on Marye's Heights, overlooking the city and a railroad line, with 78,000 men across the Rappahannock River waiting for Burnside. Once the Union Army had drawn up, with the hills in front and the river at its back, Lee had a perfect field of fire against an almost helpless foe. Burnside sent wave after wave of men up the hills in fourteen suicidal charges against the dug-in Confederates, who slaughtered them in every attempt. When the Yankees finally withdrew, with 12,700 Union troops killed, wounded, or missing, Burnside had earned the unwelcome distinction of suffering the worst defeat ever by the U.S. Army.

To the general's credit, he begged an audience with Lincoln to publicly accept blame for the defeat—the first Union general to do so. On January twenty-sixth, Lincoln fired the general who had known from the start he was in over his head, but he did so with great regret. Next in line was Fighting Joe Hooker.

Hooker's brief stint as commander exemplified all of the difficulties Lincoln had in finding a general. Whereas Burnside was incompetent but honest, Hooker was an intriguer and ladder climber who had positioned himself for command in the East from the get-go. If Burnside almost desperately tried to avoid the mantle of command, Hooker lusted after it.

With a reinforced Army of the Potomac numbering 130,000 men, Hooker planned to distract Lee with a movement at Fredericksburg, then march up the Rappahannock to attack his flank near Chancellorsville, where the Union would keep a huge reserve force. Lee ascertained the federal plan and disrupted it by sending Jeb Stuart's cavalry to take control of the roads around Chancellorsville. That blinded Hooker, who delayed his planned attack. Lee then divided his highly outnumbered forces and sent Stonewall Jackson through a thicket known as the Wilderness to the federal flank, where he achieved numerical superiority at the point of attack. Jackson's march would have been impossible for many units, but not Stonewall's trained corps. On May 2, 1863, when the Rebels emerged from the dense brush, the stunned Union troops panicked. Lee still remained in front of them with (they thought) his entire army: who were these new troops? The Union army nearly fell apart, but it held together long enough to prevent a total rout. Another telegram reached Lincoln, who could only pace back and forth, his hands behind his back, asking in despair, "My God, my God, what will the country say? What will the country say?"[99] To Stanton, Lincoln privately confided, "Our cause is lost! We are ruined. . . . This is more than I can endure."[100]

Although the Confederacy won another impressive victory, it suffered, again, heavy losses: 10,746 casualties (18.7 percent of Lee's total forces) to the Union's 11,116 (11.4 percent). By now, Lee had lost an incredible one quarter of his field force. By itself, that ratio would lead to ultimate Confederate defeat if Lee "won" eight to ten more such battles. An even more staggering loss was dealt to the

Rebel army at Chancellorsville, and not by a Yankee. Stonewall Jackson, reconnoitering well past his lines with a few of his officers, was mistakenly shot by Confederate pickets. It took him more than a week to die, removing, as it were, Lee's right hand. Jackson's value to the Confederate cause cannot be overstated. After his death, the South won only one other major battle, at Chickamauga. Another Virginian, James "Pete" Longstreet, a competent general, assumed Jackson's command, but never replaced him.

Union defeat at Chancellorsville ensured the removal of the isolated Hooker, whose female camp followers, "hookers," provided a linguistic legacy of a different sort. Lincoln was back at square one, still looking for a commanding general. In the meantime, the Confederates, perhaps sensing that their losses had started to pile up at rates they could not possibly sustain and knowing that Vicksburg was in peril, mounted one more bold and perilous invasion of the North, upon which, conceivably, hung the fate of the war.

Gettysburg

Despite triumphs in Chancellorsville, Fredericksburg, and the Wilderness, nothing in the strategic equation had changed for the Confederacy. Quite the contrary, the Rebels had over the course of four battles in the East—every one a victory—lost more than 36,000 men and come no closer to independence than when they had opened fire on Fort Sumter. Given the trend in the West, the Army of Northern Virginia could do only three things by May 1863 that might have produced the desired result of an independent CSA.

First, through an invasion Lee could capture Washington. That was a remote possibility at best. Even if the federal troops around the city were as poorly led as the forces at Fredericksburg or Bull Run, a series of forts surrounded Washington that would require a long siege. Certainly the armies in the West would instantly rush reinforcements over. Second, Lee, if he could raise enough hell in the North and agitate enough politicians, might make the war so politically unpalatable that the forces of democracy would demand Lincoln negotiate terms with the South. Perhaps some in the Confederate cabinet still clung to such fantasies, but Lee, who had seen the unwelcome reception his men received in "friendly" Maryland, knew better. The bastions of Unionism—Pennsylvania, New York, and especially Massachusetts—would see an invasion as exactly that, and civilians would respond with a predictable level of hostility and guerrilla warfare. Only the third alternative really represented a realistic chance for the Confederacy: bring the Union army—the larger part of it—into one big battle and defeat it.

Once Lee disengaged from Hooker, he turned northwest, using the Blue Ridge Mountains to cover his northerly advance into Pennsylvania. He learned through newspapers that Lincoln had sacked Hooker in June and replaced him with a corps commander, George Gordon Meade, whom the men likened to an old snapping turtle. But Lee's well-oiled machine began to slow down. First, Jeb Stuart, supposedly scouting for Lee in the Pennsylvania countryside, crossed into Maryland on May fifteenth. One of his tasks involved confusing federal intelligence as to the disposition of Lee's main forces. But Stuart, a dandy who wore plumes in his hats and perfume on his mustache, enjoyed the adulation he received in the Southern press. On June ninth, Stuart, with 10,000 of his cavalry, considered nearly invincible, ran headlong into Union forces under Alfred Pleasanton in the largest cavalry engagement in American history. As 20,000 horsemen slashed at each other and blasted away with pistols, the Union troopers were finally driven off. But in defeat, the Union cavalry knew that they had gone toe to toe with the finest the South had to offer, and under other and better circumstances, could prevail.

Stuart disengaged and then headed straight for the Union supply lines. At Rockville, Maryland, the Rebel cavalry surprised a massive wagon train and captured more than 125 wagons, which slowed down Stuart's movement. He continued to ride around the federal army, into Pennsylvania, and was out of touch with Lee for ten critical days.[101]

Seeking to intercept Lee's army, Meade had marched west into Maryland along the Taneytown Road. Already, though, advance units of both armies approached Gettysburg. Lee came up from the southwest and had ordered other divisions to swing down from the north and west. Spies informed him of the proximity of the federal army, which counted seven corps (roughly 80,000 men). Lee had approximately 75,000 men in three corps—Confederates always weighted their divisions and corps more than did the Union Army—including Stuart's cavalry, which arrived on the second day of combat. General John Buford's Union cavalry arrived on the scene to the southwest of Gettysburg. Buford instantly perceived that the ground behind the city, along Cemetery Ridge with Culp's Hill on the west and the Round Tops on the east, provided an incredibly advantageous natural defensive position. Buford commanded only 1,200 men and had in his sight 20,000 Confederates, but by holding the Rebels up for hours, Buford and his men bought critical hours for Meade.

Lee had hoped to avoid closing with the enemy until he had his entire army drawn up, but on July first it was spread all over roads in a twenty-five-mile radius around southwestern Gettysburg. By afternoon on July first, Confederate forces had driven back the Yankees. Lee's subordinates, however, hesitated to take the strong Union positions on Culp's Hill. The result was that at the end of the first day at Gettysburg, the federals held the high ground along the ridge.

On July second, Lee's forces, deployed more than a mile below Cemetery Ridge along a tree line called Seminary Ridge, faced Meade's line. The Yankees were deployed in a giant fishhook, with the barb curling around Culp's Hill, then a long line arching along Cemetery Ridge, culminating in the hook at Big Round Top and Little Round Top. Upon learning that the two hills that held the loop of the fishhook constituting the Union position, Big and Little Round Tops, were undefended, Lee sent Longstreet's division to capture the hills, then roll up the federal lines.

In fact, Meade already had started to defend the Round Tops. John Bell Hood's Texas division climbed up the hill to overrun Union positions, opposed by the very end of the Union line. There, another legend of the war was born in Maine's fighting Colonel Joshua Chamberlain. A Union regiment, the 20th Maine commanded by Chamberlain, held the farthest point of the entire fish-hook and thereby the fate of the entire army. A quiet professor of rhetoric at Bowdoin College, Chamberlain had volunteered with his Maine neighbors and his brother, who was his adjutant. Six months previously Chamberlain had charged up Marye's Heights at Fredericksburg, where he and what was left of his decimated troops were pinned down in the mud. All night, he had listened to the whiz of musket balls and the screams of the wounded, using a dead man's coat to protect him from the chilling wind.

From his position on the extreme left of the Union line, Chamberlain received word that the Confederates were advancing through the thick woods. Ordering his men to pile up brush, rocks, and anything to give them cover, the regiment beat back one attack after another by the determined Rebel troops. Suddenly a cry went out that the Confederates had marched still farther to the Union left and that they intended to flank Chamberlain's position. Whether at his order or at the suggestion of a subordinate, the 20th Maine "refused the line," bending backward at a 45-degree angle to keep the Confederates in front of its fire. By that time, Chamberlain's men were almost entirely out of ammunition. Many had only two or three rounds left. Chamberlain shouted "Bayonet! Forward to the Right!" and the 20th Maine fixed bayonets.

From its refused position, the Yankees swept down on the exhausted Confederates. The bold maneuver, combined with the shock of men racing downhill in a bayonet assault on weary attackers, shattered the Confederate advance, routing the Rebels down the hill. Although fighting raged on for hours on both ends of the fishhook, Chamberlain's men had saved the Union Army.[102] Chamberlain claimed he never felt fear in battle. "A soldier has something else to think about," he later explained. As a rule, "men stand up from one motive or another—simple manhood, force of discipline, pride, love, or bond of comradeship. . . . The instinct to seek safety is overcome by the instinct of honor."[103]

Late in the evening of July second, however, the engagement hardly seemed decisive. General George Pickett's division had just come up to join Lee, and Stuart had finally arrived. On the evening of July second, ignoring the appeals from Longstreet to disengage and find better ground, Lee risked everything on a massive attack the following day. Longstreet's final attempt to dissuade Lee was met with the stony retort that he was "tired of listening, tired of talking."[104]

After two days of vicious fighting, Lee was convinced that the federal flanks had been reinforced by taking men from the center, and that an all-out push in the middle would split their line in two. Pickett's Charge, one of the most colorful and tragic of all American military encounters, began on July third when the South initiated a two-hour artillery barrage on the middle of the Union line at Cemetery Ridge. Despite the massive artillery duel between Yankee and Rebel cannons, Lee did not know that under the withering steel torrent coming from his artillery, only about 200 Yankees had been killed and only a handful of Union guns destroyed.

At one-thirty in the afternoon, Pickett's entire division—15,000 men, at least—emerged from the orchards behind the artillery. In long and glorious well-ordered lines, a march of just under a mile began across open ground to attack the federal position. Longstreet vociferously protested: "General Lee, there never was a body of fifteen thousand men who could make that attack successfully."[105] At a thousand yards, the Union artillery opened up with canisters—tin cans filled with minié balls that flew in all directions upon impact. Row after row of Rebels fell. Then the long lines of Yankee infantry, which had lain prone beneath the artillery rounds sailing over their heads, stood or kneeled when the Rebels marched to within two hundred yards to deliver a hailstorm of lead.

Amazingly, Virginians under General Lewis Armistead reached the stone wall from which the Yankees were hurling a withering fire into their midst. Armistead stuck his general's hat on his saber and screamed, "Give them the cold steel!" Scaling the wall with about 200 Virginians following him, Armistead was killed. Known as the high-water mark of the Confederacy, it was a scene later recaptured in film and art, yet it lasted for only minutes as Union reserves poured new volleys into the exposed Confederates, then charged, reclaiming the stone wall. The attack utterly erased Pickett's division, with only half the 15,000 men who began the attack straggling back to Rebel lines in the orchards. As they ran, a chant rose up from the Yankee infantry behind the stone wall. "Fred-ricks-burg. Fred-ricks-burg."[106]

Reports trickled in to Longstreet, then Lee, who, in despair, kept repeating, "It's all my fault." The final tally revealed that the Army of Northern Virginia had taken a terrible beating at the hands of Meade: the Confederates lost 22,638, the Union, 17,684. Yet the most important phase of Gettysburg had just started. Defeated and nearly broken, could Lee escape? Would Meade blink, and prove to be another McClellan and Hooker?

Meade's son, a captain on his father's staff, wrote confidently on July seventh that "Papa will end the war," a phrase the general himself made two days later in a missive to Washington when he said, "I think the decisive battle of the war will be fought in a few days."[107] Yet Meade did not follow up, even when it appeared that nature herself demanded the war end then and there. Storms had swollen the Potomac River, temporarily blocking Lee's escape. An aggressive general could have surrounded the demoralized Confederate Army and crushed it by July 15, 1863. Instead, Lee's engineers hastily put up new pontoon bridges, and the Rebels began to slip away. When he learned the news, Lincoln wept.

Despite monumental failure, Meade also had achieved monumental success. He had done what no other Union general had done—whipped Bobbie Lee in a head-to-head battle—and shattered the Army of Northern Virginia. That, in turn, meant that Lincoln had to be careful how he dealt with Meade in public. He could not, for example, fire him outright, but the president continued his search for a general who would fight ceaselessly. When, simultaneously with Meade's victory, Ulysses S. Grant resolutely took Vicksburg in his ingenious campaign, Lincoln found his fighting general.

From Chickamauga to Charleston

Gettysburg and Vicksburg marked a congruence of the war effort, a deadly double blow to the hopes of the Confederacy, capping a string of battlefield failures that met the Confederates in 1863. By that time, Ulysses Grant commanded all the military operations in the West, and he promptly sent Sherman to open up the road to Atlanta—and the Deep South. Then, on March 10, 1864, Lincoln appointed Grant as supreme commander over all Union armies, and Grant, in turn, handed control of the western war over to Sherman.

William Tecumseh Sherman resembled Grant in many ways, not the least of which was in his utter failure in civilian life, as a banker and lawyer. How much he owed his command to political favoritism, especially the influence wielded by his powerful brother, John Sherman, the new senator from Ohio, is not clear. Unlike Grant, however, Sherman was already a Republican and a member of the Radical wing of the Republican Party that opposed slavery on moral grounds. But he was also a racist whose view of the inferiority of blacks—especially Negro troops—would bring him into constant friction with Lincoln, whom he despised. His unintended role in reelecting the president in 1864 nearly led him to switch parties, just as Grant had switched from Democrat to Republican over almost the same issues. Sherman's hatred of Lincoln, whom he labeled a black gorilla (echoing terms used by McClellan), was exceeded only by his animosity toward the Confederates.[108] Although he admitted that Lincoln was "honest & patient," he also added that Lincoln lacked "dignity, order & energy," many of the traits that McClellan also thought missing in the president.[109]

Born in Lancaster, Ohio, in 1820, Sherman had been unloaded on relatives by his widowed mother. His foster father, Thomas Ewing, proved supportive, sending Sherman to West Point, and the young red-haired soldier eventually married Ewing's daughter. The Mexican War took him to California, where he later resigned and ran a bank—poorly. By the time the Civil War broke out, he had found some measure of success running the Louisiana State Seminary and Military Academy—later known as Louisiana State University—but resigned to serve the Union after Louisiana's announcement of secession. He wrote the secretary of war requesting a colonelcy rather than a general's position, and wanted a three-year appointment, wishing to avoid the impression he was a "political general."

In late 1861, facing Confederate troops in Kentucky, Sherman became delusional, plummeting into a deep clinical depression that left him pacing his residence all night long, muttering to himself, and drinking heavily. Thus the relationship between Lincoln and Sherman—both probably manic depressives—was even more complex than either man realized. It remains one of the astounding pieces of history that the Union was saved by two depressives and a partially reformed drunk! After fighting effectively at Shiloh, Sherman received special praise from Grant and earned promotion after promotion. Grant named the red-haired Ohioan commander of all the armies in the West in the spring of 1864, with instructions to "create havoc and destruction of all resources that would be beneficial to the enemy."[110] On May 4, 1864, with almost 100,000 men, Sherman stuck a dagger into the heart of the South by attacking Atlanta. Joe Johnston's defending Confederate armies won minor engagements, but the over-whelming Union advantage in men and supplies allowed Sherman to keep up the pressure when Johnston had to resupply or rest. Jefferson Davis blamed John-ston, removing him in July in favor of John Bell Hood, but the fact was that even a mediocre general would have crushed Atlanta sooner or later. Sherman was no mediocre general.

With Yankee troops on the outskirts of Atlanta, Hood burned the railroads and withdrew, and on September 1, 1864, Union forces entered the city. Offering the Confederates the opportunity to remove all civilians, Sherman announced he would turn the city into a military base. Hood, hoping to draw the federal troops away from Atlanta, moved around him to the north, in an effort to destroy Sher-man's supply lines. Sherman scoffed that he would "supply him with rations" all the way to Ohio if Hood would keep moving in that direction. Instead, Sherman headed south, preparing to live off the land and to destroy everything the Union Army did not consume. "War is hell," he soberly noted.

Sherman's great victory at Atlanta constituted one of a trio of critical victories in late 1864, news of which reached Washington—and the voters—just as Lin-coln was under political assault. One of Lincoln's detractors thus ensured his re-election.

Politics in the North

By early 1864, in retrospect, Union victory seemed inevitable. U.S. Navy ships blockaded Southern ports, breached only occasionally (and ineffectively) by blockade runners. The Mississippi now lay open from Missouri to the Gulf, while Texas, Arkansas, and Louisiana were surgically isolated from the rest of the Con-federacy. In the far West, small important battles there had ensured that New Mexico, Utah, and California would remain in the Union and supply the federal effort with horses, cattle, gold, silver, and other raw materials. Braxton Bragg's northern defensive perimeter had shrunk from the Kentucky border on the north to Atlanta. In Virginia, Lee's army remained a viable, but critically damaged, fight-ing unit. Northern economic might had only come fully into play in 1863, and the disparities between the Union and Confederate abilities to manufacture guns, boots, clothes, ships, and, most important, to grow food, were shocking.

Given such a string of good news, Lincoln should have experienced stellar public approval and overwhelming political support. In fact, he clung to the presidency by his fingernails. Some of his weakened position emanated from his strong support of the man he had named commander of the Union armies.

Ulysses Grant and Abraham Lincoln rarely corresponded, though Grant tended to send numerous messages to Halleck, who would, he knew, read them to Lincoln. A Douglas Democrat in 1860, Grant had nonetheless gravitated toward unequivocal emancipation, though he was not a vocal abolitionist. No one seems sure when he actually changed parties. Courted by the Democrats as a potential presidential nominee in 1864, Grant refused to be drawn into politics at that time, and, in reality, never liked politics, even after he became president himself. By the fall of 1864, though, Grant endorsed Lincoln indirectly in a widely published letter.

When Hooker descended to the low expectations many had of him, Grant recommended Meade for command of the Army of the Potomac. Even after Lincoln gave Grant overall command of the army, he and the president were not particularly friendly, despite their similarities. For one thing, Mary Todd Lincoln, whose bitterness knew no bounds once it was directed at someone, despised Grant's wife, Julia.[111]

Grant intended to grind down the Confederates with a steady series of battles, even if none proved individually decisive. Grant's style caught the Rebels off guard. One Confederate soldier wrote:

> We had been accustomed to a programme which began with a Federal advance, culminating in one great battle, and ended in the retirement of the Union army, the substitution of a new Federal commander for the one beaten, and the institution of a more or less offensive campaign on our part. This was the usual order of events, and this was what we confidently expected when General Grant crossed into the Wilderness. But here was a new Federal General, fresh from the West, and so ill-informed as to the military customs in our part of the country that when the Battle of the Wilderness was over, instead of retiring to the north bank of the river and awaiting development of Lee's plans, he had the temerity to move by his left flank to a new position, there to try conclusions with us again. We were greatly disappointed with General Grant, and full of curiosity to know how long it was going to take him to perceive the impropriety of his course.[112]

The Rebels quickly realized that "the policy of pounding had begun, and would continue until our strength should be utterly worn away. . . ."[113]

The low point for Grant's reputation came in May 1864, when he launched a new offensive through the Wilderness again. Two days of bloody fighting at the Second Battle of the Wilderness ensued, and more bodies piled up. On this occasion, however, Grant immediately attacked again, and again. At Spotsylvania Court House, Lee anticipated Grant's attempt to flank him to get to Richmond, and the combat lasted twelve days. Despite the fact that Grant's armies failed to advance toward Richmond spatially, their ceaseless winnowing of the enemy continued to weaken Confederate forces and morale. It was costly, with the Union suffering 60,000 casualties in just over a month after Grant took over, and this politically damaged Lincoln.

Continuing to try to flank Lee, Grant moved to Cold Harbor, where, on June first, he sent his men against entrenched positions. One Confederate watched with astonishment what he called "inexplicable and incredible butchery."[114] Yankee troops, recognizing the futility of their assaults, pinned their names and addresses to their coats to make identification of their bodies easier. Lee saw the carnage and remarked, "This is not war, this is murder."[115] Grant lost 13,000 men to the Confederates' 2,000—the only battle in which the Army of Northern Virginia achieved any significant ratio of troops lost to the numbers engaged in the entire war.

Cold Harbor was the only action that Grant ever regretted, a grand mistake of horrific human cost. Callous as it seemed, however, Grant had, in more than a month, inflicted on the Confederates 25,000 casualties, or more than Gettysburg and Antietam put together. Shifting unexpectedly to the south, Grant struck at Petersburg, where he missed an opportunity to occupy the nearly undefended city. Instead, a long siege evolved in which "the spade took the place of the musket."[116]

Searching for a way to break through Lee's Petersburg fortifications, Grant received a plan from Colonel Henry Pleasants, a mining engineer in command of a regiment of Pennsylvania coal miners, who proposed tunneling under the fortifications and planting massive explosives to blast a hole in the Confederate defenses. On July twenty-seventh, the tunneling was completed, and tons of black powder were packed inside the tunnel. Troops prepared to follow up, including, at first, a regiment of black soldiers who, at the last minute, were replaced on Burnside's orders. When the charge detonated on July thirtieth, a massive crater was blown in the Rebel lines, but the advance troops quickly stumbled into the hole, and Confederates along the edges fired down on them. It was another disaster, costing the Union 4,000 casualties and an opportunity to smash through the Petersburg defenses.

Since 1862 Lincoln had faced turmoil inside his cabinet and criticism from both the Radical Republicans and Democrats. Prior to 1863, antislavery men were angry with Lincoln for not pursuing emancipation more aggressively. At the same time, loyal "war Democrats" or "Unionists" who remained in Congress nipped at his heels for the army's early failings, especially the debacles of McDowell, Burnside, and Hooker. Their favorite, McClellan, who scarcely had a better record, nevertheless was excused from criticism on the grounds that Lincoln had not properly supported him.

During the 1862 congressional election, criticism escalated, and the Republicans barely hung on to the House of Representatives, losing seats in five states where they had gained in 1860. These, and other Democratic gains, reversed a series of five-year gains for the Republicans, with the cruelest blow coming in Illinois, where the Democrats took nine seats to the Republicans' five and won the state legislature. Without the border states, James G. Blaine recalled, the hostile House might have overthrown his emancipation initiative.[117]

If the House losses were troublesome, Salmon Chase posed a genuine threat to the constitutional order. His financing measures had proven remarkably efficient, even if he ignored better alternatives. Yet his scheming against Seward, then Lincoln, was obvious to those outside the administration, who wrote of the Chase faction, "Their game was to drive all the cabinet out—then force . . . the [reappointment] of Mr. Chase as Premier, and form a cabinet of ultra men around him."[118] Seward, tired of the attacks, submitted his resignation without knowing the larger issues that swirled around him. Lincoln convened a meeting with several of the senators involved in the Chase schemes. Holding Seward's resignation in his hand, he demanded the resignation of all his cabinet, which he promptly placed in his top desk drawer and threatened to use if he heard of further intrigue. Lincoln's shrewd maneuver did not end the machinations by the Radicals, but it severely dampened them for the rest of the war.

An equally destabilizing issue involved the draft. Liberal Democrats and influential Republican editors like Horace Greeley opposed conscription. After announcement of the first New York conscriptees under the 1863 Enrollment Act, some fifty thousand angry Irish, who saw that they were disproportionately represented on the lists, descended upon the East Side. Mobs terrorized and looted stores, targeting blacks in particular. Between twenty-five to a hundred people died in the riots, and the mobs did $1.5 million in damage, requiring units from the U.S. Army to restore order. The new Gatling guns—the world's first machine gun, developed by American Richard Gatling—were turned on the rioting Irish.[119] The rioters were in the unfortunate circumstance of confronting troops direct from Gettysburg, who were in no mood to give them any quarter.

Another threat to the Union came from so-called Peace Democrats, known in the North as Copperheads for their treacherous, stealthy attacks. Forming secret societies, including the Knights of the Golden Circle, Copperheads forged links to the Confederacy. How far their activities went remains a matter of debate, but both Lincoln and Davis thought them significant. Copperheads propagandized Confederate success, recruited for the Rebel cause, and, in extreme situations, even stole supplies, destroyed bridges, and carried correspondence from Southern leaders. Even when arrested and convicted, Copperhead agitators often found sympathetic judges who quietly dismissed their cases and released them.

At the opposite end of the spectrum, but no less damaging to Lincoln, were the Radical Republicans. Congressional Republicans from 1861 onward clashed with the president over which branch had authority to prosecute the war. In May 1864, Radicals held a meeting in Cleveland to announce their support of John C.

Frémont as their presidential candidate in the fall elections. Rank-and-file Republicans, who eschewed any connection to the Radicals, held what would have been under other circumstances the "real" Republican convention in June, and renominated Lincoln. However, in an effort to cement the votes of "war" or "unionist" Democrats, Lincoln replaced Hannibal Hamlin, his vice president, with a new nominee, Democrat Andrew Johnson, of Tennessee.

The main source of Radical opposition to Lincoln targeted his view of reconstructing the Union. Radicals sought the utter prostration of the South. Many had looked forward to the opportunity to rub the South's nose in it, and Lincoln's moderation was not what they had in mind. Two of the most outspoken Radicals, Benjamin F. Wade of Ohio and Henry W. Davis of Maryland, authored a bill to increase the number of persons required to sign loyalty oaths to 50 percent, and to ensure black civil rights. The Wade-Davis Bill flew in the face of Lincoln's consistently stated desire to reunite the nation as quickly and peacefully as possible, and it would have provoked sufficient Southern antipathy to lengthen the war through guerrilla warfare. Yet Lincoln feared that Congress might override a veto, so he exercised a special well-timed pocket veto, in which he took no action on the bill. Congress adjourned in the meantime, effectively killing the legislation, which infuriated the Radicals even more. Wade and Davis issued the Wade-Davis Manifesto, which indicted not only Lincoln's plan for reunification but also disparaged his war leadership.

All of these factors combined to produce a remarkable development in the late summer and early fall of 1864 in which some Republican Party members started to conduct a quiet search for a nominee other than Lincoln. At the Democratic convention in August, George B. McClellan emerged as the nominee. He planned to run on a "restoration" of the Union with no change in the Confederacy except that the Richmond government would dissolve. Adopting a "peace plank," Democrats essentially declared that three years of war had been for naught—that no principles had been affirmed. Here was an astonishingly audacious and arrogant man: an incompetent and arguably traitorous Democratic general running against his former commander in chief in time of war and on a peace platform six months before the war was won! The peace plank proved so embarrassing that even McClellan soon had to disavow it. Even so, facing McClellan and the "purer" Republican Frémont, Lincoln privately expected to be voted out.

At about that time, Lincoln received welcome news that Admiral David Farragut had broken through powerful forts to capture Mobile Bay on August 5, 1864. Threatened by Confederate "torpedoes" (in reality, mines), Farragut exhorted his sailors with the famous phrase, "Damn the torpedoes. Full speed ahead." Other important Confederate ports, most notably Charleston and Wilmington on the Atlantic, held out, but remained blockaded. With Mobile safely in Union hands, the major Gulf Coast Rebel cities had surrendered. Farragut's telegrams constituted the first of three highly positive pieces of war news that ensured Lincoln's reelection. The second was Sherman's early September report of the fall of Atlanta. Sherman recommended that Grant order him to march southward from Atlanta to "cut a swath through to the sea," taking Savannah.[120] In the process, he would inflict as much damage as possible, not only on the Rebel army, but on the Southern economy and war-making capacity. A third and final boost to Lincoln's reelection came a few weeks later from the Shenandoah Valley, where General Philip Sheridan was raising havoc. Between Stuart's loss at Yellow Tavern and the destruction of the Shenandoah, Lincoln's prospects brightened considerably.

Still, he took no chances, furloughing soldiers so they could vote Republican and seeing to it that loyalists in Louisiana and Tennessee voted (even though only the Union states counted in the electoral college). McClellan, who once seemed to ride a whirlwind of support, saw it dissipate by October. Even Wade and Davis supported Lincoln, and Grant chimed in with his praise for the administration. Lincoln beat McClellan by 400,000 votes and crushed the Democrat in the electoral college, 212 to 21. McClellan's checkered career as a soldier/politician had at last sputtered to an end.

Total War and Unconditional Surrender

Fittingly, Sherman began his new offensive the day after the election. "I can make Georgia howl," he prophesied.[121] With Chattanooga and Atlanta both lost, the South lacked any major rail links to the western part of the Confederacy, causing Lee to lose what little mobility advantage he had shown in previous campaigns. "My aim then," Sherman later wrote, "was to whip the rebels, to humble their pride, to follow them to their inmost recesses, and make them fear and dread us."[122]

Graced by stunningly beautiful Dixie fall weather, Yankee troops burned cotton, confiscated livestock and food, destroyed warehouses and storage facilities, and ripped up railroads throughout Georgia. They made bonfires out of the wooden ties, then heated the iron rails over the fires, bending them around nearby telegraph poles to make "Sherman hairpins." Singing hymns as they marched—"five thousand voices could be heard singing 'Praise God from Whom All Blessings Flowed' "—the Yankee soldiers had even Sherman believing "God will take care of [these noble fellows]."[123] Sherman's army had marched to Savannah by December 1864, living off the land.[124] Despite Confederate propaganda that Sherman was "retreating—simply retreating," his western soldiers were supremely confident in their commander. "I'd rather fight under him than Grant and if he were Mahomet, we'd be devoted Mussulmen," said one midwestern private.[125] Sherman's success produced an uncomfortable relationship with Lincoln. The president wanted him to aid federal recruiting agents in enlisting newly freed slaves into the army. An insubordinate Sherman, however, insisted on using blacks as laborers or "pioneer brigades" to dig, build, and haul, but not fight.[126] "Soldiers," Sherman insisted, "must do many things without orders from their own sense. . . . Negroes are not equal to this."[127] Lincoln, unable to punish the one general who seemed to advance without interruption, could only congratulate Sherman on his conquest.

On February seventeenth, Sherman entered Columbia, South Carolina, whereupon fires swept through the city, delighting many Unionists who hoped for the total destruction of this hotbed of rebellion. Most evidence points to Sherman's vengeful soldiers as the arsonists. The following day, the Stars and Stripes was hoisted above Fort Sumter. Marching north, Sherman further compressed the tiny operating area left to Lee and Johnston. This was perfectly in sync with Grant's broad strategy of operating all the armies together on all fronts. Every army had orders to engage, a strategy to which Lincoln agreed: "Those not skinning can hold a leg."[128]

As the end neared, in December 1864, President Davis and his wife attended a "starvation party," which had no refreshments because of the food shortages. Already, Davis had sold his horses and slaves to raise money to make ends meet, and his wife had sold her carriage and team. He and other leaders knew the Confederacy did not have long to live. At that late date, Davis again proposed arming the slaves. In a sense, however, it might be said that Robert E. Lee's army was already relying heavily upon them. At the Tredegar Iron Works, the main Southern iron manufacturing facility, more than 1,200 slaves hammered out cannon barrels and bayonets, and in other wartime plants, free blacks in Alleghany, Botetourt, Henrico, and other counties shaped nails, boilers, locomotives, and a variety of instruments of war.[129] Added to that, another few thousand free blacks actually served in the Confederate Army as cooks, teamsters, and diggers, or in shoe repair or wheelwright work. Little is known of their motivation, but it appears to have been strictly economic, since the Rebel military paid more ($16 per month in Virginia) than most free blacks could ever hope to get in the South's impoverished private sector.[130] Most were impressed under state laws, including some 10,000 black Virginians immediately put to work after Bull Run throwing up breastworks in front of Confederate defensives positions. Ironically, some 286 black Virginia Confederate pensioners received benefits under Virginia law in 1926—the only slaves ever to receive any form of institutionalized compensation from their government.

Still, resistance to the use of slave soldiers was deep-seated, suggesting that Confederates well knew the implications of such policies: an 1865 Confederate House minority report stated, "The doctrine of emancipation as a reward for the services of slaves employed in the army, is antagonistic to the spirit of our institutions."[131] A Mississippi newspaper claimed that arming slaves marked "a total abandonment of the chief object of this war, and if the institution is already irretrievably undermined, the rights of the States are buried with it."[132] This constituted yet another admission that to white Southerners, the war was, after all, about slavery and not states' rights.

Of course, when possible, slaves aimed to escape to Northern lines. By 1863,

Virginia alone counted nearly 38,000 fugitives out of a population of 346,000, despite the presence of armed troops all around them.[133] Philosophically, the Confederacy placed more emphasis on recovering a black runaway than in apprehending a white deserter from the Army of Northern Virginia.

Despite the presence of a handful of Afro-Confederate volunteers, the vast majority of slaves openly celebrated their freedom once Union forces arrived. In Norfolk, Virginia, for example, new freedmen held a parade, marching through the city as they trampled and tore Confederate battle flags, finally gathering to hang Jefferson Davis in effigy.[134] Upon receiving news of emancipation, Williamsburg, Virginia, blacks literally packed up and left town. Blacks from Confederate states also joined the Union Army in large numbers. Louisiana provided 24,000, Tennessee accounted for more than 20,000, and Mississippi blacks who enlisted totaled nearly 18,000.

Grant, meanwhile, continued his relentless pursuit of Lee's army, suffocating Petersburg through siege and extending his lines around Richmond. Lee presented a desperation plan to Davis to break out of Petersburg and retreat to the southeast to link up with whatever forces remained under other Confederate commanders. Petersburg fell on April second, and, following desperate maneuvers by the Army of Northern Virginia, Grant caught up to Lee and Longstreet at Appomattox Station on April 8, 1865. Following a brief clash between the cavalry of General George Custer and General Fitzhugh Lee, the Confederates were surrounded. "I would rather die a thousand deaths," Robert E. Lee said of the action he then had to take.[135]

Opening a dialogue with Grant through letters delivered by courier, Lee met with Grant at the home of Wilmer McLean. The Confederate general dressed in a new formal gray uniform, complete with spurs, gauntlets, and epaulets, and arrived on his faithful Traveler, while Grant attended the meeting in an unbuttoned overcoat and boots splattered with mud—no sword, no designation of rank. Grant hastily wrote out the conditions, then, noticing that Lee seemed forlornly staring at the sword hanging at his side, decided on the spot that requiring the officers to formally surrender their swords was an undue humiliation. He wrote out, "This will not embrace the side-arms of the officers, nor their private horses or baggage."[136] Lee wrote a brief acceptance, glumly walked out the door and mounted Traveler, and as he began to ride off, Grant came out of the building and saluted. All the Union officers did the same. Lee sadly raised his hat in response, then rode off.

Grant had given the Confederates extremely generous terms in allowing all of the men to keep sidearms and horses, but they had to stack muskets and cannons. The men had to swear to obey the laws of the land, which would exempt them from prosecution as traitors. Grant's policy thus became the model for the surrender of all the Rebels. Fighting continued sporadically for weeks; the last actual combat of the Civil War was on May twenty-sixth, near Brownsville, Texas.

Davis had little time to ponder the cause of Confederate failure as he fled Richmond, completely detached from reality. Having already packed off his wife, arming her with a pistol and fifty rounds of ammunition, the Confederate president ran for his life. He issued a final message to the Confederacy in which he called for a massive guerrilla resistance by Confederate civilians. Expecting thousands of people to take to the Appalachians, live off the land, and fight hit-and-run style, Davis ignored the fact that not only were those sections of the South already the poorest economically—thus unable to support such a resistance—but they were also the areas where the greatest number of Union partisans and federal sentiment existed. Few read Davis's final desperate message, for by that time the Confederacy had collapsed and virtually no newspapers printed the news. Davis hid and used disguises, but to no avail. On May tenth he was captured at Irwinville, Georgia, and jailed.[137]

The call for guerrilla war inflamed Northern attitudes against Davis even further. Many wanted to hang him, and he remained in military custody at Fort Monroe, for a time in leg irons. In 1867 he was to be indicted for treason and was released to the control of a civilian court. After Horace Greeley and Cornelius Vanderbilt posted his bail, Davis languished under the cloud of a trial until December 1868, when the case was disposed of by President Andrew Johnson's proclamation of unconditional amnesty. By that time, Davis had become a political embarrassment to the administration, and his conviction—given the other amnesty provisions in place—unlikely anyway.

Lincoln's Last Days

In the two years since the Emancipation Proclamation, Maryland and Missouri had freed their slaves, the Fugitive Slave Law was repealed, and Congress had passed the Thirteenth Amendment to the Constitution, which provided that "neither slavery nor involuntary servitude, except as punishment for crime whereof the party shall have been duly convicted, shall exist within the United States, or any place subject to their jurisdiction."[138] With that amendment, Lincoln had steered the nation from a house divided over slavery to one reunited without it. Now he had two overarching goals ahead of him: ensure that the South did not reinstitute slavery in some mutated form, and at the same time, bring the former Rebels back into the Union as quickly and generously as possible.

He laid the groundwork for this approach in his second inaugural when he said, "With malice toward none; with charity for all; with firmness in the right, as God gives us to see the right, let us strive on to finish the work we are in; to bind up the nation's wounds; to care for him who shall have borne the battle, and for his widow, and his orphan—to do all which may achieve and cherish a just and lasting peace among ourselves, and with all nations."[139]

The president intended for Reconstruction to follow his "10 percent plan." By this definition, he recognized former Confederate states Tennessee, Louisiana, Arkansas, and Virginia as reconstructed in late 1864, even as Lee held out in Richmond. However, Radicals refused to seat their delegations nor to allow those states to cast electoral votes in the November 1864 election. One thing is certain: Lincoln wanted a quick and magnanimous restoration of the Union, not the Radicals' dream of a prostrate and subjugated South. When it came to traitorous Confederate leaders, Lincoln told his last cabinet secretaries, on the day he was killed, "Enough lives have been sacrificed." On matters of black economic opportunity, Lincoln was less clear. No one knows what measures Lincoln would have adopted, but his rhetoric was always several steps behind his actions in matters of race.

It is one of the tragedies of his assassination on April 15, 1865, that Abraham Lincoln did not remain in office to direct Reconstruction, for surely he would have been a towering improvement over Andrew Johnson. Tragedy befell the nation doubly so, because his murder by an arch-Confederate actor named John Wilkes Booth doused feelings of compassion and the "charity for all" that some, if not most, Northerners had indeed considered extending to the South. The details of Lincoln's death have taken on mythic status, and rightly so, for aside from George Washington, no other president—not even Jefferson—had so changed the Union.

On April fourteenth, all but a few western Confederate armies had disarmed. Mary Lincoln noticed her normally morose husband in the cheeriest of moods.[140] It was Good Friday, and Washington buzzed with the excitement that for the first time in four years citizens could celebrate an evening without the apprehension of the next day's casualty lists. Along with two guests, Major Henry Rathbone and Clara Harris, the Lincolns attended *Our American Cousin* at Ford's Theater. Lincoln did not have his bodyguard/Secret Service agent, Allan Pinkerton, with him.

At seven o'clock in the evening, with the carriage already waiting, the president's bodyguard at the White House, William Crook, was relieved three hours late by his replacement, John Porter. As always, Crook had said, "Good night, Mr. President." But that night, Crook recalled, Lincoln replied, "Good-bye, Crook," instead of the usual, "Good night, Crook." The day before, he had told Crook that he knew full well many people wanted him dead, and "if it is to be done, it is impossible to prevent it."

After intermission, Porter left his post outside the president's box and went next door to a tavern for a drink. When Act III started, John Wilkes Booth entered the unguarded anteroom leading to the president's box, braced its door with a wooden plank, opened the door to Lincoln's box slightly, and aimed the .44-caliber single-shot derringer at the back of the president's head, then fired. In the ensuing struggle with Major Rathbone, Booth leaped over the railing, where one of his boots snagged on the banner over the box. He fractured one of his legs as he hit the stage. "Sic semper tyrannis," he screamed at the stunned audience, "Thus be it ever to tyrants." Hopping out the door to his waiting horse, Booth escaped. Lincoln, carried unconscious to a nearby house, died nine hours later on the same bed John Wilkes Booth had slept in just one month prior. At one-thirty in the morning, Secretary of War Edwin Stanton made a public statement in which he said, "It is not probable the president will live through the night."[141] "Now he belongs to the ages," said Stanton on Lincoln's death.

Booth, in one maniacal act of defiance, had done more to immortalize Lincoln than all the speeches he ever made or all the laws he signed. The man who only a half year earlier stood to lose the nomination of his own party now rose, and rightfully so, to join the ranks of Washington and Jefferson in the American pavilion of political heroes. Booth worked with a group of conspirators who had hoped to knock out many more in the Washington Republican leadership, including Andrew Johnson and William Seward, that night. Seward was stabbed but the wound was not fatal. The assassins fled to Port Royal, Virginia, where Booth was trapped in a barn that was set afire. He shot himself to death. Other conspirators, quickly rounded up, were tried by a military tribunal. Three men and one woman were hanged; three others received life prison terms; and one went to jail for six years.[142] Davis, still free at the time, came under immediate suspicion for authorizing the conspiracy, but he knew nothing of it.

At ten o'clock the following morning, Andrew Johnson was sworn in as president of the United States. Walt Whitman, who had worked in the Union's hospital service, penned "O Captain, My Captain" in homage to Lincoln.[143]

Had Lincoln survived, perhaps the wounds inflicted by the war itself could have healed in a less bellicose Reconstruction. After all, only in America would a rebellion end with most of the leaders excused and the rebellious state emerging without being obliterated. Whatever damage the South suffered—and it was severe—it pales in historical comparison to the fates of other failed rebellions. Indeed, modern history is littered with *successful* rebellions (Biafra, Bangladesh) whose human cost and physical devastation exceeded that of the defeated Confederacy's. With Lincoln's death, a stream of tolerance and mercy vanished, and the divisions that brought on the war mutated into new strains of sectional, political, and racial antagonisms that gave birth to the perverted legend of "the Lost Cause."

Marxist Revisionists, Lost Cause Neo-Confederates

In the decades following the Civil War, a truly remarkable thing happened. The rebellious South, which had been utterly invaded, destroyed, and humiliated, concocted a dubious explanation of its past. This reconstruction of history reshaped every aspect of the Civil War debate, from causes (slavery was not a sectional issue) to battlefield defeats (the South only lost because of the ineptness of some of its generals, most notably James Longstreet at Gettysburg) to the legality and constitutionality of secession to the absurd notion that the South, if left to its own devices, would have eventually given up slavery.[144] The Lost Cause myth accelerated in the twentieth century when pop historians and even a few trained scholars bought into the false premises.

It is useful to recount, as historian James McPherson does, the total defeat inflicted on the South:

By 1865, the Union forces had . . . destroyed two-thirds of the assessed value of Southern wealth, two-fifths of the South's livestock, and one quarter of her white men between the ages of 20 and 40. More than half the farm machinery was ruined, and the damages to railroads and industries were incalculable . . . Southern wealth decreased by 60 percent.[145]

To that could be added the thorough destruction of the Southern banking system and the regionwide dissolution of the social structure based on slavery.[146]

Lost Cause theorists emphasized the irrelevancy of slavery as a cause of war, and sought to make the conflict about economic issues such as the tariff and cultural differences between the "honorable South" and the immoral North. They emphasized constitutional values and states' rights, not the issue of human chattel. But the record was quite different. Jefferson Davis "had frequently spoken to the United States Senate about the significance of slavery to the South and had threatened secession if what he perceived as Northern threats to the institution continued."[147] In 1861 Confederate Vice President Alexander H. Stephens called the "great truth" of slavery the "foundation" and "cornerstone" of the Confederacy.[148] The Confederate constitution specifically provided for protection of the "right of property in slaves." Far from moving toward emancipation *anywhere,* the South, as Allan Nevins pointed out, was making slavery harsher and more permanent. New laws reinforced slavery, throttled abolitionist materials, and spread the net of compliance to more and more nonslaveholding whites.[149] Indeed, the best argument against the notion that the South would have voluntarily given up slavery is that there was not the slightest indication of movement toward emancipation in any Southern state prior to 1861.

Contrary to the perpetrators of the Lost Cause story, once the Southerners saw the war on their doorstep, their defense of states' rights and principles all but vanished as the Confederacy increasingly toyed with the notion of emancipating its own slaves if they would fight for the CSA. The first such recommendations came in February 1861, but most officials dismissed them. By mid-1863, however, after Vicksburg fell, the Confederacy suddenly entertained arguments about emancipation. "Cannot we who have been raised with our Negroes and know how to command them, make them more efficient than the Yankees can?" asked one proponent of arming the slaves.[150]

The Lost Cause myth took root during Reconstruction, with pro-Southern writers emphasizing the corruption of federal occupation and the helplessness of white citizens against the power of the federal government and the proportionately large numbers of blacks who went to the polls. Neo-Confederate writers' imaginative attempts to portray the antebellum South as a utopia were outrageously distorted and ultimately destructive. They planted in a large number of Southerners (though not the majority) the notion that the Confederacy had fought for important moral principles, and they labored to move the argument away from slavery.

The modern-day voices of the Lost Cause who received new support (after the fall of the Dixiecrats in the 1960s) came from modern libertarians who, for the most part, viewed the Union government as more oppressive than the Confederacy. Emphasizing the infractions against civil and economic liberties by the Union government during and after the war, this view has maintained a dedicated but small group of adherents.[151] To these Lost Cause proponents, Lincoln remains the ultimate monster, a tyrant whose thirst for power enabled him to provoke the South into firing on Fort Sumter. Had he only let the lower Confederacy secede, their argument goes, the remaining United States would have embarked on a golden age of liberty, and the South, eventually, because of market forces (claim the libertarians) or its own noble character (as the neo-Confederates assert), would have emancipated the slaves. These views are as deceptive as they are erroneous. Virtually no evidence exists to suggest that the South would have peacefully emancipated its slaves. Indeed, since slavery was supported with the power of a Confederate government fully behind it, the institution could have survived for decades, if not perpetually. Slavery existed in some empires in the world for centuries—and still exists in parts of the Arab world today. It was seldom voluntarily eradicated from within. Equally as destructive is the notion that states—or principalities—could choose their own terms when it suited them to be in the Union.

Equally perverse is the neo-Marxist/New Left interpretation of the Civil War as merely a war "to retain the enormous national territory and market and resources" of the United States.[152] Reviving the old Charles Beard interpretations of the triumph of capitalism over an agrarian society, leftist critics find themselves in agreement with the more radical libertarian writers. Whereas the neo-Confederates harken back to an imaginary world of benign masters and happy slaves, the leftist critics complain that Lincoln was too conservative, and blocked genuinely radical (and, to them, positive) redistribution of not only plantation owners' wealth, but all wealth.

It is preposterous for Marxists to assert that capitalism enslaved free employees. Quite the contrary, the *only* hope many Southern blacks had once the Yankee armies had left for good in 1877 was the free market, where the color of money could overcome and subdue black/white racism. The government, and not the market, perpetuated Jim Crow; the government, not the market, enforced union minimum wage laws that excluded blacks from entry-level positions; and the government, not the market, passed and enforced separate-but-equal segregation laws. The market, freed from interference by racist Southern state regulations, would have desegregated the South decades before Martin Luther King Jr., the freedom riders, Harry Truman, Earl Warren, and the Civil Rights acts.

America's Civil War was ultimately and overwhelmingly about the idea of freedom: whether one group of people could restrict the God-given liberty of others. That the Republicans, in their zeal to free slaves, enacted numerous ill-advised taxes, railroad, and banking laws, is regrettable but, nevertheless, of minor consequence in the big picture. In that regard, the South perverted classic libertarianism—libertarianism did not pervert the South.

A remarkable fact of the war is that the United States divided almost evenly, fought for four bloody years, and never abandoned the *concept* of constitutional government. Quite the contrary, if one takes Southern rhetoric at face value, the war was over the definitions of that constitutionalism. But even if one rejects Southern arguments as rationalizations for slavery, the astounding fact is that the Confederacy no sooner left the Union than it set up its own constitution, modeled in most ways on that of the United States from which it had seceded. In neither section, North or South, were elections suspended or most normal workings of civilian government abandoned. In neither section was there a coup d'état. Indeed, both sides agreed that the founding ideas were worth preserving—they just disagreed over the exact composition and priority of those ideas.

And, finally, rather than a contest about capitalism, the Civil War was a struggle over the definition of union. No concept of union can survive any secession, any more than a body can survive the "secession" of its heart or lungs. The forging of the nation, undertaken in blood and faith in 1776 and culminating in the Constitution in 1787, brought the American people together as a single nation, not a country club of members who could choose to leave at the slightest sign of discomfort. The Civil War finalized that contract and gave to "all men" the promises of the Declaration and the purposes of the Constitution. And although thousands paid the ultimate price for completing that process, what emerged— truly "one nation, under God"—could never again be shattered from within.

CHAPTER TEN

Ideals and Realities of
Reconstruction, 1865–76

Hope and Despair

Less than two weeks after Lincoln's assassination more than 2,100 Union soldiers boarded the steamboat *Sultana* at Vicksburg to return to their homes via the Mississippi River. The vessel had a capacity of 376, but on that day it carried soldiers literally packed like sardines from stem to stern when, eight miles north of Memphis, a boiler exploded, collapsing the superstructure and engulfing the rest of the *Sultana* in flames. As if the ravages of war and the death of a president had not dealt the nation enough of a blow, when the dead were accounted for, more than 1,547 people had perished, making the *Sultana* explosion the worst American water-related disaster in history, exceeding the number of Americans who died on the *Lusitania* in 1915 by some 400. Their loss came as a cruel exclamation point to the end of a devastating war that had already claimed 618,000 men.

Earlier that month, just before Lee surrendered, the Army of Northern Virginia had marched out of Richmond to the sound of Rebels blowing up their own gunboats on the James River. One Confederate, S. R. Mallory, recalled that the men were "light-hearted and cheerful . . . though an empire was passing away around them." When they reached the Richmond suburbs, however, they saw "dirty-looking women, who had evidently not been improved by four year' military association, [and] dirtier-looking (if possible) children." Mallory noticed the crowds had not gathered to watch the retreat, but to pillage the burning city, looting and burning "while the standards of an empire were being taken from its capitol, and the tramp of a victorious enemy could be heard at its gates."[1]

Armies of deserters and refugees thronged to Southern cities—what was left of them—only to find that even before Union troops arrived, Confederates had set fire to many of the buildings. Union cavalry entered Richmond first, surrounded by mobs of "Confederate stragglers, negroes, and released convicts," suffocating by the air thick with smoke from the fires that swept the streets.[2] Yankee troops, cheered on by former slaves, struggled to finally bring the fires under control and to stop the looting." Northern reporters accompanying federal forces observed crowds of African Americans heading for the State House grounds, merely to walk on ground where, just days earlier, they had been prohibited from entering.[3]

Washington, meanwhile, witnessed one of the grandest illuminations ever recorded, as the entire population lit candles, flew flags, and burned lamps. The secretary of war ordered a staggering eight-hundred-gun salute—five hundred in honor of the surrender of Richmond and three hundred for Petersburg—which shook the earth as men embraced, women cheered, and, for a magical moment, old animosities evaporated in goodwill toward men. That did not last long. When word came that Richmond was aflame, cries of "Burn it! Burn it!" reverberated. Reporter Noah Brooks concluded that "a more liquorish crowd was never seen in Washington than on that night."[4]

Lincoln traveled to Petersburg to meet with the commander of the Army of the Potomac, General Grant. Perhaps appropriately, the band followed "Hail Columbia," with "We'll All Drink Stone Blind." The president congratulated the general, claiming to have had a "sneaking idea for some days" that Grant neared victory, and proceeded to confer for an hour with Grant over postwar occupation policies. It concerned many that Lincoln had walked exposed and unescorted through the streets of Petersburg, having arrived at an abandoned dock with no greeting party, and then, on April fourth, had ridden through Richmond itself, overcome by joy at seeing freed slaves shouting, "Glory to God! Glory! Glory!" Later, on the night of April fifth, aboard the *Malvern,* Lincoln jotted down his goals for reuniting the nation. He intended that all confiscated property, except slaves, would be immediately returned to its owners after a state had ceased its support of the rebellion.

Radicals in Congress who heard Lincoln's April eleventh Reconstruction speech were unimpressed. Some considered the president shallow for failing to demand "an entire moral and social transformation of the South," as if such were in the hands of any president.[5] Virtually all of Lincoln's cabinet, however, came away from his final meeting convinced he was more cheerful and happy than they had ever seen him. Lincoln had again insisted that while federal authority must be imposed and violence suppressed, private citizens in the South should be treated with courtesy and respect. Beyond that, we know little of Lincoln's specific plans, for he met his fate at Ford's Theater on April fourteenth.

The process of readmitting former members of the Confederacy to the Union, rebuilding the South, and establishing a framework for the newly freed slaves to live and work in as free men and women in a hostile environment has been termed Reconstruction. The actual political evolution of Reconstruction, however, involved three distinct phases. Under the first phase, presidential Reconstruction, Lincoln (briefly) and Andrew Johnson attempted to control the process under two broad precepts: the South should be readmitted to the Union as quickly as possible, with as little punishment as necessary for former Confederates, and the freedmen should obtain full emancipation, free from legal barriers to employment or property ownership. Beyond that, presidential Reconstruction did not attempt to make freedmen citizens, nor did it seek to compensate them for their years in bondage.

A second phase followed: in congressional Reconstruction the dominant Republican faction, the Radicals, sought full political equality for freedmen, pushed for economic compensation through the forty-acres-and-a-mule concept, and demanded more serious punishment for former Rebels. Naturally, the Radicals' distinct positions put them in conflict with President Andrew Johnson, who held to more Lincolnesque views. Congressional Reconstruction further involved a program to punish Southerners for their rebellion by denying them representation in Washington or by establishing tough requirements to regain the franchise.

In the struggle that followed, on one side stood Johnson, virtually alone, although in a pinch some Democrats and a core of so-called moderate Republicans backed him. Moderates of 1865 had strong principles—just not those of the Radicals, who favored more or less full equality of blacks. Confronting and bedeviling Johnson were Radical leaders in Congress, most notably Thaddeus Stevens and Charles Sumner (who had finally returned to his seat after his caning at the hands of Preston Brooks). They held together a shaky coalition of diverse-minded men, some of whom favored suffrage for all freedmen; others who supported a limited franchise; and still others who advocated voting rights for blacks in the South, but not the North.[6]

The third and final phase of Reconstruction occurred when Radical Reconstruction lost its steam and public support faded. At that point, Southern Democrats known as Redeemers restored white supremacy to the state governments, intimidated blacks with segregation ("Jim Crow" laws), and squeezed African Americans out of positions of power in the state governments. Reconstruction ended officially with a Redeemer victory in the Compromise of 1877, in which the final Union troops were withdrawn from the South, leaving blacks unprotected and at the mercy of Southern Democratic governments.

It is worth noting that both Lincoln and Johnson sparred with Congress over control of Reconstruction on several occasions, and thus some overlap between presidential and congressional Reconstruction occurred. Although Lincoln had enacted a few precedent-setting policies, the brunt of the initial Reconstruction efforts fell on his successor, Andrew Johnson.

Time Line

1865: Civil War ends; Lincoln assassinated; Andrew Johnson assumes presidency; Thirteenth Amendment

1866: Radical Republicans emerge in Congress; Ku Klux Klan founded

1867: Military Reconstruction Act; purchase of Alaska

1868: Johnson impeachment trial ends in acquittal; Fourteenth Amendment; Grant elected president

1870: Fifteenth Amendment

1872: Crédit Mobilier Scandal

1873: Crime of 1873; Panic of 1873

1876: Disputed presidential election between Hayes and Tilden

1877: Compromise of 1877; Hayes becomes president; Redeemers recapture Southern governments; Black Republicans in the South begin to decline

Andrew Johnson Takes the Helm

The president's death plunged the nation into grief and chaos. No other chief executive had died so suddenly, without preparation for a transition; Harrison took a month to expire, and Taylor five days. Lincoln's assassination left the nation emotionally and constitutionally unprepared, and his successor, Vice President Andrew Johnson, was detested in the North and distrusted in the South. Having stumbled through a decade of mediocre leaders in the Oval Office, the nation had risen on the greatness of Lincoln, only to deflate under the Tennessean who now took his place.

Not that Andrew Johnson was in any way dishonorable or unprincipled. Born in North Carolina in 1808, Johnson grew up in poverty not unlike that which Lincoln experienced, and, like Lincoln, he was largely self-educated. His parents worked for a local inn, although his father had also worked as a janitor at the state capitol. While a boy, Johnson was apprenticed as a tailor, but once he'd learned enough of the trade, he ran away at age thirteen to open his own shop in Greenville, Tennessee, under the sign A. JOHNSON, TAILOR. In 1827 he married Elizabeth McCardle, who helped refine and educate her husband, reading to him while he worked and improving his math and writing skills, which gave him sufficient confidence to join a debating society at a local academy. After winning the mayorship of Greenville as a Democrat, Johnson successfully ran for seats in the Tennessee House, then the Tennessee Senate, then, in 1843, he won a seat in the United States House of Representatives, where he supported fellow Tennessee Democrat James Polk and the Mexican War. After four consecutive terms in the House, Johnson ran for the governorship of Tennessee, winning that position twice before being elected to the U.S. Senate in 1857.

A Douglas Democrat, Johnson supported the Fugitive Slave Law, defended slavery, and endorsed the 1852 Homestead bill advanced by the Whigs. During his time as governor, he had not hewed a clear small-government line, increasing state spending on education and libraries. More important in defining Johnson, however, was his strict adherence to the Constitution as the final arbiter among the states and his repudiation of secessionist talk. Andrew Johnson was the only Southerner from a Confederate state to remain in the Senate. This made him Lincoln's obvious choice for military governor of Tennessee, once the federal troops had recaptured that state, and he remained there until 1864, when Lincoln tapped him to replace Hannibal Hamlin as vice president in order to preserve what Lincoln anticipated would be a thin electoral margin by attracting "war Democrats."

When Johnson was sworn in early on the morning of April 15, 1865, he assumed an office coveted by virtually every other cabinet member present, none of whom thought him ideologically or politically pure enough to step into Lincoln's shoes. To most Radicals, Lincoln himself had not been sufficiently vindictive, insisting only that blacks remain free and that the former Rebels' citizenship be restored as quickly as was feasible. His last words about the Confederates were that no one should hang or kill them. Lincoln lamented the tendency of many unionists to "Frighten them out of the country, open the gates, let down the bars, scare them off. . . . I do not share feelings of that kind."[7]

Lincoln, of course, was now gone, so at ten o'clock in the morning, at the Kirkwood Hotel, then Chief Justice Salmon Chase administered the oath of office to Johnson in the presence of the entire cabinet, save the wounded and bedridden William Seward. Each cabinet member shook Johnson's hand and promised to serve him faithfully, then Johnson settled into what everyone expected would be a harmonious and efficient continuation of the dead president's policies. It did not take long, however, for Ben Wade and other congressional Radicals to presume they had the new chief executive's ear, and to demand he form a new cabinet favorable to them. "Johnson," Wade exclaimed in one of history's worst predictions, "we have faith in you. By the gods, there will be no trouble now in running the government."[8]

Had the Radicals dominated the government as they'd wished, they would have slapped every Confederate officer in leg irons and probably executed the Rebel political leaders for treason. Instead, Lincoln's sentiments prevailed with Johnson. Aside from Booth's conspirators, only one Confederate, Major Henry Wirz, who had presided over the hell of Andersonville Prison, was executed for war crimes. Even Davis's two-year incarceration was relatively short for a man who had led a violent revolution against the United States government.

It is doubtful many Americans thought they could return to their lives as they had been before Fort Sumter. From an economic perspective alone, the Civil War's cost had been massive. The North spent $2.2 billion to win, the South just over $1 billion in losing.[9] Economists calculated that in addition to the destruction of $1.4 billion in capital, the South also lost $20 million in "undercounted labor costs associated with the draft." Estimating the lifetime earnings from soldiers had they lived an average life uninterrupted by war or wounds, economic historians affixed a value of $955 million to the Union dead, $365 million to Union wounded, and $947 million for Confederate dead and wounded. Accounting for all property, human life, decreased productivity, and other losses, the Civil War cost the nation $6.6 billion (in 1860 dollars). Translating such figures across 150 years is difficult, but in terms of that era, $6.6 billion was enough to have purchased, at average prices, every slave and provided each with a forty-acre farm—and still have had $3.5 billion left over.

Emancipation had become constitutional law with the Thirteenth Amendment, which was ratified by the states in December 1865. This amendment abolished slavery as a legal institution, in direct terminology, stating:

Section 1: Neither slavery nor involuntary servitude, except as a punishment for crime whereof the party shall have been duly convicted, shall exist within the United States, or any place subject to their jurisdiction. Section 2: Congress shall have power to enforce this article by appropriate legislation.

As part of Reconstruction, Southern states had to incorporate the Thirteenth Amendment into their state constitutions before they would be readmitted to the Union.

Other wartime costs were sure to grow as veterans began to draw their benefits. Veterans lobbied through a powerful new organization called the Grand Army of the Republic (GAR), founded by Dr. B. F. Stephenson in 1866. Organizing in "encampments," in which prospective members underwent a Masonic-type review process, the GAR constituted a huge block of votes, usually cast for the Republican Party. GAR membership peaked at just over 490,000 by 1890, and for two decades was the voice of Union veterans, who, unless wounded, made a relatively seamless transition into American society. One veteran lieutenant returned to his Illinois farm and recalled that the day after his arrival, "I doffed my uniform . . . put on some of my father's old clothes, armed myself with a corn knife, and proceeded to wage war on the standing corn."[10]

War taught many enlisted men and officers important new skills. Building railroads, bridges, and other constructions turned many soldiers into engineers; the demands of communications introduced many others to Morse code and the telegraph; keeping the army supplied taught thousands of men teamster skills; and so it went. One Chicago print shop, for example, employed forty-seven former soldiers.[11] Officers could capitalize on their postwar status, especially in politics, but also in a wide variety of commercial activities. Nothing enhanced sales like spreading the word that the proprietor was a *veteran*.

Although the Union demobilized much of the army, there still remained a largely unrepentant South to deal with, requiring about 60,000 troops to remain there. Some units were not withdrawn from Florida and Louisiana until 1876. Moreover, as movement to the West revived, a standing military force was needed to deal with Indian hostilities. Nevertheless, by August 1865 a whopping 640,000 troops had been mustered out, followed by another 160,000 by November. Reductions in force continued through 1867, when the U.S. Army counted 56,815 officers and men. The navy slashed its 700 ships down to fewer than 250, essentially mothballing many "active" vessels, including several radically advanced ironclad designs already under construction.

If the combatants who survived benefited at times from their service, the economy as a whole did not. From 1860 to 1869, the U.S. economy grew at a sluggish 2 percent annual rate, contrasted with a rate of 4.6 percent from 1840 to 1859 and 4.4 percent from 1870 to 1899. The statistics give lie to the left-wing notion that business likes wars. Quite the opposite, the manufacturing sector went into a tailspin during the war years, falling from 7.8 percent annual growth in the twenty years prior to the war to 2.3 percent from 1860 to 1869. The economy then regained steam after 1870, surging back to 6 percent annual growth. In short, there is no evidence to support the position forwarded by Charles and Mary Beard that the Civil War was a turning point and an economic watershed.[12]

A Devastated South

Where the war brought radical change was in the South. Union armies destroyed Southern croplands and towns, wrecked fences, ripped up railroads, and emancipated the slave labor force. Carl Schurz, traveling through South Carolina, witnessed a "broad black streak of ruin and desolation—the fences all gone; lonesome smoke stacks, surrounded by dark heaps of ashes and cinders, marking the spots where human habitations had stood; the fields along the road wildly overgrown by weeds, with here and there a sickly looking patch of cotton or corn cultivated by negro squatters."[13] Columbia, the capital of South Carolina, was little more than "a thin fringe of houses encircl[ing] a confused mass of charred ruins of dwellings and business buildings."[14] At the "garden spot" of Louisiana, the Bayou Teche region, once-thriving sugar fields and neat whitewashed cabins were replaced by burned fences, weeds, and bushes. Around Atlanta, some thirty-five thousand persons were dependent for their subsistence on the federal government. Discharged Confederate troops drew rations from their former Union captors. One Southern soldier expressed his surprise to see "a Government which was lately fighting us with fire, and sword, and shell, now generously feeding our poor and distressed."[15] Captain Charles Wilkes, in North Carolina, reported "whole families . . . coming in from South Carolina to seek food and obtain employment." "A more completely crushed country I have seldom witnessed," he added.[16]

Large numbers of Rebels embraced the myth of the Lost Cause, no one more dramatically than General Jubal Early, who left for Mexico before concocting an organization to promote the emigration of ex-Rebels to New Zealand. Scientist Matthew Maury also attempted an ex-Confederate colonization of Mexico. Robert E. Lee urged reconciliation and accepted a position as president of Washington College (later renamed Washington and Lee University); yet Confederate Secretary of War Judah P. Benjamin, fearing he would be unfairly linked to the Booth conspiracy, left for England, where he died. John Breckinridge also fled to Europe, where he died in 1875. Confederate colonel William H. Norris, a former U.S. senator from Alabama, organized a group of emigrant Alabama families to relocate to Brazil at the urging of Brazil's Emperor Dom Pedro II. Confederates colonized the Brazilian cities of Para, Bahia, Espirito Santo, Rio de Janeiro, and Santa Catarina. Americana, founded by Norris, only removed the Confederate battle flag from the crest of the city in 1999. Few took the course of Edmund Ruffin, a fire eater, who committed suicide. More common were the views of Amanda Worthington, a wealthy Mississippi plantation mistress, who complained, "We are no longer wealthy, . . . thanks to the yankees."[17] A bitter Virginia woman scornfully said, "Every day, every hour, that I live increases my hatred and detestation, and loathing of that race [Northerners]."[18] Many pampered plantation women expressed disgust that they had to comb their own hair and wash their own feet. "I was too delicately raised for such hard work," lamented one.[19]

Border states also suffered terrible damage stemming from the guerrilla warfare that pitted the Kansas and Missouri Jayhawkers against Rebels, spawning criminal gangs like the Quantrills and the Daltons. During the war, gangs established support networks of Confederate or Union loyalists when they could claim to be fighting for a cause, but that cloak of legitimacy fell away after 1865.

In both the Deep South and border states, the problem of maintaining law and order was compounded by the necessity to protect freedmen and deal with confiscated property. Authority over the freedmen fell under the auspices of a War Department agency, the Bureau of Refugees, Freedmen, and Abandoned Lands, established in March 1865. In addition to distributing medicine, food, and clothing to newly emancipated slaves, the Freedmen's Bureau, as it was called, supervised captured Confederate lands. In one form or another most Southern property had supported the rebellion—the Confederacy had seen to that by confiscating most of the cotton crop for secessionist purposes in the last days of the war. After the war the Union took what was left, confiscating perhaps $100 million in total Rebel property and selling it; the U.S. government received only about $30 million. This reflected the lower real values of Confederate property, and it also revealed the fantastic corruption at work in the post–Civil War agencies. All Southern agriculture had been devastated. Cotton, sugar, rice, and tobacco production did not regain their prewar harvest levels until the 1890s. Southern per capita income fell 39 percent in the 1860s, and as late as 1880, per capita income stood at only 60 percent of the national average. As late as the Great Depression, the South had yet to fully recover parity in income. In fact, the South had started a sharp economic decline (relative to the Midwest) right after Lincoln's first election.[20] A comparison of income trends in the South and Midwest from 1840 to 1880 reveals that a slight but steady decline in relative Southern income in the 1850s cascaded into a thoroughgoing collapse in the year before Fort Sumter. These economic data, among other things, suggest the South was losing ground in the 1850s, despite a much superior banking system in some states and a slave labor system. Without the war, the South's economy would have fallen further behind the North, despite the profitability of slavery itself.

Work crews repaired much of the physical damage relatively quickly. By 1870 most of the Southern transportation network had been rebuilt to prewar capacity, and manufacturing output grew by about 5 percent. In short, the view that the "prostrate South's" position could be laid entirely at the feet of Yankee pillage does not hold water.[21]

Presidential Reconstruction

Even before the term "Reconstruction" existed, the process began at the instant Union troops secured a Confederate state. Tennessee, the first to organize under Lincoln's 10 percent plan, had operated under an ostensibly civil government (with tight military supervision) since 1862. Johnson had run the state as its wartime governor until 1864, then a few months later, a state convention claimed constituent powers and issued amendments to the state constitution to abolish slavery and repudiate secession. W. G. "Parson" Brownlow was elected governor. Brownlow, whom the Confederacy had jailed when he refused to sign a pledge to the CSA, had shared prison cells with Baptist ministers who had committed "treason" against the Confederacy, one of them for shouting "Huzzah!" when Union troops came into his town.

Parson Brownlow was the epitome of what a "good Southerner" should have been by the Yankee way of thinking. Yet his presence in the governor's mansion did not mollify Radical Republicans or convince them to treat newly elected Southern representatives to Congress with respect when they arrived to take their seats in 1864. After the election that year, Radicals unceremoniously refused to admit Southern congressmen at all, although the Senate allowed the senators from Tennessee (including Andrew Johnson) to be seated. But after 1865 neither the House nor the Senate allowed any Tennessee representatives (or those from any other former Rebel state) to take their seats, denying Southerners any constitutional representation. West Virginia, which had formed in 1862 after seceding from Virginia, was recognized only reluctantly.

Southerners were doing themselves no favors. They enthusiastically and foolishly elected numerous former Confederates to political office. Georgia's legislature chose Alexander H. Stephens, the Confederacy's vice president, as one of its U.S. senators; James Orr, South Carolina's governor, had been a senator in the CSA; General Benjamin Humphreys was elected governor of Mississippi. Large majorities of the reconstituted state legislatures were ex-Confederates officeholders or military officers.

These actions outraged the Radicals, who threatened to turn parts of the South into a "frog pond." In 1865–66, though, the Radicals were a disparate group with insufficient votes to enact their threats. Most Radicals shared the view that by virtue of their rebellion, Southerners had taken themselves out from under the protection of the Constitution. The South, the Radicals argued, was a "conquered province" (Sumner said they had engaged in "state suicide"). For nearly a year Johnson's counterposition prevailed. Johnson hoped the hastily formed Unionist governments would be recognized and that Southern states following their lead would return to normalcy in due course. The reality was, however, that the vengeful congressional Radicals, led by Charles Sumner and Thaddeus Stevens—"first and foremost, good haters," as Paul Johnson observed—not only saw the former Confederacy as a festering bed of traitorous vermin to be decontaminated or extinguished, but also viewed the current occupant of the White House as completely illegitimate. A Democrat, Johnson had no leverage at all with the Republicans (least of all the Radical wing); a Southerner, he had no goodwill upon which to draw from either section, each for its own reasons eyeing him with suspicion. His only hope lay in attempting to reorganize the South quickly, in the Congressional recess, then proclaim it "done" before the lawmakers could return. That asked far too much of the South, where the majority of the population was in no mood to rush into a confession of sin. It also placed the unfortunate Johnson athwart a political structure that, for success, required skills far beyond any he possessed.

Understanding the agenda of the Radical Republicans is critical. They wanted not only to incapacitate the South as a region, but also to emasculate the Democratic Party, permanently ensuring its minority status. Indeed, many Radicals hoped the Democrats would die off entirely, like the Federalists had done decades earlier. There were two pawns in the struggle that emerged. One was the freedmen, whose fate deeply concerned many idealistic reformers in the Republican Party. At the same time, some Radicals cared not a whit about blacks, except insofar as they represented a mass bloc of voters guaranteed to loyally follow the party of emancipation. It was a view that defined people as groups and voting blocs, not individuals. In this way, first the Republicans and then seventy years later the Democrats would make a mockery of the principles of *individual* liberty for which Washington, Jefferson, Hamilton, and Lincoln had fought.

A second group of pawns were the majority of white Southerners, who felt no less manipulated by the parties. Many of them may have wished charity from the victorious Union, but had no intention of giving any in return, especially to the freedmen. Most had supported the Confederacy and, therefore, in the strictest sense were traitors. Lincoln's merciful policy, however, had insisted they be viewed as fellow citizens after they swore their loyalty to the Union. Swearing an oath did not change a lifetime of habits and prejudices, however. Few self-respecting Southerners could side with the Republicans, and thus they shut out their political options as surely as the freedmen had closed theirs. They marched in lockstep with the Southern Democrats, who were increasingly dominated by the most radical ex-Confederates.

By the time the Thirty-ninth Congress met, the Radicals had decided that no further cooperation with Johnson was possible. In December 1865, they enlisted six senators and nine representatives to investigate conditions in the South. Known as the Joint Committee on Reconstruction, this group was headed by Stevens and included congressmen John A. Bingham of Ohio, Roscoe Conkling of New York, and senators W. P. Fessenden of Maine and Reverdy Johnson of Maryland. Only three Democrats were on the committee, which planned its report for June 1866.

Meanwhile, Southern states' readmittance constitutions outraged the Radicals. South Carolina, for example, rather than declaring the ordinances of secession null and void, merely repealed them, essentially acting as though they had been legitimate when issued. In addition, rather than abolish slavery in the state constitution, the former Confederates merely noted that slavery had already been abolished by the United States government, and Texas and Mississippi refused to ratify the Thirteenth Amendment. In short, the South Carolinians were neither chastened nor remorseful. Radicals decided to take action—and to remove Johnson as an obstacle.

Four Postwar Questions

Four issues emerged in the postbellum struggle over Reconstruction: (1) What economic compensation, if any, would be given to the freedmen? (2) What would their political status be? (3) To what extent would federal laws governing either economics or politics in the South be enforced and prosecuted? And (4) Who would determine the pace and priorities of the process—the president or Congress? Disagreement existed as to which of these four issues should take priority. Although Thaddeus Stevens cautioned, "If we do not furnish [the freedmen] with homesteads, we had better left them in bondage." Frederick Douglass warned that it was the ballot that was the critical element. "Slavery is not abolished," he noted, "until the black man has the ballot."[22]

The first issue—that of economic compensation—was thoroughly intertwined with the question of amnesty for Confederates. Any widespread land distribution had to come from the former Confederates, yet to confiscate their property violated the Constitution *if,* after they had pledged their allegiance to the United States, they were once again declared citizens. Few, if any, freedmen thought equality meant owning a plantation, but virtually all of them thought it entitled them to the right, as Lincoln said, to eat the bread of their own hand. Some thought land would accompany Union occupation and emancipation. A caravan of freed blacks followed Sherman's army through Georgia, and by the time he reached South Carolina, he actually sought to institute such a forty-acres-and-a-mule program with his Special Field Order No. 15. This set aside South Carolina's Sea Islands for freedmen, giving each family forty acres and lending each an army mule. More than forty thousand freedmen settled on "Sherman Land," but the policy was ad hoc, and not approved by Lincoln, who had the prospect of Reconstruction to consider.

Breaking up the plantations followed natural rights principles of recompense when someone profited from stolen property. As a Virginia freedman explained, "We has a right to the land where we are located . . . didn't we clear the land, and raise the crops?"[23] But a Republic did not confiscate property without due process, and the Constitution explicitly prohibited ex post facto laws. For the government to have proceeded to legally confiscate slave owners' property, it would have had to charge slave owners with a crime—but what crime? Slavery had been legal and, indeed, Lincoln had been only a step away from a constitutional amendment giving it specific constitutional sanction. To have retroactively defined slaveholding as a crime, for which property confiscation was perhaps just punishment, would have opened a legal door to bedlam and, ultimately, terror. What would prevent any majority in the future from defining an action in the past as a crime for which some appropriate punishment was then needed? And

had Southern land been handed over to the freedmen, no doubt future generations of white descendants of the plantations would have concocted their own
proposals for reparations.

One option was to label all Confederates traitors, and *then* grant them conditional amnesty, based (in addition to the other requirements for regaining their
citizenship status) on a partial proportional penalty of land to each slave owned in
1861. In 1865, however, the reality was that even the towering genius of Lincoln
did not foresee the legal implications of failing to brand the Southerners traitors.
Nor was there any political support—except among the vengeful Sumner-
Stevens cabal—for such a policy. Sometimes there is no good solution to human
problems. Certainly "reparations" merely reapplies ex post facto reasoning to
modern Americans, the vast majority of whose ancestors did not own slaves and
many of whom arrived in the country long after the Civil War.

Without a land policy, many freedmen soon fell into a series of contractual
labor relationships with former owners (though often not their own) known as
sharecropping. Under the sharecropping system—in which two thirds of all
Southern sharecroppers were white—black and white laborers entered into
agreements with white plantation owners who possessed land and farm implements, but lacked workers. Typical contracts gave the landowner 50 percent of
the crop and the laborers 50 percent, although drafting a typical sharecropper
contract proved daunting. Each contract was individually negotiated, including
length, share, the nature of supervision, and so on. In some cases, "share" tenants
provided their own tools, seed, and everything except the land, whereas in others,
some freedmen worked purely as wage laborers.

Sharecropping has received rough treatment from historians, but less so from
economists for a number of reasons. First, given the strengths and weaknesses of
the former slave owners and freedmen, it represented a logical market solution,
providing land and capital for laborers who lacked both, and a labor system for
landowners without laborers. Second, the contracts were far more flexible and
competitive than once was thought. They were not lifetime agreements, but temporary arrangements. Third, both parties had to work together to adjust to
weather and market changes. Finally, given the lack of education among the
freedmen, sharecropping minimized transaction costs while at the same time extended new levels of freedom and responsibility to the ex-slaves.[24]

Still, criticisms of sharecropping are warranted because it suffered from
many deficiencies. Neither landowner nor laborer had an incentive to significantly upgrade land or implements. Rather, both had an incentive to farm the
land into barrenness or to refrain from engaging in technological or management
innovations that would improve productivity. Opportunities to gouge the sharecroppers (black and white) also abounded. In some regions, freedmen found it
difficult to move about to take advantage of better contract terms. Data on the
movement of sharecroppers suggests, however, that their movements correlated
strongly with higher-paying contracts, so the implication is that sharecroppers

knew where there were better conditions, and therefore monopoly situations occurred less frequently than some economic historians claimed.[25]

On average, though, sharecropping proved an excellent temporary market mechanism. Many freedmen did not *stay* in that situation, but moved on. Blacks acquired property and wealth more rapidly than whites (a somewhat misleading statistic, in that they began with nothing), and across the South they owned perhaps 9 percent of all land by 1880. In certain pockets, however, they achieved ownership much more slowly (in Georgia blacks only owned 2 percent of the acreage in the state by 1880) and in others, more rapidly.[26] Robert Kenzer's study of North Carolina showed that in five counties black ownership of town lots rose from 11 percent in 1875 to almost 19 percent by 1890, despite legal codes and racism.[27] Black income levels also grew more rapidly than white levels (again, in part because they began with virtually no income as it is technically defined).

It bears repeating: racism and discrimination certainly existed and unquestionably took an economic and human toll on the freedmen. But to ignore their hard-won genuine gains, or to minimize them as mere exceptions, trivializes their contributions and achievements. Moreover, it does a disservice to the freedmen to automatically view them as laborers instead of potential entrepreneurs. Historians have tended to bury stories of black entrepreneurship after the Civil War. Yet many former slaves contributed important inventions and founded useful profitable companies in the postbellum period. Alabamian Nate Shaw, an illiterate tenant farmer, moved from farm to farm, expanding his share of the crop and renting out his mules to haul lumber or do other odd jobs. Despite competition from an influx of poor whites, struggles with unscrupulous landlords who tried to defraud him of his crops, and merchants reluctant to extend him credit, Shaw persevered until he became self-sufficient and headed the Sharecroppers Union, where as an older man he led protests against land seizures by sheriffs' deputies in the 1930s.[28]

Fellow Alabamian Andrew Jackson Beard, born a slave in Jefferson County, found it too expensive to haul apples from his farm to Montgomery, whereupon he quit farming and constructed a flour mill in Hardwicks, Alabama. Experimenting with plow designs, he patented a plow in 1881, sold the patent three years later for four thousand dollars—a large sum at the time—and returned to inventing. By the 1890s, he had accumulated thirty thousand dollars and entered the real estate market, although he continued to invent, creating a rotary steam engine in 1892. He had worked previously on railroads, and he knew the dangers of joining railroad cars together—a process done entirely by hand, in which a worker would place a large metal pin in the coupling devices at exactly the right instant. Misjudgment cost railroaders their hands and fingers, and Beard himself suffered the loss of a leg crushed in a coupler accident. As a solution, in 1897 Beard came up with the famous Jenny coupler, reverse metal "hands" that fold backward on contact, then latch like hands shaking. Variants of the Jenny remain in use on railroads today, and over the years Beard's invention has saved untold thousands of railroad employees from severe personal injury.[29]

The credit records for Virginia of R. G. Dun and Co., for example, reveal that of the 1,000 enterprises about which the company kept information between 1865 and 1879, more than 220 were black owned and operated.[30] Although black businesses were usually located in areas of town with higher black populations, the advertising indicates that African American entrepreneurs appealed to white customers too. Almost 80 percent of the firms were single-owner operations, and these entrepreneurs quickly gained experience in the workplace. After 1869 the ratio of new to failed firms dropped, and even some of those that closed did so because the proprietor had died. In fact, the Virginia records showed virtually no difference in failure rates between black merchants and white merchants from 1870 to 1875, despite the presence of racism and prejudice.[31]

Attitudes of freedmen toward former masters spanned the spectrum. Some former slaves actually expressed anger at Union troops for killing and maiming their "young massas." One South Carolina slave, seeing one of the master's four sons return home from battle, "He jaw split and he teeth all shine through the cheek," was "so mad I could have kilt all de Yankees." Other slaves secretly celebrated when tragic news came to the plantation's mistress: "It made us glad to see dem cry," said one slave. "Dey made us cry so much." News that a local leader of slave patrols had been killed touched off joyous shouting in slave quarters.[32] On occasion, wartime hardships turned once-lenient masters and mistresses into monsters: one mistress, hearing of her son's death, whipped the slaves until she collapsed of exhaustion. A Virginia slave observed that treatment of blacks grew harsher as the Yankee armies came closer.

Facing blacks now as tenants and sharecroppers, more than a few whites viewed their former chattel with suspicion: "The tenants act pretty well towards us," wrote a Virginia woman, "but that doesn't prevent our being pretty certain of their intention to stampede when they get a good chance. . . . They are nothing but an ungrateful, discontented lot & I don't care how soon I get rid of mine."[33] Another owner in Texas—a "pretty good boss" as slaveowners went—made a huge mistake when informing his slaves of their emancipation, "You can jes' work on if you want to, and I'll treat you jes' like I always did." All but one family, "like birds . . . jes' flew."[34]

The Freedmen's Bureau attempted to serve as a clearinghouse for economic and family information, but its technology was too primitive and the task too Herculean. Somewhat more successful were the efforts by Northern teachers, missionaries, and administrators to assist slaves in military and contraband camps by writing letters for freedmen trying to reach relatives. After black newspapers were established in the 1870s, advertisements frequently sought information on family members separated during slavery.

The influence of black educators like Booker T. Washington was still more than a decade away. Washington, the son of a slave, had just started his teaching career in 1875, as Reconstruction wound down. Founding the Tuskegee Institute, Washington hired faculty, established productive relationships with local whites, raised money, recruited students, and set about to teach printing, carpentry, botany, cabinetmaking, farming, cooking, and other skills that would assist freedmen and their children in gaining employment quickly. He obtained benefactions from Andrew Carnegie, John D. Rockefeller, and George Eastman, and suffered insults in order to advance his view of black success. Without ignoring racial discrimination and hatred, Washington nevertheless focused on encouraging African Americans to acquire property, get education, and to live with impeccable character. In time, he believed, relations would improve. At the Atlanta Cotton States and International Exposition in September 1895, Washington delivered a speech later noted for its ambiguity and elasticity. He seemed to accept the separate-but-equal Jim Crow doctrine of the day; yet he reminded whites that blacks were not going away, and that ultimately they had to work together.[35]

Freedmen and Politics in the South

The second major question involving the freedmen—their political status—was almost immediately put to the test when, at the end of the war, blacks began to move about the South freely for the first time. This churning of human movement struck every observer, including Northern army officers who witnessed train depots and country roads crammed with people. Hungry, sick, and barely clad freedmen clogged the roads between Vicksburg and Jackson. More than 125,000 slaves had been removed to Texas when the war started, and by late 1865 they were heading home up the San Antonio Road to North Carolina and Georgia. Although much of the wandering reflected a desire to express the freedom of movement suddenly given to the former slaves, more of the travel had the purpose of searching for family members or better work.

Regardless of the motivation, any movement by free blacks terrified whites and led to the first real clash between the federal and state governments over political rights in Reconstruction policies. As the new Southern governments, created by Johnson's generous Reconstruction policies, started to function, they passed laws designed to place restraints on blacks in negotiating contracts, travel, and weapons and property ownership. Mississippi, after what Governor B. G. Humphreys called "six months of [the] administration of this black incubus," passed the South's first black codes in January 1866.[36] The legislation required annual employment contracts, prohibited movement between counties without permission, and allowed local officials to arrest any black youth on charges of vagrancy if he did not appear to have a job.

The Mississippi black code was not entirely punitive. It recognized black marriages (something not done in slavery), legitimized the Negro's right to sue in civil court, confirmed his right to property, and required that all contracts with freedmen of periods longer than a month be in writing. Some of the "guarantees" were meaningless. To freedmen, most of whom were illiterate and had never had any contact with the legal system or the courts, the right to sue was hollow. The provisions that stirred up the most revulsion among blacks, and which provoked the North to start down the road of congressional Reconstruction, involved the vagrancy provisions. Vagrants were to be fined up to a hundred dollars and imprisoned.[37] Worse, if a freedman was unable to pay the fine, he could be hired out as an "apprentice" until his fine and court costs were covered.

Another set of laws, ingeniously devised by individual states, placed huge license fees on recruiters who came in from other states to lure freedmen to work for better wages. The only purpose of the statutes was to limit blacks' freedom of movement and infringe upon their free right to contract. White state governments also received support from plumbers, barbers' unions, and medical groups—all dominated by whites—who established a variety of tests to keep blacks out of their ranks. The U.S. Supreme Court, in the so-called Slaughterhouse Cases, finally ruled that if economic regulations did not explicitly discriminate, they were valid, and not until 1905, with the decision in the case of *Lochner v. New York*, did the Court reverse itself and bar certain types of discriminatory state, union, guild, and business regulation. It was a hollow victory for the freedmen, thirty years too late to do them any good.[38]

Black codes alone, however—even without the supporting labor regulations—sufficiently alarmed Northerners, threatening no less than a backdoor reenslavement of black men, and General O. O. Howard ordered his Freedmen's Bureau to disregard the state laws. Northern newspapers editorialized against the codes, but their complaints did not stop South Carolina and Louisiana from enacting similar, though milder, versions of the black codes, and the towns of Opelousas and Franklin passed still more stringent measures. Florida, however, topped them all. By 1866, Florida's population was nearly half black, and its white legislature teetered on the brink of paranoia. Florida laws required the death penalty for *burglary,* insurrection (except when the insurrection was by ex-Confederates!), and, of course, rape of (only) white women. Freedmen were allowed to have schools—but not at state expense. Blacks were denied the right to bear arms or assemble after dark, clearly violating the provisions of the United States Constitution. At the other end of the spectrum were the lenient codes of Tennessee and Virginia. But the black codes created a major backlash in the North. Some states repealed their black codes, but it was too late. By then, congressional Radicals were arguing that the codes were further evidence the South would never reform itself.

Associated with the imposition of the black codes was the birth and growth of the Ku Klux Klan. A Pulaski, Tennessee, white-supremacy group founded in 1866, the Klan held a regional meeting a year later in Nashville, where former Confederate General Nathan Bedford Forrest became its first Grand Wizard. Wearing white sheets and hoods—not only to conceal their identities, but, they thought, to play on the "superstitious" nature of blacks—Klansmen spread a reign of terror across the South, lynching blacks and any whites who might support them. The Klan also expressed its hatred of Catholics, Jews, and immigrants, often leaving its calling card—a burning cross—at a terror scene. Eventually the Klan spread nationally through the establishment of "klaverns" (local organizations), but it had its greatest nineteenth-century influence in Tennessee, North Carolina, Georgia, Alabama, and Mississippi. Other copycat white-supremacy groups followed: the White Brotherhood, the Men of Justice, the Constitutional Union Guards, and the Knights of the White Camelia. Mayhem and violence spread. Albion Tourgee, a Northern carpetbagger who became a North Carolina judge, "counted twelve murders, nine rapes, fourteen cases of arson, and over seven hundred beatings in his political district alone."[39] Tourgee's novel, *A Fool's Errand*, exposed in fiction some of the harsh realities of Klan terror in the South.

One of the bloodiest incidents occurred in 1873 at the Colfax, Louisiana, courthouse, where a white mob attacked armed blacks, killing more than one hundred and mutilating their bodies. The federal government, after indicting ninety-eight whites, convicted only three, and even those convictions were later thrown out by the Supreme Court in the *Cruikshank* decision, which said that the Reconstruction amendments only applied to governments, not the actions of individuals. Not only had the federal government failed to give the freedmen land, but it also failed to facilitate their self-defense.

If any agency could have addressed some of the needs of the freedmen, it was the Freedmen's Bureau. Yet the history of the bureau shows it was not capable of dealing with the likes of the Ku Klux Klan or the black codes. Nevertheless, the Freedmen's Bureau provides an object lesson in the limits of both good intentions and government power.

O. O. Howard and the Freedmen's Bureau

In March 1865, Congress created the Freedmen's Bureau to help former slaves in their transition to freedom. Run by General Oliver Otis "O. O." Howard, the bureau lay for months at the center of a struggle between the Treasury and War departments over which would handle the freedmen after the war. Stanton's War Department won, as it would ultimately have to enforce any edicts, and Stanton trusted Howard as an honest and effective leader.[40] Although an executive branch agency, the Freedmen's Bureau was viewed by Congress as a wedge with which it could gain control of Reconstruction.

O. O. Howard was hardly physically intimidating. Possessing a slight build, "fidgety gestures and a shrill voice," the general was nonetheless a morally imposing figure, "proud that he was known in the nation as the 'Christian Soldier'."[41] A devout believer who insisted that his subordinates attend prayer meetings and enforced temperance among his troops, he had long opposed slavery, though he did not have the abolitionist credentials of his brother, Rowland. O.O. had studied at West Point where, before the war, criticism of slavery was prohibited. His studies, however, marked him for success. He graduated fourth, behind Robert E. Lee's son, Custis. After Fort Sumter, Howard served in several field commands in the East, then in occupation forces; he reveled in giving Christian inspirational talks to the freedmen's children at the schools established in the Sea Islands.

Howard asked the central question facing the government: "What shall we do with the Negro?" He answered by emphasizing education and Christianity.

The bureau would unleash "a great commission of compassionate Americans—teachers, ministers, farmers, superintendents—who would . . . aid and elevate the freedmen."[42]

Biblical charity, however, always came with strict stipulations: "He who will not work shall not eat," for example, and the numerous provisions in Proverbs against sloth. Howard did not see that the do-gooder instinct would unleash a monster that would spread in three separate directions. First, although the bureau definitely aided the freedmen—more than any other agency or group—it inevitably fostered dependence on government. Second, social work of this type often, if not always, tends to puff up the provider, whose role as the source of blessings inflates his own sense of worth, not to mention ego. It is not surprising, therefore, that Northerners who came South with good intentions ended up branded as "carpetbaggers," seen only as leeches sucking off Southern vitality. Third, the bureau itself, like all government institutions, was bound to be corrupted by the flow of money and the religious zeal of the participants. When nothing short of heaven on earth is at stake, the disappearance or unauthorized use of funds and equipment cannot stand in the way of progress.

As an executive office carrying out policies philosophically more in tune with those of the congressional Radicals, the Freedmen's Bureau was itself bound to become a source of controversy. For example, Howard supported key legislation during presidential Reconstruction that brought the forty-acres-and-a-mule dispute to a head. A March 3, 1865, act of Congress gave commissioners of the bureau authority to "select and set apart such confiscated and abandoned lands and property as may be deemed necessary for the immediate use of the Refugees." Howard then affixed his own Circular Order No. 13 in July saying that the Amnesty Proclamation "will not be understood to extend to the surrender of abandoned or confiscated property."[43] This amounted to nothing less than Howard's attempting to hijack Johnson's policy to meet his own (Radical) ends, and Johnson rebuked him. Undeterred, Howard instituted quiet yet forceful opposition to Johnson's policies, constituting an act of insubordination on behalf of blacks no different from Sherman's defiance of Lincoln.

With the rescinding of Circular Order No. 13, any hope for a reasonably quick march toward self-sufficiency for the freedmen vanished. Most turned their expectations from land ownership to wage labor. "The Yankees preach nothing but cotton, cotton," complained a Sea Islands freedman.[44] It was equally unrealistic, however, to expect former slaves, who had worked for nothing all their lives, to suddenly display as a group the traits of capitalist entrepreneurs who had scrimped, saved, and suffered in their own way to accumulate wealth. Entrepreneurship and capital-formation skills did not come to any group instantly or easily. The bureau did what it could, attempting to police the work contracts, but often was viewed as little more than the "planter's guards, and nothing else."[45]

Nor was the bureau an early form of Great Society welfarism. Certainly it increased the size and scope of federal government operations—for example, it supervised more than three thousand schools serving 150,000 Southern students, demanding a massive amount of oversight. And without argument the bureau wasted money and in some cases encouraged indolence. Yet in the short term, the Freedmen's Bureau was indispensable. More than 90 percent of students in Reconstruction schools were black, and they were provided with education they would never have received in elite Southern private schools. Keeping them in school, however, proved difficult. One estimate of black student attendance between 1865 and 1870 was 5 percent, and for whites it was only 20 percent of the enrollment. Reformers had an answer for that too, pushing, as they did in the North, for mandatory attendance laws, again expanding the scope of the government power.

The most enduring contribution of the Freedman's Bureau was its commitment to African Americans' self-sufficiency, if not equality, and Southerners knew it. "The black ball is in motion," lamented Mary Chestnut, and once rolling, racist whites could only slow it down, not stop it.[46] Some whites hoped that by teaching blacks to support themselves, white Southerners would quickly return to their "rightful" place atop the social lader. Johnson's Amnesty Proclamation seemed to confirm black fears when former Confederates learned that when their citizenship rights were restored, their confiscated property would be returned as well. Or, in language plain to the freedmen, no plantations would be broken up for forty acres and a mule.

Left-wing historians often leap to make the land issue solely about race. Two other important considerations, however, guided Johnson as he came to his amnesty (sans confiscation) decision. First, simply put, there were more whites than blacks in the South. At minimum, there were two potential white troublemakers for every disgruntled black. In meting out justice, however unfair, sheer numbers are always a calculation. Second, whites were voters (or in the South, potential voters) whereas blacks were not (at least, realistically, not in large numbers unless escorted by troops). No policy could survive long if Southern whites and those Northerners who feared black social equality formed a political alliance to oust Johnson and the Radicals, even if somehow they formed an unlikely united front. These were not minor considerations. To accuse Johnson of abandoning the Negro, though in essence true, nevertheless obscures the political realities confronting him. Moreover, Johnson's own preferences were to elevate poor whites, not create black competitors for them.

The Freedman's Bureau provided a qualified answer to the third Reconstruction question. The South, in an extremely limited way, could be made to comply with some of the Northern Reconstruction agenda through clear direction and, above all, heavy application of force. But in the broadest sense of racial harmony, genuine political equality, and diffuse economic growth, Reconstruction could not change either human nature or historical prejudices. At any rate, the conflict between Johnson and Howard spotlighted the last Reconstruction question: who would direct Reconstruction for the remainder of its life, the legislative or the executive branch?

A War on Four Fronts

Congress, disenchanted with Johnson's slow pace, had already started to gain control of the direction of Reconstruction. Four concurrent conflicts took place from late 1865 to 1876, and each had the potential to dramatically reshape American life.

The first battle pitted Congress against the presidency for policy dominance. Laments about Lincoln's untimely death obscure the fact that had the great man lived, it would have made little difference to Radicals in Congress who, although they may have despised the Tennessee tailor, were hardly cowed by Lincoln. A second clash involved Northerners seeking to cement their commercial and political superiority over the South into a permanent hierarchy. Third, the Republican Party intended to emasculate—if not destroy—the opposition Democratic Party. And fourth, a tension between whites and blacks over social, political, and economic equality had only started to play out in both sections, but mostly below the Mason-Dixon Line.

In this last dimension, the Radicals had, for the most part, been open and straightforward in their goals. They had argued for abolition from the beginning of the war, and they were, "if anything, somewhat *less* opportunistic in their purposes and a little *more* candid in their public utterances than the average American politician."[47] George W. Julian of Indiana, for example, lectured fellow Republicans, saying, "The real trouble is that *we hate the negro*. It is not his ignorance that offends us, but his color. . . . [Let] one rule be adopted for white and black [alike]."[48] Other Radicals warned Northerners that the rights of black and white laborers were synonymous, and, above all, they maintained a fever pitch of moral frenzy begun during the war. "*Absolute right* must prevail," said a Chicago Radical, while editor E. L. Godkin predicted that accepting the doctrine that the United States was subject to only "white man's government" would make the name of American democracy a "hissing and a byword" among the people of the earth.[49] Sentiments such as these refute the notion that the egalitarianism of Radical Reconstruction was merely a facade for Northern economic dominance.

As the new Congress considered Johnson's Reconstruction program, it became increasingly clear to Radicals that although blacks in the South could not vote, they nevertheless counted 100 percent (instead of 60 percent) toward representation in the House, giving the Southern Democrats even *more* seats in the House of Representatives than they had had before the war. As this incredible reality sank in, the Republican-dominated Congress reacted by refusing to seat the representatives of any of the Southern governments. "I am not very anxious," wrote Thaddeus Stevens in a moment of great candor, "to see [Southern] votes cast along with others to control the next election."[50] This played a crucial role in the shaping of the subsequent Fourteenth Amendment, in which the Radicals proportionately reduced representation in the House to any state denying voting rights to the freedmen.

Johnson and his Northern Democratic allies, along with the leaders of the reconstructed (neo-Confederate) governments, accepted at the outset that blacks were incapable of exercising citizenship rights. The chasm "between the two races in physical, mental, and moral characteristics," Johnson wrote in his third annual message to Congress, "will prevent an amalgamation or fusion of them together in one homogeneous mass." Blacks were "inferior," and if they gained political power, it would result in "tyranny such as this continent has never yet witnessed."[51] In February 1866, Johnson won his last victory over Congress when he vetoed an extension of the Freedmen's Bureau on the grounds that until the eleven Southern states were restored to the Union, Congress had no authority to pass such legislation. Congress sustained his veto, but the Radicals stepped up their campaign against him. Sumner described Johnson as an "insolent, drunken brute," and Stevens called him "an alien enemy of a foreign state."[52] Here was Johnson, who seldom drank, and whose loyalty to the Union was such that he was the only senator from a secessionist state to stay in office during the war, accused of drunkenness and treason.

Arrayed against Johnson and his dwindling alliance, the Radicals saw their influence grow. Thaddeus Stevens best expressed their position when he rejected the notion held by Southerners that the government of the United States was a "white man's government." "This is man's Government; the Government of all men alike," he countered.[53] He therefore advocated full political equality, though not social equality, calling it a "matter of taste" as to whether people shared their seats at their dinner table with blacks.

Between the Radicals on one side and the former Confederates on the other stood the so-called moderates. Moderates hated the black codes and wanted Republican dominance of the South, but they rejected full political equality for blacks. They agreed with the Radicals, though, that something had to be done about the laws passed by the restored—yet still rebellious—governments in the South, and together the two groups passed the Civil Rights Act of 1866, defining blacks as U.S. citizens and promising them "full and equal benefit of all laws and proceedings for the security of person and property, as is enjoyed by white citizens."[54] This law made it a federal crime to deprive someone of his civil rights and, in conjunction with a new Freedmen's Bureau law, established army tribunals to enforce civil rights cases.

Johnson promptly vetoed the bill, citing a number of objections. He disliked the absence of a period of "adjustment" to citizenship that normally occurred with alien immigrants. Social discrimination in areas such as interracial marriage, he thought, also was necessary. His main concerns, though, were over upsetting the balance of power between states and the federal government. Johnson argued that the Civil Rights Act violated the Tenth Amendment. Congress narrowly passed the Civil Rights Act over his veto, thanks to the illness of one pro-Johnson voter who stayed home and the defection of a New York Democrat.[55] Aside from Gideon Welles, all of Johnson's own cabinet opposed him.

It was increasingly clear that Andrew Johnson would not support any law that in any way significantly improved the status of African Americans. During the debate over the Fourteenth Amendment, Johnson's views would become even more transparent.

Aware that Southerners would immediately bring a court challenge to the Civil Rights Act, Republican legislators moved to make it permanent through the Fourteenth Amendment, stating, "All persons born or naturalized in the United States, and subject to the jurisdiction thereof, are citizens of the United States and the State wherein they reside." This made citizenship *national* rather than subject to state authority, marking a sea change in the understanding of the source of rights in the United States. No state could "abridge the privileges or immunities of citizens of the United States" or "deprive any person of life, liberty, or property without due process of law." Nor could any state "deny to any person within its jurisdiction the equal protection of the laws."

Subsequently, all state legislation regarding infringements on the Bill of Rights would be subjected to federal review. It was a sweeping accomplishment in defining the rights of all American citizens as equal. Some, however, were more equal than others: while granting citizenship to the freedmen, the Fourteenth Amendment simultaneously denied citizenship to high Confederate officeholders.

Meanwhile, from March to June 1866, the Joint Committee on Reconstruction held its hearings, substantially biased against the South. Calling seventy-seven Northerners living in the South, fifty-seven Southerners, and a handful of freedmen, the committee listened to hours of critical testimony, quickly dismissing hostile witnesses. Northern newspapers carried the testimony, which convinced Northern voters of Southern mistreatment of blacks. When the committee delivered its report, it convinced most objective observers that despite the lopsided way in which the committee gathered evidence, serious abuses of the freedmen continued. Worse, the committee concluded that a "state of rebellion" still existed in the South, and recommended Confederate states be denied representation in the Congress. With this report, Congress reasserted its authority over that of the executive to direct Reconstruction. Johnson remained set in his objections that no ratification process for the Fourteenth Amendment could occur until the Southern states were reinstated. He encouraged the Southern governments to reject the amendment, which they did: only Tennessee ratified it. Otherwise, the South held out for the midterm 1866 elections, which it hoped would oust the hated Radicals.

Johnson's response to the Fourteenth Amendment, combined with a maladroit campaign tour in late August, helped swing the election further to the Radicals. His obstinacy confirmed his Southern loyalties in the minds of many Northerners, and late summer race riots in New Orleans and Memphis seemed to expose the the failure of the president's program. In the fall campaign Radicals linked support of the reconstructed governments to the treason of the hated wartime Copperheads. Voters agreed, and sent a two-thirds Republican majority to each house, with more Radicals than ever filling their number. Congress had finally gained ascendancy over Reconstruction policy.

With Johnson essentially neutered, Congress proceeded to act on the joint committee's recommendations by passing the Military Reconstruction Act. Under this law governments formed under presidential Reconstruction were swept away as illegitimate, and instead, the South was divided into five military districts, each commanded by a loyal Republican general. Johnson vetoed the act of March 2, 1867, and Congress overrode his veto. Under the First Reconstruction Act (its very title implying that Johnson had not presided over any legitimate reconstruction), Southern states now had to hold new constitutional conventions. Instead of the 10 percent rule that guided the earlier conventions, these new conventions were to be selected by universal manhood suffrage. Readmission to the Union required that the new state constitutions recognize the Fourteenth Amendment and guarantee blacks the right to vote. Congress would sit as the sole judge of whether a state had complied.

The military commanders, à la the Fourteenth Amendment, prohibited high Confederate officeholders from voting or holding office, and had authority to determine what constituted a legal election. The process ensured that more blacks voted and fewer whites did. Commanders registered voters in large numbers—703,000 blacks and 627,000 whites—and in five states blacks were the majority of all voters. Military tribunals investigated a person's loyalty, and some estimates suggest as many as half a million whites were disqualified.

Thus emerged the hated triumvirate of scalawags, carpetbaggers, and black Republicans to put the Radical Southern governments in power. Scalawags, or Southerners who chose to ally with the Republicans, acted out of a variety of motivations. (The term "scalawag" was a folk expression for "mean, lousy cattle.") Many scalawags were prewar Whigs never comfortable within the Democratic Party. Some, such as Confederate General James Longstreet, saw the Republicans as the only hope for Southerners to regain control of their states. Others included Joe Brown, the governor of Georgia (who switched parties only temporarily for financial gain), and the "Grey Ghost," Virginia Colonel John Singleton Mosby. The term "carpetbaggers" referred to Northerners who came south to impose their views on Dixie. They traveled with their suitcases, or carpetbags, and were scorned by Southerners as do-gooders. Some, if not most, were well-intentioned teachers, missionaries, doctors, and administrators who all flocked to the South to assist both freedmen and the devastated white communities. But more than a few were arrogant and impulsive, caring little for the traditions they crushed or the delicate social tensions that remained. The third leg of the Reconstruction tripod, the black Republicans, were also hated by all but a few progressive Southerners. At best, Southerners saw free blacks as pawns of the Republicans and at worst, a threat to their social order.

Nevertheless, for the first time, under these Reconstruction governments, African Americans won seats in the U.S. government. Black Reconstruction, as

Southerners called it, put a number of freedmen in positions of power. Between 1869 and 1901, there were two black U.S. senators and sixteen congressmen elected. Like many of his colleagues, Blanche Kelso Bruce (1841–98), the U.S. senator from Mississippi, was highly qualified. Born into slavery in Virginia, Bruce was tutored by his master's son and worked as a printer's apprentice. When the Civil War started, he escaped north, and after the Union Army rejected his attempt to enlist, he taught school, attended Oberlin College, and worked as a steamboat porter. After the war Bruce moved to Mississippi, where he became a prosperous landowner and served in low-level elected offices. Serving as sheriff of Bolivar County, he gained the favor of the Republicans at Jackson, and after a few high-profile appointments, was elected to the Senate by the Mississippi legislature in 1874. Bruce fought against the Chinese Exclusion Act, spoke in favor of Indian rights, and became the first African American to chair a Senate committee. Once the Redeemer Democrats regained power, they ousted him, but Bruce had so impressed the national Republicans that he received a handful of votes for vice president in 1880.[56]

Another black U.S. senator, Hiram Revels, was a free man in North Carolina before attending school in the North. Ordained a minister by the African Methodist Church, Revels headed congregations in Ohio, Indiana, Illinois, Tennessee, Kentucky, Missouri, and Kansas before moving to Maryland. After April 1861 he worked for the Union cause in Maryland by organizing black regiments and then recruited African Americans to serve in Missouri. Like Bruce, he settled in Mississippi after the war and held local alderman positions, then state senator positions in Adams County before the Mississippi legislature named him to fill Jefferson Davis's seat. His appointment actually preceded Bruce's, though it was much shorter, lasting only until the end of 1871, when he returned to assume the presidency of Alcorn College, Mississippi's first black university.

Bruce, Revels, and other African Americans elected during Black Reconstruction, regardless of their qualifications, only stayed in office by the good graces of the Republican governments. More precisely, they could only hold office as long as the military allowed them to. The presence of black elected officials exaggerated the perception that the Radical governments ruled only through force. Increasingly, there was also a real awareness that some were horribly corrupt. Their legislatures issued bonds for any project, no matter how financially unstable. Virtually all the governors accepted bribes to grant charters or franchises: Governor Henry Warmoth in Louisiana, for example, reputedly stashed away a cool $100,000 from public works contracts.[57] Alabama printed $18 to $20 million worth of railroad bonds, and the overall debt of the eleven former Confederate states was estimated to exceed $132 million by 1872, yet with no tangible results for the expenditures.[58] Printing costs mysteriously soared: in South Carolina, the cost of state printing from 1868 to 1876 surpassed the total printing expenses from the entire period from 1789 to 1868! Legislators put in requests for "supplies" such as perfume, hams, ladies' bonnets, and champagne— all (obviously) essential to passing good laws.[59]

Reconstruction governments thus featured a disturbing mix of Northern reformers, Southern opportunists, and a sea of inexperienced blacks with practically no capital and little economic clout. Had all the motives of the actors been pure, the task of running the governments efficiently and without corruption would have been difficult. And without doubt, many in the Reconstruction governments sincerely wanted to improve the lives of all. They introduced the first public schools in the nation, enacted prison and asylum reforms, and enforced the Fourteenth Amendment rights of the freedmen. Without the support of Southern whites, absent their own economic base, and lacking any political experience, the governments did what governments often do: they threw money at the problems. No transportation? Issue railroad bonds that would never be paid. No education? Throw up a school and assume educated blacks would somehow be respected by their former masters.

It would be a mistake to assume that the Radicals lacked Democratic support for these measures. Even in the South, most of the railroad bond measures were bipartisan and remained so until the Panic of 1873.[60] Only after a new group of Bourbon (Redeemer) Democrats had appeared—those interested in repudiating the debts and rejecting state aid to railroad projects—did support for the measures dry up. Moreover, concern over graft and government excess grew to the point that when the Bourbons took the scene after 1870, they found voters receptive to reducing the size of government and lowering taxes.

As these trends unfolded in the South, Republicans in Washington had a veto-proof majority, although Johnson still had enforcement powers. As commander in chief of the army—the only institution capable of actually putting Reconstruction policies into practice—Johnson could still control the pace of change. He also found a surprising ally in the Supreme Court, which in the *Ex parte Milligan* case (1866) unanimously ruled against imposition of martial law in cases where civil administration still functioned. This cut the legal legs out from under the military governance in the South, and the Court proceeded to rule against loyalty oaths and allowed civil suits against military governors for damages. Congress, sensing where the Court was headed, used its discretionary powers granted in Article III of the Constitution to state that the Court had no jurisdiction in cases of habeas corpus, the issue that had been spawned by *Milligan*. Congress succeeded in evading the Constitution's stipulation that only wartime suspension of civil government was legal—the war was over—but the Court had no way to enforce its ruling. Checkmated, the Court withdrew from accepting most other Reconstruction-related decisions.

Now only Johnson stood between Congress and its vision of a prostrate South. Concerned the president might outmaneuver them by using his constitutional power as head of the executive branch to go directly through the officer corps in the Union Army, in February 1867 the Radicals passed the Tenure of Office Act, a measure that prohibited Johnson from removing federal office holders without Senate approval. This act violated a seventy-eight-year precedent and in essence handcuffed the president from removing incompetent or even dangerous officials if they had allies in the Senate. Johnson, as expected, vetoed the measure, and Congress, as expected, overrode the veto. At the same time, Congress passed the Command of the Army Act, requiring presidential orders or orders from the secretary of war (Radical sympathizer Stanton) to go through the general of the army (in that case, Ulysses S. Grant). Moreover, it stipulated Grant could not be assigned to duty in any area other than Washington (anticipating that Johnson might send him on a "fact-finding" mission to, say, China!).

In fact, Grant wanted to maintain a low profile. Although he seldom agreed with Johnson, Grant appreciated the separation of powers and understood the necessity for keeping the executive branch an independent powerful check on Congress. Although his sympathies in matters of Reconstruction favored the Republicans, he nevertheless supported Johnson's orders and attempted to execute them.

Johnson, convinced many of these congressional acts were unconstitutional, decided to challenge the Tenure of Office Act. He removed Stanton in August while Congress was adjourned, replacing him with Grant as secretary of war. He sent the Senate an explanation of his reasons in a December communication, but it was too late. The Senate rejected Johnson's statement for removing Stanton by a whopping 35 to 6 vote, and on January 14, 1868, it was time for Grant to pick up his things and vacate the War Department office. Scarcely a month later, in February 1868, Johnson dismissed Stanton a second time, and replaced him with Lorenzo Thomas.

Modern readers must note that in the nineteenth century context of separation of powers, the Congress had no constitutional right of review for executive appointment officers. In firing and hiring cabinet members, Johnson was not only fully within his constitutional rights, but he was in keeping with the actions of virtually every chief executive before him. Realistically, however, the Radicals saw Johnson as an obstacle to their programs, and neither the law nor the Constitution could be allowed to stand in the way.

At any rate, with the Thomas appointment, a truly extraordinary scene unfolded. Stanton refused to vacate his office and had a warrant issued for Thomas's arrest; whereas Johnson sent Thomas's name—the second in a few months—to the Senate for approval. This time, there was no doubt among the House Judiciary Committee members, who recommended eleven articles of impeachment for "high crimes and misdemeanors." Nine articles specifically related to Stanton's (illegal, in the eyes of the House) dismissal; one involved Johnson's speeches; and the eleventh catch-all article lumped together every charge the Radicals could find. It was Thaddeus Stevens's moment of triumph: so ill that he had to have the clerk read his speech inaugurating the impeachment committee, he was nevertheless so obsessed by enmity toward Johnson that he lashed out, "Unfortunate, unhappy man, behold your doom."[61] So spiteful was Stevens's speech that the Northern press stood back aghast. The New York *Herald* wrote that Stevens had "the bitterness and hatred of Marat, and the unscrupulousness of Robespierre."[62]

Although many historians condemn the impeachment process as rash, reckless, and unwarranted, it is significant that the full House vote was a substantial 126 to 47. This was a ratio far higher than the House impeachment vote against Bill Clinton a century later (228 to 206 on the key article of perjury following a sexual harassment suit brought against him). A Senate trial of Johnson soon followed.

Although modern Americans are slightly more familiar with the processes of impeachment because of the Clinton case, the mechanics are nevertheless worth restating. After a full House vote in favor of articles of impeachment, the president is officially impeached, but then must stand trial before the Senate. The prosecutors of the case are House managers who present the evidence for removing the chief executive. According to the Constitution, the House, and only the House, determines whether the offenses constitute "high crimes and misdemeanors"—in other words, once the House has turned out articles of impeachment, the Senate's *only* constitutional function is to determine guilt or innocence. Senators cannot (at least, according to the Constitution) determine that a president is guilty, yet conclude that removal is too great a penalty. Rather, the House has already found that *if* the president committed the acts of which he was accused, the penalty is automatic.

This structure, however, produced an unfortunate flaw in practice; namely that since the Senate would always be the second and final body to judge a president, its members could ignore the requirement that they rule on guilt or innocence only and instead reargue the question of whether the behavior fits the high-crimes-and-misdemeanors bar. Both American impeachment trials resulted in the Senates' of the respective day ignoring their constitutional charge and insinuating themselves into the powers and prerogatives of the House.

When the House managers prepared their case, John A. Bingham of Ohio headed the prosecution. Formerly opposed to impeachment, Bingham had finally concluded that Johnson had to go. Radicals dominated the prosecution team and took the most extreme positions, attempting to paint Johnson as a wild-eyed dictator bent on overthrowing the government. In a remarkable display, Senator Benjamin Butler "waved a nightshirt allegedly stained with the blood of an Ohio carpetbagger, who had been flogged by Mississippi ruffians" to show the lawlessness of the South.[63] From that point, in every election, Republicans would "wave the bloody shirt," and the tactic proved effective until the mid-1880s. It was less useful for Bingham, however.

Johnson's defense attorneys made eloquent speeches on the president's behalf. More important, no one could produce evidence of treason or truly criminal intent by Johnson, who had sought only to challenge a constitutional question. All this made the moderates uneasy about the precedent of unseating a sitting president. When the Senate voted on the catch-all Article 11, the total was 35 to convict and 19 not guilty, providing Johnson with a single-vote margin needed to keep him in office. The Senate had voted to keep an unpopular president in office on the basis that his crimes were not sufficient to warrant his removal.

Other acquittals for Johnson quickly followed, and the trial ended. Some assumed that merely the impeachment and the trial would chastise and restrain Johnson, but the stubborn Tennessean dug in his heels even more. The trial did chasten the Radicals, who realized they had pushed too hard, and they reluctantly concluded that the nation was not yet in agreement with their vision of absolute black equality or Northern domination of the South. They concluded that winning the White House again in 1868 would require someone not obviously associated with their faction and someone the public trusted. The Republican national convention in Chicago took only one ballot to choose Ulysses S. Grant as the party's nominee.

Johnson vainly attempted to form a Lincoln-type coalition, but he could not win the nomination of his own party. Instead, the Democrats turned to Horatio Seymour, New York's wartime governor who had castigated Lincoln as a dictator and despot and called the Irish draft rioters "my friends." Republicans had no trouble painting Seymour as a Copperhead, nor was he helped by a new wave of Klan racial violence in the South. Seymour's running mate, Frank P. Blair Jr. of Missouri, made matters worse by referring to the "corrupt military despotism" that still governed the South.[64] Statements such as Blair's terrified Northerners. Edward Pierrepont, a Democrat from New York City, wrote, "I cannot conceive how any intelligent man, who does not wish the Rebels returned to power . . . and the 'Lost Cause' restored, can vote against Grant."[65]

Grant hewed to the traditional Republican agenda: high tariffs, internal improvements, and, above all, stability and moderation toward Reconstruction affairs. A gold standard supporter, Grant nevertheless supported the Pendleton Plan for paying off federal bonds with greenbacks unless specifically stated that they be paid in gold. Paying for the war debt in greenbacks represented a commitment to slight inflation. For most voters, though, Grant, not the platform, was the deciding factor: his campaign slogan, "Let us have peace," appealed to people of both sections.

In the election, despite the absence of three still-unreconstructed states, 78 percent of eligible voters cast ballots. Grant received 53 percent of the popular vote, despite the fact that Seymour got almost 200,000 votes from Kentucky and Louisiana alone; Grant smashed Seymour in the electoral college 214 to 80. Some 500,000 blacks, voting for the first time, thus decided the election. Seymour took the highest electoral state (his home state of New York), but Grant took most of the North and swept the Midwest and all of the West except Oregon.

Grant and the "Era of Good Stealings"

A reluctant politician, Ulysses S. Grant was as unimpressive in person as was Johnson. Sad eyed, of average height, and possessing a low musical and penetrating voice, Grant punctuated his speech by frequently stroking his slight beard with his left hand. Courteous and capable of effusive laughter, Grant in portraits nevertheless looks as if he were attending a bullfight or a funeral. Full of personal contradictions, he puzzled even his best friends, including cartoonist Thomas Nast, who contributed mightily to the 1868 campaign. "Two things elected me," Grant later said, "the sword of Sheridan and the pencil of Thomas Nast." Early in his life Grant and Longstreet had been close, and after Fort Sumter, he came to rely heavily on Sherman. Unlike Lincoln, who never lacked confidence around men of better education or status, Grant, according to Hamilton Fish, later his secretary of state, was uncomfortable in the presence of highly literate or well-traveled men.[66] Possessed of a detailed and organized memory, Grant could tell spellbinding stories, and later wrote a military memoir considered the finest since Caesar's.[67]

When Grant claimed to be a simple soldier, he meant it. Once he put his trust in someone, he clung to them ferociously, and his loyalty led him to associate with self-interested leeches who had no compunction about betraying his faith in them. He viewed the presidency from the old Whig tradition, where the legislature made the laws, and the president merely served as a check. To that extent, Grant had failed to absorb the massive changes in federal, and presidential, power that had occurred during the Civil War.[68]

Congress was all too happy to continue to direct Reconstruction, but the Republicans' first concern involved a diagnosis of the last election, which revealed that a great deal of Democratic strength still remained in the country. Had blacks not voted in the numbers they had, or had most of the former Confederates who were legally allowed to vote not boycotted the election, the Republicans could have suffered severe setbacks. Ensuring that blacks maintained the franchise therefore emerged as the top priority for the Radicals, who sought to make black voting rights permanent. Grant had not even taken office when Congress passed the Fifteenth Amendment (February 1869) that forbade any state from depriving a citizen of his vote because of race, color, or previous condition of servitude.

The recalcitrant Southern states—Texas, Virginia, and Mississippi—that had not yet ratified the Fourteenth Amendment, finally gave in, ratifying both the Fourteenth and Fifteenth, and all three had rejoined the Union by 1870. Obedience in any of these states, however, still largely rested on the bayonets of Yankee troops. Georgia proved that in 1868, when, after federal military forces withdrew, the state legislature expelled all black legislators until the return of federal troops again imposed Northern order. Probably many Southerners otherwise harbored humane and reasonable intentions toward the freedmen, but equality enforced at bayonet point hardened their antipathy against the North even more. To most white Southerners, all of Reconstruction was a facade, a ruse to conceal the Northerners and the Republicans' true objective of crushing the South politically, economically, and culturally.

Grant had scarcely taken office, and certainly had not yet started to grapple with Reconstruction, when his unfortunate associations plunged his administration into a scandal. On September 24, 1869, in Wall Street's "Gold Room," two of the most infamous speculators in the country, Jim Fisk and Jay Gould, attempted to corner the market on gold.[69] What ensued was Black Friday, where gold prices skyrocketed, thanks to their backroom manipulations. Fisk and Gould had involved Grant's brother-in-law, Abel Corbin, who acquired insider information from Grant over dinner. Corbin relayed to the speculators that in the event of a run on gold, the federal government would not sell its gold, and thus the price would rise.

Fisk and Gould had a long history of attempting to manipulate markets. Along with Daniel Drew, they had fought Commodore Cornelius Vanderbilt over the Harlem Railroad in 1864. Now, five years later, Fisk and Gould were attempting another speculation. Armed with foreknowledge that the federal government would not sell any new gold, the conspirators started to buy all they could get at $135 an ounce. Once they had cornered the supply of gold and driven the price up to $160, they would dump gold and take the profits. For a while it appeared they would succeed. But Grant, informed of the situation by his secretary of the Treasury, ordered the Treasury to sell gold and stabilize the price. Gould escaped with several million dollars in profits, far below his expectations. Grant had in no way acted improperly, but the Fisk/Gould connection with Corbin tarnished his administration at an early stage.

A second scandal, Crédit Mobilier, tainted many congressmen and reached into Grant's administration, but did not involve him personally. The Crédit Mobilier scandal was the logical result of using massive public funding for the transcontinental railroads, specifically the Union Pacific and the Central Pacific. To that extent, the trail to Crédit Mobilier must first go through Promontory Point, Utah, where the transcontinentals met in May 1869.

Funding for the transcontinental railroads originated with a grant of 44 million acres of land and $61 million in federal loans, reflecting the urgency Congress placed on construction. Railroads could sell the land, and use the proceeds for construction. The Pacific Railroad Act of 1862 enabled the Union Pacific to lay rails westward from Omaha, while the Central Pacific started in Sacramento and headed east.[70] Congress put ridiculous incentives into the legislation: benefits given to the railroads that right-thinking legislators should have known would breed corruption on a massive scale. For example, the railroads received twenty alternating sections of federal land and, in addition, received a staggered series of cash loans for each mile of track constructed ($16,000 for flat land, $32,000 for hilly terrain, and $48,000 in mountains). Naturally, the railroads had a stake in laying as much track, on as much difficult terrain, as was humanly possible.

Historian Burton Folsom Jr. summarized how Congress's misincentives shaped the railroad companies' strategy: "They sometimes built winding, circuitous roads to collect for more mileage. . . . They used cheap and light wrought iron rails, soon to be outmoded by Bessemer rails."[71] The Union Pacific's vice president, Thomas Durant, complained to his staff members, "You are doing too much masonry. . . . [Substitute] wooden culverts for masonry whenever you can."[72] They used fragile cottonwood trees because they were handy, stealing farmers' timber with the reasoning that it was public land anyway. With government dollars backing the railroads' every move, who could argue otherwise?

Moreover, the railroads also meandered in search of mineral rights, leading the Northern Pacific through the Black Hills of South Dakota and fomenting the Sioux wars.

Union Pacific's chief engineer, Granville Dodge, laid track on ice, and the whole line had to be rebuilt in the spring. Crossing unsettled land invited Indian attacks, requiring that half the workers at any site stand guard while the other half worked. Climaxing the wasteful affair, when the Union Pacific and Central Pacific came within the vicinity of each other, work crews began gang fights and built parallel lines as long as Congress tolerated it. Finally, even the federal government had enough, and lawmakers demanded that the two lines link up. The subsidized transcontinentals linked the nation only after phenomenal waste—a task James J. Hill did without federal aid.[73] Even as the golden spike was being driven, both railroads were already planning to rebuild and even relocate the track to cover the shoddy construction. It was 1874 before the Union Pacific finished fixing the "new" track it laid five years before.

The Crédit Mobilier scandal had its roots in this perfidious use of government money. The corruption was brought into the open because the company was formed in 1864 solely as a means to prop up the sinking Union Pacific stock. The congressional charter required the railroad to sell its stock for cash at $100 par value, but the price sank almost immediately upon issue as investors questioned whether the railroad could even be built. Thomas Durant came up with the concept of forming a new credit arm, Crédit Mobilier, whose stockholders were identical to the Union Pacific's. Under the scheme, the railroad would give construction contracts to Crédit Mobilier, which then would balloon the costs of construction to double the genuine expenses. Union Pacific paid Crédit Mobilier with its own checks, which the directors of the credit company promptly used to purchase railroad stock at the par value of $100 per share. Looked at another way, Durant had managed to get the railroad to buy its own stock. He then had Crédit Mobilier sell the stock on the open market far below par.

The scam, while convoluted, nevertheless boiled down to Durant's giving stockholders "profits" from sales of Union Pacific stock on the open market, which had been sanitized up to par value by washing it through the Crédit Mobilier laundry. In the process, the directors and stockholders of Crédit Mobilier had made outrageous profits from the overbilling of the railroad—all funded by Uncle Sam's land grants and loans—and had also made profits from the resale of the watered stock. As if those gains were not enough, a number of congressmen (James A. Garfield of Ohio and James Brooks of New York), senators (James Patterson of New Jersey), and Grant administration officials, including the vice president (Schuyler Colfax), were given generous Crédit Mobilier holdings to ensure they did not turn off the money spigot. Scholars estimate that the corrupt directors and congressmen skimmed between $13 million and $23 million from the Union Pacific through Crédit Mobilier, which was finally exposed by the reporting of Charles Dana's New York *Sun* in 1872. Once again, Grant was not directly implicated, but could not escape guilt by inference.[74]

Other scandals quickly followed, including the Whiskey Ring, the Veteran's Administration scandal, and the exposure of Secretary of War William W. Belknap for accepting bribes in return for the sale of Indian trading posts. Grant's reputation suffered further blows.

Missing in the moralizing of both the pundits of the day and subsequent historians is the key issue: such corruption tracked precisely with the vast expansion of the federal bureaucracy. People acted no better, or worse, in the 1870s than they had in George Washington's day. What had changed, however, was that the *opportunity* for graft combined with the incredible profits to be gained from corruption, causing one historian to label this the "era of good stealings."[75] This malignancy owed much of its existence to the growth of government.

Scandals in the Grant era turn the liberal critique of the Gilded Age on its head. Far from laissez-faire capitalism necessitating government regulation, it was government intervention that caused the corruption and fed it. The best reform Americans could have enacted in the decade after Grant would have been to roll back to antebellum levels the subsidies, benefits, tariffs, and favorable land grants to railroads and other bonuses given to special interests. Yet the reformers learned precisely the wrong lessons from these events.

Reelection and Reform

The demise of the Democratic Party's Tweed Ring in New York City convinced many politicians in each party that not only should something be done about political corruption, but that reform measures could also be successful. The accelerating calls for political reform came as a reaction against the Radicals, and they were led by another faction of Republicans, the Liberals. These Liberals included Carl Schurz, Horace Greeley, Gideon Welles, Charles Francis Adams, and editor E. L. Godkin, who favored free trade, redeeming greenbacks in gold, a stable currency, restoring the former Confederates their rights, and civil service reform. Schurz won a Senate seat in 1872, demonstrating that the Liberals had some electoral clout and leading them to test their might in 1872, when they held a separate convention. Their emergence says something about the difficulty of applying labels in historical settings: the Liberals, like the conservative Southern Democrats, opposed further Reconstruction measures, and both were opposed by the Radical Republicans. However, the Radicals, like most Democrats, favored a continuation of the spoils system, which the Liberals wanted to end. Former conservative hard-money Democrats, after the Civil War, slowly embraced inflation and spoke favorably of greenbacks, a tool the Union government had used to win the war. Finally, Liberal Republicans and conservative Democrats both supported free trade and ending tariffs, but Radicals did not! Judging from these issues alone, any attempt to consistently apply twentieth- and twenty-first-century name tags to nineteenth-century politics is an exercise in futility.

But while the Liberals relished their name, they overestimated their importance. At their 1872 Cincinnati convention they nominated Horace Greeley (1811–72), editor of the New York *Tribune*. Greeley's true passion was reform.

He embraced every reform idea that came down the pike, and, not surprisingly, employed Karl Marx as his European correspondent. In the 1840s Greeley championed socialistic Fourierism, but finding that a political dead end, he turned to patronage and spoils—always an intelligent choice for a publisher. Alcohol, tobacco, prostitution, and gambling all earned the scornful ink of Greeley's pen. During the Mexican War he had urged, "Sign anything, ratify anything, pay anything. . . . There was never a good war or a bad peace." He seemed to have changed his view twenty years later: "On to Richmond! Crush the Rebels in blood and fire!" In 1865 the mutable Greeley contributed to the bail of Confederate president Jefferson Davis. Still, the opportunities for Democrats to ally with Liberal Republicans forced them to hand their nomination to Greeley, who was the only person of either party they thought might unseat Grant.

Had nothing unusual occurred, Greeley still would have lost the election convincingly. As it was, his wife's health deteriorated, and he judged her mentally insane. She died in the last moments of the election, essentially taking Horace with her. He had a mental or emotional breakdown and expired in an asylum three weeks after her demise. Meanwhile, the attacks on him by the Grant forces had been so relentlessly effective that even Greeley quipped he did not know if he was running for the presidency or the penitentiary. Portrayed as a crank and a disunionist, and connected by Thomas Nast to the Tweed Ring, Greeley actually accomplished something of a miracle by garnering 44 percent of the vote and 60 electoral votes. Grant smashed him with almost 300 electoral votes and beat him by three quarters of a million in the popular vote. Still, the campaign planted an important seed: Liberals started to redefine the Republican Party as the party of free trade, less government, low taxes, sound money, and the necessity for character in government. Within fifty years, a Republican presidential candidate (Warren Harding) stood for less government, lower taxes, and sound money, and in another half century Ronald Reagan embraced every one of the 1870s Liberal positions.

Meanwhile, the Radical Reconstruction program was unraveling rapidly. Democrats had not only driven out most of their number who might work for black rights, but they had also embraced former Confederates with open arms. "Virginia for the Virginians" was the campaign slogan of former Confederate general and Gettysburg veteran James L. Kemper in 1873, employing a phrase that clearly implied African Americans were not Virginians. "To save the state," said one of his lieutenants, "we must make the issue *White and Black* race against race and the canvass red hot. [italics added]"[76] To be sure, not all Southerners tolerated race-baiting, and many of the leading Southern newspapers sharply criticized establishing a color line in elections. But these were pragmatic responses by editors fearful that playing the race card would only lead to more Republican victories, and seldom reflected any genuine concern for blacks or their rights.

The revival of such attitudes emboldened the Klan, whose activities increased in number and viciousness. Violence by the Klan and other terror organizations prompted a response from Congress, which Grant wholeheartedly supported. In May 1870, under the authority of the Fifteenth Amendment, Congress passed the first Force Act. (Since the object of the legislation was to end intimidation by the Klan, this and similar acts were also called the Ku Klux Acts.) The Force Act provided heavy fines and imprisonment for anyone attempting to hinder citizens from voting. Congress reinforced the act in 1871, and then, in 1872, passed legislation even more specific in its language aimed at the Klan. Threatening or injuring witnesses, interfering with federal officers, or even going about in disguises were all prohibited. The Klansmen and their terrorist allies did not go quietly. They staged massive torchlight parades, shot at Republican offices, lynched blacks, and bullied African Americans into staying home on election day. A few blacks tried to form rifle companies to counteract the Klan, but they had little training with firearms and few weapons. Grant managed to effectively drive the Klan underground for almost a generation, but they skulked in the background, awaiting an administration in Washington less committed to black rights.

Meanwhile, by 1870, the fusion/loyalist Democrats were strongly opposed by Redeemers or Bourbons. These politicians were planters and former Confederates, like Kemper, who were determined to end Black Reconstruction. Although they also had genuine concerns for the economic collapse of their states under the Radical governments, their three main issues were race, race, and race. Redeemers found a wide audience for disenfranchising blacks. "Give us a convention," intoned Robert Toombs, "and I will fix it so that the people shall rule, and the negro shall never be heard from."[77] Opposition to the state debts, government support for business, and other Whiggish programs also played a crucial role in the Redeemers' success. Indeed, when the Bourbons got control, they did not merely reduce the debts and pay them off over time—they repudiated them.

Whether the Redeemers fully realized they were helping to condemn the South to decades more of poverty is unclear, but that certainly was the result of their policies. Repudiating debts was a sure way to guarantee no one lent Southern governments money again, and guilt by association meant that *any* Southern-originated bonds by even *private* companies would be viewed with suspicion. Or as Reconstruction historian Michael Perman observed, "Because it was fiscally untrustworthy and financially dependent, the South had, in effect, surrendered control over its future economic development."[78] Whereas the state-subsidized model of railroad and corporate support often advanced by the Whigs and Republicans proved disadvantageous (if not disastrous) to transportation and industrial progress, the Democrats' punitive redistributionist policies—little more than financial bulimia and anorexia—were equally dim-witted. The South, already bereft of railroads, banks, and manufacturing, turned to the Redeemers, who offered the region "a politics of balance, inertia, and drift."[79]

The Panic of 1873 provided the final electoral issue allowing the Democratic Redeemers to win back control of most Southern state houses in the 1874 election, and, amazingly, for the first time since 1858, Democrats won the U.S. House of Representatives. Empowered at last, Redeemers had no intention of enforcing federal civil rights laws. Just the opposite, they supported segregation statutes known as Jim Crow laws.

Interestingly, by the 1870s the free market had already made some inroads toward ending segregation when streetcars were integrated. It was government, not business (which wanted the profits from black ridership) that insisted on segregating streetcars and other public facilities.[80] With the combination of a waning federal will to enforce civil rights legislation, the return of the Redeemers, and the revival of the Klan, freedmen saw much of what they had gained in the decade after the Civil War slip away.

Diversions

Americans, especially Northern Americans, had grown increasingly weary of defending black rights and their own corrupt Reconstruction governments in the South. Less than a decade after armies marched singing, "Mine eyes have seen the glory of the coming of the Lord," Northerners wanted to know when the Lord would show up and release them from the burden of policing their white Southern neighbors.

When the Republicans lost the midterm election in 1874, it indicated support for Reconstruction was waning. Political realities of the 1870s combined to push Republicans further away from their Radical Reconstruction goals of union, emancipation, and equality, until by 1876 three of these had been reduced to two: union and emancipation. Equality had been discarded.

Events in the frontier West distracted Americans as well. The Indian wars commanded tremendous political and humanitarian energy, once solely reserved for the Negro. Reformers, having "finished" their work in the South, brushed themselves off and turned their attention to another "helpless" group, Native Americans. Indians had suffered a constant string of broken treaties, as discussed in the next chapter. Few episodes, however, shook the nation as much as the news of June 1876, when an alliance of Sioux and Cheyenne—once hated enemies—produced the worst military disaster on the western plains, the destruction of a large portion of Colonel George Custer's Seventh U.S. Cavalry. If troops were needed in the West, they had to come from the South, weakening enforcement of open polls and control over the Klan.

Economic disruption also drew attention from the South. The failure of Jay Cooke's banking house in 1873, brought about in part by his reliance on Union Pacific railroad bonds, touched off the Panic of 1873. That same year the government announced it would redeem the greenbacks in gold beginning in 1879—a policy that was in no way connected with Cooke's failure—and, at the same time, Washington announced that it would not monetize silver. Consistent with the Liberals' position of sound money, the government had refused to inflate the currency, instigating yet another howl of protest from western farmers, miners, and others who were caught in the postwar deflation, itself of international origins.

With each Union Army regiment redeployed to the West, Republican voters in the South lost a little more security. Blacks and whites alike feared for their lives as they went to the polls, which they did with less and less frequency. As a Mississippi carpetbagger governor wrote to his wife, "The Republicans are paralyzed through fear and will not act. Why should I fight a hopeless battle . . . when no possible good to the Negro or anybody else would result?"[81] A Northern Republican echoed the frustration: "The truth is our people are tired out with the worn out cry of 'Southern outrages'!! Hard times and heavy taxes make them wish the 'ever lasting nigger' were in hell or Africa."[82] Democrats and Southerners had learned an important lesson about the press: no matter how grievous the charge, deny it; then commit another wanton act, and the first behavior will be forgotten in the storm over the new one. Northern newspapers unwittingly assisted in the unraveling of Reconstruction, portraying black legislators as hopelessly corrupt. "Thieves," "orgies," "plunder"—words like these characterized reporting about the Reconstruction governments.

The first signs of surrender appeared in May 1872, when Congress passed the Amnesty Act, allowing Confederate leaders to vote and hold public office. When Southern Republicans, already disenchanted with the potential for full social equality of blacks, began to desert the party, the Reconstruction government truly became ruled by a foreign power. Democrats, having inflated Confederate currency into worthlessness and acquiesced in a government that essentially imposed a 100 percent tax on its citizens, now skillfully and disingenuously accused the Black Republicans of excessive spending and overtaxation.

As a last-gasp attempt to show its commitment, Congress passed the Civil Rights Act of 1875, a final bill pushed through the Republican-controlled lameduck Congress guaranteeing "full and equal treatment" to all persons of every race, and decreeing access to all public facilities, such as hotels, theaters, and railroads. As usual, enforcement relied on troops, and the troops had been pulled out of every Southern state except Louisiana, Florida, and South Carolina. Elsewhere, Redeemer governments had crept back in, one at a time, beginning with Tennessee in 1869, West Virginia, Missouri, and North Carolina in 1870, Georgia in 1871, Alabama, Texas, and Arkansas in 1874, and Mississippi in 1875.

What the North did, for understandable reasons, was to abandon what it started. What the South did, also for understandable reasons, was to attempt to return to its antebellum social and economic structure sans the legal institution of slavery. For Reconstruction to have worked as many had hoped, it would have required a view of government exactly opposite of the large, central behemoth that had undermined the Confederacy. It needed small, morally impeccable, and utterly efficient state governments. It needed low taxes at the state level, and abolition of those state or local regulations that gave any group advantages over another. It also required a massive infusion of banking capital, which the National Bank acts had failed to provide. Finally, it probably would have required another leader with the genius and compassion of Lincoln to pull it off. Yet even in the greatest Republic on earth, a Lincoln only comes around once a generation at best. Instead of a great leader like Lincoln, the nation's next president was a good, honest, and competent leader named Rutherford B. Hayes.

Rutherford B. Hayes: Soldier and Politician

Like his predecessor, Ulysses Grant, Rutherford B. Hayes knew combat well. During the Civil War he had been wounded five times and had four horses shot out from under him. He narrowly missed being kidnapped by Confederate raiders who absconded with Union Generals George Crook and Benjamin Franklin Kelley, then spearheaded the effort to get them back. William McKinley said of Hayes that "his whole nature seemed to change when in battle. [He went from] sunny, agreeable, the kind, generous, the gentle gentleman [to] intense and ferocious."[83] Hayes's first cousin was utopian John Humphrey Noyes, but Hayes shared none of his eccentric brand of socialism, preferring instead traditional marriage and sound capitalism. When the war ended, he had second thoughts about politics, but was, after all, a veteran and a good speaker, so much so that by the end of October 1866 he could leave his own congressional political campaigning and work to secure the election of John Sherman as an Ohio Senator.

An ardent champion of securing the rights of the freedmen, Congressman Hayes realized that only the federal government—and, with Andrew Johnson in the White House at the time, only Congress—protected the new citizens. He wrote to his wife, Lucy, about a parade celebrating the end of the war in April 1866 in which "the colored procession" marched in Washington with flags and bands. "Their cheering for the House and Senate as they passed the east front [of the Capitol] was peculiarly enthusiastic."[84] After his short stint in Congress, Hayes, waving the bloody shirt, won the gubernatorial seat in Ohio in 1867, only to find that many issues that once were the domain of state governments had been taken over by Washington. Hayes intended to emphasize black voting rights, but otherwise hoped the legislature would pass few laws. Winning a second term in 1870, Hayes especially worked to curb local taxes, which had risen five times faster in Ohio than state taxes, and sought to further reduce state indebtedness. The legislature still spent more than he requested, but Hayes managed to reduce the rate of growth, at the same time supporting increased spending on the state orphans' home, education, and penal reform.

In 1872, thinking he had retired from politics, Hayes moved back to Cincinnati, where he actively criticized Republican corruption. Called out of retirement to unite a deeply divided party, Hayes won the governorship again in mid-1876, despite a bad economy that worked against the party in power, the Republicans. No sooner had Hayes won, however, than Senator John Sherman and General Philip Sheridan both urged him to run for the presidency. Sheridan wrote Hayes endorsing his own preference for a ticket of "Hayes and Wheeler," to which Hayes remarked to his wife, "I am ashamed to say, but who is *Wheeler?*"[85] Wheeler was Congressman William A. Wheeler of New York, and the Republican convention, as fortune would have it, took place in Cincinnati, where many of the Hayes men had already infiltrated the party apparatus. Even without such inside activity, however, Hayes won support because his opponents, including Roscoe "Boss" Conkling of New York and James G. Blaine of Maine, all had significant flaws. In the general election, GOP nominee Hayes squared off against

New York Democratic governor Samuel J. Tilden, who had gained a reputation by crushing the infamous Tweed Ring.

After seeing early returns showing Tilden carrying Indiana and New York, Hayes went to bed and slept soundly, convinced he had lost the election. But the far West, including Oregon, California, and Nevada, was late to report, and all went for Hayes. In addition, there were troubling results in three Southern states: Louisiana, South Carolina, and Florida. If Hayes carried all of them, he would win by one electoral vote, even though the final popular vote showed him losing by almost a quarter million votes—a whopping 3 percent Tilden victory in ballots cast. Yet local voting boards retained the authority to determine which ballots were valid and which were fraudulent. Although he was convinced the Democrats had engaged in massive vote manipulation, Hayes nevertheless hesitated to contest the election. What sealed the matter for him was the perception that virtually all of the fraud had been perpetrated against African Americans, whose rights Hayes had fought for (almost to the exclusion of anything else) his entire political career.

As with Al Gore and George W. Bush under similar circumstances more than a century later, Tilden and Hayes engaged in the game of attempting to look presidential while their subordinates hotly contested the results. Like Gore and Bush, both men were convinced that a legitimate canvass would favor their chances. Hayes appeared to have carried South Carolina by 1,000 votes, despite the rulings from local boards there, but he had also lost Louisiana by six times that many ballots, constituting a significant challenge to his contest claim. In Florida, repeaters, ballot stuffers, and other tricksters—including those who had printed Democratic ballots with the Republican symbol on them to deceive illiterate voters—made it all but impossible to determine the true winner. Hayes probably won South Carolina and Florida, but Tilden carried Louisiana, where Republican vote tampering was probably quite high, and that was all he needed. Hayes insisted that "we are not to allow our friends to defeat one outrage and fraud by another," and demanded, "There must be nothing crooked on our part."[86] Matters had already spun out of his control, however.

The returning board in Louisiana, which was all Republican and under the supervision of J. Madison Wells, who was clearly engaged in postelection scheming for patronage, tossed out 15,000 total ballots, of which 13,000 were Democratic, giving Hayes the state by 3,000 votes. Florida's board included a Democrat, but the result was the same: Hayes won the state by 900 votes. Hayes also took the disputed South Carolina votes, giving him ostensibly 185 electoral votes to Tilden's 184 and, in turn, giving him the election.

The affair dragged on into the new year, and as provided for by the Constitution, Congress had to clean up the matter. In the interim, Hayes's forces received feelers from some Southern congressmen who floated the trial balloon of receiving "consideration" in return for their support of Hayes, meaning federal subsidies for the Texas and Pacific Railroad, an end to military occupation, and plenty of patronage. Congress settled on a fifteen-member commission made up of five senators, five congressmen, and five Supreme Court justices. Each party would have seven members, plus, ostensibly, one independent, Justice David Davis. Everyone recognized that barring a miracle, Davis would determine the election, but it was the only practical solution, and both Hayes and Tilden reluctantly approved of the commission. Then, surprising everyone, Davis refused to serve on the commission. He thought he smelled a bribe, and withdrew. By prior agreement, another Supreme Court justice had to serve, and it fell to Justice Joseph P. Bradley, a Republican, to take his place.

As with the disputed election of 2000, there was controversy over whether to accept the official returns certified by the governor and the state secretary of state or to accept other unsanctioned returns. The Democrats claimed Florida had been stolen through Republican fraud, but historian James MacPherson challenges such a contention. Voting on party lines, the commission accepted the official certified returns, and Florida went to Hayes. Similar 8-to-7 votes soon yielded to Hayes the Louisiana and South Carolina electors.

While these maneuvers were occurring, representatives from Hayes and Tilden met at Washington's Wormley Hotel to settle the election. This backstage bargain, which many historians view as having produced the Compromise of 1877, was overblown. Hayes had already made it clear he would ensure the retention of the Democratic governor of Louisiana in return for a pledge on freedmen's rights; withdraw the remaining federal troops from Louisiana, Florida, and South Carolina; and put Southerners in the cabinet. Even without a bargain, the deal was sealed, and Hayes mollified Democrats and Southerners enough to avert violence. Nevertheless, historians tout the agreement at the Wormley Hotel on February 26, 1877, as the last great sectional compromise.

On March 4, 1877—four months after the election—the nation had its new president. Hayes upheld his promise, naming a Democrat, David Key of Tennessee, as postmaster general (which remained, it should be noted, a prize political plum). The circumstances of his victory dictated that Hayes faced almost insurmountable odds against achieving much. He had not only a divided country, but also a divided party and a divided Congress. Although the Senate remained in Republican hands, the House had gone back to the Democrats in 1874 as a response to the Panic of 1873. His administration had a late start, thanks to the Tilden challenge, making it midsummer before the government even began to fill its primary positions. But most damaging, Hayes had stated that he would not run for a second term. Only through his insistence on a unified cabinet and an unwillingness to be bullied by the House did Hayes achieve as much as he did.

Protection of blacks by the bayonet in the South had run its course, and with Indian troubles on the frontier, the army was stretched too thin to keep large numbers of troops in the South as civil-rights enforcers. Withdrawal of federal troops commenced within a month, driven in part by pragmatism and in part by hope—hope that the Southerners would understand that they had entered a new era. Instead, the close election and the subsequent compromise meant that the South now acted as if it had defeated the North's legislation, if not her armies.

CHAPTER ELEVEN

Lighting Out for the Territories, 1861–90

Civilizing a Wilderness

Young Samuel Clemens (alias Mark Twain) gave up his brief career as a Mississippi steamboat pilot in 1861, setting out for the Nevada Territory aboard a stagecoach. Having tried his hand at gold and silver mining, he turned to newspaper work and a promising career as a writer. Clemens, in fact, moved west to escape the Civil War, a conflict in which he had served briefly and without distinction as a Confederate militiaman. He had no appetite for the kind of violence and devastation that consumed his fellow Missourians. Like his later literary character, Huckleberry Finn, Sam Clemens "lit out for the Territories."[1]

Many had gone before him, and many more followed. The period of manifest destiny, followed quickly by the Mormon exodus and the California Gold Rush of 1849, set the stage for a half century of migration by eastern Americans onto and across the Great Plains. Clemens was preceded by tens of thousands of anonymous fur trappers, cowboys, prostitutes, loggers, fishermen, farmers, miners, teachers, entertainers, soldiers, government officials, and business entrepreneurs, in addition to Mormons, Jesuits, Methodists, and other missionaries. In the 1860s, while the Civil War raged "back east," Clemens and a new generation headed west.[2]

In 1893 historian Frederick Jackson Turner wrote that this generation had succeeded so well that the American frontier had at last come to an end. In his brilliant essay, "The Significance of the Frontier in American History," Turner traced the course of the westward movement from Revolutionary times across the Appalachians and the Mississippi River. He pointed to the 1890 census report stating matter-of-factly that western America had achieved a density of population that rendered the term "frontier" inapplicable.[3] Turner undoubtedly portrayed America's western experience as unique—but how? Was Turner's thesis right?

Turner used the 1890 census report as a watershed to assess the impact of the frontier experience on the American people. He rejected the idea that Europeans had molded American culture and argued that it was the American frontier experience that had created a unique American civilization, providing a safety valve for the release of societal pressures. He ascribed to the West and western-ers specific character traits, most of them positive, but some unsavory. Arguing that the West made Americans democratic, egalitarian, nationalistic, pragmatic, and adaptive, Turner also contended that frontier life made them coarse, violent, anti-intellectual, and wasteful of natural resources. Yet even as he wrote, lumber-men like Frederick Weyerhaeuser, railroaders like James J. Hill, and meat packers like Gustavus Swift had begun taking extraordinary measures to preserve the en-vironment. And where Turner saw a violent, often barbaric West, the so-called Wild West may have been less violent in many respects than modern society.

Most western men were neither John Wayne types looking for a fight nor helpless citizens waiting for a frontier hero to rescue them. In regions where judges rode a circuit and came to town, with any luck, once a month, there naturally existed a tendency to take law into one's own hands. Where every animal had its claw, horn, tooth, or sting—many of them potentially fatal—and where every human had an incentive to jump a claim, steal livestock, or become offended at the slightest insult, a necessary violence literally went with the territory. Nor was the West a Marxist model of class struggle: for every saloon brawl that started over "class interests," fifty began over simple insults or alcohol.

On the other hand, frontier individualism was not ubiquitous, and western-ers could cooperate when necessary. Towns first united to bring the cattlemen in, then passed laws to keep them out; then cattlemen joined the townspeople to keep the sheepmen out; then ranchers and farmers of all types sought to keep heavy industry out. Nor were these patterns unique: a century later it was the same story: heavy industry sought to keep computers and electronics out. Those who settled the West for better and, occasionally, for worse, tamed a wild frontier. They left a legacy of romantic accomplishment that even to the present contains important messages and images for Americans.

Time Line

1843: First large Oregon Trail wagon train
1846–47: Mormon exodus to Utah
1848: Mexican War ends; New Mexico Territory, California ceded
   to United States
1849: Gold discovered at Sutter's Mill, California Gold Rush begins
1850: Compromise of 1850 admits California as a state
1853: Gadsden Purchase completes map of lower continental United States
1857: Butterfield Overland Stage provides passenger and mail route
   to California
1859: Comstock Lode discovered

    1860: Pony Express begins operations
    1861: Civil War begins
    1862: Homestead Act; Morrill Act; Plains Indian wars begin
    1864: Sand Creek massacre
1865–85: Cattle Kingdom reaches its apex
    1866: Fetterman massacre
    1867: Grange movement begins
    1869: Transcontinental railroads join at Promontory, Utah
    1876: Custer massacre
    1882: Edmunds Act
    1885: Chief Joseph and Nez Percé surrender
    1887: Dawes Severalty Act
    1890: Wounded Knee massacre
    1893: Frederick Jackson Turner declares frontier closed
    1896: Alaskan gold rush

Wagon Trains, Stagecoaches, and Steamboats

Before the completion of North America's first transcontinental railroad in 1869, westbound pioneers continued to use varied means of transport.[4] Thousands drove wagons over well-worn, often muddy trails and helped break in some new ones. An era of private road building in the early eastern frontier areas gave way to a willingness to use the state and national government to improve transportation.[5] Pony Express riders and horsemen traversed these trails, and travelers booked passage on stagecoaches. Members of the famed Mormon handcart brigades literally walked the trail west, pushing their belongings in front of them. Meanwhile, sailboats and steam-powered ocean vessels brought immigrants to the West via the coast of South America and hard-working steamboats navigated rivers. Decades after the coming of the railroad, nearly all of the above routes and means of transport endured in one form or another.

    Although the settlers of the 1830s still used muskets, increasingly the Kentucky long rifle had come into use, extending range and accuracy. After the Civil War, breech-loading Sharps, Spencer, Winchester, and Remington rifles (with repeating action) were available. The first repeaters had appeared in the Civil War, and with minimal practice a man or woman could squeeze off a dozen shots in less than thirty seconds. Many men carried sidearms—usually a Colt revolver—and knives, or tomahawks, or other weapons were always handy in case of snakes or predators.[6] When combined with circled wagons for defense, settlers had a good chance of warding off Indian attacks with such weapons.[7]

    The route north of the North Platte River became the Mormon Trail, blazed by the Mormon exodus to Utah (1846–47). Army engineers built or improved upon additional trails throughout the West, such as the Bozeman Trail, a supply route stretching north from Fort Laramie in present-day Wyoming to the Montana country. In Washington Territory the army built the 624-mile Mullan Road (named for its surveyor, Lieutenant John Mullan) between 1859 and 1862. Connecting Fort Benton, the head of Missouri River steamboat navigation, to Fort Walla Walla, near the navigable lower Columbia River, the Mullan Road was cut by the army in order to transport troops and supplies. Soon, however, hundreds of miners, missionaries, entrepreneurs, and farmer immigrants cluttered the trail, turning it into a vital route for 1860s gold seekers bound for mines in the present-day states of Washington, Idaho, and Montana.

Stagecoaches were vital common carriers—commercial transporters of mail, freight, and passengers. Like many western businesses, stagecoach companies began small and then earned enough capital to become larger firms. Eastern coach companies begun by Henry Wells (who ran a string of speech therapy schools in New York), John Butterfield, and William Fargo became the basis of the famous modern firms American Express and Wells Fargo. The Butterfield line opened its southern route running through Texas to California in 1857.[8] In 1860 the California Stage Company ran the seven-hundred-mile route between Portland, Oregon, and Sacramento, California, in an impressive six days. Beginning in 1852, Wells, Fargo & Company, California Stage's famed competitor, offered service out of San Francisco to most of the West's mining districts. In 1862, Ben Holladay, the "Stagecoach King," briefly challenged Wells and Fargo before selling out to them in 1866, and then founded the Oregon Central Railroad. For a brief moment, between the stagecoaches and the telegraph, the Pony Express filled the gap for rapid delivery of mail.

Steamboats ran the upper Missouri, Sacramento, lower Columbia, and other western rivers throughout the years before the Civil War. From 1850 to 1860 a dozen small competitors vied to haul miners and supplies along the Columbia and Snake rivers to Lewiston, in present-day Idaho. Their tough low-draft steamers symbolized a rough and ready era of independent rivermen who navigated around rocks, shoals, and numerous dangerous drift logs in swift currents, rapids, and falls. In 1860 the Oregon Steam Navigation Company bought them all out, controlling the trade (with twenty-six steamers) until 1880.[9] During this time the company built the Northwest's first railroad track, a mere six miles, to facilitate transshipment of steamboat cargoes around the Celilo Falls of the Columbia River. This little stretch of track marked the tender beginning of the western stretch of what would become the Northern Pacific Railroad.

The Iron Horse Races West

American railroads had already started to undercut prices in river traffic by the Civil War. Railroads stretched into Missouri and Wisconsin, and construction continued westward after the war. Most students of history are familiar with the subsidized transcontinental railroads that received millions of acres of federal land to support their construction. The other side of the story, however, is that hundreds of local train lines and two transcontinentals—the Great Northern and the Milwaukee Railroad—were funded and built purely with *private* capital. So, when the Union Pacific and Northern Pacific Railroads lobbied Congress after the Civil War, contending that only government could help them complete their transcontinentals, they were wrong. James J. Hill soon built a more efficient competing line without government aid, and so too did the owners of the Milwaukee Railroad. Private roads not only survived panics when subsidized roads failed, but the owners of unsubsidized lines also spent their own funds to relocate farmers (future customers) along their routes, to invest in agricultural research and livestock breeding, and to ensure that the lines, once completed, would remain healthy. And, it is worth noting, the private companies—on their own—arrived at a national railroad track width standard without any involvement of government, universally agreeing to the 4-foot-8.5-inch standard by 1886.[10]

Transcontinentals provided countless benefits, ending the isolation of many westerners and providing them with "metropolitan corridors." Life was better with easier travel for visiting friends and relatives, and leisure destinations as well as for conducting business. In thousands of western towns, the railroad station became the hub of community life, where locals eagerly awaited the daily arrival of freight and passengers, and the railroad's telegraph office became a vital link to the outside. Before radio, westerners gathered around railroad telegraphers to learn presidential election results, international news, and even the scores of football and World Series games. Railroads also contributed to the rise of America's national parks as America's first generation of ecotourists booked passage aboard special spur lines created by the Great Northern, Northern Pacific, and Southern Pacific railroads to tour Glacier, Yellowstone, and Grand Canyon National Parks. Railroad entrepreneurs like Henry Villard, in fact, plotted the routes of their lines to showcase the West's majesty, and when buffalo became a major attraction at Yellowstone Park, park officials attempted to ensure that passengers could see the buffalo herds from the train.[11]

The Natural Resources Frontier

Trends seen in the evolution of natural resource extraction industries—fur, fish, ore, timber, ranching, and agriculture—actually parallel several of the patterns of the stagecoach, steamboat, and transcontinental railroad industries. Entrepreneurs tended to start out small, but larger concerns soon came to dominate, largely because technology and capital were necessary to efficiently harvest natural resources. An important result of this efficiency, however, was a tendency to overharvest in the short term—a failure to conserve natural resources—which quickly produced higher prices and efforts to moderate extraction in the longer term.

Although historians have been quick to blame this environmental waste and destruction on the forces of free-market capitalism, once again the picture is not so clear.[12] In opposition to laissez-faire principles, the federal government often played a major role in leasing or giving federal land to miners, loggers, farmers, ranchers, and fishermen, distorting incentives by making resources cheap that, had the market had its way, would have come at a much higher cost.[13] Then, as today, federal and state governments, not market forces, regulated many natural resource extraction industries and often did so poorly, actually undercutting market forces that would have adjusted prices and, therefore, supply. Contrary to the "capitalist menace" view of the environment and extraction-related industries, it was the existence of so much *public* land—the absence of *private* property—that was the main detriment to responsible stewardship of western natural resources.[14]

As we have seen, fur trappers were the first to overharvest public lands. The American Fur Company, which flourished under the often heavy-handed direction of John Jacob Astor, began diversifying into emerging industries.[15] Before the British retreated to the forty-ninth parallel in 1846, the Hudson's Bay Company was harvesting, drying, and pickling western salmon for export to Europe. Following the Civil War, American entrepreneurs cashed in on the revolutionary changes brought by the invention of the canning process. Canned fish, especially salmon, reaped spectacular profits for large concerns like Hapgood, Hume and Company, which employed thousands of Scandinavian immigrant fishermen and Chinese cannery workers. Like the fur trappers, fishermen overharvested the public waterways; as early as 1877, trap and net fishing had interrupted and stifled salmon spawning. At the mouth of some western rivers, the armada of fishing boats was so thick during the salmon spawning season that fishermen could literally walk from deck to deck over the hundreds of fishing boats; industry technology was so efficient that it threatened its own long-term survival.

In the case of fur and fish, the early American legal system had not yet developed appropriate ways to privatize property rights so that those responsible for using the resources bore the full cost.[16] Often, industrial polluters would dump waste in streams and rivers without owning any more than a small section of waterfront land. Other industrialists, however, displayed much better stewardship: Frederick Weyerhaeuser and Gustavus Swift, for example, voluntarily monitored replacement of resources and pollution as commonsense responses to wise land management. It was simply good business to ensure a constant supply of one's raw materials, whether trees or cattle.

The rush to mine the West's rich veins of gold, silver, and copper ore also brought technology, capitalization, and environmental waste. While the Civil War raged back east, miners fanned out to seek gold in the present-day states of California, Nevada (site of the famed Comstock Lode), Washington, Idaho, and Montana. Afterward they tried their luck in Colorado, in the Black Hills of the Dakotas, and near the turn of the century, in the newly acquired Alaska. Canadian gold rushes in the Fraser River Valley of British Columbia and the Yukon Territory, saw similar patterns and usually drew the same multinational work force.

In the early stages, mining rushes were peopled by individualistic entrepreneurs—the fabled sourdoughs equipped with only a pick and shovel, a gold pan, a few months' grubstake, and a mule to carry it all to El Dorado. Very few struck it rich, and most prospectors soon gave up and moved on to better pickings. Some took advantage of collaborative efforts to strike it rich. Groups of miners replaced single panning with rockers, sluice boxes, and Long Toms, with which they channeled fast-moving river water to strain dirt and more efficiently search for gold. The crude sluices, however, soon gave way to hydraulic mining—the use of powerful pumps and water hoses to wash down and cull entire hillsides in search of ore. Hydraulics of this magnitude required capital and expertise, which brought large companies and professional management and mining engineers. This evolution was completed with lode mining—the use of dynamite and rock crushers to separate veins of gold, silver, and copper ore from hard rock buried deep within mountainsides. By the time lode mining had begun, the sourdoughs and their sluices had long departed, and many of those who had come west to strike it rich found themselves working for a paycheck in company towns like Butte, Montana, or Globe, Arizona.

While gold fever was claiming one sort of western immigrant, the thick forests, rich with spruce, cedar, pine, and Douglas fir trees, were beckoning another type, the logger. Although the Hudson's Bay Company had built a major logging and saw-milling operation in and around Fort Vancouver in 1827, smaller entrepreneurs also soon flocked to the West, drawn by the sheer abundance of natural resources. Western loggers followed water routes, floating timber down navigable rivers leading to sawmills like those at the mouth of the Columbia and Sacramento Rivers, and on Puget Sound (Port Blakely and Port Ludlow), Grays Harbor, Washington, and Coos Bay, Oregon. The railroads' need for hundreds of thousands of railroad ties provided an important early market.

This small-scale decentralized logging business was revolutionized in the 1880s with the introduction of the narrow-gauge railroad, which made it possible to cut forests far away from navigable rivers. Innovations such as crosscut saws, donkey engines, steam loaders, and steam-powered band saws, which could increase mill output tenfold, dramatically changed and improved the ways loggers felled, loaded, and processed timber.

This was all capital-intensive technology, which meant that small entrepreneurs soon gave way to larger better-financed firms like the St. Paul and Tacoma Lumber Company and the Weyerhaeuser Company, which themselves had started small. Weyerhaeuser himself went broke in 1857 but soon tried again.[17] His genius lay in his ability to see the final product and to understand the business concept of vertical integration, whereby the company owned all the various parts of the production process, from raw material to transportation to sales. By 1885 his Beef Sough Company processed some 500 million board feet of lumber. At that point he still tended to use the forests as if they were infinite, but in 1900, having purchased nearly a million acres from the Great Northern Railroad, Weyerhaeuser's inspectors found that the lands were not nearly as rich in timber as he had thought. That discovery forced him—as market forces do—to focus on reforestation, preventing soil erosion, and on fire prevention. Then, as today, more forest lands are destroyed by fires (most caused by lightning) than are lost by harvesting. (The historian of fire in America, Stephen Pyne, found that from 1940 to 1965, when fire prevention techniques were far more advanced than in Weyerhaeuser's time, lightning started some 228,000 fires in the United States, burning up to a million acres in a single forest!)[18] Weyerhaeuser and, soon, other paper giants like International Paper and Kimberly-Clark began massive re-forestation programs in which the companies planted, on average, about five times more than they consumed.[19] Kimberly-Clark, in 1902, became the first producer of paper products to embark on a long-term woodlands management program, employing hundreds of professional foresters before the U.S. government entered the arena of forest conservation.[20]

Whenever possible, of course, companies sought to use federal funds and federal lands while leasing and harvesting as many state and federal tracts as could be acquired. Interestingly, the Weyerhaeuser Company's ultimate domi-nance of northwestern logging (the company owned 26 percent and 20 percent, respectively, of all Washington and Oregon timber stands) was an indirect result of federal largesse. Frederick Weyerhaeuser bought his Northwest empire at six dollars per acre from his St. Paul, Minnesota, neighbor James J. Hill; Hill had ob-tained it when he bought the extensive federal land grants of Henry Villard's bankrupt Northern Pacific. Weyerhaeuser proceeded to build the world's largest sawmill in Everett, Washington, in 1914.[21]

A much different industry developed on the plains where, from 1865 to 1885, the West witnessed the rise and fall of the Cattle Kingdom. Prior to the Civil War, when thousands of cattle populated the Texas plains, with ranches stretch-ing into Oregon and California, ranchers had shipped cattle to New Orleans. A special breed of cow, the Texas longhorn—derisively referred to in the East as "eight pounds of hamburger on eight hundred pounds of bone and horn"—could thrive on range grasses without additional feeding, and those cattle proved espe-cially resistant to the ticks that carried Texas fever.[22] Ironically, however, the resis-tance to the fever made the Longhorn a dangerous presence in the East where the ticks fell off and soon infected other nonresistant breeds, leading to an almost-uniform quarantining of Texas Longhorns prior to the mid-1860s. Then, by accident, drovers found that freezing temperatures killed the ticks: if a herd was held over on a northern range during a frost, it could be tick free. Joseph G. McCoy, the founder of the town of Abilene, Kansas, was among the first to ap-preciate the benefits of both Abilene's cold weather and its location. He encour-aged ranchers to send their herds to the Kansas Pacific Railroad's railhead in his town, which offered transportation to eastern markets.[23] Jesse Chisholm (not to be confused with another cattle trailblazer, John Chisum) cut a trail from Texas to Abilene in 1867 (the Chisholm Trail), with his cowboys driving some 35,000 head north in the first year alone. More than 2 million cattle came up the

Chisholm Trail during the next twenty years.[24] Cattle barons like Charles Good-night and Oliver Loving established their own well-worn trails for getting herds to the railheads. Boom towns sprang up to accommodate the cattle drovers as the railroad lines extended westward.[25]

From 1865 to the 1880s, the cattle frontier was in its prime.[26] Ranches such as the King Ranch and the XIT Ranch covered thousands of acres, and tens of thousands of cattle arrived in Dodge City every year during its heyday, in the process creating one of the most thoroughly American figures in history—the cowboy.

There was something special about the American cowboy. Everything from his clothing to his entertainments to the dangers he faced seemed to represent both the best and worst of young America. Typical drives lasted weeks. During that time, upward of a dozen or more cowboys spent every day on horseback and every night on hard sod with only a saddle for a pillow. Meals came from the ever-present chuck wagon that accompanied the drives, and they usually consisted of beans, bacon, hardtack, potatoes, onions, and whatever game might be killed along the way without spooking the herd. The wagon master drove the chuck wagon, cooked, handled all sewing and repair chores for the cowboys, set up and broke down camp, and when necessary was doctor or vet. Any cattle spotted along the way that had no visible brand were immediately roped, branded, and inventoried into the herd. Cattle required water at regular intervals, and the trail boss had to make sure he did not misread a map and cause an entire herd to die of thirst. Indians or white squatters frequently had control of strategic watering holes, for whose use which they extracted a hefty tribute from the desperate cowboys.[27]

Once the herd reached the railhead, the cattle went into stockyards to await trains to the Chicago slaughterhouses while the dusty and thirsty cowboys took their pay and visited the bars and bordellos. That was what made the cattle towns so violent—a combination of liquor, guns, and men nearly crazy from the boredom of the drive. Yet outside these railhead towns, and excluding a few of the episodes of gang-type violence, the numbers of capital crimes in the West appear to be well below current violent crime rates, so the Wild West was only moderately more violent than the rest of society.[28]

Historian Roger McGrath studied the Sierra Nevada mining towns of Aurora and Bodie, which had more potential for violence than other western towns. There he found that homicide rates were high, especially among the "bad men" who hung out at the saloons, although the homicide rate was about the same as in modern-day Washington, D.C. Yet he also discovered that virtually all other crime was nonexistent, certainly due in part to the presence of an armed populace. Robberies in Aurora and Bodie were 7 percent of modern-day New York City's levels; burglary was 1 percent; and rape was unheard of.[29]

Another study, by Robert Dykstra, of five cattle towns with a reputation for violence—Abilene, Ellsworth, Wichita, Dodge City, and Caldwell—discovered that the total cumulative number of homicides was less than two per year. Again, rape and robbery—except for trains and stagecoaches—was largely unknown. Still another researcher, examining Texas frontier towns from 1875 to 1900, found murder to be rare—not counting "fair fights" staged by gunslingers. Burglary and theft were so absent that people routinely did not lock their doors. Even in the California gold fields, with all its greed, researchers found little record of violence.[30]

For a brief time it seemed as if the cattle frontier and the ubiquitous cowboys would never disappear. During the 1880s the price of beef skyrocketed, and large European investment firms entered the market; in 1883, for example, Wyoming alone hosted twelve cattle firms with $12 million in assets. But because none of these cattlemen owned the land on which their cattle grazed—the public domain—none had much interest in taking care of it. By 1885 there were far too many cattle overharvesting the grass of the public lands of the Great Plains. Tragically, the weather turned at the same time the cattle were short of feed. In the winter of 1886–87, temperatures plummeted to lows of minus 68 degrees Fahrenheit. Hundreds of thousands of cattle died of starvation, unable to graze the barren Plains.

The cowboy was usually the last in a line of characters to reach a town before civilization set in. Following the trappers, miners, soldiers, and missionaries, the cowboys inevitably gave way to the next wave of settlers, the farmers. The Homestead Act made available land in the form of 160-acre grants to 400,000 individuals and families from 1862 to 1890.[31] Total improved acreage in the United States rose from 189 million to 414 million acres, and although the Homestead grants were marked by fraud, the westward migration of legitimate farm families, and the economic and environmental impact of that migration, brought a staggering change to the demography and environment of the American West.

In true frontier fashion, new western farmers adapted to the semiarid conditions that awaited most of them. New steel-bladed John Deere plows sliced through prairie soil that had lain dormant for centuries; and barbed wire, developed by John Warne Gates, became a standard fencing material on the treeless Plains.[32] Windmills pumped ground water, and pioneers learned Mormon techniques for dryland farming and irrigation. Corn, wheat, and oat crops were complemented by alfalfa for winter feed for cattle and sheep herds; then, later, fruit, vegetables, potatoes, and sugar beets emerged as important crops in California, the Great Basin of Utah, and on the Columbia Plain.[33]

Yet frontier farmers found themselves pushed out by an emergent, highly industrialized agribusiness sector. For example, the typical farm size of 160 acres, a figure determined by unrealistic politicians in the lush eastern United States, was woefully inadequate to support Plains agriculture. Drought, harsh winters, and competition from agribusiness combined to hurt small producers. Only capitalized firms could afford the equipment—steam-powered tractors, combines, harvesters, and irrigation technology—that characterized successful farming west of the Mississippi. The small farm in America truly died more than a hundred years ago of its own inefficiency, when two thirds of all homesteaders failed. Even when farming proved profitable, life on the frontier beat down the sodbusters (who got their name from breaking ground with their plows) and their families with periods of mind-numbing boredom mixed with near-death situations. Wild animals, poisonous reptiles, deadly diseases, drought, subzero cold, and blazing heat all combined to make prairie living exceedingly hard. Sodbusters had to ward off clouds of locusts, track down stray horses, keep their wells safe, and watch out for strangers or Indians. Their nearest neighbor might be miles away, and the closest town often a day or two's ride. Generally, a prairie family would purchase supplies for a month and might not see other humans for weeks.[34] No one in a farm family had much leisure time: farm life involved backbreaking work from well before sunrise until after sunset. Farmers often ate five hearty meals a day. They rose before sunup, ate an early dawn breakfast, took a mid-morning break for another small meal, returned at lunch, had a late after-noon snack, and then ate a full-scale dinner after sundown. That meant that wives spent virtually their entire lives cooking, cleaning up from one meal, then starting another. And cleaning in a house made of sod—dirt!—itself constituted a monumental task. Despite low pay, sodbusters tried to hang on because of the in-dependence farm life offered and the opportunity they had to own land. Never-theless, most went broke, and those fortunate farmers who eventually did acquire their property after paying off the mortgage still faced problems: seldom did crop prices increase enough for them to expand operations.

But there had to be something to it: from 1860 to 1910, the number of farms in America tripled. This dynamic placed some 50 million people in an agricul-tural setting, cultivating "500 million acres, an area as large as western Europe."[35] Such farm-sector expansion was accelerated by something as small as a sharp piece of wire sticking out from a twisted wire at regular intervals—barbed wire. Joseph F. Glidden and Jacob Haish, two Illinois farmers, patented barbed wire in the mid-1870s, and by decade's end production had soared to more than 80 mil-lion pounds, costing less than $2 per 100 pounds. The appearance of barbed wire carried profound significance for the Plains, where little wood existed, and it benefited from the sales pitch of John Warne "Bet-a-Million" Gates, who trained a herd of docile steers and used them in his demonstrations. In fact, the wire worked as advertised.[36] Wire did what innumerable judges, sheriffs, and even vig-ilantes could not: it secured the property rights of the small farmer against the cattle barons. And it took little to lay new wire if a farmer was fortunate enough to expand his holdings. In the short run, this forced the constant westward migra-tion of the cattle drovers; in the long run it probably secured the viability of large agricultural operations.

Farming, milling, lumbering, mining, ranching, and harvesting of natural resources in the American West thus exhibited striking consistency. Small pro-ducers and entrepreneurs began the process, only to be superseded by large cap-italized firms that could afford the technology necessary to efficiently harvest fur, fish, timber, ore, cattle, and foodstuffs. In so doing, they produced riches that benefited millions of Americans. The evidence shows that those who enjoyed government favors and subsidies abused the resources the most; whereas those who had to pay their own way proved the best conservators of our natural heritage.

Ultimately, the story of the harvesting of natural resources in the West is far from a tragic one. Rather, it is a story of transition and adjustment. The settlement and expansion of the trans-Mississippi West exactly paralleled the rise of the Industrial Revolution and the subsequent decline of small producers and farmsteads in America toward the end of the nineteenth century and reflected a growth in manufacturing.

Without question, some of the generation that migrated west following the Civil War paid a hard price for modernity. Most never found their dream of a western Eden. Yet in the long run, a great many of them found a level of independence and prosperity unheard of in Europe. Those who did adjust, and their children after them, reaped the many benefits the Industrial Revolution and modernity brought in increased standards of living and life expectancy. Only one group was largely left out of either the rising prosperity or the expanding political freedom in the West—the original inhabitants.

The Indians' Next-to-the-Last Stand

Since colonial times, interactions between whites and Indians had followed a remarkably similar pattern, regardless of the region in which those interactions took place. Upon first contact Indians and non-Indians were often peaceful toward one another and made many important cross-cultural exchanges—food, language, religion, medicine, military techniques, and material culture (tools, weapons, clothing, and so forth). However, this initial peace was always followed by conflict over land, which would lead to a land treaty and then more misunderstanding and anger, and eventually a war, which always ended in Indian defeat. This, in turn, resulted in either the extermination or expulsion (farther West) of native Indian peoples. By the time of the Civil War, nearly all Indians east of the Mississippi were either dead, buttoned up on small reservations, or pushed westward, where this same cycle of relations had started anew.

Indians of the trans-Mississippi West were diverse regional groups inhabiting the Plains, Rocky Mountains, and the Pacific coast. Relocated tribes—eastern Indians such as the Cherokee, Creek, Delaware, Shawnee, and Miami—occupied tracts of land directly west of the Mississippi or in the Oklahoma Indian Territory. Along the Pacific shore, from Alaska to northern California, coastal Indians (Puyallup, Makah, Tlingit, Nisqualli, Chinook, and so on) lived in abundance and created sophisticated art, architecture, religion, and material culture. In the southwestern mountains, Hopi and Navajo herded livestock and farmed corn; neighboring Apache hunted and gathered on horseback like the vast majority of Columbia Plateau (Yakama, Spokane, and Nez Percé) and Great Plains Indians.

The Great Plains Indians—located in between the relocated Indians and West Coast, Plateau, and mountain tribes—constituted the most formidable barrier to white settlement.

At one time, Plains Indians had been farmers. Introduction of the horse by Europeans literally transformed the world of the Plains tribes. Once they had the horse, hunting buffalo became much easier, turning the Indians into nomads who roamed the prairie in search of the herds.[37] These herds, by any assessment, were vast at the time the first whites encountered them. Colonel Richard Dodge wrote in 1871 that "the whole country appeared one mass of buffalo," an observation similar to that by Thomas Farnham in 1839 on the Santa Fe Trail, when he watched a single herd cross his line of sight for three days.[38] To say that the animals covered the interior of America is not much of an exaggeration. They did not last long, however.

Even before the introduction of the horse, Indians had hunted bison, though not nearly as effectively. They tracked herds on foot, often setting fire to the grasslands in a massive box, surrounding a herd, except for a small opening through which the panicked animals ran—and were slaughtered by the hundreds.

Frequently, though not universally, Indians destroyed entire herds, using fire or running them off cliffs. One Indian spiritual belief held that if a single animal escaped, it would warn all other animals in the region; and other Indian concepts of animals viewed the animal population as essentially infinite, supplied by the gods.[39] Ecohistorians agree that although hunting by the Plains Indians alone did not threaten the bison with extinction, when combined with other natural factors, including fire and predators, Indian hunting may have put the buffalo on the road to extinction over time, regardless of the subsequent devastating impact of white hunters.[40]

The fatal weakness of the Plains nomads regarding the buffalo was expressed by traveler John McDougall when he wrote of the Blackfeet in 1865, "Without the buffalo they would be helpless, and yet the whole nation did not own one."[41] The crucial point is that the Indians did not herd and breed the very animal they depended on. No system of surplus accumulation existed. Since the entire source of wealth could rot and degrade, none could exist for long. Moreover, the nomadic life made it impossible to haul much baggage, and therefore personal property could not be accumulated. This led fur trader Edwin Denig to conclude that this deficiency prevented the Plains nomads from storing provisions and made them utterly dependent on European trade goods.[42]

A great ecomyth has appeared, however, about the Indians and their relationship with the buffalo, wherein Indians were portrayed as the first true ecologists and environmentalists. Nothing could be further from the truth. Traveler after traveler reported seeing herds of rotting carcasses in the sun, often with only a hump or tongue gone. While the bison was, as Tom McHugh claimed, "a tribal department store," with horns used for arrows, intestines for containers, skins and hides for teepee coverings and shields, and muscle for ropes, it is misleading to suggest that Indians did not wantonly slaughter buffalo at times.[43] Father Pierre De Smet observed an Assiniboin hunt in which two thousand to three thousand Indians surrounded an entire herd of six hundred bison and killed every one. Aside from their own deprivation—which they could only notice when it was too late to prevent—the Indians had no way of estimating or tracking the size and health of the herds, and even if they could, nomadic lifestyle "made it difficult to enforce the mandates against waste."[44]

It is also meaningless to employ terms like ecological imperialism to describe the interaction of the Europeans and the Indians. People of different races and ethnic backgrounds had come into contact with each other globally for centuries, from the Chinese in Southeast Asia to the Mongols in Europe to the Arabs in Africa. Seeds, germs, animals, viruses—all have interacted incessantly around the world for eons. (Even the European honeybee had settled as far west as St. Louis by the early 1700s.) To invoke such language is an attempt to reattach blame to Columbus and capitalism after anthropologists and historians have discovered that North American Indians had choices in how their world was shaped, and made no greater share of right—or wrong—choices than the new arrivals from Europe.[45]

Still, it is unarguable that once a market for buffalo hides, bones, and other parts developed, it paid white hunters to shoot every buffalo in sight, which they tended to do. By 1900 fewer than a couple of thousand buffalo remained, at which point the government sought to protect them on federal lands, such as Yellowstone National Park, one of the first main refuges.

Whatever the numbers, the elimination of the buffalo not only nearly exterminated a species, but it also further diminished the Plains Indians' ability to sustain themselves and pushed them into a lifestyle that made them much more likely to come into conflict with whites. Having become nomads following the herds—as opposed to landowners working farms—whatever concepts of property rights they had held vanished. So too disappeared any need for them to respect white property rights, no matter how questionably gained. After the nomadic culture overtook Plains Indian life, a new culture of hunting with an emphasis on weapons naturally infused their society.

Ironically, the nomadic lifestyle at the same time protected the Plains tribes from diseases that ravaged more stationary eastern Indian tribes, although a few, such as the Assiniboin, picked up smallpox and other diseases in neighboring villages and carried them home. It took several encounters with European diseases before the Indians discovered that humans transmitted them. But by about 1800, the "village" Indians had been decimated by diseases, whereas the nomadic tribes were relatively untouched. Thus, not only had the transformation of Indian society by bison hunting actually saved many of the Indians from an early death, but some of the techniques they practiced on the buffalo—riding and shooting, maneuvering, teamwork—also proved valuable in a challenge of a different sort: their wars against the American soldiers.

In battle, these Plains Indians could be fierce warriors. They fought while galloping at full speed, dropping and rising at will and using their horses as shields. This combination of phenomenal horsemanship and skilled marksmanship (with bow, spear, and repeating carbine rifle) proved deadly. Ultimately, the U.S. government would expend incredible resources—$1 million and 25 U.S. soldiers—for *each one* of these fierce, courageous people killed, merely exposing the complex and often contradictory problems inherent in federal Indian policy.[46]

Philosophically, American policy makers were divided into camps of preservationists, exterminationists, and assimilationists, with the latter two dominating policy debates. Preservationists such as Helen Hunt Jackson, author of *Century of Dishonor* (1885), were idealists who proposed simply leaving the Indians alone and free to roam the Plains and continue their hunting and gathering lifestyle.[47] Such romantics, of course, ignored violent Indian conquest and the documented expansion of such empires as the Lakota Sioux, who brutally smashed all opposition on the Great Plains.[48]

Equally unrealistic and less humane, intolerant exterminationists argued that preservation and assimilation were both impossible. Indians could never adjust to modernity, said exterminationists; they had to stand aside for progress because their day was done. According to this essentially racist view, any Indians who violently resisted reservation confinement should be killed, a sentiment that supposedly originated with General Philip Sheridan, who had allegedly said, "The only good Indians I ever saw were dead." In fact, Sheridan, as commander of the Division of the Missouri, supervised many reservations, and thought it important to the protection of the Indians to keep them on the agency lands, lest the whites kill them.[49] Reality was that the closer one got to the frontier, the more likely one was to see such sentiments expressed. Cleanse the Plains, roared the Nebraska *City Press*, and "exterminate the whole fraternity of redskins," whereas the Montana *Post* called notions of "civilizing" the Indians "sickly sentimentalism [that] should be consigned to novel writers. . . ."[50] If the hostiles did not end their barbarities immediately, "wipe them out," the paper intoned.

Like his predecessor at the Division of the Missouri, General William Tecumseh Sherman, Sheridan had no qualms about ruthlessly punishing Indians who strayed off the reservation to commit atrocities, and he renewed efforts to enforce confinement of tribes on reservations.[51] Certainly many soldiers, who had lost comrades in battles with the Sioux or Cheyenne, had no mercy for the Indian: "They must be hunted like wolves," Brigadier General Patrick Conner told Major General Grenville Dodge.[52]

The third group, the assimilationists, however, had a realistic view that industrialization and progress made the preservationist ideal impossible, but any effort to exterminate the natives was not only uncivilized and un-Christian, but also unconstitutional. Assimilationists argued that Indians must be put on reservations and cured of their nomadic ways for their own protection. The tribes had to learn English, embrace Christianity, and adopt the farming and ranching techniques of whites in the hope that they or their children might one day become working men and women in mainstream American civilization. This reservation system was the only "alternative to extinction," but it destroyed Indian culture as effectively as any military campaign, as critics rightly charged.[53] A glaring weakness in the assimilationist position lay in the fact that many of the so-called civilized tribes had already been forced off their lands anyway, regardless of their level of civilization.

While the assimilationist views finally prevailed, exterminationist voices remained loud in the halls of Congress, and at times federal strategy for dealing with the Indians incorporated all three viewpoints. Almost everyone, Indian and white alike, would have agreed that the approach to the Indians was confusing and contradictory. "Our whole Indian policy," wrote the editor of The Nation magazine in 1865, "is a system of mismanagement, and in many parts one of gigantic abuse."[54] In many ways, that policy only reflected the irreconcilable differences among these three strategies for dealing with the Native Americans. And although the task of moving nomadic, warlike Indian people onto reservations without incident was, in retrospect, nearly impossible, the government nevertheless commited avoidable errors.

At the root of the problems with establishing any coherent Indian policy lay a conflict of interest between the two federal agencies authorized to deal with the tribes—the Bureau of Indian Affairs (BIA) and the U.S. Army. The BIA reported to Congress, drafted Indian policy, and staffed the Indian reservation bureaucracy; the BIA planned for, governed, fed, clothed, medicated, and educated the nomads of the Plains. Created in 1824 as the Indian Bureau of the Department of War, Congress moved the agency to the newly created Interior Department in 1849. Civilian departments, which relied far less on merit than the military, by their nature spawned a thoroughgoing corruption. Christian denominations administered some agencies under the Grant Administration (and certainly they were not free from corruption either), but many other reservations landed in the hands of political hacks with get-rich-quick schemes to defraud the natives. The illegal sale of supplies, blankets, and food designated for the Indians not only deprived the tribes of necessities, but also provoked them to aggression that otherwise might have been prevented.

The other federal agency—the U.S. Army—was charged with rounding up the Indians, relocating them to their respective reservations, and keeping them there if they tried to leave.[55] Thus the army emerged as the enforcement arm of BIA policy, which was a bad arrangement under any circumstance. Frontier military forces were heavy on cavalry and infantry, and light on artillery, as dictated by the fighting style of their enemy. Other nontraditional elements soon characterized the frontier military, including scout units of Crow and other Indians, often dressed in uniform, assigned to every command. Then there were the Buffalo Soldiers, companies of African American troops whom the Indians thought had hair like bison. Stationed with the Tenth Cavalry and other regiments, the black soldiers greatly troubled the Indians, although the most interrogators could learn from Native American captives was that "Buffalo soldier no good, heap bad medicine."[56]

Despite its differences from previous armies, the U.S. Army on the frontier still had a simple mission: to engage and destroy any enemies of the United States. Fighting against the Western way of war, the natives could not win. The Native American style of war resembled the failed traditions of the Muslims at Tours or the Egyptians at the Battle of the Pyramids. It featured hit-and-run tactics, individual melee combat, personal courage in order to attain battlefield honor (as opposed to unit cohesion), and largely unsynchronized attacks.

Since most army commanders were in the exterminationist camp and most of the BIA officers espoused assimilation, there was bound to be confusion and violence. Sherman described the disconcerting tension exacted on the Indians by the policies as a "double process of peace within their reservation and war without."[57] Even before the conclusion of the Civil War, this "double process" began to take shape on the Great Plains, and it would conclude with some of the most shocking U.S. Cavalry defeats in the entire frontier period.

Sand Creek and Yellow Hair

Four major Indian wars ended once and for all the cycle of death that had characterized white-Indian contact for more than 250 years. The first, from 1864 to 1865, occurred when Cheyenne and Arapaho warriors fiercely battled U.S. troops in Colorado. During the summer of 1864, Cheyenne Chief Black Kettle led assaults on white miners, farm settlers, and travelers, but, weary of fighting, he surrendered in November. Black Kettle accepted a tribal land outside Pueblo, Colorado, and raised an American flag outside his tent, only to see his men, women, and children massacred by drunken Colorado militiamen (not U.S. regulars) in a sneak attack on November twenty-eighth at Sand Creek. One witness later testified that in this infamous Sand Creek massacre, Indians "were scalped . . . their brains knocked out; the men used their knives, ripped open women, clubbed little children, knocked them in the head with their guns [and] mutilated their bodies in every sense of the word."[58] Fighting resumed until the fall of 1865, when again the Cheyenne agreed to go to a permanent reservation.

Farther north the mighty Lakota Sioux also resisted white incursions. Their struggle began in 1862–63 in Minnesota, a theater of the war that ended when U.S. Army General John Pope achieved victory and hanged 38 Sioux warriors as punishment. Farther west, in 1866, Lieutenant Colonel William J. Fetterman, who had once boasted that he could "ride through the whole Sioux nation with 80 men," was leading a detachment of 80 men (ironically) to the relief of a wood-gathering train when a party of Oglala Sioux led by Red Cloud, and including a young warrior named Crazy Horse, annihilated his command in a precursor to the Custer massacre.[59] To anyone paying attention, the signs at the Fetterman debacle were ominous: tribes that had scarcely gotten along in the past and that controlled different regions of the Plains—Sioux, Cheyenne, and Arapaho—had simultaneously begun to resist, and to do so over vast expanses of territory. Yet during the twenty-minute Fetterman slaughter, two civilians wielding 16-shot Henry repeaters accounted for dozens of Sioux casualties. Had the Sioux appreciated the lethality of rapid-fire weapons, they would have known that even a moderate advantage in numbers would not be sufficient against similarly armed well-disciplined bluecoats.

Two years after the destruction of the Fetterman party, Sioux attacked engineers constructing a road to Fort Bozeman, in Montana. Red Cloud, by then a leading Sioux warrior, had led the incursions, but army counterattacks and subsequent promises to cease construction of the road persuaded him to retire to a Sioux reservation in the Dakotas. Following further incidents of corruption at the reservation agency, where delay in the delivery of food and supplies further antagonized the Sioux, they again bolted the reservation and renewed hostilities. By that time, a more or less constant state of war existed on the Plains, with one tribe or another constantly menacing, or being menaced by, the army. From 1868 to 1874 in the Southwest, Kiowa, Commanche, Arapaho, and Cheyenne all engaged in a series of battles against military units. Despite the number of engagements, Indians still had failed to act in concert on a large scale, allowing the army to achieve tactical superiority and feeding its overconfidence.

All this changed in June 1875. Northern Cheyenne and Sioux were once again driven to warfare by fresh white encroachments on their land. A gold rush in the Black Hills of South Dakota combined with the arrival there of the Northern Pacific Railroad to spark renewed warfare. Making matters worse in this case, the Sioux viewed the Dakota Black Hills as sacred ground, and they considered any white intrusion an act of sacrilegious trespass. Sioux leaders Sitting Bull, the diplomat father figure, and Crazy Horse, the cunning, eccentric tactician, assembled a substantial and impressive collection of tribes who reluctantly left the reservation to once again fight American soldiers. Acting as commander in chief, Sitting Bull planned the strategy.[60] Crazy Horse, whose bravery none questioned, was one of the few Indians to perceive that the Western way of war had powerful—even insurmountable—advantages: he was the only Indian observed by soldiers to dismount in order to fire his rifle, and while still a young man he had forsaken scalping.

The army knew the tribes had gathered at a general location below the Yellowstone River and its Bighorn River tributary in what is southeastern Montana. Commanding General Sheridan devised a plan to pincer the Indians south of the Yellowstone between a three-pronged American force. From the south, General George Crook would move from Wyoming Territory; from western Montana, Colonel John Gibbon would march with his men eastward along the Yellowstone River; and a third force under General Alfred Terry, supported by the entire Seventh Cavalry, would attack from the Dakotas. Since no one knew exactly where the Indians were encamped in June of 1876, the army's elaborate plan immediately began to unravel when Indians attempted to engage each wing separately. Crook was beaten in mid-June and returned to base. In late June, to find the Sioux, Terry dispatched Colonel George Custer and nearly 700 cavalry.[61] Custer, who as a Civil War hero had once held the wartime rank of brigadier general, wanted to reclaim both his former rank and glory. Attired in his famous buckskin coat with his golden locks flowing, the colonel cut a dashing figure. His wife, Elizabeth Bacon, assumed the role of his official publicist, subtly massaging the record of events in Custer's career to present him as the gallant hero at all times. Indians knew him as Son of the Morning Star or Yellow Hair, and he had impressed them in previous battles as fearless. Regular army commanders had a different opinion, considering him reckless and undisciplined. One time he rode alone into an Indian encampment to free two white female hostages; another time he'd been court-martialed for leaving his post and abusing his troops in order to return home to see his Libby.

For all his experience on the Plains, Custer grossly underestimated the size, capabilities, and leadership of the combined Sioux-Cheyenne forces arrayed against him. Against all established military doctrine, he divided his cavalry regiment into four parts—three roughly equal units commanded by himself, Major Marcus Reno, and Captain Frederick Benteen, and a small pack train—and personally led five troops of 265 men to their doom on June 25, 1876.

Despite Hollywood's subsequent depictions, the engagement had little drama: most accounts (including recent archeological mapping of cartridges and body placement) suggest the shooting from Custer's Ridge was over in less than twenty minutes. Reno's men, farther behind the main column, survived only by fleeing to a hill and digging in. There they were reinforced by the third detachment of troops and the pack train.[62] The Sioux had apparently done what no other Native Americans ever had by beating the regular U.S. Army in a head-to-head contest. But when the excited chiefs told Sitting Bull of their overwhelming victory, he reportedly noted that the white man was as numerous as the leaves on the trees, and he commanded the village to pack up and withdraw before Terry's main body arrived.

The old adage about winning the battle but losing the war is most applicable in the case of Custer's last battle. Word of Little Bighorn arrived in Washington just as the nation was preparing to celebrate the hundred-year anniversary of the American Revolution. Despite his many personal and professional flaws, Americans immediately embraced George Armstrong Custer as a martyr for the cause of American manifest destiny and sought to avenge his slaying. A mere four months after the Battle of the Little Bighorn, Sioux and Northern Cheyenne stood defeated, and they surrendered once and for all. On October 31, 1876, a new treaty sent the Sioux back to their Dakota reservation, ending the Plains Indian wars.

One more tragic, and perversely paradoxical, saga was to unfold. By 1890 the Sioux had been thoroughly demoralized. In this state of mind, they turned to spiritualism in the form of the cult of the Ghost Dance, performed in the desperate belief that dancing would banish the white men, return Indian lands, and make Indians invulnerable to bullets and cannons. Military governors, alarmed at the wild mysticism of the Ghost Dancers, ordered them to stop, and ominously sent in the Seventh Cavalry to make them desist. Two weeks earlier the Indian Agency had attempted to arrest Sitting Bull for supporting the Ghost Dancers, and in the process a gun battle broke out and the chief was killed, along with a dozen of his bodyguards and police.[63] On December 29, 1890, troops bungled their attempt to disarm the Sioux at Wounded Knee, site of the Sioux Reservation in South Dakota. In subzero temperatures shooting broke out, although both white and Indian witnesses disagreed over who started the firing. Popularly viewed as a cold-blooded massacre—some 200 Sioux men, women, and children lay dead in the snow—the army lost 25 killed and 39 wounded.[64] But it is certain that the Indians did not deliberately provoke a fight, since they could see they were surrounded by troops and artillery. Although Wounded Knee marked another dark episode in Indian-white relations, the government had already concluded that the reservation system was not working, leading to yet another direction in American Indian policy.

The Final Stages of Assimilation

The assimilation movement had gained momentum three years before Wounded Knee, with passage of the Dawes Severalty Act (1887), wherein Indian reservations (with some exceptions) were divided into approximately 160-acre plots for male family heads, with lesser amounts to individuals. Indians had four years to select their land, after which the selection was made for them by the agent. Supported strongly by President Grover Cleveland, who saw the government as a guardian to the wards of the state, the Dawes Act reflected Cleveland's personal views of the Indians, which swung from "lazy, vicious and stupid" to "industrious, peaceful, and intelligent."[65] Along with other reformers who saw the Indians as needing guidance, but who also agreed that "barbarism and civilization cannot live together," Cleveland preferred a process of civic and cultural instruction in which the Native Americans would learn English in government schools and gradually attain all the formal conventions of citizenship.[66]

In the Dawes Act, Congress also sought to move Native Americans away from the tribal system and fully into the market economy by making them landowners, but as with most dealings with the Indians, there were also ulterior, less noble, motives. Any unclaimed lands went on the open land market, which whites snapped up. But the purpose of Dawes was not to steal land—although that certainly happened—but to change the tribal organization and habits of the Indians. Supporters called it the Emancipation Proclamation for the Indian, and the Friends of the Indian (eastern religious leaders and humanitarians) also embraced the legislation. The gap between where the Indians were and where they needed to be in order to fully function in a market economy, however, was too great. Over the next decades, generations of Plains Indians born to reservation life fared little better than those who had openly fought U.S. soldiers. Alcoholism, high infant mortality, and poverty characterized the generation of Indians who struggled to make the transition from nomadic life to modernity. Congress finally gave up on the Dawes Act in the 1930s, by which time many Indians had lost their land, although others had doggedly survived and, in some cases, managed to flourish.

Change came painfully slowly: not until the middle of the twentieth century did the lives of a significant number of Indians improve. Grandchildren and great-grandchildren of the brave Plains warriors fought with distinction as American soldiers, sailors, airmen, and marines in World Wars I and II, the Korean War, Vietnam, and the Gulf and Iraq wars. (Perhaps the most famous was one of the flag raisers on Iwo Jima's Mount Suribachi, Ira Hayes.) Indians learned to speak English, embraced both Protestant and Catholic Christianity, and slowly began to assimilate into mainstream culture. Problems persisted, but by the late twentieth century, individual American Indians enjoyed success on almost every social, political, and economic front.

By that time, after three centuries of depopulation, Indians finally began to see their numbers increase. Alcoholism abated somewhat, and with that so too did infant mortality rates and fetal alcohol syndrome. Tribal elementary and secondary schools ultimately spawned tribal colleges; many Indians left to attend state and private colleges and universities. Native American politicians entered government, rising as high as the vice presidency of the United States (Republican Charles Curtis of Kansas) and the United States Senate (Republican Ben Nighthorse Campbell of Colorado). Some Indians earned law degrees and returned home to file suit and win enforcement of Indian treaty rights (including fishing) in state and federal courts. Others formed tribal corporations and harvested their reservations' natural resources—timber, ore, oil, agriculture, and fish—to vastly increase their per capita income and standard of living. Others hunted in the most fertile new grounds, the tourism market, building hunting lodges, museums, and gambling casinos to mine an increasing number of non-Indians who yearned to visit and experience "Indian Country."

Success, however, remains a relative term when describing efforts to move Native Americans into the market economy (many reservations have unemployment rates of over 40 percent). In light of these challenges, perhaps the greatest story of Native American assimilation and achievement has been that of the Mississippi Choctaw under the leadership of Chief Philip Martin. In 1975, Martin determined that the tribe's future lay in attracting private enterprise, and he convinced the tribal council to give him nearly absolute power to negotiate contracts, to enforce work rules, and to make the Choctaw reservation as competitive as any place in the private sector.[67] Using government guarantees and a couple of small federal grants, Martin constructed the infrastructure for a business park—roads, sewage, water, and other facilities. Then the tribe sent out 150 advertising packages to companies. General Motors responded, contracting the Choctaw to assemble wire harnesses for electrical parts, requiring Martin's agreement that the Indians perform as well as any white company. He dealt with employees firmly and even ruthlessly: no tardiness, no sloppy dress, and above all, perfect workmanship.

Soon a greeting card company, then Ford, then other companies began moving into Choctaw land, and Martin's positions were vindicated. Ford gave the tribe a quality performance award, and unemployment, which had reached 75 percent before Chief Martin took control, dipped to under 20 percent, a level high by white standards, but amazingly low for an Indian reservation. By 1993 the Choctaw Indian tribe was the tenth largest employer in the state of Mississippi.[68]

The Choctaw notwithstanding, it would be unwise to declare a happy ending to a four-hundred-year history of warfare, abuse, theft, and treachery by whites, and of suffering by Indians. Yet it is absolutely correct to say that the end result of Indian-white cross-acculturation has been a certain level of assimilation, an aim that had once seemed hopeless. Modern Indians are proud Americans who simultaneously embrace their Indian ethnicity and folk traditions, Christianity, western legal traditions, capitalism, and all facets of mainstream American civilization. But getting there has been a difficult, bloody, and tragic struggle.

Territorial Government and Statehood

The legal status of western territories and the means by which they were to become states in the Union is not even mentioned in the Federal Constitution. Beginning with the Northwest Ordinance of 1787, a series of Organic Acts, as they were called, set down the rules whereby frontiersmen could gain equal citizenship in the United States of America. Westerners often grew disgruntled under the rule of federally appointed territorial officials and what they saw as inordinately long territorial periods. A variety of factors weighted the length of time it took a territory to become a state: American domestic politics, foreign policy, and even social mores and religion played a role. Although most of the western states had joined the Union by 1912, it was not until 1958 and 1959 that Alaska and Hawaii at last completed their journeys through the territorial process.

Territories west of the Mississippi slowly became states in the Union before the Civil War because of the politics of slavery. Louisiana (1803), Texas (1845), and California (1850) entered under special agreements tied to American foreign policy; the remaining territories (like Oregon and Nevada, which became states in 1859 and 1864, respectively) fell under Organic Acts resembling the Northwest and Southwest Ordinances of 1787 and 1789. By the late nineteenth century, nearly all of the western territories had reached the requisite population necessary for admission to the Union. But, as before, political complications characterized their attempts to achieve statehood.

Washington Territory provides a good case study of the territorial process. Carved out of the huge Oregon Territory six years before Oregon proper became a state, Congress divided Washington Territory twice again during the nearly four decades its citizens awaited statehood. Today's Idaho, Montana, and parts of Wyoming all, at one time or another, composed the Washington Territory.

Like that of other territories, the early history of Washington was dominated by political bickering between Whigs (and Republicans) and Democrats and a strong territorial governor, Isaac Ingalls Stevens. A lifelong Democrat and West Point engineering graduate, Stevens represented the best and worst of the territorial system. He was intelligent, efficient, and tireless, and he left an indelible legacy of strong territorial government, a railroad, and a vast Indian reservation complex in the Pacific Northwest. But he ruled with an iron hand. Stevens's authoritarianism is exemplified by the fact that, during his 1853–57 term of duty, he served simultaneously as territorial governor, federal Indian superintendent, federal Indian treaty negotiator, and U.S. Army surveyor for the northern transcontinental railroad!

With this kind of authority, and conflicts of interests, Stevens engaged in an aggressive Indian policy to make way for what he sincerely viewed as God-ordained white progression onto Indian lands. Unable to resist Stevens's persuasion and intimidation, between 1854 and 1856 northwestern coastal and plateau Indians surrendered 64 million acres in return for fishing rights, a few gifts, and reservations. Yet these treaties immediately led to warfare between Stevens's troops and Indians angered by what they perceived as his duplicity and heavy-handedness. Meanwhile, Whig political opposition to Stevens resulted in a bitter court fight over his suspension of habeas corpus and declaration of martial law during the Indian war, unconstitutional actions for which Stevens was later convicted and fined fifty dollars.

When Stevens left Washington to serve as its territorial congressman in the other Washington in 1857, he had cut a wide swath across the territorial history of the Pacific Northwest. In 1861 he rejoined the army as a general. In characteristic fashion, Isaac Stevens died in a blaze of glory, carrying his Union detachment's colors in the 1862 Civil War battle of Chantilly, Virginia.[69]

Nearly four decades passed between Stevens's governorship and the final admission of Washington to the Union in 1889, even though the territory had sufficient population and could have produced an acceptable constitution by the 1870s. Why did it remain a federal territory? Most of the reasons for delay were political. First, the Civil War intervened. At war's end, as Democrats were reintegrated into national political life, Washington found its solid Republican leanings a distinct disadvantage. After 1877, Democratic congressmen mustered enough votes to thwart Washington's admission. Then too, the territory's image, true or not, as a hotbed of anti-Chinese violence, advocacy of woman suffrage, and home for socialist labor groups, definitely made federal politicians look askance.

Finally, when the Republicans won both the presidency and Congress in 1888, lame-duck Democrats decided they had antagonized westerners long enough, and in one of his last acts as president, in 1889, Cleveland signed the famed Omnibus Bill, another in the series of Organic Acts. This bill simultaneously admitted Washington, Montana, and North Dakota and South Dakota as full-fledged states in the Union. Idaho and Wyoming followed in 1890.

Unlike Washingtonians and Idahoans, Mormon Utahans usually voted as Democrats in the nineteenth century. Yet this affiliation did not win them any friends in Congress, where their religious beliefs were unacceptable to nearly all non-Mormon (Gentile) Americans. The main stumbling block was the Mormon practice of polygamy, and the Mormons' detractors vowed that Utah would remain a territory and that Mormons would be denied citizenship as long as they continued to practice this belief.[70]

Initially, Mormons had sought to entirely escape the laws of the United States by establishing independence in Mexican territory. When Americans won Utah in the Mexican-American War, the newly arrived Mormons ignored and resisted territorial government in favor of their own theocracy led by Brigham Young. In 1857, President Buchanan sent General Albert Sidney Johnston and 2,500 Army cavalry troops to enforce U.S. sovereignty in the famed (and bloodless) Mormon War. In 1858, through a negotiator, Young reached an agreement with Buchanan in which the church would recognize the United States as sovereign in all temporal matters, whereas the Mormon Church would have spiritual authority over its members. This amounted to little more than the old arrangements under which the popes and kings in Europe had operated for hundreds of years. Soon thereafter, the Mormons accepted Buchanan's territorial governor, Alfred Cumming.

Matters were not fully resolved, however. In 1862, Congress passed the Morrill Anti-Bigamy Act, abolishing plural marriage and disallowing Mormon church assets over $50,000. The Morrill law raised constitutional issues that Mormons fought out all the way to the U.S. Supreme Court. Losing in court, some Mormons (a small percentage actually) continued to practice polygamy in direct defiance of federal authority.[71]

Finally, the Edmunds Act of 1882 denied the vote and other constitutional rights to all polygamists. Moreover, it declared any children born into polygamous families after 1883 to be illegitimate, without the legal right of inheritance, which would have obliterated the Mormons' coveted family structure and stripped Mormons of all their assets. They challenged the Edmunds Act in the Supreme Court case of *Romney vs. United States* (1889) but lost again, at which point the Mormons at last surrendered and officially renounced plural marriage. Soon thereafter, in 1896, Congress admitted Utah as the forty-sixth state. New Mexico and Arizona, whose populations had lagged far behind Utah and the other western states, followed in 1912. Thus, by the early twentieth century, all of the territories in the contiguous portions of America had achieved statehood.[72]

Yet westward expansion (and the territorial and statehood systems) also included Alaska and Hawaii. Alaska became a U.S. possession (though not a territory) in 1867, when William Seward, the secretary of state, negotiated to purchase all Russian claims north of 54 degrees latitude for a mere $7.2 million. This figure seems cheap today, but at that time Seward's foes labeled the purchase of this icy acreage an act of lunacy.

Hawaii followed in 1893, when American settlers overthrew Queen Lili-uokalani and established a provisional government, which the United States rec-ognized.[73] In fact, Congress had coveted the Hawaiian Islands for several years, and the islands had been populated and influenced by a large number of Ameri-cans, but business, specifically the North American sugar industry, which feared the competition, opposed annexation. However, the new president, William McKinley, supported expansion, and an annexation resolution passed Congress in 1898.[74] Two years later, Congress created the Hawaii Territory, mainly with an eye for use as a coaling station for the new blue-water navy that the nation had started to construct. Although virtually no one saw the Far East as being of much importance in American security issues, the Spanish-American War had left the United States in control of Guam and the Philippines, creating a vast operating space for warships attempting to operate out of West Coast bases. In keeping with the naval doctrines of Alfred Thayer Mahan, the projection of seaborne forces at long distances was crucial, and, therefore so was their refueling and supply. Hawaii, with its wonderful natural harbor, fit the bill.

Alaska's legal limbo from 1867 to 1912—being neither territory nor state—only exacerbated the natural animosity colonial Americans had always felt toward the federal government. Gold rushes in the Klondike and Nome from 1896 to 1900 brought more people north—twenty thousand in the new city of Nome alone by 1900—who established some fifty new mining camp/cities in a ten-year stretch. Even though the growing population led to territorial status, Alaska's geographic isolation and low European-American population made its wait for statehood the longest of any American territory. The Alaska Railroad was built by 1923, in the process leading to the founding of Anchorage, the largest city in Alaska. Such enterprises helped, but World War II proved to be the turn-ing point. The Japanese invasion of the Aleutian Islands prompted a strong U.S. military presence in Alaska, which in turn resulted in the long-awaited comple-tion of the Alaska Highway. The Alcan, as it was called, connected the continen-tal United States and Alaska year round via a road spanning the Canadian province of British Columbia and the Yukon Territory. Meanwhile, Japan's 1941 surprise attack on Pearl Harbor brought a huge military force to the Hawaiian Islands, and simultaneously propelled that territory's efforts to achieve state-hood. Congress made Alaska the forty-ninth state in 1958, and Hawaii followed in 1959.

Alaskan and Hawaiian statehood temporarily ended the territorial story, but not for long. Debates over the territorial system continue today in Puerto Rico and other Caribbean and Pacific regions annexed by Americans during their nineteenth-century expansion under manifest destiny. And periodically the issue of statehood for the District of Columbia surfaces. Long before Alaska and

Hawaii completed the final jigsaw that is the map of the modern United States, however, the West, as a concept, had come to an end. Barbed wire, railroads, and, eventually, the invisible strands of American civilization made the West America, and America, the West.

Prairie Populism and National Radicalism

Despite abundant opportunities on the frontier, the fact was that life in the West, especially on the Plains, was hard. For every miner who hit paydirt, ten abandoned their claims and found other work. For every farmer who managed a successful homestead, several gave up and returned east. And for every cattle rancher who nurtured his herds into large holdings, dozens sold out and gave up. There was nothing new about this, except the setting, the West. Yet for the first time, significant numbers of westerners found allies in other sections of the country—people who shared their frustrations with the same economic trends.

Miners, farmers, and laborers alike grew discontented in the late nineteenth century, often for different reasons. In mining, fishing, logging, and sawmill towns, capitalism's creative destruction process caused tumultuous change, with economic panics causing unemployment rates to twice rise as high as 30 percent. Wage earners complained of low salaries and dangerous working conditions, which led to the formation of labor unions, not a few of which were steeped in violence and socialism. But even in the countryside, western farmers were growing angry over low crop prices, high railroad rates, and competition from agribusiness, expressing the sentiments of producers everywhere who found that they simply did not produce enough value for their fellow man. This realization, whether in the English spinning industry of the 1830s or the American auto industry of the 1980s, is difficult, especially for those falling behind. It did not, however, change the reality of the situation: with the availability of Homestead lands and the opening of the new territories, the number of farms exploded. There were simply too many farmers in America.

They too protested, but used the ballot not the bullet. A set of laws known as the Granger Laws, named for the farm network the Grangers (or the Patrons of Husbandry), began to take effect in the 1870s. Attempting to control railroad and grain elevator prices, maintain competition, and forestall consolidation, the Grangers achieved their greatest victory in 1876 with *Munn v. Illinois*, a case involving a grain elevator operator's fees. The U.S. Supreme Court laid down an alarming doctrine that private property in which the public has an interest must submit to public controls.[75] Under such reasoning, virtually any enterprise ever open to the public became the business of the government, a legal rendering that to a large degree stood the Constitution's property clause on its head. Fortunately, capitalism succeeded in spite of these "reforms," producing so much wealth that most working people prospered and industry expanded no matter what stifling regulatory barriers the growing federal and state bureaucracies threw up.

In western towns, as in the countryside, there was discontent. As in all emerging capitalist economies, the first generation of industrial laborers bore the brunt of rapid change. They worked, on average, sixty hours per week, with skilled laborers earning twenty cents an hour while unskilled earned half that, although these numbers could vary widely depending on industry and region.[76] Dangerous work in industries like logging, mining, and fishing offered no job security, unemployment compensation, medical insurance, or retirement pensions, nor, frequently, did even minimal safety standards exist. Moreover, laborers were not free to bargain with business owners over wages and work conditions because government stacked the deck against them. Federal and state politicians outlawed union membership, issued court injunctions to halt strikes and cripple labor activism, and sent in federal and state government troops to protect the interests of powerful businessmen.

Those who tried to improve their status by forming labor unions, often in violation of local antiunion laws, found that America's prosperity worked against them by attracting nonunion immigrants who leaped at the opportunity to receive wages considered too low by union members. An early response to the issue of low wages came from the Knights of Labor, an organization originally formed in Philadelphia in 1869, which moved west in the 1880s. The Knights sought equity in the workplace, but only for white workers; they were noted for their opposition to Chinese and African American workers. Chinese worked for wages below those Knights of Labor demanded and so the Knights, shouting, "The Chinese Must Go!" violently expelled the entire Chinese population (seven hundred) of Tacoma, Washington, in November of 1885. Later, when African American coal miners crossed the Knights' picket lines in Roslyn, Washington, the Knights again resorted to violence. In the end, however, the black strikebreakers (and the coal company) won the day, but it was a typical union response toward minorities that held sway well into the 1960s.

More radical than the Knights of Labor were the Western Federation of Miners (WFM) and the Industrial Workers of the World (IWW, the "Wobblies"). These groups took labor violence to new heights, in the process severely damaging the collective bargaining cause. Under the leadership of Ed Boyce in Kellogg, Idaho, the WFM stole a train, loaded it with dynamite, and blew up a million dollars worth of the mine owners' infrastructure. Wobblies, on the other hand, started out peacefully. Led by Big Bill Haywood, they published pamphlets, made speeches, and filled the Spokane, Washington, jail in peaceful acts of civil disobedience. Ultimately, however, the Wobblies gained fame (or infamy, depending on one's view) in violent imbroglios known as the Everett and Centralia massacres of the World War I era.

But both those unions were exceptions that proved the rule. In the main, western laborers and their unions had legitimate grievances they tried to address through the existing political system. Although saddled with unfair governmental restraints, they worked with western governors, judges, and legislators for peaceful change. Political activism, combined with the prosperity of the capitalist system, eventually brought them the improved wealth and lifestyle they sought, in the process undercutting their very reason for existence. It presented a dilemma for leaders of the union movements, just as similar circumstances would present a difficult problem for civil-rights and union leaders in the 1980s and 1990s: what do you do when, to a large degree, you have achieved your ends? The leader must either find or create new problems that need to be resolved, or admit there is no longer a purpose for him or the organization.

Meanwhile, republican political institutions addressed the complaints of the farmers and laborers, with limited success, through Populist and Progressive political movements, both of which aimed at harnessing capitalism to protect working people from its perceived dangers. Whatever gains they achieved in the courts were illusory: there is no way to mandate higher pay or greater wealth for any group. Like the mine workers, many western farmers perceived that they were on the outside looking in at the prosperity of the Industrial Revolution. Just as the small artisans and weavers of the 1820s had been overtaken by the large spinning mills and manufacturers, farmers often could not compete without large-scale, mass-production equipment like steam tractors, mechanical reapers, spreaders, and harrowers that only well-capitalized agribusiness could afford. It was the classic tale of efficiency gains forcing out the less productive members of a profession.

Farmers, of course, perceived it differently. Small landholders blamed nearly all of their problems on federal policies favoring big business: the gold standard, the tariff, and subsidization of railroads. Like all debtors, farmers wanted inflation and pursued it through any of several measures. One strategy involved reviving the greenback, which was the Civil War currency not directly backed by gold. But this flew in the face of the system of gold-backed national bank notes established to print and circulate paper money, the network of nationally chartered banks that had operated since 1863.

Another more popular option, which appealed to miners as well as farmers, called for inflation by expanding the money supply through the augmentation of the existing gold coins with silver coins. Coinage would occur at a ratio of sixteen to one (sixteen ounces of silver for an ounce of gold, or roughly sixteen silver dollars to a gold dollar), which was problematic, since silver at the time was only worth seventeen to one (that is, it would take seventeen silver dollars to exchange for one gold dollar). The "silverites" therefore wanted to force the government to purchase silver at artificially high prices—at taxpayer expense. Silverite objectives suffered a setback when, in 1873, Congress refused to monetize silver, an action that caused the prosilver factions to explode, calling it the Crime of '73.[77]

Alongside monetary policy reforms, farmers sought to create a federal regulatory agency to set railroad rates (again, more specifically, "to set them artificially low").

They rightly complained that federally subsidized railroad owners of the Union Pacific and Northern Pacific railroads gave lower rates to high-production agribusinessmen. Lost in the debate was the issue of whether those railroads should have been subsidized by the government in the first place; but once funded, the railroads, to some degree, owed their existence to Washington.[78]

Populism was born from this stiff opposition to gold and railroads, evolving from organizations such as the Grange (1867) and the Greenbacker Party (1876), then launched as a national political campaign in the 1890s. Both a southern and western agrarian political crusade, Populism gained special strength west of the Mississippi River. The Populist Party formed around a nucleus of southern and western farmers, but also enjoyed the support of ranchers, miners (especially silver miners), and townspeople and businessmen whose livelihoods were connected to agriculture. Although Populists courted the urban workingman voters, they never succeeded in stretching beyond their rural base. Socialists in the WFM and IWW thought Populists far too moderate (and religious) to create lasting change and, at root, hated the private enterprise system that the Populists merely sought to reform.

In the 1892 presidential election, Populist candidate James K. Weaver garnered 1 million popular votes, 22 electoral votes, and helped elect 12 Populist congressmen and three governors. On this base, Populists soon successfully infiltrated the Democrat Party.[79] With "Free Silver" as their rallying cry, in 1896, Populists and Democrats united to nominate William Jennings Bryan, a fiery, thirty-six-year-old Nebraska congressman, for president. Bryan roused the Populist movement to new heights when he angrily proclaimed:

> You come and tell us that the great cities are in favor of the gold standard; we reply that the great cities rest upon the broad and fertile prairies. Burn down your cities and leave our farms, and your cities will spring up again, as if by magic. But destroy our farms and the grass will grow in the streets of every city in the country. . . . Having behind us the producing masses of the nation and the world . . . the laboring interests and the toilers everywhere, we will answer their demand for a gold standard by saying to them: "You shall not press upon the brow of labor this crown of thorns; you shall not crucify mankind upon a cross of gold![80]

Yet stirring oratory never reversed a major American demographic and political shift, and the Populists simply failed to grasp the fact that in the course of the last half of the nineteenth century, political power had markedly moved from the farm to the city. This dynamic, with the farmers steadily losing clout at the polls and the marketplace, produced an angst that exaggerated the plight of the agrarians, a phenomena called psychic insecurity by historian Richard Hofstadter.[81] Although Bryan carried nearly every state in the agricultural South and the West, William McKinley still defeated him handily, 271 electoral votes to 176. The frontier had, indeed, come to an end.

Despite defeat, the Populists bequeathed a disturbing legacy to American politics and economics. Their late nineteenth-century cry for governmental regulation of the economy and monetary inflation did not vanish, but translated into a more urban-based reform movement of the early twentieth century— Progressivism.

CHAPTER TWELVE

Sinews of Democracy, 1876–96

Life After Reconstruction

With reconstruction essentially over, the nation shifted its attention from the plight of the freedmen toward other issues: settling the West, the rise of large-scale enterprise, political corruption, and the growth of large cities.

Chief among the new concerns was the corrupt spoils system. Newspapers loved graft and corruption because these topics are easy to write about, and they provided reporters with clear villains and strong morality plays. Patronage also dominated public discourse because of an aggressive wing of the Republican Party dedicated to overthrowing what it saw as vestiges of Jacksonianism. Moreover, the spoils issue and political corruption spilled over into almost all other aspects of American life: it affected the transcontinental railroads through the Crédit Mobilier scandal; it had reached into city administration in the reign of Boss Tweed; and it plagued the Bureau of Indian Affairs and its network of dishonest agencies. Large-scale businesses became targets of reformers because, in part, through their political influence they were seen as buying legislation. Rutherford B. Hayes inherited this continuing debate over spoils, and when he left the presidency, the issue had not been resolved.

Time Line

1877: *Munn v. Illinois* case; Great Railway Strike
1878: Bland-Allison Act; Knights of Labor formed
1880: James A. Garfield elected president
1881: Garfield assassinated; Chester A. Arthur becomes president
1882: Chinese Exclusion Act
1883: Pendleton Civil Service Act
1884: Mugwumps split from the Republican Party; Grover Cleveland elected president

1886: American Federation of Labor formed; Haymarket Riot

1887: Veto of the seed corn bill; Congress passes the Dependent Pension
Act; Interstate Commerce Act

1888: Benjamin Harrison defeats Cleveland for the presidency

1890: Sherman Silver Purchase Act and Sherman Antitrust Act passed;
McKinley tariff passed

1892: Cleveland defeats Harrison for the presidency; strong showing
by the Populist Party

1893: Panic of 1893 sets in; Sherman Silver Purchase Act repealed;
Coxey's Army marches on Washington

1894: Pullman strike

1895: J. P. Morgan lends U.S. government gold to stave off federal
bankruptcy

President Hayes

Having survived the closest election in American history, Rutherford Hayes—
"His Fraudulency," his opponents labeled him—may not have had Reconstruction to deal with, but other issues soon consumed him. Hayes knew that federal
intervention had reached its limits in the South, and other means would be required to change both its attitudes and reality. The nature of his own election
meant that he was compromised, and he hoped that business revitalization and
economic recovery might do for the freedmen what the government could not.

Hayes and his wife, Lemonade Lucy (as she was referred to by reporters because of her nonalcoholic table habits), interested the press far more than his actual policies. Lucy Hayes, an attractive woman, captured public fancy and her
religious stamp on the White House gave it a much different tone from that the
Grants had set.[1] Soon, however, attention turned to Hayes's actions as president.
He immediately summoned South Carolina Republican governor Daniel Chamberlain to a Washington meeting, where he reiterated his intention that the federal troops withdraw. Chamberlain, realizing the situation, agreed.

When Hayes addressed reform of civil service, he was certain to anger many
in his own party as well as in the Democratic House. Still, he set to it almost immediately, writing in April 1877, "Now for civil service reform. We must limit and
narrow the area of patronage."[2] Through an executive order, Hayes prohibited
federal officeholders from taking part "in the management of political organizations, caucuses, conventions, or election campaigns."[3] This seemed to defy logic.
After all, many of the best practitioners of spoils asked, what other reason for
winning office was there? Starting with an investigation of the New York customhouse and its excesses under Chester A. Arthur (whom Hayes removed in July
1878), Hayes sought to bring the patronage monster to heel. Both Arthur and a
naval officer whom Hayes had also removed, Alonzo Cornell, were pets of New
York's Roscoe "Boss" Conkling, and the actions sparked a revolt among the spoilsmen in Congress against the president. Conkling held up confirmation of Hayes's
replacements in the Senate, one of whom (for Arthur's spot) was Theodore

Roosevelt Sr., but Hayes prevailed. The president attempted to institute a "new tone" when it came to spoils, instructing his fellow Republicans, "Let no man be put out because he is Mr. Arthur's Friend, and no man be put in merely because he is our friend," but the words rolled right over many in the party.[4]

Still, on a variety of issues the Democratic-controlled House began to challenge or ignore the president outright, passing the Bland-Allison Act of 1878 (purchasing large quantities of silver) over his veto. At the same time, an indictment of two members of the Louisiana election board that had certified Hayes as the winner gave the Democrats the opening they needed to try to unseat him through the courts. A new spate of investigations into the 1876 fraudulent returns, sponsored by Democrats, backfired, unifying the deeply divided Republicans behind the president, who vowed to fight "rather than submit to removal by any means of the Constitutional process of impeachment."[5] He got little favorable treatment from the press, of which he disparagingly remarked that only two of God's creatures could employ the term "We": newspaper editors and men with tapeworms.[6]

No sooner had Hayes reviewed the reports of his subordinates on civil service reform than the country was racked by a series of railroad strikes over pay cuts enacted by the B&O Railroad. From Baltimore to Pittsburgh, bloodshed ensued when strikers fought strikebreakers and state militia forces, and soon clashes occurred in Ohio and New York. Honing to a strictly legalistic line, Hayes instructed federal troops to protect U.S. property, but otherwise not to interfere on either side. By midsummer 1877, the strikes had subsided. A bill to restrict Chinese laborers passed Congress, but Hayes vetoed it, further angering the labor movement. Labor unrest, coupled with the Bland-Allison veto and Republican disunity, gave the Democrats both the House and the Senate in 1878. Still, by continually forcing Hayes to use the veto, recalcitrant Republicans and disaffected Democrats gave the president more power than he would have had otherwise, since he gained both notoriety and popularity from his veto pen. His patience and decorum restored some degree of respect to the presidency. Best of all (in the eyes of voters) Hayes had avoided "Grantism." Hayes demilitarized the South, and introduced civil service reform—all remarkable achievements from a man who was a lame duck from the get-go![7]

Controlling the Spoils Beast

The Hayes tenure ended with a string of vetoes. At the Republican convention, Hayes, like others, was surprised to see a dark horse, James A. Garfield, emerge with the nomination. Old spoilsmen, known as the Stalwarts, had hoped to get Grant a third term, whereas reformers, known as the Half Breeds, supported James G. Blaine, Maine's perpetual-motion machine. Blaine was a big-picture thinker, uninterested in the details or tactics of process. Other than his commitment to reform (which was constantly under press suspicion because of his lavish lifestyle—well above his means—and his mountains of debt), Blaine had little to recommend him to the presidency. He had, for example, an empty legislative record. Hayes's favorite, John Sherman of Ohio, also sliced away votes from the front-runners. But Sherman had no chance at the presidency either: his personality was dull; his voting record was consistent for his district, but lacked vision for the nation; and his rhetoric was uninspiring. Thus Garfield emerged from the pack as the natural compromise candidate. To offset the reformers and placate the Conkling/Stalwart wing, Chester A. Arthur received the vice presidential nomination—a personal affront to Hayes, who had dismissed him.

Like Hayes, Garfield came from Ohio, where he had served as the president of Hiram College before being elected to the House of Representatives. Literate in several languages, Garfield had come from near poverty, and was the last president born in a log cabin. His father had abandoned the family while James was a toddler, so he began working at a young age, driving oxen and mule teams on Ohio's canals. He had fought in the Civil War, advancing through the officer ranks to brigadier general, but Lincoln persuaded him to resign to run for Congress. In 1880, Garfield was elected to the Senate and worked to secure the presidential nomination for Sherman, but before he could even take his seat, he agreed to be the Republican nominee, winning after 36 ballots.

The Democrats offered their own war hero, Winfield Scott Hancock, who had received wounds while fearlessly commanding Union troops from horseback on Cemetery Ridge. He lacked significant political experience, and during the campaign the Republicans published an elegantly bound large book called *Record of the Statesmanship and Achievements of General Winfield Scott Hancock*. It was filled with blank pages. The ex-soldier Hancock also managed to shoot himself in the foot by uttering words that all but sealed his doom, "The tariff question is a local question."[8] Despite a close popular vote, Garfield won a decisive electoral college victory, 214 to 155.

Arthur may have been Garfield's sop to the Stalwarts, but Senator Conkling expected far more for his support, which had handed to Garfield the critical electoral votes of New York.[9] He made clear that he expected the new president to meekly accept any nominations he put forward. Garfield had a reputation as a conciliator; he had no intention of allowing Boss Conkling to dictate federal patronage. After a power play in which Conkling resigned, New Yorkers had had enough, and the legislature retired him.

Garfield's nominations sailed through, including Lincoln's eldest son, Robert, whom Garfield appointed secretary of war.[10] No one knows what Garfield's tenure might have accomplished, since on July 2, 1881, he was shot in a Washington train station by a disgruntled office seeker, Charles Guiteau, who shouted the infamous phrase, "I am a Stalwart and Arthur is president now." Guiteau had spent time in John Humphrey Noyes's Oneida community, where he enthusiastically welcomed the doctrine of free love, although, apparently, no one reciprocated, for his nickname was Charles Gitout. Broke and mentally unstable, Guiteau had demanded the consulship to Vienna in return for voting for

Garfield.[11] The assassin's bullet did not immediately kill the president, though. Garfield lingered for weeks as doctors searched fruitlessly for the bullet; he died on September 19, 1881.

That, indeed, as Guiteau had stated, made Arthur president, even though he had been the de facto president for several months. No one was more stunned at the administration of the new president than the Stalwarts, who had insisted on his vice presidency and who now paid a heavy price in the press. Editors blamed Stalwarts for creating the climate of animosity that could produce a Guiteau, and several Stalwarts observed that they could be instantly hanged in certain cities. Meanwhile, the man associated with corruption and patronage in New York ironically proved a paragon of character as president. He vetoed a rivers and harbors bill that was nothing more than political pork barreling; he prosecuted fraud; and in 1883 he signed what most considered the deathblow to spoils, the Pendleton Civil Service Act.[12] "Elegant Arthur" was the son of a Baptist preacher from Vermont. His patronage positions had made him more a master of the actual details of government than either Hayes or Garfield. Moreover, Arthur had never personally participated in the graft, and had endeavored to make the New York custom house free of graft. But he also viewed patronage as the legitimate prerogative of elected officials and the lubricant of politics, and he wielded the appointment powers at his customs position liberally, if within the letter of the law. Thus, the charges of corruption against him technically never contained any basis in fact, but often gave Arthur the appearance of impropriety.

What surprised Republicans as much as Arthur's position on patronage was his rapid action to reduce the tariff in 1883, arguably making him the first in a long (though not uninterrupted) line of Republican tax cutters. He gained labor's favor by backing the Chinese Exclusion Act (1882). After learning he had Bright's disease, which, at the time, was inevitably debilitating and fatal, he made clear that he would not run for reelection, thereby diminishing his political clout.

Material Abundance, Social "Reform"

While the nation struggled with Reconstruction, patronage, and Indian policy, the pace of industrial production and business enterprise had rapidly accelerated. Growing industries, increasing immigration, and the gradual replacement of the family farm with the new factory system as the chief form of economic organization brought new stresses. Perhaps because the factories were located generally in the North where the intellectuals were; perhaps because the "Negro problem" had proven more difficult to solve; and perhaps because Reconstruction itself in many ways reflected the political corruption that had characterized the Tweed Ring, eastern intellectuals, upper class philanthropists, and middle-class women all gradually abandoned the quest for equality of black Americans in order to focus on goals they could more easily achieve. Emphasizing legislation that regulated large businesses (the hated trusts), these activists pursued widespread social and economic changes under the umbrella of "reform." They also embarked on a crusade to end private vices—mostly exhibited by the lower classes, particularly immigrants—including prostitution, pornography, drugs, and hard liquor.

Another group who saw itself as victims of industry and powerful interests also clamored for change, largely through the direct intervention of the federal government. Agrarians, especially in the West and South, detected what they thought was a deliberate campaign to keep them living on the margin. Convinced that railroads, banks, and grain elevator owners were all conspiring to steal their earnings, reinforced by a government policy of subsidies and deflation, they, too, clamored for reform.

The two groups—the intellectual reformers and the agrarians—had little in common, save that they both saw Uncle Sam as a combination moral evangelist and playground monitor. Whereas upper-class reformers sneered at the rural hicks who wanted to force the railroads to lower prices, they nevertheless saw the necessity to temporarily ally with them. It would be a long road to the ultimate fusion of the two groups in the Prohibition movement, and for the better part of the late nineteenth century they ran on roughly parallel rails without touching.

Part of the affinity for government action had come from experience in the cities, where individuals could not repair their own streets or clear their own harbors. Cities had become exactly what Jefferson feared, pits of political patronage built largely on immigrants and maintained by graft and spoils. Political reform, however, had proved difficult to come by. In the first place, both parties played the spoils game. Second, individuals did benefit from the political largesse, and constituents could, to some degree, be bought off. To the reformers of the late 1800s, this circumstance was eminently correctable, mainly through the expansion of the franchise and through more open and frequent use of the machinery of democracy. Efforts to allow people to bring up their own legislation (with sufficient signatures on a petition), known as an initiative—which originated in rural, Populist circles but which quickly spread to the cities—or to vote on an act of the state legislature, known as a referendum, or even to remove a problem judge or a long-term elected official (a recall) were all discussed frequently.

An equally important issue—and one the reformers thought easier to attain because they controlled the terms of the debate—involved public health. Public health, of course, is ultimately personal and not public at all, and, as the reformers found, addressing public health issues meant imposing one group's standards of hygiene and behavior upon others with, or without, their consent. But the offensive began inoffensively enough, with threats taken seriously by all: safe water and prevention of fire.

Two of the most serious enemies of safe cities in the 1800s, fire and disease, could be fought by the same weapon—water. At the end of the American Revolution, observers were struck by the cities' "almost incredible absence of the most elementary sanitary provisions."[13] At that time in New York, columns of slaves belonging to the wealthiest families each evening carried tubs filled with feces and urine to the banks of the Hudson. Most people simply "disposed of excrement by flipping it through the handiest window."[14] Piles of feces remained where they landed until either Tuesday or Friday, when a city ordinance required they be pushed or swept into the streets. In winter, however, "it lay where it landed," where it received the local appellation "corporate pudding."[15] Locals sank wells in the middle of streets, whereupon seepage drained into the drinking supply. Other sources of water included New York City's Tea Water pump, fed by the seepage from Collect Pond, which by 1783 was filled with dead dogs, cats, rodents, and further seasoned with the laundry drippings of all the shantytown residents who lived on its banks.

The United States trailed France and England in this respect. Paris had fourteen miles of sewers in 1808, and London began a massive sewer system that was substantially completed by 1865, yet Philadelphia still depended heavily on its eighty-two thousand cesspools in 1877. Nevertheless, citywide water systems spread steadily, if slowly, during the century. The resulting improved sanitation was instantly reflected in plunging death rates. By midcentury, typhoid deaths had fallen in Boston and New York, and plummeted in New Orleans and Brooklyn.[16] Digestive illness also dropped steadily. Where cholera once struck fear in the hearts of Jacksonian city dwellers, by the time of the Great Depression it had essentially been eliminated as a major public health threat. Such progress depended heavily on safe water systems.

As late as the 1830s, most citywide water systems were privately constructed: in 1800 only 5.9 percent of waterworks were publicly financed, and in 1830 a full 80 percent of the existing water systems remained in private hands, although this percentage had fallen to only 50 percent by the 1880s.[17] Chicago adopted a modified public system in which an owner of property had to show proof that he owned a lot before he could vote on any levy related to water assessments.[18]

Brooklyn (1857), Chicago (1859), Providence (1869), New Haven (1872), Boston (1876), Cincinnati (1870), and Indianapolis (1870) all had citywide planned water systems, and Worcester, Massachusetts (1890), had the country's first modern sewage disposal plant that employed chemicals to eliminate waste. By that time, nearly six hundred waterworks served more than 14.1 million urban residents. These systems, which used steam pumps, had become fairly sophisticated. Along with cast-iron pipes, these pumps provided effective protection against fire, especially when used in connection with hydrants, which were installed in New York in the early 1800s. By the middle of the century, major cities like Boston and Philadelphia had thousands of hydrants.[19]

Still, large-scale fires swept through Chicago (1871), New York (1876), Colorado Springs (1878), and in San Francisco on multiple dates, some resulting from earthquakes. Chicago suffered more than $200 million in damage—a staggering loss in the nineteenth century—in its 1871 blaze, which, according to legend, was started when Mrs. O'Leary's cow kicked over a lantern. Flames leaped thirty to forty feet into the air, spreading throughout the West Side's downtrodden shacks, then leaping the Chicago River to set most of the city afire. Even the wealthy North Side combusted when the winds carried aloft a burning board that set the district's main fire station afire. Ultimately, thousands of people sought shelter in the frigid October water of Lake Michigan.

These fires occurred in no small part because many cities still used natural gas lighting, which proved susceptible to explosions; fire could then spread easily because wood was the most common construction material in all but the largest buildings. The growing number of citywide water systems and fire departments offered a hope of reducing the number, and spread, of fires. Generally speaking, by 1900 most of the apocalyptic fires that eradicated entire towns occurred on the grasslands, where in a two-year period the Dakota towns of Leola, Jamestown, Sykeston, and Mt. Vernon were "virtually incinerated by fires rising out of the prairies."[20]

Even with fire prevention measures, plenty of water, and urban fire departments (often volunteer), fire-related disasters still plagued America well into the twentieth century. Baltimore suffered a two-day fire in 1904, and the San Francisco quakes set off fires that paved the way for a binge of looting by inhabitants of the notorious Barbary Coast section of town. Soldiers had to be called in, and authorities issued orders to shoot looters on sight.[21]

The introduction of electricity, more than the appearance of water systems, diminished the threat of fires in American cities. Before electricity, urban areas had relied on gas lighting, and a leak could turn city blocks into smoking ruins. When electric dynamos began to provide energy for lighting in the major cities, gas-originated fires naturally became less frequent. The introduction of electricity to business, however, could only ensue after several corporate giants strode onto the national stage.

Titans of Industry

In 1870 steelmaker Andrew Carnegie ordered construction of his Lucy blast furnace, completing the transition of his company into a vertical combination that controlled every aspect of product development, from raw materials to manufacturing to sales. With the Lucy furnace, Carnegie would become a supplier of pig iron to his Union Mills, and when it was completed two years later, the Lucy furnace set world records, turning out 642 tons of steel per week (the average was 350). Completion of the furnace ensured Carnegie a steady supply of raw materials for his Keystone Bridge Company, allowing him to concentrate exclusively on reducing costs. Lucy provided the springboard that Carnegie would need to become the nation's leading steelmaker and one of the wealthiest men in America—a remarkable accomplishment considering he had arrived in America penniless.

Carnegie (born 1835) had come to America from Scotland at the age of thirteen, arriving in Pittsburgh, where his mother had relatives.[22] First employed to change bobbins for $1.20 a week, Carnegie improved his skills with each new job he took. He learned to operate a telegraph and to write messages down directly without the intermediate step of translating from Morse code. His skills impressed the district superintendent of the Pennsylvania Railroad, Thomas Scott, enough that when the Pennsy opened service from Pittsburgh to Philadelphia, Scott hired Carnegie as his personal telegraph operator. The Scotsman soaked up the railroad business from Scott, learning all aspects of business management and placing him in contact with other entrepreneurs. At age twenty-four, when Scott was promoted, Carnegie took over his district supervisor job.

Seeing the railroads firsthand convinced Carnegie that the next boom would occur in the industry that supplied their bridges, leading him to found the Keystone Bridge Company (1865); he then took the next logical step of supplying iron to the bridge company through a small ironworks. In the 1860s, British iron works had turned out 6 million tons. That was B.C.—before Carnegie. After he had applied his managerial skill and innovation to his integrated steel process, the United States surged ahead of British producers as Lucy and other similar furnaces produced 2 million tons of pig iron. Hiring the best managers by offering them a share of the partnership, Carnegie brought in steel men who were innovators in their own right, including Julian Kennedy, who claimed patents on 160 inventions, half of which were in operation at the Carnegie mills during Kennedy's employ.

Carnegie viewed depressions as mere buying opportunities—a time to acquire at a bargain what others, because of circumstance, had to sell. But he ran against the grain in many other ways. Dismissing the old advice against putting all your eggs in one basket, Carnegie said, "Put all your eggs in one basket and watch that basket!" He eagerly embraced new, and foreign, technologies. When his own mills became obsolete, even if built only a few years earlier, he engaged in "creative destruction," whereby he leveled them to build new state-of-the-art facilities.[23] He obtained his own source of raw materials whenever possible: the company's demand for coal and coke had originally led Carnegie into his association with Henry Clay Frick, a titan Carnegie called "a positive genius" who operated 1,200 coke ovens before the age of thirty-five.[24]

Inexpensive steel, obtained by driving costs down through greater efficiencies in production, provided the foundation for America's rapid economic surge, but the obsession with low costs was hardly Carnegie's alone. (John D. Rockefeller had the same attitude toward kerosene when he said, "We are refining oil for the poor man and he must have it cheap and good.")[25] Carnegie put it slightly differently: two pounds of iron shipped to Pittsburgh, two pounds of coal (turned into a quarter pound of coke), a half a pound of limestone from the Alleghenies, and a small amount of Virginia manganese ore yielded one pound of steel that sold for a cent. "That's all that need be said about the steel business," Carnegie adroitly noted.[26]

Carnegie ran the company as a close partnership, rather than a modern corporation. He never fit the modern working definition of "big business," which requires that ownership be separated from management, usually because ownership consists of thousands of stockholders who elect a board of directors who in turn hire a president to run the company. As large as Carnegie Steel was, though, the Scotsman essentially managed the company himself, sometimes consulting his brother or a few close confidants. Thus, the Carnegie management style meant that Carnegie Steel had more in common with the corner drugstore than it did with Rockefeller's equally imposing Standard Oil. Yet it was this structure that gave Carnegie his flexibility and provided the dynamism that kept the company efficient and constantly pushing down prices.

With falling prices came greater sales. Carnegie Steel saw its capital rise from $20 million to $45 million from 1888 to 1898, when production tripled to 6,000 tons of steel a day. "The 4,000 men at Carnegie's Homestead works," noted Paul Johnson, "made three times as much steel in any year as the 15,000 men at the great Krupps works in Essen, supposedly the most modern in Europe."[27] Carnegie slashed the price of steel from $160 a ton for rails in 1875 to $17 a ton by 1898. To Carnegie, it all came down to finding good employees, excellent managers, and then streamlining the process.

That frequently antagonized labor unions, for whom Carnegie had little patience. It was not that he was against labor. Quite the contrary, Carnegie appreciated the value of hard work, but based on his own experience, he expected that workers would do their own negotiating and pay would be highly individualized. He wanted, for example, a sliding scale that would reward greater productivity. Such an approach was fiercely resisted by unions, which, by nature, catered to the least productive workers. Even though he was out of the country when the famous Homestead Strike (1892) occurred—Frick dealt with it—the Scotsman did not disagree with Frick's basic principles, only his tactics. Homestead was a labor-relations blunder of significant proportions, but it tarnished Carnegie's image only slightly. Even Frick, who had tried to sneak in Pinkerton strikebreakers at night to reopen the company and break the strike, became a sympathetic figure in the aftermath when an anarchist named Alexander Berkman burst into his office and shot him twice. After the maniac was subdued, Frick gritted his teeth and insisted that the company physician remove both bullets without anesthesia. The imperturbable Frick then wrote his mother a letter in which he scarcely mentioned the incident: "Was shot twice today, though not seriously."[28]

Frick had only come into the presidency of Carnegie Steel because, by that time, Carnegie was more interested in giving away his fortune and traveling in Europe than in running the company. He epitomized the captains of industry who single-handedly transformed industry after industry. His empire brought him into contact with John D. Rockefeller, who had purchased control of the rich Mesabi iron range in Minnesota, making Carnegie dependent on Rockefeller's iron ore. When Carnegie finally decided to sell his business, he sold it to the premier banker in America, J. P. Morgan, at which point Carnegie's second in command, Charles Schwab, negotiated the deal. Schwab then went on to become a powerful steel magnate in his own right. The sale of Carnegie Steel to Morgan for $450 million constituted the biggest business transaction in history, and made

Carnegie, as Morgan told him, "the richest man in the world." The Scotsman proceeded to give most of it away, distributing more than $300 million to philanthropies, art museums, community libraries, universities, and other endowments that continue to this day.

It is difficult to say which of the nineteenth-century captains of industry was most important, though certainly Carnegie is in the top three. The other two, however, would have to be both John D. Rockefeller and J. P. Morgan, each a business wizard in his own right. Rockefeller probably came in for the most scorn of the three, even described as a "brooding, cautious, secretive man" who founded the "meanest monopoly known to history."[29] When Rockefeller died, another said, "Hell must be half full."[30] One can scarcely imagine that these comments were made about a devout Baptist, a lifelong tither, and a man who did more to provide cheap energy for the masses (and, in the process, probably saved the whales from extinction) than any other person who ever walked the earth.

Rockefeller's father had been a peddler in New York before the family moved to Cleveland, where John went to school. He worked as an assistant bookkeeper, earning fifty cents per day. In that job he developed an eye for the detail of enterprise, although it was in church where he learned of a new venture in oil from a member who became one of his partners in building a refinery. In 1867, Rockefeller, along with Samuel Andrews and Henry Flagler, formed a partnership to drill for oil, but Rockefeller quickly saw that the real profits lay in oil refining. He set out to reduce the waste of the refining process by using his own timber, building his own kilns and manufacturing his own wagons to haul the kerosene, and saving money in other ways. From 1865 to 1870, Rockefeller's prices dropped by half, and the company remained profitable even as competitors failed in droves.

Reorganized as the Standard Oil Company, the firm produced kerosene at such low costs that the previous source of interior lighting, whale oil, became exorbitantly expensive, and whaling immediately began to diminish as a viable energy industry. Cheap kerosene also kept electricity at bay for a brief time, though bringing with it other dangers. Standard Oil's chemists, who were charged by Rockefeller to come up with different uses for the by-products, eventually made some three hundred different products from a single barrel of oil.

After an attempt to fix prices through a pool, which brought nothing but public outrage, Rockefeller developed a new concept in which he would purchase competitors using stock in Standard Oil Company, bringing dozens of refiners into his network. By the 1880s, Standard controlled 80 percent of the kerosene market. Since Standard shipped far more oil than anyone else, the company obtained discounts from railroads known as rebates. It is common practice in small businesses today for a frequent customer, after so many purchases, to receive a free item or a discount. Yet in the 1800s, the rebate became the symbol of unfairness and monopoly control. Most, if not all, of the complaints came from competitors unable to meet Rockefeller's efficiencies—with or without the rebates—never from consumers, whose costs plunged. When Standard obtained 90 percent of the market, kerosene prices had fallen from twenty-six cents to eight cents a gallon. By 1897, at the pinnacle of Standard's control, prices for refined oil reached "their lowest levels in the history of the petroleum industry."[31] Most customers of energy—then and now—would beg for control of that nature.

Yet Rockefeller was under no illusions that he could eliminate competition: "Competitors we must have, we must have," he said. "If we absorb them, be sure it will bring up another."[32] Citing predatory price cutting as a tool to drive out competitors, Rockefeller's critics, such as Ida Tarbell, bemoaned Standard Oil's efficiency. But when John S. McGee, a legal scholar, investigated the testimony of the competitors who claimed to have been harmed by the price cutting, he found "no evidence" to support any claims of predatory price cutting.[33]

Like Carnegie, Rockefeller excelled at philanthropy. His church tithes increased from $100,000 per year at age forty-five to $1 million per year at fifty-three, a truly staggering amount considering that many modern churches have annual budgets of less than $1 million. At eighty years of age, Rockefeller gave away $138 million, and his lifetime philanthropy was more than $540 million, exceeding that of the Scotsman. Where Carnegie had funded secular arts and education, however, Rockefeller gave most of his money to the preaching of the Gospel, although his money helped found the University of Chicago.

John Pierpont ("J.P.") Morgan, while not personally as wealthy as either Rockefeller or Carnegie, nevertheless changed the structure of business more profoundly. A contemporary of both men (Morgan was born in 1837, Rockefeller in 1839, and Carnegie in 1835), Morgan started with more advantages than either. Raised in a home as luxurious as Carnegie's was bleak and schooled in Switzerland, Morgan had nevertheless worked hard at learning the details of business. As a young man, he was strong and tall, although he later suffered from skin disorders that left his prominent nose pockmarked and red. He studied every aspect of the banking and accounting business, apprenticing at Duncan, Sherman and Company, then worked at his father's investment banking office in London. Morgan then joined several partnerships, one with Anthony Drexel that placed him at the center of many railroad reorganizations. His first real railroad deal, which consisted of a mortgage bond issue of $6.5 million for the Kansas Pacific Railroad, taught him that he needed to take a personal role in supervising any railroad to which he lent money. Within years, he was merging, disassembling, and reorganizing railroads he financed as though they were so many toy train sets.

After the Panic of 1873, the failures of several railroads led to a wave of bank bailouts by investment consortia. Most of those roads had received massive government subsidies and land grants, and were not only thoroughly inefficient, but were also laced with corruption. Only Hill's Great Northern, financed almost entirely by private funding, survived the purge. As Morgan and his partners rescued railroad after railroad, they assumed control to restore them to profitability. This was accomplished by making railroads, in essence, look much like banks.

Imposing such a structure on many of the railroads improved their operations and brought them into the managerial revolution by introducing them to modern accounting methods and line-and-staff managerial structures, and pushing them toward vertical combinations.

On one occasion, during the Panic of 1893, Morgan essentially rescued the federal government with a massive bailout, delivering 3.5 million ounces of gold to the U.S. Treasury to stave off national bankruptcy. Again, during the Panic of 1907, Morgan and his network of investment bankers helped save the banking structure, although by then he recognized that the American commercial banking system had grown too large for him to save again. By then, his completely rotund shape; stern, almost scowling, expression; and bulbous irritated nose left him a target for merciless caricatures of the "evil capitalist." Although he hardly matched the private philanthropy of Rockefeller or Carnegie, the Atlas-like Morgan had hoisted Wall Street and the entire U.S. financial world on his back several times and held it aloft until it stabilized.

If Morgan, Rockefeller, and Carnegie had been the only three prominent American business leaders to emerge in the post–Civil War era, they alone would have composed a remarkable story of industrial growth. The entrepreneurial explosion that occurred in the 1830s, however, only accelerated in the postbellum era, unleashing an army of inventors and corporate founders who enabled the United States to leapfrog past Britain and France in productivity, profitability, and innovation. From 1870 to 1900, the U. S. Patent Office granted more than four hundred thousand patents—ten times what was granted in the previous eighty years. The inventors who sparked this remarkable surge owed much to entrepreneurs who had generated a climate of risk taking unknown to the rest of the world (including capitalist Europe and England). Much of the growth derived from the new emphasis on efficiency that came with the appearance of the managerial hierarchies. The goal was to make products without waste, either in labor or in raw materials, and to sell the goods as efficiently as possible.[34]

James B. Duke, who founded the American Tobacco Company, used the Bonsack rolling machine to turn out 120,000 cigarettes per day. Charles Pillsbury, a New Hampshire bread maker, invented the purifier that made bread flour uniform in quality. In 1872 he installed a continuous rolling process similar to Duke's that mass-produced flour. By 1889 his mills were grinding 10,000 barrels of flour a day, drawing wheat from the Dakotas, processing it, then selling it in the East.[35]

Henry J. Heinz's pickle empire, Joseph Campbell's soup business, and Gustavus Swift's meat-packing plants all used mass-processing techniques, combined with innovative advertising and packaging to create household brands of food items. Heinz added a flair for advertising by giving away free pickle samples at the 1892–93 Columbian Exposition in Chicago.[36] Campbell's soups and Pillsbury's bread, along with Isaac Singer's sewing machine, saved women huge blocks of time.

So did other home products, such as soap, which now could be purchased instead of made at home, thanks to British-born soap maker William C. Procter and his brother-in-law, James Gamble. Procter and Gamble processed and sold candles and soap to the Union army, mixing and crushing products used for bar soap. By 1880, P&G, as the firm was known, was turning out daily two hundred thousand cakes of its Ivory soap. The soap, by a fluke in which an employee had left a mixing machine on for too long, was so puffed up with air that it floated. Gamble had the advertising hook he needed: "It Floats!" announced his ads, and later, when an analysis of the composition of the soap showed that it had only .56 percent impurities, the company proudly announced that its product was "99-44/100% Pure."[37]

Greed and Jealousy in the Gilded Age

Not every lumberman held to Frederick Weyerhaeuser's appreciation for replenishing the forests, and not every oilman believed as Rockefeller did that kerosene ought to be cheap and widely available for the consumer. So perhaps it was inevitable that even as wages started a sharp upward rise in the late 1800s and, more important, real purchasing power of industrial employees grew at dramatic rates, a widespread dissatisfaction with the system surfaced.

Although entrepreneurs abounded, with more appearing every day, the fact of life is that not everyone can be an entrepreneur. Most people—other than farmers—worked for someone else and often labored in a factory or a mine, usually under difficult and occasionally dangerous conditions. Workers in the late 1800s often faced tedious, repetitive, and dreary jobs. Plumbers made $3.37 a day; stonemasons, $2.58 a day; and farm laborers, $1.25 a day, usually for a fifty-four-to-sixty-hour work week.[38]

In terms of that era's cost of living, these wages were sufficient, though certainly not generous. Eleven pounds of coffee went for $1.00, a box of chocolate bonbons sold for $0.60, a shirt might cost $1.50 or a pair of boots $0.60, and a cigar (naturally) $0.05.[39] A typical city family in Atlanta would pay, on average, about $120 per year for food, and all other expenses, including medical care, books, vacations, or entertainments, would cost perhaps $85.

Consider a Scots-Irish family in Atlanta in 1890 with one child—the McGloins—whose main source of income came from the father's job in a textile mill, supplemented by his wife's sewing and rent from a boarder. The husband's textile job brought in $312 a year; the wife's sewing added $40 and the boarder's rents another $10. In a typical year, though, the family spent nearly $400, paying for the extra expenses out of credit at the mill store. The McGloins heated their home with wood, used oil lamps for indoor lighting, gave to their church (but only 1 percent), spent no more than $40 per year for clothes, and dealt frequently with roundworm and, in the case of the child, croup.[40]

The life of the McGloins contrasted sharply with the top end of the income scale, a fact that lay at the root of some of the bitterness and anxiety prevalent in the late nineteenth century. Greed and jealousy worked from opposite ends to create strife. Greed on the part of owners and industrialists could be seen in the lavish and (to most people) outrageous expenditures that seemed obscene. Certainly nothing seemed more ostentatious than the mansions erected at Newport, Rhode Island, where the on-site cleaning staff lived in houses larger than those owned by most Americans. Newport's "froth of castles," as one critic described it, often had more rooms than large hotels. Yet the Newport crowd, in truth, did not seek to impress the proletariat as much as each other: they threw extravagant parties replete with party favors consisting of diamond necklaces. Attendees lit cigars with hundred-dollar bills while hosts showered gifts on children, friends, and even pets (one owner had a dinner for the family dog, giving the pooch a necklace worth fifteen thousand dollars). One "castle" had Champagne flowing from its faucets, and one millionaire had his teeth drilled and filled with diamonds so that he literally flashed a million-dollar-smile![41]

America's wealthiest people held between three hundred and four hundred times the capital of ordinary line workers, creating perhaps the greatest wealth gap between the rich and middle class that the nation has ever witnessed. The good news was that there were more of the wealthy: from 1865 to 1892, the number of millionaires in the nation rose from a handful to more than four thousand. That type of upward mobility seemed inconceivable to farmers who faced foreclosure or to factory workers who, despite the fact they actually had more purchasing power, saw their paychecks stagnating. It nevertheless meant that more than ever America was the land of rags to riches.

Still, frustration and jealousy boiled over in the form of calls for specific remedial legislation for what many considered business excesses. Railroads, for example, were excoriated by farmers for the rates they charged, often under the allegation that they enjoyed "monopoly control."

Farmers also suffered more than any other group when falling prices gripped the economy. Farm owners held mortgages whose rates did not change when they were getting less for their crops. Others argued, they could not even *get* mortgages because of the lack of competition, since banks and lending agencies were (in theory) so scarce in the West. Unquestionably, individuals suffered in some circumstances. But setting anecdotes aside, our measure of the condition of farmers and shippers must be judged by the overall statistics and, when possible, application of microlevel studies. Given those criteria, the charges of widespread distress in the late 1800s must be attributed to perception more than reality. For example, numerous studies exist on the mortgage market that demonstrate that mortgages, which only ran for five years in that period, were readjusted in current dollars with each renewal and that statistics of foreclosures show that "the risk of individual foreclosure was quite small," as low as 0.61 percent in Illinois in 1880 and 1.55 percent in Minnesota in 1891.[42] Other statistics suggest that large numbers of farmers failed, although many may have owned their land free and clear at the time of bankruptcy. Most, however, should not have been farming. Again, government subsidies in the form of absurdly cheap (and free) land through the Homestead Acts encouraged westward migration and farming by millions of Americans who, truth be told, were not good farmers. The Homestead Act was in keeping with Jefferson's ideals, but realistically it was going to be accompanied by large numbers of failures.

What about factory laborers? What was their real status and condition? Because anecdotal evidence is unreliable, we have to depend on more sterile statistical analysis, such as that of economic historian Stanley Lebergott. He traced the real earnings of the era, based on two series of statistics. It is clear that regardless which series is used, "With a brief downturn between 1870 and 1880, real nonfarm earnings rose more than 60 percent from 1870 to 1900," and rose more rapidly after the Civil War than ever before.[43] A similar study by Kenneth Sokoloff and Georgia Villafor concluded that real wages during the period 1865 to 1900 rose about 1.4 percent per year—which may seem inconsequential until it is remembered that this was a period of *deflation,* and all other prices were falling. Still other investigations of wages, by Clarence D. Long and Paul Douglas, showed real wages hitting a trough in 1867, then rising almost unbroken until the Panic of 1893—from $1.00 to $1.90.[44] Thus, the average laborer gained consistently and substantially during the postbellum period.[45] Moreover, Joseph Schumpeter noted that "creative destruction" of capitalism often produces benefits to second-generation wage laborers, while the first generation suffered. Averages conceal the angst and poverty that genuinely afflicted many wage laborers, but such is the case in all societies at all times. The issue ultimately comes down to defining the *average* worker, and the evidence is conclusive that American laborers were well paid and their standard of living getting better by the decade.

Even with the cost of higher wages, unprecedented breakthroughs in machinery made businessmen as a class 112 times more productive than the class of lowest-paid laborers. Much of the gain came from the relentless absorption of smaller firms by larger corporations. More, perhaps, came from the application of new technology. Unfortunately, many social critics contended that the ownership of land and factories alone had given the rich their wealth, despite the fact that the sons of the wealthy rarely equaled the success of their fathers and soon saw their fortunes fade.[46] Henry George, for example, in his *Progress and Poverty* (1879) originated the phrase "unearned income" to describe profits from land. Less than a decade later, Edward Bellamy's *Looking Backward* (1888) romanticized about a man who fell asleep in 1887 and woke up a hundred years later to a socialist utopia. One of the most famous children's books of all time, *The Wonderful Wizard of Oz*, by Frank Baum embraced the themes of downtrodden labor and insufficient money. Henry Lloyd's *Wealth Against Commonwealth* (1894) claimed that large consolidations constituted an antidemocratic force that should be smashed by the federal government.[47]

Whether or not the historical statistics support the assertions of farm and labor groups, their perceptions shaped their worldview, and their perception was that the rich were getting richer. In 1899, differences in social strata inspired

Thorstein Veblen, an immigrant social scientist, to publish his *Theory of the Leisure Class*, in which he claimed that the rich had a compulsion toward "conspicuous consumption," or the need to consume ostentatiously in order to, in popular vernacular, rub it in. Although social critics juxtapose the most wealthy with the most desperate, at every level someone had more—or less—than someone else. Such was, after all, the nature of America and capitalism. The urban slum dweller saw the couple living in a duplex as phenomenally blessed; they, in turn, looked at those in the penthouses; and they, in turn, envied the ultrarich in their country manors.

Undoubtedly the reports of Mrs. Vanderbilt's bedroom, which was a replica of Louis XV's wife's room, or the du Pont house, with its electric water-sprinkling systems, its central heating system, and its self-contained drink-bottling plant, stunned many and disgusted others. But there were more than a few who ascribed it to the natural order of things, and still more who saw it as evidence that in America, anything was possible.[48]

Regardless of why the rich behaved the way they did, or whether disparities were as great as some claimed, it is a fact that by the 1880s, farmers and factory laborers increasingly felt a sense of alienation and anxiety and searched for new forms of political expression. The most prominent of these political outlets were in the form of unions and new political organizations.

"Your Masters Sent Out Their Bloodhounds"

Unions had been declared by several courts to be illegal conspiracies until 1842, when the U.S. Supreme Court ruled in *Commonwealth v. Hunt* that unions could legally operate. Even then, however, state conspiracy laws kept unions essentially illegal. Then, after 1890, the Sherman Act was wielded against labor. Employer resistance, pride in the independence of individual workers, and the unfamiliarity with mass movements tended to limit the spread of unionism in the United States prior to 1900, when only 3 percent of the entire industrial workforce was unionized. High wages also diminished the appeal of organized labor. But as might be expected, the expansion of mass production after the Civil War, combined with the discontent over money and nominal, that is, face-value as opposed to real or actual decline in wages, led to a renewed interest in labor organizations.

One of the most successful was Ulrich S. Stephens and Terence V. Powderly's previously mentioned Knights of Labor, founded in 1869. An "essentially secret society" almost like the Freemasons (although it became more open over time), its mysterious origins and secretive overtones derived in part from the earlier suppression of unions.[49] Although the Knights of Labor was not the first national labor organization, it claimed the title and grew the most rapidly. Powderly's strategy involved enlisting everyone—skilled, unskilled, farmers—in order to make the union as large as possible. By 1886, the Knights numbered more than seven hundred thousand, and they successfully struck the Denver Union Pacific railroads and achieved their greatest victory with a strike against Jay Gould's Missouri, Kansas, Texas, and Wabash Railroads, as well as the related Missouri-

Pacific. In the face of such disciplined opposition, Gould had to restore the pay cuts he had made earlier.

A more disastrous incident occurred at Chicago's Haymarket Square in 1886, where the Knights protested at the McCormick Reaper Works for an eight-hour day. On May third, two hundred policemen were watching an angry, but still orderly crowd of six thousand when the work day ended and strikebreakers left the plant. As the strikers converged on them, the police assumed the worst and began clubbing and shooting the strikers. Calling for a new mass meeting on May fourth, radical editors like August Spies set the table for more violence: "Revenge! Workingmen, to arms! Your masters sent out their bloodhounds!"[50] At the meeting the next day, a bomb exploded, killing seven policemen and leaving more than sixty wounded, and the city was placed under martial law for what became known as the Haymarket Riot. Subsequent trials produced evidence that anarchists only loosely associated with the Knights had been involved, but a jury nevertheless convicted eight Knights of murder. Governor John Peter Altgeld, in 1893, pardoned three of the men.

The affair marked the end of the Knights as a force in organized labor (as well as the anarchist threat in America), but they appeared to have peaked anyway: Powderly's strategy of admitting anyone could not succeed in sustaining strikes by the highly skilled workers for the unskilled, and farmers never had a clear role in the organization.

A more powerful and effective union movement came out of the efforts of a former Knight, Samuel Gompers, who in 1886 founded a rival union, the American Federation of Labor (AFL). Like Carnegie, he had started his career at age thirteen, moving to New York from London, where he had been born into a family of Dutch Jews. (Karl Marx, another Jewish refugee, arrived in London the year before Gompers was born.)[51] While still a boy in England, Gompers had watched his father work as a cigar maker, and he became enamored of the union organization, seeing it as the locus of social interaction and security. Indeed, even before he left for America, Samuel Gompers treated the union as a creed or a religion. Unlike many laborers, though, Gompers acquired a broad education, learning the rudiments of several languages, the basics of geography and politics, and even dabbling in logic and ethical philosophy. He arrived in New York City in the middle of the Civil War, disembarking only a few weeks after the draft riots there.

Working his way through the Cigar Makers Union, Gompers came to reject the radical ideologies of the socialists. On one occasion he grew so agitated by a socialist diatribe that he grabbed the speaker by the throat with the intent to kill him, only to be dragged off by other patrons.[52] Gompers rejected socialism, often voicing his anger at agitators who he knew had never set foot on a shop floor. For Gompers, pragmatism had become the objective: "We are fighting only for immediate objects," he told the U.S. Senate, by which he meant his staples of wages and hours.[53]

By 1877, when he took over as president of the New York local, he was a stocky man with a thick handlebar mustache. Already he had surpassed Powderly as a strategist on a number of levels. He could drink with his fellow workers on the shop floor one moment, and negotiate boundaries between rival shops the next. He understood that the strength of the unions lay in the skilled labor and craft unions, not in the unskilled masses. Above all, he kept his eye on the ball: wages and hours.

Gompers also kept American unions (in theory, at least) apolitical. This was common sense, given the small percentage of trade unionists in the country, who by 1880 accounted for less than 2.3 percent of the nonfarm labor force. For employees to have power, he believed, they had to be organized, strike infrequently (and only for the most significant of objectives), and maintain perfect discipline. Work stoppages in opposition to the introduction of new machinery not only were ineffective, but they also ran against the tide of history and human progress. In addition, uncoordinated strikes—especially when the unions had not properly prepared a war chest to see the members through the lean times—were worse than ineffective, posing the threat of destroying the union altogether. Gompers knew hardship first hand. In the 1877 strike, Gompers, with six children, pawned everything he had except his wife's wedding ring, and the family "had nothing to eat but a soup of flour, water, salt, and pepper."[54] Even though that strike failed, it convinced Gompers more than ever that a unified and prepared union could succeed. Equally important, Gompers had accidentally hit upon the confederation structure, which allowed employees of new and evolving industries to join the organization essentially with equality to the established trades, thus allowing continued growth and development rather than a calcification around aging and soon-to-be obsolete enterprises.

What Gompers and his unions did not endorse were third-party movements, since he appreciated the winner-take-all/single-member-district structure of American politics. Specifically, for Gompers, that meant avoiding the new Populist movement, despite its appeals and the Populist leaders' efforts at recruiting among the unions.

Raising Less Corn, and More Hell

Farm organization efforts began as early as 1867 with the founding of the Patrons of Husbandry, more popularly known as the Grangers. Grange chapters spread rapidly, gaining momentum until the Grange had a membership of 1.5 million by 1874. Originally seen as a means to promote farm cooperatives—facilitating the purchase and sales of other farmers' products at lower prices—the Grange soon engaged in political lobbying on behalf of various regulations aimed at railroads and grain elevators. The Grangers managed to pass laws in five states that were challenged by the railroad and elevator owners, including the partners in a Chicago warehouse firm, Ira Y. Munn and George Scott, in the *Munn v. Illinois* case, where the Illinois Supreme Court held that the state legislature had broad powers to fix prices on everything from cab fares to bread prices.[55] Munn and

Scott were found guilty by an Illinois court of fixing prices, and Munn appealed, arguing that any arbitrary definition by the state about what constituted a maximum price violated the Constitution's takings clause and the Fifth and Fourteenth Amendments.[56] The Supreme Court held that states could regulate property for the public good under the police powers provisions if it could be shown that the enterprise in question benefited from its public context. Unfortunately, the court did not consider the state's "evidence" that grain elevators had constituted a monopoly, and it ruled exclusively on the appeal of state authority to regulate.

The Grangers had already moved into a political activism that peaked with the election of 1880, and they soon faded, replaced by the Farmers' Alliances. This movement emphasized similar cooperative efforts but also stressed mainstream political participation and organization. Led by a host of colorful characters, including Mary Elizabeth Lease, a Kansas schoolteacher and lawyer famous for her recommendation that farmers should "raise less corn, and more hell," the Alliance sought to appeal to blacks to widen its base.[57] White Southerners, however, never supported the Colored Farmers' Alliance, and it disappeared within a few years. Meanwhile, every move to expand the appeal of the agrarians to one group, such as the freedmen, alienated other races or ethnic groups.

Despite the flamboyance of characters like Lease and Sockless Jerry Simpson, it was Charles W. Macune, the Alliance president, who formulated a genuine political plan of action.[58] Macune advocated government loans monetized by the issue of new greenbacks or other types of government legal-tender notes, thus inflating the currency. The idea of inflation, either by the monetization of silver or through creation of new fiat money issued by the government, took on a life of its own as the end all of agrarian unrest. Farmers, sharecroppers, and any of the southern or western poor, for that matter, had become indoctrinated by pamphlets and incessant speeches that the solution to their problems was merely more money, with little instruction about the ramifications of money creation at the government level. William "Coin" Harvey, for example, in his popular book *Coin's Financial School* (1894), offered a conspiratorial worldview of a money system controlled by sinister (often Jewish) bankers who, like the octopus (a favorite conspiracy symbol) had their tentacles throughout the international banking system.[59] Other conspiracy-oriented books included *Seven Financial Conspiracies Which Have Enslaved the American People*, by Sarah E. V. Emery (1887), and Mary Lease's *The Problem of Civilization Solved* (1895), which raised the specter of both international banking cartels and racial pollution as the cause of American farmers' plight.[60] In these scenarios, the Rothschilds and other Jews of Europe, operating through a nebulous network in London (sometimes with the aid of the Bank of England and Wall Street), conspired to contract the money supply to benefit the lending classes.[61]

The developments surrounding the silver and money issue in the late nineteenth century originated with an international deflation that set in during the 1870s, but were in no way the work of the Rothschilds or other allegedly nefarious groups. These international forces were largely hidden from domestic critics and inflationists, who thought that increasing wage levels allowed them to pay back fixed debts with increasingly cheap dollars. (They ignored the fact that all other prices rise, and that although mortgages may stay constant, the price of seed, tools, farm implements, clothing, and fuel increases, eating up whatever savings are "gained" through the temporary artificial advantage in the mortgage payments.) Nevertheless, at the time, the postbellum policies of the U.S. government appeared to cause agrarian and labor distress.

It began with Congress's 1873 decision not to monetize silver but to resume redemption of the Civil War–era greenbacks in 1879, putting the country on a de facto gold standard. This followed a decade's worth of increased silver production, originating with the Comstock Lode in 1859, that had changed the ratio of exchange between silver and gold. Gold became more expensive, but the cheaper, more abundant silver was more widely available. This seemed to offer an opportunity for government action: if the government could be forced to purchase silver at fixed prices (higher than the market price) and coin it, silver miners would receive artificial price increases, and new silver coins would flood the West and South, providing a solution (it was thought) to the money question. When Congress rejected this scenario, silverites labeled the action the crime of '73.

Meanwhile, the Treasury, under John Sherman, had carefully accumulated enough gold that the resumption occurred smoothly. Prior to the resumption, pressures from westerners and southerners to counteract the slow deflation that had gripped the economy led to calls for new issues of greenbacks. Alliance-related greenbackers even succeeded in electing forty-four congressmen sympathetic to the movement and four pro-Alliance governors in the years preceding 1892. The farmers increasingly found their calls for regulation and control of business drowned out by a larger new coalition of westerners and southerners who wanted the monetization of silver as the cure to all agrarian ills.

Since the early 1870s, worldwide deflationary pressures had forced prices down. Farm prices fell more than others, or so it seemed. Actually, it depended entirely on the crop as to whether prices genuinely dropped or stayed relatively even with other products. Despite the roundly criticized "crime," the U.S. government had little impact on the price level, except when it came to bank notes. Since the Civil War, national banks had been the sole sources of note issue in the United States. That meant that notes tended to be more plentiful where there were many national banks, and less so where there were fewer. Both the South and the West were at a disadvantage in that case, the South because the comptroller of the currency was unlikely to give a bank charter to either former Confederates or freedmen, and the West because of the sparse population. Each region clamored for more money.

When the western silver mines proved richer than even the original prospectors had dreamed, both regions saw silver as a means to address the shortfall. In 1878, Richard "Silver Dick" Bland of Missouri and William Allison of Iowa introduced a measure for "free and unlimited coinage of silver" at a ratio of sixteen silver ounces for one gold ounce. Fearing a veto from President Hayes, Allison introduced amendments that limited the total silver purchased to $4 million per month at market prices. Allison's amendments essentially took the teeth from the bill by robbing it of its artificial advantages for the holders of silver. Nevertheless, it reflected the new West/South coalition around "free silver," meaning the purchase of all the western silver that could be mined, and its coinage at the inflated rate of sixteen ounces of silver to every ounce of gold. This was stated in the parlance of the day as sixteen to one, when the real relationship between silver and gold was seventeen to one. Put another way, silverites would be subsidized at taxpayers' expense.

By Cleveland's time, the federal mints had coined 215 million silver dollars, with more than three quarters of them in government vaults and only $50 million in actual circulation. Meanwhile, as miners hauled more silver in to exchange for gold, the government saw its gold supply dwindle steadily. Had the government circulated all the silver coins, it would not have produced prosperity, but inflation. Prices on existing goods would have gone up, but there would have been no new incentive to produce new goods. Instead, a different problem arose: the government had to pay gold to its creditors (mostly foreign) but had to accept the less valuable silver from its debtors. Congress formed into two camps, one around free silver, intending to increase the silver purchases and push for full bimetallism, and another around the gold standard. Cleveland was in the latter group. With a hostile president, and enough goldbugs in the House and Senate to prevent veto overrides, the silver issue stalled throughout the remainder of Cleveland's term, but it would resurface with a vengeance under Harrison.

Shame of the Cities

While farmers agitated over silver, another large group of people—immigrants—flooded into the seaport cities in search of a new life. Occasionally, they were fleeced or organized by local politicians when they arrived. Often they melted into the American pot by starting businesses, shaping the culture, and transforming urban areas. In the process the cities lost their antebellum identities, becoming true centers of commerce, arts, and the economy, as well as hotbeds of crime, corruption and degeneracy—"a serious menace to our civilization," warned the Reverend Josiah Strong in 1885.[62] The cities, he intoned, were "where the forces of evil are massed," and they were under attack by "the demoralizing and pauperizing power of the saloons and their debauching influence in politics," not to mention the population, whose character was "so largely foreign, [and where] Romanism finds its chief strength."[63] The clergyman probably underestimated the decay: in 1873, within three miles of New York's city hall, one survey counted more than four hundred brothels housing ten times that number of prostitutes.[64] Such illicit behavior coincided with the highest alcohol consumption levels since the turn of the century, or a quart of whiskey a week for every adult American.

Some level of social and political pathology was inevitable in any population, but it was exacerbated by the gigantic size of the cities. By the 1850s, the more partisan of the cities, especially New York and Boston, achieved growth in spite of the graft of the machines and the hooliganism. New York (the largest American city after 1820), Chicago, Philadelphia, and Boston emerged as commercial hubs, with a second tier of cities, including New Orleans, Cincinnati, Providence, Atlanta, Richmond, Pittsburgh, and Cleveland developing strong urban areas of their own. But New York, Boston, Chicago, and New Orleans, especially, also benefited from being regional money centers, further accelerating their influence by bringing to the cities herds of accountants, bankers, lawyers, and related professionals.

By the mid-1800s, multistory buildings were commonplace, predating the pure skyscraper conceived by Louis Sullivan in 1890. Even before then, by mid-century two-story developments and multiuse buildings done in the London style had proliferated. These warehouses and factories soon yielded to larger structures made of brick (such as the Montauk buildings of Chicago in 1882) or combinations of masonry hung on a metal structure. Then, after Andrew Carnegie managed to produce good cheap steel, buildings were constructed out of that metal. More than a few stories, however, required another invention, the electric safety-brake-equipped elevator conceived by Elisha Otis. After Otis demonstrated his safety brake in 1887, tall buildings with convenient access proliferated, including the Burnham & Root, Adler & Sullivan, and Holabird & Roche buildings in Chicago, all of which featured steel frames. Large buildings not only housed businesses, but also entertainments: the Chicago Auditorium (1890) was ten stories high and included a hotel. After 1893 the Chicago city government prohibited buildings of more than ten stories, a prohibition that lasted for several decades.

If the cities of the late 1800s fulfilled Jefferson's worst nightmares, they might have been worse had the crime and graft not been constrained by a new religious awakening.

Intellectuals, Reform, and the Foundations of Progressivism
The "age of reform," as historian Richard Hofstadter put it, bloomed at the turn of the century, but it owed its heritage to the intellectuals of the 1880s reform movements. These reformers embodied a worldview that saw man as inherently perfectible. Only his environment, especially the roles cast on him by society, prevented him (or her) from obtaining that perfect state.[65] Whereas many of the intellectuals of the late nineteenth century came from mainstream Christian religions, few—if any—traced their roots to the more fundamentalist doctrines of the Baptists or traditional Methodists. Instead, they were the intellectual heirs of Emerson and Unitarianism, but with a decidedly secular bent. Reformer Jane Addams, for example, had a Quaker background, but absorbed little Christianity. "Christ don't help me in the least . . . ," she claimed.[66] After her father died and she fell into a horrendous depression, Addams gained no support from Christian-

ity: "When I am needing something more, I find myself approaching a crisis, & look rather wistfully to my friends for help."[67] Henry Demarest Lloyd, whose series of *Atlantic Monthly* articles in 1881 made him the original muckraker, was born to a Dutch Reformed minister-turned-bookseller. Lloyd himself was religious, though well educated (at Columbia). Like most of the early reformers, he had received a first-class education.

Indeed, the reformers almost always came from families of wealthy means, and were people who seldom experienced hardship firsthand. Mabel Dodge Luhan, the daughter of a Buffalo banker, attended all the best schools before coming to the conclusion that she could not trust her thoughts, only her senses. Lincoln Steffens's father was an affluent merchant who could afford to send his son to universities in Europe, where he "acquired a taste for expensive clothes" and "dabbled in philosophy and aesthetics."[68] Upton Sinclair and Jack London proved exceptions to this rule. Sinclair's family came from wealth on his mother's side, but Sinclair's father, a ruined former Southern aristocrat, had descended into alcoholism and supported the family by selling liquor, then hats. Unlike most of the other reformer intellectuals, Sinclair actually worked, selling dime novels to put himself through Columbia University before turning out the muckraker's call to arms, *The Jungle*. London, a socialist, adventurer, sailor, gold seeker, and famous novelist whose *Call of the Wild* became a classic, had grown up poor, and had as a youth worked a wide range of jobs. More typical than either of these writers was Ida Tarbell, considered the original muckraker, whose father, Franklin, had a thriving oil tank-building business, providing her with a first-class education at the Sorbonne.

Another aspect of the social gospelers is worth mentioning here: with some two to three million fathers absent from the home during the Civil War and hundreds of thousands of fathers dead, literally millions of young boys were raised in households of women. Rather than learning masculine behaviors, they had "been raised by mothers who taught nurturing and caring," in the process turning "to the ways of their mothers and took Christianity out of the home to save the world."[69] It is not a stretch to suggest that the casualty lists of Gettysburg and Chancellorsville produced a feminized, Progressive worldview among the emerging generation of reformers.

Best known for his association with the phrase "social Darwinism," Sumner's views were slightly more complicated. Writing in the *Independent* in 1887, Sumner identified the central threat to the nation as "plutocracy," which was controlled by the wealthy who had the bourgeois tastes of the middle class. Embracing Malthusian views of overpopulation, Sumner expressed concern for the negative impact of charity and government policy, arguing in his "Forgotten Man" character introduced in his 1884 book, *What the Social Classes Owe to Each Other*. The danger, was as follows:

> The type and formula of most schemes of philanthropy or humanitarianism is this: A and B put their heads together to decide what C shall be

made to do for D. The radical vice of all these schemes, from a sociological point of view, is that C is not allowed a voice in the matter, and his position, character, and interests, as well as the ultimate effects on society through C's interests, are entirely overlooked. I call C the Forgotten Man.[70]

Benevolence, he argued, stole resources from those who would actually use funds to improve the lot of all in society. "Every bit of capital," he argued, "which is given to a shiftless and inefficient member of society, who makes no return for it, is diverted from a reproductive use; but if it was put into reproductive use, it would have to be granted in wages to an efficient and productive laborer."[71] What the social classes "owed to each other" was to not create new impediments to the natural laws and laissez-faire capitalism that already functioned well.

Critics latched on to Sumner's phrases, such as the "competition for life" and "struggle" to apply the natural science ideas of natural selection advanced by Charles Darwin. Yet Sumner had specifically warned against plutocracy and acquisition for its own sake. To Sumner, social classes best helped each other by performing their tasks with efficiency, honed by competition. That did not stop Sinclair from claiming that Sumner took "ghoulish delight" in "glorifying commercialism," or prevent historian Richard Hofstadter from calling Sumner a "Social Darwinist" in his 1944 book, *Social Darwinism in American Thought*.[72] Like other intellectuals and academics, Sumner ultimately relied on a scientific view of human behavior to explain (and defend) policy. And, like other intellectuals and academics, who at one time had as their central purpose the search for truth, Sumner had (at least in part) taken on the new vocation of social moralist.[73] The emergence of this class was a phenomenon made possible only by the fantastic productive capabilities of capitalism, which provided the time and goods to allow people, essentially, to think for a living.

Grover Cleveland, Presidential Giant

Perhaps because his terms were separated by the administration of the opposing party under Benjamin Harrison, or perhaps because he simply refrained from the massive types of executive intervention that so attract modern big-government-oriented scholars, Grover Cleveland has been pushed well down the list of greatness in American presidents as measured by most modern surveys (although in older polls of historians he routinely ranked in the top ten). Republicans have ignored him because he was a Democrat; Democrats downplayed his administration because he governed like a modern Republican. Uncle Jumbo, as his nephews called him, had served as mayor of Buffalo, New York, in 1881, and the following year won election as governor of the state. Cleveland's rise to prominence was nothing short of meteoric: he claimed the mayorship of Buffalo, the governorship of New York, and the presidency within a four-year period.

Cleveland's image has enjoyed a revival in the late twentieth century because of new interest by conservative and libertarian scholars who see in him one of the few presidents whose every action seemed to be genuinely dictated by Constitutional principle. He was the last president to answer the White House door himself or to write the checks to pay the White House bills. Displaying a willingness to completely disregard either public opinion or Congressional influence to do what he thought morally and Constitutionally right, Cleveland supported the Dawes Severalty Act—which turned out to be disastrous—and alienated many in his own party through his loyalty to the gold standard. A man whose personal character, like that of his friendly New York rival, Theodore Roosevelt, stood above all other considerations, Cleveland repeatedly squelched attempts by outsiders to influence his policies for political favors.

Above all, Cleveland saw himself as the guardian of the people's money. He fought to reduce the tariff and to whittle down the pension system that had bloated government balance sheets. Cultivating a reputation in New York as "the veto governor," Cleveland peppered every veto, whether to the legislators in Albany or, later, to their counterparts in Washington, with principled reasons for not acting based on a Beardian class-based reading of the Constitution. It must be remembered, however, that the federal government of Cleveland's era, leaving aside the pensioners and the Post Office, was tiny by modern comparisons. Congress did not have even a single clerk in 1856, and fifteen years later Grant operated the executive branch of government with a staff of three assistants. The total federal bureaucracy, even including the Post Office and customs inspectors, numbered only about fifty thousand.[74]

In the election of 1884, Cleveland won a narrow victory over Republican James G. Blaine of Maine (219 to 182 electoral votes and 4.875 million to 4.852 million in the popular vote). A mere 600 votes in crucial New York would have given the election to Blaine. The campaign had been one of the dirtiest in American history: Blaine supporters accused Cleveland of coming from the party of "Rum, Romanism and Rebellion" (referring to the perceived affinity between immigrants and alcohol, the Catholicism of many Democratic voters, and the Confederacy). The charges backfired on the Republicans by propelling Irish and Italians to the polls in large numbers. Blaine's troops also sought to tar Cleveland with the charge that he had fathered an illegitimate child, generating the slogan, "Ma, Ma, Where's my pa?" This related to a child named Oscar born to Maria Halpin, who she said belonged to Cleveland. The governor had never denied possibly fathering the child, but the woman's record of promiscuity allowed for any of several men to be the father. At any rate, Cleveland agreed to provide for the boy, and eventually arranged for the child's adoption after the mother drifted into drunkenness and insanity. He never maintained contact with the boy, or even met him again after the adoption. In any event, the charges had failed to gain traction with the voters.

Blaine, a notorious spoilsman, "wallowed in spoils like a rhinoceros at a pool," complained New York *Evening Post* editor Lawrence Godkin.[75] In contrast, when a man approached the Cleveland camp about purchasing documents that proved Blaine had had an affair, Cleveland bought the documents—then promptly destroyed them in front of the man, who nevertheless tried to peddle the story to the papers. Cleveland was not perfect. Like Rockefeller, he had purchased a substitute during the Civil War, making him the first draft-dodger president, no matter the legality of the purchase. Nevertheless, draft evasion never seemed to damage Cleveland.

Once in office, Cleveland announced he would enforce the Pendleton Act scrupulously, finding allies in the new reform wing of the Republican Party. If anyone appreciated Henry Adams's criticisms of legislators—"You can't use tact with a Congressman! A Congressman is a hog! You must take a stick and hit him on the snout!"—it was Cleveland.[76] When he assumed office, he found a system corrupt to the core. Temporary employees were shifted from job to job within the administration in what was called rotation, rather than eliminate unneeded positions. (This put a completely new twist on the Jacksonian concept of rotation in office!) Customs collectors, postal officials, and other federal bureaucrats recycled thousands of people through the system in this manner: when one clerk making $1,800 was released, three more temporary employees making $600 each were hired, while the original employee went into a queue to be rehired.

What made his reforms stick was the fact that Cleveland imposed the same standards on his own party as on the Republicans, who had just been kicked out of office. Only once did a delegation of Democrats approach Cleveland about tossing a capable Republican from a position in order to fill it with a member of their own party, and the president dismissed them.

No battle demonstrated more clearly Cleveland's determination to combat corruption in government than the fight over pensions, in which he took on a key part of the Republican voting bloc, the Grand Army of the Republic (GAR). Founded by B. F. Stephenson in 1866, this veterans' organization had quickly become the most powerful special interest lobbying group in the United States. Membership was limited to those who had served during the Civil War, and although the GAR had built soldiers' homes and managed to have Memorial Day declared a national holiday, the organization's main raison d'être consisted of increasing the value of pensions and expanding the number of those eligible for Civil War pensions.[77] Although eligibility for the pensions was supposedly restricted to those suffering from disabilities in military service, congressmen encouraged fraud by introducing private pension bills for constituents.

Presidents, not wishing to alienate voters, simply signed off on the legislation—until Cleveland, who not only inspected the claims but also rejected three out of four. One claimant had broken his leg picking dandelions, yet wanted a government pension; another had a heart problem fourteen years after the war's end; and another wanted recompense for injuries received twenty-three years *before* the war from the explosion of a Fourth of July cannon. Still others had deserted or mustered out with no evidence of disability until long after the war, when Congress opened the federal Treasury.

By confronting the pension question head on, Cleveland addressed an outrageous scandal, but one cloaked in the rhetoric of the war. In 1866 just over

125,000 veterans received pensions accounting for an annual total of $13.5 million from the Treasury. But seven years later the numbers had *risen* to 238,411, despite the fact that many of the pensioners were getting older and should have been dying off![78] Supported by—indeed, agitated by—the GAR, pensioners lobbied Congress for ever-widening definitions of who was a veteran, and to make provisions for widows, orphans, and ultimately even *Confederate* veterans. When the pension numbers finally began to decline (which should have occurred in the 1870s), Congress introduced the Arrears of Pensions Act, which allowed claimants to discover wounds or diseases, then file retroactively for pension benefits that had been granted when they served. "Men who suffered an attack of fever while on active duty became 'convinced' the fever was in fact the root cause of every ill they suffered since separation from the service," observed Cleveland's biographer.[79] New claims shot up from 19,000 per year to 19,000 per *month*.

Cleveland would have none of it. He had no reluctance to give legitimate pensioners what was due them, but he considered most of the claims an outrage. Congress had learned to enact special pension bills late on Friday nights—on one night alone the Senate enacted four hundred special pension grants. Worse, each "bill" required that Cleveland sign or veto it personally. This absorbed monumental amounts of the president's time and energy. Cleveland had enough and vetoed as many as he could, finally delivering the death blow to the bogus pension system in 1887. His veto of the so-called Blair bill, which represented a massive expansion of federal benefits, was sustained. After that, a chastened Congress submitted no more pension legislation.

In 1888 the Republicans nominated Benjamin Harrison, the grandson of William Henry Harrison and the second of four pairs of family presidents (the Adamses, the Harrisons, the Roosevelts, and the Bushes). "Little Ben" stood five feet six inches tall, was strong yet chubby, and grew up on a farm. He attended Miami University in Ohio, the "Yale of the West," then settled with his wife, Carrie, in Indianapolis. There he practiced law and worked a second job as a court crier that paid $2.50 a day. The couple had a son and daughter (a third child died in infancy), and Harrison made important political connections. When the Civil War came, Harrison was a colonel in the infantry, fighting at Atlanta and Nashville and earning a promotion to brigadier general. Returning as a war hero, Harrison nevertheless lost a race for the governorship of Indiana in 1876, but four years later he was elected by the state legislature to the U.S. Senate.

Garfield offered him a cabinet spot, but he declined because he had just taken his seat as a senator. From the floor of the upper house, he impressed the Republican hierarchy with his stinging criticisms of Cleveland. When James G. Blaine refused to be the Republican candidate in 1888, Harrison's name came forward as having the prerequisite military and political experience.

Republican Interlude

Whereas Grover Cleveland had antagonized many Democrats in his first term, Harrison ran a remarkably error-free campaign. Running from his front porch in

Indianapolis, where he granted interviews and spoke to the more than 300,000 people who came to see him, Harrison emphasized the tariff. As had been the case four years earlier, the margin of victory in 1888 was remarkably slim. For example, Harrison received only 2,300 more votes in his home state than had Cleveland, who lost Connecticut by 336 votes. In the end Cleveland learned the hard way that America is a republic, not a democracy: he won the popular vote, but Harrison became president with a majority in the electoral college (this also happened in 1824, 1876, and 2000).

The electoral situation in America was quite simple: the two parties geographically split the nation east of the Mississippi. Whereas Republicans could count on the votes of freedmen—a shrinking vote because of intimidation, literacy tests, and poll taxes in the South—the Democrats in the North drew support from city immigrants, debtor groups angry at hard money, and from labor. Cleveland had offended the second group of Democratic voters with his monetary policies, throwing a wild card into the deck. With this sectional division, from 1876 to 1896, the West, including parts of the Old Northwest as well as the new plains areas and Pacific states, became the fulcrum on which elections swung. Historian Paul Kleppner has pinned down the swing areas to specific counties within some of these states, and further identified the source of change as essentially religious, between Catholics and two variants of Lutherans.[80] No doubt these ethnocultural factors existed, but probably they shaped, and were shaped by, other important views. The fact was, white Southerners wanted nothing to do with the party of emancipation, and freedmen and veterans of the Union Army would never vote for the Democrats. That put each election into the hands of farmers and immigrants who saw much to applaud and condemn in each party. Republicans still stood for the tariff and the gold standard, which seemed oppressive to low-income groups. Democrats wanted cheap money, which frightened eastern businessmen. Each party contained advocates of patronage reform. Thus, the elections were close, contested, and often came down to which candidate had the best party machine in key states on election day.

Harrison, therefore, entered the presidency as had many of his immediate predecessors—without a clear mandate. In 1889 the Republicans had a ten-seat advantage in the Senate and a bare twelve-seat majority in the House. Harrison's cabinet—entirely Presbyterian, with four Missourians and several war heroes—was politically obscure. Worse, he had ignored the party bosses, touching off an immediate battle between Congress and the president over spoils. When considering John Hay, Lincoln's private secretary, for an appointment, Harrison observed, "This would be a fine appointment, . . . but there isn't any politics in it."[81] Seeking to sustain the patronage reforms, Harrison placed Theodore Roosevelt on the Civil Service Commission, whereupon the New Yorker promptly irritated and aggravated his fellow members with his energetic but abrasive style. As president, Harrison hoped to restrain the growth of government. But his administration overall constituted a remarkable inversion of the parties' positions. He signed the inflationary Sherman Silver Purchase Act and enthusiastically supported the Sherman Antitrust Act (both signed in July 1890). This was ironic, in that Grover Cleveland, Harrison's Democratic opponent, essentially supported the gold standard and was more favorable toward business than Harrison. Yet neither bill's passage came as a surprise.

Sherman's antitrust legislation had overwhelming support (52 to 1 in the Senate, and passed without dissent in the House). The bill lacked specifics, which was common in state antitrust law and corporate regulation, but it played to the public's demand that government "do something" about unfair business practices. Yet backers of the Sherman Act, with language prohibiting combinations "in restraint of trade" and its focus on the trust as a business organization, unwittingly placed more power than ever in the hands of big business. Since the railroad age, businesses had grown by attracting capital through sales of stocks. Multiplying the number of stockholder-owners, in turn, required that professional managers take over the operations of the companies. Obsessed with efficiency and cost control (which then meant profits), the managers looked for ways to essentially guarantee prices. They tried a number of unsuccessful forms, including pools, whereby competitors would jointly contribute to a member who agreed to maintain a higher price, but who lost money doing so, and territorial enforcement of markets, in which members would agree not to compete past certain geographic boundaries. Then there was the famous horizontal combination, which is the form of business most people associate with monopoly control. Under a horizontal combination a competitor seeks to eliminate all other firms in the field. Rockefeller's Standard Oil was accused of acquiring competing refineries to achieve such a monopoly.

Unfortunately for the monopolists—but luckily for the public—none of these arrangements ever achieved anything but the most temporary gains. At the time that Rockefeller's Standard Oil controlled upward of 90 percent of the refining capacity, oil prices were steadily falling. If there was a theoretical monopoly price to be gained, no company in the late 1800s had successfully demonstrated it in practice, and certainly none had capitalized on one through higher prices.[82]

Indeed, the best evidence that none of these arrangements worked is that firms had to constantly keep coming up with other gimmicks. One of the most hated was the trust company, the brainchild of Standard Oil attorney S.C.T. Dodd, who suggested using a standard legal fiduciary device to manage the property of another to trade stock in a voting trust. In a trust arrangement, a company creates a new business organization that exchanges shares of its trust certificates for shares in the stock of the acquired companies. Essentially, smaller businesses give 100 percent control of their company to a trust in return for trust certificates of equal value. The owners of any new firms the trust company acquires do not lose money, but do lose control. Standard Oil formed its trust in Ohio in 1879, and within three years forty companies had exchanged their stock for Standard Oil trust shares. It was all quite reasonable to Rockefeller. Soon, large-scale trusts existed in almost every manufacturing industry, including sugar, whiskey, paint, lead, and petroleum.

To legislators this apparatus seemed dishonest and shifty—a mere paper creation to hide control by "wealthy monopolists."[83] Congress thus felt compelled to pass the Sherman Act to constrain these entities, at which time corporations merely turned to another form of organization called a holding company, which acquired special chartering legislation from the state government (that many trusts lacked) allowing one company to hold stock in another. New Jersey liberalized its general incorporation laws in 1889 permitting companies to "hold" other companies, even if the "held" companies were located in other states. Within a decade, several companies established themselves in New Jersey, including the newly recapitalized Standard Oil.

Long before that, however, professional managers had already started to abandon the horizontal combination and the trust in favor of yet another, far more efficient and profitable structure, the vertical combination.[84] Rather than concerning themselves with competitors, the vertical combinations focused exclusively on achieving efficiencies in their own products by acquiring sources of raw materials, transportation, warehousing, and sales. Standard Oil, for example, not only had its own oil in the ground, but also made its own barrels, refined the oil itself, had its own railroad cars and ships, and literally controlled the oil from the ground to its final form as refined kerosene. Similarly, Gustavus Swift, the meatpacker, owned his own cattle ranches, transportation networks, slaughterhouses, refrigerated railroad cars, and even wholesale meat distributors.[85] Managers could take advantage of the top-to-bottom control to reduce costs and, above all, plan for the acquisition of new raw materials and factories.

In the 1890s, the Sherman Act was only marginally employed against corporations, but as it came into use, it drove firms out of the inefficient trusts and into the more efficient vertical combinations. With trusts prohibited, even those firms not inclined to adopt vertical combinations abandoned other forms of organization. Sherman, paradoxically, forced American business into an organizational structure that made it larger and more powerful than it otherwise would have been, funneling the corporation into the most efficient form it could possibly take, making the average industrial firm several times larger than if it had adopted either a horizontal combination or a trust structure. Thanks to Sherman, American industry embarked on the first great merger wave toward truly giant-sized companies. The most famous of these was Morgan's reorganization of Carnegie Steel, which, when merged with John Warne Gates's American Wire Company and other smaller businesses, became U.S. Steel, the world's first billion-dollar corporation. Most of the mergers took place under the administration of McKinley, but it was the Sherman Act that had slammed shut alternative paths.[86]

Meanwhile, Sherman's other bill, the Silver Purchase Act, was nearly fatal to the nation's economy in Harrison's tenure. Sherman authorized the government to purchase 4.5 million ounces of silver a month at the stipulated price of 16½ to 1—not enough to ensure the inflation the silverites wanted, but just enough to turn the arbitragers loose. Over the subsequent three years the government purchased $147 million worth of silver, often paying for it in gold, bringing into play Gresham's Law, which postulated that "bad money drives out good." Prosilver forces set into motion a dynamic of arbitrage that would encourage speculators to exchange cheap silver for undervalued gold. Harrison would escape blame for the brunt of the damage—which occurred under the unfortunate Cleveland's second term—but he had set those forces loose.

One of Harrison's most successful programs involved his rebuilding of U.S. naval power. When Harrison took office, a series of modern steel cruisers had been authorized (in 1885) by Congress—the so-called A, B, C, D ships (*Atlanta*, *Boston*, *Chicago*, and *Dolphin*)—to supplement five medium-sized cruisers, two large cruisers, and two battleships. But at the time Harrison assumed office, only the *Atlanta* and *Boston* were seaworthy, and soon the nation was stunned by a major storm that devastated three ships, or 10 percent of the active fleet, including the *Trenton*, the navy's newest vessel aside from the A, B, C, D ships. Brigadier General Benjamin Franklin Tracy, the secretary of the navy, took the initiative to reinvigorate the navy, beginning with support for the Naval War College and naming Alfred Thayer Mahan as its president. As soon as the *Chicago* became operational, Tracy had its squadron perform in several displays designed to raise public awareness and generate congressional support. Even so, the United States, with the new cruisers, would be, at best, the twelfth-ranked naval power in the world, behind "powerhouses" like Chile and Turkey!

Independent of the Department of the Navy, a commission called the Naval Policy Board had come to similar conclusions, advocating a navy that would rank second only to Great Britain's. The result was the Naval Act of 1890, which authorized the *Indiana*, *Massachusetts*, and *Oregon*, all 10,000-ton battleships, supplemented with other large cruisers. To meet the new demand, the navy negotiated a contract with Carnegie Steel for armor plating. Although Congress did not fund every ship, by 1899, Harrison had jumped the U.S. Navy up to the sixth position in the world, behind the traditional European powers of Great Britain, France, Russia, Italy, and Germany. Within just a few more years, new construction programs would lift the American fleet up to the second spot—just behind Britain.

Seed Corn and Cleveland's Return

Harrison might have won reelection if he'd had only the sour economy to contend with. Other factors worked in favor of Cleveland, who squared off against him again. The summer of 1892 brought several bloody strikes, including the Coeur d'Alene violence in Idaho and the Homestead strike. Despite Harrison's prosilver attitudes, the cheap-money forces were not assuaged. The McKinley Tariff alienated southerners and westerners; the Sherman Act had laid the groundwork for upheaval in the economy.

The Populist Party nominated James B. Weaver of Iowa, who received 1 million votes. In an election decided by 380,000 votes out of 10.6 million, the

Populists split the silver vote enough to ensure Cleveland's election. In the electoral college, Cleveland's victory was more pronounced. Harrison spent his final months unsuccessfully attempting to annex Hawaii. As the last Civil War general to hold office, Harrison had pushed the United States onto the world stage—a position it would grab enthusiastically in 1898.

In office for the second time, Cleveland again proved a model of character and firmness on issues. His seed corn veto—a prime act of political courage in that he had everything to gain by signing it and nothing to lose—blocked the provision of millions of dollars in loans for midwestern farmers to buy seed; Cleveland said that no such federal power was sanctioned by the Constitution. Private charity should take care of the farmers, he argued, and it did. Private organizations raised many times the amount that the feds would have provided.

Cleveland nonetheless failed to contain the bloating federal bureaucracy. By the time William McKinley entered the White House, Cleveland's administration had seen the number of Civil Service jobs doubled. Whether or not the new professional civil servants were more qualified, the Pendleton Act had dramatically increased their ranks.

Of more immediate concern to Cleveland was the massive gold drain and collapse in railroad stocks, which sent the economy into a full-fledged panic in 1893. In a month one fourth of the nation's railroads had met with financial disaster, dissipating $2.5 billion in capital and sending waves through the economy that culminated in more than 2 million unemployed. More than six hundred banks failed, along with mines, factories, and brokerage houses. At the peak of the depression, Jacob Coxey, an Ohio reformer, set out from Massillon, Ohio, with twenty thousand marchers for Washington, although some came from as far away as the West Coast. They planned to stage a protest at the nation's capital. The hungry "soldiers" in "Coxey's Army" descended on Washington and attempted to force their way into the Capitol, whereupon police charged and scattered the marchers.

To continue paying artificially high prices for silver threatened to bankrupt the U.S. Treasury. Cleveland therefore called a special session of Congress for the purpose of repealing the Sherman Silver Purchase Act. Silver interests demonized Cleveland. Pitchfork Ben Tillman, a fellow Democrat campaigning for the Senate, called Cleveland "an old bag of beef," who was acting worse than "when Judas betrayed Christ."[87] Only later was Cleveland praised by the press for standing firm on gold. Although the silver act was repealed, outstanding silver notes continued to be presented for redemption in gold. In 1892 the U.S. gold reserve was $84 million, but by 1894 it had fallen to $69 million.

It appeared the economy might stagger to a recovery when, in 1895, a new panic swept through the banking community. More than $20 million in gold had flowed out of the Treasury in just over a week. To the rescue rode Morgan. He had spoken by telephone to Cleveland about a massive loan to the government when the president mentioned that there was only $9 million left in the New York subtreasury. Morgan, through his sources, "was aware of a large [$10 million] draft about to be presented for payment," which essentially would have put the U.S. government in default.[88] A default would have triggered a nationwide panic and, essentially, bankrupted the government. Morgan recommended immediately forming a syndicate with European bankers to buy 3.5 million ounces of gold for $65 million in long-term bonds. For literally saving the national economy, Morgan and Cleveland were both heaped with abuse—Morgan for the profits he made (approximately $7 million) and Cleveland for having cut a deal with the gold devil. Lost in the debate was the fact that Morgan was already wealthy, and the collapse of the U.S. government would have only inconvenienced him. He could have sailed for England or France with his remaining fortune. Instead, he acted in concert with a sensible president to save the country from the silverites' idiocy.

The economy and the silver issue dominated the national parties' conventions in 1896. Silver Democrats continued to heap scorn on Cleveland, with Tillman taking the Senate floor to call him a "besotted tyrant."[89] Whatever hopes Cleveland had of running for a third term were dashed at the Democratic convention in Chicago, where the Cleveland supporters saw the streets lined with crowds sporting silver badges and waving silver banners. A new star now took the political stage, Congressman William Jennings Bryan of Nebraska. Bryan had run for the U.S. Senate in 1894 and been defeated, but he had used his time out of politics to reach wide audiences on the Chautauqua speaking circuit. A devout Christian and stirring orator, Bryan captivated the 1896 Democratic convention with his famous "Cross of Gold" speech in which he used the metaphor of Christ's crucifixion to describe Americans' enslavement to hard money. The convention voted two to one for a plank calling for taking the country off the gold standard. It sickened Cleveland, who years later still referred to "Bryanism": "I do not regard it as Democracy," he told a reporter.[90] Cleveland's departure from American politics ensured a string of defeats for the Democrats, and he was the last small-government candidate the Democrats would ever run.

Inching Toward a Modern America

Harrison and Cleveland saw innumerable changes in the nation in their combined twelve-year tenure. By the time of Cleveland's second term, telephones were widely available, although the president still functioned without a full-time operator, instead relying on a telegrapher assigned to the chief executive. Most of the daily executive office work was carried out by three clerks, a pair of doormen, and a handful of military aides and attachés. Harrison met with his cabinet twice a week, but the days when a president could run the government single-handedly from the White House were all but gone.

Something else had passed too. The Civil War generation had largely disappeared during Harrison's term. In 1893 alone, Jefferson Davis, David Porter, William T. Sherman, Lincoln's former vice president Hannibal Hamlin, Supreme Court Justice Lucius Q. C. Lamar, James Blaine, and Rutherford Hayes all died. In their place came a new generation of politicians, including Teddy Roosevelt,

William Jennings Bryan, and Woodrow Wilson, and industrialists like Henry Ford, Henry Leland, and Billy Durant, all born during or after the Civil War and too young to remember it. For this generation, "waving the bloody shirt" would not only prove ineffective (at least in the North), but it would also appear to many Americans as anachronistic.

William McKinley was perhaps the first president ever to even obliquely appreciate the staggering changes that had occurred. He captured the direction of the new reality with his pithy campaign slogan, "A Full Dinner Pail." Far from the end of the Van Buren-originated spoils system, the post-Pendleton era in American politics marked a malignant mutation of the concept of patronage, pushing it down one level further, directly to the voters themselves.

CHAPTER THIRTEEN

"Building Best, Building Greatly,"
1896–1912

Average Americans at the Turn of the Century

A popular 1901 magazine, *Current Literature,* collated available census data about American males at the turn of the century. It reported that the typical American man was British by ancestry, with traces of German; was five feet nine inches tall (or about two inches taller than average European males); and had three living children and one who had died in infancy. A Protestant, the average American male was a Republican, subscribed to a newspaper, and lived in a two-story, seven-room house. His estate was valued at about $5,000, of which $750 was in a bank account or other equities. He drank more than seven gallons of liquor a year, consumed seventy-five gallons of beer, and smoked twenty pounds of tobacco. City males earned about $750 a year, farmers about $550, and they paid only 3 percent of their income in taxes. Compared to their European counterparts, Americans were vastly better off, leading the world with a per capita income of $227 as opposed to the British male's $181 and a Frenchman's $161— partially because of lower taxes (British men paid 9 percent of their income, and the French, 12 percent).[1]

Standard income for industrial workers averaged $559 per year; gas and electricity workers earned $543 per year; and even lower-skilled labor was receiving $484 a year.[2] Of course, people in unusual or exceptional jobs could make a lot more money. Actress Sarah Bernhardt in 1906 earned $1 million for her movies, and heavyweight boxer Jack Johnson took home a purse of $5,000 when he won the Heavyweight Boxing Championship of 1908. Even more "normal" (yet still specialized) jobs brought high earnings. The manager of a farm-implement department could command $2,000 per year in 1905 or an actuary familiar with western insurance could make up to $12,000 annually, according to ads in the New York *Times.*[3]

What did that buy? An American in 1900 spent $30 a year on clothes, $82 for food, $4 for doctors and dentists, and gave $9 to religion and welfare. A statistic that might horrify modern readers, however, shows that tobacco expenditures averaged more than $6, or more than personal care and furniture put together! A quart of milk went for 6 cents, a pound of pork for nearly 17 cents, and a pound of rice for 8 cents; for entertainment, a good wrestling match in South Carolina cost 25 cents, and a New York opera ticket to *Die Meistersinger* cost $1.50.

A working woman earned about $365 a year, and she spent $55 on clothes, $78 on food, and $208 on room and board.[4] Consider the example of Mary Kennealy, an unmarried Irish American clerk in Boston, who made $7 a week (plus commissions) and shared a bedroom with one of the children in the family she boarded with. (The family of seven, headed by a loom repairman, earned just over $1,000 a year, and had a five-room house with no electricity or running water.) At work Kennealy was not permitted to sit; she put in twelve to sixteen hours a day during a holiday season. Although more than 80 percent of the clerks were women, they were managed by men, who trusted them implicitly. One executive said, "We never had but four dishonest girls, and we've had to discharge over 40 boys in the same time." "Boys smoke and lose at cards," the manager dourly noted.[5]

Time Line

1896: McKinley elected

1898: Spanish-American War; Hawaii annexed; Open Door Note

1900: McKinley reelected

1901: McKinley assassinated; Theodore Roosevelt becomes president

1902: Northern Securities suit; Newlands Reclamation Act

1903: Acquisition of Panama Canal Zone; Roosevelt Corollary delivered

1904: Roosevelt elected president

1908: Taft elected president

1909–11: Ballinger-Pinchot Controversy

1911: Standard Oil Supreme Court Decision

1912: Roosevelt forms Bull Moose/Progressive Party; Wilson elected president

Until 1900, employees like Kennealy usually took electric trolleys to work, although Boston opened the first subway in the United States in 1898, and low-paid workers could enjoy the many public parks—Boston was among the nation's leaders in playground and park space. Bicycles, though available, remained expensive (about a hundred dollars, or more than a quarter of a year's wage for someone like Kennealy), and thus most people still depended on either city transportation or their own feet to get them to work.

Nevertheless, the economic progress was astonishing. Here were working-class women whose wages and lifestyle exceeded that of most European *men* by the end of Teddy Roosevelt's second term. The improvement in the living conditions of average Americans was so overwhelming that even one of the godfathers of communism, Leon Trotsky, who lived in New York City just a few years later, in 1917, recalled:

> We rented an apartment in a workers' district, and furnished it on the installment plan. That apartment, at $18 a month, was equipped with all sorts of conveniences that we Europeans were quite unused to: electric lights, gas cooking-range, bath, telephone, automatic service-elevator, and even a chute for the garbage.[6]

This prosperity baffled socialists like the German August Bebel, who predicted in 1907, "Americans will be the first to usher in a Socialist republic."[7] Yet by the year 2000, two historians of socialism in America concluded, "No socialist candidate has ever become a vehicle for major protest in the United States."[8]

The prosperity that short-circuited the socialists and dumbfounded the communists was the end product of a thirty-year spurt, marred only by the two panics. During that burst, American steel producers climbed atop world markets. National wealth doubled in the 1890s, and in 1892 the United States attained a favorable balance of trade. By 1908, American investments overseas reached $2.5 billion, and would soar to $3.5 billion in less than a decade. The president of the American Bankers' Association boasted in 1898, "We hold . . . three of the winning cards in the game of commercial greatness, to wit—iron, steel, and coal."[9]

The excesses of the Gilded Age, both outrageous and mesmerizing, concealed, as most people knew, a widespread prosperity generated by the most amazing engine of growth ever seen. The number of patents, which passed the one-million mark in 1911, rewarded invention and innovation. Brilliant engineers like Carnegie's Julian Kennedy had more than half of his hundred patents in actual operation in Carnegie's steel mills during his lifetime. American innovation enabled factory workers to maintain rising real wages, enabled agriculture to consistently expand production, and generated enough wealth that waves of immigrants came in, and kept on coming. It was something Upton Sinclair's *The Jungle* could not explain: if things were so bad, why did people so desperately try to get here?

"Professionalism" and "scientific" became the buzzwords of the day. To many, science had become the new god, and the theories of Darwin, Freud, and Marx convinced people that only those things one could prove through experimentation were valid—despite the fact that Darwin, Marx, or Freud had never proven anything scientifically. Even Roosevelt, usually levelheaded if somewhat impulsive, called for "scientific management" of the tariff. Although Frederick W. Taylor did not introduce his concepts of labor effectiveness until 1915, when he wrote *Principles of Scientific Management*, the bible of productivity studies, he had already perfected his practices at Midvale Steel Company. Everywhere, however, science and professionalism were mated to the reform impulse to convince the public that a solution existed to all problems.

Two of the most prominent writers of the day, Walter Lippmann and William James, contributed to the broadening consensus that man was in control. Lippmann, publishing *Drift and Mastery* in 1914, celebrated the introduction of scientific discipline into human affairs. As his title implied, all previous human history had been "drift," until saved by the planners. James, who wrote *Principles of Psychology* (1890) and *The Will to Believe* (1897), introduced the philosophy of pragmatism in which man controlled his own fate. "Truth *happens* to an idea," James argued in *Pragmatism* (1907): "It *becomes* true, is *made* true by events."[10] It was deliciously ironic: by his own definition, James "invented" the "truth" of pragmatism!

James shared with Theodore Roosevelt and Woodrow Wilson the Progressive view that government should reside in the hands of "true men" and trusted reformers who could focus their "battle-instinct" on the social issues of the day.[11] Like Roosevelt's, James's father had come from wealth, providing the time and leisure to denounce Americans' worship of "the bitch-goddess SUCCESS," even though he obsessively pursued money himself.[12]

William James absorbed his father's writings (Henry James worked for Brook Farm founder George Ripley). He also was exposed to the ideas of European intellectuals he met on trips to the Continent. After settling on psychology as a field, the young man expressed an interest in studying "ghosts, second sight, spiritualism, & all sorts of hobgoblins."[13] Yet despite his thirst for God and his fascination with the supernatural, he steadily moved further away from spirituality, seeking to satisfy the "urgent demand of common sense."[14] The result was his *Principles of Psychology*, which addressed issues of personal consciousness, the expression of one's self to others, and of the necessity for action causing experiences "in the direction of habits you aspire to gain."[15] James's famous *Pragmatism* (1907) was the culmination of his attempt to link human action to eternal dispositions. Beliefs, he maintained, were really "rules for action," which often led him to support social reform and to oppose the war in the Philippines.[16]

On the other end of the spectrum of religious/spiritual thought in the late 1800s came a new wave of cults that spread through the nation under the auspices of Christianity—all well outside the mainstream of traditional Biblical teachings. Mary Baker Eddy's Christian Science thrived during this era, as did other mind cure/New Thought doctrines that incorporated pseudowitchcraft practices like Eddy's "Malicious Animal Magnetism," whereby a follower could inflict occult harm on others at a distance.[17] Theosophy, with overtones of Hinduism and Asian mysticism, also surged at this time. Perhaps the most rapidly growing sect, started by Charles Taze Russell, was the Watch Tower Bible Society, otherwise known as the Jehovah's Witnesses. Russell had come out of Adventist influences, but diverted sharply from the teachings of Ellen White to claim that God had two sons, Jesus and Lucifer.

A virtual who's who of mystical and religious figures were born between 1874 and 1890, including Harry Houdini, Aleister Crowley, Edgar Cayce, Father Divine, Aimee Semple McPherson, and H. P. Lovecraft. They reflected a continued trend away from the intellectual and academic search for God posed by thinkers like James. Yet the nature of their ideas necessarily tended to cut them off from mainstream social action through government. Indeed, rather than attracting the emotional, esoteric followers who gravitated to Father Divine and Mary Baker Eddy, the Progressives found a legion of willing allies in a different camp, journalists. After all, journalism had once been the home of religious newspapers, and a few of the sect newspapers not only survived but flourished, including the *Christian Science Monitor*.

In general, journalism had secularized at a shocking rate by the late 1800s. The separation of fact from partisanship had imposed on newspapers a little-understood requirement that they also cleave fact from values. So journalism returned to the notions of science, planning, and human control already prevailing in government and business. Typical of the new journalistic Progressives was Walter Lippmann. A former socialist—indeed, the founder of the Harvard Socialist Club—Lippmann served as Lincoln Steffens's secretary. By the early 1900s, however, he had abandoned his socialism in favor of more moderate Progressivism, supporting Teddy Roosevelt in 1912.

Despite many similarities in their views, Lippmann and James came from different eras. Lippmann's generation came on the tail end of the mystic boom, and included Babe Ruth (born 1895), Sinclair Lewis (born 1885), Irving Berlin (born 1888), Al Capone (born 1899), and F. Scott Fitzgerald (born 1896). A generation straddled by wars, it differed significantly from William James's, whose earlier generation included William McKinley, Woodrow Wilson, Frederick Taylor, and Booker T. Washington. Lippmann and James did share a certain relativistic belief that no value could exist for long. Whatever proved effective today would still be subject to time and place, and therefore not valid as eternal truth.

Intellectuals may have bought the new pragmatism and secular scientific approach to life's challenges, but middle America had not. Jean Pierre Godet, a Belgian immigrant in Cedar Falls, Iowa, reflected the turn-of-the-century faith that still gripped most Americans with this simple prayer:

> Dear God, thanks for Cedar Falls and all 391 residents [and for] this good piece of farmland two miles outside of town. From there I can watch the rest of the people with a little perspective. I'd like to learn to be like the best of them and avoid the bad habits of the worst of them. I'd like to pay off my bank mortgage as fast as I can and still have time to sit down with my neighbors. . . . And if You don't mind, I think I'll keep the mortgage in the family Bible . . . [to] let You remind me that I have some debts to pay . . . while I remember that honesty is the never-ending rehearsal of those who want to be the friends of God and the 391 people in the good little section of the Kingdom where we live.[18]

Citizens in Godet's "little section" of Cedar Falls exulted in sharing their freedom with others. Life, liberty, and the pursuit of happiness could never be impositions or values foisted on unwilling recipients. Quite the contrary, they were the embodiment of Americanism. "I have fallen in love with American names," Stephen Vincent Benét once wrote. "The sharp names that never get fat, the Snakeskin titles of mining claims, the Plumed War-bonnet of Medicine Hat, Tucson and Deadwood and Lost Mule Flat."[19] The words of immigrants like Godet, "I love America for giving so many of us the right to dream a new dream," were as lost on the muckrakers as they were on many modern historians obsessed by class, race, and gender oppression.[20] Yet they have never been lost on those who would lead: "An American," John F. Kennedy said decades later, "by nature is an optimist. He is experimental, an inventor and builder, who builds best when called upon to build greatly."[21]

Operating under such assumptions, overseas expansion—whether in Hawaii, Panama, or Cuba—could prove only beneficial to whatever people were assimilated. Consequently, the era of American imperialism could just as easily be relabeled the era of optimism. Emerging from the lingering effects of a depression, still healing from the ravages of the Civil War, and divided over a broad spectrum of issues, Americans nevertheless remained a people of vision and unselfishness. The liberties they enjoyed belonged by right, they thought, to everyone. If manifest destiny itself was dead, the concept of an American presence in the world, of Americans who "build greatly," had only just started.

Major McKinley

Save Cleveland, few American politicians have so consistently upheld high standards of personal character, and yet at the same time so consistently been on the wrong side of important issues, as William McKinley. Born in Niles, Ohio (1843), and raised in Poland, Ohio, McKinley absorbed a sense of spiritual design for his life from his Methodist mother. In this he resembled Lincoln, convinced that God had important plans for his life, and he professed his Christian faith at age sixteen. He also inherited from his mother a strong abolitionist sentiment and a commitment to the Union. When the Civil War came, McKinley was working in his hometown, but he quickly joined the Ohio Volunteer Infantry Regiment under the-then major Rutherford B. Hayes, whom he greatly admired. "Application, not brilliance, carried him," remarked his biographer, and certainly McKinley displayed an appreciation for doing the little things right.[22] When opportunity came, he literally grabbed it by the reins.

Assigned to commissary duty, at the Battle of Antietam, McKinley grew concerned about his regiment, which had left at daybreak, when he saw stragglers returning to camp. Reasoning that his comrades were probably under fire and without supplies, he organized a group of wagons, one of which he drove himself, to carry food, coffee, and other supplies to the front. Racing the horses through the blizzard of musket and cannon fire, McKinley provided welcome rations to his regiment, earning him a battlefield promotion to lieutenant. Before the end of the war, he was further promoted to captain, then major. Hence he remained, from that time on, Major McKinley to his friends and admirers.

Returning to Ohio after the war, McKinley met his wife, Ida—like Lemonade Lucy Hayes, an ardent prohibitionist—further instilling in him another Progressive notion that had started to influence many of the intellectuals and politicians of the day. Self-effacing, genuinely unaffected by money and its lures, and deeply committed to his sickly wife, McKinley went into law in Canton, where his penchant for taking cases from groups other lawyers often ignored, like the Masons and Catholics, attracted the attention of the Republican Party. He won a seat in the U.S. House of Representatives in 1876, joining such future political notables as Joe Cannon and James Garfield alongside a Senate class that featured James G. Blaine, Roscoe Conkling, and Lucius Quincy Lamar. In the House, McKinley fought tenaciously for the protective tariff, opposing the "tariff for revenue only" crowd. The Major was convinced that tariffs protected laborers, and brought prosperity for all. Only after he had won the presidency, and had to deal with the reciprocity of trade with Canada, did McKinley begin to appreciate the value of free and open trade. He was equally committed to sound money, although he entertained arguments for bimetallism as long as silver's value remained fixed to gold.

His friendship with his old military superior, Rutherford Hayes, grew while Hayes was in the White House, and the McKinleys were frequent dinner guests. McKinley and fellow Ohioan John Sherman (with whom he disagreed sharply over silver) escorted Chester Arthur to his Congressional address following the assassination of Garfield. By 1890, after guiding a new protective tariff—the McKinley Tariff—through the House, the Major had arrived on the national stage. Nevertheless, local district politics led to his defeat that year for the House, after which he promptly was elected governor of Ohio. In sum, McKinley paid his dues and greased his own skids.

Although a McKinley presidential boomlet had occurred in 1892, it was not yet his time. In 1896, however, he was ready for a full run at the White House, aided by Marcus A. Hannah, his political mentor.[23] Mounting a "front porch" campaign, in which people literally traveled to his house to hear his ideas, McKinley spoke to 750,000 people from thirty states. His denuded yard, tramped over by so many feet, became a sea of mud in the rain. But his work was effective, and the lag between William Jennings Bryan's burst of energy following the "Cross of Gold" speech and the election provided just enough cushion for the Republican to win. The closeness of the electoral vote, 271 to 176, and the popular vote, 7.1 million to 6.5 million, between two candidates with such strikingly opposite views, reflected the sharp divisions within the country over the money question, the tariff, and, most recently, the depression and its cures. McKinley did not get a single electoral vote south of the Mason-Dixon Line, and only won California, North Dakota, Iowa, and Oregon out of the entire West.

Nevertheless, political scientists have long considered the election of 1896 a critical realignment, in that pro-Republican voters remained a solid bloc for the next twenty-six years. This bloc would elect one Republican president after another—interrupted only by the 1912 election, in which two Republicans split the vote and allowed Woodrow Wilson to win. Not only would Minnesota, Iowa, and Oregon generally remain in the Republican column, but in 1900, McKinley would add South Dakota, Nebraska, Kansas, Wyoming, Utah, and Washington after the realignment. Four years later, in 1904, Republicans added Idaho, Nevada, and Colorado, giving them not only the solid North, but also the entire West, except for the former Confederate state of Texas. Only when Teddy Roosevelt stepped down did the Democrats again recover momentum in the West.

At first, however, such a massive shift was not obvious in the conduct of the new administration. McKinley impressed no one after naming his cabinet ("a fine old hospital," Henry Adams remarked).[24] The last president to write his own speeches or, at least, dictate them, McKinley won no accolades for inspirational rhetoric. And as a committed husband to an ailing wife, McKinley hardly fed the social appetites of the Washington elites. Ida McKinley spent her days secluded in her room, entirely miserable. When in public, she was prone to seizures and fainting, perhaps an undiagnosed narcolepsy; a platoon of doctors—legitimate and quacks—never managed to control her condition. Yet the Major could continue a conversation right through one of Ida's seizures as though nothing had happened.

Foreign affairs crept into the spotlight during McKinley's term, particularly American dealings with Hawaii and Cuba. Harrison and Cleveland had left the Hawaiian problem unsettled. Located two thousand miles west of California, the Hawaiian Islands (also called the Sandwich Islands) had played host to American sailors, traders, and missionaries in the 1800s. Rich in sugar, fruit, and other products, the United States had extended tariff favors to Hawaii, and American business interests soon controlled important sugar plantations, often dominating the islands' economies. In 1893, with tacit U.S. support, republican forces on the islands staged a rebellion against Queen Liliuokalani, who had gained the throne two years earlier when David Kalakaua, her brother, died. Liliuokalana inherited charges of corruption, including special favors to sugar magnate Claus Spreckels. Her brother had also repealed laws prohibiting sales of liquor and opium to Hawaiians. An antimonarchy movement, spearheaded by the Reform Party, forced Kalakaua to sign the "Bayonet constitution" in 1887—so named because it was signed under threat of an armed uprising. The constitution gave foreigners the right to vote. When Liliuokalani ascended to the throne, ostensibly to maintain and protect the constitution, she immediately sought to overthrow it. Thus the rebellion of 1893, while certainly supported by whites, was a response to the queen's poor judgment as much as it was an American plot.

The new government sent a treaty of annexation to Washington, but the lame duck Harrison forwarded it to the Senate. When the antiexpansionist Cleveland came into office, he dispatched a team to Hawaii to determine if the revolution was genuine or an American-contrived plot. Based on its findings, Cleveland concluded that the latter was the case. He determined that although

Liliuokalani had indeed planned to elevate herself again above the constitution, a group of eighteen Hawaiians, including some sugar farmers, with the aid of U.S. Marines, had overthrown her and named themselves as a provisional government.

What is often missed is at least one earlier attempt by Hawaii to become a part of the United States: in 1851, King Kamehameha III had secretly asked the United States to annex Hawaii, but Secretary of State Daniel Webster declined, saying, "No power ought to take possession of the islands as a conquest . . . or colonization." Webster, preoccupied by slavery, was unwilling to set a precedent that might allow more slave territory into the Union.

By the time the issue reached McKinley's desk, another concern complicated the Hawaiian question: Japan. The Empire of Japan had started to assert itself in the Pacific and, seeing Hawaii as a threat to her sphere of interest, sent warships to Hawaii and encouraged emigration there. This greatly troubled Theodore Roosevelt, among others, who energetically warned Americans that they could not allow Japan to claim the islands. McKinley, in private, agreed with Roosevelt, though he was coy when it came to stating so publicly. Before he assumed office, McKinley had told representatives from Hawaii, "Of course I have my ideas about Hawaii, but consider that it best at the present time not to make known what my policy is."[25] Nevertheless, once in office he pointed out that if nothing was done, "there will be before long another Revolution, and Japan will get control."[26] "We cannot let those islands go to Japan," McKinley bluntly told Senator George Hoar.[27]

Indeed, it was Hawaii herself that, in June 1897, refused to admit a new contingent of Japanese laborers, prompting a visit from Imperial warships. And it was not big business that supported Hawaiian annexation—quite the contrary, the western sugar beet interests opposed the infusion of Hawaiian cane sugar. At the same time, McKinley knew that an annexation treaty likely lacked the two-thirds Senate majority to pass, since most of the Southern Democrats disliked the notion of bringing in as citizens more Asians and brown-skinned Hawaiians. Therefore, to avoid dealing with the insufficient Senate majority, the Republicans introduced a joint resolution to annex Hawaii, apart from the original (withdrawn) treaty. On July 7, 1898, McKinley signed the joint resolution of Congress annexing the Hawaiian islands.

Cuba Libre!

A far more difficult problem that McKinley had inherited was a growing tension with Spain over Cuba. A Spanish possession, Cuba lay only ninety miles off the coast of Florida. At one time it had been both gatekeeper and customhouse for Spain's New World empire, but, like Spain herself, Cuba had lost influence. The Cubans desired freedom and autonomy, as illustrated by revolts that erupted in 1868, 1878, and 1895, all suppressed by the 160,000 Spanish soldiers on the island. General Valeriano Weyler, who governed the island, had a reputation for unusual cruelty, leading to his nickname the Butcher. For forty years the United

States had entertained notions of purchasing Cuba, but Spain had no intention of selling, and the installation of Weyler sounded a requiem for negotiations to acquire the Pearl of the Antilles.

American concerns were threefold. First, there was the political component, in which Americans sympathized with the Cubans' yearning for independence. Second, businessmen had important interests on the island, cultivated over several decades. Sugar, railroads, shipping, and other enterprises gave the United States an undeniable economic interest in Cuba, while at the same time putting Americans in a potential crossfire. Third, there was the moral issue of Weyler's treatment of the Cubans, which appealed to American humanitarianism.

It might have ended at that—with Americans expressing their support for the rebels from afar—if not for the efforts of two newspapermen, Joseph Pulitzer and William Randolph Hearst. Pulitzer, an Austro-Hungarian immigrant, had worked as a mule driver before being recruited by Carl Schurz to write for a German-language daily. A Radical Missouri Republican, Pulitzer had purchased the St. Louis *Post* and *Dispatch* newspapers, using them as a base for the reformist agenda that included issues of prohibition, tax fraud, and gambling. His most important acquisition, however, the New York *World*, emphasized sensation, scandal, and human interest stories. For all of its innovation and success, the New York *World* remains best known for a color supplement it started to run in 1896 on cheap yellow paper featuring a cartoon character known as *The Yellow Kid,* which led to the phrase, "yellow press."[28]

Hearst, born to California millionaire rancher George Hearst, obtained the San Francisco *Examiner* to satisfy a gambling debt. He admired Pulitzer and tailored the *Examiner* to resemble Pulitzer's paper. Emphasizing investigative reporting combined with reformism and sensationalism, Hearst employed the best writers he could find, including Ambrose Bierce, Stephen Crane, Mark Twain, and Jack London. Purchasing the New York *Journal* in 1895, Hearst became Pulitzer's competitor. The two men had much in common, though. Both saw the chaos and tragedy of Cuba purely in terms of expanded circulation. Cuban suffering advanced sales, but a war would be even better. Hearst assigned the brilliant artist Frederic Remington to Cuba to provide battle sketches, well before any hostilities were announced. When Remington arrived in Cuba, he cabled back to Hearst that there was no war to illustrate. "You furnish the pictures," Hearst wired. "I'll furnish the war."[29]

Each publisher sought to outdo the other with Spanish horror stories, giving Weyler his nickname and referring to Cuba as a prison. (Ironically, eighty years later, when Castro's Cuba genuinely became such a prison, no national newspaper dared call it as much.)

Nevertheless, the influence of the press in fomenting war has been overemphasized. Cuban expatriates had already circulated in major U.S. cities attempting to raise awareness and money. Moreover, mainstream papers, such as the New York *Times*, supported McKinley's caution. The role of business in beating the drums for war has also been exaggerated, since as many businesses opposed any support for the revolution as supported it. Prosperity had only recently returned to the nation, and industrialists wished to avoid any disruption of markets that war might bring. Certainly an intellectual case for war, embraced by Alfred Thayer Mahan, John Hay, and Roosevelt, needed no support from the yellow press. Their arguments combined the need for humanitarian relief for the suffering Cubans with the necessity for naval bases and eviction of Old World powers from the Caribbean, as well as good old-fashioned expansionism.

If the yellow press needed any help in "furnishing" the war, Spanish minister to Washington Dupuy de Lome provided it with a letter he wrote in February 1897. De Lome's letter ended up on a desk at the New York *Journal*, thanks to the Cuban rebels and their contacts in New York, and of course the paper gleefully printed its contents with the headline WORST INSULT TO THE UNITED STATES IN ITS HISTORY. The minister called McKinley "weak and a bidder for the admiration of the crowd" who played both sides of the war issue.[30] He further announced his intention to propagandize among American senators and "others in opposition to the junta."[31] McKinley demanded a formal apology, and even though Spain generally agreed with American conditions, the Spanish delay in issuing the apology made them look belligerent. Nevertheless, it appeared relations might be restored, and as part of the reconciliation, McKinley dispatched the battleship USS *Maine* to make a courtesy call to Havana.

At anchor in Havana, the *Maine*'s presence seemed uncontroversial. Sailors routinely walked the streets, fraternizing with sailors of the Spanish navy and purchasing Cuban goods to take home. On the evening of February 15, 1898, however, a massive explosion rocked the vessel, which slowly sank, killing 260 crewmen. News reached McKinley at three o'clock in the morning. Coming on the heels of the de Lome letter—which had actually been written many months earlier—McKinley assumed that the two were linked, but he hoped to avoid a rush to war. He ordered an investigation of the explosion, knowing that a conclusion showing the blast had originated from the outside would tend to implicate Spain (although certainly the rebels had a stake in trying to involve the United States). Americans, however, already seemed convinced of Spain's complicity, and increasingly McKinley was viewed as blocking a necessary war.

Although no proof was offered of Spain's culpability (and not until 1910 did an official inquiry on the remains of the ship seem to confirm that the explosion was caused by a mine), on April 20, 1898, Congress handed McKinley a war resolution, along with the Teller Amendment to liberate Cuba within five years of occupation. For those historians who claimed the United States desired an empire, American behavior was odd: what other empires legally bind themselves to abandoning conquered lands the instant they acquire them? Spain's sudden conciliatory attitude notwithstanding, the pieces fit too conveniently for many Americans to arrive at any other conclusion than that the Spanish were responsible for the sinking of the *Maine*. From Spain it was much too little, too late, and for the

United States it was another opportunity to teach the pompous European state a lesson. On April twenty-first, the Spanish severed diplomatic ties. Four days later, Congress declared war.

Just as the world powers had fully expected Mexico to easily defeat the United States in the Mexican War, Europeans again overestimated the decrepit Spanish empire's strengths and virtually ignored American technology and resolve. The U.S. Army was small and largely untrained. Many units were volunteers; those who had fighting experience came from the frontier, where the Sioux and the Apache presented much different challenges than the more conventional Spanish foe.

McKinley made plans to gather the forces at Tampa and other Florida ports, then land at several points in Cuba. He called for 200,000 volunteers to expand the small 28,000-man army, and by the end of November 1898, 223,000 volunteers had swelled the ranks. These volunteers included the famous Theodore Roosevelt (who had resigned his position as assistant secretary of the navy) and his Rough Riders, an assortment of Indians and scouts, miners and marauders, and even the famous Prescott, Arizona, lawman Bucky O'Neill. But the regiment also included James Robb Church, a star football player at Princeton; New York socialite Hamilton Fish; and the cream of Harvard and Yale. Everyone wanted to join, including the creator of the famous *Tarzan* series, Edgar Rice Burroughs, whom Roosevelt rejected.[32]

Equipping and transporting this army of volunteers was a difficult matter. A new Krag .308 rifle that fired smokeless shells was available, but few units had it; troops called the poor food they received "embalmed beef"; and the atrocious state of medical facilities contributed to the deaths of 2,565 men from disease—more than seven times the 345 men who died in combat.[33] The Rough Riders found they could not even take their horses to Cuba. For good or ill, though, one thing was certain: the press would cover this war. Hearst had seen to that. In addition to Remington with his sketchbooks, author Stephen Crane, whose Civil War tale, *The Red Badge of Courage* (1895), had already become a classic, traveled with the troops to Cuba.

America may have trailed Spain in rifle quality and even the training of her ground forces, but the United States had a decided advantage at sea. There the white cruisers *Olympia, Boston, Raleigh, Concord,* and *Baltimore* outranged and outgunned all of the Spanish vessels. Deploying the fleet to Hong Kong, however, was entirely Roosevelt's doing; he had given the order when the secretary of the navy had gone out of the office for a doctor's appointment. European observers, as always, underestimated Yankee capabilities. Commodore George Dewey, who headed the U.S. Asiatic squadron, reported strong betting at the Hong Kong Club against the Americans, even at considerable odds.

The American battle plan was sound, however. First, Roosevelt ordered Dewey's squadron to Hong Kong even before a declaration of war, in case hostilities broke out. In April, Dewey headed to sea, where he prepared for battle. Spain had seven vessels to Dewey's six in Manila Bay, but they were inferior, and their commander, Rear Admiral Patricio Passaron, knew it. Lined up in Manila Bay, Passaron, in a state of gloom, resigned himself to going down with guns blazing. After the declaration of war, Dewey had sailed for Manila Bay. Spanish guns fired first, prompting shouts of "Remember the Maine" from the American decks, but Dewey uttered his classic line, repeated afterward in countless cartoons, when he told the *Olympia*'s captain, "You may fire when ready, Gridley." At a range of more than five thousand yards—outside the Spaniards' range—U.S. guns shattered the helpless Spanish ships.[34] Dewey did not lose a single man.[35]

A two-pronged assault on Cuba was the second piece of the U.S. strategy, and it was aimed at forcing the Spanish Caribbean fleet to exit its port while American troops advanced overland to Havana. The grand assault was led by the three-hundred-pound General William Shafter, whose forces landed on June twenty-second at Daquiri, unopposed and unscathed. The only U.S. casualties were five drowned horses.

Ex-Rebel General Joseph Wheeler, in his first encounter with Spanish troops, shouted, "We've got the damned Yankees on the run!"[36] But his men knew what he meant, and they proceeded to link up with Shafter's forces. By that time, Shafter had fallen ill, to the point where he was unable to ride. After driving the Spaniards out of several positions, American troops converged on the main target, San Juan Heights.

Faced with two hills, San Juan and Kettle, Leonard Wood's regiments—including the Rough Riders (whose horses were still back in Tampa) and Lieutenant John J. Pershing's 10th Cavalry buffalo soldiers—crossed the river in front of Kettle Hill. Organizing both the regiments, Teddy Roosevelt, a mounted sitting target, spurred his horse Little Texas in front of his men charging on foot. The units storming Kettle Hill raised a cheer from the American forces still pinned under fire below San Juan Heights.

Spanish positions on San Juan Heights still proved impenetrable until a courageous captain, G. S. Grimes, drove three batteries of Gatling guns to within six hundred yards of the Spanish lines and poured fire at them. (Remington captured the moment in a memorable painting). That was enough to spark the actual "charge up San Juan Hill." Roosevelt had already led his men up *Kettle Hill* and was not among those advancing on San Juan's positions, and the "charge" was an orderly, steady advance into heavy fire.

At the same time, Roosevelt's Rough Riders, pouring machine gun fire into the Spanish flank, charged down the mild slope of Kettle Hill directly into the Spanish positions. Spanish resistance disintegrated. Later, Pershing wrote his recollections of the attack: "White regiments, black regiments, regulars and Rough Riders, representing the young manhood of the North and the South, fought shoulder to shoulder, unmindful of race or color, unmindful of whether commanded by ex-Confederate or not, and mindful of only their common duty as Americans."[37] The Spanish general Joaquin Vara del Rey had the gross misfortune of being shot through both legs; then, as his men carried him on a stretcher to safety, he was hit again, through the head. Roosevelt, recommended for a

Medal of Honor for his actions by both commanding officers, Shafter and Wood, was denied the recognition by political enemies until January 2001, when Congress finally awarded it to him posthumously.

Shafter, still battling gout and heat, now surrounded Santiago and squeezed Admiral Pascual Cervera's fleet out of the harbor, where it had to run the gauntlet of Admiral William Sampson's American vessels. On July 3, 1898, Cervera's fleet sailed out, much to the surprise of Sampson. The Spanish knew what awaited them. "Poor Spain," said a captain aboard the *Theresa* to Admiral Cervera. The sound of the ship bugles meant that Spain had become "a nation of the fourth class."[38] After a brief running battle with the far superior American ships, in which the U.S. Navy badly damaged all of Cervera's vessels, the Spanish fleet hauled down its colors. "The fleet under my command," telegraphed Admiral Sampson to Washington, "offers the nation, as a Fourth of July present, the whole of Cervera's fleet."[39] Spain quickly capitulated. Despite the loss of only 400 men in combat, the Spanish-American War had proven costly. The government had mobilized thousands of soldiers who never saw action, but who ultimately would draw pensions valued at $5 billion. At the end of sixty years, the pensions from the Spanish-American War still cost the United States $160 million annually.

Final negotiations left the United States in control of the Philippines, Cuba, and Puerto Rico. The Senate had insisted that Cuba be free and not a U.S. possession, but the United States paid $20 million for Guam, the Philippines, and Puerto Rico. The disposition of these other territories, however, was not so clear. Two other nations, in addition to the Filipinos themselves, had an interest in the Philippines. Filipino freedom fighters, led by Emilio Aguinaldo, had been brought by Dewey from Hong Kong to help liberate the Philippines. Aguinaldo's ten thousand insurgents had helped to capture Manila. Under other circumstances, it is highly likely the United States would have washed its hands of the Philippines and hastily departed.

By 1898, however, there were other considerations. Roosevelt, Alfred Thayer Mahan, and others had already started to push the United States onto the world stage, and as a world power the nation needed overseas coaling stations. With the annexation of Hawaii in July, the Philippines suddenly became a logical extension of American naval bases.

Combined with the presence of British and German fleets, the fate of the Philippines as an American protectorate was sealed. Britain and Germany both had fleets in the region. Germany, in particular, thought little of the United States, saying, "God favored drunkards, fools, and the United States of America." Either nation could have controlled the Philippines the moment the American fleet left, although whether they would have fought each other is conjecture. At any rate, McKinley explained his reasoning as follows:

> . . . one night it came to me this way . . . (1) we could not give them [the Philippines] back to Spain—that would be cowardly and dishonorable; (2) that we could not turn them over to France or Germany—our com-

mercial rivals in the Orient—that would be bad business and discreditable; (3) that we could not leave them to themselves—they were unfit for self-government—and they would soon have anarchy and misrule over there worse than Spain's was; and (4) that there was nothing left for us to do but to take them all, and to educate the Filipinos, and uplift and civilize and Christianize them.[40]

The last point, although it played a minor part in the president's decision, had been on the minds of Protestant Americans, whose missionary societies had sent many evangelists to the islands. Methodists, in particular, wrote of saving the "little brown brother."[41] Some historians dismiss these expressions of concern for the Filipinos as insincere excuses for national economic expansion, but, as usual, they ignore the genuine doctrinal commitment of most Christian groups to evangelize.

McKinley realized that the choice he faced was not whether to liberate the islands, but which of three nations—the United States, Germany, or Britain— would control them. Predictably, when the Stars and Stripes went up in Manila, sending the European fleets packing, it ensured a response from the eighty thousand Filipinos under Aguinaldo, who felt betrayed. An insurrection ensued, and for a year and a half, a guerrilla war of brutal proportions witnessed both sides engaging in torture and atrocities. McKinley, aware that the occupation required the support of the Filipino people, persuaded William Howard Taft to lead a five-man commission to Manila in April 1900. Taft, who liked the Filipinos, earned their respect and soon produced reasonable, concrete steps to reduce opposition.

McKinley's policy opened the door to anti-imperialists, such as William Jennings Bryan, the Populists, and the Anti-Imperialist League. League members handed out leaflets to soldiers in the Philippines, urging them not to reenlist. Some of the more extreme members of the League compared McKinley to a mass murderer and issued wild predictions that eight thousand Americans would die trying to hold the islands. The insurgents quoted Bryan and fellow anti-imperialist Edward Atkinson, thus inspiring the rebels and, possibly, prolonging the conflict, thereby contributing to the deaths of U.S. soldiers.

Aguinaldo himself remained elusive, despite unceasing American attempts to locate and capture him. Finally, with the assistance of an anti-insurrectionist Filipino group called the Maccabees, Aguinaldo was captured, and in April 1901 he swore an oath of allegiance to the United States. Three months later the military government ended, replaced by a provincial government under Taft.

The islands remained U.S. possessions until World War II, although in 1916, the Jones Act announced American intentions to grant Philippine independence as soon as practicable. In 1934, the Tydings-McDuffie Act provided a tutelage period of ten more years, setting the date for independence as 1944, and providing an election in which Manuel Quezon became the first president of the Philippines. Although Japanese occupation of the islands delayed independence beyond the 1944 target, in 1946 the United States granted independence to the

Philippines on the Fourth of July, once again proving wrong the critics of America who saw imperial interests as the reason for overseas expansion. Never before in history had a nation so willingly and, in general, so peacefully rescinded control over so much territory and so many conquered people as in the case of the possessions taken in the Spanish-American War.

The "Full Dinner Pail" and Assassination

Not long after the war ended, Vice President Garret A. Hobart died in office. McKinley and the Republicans knew they might have a popular replacement in Teddy Roosevelt, who had recently been elected governor of New York. McKinley had met Roosevelt when he went to Montauk to congratulate General Shafter and his troops; when the president saw Roosevelt, he stopped the carriage and extended his hand. The ebullient Roosevelt struggled to pull his glove off, finally grabbing it in his teeth before pumping McKinley's hand. Thus, with Hobart out, the Republicans approached Roosevelt—who really wanted no job save the president's—to replace the deceased vice president.

Political realities, however, created an inexorable momentum toward the vice presidential nomination. As Boss Platt quipped, "Roosevelt might as well stand under Niagara Falls and try to spit water back as to stop his nomination by this convention."[42] With Teddy on the ballot, a good economy, and the conclusion of a successful war, McKinley was unbeatable. His slogan, a "full dinner pail," spoke to the economic well-being of millions without committing the government to engage in specific action. McKinley beat the Democrat, William Jennings Bryan, worse than he had in 1896, winning the popular vote 7.2 million to 6.3 million, and taking the electoral vote, 292 to 155. While McKinley looked forward to serving as "President of the whole people," Roosevelt committed himself to being a "dignified nonentity for four years."[43]

The president had undertaken few new programs (aside from turning the Northern Security Trust issue over to Roosevelt to handle) when he made a trip to the Pan American Exposition in Buffalo on September 6, 1901. Just as a premonition of disaster had gripped many around Lincoln in his final days, so too did McKinley's staff grow increasingly uneasy as he headed to Buffalo. Several crank letters threatening assassination had arrived during the campaign, but McKinley dismissed them. The threats, however, alarmed his private secretary, George Cortelyou, who on his own started a screening process for visitors. In addition, a private investigator dogged the president's steps, and Buffalo police were on alert. McKinley refused to allow his aides to seal him off from the public, thus agreeing to a long reception line at one of the exposition buildings, the Music Temple. While a line of well-wishers streamed in to a Bach organ sonata, Leon Czolgosz, the anarchist assassin, joined them, concealing a pistol in his bandaged right hand. As McKinley shook the man's left hand, Czolgosz shot the president twice. The stricken Major slumped backward to a chair, urging Cortelyou to "be careful" how he informed Mrs. McKinley her husband was dead.[44]

In fact, he remained alive, unconscious. A bullet had gone through his stomach and into his back; efforts to locate it failed, despite the presence at the exposition of a new X-ray machine, which was not used. Doctors cleansed and closed the wound without extracting the bullet. Over the next few days, McKinley regained consciousness, giving everyone around him hope, but he drifted away a week after the attack. New York City papers, which had earlier published editorials calling for McKinley's removal—Hearst had even said, "assassination can be a good thing"—engaged in finger-pointing as to whether the press should share blame in the president's death.[45]

McKinley became the third president in thirty-five years to be killed by an assassin, and for the first time, both a president and a vice president from the same administration (1896–1900) died in office. His killer, who wanted to cause all government to collapse, only succeeded in replacing a successful president with a legendary one.

A Brilliant Madman, Born a Century Too Soon

By 1907, Theodore Roosevelt—he hated the sobriquet Teddy, and although resigned to it, allowed none to call him that in person—stood five feet eight inches tall and weighed two hundred pounds, mostly muscle. His heavyweight sparring partner described him as a "strong, tough man; hard to hurt and harder to stop."[46] It was a remarkable transformation for the skinny kid who had entered Harvard in the mid-1870s. Yet for such a powerful man, he was small boned, with delicate feet and hands that contrasted with the heavy girth and jowls. His famous teeth, not as prominent as the caricatures, lent a distinctiveness to his speech, which was clipped, raspy, and likened to a man "biting tenpenny nails."[47] Roosevelt's pronunciation added another distinguishing tone to his speech, wherein he pronounced "I" as "Aieee" and punctuated his sentences with his favorite word, "deeeee-lighted." Albany legislators had made legend his habit of running up to the podium waving a finger and shouting, "Mister Spee-kar." Asthmatic and bespectacled with his famous pince-nez, Roosevelt was a swirl of energy. He burst into rooms, descending on friends and foes like a thunderstorm, leading English writer John Morely to call Niagara Falls and Theodore Roosevelt "great works of nature."[48] Bram Stoker, the author of *Dracula*, once meeting Roosevelt, noted in his diary, "Must be President some day. A man you can't cajole, can't frighten, can't buy."[49]

Long before he became president, Roosevelt impressed people with his sharp mind and his ability to discuss intelligently almost any subject—his entrance exams at Harvard testify to his mental capacities. Obsessed with reading (he referred to it as a disease with him), Roosevelt had consumed such mammoth tomes as David Livingstone's *Missionary Travels*. Well traveled in Europe, Africa, and America, Roosevelt marveled at the written word as much as at the visual image.

A frail child, Roosevelt spent summers working out and boxing as a means to build his body. He boxed during his Harvard years, but just as often he fought outside the ring, often decking political rivals who made fun of him. The intellectual

Roosevelt, however, could penetrate to the heart of intricate legislative matters, often offending everyone in the process of doing the right thing. He spearheaded several municipal reform bills, nearly pulling off an investigation of New York corruption before witnesses developed "memory loss." New York assemblyman Newton Curtis called him a "brilliant madman, born a century too soon."[50]

Having overcome asthma, poor eyesight, and his own impetuous moods, Roosevelt was struck by sudden and nearly unbearable grief in February 1884, when his wife died after giving birth only a few hours after Roosevelt's mother, who had been in the same house, expired of typhoid fever. "There is a curse on this house," his brother Elliott had told him, and Roosevelt began to believe it. That curse would claim the alcoholic Elliott in 1891, when he had to be committed to an asylum.

To drown his grief after his wife's death, the hyper Roosevelt left politics for his cattle ranch in Elkhorn, North Dakota, where he served as a deputy sheriff and helped track down a trio of horse thieves. Then, in 1889, after he was appointed by President Harrison to the Civil Service Commission, he returned to New York, where he developed a feud with the-then New York Governor Grover Cleveland. As in the case of the bitter antagonism between Adams and Jefferson, Jefferson and Hamilton, and Sherman and Lincoln, the Cleveland-Roosevelt feud (lopsided in Cleveland's favor as it was) was regrettable. Here was another example of two figures of towering character and, in many instances, clear vision, disagreeing over the proper implementation of their ideals. Yet such debates refined American democracy, and were of no small import.

Even before his appointment to the Civil Service Commission, Roosevelt had started to develop a national name with his authorship of books on the West, including *Hunting Trips* (1885) and *The Winning of the West* (1889), as well as ten other works. While far from an inexorable march to the presidency, Roosevelt's steps seem measured by a certain sense of relentlessness or Providence. He entered New York City politics as police commissioner, a position that called for him to walk the slums and meet with future muckraker Lincoln Steffens and a police reporter named Jacob Riis. Roosevelt fit right in with the two men. (Riis soon gravitated from his job with the New York *Tribune* to work on housing reform, which was the basis for his popular book *How the Other Half Lives* [1890]. Steffens, whose wealthy father had instructed him to "stay in New York and hustle," instead also became a reporter, but with the New York *Evening Post*.)[51] Roosevelt took Steffens seriously enough to initiate legislation based on his writings, although Roosevelt was dead by the time Steffens visited the Soviet Union, in 1921, and uttered the preposterous comment, "I have seen the future, and it works."

Even as a young state assemblyman in the 1880s, Roosevelt was consumed by reform in his public career. His progressivism embraced an activist government to alleviate social ills.

For many reformers, words like "ethics" and phrases about "uplifting the masses" were only so much window dressing for their real agenda of social architecture. Not Roosevelt. He genuinely believed that "no people were ever benefited by riches if their prosperity corrupted their virtue. It is," he added, "more important that we should show ourselves honest, brave, truthful, and intelligent than we should own all the railways and grain elevators in the world."[52] Roosevelt came from "old money," and despite such sentiment, he never entirely lost his patrician biases.

This in part explains his antipathy toward corporations, most of whose founders came from "new" money. Rockefeller and Carnegie were self-made men who had built their fortunes the hard way. Roosevelt could never be accused of being afraid to dirty his hands, but his animosity toward businessmen like Edward H. Harriman suggested that in some ways he envied the corporate captains who had worked their way up from the bottom. To have never had the opportunity to succeed in business troubled Roosevelt. It was all the more paradoxical coming from the man whose classic "Man in the Arena" speech still retains its wisdom and dignity:

> It is not the critic who counts: not the man who points out how the strong man stumbles or where the doer of deeds could have done better. The credit belongs to the man who is actually in the arena, whose face is marred by dust and sweat and blood, who strives valiantly, who errs and comes up short again and again, because there is no effort without error or shortcoming, but who knows the great enthusiasms, the great devotions, who spends himself for a worthy cause; who, at the best, knows, in the end, the triumph of high achievement, and who, at the worst, if he fails, at least he fails while daring greatly, so that his place shall never be with those cold and timid souls who knew neither victory nor defeat.[53]

Roosevelt had succeeded at everything he ever attempted—improving his physical strength and athletic prowess, courting and winning his wife, leading men in combat, and running for office.

By the time he became president then, Theodore Roosevelt had prepared himself for the office in every aspect necessary to the job, save one: understanding capitalism, private enterprise, and the industrial nature of modern America. For someone steeped in the romantic images of the West, Roosevelt should have favored the "rugged individualism" of a Carnegie, but his reform impulse possessed him. As a result, he became the most activist president since Andrew Jackson, doing more to impede business than any president since Old Hickory.

Trust-busting, Business Bashing

An indication of where Roosevelt planned to go with his agenda of corporate regulation could be gleaned from his brief stint as New York governor, where he pushed through a measure taxing corporations. A social Darwinist, Roosevelt liked the notion that there existed an intellectual hierarchy among men, and that only the "best and the brightest" should lead. This same Roosevelt fancied himself the friend of the oppressed and thought farmers, mechanics, and small business owners were his "natural allies."[54] But in Roosevelt's mind, if the brilliant individual or the visionary man knew best how to reform society, he should do so with whatever tools he had at his disposal, including government. Consequently, it surprised no one who knew him that Roosevelt favored an activist federal presence. William Howard Taft said that he never met a man "more strongly in favor of strong government" than Roosevelt.[55]

In his first inaugural, Roosevelt spoke favorably of great corporations and endorsed the idea of expanding markets. To this he added that trusts had gone beyond the capacity of existing laws to deal with them, and that old laws and traditions could not sufficiently contain concentrations of wealth and power. Congress sensed the change, passing the Elkins Act in 1903, which prohibited railroads from giving rebates—essentially volume discounts—to large corporations. The notion that businesses were different from individual behavior, or needed to be penalized for success beyond what was "reasonable," was a Progressive principle that soon emerged in many regulations.

Epitomizing the direction of Roosevelt's new policies was the Northern Securities suit of 1902. This followed a legal ruling in the E. C. Knight sugar refiner case of 1895, where the Supreme Court declared the regulation of manufacturing a state responsibility; since the manufacturing was within a state's boundaries, any successful suit had to involve interstate commerce. Since Northern Securities involved railroads crossing state lines, it met the requirements. Roosevelt thought he had an opening, and instructed the attorney general, Philander C. Knox, to file a Sherman antitrust suit against Northern Securities, a holding company for the Northern Pacific, Great Northern, and Chicago, Burlington, and Quincy railroads. J. P. Morgan, James J. Hill, E. H. Harriman, and representatives of Standard Oil Company had combined the northwestern railroad lines into Northern Securities, a single holding company worth $400 million. What made the Northern Securities suit different was that although the government claimed that Northern Securities sought to create a monopoly, no higher rates had actually emerged, only the "threat" of "restraint of trade." For the first time, then, the federal government acted against commerce only on a *potential* threat, not genuine behavior, thus debunking the myth that corporations are "like individuals," whom the law treats as "innocent until proven guilty."[56]

Thanks largely to the Northern Securities case, Roosevelt—whose nickname Teddy had been popularized after a toy manufacturer named a stuffed bear for him—now earned the moniker "Trustbuster." He followed up the victory with an assault on Rockefeller's Standard Oil, although it was the administration of TR's successor, William Howard Taft, that eventually witnessed the final disposition of that case—the breakup of the oil giant into several smaller companies. Already, however, the inconsistencies and contradictions of the Sherman Act had become apparent to even some reformers. Research by George Bitlingmayer found that far from helping the little guy, antitrust actions tended to hurt small businesses by driving down profits in the entire sector, presumably those businesses most helped by reducing "monopolistic" competition.[57]

Roosevelt got away with his assault on corporations by balancing it with rhetoric about the need to control labor radicalism. Only the presidency was exempted from Roosevelt's concern about the abuse of power. Congress, all too willing to contain the "excesses" of corporations, passed the Expedition Act of 1903, requiring courts to put antitrust cases on a fast track, then created a new department, Commerce and Labor, within which was established a Bureau of Corporations to investigate violations of interstate commerce. All of this legislation came on top of the aforementioned Elkins Act, and represented an attempt by Congress to appear to be doing something. Roosevelt, however, grabbed the headlines, invoking the Sherman Act twenty-five times during his administration.

When it came to action, though, Roosevelt sided substantially with labor. In 1902 he intervened in a strike by Pennsylvania coal miners, who wanted recognition of their union as well as the expected higher wages and lower work hours. Publicly, Roosevelt expressed sympathy for the miners, and then he invited both United Mine Worker (UMW) leaders and mine owners to the White House in order to avert a coal shortage. Mine owners, led by George F. Baer of the Reading Railroad, alienated both the miners and the president, who grew so irritated that he wanted to grab Baer "by the seat of the breeches" and "chuck him out [a window]."[58] The owners were "wooden-headed," whose "arrogant stupidity" made arbitration more difficult.[59] He warned that he would send 10,000 federal troops to take over coal production in the mines if the two sides did not reach an arrangement, a move of "dubious legality," which prompted Roosevelt to snap, "To hell with the Constitution when the people want coal!"[60] TR's bluster finally produced concessions, with both sides agreeing to an arbitration commission named by the president, and led to higher wages (below what the strikers wanted), fewer work hours (though above what the strikers sought), and no UMW recognition. It was enough for Roosevelt to claim that he had brokered a "square deal," which later provided a popular campaign phrase for the president.

Most presidential clout, though, was reserved for corporations, not labor. "We don't wish to destroy corporations," he generously noted, "but we do wish to make them subserve the public good."[61] Implied in Roosevelt's comment was the astonishing view that corporations do not serve the public good on their own— that they must be made to—and that furnishing jobs, paying taxes, and creating new wealth did not constitute a sufficient public benefit. It was a position even more astonishing coming from the so-called "party of big business." TR despised what he called "the tyranny of mere wealth."[62] Yet like other presidents who inherited wealth—his cousin, Franklin Roosevelt, and John F. Kennedy—Teddy never appreciated what it took to meet a payroll or to balance a firm's books. Roosevelt knew that in the 1904 election he might lose the support of key Republican constituencies, and therefore he spent the last months mending fences, corresponding with Morgan and other business leaders, and supporting the

GOP's probusiness platform. It served him well. Already a popular leader, Roosevelt knew that the Democrats had allied themselves with radical elements of labor and the farm sectors.

Democrats knew it too, and they beat a hasty retreat from William Jennings Bryan's more explosive rhetoric, endorsing the gold standard and selecting as their nominee a conservative New York judge, Alton B. Parker. With a socialist candidate, Eugene V. Debs, siphoning off 400,000 votes, the Democrats did not stand a chance of unseating the popular Teddy. Roosevelt crushed Parker and, more impressively, carried every single state except the South and Maryland, solidifying the western base brought in by McKinley.

The day before his inauguration, Roosevelt said, "Tomorrow I shall come into the office in my own right. Then watch out for me."[63] Safely reelected, Roosevelt again turned on the business community, especially the railroads. He supported the Hepburn Act, called "a landmark in the evolution of federal control of private industry."[64] It allowed the Interstate Commerce Act to set railroad rates. As part of the compromise to obtain passage of Hepburn, Roosevelt agreed to delay tariff reform, which became the central issue of his successor's administration. In 1905, at his urging, Congress passed the Pure Food and Drug Act, prohibiting companies from selling adulterated foods, or foods or medicines that contained ingredients the FDA deemed harmful. Like most laws, the Food and Drug Act originated out of noble intentions. Americans had already been sufficiently alarmed about the dangers of cocaine, which had forced Coca-Cola to change its secret formula, and, after Sinclair's horrifying novel, an even greater public outcry over tainted meat led to the Meat Inspection Act.

Summer Camps and Saving the Bison

At the turn of the century, a movement for conserving America's natural resources sprang up. The first conservation legislation, in 1891, authorized President Harrison to designate public lands as forest reserves, allowing Harrison and Cleveland to reserve 35 million acres. Popular tastes had increasingly embraced a wilderness infatuation, especially among elite eastern groups. Writers had romanticized the wilderness since the Revolution's Hector St. John and the early national era writings of James Fenimore Cooper and Henry David Thoreau. Interest accelerated with the summer camp movement of the 1890s. Roosevelt institutionalized the conservation movement, creating the U.S. Forest Service in 1905 and appointing Yale University's first professional forester, Gifford Pinchot, to head the agency.

Roosevelt's action marked the culmination of the efforts of naturalists, artists, and anthropologists who had argued for application of Progressive management techniques to natural resources. That movement also had its origins in the efforts of John Muir, an Indianapolis carriage worker who was nearly blinded in a factory accident. When his sight returned, Muir resolved to turn his gaze to America's natural wonders. In the late 1860s, a trip to Yosemite and the Sierra Nevada mountains led him to produce a series of articles called "Studies in the

Sierra," before exploring Alaska and Glacier Bay. It was in his series of articles appearing in *Century* magazine that Muir drew attention to the devastation of mountain meadows and forests by sheep and cattle. Robert Underwood Johnson, the editor of *Century*, joined with Muir to form the Sierra Club in 1892 to protect natural resources and public parks.[65]

Important differences separated Roosevelt and Muir, even though the two were friends and even camped together in Yosemite in 1903. Muir was a preservationist who envisioned maintenance of a pristine, sacred natural world in which any development was prohibited. He was also proven wrong in some of his more apocalyptic prophecies, such as his claim that the damming of the river in the Hetch Hetchy Valley would doom Yosemite.

Needless to say, Roosevelt did not share the view that water for people's cities was the practical equivalent of water for trees. It would be the same mentality that a century later would consign hundreds of Klamath, Oregon, farmers to poverty and financial ruin when an endangered fish was discovered in the basin, causing the federal government to shut off all water use.

The first most practical effect of the new conservation movement came in 1901, when thirty western senators and congressmen from seventeen western states agreed to a plan by Senator Francis Newlands of Wyoming to apply a portion of public lands receipts to reclamation, dam construction, and other water projects. Roosevelt jumped on the Newlands bandwagon and secured passage of the bill, which, without question, taxed some western farmers who lived in areas with heavier rainfall for others who did not. Roosevelt rejected the pristine view, signing the National Reclamation Act of 1902, which made possible the settlement and managed use of a vast, mostly barren, landscape.

As conservationists, Roosevelt and Pinchot saw the use of nature by people as the primary reason for preserving nature. In 1910, Pinchot—in sharp contrast to Muir—wrote that the first principle of conservation was "development, the use of natural resources now existing on this continent for the benefit of *people who live here now* [emphasis added]."[66]

Roosevelt, however, soon went too far, setting aside 200 million acres of public land (more than one third of it in Alaska) as national forests or other reserved sites. After being confronted by angry western legislators, Roosevelt backed down and rescinded the set-aside program—but not before tacking on another 16 million acres to the public lands map. Roosevelt overthrew the Jeffersonian principle that the land belonged in the hands of the people individually rather than the people as a whole. Only the public sector, he thought, could regulate the political entrepreneurs and their harvesting of ore and timber by enclosing public lands. This was Roosevelt's elite, Progressive side taking over. His own experiences as a wealthy hunter won out over the principle that individuals should own, and work, their own land.

One of the most hidden facts of the conservation movement—perhaps deliberately buried by modern environmental extremists—involved the fate of the buffalo. When we last examined the Plains buffalo, white hunters had nearly ex-

terminated the herds. Ranchers, noticing fewer buffalo, concluded that ownership of a scarce resource would produce profits. A handful of western American
and Canadian ranchers, therefore, began to round up, care for, and breed the remaining buffalo. The federal government's Yellowstone National Park purchased
these bison in 1902, and other government parks were also soon established,
including the Oklahoma Wichita Mountains Park, Montana's National Bison
Range, and Nebraska's National Wildlife Refuge.[67]

Yet public control of natural resources contrasted with the fact that in many
areas, TR had abandoned antibusiness inclinations in his second term. For example, he had slowly gravitated more toward free trade when it came to the tariff.
During McKinley's short second term, the Major had drifted toward an appreciation for lower tariff duties, speaking in favor of reciprocity, whereby the United
States would reduce rates on certain imported goods if foreign countries would
do the same on American imports. Roosevelt saw the logic in lower tariffs, especially after the 1902 Dingley Tariff provoked foreign responses in the form of
higher rates on all American goods. One industry at a time, former advocates of
high duties saw the light and swung behind lower tariffs. Iron, steel, foodstuffs,
manufactured items—all were represented by important lobbies that gradually
started to argue on behalf of lower duties.

As president, Roosevelt, who had in the past fought for lower duties, suddenly became cautious. He decided to do nothing on broad-based tariff reform.
With his war on the trusts, the new emphasis on conservation of the resources,
and the growing need for a water route linking the oceans through Central
America, Roosevelt had a full plate, and he left the tariff issue to be taken up by
his successor.

"Speak Softly . . ."

Most Americans are familiar with Roosevelt's comment on international relations, "Speak softly and carry a big stick." As a Progressive, Roosevelt believed in
the principle of human advance, morally and ethically, which translated into a
foreign policy of aggressive intervention. He kept a wary eye on England and her
ability to maintain a balance of power, but knew that the United States had to
step in if Britain faltered. Roosevelt appreciated the value of ships and the power
they could project. During his first administration, he pressed Congress for new
expenditures, resulting in a near doubling of the navy by the end of his second
term.

Both the strength and weakness of America, and the navy in particular, lay in
the fact that two massive oceans protected the United States. Any blue-water
fleet had to be capable of conducting operations in both the Atlantic and Pacific
nearly simultaneously. That was before a short-cut route connecting the two
oceans was conceived. For several decades, transit across Panama, a territory of
Colombia, had required a stop on one side, unloading and transporting people
and goods by rail to the other side, then reloading them to continue the journey.
Warships had to sail all the way around South America to get from the Atlantic

to the Pacific, and vice versa. The concept of a canal was obvious, and despite the presence of powerful American interests, a French company had acquired rights to build a canal across the Isthmus of Panama in 1879. After ten years and $400 million, the French gave up, leaving the canal only partially finished. Desperately in debt, the French attempted to sell the assets, including the concession, to the United States for $109 million, but the United States balked at the steep price. An alternate route, through Nicaragua, offered the less difficult construction chore of merely linking several large lakes together, taking advantage of nature's own "canal." But Nicaragua had its own problems, including earthquakes, so the French, eager for any return on the investment, lowered the price to $40 million.

Congress liked that price, as did Roosevelt, who dispatched the new secretary of state John Hay to negotiate the final agreement with Tomás Herrán, Colombia's representative, wherein the United States received a ninety-nine-year lease on the Canal Zone for $10 million down and $250,000 per year. The ensuing events brought out Roosevelt's darker side, part of which he had revealed years earlier in his *Winning of the West.* "The most righteous of all wars," he wrote, "is a war with savages, though it is apt to be also the most terrible and inhuman. The rude, fierce settler who drives the savage from the land lays all civilized mankind under debt to him."[68]

When Colombia heard of the new Hay agreement, the government rejected it, offering several possible replacements. One had Colombia receiving $20 million from the United States and $10 million from the French company. Roosevelt had no intention of renegotiating a deal he thought was his. By October 1903, his rhetoric had left no doubt where he stood on the Panama issue, calling the Colombian representatives "homicidal corruptionists" and "greedy little arthropoids."[69] The president saw Colombians as blackmailers. Although he had not been pressed to somehow intervene in Panama, "so as to secure the Panama route," neither did he silence his friends, including *The Outlook,* which editorialized about the desirability of an internal revolution in Panama that might result in secession from Colombia.[70] Although Roosevelt planned in his annual message to Congress to recommend that the United States take the Isthmus of Panama, he never sent it, nor was it needed: a November revolution in Panama, headed by a New Yorker named Philippe Bunau-Varilla, overthrew the Colombian government there and declared an independent state of Panama.

As soon as Bunau-Varilla and his associates ousted the Colombian authorities in Panama, the USS *Nashville* arrived to intimidate reinforcements from Columbia, since the United States had recognized Bunau-Varilla's group as Panama's official government. Bunau-Varilla, an agent of the French Canal Company, had lobbied Congress for the Panama route after the French enterprise ran out of money, and he helped insert a clause in the new treaty that gave the United States the ten-milewide Canal Zone for $40 million, protection against any recovery of money owed to Colombia. Some suggested that part of the deal was an under-the-table cash payoff of the French as well. Roosevelt denied any wrongdoing, but ultimately admitted, "I took the Canal Zone."[71] Yet his logic was commendable: "I . . . left [it to] Congress, not to debate the Canal, but to debate me."[72]

Construction across the fifty miles of the isthmus is one of the miracles of human engineering. It completed the work begun in 1878 by Ferdinand de Lesseps, the French engineer who had constructed the Suez Canal. Once the Canal treaty was finalized, Roosevelt authorized U.S. Army engineers to start digging. John. F. Wallace supervised most of the work. He spent two years assembling supplies and creating the massive infrastructure the project needed. He oversaw the construction of entire towns with plank walkways, hospitals, mess halls, and general stores—all dug out of the Panamanian mud. When it came down to the Canal, though, he could not drum up any enthusiasm: "To me," he told Roosevelt, "the canal is only a big ditch."[73] By 1907 he realized that a sea-level canal would be too difficult, and instead proposed a series of locks to raise vessels from the Atlantic about thirty yards above sea level to Gatún Lake, then to the famous eight-mile-long Calebra Cut—one of the most daunting engineering feats in modern history. Roosevelt then brought in Colonel George Goethals, who by then also had the benefit of Colonel William Gorgas's medical research on malaria, to direct the project.

Goethals infused the effort with new energy, even as he confronted the Calebra Cut, using more than 2,500 men to dynamite mountain walls, excavating more than 200 million yards of dirt and rock, which was hauled away by 4,000 wagons. Despite the use of 19 million pounds of explosives, only eight men perished in accidents. In 1913 the final part of the Calebra Cut was completed, and on the other side lay the locks at Pedro Miguel, which lower ships to the Pacific's level. When the Canal finally opened, on August 15, 1914, Roosevelt was out of politics, but he could claim substantial responsibility for the greatest engineering feat in history.

The acquisition of the Canal Zone and the construction of the Panama Canal typified Roosevelt's "big stick" attitude toward foreign policy. He was determined to keep Europeans out of the New World, largely in order to preserve some of it, particularly the Caribbean, for American expansion. When Germany tried to strong-arm Venezuela in December 1902 into repaying debts by threatening to blockade Venezuelan ports, Roosevelt stepped in. Eyeing the Germans suspiciously, Roosevelt decided that the United States could not allow them or any other European power to intervene in Latin America.

The resulting Roosevelt Corollary to the Monroe Doctrine, delivered when Elihu Root read a letter from Roosevelt at the Cuban independence anniversary dinner in 1904, promised no interference with a country conducting itself "with decency" in matters of trade and politics. But the United States would not tolerate "brutal wrongdoing," or behavior that "results in a general loosening of the ties of civilized society." Such activity would require "intervention by some civilized nation, and in the Western Hemisphere the United States cannot ignore this duty."[74] This sentiment formed the basis of a worldview that saw any unrest in the Western Hemisphere as a potential threat to U.S. interests. Roosevelt's foreign policy blended Progressive reformism, a lingering sense of manifest destiny, and a refereshing unwillingness to tolerate thugs and brigands just because they happened to be outside American borders. In truth, his role as hemispheric policeman differed little from his approach to businesses and corporations. He demanded that they act morally (as he and his fellow Progressives defined "morality") and viewed their refusal as endangering the American people when they did not.

Black and White in Progressive America

Shortly after he had succeeded McKinley, Roosevelt invited black leader Booker T. Washington to a personal, formal dinner at the White House. The affair shocked many Americans, some of whom treated it like a scandal, and Roosevelt, though he maintained that Washington remained an adviser, never asked him to return. Still, the event showed both how far America had come, and how far it had to go.

Washington's dinner invitation seemed trivial next to the Brownsville, Texas, shooting spree of August 1906, in which black soldiers, angered by their treatment at the hands of Brownsville citizens, started shooting up the town, killing a civilian, then managing to return to the base unobserved. None of the 160 members of the black units would provide a name to investigators, and after three months, Roosevelt discharged all 160 men, including six Medal of Honor winners. All the dishonorably discharged men would be disqualified from receiving their pensions (they were reinstated and all military honors restored by Congress in 1972). Northerners came to the defense of the soldiers, although the South was outraged at their behavior.

Since the end of Reconstruction, the South had degenerated into a two-tiered segregated society of Jim Crow laws ensuring the separation of blacks and whites in virtually every aspect of social life. Even in the North, however, Progressives used IQ tests to segregate education and keep the races apart.[75] The federal government contributed to this with the 1896 Supreme Court decision, *Plessy v. Ferguson*, in which the Court ruled that the establishment of "separate but equal" facilities, including schools, was legal and acceptable. A case originating in Louisiana when a black man, Homer Plessy, rode home in a "whites only" railroad car (thus violating state law), *Plessy v. Ferguson* held of the intent of the Fourteenth Amendment that:

> it could not have been intended to abolish distinctions based on color, or to enforce social, as distinguished from political equality, or a commingling of the two races upon terms unsatisfactory to either. Laws permitting, and even requiring, that separation in places where they are liable to be brought into contact do not necessarily imply the inferiority of

either race to the other, and have been generally, if not universally, recognized as within the competency of the state legislatures in the exercise of their police power.[76]

A split in black leadership occurred, with some arguing for the community to apply its limited resources to ensuring political rights rather than, for the time being, guaranteeing full access to other aspects of society. In 1910, alongside white Progressives, a group of blacks known as the Black Niagara Movement combined to found the National Association for the Advancement of Colored People (NAACP). Using the court system, NAACP lawyers waged a long struggle to eliminate state voting laws designed to prohibit blacks from voting, winning an important victory in the *Guinn v. United States* case in Oklahoma (1915), although it failed to obtain an antilynching law until the 1930s.[77] In 1917 the *Buchanan v. Worley* decision stated that Louisville, Kentucky, laws requiring that blacks and whites live in separate communities were unconstitutional.

Without resorting directly to the law, white property owners in New York's Harlem area, under John C. Taylor, organized to keep blacks from settling in their neighborhoods from Seventh Avenue to Fifth Avenue (although parts extended to the Harlem River) and from 139th Street to 130th Street. Taylor's Harlem Property Owners' Improvement Corporation attempted to force blacks to "colonize" on land outside the city (much like an Indian reservation) and encouraged residents to erect twenty-four-foot-tall fences to seal off white zones. On the other side of the issue stood a white Southern real estate developer named Phil Payton, who formed the Afro-American Realty Corporation in 1904 with the purpose of acquiring five-year leases on white properties and renting them to blacks. Payton's company folded after four years, but he broke the race barrier, and opened the door to black residency.

Blacks began to settle in Harlem in 1902, and over the next two decades, Harlem got both blacker and poorer. Other disconcerting trends had appeared as well: W.E.B. Du Bois noted that in 1901 there were twice as many black women as men in New York, and that the rate of illegitimacy was high.[78] Corruption, graft, and prostitution were rampant. One neighborhood, called by the preachers the Terrible Tenderloin—because the bribes paid to police to ignore the prostitution were so great that a captain could live on tenderloin steaks for a year—housed one of the worst red-light districts in the nation. The Reverend Adam Clayton Powell Sr., of the Abyssinian Baptist Church, recalled that prostitutes lived "over me and all around me" and he shelled "pimps, prostitutes, and keepers of dives" with "gospel bombardments."[79] The audacity of the harlots and the susceptibility of the Johns, knew no bounds: Powell observed that they stood across the street from his church on Sunday evenings, shirts unbuttoned, soliciting male churchgoers on their way out of the service! It seemed surreal that only eleven years earlier there had been a Harlem Yacht Club, a Philharmonic Society, and a Harlem Literary Society.

More than 90 percent of blacks in New York worked in menial services.

Many of the higher-paid black businesses had been replaced by foreign-born whites, especially in catering, where blacks had gained a solid reputation in the city.

As the black population of New York City rose from just under 92,000 in 1910 to more than 150,000 by 1920, virtually all of it in Harlem, it grew more dense. The city's white population fell by 18 percent, whereas the black population soared by 106 percent, with blacks comprising 12 percent of Manhattan's population, despite being just under 5 percent of the city's population. By 1930, eleven of the twelve blocks from Park Avenue and West 126th Street to West 153rd Street on the River were 90 percent black. Nor were all the new arrivals in Harlem African Americans. Many came from Jamaica, Barbados, and other parts of the West Indies—more than 40,000 of them—joined in the 1920s by 45,000 Puerto Ricans in what was called the Harlem ghetto.

The crush of people, most of them with few assets, made for one of the highest-density areas in America: by 1930, 72 percent of all blacks in New York City lived in Harlem (164,566).[80] That gave Harlem a population density of 336 people to an acre, contrasted with Philadelphia (ranking second in black population in the United States) at 111 per acre, or Chicago, with 67 per acre.[81] Predictably, with such densities—including two of the most crowded city streets in the entire world—black sections of New York were among the sickest in the nation, with death rates 42 percent higher than the city's average. In a harbinger of the late twentieth century, black-on-black violence rose 60 percent between 1900 and 1925.[82]

Outside of the largest cities, blacks found that although the law was infrequently an effective weapon for addressing racial injustice, the wallet worked somewhat better. African Americans realized that their buying power gave them important leverage against white businesses, such as when they staged boycotts against transportation companies in Georgia, foreshadowing the Montgomery bus boycott of the 1950s. African Americans set up their own insurance and banking companies, developed important networks, and formed their own all-black labor unions when barred by white unions. They had their greatest success in the South, where Georgia blacks built 1,544 schools that educated more than eleven thousand students, despite resistance from local cities and towns against building black schools. Long segregated from white Protestant churches, blacks had established the African Methodist Episcopal Church (AME) in 1816, and by the end of the Progressive era, it had grown dramatically.

Blacks created all-black universities, such as Howard (1867), Spelman (1881), Fisk (1866), Tuskegee (1881), Morehouse (1867), Lincoln (1854), Atlanta (1865), and Hampton (1868)—the so-called black Ivy League or the elite eight—to overcome the reluctance of white universities to admit and educate black students. *Plessy v. Ferguson* spawned and bolstered several black public colleges, such as Alcorn State, North Carolina A&T, Tennessee State, Grambling,

Delaware State, Southern University, Florida A&M, and Prairie View. These schools, while grossly underfunded, stood in the gap until mainstream white universities desegregated.[83]

Blacks held varied philosophies on how best to attain equality, and some even questioned whether equality with whites was a goal worth pursuing. Generally, the divisions broke down into three groups. Booker T. Washington, a former slave, preached a message of slow, steady economic progress. Blacks and whites would accommodate each other, gradually wearing their chafing conflict into comfortable communities. Yet Washington was no sellout—nor, in the modern (wrongly referenced) term, an Uncle Tom. He was under no illusions of white goodness, and his accomodationist message carried a quid pro quo: in return for black cooperation, whites would eliminate lynching and end segregation. Nevertheless, many African Americans found his tactics insufficient and his pace too slow. W.E.B. Du Bois (1868–1963), a Boston-born, Harvard-educated black who had studied under William James, adopted the social-science methodology that had gripped so many of his generation. One of the founders of the NAACP, Du Bois taught at Atlanta University, where he emerged as an accomodationist. Du Bois rejected Washington's approach, instead urging blacks to advance their economic and political power through what he called the Talented Tenth—a black intellectual and economic elite (with members like himself) who could lift the 90 percent to a position of full citizenship. His ideas foundered, partly because there were few blacks or whites as well educated as Du Bois, and partly because blacks were not only a small minority nationally, but were also disproportionately clustered in the Deep South, where the full weight of the political structures and economic trends were against them.

Younger than either Washington or Du Bois, Marcus Garvey offered a third road to black empowerment. A Jamaican, once inspired by Washington's *Up From Slavery,* Garvey founded the Universal Negro Improvement Association in 1914, but he soon parted with Washington's moderate approach. Instead of living with whites, he maintained, blacks needed to reclaim their home continent, Africa, and establish themselves internationally through achievements that emanated solely from a black culture. A complex man, Garvey spoke with derision of Africans who lived on the Continent, arguing that American blacks could return to Africa and lift up the natives. Advocating a black nationalism in which American blacks separated to succeed, Garvey frequently appeared in a Napoleonic-type military uniform while attaching to himself a variety of quasi-religious titles, including reverend. He blended Jamaican Rastafarianism, New England reformist Unitarianism, and popular one-world notions, but with little consistency. His movement swelled rapidly, then declined just as rapidly after Garvey was finally imprisoned on charges of mail fraud. Unlike Washington, Garvey argued that the former status of slavery itself prohibited the two races from living together harmoniously: there was no example in history, he maintained, of a "slave race" ever rising to political equality with its masters, and thus American blacks had to leave—to reclaim Africa before they could prosper.

Theodore Roosevelt's single dinner with Washington and his slighting of the role of the Tenth Cavalry regiment in his memoirs of Cuba hardly qualified him as a champion of race relations. In his racial attitudes, Roosevelt differed little from the vast majority of Americans at the turn of the century. The fact that the "slave race" had founded its own universities and businesses and had developed a sophisticated debate over the nature of a full and equal place for African Americans in society said just as much about the progress of blacks as Jim Crow, *Plessy v. Ferguson*, and the often two-tiered society said about the lack of progress in racial matters.

Despite the continued struggles of blacks, it was nevertheless the case that America by 1910 had successfully blended more—and more radically different— people than any other society in human history, and had spread over the lot of them a broad blanket of public protections, civil rights, educational support, and, equally important, civic expectations. In World War I, the willingness of German-Americans to fight against Germany, for example, convinced many of their complete Americanization. In addition, the fact that a Catholic could run for the presidency just a decade after that further underscored the melting-pot principle. Unfortunately, African Americans remained largely excluded from the "pot" for several decades, despite pandering by the administration of Teddy Roosevelt's cousin Franklin. Well into the twentieth century, blacks remained divided over which of the three paths to follow—Washington's, Du Bois's, or Garvey's.

Ballinger and Pinchot

A largely prosperous economy had insulated Roosevelt's economic policies and corporate attacks for several years, but that threatened to change in 1907. The economy weakened in March of that year, the real blow coming in October, when the Knickerbocker Trust Company in New York closed. New York bankers shifted funds from bank to bank, staving off runs, until J. P. Morgan could step in. The panic dissipated, but in the process Roosevelt labeled businessmen "malefactors of great wealth."[84] By 1908 more than a few Republicans had concluded that Roosevelt's antibusiness views had contributed to the effects of the downturn and damaged American enterprise.

At the same time, Roosevelt either ignored or contributed to (depending on the historical source) a deepening rift with Congress. A conservative majority felt betrayed by many of his actions, whereas the Progressive minority had grown increasingly restless at its inability to change policy fast enough. Riding his own personal popularity, Roosevelt assumed that he could bully his foes or, at worst, sidestep them. But the chaos he left ensured that anyone following Roosevelt was in for a tough term. That is, *if* Roosevelt did not run again . . .

The most critical indicator that he would not was his 1904 promise not to seek another term. Above all, Roosevelt stood for integrity, and despite his occasional theatrics, he understood checks and balances too. Having "used every ounce of power there was in office," Roosevelt wanted to make that influence permanent by stepping down.[85] To have run again would have tainted his integrity and, though he did not admit it, diminished his well-crafted image, making him little more than the power-grubbing pols he supposedly towered above. Therefore, Roosevelt decided to select his own successor, his secretary of war, William Howard Taft of Ohio.

The president had already placed considerable patronage selection in Taft's hands. Aside from Elihu Root, who was too old, and Charles Evans Hughes, who was insufficiently aligned with the Progressive agenda, Taft had no real internal opposition. Known as a competent jurist from a Republican political family, Taft had worked his way up the party through a series of judicial appointments. Under Harrison, he had served as solicitor general. Under McKinley, Taft had his finest hour when he had served as civil administrator of the Philippines, where he improved the country's roads, schools, and medical facilities, helping to extinguish the *insurrecciós* there. This was made possible in part by Taft's utter lack of prejudice, and willingness to incorporate the Filipinos into the islands' government.

Then came Roosevelt's "investiture" of Taft, placing the good-humored giant in a difficult position. He had already told his wife he did not want to be president, but his wife and family insisted. Actually, Taft had a longing for a seat on the U.S. Supreme Court, and Roosevelt offered him the position on three occasions, but each time Helen Taft pushed him away from it, largely because she wanted to inhabit the executive mansion. Somewhat unenthusiastically, then, Taft ran for the presidency. His opponent, the twice-beaten William Jennings Bryan, elicited only a tepid fraction of the enthusiasm he had had in 1896. Taft easily beat Bryan, even as the Republicans lost several congressional seats and governorships.

Upon assuming the presidency, Taft promptly packed his cabinet with as many lawyers as he could find, selecting them almost entirely without party input. Although a relatively obscure group, the cabinet members proved reasonably effective, possibly because they lacked outside obligations. He set to law the Roosevelt legacy and was every bit the Progressive TR was.

Taft found that Roosevelt had left him plenty of problems to clean up, not the least of which was the tariff. Tied up with the tariff came the thorny personality of Joe Cannon, the Republican Speaker of the House. A high-tariff man, Cannon wielded the rules of the House like no one since Henry Clay a century earlier, stalling legislation here, speeding it along there, depending on his fancy. Taft called him "dirty and vulgar," welcoming the news that many House Republicans would not vote for him as Speaker.[86] Openly siding with the "insurgents," as the anti-Cannon forces were called, was dangerous. Roosevelt cautioned against it, but Taft plunged into the melee, convinced Cannon had betrayed the party's lower-tariff platform. The insurgents held just enough of a margin to swing the vote away from Cannon on a critical procedural issue. Again, Taft shortsightedly offered them his support.

But Cannon had not achieved his position of power by meekly acceding to the wishes of others. He let it be known that if the president did not side with him, the tariff bill would be held hostage by his allies. Taft had no choice but to retreat, abandoning the insurgents and acquiescing to Cannon's reelection as Speaker. This placed Taft in the unpleasant position of supporting a Speaker who despised him while alienating the insurgents, who now distrusted him.

Whether Roosevelt would have handled the insurgent question differently is debatable, but there is little doubt that he would have surmised Cannon would double-cross him at the first opportunity. The naïve Taft did not. Worse, when the House committee assignments came out, the thirty insurgents found themselves stripped of all committee power, and the Republican Party announced that it would support "loyal" candidates in the forthcoming primaries against any insurgents. Taft's political ineptness had cut the rebel faction off at the knees.

Meanwhile, three defining elements of Taft's administration took shape. The first was the tariff revision. A topic that is decidedly unexciting to modern Americans, the tariff remained a political hot potato. Even many former supporters had come to see that it had outlived whatever economic usefulness it ever had (and many argued that it had never achieved the gains attributed to it). But getting rid of it was a different matter. For one thing, since Roosevelt had started to set aside large chunks of federal land, government revenues from land sales had dwindled. They were already shrinking, since all but Arizona and New Mexico had achieved statehood and most of the West had been settled by 1910. Ending the tariff meant replacing it with some form of revenue system that had not yet generated much enthusiasm—direct taxation, probably in the form of income taxes (which had been declared unconstitutional).

Nevertheless, the Payne bill was introduced into the House of Representatives in April 1909, passing easily, despite resistance from the insurgents. A Senate version, the Aldrich bill, featured some eight hundred revisions of the low House rates, raising almost all rates. Many Progressive senators, including Robert LaFollette of Wisconsin and William Borah of Idaho, resisted the higher rates. These Progressives were remarkably homogeneous: most came to the Senate in 1906; none had attended an eastern university; and they all came from primarily agricultural Midwestern states. Together they "took the floor of the Senate to launch perhaps the most destructive criticism of high tariffs that had been made by the elected representatives of the Republican party."[87] The Senate rebels put Taft in a box just as had the House insurgents, forcing him to choose between the lower tariffs, which he believed in, or supporting the Senate organization under Nelson Aldrich.

Ultimately, the Payne-Aldrich bill passed, reducing rates somewhat, but leaving Taft weaker than ever. Taft had to some degree staked his presidency on the tariff—that, and trust-busting. Nevertheless, in the jumble of rates, the new tariff probably favored the large eastern industrialists at the expense of western raw materials producers.

A second emphasis of the Taft administration, a continuation of trust-busting, actually saw Taft outdo his predecessor. Having bumped Roosevelt's attorney general, Philander Knox, up to secretary of state, Taft appointed George Wickersham as his new chief law enforcement officer charged with prosecuting antitrust violations. Wickersham concluded Roosevelt's campaign against Standard Oil, finally succeeding in 1911, in getting the Supreme Court to break up the oil giant into several smaller companies. "A bad trust," Roosevelt had called it, distinguishing from a "good trust." That statement alone indicated the futility of government determining when a business was succeeding too much. Under subsequent antitrust laws, such as Clayton (1914) and others, a company could be hauled into court for cutting prices too low (predatory pricing), raising prices too high (monopolistic pricing), or having prices the same as all other competitors (collusion)! Undeterred, Taft more than tripled the number of antitrust cases compared to Roosevelt's.

Now Taft stumbled into the position of attacking the popular Roosevelt when he pursued the U.S. Steel antitrust case, unaware Roosevelt had approved the combination. In the process, TR was summoned before a House committee to explain himself. The matter embarrassed Roosevelt, who had to admit he was aware of the monopolistic tendencies inherent in the acquisition. Teddy had remained subdued in his criticisms until the congressional testimony. Now his remarks about Taft became positively toxic. A third issue, the Ballinger-Pinchot controversy, sealed the breach with Roosevelt.

As head of the Forestry Service, Gifford Pinchot, Roosevelt's friend and eastern-born soul mate, shared his attitudes toward conservation policy. Indeed, he probably exceeded Roosevelt's zealous approach to preserving the environment. "Sir Galahad of the woodlands," Harold Ickes later called him.[88] In stark contrast stood Richard Ballinger, a westerner from Seattle, who had replaced James Garfield as secretary of the interior. Ballinger brought a different attitude to the Roosevelt/Pinchot "pristine" approach, preferring development and use of government lands.

Ballinger thought setting aside the lands was illegal, reopening the lands to public entry, whereupon Pinchot branded him an enemy of conservation. A further allegation against Ballinger came from an Interior Department employee, Louis Glavis, who asserted that Ballinger had given rights to Alaskan coal lands to Seattle business interests, including some he had done legal work for in the past. Pinchot urged Glavis to take the matter to Taft. The president examined the charges, concluded that Ballinger had acted properly, and fired Glavis as much for disloyalty as any other reason. Afterward, Glavis attempted to destroy Ballinger and Taft, writing an exposé of the land/coal deal in *Collier's* (1909). Up to that point, Taft had attempted to keep Pinchot out of the controversy, writing a letter to the Forestry chief urging him to stay clear of the Glavis affair. Instead, Pinchot supplied the material for Glavis's articles from his own office, then, seeking a martyrdom for conservation, he gave Congress evidence that he had been the leaker. Taft had no choice but to sack Pinchot as well.

At no time did Taft want matters to come to that. With Roosevelt out of the country, Pinchot was the face of the administration's conservation movement. Subsequent investigations proved Ballinger innocent of all charges. He was, in the truest sense, a genuine conservationist seeking to conserve and use public lands and to put as much real estate as possible in the hands of the public. Tremendous damage had been done to Taft, though, especially in the Midwest, accelerating Taft's "almost unerring penchant for creating powerful enemies."[89] By that time, Ballinger had become such a political liability to Taft that he resigned in March 1911, giving the Pinchot forces a late-inning victory.

Taft's political ineptness, combined with the Ballinger-Pinchot controversy and his decision to oppose the insurgents left him weakened. Democrats captured the House in 1910, dealing him yet another defeat, and the Senate, although technically controlled by the Republicans, was in the hands of an axis of Republican insurgents and Democrats. By 1912, Republican governors were actively calling for Roosevelt to come out of retirement. Feigning a lack of enthusiasm, Roosevelt nevertheless jumped at the chance to regain the presidency, and entered the primaries. To oppose Taft, TR had to move left, abandoning the conservative elements of his own presidency.[90] His entrance into the race doomed Taft, and opened the door to Democrat Woodrow Wilson in the general election. Yet Wilson had more in common with the two Republicans he would succeed than he did with many Democrats of the past, including the thrice-beaten Bryan, just as Roosevelt and Taft had more in common with him than they did with either McKinley or Harrison. The Progressive movement had reached its apex, temporarily eclipsing even party ideology and producing both domestic and international upheavals of mammoth proportions.

CHAPTER FOURTEEN

War, Wilson, and Internationalism, 1912–20

The Dawn of Dreams

At the turn of the century, the United States had joined much of the industrialized world in expecting that the fantastic progress and wondrous advances in science and technology would produce not only more affluence, but peace and brotherhood. That, after all, had been the dream of the Progressive movement and its myriad reforms under Theodore Roosevelt and William Howard Taft. Unions continued to press for government support against business, women maintained pressure for the franchise, and blacks examined ways to reclaim the rights guaranteed by the Thirteenth, Fourteenth, and Fifteenth amendments that had been suppressed after 1877. The slow realization of some of these dreams offered a strong lesson to those willing to learn: human nature changes slowly, if at all.

Such was the case in Europe. The euphoria of goodwill brought about by international scientific exchanges in the 1890s, combined with the absence of a European land war involving the major powers since 1871, provided the illusion that conflict had somehow disappeared once and for all. Was peace at hand? Many Europeans thought so, and the ever-optimistic Americans wanted to accept the judgment of their Continental friends in this matter. British writer Norman Angell, in his 1909 book *Europe's Optical Illusion*—better known by its 1910 reissued title, *The Great Illusion*—contended that the industrialized nations were losing the "psychological impulse to war."[1] One diplomat involved in a commission settling a conflict in the Balkans thought the resulting 1913 peace treaty represented the end of warfare. Increased communications, fear of socialist revolutions, resistance of taxpayers, and international market competition all forced the Great Powers to the point where they were manifestly unwilling to make war.[2]

A young Winston Churchill, then a member of Parliament, rose for his first speech and agreed with this assessment. "In former days," he intoned, "when wars arose from individual causes, from the policy of a Minister or the passion of a King, when they were fought by small regular armies . . . it was possible to limit the liabilities of the combatants. But now, when mighty populations are impelled on each other . . . when the resources of science and civilization sweep away everything that might mitigate their fury, a European war can only end in the ruin of the vanquished and the . . . commercial dislocation and exhaustion of the conquerors."[3] Churchill, who had seen combat at Omdurman as a lieutenant in the 24th Lancers, witnessed firsthand the lethality of modern rapid-fire rifles, Maxim machine guns, and long-range artillery.

Other military experts chimed in, including Ivan S. Bloch, who, even before the Boer War had concluded, predicted that the combination of automatic weapons and trenches would give a decided edge to the defense, so as to increase the bloodshed in a subsequent war to unfathomable levels.[4] *Is War Impossible?* asked the subtitle of Bloch's book. Many thought so. Americans knew from the losses in the Spanish-American War that the slightest technological advantage, such as smokeless powder, could translate into massive combat losses.

Two factors obscured the horrendous reality of conflicts. First, although combat that pitted one European power against another, or Americans against each other, resulted in massive bloodletting—more Americans were killed on the third day of Gettysburg than in all the frontier wars put together—all too often American and European papers carried lopsided news of the carnage in the colonies when western forces crushed native armies. Britain, ignoring severe losses in the Boer War, instead pointed to the overwhelming victories at Ulundi (1879) or Omdurman (1898). Americans discounted the losses to Spanish bullets and overemphasized the success at smashing Apache, Nez Percé, and the Sioux.

The idealistic notion that war itself had been banished from human society was even dangerous. Teddy Roosevelt's success at bringing the Russians and Japanese together with the Portsmouth Treaty, combined with the unprecedented affluence of the United States, fooled many into thinking that a new age had indeed dawned. A certain faith in technology and affluence buttressed these notions. Americans certainly should have realized, and rejected, the pattern: the very same principles—that if only there is enough wealth spread around, people will refuse to fight over ideological or cultural differences—had failed to prevent the Civil War. Or put in the crass terms of Jacksonianism, as long as wallets are fat and bellies are full, ideas do not matter.

At almost the same moment that *Europe's Optical Illusion* reached the publisher, a former German chief of staff, Count Alfred von Schlieffen, wrote an article with a vastly different conclusion, suggesting that in the near future four powers— France, Russia, Italy, and Britain—would combine for a "concentrated attack" on Germany. Schlieffen had already prepared a detailed battle plan for such an eventuality, calling for the rapid swing of German troops through neutral Belgium to defeat the alliance before it could coordinate against the empire of Germany. Thus, whereas some in England and America prophesied peace, others were already sharpening the swords of war.

Time Line

1912: Woodrow Wilson elected president

1913: Federal Reserve Act passed; Sixteenth Amendment (income tax) passed; Seventeenth Amendment (direct election of U.S. senators) passed

1914: World War I breaks out in Europe; revolution in Mexico leads to landing of U.S. troops at Vera Cruz; Clayton Act passed

1915: Sinking of the *Lusitania* prompts sharp response from United States to Germany

1916: Woodrow Wilson reelected; U.S. forces under General John Pershing chase Pancho Villa in Mexico

1917: Zimmerman telegram; United States declares war on Germany and the Central Powers; Noncommunist revolution in Russia (March) followed by a communist revolution in Russia (October)

1918: American forces in key battles at Belleau Wood, the Ardennes; Armistice (November eleventh)

1919: Versailles peace conference; Wilson offers Fourteen Points; Versailles Treaty; Lodge reservations to treaty introduced in the Senate; Eighteenth Amendment (Prohibition) ratified

1920: Wilson suffers stroke; Nineteenth Amendment (Woman suffrage) ratified; U.S. economy enters recession

Marvels in the Earth and Skies

The technology that made killing so easy from 1914 to 1918 had offered only hope and promise a few years earlier. Many of the new gizmos and gadgets had come from American inventors. The United States blew past the established European industrial giants largely because of the openness of the system and the innovation that had come from generations of farmers and mechanics who translated their constant tinkering into immense technological breakthroughs. Auto wizard Henry Ford was such a man.[5]

An electrical mechanic with Edison Electric in Michigan in the 1890s, Henry Ford spent his nights reading manuals about a new internal combustion engine, and by 1896 he had imagined ways to mate it to a carriage. In fact, many others had already done so. At the Chicago Exposition of 1893, no fewer than a half dozen horseless carriages were on display; and four years later Charles Duryea demonstrated the feasibility of cross-country travel when he drove a "car" from Cleveland to New York. Now Ford welded a larger four-cycle engine to a carriage frame and called it a quadricycle. It was scarcely bigger than a child's red wagon, with a single seat with barely enough room for two adults. Even at that, it was too large to get through the door in the shed where Ford constructed it, and he had to take an ax to the walls to free his creation.

Henry Ford lacked any formal education. He adapted his ideas through trial and error and recruited the best help, combining ideas and developing his own engine and wheels. His closest associates always noted that Ford seemed to have an idea when the experts did not. After testing the car for three years, Ford finally decided he was ready to mass-produce automobiles.

Like other visionaries, Ford looked well beyond the horseless carriage to a mobile society with millions of people using automobiles. Scoffers had their own opinions. Woodrow Wilson called the car the "new symbol of wealth's arrogance," and when Ford asked for a loan in 1903 to build his contraption, the president of the Michigan Savings Bank told Ford's lawyer that "the horse is here to stay, but the automobile is only a novelty—a fad."[6] Like countless other successful entrepreneurs, Ford opened his first car company only to have it fail in 1900; then he opened another, and it, too, collapsed; on the third try, in 1903, the Ford Motor Company finally opened for good.

Unable to read blueprints himself, Ford nevertheless contributed all the major ideas to the automobile, including the use of vanadium steel, the design of the transmission's planetary gears, and the decision to use a detachable head for the block, even though no one knew how to build a head gasket strong enough to withstand the pressure.[7] His plants mass-produced eight different models of cars, but lost money on several, leading Ford to conclude that he should focus on a single variant, the Model T. All other models were eliminated from the Ford production lines. This allowed Ford to emphasize lower cost over speed, which was not needed anyway (Detroit had a speed limit of eight miles an hour and fines of $100—two months' wages—for a single violation!). "I will build a motor car for the great multitude," he announced. "It will be so low in price that no man making a good salary will be unable to own one."[8] As the price fell to $850, Ford sold twelve thousand Model Ts in twelve months, continually pressing the prices downward. By the 1920s, he estimated that for every dollar he chopped off the price he sold another thousand cars.[9]

Ford's great twist to Eli Whitney's mass-production techniques came when he applied electric power at his Highland Park facility to move the car from one station to another, reducing work time and wasted effort. Ford also understood that economy was obtained through simplicity, another of Whitney's lessons. He therefore concentrated entirely on the T, or the Tin Lizzy, as some called it, and made it as simple as possible. It had no starter, no heater, no side windows, and was available only in black. But it was cheap. Ford's own line workers could purchase one with savings from the remarkably high wages Ford paid. Partly to prevent unionization and partly to attract the best workforce in Michigan, Ford introduced the $5-a-day wage in 1914. This was nearly double what his most generous competitors paid, and it cut the legs out from under the union. Yet even at these wages, Ford drove down the price to $345 in 1916.

The automaker's personal life was more complex than the design of the Tin Lizzy, however. Famous for saying, "History is bunk," Ford actually spent millions of dollars collecting and preserving historical artifacts. And he could be a master of the gaffe. While making a speech at Sing Sing prison in New York, Ford opened by saying, "Boys, I'm glad to see you here."[10] But as an internationalist/utopian in the mold of Alfred Nobel, Ford put his money where his mouth was, financing a "peace ship" in 1915 to haul himself and other peace activists to Germany to instruct Kaiser Wilhelm to call off the war. His anti-Semitism was well known, and to his great discredit he financed an anti-Jewish newspaper in Detroit, to which he frequently contributed. After Adolf Hitler came to power in Germany, Ford expressed admiration for *der Führer,* who supposedly had a picture of the American on his wall.

At the same time Henry Ford struggled with the automobile, another fantastic machine appeared on the scene when two bicycle manufacturers from Dayton, Ohio, Wilbur and Orville Wright, sought to use the laws of aerodynamics to produce machine-powered, human-controlled flight at Kitty Hawk, North Carolina. Although the Wright Brothers' maiden voyage on December 17, 1903, lasted just twelve seconds and covered only 120 feet—"you could have thrown a ball farther"—it displayed the possibility of conquering air itself to the world.[11] The flight proved highly embarrassing to the U.S. government, which through the army had given seed money to a similar program under the direction of Samuel P. Langley. But Langley's government-funded aircraft crashed ignominiously, and after the Wright Brothers' success, he stood to lose his funding. He therefore claimed that the Wright Brothers' flight had not been "powered flight" at all, but gliding. The Wrights contributed to the suspicion with their secrecy about the designs, fearing patent infringements of the type that had afflicted Whitney. Already, Glenn Curtiss and others had taken elements of the Wright flyer and applied them to their own craft. Thus the Wrights hesitated to publicly display the aircraft and, for several years, to conduct highly visible trials. President Roosevelt intervened to settle the issue, insisting on a carefully monitored test in which Langley was proven wrong and the Wright Brothers, right.

In a 1908 summer flight at Le Mans, France, Wilbur flew an airplane for an hour and a half, covering more than forty miles. *Le Figaro,* France's premier newspaper, gushed that it had witnessed "Wilbur Wright and his great white bird, the beautiful mechanical bird . . . there is no doubt! Wilbur and Orville Wright have well and truly flown."[12] Convinced, in 1909 the army gave the Wright Brothers a contract for $30,000 per machine.

The auto and the airplane were still in their infancy, and only the most eccentric dreamers could envision an America crisscrossed by thousands of miles of asphalt and dotted by hundreds of airports. Dreamers of another sort remained hard at work, though, in the realm of social engineering.

Progressive Reformers

While the Wright Brothers aspired to reach the heavens, quite literally, through technology, another movement sought the kingdom of heaven through more spiritual means. Revivals, of course, had played a prominent role in the First and Second Great Awakenings of the colonial era and Jacksonian periods. Following in the paths blazed by evangelists such as Charles G. Finney and Holiness leader Charles Parnham, evangelists routinely hit the dusty trails to rouse the morally sleeping masses for the Lord. In the late 1800s, many Americans had adopted either a more formal liturgical stance aligned with the major traditional churches or had joined the growing sea of secularists. But in 1905 spiritual shock waves hit Los Angeles, spread from a revival in Wales. The Welsh revival was so powerful that the number of drunkenness arrests fell over a three-year period, and the miners cleaned up their language so much that their horses reportedly could no longer understand the commands. The revival reached the United States through traveling ministers to the American Holiness churches, where a number of prophecies foretold a massive revival that would descend on California.[13]

A year later, in April 1906, at a church on Azusa Street in Los Angeles, as Elder William Seymour began praying with local church members, the Azusa Christians began to speak in other tongues (technically called glossolalia). This was a biblical phenomenon that occurred at Pentecost, when the Holy Spirit filled the believers, and at that time they spoke in other tongues—that is, they spoke in languages they did not know. Crowds packed the area around the house, growing so large that the foundation of the front porch collapsed. Eventually the prayer services—which, by now, were going on for twenty-four hours a day—had to be moved to an old African Methodist Episcopal (AME) church nearby. As word of the Azusa Street revival spread, it became clear that this was an interracial event, often with women conducting important parts of the services or prayers. Inevitably, divisions and schisms appeared, and some of the early members left or otherwise lost their influence, until finally, between 1909 and 1913 (depending on whether one counts a second revival that occurred at the same location), the revival ended. The Azusa Street revival gave birth to the modern charismatic/Pentecostal movement in America, setting the spiritual stage for dozens of charismatic denominations in the United States.

An even larger movement, that of the Social Gospel, sprang from mainstream Protestant ministers who emphasized social justice over perfecting the inner man, and the relationship of Christians to others in society. Social Gospel advocates included Washington Gladden, an Ohio Congregational minister; Walter Rauschenbusch, a New York Baptist preacher; and Kansan Charles Sheldon, whose *In His Steps* sold 23 million copies and was a precursor to the twenty-first-century WWJD (What Would Jesus Do?) movement. Most Social Gospelers endorsed minimum wage and child labor laws, favored a redistribution of wealth, and generally embraced state regulation of business.[14] To do so usually involved significant revisions of the Bible, and many (though not all) Social Gospelers abandoned any claims about scripture's literal accuracy. Instead, the Social Gospelers viewed the Bible as a moral guidebook—but no more than that. These modernists also "abandoned theological dogmatism for greater tolerance of other faiths."[15]

Secularist reformers continued the quest for perfectionism with something like a religious zeal. They wielded great influence in the first decade of the new century. By 1912, Progressives found adherents in both political parties and had substantial support from women, who supported health and safety laws and prohibition and temperance legislation. In turn, woman suffrage became a centerpiece of all Progressive reform. Theodore Roosevelt had done much to dull the campaign issues of food and drug reform and trust-busting. Individual states initiated many Progressive ideas for direct election of judges, popular initiative for legislation that the state assembly did not wish to bring up, public referenda on unpopular bills advanced by the legislatures, and recall of public officials. (Indeed, Arizona's statehood had been held up until 1912 because its constitution had all these features.)

Reform impulse sprang up as much in the West as in the big cities of the East. Arizona, California, Nevada, Oregon, Washington, New Mexico, Texas, Kansas, Montana, Wyoming, Utah, Idaho, Oklahoma, and South Dakota all had enacted woman suffrage by 1919. Progressive ideas were in the air everywhere: from Virginia to Wisconsin, professional city managers replaced city councils, and new campaigns to reform government swept from South Dakota to Texas. There was a certain illogic to the whole reform mentality. Full-time career politicians were venal, and thus needed to be replaced with professional managers. But professional managers were also untrustworthy because they wanted the job in the first place! Jefferson and Madison's dream of part-time citizen legislators, who would convene at the capital, do their business, and then go home to their constituents, under assault since the Jacksonian party system, now yielded further to demands for the professionalization of politics. This professionalization hardly eliminated corruption. Rather, it changed the names of those controlling the graft.

Under ordinary circumstances, immigrants were the object of considerable pandering, but election days brought even more extreme treatment for those who had newly arrived on American shores. Bosses trucked the immigrants to polls and paid them to vote for the machine. When possible, party loyalists voted multiple times, honoring Tweed's maxim to "vote early and often." Supporters stuffed ballot boxes with the names of dead voters, wrote in fictitious residents, or, conversely, helped lose ballot boxes from areas where the opposing party might do well. Secret ballots, of course, undercut this power by hampering vote buying and also by preventing illiterate citizens from voting, since they could no longer take a colored card that indicated party preference, but had to actually read a ballot.

All the while a climate of violence and larceny—and, not surprisingly, organized crime—hovered around the perimeter of political machines, occasionally swooping in to grab a contract or blackmail an official. Every ethnic group in a large city had its own mob. The Italian Mafia was merely the most notorious of these; the Irish, Jews, and, in subsequent decades, blacks, Puerto Ricans, Chinese, and Jamaicans had gangs, and every gang battled every other, often in bloody shootouts. Corruption filtered down into police departments, where being on the take was viewed as a legitimate bonus as long as it did not interfere with prosecuting real criminals. Law enforcement officials routinely winked at brothels, gambling rooms, even opium dens—as long as the users remained blissfully pacific—in return for payola envelopes that appeared in the officers' coat pockets during their daily rounds.

In 1911 the Chicago Metropolitan Vice Commission conducted a thorough study of prostitution, which shocked the investigators. At least five thousand full-time prostitutes worked the city—one for every two hundred women in Chicago—although that number, the commission estimated, might have represented a conservative guess that did not include so-called clandestine prostitutes, such as married women making part-time money. Equally stunning, the prostitution business (when counting procurers, pimps, tavern owners, thugs, and crime lords who ran the districts) probably generated upward of $15 million in annual revenues.[16]

Had the money stayed only with the criminals, it would have been easier to deal with. But as the commission reported, the graft was so widespread that prostitution income found its way into the hands not only of the owners of the bordellos, but also of the police, judges handling the cases, and politicians appointing the judges.

Progressive-era reformers tried to remedy such social ills and vices through education, their most valued weapon. Public education in such areas as hygiene, they contended, would solve the problems of venereal disease and alcoholism. Only a few groups, such as the Catholic Church, pointed out that a wide gap existed between education and morality, or that secular knowledge did not equate with spiritual wisdom. Reformers silenced those voices with ridicule and embarrassment.

Reformers such as Jane Addams firmly believed all urban dwellers should conform to certain Progressive ideals regarding living spaces ("clean" and not too crowded), personal behavior (eschewing hard liquor, prostitution, gambling, and other vices), and civic equality (women should vote and be educated). The fact that they were imposing what were, in reality, upper-class values on people who did not have the means to maintain them did not stop the reformers.[17]

Social activists found that they needed more than good intentions to gain the upper ground in the reform debates—they needed an aura of expertise. Consequently, intellectuals and academics appropriated the concept of professionalism and special insight based on science and numbers, and now they applied a strange twist. To claim superior understanding of urban issues, reformers could not rely on established fields of learning, so they created entirely new subjects in which they could claim mastery. These social sciences by their very name asserted *scientific* explanations for human behavior. The new social scientists found that if, in addition to numbers, they could invoke esoteric and virtually indecipherable theories, their claims to special insight became even more believable. Many Americans would dismiss them immediately as cranks, while some (especially the elites and other intellectuals) would find them to be on the cutting edge and revolutionary and would feed their ideas back into the system. Thorsten Veblen was one of the first sociologists to emerge from the new disciplines. Writing *A Theory of the Leisure Class* (1899), a predictably antibusiness book, Veblen proposed a new economic system in which power would reside in the hands of highly trained engineers, including, one suspects, himself.[18] Famous (or, perhaps, notorious) for his theory of conspicuous consumption, Veblen viewed the economic world as a zero-sum scenario in which one person's consumption decreased the amount of goods available to someone else. In that sense, he reinforced the positions of Progressive social scientists, who sought to use science to bolster their antivice crusades. Social scientists managed to exert great influence on lower levels of society by inserting Progressive views of morality and behavior into the public education system through the social hygiene movement. Who, after all, could oppose cleanliness and good health? And whom better to target than children?

Cleaning up individual morality still took a backseat to the central task of eliminating corruption of the city and state governments. Obsessed with perfecting the political system at all levels, Progressives were responsible for the bookends that touched on each end of reform. The first, the income tax, represented a continued irrational antipathy toward wealthy Americans. Hostility toward the rich had characterized the Populists' platforms, and had never completely disappeared after the 1890s. The interesting twist now was that guilty Progressive elites sought to take wealth from other non-Progressive elites by appealing to still other strata in society. Concerns over inequities in wealth distribution and banking reform were the central features of the Progressives' agenda. The second, temperance, which had receded temporarily as an issue after the Civil War, found renewed interest in the early twentieth century.

In the 1960s former Alabama governor George Wallace, running as a third-party candidate, complained that there wasn't a dime's worth of difference between the Republicans and the Democrats. He would have been right in 1912, when not one, and not two, but all three of the major candidates to one degree or another embraced the agenda of Progressivism. The incumbent William Howard Taft, the Democratic challenger Woodrow Wilson, and the former president Theodore Roosevelt, now an insurgent seeking to unseat Taft, all professed their belief in strong antitrust actions, tariff reform, direct taxation, and more equitable wealth distribution. Of the three, Wilson (perhaps) was the most idealistic, but given the nature of Progressivism itself, all three suffered from a skepticism of free markets and an affinity for government intervention in public health.

Roosevelt held the key to the election. No successor would have satisfied him. "Theodore Rex," as one recent biographer called him, had an ego that precluded yielding the spotlight.[19] Few leaders inherently combined such raw frontier aggressiveness with an upper-class Progressive reform mentality. Roosevelt was a fusion of human diversity as opposite as Arnold Schwarzenegger is from Ralph Nader. Certainly Taft, despite his intention to continue TR's Progressive agenda, could not measure up. Roosevelt was at his best when campaigning against something, or someone, even if it was his own successor.

He selected Taft as his heir, then ran off to Africa on a safari, only to be hunted down himself by Pinchot and other malcontents who disliked the new president. Within two years of anointing Taft, Roosevelt had second thoughts. The president had a poor public image, despite an activist agenda that would have made even Roosevelt blanch. He had brought eighty antitrust suits (compared to TR's twenty-five) and declared more lands for public use (that is, yanking them from the private sector) than Roosevelt. Many Republicans, however, disliked Taft, partly out of his sour relations with Congress, partly out of a concern for his weak public image, but most of all because he was not Roosevelt. Consequently, a group of Republican leaders contacted Roosevelt about running in the 1912 election, which the former president greeted with his characteristic toothy smile. Roosevelt planned to enter the primaries, gaining enough convention delegates to wrest the nomination from the incumbent Taft.

Party hierarchies, though, do not embrace change any more readily than the professional business managers on whom they pattern themselves. Unpopular incumbents, whether Taft in 1912, Hoover in 1932, or Ford in 1976, generally maintain sufficient control over the machinery of the party to prevent a coup, no matter how attractive the alternative candidate. Roosevelt should have recalled his own dominance of the procedures in 1904, when he had quashed an insurgent movement to replace him at the top of the ticket. Taft's men knew the same tricks. TR needed only 100 votes to win the nomination, but it may as well have been a thousand. The Taft forces controlled the procedures, and the president emerged as the party's nominee. Unwilling to bow out gracefully, Roosevelt declared war on Taft, forming his own new party, the Progressive Party (which had as its logo the Bull Moose). Roosevelt invoked thoroughly Progressive positions, moving to the left of Taft by advocating an income tax and further regulation of business. This not only stole votes that normally would have gone to Taft, but it also allowed Democrat Woodrow Wilson to appear more sensible and moderate.[20]

Roosevelt won 4.1 million votes and 88 electoral college votes, compared to 3.4 million for Taft (and 8 electoral votes). This gave Wilson an electoral victory despite taking only 6.2 million popular votes (45 percent of the total), a number lower than any other victorious president since Lincoln had won with less than half the country in 1860. TR effectively denied the White House to Taft, allowing the second Democrat since Reconstruction to be elected president.

An ominous note was sounded by the candidacy of the avowed socialist Eugene V. Debs, who received nearly a million votes. Uniting the anarchists, Populists, Grangers, and Single Taxers, the Socialist Party had witnessed a rapid growth, from 10,000 in 1901 to 58,000 in 1908 to its peak of just under 1 million votes, or 6 percent of the total vote cast, in the 1912 election. Debs, whom fellow socialist Margaret Sanger once dubbed a silly silk-hat radical, was the glue that held together the disparate groups.[21] Despite their meteoric rise, however, the socialists flattened out against the hard demands of industry in World War I.

One could not miss the contrast of the American election, where the winner had only a plurality and where there was no challenge whatsoever to the legitimacy of the election, with the events in Spain the same year, where not one but two prime ministers in succession were assassinated; or in Paraguay, where two successive presidents were overthrown in coups (one hunted down and killed); or in neighboring Mexico, where Francisco Madero overthrew President Porfirio Díaz, but who lasted only a few months himself before being overthrown by Victoriano Huerta. In short, America's remarkable stability and willingness to peacefully abide by the lawful results of elections was a glaring exception to the pattern seen in most of the world.

Woodrow Wilson was a throwback in many ways to the old Van Buren ideal, or rather, the reverse of it—a Southern man of Northern principles. Born in 1856, Wilson grew up in Georgia, where he saw the Civil War firsthand as a boy. His Presbyterian minister father sent Woodrow to Princeton, then to the University of Virginia Law School, then to Johns Hopkins, where he earned a doctorate. Throwing himself into academia, Wilson became a political science professor at Princeton, then, in 1902, its president. His 1889 book, *The State,* adopted a strangely Darwinian view of government. He called for regulation of trade and industry, regulation of labor, care of the poor and incapable, sumptuary laws, as well as prohibition laws.[22] With great pride, Wilson observed that government did whatever experience permits or the times demand, and he advocated a "middle ground" between individuals and socialism. Wilson argued that "*all combination* [emphasis added] which leads to monopoly" must be under the direct or indirect control of society.

Both Wilson's Progressive positions and his prominent place at Princeton made him a prime prospect for the New Jersey governorship, which he won in 1910 on a platform of ending corruption in state government. By the time he ran for president in 1912, Wilson could claim roots in both the South and North, blending the two under the banner of Progressive idealism.

Wilsonian Progressivism

Timing is a large part of any presidency. Presidents receive credit for programs long under way before their arrival, or pay the penalty for circumstances they inherit. As a Progressive president, Wilson benefited from ideas already percolating through the system, including the income tax and reform of the national banking system. This one-two punch, it could be argued, did more to fundamentally reorder American economic life than any other package of legislation passed anytime thereafter, including the New Deal and Great Society programs. Both received the enthusiastic support of Wilson's secretary of the treasury, William Gibbs McAdoo, who helped craft the banking reform, which he called a "blow in the solar-plexus of the money monopoly."[23] A Georgia Populist/Progressive lawyer, McAdoo stood firmly on the side of reform, whether it was food and product safety, taxes, or banking, and as a Southerner, he bridged the old Confederacy gap by invoking the name of Lincoln favorably while touting Wilson as a Southerner. However, he abandoned states' rights entirely by hastening the transfer of financial power from New York to Washington through both taxation and banking policies.[24]

America's banking system had suffered criticism since the Civil War. It was too elastic. It was not elastic enough. It was too centralized in New York. It was not centralized enough in New York. For twenty years, it had seemed that the colossus J. P. Morgan alone might carry the nation's banking community on his shoulders like Atlas. He did so in 1893, then again in 1907, at which time he announced that even with support from other syndicate members, including some foreign bankers, the next panic would sink him and the country. Consequently, by the turn of the century most of the so-called bank reformers—including numerous bankers from the Midwest who feared for their own smaller institutions if large East Coast banks got into trouble—agreed on three main principles for shoring up the system.

First, genuine bank reform needed (in their view) to fill the void left by the old BUS as a central bank. Never mind that the BUS had never fulfilled that function. Collective memory inaccurately said that the Bank had restrained the inflationary impulses of the state banks, and thus provided a crucial check on the system in times of stress. The new central bank above all should be a lender of last resort, that is, it should provide cash (liquidity) when there were isolated bank runs.

Second, bank reformers concluded that an elastic money supply was needed in which credit and cash could expand in good times and contract in bad. This was a main complaint about the money supply under the National Bank Act—that the national banks lacked the ability to rapidly issue new banknotes or any mechanism for withdrawing them from circulation. Of course, any elastic powers would centralize even further the money supply in the hands of one source, as opposed to the many national banks who each issued their own notes, providing some tiny measure of competition.

Third, all but a few of the most conservative East Coast bankers wanted to reduce the power of New York's financial community. A certain element of anti-Semitism accompanied this because the phrase "New York bankers" was really code for "New York Jewish bankers." It regurgitated the old fears of the Roth-schilds and their "world money power," but even well-meaning midwestern bankers looked suspiciously at the influence eastern banking houses had over affairs in Kansas or Colorado. It seemed unfair to them that an East Coast panic could close banks in Littletown or Salina.

Critics noted another problem, namely, that national banks could not just print money willy-nilly. To expand the number of notes they issued, the national banks had to purchase additional U.S. government bonds, a process that could take several months. Certainly the structure did not enhance elasticity. On the other hand, states permitted branch banking (which enhanced stability and solvency), whereas national banks were denied branching privileges.[25]

The entire banking structure still relied on gold as a reserve. For gold to effectively police international transactions, all nations had to abide by the rules of the game. If one nation had a trade deficit with another, it would make up the difference in gold. But this meant a decrease in that nation's gold reserve, in turn decreasing the amount of money issued by that nation's central bank, causing a recession. As prices fell, the terms of trade would then swing back in that country's favor, whereupon gold would flow in, and the cycle would reverse.

The difficulty with the gold standard was not financial, but political: a nation in recession always had an incentive to go off the gold standard. However, from 1900 to 1912 most nations faithfully submitted to the discipline of gold in a time of prosperity. Such false optimism cloaked the fact that when the pressure of national recessions began, the temptation would be for each country to leave the gold standard before another. In the meantime, however, it reinforced the desire on the part of American reformers to create a financial system with a central bank along the lines of the European model.

Following the many plans and proposals drawn up by bankers' organizations over the previous thirty years, in November 1910 five men met in secrecy on Jekyll Island, Georgia, to design a new financial system for the nation. Frank Vanderlip (president of National City Bank), Paul Warburg (a powerful partner in Kuhn, Loeb and Company), Henry Davison (a partner in the Morgan bank), Harvard professor A. Piatt Andrew, and Senator Nelson Aldrich of Rhode Island outlined the plan that became the Federal Reserve System. They presented their completed plan to Congress, where it stagnated. Many viewed it as too centralized, and others complained that it did not deal with the "money power" of New York's banks.

Meanwhile, the House held hearings in 1912 that dragged J. P. Morgan and other prominent bankers before the Banking and Currency Committee. Morgan was accused of "consolidation" and stifling competition. In fact, Morgan and his contemporaries had strengthened the system and protected depositors by establishing combinations and utilizing clearinghouses, which were private organizations that reduced the likelihood of panics and provided a setting for effective information exchange. House members pontificated about the evils of consolidation—an incredible irony given that in the 1930s, after the Great Depression, another set of congressional investigators would complain that the competitiveness within the securities industry helped cause the stock market crash. Thus, bankers were criticized for competing and criticized for combining![26]

Congressional interest in the Jekyll Island proposal revived, but with emphasis on decentralizing the system and in reducing the influence of New York's banks. The result was the Federal Reserve Act, passed by Congress in 1913. Under the act, twelve Federal Reserve banks would be established across the country, diminishing New York's financial clout. Atlanta, Boston, Dallas, San Francisco, Minneapolis, Chicago, Cleveland, Philadelphia, and Richmond all received Federal Reserve Banks, and Missouri got two—St. Louis and Kansas City. Each bank was a corporation owned by the commercial banks in its region and funded by their required deposits. In return, the member banks could borrow from the Reserve bank in their region. A separate board of governors, housed in Washington, D.C., consisting of representatives from each bank, was to set policy, but in reality, each bank tended to go its own way. These characteristics allowed the Federal Reserve System to appear to be independent of the government and nonpartisan.

While decentralizing the financial system answered one critical need demanded by the reformers, the Fed (as it became known) also met another in that it served as the lender of last resort. The district banks were to step in during emergencies to rescue failing private banks, but if the crisis grew too severe, one Federal Reserve bank could obtain help from the Reserve bank in another region (or all regions, if necessary). Few really imagined that even under the new system, there might exist an emergency so broad that every Federal Reserve District would come under siege at the same time. But the reformers had ignored the single most important corrective: introducing interstate branch banking.[27] This disadvantage kept large branch-bank systems from becoming member banks, especially A. P. Giannini's powerful Bank of America and Joseph Sartori's First Security Bank and Trust, both in California. To rectify this problem, Congress passed the McFadden Act in 1927, which permitted national banks to have branches in states where the state laws permitted branching, thus allowing both Giannini and Sartori to join the Federal Reserve System as members. But Giannini's dream of nationwide interstate banking was never reached, contributing to the collapse of the banking system during the Great Depression.

Contrary to all intentions, the New York Federal Reserve Bank quickly emerged as the most powerful influence in the new Fed system. The creation of the Fed also marked the end of any form of competition in money, since the new Federal Reserve notes eventually replaced money specifically (and legally) backed by gold or silver.

Another pillar of Progressivism came to fruition on Wilson's watch. The idea of an income tax had long been cherished by socialists, and it was one of the ten planks desired by the Communist Party in Karl Marx's *Communist Manifesto*. During the Civil War, the Republicans had imposed a 3 percent tax on all incomes over $800, then raised it twice thereafter. Several utopian socialists called for income taxes in the postwar years, and both the Populists and the Democrats advocated an income tax in the 1890s. But not until 1894 did Congress pass a 2 percent tax on all incomes above $4,000. Within a year, the Supreme Court struck down the measure as unconstitutional—which it clearly was.[28]

For several decades, the tariff (and land sales) had provided most of the revenue for running the operations of the government, which was adequate as long as the government remained small. However, tariffs carried tremendous political baggage. They pitted one group of Americans against another, usually by section. Northern manufacturers, who obtained a tariff on manufactured imports, received artificially higher prices for their goods at the expense of all other Americans; southern sugar planters, who obtained a tariff on sugar, could raise prices for all sugar consumers; and so on. While some argued that the tariff burdens balanced out—that in one way or another everyone was hurt, and everyone benefited—each tariff bill focused the debate on specific groups who gained and lost. In this regard, the substitution of income taxes for tariffs "efficiently conserved legislative energies: Life became simpler for Congress [because] the battle against tariffs had always involved direct, urgent, and threatening lobbies."[29] The proposed income tax, on the other hand, only affected a small group of the wealthy.

Proponents also designed the first proposed tax with two features that would reduce resistance to it. The tax rates would be extremely low, even for wealthy groups, and the filing process would be absurdly simple—only a few pages were required for the first income tax. Since people had become convinced that equal taxes meant proportional taxes—which was surely untrue—then the income tax promised to "equalize tax burdens borne by the various classes . . . and to ensure it was paid by the wealthiest classes."[30] To underscore this fact, the income tax had "little to do with revenue and everything to do with reform."[31]

There was one small hurdle—the Constitution. Since income taxes were uncon-stitutional, imposing the new tax demanded the Sixteenth Amendment, which was ratified in 1913. Reformers gained support using three major strategies: (1) they emphasized the extremely low nature of the tax and the fact that many Americans would pay no tax at all; (2) they stressed its simplicity; and (3) they pointed to the problems and controversies surrounding tariffs. The original tax exempted anyone earning less than $3,000 per year or married couples earning less than $4,000 per year; whereas those earning between $20,000 and $50,000 paid only 2 percent. For the richest of the rich, those earning over $500,000, the top rate was 7 percent. Contrasted with taxes in the twenty-first century, the *state* tax rates alone in many states exceeds the *top rates* exacted by the federal govern-ment in 1913. Although some liberal historians claimed that the income tax was a "conservative measure designed to placate the lower classes with a form of pre-tend punishment of the rich," it certainly did not help the workingman by any stretch of the imagination. By the year 2000 the average American worked until *May* of every year to pay just his federal taxes; whereas that same American worked only nineteen days to purchase all the food he would eat in a year![32]

Income taxes introduced a significant danger to American life, especially through the hidden growth of the federal government. Minor rate changes in the tax would be enacted without any public reaction; then, after World War II, they were deducted directly from workers' paychecks so that they never saw the dam-age. Moreover, during an emergency, rate increases became substantial, and even if lowered later, never returned to the preemergency levels. Economist Robert Higgs described this as a "ratchet effect" in which government power grew with each crisis.[33] At the end of World War I, the top tax rate would rise by a *factor of ten,* illustrating the grave danger inherent in the structure.

Wilson's reduction of tariff rates was inconsequential and irrelevant after passage of the income tax. He was a big-government Progressive, and his inclinations were on display in numerous other policies, especially the creation of the Federal Trade Commission, a group appointed by the president to review and investigate business practices. Ostensibly, the FTC was to prevent the formation of monopo-listic combinations, using its cease-and-desist orders, augmented by the 1914 Clayton Antitrust Act. A follow-up to the Sherman Antitrust Act, it prohibited in-terlocking directorates and tying clauses, whereby a producer could tie the sale of a desired product it made to another product the buyer did not particularly want.

Both the FTC and Clayton, in the truest style of Teddy Roosevelt, targeted big business and trusts. Unfortunately, like taxes, the burden of regulations fell on unintended groups, whereas those usually targeted by the regulations and taxes escaped. Such was the case with the Clayton Act. A study of antitrust laws and their effect on overall business activity revealed that the antitrust actions against large firms coincided with business downturns, suggesting that the downturns *resulted* from the attacks on a few large firms.[34] (These results were repeated in the 1990s when an antitrust suit against Microsoft sparked a massive sell-off in tech stocks, adding support to the argument that antitrust law had done little to encourage competition and had inflicted substantial damage to the U.S. economy for more than a century.)[35] While creation of the Fed and the passage of the income tax amendment characterized Progressivism at home, events in Mexico gave a brief glimpse of Wilson's vision for Progressivism abroad.

South of the Border

Even before Wilson assumed office, in 1910, Mexico had entered a period of constant chaos. That year the Mexican dictator of thirty-three years, Porfirio Díaz, was overthrown in a coup led by Francisco Madero, ostensibly a democrat. Within three years, however, Madero was in turn unseated by General Victoriano Huerta, who promised a favorable climate for American businesses operating in Mexico. Huerta received support from the U.S. ambassador, Henry Lane Wilson. Aside from the protection of American firms' operations and personnel, the United States really had little interest in the internal affairs of Mexico.

Taft had expressed a willingness to recognize Huerta, but Huerta's forces killed Madero just before Wilson took over, whereupon the president stated that he would not recognize "a government of butchers."[36] Wilson's idealism took over as he openly supported Venustiano Carranza and Francisco (Pancho) Villa, two rebel generals who opposed Huerta. In April 1914 a Mexican officer in Tampico arrested American sailors from the USS *Dolphin*, when they disturbed the public peace on shore leave. When the American naval officers protested, the Mexicans immediately released the sailors, but did not apologize sufficiently to please the admiral.

Wilson saw an opportunity to intervene against Huerta. He dispatched a fleet to Vera Cruz, purportedly to intercept a German vessel delivering munitions to Huerta's army. Events spun out of control, and American warships shelled the city. Carranza soaked all this in and recognized that an overt alliance with Wilson would taint his regime in the eyes of the Mexican people. From that point on, he continued to buy arms from the U.S. government, but he otherwise kept his distance. When the fighting at Vera Cruz weakened Huerta, Carranza took over in August, then promptly gave the cold shoulder to Wilson's overtures to assist in forming the new Mexican administration.

Having failed to woo Carranza, Wilson turned to the other revolutionary general, Villa, whose army held much of northern Mexico. By that time, Villa was something of a celebrity in America, gaining notoriety among journalists and filmmakers as the personification of the "new democrat" in Mexico. He was also now Carranza's enemy, and government troops defeated Villa in April 1915, whereupon the rebel leader lost much of his luster. This victory forced Wilson to reconsider Carranza's legitimacy. In frustration, he recognized Carranza as the de facto leader of Mexico without offering official recognition, which, in turn, outraged the jilted Villa. Seeing his hopes of running Mexico melt away, Villa launched a series of revenge raids directed at Americans across northern Mexico. He killed eighteen Americans on a train and then crossed the border in 1916 at Columbus, New Mexico, murdering another seventeen U.S. citizens.

The president of Mexico lacked the resources (as well as the will) to pursue Villa in his own territory. Wilson did not. He sent American troops under General John "Black Jack" Pershing on a punitive expedition into Mexico to capture Villa. Entering Mexico in the spring of 1916 with more than 15,000 men, armored cars (one commanded by a young cavalry officer named George Patton), and reconnaissance aircraft, Pershing hunted Villa across more than three hundred miles of Mexican desert. Although Patton's lead units engaged some of the Villistas, Pershing never truly came close to the main body of Villa's troops, and he finally informed Wilson that the best course of action would be to occupy all of northern Mexico.

The Pershing invasion revived fears of the "Colossus of the North" again marching on Mexican soil, causing Villa's forces to grow and turning the bloodthirsty killer into a cult hero in parts of Mexico. And while Carranza certainly wanted Villa dead, he did not intend to let the Yankees simply walk into sovereign Mexican territory. In June 1916, Carranza's and Pershing's forces clashed, bringing the two nations to the precipice of war. The president considered Pershing's recommendation for an American occupation of parts of Mexico, and even drafted a message to Congress outlining the proposed occupation, but then scrapped it.

With the public's attention increasingly focused on Europe, few people wanted a war with Mexico, especially under such confused circumstances (in which Villa could in no way be viewed as a legitimate agent of the official Mexican government). Given his own culpability in destabilizing the Mexican regime under the guise of promoting democracy, Wilson looked for a graceful exit, agreeing to an international commission to negotiate a settlement. The troops came home from the Mexican desert, just in time to board steamers for France.

The episode was rife with foreign policy and military lessons for those willing to learn. First, American troops had been committed with no reasonable assurance of achieving their mission, nor was there much public support. Second, Wilson had not exhausted—or really even tried—other methods to secure the U.S. border against Villa's incursions. Third, by arbitrarily and hastily invading Mexico, twice, Wilson turned a natural ally into a wary neighbor. Last, Wilson's insistence on American-style democracy in a primitive country—without concurrent supervision through occupation, as in post–World War II Japan or Iraq—was fraught with peril. Mexico did not have fully developed property rights or other essential concepts of government. Wilson did learn some of the lessons. The next time he had to send American forces into foreign lands, it would be for unimpeachable reasons.

He Kept Us Out of War

On September 29, 1913, Turkey, Greece, and Bulgaria signed a Treaty of Peace that many saw as an omen for world amity. Yet over the next year, Europe's diplomats and clear thinkers sank, buried beneath a wave of war mobilizations over which they seemingly had no control.

The June 1914 assassination of Austrian Archduke Franz Ferdinand launched these forces on their course. A Serbian nationalist has been blamed for the assassination, although controversy exists as to whether he was a member of the terrorist Black Hand group. Regardless, Austria, with the full support of Germany, immediately moved to retaliate. Serbia invoked a secret agreement with Russia, mobilizing the Russian army, which in turn prompted a reaction from Germany, then a counterreaction from France, who in turn brought in the British. Within a matter of weeks, the armies of Europe were fully mobilized on enemy borders, trigger fingers itchy, and without any comprehension of why they were going to fight.

Germany's Schlieffen Plan, however, demanded that Germany not wait for a full-scale Russian mobilization before striking the Allies. On August 3, 1914, German forces crossed the Belgian border, thereby touching off the Great War. Britain, France, and Russia (called the Triple Entente or Allies) soon declared war on Germany and Austria-Hungary (soon known as the Central Powers). Before long a host of second-tier states had been sucked into the war as well, essentially pulling the entire world into the conflict in one form or another—all except the United States.

When German guns opened their barrage against Belgium, Wilson warned Americans against that "deepest, most subtle, most essential breach of neutrality which may spring out of partisanship, out of passionately taking sides."[37] Roosevelt immediately broke with him, arguing that the nation should take the position of a "just man armed," and he wrote angrily of Wilson's reluctance to stand up for the wrongs Belgium had suffered. Wilson, instead, implored the nation to be "neutral in fact as well as name." Already, in January 1915, the Central Powers had launched the world's first zeppelin attacks against England and had finalized plans to cut off Britain's lifeline at sea to the United States.

As is often the case, experts on both sides mistakenly foresaw a quick end to the war. British forward observers at Neuve-Chapelle were dumbfounded when their initial probing assault, led by 1,000 men, was entirely obliterated. They had another surprise when, in April 1915, the Germans used poison gas for the first time, choking French African troops who could only cough and point to their throats. The British had barely absorbed the threats posed by gas when, in July, the Germans introduced another horror—the flamethrower.

The news got worse. Seeking an end run to link up with the Russians and come at the Central Powers from the Black Sea, Britain attempted to break through the Dardanelles Strait. Even the powerful Royal Navy could not punch through the defenses of Germany's allies, the Ottoman Turks. Underestimating the enemy and the geography, the Allies staged a massive invasion of the narrow beaches at Gallipoli at the foot of the Dardanelles. British, Australian, and New Zealand troops were staggered when, rather than running, the Turks stood their ground to repulse attack after attack up bloody hills. Over a nine-month period, British, French, Australians, and New Zealanders lost 48,000 men yet gained nothing. Only then did it begin to dawn on the military minds that the machine gun, combined with trench warfare, barbed wire, and long-range artillery, had made the massed infantry charges of the day utterly useless.

This was a lesson it had taken the Americans in both the Union Army (Fredericksburg) and Confederate Army (Gettysburg) thousands of battlefield deaths to learn, but finally the message had sunk in. Battles in Europe soon claimed a half million dead and wounded in a single day, then three quarters of a million, then a million casualties in battles that lasted weeks over a few acres of ground. British units lost 60 percent of their officers in a single day's combat. At the Somme, in June 1916, despite the fact that the British fired a quarter million shells at the German trenches—sixty artillery shells *every second*—20,000 men and 1,000 officers died in a few hours. Entire companies literally vanished in unending sprays of bullets and shells.

The Germans misjudged their enemies even worse than the Allies, predicting that the colonies would rise up, that Ireland would rebel, or that the British population would demand peace at any price. None of that materialized. Next, the Germans expected the Americans to suffer indignity after indignity and gambled that they could kill U.S. citizens, incite Mexico to go to war with the United States, and flagrantly disregard Wilson's repeated warnings. They were wrong about England, and they were wrong about America.

Still, after a full year of watching the carnage from afar, Americans shook their heads in wonder. Until May 1915, many still held out hope their nation could avoid taking sides. Wilson even offered to mediate. But forces were already in motion to ensure American entry sooner or later. Germany doubted her High Seas Fleet could compete with England for control of the oceans and early on had employed U-boats (submarines) to intercept and destroy trade bound for England. U-boat warfare proved phenomenally effective, if mistake prone. U-boat captains had difficulty establishing the colors of vessels at sea through their periscopes, and, to make matters worse, the British fraudulently flew neutral flags on their own merchantmen, which violated the very essence of neutrality. Before any real enmity could appear between the United States and England over the neutral flag issue, the Germans blundered by sinking the passenger liner *Lusitania* in May 1915, killing 1,198, including 128 Americans.

Between its zeppelin and U-boat attacks, the German government helped shift American public opinion to the Allies, prompting leading newspapers such as the New York *Herald* to refer to the sinking of the *Lusitania* as "wholesale murder" and the New York *Times* to compare the Germans to "savages drunk with blood."

Wilson already had justification for joining the Allies at that point, and had the United States done so, it might have shortened the war and short-circuited Russian communism. Certainly Vladimir Ilich Ulyanov Lenin, exiled in Switzerland when the war started, would have remained an insignificant figure in human history, not the mass murderer who directed the Red October Revolution in Russia. Instead, Wilson opted for the safe, and cheap, response. He demanded and secured German assurances that "such atrocities would never be repeated," although within a few months the Reichstag would formalize the policy of unrestricted submarine warfare, dooming the *Sussex,* a Channel ferry, to torpedoing and the loss of another fifty passengers, including two more Americans.

Wilson again issued strong protests, to which the Germans again responded by promising to behave. In truth, Erich Ludendorff, the industrial supremo who directed the U-boat campaign, had no intention of curtailing his effective submarine war, even less so after May 1916, when the outnumbered High Seas Fleet failed to break the blockade at Jutland. In a gigantic battle that pitted more than 100 German warships against more than 150 British vessels, some 6,000 British sailors were killed and 2,500 German seamen went down. The German High Seas Fleet had engaged a force significantly larger than its own, inflicted more than twice as many casualties, and yet after the battle, German Admiral Reinhard Scheer informed the kaiser that the surface fleet could not defeat the English. Only U-boats could shut down transatlantic trade. They continued to ignore previous promises made to Wilson.

Wilson used his (so far) successful efforts at neutrality as a campaign motif in 1916. With the slogan "He kept us out of war," Wilson squeaked out an electoral victory in the November elections against the Republican Charles Evans Hughes, a former governor of New York who had the support of Teddy Roosevelt. In the electoral college, Wilson won 277 to 254, although he enjoyed a wider popular vote margin of about half a million. Americans wanted to give him the benefit of the doubt. Certainly he received support from the peace movement, which was largely, though not entirely, sponsored by the Socialist Party, from whom Wilson drew large numbers of votes. Antiwar groups appeared—the American Union Against Militarism and the Women's Peace Party, for example— and some 1,500 women marched down Fifth Avenue in New York in August 1914 to protest against intervention. House Democrats broke away from the White House to block even modest preparations for war, and celebrities such as Jane Addams and Henry Ford publicly announced their opposition to involvement in "Europe's fight."

There was one small problem: the Germans would not cooperate. In October 1916, Kaiser Wilhelm celebrated the U-boats' feat of sinking a million tons of Allied shipping, and a week later five Allied ships were torpedoed within sight of Nantucket Island.[38] Only a few days before the election, a U-boat sank the Brit-

ish liner *Marina* (six Americans died) and then, in an act of astounding recklessness, the Germans sank the *Lanao*, a U.S.-chartered vessel, off Portugal. Victories
on the ground further bolstered the German outlook on the war, despite the fact
that on the Western Front alone men were dying at the rate of 3,000 per day (including, since 1914, 800,000 Germans). By late 1916, German or German-
backed Austro-Hungarian forces controlled Serbia, Montenegro, and Galicia; had
dismantled Romania, soundly thrashed the French army at Verdun, and turned
back Allied offensives at the Somme; and occupied much of the western section
of Russia. Moreover, the Austrians had dealt defeat after defeat to the Italians
(who had come in on the side of the Allies). Under such circumstances, a little
risk of offending the United States seemed harmless, especially since Wilson had
not demonstrated that he was a man of action when it came to Germany.

In December 1916, Wilson made yet another effort to mediate, issuing a
Peace Note to the belligerents that first raised the prospect of a league of nations
that might "preserve peace throughout the world." He also offended and irritated
both sides by claiming that the United States "was too proud to fight."[39] For their
part, the Germans had no intention of giving up territory they already held under
any Wilsonian-brokered agreement. And Germany rightly perceived that Russia
was coming apart. It probably would not remain in the war much longer, in which
case a France that was already bled white would, the Germans thought, offer little final resistance.

Here again, Wilson's potential impact on the calculations of the warring parties
was critical. Had Germany in 1915 or even 1916 seriously thought that several
million American troops would replenish the French, the Germans might have
come to the negotiating table sooner. Wilson's reluctance to fight over the just
cause of the sinking of several American ships hardened, rather than softened,
the foe. Sensing they could turn the war, the German leaders made two critical
errors in January 1917.

The first involved a resumption of the de facto policy of unrestricted submarine warfare. Now the Germans admitted publicly that U-boats would attack
anything and everything at sea—belligerents, civilian vessels, neutrals. All shipping was fair game. Even if that brought the United States into the war, they reasoned, it would be over before American armies could mobilize and arrive in
Europe. Perhaps the second error was an even greater blunder in that it directly
(if weakly) threatened Americans in the homeland.

Noting that Pershing's expedition against Pancho Villa had soured relations
between the United States and Mexico, the German foreign minister, Alfred von
Zimmerman, sent a coded radio message to Carranza's government, essentially
urging Mexico to declare war on America. In return, Germany would recognize
Mexico's reconquest of Arizona, New Mexico, and other parts of the Southwest.
American agents in London deciphered the code, showed it to an American
diplomat, then forwarded it to the White House. Washington made the message

public, generating the expected indignation. Henry Cabot Lodge of Massachusetts knew immediately that the Zimmerman note would arouse the country more than any other event.[40]

Sensing that the public mood had shifted, Wilson issued an order authorizing the arming of merchant ships for self-protection—a symbolic act with no substance. After seven more merchantmen went down, and following massive prowar demonstrations in the nation's major cities, Wilson spoke to a special session of Congress on April second. He asked for a declaration of war, laying out the unlawful attacks on American persons and property. That would have been enough: Congress would have given him the declaration, and matters would have been simple. Ever the idealist, however, Wilson drifted into grandiloquent terms, seeing the struggle as about making the world safe for democracy. It was of the utmost convenience that only a few weeks earlier a revolution in Russia had dethroned the czar, for Wilson would have placed himself in the difficult position of explaining why, if America was fighting for democracy, the nation was allied with a near-feudal monarchy. Fortunately, the Russians had (temporarily, as it turned out) established a constitutional democracy under Alexander Kerensky, giving Wilson the cover of philosophical consistency.

The war fanned the righteous indignation of an aroused public even more through an intense propaganda campaign. American strategy, like Grant's fifty years earlier, involved wearing down the enemy with superior numbers and quality of arms. And finally, the war effort ensured that the world's dominant economy was sufficiently mobilized on the one hand, yet not too centralized on the other. Committing to a European land war, nevertheless, was not easy. The very nature of civilian control of the U.S. military, its demobilized force structure, and the American optimistic willingness to see negotiation and compromise as possible in the most impossible circumstances all inhibited the quick and capricious use of armies and navies. Once Americans become convinced that force is the only option, however, they have proven that they can turn 180 degrees and implement it with wicked effectiveness.

Flexing Democracy's Muscles

In spite of the nation's original neutral position—Wilson's strict neutrality "in thought and deed"—the administration now suddenly had to convince Americans that in fact one side was brutal and ruthless. Citizens who only a year earlier had been cautioned to curtail their anti-German feelings were now encouraged, openly and often, to indulge them. The government launched an all-out propaganda offensive, depicting the Germans in posters as the Hun—apelike, fanged creatures wearing spiked German helmets and carrying off women. A culture sanitization occurred in which products or foods with Germanic- or Teutonic-sounding names were replaced by American phrases: hamburgers became liberty sandwiches, and sauerkraut was called liberty cabbage. Any identification with

German culture was proscribed: Berlin, Iowa, became Lincoln; Kaiser Street became Maine Way; Germantown, Nebraska, was renamed Garland; Hamburg Avenue in Brooklyn was changed to Wilson Avenue; and even the famous German shepherd dog received a new name, the Alsatian shepherd.

Scholars often deride such efforts as "brainwashing," failing to understand that in democracies, citizens view war as a last resort, something abnormal. Contrary to how propaganda is portrayed—manipulating the public to do something against its collective will—wartime propaganda is often obviously accepted and enthusiastically received as a means of preparing a republic for the grim task ahead.

George Creel, a Denver journalist, supported this effort with his Committee on Public Information, which provided posters and distributed war literature. The committee encouraged citizens to report anyone engaging in antiwar behavior to the Justice Department. Creel used his contacts in journalism to encourage fellow reporters to monitor their coverage of the war.

Of course abuses occurred. Germans in the United States became the objects of suspicion and, occasionally, violence. One German immigrant was lynched in St. Louis. Ultimately, the distrust spread to all immigrants, as seen in the Immigration Restriction Act of 1917, which refused admission to any adult immigrant who could not pass a basic reading test. (Prohibition, in part, reflected the anti-immigrant attitudes fanned by the war because of a belief that Germans and others brought a "drinking culture" to the United States.) And the most significant piece of legislation, the Espionage, Sabotage, and Sedition Acts of 1917 and 1918, extended the bounds of what was considered sabotage or espionage to include slandering the Constitution or the military. The postmaster general blocked mailings of Socialist Party materials. But even if somewhat censored, the press continued to report, Congress continued to meet and pass laws (in fact, Wilson vetoed the Immigration Act), and people still experienced a level of freedom unseen in most of the world during *peacetime*.

With the public support of combat sufficiently ratcheted up, the administration turned to financing and supply. The Federal Reserve facilitated bond sales and helped prevent wartime profiteering, and income tax rates skyrocketed to provide further cash (and only later was it discovered that the revenues collected from the rich plummeted with each rate increase).

Much of the credit for organizing the finance and supply effort at home went to the secretary of the treasury, William McAdoo, who organized the War Finance Corporation (WFC). The idea was to facilitate the conversion of civilian production—such as Ford's motor plants—into factories turning out war matériel. At first, however, even with McAdoo's genius, the WFC's effort was helter-skelter. Companies made too many of the same parts; there were no priorities established; and the government lacked an overall strategy concerning which items to buy, and in what order. To be sure, this fostered some profiteering (the infamous "merchants of death"), but in most cases the lack of direction caused redundancies and inefficiency. It took almost a year before McAdoo figured it out, handing the job over, in March 1918, to a new organization, the War Industries Board (WIB), under the direction of South Carolina millionaire and Wall Street tycoon, Bernard Baruch.

The new boss, who had come from the business sector and was not a lifetime bureaucrat, immediately perceived that besides priorities, what the government lacked was a business approach to procurement. He also knew that business leaders needed to take control of the production if it was to have any chance of succeeding. Reviving the successful productive practices of the Civil War, when government encouraged private enterprise to provide the weapons of war, Baruch "permitted industrialists to charge high prices for their products," a feature that would be repeated yet again with equally stunning success in the next world war.[41] He persuaded Wilson's Justice Department to call off the antitrust dogs, exempting many businesses from investigation as monopolies, while at the same time chastising any companies that did not comply with WIB requests.

Baruch also persuaded successful corporate leaders to head up important procurement agencies and boards for a token fee of a dollar a year—hence their name, the Dollar-a-Year Men. The approach worked. In short order the businessmen had the war industry churning out supplies and machines, all according to a master plan Baruch and McAdoo had mapped out with Wilson and the War Department.

Raising a legitimate ground force capable of going toe to toe with the Germans presented a equally daunting challenge. The U.S. Army, except for the Civil War, had never been particularly large and had atrophied since the Spanish-American War. Total numbers, including reserves, reached perhaps 200,000. For perspective, one should consider that at the Somme offensive in 1916, the British lost more than 95,000 dead (including 20,000 on the first day); the French, 50,000; and the Germans, 160,000. Put another way, in just under four months the combatants had lost more men than even existed in the entire U.S. Army of 1917.

Not only was the army small, it was inexperienced, although many troops had fought in Cuba and the Filipino rebellion. But only a few commanders had had wartime experience in Cuba, the Philippines, or the Mexico expedition, most notably George Catlett Marshall, Douglas MacArthur, and Black Jack Pershing. Another Pancho Villa chaser who joined Pershing's American Expeditionary Force was cavalry officer George S. Patton, already training in the revolutionary war vehicle known as the tank. Roosevelt, as he had in the Spanish-American War, offered to raise another regiment of troops, but Wilson politely refused.[42]

To meet the need for men, Wilson and Secretary of War Newton Baker pushed through Congress the Selective Service Act, or a draft. Three million men came into the army through the draft, and two million more volunteered for service. More than 240,000 black troops entered the armed services, with most of them serving in France. Blacks had a greater chance of being drafted, but a far smaller likelihood than whites of seeing combat. Nevertheless, one of the most famous black combat outfits—the 369th Infantry—was in the trenches for almost two hundred days, and the entire regiment received the Croix de Guerre for heroism from the French government. In addition, 171 individual soldiers and officers were cited for their courage under fire.

Other ethnic groups served in disproportionate numbers, especially German-Americans, and overall, 20 percent of the draftees were born in another country. A typical draftee was a second- or third-generation immigrant like Jean Pierre Godet, who enlisted in the army in November 1917. At the time of Godet's enlistment, the young man's unnamed father wrote to his sister the conflicting emotions that gripped every soldier's parent at that moment:

> Today is November 3 . . . and Jean Pierre was sworn into the infantry. . . .
> I cannot tell you the mixed sense of joy and pain I have felt upon his
> leaving for the war. I cannot withhold Jean Pierre and forbid him to take
> part in the army, for the importance of this war is hard to estimate. I feel
> a strange contradiction between my love for Jean Pierre and my love for
> America. It is difficult to surrender my son that my country may be free.
> On the other hand, without the willingness of all Americans to make
> these kinds of sacrifices neither the country nor the world would long remain free.[43]

Thousands more did not fight but served in, or worked to advance, the Red Cross, including Lewis Douglas, future budget director under Franklin Roosevelt; advertising executive Bruce Barton; and a budding artist named Walt Disney. Indeed, two of the men most responsible for the symbolic view of America that evolved by the 1960s, Disney and McDonald's founder Ray Kroc, crossed each other's path in the Red Cross in France.[44] Still thousands more "Plowed to the fence for national defense" on their farms and raised beef and sheep on their ranches.

Britain and France had few doubts that the doughboys would arrive and weigh heavily on the scale of battle. Their concern, however, was that the war at sea would be lost before the Americans ever set foot in France. America's Rear Admiral William S. Sims, after meeting with Sir John Jellicoe in London regarding the shipping situation, admitted that the German U-boat campaign was succeeding. At the-then-current rates of losses, by fall of 1917 the U-boats would be sinking more vessels than could be built. Sims then helped design the convoy system (akin to the frontier wagon trains), making it easier to protect merchant ships.

The convoy system worked like a charm because it turned the chief strength of the U-boats—their stealth—into a weakness by forcing them to reveal themselves in an attack.[45] Once they struck, U-boats could not escape the escort vessels easily. This turn of events and the addition of American ships had a decided effect, drastically reducing losses from submarines. In April 1917 alone, before the United States joined the war, the Allies lost nine hundred thousand tons of shipping, but by December the convoy system had cut that monthly number to four hundred thousand. Thus, even before American soldiers could make a difference on the ground, the U.S. Navy had ensured Germany could not win at sea.

With the seas under Allied control, American troops departed for Europe. In July 1917 the U.S. First Infantry Division left for France, where it was greeted by Pershing himself. Pershing, lacking oratory skill, sent Colonel Charles Stanton to meet the men, and it was he who uttered the famous phrase, "Lafayette, we are here." Black Jack did not need flowery or emotional speeches. He had gained his fame in the Spanish-American War, charging San Juan Hill next to Roosevelt's Rough Riders. Pershing kept himself in almost robotlike control, and even his voice was monotone. But he was as fine a commander as any nation put in the field. Above all, the general understood that he could not allow the French to incorporate small untrained American units into French forces as mere reinforcements. He certainly did not intend for them to be chewed up in frontal assaults as the best of European manhood had been in the previous three years. Nor would a single division tilt the scales much. Pershing intended to deploy 3 million American troops in France by May 1918, but until then, the American Expeditionary Force had to resist sending brigade-sized replacements to the British or French. After 100,000 Yanks had arrived, they took up positions near the Swiss border, and on October 23, 1917, Alex Arch, an artillery sergeant, fired the first American shots at the Germans, and a few nights later the United States took her first war casualties.

By that time, virtually every aspect of the war was working against Germany. The U-boat war had failed and would never reach the level of effectiveness it had had in the spring of 1917. At the same time, the British blockade was starving Germany. In late 1917 the British unleashed a massive attack spearheaded by three hundred of the new wonder weapons, the tanks, gaining more ground in a single day than in months of fighting in previous battles. Although the Germans regrouped, the carefully deployed and supported tank units doomed trench warfare once and for all. This made the Germans increasingly desperate, accounting for their offensive in early 1918.

Pershing appreciated the delicate situation in which either Germany or France could collapse. Writing Wilson's adviser, Colonel Edward House, he stated, "The Allies are done for, and the only thing that will hold them (especially France) in the war will be the assurance that we have enough forces to assume the initiative."[46] By midsummer 1918, French officers rejoiced at the sight of

American armies: "Life was coming in floods to re-animate the dying body of France."[47] Indeed, that May, with the additional U.S. troops, the Allies now had about 3 million men on the Western Front facing 3.5 million Germans.

The German advance of 42 divisions in mid-1918 swept away British troops and came within eighty miles of Paris, which began a general evacuation until American marines appeared on the roads. They were thrown into a gap at Château-Thierry and Belleau Wood, and when the marines took up their positions, they dug no trenches for fallback positions. "The Marines will hold where they stand," said Brigadier General James Harbord, and they did, although the press misidentified the men as army doughboys, starting a friendly rivalry between regular army and marines, each seeking to outdo the other in military glory. American troops counterattacked on June twenty-sixth, driving the Germans out of the areas near Paris and stunning the German general staff, which had to reconsider its offensive. General Erich Ludendorff, in charge of war production, ordered aircraft production doubled to offset the Yankee units.

More desperate German offensives followed. Douglas MacArthur, an American officer facing the June-July attacks, witnessed one of the final German assaults on the Western Front. Despite a barrage of more than half a million gas shells, the Germans could not break through. German forces slammed into unbroken barbed-wire barriers defended by U.S. doughboys blazing away with machine guns. MacArthur, who would be criticized for his seeming absence of compassion in the Bonus Army charge, later recalled that he was "haunted by the vision of those writhing bodies hanging from the barbed wire." When the Allied forces counterattacked, MacArthur found the enemy "exhausted, uncoordinated, and shattered."[48] Across the lines, one of those exhausted and shattered soldiers, Corporal Adolf Hitler, was awarded an Iron Cross Second Class for personal bravery by a Jew, Captain Hugo Gutmann. And at the time Gutmann decorated Adolf Hitler, the American assistant secretary of the navy, Franklin Delano Roosevelt, visited the battle zone and fired an artillery piece in Hitler's direction. A few hours later Roosevelt watched 200 tired and wounded American soldiers moving to the rear—all that remained of a regiment of 1,000 that had advanced merely two days before.[49]

In Shermanesque fashion the American troops continued to advance, not giving the German army a chance to regroup. In early September, at Saint-Mihiel, American forces slammed into retreating German units and probably could have taken Metz. But Field Marshal Foch, the commander in chief of the Allied troops, had another strategy that shifted the American First Army west to the Meuse-Argonne forest along a massive, and broad, front. It was here that the greatest tale of American heroism from the Great War emerged. Sergeant Alvin York was a Tennessee turkey-shooting champion and conscientious objector when the war began, but he was persuaded by his pastor to join the war effort. Part of the 82nd Division, York's platoon became separated from the main body, and fighting his way back with only a handful of men, York killed 25 enemy soldiers, took out thirty-five German machine guns, and took 132 prisoners. Germans' heads, the Tennessean noted, were "so much bigger than turkeys' heads."[50] Even York's heroism paled beside that of Dan Edwards, whose arm was pinned beneath a tree by artillery fire. When he saw eight Germans advancing toward him, he shot four with his revolver and took the other four prisoner—his arm still pinned. Using his bayonet to cut off his crushed arm, he applied a tourniquet and, using one hand, herded the Germans back to his lines. When yet another explosion broke his leg, he ordered the Germans to carry him!

The offensive had broken the back of the German army, and Ludendorff knew it. Only months earlier French troops had mutinied, but now riots occurred in German shipyards and cities. In August the Austrian foreign minister informed the Germans that his nation would seek a separate peace negotiation. German troops were ordered to evacuate forward positions rather than face encirclement and death. As the kaiser's inner circle grew more desperate for an armistice, they told the insecure Wilhelm that peace feelers they had sent to Wilson had been squelched by the demand that the kaiser step down as a precondition to an armistice. A shaken Wilhelm, whose cousin Czar Nicholas II had recently been executed by Lenin's Bolsheviks, agreed to change the German constitution to allow for a parliamentary government. On November 9, 1918, a new republic was established in Berlin, and the kaiser boarded an imperial train for neutral Holland. Pershing warned that the fighting needed to continue until the Allies obtained an unconditional surrender, not a cease-fire. "What I dread is that Germany doesn't know that she is licked. Had they given us another week, we'd have *taught* them."[51] But it was out of his hands. At 11:00 A.M. on November 11, 1918, a silence fell over the bloody battlefields of Europe, ending the costliest war in human history.

The cease-fire was announced around five o' clock in the morning Paris time, indicating eleven o'clock as the appointed Armistice hour. Harry Truman, commanding a battery of the 129th Field Artillery, fired his last shell just a few minutes before the set time, having received orders to keep fighting until the actual Armistice hour. Ironically, Truman, at least indirectly, may have fired the last shots of *both* world wars—one at his artillery station in France and another through his order to drop the second atomic bomb on Nagasaki, in Japan.

When the shooting stopped, the United States was fortunate that its casualty lists were considerably shorter than those of the other participants. The numbers of dead were mind-numbing: 1.8 million Germans, 1.7 million Russians, 1.4 million French, 1.3 million Austrians, and 947,000 British or Commonwealth troops. American losses were staggeringly light by comparison. The nation soberly absorbed the actual battle deaths for the American Expeditionary Force, which stood at 48,909, although a total of 112,432 soldiers and sailors had died in all theaters of all causes in a conflict not of their own making.

Wilson, meanwhile, had already outlined a proposal for ensuring (in his mind) that another such war would never occur. He had labeled his program the Fourteen Points, yet even before the Armistice had taken effect, eleven German cities were flying the communist red flag of revolution. Germany had deteriorated into chaos before Wilson even boarded the vessel sailing to France for the peace conference. Germany was not the only European power whose collapse involved the United States. To the east, Russia had disintegrated in the face of antiwar protests and the skillful maneuvering of the diabolical V. I. Lenin, Russia's "Red Son," who would spawn the first communist state of the twentieth century."

Red Son Rising

Amid the sea of blood and America's entry into the Great War, Russia's second revolution went almost unnoticed. But not for long. In October 1917, Vladimir Lenin and a tiny core of radically committed Bolshevik communists, took the Russian government by force, grabbing the key centers of communication and controlling the legislature. Estimates put the number of loyal Leninist supporters in Russia at no more than twenty thousand—in a nation of 160 million—but with zealous fervor and unshakable focus, the Bolsheviks seized near-total power in a few months. Lenin's puppet legislature announced an immediate end to hostilities with Germany, freeing millions of Germany's Eastern Front troops for service against the newly arrived Yankee forces.

During the civil war that followed between Communist forces (Reds) and non-Communists (Whites), the United States and the Allies sought to ensure supply lines. Anglo-American troops landed to secure objectives imperative to the Allies' war effort. When the Bolsheviks finally won, and had pulled Russia out of the war with the Treaty of Brest Litovsk (1918), these actions later aided the Soviet propaganda line that the United States and other capitalist nations had arrayed themselves against Communism in its infancy.

Few Euopeans or Americans—Churchill excepted—saw the menace posed by a Communist government in such a large resource-rich nation. Quite the contrary, many American intellectuals welcomed the Communist movement in Russia as a harbinger of what "should" happen next in America. It did not matter that Joseph Stalin's minister Vyacheslav Molotov "could sign the death sentences of 3,187 people in just one night and then watch Western movies with Stalin with a pure conscience."[52] When Stalin later claimed his show trials were fair, the *New Republic* accepted his explanations at face value. Owen Lattimore commented that "the executions of dissidents sounds like democracy to me."[53] (Lattimore would be revealed in the 1950s as a Soviet accomplice, if not outright agent.) Harry Ward, a professor of Christian ethics at Union Theological Seminary in New York, compared the Soviet system with the teachings of Jesus. From 1919 on, large numbers of the intelligentsia in the United States ignored or down-played Lenin's and Stalin's atrocities, hiding behind the lack of firsthand evidence about the actual brutality of the regime.

At home, however, the Communist movement could not cover up its activi-ties. In April 1919, New York City postal clerks found twenty package bombs addressed to public officials and caught all but two of the saboteurs. The unde-tected bombs exploded at the attorney general's house, blowing a deliveryman to pieces, and another exploded at a U.S. senator's house, shattering the arm of a maid. Outraged citizens supported immediate action, which, with Senate ap-proval, the Justice Department took by launching a series of raids on suspected communists. Authorized by Attorney General Mitchell Palmer, the raids, directed by Palmer's assistant J. Edgar Hoover, smashed the Communist movement in the United States. A team of lawyers claiming that the government's attacks endan-gered civil liberties for all citizens resisted the raids and eventually forced Palmer's resignation but not before he had reduced membership in the American Communist party and its allies by 80 percent.

The remaining Communists might have remained underground and harm-less after the war, but for a sensational murder trial of two anarchists, Nicola Sacco and Bartolomeo Vanzetti, who were convicted of a Braintree, Massachu-setts, robbery and murder in 1921. Both supporters and opponents misidentified the pair as Communists (when in fact they were anarchists), and both sides saw the case as a test of the government's position on radicals. The two were executed on solid evidence, and attempts to portray the trial as rigged have not stood up. In any event, the prosperity of the 1920s soon combined with the concerns about anarchism to blunt any further spread of communism in the United States. "Sacco and Vanzetti forged an important bond between Communists and their liberal sympathizers," a bond that resurfaced during the Great Depression and the rise of fascism in the 1930s.[54]

Versailles and the Fourteen Points

As events in Bolshevik Russia unfolded, they had a direct impact on Wilson's phi-losophy of foreign policy. Lenin had already (in December 1917) issued a decla-ration of his government's war aims, which was in many ways a formality: he intended to get out of the war as quickly as possible. Partly in response to the So-viet proposals, in January 1918 Wilson offered his own program, known as the Fourteen Points, which in some ways mirrored Lenin's suggestions. Although the president hoped Russia could be persuaded to stay in the war, he soon "realized that Lenin was now a competitor in the effort to lead the postwar order."[55]

In 1918, Wilson the social scientist had convened a panel of 150 academic ex-perts to craft a peace plan under the direction of his close adviser, Colonel Ed-ward House. Some observers, including British diplomatic historian Harold Nicolson, were impressed by this illustrious group, asserting it had produced one of the "wisest documents in history."[56] Others remained skeptical of foreign policy drafted by an academic elite. Attracted to numbers and categories, Wilson outlined five points that related to international relations, including "open covenants" (a concession to Lenin, who had already made public all the treaties Russia had secretly made prior to the revolution), freedom of the seas, free trade, arms reductions, and review of colonial policies with an eye toward justice for the colonized peoples. Then Wilson added eight more points addressing territorial claims after the war, including the return of Alsace-Lorraine to France, recovery of Russian and Italian territory from the Central Powers, establishment of a new Polish nation, and modifications in the Ottoman Empire to separate ethnic minorities into their own countries under the rubric of the Wilsonian phrase, "national self-determination." That made thirteen points, with the fourteenth consisting of a call for an international congress to discuss and deliberate, even to act as an international policeman to prevent future wars.

Before anyone in the international community could absorb even a few of the Fourteen Points, Wilson inundated them with still more. In February, the Four Principles followed, then in September 1918, the Five Particulars. All of this relentless drafting, pontificating, and, above all, *numbering* came during the bloody final months of the war, when some 9 million Germans still faced the Allied-American armies now without regard to the Eastern Front. The constant stream of points and principles and particulars gave the Germans the impression that the basis of an armistice was constantly in flux and negotiable. Consequently, in early October 1918, German and Austrian diplomats agreed to what they thought Wilson had offered—the Fourteen Points.

More accurately, the Fourteen Points should have been called the *American* Fourteen Points. Certainly the British and the French did not sign off on them, and no sooner had the Central Powers agreed to the stipulations than a secret meeting occurred between House and Anglo-French leaders where they introduced numerous caveats. The Allies changed or amended many of the most important passages. This "Anglo-French Commentary," as it was called, left the Allies everything and the Central Powers virtually nothing. It created a "Polish Corridor" that divided Prussia; it broke up the Austro-Hungarian Empire and stripped Germany of overseas colonies; it changed Wilson's word "compensation" to a more harsh-sounding "reparations," opening the door for the hated war-guilt clause.

Perhaps the worst feature of the Fourteen Points (besides deceiving Germany after a deal had been offered and accepted) was that it proffered a phony explanation of the war itself with the Central Powers the sole villains. It excused Britain and France from their own desire for territory and dominance. To be sure, Germany had struck first; the Germans had engaged in unrestricted submarine warfare, which had already been demonized as "inhuman"; Germany had used zeppelins to bomb London civilians, and had introduced the flamethrower; and Germany had smugly thought she could launch a last-minute offensive and smash France as late as 1918. But it would be unrealistic to ignore the British and French (not to mention Russian and Serbian) culpability in starting the war. Indeed, when comparing the relatively mild treatment post-Napoleonic France had received after Waterloo by the Congress of Vienna—which followed a period of constant war that lasted three times longer than World War I—Germany was unfairly punished in 1919.

Wilson set the stage for such international malfeasance by his make-the-world-safe-for-democracy comments in the original war message, indicating he would not be satisfied until he had reshaped the world in the image of America. The Central Powers should have listened then. Instead, having accepted the Fourteen Points as the grounds for the November 1918 Armistice, they now found themselves excluded from the treaty process entirely, to be handed a Carthaginian peace.

Nevertheless, when Wilson sailed for the peace conference in Paris on December 4, 1918, it is safe to say that he took the hopes of much of the world with him. His arrival in Europe was messianic in tone, the cheers of the people echoing a desperate longing that this American leader might end centuries of Continental conflict. The "stiff-necked, humorless, self-righteous, and puritan" Wilson lapped up the adulation.[57] European leaders may have privately scoffed at the president—the French Premier Georges Clemenceau dourly said, "The Fourteen Points bore me ... God Almighty has only ten!"—but the masses embraced him.[58] Wilson's reception, in part, involved a natural euphoria over the termination of the war, akin to the brief Era of Good Feelings that had surfaced between the North and South in the weeks following Appomattox.

Personally attending the conference, while good for Wilson's ego, proved a fatal political mistake. Other representatives, by nature of their parliamentary systems, already had the support of their legislatures. The Constitution, however, required the president to obtain Senate ratification of treaties. By participating personally, Wilson lost some of the aura of a deity from a distance that had won him the adoration of the French.

Unfortunately, Wilson's lofty phrases did not easily translate into genuine policy with teeth. For example, national self-determination, while apparently sensible, was an idea fraught with danger. Carving a new Poland out of parts of Germany and Russia failed to take into account the many decades when an aggressive Poland had waged war to expand *her* boundaries in the past. Nor did the Ottoman Empire get off easily: Palestine, Mesopotamia (later Iraq), and Syria were sliced off and handed to the League of Nations as trust territories, as was Armenia, though too late to save the half million Armenian civilians slaughtered by the Turkish government. Wilson did not originally insist on establishing completely new states of Romania, Serbia, and Montenegro—only "autonomy" within empires—but by October 16, 1918, while the guns still blazed, Wilson had upped the ante to require statehood status. Perversely, the Allies now lobbied for entire Slavic and Slovakian states that would themselves subordinate Serbs,

Croats, Slovenians, Albanians, and other groups trapped within the new nation-alities. Wilson had moved in less than four years from neutral in thought and deed to outright hostility toward Germany and Austria-Hungary.

Other punitive clauses reduced the army to a rump, eliminated Germany's navy as well as stripped her rich industrial territories, and imposed massive repa-rations. These included not only direct gold payments, but also the construction of ships and railroad cars that the Germans had to offer to the British and French free of charge. All of these constituted massive (and foolish) economic disloca-tions that helped send Europe into a depression within a few years.

Where the treaty was not self-contradictory, it was mean, vindictive, and, at the same time, ambiguous. The phrases avoided specifics, falling back on the re-formist language of freedom, respect, and observing the rights of nations. Which were? Wilson could not, or at least did not, say. Nations had to be respected, ex-cept for Germany, which had to be taught a lesson. In that regard, the French were much more pragmatic, seeking a mutual security pact with the United States and Britain. Instead, Wilson pressed for universal participation in the League of Nations, which, the French knew, would soon include France's ene-mies. More damaging (at least in the eyes of U.S. Senate critics of the treaty), the League threatened to draw the United States into colonial conflicts to maintain the Europeans' grip in Africa and Asia—a concept fundamentally at odds with America's heritage of revolution and independence.

Satisfied they had emasculated the Central Powers and at the same time made the world safe for democracy, Great Britain, France, the United States, Italy, and other participants signed the Treaty of Versailles in June 1919. Within ten years, its provisions would accelerate German economic chaos, European unemployment, and at least indirectly, the rise of Adolf Hitler and Benito Mussolini.

Returning to the United States with the treaty in hand, Wilson faced a skeptical Senate—now in the hands of the Republicans, who had won both houses in the 1918 off-year elections (despite Wilson's claim that a Republican election would embarrass the nation). Opposition to the treaty in the Senate was led by Henry Cabot Lodge (Massachusetts) and William Borah (Idaho). Lodge, chairman of the Senate Armed Forces Committee, disagreed less with the intent of the treaty or its likelihood to involve the nation in foreign conflicts than he did with the im-precision of its wording, which was, in his opinion, too open ended. The public agreed with the general premise of a worldwide peacekeeping body, but needed to be convinced that the League would be feasible and effective. Attempting to add specificity, Lodge introduced his own reservations to the treaty. Other oppo-nents, however, including the Progressive wing of the party led by Robert La Fol-lette, Hiram Johnson, and Borah, had voted against going to war in the first place, and continued to reject any postwar European involvement.

Many Democrats, including Bryan and Colonel House, as well as members of Wilson's own cabinet, such as Herbert Hoover, echoed the reservations. Some argued that the League of Nations committed American boys to dying for nebulous and ill-defined international causes. This in itself violated the Constitution, and no American sailor, soldier, or marine had ever taken a vow to defend the League of Nations. Since virtually none of the opponents had been present at Versailles when Wilson had negotiated the final points, they didn't realize that he had already traded away the substance of any legitimate leverage the United States might have had in return for the shadow of a peace enforced by international means.

Lodge rightly recognized that the notion that every separate ethnic group should have its own nation was hopelessly naïve. Was French Quebec to declare independence from English Canada? Should the Mexican-dominated American Southwest attempt to create Aztlan? Branded an obstructionist, Lodge in fact controlled only 49 votes, some of which could have been swung by reasonable negotiations by Wilson. Instead, the stubborn president sought to go over the heads of the senators, making a whistle-stop tour touting the treaty. Speaking on behalf of the treaty, Wilson covered a remarkable eight thousand miles in three weeks, often from the back of his train at thirty-seven different locations. Occasionally he spoke four times a day, sometimes an hour at a time. Yet even in our age of instantaneous mass communication, such a strategy would involve great risk: presidents are important, but not supreme. Wilson could count on reaching only a small handful of the population, and certainly not with the effect needed to shift entire blocs of votes in the Senate.

Wilson was already in poor health, having suffered a stroke in April 1919 while still in Paris, and concealing it from the public. In September he had another stroke, then, on October second, yet another. After the final stroke, Wilson remained debilitated and bedridden, out of touch with the American voter. Mrs. Edith Wilson thus became, in a manner of speaking, the first female president of the United States, though her role, again, was unknown to the general public. For more than a year she determined who Wilson saw, what he said, and what he wanted through notes that she crafted in a clumsy hand. When he was lucid, Edith arranged for Wilson to meet with staff and members of Congress, but most of the time he looked distant and dull. His speech was slurred, and he remained partly paralyzed, especially on his left side. Whether the stroke accounted for his unwillingness to negotiate any of the Lodge criticisms is uncertain, but whatever the cause, his cadre of supporters in the Senate failed to persuade a single vote to switch, sending the treaty down to defeat. And because Wilson would not entertain any of the Lodge reservations, indeed had ordered his loyal senators to vote against the Lodge version, in March 1920 the amended treaty also failed to pass. The defeated treaty symbolized the high water mark of international Progressivism. Although it would take several years, a new, more realistic foreign policy would set in at the end of the Coolidge administration. If the Progressives had failed in foreign policy, they were just getting started in areas of social reform, especially when it came to public health and women's suffrage.

Progressive Fervor and the Real Thing

America's war against alcohol began, oddly enough, with an attack on Coca-Cola. One of the first products challenged under the 1906 Food and Drug Act, Coke had eliminated even the minute portions of cocaine it had once used in the cooking process years before.[59] The drink had originated with an Atlanta pharmacist, Dr. John Pemberton, and his Yankee advertiser, Frank Robinson, from a desire to create a cold drink that could be served over ice in the South to compete with hot coffee and tea. Pemberton had concocted the mixture from kola nuts, sugar, caffeine, caramel, citric acid, and a fluid extract of cocaine for a little euphoria. After Pemberton fell ill—one biographer claims of a cocaine addiction—Asa Griggs Candler, another pharmacist who suffered from frequent headaches, took over after discovering that Coke alleviated his pain. By that time, pharmaceutical tests had showed that Coca-Cola contained about one thirtieth of a *grain* of cocaine, or so little that even the most sensitive person would not feel any effects short of a half dozen drinks. Candler thought it unethical to advertise a product as Coca-Cola without any cocaine in the contents, but he realized that the growing public clamor for drug regulation could destroy the company. He therefore arrived at a secret formula that began with a tiny portion of cocaine that through the process of cooking and distilling was ultimately removed.

Since the late 1890s, Coke had been the subject of attacks by health activists and temperance advocates. Many Progressives, especially Dr. Harvey Wiley, the leader of the government's case brought by the Food and Drug Administration in 1909–10, recklessly endorsed some products and condemned others. Wiley sought to expand his domain as much as possible and initiated a highly publicized case against Coke that culminated in a 1911 Chattanooga trial. By that time, there were no trace elements of cocaine in the drink at all, and the government's own tests had proved it.[60] This prompted Wiley to switch strategies by claiming that Coke's advertising was fraudulent because Coca-Cola did *not* contain cocaine!

The effort to prosecute Coke went flat, but convinced Progressive reformers that government could successfully litigate against products with "proven" health risks. Wiley's effort to get Coke was a test run for the Eighteenth Amendment, or the "noble experiment" of Prohibition, which involved the direct intervention of government against both social mores and market forces and, more than any other movement, epitomized the reform tradition.[61]

Temperance had a long history in American politics. Maine passed the first state law banning the sale of alcohol in 1851, based on the studies of Neal Dow, a Portland businessman who claimed to have found a link between booze and family violence, crime, and poverty.[62] Abraham Lincoln had run on a platform of temperance. For a while, eliminating alcohol seemed a necessary component of the women's movement as a means to rescue wives from drunken abuse and to keep the family wages from the saloon keeper. Alcohol, by way of the saloons, was linked to prostitution, and prostitution to the epidemic of venereal disease. "Today," declared Dr. Prince Morrow, a specialist on sexually transmitted diseases, "we recognize [gonorrhea] not only as the most widespread but also one of the most serious of infective diseases; it has risen to the dignity of a public peril."[63] Convinced that unfaithful husbands were bringing home syphilis, doctors warned of the "syphilis of the innocent"—infected wives and children. Then there was the alcohol-related problem of white slavery, brought before the public eye in the 1913 play *Damaged*.[64] At that point a public clamor arose, and Congress reacted by passing the Mann Act of 1910, which prohibited the transport of women across state lines for the purpose of prostitution.

When Prince Morrow died, groups such as the American Social Hygiene Association persuaded John D. Rockefeller Jr. and Grace Dodge to take over the leadership of the movement. Rockefeller, who had given thousands of dollars for studies and provided much of the annual budget, had served on special grand juries in New York investigating the white-slave trade. Although the juries found no evidence of a syndicate, the experience convinced Rockefeller that there were responsible concerns about the damage done to society by venereal disease. He thus joined the thousands of other moral crusaders of the day, further cementing the relationship between planning, professionalism, and social reform. As one press release aptly put it, "The name Rockefeller stands for a type of efficiency and thoroughness of work."[65]

All of these streams of reform and the application of science and professional solutions came to a confluence over alcohol, particularly because the saloon was perceived as the hotbed of prostitution. Even the direct democracy movement played a significant role in eliminating booze. At the elementary school level, thanks to Massachusetts housewife Mary Hunt, a movement called Scientific Temperance Instruction swept the nation in the 1880s, providing a forerunner to Nancy Reagan's "Just Say No" antidrug campaign a century later.[66] Enlisting anti-alcohol crusaders from Connecticut to California, Scientific Temperance Instruction in classrooms introduced scientific experts to support its Prohibition position, leading a popular democratic movement to influence curricula. The Anti-Saloon League, founded in the 1890s, joined with the Women's Christian Temperance Union to use local laws to excise saloons within city boundaries, isolating them in wet areas. More than 40 percent of the population lived in dry communities by 1906, thanks to such local legislation, and within three years the dry movement had spread to a dozen states, again through grassroots activism.[67]

Prohibition puts modern liberal historians in a quandary: on the one hand, they have approved of its use of federal power for social engineering for a purpose they deem desirable; but on the other hand, it ran counter to their unwillingness to pursue any policies based on morals or values. Consequently, historians have mischaracterized Prohibition as "cultural and class legislation," wherein Progressive upper classes and Anglo-Saxons "imposed their Puritanical will on benign but besotted immigrants to mold an America that reflected their values," as one text described the Progressives' efforts.[68] Historian Richard Hofstadter called

Prohibition a "parochial substitute for genuine reform, carried about America by the rural-evangelical virus."[69] Such a view erred by lumping together two substantially different groups, the Progressives and the rural Populists. A stronger correlation existed with women and Prohibition, leading dry counties to also permit universal suffrage. Only after Prohibition failed was there a deliberate effort to reinterpret the essentially Progressive flavor of Prohibition as the work of wild-eyed Christian evangelists and Populists or, as H. L. Mencken sneeringly put it, "ignorant bumpkins of the cow states."[70] The amendment gained broad supermajority support from a wide range of groups, as was obvious by the fact that it was an amendment and not a statutory law. As Prohibition historian Norman Clark wrote, "A majority of the people in a majority of the states wanted this truly national effort to influence national morality."[71] Doctors, teachers, upper-class reformers, rural preachers, labor leaders, and businessmen of all sorts supported Prohibition.

Under the amendment, the manufacture, sale, or transportation of intoxicating liquors (consisting of any beverage with more than .5 percent alcohol) was prohibited. Unlike later laws against drug use, actually consuming alcohol was not a crime, and had enforcement been even remotely possible, Prohibition may not have passed. Although a large majority of Americans (for a variety of motivations) supported the concept, it was not clear how many wished to provide the government with the means and the license to ensure compliance.[72]

A revealing look at the Janus-faced nature of Progressive policy can be gleaned from the approach to enforcement of the antialcohol campaign. The Volstead Act, passed in 1919 over Wilson's veto, provided an enforcement mechanism, but instead of placing the Prohibition Bureau inside the Justice Department, where it belonged, Volstead made it a part of the Treasury Department. "Revenooers" broke up illegal stills, and agents crashed into speakeasies; and when the government had no other evidence, it charged mobsters with income tax evasion, which was what finally put Al Capone behind bars.

Reform zeal during this time led to the formation of an antituberculosis league in 1897, the American Conference for the Prevention of Infant Mortality in 1909, the National Mental Hygiene Committee that same year, the National Society for the Prevention of Blindness in 1915, and a half dozen more.[73] The founding of the American Eugenics Society in 1923 by biologist Charles Davenport, Alexander Graham Bell, and Luther Burbank was more chilling.[74] Indiana and California mandated sterilization of confirmed "criminals, idiots, rapists, and imbeciles" whose condition was viewed as "incurable" based on the recommendation of three physicians.[75] All of these organizations and movements captured the Progressive view that disease and imperfection of any kind could be "reformed" through human action.

As with most other reform movements in America, Prohibition started among upper-class females, and, as was often the case, the targets ultimately were lower-class men. According to the pietistic conscience, the lower classes were naturally the morally weaker classes, but predictably it was pietist women who after 1870 rushed toward political and social protest to save the family.[76] And who could be numbered among these "morally weaker classes"? None other than immigrants, Irish, Italians, and Poles. In the eyes of Progressive reformers, the drinking habits of the foreigners reinforced the political corruption where fat, cigar-smoking backroom pols mobilized armies of drunken immigrants to pad their machine's vote.

Whether temperance itself was ever the sole objective of the women's groups who participated in the Prohibition movement invites skepticism. Many feminist leaders latched on to Prohibition only as an organizational tool that would permit them to mobilize for the "real" effort, women's suffrage.

Suffering for Suffrage

Voting rights for women, another Progressive plank, had a long history. Since the Seneca Falls Convention in 1848, calls for the Declaration of Independence to be applied to all people, not just all men, had increased in frequency and intensity. Elizabeth Cady Stanton, who had organized the Seneca Women's Rights Convention, labeled it the "duty of women . . . to secure . . . their sacred right to the elective franchise."[77] Shortly after the Civil War, Stanton had formed the National Woman Suffrage Association, which wanted a constitutional amendment for female suffrage. That association soon pressed for other objectives, including birth control and easier divorce laws, and alienated some women who merely wanted the vote, and who in turn formed the American Woman Suffrage Association. The two merged in 1890 as the National American Woman Suffrage Association, largely made up of middle- and upper-class reform-minded people of both sexes.

The Wyoming Territory had granted voting rights to women in 1869, and when Wyoming petitioned to enter the Union twenty years later, Congress allowed the women's vote clause to stand in the new state constitution. In 1916, Wyoming's neighbor, Montana, elected Jeannette Pickering Rankin as the first woman to serve in the U.S. House of Representatives. Colorado voters changed their state's law in 1893 to permit female suffrage, and were soon joined by their neighbors in Utah, which became a state in 1896 with women's suffrage. The trend seemed inevitable, and in 1919, Congress introduced the Nineteenth Amendment to enfranchise adult women. The states ratified the amendment in 1920. Over the years, one of the most significant impacts of female voting rights has been a corollary increase in the size of government.[78]

Voting rights for women might have come sooner had the issue been restricted to the franchise alone. But activists such as Margaret Sanger from New York City had associated feminism with such controversial practices as birth control and eugenics. Sanger, one of eleven children, was deeply affected by the death of her tubercular mother. Instead of blaming the disease, Sanger blamed the rigors of childbirth for her mother's death. The difficult delivery of her own baby convinced her of the dangers of the birth process and the problems of poverty she associated with large families.

Sanger quickly fell in with New York radicals and met all the important socialists, including Debs, "Big Bill" Haywood, John Reed, Clarence Darrow, Will Durant, and Upton Sinclair. She seemed "supremely unimpressed" by her fellow travelers: in addition to her disparaging remarks about Haywood and her "silk hat radical" reference to Debs, she called Alexander Beckman, a labor organizer, "a hack, armchair socialist—full of hot air but likely little else."[79] Sanger bitterly attacked any fellow travelers, characterizing members of the Socialist Party as "losers, complainers, and perpetual victims—unwilling or unable to do for themselves, much less society at large."[80] What kept her in the good graces of the radical community was her libertine attitude and, above all, her willingness to link socialism to sexual liberation.

After a failed attempt to open an abortion clinic, Sanger published a paper called *The Woman Rebel* that denounced marriage as a "degenerate institution," openly advocated abortion, and endorsed political assassinations.[81] Her writings clearly violated the Comstock Laws, enacted in 1873 to prohibit the transmission of pornography or other obscene materials through the mail, and she was indicted. Rather than submit to jail, Sanger fled to England, where she absorbed the already discredited overpopulation ideas of Malthus. Suddenly she found a way to package birth control in the less offensive wrapping of concern for population pressures. Although relabeling her program as family planning, in reality Sanger associated birth control with population control, particularly among the unfit. The most merciful thing a large family could do to a new baby, she suggested, was to kill it.[82] She attacked charity as enabling the dregs of society to escape natural selection: "My criticism . . . is not directed at the failure of philanthropy, but rather at its success. The dangers inherent in the very idea of humanitarianism and altruism . . . have today produced their full harvest of human waste."[83] Benevolence encouraged the "perpetuation of defectives, delinquents, and dependents."[84] Birth control and sterilization could be used to weed out the poor (and, she noted, blacks and Chinese, whom she likened to a "plague"). She viewed birth control as a means of "weeding out the unfit," aiming at the "creation of a superman."[85]

Founding the *Birth Control Review* in 1917, Sanger published a number of proeugenics articles: "Some Moral Aspects of Eugenics" (June 1920), "The Eugenic Conscience" (February 1921), "The Purpose of Eugenics" (December 1924), "Birth Control and Positive Eugenics" (July 1925), and "Birth Control: The True Eugenics" (August 1928). One of her regular contributors, Norman Hines, repeatedly claimed that Catholic stock (that is, people from predominantly Catholic nations) was inferior to Protestant stock. Perhaps the most outrageous article published in *Birth Control Review* was a favorable book review of Lothrop Stoddard's *The Rising Tide of Color Against White World Supremacy*

(1923)—a book that became a model for fascist eugenics in Europe. Claiming that black children were "destined to be a burden to themselves, to their family, and ultimately to the nation," Sanger revealed herself as a full-fledged racist.[86]

Mainstream feminists recognized the dangers posed by any association with the eugenics movement, and distanced themselves from her views sufficiently enough to ensure passage of the Nineteenth Amendment. Only later would they revive Sanger's positions under the benign-sounding name Planned Parenthood.

The Dark Bargain

By 1920 the United States looked vastly different than it had at the turn of the century. Technology had changed life in dramatic ways; Progressive reforms had affected almost every aspect of daily life; and the large-scale economic reorganization that had started in the 1860s had reached maturity. Although the end of the war brought a large-scale depression in the agricultural sector, the nation nevertheless was perched to spread its wings. However, flight would require a drastic withdrawal from Progressive wartime assumptions and structures in every area of life. Candidate Warren G. Harding would call it a return to normalcy, but regardless of the term, exorbitant tax rates, large government debt, and price fixing would need to go.

Wilson's exit marked the last gasp of Progressivism until, arguably, 1933. That would have surprised many, especially since the polestar of Progressive policy, Prohibition, had just been enacted. Yet the contradictions of Progressivism were precisely what had doomed it as a viable American political theory. Progressives had made a dark bargain with the voters. On the one hand, they sought women's rights, which liberated women (often) to act as men; on the other hand, they sought to constrain liberties across a wide range of economic, social, and behavioral issues. Women could vote, but now they could not drink. They could start businesses, but could not expand those companies lest they fall prey to antitrust fervor. Likewise, men found that Progressive policies had freed them from the dominance of the state legislators when it came to electing their senators, but then they learned that the states lacked the power to insulate them from arbitrary action by the federal government. Voters could recall their judges, but at the cost of allowing them to make tough, unpopular decisions. They could initiate legislation, swamping ballots with scores of legal-sounding and unfathomable proposals. And the income tax, hailed as the measure to redistribute wealth, succeeded only in taking more wealth than ever from those least able to pay it. Small wonder that in 1920 Americans, for the most part, were ready to ditch Progressivism.

CHAPTER FIFTEEN

The Roaring Twenties and the Great Crash, 1920–32

The Twenties Myth

Many recent histories—including textbooks—have developed a mythology about the Roaring Twenties and the Great Crash of 1929. Although it is tempting to call this mythology the Liberal Legend, it would be inaccurate because elements of it have been echoed by conservative historians, most recently Paul Johnson, and to some extent, by libertarian economists like Murray Rothbard. By and large, however, the essentials of this story are the same.[1]

During the 1920s, the story goes, the wild speculation in the stock market led to a maladjustment of wealth on the one hand and too much investment on the other. Average Americans could not buy enough durable goods—autos, radios, and other big ticket items—and as a consequence, sales in automobiles and other manufactured items tailed off. The Federal Reserve Board, in thrall to the Republican probusiness clique, did not curtail bank lending to securities affiliates, as the banks' securities arms were called, until it was too late. Instead, throughout much of the 1920s the Fed actually expanded the money supply, allowing stock prices to soar in a wild orgy of speculation.

At this point in the mythology, Herbert Hoover enters the picture, thoroughly bamboozled by the developments and too uninventive to correct the problems. Lacking the vision of Franklin Roosevelt, Hoover simply allowed things to deteriorate, and he deserved the embarrassment from appellations like "Hoovervilles" (given to tent cities) and "Hoover hankies" (given to empty pockets turned inside out). Unwilling to use the power of the federal government to "fix" the economy, the befuddled Hoover deservedly lost the 1932 election to Franklin Roosevelt, at which point everything improved. Roosevelt's vision and courage, through the creation of the New Deal, led America out of the Depression.

Little of this mythology is true. Consider the notion that the stock market was one gigantic speculative bubble: there is virtually no evidence for that in numerous studies by economic historians. The most any economists come up with is a tiny layer of speculation at the top, one incapable of affecting either stock prices or attitudes toward buying securities.[2] If anything, the market accurately reflected the fantastic growth in American industry. The most rapidly rising stocks in the 1920s had been electric utilities, radios, and autos. Since 1899 industrial use of electricity had zoomed upward by nearly 300 percent. Little else needs to be said about the impact of autos on America's culture and economy. Certainly the auto industry was not indicative of speculation.

In fact, several elements would have had to be present to make a case for speculation. First, people would have had to invest with little or no information about the securities they were purchasing. That has not been demonstrated. Quite the opposite, studies have shown that most investors were well informed, especially about foreign bonds that supposedly had dragged down the large banks. As just one example, Charles E. Merrill, the securities genius who perceived that the markets of the future would lie with the vast middle class, constructed his firm's reputation on accurate and honest appraisals of securities.[3] Second, to make the case for speculation, as John Kenneth Galbraith attempted to do, it has to be shown that the maldistribution of wealth resulted in most of the trading's being conducted by the wealthy. Yet analyses of bond issues of the day showed that a broad cross section of Americans snapped up the latest bonds, with the most prominent occupations of the purchasers being schoolteachers, cabbies, and maids.

But even the notion that the stock market crash caused the Depression itself is egregiously wrong. Although the market may have temporarily reflected a downturn in the economy, the Depression was a confluence of several dramatic shocks (especially the Smoot-Hawley Tariff Act), which were made worse by foolish Federal Reserve Board policies and then rapidly accelerated into the abyss by government attempts to "solve" the problems. We begin to correct the host of thoroughly confused writings about the nation's worst economic episode with an accurate appraisal of the 1920s.

Time Line

1920: Warren Harding elected president

1922: Washington Conference

1923: Harding dies in office; Calvin Coolidge assumes presidency

1923–24: Upheaval in Germany; near collapse of Weimar Republic

1924: Coolidge reelected

1926: Locarno Pact

1928: Kellogg-Briand Treaty; Herbert Hoover elected president

1929: Stock market crash

1930: Smoot-Hawley Tariff passes Congress; Reconstruction Finance Corporation started

1930–32: Bank collapse; money supply contracts by one third

1932: Franklin Roosevelt elected president

Return to Normalcy

Anyone looking at the American economy from 1919 to 1921 might have been completely misled about the future. The end of World War I brought the return of millions of soldiers and sailors to farms and factories in the United States and Europe, and the destruction wreaked by several years of combat had disrupted normal economic activities, fattened the U.S. government, and glutted the job markets. Farmers were especially devastated, with farm prices plummeting after the European farmers—who had been holding rifles instead of hoes just months earlier—abruptly returned to the land. In the United States, the weakening of the agricultural sector, although not in itself debilitating, had severe but largely hidden repercussions.

After 1921, however, the nation made a sharp U-turn. First came a new administration when Warren G. Harding defeated Woodrow Wilson's handpicked successor, James M. Cox. Cox, a Dayton, Ohio, newspaper publisher and governor of Ohio, saw economic activity in a static bureaucratic way. In his view, the high national debt needed for the war had to be paid off by high taxes. He could not have been more wrong. Andrew Mellon, Harding's secretary of the treasury, commissioned a study of why the wealthier classes had paid less and less in taxes as the government raised the tax rate on them repeatedly. He found that high tax rates actually drove money underground. The rich tended to invest abroad rather than build new factories and mills in the United States and then suffer from the 73 percent tax on any income from those investments. At any rate, Cox's misfortune to be with the incumbent party during a recession was not aided in any way by his view that a correction required more of the same. Wilson's League of Nations had proven equally unpopular, and the infirm president could not campaign for his would-be successor.

Oddly enough, Warren Harding (1865–1923), the winner in the 1920 election, would die before the ailing Wilson, whose series of strokes had left him little more than a figurehead during his final months in office. (Wilson hung on until 1924.) Harding had defeated Cox by the largest plurality up to that time in history, 16.1 million to 9.1 million (the electoral college vote was 404 to 127). The election was also notable for the showing of socialist Eugene V. Debs, who, while in jail, had still pulled almost 1 million votes, as he had in 1912 and 1916.

Debs had "run" for office from the hoosegow while Senator Harding essentially campaigned from his home in Marion, Ohio. A self-made man, Harding, like Cox, created a successful newspaper (*The Marion Star*). After his nomination by the Republicans, Harding copied Harrison, campaigning from his Marion front porch and greeting the more than six hundred thousand people who had made the pilgrimage. He invited many reporters to join him in a chew of tobacco or a shot of whiskey. When Harding finally hit the campaign trail, he told a Boston crowd that America needed "not nostrums but normalcy," thus coining the phrase that became his unintended theme. His association with Madison Avenue marketing whiz Albert Lasker led him to introduce state-of-the-art advertising.[4]

Without a doubt, Harding's most astute appointment was Andrew Mellon at Treasury. Mellon, whose Pittsburgh family had generated a fortune from oil and banking, understood business better than any Treasury secretary since Hamilton. After his study of falling tax revenues revealed that the amont of money gleaned from the upper classes had declined with each new rate increase, Mellon concluded that *lowering* the rates on everyone, especially the wealthiest classes, would actually result in their paying more taxes. From 1921 to 1926, Congress reduced rates from 73 percent on the top income earners and 4 percent on the lowest taxpayers to 25 percent and 1.5 percent, respectively, then down even further in 1929. Unexpectedly, to everyone except Mellon, the tax take from the wealthy almost tripled, but the poorer classes saw their share of taxes fall substantially. The nation as a whole benefited as the national debt fell by one third (from $24 billion to $18 billion) in five years.

Mellon's tax policies set the stage for the most amazing growth yet seen in America's already impressive economy. Had Harding appointed a dozen Mellons, he would have been remembered as a great president, but he did not, of course, and many of his appointees were of less than stellar character.

A Scandal for Every Occasion

Self-discipline and trustworthiness proved to be lacking in Harry Daugherty, the attorney general; Charles Forbes of the Veterans Bureau; and Albert Fall, the interior secretary—all of whom either directly or indirectly fleeced the government. Forbes resigned after a scandal in which he sold U.S. veterans hospital supplies to his friends; Fall resigned after the infamous Teapot Dome scandal, during which he granted favorable leases for government oil fields in Elk Hills, California, and Teapot Dome, Wyoming, in return for kickbacks totaling $400,000. Teapot Dome would join Crédit Mobilier as among the worst scandals in American history. It had its origins in a fight over the environment between "developmentalists" and "conservationists."[5] Had the conservationist wing of the Republican Party not become aware of the leases, which it opposed, and thus made a public issue of them, it is unlikely that the newspapers would have picked up on the issue or that the public would have exhibited such outrage. It would not be the last time that environmental issues would color the political debate over economic development.

Any one of the three scandals alone might not have damaged Harding. Taken together, however, the impact tainted his entire administration. Worse, swirling amid those scandals were the suicides of Charles Cramer, the counsel for the Veterans Bureau, and Jess Smith, an associate of Daugherty's. An odor of corruption started to cling to Harding, who, Grant-like, had a knack for appointing crooks and bunglers. Harding commented after the unwelcome publicity that followed one suicide, "I can take care of my enemies all right. But my damned friends . . . they're the ones who keep me walking the floor nights."

In 1923, before any image restoration could occur, Harding died of a heart attack. His successor, Calvin Coolidge, although eminently capable, had altogether the wrong personality for using the public relations machinery of the White House to rebuild his predecessor's image. On the other hand, as historian Robert Maddox concludes, " 'Silent Cal' was in fact the only public figure to come away from the mess with his reputation enhanced."[6]

As part of the twenties myth, Coolidge has been ridiculed as lazy, with one text even claiming that he "spent only about four hours daily on his executive duties," and another offering without qualification that "Coolidge hardly worked at all: he napped in the mornings before lunch, dozed a bit after eating, [and then he] lay down for a few minutes prior to dinner."[7] Yet his work habits reflected the view of government's role in American life, and he also refused to play the public relations game that most politicians practiced. Coolidge had a remarkable ability to refrain from small talk. Known as Silent Cal, Coolidge was once the subject of a bet by two dinner guests: one woman bet another she could get Coolidge to say three words in succession. After several unsuccessful tries, she explained the bet to Coolidge, who said, "You lose." Coolidge may not have been a friend of the elites, and he probably was not the quotable, boisterous type the public had become accustomed to with Roosevelt, but he was thoroughly American.

Literally born on the Fourth of July in 1872, Coolidge grew up on a Vermont farm. A redheaded youngster prone to allergies, Coolidge experienced a constant loneliness that stemmed first from punishments at the hands of his grandmother, then later, in 1890, from the death of his sister Abbie from appendicitis. These and other events contributed to Coolidge's famous shyness and standoffish nature.

Young Coolidge moved off the farm, studied law, and advanced up the ranks in the Massachusetts Republican Party. He became governor of Massachusetts, where he demonstrated his approach to limited government. Explaining that public institutions could never take the place of the private sector and hard work, Coolidge saw self-government as meaning self-support. As Harding's vice president, Coolidge avoided the scandals that had enveloped other members of the administration and remained clean. Appropriately enough, he was asleep at his father's farmhouse the night that a postal messenger arrived with the telegram informing Coolidge that Harding had died, and he needed to take the oath of office immediately. The Coolidge home did not have a telephone, but it did have a notary public (Calvin's father) to administer the oath of office by kerosene lamp. Silent Cal pulled off a silent coup within the GOP itself, effectively overthrowing the old guard in that party that had stood with Harding. In his inaugural address—an astoundingly brief 102 words—Coolidge warned Americans not to expect to build up the weak by pulling down the strong, and not to be in a hurry to legislate. When a business or union endangered the public, however, Coolidge acted with decisiveness and skill. During the 1919 Boston Police strike, the then-governor Coolidge had given the strikers enough rope to hang themselves when public opinion ultimately turned against them. At that point he summoned the National Guard, stating that there was no right to strike "against the public safety at any time."[8] That perspective remained with President Coolidge, and it sent a message to business and consumers that he would protect private property from government confiscation.

Government expenditures plummeted under the Republicans, falling almost to 1916 levels. Outlays remained low under both Harding and Coolidge (though they soared under Herbert Hoover), and even after defense expenditures were factored in, real per capita federal expenditures dropped from $170 per year in 1920 to a low of $70 in 1924, and remained well below $100 until 1930, when they reached $101.[9]

Coolidge's reluctance to involve the government in labor disputes combined with general prosperity to drive down union membership. Unemployment reached the unheard-of low mark of less than 2 percent under Coolidge, and workers, overall, had little to complain about. The AFL's membership dropped by 4 million during the decade, and overall union membership shrank slightly faster. Union leaders shook their heads and complained that affluence and luxury produced by the economy had made unions seem irrelevant. But business had contributed to the weakening of unions as well through a strategy called welfare capitalism, preemptively providing employees with a wide range of benefits without pressure from unions. Government refused to support strikers, and when the Railway Brotherhoods rejected the Railway Labor Board's 12 percent reduction in wages for shop men, the subsequent labor stoppage was met with an injunction from Attorney General Harry Daugherty.

Government's shifting attitude toward workers, which had been increasingly favorable prior to the 1920s, reflected the difficulty of having Washington involved at all in such matters as setting private sector wages. Many such episodes of the government's refusing to act clearly illustrated the central belief during the Harding-Coolidge years that the government should butt out. The Supreme Court largely agreed, ruling on a number of issues related to government interference: whether to impose taxes on "undesirable" products (those manufactured by children), *Bailey v. Drexel Furniture Company* (1922), or to require that companies pay minimum wages, *Adkins v. Children's Hospital* (1923). In so doing, the Court reflected the culture of the day in which children often assumed adult roles in their early teens, and although adolescents were victimized in some instances, the workplace often remained the only path to upward mobility for those who lacked the opportunity to attend college. In addition, the refusal to allow government to set minimum wages for women, far from aiming at depriving women of better-paying jobs, was designed to strengthen the role of the husbands who were primary breadwinners in families.

An Economic (and Cultural) Goliath

Harding's scandals and untimely death did nothing to impede the steadily expanding economy. Both Harding and Coolidge proved to be good friends to business if only because they moved the federal government out of the way of economic growth. The main fact was this: unleashed, and with government playing only a small role in people's everyday affairs, American entrepreneurs produced the most vibrant eight-year burst of manufacturing and innovation in the nation's history. It was a period that easily compared with any other eight-year period at any time, anywhere, including during the Industrial Revolution.

American businesses did more than simply turn out more goods, as is implied by critics of the Roaring Twenties. They fostered an environment that enabled the invention of breakthrough devices and products that fundamentally changed the structure of society, perhaps more than the Industrial Revolution itself. Consider the automobile. Prior to the widespread availability of cars—made possible in large part by Henry Ford's moving assembly line and his keen understanding that what people needed was an affordable automobile—people either walked, took trains, or sailed on ships and riverboats. Auto registration rose from just over 9 million in 1921 to 23 million by 1929, whereas automobile production soared 225 percent during the decade. Ford, of course, had already seen demand for his own product peak prior to the war, when the price of a Ford Model T stood at $345, allowing Ford to sell 734,000 units.

Ford's company already was being eclipsed by a new giant, General Motors (GM), a merger of Chevrolet, Oldsmobile, Buick, Cadillac, Fisher Body, Delco, and other firms. Between 1918 and 1920, William Durant, GM's founder, created a company that could satisfy all tastes (whereas with Ford's Model T, "You could have any color you wanted as long as it was black"). Durant, however, was unable to manage the monster he had created, yielding control to Alfred P. Sloan Jr., who led GM's surge past Ford during the decade. Whether a Ford or a Chevrolet, however, it was irrelevant *which* auto Americans drove. What was important was that they were driving more than ever before, generating an unprecedented demand for a wide variety of related materials—metal, lumber, steel, cotton, leather, paint, rubber, glass, and, of course, gasoline. Production of a vast legion of auxiliary items sparked expansion in those businesses as well as in all the firms needed to supply them. Cement plants, housing construction, gasoline, and spare parts firms grew at a dramatic rate. Moreover, the demand for autos led to a related clamoring on the part of drivers that cities and states build roads. State highway road construction soared tenfold between 1918 and 1930. As politicians moved to meet the public need for roads, often through bond financing, states and municipalities often turned to Wall Street either to supply the capital directly or to place the bond issues.

In ways less visible, though, the auto also encouraged opportunity and occupational freedom never before seen in American history. People were no longer tied to inner-city jobs or to sharecropper farms. Instead, they had hope that good jobs awaited just down the road or in California, which itself became a success story during the decade.

Another new technology, the radio, had also leaped onto the scene. The Radio Corporation of America (RCA) had been formed in 1919 to take over the assets of the American Marconi Company. The new radio medium utilized broadcasting in which the transmitter sent signals out over the airwaves for whoever wanted to pick them up, as opposed to the two-way wireless communication associated with a walkie-talkie. RCA expected that it could make money by providing the broadcasting free and selling the radio sets. In 1920, Westinghouse, one of the RCA partners, applied for the first radio station license, in Pittsburgh, and on November second of that year some five hundred listeners tuned in to coverage of Harding's presidential victory. The following week the first World Series broadcast was heard. By 1922 more than two hundred stations were operating, and radio soon began to feature paid advertisements for products, giving birth to the modern practice of sponsor payment for programming on public airwaves.

Perhaps it was no coincidence that the best-known baseball player of all time, and perhaps the most dominant athlete in any sport at any time in American history, George Herman "Babe" Ruth (1895–1948), captured America's imagination just as radio could broadcast his exploits, among which was setting the record, in 1927, of sixty home runs in a single season. A larger-than-life figure, Ruth not only led all of baseball in both home runs and strikeouts, but according to most contemporary newspaper accounts, he also surpassed any other player in his ability to party all night, carouse, smoke cigars, and then play a doubleheader.[10]

Motion pictures, another new technology, competed with radio as a main source of public entertainment. "Movies" originated with Thomas Edison in the late 1880s, and in 1903 *The Great Train Robbery* became "the first movie with a recognizable plot."[11] Almost a decade later, D. W. Griffith produced *The Birth of a Nation*, about the Civil War, arguably creating the first true modern-era motion picture. But the greatest motion picture director of all, Cecil B. DeMille, captured the grand sweep of the 1920s with his epics *The Ten Commandments* (1923) and *King of Kings* (1927).[12]

Warner Bros., however, provided the decade's key breakthrough when Al Jolson appeared in the first film with a sound track, *The Jazz Singer* (1927). Previously, movies had relied on written text to move the plot along, although posher theaters featured live organists or even orchestras playing along with the screen action. Jolson's breakthrough opened the floodgates for the "talkies," instantly ending the careers of many silent film artists who looked appealing, but sounded bad, and demanding more overall of the actor's craft. With the industry producing up to five hundred movies a year, in a short time Mary Pickford, Douglas Fairbanks, Rudolph Valentino, Charlie Chaplin, and Clara Bow would epitomize the lavish lifestyles and celebrity culture that later was synonymous with Hollywood. Next to *The Jazz Singer*, though, was the other revolutionary motion picture of the decade—this one starring a mouse. Walter Elias "Walt" Disney, an illustrator and animator, had dreamed of producing a full-length motion picture cartoon. He took a giant step toward fulfilling that dream with *Steamboat Willie* in 1928, which introduced the world to a whistling Mickey Mouse. Motion pictures and radios were joined by another new consumer item—the telephone. In 1920, for every 1,000 city dwellers there were 61 telephones; by 1928 the number had risen to 92 per 1,000.[13]

Wets Versus Drys

As the idealism of Prohibition faded, and the reality of crime associated with bootlegging set in, the effort to ban alcohol began to unravel. One reason was that enforcement mechanisms were pitifully weak. The government had hired only fifteen hundred agents to support local police, compared to the thousand gunmen in Al Capone's employ added to the dozens of other gangs of comparable size. Gunplay and violence, as law enforcement agents tried to shut down bootlegging operations, led to countless deaths. Intergang warfare killed hundreds in Chicago alone between 1920 and 1927. By some estimates, the number of bootleggers and illegal saloons went up after Prohibition. Washington, D.C., and Boston both saw the stratospheric increase in the number of liquor joints. Kansas, the origin of the dry movement, did not have a town where alcohol could not be obtained, at least according to an expert witness before the House Judiciary Committee.[14]

The leadership of the early Prohibition movement included many famous women, such as Carry Nation, who were concerned with protecting the nuclear family from the assault by liquor and prostitution. She was wrong in her assessment of the problem. Far from protecting women by improving the character of men, Prohibition perversely led women down to the saloon. Cocktails, especially, were in vogue among these "liberated" women, who, like their reformer sisters, came from the ranks of the well-to-do.

Liquor spread through organized crime into the hands (or bellies) of the lower classes only gradually in the 1920s, eventually entering into the political arena with the presidential campaign of Al Smith. By that time, much of the support for Prohibition had disappeared because several factors had coalesced to destroy the dry coalition. First, the drys lost some of their flexible and dynamic leaders, who in turn were replaced with more dogmatic and less imaginative types. Second, dry politicians, who were already in power, bore much of the blame for the economic fallout associated with the market crash in 1929. Third, public tastes had shifted (literally in some cases) to accommodate the new freedom of the age represented by the automobile and the radio. Restricting individual choices about anything did not fit well with those new icons. Finally, states chafed under federal laws. Above all, the liquor industry pumped massive resources into the repeal campaign, obtaining a "monopoly on . . . press coverage by providing reporters with reliable—and constant—information."[15] By the late 1920s and early 1930s, "it was unusual to find a story about prohibition in small local papers that did not have its origin with the [anti-Prohibition forces]."[16]

Not to be discounted, either, was the fact that the intelligentsia turned against Prohibition. Neo-Freudians—the rage in psychology circles—scorned the reformers, in sharp contrast to the pre–World War I sympathy they'd enjoyed in intellectual circles. Psychologists now saw Progressive reformers as sexually repressed meddlers.

All of these factors led toward the inexorable repeal of Prohibition with the

Twenty-first Amendment in 1933. Still, for history written since the 1960s, where an open society was deemed the highest good and any restrictions on personal freedom were viewed as inherently autocratic, Prohibition left a more mixed legacy than is commonly portrayed. In the first place, it was not designed to stop private individuals from drinking, but only to eliminate the source of (as the reformers saw it) evil and misery, the saloon. Moreover, historians have displayed a nearly irresistible urge to saddle white rural Protestants with Prohibition, despite its female, upper- to upper-middle-class urban origins. A concurrent lack of attention was given to the measurable results of Prohibition. The U.S. Department of Health, Education and Welfare, for example, prepared a report called "Alcohol and Health" in 1971, which showed that per capita consumption of alcoholic beverages fell by at least 40 percent in 1920, marking a permanent reduction in drinking.[17] Economist Clark Warburton's 1932 study analyzed a wide array of data, all of which were refined further by other economists in 1948. The conclusion of these studies was that alcohol consumption declined by 30 to 50 percent, or roughly what the 1971 HEW report had claimed.

Other benefits of Prohibition are overstated. Arrests for public drunkenness fell, leading to lower public expenses for dealing with drunks; the rates of alcoholic psychoses fell; and medical problems related to drinking in almost every category plummeted so much that medical journals scarcely mentioned it as a public health problem.[18] Yet these statistics ignored a lag time of disease—especially illnesses such as psychoses and liver problems, which are cumulative and would not have shown up until the late 1920s, if then.

What about the crime wave associated with Prohibition? Norman Clark points out, "There is no reason to suppose that the speakeasy . . . in any quantifiable way, replaced the saloon. In fact . . . most Americans outside the larger cities never knew a bootlegger, never saw a speakeasy, and would not have known where to look for one."[19] Federal expenditures for law enforcement rose at an annual rate of 17.5 percent during the Prohibition years, with liquor-related enforcement costs exceeding budgets and revenues from licenses every year.[20] Defenders of Prohibition argued that crime was growing anyway, and that gambling, not liquor, remained organized crime's major money source. Prohibition may have accelerated the rise of the gangsters, but it did not cause the rise of organized crime.

Prohibition therefore provided ammunition for both sides of the public health debate in subsequent generations; thus it usually came down to issues about personal rights. Critics pointed to its later failures; supporters, to its early successes.

Bulls and . . . Bulls

Prohibition's social sideshow had little effect on the continued technological advances of the twenties and their spillover effect on the stock market and the American economy. Improved productivity in the brokerage and investment firms expanded their ability to provide capital for the growing number of auto factories, glassworks, cement plants, tire manufacturers, and dozens of other complementary enterprises. Moreover, both traditional manufacturing and the new industries of radio, movies, finance, and telephones all required electricity. With electric power applied as never before, the utilities industries also witnessed a boom. In 1899, for example, electrical motors accounted for only 5 percent of all the installed horsepower in the United States, but thirty years later electrical power accounted for 80 percent of the installed horsepower. One estimate found that electricity could increase productivity on a given task by two thirds.

That automobile/electrical nexus probably would have sustained the Great Bull Market by itself; but added to it were several other unrelated industries, including radio broadcasters, who reached 7.5 million sets by 1928. Radio broadcasting stood uniquely among all industries in that it depended entirely on advertising for its sustenance. Advertising revenues on radio had accounted for $350 million by the middle of the decade, reflecting the growing power of Madison Avenue and professional advertising. For the first time, advertising and professional marketing entered the mainstream of American society, shucking the aura of hucksterism associated with P. T. Barnum.

All this growth, energy, and American industrial success alarmed the Europeans. In 1927 at the International Economic Conference in Geneva, which met at the behest of the French, proposals were put forward for "an economic League of Nations whose long-term goal . . . is the creation of a United States of Europe." This was, according to the chairman, "the sole economic formula which can effectively fight against the United States of America."[21] English writer J. B. Priestley complained a few years later that British roads "only differ in a few minor details from a few thousand such roads in the United States, where the same toothpastes and soaps and gramophone records are being sold, the very same films are being shown [here]."[22] Europeans seemed uniformly wary of the rising American economic might, with books such as *America Coming of Age* (1927) warning of the rising giant across the Atlantic. We should not discount these reactions, because they underscored the fact that the U.S. economy was robust and reinforced evidence that the stock market boom was not an illusion.

Rather than a frenzy of speculation, the Great Bull Market reflected the fantastic growth in genuine production, which did not fall; consequently, stocks did not fall either. Using an index of common stock prices for the year 1900 equaling 100, the index topped 130 in 1922, 140 in 1924, 320 in 1928, and 423 in October 1929. Individual stocks refused to go down. Radio Corporation of America (RCA) never paid a single dividend, yet its stock went from $85 a share to $289 in 1928 alone. General Motors stock that was worth $25,000 in 1921 was valued at $1 million in 1929. Was that all speculation? It is doubtful: GM produced $200 million in profits in 1929 alone; and electricity, which was ubiquitous by 1925, promised only steady gains in utilities securities.

Certainly the securities firms gave the market a push whenever possible, mostly through margin sales in which an individual could put down as little as 10 percent early in the decade to purchase stock, using the stock itself as collateral for the 90 percent borrowed from the broker. By middecade, most firms had raised their margins to 15 percent, yet margin buying continued to accelerate, going from $1 billion in 1921 to $8 billion in 1929. But it wasn't only the rich investing in the market. In 1900, 15 percent of American families owned stock; by 1929, 28 percent of American families held stock. One analysis of those buying at least fifty shares of stock in one large utility issue showed that the most numerous purchasers, in order, were housekeepers, clerks, factory workers, merchants, chauffeurs and drivers, electricians, mechanics, and foremen—in other words, hardly the wealthy speculators that critics of the twenties would suggest.[23]

The fact that many Americans were better off than they had ever been before deeply disturbed some, partly because the middle class was rapidly closing in on the monied elites. Writers like F. Scott Fitzgerald sneered that Americans had engaged in the "greatest, gaudiest spree in history." Others, employing religious models, viewed the prosperity of the 1920s as a materialist binge that required a disciplinary correction. But the facts of the consumer-durables revolution reflected both the width and depth of the wealth explosion: by 1928, American homes had 15 million irons, 6.8 million vacuum cleaners, 5 million washers, 4.5 million toasters, and 750,000 electric refrigerators. Housing construction reached record levels, beginning in 1920, when the United States embarked on the longest building boom in history. By the middle of the decade, more than 11 million families had acquired homes, three fourths of which had electrical power by 1930. During the 1920s, total electrical-product sales had increased to $2.4 billion. Per capita income had increased from $522 to $716 between 1921 and 1929 in real terms, and such a rising tide of affluence allowed people to save and invest as never before, acquiring such instruments of savings as life insurance policies.

Indeed, the notion—first offered by John Maynard Keynes in his *General Theory of Employment, Interest, and Money* (1936) and later championed by John Kenneth Galbraith in *The Great Crash* (1955)—that consumer purchasing fell behind the productivity increases, causing a glut of goods late in the decade, doesn't wash. In 1921 the consumer share of GNP was $54 billion, and it quickly rose to $73 billion, adding 5 percent at a time when consumer prices were falling. It gave consumers the available cash to own not only stocks and bonds, but also to control five sixths of the world's production of autos—one car for every five people in America—and allowed a growing number of people to engage in travel by air. In 1920 there were only 40,000 air passengers, but by 1930 the number had leaped to 417,000, and it shot up again, to 3.1 million, by 1940.

The soaring level of investment in securities and the business boom fostered the legend that both Harding and Coolidge were rabid probusiness types. Attackers have especially, and selectively, repeated Coolidge's comment that "the business of America is business" and his suggestion that "the man who builds a factory builds a temple." What did Coolidge *really* say about business when all of his comments were put into context? "We live in an age of . . . abounding accumulation of material things. These did not create our Declaration. Our Declaration created them. *The things of the spirit come first.*"[24]

Criticized by historian Arthur Schlesinger Jr., who served as the "court historian" for Franklin Roosevelt and John Kennedy, as wanting a "business government," Coolidge in fact said that America needed a government that "will understand business. I mean a government able to establish the best possible relations between the people in their business capacity and the people in their social capacity."[25]

Silent Cal had a few weaknesses, including his intolerance for the insubordinate (but ultimately accurate) predictions of Colonel Billy Mitchell and his support of tariffs. Overall, though, it was Coolidge's moral compass and self-control over executive power that allowed the bulls to dominate Wall Street. Contributing to the Great Bull Market, however, were successful foreign policies that also helped usher in a decade of peace that contributed to the prosperity.

A "Tornado of Cheering"

Following the Great War—the worst war in human history up to that point—few nations had the resources or the desire to fan even the smallest embers of conflict. The Republican administrations sought to go even further, however, by ensuring peace through active negotiations to limit weapons, encouraging discussions among the former enemies, and assisting the German Weimar Republic when it experienced rampant inflation in the mid-1920s. These were not isolationist positions in the least, nor did they characterize small-government views associated with the Republicans, especially when it came to the German question.

Germany, saddled with tremendous (and, in many ways, unreasonable) war reparation debts from World War I, had been consigned to a form of national servitude to Britain and France after the conflict. Among other penalties, Germany had to provide France with thousands of locomotives and railroad cars, free, and give to Britain hundreds of thousands of tons of shipping—again, at no cost. Because the Treaty of Versailles demanded that Germany pay billions of marks to France, Germany simply devalued the mark and printed currency in geometric increments, handing the French, in essence, worthless money. When the French converted the marks into francs and then shipped the converted marks back home to Germany, hyperinflation ensued. In a matter of months, German currency plummeted to such lows in value that people burned money in fireplaces and stoves because it was cheaper than using the money to buy wood.

France moved in to take over German industries in the Ruhr Valley, and tensions escalated. Fearing another war, the United States devised a 1924 plan implemented by Charles G. Dawes. A banker who had coordinated procurement in Europe during the war, Dawes had become a household name following his kinetic postwar testimony before Congress. Grilled about paying top dollar for supplies, Dawes leaped from the witness chair, shouting "Helen Maria! I would have paid horse prices for sheep, if sheep could have pulled artillery to the front!"[26] When the wire services carried the line, they garbled the "Helen Maria" phrase— a Nebraska farm saying—so it read "Hell 'n' Maria." Dawes quickly became an icon in American pop culture. Such a man was perfect to head the committee to untangle the reparations mess. Coolidge, admonishing the members before they left, said, "Just remember that you are Americans!"[27]

By April 1924, the Dawes committee had completed its work. It proposed that German reparations be lowered, that the Deutschemark be pegged to the gold-based American dollar, that half of future reparations come from taxes, and that the United States lend Germany some of the money to get back on its feet. Dawes thus defused the situation, sharing the Nobel Peace Prize the following year with Sir Josiah Stamp, another member of the delegation (who had done the number crunching). The Dawes Plan perhaps staved off war, and certainly the loans returned to American business to purchase U.S. products.[28]

Concerns over naval power also dominated postwar policy. After the war, Congress had refused to continue to appropriate money for the Naval Act, which would have created the largest fleet in the world. Secretary of State Charles Evans Hughes rightly saw naval affairs as the most critical elements of America's near-term security. No nation in the world could have launched air attacks on the United States in the 1920s, and landing any ground troops would have required an armada as yet unseen in human history. Increasingly, however, America depended on trade, and any threat to U.S. trade routes concerned Washington.

Delegates from the major naval powers of the world were invited to a conference in Washington in 1921. Hughes directed the tenor and direction of the meeting toward arms limitations, especially on what some had called "the ultimate weapon," the battleship. Like many arms control agreements that followed, the Five Power Pact that emerged from the Washington conference relied on maintaining rough equality of weapons among the participants, enforcing a sort of balance of terror. Signatories agreed to limits on the tonnage (that is, tons of water displaced as an indicator of the size, and often type, of ship) each nation would build. For every 525,000 tons of capital ships the United States built, England could build the same amount; Japan could build 315,000 tons; and France and Italy, 175,000 tons each. Over time, the agreement came to be referred to by a sort of shorthand reference to the tonnage limitations, namely the 5-5-3 ratio. Moreover, Hughes urged the delegates to cancel production entirely on all those battleships currently under construction.

Met with a "tornado of cheering" as "delegates whooped and embraced," the agreement was a typically utopian and wrongheaded approach to maintaining peace.[29] Nations indeed limited the *tonnage* of ships, but instantly cheated by changing both the character and lethality of such vessels. On the one hand, they shifted production to a newer ship type that would soon prove far more potent, the aircraft carrier (which had not been covered in the agreement), and on the other, they simply installed more, and bigger, guns on existing platforms. Indeed, many of the Japanese carriers that struck Pearl Harbor were battleship hulls converted in the wake of the Washington agreements and retrofitted with carrier decks. And it was no accident that the size of long-range guns mounted on existing battleships and cruisers increased, from twelve to fourteen inches aboard the USS *Arizona*, sunk at Pearl Harbor, to the sixteen-inch guns of the USS *Missouri* and the eighteen-inch guns of the German superbattleships *Bismarck* and *Tirpiz*. Japan topped everyone with its massive battleships *Yamato* and *Musashi*, each featuring nine eighteen-inch guns. All nations reinvigorated their submarine programs as well. Thus the Washington conference had the ironic effect of encouraging the development of two new weapons—the carrier and the submarine—that would prove far more effective than the increasingly obsolete battleships the treaties sought to control.

Few paid any attention to such realities. The euphoria of arms control reached its absurd conclusion in 1928 with the Kellogg-Briand pact (named for Frank Kellogg, U.S. secretary of state, and Aristide Briand, French foreign minister), which outlawed war. War was now illegal! One wonders if the delegates had considered repealing the law of gravity while they were at it. The ink on this incredible document, signed with a foot-long pen of gold, remained dry for scarcely a decade before Adolf Hitler plunged the world into the most catastrophic war in human history.

Coolidge refused to be sucked into the orbit of the "outlawrists." He did not oppose arms limitations on general grounds, but rather doubted that the European powers would limit their own numbers of ships in any significant way. He had the luxury of knowing that in a practical sense, the *only* way the United States was vulnerable to a direct attack was by sea, and therefore American security could be achieved by reducing the ability of others to build capital ships. Coolidge also saw the potential for arms reductions to further limit the size of government expenditures and thus the size of government—something he always considered worthwhile.

Significantly, after a brief foray into an international arms reduction agreement in 1926–27, Coolidge realized that foreign powers were not about to sacrifice any advantages they held. In 1927 he therefore recommended a nine-year naval development program, and although he "never completely surrendered hope that the powers could . . . restrict their sea strength . . . he could take no chances with his country's defenses."[30] It was vintage Coolidge: reduce government, promote peace, but protect yourself and stand firm when necessary.

The New Deal Writ Small

Coolidge could have stood for reelection, but he chose not to. In his *Autobiography*, he pointed to the fact that presidents who served eight years were not effective in the latter parts of their term. Some suspect Coolidge sensed that an economic downturn lay ahead. Still others point to odd statements by Coolidge, whose son died in 1924 of an infected blister on his foot, suggesting the president believed his death was some sort of spiritual "price exacted for occupying the White House."[31] Whatever the reason, with typical Coolidge brusqueness, during a press conference, the president quietly marched down a line of newsmen, handing them each a little strip of paper with the words, "I do not choose to run for President in nineteen twenty-eight."[32]

His successor, Herbert Clark Hoover (1874–1964), could not have been more different from Silent Cal. The secretary of commerce who had headed the Food Administration during the First World War, Hoover represented the latest in a long line of Republican Progressives whom Coolidge despised. Hoover thus inherited the Teddy Roosevelt/William Howard Taft wing of the Republican Party. In some ways, this progressivism, especially as exhibited by Hoover, was a type of devout religiosity, with an emphasis on perfection of this world, as opposed to the traditional Christianity practiced by Coolidge, with its presumption of man's sinful nature.

Certainly, Hoover *was* religious. He was born of Iowa Quaker stock, and his church training stayed with him to the point where he refused to play in Harding's White House poker games. Far from being conservative in the nineteenth-century sense of the word, Hoover's views entitled him to be described by one biographer as a "forgotten Progressive."[33] He displayed his "forward-looking" views across a wide spectrum of policies, telling his confidants that he wanted "very much to appoint a woman to a distinguished position" only a decade after women had received the franchise, adding, "if I could find a distinguished woman to appoint." His policies anticipated most aspects of Franklin Roosevelt's New Deal Depression remedies.[34]

Of course, many of the comments hailing Hoover as a Progressive come from a liberal historical school that endorsed the expansion of government, and by any yardstick, Hoover was a big-government type. The Department of Commerce increased its bureaucracy under Hoover, growing by more than two thousand employees and $13 million at a time when every other department in government was shrinking. He was the quintessential manager, in both the best and worst senses of the word, coining new phrases and generating streams of new reports. It should not be a surprise that, before running against him in an election, Franklin D. Roosevelt called him "a wonder" and added, "I wish we could make him President. . . . There couldn't be a better one."[35] Those same traits—his obsession with paperwork and bureaucratic forms—caused Coolidge to hold him in contempt, calling him "wonder boy" and noting that Hoover had given him "unsolicited advice for six years, all of it bad."[36] Hoover was too entrenched to kick out, but Silent Cal had scarcely said a good word about him, even during the campaign.[37]

Hoover's work with the bureaucracy took his natural affinity for capitalism and seasoned it with a dose of corporatism, the notion that large-scale planned organizations could direct outcomes better than a laissez-faire method. But perhaps a better word for describing Hoover's approach to government than "corporatism"—which often suggested a form of Benito Mussolini's fascism—was "activism" or even a revival of the old mercantilist view of the world. As commerce secretary, he sought to "rationalize" the coal industry, an approach that would have horrified Lincoln or Jefferson. He concocted a scheme reminiscent of Albert Gallatin's inland waterway plan, proposing a "comprehensive system of inland waterways that would aid the farmer."[38] These private/public "cooperation" policies allowed biographers to claim that Hoover's presidency incorporated "a philosophy of individualism through the coordination of capital, government, and labor."[39]

Despite his willingness to employ the federal government to solve problems, Hoover's name, especially after the Depression, was almost exclusively associated with "rugged individualism" in a negative sense. As the economic collapse deepened, people assumed he did not care for their plight, despite the fact that he had pushed federal involvement in the private sector to unprecedented peacetime levels. It did not help that he had written a book called *American Individualism* in 1922.[40] Unlike Coolidge, who had no compunction about allowing a recession to lower wages, Hoover saw high wages as critical to maintaining prosperity. In that respect, he displayed the classic Keynesian approach to economics that would soon captivate policy makers in the West: demand was what counted, not supply.

Hoover won in 1928 because of Coolidge's peace and prosperity—always a tough row to hoe for a political opponent. The opponent, Democratic candidate Alfred E. Smith, governor of New York, represented the growing anti-Prohibition movement. Smith, a Catholic, suffered from anti-Catholic prejudices and the American distrust of New York urbanites, which helped Hoover, as did his Quaker moralism and his seeming concern for common Americans. "A chicken for every pot and a car for every garage," he intoned, and the press that he had carefully cultivated carried his proclamations with enthusiasm. Major newspapers endorsed him wholeheartedly. Some of their commentary seems absurd, given the scorn the nation heaped on him just four years later: he was called the "most useful American citizen now alive," "a new force in economic and social life," associated with unfailing integrity, and even "a genius."[41] In some ways, Smith held positions more conservative (and more in line with Harding and Coolidge) than did Hoover: he opposed government interference with business and the rising expenditures of federal agencies, and he favored restraining or cutting back the Washington bureaucracy.

More Americans voted in the presidential election of 1928 than ever before (67.5 percent of those eligible), and Hoover won in a landslide, 444 electoral votes to Smith's 87, racking up more than 21.3 million popular votes in the process. Yet Smith virtually swept the big cities—St. Louis, Cleveland, San Francisco, New York, Boston, Philadelphia, Chicago, Detroit, and so on—laying the groundwork for the Roosevelt coalition four years later. It marked the first time in the twentieth century that the big urban areas went overwhelmingly Democratic, a position they had not relinquished by the year 2000.

From the hindsight of nearly seventy years, it would appear that when Hoover was inaugurated in 1929, he had jumped behind the wheel of a flaming gasoline truck with no brakes headed over a cliff. But only in hindsight. Hoover's perspective was that he had the opportunity to end the business cycle once and for all—to use the tools of government to manage minor dips and hiccups. Given the emphasis on planning, could not any obstacle be overcome? With enough information, could not even the economy be controlled?

Crash and Depression

On October 29, 1929, the economy just dropped off the table. Or so the story goes. In fact, several sectors of the economy had experienced slow growth or even stagnation in the 1920s. Then there was the Federal Reserve, which failed to expand the money supply at a pace that would support the growth over the long haul. The slow drain caused by the weakened agricultural sector had started to afflict the financial structure. Manufacturing indices started a natural slowdown by mid-1928. These rather hidden factors were greatly exacerbated by the Smoot-Hawley Tariff; then, once the crash occurred, the government made almost every poor policy decision possible.

Farming had never recovered from the end of World War I. By 1927, farm bankruptcies stood at about 1.8 per 100, a rate lower than all American businesses. And farm income averaged $7 billion from 1923 to 1929, after averaging only $4.6 billion during the boom of World War I.[42] Only later, in the midst of the Depression, did economist Joseph S. Davis observe that "in retrospect, in the light of revised data and a truer perspective, [the mid- to late-1920s] should properly be regarded as moderately prosperous and relatively normal for agriculture."[43] Much anxiety came from the so-called parity formula developed by the U.S. Department of Agriculture and pushed by a pair of farm industrialists, George N. Peek and Hugh S. Johnson of Moline, Illinois. They sought to maintain a relationship between the prices of farm and nonfarm goods. The idea was deeply flawed in that no fixed relationships exist between *any* goods or services, but rather are always subject to laws of supply and demand. Worse, not only did the USDA's parity formula understate farm income, it also failed to take into account the revolution in mechanical motorized farm equipment, which essentially combined the genius of Henry Ford, John Deere, and Cyrus McCormick. That equipment tended to increase production as farmers plowed far more land, which was good, but depressed prices, which was a continued source of concern. American farmers could overcome price declines with higher overall sales, but that required open markets, and increasingly the Europeans had erected tariff barriers to imported goods that limited American agriculture's foreign sales.

The drop in agricultural prices gave the impression that farms in general were in trouble when that was not true, but added to the price decline came several natural shocks that destroyed the livestock and farm economies of several specific regions. Wyoming experienced such a terrible winter in the mid-1920s that bankbooks literally froze in their cabinets and livestock herds were decimated. As the collateral for livestock loans disappeared, banks in agricultural sectors started to struggle, with many of them closing. A similar set of natural weather and insect phenomena struck the Deep South, destroying huge swaths of rice and cotton farms. Coolidge resisted McNary-Haugenism, a movement named for the sponsors of several bills (Senator Charles L. McNary of Oregon and Representative Gilbert N. Haugen of Iowa) to have the government purchase surplus agricultural production to maintain the parity prices. He vetoed two such bills, arguing that they would encourage one-crop farming, and he made the vetoes stick.

Pockets where farming was collapsing, especially in the Midwest, certainly weakened the banking system by saddling banks with a mountain of bad debts. Bank distress then contributed to the second problem that developed in the 1920s, namely, the slow growth of the money supply. Although no nationally known banks failed before 1930, state banks in the West and South had failed in droves in the decade. Many of those institutions had small, even minuscule, capital, and they passed away without notice. But just as banks "create" money through fractional reserve banking when people make deposits, the banking system "destroys" money when banks fail. The Federal Reserve should have deliberately offset those failures—and the contraction of the money supply caused by them—by reducing the interest rate it charged member banks and making it easier for banks to borrow money. Yet it did not: quite the opposite, the Fed had not even been keeping up with the growth indicators of industry, regardless of the drain posed by the agricultural sector.

The nation's money supply, contrary to the claims of many economists and historians, simply failed to keep up with output. One reason even conservative historians like Paul Johnson and mainstream textbook writers have failed to discern this fact is that, once again, they have become obsessed with stock prices. This even led the conservative writer Paul Johnson to claim that the market was "pure speculation, calculated on the assumption that capital gains would continue to be made indefinitely."[44] Many authors cite the price of RCA stock, which went from $85 to $420 a share in 1928, with Johnson noting that RCA had not paid a dividend. But Carnegie Steel had never paid a dividend either when its value had soared fifty years earlier. Radio sales had expanded far faster than stock prices rose, and an argument could be made that RCA stock was still *undervalued* even after its spectacular rise. At any rate, securities provided only one snapshot of the economy, whereas the money supply touched everyone from the dockworker to the dentist, and from the typist to the tycoon. As the availability of loans shrank, business had less cash with which to continue to grow.

That was seen in a third factor, the slowing of the manufacturing sector in mid-1928. Contrary to demand-side economists like John Kenneth Galbraith and the renowned John Maynard Keynes, demand did not disappear in the late 1920s, and wages remained high enough to purchase most of the vast number of new conveniences or entertainments. But firms could not add new production facilities without bank loans, which, instead of increasing, tightened when the Fed grew concerned about speculation. Members of the Fed's board of governors mistakenly thought banks were funneling depositors' money into the stock market, and further dried up credit, instigating a shrinkage of the money supply that would not stop until 1932, when it had squeezed one dollar in three out of the system. Evidence suggests that corporations sensed the tightening money supply, and cut back in anticipation of further credit contraction.[45]

One factor that can account for the sudden nature of the crash, however, was the Smoot-Hawley Tariff. This tariff increased rates already enacted under the Fordney-McCumber Tariff, by about 20 percent on average, but rates were increased much higher on some specific goods. Obviously, the passage of the tariff in 1930 discredits assertions that it shaped perceptions in late 1929—unless one takes into account the legislative process. Former *Wall Street Journal* writer Jude Wanniski raised the argument in 1978 with his book *The Way the World Works* that uncertainties over the effects of the tariff may have triggered the stock market sell-off.[46] In the 1990s a new generation of scholars interested in trade revisited Wanniski's views, with Robert Archibald and David Feldman finding that the politics of the tariff generated significant business uncertainty, and that the uncertainty began in 1928 (when manufacturing turned down) and grew worse in late 1929.[47]

The timing is crucial. The bill cleared key hurdles in committees in the autumn of 1929, with key votes coming just prior to the Great Crash. Certainly if business leaders became convinced that the tariff, which promised to raise the tax on imports of virtually all items by as much as 30 percent, would drive production costs up, and thus reduce sales, they would have prepared for it as soon as possible. From that perspective, it is entirely possible that expectations that Smoot-Hawley would pass may have caused a massive sell-off in October 1929. And after the crash the worst fears of the Smoot-Hawley opponents came to pass as European nations enacted higher tariffs on American goods, forcing prices on those imports up further and reducing demand. Companies' expectations were, in fact, critical. If companies believed that the tariff would pass, and if they therefore expected hard times in 1930, it stands to reason that among other precautions they would take, firms would increase liquidity by selling off some of their own stock. Such sales alone could have sent dangerous signals to average investors, which then could have sparked the general panic.

Were businesses right to expect problems associated with Smoot-Hawley? Hadn't business interests lobbied for many of the duties that Congress tacked on to the original bill? Business had indeed favored tariffs for decades, but favoring something in general and specifically assessing its impact are completely different. It becomes easier to discover the source of industry's unease from hindsight. Among other things recent research has shown, the tariff reduced imports by 4 to 8 percent in nominal terms, but when deflationary effects are factored in—and it seems that almost everyone in the country except the Federal Reserve understood that some degree of deflation had set in by late 1929—the real decline in trade attributable to Smoot-Hawley accounts for one quarter of the 40 percent decline in imports after 1930.[48]

Other research has shown that changes in trade had a ripple effect throughout the economy, and the tariff alone could have reduced the U.S. GNP by 2 percent in the 1930s. Moreover, "had such tariffs been introduced in any other time period they could have brought about a recession all by themselves."[49] Thus we are left with some fairly obvious conclusions: (1) the Smoot-Hawley Tariff had important disruptive effects; (2) few people knew exactly what form those disruptive effects would take; and (3) unknown to anyone at the time, the Fed made the harmful effects even worse through its policy of deflation. The only link that seems to remain for further research is how much the perceptions of impending chaos affected securities sales prior to the Great Crash.

The combination of concerns about Smoot-Hawley; the need for a real, but not necessarily large, correction; and the rapid sell-off by speculators triggered a sharp decline. On Tuesday, October twenty-ninth, the market traded more than 16 million shares (compared to a normal day's 3 million shares traded), and the indexes fell sharply. For the month of October alone, the New York Stock Exchange (NYSE) dropped almost 40 percent in value. By March, manufacturing orders (which had already slowed nearly a year before) dried up. Enter Herbert Hoover, who now turned a bad, but cyclical, recession into the nation's worst depression.

Hoover Accelerates the Decline

Almost immediately upon assuming office, Hoover tried to prop up farm prices, creating another new federal agency with the Agriculture Marketing Act of 1929. Then he turned his attention to the tariff, where Congress had expanded the number of items in the tariff bill and had also substantially increased rates on many other items. Once the crash hit, the banking crisis followed. When the Bank of the United States in New York failed in 1930, followed by the collapse of Caldwell and Company in Nashville, the sense of panic spread. People pulled out their deposits, and the Fed proved unable or unwilling to break the runs. Indeed, contrary to one of the tenets of its charter, the Fed did not even rescue the bank of the United States.[50]

Hoover did cut taxes, but on an across-the-board basis that made it appear he cared for average Americans, lowering the taxes of a family with an income of $4,000 by two thirds. As a symbol, it may have been laudable, but in substance it offered no incentives to the wealthy to invest in new plants to stimulate hiring. It was, again, a quintessential Keynesian response—addressing demand. For the first time since the war, the 1930 U.S. government ran a deficit, a fact that further destabilized markets. On the other side of the coin, however, Hoover taxed bank checks, which acclerated the decline in the availability of money by penalizing people for writing checks.[51]

Even after the initial panic subsided, the economic downturn continued. Smoot-Hawley made selling goods overseas more difficult than ever; and the public quickly went through the tiny tax cut—whereas a steep cut on the upper tier of taxpayers would have resulted in renewed investment and plant openings, thus more employment. Worse, Hoover never inspired confidence. When the Democrats won the off-term election, taking control of the House, it meant that any consistent policy, even if Hoover had had one, was doomed. As the unemployed and poverty stricken lost their houses and cars, a string of appellations beginning with "Hoover" characterized all aspects of the economic collapse. Shantytowns erected on the outskirts of cities were Hoovervilles, and a broken-down car pulled by a team of horses was dubbed a Hoover Wagon.

The most significant response by the Hoover administration was the Reconstruction Finance Corporation (RFC), created in January 1932. Viewed by Hoover as a temporary measure, the RFC provided $2 billion in funds for financial institutions that were teetering on the brink. Although the RFC made loans (which, for the time, seemed massive) to private businesses, conditions of the loans actually *generated* instability in the firms the RFC sought to save. Federal regulations required publication of the names of businesses and banks receiving RFC loans. Banks, which were in trouble because of the collapse in customer confidence anyway, suffered a terrific blow by public notice that they needed RFC funds. This sent depositors scrambling to remove their money, weakening the banks even further. Despite a doubling of its funding, the RFC was a fatally unsound program.

Having passed a "demand-side" tax cut in June 1932, Hoover then signed the largest peacetime tax increase in history. Whereas the earlier tax cut had proved ineffective because it had dribbled small reductions across too large a population, the tax hike took the form of a sales tax that threatened to further burden already-struggling middle-class and lower-class families. A tax revolt ensued in the House, and when Hoover signed the bill, he further alienated middle America and produced one of the most vibrant tax rebellions since the early national period.[52]

Banks found their positions going from bad to desperate. As banks failed, they "destroyed" money, not only their depositors' accounts, but also whatever new loans those deposits would have supported. Without prompt Fed action, which never came, between 1929 and 1932 the U.S. money supply fell by *one third*. Had no other factors been at work—no Smoot-Hawley, no RFC, no government deficits—this alone would have pushed the economy over the edge.

By 1933, the numbers produced by this comedy of errors were staggering: national unemployment rates reached 25 percent, but within some individual cities, the statistics seemed beyond comprehension. Cleveland reported that 50 percent of its labor force was unemployed; Toledo, 80 percent; and some states even averaged over 40 percent.[53] Because of the dual-edged sword of declining revenues and increasing welfare demands, the burden on the cities pushed many municipalities to the brink. Schools in New York shut down, and teachers in Chicago were owed some $20 million. Private schools, in many cases, failed completely. One government study found that by 1933 some fifteen hundred colleges had gone belly-up, and book sales plummeted. Chicago's library system did not purchase a single book in a year-long period.

Hoover, wedded to the idea of balanced budgets, refused to pay military service bonuses to unemployed veterans of World War I. The bonuses were not due until

1945, but the so-called Bonus Army wanted the money early. When Hoover refused, the vets erected a shack city on the outskirts of Washington. The police shied away from a confrontation, but the U.S. Army under General Douglas MacArthur was called in to disperse the Bonus Army in July 1932. Naturally, MacArthur's actions were portrayed in the popular press as bloodthirsty and overzealous, but in fact the protesters' claims had no basis in law, and their deliberate disruption and drain on the resources of an already depleted D.C. metropolitan area represented an attempt to foist off onto others their own desire for special privileges.

In subsequent decades Hoover would be assailed for his unwillingness to use the powers of government to halt the Depression, but the truth is that his activist policies deepened and prolonged the business downturn. Surprisingly, in subsequent decades, even Republicans came to buy the assertion that Hoover had stood for small government, when in fact he had more in common with Franklin Roosevelt than with Coolidge and Mellon.

Hoover planned to run for reelection, casting a gloom over the Republicans. The Democrats realized that almost any candidate could defeat Hoover in 1932. It happened that they chose the governor of New York, a wealthy man of an elite and established American family with a familiar presidential name. In Franklin Delano Roosevelt, the Democrats did not merely nominate *anybody*, but had instead put forth a formidable candidate. FDR, as he came to be known, was the first U.S. president who had never been obligated to work for a living because of his inherited wealth. After an education at Harvard and Columbia Law School, he served in the New York Senate, then, during World War I, he was the assistant secretary of the navy, where he had served well in organizing the supply efforts for the Allies over the ocean.

Franklin shared with his cousin Teddy the disadvantage of never having had to run or manage a business. He evinced a disdain for commerce; at best he held an aloof attitude toward enterprise and instead developed a penchant for wielding public funds, whether with the navy or as governor of New York. To that end, he had learned how to manipulate patronage better than any politician since Boss Tweed. But FDR also had distinctly admirable characteristics, not the least of which was his personal courage in overcoming polio, which at the time was a permanently crippling disease that frequently put victims in iron lungs to help them breathe. Yet Roosevelt never used his disability for political gain, and whenever possible he kept the disease private after it struck him in 1921.[54]

Tutored privately as a child, he went on to attend Groton prep school. There he absorbed the "social gospel," a milk water socialism combined with social universalism, which was "the belief that it was unfair for anyone to be poor, and that government's task was to eliminate this unfairness by siding with poorer over richer, worker over capitalist."[55] How much of this he really absorbed remains a matter of debate, but in a 1912 speech Roosevelt revived the themes of community over individual, emphasizing a new era of regulation. He proved less adept at managing his marriage to the plain Eleanor Roosevelt, carrying on with a social secretary (Lucy Mercer) as early as 1914. Alice Roosevelt Longworth, Eleanor's acerbic cousin, had actually encouraged the illicit sex, inviting the couple to her home for dinner without Eleanor, noting sympathetically that Franklin "deserved a good time. He was married to Eleanor."[56] By 1918 Eleanor had confirmed her suspicions, discovering letters from Lucy to Franklin in a suitcase, and she offered FDR a divorce. Family and political considerations led him to an arrangement with his wife, wherein he would terminate his meetings with Lucy and keep his hands off Eleanor as well.

After a period of depression, FDR used his rehabilitation from polio to develop qualities he had never had before, including a sense of timing and patience to let political enemies hang themselves. Most of all, his rehabilitation had conferred on him a discipline that he never could have mastered otherwise, committing himself to details and studying public perceptions.

Best known in the context of his fireside chats as president, Roosevelt successfully used radio, beginning with the 1928 nominating speech for Al Smith, which in a manner, he admitted, he directed specifically to the radio audience. One of his most important speeches, during his first run for the presidency, came on the *Lucky Strike Hour*, sponsored by the American Tobacco Company. But it was the fireside chats that allowed Roosevelt to connect with large numbers of Americans. He deliberately slowed his speech to about 120 words per minute, well below that of the 170 words per minute at which most radio orators spoke.[57] Despite an elite northeastern accent, Roosevelt came across as an ordinary American. One summer night in Washington, he asked, on air, "Where's that glass of water?" and, after a brief pause in which he poured and drank the water, said, "My friends, it's very hot here in Washington tonight."[58] Realizing that familiarity breeds contempt, however, FDR carefully spaced his talks in order to avoid losing their effectiveness, aiming for a schedule of one every five or six weeks.

FDR's adroit manipulation of the media became all the more important when combined with his pliable approach to the truth. The Depression, he claimed, stemmed from the "lure of profit," and he decried the "unscrupulous money changers"—warmed-over Populist rhetoric that always played well in tough economic times.[59] He knew, certainly, or at least his advisers must have told him, that it was an arm of government, the Fed, which had tightened money, making the Depression worse. One hardly thinks Roosevelt had the Fed in mind when he spoke of "unscrupulous money changers."

Once he won the nomination, he had an opportunity to solidify the markets and restore at least some confidence in the economy by stating the truth—that many of his policies would simply continue Hoover's. But he would not. Between November and the inauguration, Roosevelt kept silent when a few endorsements of Hoover's policies might have made the difference between continued misery and a recovery. These deceptions illustrated Roosevelt's continued facility with lying. Nor was he above pure hypocrisy: during the campaign, FDR, a man whose presidency would feature by far the largest expansion of the federal government ever, called for a balanced budget and accused Hoover of heading "the greatest spending Administration in . . . all our history [which] has piled bureau on bureau, commission on commission."[60] Honest observers can find little difference between his programs and Hoover's. His own advisers admitted as much. Rexford Tugwell, for example, noted, "We didn't admit it at the time, but practically the whole New Deal was extrapolated from programs that Hoover started."[61]

CHAPTER SIXTEEN

Enlarging the Public Sector, 1932–40

Economic Chaos

In addition to all his natural advantages—the flashy smile, personal courage, and his family name—Franklin Roosevelt also had good old-fashioned luck. After narrowly escaping an assassination attempt in Miami, Roosevelt took the controls of the U.S. government just as repeal of Prohibition had cleared Congress, leading to the slogan, "Beer by Easter." If nothing else, the free flow of alcohol seemed to liven the spirits of the nation. (It also filled the federal coffers, providing new sources of revenue that the Roosevelt administration desperately needed.)

When voters went to the polls in November 1932, they handed Roosevelt a landslide victory, giving him the entire West and South. Roosevelt received 22.8 million votes to Hoover's 15.7 million, a remarkably strong showing for the loser considering the circumstances of the Depression. Roosevelt heaped dishonor on the defeated Hoover, denying him even a Secret Service guard out of town. Congress paid a price as well, having done nothing during the lame-duck session because many members knew the new president would purposely torpedo any actions they took.

In fact, Roosevelt hoped to capitalize on the terrifying collapse of the economy, his own absence of preelection promises, and a timid Congress to bulldoze through a set of policies that fundamentally rearranged the business and welfare foundations of American life. Many of FDR's programs—undertaken under the rubric of a "New Deal" for Americans—came as spur-of-the-moment reactions to the latest crisis. The absence of internal consistency has thus produced confusion over whether there was a single New Deal or two distinct programs that were dramatically different.

Time Line

1932: Roosevelt elected; Japanese aggression in China

1933: The Hundred Days; New Deal legislation passed; Bank Holiday; Prohibition repealed; FDR takes nation off gold standard; National Industrial Recovery Act; Adolf Hitler named Chancellor in Germany

1934: Securities and Exchange Commission established; temporary minimum wage law passed

1935: Glass-Steagall Act; Wagner Act; Works Progress Administration; Social Security program created; Neutrality Act passed

1936: Roosevelt reelected

1937: Rape of Nanking by Japanese troops; U.S. gunboat *Panay* sunk

1938: German expansion in Czechoslovakia; U.S. unemployment soars again

1939: "Golden year" for American cinema; Hitler invades Poland, starting World War II

1940: Roosevelt reelected

1941: Lend-Lease Act passed; Japanese bomb Pearl Harbor; United States declares war on Axis powers

Were There Two New Deals?

Just as a fable developed about business failures causing the stock market collapse and the subsequent recession, a similar tale arose about Roosevelt's New Deal program to rescue America. Although most scholars have maintained that there were two New Deals, not one, they differ on the direction and extent of the changes between the first and second. According to one tradition, Roosevelt came into office with a dramatically different plan from Hoover's "do-nothing-ism," and the president set out to restore health to the American economy by "saving capitalism." However, although the first phase of FDR's master plan—roughly between 1933 and 1935—consisted of adopting a widespread series of measures at the national level that emphasized relief, around 1936 he shifted the legislation toward reform.

Another variant of this theory saw the early measures as designed to keep capitalism afloat, especially the banking legislation, with a deliberate attempt to introduce planning into the economy. Rexford Tugwell subscribed to this interpretation, complaining that conservative elements stifled attempts to centralize control over the economy in the federal government's hands. At the point where FDR had found that more radical redistributions of wealth could not be attained, a second, more conservative New Deal evolved that emphasized piecemeal measures. Generally speaking, the Tugwell interpretation is endorsed by the Left, which suggests that FDR saved capitalism from itself by entrenching a number of regulatory measures and social programs that kept the market economy from its own "excesses."

That there is confusion about how many New Deals there were reflected the utter lack of a blueprint or consistency to Roosevelt's programs. Rather, a single theme underlay all of them, namely that government could and should do things that citizens previously had done themselves. In fact, FDR's policies were haphazard, fluctuating with whichever advisers happened to be on the ascent at the time.

Then Nazi Germany invaded Poland, and many New Dealers realized that in a coming war—if it came—they needed capitalists. World War II in a sense saved the nation from the New Deal by unleashing the power of the private sector to make implements of war—rather than the New Deal saved capitalism.

The two–New Deals interpretation has allowed scholars to deal simultaneously with the relative ineffectiveness of FDR's policies to extricate the nation from the Depression and to explain the contradictions of FDR's first half-dozen years in office.[1] For example, he often claimed that he was committed to a balanced budget, yet he ran what were—and remain to the present, in real terms—all-time record deficits. Those deficits came in spite of the Revenue Act of 1935 that raised the tax rates on the upper classes from the already high level of 59 percent to 75 percent. More than anything, the two New Deals view paralleled the ascendance and decline of different groups within the administration, revealing policy influences on Roosevelt from among a staff who spanned the ideological spectrum.

At the advice of Raymond Moley, a Columbia University professor, Roosevelt sought to raid the nation's universities to produce a "Brain Trust" of intellectuals, then mix in a cross section of business leaders or career politicians from around the country. Moley became FDR's trusted adviser and speechwriter, and he later served in the State Department. Roosevelt's administration also included Texan Jessie H. Jones (head of the Reconstruction Finance Corporation); two Columbia University professors, Rexford Tugwell (assistant secretary of agriculture) and Adolph Berle (a member of the Brain Trust); Arizonan Lewis Douglas (director of the budget); Louis Brandeis (associate justice of the Supreme Court); and Harry Hopkins. Some, such as Budget Director Douglas, were budget balancers, pure and simple. When Roosevelt took the nation off the gold standard, Douglas envisioned waves of inflation sweeping through the country, at which point someone suggested to him that they change the inscription on money from "In God We Trust" to "I Hope That My Redeemer Liveth." Tugwell was an intellectual and scholar who had written on economics. In 1939, summing up his views as the New Deal began, he exposed what he called the "myths" of laissez-faire, stating flatly, "The jig is up. There is no invisible hand. There never was."[2]

Others, such as Jones, who headed the RFC—a New Deal holdover from the Hoover years—were big government activists extolling the efficiencies of government/business partnerships. Still others, like Hugh Johnson, who ran the National Industrial Recovery Agency (NIRA), was an antibusiness bully who threatened corporate leaders who resisted his "voluntary" programs with "a sock right on the nose."[3]

Most of these policy makers subscribed in one way or another to the theories of English economist John Maynard Keynes, whose book *The General Theory of Employment, Interest and Money* had appeared in 1936. Long before Keynes had published the *General Theory*, however, his papers had circulated and his basic premises—that government spending would spur demand and thus pull a nation out of a depression—had thoroughly seasoned the thinking of the Brain Trust members. As Treasury Secretary Henry Morgenthau noted, a number of acolytes already labored within the government to ensure that federal spending was transformed "from a temporary expedient to a permanent instrument of government."[4] Traditionalists, including Morgenthau and Budget Director Douglas, instead argued for cutting government spending to encourage private investment. For weeks (the nature of the crisis had compressed the time available for considering the positions), the two camps fought over Roosevelt's soul, but the president sided with the Keynesians, and the race to spend federal money was on.

Given these disparate influences on Roosevelt, it became possible for sympathetic writers at the time, and to historians subsequently, to portray FDR as either a conservative corporatist intent on saving the free enterprise system through regulation or as a revolutionary who understood the limits of genuine reform. But there is another alternative, namely, that the New Deal—or either of them, if one prefers—had no overarching principles, no long-term vision, no guiding fundamentals, but was rather a reactive network of plans designed to "get" business. Many members of Roosevelt's New Deal Brain Trust could not identify any coherent precepts even years later—certainly nothing of majestic civic virtue or high moral cause. Quite the contrary, whatever clear policies could be identified, such as electric-power policy, the administration's aims were crudely simple: "One objective [of New Deal power policy] was to enlarge the publicly owned sector of the power industry . . . as a means of diminishing private control over the necessities of life."[5]

It did not help that FDR had few business leaders among his advisers. He distrusted them. Roosevelt told Moley that he "had talked to a great many business men, in fact to more . . . than any other President, and that they are generally stupid."[6] Roosevelt cared nothing about the effects of the class warfare that he had started. When Moley questioned how the welfare of the country could be served by "totally discrediting business to the people," he concluded that Roosevelt "was thinking merely in terms of the political advantage to him in creating the impression through the country that he was being unjustly attacked by business men."[7] FDR specifically looked for "high spots" in his speeches to get in "a dig at his enemies." More than by the president's vindictiveness, Moley was "impressed as never before by the utter lack of logic of the man, the scantiness of his precise knowledge of things that he was talking about [and] by the immense and growing egotism that came from his office."[8]

It is true that "the New Dealers shared John Dewey's conviction that organized social intelligence could shape society, and some, like [Adoph] Berle, reflected the hope of the Social Gospel of creating a Kingdom of God on earth."[9]

Roosevelt, however, had enough vision to know that the public would not share in his enthusiasm for many large-scale programs. Tugwell observed that the president engaged in "secret amputation" when it came to introducing programs that might generate opposition: "If you have to do some social reorganizing," Tugwell noted, "you do it as quietly as possible. You play down its implications."[10] Mixing Hooverism with spot emergency measures, applied to selective sectors of the economy, then combining them with stealth social engineering, the New Deal took on a variegated appearance, and perhaps the only thread that ran through it emanated from the Keynesian policy recommendations.

By the time the New Deal got underway, Keynes had already established a spectacular scholarly reputation as well as a talent for turning quick profits in the British stock market. His *General Theory* did not appear until 1936, but Keynes had published the essentials in scholarly studies and white papers that found their way to the United States through academia. They had thoroughly penetrated American economic thinking even while Hoover was in the Oval Office.

Few seemed troubled by the fact that Britain had pursued Keynesian policies with little success for some time prior to Roosevelt's election. Moreover, people pointed to Roosevelt's comments about the need to balance the budget, and his choice of Douglas (a budget balancer par excellence) as budget director, as evidence that Roosevelt never endorsed Keynesian economics. But the deficits told a different story, and between 1932 and 1939, the federal debt—the accumulated deficits—had leaped from $3 billion to $9 billion, and the national debt had soared to real levels unmatched to this day. Insiders with Roosevelt's ear, such as Tugwell, saw the only hope for escaping the Depression as lying with increasing purchasing power on the part of ordinary Americans, not with stimulating business investment.

Thus, the New Deal contained little in the way of a guiding philosophy, except that government should "do something." Equally as important as the lack of direction, virtually all of the New Dealers shared, to one degree or another, a distrust of business and entrepreneurship that they thought had landed the nation in its current distressed condition. Above all, emergency measures needed to be done quickly before opposition could mount to many of these breathtaking challenges to the Constitution.

The Hundred Days

Although many historians characterize the New Deal programs as divided into categories of relief, reform, and recovery, such a neat compartmentalization of the programs clouds the fact that they were passed in haste—occasionally, even frenzy—and that no one in 1933 knew that any of the programs would be effective or politically beneficial. Rather, the Hundred Days especially addressed areas of the economy that seemed to be most distressed. The banking system had to be stabilized, and wages (including farm income) increased. And the only calculated policy Roosevelt had, namely, to somehow restore the morale of the nation, rested almost entirely on intangibles such as public emotion and a willingness to believe change would occur. When FDR addressed the nation in his first inaugural, his comment that "the only thing we have to fear is fear itself" embodied the single most important element of Roosevelt's recovery program, a sense of confidence at the top.

Bolstering optimism was no small task. Roosevelt excelled at projecting a reassurance to the public, and, surprisingly to some, most Americans neither lost hope nor drifted into lethargy.[11] Many of the groups hardest hit—the Okies and African Americans—remained hopeful and sanguine that despite the impediments, a better future lay ahead.

By far, the bank collapse was the most serious threat to the nation. Some 5,500 banks had closed in a three-year period, stimulated by the outflow of gold, which had undergirded the banking structure. Roosevelt immediately called Congress into special session and requested broad executive powers. Even before the session was convened, FDR announced on March 5, 1933, a national bank holiday in which all state and national banks would be closed and then examined. After the examiners found that the banks were solvent, they would be allowed to reopen. Banks that still might be in danger, but which were fundamentally strong, could reopen with government support. Weak banks would be closed. Congress, convening a few days later, approved the measures. The bank holiday, obviously, stopped the runs by closing the banks. In his first fireside chat radio address on March twelfth, Roosevelt reassured the nation that the government had stepped in to protect the banks, and when banks began reopening on the thirteenth, deposits returned, leaving Raymond Moley to pontificate, "Capitalism was saved in eight days."[12]

While not publicly tied to the bank holiday, Roosevelt's most important single act in saving the banking system occurred when he took the United States off the gold standard in April 1933, ending the requirement that all U.S. dollars be converted into gold upon request. Other countries not on the gold standard could convert dollars to gold, but the United States could not convert francs or pound sterling notes to gold. Foreign notes flowed in, then were converted to gold, which flowed out. That destabilized the banks in the most fundamental sense by kicking out from under them the gold reserve that propped them up. By protecting the gold reserves, FDR ended the drain, and quietly and immediately restored viability to the financial structure. All along, the banking/gold destabilization had been a response to government manipulation of market forces in which Europeans sought to gain an advantage by going off gold. If all nations had remained on gold, the market would have gradually reestablished stability; or if none remained on gold the same result would have been achieved. America's bank destabilization occurred in part because *only* the United States continued to honor gold contracts, which was akin to being the only bank in town to remain open during a run, whereupon sooner or later it, too, would run out of money. This single positive action by FDR is widely overlooked.[13]

Over the Hundred Days, FDR unleashed a torrent of presidential initiatives focused mainly on raising wages or providing jobs. Congress turned out the legislation, creating what was referred to as the "alphabet soup" agencies because of the abbreviations of the host of new offices and acts. The Civilian Conservation Corps (CCC) and the Public Works Administration (PWA) both promised to put people (mostly young men) to work in government-paid make-work jobs. The CCC paid boys from the cities to work in the forests planting trees, cutting firebreaks, and in general doing something that would justify the government paying them. Two million jobs were created, and it made great press. As supporters said, Roosevelt sent "boys into the forests to get us out of the woods."

Two Roosevelt Brain Trusters, Harry Hopkins and Harold Ickes, battled for control of the piles of new public monies. Ickes, who headed the PWA, insisted that the jobs involve meaningful work and that they pay a wage that would allow the employees to purchase goods, stimulating consumption. The PWA, therefore, tended toward large-scale public works such as new school buildings, hospitals, city halls, sewage plants, and courthouses. Many of these might have constituted worthwhile additions to the infrastructure under normal circumstances, and perhaps a few genuinely fell in the domain of the public sector. But the necessary tradeoff of taxes for public works was missing. At the same time, schools were closing at a record pace because of the inability of local districts to pay teachers and buy books; and pouring money into courthouses and city halls rekindled memories of the Tweed Ring's abuses. Indeed, had every dollar dumped into public facilities (for which there still existed no funding for the people to *operate* the facilities) remained in private hands, the private sector would have rebounded in a more healthy, but far less flamboyant, way. And grandiose these projects were: the PWA constructed the Lincoln Tunnel, the Triborough Bridge, and linked Florida's mainland with Key West. PWA money also paid for construction of the navy's aircraft carriers *Yorktown* and *Enterprise*.

On the surface, large-scale projects brought some measure of hope and demonstrated that the government was *doing* something—that America was building again. And, no question, the projects were impressive. Yet what could not be seen was that the capital for these projects came from the private sector, where it would have generated a similar amount of economic activity, but activity that was demanded by the market.

But the job not seen is a vote not won, and therefore public activities had to be . . . well, *public*. Harry Hopkins's Works Progress Administration (WPA), which had come out of the Emergency Relief Appropriation Act (1935), extended some of the initiatives of the Civil Works Administration begun a year earlier that had given jobs to some 4 million people. The WPA came about even as Roosevelt warned Congress that welfare was "a narcotic, a subtle destroyer of the human spirit." Yet the WPA generated jobs of far more dubious value than the PWA.[14] There is no question that the WPA (which critics label We Piddle Around) produced benefits in the public sector. By 1940, the WPA could claim a half million miles of roads, 100,000 bridges and public buildings, 18,000 miles of storm drains and sewers, 200 airfields, and other worthwhile projects. It also generated a certain temporary measure of self-respect: unemployed men could look their children in their faces as breadwinners. In an era in which most people took any work seriously, and infused it with pride, even make-work programs had some virtue. But it also built opera houses, hired writers to design travel guides, and paid for traveling circuses.[15]

Over the long haul, however, government's attempt to endow work with true market value proved as futile for Roosevelt's New Dealers as for Robert Owens's utopians in New Harmony or the Brook Farm communalists. The inescapable conclusion was that if a task was valuable, someone in the private sector would have paid to have it done, or, at least, citizens would have imposed taxes on themselves to pay for it in the first place. If Roosevelt's New Dealers thought that they could shift the tax burden for all these projects onto the wealthy, they were wrong. As always, the rich could hide much of their income from taxation. What the Brain Trusters did not take into account was the depressing drain on the overall economy by the disincentives to invest and make profits. Virtually all private investment stopped as industry felt punished.

Another act, designed to work in conjunction with employment measures, the National Industrial Recovery Act (NIRA) of 1933, was directed by the National Recovery Administration (NRA) under the hand of Hugh Johnson. A man given to a robust vocabulary of profanity, Johnson had been a lawyer and businessman as well as a soldier, and was capable of using his dynamic genius and exceptional energy to design and administer large-scale military-style operations such as the NRA. Symbolized by a blue eagle—a bright military badge, to Johnson—the NRA authorized industrial and trade associations to establish production codes (based on a blanket code), set prices and wages, and otherwise collude. The NIRA completely reversed the TR–Taft antitrust legislation, suspending antitrust acts, and recognized (from the federal level) the rights of employees to organize unions and bargain collectively, effectively cementing organized labor as a permanent voting bloc for the Democratic Party.

It was unclear, however, how merely allowing corporations to become larger through nonmarket forces and to fix prices would restore vitality to the system. Eventually the collusive effects of the NIRA sparked intense opposition, especially from small employers, who referred to the Blue Eagle as a Soviet duck or a fascist pigeon, culminating with the Supreme Court's declaring the act unconstitutional in 1935. But in the meantime, it did what most New Deal programs did: it spent money on a large scale. The NRA became so corrupt that Johnson himself persuaded the Senate to name a committee to investigate, headed by the famous attorney Clarence Darrow. The committee's report, delivered in May 1934, called the NRA, among other things, "ghastly," "preposterous," "savage," "wolfish," "monopolistic," and "invasive."[16]

Labor and Leviathan

By that time, however, the Democratic Party realized that it had struck gold in the votes of the labor unions, which it courted even more intensively after 1934, when the midterm elections gave the Democrats an even larger majority. The new House had 322 Democrats to only 103 Republicans and fewer than a dozen third- and fourth-party representatives. The Democrats held more than a two-thirds majority in the Senate as well. It was the closest a single party had come to dominating the government since the Southern Democrats had walked out during secession. Traditional Democratic supporters, such as the unions, saw their opportunity to seize power on a more or less permanent basis, and even the split of the unions in 1935, when John L. Lewis left the older, more established American Federation of Labor, did not damage the Democrats' support with organized labor. Lewis's new union, the Congress of Industrial Organizations (CIO), drew together industrial unions like the United Mine Workers, the Ladies Garment Workers, and the Amalgamated Clothing Workers. In 1934, however, the unions overplayed their hand. A series of violent strikes, many of them initiated by radical elements, resulted in a wave of looting, burning, and general rioting in New York, Philadelphia, and Milwaukee. That was even before the textile workers began a strike of monstrous proportions, slamming shut factory gates in twenty states and setting off armed conflicts when police and troops battled strikers. Roosevelt conveniently was out of the country at the time, arriving home (with his characteristic good fortune) after the strike had ended.

If anything, labor unrest only encouraged the more radical elements of the Democratic Party to press for more extreme demands within their new majority. Many viewed the period after the 1934 elections as a chance to entrench programs that only a decade earlier might have seemed unattainable, locking their party into power for the foreseeable future.[17] Harry Hopkins sensed the critical timing, declaring desperately, "We've got to get everything we want—a works program, social security, wages and hours, everything—now or never."[18] Securing the loyalty of the labor unions was crucial to establishing the Democrats permanently as the majority party; thus the new Congress passed the National Labor Relations Act, known for its author, Robert Wagner of New York, as the Wagner Act, which protected the right to organize unions and prohibited firing union activists. More important, perhaps, Congress established the National Labor Relations Board (NLRB) to bring management and labor together, at least in theory. In practical terms, however, management had to bargain in good faith, meaning that anytime the NLRB decided management was not acting in good faith, it could impose sanctions. The Wagner Act thus threw the entire weight of government behind the unions—a 180-degree turn from the government's position in the late 1800s.

Similar prolabor legislation involved the Fair Labor Standards Act, which established a minimum wage. With the legislators' focus on raising the wages of employees, especially male family heads, little attention was directed at the natural business reaction, which was to trim workforces. More than any other single policy, the minimum wage law cemented unemployment levels that were nearly twice those of 1929, ensuring that many Americans who wanted jobs could not accept any wage offered by industry, but could only work for the approved government wage. After the law, in order to pay minimum wage to a workforce that had previously consisted of ten employees, the employer now could only retain eight. The problem was that *no* set wage level creates wealth; it only reflects it.

Employment recovery represented the industrial side of job relief, whereas raising income in the agricultural sector was the aim of the Agricultural Adjustment Administration (AAA), which sought to drive up prices by restricting farm output. Aimed at addressing the central problem of agriculture in the 1920s—overproduction, which had resulted in lower prices—the AAA subsidized farmers *not* to produce, that is, to restrict production. In one summer southern farmers received funds to plow up 10 million acres of cotton, and midwestern farmers were paid to eliminate 9 million pounds of pork, all at a time when unemployed starving people stood in soup lines. Farm income indeed rose, but only because farmers took the government subsidies *and* kept their production levels up, occasionally double planting on the remaining acreage. Large corporate producers did well in the new system, receiving substantial government checks, with a large sugar company receiving more than $1 million not to produce sugar. But the farm programs worked in favor of the Democrats, adding to the Roosevelt coalition. Even after the Supreme Court declared the AAA unconstitutional, the administration shuffled the subsidies off to existing soil conservation programs, where in one form or another they remained until the 1990s, when Congress finally eliminated most of them.

Still other parts of the Hundred Days incorporated more direct state planning, such as the Tennessee Valley Authority (TVA) Act, which authorized public money for multipurpose dams to generate power for rural areas. The authority would build a 650-mile canal from Knoxville, Tennessee, to Paducah, Kentucky, and marked a further insinuation of government into private markets.

Although most of the recovery efforts could be, and were, justified as necessary to pull the nation out of the Depression, it would be naive to ignore the political implications of the measures, especially for the Democratic Party. With each new government initiative, reliance on the federal government grew, and the party that would promise to maintain, or even expand, government assistance, could count on the votes of large numbers of Americans who saw the opportunity to tax others for their own benefit. Such was the case with the Home Owners' Loan Act of June 1933, in which the government guaranteed home loans. This legislation had the effect of benefiting new home buyers by making it less risky for a lender to extend credit, but it created a new quasi-dependent class of people who assumed it was the government's responsibility to guarantee that everyone could own a home. Supports of this type were expanded under similar Federal

Housing Administration (FHA) and, after World War II, Veterans Administration (VA) loans, all under the guise of making home ownership a right.[19]

All these acts carried the potentially fatal risk that at some point a majority of Americans would see the path to prosperity as running through the government—essentially taking from their neighbors to pad their own pockets—and at that point the game would be up. All politics would disintegrate into a contest of promising to dispense more goodies than the other fellow.

Regardless, the political and economic policies of the New Deal almost without exception created long-term unintended effects that severely damaged the nation (see below, The New Deal: Immediate Goals, Unintended Results). Only a half century later did Americans pay attention to the warnings given by conservatives in the 1930s about the dangers posed by introducing such massively destructive social and economic incentives into American life. In almost every case, the temporary fix offered by the New Deal program resulted in substantial long-term disruptions of labor markets and financial structures and reduced American competitiveness. Whether or not they led to an inflationary state (as some conservatives contend) is unproved, but without question they saddled future generations with mountains of unfunded obligations (like Social Security), and laid the groundwork for destroying the black family through AFDC and other welfare policies.

The New Deal: Immediate Goals, Unintended Results

NEW DEAL PROGRAM	INTENDED EFFECT AND/OR IMMEDIATE RESULT	LONG-TERM EFFECT AFTER 50 YEARS
Civilian Conservation Corps	To provide employment to 2.5 million; address conservation issues.	Negligible. Program ended in 1942.
Agricultural Adjustment Act	To control production; raise prices by offering subsidies to farmers. Farm income rose 51%, but did not return to 1929 levels until 1941.	Farm subsidies raised prices to consumers, benefited large agribusinesses, and encouraged overproduction. In 1995, Congress ended most agricultural subsidies because of cost, inefficiency, and discrimination against both consumers and small farmers. Subsidies on dairy products and sugar remained.
Glass-Steagell Act (1935)	To seperate investment banking (brokerage of stocks and bonds) from	Allowed financial institutions other than banks (e.g., insurance companies) to

	commercial banking (loans, checking, and savings accounts)	compete with banks in a wide range of services, such as checking and insurance; limited American banks' ability to compete in world markets and to diversify.
Tennessee Valley Authority Act	To create the TVA and provide government-subsidized electric power to private citizens.	Developed Tennessee River Valley hydroelectric dams with locks; increased government's intrusion into private sector electric utility operations; fostered monopolies in electric power.
Federal Deposit Insurance Corporation (1934)	To insure all bank deposits up to $5,000 per account; bring stability to the banking system.	Sister agency, Federal Savings and Loan Insurance Corporation (FSLIC), contributed to the collapse of the S&L industry in the 1970s and 1980s by encouraging risky investments by managers and owners. Total tab: $800 billion.
Revenue Act of 1935	To offset huge federal deficits under FDR by enacting huge tax hikes and estate taxes.	Accelerated progressive notions of redistribution by targeting upper classes. Did not offset deficits, but rather ensured that the rich would continue to avoid taxes by being able to move money offshore or purchase tax-free municipal bonds, shifting the real burden onto the poor and middle classes. Concept remained in place until John Kennedy's and Ronald Reagan's cuts, both of which increased the amount paid by the wealthy.
Works Progress Administration (1935)	To create public works jobs for 9 million to construct bridges, sidewalks, art theaters, opera houses, and other projects.	Ended in 1943 during World War II. By 1937, though, unemployment had again soared to 14 million. Many WPA projects were unnecessary economically and often catered to the elites (opera houses, art galleries, etc.) and subsidized via deficits.

Social Security Act (1935)	To provide a supplemental old-age pension and emergency unemployment compensation as well as aid to families with dependent children (AFDC).	Because of cross-generational transfers, the Social Security Trust Fund, while solvent during the baby boom years, is projected to be in severe deficit by 2020, and, depending on the economic conditions, bankrupt not long after that, even according to the most optimistic estimates. The system faces massive overhaul, with higher taxes, lower benefits, or privatization. One result of AFDC was the "illegitimacy explosion" of the 1960s–1970s and was substantially curtailed in 1995 as part of the welfare reform bill.
Fair Labor Standards Act (1934)	To set minimum wages and maximum hours that could be worked; raised wages in industry while reducing employment overall.	New studies suggest this might have prolonged the Great Depression; minimum wage laws in the 1950s and 1960s were closely correlated with minority teenage unemployment at the time, suggesting the laws encouraged discrimination.

Moreover, the New Deal caused a new influx of corporate money into politics unlike anything seen before. What stands out is how little business gave to either political party prior to the Great Depression and the manipulation of the tax code that politicians wrought in an attempt to combat it.[20] Sociologist Michael Webber has conducted a study of the contributions of corporate boards of directors in 1936, finding that region and religion—not class identity—determined who gave how much to either the Democrats or the Republicans. Instead, the lesson corporate donors learned in 1936 was that government had put itself in the position of picking winners and losers in the tax code, making it critical, for the first time, to influence politicians with money.

Social Change in the Great Depression

With the end of Prohibition, the saloon business mushroomed—one of the few growing areas of enterprise in the 1930s. Another growing industry, which served somewhat the same purpose with less destructive physical effects, was motion pictures. Although several studios met with hard times during the Depression, movies became more popular than ever, providing a low-cost way for people to escape reality temporarily. Some 60 to 90 million Americans went to the movies every week, seeing classic stars such as Greta Garbo, Jean Harlow, Clark Gable, Cary Grant, and Joan Crawford, as well as a relatively new use of the silver screen for full-length animated features, pioneered by Walt Disney's *Snow White and the Seven Dwarfs* (1937). Walt Disney Studios, MGM, Warner Bros., and many others cranked out formula pictures from the famous studio system in which a motion picture company signed artists and directors to long-term contracts, making them (in some cases) little more than assembly-line employees. The assembly-line process of making movies led to great names in the industry being shuffled in and out of pictures like the interchangeable bolts and screws in Eli Whitney's factory.

For all its detractors, the studio system attained, at least briefly, a level of quality that has never been matched. Consider the stunning releases of 1939— by far the best year in motion picture history, with no other coming close. Several notable pictures received Academy Award nominations, including *Dark Victory, Of Mice and Men,* and *Wuthering Heights.* At least five of the nominees rank among the greatest films ever to grace the silver screen: *The Wizard of Oz, Stagecoach, Mr. Smith Goes to Washington, Goodbye Mr. Chips,* and, of course, the picture that swept the Academy Awards, *Gone With the Wind.* That year, John Wayne, Judy Garland, Jimmy Stewart, and Clark Gable all appeared in roles that defined their careers. Even B-list movies from that year, such as *Beau Geste,* are considered classics.

Radio broadcasting also reached new heights, with more than 39 million households owning radios by the end of the 1930s. They heard stars like comedians Jack Benny and Edgar Bergen, or listened to adventure shows such as *The Lone Ranger.* Perhaps the event that best demonstrated radio's tremendous influence was Orson Welles's broadcast of "The War of the Worlds" on October 30, 1938, on *The Mercury Theatre on the Air.* The broadcast induced mass panic as Welles convinced thousands of Americans that Martians had landed and had laid waste to major cities in an intergalactic war.

The popularity of radio and movies said much about the desire of Americans to escape from the circumstances of the Depression and also from the relentless criticism of American life that emanated from intellectual circles. Such attacks on American institutions commonly appeared in many of the books deemed classics today, but which inspired few at the time. Chief among the critical writers of the day, John Steinbeck (*Grapes of Wrath,* 1939, and *Tortilla Flat,* 1935) and John Dos Passos (*Adventures of a Young Man,* 1939) won literary acclaim, but the general public passed their books on the way to purchase Margaret Mitchell's *Gone With the Wind* (1936). Americans showed that they needed chicken soup for the soul—stories of courage, hope, and optimism—not another application of leeches or a dose of castor oil masquerading as social commentary.

The First Referendum

After four years of the New Deal, many of the programs had shown positive short-term results. Unemployment had dropped from 12 million to about 8 million; the banking system had been saved; and the panic mentality associated with the stock market crash had ebbed. Most important, Roosevelt's flurry of activity convinced average Americans that he cared about their circumstances, and that the administration was at least trying to solve the nation's economic woes. On the other hand, most of the long-term dangers and structural damage done by New Deal programs remained hidden. Even business still hesitated to attack Roosevelt's statism, which provided a chance for those companies still operating to solidify their hold on the market, free of new competitors. Thus, Roosevelt stood little chance of being unseated by any candidate in 1936. The Republicans ran Alf Landon, governor of Kansas, who all but endorsed Roosevelt with a me-too-only-better attitude, as a sacrificial candidate. Landon was trounced, receiving only the electoral votes of Maine and Vermont.

The Democratic Party completed its remarkable comeback from the depths of Reconstruction by forging a new coalition. Despite the hardships caused by the New Deal's agricultural programs, farmers—especially in the South and West—still remained loyal to the party. Unionized labor's votes were cemented through the minimum wage legislation and the Wagner Act, whereas ethnic groups, such as Italian Catholics and Jews, were enticed by large numbers of political appointments and repelled by memories of the Republicans' Prohibition policies. But the newest group to complete the coalition was comprised of blacks, who had supported the GOP since Reconstruction. The shift of the black vote provided the Democratic Party with its single most loyal constituency well after the millennium. Eleanor Roosevelt, in particular, publicly courted black voters for her husband, and public education programs temporarily provided a stimulus for reducing black illiteracy. New Deal public health programs also proved popular, and Roosevelt's rhetoric, if not his actions, was supportive and sympathetic to black concerns. Republicans, who had essentially abandoned blacks after 1877 and refused to challenge *Plessy*, lost their appeal to black citizens who still labored under strict segregation in parts of the country and blatant racial discrimination virtually everywhere. A combination of blacks, unions, ethnic groups, and big-city intellectual elites ensured Democratic dominance over both houses of Congress for more than forty years, ensuring a total grip on public policy agendas, even when Republican presidents were in office.

Roosevelt's Second Hundred Days promised to exceed the ambitions of the first term, building on the huge congressional majorities and his reelection landslide. The president proposed a new set of radical taxes and redistributionist measures aimed at ending inheritance, penalizing successful corporations, and beginning a steady attack on top-bracket individual fortunes.[21]

It is worth reiterating, however, that New Deal policies were only aimed *in part* at restoring the American economy, just as Reconstruction policies were only directed, in part, at helping the freedmen. One important objective always lurked just below the smooth waters of Roosevelt's rhetoric, and that was the ability of his policies to maintain the Democratic Party in power for the next several generations. Virtually every one of the New Deal programs in some way made people more dependent on government—not more independent, or self-sufficient—and when the government was run by Democrats, the logical conclusion voters had to draw was that whatever they "got" from government "came" from the Democrats. Social Security, farm subsidies, special favors for labor—they all targeted separate groups and played on their specific fears, and all problems were "solved" only through the efforts of Democratic politicians in Washington. Merely to raise the question of whether such policies were wise invited attack at election time, usually in the form of a question to the (usually Republican) opponent: "Why do you want to (fill in the blank with 'take food away from the elderly,' 'keep farmers poor,' and so on)." Roosevelt had created a sea change, therefore, not only in dealing with a national economic crisis, but also by establishing an entirely new political culture of Democratic dominance for decades to come.

The New Deal Stalls

Just as it appeared that the New Deal might enter a higher orbit in the universe of policy making, several events brought the Roosevelt administration down to earth. First, the Supreme Court, with a string of rulings, found that many components of the New Deal, including the NRA, the AAA, and a number of smaller New Deal acts, or state variants of New Deal laws, were unconstitutional. Seeing the Supreme Court as standing athwart the tide of progressive history, FDR found an obscure precedent in the British system that, he thought, allowed him to diminish the relative vote of the four hard-core conservatives on the Supreme Court by simply adding more members—the judicial equivalent of watering down soup. Roosevelt justified his bold attempt by arguing that the justices were overworked, proposing that for every justice of at least ten years' experience over the age of seventy, the president should be allowed to appoint a new one. Here FDR not only alienated many of his congressional supporters, who were themselves in their sixties and seventies, but also positioned himself against the checks-and-balances system of the federal government.

The issue threatened to erode much of Roosevelt's support in Congress until, abruptly, the Supreme Court issued several decisions favorable to the New Deal, and at the same time one of the conservative justices announced his retirement. A more pliable court—in the eyes of the New Dealers—killed the court reform bill before it caused FDR further damage. Over the next three years, Roosevelt appointed five of his own men, all Democrats, to the Supreme Court, making it a true Roosevelt Court and further molding Washington into a one-party town.

Roosevelt was preparing to launch another round of legislation when a second development hammered the administration on the economic front. In 1937, the nation had finally squeaked past the output levels attained before the crash, marking seven years' worth of complete stagnation. Then, suddenly, the business index plummeted, dropping below 1935 levels. Steel production dropped from

80 percent of capacity to below 20 percent, and government deficits shot up despite all-time-high levels of taxation. Some in the Brain Trust rightly perceived that business had been terrorized, but the timing wasn't right. No particular act had just been implemented. What had so frightened industry? The answer was that the cumulative effects of the minimum wage law, the Wagner Act, high taxation, and Keynesian inflationist policies all combined with what now appeared to be unchecked power in FDR's hands. Hearing a new explosion of heated antimonopolist rhetoric by Roosevelt's advisers, business began to question how long it could absorb further punishment. Although in the early 1930s American business had supported some of the relief programs to keep from being the scapegoats of the Depression, by late in the decade, the business community feared that even the most radical social and political reorganization was not beyond consideration by the New Dealers. Assistant Attorney General Robert Jackson singled out by name leading industrialists and criticized their salaries; Harold Ickes charged that "sixty families" sought to establish control over the nation and that the struggle "must be fought through to a finish."[22] Roosevelt's New Dealers had taken Reconstruction-era sectional antagonisms, repackaged them as class envy, and offered them up on an apocalyptic scale that was the Great Depression equivalent of "waving the bloody shirt" or, perhaps more fittingly, waving the unemployment compensation check.

The New Dealers' comments made business more skittish than it already was, and precipitated the Roosevelt recession. Between October 1937 and May 1938, WPA relief rolls in the auto towns in the Midwest swelled, increasing 194 percent in Toledo and 434 percent in Detroit. St. Louis, Cleveland, Omaha, and Chicago all eliminated or drastically curtailed welfare and unemployment payments. Nationally, unemployment rose from near 12 percent back to 19 percent. The ranks of organizations like the National Association of Manufacturers, which opposed the New Deal, started to swell. Roosevelt, nevertheless, remarked, "We are on our way back . . . we planned it that way."[23] What FDR did not understand was that although many people accepted some New Deal programs as necessary, they saw them as only *temporary* expedients. Meanwhile, "the New Dealers were never able to develop an adequate reform ideology to challenge the business rhetoricians."[24] A third shift against the New Deal came at the ballot box. The public grew concerned enough about the unchecked power of the Democrats that in the 1938 midterm elections the Republicans picked up eighty-one seats in the House, eight in the Senate, and thirteen governorships. It was a stinging rebuke to New Deal excesses and was achieved despite the fact that the Democrats had started to call in their patronage markers. This meshing of politics and jobs during the 1938 congressional elections raised another unsettling aspect of the New Deal. Allegations that WPA funds had been used in a Kentucky campaign prompted a Senate investigation, which raised questions about the potential abuse of federal offices for electioneering. As a consequence, the Hatch Act, prohibiting political activity by federal officials or campaign activities on federal property (and named for Senator Carl Hatch of New Mexico), was passed in 1939.

Fourth, Roosevelt had caused more than a little concern when he introduced a benign-appearing reorganization bill in Congress. At first it appeared to be a routine reshuffling of bureaucratic agencies. But by the time Congress (which was now more Republican) debated the bill, in 1938, the Court-packing scheme was fresh in the legislators' minds, as was the fascist takeover of the Weimar Republic in Germany. No one thought FDR was Hitler, but papers were increasingly using the term "dictator" when they referred to the president. Congress decided that Roosevelt had started to infringe on constitutional separation of powers. Shocking the president, 108 Democrats crossed the aisle to defeat the reorganization bill in the House, prodded by thousands of telegrams from home.

Reaction to Roosevelt's power grab revealed how deeply entrenched values regarding private property, opportunity, and upward mobility still were. Despite six years of controlling the American economy, of dominating the political appointment process, of rigging the system with government bribes to special interest groups, and of generally favorable press, the public still resisted attempts to socialize the industrial system or to hand the president more power. It was a healthy sign—one not seen across the oceans, where dark forces snuffed out the light of freedom.

Demons Unleashed

As the nation struggled in its economic morass, events in Europe and Asia had posed an additional and even more serious threat than the Depression. For more than a decade, Americans had enjoyed relative peace in foreign affairs and had taken the lead in forging so-called arms control agreements. This was not out of altruism or pacifism, but out of a practical awareness that in the Atlantic the United States could keep up with Great Britain, but only at the expense of ceding the Pacific to the rising Empire of Japan.

America's relationship with Japan had been deteriorating for years. In 1915, Japan had stated in its Twenty-one Demands that it had a special position in China. Two years later, with the United States at war in Europe, Japanese negotiators upped the ante in their bid for dominance of China when Viscount Kikujiro Ishii met with Robert Lansing, the secretary of state. In the resulting Lansing-Ishii Agreement, the United States acknowledged that Japan had special interests in China, essentially abandoning the Open Door won just twenty years earlier. Reining in the Japanese in China had to involve obtaining naval parity in the Pacific. That proved to be no small task.

The Empire of Japan had emerged victorious in two major naval actions in the Russo-Japanese War. Although the Japanese also captured Port Arthur on the Russian Pacific coast, the victory had come at a terrible cost, revealing that Japan would face severe difficulties if it ever engaged in a full-scale land war with Russia. Although Japan had courted both British and American favor during the first decade of the 1900s, by the 1930s, stung by what it viewed as discriminatory treatment in the Washington Conference agreements, Japan increasingly looked to herself.

America had competitors—and perhaps enemies—on each ocean, and the most practical method of leveling the playing field was to restrain naval construction. That was the thought behind the Washington Conference. Ever since Lansing-Ishii, Japanese strategy had emphasized large-scale naval battles that sought to bring the enemy into one climactic engagement. But Japanese planners recognized that it would be years before they could produce a fleet comparable to that of either the British or the Americans, and so although they chafed at the inequitable provisions of the Washington Conference, "arms limitations" temporarily provided a means to tie up potential adversaries in meaningless agreements while quietly catching up technologically where it really mattered.

All signatories to the Washington Pact accepted as fact the continued dominance of the battleship in future naval actions. In doing so, they all but ignored a series of critical tests in 1921 when an Army Air Force colonel, William "Billy" Mitchell, staged a demonstration that flabbergasted army and navy brass. Using the *Ostfriesland*, a German battleship acquired by the U.S. Navy in the Treaty of Versailles, as a target, Mitchell managed to sink the ship with bomber aircraft while the vessel was steaming in the open sea. Many, if not most, of the "battleship admirals" considered this an impossibility, and even after the fact, the astonished naval officers still refused to believe that it was anything other than a trick.

Four years later, in 1925, navy aircraft attacked a U.S. fleet in simulated bombing runs and "destroyed" some sixty ships, all without the antiaircraft guns scoring a single hit on the towed targets. This pathetic performance occurred despite the fact that naval gunners fired off 880 rounds against the attackers.[25] The episode so embarrassed the navy that in subsequent tests antiaircraft guns scored a large number of hits, only to be exposed by Colonel Mitchell as bunk because the aircraft had been limited to flying at a mere thirty-three miles per hour. Mitchell was later court-martialed for his comments on the culpability of the government when it had failed to provide weather stations after the lightning-induced destruction of the blimp *Shenandoah*. Mitchell also outlined how an Asian enemy—he said, "the Empire of Japan"—could launch a surprise attack on Pearl Harbor and expect complete success. Japan took notes on Mitchell's concepts, and the attack on Pearl Harbor bore an eerie resemblance to his scenario.

By the time of his death in 1936, few besides Mitchell considered Japan any kind of serious threat. And no one thought much could come from a revived Italy led by Benito Mussolini and his Fascist Party. Mussolini was the son of a blacksmith and, in all respects, a problem child who was expelled from school. A Socialist Party member, Mussolini had taught school, served at the front in World War I (where he was wounded), and become a newspaper editor. Along with Antonio Gramsci, Mussolini formed a new political movement—a hybrid of state corporatism, nationalism, and socialism—called fascism.

The Fascists' economic doctrines lacked any cohesion except that they wedged a layer of corporate leaders between state planning and the rest of the economy. There was no operation of the free market in fascism, but rather the illusion of a group of independent corporate leaders who, in reality, acted as extensions of the state and were allowed to keep impressive salaries as a payoff. Even there, however, the Italian state bought large stock holdings in the major banks and other companies, making it the leading stockholder in ventures controlling 70 percent of iron production and almost half of all steel production. It was as close to communism as one could get without collectivizing all industry, and fascism certainly shared with communism a bent for terrorism and violence. There was "no life without shedding blood," according to Mussolini.[26]

Mussolini himself had not broken with the Socialists over economic issues, but over Italy's participation in World War I, and he seized as the symbol of his Fascist Party the Roman fasces—a bundle of sticks tied around an ax, representing authority and strength. From its origins, fascism was never anything but convoluted socialism—a point obscured still further by Adolf Hitler in Germany with his incessant attacks on both capitalism and communism. Seeing Jews behind each allowed him to conceal fascism's close similarity to Stalin's Soviet system.

In 1922, Mussolini's followers staged a march on Rome, handing him the Italian government, after which the Italian king named *Il Duce* (the leader) prime minister of Italy. Mussolini thus took by intimidation what he could not win at the ballot box. Within two years, after censoring press opposition (but not completely closing down antagonistic publishers) and manipulating the voting laws, he consolidated all power into his party's hands, with himself as dictator, albeit one far weaker than the Nazi leader. Fables that he made the trains run on time and worked other economic miracles were more publicity and propaganda than fact, but they attracted the attention of many Americans, especially before the German Nazis started to enact their anti-Jewish legislation. Among those who lauded Mussolini was Breckinridge Long, ambassador to Italy, who called fascism "the most interesting experiment in government to come above the horizon since the formulation of our Constitution."[27] Long praised the "Fascisti in their black shirts. . . . They are dapper and well dressed and stand up straight and lend an atmosphere of individuality and importance to their surroundings."[28] A young American diplomat named George Kennan, far from being repulsed by the Fascists, concluded that "benevolent despotism had greater possibilities for good" than did democracy, and that the United States needed to travel "along the road which leads through consitutional change to the authoritarian state."[29] Meanwhile, Mussolini grew in popularity by promising the Italian people that he would restore the Roman Empire. With most of the former Roman Empire occupied by the French, Spaniards, Austrians, and others, Mussolini picked out the path of least resistance—parts of Africa not occupied by Europe, like Ethiopia. In 1935,

Italian armies armed with the latest weapons, including aircraft, trucks, tanks, and machine guns, invaded a backward Ethiopia, whose emperor begged the League of Nations to intervene. Except for minor sanctions, the League turned a deaf ear, and Italian forces captured the Ethiopian capital in 1936. (Breckinridge Long, Il Duce's cheerleader in the administration, referred to Italy's crushing of backward Ethiopia as the "fruitful harvest of Mussolini's enterprise.")

Like Mussolini, Adolf Hitler had had a troubled childhood. The son of a customs inspector, Hitler had dropped out of high school and worked as an artist in Vienna prior to World War I. He proved a failure at art, was twice rejected for architectural school, then finally enlisted in the German army at the start of the Great War. After the war he joined the German Workers' Party, a socialist but anti-Marxist organization that emphasized nationalism and anti-Semitism. There Hitler found his niche, developing the skills of a hypnotic speaker and emotional actor for the party, which had taken a new name, the National Socialist German Workers' Party, or Nazis.

Hitler toiled within the Nazi Party until the German hyperinflation of 1923 nearly caused the collapse of the Weimar Republic. Seeing his opportunity, Hitler led an attempted takeover, or *putsch*, but the police were ready for him. Arrested and sentenced to five years in prison, he wrote *Mein Kampf* (*My Struggle*) from behind bars. A rambling book that detailed his hatred for Jews; his intentions to create a new German Reich, or empire; and his economic policies—which were as contradictory and confused as Mussolini's—*Mein Kampf* provided a road map for anyone willing to take it seriously. For example, he alerted everyone to his intentions of subjecting even the innocent to violence by stating that early in his political career, "the importance of physical terror became clear to me." Hitler gained his release after only a few months in confinement, by which time the Nazis had emerged as a powerful force in German politics. He gained control of the party within two years. When Germany started to slide into the economic depression that gripped the rest of the world, Hitler had the issue he needed to appeal to large numbers of Germans, who responded to his calls for a socialist reordering of society along the lines of Mussolini's corporatism.

The Rome/Berlin Axis used a revolution in Spain as a warm-up to test its weapons and armies in combat. Playing on Japan's fears of an expansionist Soviet Union in the Far East, Hitler pulled Japan into the Axis as a de facto member with the Anti-Comintern Pact (1935). Japan thus threw her lot in with an ideological cause for which the Japanese people had no connection or affinity except for apprehension about Soviet Russia. Still, the Japanese warlords resembled the fascists in their utter brutality, and the European fascist states and Japan did have one important trait in common: a growing comfort level with totalitarianism. The United States certainly wanted nothing to do with Mussolini's invasion of Ethiopia—a desert war over the questionable independence of some obscure African nation. Nor were the sides clear in Spain. How to choose, for example, between Hitler (who had yet to engage in mass murder) and Stalin (where reports of millions of deaths at his hands had already leaked out)? Still, hundreds of idealistic Americans volunteered to fight in Spain against Franco, who had Fascist ties but was no ally of Hitler's. Official noninvolvement by the United States and Britain, however, set a pattern: the democracies would not intervene, no matter who the villains were or how egregious their atrocities.

The plea by Ethiopia to the League of Nations for help against Mussolini resembled an appeal two years earlier from halfway across the globe, from China, where American interests stood out more clearly. There the Empire of Japan had expanded its foothold in Manchuria (gained in the Russo-Japanese War, 1904–5). Although Manchuria, in theory, was independent, Japan occupied it as a protectorate. Then in September 1931 it ostensibly staged an attack on a Japanese railroad at Mukden as an excuse to send in the army. Within a few months, Japan had complete control over Manchuria (renaming it Manchukuo), which provided a jumping-off point for invading other areas of China, whose pleas for assistance the League ignored.

Japan's actions came as its military was increasingly usurping civilian control of the government. Assassination of public officials began to match the levels associated with modern-day Colombia, but instead of criminal or drug gangs doing the killing, they were fanatical Japanese nationalists. In 1933 the emperor himself was nearly assassinated—a remarkable event, considering that the Japanese people viewed him as a god incarnate. Chicago-style gangsters often controlled the streets, replete with zoot-suit garb and Thompson-style submachine guns. The more dangerous gangsters, however, roamed the palace halls and the military barracks. After a temporary recovery of parliamentary government in 1936, the military staged a coup attempt during which assassination squads and regular infantry units surrounded the imperial palace and attempted to assassinate the civilian leadership of Japan. They killed the finance and education ministers, injured the chamberlain (Admiral Kantaro Suzuki), and killed several other administrators. They failed to kill the prime minister, whose wife locked him in a cupboard, but assassins shot his brother by mistake. Another prime target, the emperor, also survived, and within days order had been restored. But no civilian leaders forgot, nor did the military, which was now calling the shots. Indeed, many of Japan's "saviors" merely looked for their own opportunity to grab power, which they saw increasingly as coming from expansion in China. It is significant that Japan—at a crossroads between expansion in China and Russia, her traditional rival to the north—chose China, which engaged Japanese forces in a quagmire.

By 1937, Japanese troops had ruthlessly destroyed Shanghai and Canton, and slaughtered 300,000 civilians in Nanking. At one point in the Rape of Nanking, as it was called in part because of the systematic atrocities against women, the Japanese marched some 20,000 young Chinese outside the city and machine-gunned them. In retrospect, the League's refusal to intervene in China and Ethiopia proved to be a costly error. American policy was pro-China in sentiment, thanks to a large China lobby in Washington, but in action America remained steadfastly aloof from the atrocities. Even after reports that the Chinese were hunted like rabbits in Nanking and that anything that moved was shot, and despite the fact that in addition to Chiang's pro-Western army, Mao Tse-tung had a large communist army dedicated to evicting the Japanese, the United States did not offer even token help.

As in Spain, several idealistic aviators, flying nearly obsolete P-40 War Hawks, went to China to earn enduring acclaim as the Flying Tigers, but a handful of fighter pilots simply proved inadequate against the Rising Sun. The democracies' inaction only whetted the appetites of the dogs of war, encouraging Italy, Germany, and Japan to seek other conquests.

At one point in 1937 it appeared that the Japanese had become too brazen and careless: on December twelfth, imperial Japanese war planes strafed and bombed several ships on the Yangtze River. Three of them were Standard Oil tankers, and the fourth, a U.S. gunboat, the *Panay*, was sunk despite flying a large American flag and having Old Glory spread out on the awnings. Two crewmen and an Italian journalist were killed, and another eleven were wounded. Even with a deliberate attack in broad daylight, however, popular sentiment resisted any thought of war. Roosevelt only asked his aides to examine whether the Japanese could be held liable for monetary damages. Several admirals argued that Japan intended a war with the United States, but they were ignored by all except Harold Ickes, who noted, "Certainly war with Japan is inevitable sooner or later, and if we have to fight her, isn't this the best possible time?"[30] Upon reflection, the Japanese knew they had made a potentially disastrous miscalculation—one that could push them into a war with America years before they were ready. Consequently, Tokyo issued a thorough apology, promising to pay every cent in indemnities and recalling the commander of the Japanese naval forces. The measures satisfied most Americans, with newspapers such as the *Christian Science Monitor* urging its readers to differentiate between the *Panay* incident and the sinking of the *Maine*.

Japan further saw that Britain would be tied up with Hitler, should he press matters in Europe, opening up Malaya and, farther to the southeast, Indonesia and the rich Dutch oil fields. If the cards fell right, many strategists suggested, the Japanese might not have to deal with Great Britain at all. In this context, America's response would prove critical. The U.S. presence in the Philippines, Wake Island, Guam, and Hawaii meant that eventually Japan would have to negotiate or fight to expand her empire to the south and west. Instead, the United States compounded the disarmament mistakes of the 1920s by slumping into an isolationist funk.

Isolationism Ascendant

The very fact that the British hid behind their navy, and the French behind their massive fortifications along the German border (the Maginot Line), indicated that the major Western powers never believed their own arms control promises. As in the United States, a malaise developed in these nations out of the Great Depression, producing a helplessness and lethargy. In many circles, a perception existed that nothing could be done to stop the Italian, German, and Japanese expansionists, at least within Europe and Asia. Moreover, the U.S. Senate's Nye Committee had investigated the munitions industry, the "merchants of death" that supposedly had driven the nation into World War I, adding to suspicions of those calling for military readiness.

Britain remained the most important trading partner for American firms in the 1930s, but overseas trade was relatively insignificant to the domestic U.S. market, and the loss of that trade, while undesirable, was not crucial except to the British, who desperately needed war goods. High tariffs remained the rule of the day, reflecting the prevailing doctrine that one nation could "tax" the work of another to its own benefit. That view changed sharply after Cordell Hull became secretary of state under Roosevelt. A free trader who favored lower tariffs, his views would have been entirely appropriate for the 1920s and might have provided a firewall against the economic collapse. But by the mid-1930s, with the dictators firmly entrenched, the circumstances had changed dramatically enough to work against the doctrine of free trade. Indeed, at that point the trade weapon had to be used, and events demanded that free nations play favorites in resisting aggressors.

As the economic expansion of the 1920s gave way to the Great Depression, even stronger impulses toward isolation arose, as symbolized by the First Neutrality Act (1935), issued in response to Ethiopia's plea for help. Further congressional action in early 1937 prohibited supplying arms to either side of the Spanish Civil War. Isolationists of every political stripe tended to portray all sides in a conflict as "belligerents," thus removing any moral judgments about who might be the aggressor. The ambassador to Great Britain, Joseph Kennedy, went so far as to suggest that the democracies and the Axis powers put aside their minor disagreements and, in so many words, just get along.

Cordell Hull was among the few who saw the unprecedented evil inherent in the Nazi regime. In the wake of the disastrous Munich Agreement of 1938, which handed the sovereign nation of Czechoslovakia to Nazi Germany—having already ceded the Sudetenland territory—Hull told Roosevelt in confidence that war would follow. Speaking off the record to members of the Senate Foreign Relations Committee, Hull bluntly warned them that the coming war would not be "another goddam piddling dispute over a boundary line," but a full-scale assault on world order by "powerful nations, armed to the teeth, preaching a doctrine of naked force and practicing a philosophy of barbarism."[31]

Hull favored a cash-and-carry policy, which he thought would allow Britain to purchase whatever war materials were needed. In reality, however, at the time that the British desperately needed arms, food, and machinery, her accounts had sunk so low that she scarcely had the hard currency needed to actually purchase the goods. Hull's policy seemed a magnanimous gesture, but by then, much more generous terms were needed. Indeed, the neutrality acts often punished the states (Ethiopia or China) that had attempted to resist the Italian and Japanese aggressors. Such was the case with the 1937 cash-and-carry legislation, which sold American goods to any belligerent that could pay cash and ship the materials in its own vessels. Clearly, Britain, with her navy, benefited from this legislation the most; but Italy, Japan, and Germany fared well too.

The isolationist mood was encouraged by the intelligentsia, which, although supporting the procommunist Republican forces in the Spanish Civil War, otherwise viewed any overseas escapades as inherently imperialistic. American leftists Walter Duranty, Upton Sinclair, Langston Hughes, E. W. Scripps, Alger Hiss, and Edmund Wilson had made excuses for Lenin's Red terror and Stalin's "harvest of sorrow"—despite full knowledge that millions of Soviet citizens were being exterminated—and refused to engage in any public policy debates over the morality of one side or another.

International communist movements also condemned any involvement against the Axis powers as imperialistic, at least until the Soviet Union herself became a target of Hitler's invasion in June 1941. For example, in 1940, communist-dominated delegations to the Emergency Peace Mobilization, which met in Chicago, refused to criticize the Axis powers, but managed to scorn the "war policies" of Roosevelt.[32] Only after Operation Barbarossa and the Nazi advance into Russia, did the peace groups change their tune.

Against all these forces, solid leadership from Roosevelt's advisers—especially in the diplomatic corps—still might have convinced him and Congress that the fascists and the Japanese imperialists only understood power. Ickes, for example, lobbied for more severe sanctions against the Japanese. Other appointments proved colossally inappropriate, particularly the ambassadors to Britain and the Soviet Union. Joseph P. Kennedy, for example, the "thief" that FDR had chosen as head of the Securities and Exchange Commission "to catch a thief," received an appointment as ambassador to Britain, despite his outspoken anti-British views. Kennedy suspected every British move, convinced that England was manipulating Germany into another war.

Joseph Davies, Roosevelt's ambassador to Russia, on the other hand, completely refused to criticize one of the most vile regimes on the planet. He said Joseph Stalin, despite exterminating all opponents within the Communist Party, "is the 'easy boss' type—quiet, self-effacing, personally kindly. Like all the other Soviet leaders, Stalin works hard, lives simply, and administers his job with complete honesty."[33] The ambassador's naive characterizations extended to Stalin's subordinates, who, like Stalin, worked hard and lived simply, performing their tasks without corruption. "It is generally admitted that no graft exits in high places in Moscow," he claimed.[34]

Even where Roosevelt appointed capable men, they were ill suited for the time. Secretary of State Hull, a former judge and congressman from Tennessee, often seemed as anti-British as Kennedy, exactly at the time that the situation required the Western powers to resist aggression together. Instead of squarely facing the Axis threat in Europe, Hull sought to erode British trading influence in the Pacific to open more markets for U.S. goods. To his credit, treasury secretary Henry Morgenthau battled to sell both France and Britain top-of-the-line aircraft, to which Roosevelt finally agreed in late 1938, although whether Morgenthau favored the sales because they genuinely helped the Allies or because, as he put it, "Our aircraft industry desperately neede[ed] a shot in the arm [and] here was the hypodermic poised."[35] Between 1937 and 1940, then, Roosevelt, prompted by Hull and Kennedy, provided only a modicum of support to Britain under exorbitant terms compared to the boatloads of materials later handed out to the Soviets at much lower costs. Yet even that small level of support enabled Britain to hold out during 1940–41.

Desperate to avoid even the appearance of forming an alliance against the fascist powers, American diplomats blamed Britain and France for refusing to stand up to Hitler and therefore, in essence for saving Americans from having to confront the evil empires as well. Kennedy argued for giving Hitler a free hand in Eastern Europe; ambassador to France William Bullitt urged a Franco-German accommodation; and Breckinridge Long, the former American ambassador to Italy, blamed Britain for treating Mussolini unfairly. Roosevelt looked for any assurance from Hitler that he would behave, in 1939 sending a message asking Hitler and Mussolini if they would promise not to attack some thirty-one nations named in the letter. Hitler responded by reading it to the Reichstag, mockingly ticking off "Finland . . . Lithuania . . . Juden," to howls of laughter from the delegates, few of whom would have guessed that in the next few years he would seek to control or capture parts or all of these nations and peoples.[36]

In September 1939, Hitler's armies rolled into one of the nations he claimed to have no interest in invading—Poland. World War II had begun in Europe. America remained steadfastly neutral as the blitzkrieg, or lightning war, swept through the Polish armies, then turned on Denmark, Norway, Belgium, the Netherlands, Luxembourg, and France, all in less than a year. Even as Nazi tanks smashed French forces and trapped nearly half a million British and French troops at Dunkirk, Cordell Hull characterized French cries for U.S. support as "hysterical appeals," and Joseph Kennedy bluntly told the British that they could expect "zero support."[37] Hull and Kennedy had their own agendas, but they probably reflected the fact that many, if not most, Americans wanted nothing to do with war.

Just two years after Neville Chamberlain, the British prime minister, had returned from Munich with an agreement with Hitler that, he said, ensured "peace in our time," all of mainland Europe was under the iron grip of the Nazis, Italian Fascists, their allies, or the Communist Soviets, whose behavior in taking half of Poland, as well as Latvia, Lithuania, Estonia, and part of Finland somehow escaped the ire of the West.[38] Britain stood alone. Nearly broke, with national reserves down to $12 million, Britain could no longer buy war materials or food. Prime Minister Winston Churchill begged Roosevelt to "lend" fifty aged World War I destroyers for antisubmarine patrols, and FDR finally came around. "I have been thinking very hard . . . what we should do for England. . . . The thing to do is to get away from a dollar sign."[39] The answer was an exchange of weapons for long-term leases for several British bases, mostly in the Caribbean, although Roosevelt turned down a suggestion that would have included British ships in the West Indies, noting that they would be antiquated. He also rejected as too big a burden, both on himself and the nation, the suggestion that the United States take the West Indies themselves. The final legislation, which passed in March 1941, was known as the Lend-Lease Act. It assisted the British in protecting their sea-lanes.

Isolationists (more accurately, noninterventionists) claimed Lend-Lease would drag the United States into the war.[40] Senator Burton K. Wheeler called it the "New Deal's triple A foreign policy: it will plow under every fourth American boy."[41] Significantly, Roosevelt had rejected appeals from Norway and France, citing the fact that leasing ships to belligerents would violate international law. The destroyer deal reflected less a commitment to principle than an admission that the public mood was beginning to shift, and again demonstrated that far from leading from principle, FDR waited for the political winds to swing in his direction.

Those winds had a considerably stealthy boost from British agents in the United States. Believing the Nazis a menace to their very existence, the British hardly played by the rules in attempting to lure America into the conflict as an ally. The British used deception and craftily tailored propaganda to swing American public opinion into bringing the United States into the war, engaging in covert manipulation of democratic processes to achieve their ends.[42]

Backed by a number of American pan-Atlanticists in newspapers, Congress, and even polling organizations, British agents conducted a silent war to persuade U.S. lawmakers to enact a peacetime draft; support Lend-Lease; and, they hoped, eventually ally the United States against Hitler. The most shocking and effective aspect of British covert operations in America involved shaping public opinion through polls. It is important to note that polls, which were supposedly designed to *reflect* the public's mood, in fact were used as tools to create a mandate for positions the pollsters wanted. Although this was the first documented time that polls would be used in such a way, it certainly wouldn't be the last. British agents working for Gallup and Roper, as well as other American polling organizations, alternatively suppressed or publicized polls that supported America's entry into the war. One American pollster, sympathetic to the British, admitted "cooking" polls by "suggesting issues and questions the vote on which I was fairly sure would be on the right side."[43] In November 1941 the Fight for Freedom Committee, an interventionist group, ran a rigged poll at the Congress of Industrial Organization's national convention, taking "great care . . . beforehand to make certain the poll results would turn out as desired."[44] Another poll found 81 percent of young men facing the draft favored compulsory military service, an astoundingly high figure given that congressional mail ran "overwhelmingly" against conscription.[45]

On the other side of the argument were a few outright loonies, of course, including discredited socialists, and the entire front for the American Communist Party. The American Peace Mobilization Committee, for example, had peace marches right up to the day that Hitler invaded the USSR, when signs protesting American involvement in the war were literally changed on the spot to read OPEN THE SECOND FRONT![46] Where five minutes earlier American communists had opposed American involvement, once Stalin's bacon was in the fire they demanded U.S. intervention.

Besides these fringe groups, however, were millions of well-intentioned Americans who sincerely wanted to avoid another European entanglement. Senator Arthur H. Vandenberg, Republican of Michigan, aptly expressed the views of the vast majority of so-called isolationists when he wrote in his diary, "I hate Hitlerism and Naziism and Communism as completely as any person living. But I decline to embrace the opportunist idea . . . that *we* can stop these things in *Europe* without entering the conflict with everything at our command. . . . There is no middle ground. We are either *all the way in* or *all the way out.*"[47]

Indeed, the dirty little secret of the prewar period was that polls, when not doctored by the British, showed that most Americans agreed with aviator Charles Lindbergh's antiwar position. A few months later, in February 1941, the "Lone Eagle" testified before Congress about his firsthand inspection of Hitler's Luftwaffe. Roosevelt, convinced the aviator was attempting to undermine his Lend-Lease program, launched a campaign through subordinates to convince Americans that Lindbergh was a Nazi.[48] The entire saga showed how far the corruption of Hitler, Italian fascism, Japanese militarism, and Soviet communism had spread: the British conducted widespread spying and manipulations inside the borders of their closest ally; an American hero was tarred with the appellation Nazi for holding a position different from the president's about the best way to *defeat* the Nazis; and the Roosevelt administration increasingly had to accommodate an utterly evil Stalinist regime in Russia for the sole reason that the Soviets were fighting the Nazis.

Roosevelt, then, governed a nation that wanted to remain out of the conflict, yet despised the Axis and possessed deep sympathies for the English. Public attitudes required a clear presentation of both the costs of involvement and the dangers of neutrality, but FDR's foreign policy appointees lacked the skill to deal with either the British or the Axis.

In that context, by 1940 the isolationists certainly had drifted into a never-never land of illusion, thereby risking essential strategic advantages that, if conceded, could indeed have threatened the U.S. mainland. Isolationists, unfortunately, probably had a point when they complained that the French and Belgians "deserved" their fate. As Nazi tanks rolled over Europe, one European countess lamented that "these European peoples themselves have become indifferent to democracy. . . . I saw that not more than ten percent of the people on the European continent cared for individual freedom or were vitally interested in it to fight for its preservation."[49]

Yet in many ways, the only difference between the French and the isolationist Americans, who obsessed about the depressed economy, was one of geography: France was "over there," with Hitler, and Americans were not—yet. Thus, Roosevelt's dilemma lay in controlling the British covert agents (whose methods were illegal and repugnant, but whose cause was just) while preparing the reluctant public for an inevitable war and demonstrating that the isolationists had lost touch with strategic reality (without questioning their patriotism or motives)—all the while overcoming ambassadorial appointees who sabotaged any coherent policies.

In any event, he had a responsibility to rapidly upgrade the military by using the bully pulpit to prepare Americans for war. Instead, he chose the politically expedient course. He rebuilt the navy—a wise policy—but by stealth, shifting NIRA funds and other government slush money into ship construction. The United States took important strategic steps to ensure our sea-lanes to Britain, assuming control of Greenland in April 1941 and, three months later, occupying Iceland, allowing the British garrison there to deploy elsewhere. But these, and even the shoot-on-sight orders given to U.S. warships protecting convoys across half of the Atlantic, never required the voters to confront reality, which Roosevelt could have done prior to Pearl Harbor without alienating the isolationists. By waiting for the public to lead on the issue of war, Roosevelt reaped the worst of all worlds: he allowed the British to manipulate the United States and at the same time failed to prepare either the military or the public adequately for a forthcoming conflict. In 1939 he had argued forcefully for a repeal of the arms embargo against Britain, and he won. But a month later FDR defined the combat zone as the Baltic and the Atlantic Ocean from Norway to Spain. In essence, Roosevelt took American ships off any oceans where they might have to defend freedom of the seas, handing a major victory to the isolationists. He also delayed aid to Finland, which had heroically tried to hold off the giant Soviet army in the dead of winter, until a large chunk of that nation had fallen under Soviet tyranny.

In short, the Roosevelt war legacy is mixed: although he clearly (and more than most American political leaders) appreciated the threat posed by Hitler, he failed to mobilize public opinion, waiting instead for events to do so. He never found the Soviets guilty of any of the territorial violations that he had criticized. Just as the war saved Roosevelt from a final verdict on the effectiveness of his New Deal policies, so too did Pearl Harbor ensure that history could not effectively evaluate his wartime preparations oriented toward the Atlantic. One could say the Roosevelt legacy was twice saved by the same war.

Reelection and Inevitability

Roosevelt kept his intentions to run for reelection a secret for as long as he could. Faced with the war in Europe, FDR had decided to run, but he wanted his candidacy to appear as a draft-Roosevelt movement. He even allowed a spokesman to read an announcement to the Democratic National Committee stating that he did not want to run. It was grandstanding at its worst, but it had the desired result: echoes of "We want Roosevelt" rang out in the convention hall. The "draft" worked, and FDR selected Henry Wallace, the secretary of agriculture and a man to the left of Roosevelt, as a new vice president. Against the incumbent president, the Republicans nominated Wendell Willkie, chief executive of the Commonwealth and Southern Corporation, a utility company. Willkie, in addition to being a businessman, was also an Indiana lawyer and farmer, owning "two farms he actually farmed," in contrast to the country squire Roosevelt.[50] Willkie actually managed to gain some traction against Roosevelt on the economic front, arguing that the New Deal had failed to eliminate mass unemployment; still later, he tried to paint FDR as a warmonger. Without a clear vision for a smaller-state America, Willkie was doomed. In the reelection, Roosevelt racked up another electoral college victory with a margin of 449 to 82, but in the popular vote, the Republicans narrowed the margin considerably, with 22 million votes to FDR's 27 million. Once again the Democrats controlled the big cities with their combination of political machines and government funds.

In charging Roosevelt with desiring war, Willkie failed to appreciate the complex forces at work in the United States or the president's lack of a well-thought-out strategy. Throughout 1939–40, Roosevelt seemed to appreciate the dangers posed by the fascist states, though never Japan. However, he never made a clear case for war with Germany or Italy, having been lulled into a false sense of security by the Royal Navy's control of the Atlantic. When he finally did risk his popularity by taking the case to the public in early 1940, Congress gave him everything he asked for and more, giving lie to the position that Congress wouldn't have supported him even if he had provided leadership. Quite the contrary: Congress authorized 1.3 million tons of new fighting ships (some of which went to sea at the very time Japan stood poised to overrun the Pacific), and overall Congress voted $17 billion for defense. The president appointed two prominent Republicans to defense positions, naming Henry Stimson as secretary of war and Frank Knox as secretary of the navy. Both those men advocated much more militant positions than did Roosevelt, favoring, for example, armed escorts for U.S. shipping to Britain.

One sound argument for giving less aid to England did emerge. American forces were so unprepared after a decade's worth of neglect that if the United States energetically threw its military behind England (say, by sending aircraft and antiaircraft guns), and if, despite the help, the British surrendered, America would be left essentially defenseless. Only 160 P-40 War Hawks were in working order, and the army lacked antiaircraft ammunition, which would not be available for six more months. Advisers close to Roosevelt glumly expected Britain to fall.

Hitler's massive air attacks on England, known as the Battle of Britain, began in July 1940 to prepare for Germany's Operation Sea Lion, the invasion of England. Use of radar, combined with Churchill's timely attacks on Germany by long-range bombers, saved the day. By October, the Royal Air Force had turned back the Luftwaffe, but Britain remained isolated, broke, and under increasing danger of starvation because of U-boat attacks on merchant vessels. At about the time the British had survived Germany's aerial attacks, Mussolini attempted to expand the southern front by invading Greece. With British support, the Greeks repulsed the Italians; Britain then counterattacked in Africa, striking at the Italian forces in Libya. Mussolini's foolishness brought the Nazi armies into North Africa, and with great success at first. General Erwin Rommel took only eleven days to defeat the British and chase them back to Egypt. Yugoslavia, Greece, and Crete also fell, joining Hungary, Romania, and Bulgaria under German rule.

At that point, during a critical juncture in world history, two factors made American intervention to save Britain unnecessary in military terms and yet critical in the long run for stabilizing Western Europe for decades. First, following a November 1940 raid by the Royal Navy, the Italian fleet at Taranto had to withdraw to its ports, ceding sea control of the Mediterranean to the British. This made it difficult, though not impossible, for Hitler to consider smashing the British ground troops in Egypt and marching eastward toward India, where he entertained some thoughts of linking up with the Japanese. As long as the British had free reign of the Mediterranean, however, resupply of such an effort would have to be conducted overland. This prospect led to the second critical development, Hitler's decision to invade the Soviet Union in June 1941. In part, the Soviet invasion was inevitable in Hitler's mind. Since *Mein Kampf*, he had clung to the notion that Poland and western Russia represented the only hope for Germany's "overpopulation" (in his mind).

As a result, when the bombs fell in Hawaii on December 7, 1941, the shocking unpreparedness of American forces and the disastrous defeat at Pearl Harbor provided just enough evidence for critics of the president to claim that he had what he had wanted all along, a war in Europe through the back door of Asia. Here the critics missed the mark: FDR had had no advance warning about Pearl Harbor. Nevertheless, his unwillingness to stand clearly in favor of rebuilding the military at the risk of losing at the ballot box ensured that, despite Roosevelt's otherwise good inclinations, somewhere, at some time, U.S. military forces would take a beating.

CHAPTER SEVENTEEN

Democracy's Finest Hour, 1941–45

Democracy in Peril

World War II presented an unparalleled challenge to the United States because, for the first time, two capable and determined enemies faced America simultaneously. These foreign enemies were not merely seeking to maintain colonial empires, nor were they interested in traditional balance-of-power concerns. They were, rather, thoroughly and unmistakably evil foes. Nazi Germany had the potential technological capability to launch devastating attacks on the American mainland. The Empire of Japan had gained more territory and controlled more people in a shorter time than the Romans, the Mongols, or the Muslim empires.

Also for the first time, the United States had to fight with a true coalition. Unlike World War I, when Americans were akin to modern free agents entering the war at the last minute, the United States was allied with England, France, and Russia. The USSR was the dominant power west of the Urals, and the United States was instantly accorded the role of leadership on the Western Front. Although America was substantially free from enemy attack (aside from Pearl Harbor), the conflict brought the nation closer to a total-war footing than at any other time in its history. But as in previous wars, the business leaders of the country again took the lead, burying the Axis powers in mountains of planes, ships, tanks, and trucks. Emerging from the war as the world's dominant power, imbued with both military force and moral certainty of cause, the United States stood firm in democracy's finest hour.

"The Americans Will Be Overawed"

"Blitzkrieg," or lightning war, became a familiar word as the Nazi panzer (tank) armies slashed through Poland in 1939, then France in 1940. Technically a *tactic* (a method to obtain an objective), blitzkrieg also constituted a *strategy,* that is, a large sweeping plan for victory in war. Few recognized in 1941 that both Germany and Japan had adopted blitzkrieg because of the perception that without access to vital oil supplies, they would quickly lose, but Germany had slashed through to the Caucasus oil reserves in southern Russia, and Japan had seized oil-rich Indonesia.

There were key differences in the two foes, though. Germany's productive industry and technological capabilities might have sustained her for several years. Japanese planners harbored no such illusions about their chances of success. Admiral Nagano Osami, who had strongly supported war with America well before the Pearl Harbor plan was formulated, grimly promised to "put up a tough fight for the first six months," but if the war went for two or three years he had "no confidence" in Japan's ability to win.[1] Just two months before Pearl Harbor, Nagano again said that the imperial navy could hold its own for about two years; other voices in the military thought a year was more realistic. Asked point-blank if Japan could win a quick-strike war similar to the Russo-Japanese War nearly forty years earlier, Nagano stated flatly that "it was doubtful whether we could even win," let alone come close to the success of 1904.[2] But the army dictated strategy, and the Bushido warrior code, combined with the assassination of dissenters, sealed Japan's doom. In retrospect, Japan essentially marched grimly into a disaster with most of its leaders fully aware that, even with extreme luck, victory was next to impossible.

By 1939, Japan's army had already wallowed for three years in China, helping itself to Chinese resources. Despite the fact that China, a pitiful giant, was too divided among feuding factions and too backward to resist effectively, Japan had trouble subduing the mainland. By 1940, the Japanese occupied all the major population centers with a ruthlessness resembling that of the Nazis, yet they still could not claim total victory. Imperial policy exacted great costs. In July 1939 the United States revoked the most-favored-nation trading status provided by a commercial treaty of 1911, and a month later, in a dispute little noticed in the West, the Soviets defeated Japanese troops in Mongolia.

Japan's China policy stemmed in part from the perverse power of the military in a civilian government on the home islands, where any civilian or military leaders who interfered with the expansionism of the army or navy were muffled or assassinated. Yet for all their recklessness, many in the empire's inner circle viewed any strategy of engaging the United States in a full-scale war as utter lunacy. One logistics expert starkly laid out production differentials between America and Japan: steel, twenty to one; oil, one hundred to one; aircraft, five to one; and so on. His arguments fell on deaf ears. By 1940, no Japanese official openly criticized the momentum toward war. The American-educated Admiral Isoroku Yamamoto came the closest to outright opposition. He had flown across the United States once and soberly observed America's awesome productive capability. His visit to Dayton's Wright Field, while opening his imagination to the potential for long-range air strikes, also reminded him of the vast gulf between the two nations. When he raised such concerns with the imperial warlords, they transferred him to sea duty.

Military ascendancy was complete by October 1941, when Japan installed as prime minister General Hideki Tojo, known to the British press as the Razor. A stubborn, uncompromising man, Tojo's ascension to power essentially ended all hopes of a diplomatic solution to the Asian situation. Tojo became enamored of a quick knockout blow to the United States, advocating a strike in which "the Americans [would] be so overawed from the start as to cause them to shrink from continuing the war. Faced with [the destruction of] their entire Pacific fleet in a single assault delivered at a range of over three thousand miles, they would be forced to consider what chance there would be of beating this same enemy [across] an impregnable ring of defensive positions."[3]

Americans had little appreciation for a society steeped in a tradition of extreme nationalism, reinforced through indoctrination in its public education system and replete with military training of children from the time they could walk.[4] Nor did most westerners even begin to grasp Bushido, the Japanese warrior code that demanded death over the "loss of face." It simply did not register on Main Street, U.S.A., that Japan might pose a genuine threat to U.S. security. Quite the contrary, in February 1941, *Time* publisher Henry Luce declared the dawning of the "American Century," reflecting the views of probably a majority of Americans.

Americans may have misjudged their enemy, but the delusion in Japan was worse. Withdrawing from Indochina and China, to them, was simply an unacceptable loss of honor. Therefore, by mid-1941, Japan's civilian and military leadership had settled on a course of war with the United States. Most agreed, however, that Japan's only hope of victory was a massive all-Asian offensive with a key surprise strike at the U.S. Navy's main Pacific base at Pearl Harbor, Hawaii, with simultaneous attacks in the American-held Philippine islands, British Singapore, and Hong Kong. Never in human history had military forces undertaken such sweeping and ambitious operations, let alone attempted such strikes simultaneously. Most astounding of all, not only did Japan make the attempt to swallow all of Asia in a single gulp, she came within a hair of succeeding.

Time Line

Sept. 1939: Hitler invades Poland, and World War II begins in Europe

1940: Germany defeats French and British forces in France; France surrenders and is occupied; Norway occupied; Battle of Britain

Dec. 7, 1941: Japan attacks Pearl Harbor

1942: United States and Britain invade North Africa; Jimmy Doolittle bombs Tokyo (February); Battles of Coral Sea (May) and Midway (June)

1943: Allies begin bombing Europe, defeat the Afrika Korps at the battle of Kasserine Pass (February), and invade Sicily and Italy (July)

1944: Invasion of France (June sixth); Paris liberated (August); Battle of the Bulge (December); invasion of the Philippines and Battle of Leyte Gulf (October)

1945: Germany surrenders (May); landings on Iwo Jima and Okinawa (March-June); Trinity test of atomic bomb (July); atomic bombing of Hiroshima and Nagasaki (August sixth and ninth); Japan surrenders (August twelfth)

1946: "Iron Curtain" speech by Winston Churchill, Cold War begins

1947: Marshall Plan, North Atlantic Treaty Organization founded

Back Door to War?

Hitler's quick conquest of France in 1940 put French possessions in the Far East up for grabs. After Vichy France permitted the Japanese to build airfields in northern Indochina, the United States passed the Export Control Act (July 1940), restricting sales of arms and other materials to Japan. Over time, scrap iron, gasoline, and other products were added to the strategic embargo. The Japanese warlords spoke of a Greater East Asia Co-Prosperity Sphere, a term they used to describe an Asia dominated by the Japanese Empire. The fly in the ointment remained oil, since Japan had *no* domestic oil reserves. This made the empire fully dependent on foreign energy sources, a fact that had shaped Japan's war planning.

In September 1940, Tokyo made a colossal blunder by signing the Tripartite Pact with Germany and Italy, mainly as a way to acquire British Far Eastern possessions that would be available if Hitler conquered Britain. Japan's dalliance with Germany had run both hot and cold, but now the Japanese threw in their lot with the Nazis. In the eyes of many westerners, this confirmed that the Japanese warlords were no different from Hitler or Mussolini. The alliance albatross hung around Japan's neck for the entire war. Hitler hoped to lure Japan into opening a second front in Siberia against the Soviets, but Japan, remembering the ill-fated land campaign of 1904, instead planned to move south for oil. To eliminate interference from the Russians, Japan signed a nonaggression pact with the Soviets in April 1941.

The nonaggression pact freed Japanese troops in Manchuria to move south, whereupon Japan announced its intention to control all of Indochina. Roosevelt had had enough. He restricted all exports of oil to Japan and froze Japanese assets in the United States, which had the effect of choking off Japanese credit and making it nearly impossible for Japan to buy imported oil from other countries.

Freezing Japan's assets left the empire with a two-year supply of oil under peacetime conditions, but less than a year's worth of "war oil" because the consumption of fuel by carriers, battleships, and aircraft would rapidly deplete Japan's reserves. Thus, FDR's efforts to coerce Japan into withdrawing from Indochina had the opposite effect and certainly increased pressure to go to war. However, notions that Roosevelt provoked Japan are absurd. Japan was already on a timetable for war. Even before the embargo, "Japan was trading at a rate, and with trade deficits, which ensured that she would have exhausted her gold and foreign currency reserves some time in early spring 1942."[5] Put another way, with or without the frozen assets, Japan faced national bankruptcy in mid-1942, making the "crisis entirely of Japan's own making."[6] Equally important, based on ship-building ratios then in place, the imperial navy was in a once-in-a-lifetime position of strength relative to the Americans. (Even without combat losses, by 1944, the imperial navy would have fallen to 30 percent of U.S. naval strength, which, as a result of the Two-Ocean Naval Expansion Act of 1940, would include enough vessels to render the Japanese naval forces "nothing more than an impotent irrelevance, wholly deprived of any prospect of giving battle with any hope of success.")[7]

Contrary to the back-door-to-war theories of the Roosevelt haters, Japan's warlords had all but committed themselves to a conflict with the United States in January 1941, well before the freezing of the assets. Moreover, there is some question as to how badly the embargo hurt Japan: from July 1940 to April 1941, when petroleum supposedly was locked up, American oil companies sold 9.2 million barrels of crude to Japan, and permits were approved for 2 million additional barrels. It is hard to argue that under such circumstances the United States was squeezing the Japanese economy to death.[8]

Additional warning signs came from American code breakers, who in December 1940 deciphered the Japanese diplomatic code, called Purple. This allowed the United States to read Japan's mail for over a year. From these intercepts it was clear that Japan intended to expand to the southwest (Singapore, a British possession), the south (the Philippines), the east (striking at Pearl Harbor), or all three. A final, failed negotiation included an offer to resume full trade with Japan in return for her withdrawal from China, after which the imperial fleets raised anchor, placing the 7th Fleet at Pearl Harbor in the center of Yamamoto's crosshairs.

"A Date Which Will Live in Infamy"

Japanese strategists began planning an air attack on the U.S. naval base in Hawaii in the summer of 1941. Japanese preparations for the Pearl Harbor strike comprised only *one third* of the overall military operation, which included two simultaneous invasions of the Philippines and Malaysia. Any one of the three prongs of attack would have been a major military undertaking—especially for a small island nation with limited resources—but coordination of all three spoke volumes about Japan's delusion and her desperation. The goal of the ambitious strategy was for no less than a knockout blow aimed at all the remaining allied powers in Asia except for India and Australia. Despite the interception of Japanese messages, no one had dreamed that this small island nation, which had never won a major war against European powers, could execute three separate military operations spanning thousands of miles and engaging two of the most powerful nations on earth as well as nearly a dozen regional military forces.

Western intelligence did know that Japanese troops and fleets were on the move somewhere. But where? Most trackers had them headed south, toward Singapore, which led to some complacency at Pearl Harbor, where Admiral Husband Kimmel and General Walter Short shared responsibilities for the defense of the Hawaiian Islands. The officers had never worked out an effective division of command authority and had failed to schedule appropriate air reconnaissance. Despite repeated war warnings, Kimmel and Short had never put the fleet or airfields on full alert. As a result, American ships were sitting ducks on December seventh.

Japan attacked methodically and with deadly efficiency. Bombers, torpedo planes, dive bombers—all covered by Mitsubishi Zero fighter planes—took out American air power, then hit the battleships on "battleship row," sinking or severely damaging every one. The worst casualty, the USS *Arizona*, went down in ten minutes with a thousand sailors. Few ships of any sort escaped damage of some type. Even civilian quarters suffered collateral damage from the attack, including large numbers hit by American antiaircraft rounds that fell back to earth.[9]

Despite the phenomenal success of the attack, Yamamoto did not achieve total victory because three key targets, the American aircraft carriers, had been out on maneuvers. Going in, Yamamoto had expected to lose 30 percent of his entire force—ships included—yet he lost nothing larger than a midget sub and only a handful of aircraft. In a critical error of judgment, Yamamoto took his winnings and left the table without the carriers. Although unforeseen at the time, all the battleships except the *Arizona* would be salvaged and returned to action during the war. More important, by leaving the oil storage facilities undamaged, Yamamoto allowed U.S. forces to continue to operate out of Hawaii and not San Diego or San Francisco. The attack at Pearl Harbor had indeed been a crushing defeat for the United States, but the price at which the Japanese acquired their victory could not be measured in ships or men. An outraged American public had been galvanized and united.

Did Roosevelt Have Advance Knowledge About the Pearl Harbor Attack?

Even as the last smoke billowed from the sinking or capsized ships in Hawaii, many people were asking how the United States could have been so unprepared. Historian Charles Tansill suggested that the debacle could only have occurred with Franklin Roosevelt's foreknowledge. Clearly, if a president in possession of advance warning had allowed hundreds of sailors and soldiers to die in a surprise attack, it would have constituted high treason. Why would any chief executive permit such a strike?

In his famous book, *Back Door to War* (1952), Tansill accused Roosevelt of allowing a Japanese attack at Pearl Harbor to provide the United States with the motivation and justification to enter the war against Hitler in Europe. A number of historians and writers added to the Tansill thesis over the years, but little new evidence was produced until the 1980s, when John Toland published *Infamy*, wherein he claimed to have located a navy witness who, while on duty in San Francisco, received transmissions locating the Japanese carriers and forwarded the information to Washington.

Adding to Toland's revelations, a "Notes and Documents" piece in the *American Historical Review* disclosed that the FBI had acquired information from an Axis double agent named Duskow Popov ("Tricycle"), who had information on a microdot about the attack.[10] Although Toland and others maintained that Popov's documents included a detailed plan of the Japanese air attack, it did no such thing. Tricycle's data dealt almost exclusively with buildings and installations, but had nothing on ships, aircraft, scouting patterns, or any of the rather important items that one would expect from a "detailed plan."[11]

In 1981, Asian historian Gordon Prange published *At Dawn We Slept*; following his death, his students Donald Goldstein and Katherine Dillon completed his work with new Pearl Harbor claims in *Pearl Harbor: The Verdict of History*. The authors found Toland's mystery sailor, Robert Ogg, who emphatically rejected Toland's assertion that he had said he had intercepted massive Japanese radio traffic. Meanwhile, documents acquired from Japanese archives raised a more serious problem for the conspiracy theorists because they proved the Japanese fleet had been under strict radio silence during the attack voyage to Pearl Harbor.

The controversy refused to go away. In 1999, Robert B. Stinnett's *Day of Deceit* revived the argument that Roosevelt had prior knowledge of the attack with important new code-breaking information. But the crucial pieces of "evidence" that Stinnett employed often proved the opposite of what he claimed. He used precise intelligence terms—code breaking, interception, translation, analysis—interchangeably, which produced massive errors: an intercepted document is not necessarily broken, and if intercepted and broken, it may not be translated, and if intercepted, broken, and translated, it may not be analyzed for days, weeks, or even years. Some of the intercepts in November 1941 were indeed broken, but not translated or analyzed until . . . 1945!

The entire argument of the revisionists hinges on the notion that FDR couldn't get into the war with Germany without a pretext. But Roosevelt had already had ample cause, if he'd wanted it, to ask for a declaration of war against Germany. Nazi U-boats had sunk American ships, killed American sailors, and in all ways shown themselves hostile. Against a nation that had declared war on Mexico over a handful of cavalry troopers or that had declared war on Spain for the questionable destruction of a single ship, Germany had long since crossed the line needed for a declaration of war. Despite the isolationist elements in Congress, it is entirely possible that FDR could have asked for a declaration of war after the sinking of the *Reuben James* or other such attacks. Certainly the U-boats were not going to stop, and it was only a matter of time before more Americans died. Pearl Harbor was a tragedy, but not a conspiracy.

Sources: Charles Beard, *President Roosevelt and the Coming of the War* (New Haven, Connecticut: Yale University Press, 1948); Walter Millis, *This Is Pearl!* (New York: William Morrow, 1947); Charles C. Tansill, *Back Door to War* (Chicago: Regnery, 1952); Gordon W. Prange with Donald M. Goldstein and Katherine V. Dillon, *At Dawn We Slept* (New York: McGraw-Hill, 1981); John Toland, *Infamy* (New York: Doubleday, 1982); Dusko Popov, *Spy/Counterspy* (New York: Grosset & Dunlap, 1974); Harry Elmer Barnes, "Pearl Harbor After a Quarter of a Century," *Left and Right*, IV (1968); Roberta Wohlstetter, *Pearl Harbor* (Stanford, California: Stanford University Press, 1962); Robert B. Stinnett, *Day of Deceit* (New York: Free Press, 2000).

On December eighth, Roosevelt, appearing before the jointly assembled House and Senate, called December 7, 1941, a "date which will live in infamy" as he asked Congress for a declaration of war against Japan. Four days later Germany and Italy declared war on the United States. With a declaration of war only against Japan, it appeared to some isolationists that it still might be possible to avoid entering the war in Europe. Hitler refused to oblige them and rushed head-long at the United States and the USSR simultaneously.

Indeed, Hitler, at the recommendation of his foreign minister, Joachim von Ribbentrop, had no intention of allowing the United States to get its declaration of war in ahead of his own. "A great power does not allow itself to be declared war upon," Ribbentrop purportedly said. "It declares war on others."[12] War with Germany had been far closer than many isolationists imagined: in May 1941, the Nazis sank the freighter *Robin Moor*, prompting Roosevelt to extend American neutral waters to Iceland and allow American warships to escort U.S. merchant-men farther out to sea. A few months later, German vessels attacked the USS *Greer*; and in October 1941 they torpedoed the destroyer *Kearney*, which man-aged to make it back to port. The House of Representatives voted the next day to arm American merchant ships. Then, on Halloween, Germans sank the destroyer *Reuben James*, killing 115 Americans. At that point, the United States would have been fully justified by international law in declaring war on Germany and her al-lies, but Roosevelt was still unconvinced that the American public would support him. Yet even if Japan had not bombed Pearl Harbor, it is inconceivable that ten-sions with Nazi Germany would have subsided. Rather, more casualties and di-rect German attacks would have provoked the United States into declaring war on the Axis powers anyway.

Congress had consistently failed to appreciate the danger posed by both the Nazi regime and the perception of U.S. weakness propagated in the Japanese mind by Hitler's repeated incursions. Americans came to war with Hitler reluc-tantly and only as a last resort. At no time prior to Pearl Harbor did anywhere close to a majority of citizens think the events in Europe sufficiently threatened U.S. national interests. Roosevelt, on the other hand, recognized both the moral evil of Hitler and the near-term threat to American security posed by Nazi Germany. However, he nevertheless refused to sacrifice his personal popu-larity to lead the United States into the war sooner, knowing full well it would come eventually—and at a higher cost.

Had the United States deliberately and forcefully entered the war in Europe earlier, on its own timetable, perhaps some of Hitler's strategic victories (and, possibly, much of the Holocaust) might have been avoided. For example, Ameri-can aircraft would have already been in England by 1940, meaning that the Bat-tle of Britain would not have been close. Moreover, a European buildup almost certainly would have brought the Pacific military forces into a higher stage of alert. And, most important, an American presence well before 1942 might have been just enough to force Hitler into scrapping the German invasion of Russia.

Isolationist critics from the Right have argued that American entry in Europe was needless even after Pearl Harbor and that the Soviets had all but won the war by the time the United States got involved in any significant way.[13] This view not only distorts battlefield realities—the Eastern Front was not decided completely until after Kursk in 1943—but it also ignores the fact that American aid may have tipped the balance for the Soviets between 1942 and 1944. Moreover, it should be noted that Stalin offered to negotiate with Hitler in December 1942, a full year after Pearl Harbor, and again in the summer of 1943—hardly the act of a man confident of victory on the field. Stalin was as suspicious of Churchill and Roosevelt as he was of Hitler, and he feared that the Anglo-American powers would encourage a Nazi-Soviet war of exhaustion.[14] Certainly the Soviets wore out the *Wehrmacht* in the east, and they absorbed a disproportionate amount of Nazi resources in some areas, especially men and tanks. But those contributions have to be seen in the context of the entire conflict, and not just in the battles on the Eastern Front. When the bigger picture is revealed, it is clear the U.S. economy won the war.

Putting the Ax to the Axis

Unlike during the Vietnam conflict some thirty years later, in December 1941 the only Americans lying about their ages or searching for sympathetic doctors for notes were trying to fake their way *into* the armed forces. Men too old and boys too young to be eligible for service managed to slip past the recruitment authorities. It was easy to do with more than 16 million males enlisting or being drafted into the armed forces. Another 245,000 women in the Women's Army Corps (WACS) and WAVES (Women Accepted for Voluntary Emergency Services, which was the women's naval auxiliary created largely through the efforts of Senator Margaret Chase Smith), supported the effort. Other women, such as actress Ida Lupino, joined the ambulance and nurse corps, and Julia Child, later to be a cooking guru, served with the Office of Strategic Services in Ceylon. Ethnic minorities like the Japanese and blacks, discriminated against at home, brushed off their mistreatment to enlist, winning battle honors. The Japanese American 442nd Regimental Combat Team became the most decorated American division of the war, and included future U.S. Senator Daniel K. Inouye, who lost an arm in combat. The all-black 99th Fighter Squadron saw action in Italy.

Celebrities of the day did not hesitate to enter the armed forces. Even before Pearl Harbor, many well-known personalities had signed up for the reserves, including Major Cecil B. DeMille, Brigadier General Cornelius Vanderbilt III, and Colonel David Sarnoff. And once war broke out, rather than seeking safety behind the lines, a number of movie stars and sons of elite families gave up their prestige and the protections of wealth to actively pursue combat assignments. Theodore Roosevelt Jr. quit his job in 1941 to go on active duty as a colonel and later saw action on D-Day.[15] Academy Award winner Van Heflin joined the army as an artilleryman; television's *Gunsmoke* hero, James Arness, was in the army and wounded at Anzio, earning a Bronze Star; Eddie Albert, wounded at Tarawa, also earned a Bronze Star rescuing wounded and stranded marines from the beach; *Get Smart*'s Don Adams, a marine, contracted malaria at Guadalcanal; Charleton Heston was a radio operator on B-25 bombers; Art Carney, sidekick of Jackie Gleason on *The Honeymooners*, suffered a shrapnel wound at Saint-Lô before he could fire a shot. Ernest Borgnine, who later would play fictional

Lieutenant Commander McHale in *McHale's Navy*, had already served in the navy for twelve years before World War II; Lucille Ball's famous Cuban husband, Desi Arnaz, was offered a commission in the Cuban navy, where, as an officer, he would be relatively safe on patrol in the Caribbean. He refused, choosing instead to enlist in the U.S. Navy, where he was rejected on the grounds that he was a noncitizen. Nevertheless, he could be drafted—and was—and despite failing the physical, went into the infantry, where he injured his knees. He finished the war entertaining troops.

Other young men went on to literary or theatrical fame after the war. Novelist Norman Mailer went ashore with his infantry regiment in the Philippines, and western writer Louis L'Amour hit the beaches with his tank destroyer on D-Day. Alex Haley, later a famous novelist, served in the U.S. Coast Guard; and author William Manchester was wounded and left for dead, recovering after five months in a hospital. Tony Bennet, serving as an infantryman in Europe, got his first chance to sing while in the army. Men who later would become Hollywood stars, including William Holden, Charles Bronson, Jack Lemmon, and Karl Malden, signed up. Holden flew bombers over Germany; Ed McMahon was a U.S. Marine fighter pilot; and George Kennedy served under General George Patton. Football great Tom Landry, coach of the Dallas Cowboys, flew B-17s with the Eighth Army; and baseball legend Yogi Berra served as a gunner on a navy bombardment ship. More than a few became heroes. Future director Mel Brooks fought at the Battle of the Bulge; Tony Curtis served on a submarine; and an underage Telly Savalas, later known for his television cop-show role as Kojak, was critically wounded in action and told he would never walk again. Academy Award winner Lee Marvin assaulted more than twenty beaches in the Pacific with his marine unit, and after one battle, only Marvin and 5 others out of 247 had survived. Walter Matthau, famous for his roles in *The Odd Couple* and *The Bad News Bears*, won an impressive six Silver Stars as an air force gunner. None was more decorated than Audie Murphy, who became an actor after the war based on his incredible career. Murphy was the most decorated soldier in World War II, having been awarded the Medal of Honor and twenty-seven other medals as well as the French Legion of Honor and the Croix de Guerre.

Others, such as directors John Huston and John Ford, entered combat situations armed with movie cameras instead of guns, shooting war documentaries for propaganda. Captain Ronald Reagan commanded a Hollywood documentary film company that, among its varied duties, filmed the aftermath of the European war, including the Nazi death camps. Science fiction writer Ray Bradbury honed his skills writing patriotic radio commercials. Jazz great Al Hirt entertained troops as part of the 82nd Army Band, and bandleader Glenn Miller, who had enlisted in the air force and was commissioned a captain, died while flying to Europe to entertain troops. Even civilians, at home or in service at the front, occasionally made the ultimate sacrifice, as when actress Carole Lombard died in an airplane crash on a tour selling war bonds. Ironically, one of the heroes most frequently associated with the military, John Wayne, was not drafted because of his large family, although he made several war movies that boosted morale immeasurably.

Movie studios, including Walt Disney's cartoon factory, which had made a war hero out of Donald Duck, increased production fivefold. Under the tight control of wartime bureaucrats, costs for producing a typical film dropped from $200 per foot of film shot to $4 as the Disney studios released a torrent of training projects for the military: *Dental Health, Operation of the C-1 Auto Pilot, High Level Precision Bombing,* and *Food Will Win the War* for civilians. (Reagan was prominent in many of these military training films.) Probably the most successful war cartoon ever, *Der Fuehrer's Face* (1943), with Donald Duck, won an Academy Award. The music industry kicked in too. New York's song-writing mecca, Tin Pan Alley, cranked out propaganda ditties like "It's Our Pacific, to Be Specific" and "Let's Put the Ax to the Axis" as well as some racist tunes like "When the Cohens and the Kellys Meet the Little Yellow Bellies" and "Let's Find the Fellow Who Is Yellow and Beat Him 'til He's Red, White, and Blue." Germans, as they had been in World War I, were routinely portrayed as Huns, replete with blood-drenched fangs and bearskin clothes. Yet it would be a mistake to overly criticize the necessity of such propaganda. Americans, as a rule, were not natural-born killers. Once aroused, the essence of civic militarism produced a warrior who displayed individuality, determination to stay alive (as opposed to die gloriously), and constant adaptation to circumstances (as opposed to unbending obedience to doctrine).[16]

Many of these young men came from a generation whose parents had never seen an ocean, and the longest journey they had ever made was from one state to another. They came from a time when homes did not even have locks on the doors. Most knew little of fascism, except that they instinctively hated Hitler— the "paper hangin' son of a bitch," Patton called him. The sneak attack on Pearl Harbor struck deeply at their sense of right and wrong and, in their way of thinking, put the Nazis, Italians, and Japanese all in the same category.[17]

America's soldiers were not just motivated; they were also the best educated in the world and arrived at induction centers highly skilled. The U.S. Army put soldiers into the field who often were well versed in the use of motor vehicles and mechanized farm implements, meaning that they could not only drive them, but could often rebuild and repair them with little training. Prior to the war, America had had a motor vehicle ratio of four people to one car, whereas Germany's ratio was thirty-seven to one. The GI was four to seven times more likely to have driven a motor vehicle than any of his allies or opponents.[18] Americans were the highest paid and best fed soldiers in the war, and they received, by far, the best medical attention of any army in history. When that was combined with the good—and improving—training they received, American warriors possessed decided advantages. They soon benefited from an industrial tsunami from the capitalists back home.

Democracy's Industrial Tsunami

Aside from the obvious self-sacrifice of the soldiers and sailors who fought, the key contribution to winning the war came not from Hollywood or Tin Pan Alley, but from American industry, which had unleashed a tidal wave of war materials, paid for with $80 billion from Uncle Sam. "Capitalism, U.S.A." buried the fascists and imperialists under a mountain of fighter planes, tanks, and ships. Yankee factories turned out war materials at nearly incomprehensible levels: 221,000 aircraft and more than 1,500 warships, doubling the entire military production of the Axis powers combined by 1944. Indeed, American business produced almost as much as all other nations of the *world* combined. From 1941 to 1945, the U.S. Navy commissioned 18 fleet carriers, 9 light carriers, 77 escort carriers, 8 battleships (and repaired all the battleships damaged at Pearl Harbor except the *Arizona*), 46 cruisers, 349 destroyers, 420 destroyer escorts, and more than 200 submarines. In the Battle of Leyte Gulf, the United States had more destroyers deployed than the Japanese had carrier aircraft!

Obviously, the United States had an enormous advantage in sheer economic capability, even despite the Great Depression. American gross domestic product (1990 prices) topped $1.4 trillion, whereas Japan, Germany, and Italy mustered barely half that. But whereas Germany had had five years to gear up for war, and Italy had had close to fifteen, the United States had accelerated to its phenomenal production capacity within a matter of months. Between 1942 and 1943, GDP rose nearly $200 billion—more than Japan's entire economy.

After only a year of war, the United States had gone from a handful of fighter planes to 78,000, from 900 tanks to 65,000, and from 544 major naval vessels to 4,500.[19] American shipyards turned out 16 warships for every 1 Japan built. The Soviet Union—often held up as the model of wartime production—turned out 80,000 fewer aircraft than did the United States, and well into mid-1943, the "top Soviet Aces flew Lend-Lease aircraft such as the P-39 Airacobra."[20]

The relationship between Russian blood and American dollars in the "grand alliance" cannot be overstated. Both were necessary in the watershed year 1943. Although the German army had been blunted at Moscow and Stalingrad, the outcome was not sealed until Kursk and, on the Western Front, until the invasion of Sicily, when Hitler was finally forced to fight a two-front war. Thus, it behooves us to consider the mind-boggling war production of the United States as part and parcel of the Soviet offensives of 1943. For example, by that time, the bulk of German air power in the East had been withdrawn to defend against Allied bombing in the West, and it is no surprise that only after German air power had been siphoned off to contest the Anglo-American bombers did the Soviets consistently win large offensive armored battles.

It is true that Soviet industry made plenty of tanks. But by the pivotal battle of Kursk in July 1943, some 20 percent of Soviet armored brigades already consisted of Lend-Lease American-made tanks.[21] Trucks and other vehicles proved even more important: by June 1943 the USSR had received 90,000 trucks and

17,000 jeeps, again giving the Red Army important advantages. At Kursk, one new study has concluded, "Lend-Lease trucks and jeeps made a major contribution," and even today, "Studebaker" and "Villies" (Willys) are familiar words to Russian veterans of the Great Patriotic War.[22] Then there was the American contribution of 100-octane aviation fuel, which by itself improved the performance of Soviet aircraft against the Germans, and waterproof telephone wire, which the Soviets could not produce and which they relied on heavily.[23] Despite the reputation of the Red Army for turning out armored vehicles, the United States nearly matched the USSR in tank/personnel carrier output (99,500 to 102,800), while constructing some 8,700 *more* ships—all the while secretly pouring seemingly limitless funds into the Manhattan Project's development of the atomic bomb.

Once American businesses saw that FDR would not undercut them with government policies, they responded with mind-boggling speed. Uncle Sam came up with the money by borrowing both from current citizens and from generations unborn; then it provided the buildings (through the Defense Plant Corporation); then it got out of the way, authorizing the titans of business to make good arms and fast ships. Newport News, Litton Ingalls, and other shipbuilders could put a completed aircraft carrier in the water fifteen months from keel laying (compared to nearly ten years in 1999); and a tank rolled off the assembly line in less than five hours, fabricated from scratch. Perhaps the most miraculous construction efforts came in the form of Liberty Ships, the simple freighters designed to carry food, munitions, and other supplies in convoys to England.

Henry Kaiser, who had supervised construction of the Boulder Dam, received an order from Roosevelt to build ships as fast as possible, regardless of cost. He opened several California shipyards, importing inner-city workers from Chicago, Detroit, and the East Coast, paying them the highest wages. Aware that the ship workers would have no place to live, Kaiser developed the world's first modular homes, which allowed him to attract employees, and he provided day care for the children of working mothers. Once shipyards had begun production, Kaiser was able to slash the building time of a Liberty Ship from 196 days to 27, setting a record in turning out the *Robert E. Peary*, from its keel laying to christening, in 4.5 days. By 1943, the Kaiser yards were spitting out a Liberty Ship nearly every 2 days.

The early Kaiser ships were not given the best steel, however, because of military requirements that sent the higher-quality steel to "pure" warships. As a result, several of the first Liberty Ships literally split in half at sea, especially on runs to Murmansk. Concerned investigators found no fault with the Kaiser production techniques, but they learned that the cheaper grade of steel mandated by the government became exceedingly brittle in icy water. Upon learning of the brittleness problem, Kaiser adopted a simple solution, which was to weld an additional huge steel support beam on each side of a ship's hull, thereby ending that particular problem. Indeed, Kaiser's original innovation had been to weld the

Liberty Ships instead of using rivets because welding took far less time and permitted crews to construct entire sections in a modular process, literally hoisting entire prefabricated deckhouses into position on a finished hull.

Another shipbuilder, Andrew Jackson Higgins, designed new shallow-draft wooden boats specifically for invading the sandy beaches and coral atolls in the Pacific. Higgins, who hailed from land-locked Nebraska, had built fishing and pleasure craft before the war. When the war started, the navy found it had a desperate need for Higgins boats, which featured a flat lip on the bow that dropped down as the vessel reached shore, affording the troops a ramp from which to run onto the beach. After the war a reporter asked Dwight Eisenhower who had proved most valuable to the Allies' victory, fully expecting Ike would name generals like George Patton or Douglas MacArthur or a naval commander like Admiral Chester Nimitz. Instead, Eisenhower said Higgins was "the man who won the war."

Without question, though, countless Americans played a part and voluntarily would have done even more. A Roper poll in 1941, *prior* to Pearl Harbor, showed that 89 percent of American men would spend one day a week training for homeland defense and that 78 percent of all Americans would "willingly" pay a sales tax on everything and cut gasoline consumption by a third in the event of war.[24] By 1945, pollster George Gallup had found that more than two thirds of Americans thought they had not made any "real sacrifice" for the war, and 44 percent of the respondents in a 1943 Gallup poll said that the government had not gone "far enough" in asking people to make sacrifices for the war (40 percent said the government's demands were "about right.")[25] Despite the largest commitment in history by both the U.S. civilian and military sectors, large numbers of Americans thought they still could do more!

In reality, civilians did far more than they imagined. Important equipment like the jeep came from civilian-submitted designs, not government bureaucracy. Farmers pushed their productivity up 30 percent, and average citizens added 8 million more tons of food to the effort through backyard "victory" gardens. Scrap drives became outlets for patriotic frenzy, and a thirteen-year-old in Maywood, Illinois, collected more than 100 tons of paper from 1942 to 1943.[26] Some 40 percent of the nation's retirees returned to the workplace. It was as close to a total-war effort as the United States has ever seen.

Is This Trip Really Necessary?

The war allowed Roosevelt to accelerate implementation of some of his New Deal goals. In 1941, FDR proposed a 99.5 percent marginal tax rate on all incomes over $100,000. The measure failed, but undaunted, he issued an executive order to "tax all income over $25,000 at the astonishing rate of *100 percent*."[27] Other insidious changes in taxation found their way into the code, the most damaging of which involved the introduction in July 1943 of withholding taxes from the paychecks of employees. That subtle shift, described sympathetically by one text as an "innovative feature" where "no longer would taxpayers have to set aside money to pay their total tax bill . . . at the end of the year," in fact allowed the government to conceal the total tax burden from the public and make it easier to steadily raise taxes, not just during the war, but for decades.[28] It was that burden of laying aside the money that had focused the public's attention on taxation levels. Subsequently, many limited-government critics have argued that the single most effective change in regaining control of the bloated tax code would be to abolish withholding and require that all individuals make a one-time tax payment per year, due the last week in October—right before the November elections.

When it came to applying taxes and regulations, however, the administration took care not to unnecessarily cripple or alienate business leaders and entrepreneurs. Some obvious restrictions were necessary. War-critical products such as oil, gasoline, cotton, rubber, tin, and aluminum were rationed. (A popular phrase of the day, and one that made its way into most cartoons and movies, was "Is this trip really necessary?") Various food items, especially meat and coffee, also went on the ration lists. Civilians enthusiastically pitched in with tin can drives, rounded up mountains of old tires for recycling, and collected used toothpaste tubes for their aluminum content.

To manage the war production and procurement system, Roosevelt named Sears, Roebuck president Donald M. Nelson as the head of the War Production Board (WPB), which coordinated the effort. The WPB immediately ordered all civilian car and truck production halted to convert the factories to the manufacturing of tanks and armored personnel carriers. In theory, the WPB was to have exercised the same types of powers that the WIB under Bernard Baruch had in World War I. But Nelson was not Baruch, and the demands of this war were much steeper.

Realizing the nation needed a single source of direction for the production effort, in 1943 Roosevelt created the Office of War Management (OWM), headed by former Supreme Court Justice (and FDR crony) James Byrnes. Byrnes soon demonstrated such great access to the president that people referred to him as the president's assistant. Byrnes got the job done, allowing larger companies to make as much as they could, with profits tied strictly to numbers of units produced. The government had little regard for the cost of specific items—only performance and delivery mattered. The United States was rich enough to survive postwar debt and inflation, but there would be no surviving a victorious Hitler.

War costs demanded the largest loan the American government had ever received from its people, in the form of war bonds. Bond drives resulted in a deluge of money for the war. Yet it paled beside the demands for cash—$8 billion a month!—to combat the Axis. Between 1941 and 1945 the national debt skyrocketed, from $48 billion to $247 billion. As a share of GNP measured in constant dollars, this represented a 120-fold increase over precrash 1929 debt levels.[29] This debt growth illustrated one reason isolationists were wary of war in the first place, and it also confirmed their fears about the rise of a permanent engorged bureaucracy.[30]

In another area, that of domestic surveillance and intelligence gathering, people sacrificed liberty for the war effort. Keeping tabs on the enemy and foreign agents led the government to nearly triple the budget of the Federal Bureau of Investigation in just two years. Domestic surveillance increased as the attorney general authorized extensive wiretapping in cases of espionage. A new propaganda agency, the Office of War Information, coordinated the information campaign. The Joint Chiefs of Staff also needed information on the enemy, so they formed the Office of Strategic Services (OSS), which would be the forerunner of the Central Intelligence Agency, to gather intelligence and to conduct psychological warfare against the enemy. After Americans began to take large numbers of enemy prisoners, the United States had to establish camps in the Arizona desert to house the POWs. (One U-boat commander, determined to escape, broke out of the Papago POW compound near Scottsdale, Arizona, only to find himself confronted with desert as far as his eyes could see. He was recaptured after holing up in the dry Arizona buttes for several days.)

Ironically, the very traits often denounced by the New Dealers—individual effort, self-reliance, and capitalism—were now needed to fight the war. Government-backed science, however, did succeed in delivering what no individual could, the "ultimate weapon," although the atomic bomb remained one of the best-kept secrets of the war until August 1945.

The Gadget

Experiments with splitting the atom had taken place in England in 1932, and by the time Hitler invaded Poland, most of the world's scientists understood that a man-made atomic explosion could be accomplished. How long before the actual fabrication of such a device could occur, however, no one knew. Roosevelt had already received a letter from one of the world's leading pacifists, Albert Einstein, urging him to build a uranium bomb before the Nazis did. FDR set up a Uranium Committee in October 1939, which gained momentum less than a year later when British scientists, fearing their island might fall to the Nazis, arrived in America with a black box containing British atomic secrets.[31] After mid-1941, when it was established, the Office of Scientific Research and Development (OSRD), headed by Vannevar Bush, was investigating the bomb's feasibility.

Kept out of the loop by Bush, who feared he was a security risk, Einstein used his influence to nudge FDR toward the bomb project. Recent evidence suggests Einstein's role in bringing the problem to Roosevelt's attention was even greater than previously thought.[32] Ironically, as Einstein's biographer has pointed out, without the genius's support, the bombs would have been built anyway, but not in time for use against Japan. Instead, with civilian and military authorities insufficiently aware of the vast destructiveness of such weapons in real situations, they may well have been used in Korea, at a time when the Soviet Union would have had its own bombs for counterattack, thus offering the terrifying possibility of a nuclear conflict over Korea. By wielding his considerable influence in 1939 and 1940, Einstein may have saved innumerable lives, beyond those of the

Americans and Japanese who would have clashed in Operation Olympic, the invasion of the Japanese home islands.[33]

No one knew the status of Hitler's bomb project—only that there was one. As late as 1944, American intelligence was still seeking to assassinate Walter Heisenberg (head of the Nazi bomb project), among others, unaware at the time that the German bomb was all but kaput. In total secrecy, then, the Manhattan Project, placed under the U.S. Army's Corps of Engineers and begun in the Borough of Manhattan, was directed by a general, Leslie Groves, a man with an appreciation for the fruits of capitalism. He scarcely blinked at the incredible demands for material, requiring thousands of tons of silver for wiring, only to be told, "In the Treasury [Department] we do not speak of tons of silver. Our unit is the troy ounce."[34] Yet Groves got his silver and everything else he required. Roosevelt made sure the Manhattan Project lacked for nothing, although Roosevelt himself died before seeing the terrible fruition of the Manhattan Project's deadly labors.

War Strategy: Casablanca

The intense concern both Roosevelt and the British displayed over producing the bomb reflected their deepest fear that Hitler's Germany would soon develop its own weapon of mass destruction. They did not know that Germany would soon begin plans for the A-9/A-10 100–ton intercontinental rocket. In retrospect, if the intercontinental rocket had been mated to atomic warheads, the war might have ended much differently. Allied spies were unaware of other potential threats to the U.S. mainland: Germany flew the four-engine Me-264 Amerika bomber in 1942, which later was converted into a jet bomber capable of 500-miles-per-hour speeds. The Nazis had already flown a Ju-290 reconnaissance plane to New York and back, taking pictures and proving that a bomber could attack New York. With their fears of known German technology combined with Stalin's pleas for a second front, Churchill and Roosevelt knew that they had to focus on defeating Germany, not Japan, first.

On New Year's Day, 1942, the representatives of twenty-six nations at war with the Axis powers signed a Declaration of the United Nations based on the principles of the Atlantic Charter. They promised not to make a separate peace with any of the Axis powers and agreed to defeat Germany first. That decision only formalized what British prime minister Winston Churchill and Roosevelt had already concluded in private talks. Churchill, one of the few Western leaders to fully appreciate the barbarity and evil of Soviet communism, repeatedly expressed his concerns to FDR. But the president, based in part on the naïve reports of his ambassador, Joseph Davies, trusted Stalin to behave rationally; thus Churchill, who desperately needed American war matériel, could do little to talk Roosevelt into a more sober assessment of Russia's overall aims. In January 1943, Churchill, Roosevelt, and the Combined Chiefs of Staff met at Casablanca to discuss war strategy. Stalin did not attend. The meeting produced the defeat-Germany-first decision and directed the resources to the European war. It also resulted in a commitment on the part of the Allies to demand unconditional surrender from all Axis parties.[35]

Consequently, the Anglo-American leaders agreed that nearly 80 percent of America's war capacity would go toward the European theater and, especially in the early days, the bombing campaign aimed to soften up Germany for the necessary amphibious invasion. Churchill saw bombing as a way to draw in the United States and use her massive economic output, but at the same time minimize the loss of American lives and avoid early public hostility.

Since the prospects for invading the European mainland in 1942 were remote, about all Britain and America could do while building up was launch devastating air strikes on German manufacturing, especially on those industries related to aircraft production. The goal was to ensure total domination of the skies over whatever landing area the Allies would choose at some future point. Much debate has ensued over the supposed ineffectiveness of the air campaign that dropped between 1.5 and 2.6 million tons of bombs (depending on which aircraft are included in the survey) on Germany and related European targets. Many analysts have labeled strategic bombing a failure. It is true that Germany's production actually increased between 1942 and 1944, and bombing was costly, in both lives and money. Several factors must be weighed, however. Nazi production increased because until late in the war Hitler had ordered his production chief Albert Speer to keep German civilian life as normal as possible. This meant that Germany retained excess capacity in her factories until near the end, having never put the nation on a total-war footing. Some of the continued buildup during the bombing reflected not a failure of bombing, but of Germany's unwillingness to fully mobilize earlier.

Second, in the early stages of the bombing campaign, neither Great Britain nor the United States had fighter planes with enough range to escort the bombers, so raids were conducted over enemy skies amid swarms of Luftwaffe aircraft, resulting in substantial losses. The United States agreed to fly missions during the day, based in part on the availability of the superior (and secret) Norden bombsight, which allowed the Americans to engage in pinpoint bombing as opposed to area or carpet bombing.[36] That meant the loss of American aircraft and life would be higher than that of the British, who bombed at night. B-17 Flying Fortress bombers began regular raids on European targets in August 1942, striking targets in France. Then, in January 1943, the Eighth Army Air Force began missions against Germany itself.[37] Even when flying in tight box formations, B-17s suffered tremendous losses, especially when out of escort range. Nevertheless, Germany had to commit increasingly greater resources to countering the bombers, thus diverting crucial resources from antitank tactical aircraft for the Eastern Front.

Despite the high cost in men and planes, the strategic bombing campaign achieved a decisive victory almost from its inception. Surprisingly, even the U.S. government's own "Strategic Bombing Survey" after the war tended to obscure the overwhelming success in the skies. In retrospect the devastation caused by Allied bombing, and its key role in the war, is clear. First, German aircraft were siphoned away from the Eastern Front, where they could have made the difference against Russian tanks. Second, the bombing hindered the Third Reich's war production, especially of transport and oil, and there is no way of telling how many more aircraft, submarines, or tanks could have been produced without the bombing. Germany tied up nearly 20 percent of its nonagricultural workforce in air defense activities, and bombing reduced reserves of aviation gas by 90 percent. This represented millions of combat troops and civilians, not to mention pilots, who were pinned down by part-time defense duty. Existing statistics may even substantially understate the percentage of workers absorbed by the bombing because many were foreign slaves and POWs. Rail transportation—absolutely critical for getting larger Tiger tanks to the Russian front—plummeted by 75 percent in a five-month period because of the impact of air power.[38]

Third, even before the long-range fighter aircraft appeared on the scene in 1943, the Luftwaffe had lost large numbers of fighter planes in its attempts to defend against bomber attacks. Every time a Messerschmitt went down, however, it took with it a pilot; and although most German pilots bailed out over friendly territory, not all survived. Pilot training took years, placing a huge burden on the Luftwaffe when it had to send up inexperienced youngsters to stop the waves of bombers over German skies. That had a cascading effect: inexperienced pilots were easier to shoot down. In short, the strategic bombing campaign worked more effectively than anyone had dreamed. By June 6, 1944, in the skies over Normandy on D-Day, the Allies could put eleven thousand aircraft over the battlefield. The Germans responded with two, a pair of desperate Messerschmitt pilots who made a single pass over Normandy before fleeing with the satisfaction that "the Luftwaffe has had its day!"[39]

"Remember Bataan!"

But the road to D-Day was long and rugged. Despite the strategic concern with Hitler, most Americans had turned their attention first, in 1942, to events in the Pacific, where Japan continued to crush opposition. Singapore, Britain's powerful naval base in Malaysia, fell in February 1942, when Japanese armies cut off the city's water supplies, having used bicycles to negotiate the dense impregnable jungle. When they arrived, they were short on food and water, and they took the base largely through bluff and luck. Moreover, the Japanese soldiers only had a hundred rounds of ammunition per man left. A vigorous defense of the city would have rendered General Tomoyuki Yamashita's troops virtually unarmed, but the legend of the invincible Japanese soldier already had started to set in, and the British surrendered.

By that time, Japan had eliminated virtually all Allied naval forces east of Pearl Harbor. The British battleships *Repulse* and *Prince of Wales* had left Singapore, only to be destroyed by air strikes in December. Australia to the south and Pearl Harbor to the east lay open to Japanese invasion, and Australia found itself hamstrung by its own socialist policies and labor unions, whose stevedores "refused to modify their union contracts in order to aid the war effort," including clauses that "allowed the laborers to refuse work when it was raining."[40] American forces in the Philippines held out until April ninth, but before the surrender President Roosevelt ordered the American commander, General Douglas MacArthur, to relocate in Australia, where, as commander in chief of Allied forces in the Pacific, he organized a more tenacious defense. Following the surrender of the American island bastion of Corregidor, some eleven thousand Americans on the Bataan Peninsula were marched inland on hot jungle roads with no food or water. This Bataan Death March revealed the Japanese to be every bit as vicious as the Nazis. Japanese soldiers bayoneted American soldiers who fell by the wayside or tied them up in barbed wire to be eaten by ants. "Remember Bataan" and "Remember Pearl Harbor" would soon become the battle cries of GIs who stormed the beaches of Japanese-held islands.

The constant drumbeat of disasters enhanced the image of superhuman Japanese fighting forces. When a Japanese sub surfaced off the coast of Oregon to lob shells harmlessly onto continental U.S. soil, American planners anticipated that it indicated an imminent invasion of San Francisco, San Diego, or the Los Angeles area. Bunkers were thrown up at Santa Barbara; skyscrapers in Los Angeles sported antiaircraft guns on their roofs; and lights on all high-rise buildings were extinguished or covered at night to make it more difficult for imperial bombers to hit their targets. Local rodeo associations and the Shrine Mounted Patrol conducted routine reconnaissance of mountains, foothills, and deserts, checking for infiltrators. No one could guess that this shocking string of victories actually marked the high tide of imperial Japanese success, not the beginning.

Understanding the psychological impact of the Japanese successes in 1942 is critical to explaining Roosevelt's decision to put Japanese American citizens of California, Oregon, and Washington State into "relocation camps." Some 110,000 Japanese Americans, most of them citizens, were removed from their homes and moved to inland centers in Idaho, Wyoming, Nevada, California, and Arizona.[41] Opponents of the internment of Japanese Americans formed an odd political mix. Conservatives included FBI Director J. Edgar Hoover, who thought the move unnecessary, and Robert Taft of Ohio, who was the only congressman to vote in opposition to the 1942 bill. Liberal critics included Supreme Court Justices Felix Frankfurter and Hugo Black and future Chief Justice Earl Warren (California's Republican governor).

Liberal historians have ascribed racist motives to the Japanese American relocation, pointing to the fact that the same thing was not done to German Americans or Italian Americans on the East Coast.[42] In fact, both groups already had been under close scrutiny by the FBI and other agencies, a holdover policy from World War I, when German Americans had indeed experienced persecution and been denied fundamental civil liberties. Yet the comparison of the two is otherwise untenable. Although Germany had for a short time threatened the eastern U.S. coastline, by 1942 the Germans not only lacked a blue-water fleet, but also had not staged a successful amphibious invasion in two years. Germany had no aircraft carriers and no troopships. And Germany had certainly not launched an air strike two thousand miles from its home base across an ocean as had Japan at Pearl Harbor.

Today, with the benefit of hindsight, most can agree that the relocation of Japanese Americans during World War II was an unfair and mistaken policy. Although the wartime Supreme Court supported Roosevelt's policy (Executive Order 9066), a subsequent ruling vacated the World War II decision, making the relocation order inoperable (but stopping short of overturning it). Subsequently, Nisei internees were awarded $1.25 billion in reparations during the Reagan administration. Yet with the benefit of the same hindsight, one must say that the relocation was not, as two historians label it, a policy of "hysterical racial repression."[43] Instead, Roosevelt took understandable precautions to protect national security in the face of what most Americans firmly believed was an impending attack.

A few contemporary liberal scholars continue to call the Japanese American internment camps concentration camps. Considering that this same term is also applied to the Nazi and Japanese camps, its usage is loaded indeed. In fact, there existed critical and simple distinctions between the two. Can anyone honestly compare the American camps—where perseverant, brave, and industrious Japanese Americans grew vegetables and flowers, published their own newspapers, established schools, and organized glee clubs and Little League baseball teams for their children—to Auschwitz and Bataan? Can anyone forget the brave Nisei men who, despite the wrongs they had suffered, left the camps to join and fight bravely in the U.S. Army's European theater? Moreoever, had Germany won the war, does anyone actually believe the inmates in the Nazi camps would have been released—let alone paid reparations? The fact that the United States not only addressed the constitutional violations with shame, and ultimately attempted to make restitution speaks volumes about the fundamental differences in worldviews between America and the Axis.

Yet the constant string of bad news that produced the internment camps, and the apparent Japanese invincibility, masked a fatal flaw in the Japanese war mentality. Like other non-Western cultures, Japan, despite her rapid modernization in the early twentieth century, had not adopted the fundamentals of a free society that produces westernized soldiers. Bushido, the warrior code, combined with the Shinto religion to saddle Japan with a fatal strategy employing surprise and quick strikes—all aimed at forcing the United States to exit the war with a treaty. Japan did not understand that it was at war with a westernized democracy with a tradition of civic militarism—an American nation that fought with intense discipline, yet incorporated the flexibility of individuality. Whereas Japanese admirals went down with their ships, American admirals transferred to other vessels, realizing that long after their ships were gone, the navy would still need their talent. Junior officers of all ranks respectfully criticized war plans and offered suggestions, providing a self-evaluation for the armed forces that did not exist in Germany or Japan. Above all, the Western way of war, with its emphasis on the value of the individual and his life, demanded an unrelenting campaign to the finish—a war of annihilation or total surrender, without a face-saving honorable exit.

American victory, however, seemed in the far distance as Japan conquered Burma, closing the Burma supply road to China; captured Wake Island; and threatened Port Moresby in New Guinea. In its relentless march of conquest, Japan had grabbed more territory and subjugated more people than any other empire in history and, for the most part, had accomplished all this in a matter of months—all for the net cost of one hundred aircraft, a few destroyers, and minor casualties in the army. Threats still remained, however. Destroying the four American aircraft carriers in the Pacific, which had escaped the Pearl Harbor massacre, remained a prime strategic objective for the imperial fleet, especially after the shocking bombing of Tokyo in April 1942 by Colonel Jimmy Doolittle's force.

Doolittle, convinced that the United States needed a victory of some sort to regain its confidence, conceived a mission in which highly modified B-25 bombers (fittingly named the Mitchell bombers for Colonel Billy Mitchell) would take off from a carrier, bomb Tokyo, then continue on to safe airfields inside China. Even in the planning stages, Doolittle doubted that most of his aircraft would make it to China. Their chances grew slimmer when the *Hornet's* task force was discovered and Doolittle had to launch early. Nevertheless, the strike force attacked Tokyo in broad daylight as flabbergasted Japanese warlords looked on (described in Ted Lawson's famous book, *Thirty Seconds over Tokyo*).[44] Although some of the crews were killed or captured—three were beheaded after Japanese trials—the raid exceeded American expectations.

Not only did Doolittle's brave crews buck up morale, but the attack also so incensed imperial planners that it goaded them into reckless attacks in the Coral Sea and near Port Moresby. And it convinced Yamamoto that Midway Island was a strategic target. At the Battle of the Coral Sea, American and Japanese fleets engaged in the first naval engagement in history fought solely by carrier-launched aircraft. Most history books call the battle a draw, with both sides losing a carrier and the American carrier *Yorktown* suffering what most thought was crippling damage. In fact, however, the loss of the *Yorktown*, which headed for an expected two-month repair job at Pearl Harbor, left the Allies with exactly two undamaged capital ships—carriers *Lexington* and *Hornet*—in the eastern Pacific to confront the entire Japanese fleet.

Miracle at Midway

What occurred next was nothing short of what historian Gordon Prange termed a "Miracle at Midway." Determined to force the last two carriers out in the open and destroy them, Yamamoto moved an invasion force toward Midway Island. His real goal, though, was to lure the American carriers into positions for destruction. Midway's airfield had to be eliminated first. Japanese attacks failed to knock out the airfield, requiring second strikes. But where were the carriers? After receiving reports from scout planes he had sent in an arc around Midway, Yamamoto ordered a second attack on the island. Only one scout had yet to report when Ya-mamoto rolled the dice and ordered his tactical bombers to rearm for another attack on the island.

In the midst of this tedious reloading process, word arrived from the last scout: the American carrier fleet was right below him! At that point, Yamamoto countermanded his previous order and then instructed the aircraft to prepare for attacking the carriers (which required a complete change in the types of armaments on the planes). Apparently out of nowhere, several squadrons of American planes from the two U.S. carriers—launched independently and groping blindly for the Japanese fleet—all converged at the same instant. They all were shot down. This, actually, was good news in disguise.

In the process of wiping out the attackers, the Japanese Zeros ran out of fuel, and there was another delay as they landed and refueled. Suddenly another squadron of American dive-bombers appeared above the Japanese fleet, which, with no fighter cover and all its planes, bombs, and fuel sitting exposed on its carrier decks, was a giant target in a shooting gallery. The American aircraft, astoundingly enough, had come from the *Yorktown*, her two-week repair job completed in forty-eight hours by some twelve hundred technicians working nonstop. In a matter of minutes, *Yorktown*'s aircraft had sunk three of the carriers, and a follow-up strike by the other U.S. carriers' reserves destroyed the fourth. *Yorktown* herself was again badly damaged, so much so that she had to be sunk by a U.S. sub on her way back to Pearl, but the United States had pulled off its miracle. Not only did Japan lose four modern carriers, but more important, more than three hundred trained pilots died when the ships sank. Japan never recovered, and in the blink of an eye, the empire's hopes for victory had vanished. The Japanese never won another substantial victory, and even though bloody fighting continued on many islands, Japan lost the war in June 1942.

The End of the "Thousand-Year Reich"

Germany's invasion of Russia in May 1941 led to a string of victories as sweeping and unrelenting as Japan's early conquest of Asia, putting Nazi forces just ten miles outside Moscow. In retrospect the German assault on Russia was a huge blunder, pitting Nazi armies against the bottomless pit of Soviet manpower and the vastness of Russian geography. At the time, even many Wehrmacht officers knew they lacked the resources to pull off such a military operation. Germany's supply lines were widely overextended; and Hitler's generals, who had warned him they needed far more trucks and tanks, displayed astonishment at the incredible size of Russia, which seemed to swallow up their army.

Nevertheless, Nazi successes led Stalin's diplomats to press the British and Americans for immediate relief through an invasion of Europe. As of 1942, neither the United States nor Britain (nor, certainly, the limited Free French or Polish forces that had retreated to England) had nearly enough men or matériel in place to achieve a successful invasion of France from the English Channel. In August 1942 the British tried a mini-invasion, called a reconnaissance-in-force, at Dieppe, which proved a disaster. The debacle did, however, alert Eisenhower to the difficulties of breaching Hitler's defenses, called the Atlantic Wall, which was a gigantic series of concrete barriers, pillboxes, barbed wire, minefields, and tank traps built by tens of thousands of slave laborers and prisoners of war.

Between January 1942 and July 1943, the war continued on another hidden, but absolutely vital, front. Germany's U-boats had conducted a devastating undersea war against shipping from America to Britain and the Soviet Union. Whatever industrial might the United States had was meaningless if it was unable to get war materials and food to England and Russia. In January 1942 a German submarine force of only six vessels unleashed a ferocious series of attacks on ships leaving U.S. ports. Many were sunk within sight of the coast, their silhouettes having marked them as easy targets against the lights of the cities. During a six-month period, a handful of U-boats sank 568 Allied ships. Carefully moving his forces around, German Admiral Karl Doenitz kept the Allies off balance, returning to the North Atlantic in November 1942, when many escorts had been diverted to support the landings in Africa. That month, Doenitz's U-boats sank 117 ships. This rate of sinking exceeded even Henry Kaiser's incredible capacity to build Liberty Ships.

Finally, under the direction of Admiral Ernest King, a combination of air cover, added escorts (including small carrier escorts that could launch antisubmarine aircraft quickly), and the convoy system, the United States slowly turned the U-boat war around. New location devices—sonar and radar—aided in the search for subs. By May 1943, when thirty U-boats were sunk, the Allies had made the sea-lanes relatively safe. Again, however, only a narrow margin separated victory from defeat: a handful of subs had come close to winning the war in the Atlantic. Had Hitler shifted even a minimal amount of resources to building additional subs in 1941–42, there could have been disastrous consequences for the Allies.

In the meantime, Germany's success in Africa under General Erwin Rommel, the "Desert Fox," had convinced General Dwight D. "Ike" Eisenhower, commander of the Allied forces in Northwest Africa, that the British plan for retaking North Africa was both necessary and feasible. Ike commanded a multinational force, with the November 1942 landings in Casablanca (French Morocco), Algiers, and Oran (French Algeria) now opening a true second front in Africa. American and British forces now closed in on Rommel from the west, while British general Bernard Montgomery's Desert Rats of the Eighth Army pushed out from Egypt through Libya in the east. Superior American and British naval power pounded the Germans and Italians from the sea, and Allied control of the air soon left the Axis forces in Africa reeling, leaving them holding only Tunisia. Operation Torch ended any hopes Germany had of extending eastward to link up with the Japanese. In May 1943 more than a quarter of a million German and Italian soldiers surrendered, dealing Hitler his first serious defeat and securing the Mediterranean for Allied navies once and for all. But Allied forces failed to bag the Desert Fox, who escaped to supervise construction of the Atlantic Wall that the Allies would have to breach in June 1944.

Germany's defeat in North Africa technically opened for Stalin his much-desired second front, but to little avail. Hitler had dedicated no more than a small portion of Germany's resources to Africa. However, Sicily, and later mainland Italy, now lay open for invasion. In July 1943, after deceiving the Germans with an elaborate hoax involving a corpse that washed ashore in Spain with information that the invasion would occur in Greece, Patton and Montgomery invaded Sicily at different spots on the island. The ruse worked: Hitler had reinforced Greece, and advancing American troops encountered enthusiastic Italian citizens who greeted the liberators with cries of "Down with Mussolini!" and "Long live America!" Italian soldiers surrendered by the thousands, and townspeople threw flowers at GIs and gave them wine and bread. If the Italian army no longer posed a threat to the invaders, the German troops that remained proved far more determined and skillful, mining roads, blowing up bridges, and otherwise successfully delaying the Allied advances long enough to escape back to the Italian mainland.

The defeat on Sicily coincided with increased Italian dissatisfaction with Mussolini and his unpopular war, and it occurred at a pivotal moment during the struggle in the East. Hitler, weighing whether to continue the offensive at Kursk with reinforcements or to divert them to Italy, chose the latter. His concerns about Italian allegiance were well founded. While the forces were en route, Allied aircraft dropped propaganda leaflets urging the Italian people to abandon the regime, and on July 24, 1943, even the Fascist ministers in the Grand Council agreed to hand control of the Italian army back to the king, Victor Emmanuel III, who accepted Mussolini's resignation. Marshal Pietro Badoglio, Il Duce's successor, signed an unconditional surrender in September 1943. Germany reacted before the Allies could actually occupy the mainland of Italy or before Mussolini himself could be captured, but the second front had in fact helped ensure Soviet victory at Kursk.

The Nazis' thirteen divisions—more than 100,000 men—arrived, seized Rome and other major cities, and freed Mussolini from his house arrest, reinstalling him as a puppet dictator. That meant, of course, that Hitler was then calling the shots for all of Italy. German general Albert Kesselring, who directed the German defense, instructed his troops to dig in across the rocky northern part of the country and fortify every pass. Patton's open-field tank tactics would have been useless even if he had remained in command, but an incident in which he slapped soldiers for cowardice on two separate occasions prompted Eisenhower to discipline him. Patton's temper tantrum (which his biographer suggests may have been caused by the general's own battle fatigue) was a blessing in disguise because it saved him from a slow and bloody slog up the Italian coast. Murderous fire and dogged resistance by the Germans delayed the American conquest of Italy, which had other unintended effects. A rapid Italian campaign would have enabled the Anglo-American forces to invade the Balkans, preventing Eastern

Europe from falling into the grasp of the Red Army. Instead, Naples fell on September 30, 1943, after which Allied troops plodded inch by inch up the coast, covering less than a hundred miles by June 1944, when Rome was liberated, only two days before the D-Day invasion.

The Longest Day

Thanks to Admiral King's effective anti-U-boat campaign, and air superiority, by 1943 the United States had turned a trickle of supplies, maintained by a tenuous lifeline through the submarine packs, into a flood that poured through open-ocean pipelines. On any given day, more than thirty convoys were at sea with more than 650 merchant ships and 140 escorts. After midyear, virtually none of the troopships were lost to torpedoes. This stream of materials and men had made possible the invasion of Sicily and Italy, and now it opened the door for the invasion of France.

All along, Roosevelt and Churchill, despite their hopes for a quick surge up the coast of Italy, knew that talk of the "soft underbelly of Europe" was just that, and an invasion of France by sea was necessary. Planners had concluded that an invasion could only occur during summer months, given the tides along the beaches at Normandy where the Allies wanted to land and the weather that would permit air cover. In December 1943, Roosevelt and Churchill appointed General Eisenhower commander of the Supreme Headquarters Allied Expeditionary Force (SHAEF), headquartered in London. As a masterful diversion, Patton, who had been languishing in Eisenhower's doghouse because of his Sicilian slaps, was ordered to set up a vast—and completely phony—"army" poised to attack the Pas-de-Calais, exactly where Hitler had determined the Allies would strike. But Ike had other ideas. The real invasion was to occur two hundred miles away, on the beaches of Normandy, where there was more room and fewer German ports or defenses. Operation Overlord involved more than 1.6 million American soldiers as well as British, Canadians, Poles, and Free French.

In retrospect, the invasion seemed destined for success from the outset: the Allies owned the air and sea-lanes; they vastly outnumbered the defenders—some of whom were the unlikeliest of conscripts (including a handful of Korean POWs)—and they had the French and Belgian resistance movements to assist behind the lines. At the time, however, the invasion presented countless dangers and could have collapsed at any of a number of points. Lingering in the minds of Allied planners was the Canadian disaster at Dieppe and the ill-fated landing at Anzio. Churchill worried about another potential catastrophe, perhaps a new Dunkirk, and Ike's own advisers estimated the odds of success at no better than even.[45]

Nevertheless, the Allies possessed overwhelming air and sea superiority, large numbers of fresh troops, and the element of surprise. They read the German secret Enigma codes, which provided crucial, often pinpoint, intelligence. The bombing campaign had already severely winnowed not only the Luftwaffe, but the regular army and defensive positions. Both the British and American forces had good field commanders like General Montgomery, General Omar Bradley, and Lieutenant General Theodore Roosevelt Jr. , the son of President Teddy Roosevelt. Facing them, the German commander was no less than the famed Desert Fox, Rommel himself, who had organized a thorough network of coastal defenses including mines, barbed wire, tank traps, bunkers, and pillboxes—all topped off with a series of trenches running along the high ground above the beaches. Rommel had strenuously argued for concentrating his forces—including the reserves of Panzers—close to the beaches and fighting at the water's edge. His superior, Field Marshal Gerd von Rundstedt, favored allowing the enemy to land, then striking before they could consolidate. As a result, the Germans had infantry at the beaches, tanks in the rear, and little coordination between them. Rommel appreciated the difficulty of the situation and prophesied that there would only be one chance to defeat the invasion, and perhaps, decide the entire war: "The war will be won or lost on the beaches. . . . We'll have only one chance to stop the enemy and that's while he's in the water." It would be, he observed, "the longest day" of the war.[46]

Eisenhower had to consider another enemy: the weather, which could do as much damage to the invasion fleet as the Germans. On June fourth, when he had originally planned to launch Overlord, strong winds, rain, and waves scuttled the landings. Weather forecasts suggested that they had a thirty-six-hour window to invade, or risk delaying another month, and that, in turn, could hang up Allied troops on the Siegfried line in winter.

More than 2,700 ships headed across the Channel, and on the night of June fifth, thousands of airborne and glider troops of the 101st Airborne and 82nd Airborne dropped in behind the beaches to disrupt communications and transportation, and to hold key bridges. Although some units were blown as far as thirty-five miles off course by high winds, most of them secured the important causeways and bridges, aided by thousands of human-looking one-third-scale dummy paratroopers that fell from the sky along with the real soldiers. The dummies contributed to the confusion and chaos of German forces holding key towns. Next, at dawn on D-Day, June 6, 1944, came more than 11,000 aircraft, pounding targets and raining bombs onto the German positions. Unfortunately, clouds and smoke obscured the targets, and the air cover contributed little to relieving the hell on the beaches when the first units went ashore.

Fighting on parts of Omaha Beach proved particularly gruesome. Hundreds of men drowned in the choppy Channel water; German gunners peppered the ramps of the landing boats with machine-gun and sniper fire even before they dropped, pinning the helpless men behind the dead and wounded in front of them; and a murderous cross fire slaughtered 197 out of 205 men in a single rifle company. Even if the men leaped over the side of the Higgins boats, the rain of fire from the bluffs raked the water mercilessly—if the weight of their own packs and equipment did not drown them first. All the troops could do was frantically run or crawl to the sand dunes at the base of the Atlantic Wall, where they were temporarily immune from fire, but where they also remained helpless to strike back. One heroic tank group, whose Higgins boat was unable to get any closer than three miles from shore, insisted on plunging into the water. All the tankers drowned trying to reach land.

Meanwhile, those trapped ashore had to attack or die. Rising as if one, thousands of Americans on the beaches rose at the urging of brave captains, lieutenants, and sergeants and assaulted the defenses. One colonel urged his men on, screaming, "There are only two kinds of people on this beach. Those who are dead and those who will be. Move in!"[47] Slowly, the enemy positions collapsed, and as each fell, the overlapping fields of fire vanished, allowing still more GIs to pour ashore. By the end of the day, Allied beachheads penetrated as far inland as seven miles. What Rommel had predicted would be the longest day of the war was over, and the Allies held the field, but more than 10,000 Allied soldiers were dead or wounded. Despite the carnage on Omaha, however, the inability of the Atlantic Wall to contain the invaders had to be considered one of the greatest military failures of the war.

Churchill hailed the invasion. "What a plan!" he said to Parliament, and even Stalin called the invasion unprecedented in history, with its "vast conception and its orderly execution."[48] All along, though, Ike had known that the Normandy invasion contained enormous risks for potential disaster. He had therefore drafted a statement in the afternoon of June fifth, hours before the first airborne troops would touch European soil: "Our landings . . . have failed and I have withdrawn the troops. . . . Any blame . . . is mine alone."[49] In failure Eisenhower was willing to shoulder all the blame, yet in victory he gladly shared credit with his commanders and his troops. "It just shows what free men will do rather than be slaves," he told reporter Walter Cronkite in 1964.[50]

Within two months, the Allies held a tactical beachhead and had brought in enough supplies that at the end of July they could attempt a breakout. Using a devastating air bombardment—this time extremely effective—Bradley's troops punched out at Saint-Lô. With the Americans coming down from the northeast (behind the enemy), and the British and Americans from the west, the German Seventh Army was nearly encircled. Hitler ordered a counterattack to drive between the armies, but once again, Ultra, the code-breaking operation, allowed the Allies to place antitank guns in defensive positions to slaughter the advancing panzers. Hitler finally ordered a retreat. German forces now rushed to escape complete encirclement. Thanks to a rearguard defense at the Falaise Gap, one third of the German forces escaped the pincer, but overall, the disaster "was the worst German defeat since Stalingrad," and it ensured the liberation of France.[51] Moreover, Patton, reassigned to command of the U.S. Third Army, was now in his element—in the open fields of France with plenty of gas. By that time, the U.S. Seventh Army had invaded southern France and driven north to link up. The delay in unifying the northern and southern command in France ensured the communist domination of southeastern Europe. Already the

Soviets had taken Poland and other territories. Churchill urged the United States to divert forces from the southern French landings to an amphibious invasion on the Adriatic side of Italy, where the Anglo-American forces could swing east and save large parts of the Balkans from Soviet conquest. But at the Tehran Conference in 1943, Roosevelt had promised eastern Europe to Stalin.

Meanwhile, Patton launched his armored invasion, bypassing Paris in pursuit of the fleeing German army, capturing an astounding 2,700 Germans per day. This allowed French partisans, in conjunction with the French Second Armored Division, to liberate the City of Light. General Charles de Gaulle led the procession down the Champs-Élysées in August 1944. With Bradley's armies gulping enormous quantities of fuel and consuming vast stockpiles of supplies, the Red Ball Express, a continuous trucking route from the beaches to the front, tried to maintain a flow of materials.

Here Eisenhower's good judgment failed him. Montgomery from the north and Bradley in the center-south both demanded supplies, and the Allies had enough to keep only one of the two groups moving decisively. Either group probably could have punched through to Berlin, perhaps ahead of the Soviets. True to his diplomatic evenhandedness throughout the invasion effort, however, Ike refused to focus all the emphasis on one spearhead, choosing to advance slowly across a broad front. Perhaps because he realized that the Anglo-American forces were capable of a bolder stroke, Eisenhower approved Montgomery's plan for Operation Market Garden, an overly ambitious airborne drop intended to capture six key bridges in Holland leading into Germany. But advancing British armored units could not seize the bridge at Arnhem in time, and the operation failed. Weather, not Hitler, slowed the Allies. Over Christmas, 1944, American armies settled down for a hibernal regrouping.

A Contrast in Governments

Meanwhile, a political nonevent occurred back home. In November 1944, Roosevelt ran for a fourth term. Governor Thomas A. Dewey of New York, the Republican nominee, came remarkably close in the popular vote (22 million to FDR's 25 million), but suffered a blowout in the electoral college (432 to 99). Dewey and the Republicans had virtually no platform. They supported the war and could hardly complain about FDR's wartime leadership. Roosevelt, by virtue of his control over presidential events at a time when gas and even newsreels were "war materials," could overwhelm any foe with a propaganda blitz. To appease the party bosses, however, Roosevelt ditched left-wing vice president Henry Wallace, who was certainly the most radical politician ever to hold that office, and replaced him with someone more politically appealing, Senator Harry S. Truman of Missouri.

An "election" of sorts was also being held in Germany, where, not long after D-Day, a cadre of German officers attempted to assassinate Hitler with a bomb at his Wolf's Lair bunker. They failed. He had the ringleaders brutally executed.

The contrast between the two episodes of choosing leadership—one in

America, one in Nazi Germany—could not be clearer. In the totalitarian state, where death reigned, Hitler escaped removal through luck, terror, and total control of the state media. But in the United States, even during a major war whose outcome still had not been decided, regular elections took place, and the Republican opponent mounted a substantial challenge to a popular incumbent.

The Wolf's Lair assassination attempt reflected the desperation of the professional officer class in Germany, which was in sharp contrast to the deluded Hitler's fantasies of victory. Despite the increasing collapse of the Eastern Front, Hitler remained convinced that a sharp victory would turn American public opinion against the war and allow him to regain the initiative. He therefore stockpiled some 2,000 tanks, including the new Tiger IIs, an equal number of planes, and three full armies for a massive counterattack through Belgium under the cover of winter weather. Hitler still fantasized that he could split Allied lines, somehow force the United States to withdraw from the war, and defeat the Soviets in the East without pressure from the Western Front. In December 1944, the Battle of the Bulge began as Germans ripped a hole forty-five miles wide in Allied lines. Devoid of air cover, Allied troops rushed poorly supplied units, such as the 82nd Airborne, under General Anthony McAuliffe, to key spots like Bastogne. Lacking winter gear, and often without ammunition, the airborne forces nevertheless somehow held out as an isolated pocket in the German rear. When German negotiators approached, asking McAuliffe to surrender, he responded with the one-word reply, "Nuts!" Then the weather cleared, and the Nazi advance ground to a halt. Eisenhower's staff quickly assembled 11,000 trucks and 60,000 men to throw into the breach on a single day. Again, American productivity and volume of equipment overcame temporary tactical disadvantages as the American forces hurled a quarter of a million men at the German troops, spearheaded by Patton's Third Army, which arrived to rescue the 82nd.[52] To this day, living members of the 82nd reject the notion that they needed rescuing. Either way, the outcome in the West was no longer in doubt.

In another sense, however, the Battle of the Bulge was a postwar defeat for the United States: by shifting massive forces away from the Eastern Front, Hitler had ensured that the Soviets and not the Anglo-Americans would capture Berlin. Attacking just weeks after Bastogne was relieved, the Red Army swept through Poland, moved into East Prussia, and slowed only thirty miles from Berlin. Eisenhower's resupplied troops crossed the Rhine River (Patton ceremoniously urinated in the river), capturing the bridge at Remagen that the Germans had intended, but failed, to destroy. While the Russians regrouped on the Oder River east of Berlin, Patton swung into Czechoslovakia, and other Allied units reached the Elbe River. There Ike ordered the troops to halt. He had received a mandate from Roosevelt that Prague and Berlin were to be captured by Soviet forces. Patton fumed, arguing that he should march into the German capital before the Red army, but Ike, wishing to keep out of the geopolitics, blundered by allowing the communists to bring historic and strategic cities into their empire.

Shaping the Postwar World

Soviet forces closed to within fifty miles of Berlin by February 1945, establishing communist regimes in Poland, Czechoslovakia, and Hungary. Austria was poised to collapse, and much of Finland lay in Soviet hands. In Eastern Europe, only Greece, where Churchill had dispatched British troops to prevent a communist takeover, remained out of Stalin's orbit. The communist dictator arrived at Yalta in the Crimea for a meeting with the other members of the Big Three, Churchill and Roosevelt, able to deal from a position of strength. From February fourth to the eleventh, the three men deliberated the fate of postwar Europe. Stalin told the western leaders he would brook no unfriendly governments on his borders. Yet what, exactly, constituted the borders of an expansionist Soviet state? The boundaries of prewar Russia? Germany? Stalin did not elaborate. In fact, the Soviets, stung by the loss of millions of lives during World War II and fueled by communist self-righteousness, fully intended to impose a buffer zone across all of Eastern Europe.

Roosevelt had entered the alliance with a naïve view of Stalin, believing his advisers' reports that the dictator was interested in traditional balance-of-power concerns, not a buffer zone or an expansionist communist ideology. Roosevelt ignored the reality of Stalin's mass exterminations—which had exceeded Hitler's—going so far as to tell Churchill, "I think I can personally handle Stalin better than either your Foreign Office or my State Department."[53] Roosevelt even admitted planning to give Stalin "everything I possibly can and ask nothing from him in return [and therefore] he won't try to annex anything and will work with me for a world of democracy and peace."[54] This, of course, was Roosevelt admitting that he would violate the principles of the Atlantic Charter of August 1941, which he himself had codrafted, and which prohibited turning territories over to occupying countries without the "freely expressed wishes of the people concerned."

No doubt his failing health contributed to the mistaken notion that he could "control" Stalin. Stalin promised "free and unfettered elections" in Poland at the earliest convenience, but neither there, nor in other areas seized by the Red Army, did the USSR take the slightest step to withdraw. Roosevelt, on the other hand, seemed obsessed with drawing the Soviets into the war with Japan, perhaps fearing the high casualties that he knew a full-scale invasion of the home islands would produce and hoping that the Red Army would absorb its share. And at the time, FDR did not know with confidence that the atomic bomb would be ready anytime soon; he knew only that American scientists were working on it. He informed Stalin of the existence of such a program, to which Stalin responded with a shrug of indifference. The Russian dictator already knew about it, of course, through his spies; but that would only become apparent after the war.

Among other agreements at Yalta, the Big Three decided to try German and Japanese principals as war criminals, creating for the first time in history a dubious new category of villainy for the losers of a conflict. The Holocaust notwithstanding, it set a dangerous and perverse precedent, for at anytime in the future, heads of state on the wrong side of a military outcome could be easily demonized and tried for "crimes against humanity." Worse, unpopular winners could now find themselves accused of war crimes by losers whose religion or politics were shared by whatever majority of the international governing body happened, at the time, to be overseeing such nonsense. Predictably, critics of American policy in the Vietnam War some twenty years later would employ the same language against Presidents Lyndon Johnson and Richard Nixon.

Yalta also produced an agreement to hold a United Nations conference in San Francisco in April 1945, with the objective of creating an effective successor to the old League of Nations. To Roosevelt, these "concessions" by Stalin indicated his willingness to work for peace. Little did he know that Soviet spies in the United States had already provided the Russian dictator with all the information he needed about the American positions, and thus he easily outnegotiated the "woolly and wobbly" Roosevelt.[55] Others, however, noted that Stalin traded words and promises for carte blanche within territory he already held, and that having lost more than 20 million defeating Hitler, Stalin felt a few more casualties in the invasion of Japan seemed a cheap price in exchange for occupying large chunks of China, Korea, and northern Japan.

Whether or not the Soviets would actually enter the conflict in the Far East remained a matter of doubt. What was not in doubt was the complete collapse of the Axis and the inglorious deaths of the fascist dictators. Allied armies closed in on Mussolini at Milan; he fled, only to be captured by Italian communist partisans who killed the dictator and his mistress. Then, with the Red Army entering Berlin, Hitler married his mistress and the two committed suicide. On May 7, 1945, General Alfred Jodl, chief of staff of the German armed forces, surrendered unconditionally. VE Day (Victory in Europe Day), May 8, 1945, generated huge celebrations. These, however, would be tempered in relatively short order with revelations of the Holocaust and of the vast empire that the Soviets had now established. It cannot be ignored that "more Jews would be gassed from the time Patton closed in on the German border in late summer 1944 until May 1945 than had been killed during the entire first four years of the war."[56] Thus, there is some evidence to support the notion that a "narrow front" might have saved countless Jewish lives.

The Holocaust and American Jews

Roosevelt's Soviet policy, which gave the Communists undeniable advantages in postwar Europe, must be seen in the context of another issue in which pressures existed to divert resources from purely military aims, namely, a steady stream of information reaching the United States about the mass murder of Jews by the Nazis. America's response to news of this genocide, the Holocaust, patterned exactly FDR's approach to the Soviet advances and demonstrated remarkable consistency by the American government. In each case, the goal remained winning the war as quickly as possible. Roosevelt refused to veer off into any other direction, whether it involved denying the Soviets postwar footholds in the Balkans or diverting air power to bomb railroads leading to the Nazi death camps. In retrospect, however, the two issues were vastly different, and required separate analysis and solutions.

Hitler had made clear to anyone willing to read his writings or listen to his speeches that from at least 1919 he intended a *Judenfrei* (Jewish-free) Germany. Those who suggest he did not intend the physical extermination of the Jews ignore the consistency with which Hitler operated and the single-minded relentlessness of the Nuremberg Laws and other anti-Semitic legislation. Most of all, they ignore Hitler's own language: he referred to Jews as subhuman, a "bacillus," or as "parasites" on the German body. One does not reform a parasite or educate a bacillus. From his earliest speeches, he compared Jews to a disease. One does not exile a disease; one eradicates any sign of it.

Hitler's anti-Semitism has been explained by a variety of factors, none completely convincing. His motivations are irrelevant in the long run. Hitler made clear he would elevate destruction of the Jews above even winning the war.

Following a relentless and incremental program to isolate and dehumanize Jews, Germany began systematic extermination during the invasion of Russia, where killing squads called *Einsatzgruppen* followed closely behind the regular army units and massacred Jews in captured towns. Hitler carefully avoided written orders on the Holocaust, and apparently other participants received unmistakable directions to keep as much as possible out of the written record. The Nazi leader Alfred Rosenberg, after a meeting with Hitler on the Jewish issue, commented on the secrecy of the program.[57] Hitler's reluctance to document his killing program, or even discuss it publicly, is demonstrated in Himmler's speech to a group of SS officers in 1943, wherein he urged that they all "take this secret with us to the grave."[58]

In July 1941, Hitler ordered (through his propaganda head Josef Goebbels) Reinhard Heydrich to enact the "final solution," at which time some 500,000 Russian Jews already had been executed by firing squads. The term "final solution," which some Holocaust deniers lamely have tried to argue meant relocation, was defined by Goebbels—on Hitler's orders—to Heydrich. According to Heydrich's assistant, Adolf Eichmann, the term meant "the planned biological destruction of the Jewish race in the Eastern territories."[59] At the time the Japanese bombed Pearl Harbor, Hitler already controlled more than 8.7 million Jews in Europe, with orders going out the following April to round up all Jews into concentration camps.

When, exactly, FDR learned of the Holocaust remains murky. Reports had already reached public newspapers by 1942, and it is likely he knew at that time. At least one early cable, to the State Department's European Division, detailed the atrocities, yet was met with "universal disbelief," and was suppressed by Paul Culbertson, the assistant division chief.[60] Certainly the latest date at which Roosevelt could claim ignorance was November 1942, by which time "an impressive collection of affidavits and personal testimony" had descended upon the State Department.[61] Most scholars agree that by 1943 at the latest he had solid information that Hitler planned to exterminate the entire Jewish population of Europe even if it cost him the war to do so. Polls showed that more than 40 percent of all Americans at the time thought Hitler was systematically slaughtering the Jews.

For years, Roosevelt had "devoted a good deal of rhetorical sympathy to the Jews, but did nothing practical to help them get into America."[62] He had at his disposal a multitude of executive orders, bureaucratic options, and even arm-twisting with Congress, yet FDR—often accused by critics of being blatantly pro-Jewish—turned his back on Europe's Jews in their darkest hour. No special immigration waivers, exemptions, or other administrative manipulations were employed; no lobbying of allies in Latin America or elsewhere occurred, asking them to accept more Jewish immigrants.[63] The Anglo-American Bermuda Conference, ostensibly called to offer some relief, was a "mandate for inaction."[64] Roosevelt claimed that attempting to change immigration policies would result in a lengthy and bitter debate in Congress. Backed by a Treasury Department report, and amid growing public concerns that the United States should act, FDR established a War Refugee Board with limited resources and a broad mandate not specifically directed at Jews. While it facilitated the escape of perhaps two hundred thousand Jews, the government did little else.

The most recent student of the failed refugee policies, David Wyman, concludes, "The American State Department . . . had no intention of rescuing large numbers of European Jews." He points out that even under existing administrative policies, the United States admitted only 10 percent of the number of Jews who legally could have been allowed in.[65] Roosevelt's indifference was so "momentous" that it constituted the "worst failure of [his] presidency."[66] That said, FDR's policy nevertheless demonstrated rigid consistency: he pursued victory over German armies in the field in the most narrow sense, pushing aside all other considerations.

Ironically, Roosevelt's lack of concern for the Jews seemed to matter little to his Jewish supporters, who remained loyal to the Democratic Party despite the president's unenthusiastic responses to Zionist calls for the creation of the state of Israel. Had FDR not died in April 1945, it is doubtful whether Israel would have come into existence at all, as one of his assistants noted.[67] Neither he nor his State Department supported the formation of a Jewish state in Palestine. The British Foreign Office opposed it, despite signing the Balfour Declaration in 1921 guaranteeing the creation of a Zionist state; the defense departments in both the United States and Britain opposed it; and most business interests opposed it, wishing to avoid any disruption of Middle Eastern oil flow. Many American politicians worried about the influence of the "Jewish lobby." Secretary of Defense James Forrestal referred specifically to American Jews when he wrote that no group should "be permitted to influence our policy to the point where it could endanger our national security."[68]

On April 12, 1945, Franklin Roosevelt, in Warm Springs, Georgia, to prepare for the upcoming United Nations conference, died of a cerebral hemorrhage. Hitler, delusional to the end, thought that with FDR's death, the Americans would pack up and go home. Instead, the constitutional process worked perfectly, as Vice President Harry S. Truman took the oath of office as the new president. Repeatedly underestimated, Truman hardly elicited confidence from the New Deal inner circle. David Lilienthal, head of the TVA, described in his diary a "sick, hapless feeling" when it dawned on him who would replace Roosevelt.[69] Harold Ickes, the secretary of the interior, worried that Truman "doesn't have great depth mentally."[70] Truman, as dogged as Roosevelt about bringing the war to an end, nevertheless differed from FDR in his view of the Soviets—he neither liked nor trusted them—and was much more supportive of an Israeli state. By then it was too late to do much about the Holocaust, or about the communist occupation of most of Eastern Europe.

Thus, the two nonmilitary issues that could have shaped American strategy in World War II, Soviet empire building and the Holocaust, both turned on the decision by the U.S. government—from the president through the chief of staff to Eisenhower—to concentrate narrowly upon winning the war as quickly as possible. That view no doubt had its roots in the significant isolationism before the war. The United States defined the Second World War in strictly military terms, and remained completely consistent in the pursuit of military victory to the war's last days and through two different presidents. In the Pacific, the narrow focus maintained a relentless demand for the unconditional surrender of the Empire of Japan. Japanese leaders ignored those demands at a terrifying cost.

On to Japan!

Following Midway, Admiral Chester Nimitz and General Douglas MacArthur controlled the skies in the Pacific and, for the most part, the seas. Japan had lost too many trained pilots and too many ships and aircraft at Midway to oppose the steady string of island invasions that followed. Instead, Admirals Yamamoto and Nagumo conserved their naval forces, still hoping for a single Tsushima-style "big battle" that would give them a decisive victory.[71]

Guadalcanal, some six hundred miles southeast of the main Japanese staging base at Rabaul, soon emerged as the key to driving the Japanese out of the island chains. Japan had tried to build an airfield there, leading the United States to send 19,000 marines to eliminate the threat. In August 1942, less than a year after the Japanese thought they had put the American fleet out of action, eighty-nine American ships landed thousands of marines on Guadalcanal. Japan launched an immediate counterattack by the imperial navy, forcing the American support fleet to withdraw. The stranded marines were on their own. For four long months, Japanese banzai attacks hammered the leathernecks until they were rescued by Admiral William "Bull" Halsey. After the Japanese defeat, and their failure to retain the airstrip, in just over twenty-four hours the Seabees (navy construction batallions) had aircraft flying out of Guadalcanal. The victory was as momentous as the Midway success farther to the north in May, and it was quickly followed by the Australian-American invasion of Port Moresby on New Guinea.

Provided with air cover from New Guinea and Guadalcanal, MacArthur implemented his strategy of bypassing many of the more entrenched Japanese fortifications and cutting off their lines of supply and communications. Island hopping played to American strengths in numbers of aircraft and ships while at the same time minimizing U.S. casualties. In several encounters, American air superiority caused devastating losses for Japan. An important blow was delivered to the Japanese at Tarawa, an island defended to the death by forces dug into honeycombs of caves and tunnels. "A million men cannot take Tarawa in a hundred years," boasted its commander, but it took only 12,000 Marines four days to secure the island.[72] It was not easy. At "Bloody Tarawa," the United States suffered one of its highest casualty tolls, losing 983 marines killed and 2,186 wounded, but positioning American forces to strike the key Japanese naval base at Truk.[73] All but about 100 of the nearly 5,000 defenders died, refusing to surrender. "Here was an army unique in history, not because it was sworn to fight to the last man, but because it very nearly did."[74]

Japan tried one last time to deliver a crushing blow at sea to the U.S. Navy, in June 1944. Admiral Soemu Toyoda, by then in charge, planned an ambitious attack with his heaviest battleships and waves of aircraft. Before the Japanese could even get into action, American ships had sunk two carriers, and waves of Japanese strike aircraft were shot down in what was labeled the "Marianas Turkey Shoot." Japan lost 445 pilots, which, when combined with the losses at Midway, virtually eliminated any Japanese naval air activity for the rest of the war. Then, in the fall of 1944, the U.S. Navy wiped out the remainder of the Japanese fleet at the Battle of the Philippine Sea.

Bloody struggles over Iwo Jima and Okinawa remained. Despite heavy losses in each battle, MacArthur's casualty ratio in the Pacific was lower than any other general's in any theater. The success of island hopping reflected the clear superiority of American technology and U.S. wartime manufacturing capability, and enabled U.S. forces to achieve casualty ratios similar to those of Europe's colonial era. At the same time, the staggering number of American casualties on Okinawa convinced U.S. planners that an invasion of the Japanese home islands would be extremely costly, and in the long run the lists of dead from Okinawa made Truman's decision on the atomic bomb fairly easy.[75]

Since November 1944, American bombers (the new B-29 Superfortresses) had attacked the Japanese home islands from bases in the Marianas. Japanese radar installations on Iwo Jima alerted interceptor aircraft of the approaching B-29 formations, and the defenders inflicted sharp losses on the bombers. Iwo Jima not only provided an early warning system for the Japanese, but it also offered the potential of a landing field for the B-29s if it could be captured. The four-mile-long island, defended to the death by the 21,000–man garrison, featured a honeycomb of caves in which the Japanese hid. In February 1945, U.S. Marines stormed ashore to little resistance. Ordered to hold their fire until the invaders actually got on the beaches, the defenders sat through an awesome bombardment, which nevertheless did little damage to the entrenched and camouflaged Japanese troops. Once the marines were on the beaches, however, the U.S. Navy had to lift much of its bombardment, allowing the Japanese to open fire. Still, the marines moved in steadily, and on February twenty-third, a patrol scrambled its way to the top of Mount Suribachi, where it raised a small American flag—too small to be seen by the troops below. Later, another larger flag appeared; five marines and a navy medic raised the flag, captured in the classic photo by Joe Rosenthal of the Associated Press, and later reproduced as the bronze memorial to the U.S. Marines at Arlington Cemetery. Taking the island had indeed exacted the fearful cost the Japanese general had expected, with some 7,000 Americans killed, including 5,900 marines. Only 200 of the 21,000 defenders surrendered.

With Iwo Jima as a base, the bombings of Japan intensified. In March a B-29 raid on Tokyo destroyed a quarter of a million homes in the most destructive single bombing mission of the war. Astonishingly, the Japanese still refused to surrender. That required the invasion of Okinawa, just 350 miles south of Japan. Like Iwo Jima, Okinawa was defended with suicidal fervor, including generous use of the kamikaze (divine wind) suicide planes. Contrary to the myth that Japanese airmen had to be forcibly strapped into the planes, the pilots of the kamikazes volunteered for missions in which they would crash their small aircraft full of bombs into an enemy ship. One life for a thousand, the strategic reasoning went. The standard kamikaze aircraft, called *baka* bombs by the Americans (*baka* is Japanese for idiot), consisted of four-thousand-pound rocket vehicles dropped from manned bombers to be guided by their human pilots to a divine explosion on the deck of a U.S. carrier. Clouds of kamikazes—up to 350 at a time—swept down on the Okinawa landing force. Gunners shot down the incoming suicide planes in vast numbers, but enough got through that 34 ships were sunk and another 368 damaged. The attacks just about emptied Japan's arsenal, since more than 4,200 were shot down. Meanwhile, the American invasion forces pressed on, and by June, Okinawa was secured.

By that time, only Emperor Hirohito was pressing his Supreme War Council to seek peace, although recently released Japanese documents have questioned how sincere this "peace offensive" was. Hirohito himself vacillated between resistance and surrender.[76] Surrounded by American submarines, which had completely sealed off Japan and prevented importation of any raw materials from China, the country was now subjected to heavy air bombardment; and having lost virtually its entire navy, it faced direct invasion. Within the Japanese hierarchy, however, a sharp division arose between the military commanders directing the war, who had no intention of surrendering, and a peace or moderate faction. The warlords carried the day.

In June 1945, Japanese military leaders issued Operation Decision, a massive defense plan of the home islands in which some 2.5 million troops, backed by a civilian militia of 28 million, would resist the American invaders with muzzle loaders if necessary. Women "practiced how to face American tanks with bamboo spears," according to Japanese historian Sadao Asada.[77] Almost 1 million soldiers would attack the Americans on the beaches, supported by midget submarines used as manned torpedoes and more than ten thousand suicide aircraft, many of them converted trainer planes.

Aware that no hope for victory remained, the warlords promised to fight to the bitter end, and they treated the Potsdam Proclamation, issued in July by the United States, Britain, and China, with utter contempt. Although the Potsdam Proclamation stated that the term "unconditional surrender" applied only to military forces, it also made clear that Japan's home islands would be occupied, that she would lose all overseas possessions, and that a new elected government would have to replace the imperial military rule. One sticking point that remained was the fate of Emperor Hirohito, whom the Japanese people, in the tradition of the Shinto religion, regarded as a god. Would he be a war criminal subjected to the same kinds of trials as the Nazi killers, even though the Allies had specifically exempted Hirohito from reprisals? And even if he was exempted, would that change the opinion of the same warlords who had ordered the Rape of Nanking or the Bataan Death March? Reports had already leaked out about Japanese treatment of prisoners of war and Asians trapped inside the Japanese Empire. As the Allied noose tightened, the Japanese became even more brutal toward their prisoners. In Burma and elsewhere, Japanese slave-labor camps, though lacking the merciless efficiency of the Nazis, nevertheless imitated them in a more primitive form, stacking masses of bodies on teak logs and firing the pyres. As one observer reported,

> When the bodies started to char, their arms and legs twitched, and they sat up as if they were alive. Smoke came out of their burned-out eyes, their mouths opened, and licks of flames came out. . . .[78]

Ground Zero

On July 16, 1945, at a desolate spot 160 miles from Los Alamos, New Mexico, the United States tested a weapon that would make even the most hardened and suicidal Japanese leaders change their minds. The device, referred to by the Los Alamos technicians as the gadget (and never as an atomic bomb), represented an astounding technological leap and an acceleration of the normal peacetime process needed to do the job by a factor of three, compressing some fifteen to twenty years of work into five. Yet the test was only that, a test. No bomb was actually dropped. Instead, a device sitting atop a huge tower in the New Mexico desert was detonated through cables and wires from bunkers thousands of yards away. Few, however, were prepared for the fantastic destructive power released at the Trinity bomb site on July sixteenth. A fireball with temperatures four times the heat of the sun's center produced a cloud that reached thirty-eight thousand feet into the sky while simultaneously turning the sand below into glass. The cloud was followed by a shock wave that shattered windows two hundred miles away and hurricane-strength winds carrying deadly radioactive dust, the dangers of which few perceived at the time. Brigadier General Thomas Farrell reported that the air blast that came after the fireball was "followed almost immediately by the strong, sustained, awesome roar which warned of doomsday and made us feel that we were puny things, were blasphemous to dare tamper with the forces heretofore reserved to The Almighty."[79]

All along, the U.S. government had intended to use the weapon as soon as it became available on any of the Axis powers still in the war. Truman said he "regarded the bomb as a military weapon and never had any doubt that it should be used."[80] Nor did he find the actual decision to use the bomb difficult. The former army artillery major recalled that giving authority to use the atomic bomb "was no great decision, not any decision you had to worry about," but rather called the bomb "merely another powerful weapon in the arsenal of righteousnss."[81] Thus, both the condition and the attitude of Japan in late July, as the invasion and the bombs were being readied, remains the key issue in determining how necessary the use of the bombs was. At the same time, the American public had started to expect some of the troops in Europe to come home, forcing the army to adopt a point system based on a soldier's length of service, military honors, and participation in campaigns. The perverse effect of this was that "for the first time in their army careers, the officers and men became seriously concerned with medals."[82] Having defeated the Germans, few servicemen wanted to be transferred to fight the Japanese, which was an increasingly likely prospect.

Regardless of the fact that Japan had launched no new offensives, their capability to resist a large-scale invasion, with bloody results, still remained. No one doubts that in the absence of the bombs an invasion would have occurred.[83] Instead, liberal critics challenge the casualty estimates of the American planners. Based on Japan's remaining military forces, and using Iwo Jima and Okinawa casualty rates as a barometer, strategists concluded that between 100,000 and 1 million American soldiers and sailors would die in a full-scale invasion. In addition, using as a guide the civilian casualties at Manila, Okinawa, and other densely populated areas that the U.S. had reconquered during the war, the numbers of Japanese civilians expected to die in such an invasion were put at between 1 and 9 million. Critics charge that these numbers represented only the highest initial estimates, and that expected casualty rates were scaled down.

In fact, however, the estimates were probably low.[84] The figures only included ground-battle casualties, not *total* expected losses to such deadly weapons as kamikazes. Moreover, the Joint Chiefs of Staff considered its estimates, at best, only educated guesses and that the projections of Japanese resistance severely understated the number of Japanese troops.[85] Equally distressing, intercepts of Japanese secret documents revealed that Japan had concentrated all of its troops near the southern beaches, the location where the invasion was planned to begin.[86] This proved particularly troubling because the first round of casualty guesses in June was based on the anticipation that Japan's forces would be dispersed. Indeed, there were probably far more than 350,000 Japanese troops in the southern part of Kyushu—a fact that could yield at least 900,000 American combat casualties.

Other models used for estimates produced even more sobering predictors of Japanese resistance. At Tarawa, of 2,571 enemy soldiers on the island when the U.S. Marines landed, only 8 men were captured alive, indicating a shocking casualty rate of 99.7 percent; and in the Aleutians, only 29 out of 2,350 surrendered, for a fatality rate of 98.8 percent. Worse, on Saipan, hundreds of civilians refused to surrender. Marines watched whole families wade into the ocean to drown together or huddle around grenades; parents "tossed their children off cliffs before leaping to join them in death."[87] It seems clear, then, that no matter which estimates are employed, more than a million soldiers and civilians at least would die in an invasion under even the rosiest scenarios. If the bomb could save lives in the end, the morality of dropping it was clear. Perhaps more important than the what-ifs, the Japanese reaction provides sobering testimony of the bombs' value, because even *after* the first bomb fell, the Japanese made no effort whatsoever to surrender.

Recent research in classified Japanese governmental documents confirms the wisdom of Truman's decision. Historian Sadao Asada argues that it was most likely the atom bomb that finally overcame the warlords' tenacious (and suicidal) opposition to surrender. Asada concludes from postwar memoranda left by the inner councils that "the atomic bombing was crucial in accelerating the peace process." Although some hard-liners were also concerned about the possibility of a concurrent Soviet/U.S. invasion, that fear merely served as the coup de grâce. The memoirs of the deputy chief of the Army General Staff confirm this when he noted, "There is nothing we can do about the . . . atomic bomb. That nullifies everything."[88]

Truman never had the slightest hesitation about using the bomb, leaving left-wing scholars to scour his memoirs and letters for even the slightest evidence of second thoughts. He promptly gave his approval as soon as the Trinity test proved successful. Moreover, Truman planned to drop the existing bombs in a fairly rapid sequence if the warlords did not surrender, in order to convince Japan that Americans had a plentiful supply.

On August 6, 1945, two B-29s flew over Hiroshima, one of them a reconnaissance/photo plane, another the *Enola Gay*, under the command of Colonel Paul Tibbets, which carried the atomic bomb. American aircraft two days earlier had dropped three-quarters of a million warning leaflets informing citizens of Hiroshima that the city would be obliterated, but few Japanese had heeded the message. Rumors that Truman's mother had once lived nearby or that the United States planned to make the city an occupation center or just plain stubbornness contributed to the fatal decision of most inhabitants to remain.

Tibbets's payload produced an explosion about the size of 20,000 tons of TNT, or about three times the size of the August first raid, when 820 B-29 bombers had dropped 6,600 tons of TNT on several cities. More than 66,000 people in Hiroshima died instantly or soon after the explosion; some 80,000 more were injured; and another 300,000 were exposed to radiation. The Japanese government reacted by calling in its own top atomic scientist, Dr. Yoshio Nishina, inquiring whether Japan could make such a weapon in a short period.[89] Clearly, this was not the response of a "defeated" nation seeking an end to hostilities. After nothing but a deafening silence had emanated from Tokyo, Truman ordered the second bomb to be dropped. On August ninth, Nagasaki, an alternative target to Kokura, was hit. (The B-29 pilot, ordered to strike a clear target, had to abandon munitions-rich Kokura because of cloud conditions.) The deadly results were similar to those in Hiroshima: nearly 75,000 dead.

After Nagasaki, Japanese officials cabled a message that they accepted in principle the terms of unconditional surrender. Still, that cable did not itself constitute a surrender. Truman halted atomic warfare (an act that in itself was a bluff, since the United States had no more bombs immediately ready), but conventional raids continued while the Japanese officials argued heatedly about their course of action. Indeed, for a brief time on August tenth, even though no Japanese reply had surfaced, Marshall ordered a halt to the strategic bombing. On August fourteenth, the Japanese cabinet was still divided over the prospect of surrender, with the war minister and members of the chiefs of staff still opposing it.

Only when that gridlock prevented a decision did the new prime minister, Kantaro Suzuki, ask Emperor Hirohito to intervene. By Japanese tradition, he had to remain silent until that moment, but allowed to speak, he quickly sided with those favoring surrender. Hirohito's decision, broadcast on radio, was an amazing occurrence. Most Japanese people had never before heard the voice of this "god," so to lessen the trauma the emperor had recorded the message, instructing his citizens that they had to "endure the unendurable" and allow American occupation because the only alternative was the "total extinction of human civilization."[90] Even then, aides worried that militarists would attempt to assassinate him before he could record the message. He told his subjects, "The time has come when we must bear the unbearable. . . . I swallow my own tears and give my sanction to the proposal to accept the Allied proclamation."[91] Even in defeat, however, the emperor's comments gave insight into the nature of the Japanese thinking that had started the war in the first place: the massacre of two hundred thousand Chinese at Nanking apparently did not count when it came to "human civilization"—only Japanese dead. American commanders ordered their forces to cease fire on August fifteenth, and on September second, aboard the USS *Missouri* in Tokyo Bay, General MacArthur and Admiral Nimitz, along with representatives of the other Allied powers in the Pacific, accepted the Japanese surrender. American planes blackened the skies above, and most of the ships in the Pacific fleet sailed by in a massive display of might. As one veteran at the ceremonies observed, "We wanted to make sure they knew who won the war."[92]

Most Americans seemed undisturbed by the use of atomic weapons to end the war. Far from causing "nuclear nightmares," as activists liked to imply later, some 65 percent of Gallup Poll respondents claimed they were not concerned about the bomb or its implications.[93] Truman remained unmoved in his view that the bomb's use was thoroughly justified. When the head of the atomic bomb project, J. Robert Oppenheimer, commented to Truman that some of the scientists "felt like they had blood on their hands . . . , [Truman] offered him a handkerchief and said: 'Well, here, would you like to wipe off your hands?' "[94] Years later, when a crew filming a documentary on Hiroshima asked Truman if he would consider a pilgrimage to ground zero, he caustically responded, "I'll go to Japan if that's what you want. But I won't kiss their ass."[95]

In retrospect, three central reasons justified the dropping of the atomic bombs. First, and most important, the invasion of Japan would cost more American lives—up to a million, perhaps far more. The interests of the United States demanded that the government do everything in its power to see that not one more American soldier or sailor died than was absolutely necessary, and the atomic bombs ensured that result. Second, Japan would not surrender, nor did its leaders give any indication whatsoever that they would surrender short of annihilation. One can engage in hypothetical discussions about possible intentions, but public statements such as the fight-to-the-bitter-end comment and the summoning of Japan's top atomic scientist after the Hiroshima bomb was dropped demonstrate rather conclusively that the empire planned to fight on. Third, the depredations of the Japanese equaled those of the Nazis. The Allies, therefore, were justified in nothing less than unconditional surrender and a complete dismantling of the samurai Bushido as a requirement for peace.

Only in the aftermath, when the prisoner-of-war camps were opened, did it become apparent that the Japanese regime had been every bit as brutal as the Nazis, if less focused on particular groups. Thousands of prisoners died working on the Siam railway, and field commanders had working instructions to kill any prisoners incapable of labor. (Guards routinely forced fistfuls of rice down prisoners' throats, then filled them with water, then as their stomachs swelled, punched or kicked the men's bellies.)[96] Almost five times as many Anglo-American POWs died in Japanese hands as in the Nazi camps, which reflected almost benign treatment in comparison to what Chinese and other Asians received at the hands of the Japanese. As with the Nazis, such horrors illustrated not only individuals' capacity for evil but, more important, they also illustrated the nature of the brutal system that had produced a view of non-Japanese as "subhumans."

At the same time, Japan's fanaticism led to a paralysis of government that prevented the nation from surrendering. The outcome of the war, evident after Midway, was probably decided even before. In February 1942, advisers had told the emperor that Japan could not possibly win. Human suicide bombers were used in 1944 with no end of the war in sight. Fanaticism of that type mirrored the fiendish Nazi ideology, and in the end, the Japanese warlords and Nazi despots had made the Second World War a contest between barbarism and civilization. Civilization won.

CHAPTER EIGHTEEN

America's "Happy Days," 1946–59

Atoms for Peace

Having defeated the totalitarians and vanquished the Great Depression, it was inevitable that the United States would develop a can-do optimism and problem-solving confidence at the end of World War II. Threats remained, at home and abroad, yet were these not minor compared to the victories already achieved? By 1960, however, many would reflect on the immediate postwar years soberly, reevaluating their optimism. For by that time the civil rights movement would have exposed racism and the lingering effects of Jim Crow; the Soviet Union would have shown itself to be a dangerous and well-armed enemy; and the role of world leader meant that America could afford few mistakes—politically, morally, or culturally.

Having just fought and bled a second time in thirty years, having witnessed a massive—though many at the time thought necessary—shift of power to the executive branch, and having seen inflation and high taxes eat away at the prosperity that they anticipated would come from defeating the Axis powers, Americans were open to change in 1946. Government had grown rapidly in the period following the Great Crash, and the size of the federal government doubled in a scant three years from 1939 to 1942, ballooning to almost 2 million employees! More than 250,000 government workers lived in the Washington area alone, up from a mere 73,000 in 1932.

The 1946 elections, in which Republicans ran against "big government, big labor, big regulation, and the New Deal's links to communism" produced a rout in which the GOP captured control of both houses of Congress for the first time since before the Great Depression.[1] Not only had the Republicans whipped the Democrats, but they also virtually annihilated the liberal wing of the Democratic machine, sending 37 of 69 liberal Democrats in Congress down to defeat, shattering the Left-laborite coalition that had sustained FDR.

Part of the Republican victory could be attributed to the high taxes and heavy regulation imposed by the New Deal and the war. *U.S. News & World Report's* headlines blared THE HANDOUT ERA IS OVER as the can-do attitude that character-ized the war effort quickly replaced the helplessness of the New Deal.[2] National security and communism also concerned the public. Shortly after Germany sur-rendered, the nation was shocked by the discovery that the magazine *Amerasia* had been passing highly classified documents to the Soviets. In June of 1945, the FBI traced the documents to a massive Soviet espionage ring in the United States.[3] When word of that leaked, it gave credence to allegations that the Roo-sevelt administration had been soft on communists. Consequently, the Republi-can Congress came in, as Representative Clarence Brown put it, to "open with a prayer, and close with a probe."[4] Far from being paranoid, most Americans cor-rectly perceived that Soviet espionage and domestic subversion was a serious a threat.

President Harry Truman eventually made hay campaigning against the Re-publican "do-nothing Congress," but in fact it did a great deal—just nothing that Truman liked. The Eightieth Congress passed the first balanced budget since the Great Crash; chopped taxes by nearly $5 billion (while at the same time exempt-ing millions of low-income working-class Americans from taxation); quashed a socialist national health-care scheme; passed the Taft-Hartley freedom-to-work act over the president's veto; and closed the Office of Price Administration, which had fixed prices since the beginning of the war. In a massive reorganization of government, Congress folded the departments of the army and navy into a new Department of Defense, and the National Security Act created the Central Intel-ligence Agency (CIA) out of the former OSS. In international affairs, Congress funded the Marshall Plan and America's commitment to the new North Atlantic Treaty Organization (NATO) and the United Nations.

An Atomic World

In a sense, World War II did not end with the surrender of Germany in May 1945, or even of Japan in August 1945, but rather continued until the 1990s, when the Soviet communist state fell. The Second World War, after all, was a struggle between barbarism and civilization, and it only moved from an active heated battle in 1945 into a quieter, but equally dangerous phase thereafter. In-deed, instead of a true two-sided conflict, World War II had been a triangular struggle pitting Hitler and his demonic allies in one corner, Stalin and his com-munist accomplices in another, and the Western democracies in a third. Keep in mind that until Hitler invaded Russia in 1941, he and Stalin were de facto allies, and American communists, such as the American Peace Mobilization and the Communist Party of the United States of America (CPUSA), had lobbied hard for nonintervention.[5]

Shaking off the shortsightedness of Roosevelt and other policy makers, by 1946 a few advisers in the Truman administration had recognized the dangers posed by an expansionist Soviet Union. Truman himself required more convinc-ing. As late as 1945 the president had referred privately to Stalin as "a fine man who wanted to do the right thing"—this about a dictator whose mass murders had exceeded those of Hitler and Tojo combined.[6] Stalin was, said Truman, "an honest man who is easy to get along with—who arrives at sound decisions."[7] Well before the Missourian spoke those words, however, this "fine man" had started work on a Soviet atomic bomb—developing the weapon in the middle of the Battle of Stalingrad, when it was apparent it could not be ready in time to assist in the destruction of Germany. Stalin was already looking ahead to the postwar world and his new enemies, the United States and Great Britain.[8]

Over time, Truman formulated a different assessment of the Soviet dictator, recognizing the dangers posed by an expansionist Soviet Union. For the next forty-five years the ensuing cold war in many ways required more national commitment than was ever before seen in American history. By 1991 the Soviet system had collapsed, and the United States and the West could claim victory. In a sense, this constituted the unfinished conclusion of World War II's struggle against tyranny. Victory had several architects, including Americans Harry Truman, George Kennan, Dwight Eisenhower, John Kennedy, Richard Nixon, Ronald Reagan, and George Bush as well as British allies Winston Churchill and Margaret Thatcher.

Only the most prescient foresaw that conflict. By the time the atomic bombs had fallen on Japan, the United States had lost 280,677 men in Europe, 41,322 in the Pacific, and 115,187 in training accidents and noncombat losses along with 10,650 deceased POWs (about one fourth of all American prisoners held by the Japanese) for a total of 447,836 dead and 971,801 wounded. The war drove the national debt up (constant dollars, as a share of GNP) to a level two and a half times larger than the $5 trillion national debt of the United States in the 1990s. Although the domestic economy recovered during the war, a complete rebound from the Great Depression may not have occurred until 1946.[9]

Dropping the atomic bombs had the unintended effect of showing the rest of the world the power of nuclear weapons and made clear that, at least until 1949, America had a monopoly over such weapons. The United States had successfully bluffed other nations into thinking it could deliver large numbers of atomic bombs, even deep into the Soviet Union. In reality, however, America's nuclear arsenal remained a hollow threat until the early 1950s because of the limited range of strategic aircraft and the small number of available nuclear bombs.[10] By the time of the Korean War, nuclear capability had caught up to the perception, and the United States never looked back. It "had a force . . . with potential to deliver a smashing blow against Soviet cities," consisting of some hundred atomic bombs and two hundred aircraft capable of hitting Russia from mainland American bases through the use of aerial refueling.[11] Despite a new threat that emerged when the USSR exploded its own atomic bomb in 1949, Truman and Eisenhower maintained American nuclear superiority.

Time Line

1945: Harry Truman ascends to the U.S. presidency upon the death of Franklin D. Roosevelt

1946: Republicans capture both the House and Senate in midterm elections

1947: Truman Doctrine implemented; cold war begins; Marshall Plan instituted; Taft-Hartley Act

1948: Berlin airlift; Truman reelected

1949: NATO formed; Communists take control of China

1950: Alger Hiss convicted; Korean War begins

1952: Dwight D. Eisenhower elected

1953: Korean War ends

1954: *Brown v. Board of Education*

1955: SEATO formed

1956: Soviets crush Hungarian uprising; Eisenhower reelected

1957: Eisenhower orders federal troops to desegregate Little Rock High School; Soviets launch *Sputnik*

1959: Castro captures Cuba

1960: John F. Kennedy elected president

The Iron Curtain and the Cold War

Soviet domination of Eastern Europe, along with the potential for communist regimes in Greece, Italy, and even France posed a new communist version of the old Nazi threat. In key elements, communism and fascism looked remarkably similar: totalitarian control of the economy, communication, and information centers; a national identity based on a single characteristic (race with the Nazis, class with the communists); the obsession over existence of an enemy, whose very presence supposedly prevented the appearance of the ideological utopia; and all power relegated to a dangerous and ambitious dictator. It is true that the Soviets, who lost millions of lives in World War II, had good reason to strike a strong defensive posture after the war, but that does not justify their takeover of sovereign nations. Mistakenly, most of the Allies—again, Churchill was the lone exception—hoped the USSR really did not mean its rhetoric about international revolution and the destruction of the international bourgeoisie. When it became clear that the Soviets had no intention of leaving occupied areas, but rather planned to incorporate them into a new Soviet empire, a belated light went on in the heads of many in the State Department.

Churchill had been sounding the alarm about the communists for years. Roosevelt, however, naively expressed his confidence in his one-on-one ability to handle Stalin, eerily echoing the attitudes of Neville Chamberlain, who thought he could handle Hitler at Munich. Once again, FDR's own prejudices had been amplified by rosy reports from the U.S. ambassador to the USSR, Joseph Davies, who instructed the president that to "distrust Stalin was 'bad Christianity, bad sportsmanship, bad sense.'"[12] By 1945, Churchill was shrewdly trying to manipulate American power like a "great unwieldy barge," steering it into the "right harbor," lest it "wallow in the ocean."[13] Churchill remained clear eyed about the long-term threat posed by an expansionist, communist Soviet Union. His March 5, 1946, speech to Westminster College in Missouri proclaimed that "an iron curtain has descended across the continent," placing the nations of Eastern Europe under a "high and in many cases increasing measure of control from Moscow."[14] Truman refused to endorse Churchill's position, continuing to refer to the Soviets as "friends," even offering Stalin a chance to deliver a rebuttal to the students at Westminster! Yet beneath the surface, Truman's attitudes had started to change.

Harry Truman was born in Independence, Missouri, to a life of great contrasts. Raised in a Southern Baptist tradition, steeped in Victorian morality, he wrote in his diary in the 1930s that America needed a "reformation of the heart." At the same time, he used profanity with staggering deftness, and in any company. One Roosevelt appointee, Chester Bowles, expressed his shock at the emotional discussions he had had with Truman in a half-hour conversation "punctuated by extraordinary profanity."[15]

Truman's World War I combat experience gave him what no president since Teddy Roosevelt had possessed—firsthand knowledge of the horrors of war. Perhaps that fact accounts for both men's willingness to support a strong peacetime military force, when others, including Coolidge, had failed to see the need for such investments. After the war Truman moved to Kansas City, where he opened a haberdashery. That, like most of his other business attempts, failed.

Business failure led Truman to his true calling in politics. Taken under the wing of Thomas J. Pendergast's Kansas City Democratic machine, Truman won election as a judge on the Jackson County Court in 1922, with the unusual job (for a jurist) of overseeing the Kansas City road system and supervising its (largely corrupt) paymasters. This was akin to trying to stay sweet smelling in a fertilizer factory! Truman pulled it off, largely by throwing himself into the legitimate aspects of the road programs. Truman's frugal lower-middle-class lifestyle testified to his fundamental honesty. When his mentor, Pendergast, was tagged with a $350,000 fine and fifteen months in Leavenworth Federal Prison for graft, Truman wrote Bess, "Looks like everyone got rich in Jackson County but me."[16]

Voters rewarded his independence in 1934, electing him to a U.S. Senate seat, but six years later the association with Pendergast still threatened his reelection. Then, at the very moment when Truman might have fallen off the pages of history, an odd serendipity intervened. The county seized the Truman family farm, making it abundantly clear that he had not profited from his public service, and he was reelected. In his second term he headed the Truman Committee investigation of price gouging by defense contractors during the war. His turning up numerous examples of fraud and waste made him a national figure and put his name before the Democratic Party power brokers, who in turn urged him on Roosevelt in 1944. FDR's death, of course, catapulted the humble Missourian into history.

President Harry Truman knew in 1946 that the American public would not tolerate another new conflict, especially over Poland, Latvia, Lithuania, and Estonia. On the other hand, he wished to avoid encouraging another Hitler to swallow up other European countries. When the Soviets failed to withdraw from Iran on deadline, as they had promised, Truman viewed it as the first test of Western resolve. "This may lead to war," he told his commerce secretary.[17] Subordinates pressed the matter strongly in the United Nations Security Council, at which time the Soviets reluctantly accepted the fact that they could not pull off a Munich. Negotiations between the Iranians and Soviets resulted in the Russians pulling out, but there is little question they did so because they realized Truman, although no Churchill, was no Chamberlain either. Whether he fully appreciated it or not, Truman had sided with those who viewed the Soviet Union as fundamentally different from other Russian empires. Stalin's USSR was an ideological expansionist state, not just a traditional big power seeking to protect its borders.

A third group remained active in government, however—those who saw the USSR as a potential model for human development. Many of the New Dealers, including Rexford Tugwell and Roosevelt's agriculture secretary (and later, vice president), Henry Wallace, profoundly admired Stalin, and most of these intellectuals favored complete pacifism and disarmament in the face of Soviet expansion. To a far greater extent than many Americans want to believe, communist agents had penetrated the Roosevelt administration and reached high levels: Harold Ware had staffed his AAA agency with communist sympathizers; Ware and his AAA colleagues John Abt, Lee Pressman, and Nathan Witt (all devout communists) worked with spy Alger Hiss. Other underground agents worked in the Office of Price Administration (Victor Perlo), the NRA (Henry Collins), and the Farm Security Administration (Nathan Silvermaster). There were communist agents in the Treasury, State, and Interior departments, and even in the nation's spy agency, the OSS. Duncan Lee, the chief of staff for the OSS, was a KGB agent.[18]

Perhaps the most dangerous of these characters was Wallace, whom Roosevelt named as commerce secretary after he was dropped from the 1944 ticket to make room for Truman. Wallace pulled the department further to the left during the New Deal, when he expressed his admiration for Stalin's economic achievements. By the time Truman replaced him, Wallace was leader of the progressive/socialist wing of the Democratic Party.[19]

It did not take long for the former veep to make waves. He wrote the president a long memo in July 1945, advocating unilateral disarmament, then leaked the contents to the press in a startling display of presumptuousness and contempt for the chain of command. Many in Roosevelt's administration viewed Wallace as a mystic, a wild spender who would "give every Hottentot a pint of American milk every day."[20] Wallace seriously entertained notions that groups of generals were scheming to stage a coup against the president. Truman bluntly called Wallace a "cat bastard."[21] To have such an apologist for the Soviets in a cabinet-level position shocked Truman: "Wallace is a pacifist 100 per cent. He wants us to disband our armed forces, give Russia our atomic secrets and trust a bunch of adventurers in the Politburo."[22]

Extremist New Dealers viewed Wallace as the genuine heir to the Roosevelt mantle; Truman was an unsatisfactory substitute. Truman's unexpected ascension to the presidency dramatically altered the expected steady march of the New Deal. One historian called Wallace "the closest the Soviets ever came to choosing and nominating a candidate for the American presidency."[23] Recently released KGB archive material has revealed that at the time, Harry Dexter White, in the Treasury Department, and Lawrence Duggan were Soviet agents. Wallace later said that had he become president, White would have been his treasury secretary and Duggan his secretary of state.[24] Furthermore, Wallace's Progressive Party had active Soviet agents at every level of its organization, including platform committee chairman, recording secretary, and Wallace's chief speechwriter. A Wallace presidency probably would have led to new rounds of Soviet expansionism, most likely in Europe. Given the determination of the French and British to remain independent, and the fact that they were both nuclear players by the mid-1950s, it is not unreasonable to conclude that nuclear weapons would have been used at some point against Soviet incursions. By naming the hard-line Truman, FDR may have prevented a nuclear war in more ways than one.

Attacking Communism with a Two-Edged Sword . . . and a Saxophone!

Most American policy analysts agreed that the United States, even with the full support of the European allies, was not militarily capable of pushing the Soviets out of their occupied areas. Therefore, the United States needed another strategy of resistance. Truman had kept his eye on British efforts to support the Greek government against communist guerrillas since March 1946, but by early 1947, England was running out of money. Her own economy had suffered, the empire was in disarray, and the war had simply sapped the will of the British citizenry in such matters.

In February 1947, Truman, George Marshall (army chief of staff and now secretary of state), George Kennan (head of the Policy Planning Staff), and Dean Acheson (undersecretary of state) met with leaders from the newly elected Republican-dominated Congress, whose support would be essential. In the past they had resisted overseas involvement. Senator Arthur Vandenberg assured Truman that the Republicans would support him, but that the president would have to take his case directly to the American people too. Consequently, Truman laid out the Truman Doctrine, establishing as American policy the support of "free peoples who are resisting attempted subjugation by armed minorities or by outside pressure." The cold war had begun.

Aid to Greece and Turkey solved the immediate problem, but the whole dam threatened to break unless extensive support was extended to the rest of Western Europe. Communists gained ground in the 1947 French and Italian elections as both nations struggled to recover from the ravages of war. Stopping Soviet expansionism would require the United States to inject capital, expertise, and economic support of every type into Europe in order to revive the free economies there. The Marshall Plan, outlined in June 1947, proved exactly the right remedy. European nations requested $17 billion over a four-year period. It joined the Truman Doctrine as a basis for America's cold war strategy.

The coup in Czechoslovakia and the near collapse of Greece led Kennan to conceive a framework for resisting communism that involved neither appeasement nor full-scale conflict. Kennan had trod a remarkable intellectual journey since the prewar years. Four years of war against fascist troops had given Kennan a keen knowledge of the grave threat posed by totalitarian dictatorships, especially the USSR.[25] In July 1947, Kennan wrote an article under the pseudonym Mr. X for *Foreign Affairs* entitled "The Sources of Soviet Conduct," which outlined a strategy for dealing with an aggressive Soviet Union.[26] The key to winning the cold war, Kennan wrote, lay in a strategy of "containment," in which the United States did not seek to roll back Soviet gains as much as to build a giant economic/military/political fence around the communist state so that it could not expand farther. America should respond to Soviet advances with "the adroit and vigilant application of counterforce at a series of constantly shifting geographical and political points," Kennan wrote.[27]

Curiously, containment introduced a diametric inversion of V. I. Lenin's own Marxist hypotheses from the turn of the century, when European nations still engaged in creating overseas empires. Lenin's *Imperialism* sought to explain why there were no communist revolutions in capitalist nations, as predicted by Marx. According to Marx, the overproduction of the capitalist's boom-and-bust business cycle would lead to a wide depression, yet no such revolutions had occurred. Why? Lenin reasoned that imperialism explained this glitch—that capitalist countries exported their surpluses to the underdeveloped sections of the globe through the process of acquiring empires. Without this expansion, capitalism would die.

Kennan's containment doctrine stood Lenin's thesis on its head. It was the Soviet Union—not the capitalist countries—that needed to expand to survive. Without expansion to justify totalitarian controls, a huge secret police, and massive expenditures on the military, the USSR and its leaders would have to explain to the people why they had virtually no cars, little good food, and a staggering lack of basic items such as soap and toilet paper. Containing the Soviets and stifling their expansionist ventures would focus Russian attention on their sad domestic economy, which was accelerating the collapse of communism through its own dead weight. Containment would make the communists, not the capitalists, their own grave diggers. The second edge of the sword, then, became a military alliance with the free countries of Europe. Several European countries—England, France, Belgium, the Netherlands, and Luxembourg—had signed a collective defense pact in 1948. Now Truman sought to join and expand and strengthen it. Norway and Italy were invited to join along with Canada. On April 4, 1949, the North Atlantic Treaty Organization (NATO) was established, linking America directly to European entanglements for the first time since the Revolution. Under the agreement, an "armed attack against one" would be considered an attack upon all. Since the United States already had established the fact that any attack on American assets was an act of war, to which the response could be atomic bombing, the NATO treaty effectively linked the Western European powers to the U.S. atomic umbrella. To more firmly cement this relationship, Truman ordered four U.S. divisions to Europe for permanent duty there—with the Allies' consent—in essence, putting American bodies in the line of fire to ensure full participation by the United States.

Leftist scholars have sought to paint the Soviets as victims and NATO as the villain. One mainstream text argues that "there was no evidence of any Russian plan to invade Western Europe, and in the face of the American atomic bomb, none was likely."[28] This is simply fantasy, as recent documents from the former Soviet states have revealed. The Warsaw Pact had a plan in place for an invasion of the West that included a barrage of tactical nuclear weapons just ahead of the Soviet advance. More important, the Soviets' espionage network informed them fully that American atomic bombs could not be delivered in sufficient numbers against targets in the USSR—and certainly could not be dropped on Western European soil without a massive backlash that probably would split the alliance. Pro-Soviet historians ignore the incredible buildup of *offensive* forces by the USSR, giving the lie to the notion that the massive Soviet arms expansion was defensive. Almost immediately, Stalin, in June 1948, probed into the Allied belly at Berlin.

The former German capital, fully surrounded by communist East Germany, remained an isolated outpost of liberty in an ocean of totalitarian control. West Germany had limited access to the western sectors of Berlin while the Soviets controlled the other half of the city, making Berlin an outpost in enemy territory. If such a metropolitan region became prosperous, as was the tendency of capitalist areas, it would pose a startling shining contrast to whatever Marx's ghost offered. On June 20, 1948, Stalin sought to eliminate this potential threat by cutting off the railroad and traffic lines into West Berlin.

Stalin's move came at a key point in the election cycle—just as Truman was engaged in a tough reelection fight not only against the Republican, New York governor Thomas E. Dewey, but also against two renegades from his own party: Dixiecrat Strom Thurmond, who headed a states' rights wing of the Democratic Party, and Henry Wallace, who appealed to the party's disaffected radicals as the Progressive Party candidate. Wallace ran a phenomenally expensive campaign, spending $3 million as a third-party candidate—easily the most costly and least-productive-per-dollar presidential run ever attempted, generating only 2.4 percent of the vote.

As usual, everyone underestimated Truman, who threw himself into a whistle-stop campaign as only an American president could do.[29] At one campaign stop, a supporter yelled, "Give 'em hell, Harry." Truman shot back, "I only tell the truth and they think it's hell." The electorate appreciated his candid approach, even if the media discounted him. When *Newsweek* magazine ran a survey of fifty journalists, all of whom predicted Truman would lose, the president countered, "I know every one of those fifty fellows and not one of them has enough sense to pound sand into a rathole."[30] The epitome of media goofs occurred when the Chicago *Tribune* prematurely ran a banner headline reading DEWEY DEFEATS TRUMAN. It wouldn't be the last time the mainstream media was embarrassed on election night.

Once again, the country had rallied around an incumbent in a crisis. Stalin had to deal with a tenacious Truman rather than a conciliatory Dewey. Truman refused to give up Berlin, but had to do so without touching off World War III. He found a middle ground that forced the Soviets into the position of having to fire the first shot.

Truman deployed three squadrons of B-29 bombers to Europe, hoping that Stalin would think they were equipped with atomic bombs (they were not). Rejecting General Lucius Clay's proposal to resupply Berlin by truck, Truman opted for a massive airlift. From December 1948 to the spring of 1949, American C-47s, C-52s, and escorts shuttled in up to seven thousand tons of supplies a day, demonstrating the Allies' resolve and impressing upon the Soviets the size and quality of U.S. air superiority. The Soviet dictator realized he could not order any planes shot down—that would be an act of war—and accepted, temporarily, that he was beaten, removing Soviet barricades and roadblocks to Berlin from the West in May 1949.

Most advisers realized they had to rapidly rebuild the armed forces to counter the the 2.5-million-man Soviet army. The cold war would be a long one, one not decided by a few early skirmishes like Berlin. In fact, Stalin had made a critical error by greedily attempting to seize Berlin. Had he waited, the United States might have disarmed so thoroughly that rearming would have been politically impossible. His divisions might have simply walked into Berlin, but Eisenhower saw the danger and stepped in to support the president by conducting a swing through NATO capitals. He then returned to Washington to argue for decisive commitments to NATO. Eisenhower's speeches convinced Americans and Europeans that resisting the Soviets required them to act together.

So Truman, occasionally in spite of himself, managed to win early victories on the political and military fronts, but there was yet one more battlefield for the cold war—that of culture. America faced a serious propaganda hurdle when the communists could point to segregation of blacks within parts of the American South, and claim that the democratic ideals held out to other regions of the globe were empty words. A series of programs sponsored by the U.S. State Department that sent American jazz musicians overseas proved important in that regard. American jazz was already extremely popular in Europe, with a ready-built audience for jazzmen like Dizzy Gillespie, Benny Goodman, and Louis Armstrong, who made tours of Europe, the Middle East, and Latin America. Jazz opened doors no diplomats could. As Eisenhower's vice president, Richard Nixon had encountered crowds in Latin America that spit on him and threw rocks at his car. But Louis Armstrong drew crowds that greeted him with standing ovations. Jazz bands carried understated, but obvious, messages without the need for speeches. First, many of the bands were integrated. Black, white, Jewish, and Hispanic musicians played alongside each other. Second, the very nature of jazz (and later, rock and roll) epitomized democracy: the whole band played together in the opening verses and choruses, then a soloist would depart from the band to do his own thing while the rest of the group held the song together. Ultimately, the soloist would return to the scripted parts, reflecting the notion that in a democracy people can cooperate, yet have infinite individuality.

Louis "Satchmo" Armstrong symbolized, as a band leader, that African Americans could attain leadership positions in American culture. Armstrong knew America had its faults—he had criticized the American government during the 1950s school desegregation crisis and the Civil Rights era—yet he was also a proud American. He gained such fame that he became known as the U.S. Ambassador of Jazz. In 1965 his band toured Eastern Europe, taking American jazz behind the Iron Curtain. Twenty years later, when Ronald Reagan brought down the Soviet empire, another American music form, rock and roll, played no small role in undermining communism's grip on the minds of the young.

Containment and Korea

When Roosevelt, Churchill, and Stalin met at Yalta, they agreed to maintain spheres of influence in Asia, with the Russians taking the northeastern part of Asia, including North Korea, and the Americans dominating the southern part of China and South Korea below the thirty-eighth parallel. Mao Tse-tung, the communist Chinese leader in the north, had the advantage of a unified command of a large patriotic army and virtual sovereignty in Manchuria after the Soviets pulled out (taking all the machinery and hardware they could carry with them). His opponent, Chiang Kai-shek, leader of the Nationalist camp, had some American support, but he suffered from internal dissension among his officers, terrible economic conditions inherited from the Japanese, and corruption. Chiang had squandered vast piles of American assistance, which totaled $2 billion from 1945 to 1949 (although much of it simply vanished through the skyrocketing inflation inside China). Other factors much more insidious also helped undercut Chiang, including the State Department's pro-Mao tilt that consistently painted Chiang in the worst possible light and depicted Mao as a peasant freedom fighter. The result was that aid earmarked for Chiang—especially gold that could have stabilized the inflation—was delayed at critical times. All of this would surface later, yet the question of how U.S. policy toward China was bent toward Mao's forces went essentially unexamined.

In 1949, Mao's troops crossed the Yangtze, capturing the capital city, Nanking, after which all but the most loyal of Chiang's army disintegrated and was pushed entirely off the mainland to the island of Taiwan (Formosa). There the refractory Chiang established the "true" Chinese government in exile and vowed a return to the mainland. Amid all this communist expansion, where was the United States?

Secretary of State Dean Acheson produced a white paper explaining that the United States had no hope of affecting the outcome of the Chinese "civil war," and that getting American troops into a land war in China would be a disaster. Republicans, still isolationist at the core, nevertheless reveled in seeing the Democratic administration stumble so badly. Congress blamed the "loss of China" on policy errors and incompetent diplomacy. In truth, Acheson was right. Despite having utterly demolished the Japanese just four years earlier, the United States had played almost no role in actual mainland fighting—that had been conducted by the Chinese of both groups and the British, Australians, New Zealanders, and Indians. The forces that had existed in the Far East at the end of World War II had for the most part been decommissioned or reassigned. Any serious attempt to intervene would have required a full-scale buildup equivalent to that of 1942, combined with unrelenting use of atomic bombs, and then only if Russia stood by.

No sooner had the world readjusted its maps to the new People's Republic of China than Acheson gave an unfortunate speech to the National Press Club. There he implied that Korea was no longer considered within the U.S. containment fence, thus suggesting to Kim Il-sung of North Korea that the southern part of the Korean peninsula might be obtained at a minimal price. Using the justification that the Nationalist leader of the South, Syngman Rhee, would try to unify the two Koreas, Kim launched a general attack on June 25, 1950, quickly pummeling the Republic of Korea (ROK) forces. Truman had not backed down in Berlin, and would not now hand over Korea to the communists. "We've go to stop the sons-of-bitches no matter what," he told Acheson. Whereas the military and politicians alike shied away from a land war in China, Korea was different. Its small size and abundant coastline played to America's greatest advantages, mobile amphibious attacks, carrier-based air power, and easy defense of choke points. Truman also appreciated the fact that unlike the Berlin crisis four years earlier, the United States now had an ample stockpile of atomic weapons and long-range delivery aircraft.

Here, Stalin sought to play the Chinese against the Americans, warning Kim that the USSR wouldn't "lift a finger" if the North got "kicked in the teeth" by the United States. Instead, he admonished Kim, "ask Mao for all the help."[31] The Soviet dictator now joined the press and Truman's political opponents in underestimating Truman. Even so, Stalin was startled by the timing of Kim's invasion. The Soviets had been engaged in a walkout of the United Nations Security Council over another matter, meaning that for one of only a handful of times in its history, the Security Council voted with the United States on a major international issue. While the UN vote was desirable, and put all forces in Korea under United Nations command, it could not conceal the obvious: the Americans would provide the bulk of the forces as well as the supreme commander of the UN forces, General Douglas MacArthur.

Even after the arrival of American forces, the North Koreans continued to push the ROK forces back toward Seoul. Finally, the UN/ROK troops managed to stabilize a perimeter near Pusan. To gain that territory, the communists had overextended their lines, which they could neither defend nor patrol effectively. Taking advantage of U.S. seapower, MacArthur staged a daring amphibious invasion at Inchon, behind North Korean lines, threatening to encircle and exterminate the entire North Korean army. His risky gambit is considered one of the most daring invasions in military history.[32] The geography of the location alone presented almost insurmountable challenges. The tidal swell at Inchon was thirty-seven feet, meaning that although high-tide landings would be relatively easy, at low tide ships would be stuck in mud. Initial troops would have to hold for twelve hours before reinforcements could again arrive. Wolmido Island, which controlled the harbor, had to be taken first, which would alert enemy forces to the attack when surprise was of the essence.[33]

American marines took the island in forty-five minutes, eliminated all the dug-in defenders, and did so without a single American death. MacArthur then defeated Korean troops that numbered 5,000 to 6,000 in the harbor and surrounding areas. In less than two weeks, Allied troops cut all the way across Korea, regaining the thirty-eighth parallel line—the original border whose violation had sparked the war. But MacArthur had proceeded farther north. For reasons of temperament and political ambition, MacArthur would have liked to have pursued the war beyond the thirty-eighth parallel anyway, but he had also received clear instructions from Secretary of Defense Marshall to "feel unhampered tactically and strategically *to proceed north of the 38th parallel* [emphasis added]."[34] Both MacArthur and Acheson had assured Truman that the Chinese would not intervene, with the general predicting a slaughter if Chinese troops crossed the Yalu River. When the Chinese did launch a massive counterattack in November 1950, the UN struggled to hold the line at the thirty-eighth parallel.

MacArthur, meanwhile, had grown increasingly critical of the president. He urged bringing the Taiwanese into the war, called for intensive bombing of Chinese bases, and a thorough blockade of the People's Republic. General Omar Bradley, among others, warned Truman that a full-scale war in China would be the "wrong war, in the wrong place, at the wrong time," and the president wisely refused to expand the conflict. Meanwhile, MacArthur's "rank insubordination," as Truman called it, was not only undesirable but dangerous, unconstitutional, and counter to the American tradition of keeping the military under control of civilians. In a bold and necessary stroke, Truman relieved MacArthur, sparking a public firestorm that even he misjudged. MacArthur returned like a Roman conqueror to address Congress to thunderous ovations as he bade farewell, saying, "Old soldiers never die. They just fade away."

Relieving MacArthur had placed Truman in the crucible of public criticism, which naturally did not faze the president. "What would Jesus Christ have preached if he had taken a poll in the land of Israel?" he asked. "It isn't [polls] that count. It is right and wrong, and leadership."[35] Despite his frequent underestimation of the communist threat, the feisty Missourian protected the integrity of the presidency and squelched permanently any notion that military leaders could dictate public policy. Not since Washington had a general come so close to wielding as much power with public opinion as had MacArthur. It was a battle Truman had to engage in.

The Korean conflict ended in a cease-fire in July 1953 (no peace treaty was ever negotiated), and as late as the 1990s, the Demilitarized Zone between the two Koreas constantly threatened to erupt into widespread violence. The war had not been cheap. Some 33,000 Americans died in battle, in addition to more than 100,000 wounded and 15,000 missing or made prisoners. The Korean War, like Vietnam, featured dozens of bloody engagements and few memorable battles. Hills often had numbers, not names, and the most successful offensive of the war, devised by General Matthew Ridgway, was aptly named the meatgrinder. The most oft-referenced geographic spot was not a battlefield such as Gettysburg, where a great victory had occurred, but the Yalu River, which American pursuit aircraft were not to cross. It was, according to one soldier, "the war we can't win, we can't lose, and we can't quit."[36]

The war was the high-water mark of Truman's administration, which was noteworthy for its foreign policy successes. But his presidency was far from perfect. Economic growth remained sporadic, and high inflation had left Truman with the nickname Horsemeat Harry for the meats housewives had to substitute when beef prices rose too high. Labor battles had shut down several industries. All of this could have been treated easily, however, by application of basic free-market economics, had Truman been so inclined. More problematic, Truman inherited a raft of Roosevelt appointees who were sympathetic to communists at best or who engaged in treasonous activities and espionage at worst. Revelations about Soviet spies in America severely damaged Truman's otherwise well-earned reputation.

Soviet Espionage in 1950s America

Soviet spies in America had been active for more than two decades, of course, just as Americans themselves conducted intelligence operations in most major foreign countries. What the Soviets gained through their American agents, however, was substantial. One new study concludes that contrary to the claims of liberals for many years, physicist Robert Oppenheimer, the father of the atomic bomb, helped write American Communist Party literature at the University of California and may have been a party member.[37] Another recent study of Soviet agents in America, based on newly released KGB documents and coauthored by a former Soviet agent, revealed that Russian intelligence agencies "received substantial and sometimes critical information (including many classified documents) concerning U.S. government policies on highly sensitive subjects, its confidential negotiating strategies, and secret weapons development, including essential processes involved in building the atomic bomb."[38] The agents' skills ranged from those of practiced professionals to bumbling amateurs, but, significantly, their level of penetration into the U.S. government is no longer in doubt.

Ironically, by the time Senator Joseph McCarthy, Republican of Wisconsin, got around to discovering the presence of this underground network, it had been shut down for several years because of the defection of a single mentally depressed female agent. McCarthy, whose name has sloppily been linked to hysteria and totalitarianism, was a complex figure.[39] The last major American political figure raised in a log cabin, the Irish Democrat had switched parties after the Second World War, winning a judgeship, then the Senate seat that had belonged to Robert LaFollette. He came into the Senate with his two friends John Kennedy and Richard Nixon. Joe Kennedy liked McCarthy, and Robert F. Kennedy worked as the senator's staffer during his investigations.

Like Joe Kennedy, McCarthy was blue collar, rough, and viewed as an outsider. Given to both overdrinking and overwork, McCarthy had a strong record on civil rights and support of Wisconsin's farmers, but he tended to operate within the committee on which he was seated, the Permanent Subcommittee on Investigations (PSI). The PSI resembled the House Un-American Activities Committee (HUAC), which had commenced operation in 1938 to deal with both Nazi and Communist subversion. McCarthy failed to appreciate—or capitalize on—his own evidence that indicated America's national security had been penetrated at the highest levels under Roosevelt. The Agricultural Adjustment Administration had provided a breeding ground for young communist agents, sympathizers, and radicals in the 1930s, including John Abt, Lee Pressman, Nathan Witt, Harold Ware, and Alger Hiss. Ware, for example, had already set up a network in Washington with seven cells, all linked to the USSR. Though opposed by his Senate committee, McCarthy, soon assisted on his own staff by young Robert F. Kennedy, and on the House side by Congressman Richard Nixon (pursuing Alger Hiss), succeeded in grabbing headlines and sounding a warning. Too often McCarthy's willingness to tout any unverified piece of information or to act before he had proof obscured the fact that the genuine damage already had been done to American security.

Alleging that the U.S. Army itself had security issues, McCarthy challenged the integrity of General George Marshall, at which point Americans' patience ran out. Many of his supporters turned against him; the Senate censured him in 1954; and his health deteriorated until his death three years later after long bouts with alcoholism.

"McCarthyism" subsequently became a term synonymous with repression and terror—an amazing development considering that not one of the people subpoenaed by the senator to testify lacked legal counsel; none were arrested or detained without due process; and no one went to jail without a trial. "All through the 'worst' of the McCarthy period, the Communist Party itself was never outlawed, membership in the party was never declared a crime, and it continued to maintain public offices, publish books and the *Daily Worker*," wrote McCarthy biographer Arthur Herman.[40] If anything, McCarthy's investigations *underesti-mated* the number of active Soviet agents in the country. At one time or another, the KGB regularly debriefed not only Harry Dexter White and Laurence Duggan, but also Michael Straight in the State Department; an agent known as Moris (thought to be John Abt in the Justice Department); Boris Morros, a Hollywood producer; and well-known columnist Walter Lippmann. Some, such as Duggan and White, deliberately and frequently shaped their internal policy memos to best benefit the USSR, not the United States, according to recently released KGB material from the Soviet Archives.[41]

Even though the Eisenhower administration quietly abandoned the search for communists in the government, the assault on American communists became broader and, one could say, "more democratic," as communists found themselves harassed, prosecuted, and hunted by the government with the enthusiastic support of large segments of the public. Unions, led by Walter Reuther of the United Auto Workers and Philip Murray of the CIO, had kicked known communists out even before McCarthy started his famous hearings. J. Edgar Hoover, the director of the FBI, turned anticommunism at the Bureau into a nearly personal vendetta: from its 1944 peak of eighty thousand members, the American Communist Party had shrunk to below twenty thousand in 1956 and fewer than three thousand in 1971.[42] Hoover had considerable help, however. Public officials often ignored or violated the constitutional rights of Communist Party members, and more extreme groups encouraged vigilante activity against known communists. Harvard University stated in May 1953 that "membership in the Communist Party is beyond the scope of academic freedom," and constituted "grave misconduct justifying dismissal."[43] That said, the fundamental fact was that overall the constitutional protections and the fair play and ethics of the majority of citizens restrained and limited anticommunist zeal.

Without doubt, the public was hostile to communism and suspicious of fellow travelers (nonparty members who abetted communism). In its last burst of pro-America activism, Hollywood chipped in with movies such as *I Married a Communist* and *The Red Menace,* produced between 1947 and 1949. The blacklisting of the Hollywood Ten is well known. Hearings into the movie industry saw one resolute witness, a young Ronald Reagan, defend the industry and question the attacks on civil liberties. Public schools promoted prodemocracy programs, and tell-all books by former communists abounded.

The bottom line, however, was that anticommunism was a serious response to genuine threats on many levels than it was a form of paranoia. And overall, the dislocations attributed to anticommunist movements were and are exaggerated. As historians of the American communist movement noted, "Even during the early 1950s, the high tide of McCarthyism, the Communist party functioned legally, its spokesmen publicly advocated its doctrines, its recruiters brought in new members, and its press published daily and weekly newspapers, journals, pamphlets, and books in the millions of copies."[44] University purges were rare. Of the 1,850 colleges and universities with nearly 300,000 faculty in the 1950s, there were 126 cases of professors (at 58 institutions) dismissed or threatened with dismissal for their communist affiliation.

The truly bad news was that the spy scandals in the United States and Britain indicated that communist infiltration into national security and the State Department was far worse than imagined. The spy revelations, combined with the invasion of South Korea by communist North Korea and the fall of China to communist dictator Mao Tse-tung in 1949, led to sharp concern over Soviet espionage activities in the United States. Labeling this the Red scare, or hysteria, is a gross exaggeration. Hysteria is an ungrounded fear, as opposed to concern based on genuine threats. As newly released Soviet documents confirm without question, the USSR had penetrated virtually every important division of the U.S. government related to military, diplomatic, and security issues. Certainly the opposition to the cold war and agitation by so-called peace movements in America was manipulated by the Soviets. Ironically, evidence for this Soviet involvement in domestic peace organizations comes from a historian sympathetic to the Left, Robbie Lieberman, who admits that American Communists "saw peace as bound up with the fortunes of the Soviet Union."[45] As Lieberman noted, "Communist agitation for peace was bound up with defending the interests of the Soviet Union, especially guaranteeing its . . . power (nuclear and otherwise) vis-à-vis the United States."[46]

The nation was quite rational in exhibiting serious concerns about such developments and, at the same time, was fortunate to have a war hero and level-headed Kansan as its new president—a man who could stand up to the excesses of McCarthy without in any way backing down from the commitment to containment abroad. What is less clear is how seriously Eisenhower took the threat of communist infiltration into the Roosevelt and Truman administrations: he appeared more embarrassed by McCarthy than concerned with the likes of Owen Lattimore and Alger Hiss. Some of Eisenhower's approach must in part be attributed to strategy, not wishing to expend little of his administration's energy pounding on the errors of his predecessor. Some of it must be chalked up to a certain (and in this case, wrong) American presumption that large numbers of fellow citizens would not be traitors. Whatever the reason, Ike's unwillingness to be even slightly associated with McCarthy's cause led the new president to miss a golden opportunity to clean house of Soviet agents and, in the process, reinvigorate the conservative movement without the taint of extremism associated with the John Birch Society (a far-right anticommunist group) or McCarthy.[47]

The Eisenhower Smile
It was natural that Americans considered military service a training ground for the presidency—most presidents had served in the armed forces, many as successful generals—and both Eisenhower and MacArthur entertained thoughts of a political career. For Dwight Eisenhower, one potential roadblock was that he had not been particularly political in his life, nor did the public even know what party he favored, although he had voted Republican those times that he did vote.

Ike encouraged the impression among the media elites that he was somehow detached from the partisan wrangling of the day. Supporters lobbied him to run for office the minute he came home from Europe, but he demurred. He even indicated that he would have been happy supporting the party favorite, Robert Taft of Ohio (1889–1953) if "Mr. Republican" had endorsed NATO. Yet in a meeting with Eisenhower, Taft rejected American involvement in collective security for Europe, sealing Ike's decision to run. Like Truman, Ike did not mind being underestimated. Elites rallied to the Democratic candidate, Adlai E. Stevenson of Illinois (1900–65), but Eisenhower appealed to the common man.

Seeking to blunt attacks from the McCarthy wing of the GOP, Ike named Congressman Richard Nixon of California as his running mate. In the campaign, Democrats charged Nixon with financial irregularities and corruption. The resilient Nixon, in one of the most famous political television addresses ever, carefully reviewed his finances, noting that he and his family had few luxuries, that his wife Pat did not have fur coats but a "good Republican cloth coat." They had accepted one gift—a cocker spaniel named Checkers, and with a tear in his eye Nixon stated he would not give up the family dog. Unswayed, Ike certainly stood ready to dump Nixon if popular support didn't materialize, but the speech grabbed the nation's heartstrings, and he stayed on the ticket. Eisenhower buried Stevenson in the popular vote, garnering nearly 10 percent more votes and overwhelming him in the electoral college, 457 to 73.

Liberal journalists and academics have attempted to portray the election as one in which the lesser man won—that "smart" people voted for Stevenson, but were swamped by the rubes. In fact, Stevenson was an avid *non*reader, and the only book at his nightstand when he died was *The Social Register*.[48] Voter statistics revealed that the more education someone had, the more likely the person was to vote for Eisenhower. Oddly, Ike irked the press by smiling a lot. But he also worked hard and long, and despite his demeanor, in some ways he lived hard too. No soldier could achieve what Ike had without some rough edges. During the war he drank twenty cups of coffee a day, smoked four packs of cigarettes a day, and lived with myriad constant health problems.[49] Ike played politics with the best, often opting for the indirect route that kept his friends and foes alike baffled and, like Ronald Reagan after him, he delegated duties effectively.

Unlike his successors Kennedy and Nixon, Eisenhower had no love for the power or status of the office itself. Being president provided the means to improve the nation, and more broadly, the world. Adviser George Kennan found that in small meetings, especially on foreign affairs, Ike was "a man of keen political intelligence and penetration [who] spoke of matters seriously . . . insights of a high order flashed out time after time."[50] When he wished to avoid a direct answer, Eisenhower employed military jargon to obfuscate, and even pretended not to understand his own translator to deflect foreign queries. Most of all, Ike's animated face fit the times, like Lincoln's solemn demeanor fit his own.

The Eisenhower smile "was a political statement: America was *good;* unlike Hitler or Stalin, America was offering to the world a *good* man. . . . Understandably, it drove fanatics and the alienated up the wall."[51] He responded with straightforward and simple answers:

Q. Can you bring taxes down?
A. Yes. We will work to cut billions . . . and bring your taxes down.[52]

A low inflation rate (just over 1 percent) and virtual full employment (3 percent unemployment) contributed to Eisenhower's popularity. He balanced his budget three of eight times, and the other years had only minor deficits. Long before Ronald Reagan established the Eleventh Commandment—Thou shalt not speak ill of another Republican—Ike had absorbed that principle. If he needed to bash a particular GOP opponent, he did so through references to general characteristics, not by name. When it came to the Democrats, however, Ike could be brutal. And when it came to foreign enemies, Eisenhower took another tack, speaking in paradoxes and inscrutable philosophizing.

The "Fair Deal" Becomes "Dynamic Conservatism"

A central, lingering domestic question that both Truman and Eisenhower had to deal with involved the continuation of the New Deal—or rolling it back, as some hoped. Welfare-state liberalism had become entrenched by 1946, and despite his triumph over Wallace, Truman did little to slow the extension of federal programs. Truman raised the minimum wage, made an additional 10 million people eligible for new Social Security benefits, embarked on federal slum clearance, and proposed a large farm-income program. Truman's domestic program—dubbed the Fair Deal in honor of his Progressive forebears—also included 810,000 federally subsidized housing units. At almost every point Truman allied with the big-government forces.

In 1953, therefore, Eisenhower had a remarkable opportunity. As the first GOP president since Hoover, he was in a position to limit or end some of the New Deal policies, especially with the House and Senate under Republican control for a brief time. Nevertheless, Ike recognized that part of his appeal rested on his bipartisan image. He had not run as anti-Roosevelt, and was indeed far too progressive for some in the Republican Party, including "Mr. Republican," Senator Taft of Ohio. Many voters thought Taft and other conservatives overemphasized anticommunism to the exclusion of other issues (although Taft is perhaps best known for his sponsorship of the Taft-Hartley Act of 1946, prohibiting closed-shop, union-only, workplaces). Taft's insurgency failed, and the senator died in 1953, removing the most significant Republican opposing voice to Ike's policies, although remaining GOP insurgents forced the president to moderate the rate of growth of New Deal programs. Where Ike did reverse New Deal policies was in his cabinet selections, who were mostly businessmen. Among the group was the devout Mormon, Ezra Taft Benson, who cut back federal ownership of hydroelectric power businesses and limited regulation of offshore oil leases. But Eisenhower did not hesitate to spend: the National Highway Act of 1956 used federal money to link the nation's cities, thus lowering (private) transportation costs. Blasted as "corporate socialism" for Detroit, the act reflected Ike's World War II experience, which impressed on him the need for a highway system for defense.

His domestic strategy, called dynamic conservatism, was a policy that shed the criticism that conservatives were only against something and offered nothing positive. The minimum wage rose to a dollar an hour under Eisenhower and federal aid to education increased through the National Defense Education Act. Social Security benefits likewise rose, and Ike created a new superagency—the Department of Health, Education, and Welfare—to continue to administer the New Deal welfare-state programs. Eisenhower did not end the New Deal, but he slowed its growth.

The Atomic Genie

Both Truman and Eisenhower maintained a consistency in dealing with atomic energy and atomic weapons. Realizing that atomic power provided not only new terrors, but also new sources of relatively clean energy for civilian use, Congress authorized the Atomic Energy Commission under civilian control to examine peaceful uses of nuclear power. Bernard Baruch, head of the War Industries Board in World War I, became the American delegate to the newly formed United Nations Atomic Energy Commission. To control the spread of nuclear weapons—which could easily grow out of the unchecked expansion of peaceful nuclear power—the UN proposed an international agency to supervise all atomic development. Baruch even submitted a plan to have the United States hand over atomic secrets to the UN, on the condition that the United States, the USSR, and other nations likely to develop nuclear power would agree to allow international inspections at atomic installations. The United States, under those conditions, would agree to destroy its nuclear stockpile. The Soviets had already secretly started construction of their own atomic bombs, and they had no intention of allowing free access by international inspectors to anything.

H-bomb testing produced fallout of a different sort when a national meeting of church leaders, scientists, authors, and other notables in June 1957 led to the formation of the National Committee for a Sane Nuclear Policy (SANE). Emphasizing the "human community," SANE placed ads in major papers protesting the H-bomb tests, but soon its agenda included international control over all U.S. weapons.

By 1948, even before the USSR had detonated its own atomic bomb, the Joint Chiefs of Staff and Truman's security advisers understood that temporarily the only way to protect Europe from further Soviet expansion was the threat, sometimes subtle, sometimes not, of the use of nuclear weapons by the United States in the event of aggression against any of the NATO allies. In a document called NSC-30, "the first formal expression of American atomic policy," the United States deliberately left its options open regarding the use of nuclear weapons.[53] After NSC-30, which effectively established the principle of linkage,

America's enemies knew that the atomic weapons in the arsenals of democracy would not just sit by while Europe or Asia was being overrun.

At about the same time, an independent group of civilians established the Research and Development Corporation (RAND) as a think tank to study problems associated with nuclear warfare. RAND employees John D. Williams, mathematician John von Neumann, and others concluded that nuclear war was not "unthinkable"; quite the contrary, to prevent it, someone *should* think about it. RAND developed studies that crystallized the armed forces' concepts of how to use, and how to prevent the use of, nuclear weapons, essentially forming the theoretical basis for mutual assured destruction, or MAD.[54]

Eisenhower, along with Secretary of State John Foster Dulles, further delineated America's strategy in 1954 by making it clear the United States would, if necessary, use nuclear weapons even on nonnuclear countries that threatened American national interests. To the Soviets—who by then had their own nuclear arsenal—this sent a clear message that the United States would not be bullied. Wishing to keep the nuclear genie in his bottle, however, Eisenhower introduced a flexible response that allowed for a wide range of military options when confronted with local or regional threats.[55] In short, Ike kept America's enemies guessing and off balance, never sure if aggression might invoke a nuclear response. This tended to keep rogue nations cautious and, for the most part, peaceful.

Secretly, Eisenhower prepared the nation to win a nuclear war far more than historians have previously thought, going so far as to disperse nuclear weapons to the soil of allies such as Canada, then later to Greenland, Iceland, Greece, Italy, and Japan, beginning in the 1950s.[56] America kept ahead of the Soviets and far ahead of the Chinese, as seen in the 1958 confrontation with China over the islands of Quemoy and Matsu in the Formosa Straits. The Nationalist government claimed these islands, as did the communist mainland, which made plans to invade them. Quiet diplomacy provided an agreement, but looming over the discussions was the fact that the United States had an "ace in the hole," as historian Timothy Botti called the nuclear weapons. Time and again, this nuclear backstop enabled the United States to pursue its national interests in ways that few large states in previous eras ever could have imagined. In short, the implicit threat of its large nuclear arsenal permitted the United States to engage in less than total war and to pursue localized, or limited, wars on several occasions.

Eisenhower also sought to develop a broader nuclear policy that would make use of atomic energy for peaceful purposes. In December 1953, Ike delivered his "Atoms for Peace" speech at the United Nations in New York City in hopes of breaking the deadlock over establishing international supervision of fissionable materials, and of approving an amendment to the Atomic Energy Act of 1946 that provided for research in nuclear energy in civilian areas under the direction of the National Security Council.[57] Thus, the federal government assumed authority for the safety and regulation of all civilian nuclear plants in the nation. This expanded federal power on the one hand, but it opened up an untapped resource to be used with confidence on the other.

Sputnik: Cold War in Space

To America's shock, in August 1957 the cold war took a new turn or, more appropriately, an upward arc when the USSR announced it had successfully tested an intercontinental ballistic missile (ICBM), a rocket fired upward out of the earth's atmosphere on an arc that would descend on a target and release warheads. Although the public did not immediately appreciate the import of these tests, in October the Soviet Union claimed the lead in the space race by launching *Sputnik I* into orbit, using a launcher similar to that on their ICBMs. To the man on the street, *Sputnik* represented little more than a Soviet scientific feat, but added to the ICBM test, *Sputnik's* successful orbit suggested that now the USSR had the capability of raining atomic bombs on American soil safely from within bases inside Russia.

Realistically, the Soviets had merely skipped a step in the development of nuclear weapons, temporarily forgoing construction of a long-range bomber fleet. Eisenhower personally seemed unconcerned. Not so the general public. Popular media publications such as *Life* magazine headlined its post-*Sputnik* issue with THE CASE FOR BEING PANICKY. The public did not know that General Curtis LeMay, of the Strategic Air Command, in an internal study reviewing the results of a simulated missile attack on American bomber bases, had concluded that the Soviet Union could have wiped out sixty of the major U.S. bases with a coordinated attack. *Sputnik* persuaded the United States to keep a force of long-range reconnaissance aircraft—the U-2 spy planes—in the skies over the USSR at all times to detect enemy preparations for an attack. Eisenhower also offered intermediate-range ballistic missiles to NATO allies, such as Britain, Turkey, and Italy.

Nevertheless, the public demanded a response to the threat of ICBMs. This came in a crash program aimed in two directions. First, money poured into education, particularly into universities and colleges for engineering, science, and math programs. Through the National Defense Education Act (1958), Congress "authorized grants for training in mathematics, science, and modern languages."[58] That might have kept the money in the labs where Congress intended it, but by also funding student loans and fellowships, the federal government flooded the humanities and other university departments with cash, providing the financial base for the student rebellions that would dominate the late 1960s.

Second, the United States moved with urgency to develop its own solid- and liquid-fueled rockets, resulting in some early spectacular crashes as American technology exploded on launching pads or flew apart in flight. Defense spending surged, and Congress turned the National Advisory Council on Aeronautics (NACA, created in 1915 by President Woodrow Wilson) into a larger, more powerful agency, the National Aeronautics and Space Administration (NASA). In

May 1961, Commander Alan B. Shepard Jr. became the first American into space; then, in February 1962, Colonel John Glenn was launched into orbit aboard a Mercury rocket. In both cases the Soviets beat the United States to the punch, placing their own "astronauts"—a new term coined to describe space travelers, although the Russian "cosmonauts" preceded American astronauts—into space, then into orbit. To the public, these activities merely confirmed that the communists continued to lead in the space race. The images of exploding American rockets remained fresh, and even with Glenn's flight, American scientists feared the worst while they hoped (and planned) for the best. Military planners even had a plan (Operation Dirty Trick) that would blame Cuban communists if the Mercury flight failed.[59] Soviet victories in space contributed to the cloud of anxiety that hung over what otherwise was a decade of prosperity and growth.

Happy Days: Myth or Reality?

A popular television sitcom called *Happy Days* appeared from 1974 to 1984 and depicted life in 1950s America as lighthearted and easy, with intact families, supportive communities, and teenagers who, although prone to an occasional prank or misstep, nevertheless behaved like upstanding citizens. Even the antihero, the Fonz (Vincent Fonzarelli, played by Henry Winkler), who sported a motorcycle jacket and a tough-guy mystique, possessed a heart of gold and displayed loyalty, courage, and wisdom. Of course, in the cynical 1970s, critics salivated at the opportunity to lampoon *Happy Days.* They pointed out that the show did not deal at any length with racial prejudice (it did not, although Asian actor Pat Morita was the original owner of the diner) or family problems such as alcoholism and divorce (again, guilty as charged). But the very fact that so many critics, especially of the Left, responded so vehemently to *Happy Days* suggests that the show touched a raw nerve. Despite genuine social problems and hidden pathologies, despite racial discrimination and so-called traditional roles for women, and despite the threat of atomic warfare, for the vast majority of Americans, the 1950s *were* happy days.

One view of the 1950s, focused on those who had entered adulthood in the decade or slightly before, comes from generational pundits William Strauss and Neil Howe. They label the group born from 1901 to 1924 the GI generation. By 1946, GIs would have reached twenty-two at the youngest and forty-five at the oldest, putting them at the prime earning years of their lives. That coincided with the postwar economic boom that fitted together a generation viewed as "fearless but not reckless," replete with heroes and full of problem solvers.[60] As the inscription on the Iwo Jima shrine (itself a testament to their courage) puts it, "Uncommon valor was a common virtue."

Adults of the 1950s included many of America's greatest achievers, including Walt Disney, Ronald Reagan, Lee Iacocca, Lyndon Johnson, George Bush, Bob Hope, John Wayne, Katharine Hepburn, Ann Landers, Billy Graham, Sidney Poitier, Walter Cronkite, Jimmy Stewart, Charles Lindbergh, and Joe DiMaggio. They produced such cultural monuments as Herman Wouk's *The Caine Mutiny,*

Leonard Bernstein's *West Side Story*, Jackie Gleason's *The Honeymooners*, and Walt Disney's *Lady and the Tramp* and *Bambi*. They initiated a spiritual revival that spread the Gospel of Christianity more broadly through Billy Graham and the ministry of Oral Roberts. Epitomizing the spirit of the decade, the best-known comic strip character, Superman, fought for "truth, justice, and the American way."

Nineteen fifties Americans received the benefit of the largest one-generation jump in educational achievement in the nation's history; they had learned the importance of work, yet had worked less outside the home than any other group; and as a generation they had an uncanny knack for backing the winning candidate in every single major election. As adults, they won two thirds of all Nobel prizes ever won by Americans, including all fourteen prizes in economics. Supported in some of their affluence by grateful taxpayers, they received housing subsidies through mortgage interest deductions on taxes, and through the Veterans Administration, they received guaranteed mortgage loans to purchase houses. This group of adults also effectively changed the debate about racial segregation, with black intellectuals like Ralph Ellison (*Invisible Man*) arguing that segregation not only was morally wrong, but also economically inefficient. By 1965, *Look* magazine would say—speaking mainly of the adults in society—"Americans today bear themselves like victory-addicted champions. . . . They are accustomed to meeting, and beating, tests."[61]

This optimism hid a spiritual emptiness that characterized many of this generation, the efforts of preachers such as Billy Graham, Norman Vincent Peale, and Oral Roberts notwithstanding. Later surveys would show the 1950s generation to be in many ways one of the least religious groups in American history, and this may in part account for why their success—while genuine and admirable in many cases—was fleeting. Sooner or later, a sandy foundation of civic virtue, unsupported by deeper spiritual commitments, would crumble.

What is amazing about all this is that the 1950s still had plenty of structure. Marriage and motherhood were considered the main destiny of young women—with teaching and nursing considered their only "acceptable" careers—and magazines such as *Seventeen* or *Mademoiselle* or popular books such as Mary McGee Williams's *On Becoming a Woman* all operated under this assumption. "It's Not Too Soon to Dream of Marriage" ran a typical chapter title in Williams's book. Yet at the same time, the prominent female movie stars were the sexy Marilyn Monroe, Jayne Mansfield, Jane Russell, and Brigitte Bardot. Alfred Kinsey's *Sexual Behavior in the Human Female*, which appeared in 1953, even if tainted by flawed data still indicated that women were having sex before marriage in large numbers, perhaps—if Kinsey's statistics were to be believed—up to half of the six thousand women he had interviewed. Certainly men thought about sex all the time, or at least that was the premise behind the launch of Hugh Hefner's *Playboy* magazine in 1953, wherein photos of nude women were legitimized for viewing by middle-class men by packaging them with interviews, fiction, and "serious reporting." The standard joke of the day was that a male, when caught in possession of a *Playboy*, would claim to read it "just for the articles." As if to follow Hefner's lead, in 1957 the Searle pharmaceutical company brought out the birth-control pill, which proved instrumental in delinking sexual intercourse from childbearing or, put another way, in separating consequences from actions.

Before the Pill, in the early 1950s, young adults, especially those married in the late 1940s, produced the largest boom in childbirths ever witnessed in the United States. Aptly labeled baby boomers, these children grew up in unprecedented affluence by the standards of the day. Adult expectations were that the boomers stood "on the fringe of a golden era" and would "lay out blight proof, smog-free cities, enrich the underdeveloped world, and, no doubt, write *finis* to poverty and war."[62] New foods developed specifically for babies had experienced slow growth before the boomers began consuming boxcars full of Frank Gerber's baby products and pediatrics "reached its height of physical aggressiveness: No generation of kids got more shots or operations."[63]

Clothes designers targeted babies and children as distinct consumer groups rather than viewing them as little adults. Manufacturers made clothes tailored for babies' and children's bodies, for play, and for, well . . . accidents. Barbie dolls, Hula-Hoops, Davy Crockett coonskin caps, and other toys aimed at children appeared on the market, and other toys invented earlier, like Tinkertoys and Lionel trains, saw their sales soar. In short, the baby boomers in general wanted for no material thing.

In addition to growing up in abundance, the boom generation also was raised on the theories of the best-selling baby book of all time, Dr. Benjamin Spock's *Common Sense Book of Baby and Child Care* (1946). Spock, thoroughly steeped in psychoanalysis and Freudianism, had been a Coolidge Republican in early adulthood, but along with his wife had moved steadily leftward, advocating positions that would have made Coolidge quiver. He advised parents to refrain from disciplining their children and to let children determine when and where everything took place, from bathroom habits to education. American homes overnight became child centered, whereas spanking and other physical discipline was viewed as psychologically unhealthy. The dangerous combination of material comfort and loose control made for a generation that lacked toughness, one that literally fell apart under the pressures of civil rights, the Vietnam War, and economic stagnation. Not surprisingly, boomers turned to drugs and sex in record numbers, and divorce among the generation skyrocketed.

Along with the permissiveness at home came an unparalleled freedom of travel and movement. Some of this movement was permanent relocation for jobs or better living conditions, including climate. Most of it was from north and east to south and west: between 1947 and 1960, a quarter of a million Americans left the Great Lakes region and the mid-Atlantic/New England areas for the far West, Southwest, and Southeast. At the same time, only twenty-one thousand— virtually all black—left the South for higher wages and greater social freedom in the North. Thus, the Sun Belt regions netted a huge population gain in just over a decade, dramatically shifting both the economy and political balance of the country.

Central cities saw their rate of growth slow as suburbs appeared around all the major metropolitan areas. Levittown, New York—built by William Levitt in 1947—created such a demand that by the time it was finished in 1951, it covered 1,200 acres with more than 17,000 homes, most of them owned by young families. Levittown quickly acquired the nickname Fertility Valley. Levitt's basic house consisted of a 720-square-foot Cape Cod, constructed on a concrete slab, including a kitchen, two bedrooms, a bath, a living room with fireplace, and an attic with the potential for conversion into two more bedrooms. Basic models sold for just under $7,000, whereas larger versions went for $10,000.

Many communities like Levittown were planned cities that sought to control the types of businesses, architecture, and developments that were permitted in an attempt to beautify the environment.[64] Oversight by professionals in city planning represented the culmination of the dreams of the Progressives who had once thought that central cities would evolve into what the suburbs, in fact, became. Yet once the planned communities arose, criticism of them from academics and urban advocates sprang up almost as fast: the "soulless" suburbs, it was said, were draining away the talent and wealth from the inner cities. Instead of praising lower crime rates in the suburbs, critics blamed the suburbanites for abandoning the core city.[65] They failed to understand the basic human desire for security, privacy, and property.

Travel for business and pleasure also expanded at geometric rates, thanks to the widespread availability of the family automobile. Autos had started to permeate American culture in the 1920s, but the expansion of auto travel slowed during the Depression and war. After 1946, however, people had several years' worth of wartime savings to spend, and General Motors and Ford, the giants, began to offer their own financing programs, making it still easier to acquire dependable transportation. A feedback loop—a self-reinforcing cycle—occurred as it had in the 1920s: as more people obtained autos, they demanded better roads, which state governments started to provide; and as more roads were laid, reaching more towns and cities, more people wanted cars. The Big Three automakers (GM, Ford, and Chrysler) dominated the market, but many other small companies remained competitive, such as Jeep, Rambler, Nash, Checker, Willys, and the short-lived (but high-selling) Kaiser-Frazer cars. In the 1950s, U.S. auto production exceeded that of Great Britain, France, Japan, Sweden, and all other nations *put together several times over,* and Ford and GM—both of which produced their 50 millionth vehicles in the 1950s—posted healthy profits.

Even before the 1956 National Highway Act was passed, building 41,000 miles of interstates, 60 percent of all American households owned a car, but most trips were local. The nation's more than 40 million cars traveled on some 1.6 million miles of surfaced highways, testifying to the fact that auto ownership had become common. Average annual highway driving rose 400 percent after the act, making interstate travel commonplace. But on the negative side, the fuel taxes remained in place long after the highway construction ended, and nearly fifty years later, almost half of the price of a gallon of gasoline consisted of federal, state, and local taxes. Indeed, the leftist notion that roads use tax dollars to subsidize auto travel fails to confront the reality that gasoline taxes ensured that the people who used the highways would, in fact, pay for them—even as they were also paying for the mass transit systems that the "experts" promoted. The unbridled liberty of the automobile irks those enamored of planning and control, those who see government-dominated mass transit systems as an ordered and structured alternative.

Air travel also entered a new democratic age. While still expensive, passenger flights became increasingly more available to more people. Air carriers, such as Trans World Airlines, American, Pan Am, and others, flew enough routes at low enough prices that by the late 1950s average American families could consider taking an airplane flight to a vacation site or to see relatives. Juan Trippe's Pan American World Airways, which had flown directly to England by the 1930s and had mapped South American routes for security purposes during the war, emerged as a leading overseas carrier. Howard Hughes, who owned enough of Trans World Airlines (TWA) to assume hands-on management, started designing his own giant passenger aircraft even before the war, resulting in the Lockheed Constellation, which set an "industry standard for size, comfort, and range."[66] New technology converged with a glut of war-trained pilots who came on the market after 1945, producing lower fares. Eastern, American, and TWA offered coach-class tickets that made air travel competitive with rail travel, resulting in a doubling of airplane passengers between 1951 and 1958. The ease with which people traveled by air was, ironically, symbolized by the first air traffic jam over New York City in 1954, when three hundred airliners lined up in holding patterns in the airspace around the metropolis, involving forty-five thousand passengers in delays.

After Pan Am introduced a new transatlantic airliner designed specifically for passengers, the Douglas DC-7, Boeing matched it with the famous 707 jetliner, providing competition in passenger-aircraft production that drove down prices. The frequency of air travel even produced a new term in the language, a physical and mental malady called jet lag.

It goes without saying that Americans could fly and drive because their paychecks purchased more than ever before. In 1955 the average income for all industries, excluding farm labor, topped $4,220 per year, and by 1959 that had increased by another 10 percent. A New Orleans salesman with a high school education earned $400 per month; a Chicago private secretary pulled in about the same; and a Charlotte housekeeper received about $140 a month. Marilyn Monroe could command $100,000 a picture—just a little more than the $90,000 annual income earned by *Peanuts* cartoonist Charles Schulz.[67] Such high wages bought a lot of potatoes at $.51 per pound, or rice at $.19 per pound, and even new electronics gadgets like movie projectors were within reach at $89. Chevrolet's Corvette—arguably the hottest car of the 1950s—had a sticker price of $3,670, or below the average annual salary in America.

Cookie-Cutter America?

The newfound freedom on the highways and airways held a threat as well as a promise, for although people could break the restraints of their geography, social class, background, and family more easily than ever, they also were exposed to new and unfamiliar, often uncomfortable social settings and customs. People responded by seeking a balance, embracing similar—almost uniform—housing on the one hand and enjoying their visits to other parts of the country on the other. The popularity of the famous Levittown subdivisions, where all houses were almost identical, have led some historians to mistake this need for order, and the cost advantages resulting from economics of scale, for an overarching quest for conformity. It was no such thing at all. Just as the adventurous pilot scans the landscape for a familiar topography every now and then, so too did Americans embrace individualism while they retained some sense of order.

To see this, all one has to do is examine American travel patterns to observe how people eagerly entered into parts of the country that were in many ways foreign to them, even threatening. Yankees heading to Florida's vacation spots for the first time crossed through the redneck backwoods of the Old South. Easterners visiting California often encountered Asians for the first time; and midwesterners taking new jobs in the Southwest were exposed to Indian or Mexican cultures and probably ate their first taco or tasted their first salsa. Even such things as housing—in Arizona few multilevel homes were built because of the heat—food, and beverages differed greatly from place to place. Southern iced tea, for example, was always presweetened, and so-called Mexican food in Texas hardly resembled Mexican food in California. Midwesterners, who battled snows and rains all winter and spring, had trouble relating to water politics in the West, where titanic struggles over the Colorado River consumed lawmakers and citizens.

Food rapidly democratized and diversified, with the specialized dishes of the elites spreading to the middle class throughout the country. Soldiers who had come back from Italy had a yearning for pasta; New Yorkers who knew Coney Island learned the magic of the hot dog and took the concept with them as they traveled. Asian recipes moved inward from the coasts as Mexican cuisine surged northward. America's eating establishments became the most richly textured on the planet, with the most varied menus anywhere in the world. Within thirty years, Jamaican hot peppers, Indian curry sauce, flour tortillas, lox, teriyaki sauce, Dutch chocolates, innumerable pasta variations, and spices of all descriptions flooded the shelves of American grocers, allowing a cook in North Dakota to specialize in cashew chicken, N'Awlins shrimp, or enchiladas. Not surprisingly, some of the most celebrated chefs to come out of this era drew upon their ethnic roots or experiences for their cooking. Martha Stewart (born Martha Kostyra) frequently prepared Polish dishes. And Julia Child, who worked in Asia with the Office of Strategic Services and then lived in Paris (where she learned to cook), had a broad firsthand exposure to foreign cuisine. Emeril Lagasse, another future star, born in the early 1960s, earned his chef's apron in his parents' Portuguese bakery.

Far from a decade of conformity, as expressed in the lamentations of books on corporate America, such as William Whyte's *The Organization Man* (1956) or Sloan Wilson's *The Man in the Gray Flannel Suit* (1955), the population had entered a period of sharp transition where technology was the handmaiden of turmoil. These books and others, such as David Reisman's *The Lonely Crowd* (1950), emphasized a shift from rugged individualism to a team or corporate orientation. Reality was quite different: American conformity in fact kept the sudden and difficult transitions of the postwar world from careening out of control. It is not surprising that the two most popular movie stars of the day—the establishment's John Wayne and the counterculture's James Dean—in different ways celebrated rugged individualism, not conformity.

No one symbolized the effort to maintain continuity between 1950s America and its small-town roots and patriotic past more than painter Norman Rockwell (1894–1978), who in some ways was the most important and significant American artist in the history of the Republic. Born in New York, Rockwell left school in 1910 to study at the National Academy of Design. Almost immediately his work found an audience and a market. He painted Christmas cards before he was sixteen, and while still a teenager was hired to paint the covers of *Boys' Life*, the official publication of the Boy Scouts of America.[68] Setting up a studio in New Rochelle, Rockwell worked for a number of magazines until he received a job in 1916 painting covers for *The Saturday Evening Post*, a magazine Rockwell called the "greatest show window in America." In all, Rockwell painted 322 covers for the *Post*, and illustrated children's books before he began painting for *Look* magazine.

Critics despised Rockwell because he presented an honest, yet sympathetic and loving, view of America.[69] He insisted on painting those scenes that captured the American spirit of family—independence, patriotism, and commitment to worship. Inspired by one of Franklin Roosevelt's speeches, Rockwell produced his masterpieces, the *Four Freedoms*, which ran in consecutive issues of the *Post* in 1943 along with interpretive essays by contemporary writers. *Freedom from Want* was inspired by his family's cook presenting a turkey at Thanksgiving. *Freedom of Speech*, possibly the best known Rockwell painting of all, featured a small-town meeting in which a laborer in a brown leather jacket speaks with confidence about a bill or proposal tucked in his pocket.

Rockwell did not ignore the serious deficiencies of American society. His 1964 *Look* painting *The Problem We All Live With* remains one of the most powerful indictments of racial discrimination ever produced. Depicting the desegregation of a New Orleans school district in 1960, Rockwell painted a little black girl, Ruby Bridges, being escorted into the formerly all-white school by four federal marshals. The wall in the background has the splattered remains of a tomato just under the graffito NIGGER that appears above her head. *New Kids in the Neighborhood* (1967) pictures a moving van with two African American kids standing beside it—the new kids staring at three white children who are looking at them with curiosity, not anger or fear.

Rockwell's paintings capture a stability in a sea of unraveling social and regional bonds. Religion tried to adapt to these changes but failed. It took outsiders, such as Billy Graham and Oral Roberts, to cut through the serenity, comfort, and even sloth of the mainstream religions to get Christianity focused again on saving the lost and empowering the body of Christ. Clinging to stability and eschewing change came at a price: the lack of passion and avoidance of contention in many denominations triggered a staggering decline in membership. One researcher found that starting in 1955, the Methodist Church lost an average of a thousand members every week for the next thirty years.[70] In the mid-1950s, churches responded by becoming more traditional and turning down the doctrinal voltage.

As religion grew less denominationally contentious, thus making it less important to live near those of a similar denomination, Americans found one less impediment to relocating to other cities or regions of the country. The market played a role in this sense of regional familiarity too. Entire industries sprang up to meet the demands of an increasingly mobile population. For example, Kemmons Wilson, a Tennessee architect, traveled with his family extensively and was irritated by the quality of hotels and the fact that most hotels or motels charged extra for children. Wilson and his wife embarked on a cross-country trip in which they took copious notes about every motel and hotel where they stayed: size of rooms, facilities, cost, and so on. He then returned home to design the model motel of optimal size, comfort, and pricing—with kids staying free. The result—Holiday Inn—succeeded beyond Wilson's wildest dreams. By 1962, Wilson had 250 motels in some 35 states. Wilson saw standardization as the key. Each Holiday Inn had to be the same, more or less, as any other. That way, travelers could always count on a "good night's sleep," as he said later. Americans' quest for familiar products, foods, and even fuel and music in an age of growing mobility produced a vast market waiting to be tapped.[71]

Ray Kroc saw that potential. A middle-aged paper-cup salesman who had invented a multiple-milk-shake mixer, Kroc was impressed with a California hamburger stand owned by a pair of brothers named McDonald. He purchased the rights to the name and the recipes and standardized the food. All burgers, fries, and milk shakes at all locations had to be made in exactly the same way. In 1954 he opened the first McDonald's drive-in restaurant in Des Planes, Illinois, replete with its characteristic golden arches. After five years, there were two hundred McDonald's restaurants in the United States, and Kroc was opening a hundred more per year.[72] By the twenty-first century, "fast food" had become a derogatory term. But fifty years earlier, when truckers planned their stops at roadside truck cafés, the appearance of a McDonald's restaurant in the distance, with its consistent level of food quality, brought nothing but smiles.

What Norman Rockwell had done for canvas, Kroc and Wilson did for food and lodging, in the sense that they provided buoys of familiarity in a sea of turbulence and international threats. Americans needed—indeed, demanded—a number of consistent threads, from music to meals, from autos to dwellings, within which to navigate the sea of transformation in which they found themselves.

The Invisible Man

One of the main arenas where Americans confronted radical change in the 1950s was in race relations. The continued injustice of a segregated society in which black people were either second-class citizens or, in more "sophisticated" cities, merely invisible, had finally started to change. Ralph Ellison's novel *The Invisible Man* eloquently captured the fact that to most white Americans, blacks simply did not exist. Television shows never depicted blacks in central roles; black or "nigger" music, as white-dominated radio stations called it, was banned from playlists (as was Elvis Presley, whom disc jockeys thought was black, early on). One could search in vain for African American executives heading major white-owned companies.

Few blacks were even remotely equal to whites in economic, political, or cultural power. This situation existed across the nation, where it was winked at or deliberately ignored by most whites. But in the South racism was open and institutionalized in state and local laws. Since *Plessy v. Ferguson* the doctrine of "separate but equal" had been applied to southern public facilities, including schools, transportation, public restrooms and drinking fountains, and in the vast majority of private restaurants and in the housing market. On municipal buses, for example, blacks were *required* to give up their seats to whites, and were always expected to go to the back or middle of the bus. Segregation of the races divided everything from church services to whites-only diners. State universities in many southern states would not admit blacks, nor was any black—no matter how affluent—permitted to join country clubs or civic groups. Indeed, even as late as the 1990s, when the black/Asian golfer Tiger Woods became the youngest pro golfer to win the Masters, he was prohibited from joining some of the private golf clubs at which he had played as part of the Professional Golfers' Association tour. Also in the 1990s, famous televangelist pastor Frederick K. C. Price was not invited to speak at certain churches because of his skin color.

Large numbers—if not the vast majority—of whites entertained some racial prejudices if not outright racism. Confederate flag-wavers, white-robed Ku Klux Klansmen (whose organization had plummeted in membership since the 1920s), and potbellied southern sheriffs still stood out as not-so-comical symbols of white racism. Equally dangerous to blacks, though, were well-meaning whites, especially northeastern liberals, who practiced a quiet, and perhaps equally systematic, racism. Those northern white elites would enthusiastically and aggressively support the fight for civil rights in the South while carefully segregating their own children at all-white private schools. They overwhelmingly supported public school systems with their votes and their editorials, but insulated their own children from exposure to other races by sending them to Andover or Sidwell Friends. Few had personal acquaintances who were black, and fewer still, when it was in their power, appointed or promoted blacks to corporate, church, or community positions.

Not surprisingly, this subterranean prejudice was at its worst in liberal meccas such as Hollywood and New York City, where television production headquarters selected the programming for virtually all TV broadcasting in the 1950s and early 1960s. With the notable exception of the radio show *Amos and Andy*—whose actors were actually white!—black television characters were nonexistent except as occasional servants or for comic relief or as dancers. There were no black heroes on television; worse, there were no black families. Black children did not have many good role models on television, and those African Americans they did see were seldom entrepreneurs, political leaders, or professionals. Perhaps not surprisingly, the wholesale exclusion of blacks from large segments of American society made African Americans suspicious of the few who did achieve positions of importance in white business or culture. Ellison's *Invisible Man* appropriately captured white America's treatment of more than 10 percent of its population.

Hardly in the vanguard of civil rights, Eisenhower shielded himself from controversy behind the separation of powers. His position, while perhaps appropriate at times, nevertheless contradicted the constitutionally protected civil rights of blacks and cemented the view among black politicians that their only source of support was the Democratic Party. It is ironic, then, that two key events in America's racial history occurred during Eisenhower's presidency. The Legal Defense and Educational Fund of the NAACP (National Association for the Advancement of Colored People), led by its director, attorney Thurgood Marshall, earlier had started to take on the "separate but equal" *Plessy* decision. Marshall had laid the groundwork with a Texas case, *Sweatt v. Painter* (1950), in which the Supreme Court found that intangible factors, such as isolation from the legal market, constituted inequality. The real breakthrough, however, came in 1954 through a case from Topeka, Kansas, in which the Supreme Court's ruling in *Brown v. Board of Education* overturned *Plessy v. Ferguson* and prohibited state-supported racial discrimination.

The Reverend Oliver Brown, whose daughter Linda had to walk past a white school to catch her bus to a black school, had brought a suit against the Board of Education of Topeka, Kansas.[73] The board argued that its schools were separate, but equal (à la *Plessy*). In 1953, President Eisenhower had appointed a Republican, Earl Warren of California, as chief justice. This brought about a shift in the Court against *Plessy*, which the Court found inherently unequal. A year later, the Court required that states with segregated districts (twenty-one states and the District of Columbia) desegregate with "all deliberate speed." In 1956, Southern states dominated by the Democrats issued a defiant "Southern Manifesto," in which nineteen senators and eighty-one congressmen promised to use "all lawful means" to reinstate segregation.

The Court's language and rulings after the case generated confusion, uncertainty, and resistance. Racist whites would argue that they were moving with "all deliberate speed" decades after the decision. Equally damaging on the other end of the scale, the Court had stated that segregation "generates a feeling of inferiority" by blacks within the community, which implied that the only way blacks could overcome "inferiority" was to "sit next to whites"—a position that by the 1980s, blacks came to ridicule. It further suggested that in *any* situation, even voluntary arrangements in which some preordained proportion of races was not achieved, it would "generate a feeling of inferiority." Eisenhower thought the *Brown* decision set back racial progress, arguing that real integration could not be brought about by force.

White resistance to integration involved citizens councils, organizations that threatened blacks whose children attended white schools with economic retaliation, job loss, and other veiled intimidation. States that had made up the border areas in the Civil War—Maryland, Delaware, Kentucky, Missouri, Oklahoma, Kansas—grudgingly began to desegregate. Farther south, though, in the heart of Dixie, a full-scale offensive against desegregation ensued. Latching onto the Supreme Court's wording of "all deliberate speed," the Deep South engaged in a massive foot-dragging campaign.

In Little Rock, Arkansas, the city school board admitted nine black students to Central High School. In response, Governor Orval Faubus, citing the likelihood of violence, encircled the high school with national guard troops to prevent the students from entering. Eisenhower, after conferring with Faubus, concluded the Arkansas governor would remain intransigent. A federal court order forced the national guard to withdraw, at which point the students again sought to enter the school. White mobs threatened to drag the students out and intimidated the authorities into removing the black students. A stunned Ike, who had only months earlier said he could not imagine sending federal troops to enforce integration, nationalized the Arkansas Guard and sent in a thousand paratroopers to ensure the students' safety. Faubus then closed the schools, requiring yet another court ruling to pry them open. Further efforts at "massive resistance," a phrase coined by Democrat senator Harry F. Byrd of Virginia, led to state attempts to defund desegregated schools. But state and federal courts held firm, and supported with minimal enthusiasm by Eisenhower and then by Kennedy, the segregated structure finally began to fracture.

As with much of the history of slavery and racism in America, the desegregation of schools ultimately had required a perversion of the apparatus of the state in order to get people to act responsibly and justly. The Founders never imagined in their wildest dreams that federal courts would be determining the makeup of student bodies in a local high school, yet the utter collapse of the state legislative process to act morally—or at the very least, even effectively—pushed the courts into action. It was a cautionary tale. At every point in the past, the continued refusal of any group to abide by a modicum of decency and tolerance inevitably brought change, but also brought vast expansions of federal power that afflicted all, including the groups that initially benefited from the needed change.

If lawsuits and federal action constituted one front in the struggle for civil rights, the wallet and the heart were two other critical battlefields. On December 1, 1955, in Montgomery, Alabama, police arrested a black seamstress, Rosa Parks, for refusing to give up her seat in the middle of the bus to a white man in defiance of a local ordinance. (Blacks could sit in the middle, but only if no whites wanted the seat.) "Back of the bus" not only embodied the actual laws of many Southern states, but it also represented a societywide attitude toward blacks.

Parks, along with other black female activists, members of the Montgomery Women's Political Council, had looked for the proper ordinance to challenge. Her refusal to "get back" sparked an organized protest by the black community. Local black leaders met the following night in a Baptist church to use the power of the market to bring justice to Montgomery. They organized a boycott of the bus system under the leadership of Martin Luther King Jr., a young Atlanta-born pastor who had studied Thoreau and Gandhi as well as the Gospels. Contrary to a widely held view that later developed among conservatives, King specifically condemned and repudiated communism. A man with a mighty presence and a charismatic speaker, King had discerned that the battle was not about Montgomery—that was only a skirmish in the war for justice—and he developed a brilliant plan to use the innate goodness of many, if not most, Americans to turn the system.

King promised his enemies to "wear you down by our capacity to suffer, and in winning our freedom we will so appeal to your heart and conscience that we will win you in the process."[74] "We are determined," he stated, "to work and fight until justice runs down like water, and righteousness like a mighty stream."[75] King's gamble hinged on the essential decency of Americans, and for every racist he thought could elicit the support of five nonracists. King also appreciated that for all its serious defects, the American system could actually work in his favor. Police might unleash dogs, fire hoses, and nightsticks, but (at least in daytime, under the watchful eye of the press) they would not dare kill unarmed protesters. While these strategies germinated in his mind he set to the task of leading the boycott.

Blacks constituted the majority of riders on the Montgomery buses, and the protesters used car pools or simply walked as the income plummeted for the privately owned bus company. The boycott continued for months, and eventually the media began to notice. Finally, after a year, the Supreme Court let stand a lower court ruling stating that the "separate but equal" clause was no longer valid. Montgomery blacks, led by King, boarded buses and sat where they pleased. The episode illustrated the power of the market and the colorblind processes in capitalism.

The moral issues in the initial civil rights cases in the 1950s and 1960s were crystal clear. But the steady encroachment of government into race relations later raised difficult issues about freedom of choice in America. Black economist Walter Williams has referred to "forced association laws," noting that the logical outcome of defining every business as "public" increasingly restricts a person's freedom to choose those with whom he or she wishes to associate. In cases of genuinely public facilities, the issue is clear: all citizens pay taxes, and thus all citizens must have access without regard for race or color. But where was the line drawn? Private clubs? The logic of the issue transcended race. Did Christians or others whose religion dictated that they not aid and abet sin have to rent apartments to unmarried couples living together? Did Augusta National Golf Club—a private club—have to admit women, contrary to its rules? Likewise, the firewall of states' rights also deteriorated in the civil rights clashes. A phrase used all too often by racist whites, the fact is that "states' rights" still represented a structural safeguard for all citizens of a state against direct federal action.

Both the bus boycott and the *Brown* decision represented significant steps toward full equality for all citizens, but as always the real lever of power remained the ballot. Since Reconstruction, Southern whites had systematically prevented blacks from voting or had made them pay dearly for going to the polls through intimidation, threats, and often outright violence. Poll taxes sought to eliminate poorer voters, and literacy tests could be easily manipulated, for instance, by allowing a white person to read only his name, whereas a black person would be required to interpret *Beowulf* or a Shakespearean play.

Eisenhower offered the first civil rights law since Reconstruction, the Civil Rights Act of 1957. It established a Civil Rights Commission and created a Civil Rights Division inside the Justice Department specifically charged with prosecuting election crimes. Most Southern Democrats opposed the bill, and Southern Democratic governors would not support the law, leaving enforcement to the federal government, which was not equipped to police every precinct in the South. Far from revealing Ike's lack of commitment to civil rights, the president's position stated a reality that, again, underscored the basic structure of the federal system, which never intended Washington, D.C., to supervise voting in New Orleans or Richmond. More widespread change depended on a transformation of hearts and attitudes. When the next round of civil rights legislation emerged from Congress in 1964, public perceptions of race and racism had changed enough that large numbers of whites, both in the South and from the North, assisted in making it possible to enforce the laws.[76]

Black leaders did not simply wait timidly for attitudes to change. They actively worked to place racism and discrimination squarely in front of the American public. Following the successful bus boycott, Martin Luther King assembled some hundred black Christian ministers to establish the Southern Christian Leadership Conference (SCLC). Assisted by another minister, Ralph Abernathy,

King called on the leaders to engage in the struggle for equality with nonviolence, not as a symbol of weakness or cowardice, but with courage and persistence. Formation of the SCLC transferred leadership of the civil rights movements from the descendants of northern freemen of color to the Southerners who had to live daily with discrimination.[77]

From Boring to Booming? Expectations at Decade's End

Given America's position in the world, its tremendous wealth, the success with which it had resisted communism, and the fact that it had at least begun to confront some of its greatest domestic problems, most observers in 1959 would have predicted a marvelous decade ahead for the United States. Few would have imagined that within ten years the American economy would be nearly flat; that a continued foreign war would absorb tremendous amounts of blood and treasure; that society would find itself ripped asunder and torn by race, generation, and ideology. Fewer still would have foreseen the earthquake generated by the coming of age of the massive baby-boom generation.

The United States had gone through a particularly turbulent era whose dynamic upheavals and impetus toward freedom and individualism had been effectively masked and less effectively contained by powerful pressures of order. In the resulting cookie-cutter America, the outward signs of conformity concealed a decade of dramatic change in lifestyle, income, social mobility, religion, and racial attitudes. The seeds of virtually all of the revolutionary developments of the 1960s had already started to bloom before Eisenhower ever left the presidency.

CHAPTER NINETEEN

The Age of Upheaval, 1960–74

The Fractured Decade

Following the perceived stability of the 1950s—a decade which, in reality, involved deep social change and substantial foreign threats—the 1960s were marked by unmistakable turmoil and conflict from policy divisions, racial clashes, and generational strife unseen in many generations. Much of the division came from the increasingly vocal presence of the baby boomers—exaggerated and sharpened by a foreign war—the assassination of a president, and, toward the end of the decade, economic stagnation that had not been seen since the end of World War II. The "fractured decade" of the sixties brought some needed social reforms, but also saddled the nation with long-term problems stemming directly from the very policies adopted during the period.

Except, perhaps, for the decade between 1935 and 1945, the 1960s changed American life and culture more profoundly than any other ten-year period in the twentieth century. Modern society continues to deal with many of the pathologies generated by the era of "free love," "tune in, turn on, and drop out," and rebellion.[1] Every aspect of America's fabric, from national image and reputation to family life, experienced distasteful side effects from the upheaval that began when John F. Kennedy won the presidential election over Richard Nixon.

Time Line

1960: John F. Kennedy elected president

1961: Bay of Pigs invasion of Cuba; Soviet Union erects Berlin Wall

1962: Cuban Missile Crisis

1963: John F. Kennedy assassinated; Lyndon B. Johnson assumes presidency

1964: Johnson introduces Great Society legislation; Civil Rights Act passed; Tonkin Gulf Resolution; Ronald Reagan campaigns for Barry Goldwater's presidential campaign; Johnson defeats Goldwater

1965: Johnson sends combat troops to Vietnam

1968: Martin Luther King Jr. and Robert F. Kennedy assassinated; Richard Nixon elected president

1969: United States lands man on the moon

1971: Twenty-sixth Amendment to the Constitution; wage and price controls

1972: Nixon visits China; Watergate break-in; Nixon reelected

1973: Nixon withdraws last of American troops from Vietnam; *Roe v. Wade* case decided

1974: Nixon resigns; Gerald Ford assumes the presidency

It might have appeared that Richard Nixon should have waltzed to victory in 1960. He had numerous advantages. As vice president, he was associated with eight years of peace and prosperity bestowed on the nation by Eisenhower. A former congressman with a record of being tough on communists, Nixon would be hard to attack on defense or national security issues. A well-read man and a solid, though hardly eloquent, speaker, Nixon had held his own in debates with the soviet premier Nikita Khruschev. Yet Nixon began the campaign as the underdog for several reasons.

First, Eisenhower was no traditional Republican and more of a moderate. In his eight years, he posed no threat to Roosevelt's legacy. Nixon, on the other hand, appeared to represent more of a break from the New Deal (although, in reality, his social and economic programs had far more in common with FDR than with a true conservative like Ronald Reagan).[2] Second, public affection for Ike was personal, but Nixon generated little fondness. He seemed to have had only one or two genuine friends in his entire adult life. Twenty years later, even those Nixon subordinates who had been caught up in the Watergate scandal—men who received jail sentences and had their careers destroyed—operated out of loyalty to the cause more than out of love for the man. Third, Nixon suffered from plain old bad timing. Whereas the congenial Eisenhower (who did a great deal quietly) had met Americans' desire for a caretaker, the nation, having caught its breath, now gathered itself for another step in the ascent to greatness—or so many believed. Any candidate who could give voice to those aspirations, anyone who could lay out a vision, whether he had any intentions of acting on the promises or not, would have the edge in such a climate.

Another factor worked against Nixon: television. Nixon was the first public figure to use a television appearance to swing an election his way with his famous 1952 "Checkers" speech, but the tube became his enemy. It automatically benefited the more handsome and photogenic candidate. Television news favored the man better suited to deliver a "sound bite" (although the term had not yet been coined). Neither case fit Nixon. For the first time in American history physical appearance played a large part in the selection of a president. Finally, Nixon had never viewed the press as his friends, and beginning with the 1960 election the media actively worked against him. Eisenhower would be the last Republican president to receive favorable, or even balanced and fair, treatment by the increasingly liberal national mainstream press.

An irony of the election was that Richard Nixon and Jack Kennedy were friends, far more so than Nixon and Ike, or Kennedy and his running mate, Lyndon Johnson. When JFK was in the hospital with back surgery, and close to death (it was thought), Nixon wept. Kennedy, for his part, told loyalists that if he did not get the Democratic nomination, he would be voting for Nixon in the November general election.[3] Friendship, however, did not stand in the way of winning.

As it turned out, Kennedy did not have to go against his party. He carried an incredibly close election, but it is questionable whether he won the popular vote. Typical reports had Kennedy winning by about 120,000 votes. Little known electoral quirks in Alabama and Georgia reduced Kennedy's popular totals. Unpledged Democratic votes for segregationist Democrat Henry F. Byrd and others, totaling 292,121, were lumped eventually with JFK's totals, giving him the final edge.[4]

Republican leaders, detecting fraud in two states, Texas and Illinois, urged Nixon to file a formal legal challenge and demand a recount. Earl Mazo, the national political correspondent for the New York *Herald Tribune*, examining the election returns in Texas, found that huge numbers of votes were dismissed on technicalities, whereas Kennedy had gained some 100,000 phantom ballots. Nixon lost the state by 46,000 votes, and then lost Illinois by less than 9,000 votes. Robert Finch, a Nixon confidant who later served as secretary of health, education, and welfare, said flatly that fraud had carried Texas and Illinois, and that Kennedy "needed Missouri, too, which was very close, but we didn't think he stole that."[5] In one district in Texas, where 86 people were registered to vote, Nixon got 24 votes. JFK got 148.

Nixon refused to protest any of these states, saying an electoral crisis had to be avoided. It would take a year to get a full recount of Illinois, and Nixon did not want to put the country through the ordeal. He not only accepted the electoral college verdict, but also contacted the *Herald Tribune* to insist that it abort a planned twelve-article series detailing the fraud. It was a remarkable and civic-minded position taken by a man later excoriated for abusing power, and stands in stark relief to the actions of Al Gore in the 2000 election. Nixon never fully realized that in the contest with his friend JFK he was pitted against one of the most ruthless candidates—and political families—in the twentieth century.

Kennedy and Crisis

John Kennedy's father, Joseph P. Kennedy, or "old Joe," as friends called him, had risen from poverty to great wealth primarily through booze running during Prohibition. Having accumulated a black-market fortune, Joe "went legit" during the market crash of 1929, buying when stock prices bottomed out and becoming a multimillionaire when stock values returned. By then he had already decided his oldest son, Joseph P. Kennedy Jr., would one day become president of the United States.

Roosevelt appointed Joseph senior ambassador to Great Britain (an odd choice, given that the Irish Kennedy hated the British), and John Fitzgerald, the second oldest son, studied in England. As war loomed, Joseph routinely blamed the British for failing to accommodate Hitler, as if the occupation of Czechoslovakia and the invasion of Poland occurred because Britain had not given Hitler enough concessions. John Kennedy supported his father, producing an undergraduate thesis on the arrival of war, called *Why England Slept*, an oddly pro-German treatment of the Munich Agreement, later made into a book by an affiliate of Joseph's and published as Kennedy's original work.[6]

During the war—at a time when all future political leaders were expected to do their military duty—Joseph junior went to fly patrol bombers in England. John had a safe position in naval intelligence in Washington. There he struck up a sexual relationship with a woman named Inga Arvad, who was suspected by the FBI of being a Nazi spy. Aware of the potential danger to Jack (as John F. was called), Joe Kennedy arranged a sudden transfer several thousand miles from "Inga Binga" (as the FBI referred to her) to the South Pacific, where he added to his own legend.

As commander of PT-109, Kennedy was engaged in an escort mission at night when a Japanese destroyer rammed through the ship. The young commander apparently had posted no lookouts and had only one of three engines in gear, making escape impossible. Surviving crew members drifted throughout the night, then made it to a nearby atoll, whereupon Kennedy again swam back into the adjacent waters to try to flag down a U.S. ship. Eventually a British coastal naval watcher facilitated the rescue. When search parties arrived, they had reporters with them—alerted by Joe Kennedy—and when the group finally reached safety, the British naval watcher was conveniently forgotten in place of the ambassador's heroic son. Jack certainly exemplified courage, endurance, and physical prowess in getting his crew to the island. A story on PT-109, turned into a *Reader's Digest* article that made JFK a war hero, led him to comment, "My story about the collision is getting better all the time."[7] Not long after, Joseph junior died in a risky flight, making John next in line for political office in the eyes of his father.

Upon his discharge, Jack entered politics, winning a House seat, then taking the 1952 Massachusetts Senate seat. JFK suffered from severe back problems, which required surgery that fused some of his vertebrae. While recuperating, he managed to write another book, *Profiles in Courage*. Or so went the story. In fact, most of the actual research and writing came from a veritable *Who's Who* of academics, including historians Arthur Schlesinger Jr. and Allan Nevins, government professor James Burns, and reliable speechwriter Ted Sorensen (who would later be JFK's press secretary). Despite writing only a tiny fraction of the manuscript, Kennedy acted as though it were fully his, accepting the 1957 Pulitzer Prize for biography for it.[8]

There is no question Kennedy inherited several foreign policy messes from his predecessor, chief among them the recent overthrow of Cuban dictator Fulgencio Batista by communist rebel Fidel Castro in 1959. Advisers to both Ike and JFK argued that the Maximum Leader, as Castro called himself, was merely an ardent nationalist and opportunist, much the way Ho Chi Minh of North Vietnam was later depicted. Castro encouraged such mischaracterizations, even though he claimed to have been a Marxist-Leninist when he started his guerrilla activities.[9] Unfortunately, Eisenhower had offered diplomatic recognition to Castro's government. Within a few months, the administration realized it had blundered and that a new Iron Curtain had dropped over Cuba, behind which stood a communist dictatorship easily as oppressive as any in Europe. Eisenhower also approved a CIA plan in March 1960 to organize an army of Cuban exiles, recruited mostly in Miami and based in Guatemala. At the same time, the CIA plotted Castro's assassination, a project at which the agency proved so inept that it recruited Mafia dons John Roselli, Santos Trafficante, and Sam Giancana to provide hit men to take out Castro. Although some of these more radical operations originated in the Eisenhower administration (unapproved by the president), Kennedy was fully briefed on all of them and through surrogates issued his complete consent. He supposedly told a reporter that he was "under terrific pressure" from his advisers to have Castro assassinated. His brother, Robert F. "Bobby" Kennedy was deeply involved in the intrigue: He knew about his brother's close ties to the mob through a sex partner named Judy Exner, whom Kennedy shared with Sam Giancana.[10]

The first flashpoint, however, involved not the assassination of Castro but an invasion by the exiles at the Bay of Pigs, which occurred three months after the inauguration. Again, JFK reviewed and approved the operation.[11] Castro had anticipated an invasion, having told Radio Havana that the State of the Union address had indicated "a new attack on Cuba by the United States."[12] Success for any invasion depended entirely on getting Castro out of the way first. As John Davis noted, the dictator's assassination was "the very lynchpin" of the plan—"an integral part," as Arthur Schlesinger had termed it.[13] Kennedy even met with the Cuban national hired by the Mafia to eliminate Castro, indicating he knew *exactly* whom to contact.[14]

On April 17, 1961, a small army of 1,400 Cuban exiles landed at the Bay of Pigs, where, they were assured, the U.S. fleet and CIA-operated warplanes would support the invasion. When things went badly, however, Kennedy suddenly withheld the promised support, dooming the invasion and sentencing the invaders to prison or death at Castro's hands. Anti-Castro elements never forgot that JFK had betrayed them. American public opinion "was outraged by the Bay of Pigs failure and would have supported direct intervention."[15] Chester Bowles, a senior member of the Kennedy administration, said that "at least 90 percent of the people" would have supported a decision to send troops into Cuba or otherwise overthrow Castro.[16] Soviet Premier Nikita Khrushchev viewed Kennedy's vacillation as weakness and decided to probe further.

Khrushchev began testing Kennedy in Berlin, where the western half of the divided city offered an escape from communism. West German Chancellor

Konrad Adenauer had encouraged the refugees coming across the borders, at a rate of a thousand a day by July 1961. To stanch this hemorrhage, the East Germans, with Soviet permission, erected the massive Berlin Wall separating the two sections of the city. It was left to America to act. A Polk or a Teddy Roosevelt would have destroyed the wall immediately. Kennedy called up reservists and began a small-scale mobilization, but otherwise did nothing about the wall itself, which became a physical symbol of the cold war. Its barbed wire, minefields, and tank traps—all facing inward—clearly illustrated that the chief task of communism was to keep people from leaving, not to keep invaders from entering.

Kennedy's weakness in Berlin convinced Khrushchev that the United States would not resist communist expansion elsewhere. At Castro's urging, the Soviet Union had begun to place intermediate range ballistic missiles (IRBMs) in Cuba. Subsequent letters have surfaced that reveal a wild, almost fanatical Castro hoping to goad the United States into a nuclear war. The IRBMs placed in Cuba posed a huge threat: these weapons had a fifteen-minute flight time to major United States cities, and their launch would provide only a few minutes for actual confirmation and warning, unlike Soviet land-based ICBMs that would have a thirty-minute flight time. Khrushchev lied about the missiles to Kennedy, claiming they were antiaircraft missiles. U-2 spy planes soon revealed the truth. A flight in mid-October 1962 provided photographic confirmation, not only of the IRBMs, but also of the surface-to-air (SAM) missiles protecting the nuclear missile sites.

Kennedy's cabinet divided almost evenly. Some wanted to strike immediately with a full air attack and even an invasion, whereas others advocated going to the United Nations and invoking sanctions. Robert Kennedy came up with a third alternative, a quarantine, or blockade, of Cuba to keep incomplete weapons from being finished. It provided time to allow the Russians to back down gracefully. Kennedy announced the quarantine on October twenty-second, with a deadline on October twenty-fourth, cabling Khrushchev to return to the "earlier situation" before the missiles. Negotiating through an ABC newsman, John Scali, the Kennedy administration and the Russians floated several mutual solutions. On October twenty-sixth, Khrushchev in a secret letter offered to withdraw the missiles in return for a pledge by the United States not to invade Cuba.[17] Shortly after the letter was tendered, the hard-liners inside the Kremlin demanded that Khrushchev gain deeper concessions, which he submitted in a second letter insisting on the removal of the U.S. missiles deployed in Turkey. Kennedy brilliantly pretended not to have received the second letter, then publicly acknowledged the first, offering the Soviet leader a way out, which he accepted.[18] Castro reportedly responded by flying into a rage. His communist sidekick, Che Guevara, watched as Castro swore, smashed a mirror, and kicked a hole in a wall.

Meanwhile, the Soviets had been embarrassed by allowing the Cuban dictator to egg them on, then were humiliated a second time when their postoperation intelligence showed that the U.S. Navy could have utterly destroyed the Soviet Atlantic fleet in a matter of minutes had hostilities broken out. From that point on, the USSR set a policy of building a world-class navy capable of blue-water operations under Admiral Sergei Gorshkov.

But reality matched neither the euphoria of Kennedy's "victory" nor the "embarrassment" of the USSR. The United States had now failed—twice—to evict communists from Cuba. Millions of Cubans voted with their feet and relocated to the United States. Most of them moved to Florida, where they thrived in a capitalist economy, whereas Cuba continued to languish in utter poverty. Castro, over the next thirty years, would prove the single most irritating communist leader on the planet, launching military operations in Nicaragua, El Salvador, and even Angola, destabilizing much of Central America and fomenting revolution in Africa. No other great power had permitted an enemy outpost to exist in such proximity when it had the military might to eliminate it. Nevertheless, JFK emerged with a public relations victory, heralded as the tough young president who had forced the Russians to back down. In fact, he was on the run on other fronts, such as space.

Where Can We Catch Them?

Eisenhower's concern over *Sputnik* had led to the massive, if ill-directed, flood of federal money into universities. Another blow to American prestige occurred in April 1961, when the USSR put the first human in orbit, sending Yuri Gagarin up some four weeks ahead of an American astronaut. Two days later Kennedy held a meeting in which he desperately questioned his advisers: "Is there any place where we can catch them [the Soviets]? What can we do? Can we go around the Moon before them? Can we put a man on the Moon before them?"[19] What Kennedy did not know was that between *Sputnik* and Gagarin's flight, at least three Soviet test pilots had died, having been fired into the outer atmosphere only to drop back down like flaming meteors. Another had burned up in a test chamber in 1961. Even with Gagarin's flight, the Soviet government was so unsure he would survive that it generated a news release for the cosmonaut's death in advance, to be read by the official TASS news agency if Gagarin did not return alive. The Soviet citizenry was, as usual, not informed of any of these events.[20]

In May 1961, after a frenzied study session with NASA administrators, Kennedy committed the United States to putting a man on the moon by the end of the decade, resulting in an expenditure of $5 billion per year on space until 1969. The Soviets had recognized the propaganda aspects of space, and they now hustled to add a wooden seat for a third cosmonaut to a two-man capsule in order to again beat the U.S. Apollo three-man spacecraft into orbit.[21] It was characteristic of Soviet mentality when it came to science and technology to ignore human safety or environmental concerns in favor of a public relations coup.

Kennedy hardly held a more idealistic position. Newly released tapes from the Kennedy library of a key 1962 discussion with NASA administrator James Webb revealed that Webb repeatedly resisted Kennedy's efforts to turn the U.S. space program into a narrowly focused lunar expedition. Another legend soon exploded—that of Kennedy's great vision in putting a man on the moon. JFK wanted a propaganda victory, pure and simple: "Everything we do [in space] ought to be tied into getting to the moon ahead of the Russians."[22] He then laid it on the table for the NASA administrator, saying that beating the Russians to the moon "is the top priority of the [space] agency and . . . except for defense, the top priority of the United States government. Otherwise, we shouldn't be spending this kind of money, because *I'm not that interested in space* [emphasis ours]."[23]

Once committed, however, the sheer technological prowess and economic might of the United States closed the gap. When Apollo 11 landed Neil Armstrong, Michael Collins, and Edwin Aldrin on the moon on July 20, 1969, the Russians knew they had met their match. More important, the Soviets had concluded that the advantages of space-based weaponry—especially given their relative technological backwardness compared to the West—were minimal and that military money could best be used in nuclear missiles and submarines. *Apollo 11* thus marked a victory of sorts in the cold war, with the Soviets slowly and quietly scaling down their space efforts.

In broader terms, the space program presented troubling confirmation of government centralization in America, having turned space into a public domain wherein private access was retarded through subsidization of orbital launches by taxpayer dollars.[24] National security concerns engendered layers of bureaucracy, bringing parts of NASA's supposedly civilian operations under the oversight of the Pentagon. Space launch was never debated on its own merits, and it was never placed against other policy options or even other uses of its massive resources. Kennedy's "vision" of putting a man on the moon reaped the headlines, whereas the practical utility of space access had yet to be attained despite extraordinary financial and social costs.

Having done what some considered impossible, NASA proceeded to flounder during the Nixon and Carter years as it struggled to achieve routine space launch through a questionable commitment to the expensive and generally inefficient space shuttle.[25] To contrast the promise and the reality of the space program, one has only to look at such films as Stanley Kubrick's fantasy, *2001: A Space Odyssey*, in which spacecraft docked with a wheel-shaped space station to the tune of the "Blue Danube Waltz" as it prepared for deep-space missions. In fact, by the end of 2001, the United States did not have anything resembling a fully operational space-based launch platform in orbit, although the Russian Mir space station had already worn out and was positioning itself to crash into an ocean. Worse, the United States had no routine way to get to a space station even in emergencies.[26]

Tax Cuts and Growth

Whether it involved the space or antipoverty efforts, already a mind-set had taken root in Washington that money, education, and research could solve any problem. This marked the final evolution of the Progressive-era embrace of education as the answer to all challenges, invoking an unquestioning trust of the New Deal assumptions that the federal government could overcome any obstacle. Well before

Kennedy took office, Ike's Department of Health, Education, and Welfare (HEW) had spent $46 million on research unrelated to health. Then that number exploded: by 1966, Johnson had kicked it up to $154 million; then, in a single year, the budget jumped to $313 million. Much of this "research" became circular: defending, reporting, or "explaining" what federal programs were doing by internal and anonymous literature circulated in obscure journals or by photocopy. For whoever read it, the results could not have been inspiring. One Oakland job-training program designed to raise wages by teaching new skills to the poor was at first a Kennedy showpiece. Years later, when the first internal studies became public, it was revealed that male trainees gained all of $150 to $500 per *year* in income—for a per capita expenditure of thousands.[27]

One reason government-oriented elites thought that they could solve problems with money was that the wealth existed, and the government's take had increased after the JFK tax cuts of 1961–62. West German Chancellor Ludwig Erhard had impressed the idea on Kennedy during his visit to Germany in 1961, instructing JFK to avoid the British model of high taxes, which had all but killed economic growth in England. Obviously frustrating liberals in his own party, Kennedy delivered a speech to the Economic Club of New York in which he rebuked the critics: "Our true choice is not between tax reduction . . . and the avoidance of large federal deficits. . . . It is increasingly clear that . . . an economy hampered by restrictive tax rates will never produce enough revenue to balance the budget—just as it will never produce enough jobs or enough profits."[28]

JFK favored tax cuts, but *not* to jump-start the economy, which was not in recession, but to generate wealth that would produce more tax revenues. Put simply, Kennedy realized that government could *grow* with tax cuts if there were no corresponding spending cuts. He therefore proposed a two-year across-the-board reduction from 91 percent to 70 percent on the top rates and from 20 percent to 14 percent on the bottom rates. He added depreciation incentives for new plant and equipment purchases, framed in Keynesian defenses. Yet it was pure Mellonism: giving those at the top a large cut so that they could invest, start new firms, and add production facilities, employing still others who themselves would pay taxes. Critics typically called it trickle-down economics, but it was common sense—and it worked. Over the next six years, personal savings rose from a 2 percent annual growth rate to 9 percent; business investment rose from an annual rate of 2 percent to 8 percent; GNP rose by 40 percent in two years; job growth doubled; and unemployment fell by one third.[29]

Federal revenues rose, and Walter Heller, a Keynesian economist who had tried to talk Kennedy out of the tax cut, admitted in testimony to the Joint Economic Committee in 1977 that the tax cut paid "for itself in increased revenues . . . [because] it did seem to have a tremendously stimulative effect."[30] But if Kennedy achieved his objective of spurring economic growth with lower tax rates, his other policies had tragically unintended consequences, most notably the increasingly dangerous situation in Southeast Asia.

Origins of the Vietnam Quagmire

Just as the space race had its roots in concerns over Soviet ability to strike the United States with atomic weapons, so too did the disaster in Southeast Asia known as the Vietnam War. As he does for Soviet space supremacy, Eisenhower bears much of the blame for failing to address the problems in Vietnam. He failed to lead decisively in the 1954 accords that ended the French presence in Vietnam (by which time America already was paying 80 percent of the French effort there).[31] The communist boss from the North, Ho Chi Minh, or "He Who Shines," had received extensive support from the U.S. wartime spy agency, the OSS (forerunner to the Central Intelligence Agency).[32] By 1954, most analysts agree, open and fair elections throughout the whole of Vietnam would have placed Ho in power—an unacceptable outcome to most cold war State Department officials. It is also true, however, that when the partition did take place, some nine hundred thousand residents of the North decided to escape the blessings of "enlightenment" offered by the new communist regime and headed south.

Eisenhower helped entrench the view that Vietnam's fall might topple other "dominoes" in the region. History proved Eisenhower partially correct in this regard: after South Vietnam fell, Cambodia and Laos soon followed. But then the dominoes stopped falling for a number of reasons, including the split between China and the Soviet Union that turned off the funding faucet to the North's regime.

Meanwhile, even with the scant attention the United States had paid to Vietnam under Eisenhower, the country made progress under its premier, Ngo Dinh Diem (a French-educated Catholic in a primarily Buddhist nation). Advances were so rapid that after a visit to the South in 1958, North Vietnamese commissar Le Doan returned with alarming news that conditions in the South were improving at such a pace that in the near future insufficient sentiment for a communist revolution would exist. Here was the communist bottom line: their cause was only advanced out of misery, and when average people improved their lot, communism came out a loser. To ensure that progress stopped, Viet Cong (VC) guerrillas assassinated government disease-control squads sent out to spray malarial swamps; they killed doctors traveling away from their hospitals en route to the villages; and killed progovernment village chiefs after hacking off the arms of their children, displaying all the impaled heads on stakes outside the village as a warning to others.

Eisenhower had utterly failed to equip and support the interior defense forces in the South. Kennedy, however, wanted to establish the image of a young "cold warrior." He promised in his inaugural address that the United States would "pay any price" and "bear any burden" in the cause of liberty. After failing to support the Bay of Pigs invasion, Kennedy could not afford another foreign policy flop. More than any other twentieth-century president before him, JFK paid attention to propaganda and world opinion. He increased the funding and authority of the

U.S. Information Agency, actively challenging foreign governments by market research and advertising.[33] His Peace Corps fought communism with shovels and spades instead of guns. Kennedy's appraisal of communism was not at issue.

Even after the Cuban missile crisis, questions remained about whether he (and America) had the patience to stay the course in a conflict involving international communism. The first threat in Southeast Asia had come in Laos, where again Eisenhower's failure to commit troops had sealed a country's fate. Kennedy had to negotiate, leading one of the communist leaders of North Vietnam to note approvingly that "the American government . . . has fallen entirely within the scope of Communist strategy in Laos."[34] That left Vietnam, and Kennedy made clear that he would not abandon this domino. When, after the disastrous decade-long Vietnam War resulted in public criticism and assignment of responsibility, Kennedy should have been at the top of the blame list. Why he was not is itself an interesting twist in American history.

Just as in later years writers and historians would ascribe to JFK a zeal to rectify economic and racial disparities that he had never displayed while alive, so too they would later seek to insulate him from criticism over his Vietnam policy. John Roche, special consultant to Lyndon Johnson and an adviser to Vice President Hubert H. Humphrey, recalled that the revival of Kennedy's Vietnam record began in 1965–66 by a group Roche labeled the Jackobites.[35] As Roche recalled, "Odd stories surfaced: 'Jack Kennedy had [whispered to speechwriter Kenny O'Donnell] that once he was re-elected in 1964 he'd get out of Vietnam.' . . . The point of all these tales was that Johnson had betrayed the Kennedy trust, had gone off on a crazy Texas-style military adventure. . . ."[36]

An "alternative history"—having JFK withdraw from Vietnam right after his reelection—has appeared, and some have argued that his strong stance prior to the election was a deception. Whether Kennedy planned to follow through on his "deception," or whether he ever intended to withdraw from Vietnam remains a matter of high controversy, with two recent books vigorously arguing that JFK would have withdrawn.[37] The evidence, however, paints a much different picture.

After JFK's election, American liberals running the war emphasized "winning the hearts and minds of the people" through material prosperity and general progress. But such progress depended on a climate of security, which Vietnam did not possess. The VC were not impressed, and without American or ARVN (Army of the Republic of Vietnam) troops actually present, full time, to protect villages, locals swung their allegiance to their only alternative for survival, the Viet Cong.

No president did more to ensure the quagmire of Vietnam than John Kennedy. Fully briefed by Eisenhower even before the election of 1960, JFK had been informed that the Joint Chiefs of Staff had already estimated that 40,000 American soldiers would be needed to combat the estimated 17,000 Viet Cong rebels. If the North Vietnamese got involved, the Joint Chiefs warned, it would take three times that many men. Kennedy was the first to order U.S. military troops into Vietnam—not merely CIA advisers—when he secretly dispatched 500 Green Berets (a new unit of highly trained counterinsurgency soldiers that Kennedy also had formed) into Southeast Asia. He also escalated the buildup of American forces faster than any other president, so that by 1963 almost 17,000 U.S. military forces were stationed in South Vietnam, augmented by American helicopters and countless naval units not included in the official commitment levels.[38] At his final press conference, Kennedy said, "For us to withdraw . . . would mean a collapse not only of South Vietnam but Southeast Asia. . . . So we are going to stay there."[39] All his principal military advisers favored not only remaining, but also increasing the U.S. commitment. Only the Kennedy image machine spun the notion that Vietnam "wasn't Jack's fault."

The commitment to Vietnam involved more than military forces. Kennedy and his advisers had come to the conclusion that they could not effectively control South Vietnamese Premier Diem, who had received sharp Western press criticism for persecuting Buddhists. Far from being the "Jefferson of Asia," Diem had engaged in a number of distasteful practices. The extent of Diem's anti-Buddhist policies remains in dispute, but little doubt exists that he oppressed Buddhist leaders. Kennedy worried less about the actual oppression and more about the public relations image. By 1963 he was looking for an opportunity to replace Diem with someone more tolerant and malleable, so the United States quietly began searching for South Vietnamese generals who would perform a coup.[40]

On November 2, 1963, with full support of the United States and using cash supplied by the CIA, South Vietnamese generals overthrew Diem. Coup ringleader Duong Van Minh, or "Big Minh" (no relation to Ho), described by anti-Diem American reporters as a "deceptively gentle man, . . . [who] when he spoke of the coup d'état that lifted him into office, . . . [had] a discernable tone of apology in his voice," nevertheless managed to make sure that Diem and his brother were shot and knifed several times en route to their exile, having given the pair assurances they would be allowed to live.[41] Despite the administration's support of the coup, Kennedy expressed shock that Diem had been assassinated, having fooled himself into thinking that America could topple a regime in a third-world country and expect the participants to behave as though they were in Harvard Yard. Meanwhile, the leader of the Viet Cong called Diem's assassination a "gift from Heaven for us."[42] It wasn't the only gift the United States would hand Ho.

Kennedy's secretary of defense and former Ford executive, Robert McNamara, arrived in Washington with a long record of mastering statistics for his own purposes. In World War II he and other whiz kids had put their talents to great use, calculating the most efficient use of bombing by doing target analysis. After the war, McNamara had used his facility with statistics to win almost every internal debate at Ford.[43]

Kennedy and McNamara rapidly moved to isolate and weaken the Joint Chiefs of Staff (JCS).[44] Often, the JCS did not receive reports critical of the war effort or even objective briefings because of direct intervention by the secretary of defense, the president, or the chairman of the Joint Chiefs. By the time of the Kennedy assassination, the military had to a great extent been cut out of all substantive planning for a war it was expected to fight and win. And JCS policy recommendations were in disarray because each service branch sought to take the lead in the Vietnam conflict, and often refused to support the recommendations of other branches. All of these issues, however, were largely obscured by the confused and tragic nature of the events in Dallas in November 1963, less than a month after Diem's assassination.

The Crime of the Century

No sooner had the blood dried on Diem's corpse than the American public was shocked by another assassination—that of its own president, on home soil, virtually on national television. By 1963, John Kennedy, having elicited the hatred of Fidel Castro, anti-Castro Americanized Cubans, the Mafia, and many right-wingers because of the Bay of Pigs fiasco and his fondness (in their view) for using the United Nations to solve problems, had any number of people who wished him dead. To say otherwise would be to ignore reality.

On November twenty-second, Kennedy had gone to Dallas to talk up his nuclear test ban treaty and also to firm up support with Texas Democrats with an eye toward reelection. The visit included a ten-mile motorcade through Dallas, an area termed by Kennedy "nut country." The Kennedys were greatly troubled by what they saw as the right wing. But the lunatic fringe of the right wing was only one group after JFK's scalp. Both sides of the Cuban imbroglio felt betrayed by him, as did the mob. He had already received death threats from Miami and other spots, and Kennedy did not take even the most minimal security precautions, riding in an open limo after ordering the protective bubble removed. Near the end of the route, Kennedy's car passed by the Texas Book Depository building, where a gunman, Lee Harvey Oswald, an odd individual, shot him twice. Although the limo immediately sped to Parkland Hospital just a few miles away, the president was pronounced dead within minutes of arrival.

Oswald was arrested just two hours after the shooting, precluding a long investigation that surely would have unearthed a number of facts the Kennedys wanted to remain secret. Indeed, Oswald's capture had come about after he was first charged with killing a Dallas police officer, J. D. Tippitt, who had detained him for questioning after news of the assassination had been broadcast. Later charged with killing Kennedy, Oswald was himself shot at point-blank range two days after his arrest by Dallas nightclub owner Jack Ruby as he was being transferred from one facility to another.

A number of things were suspicious about the Kennedy assassination. The police never conducted a thorough investigation—having caught Oswald so quickly—and the justice system never held a trial because Oswald had been killed. Worse, facts of Oswald's checkered past leaked out, providing grist for the mill of "researchers" with almost any political viewpoint. Oswald, for example, had become a Soviet citizen in 1959 and had handed out pro-Castro tracts in New Orleans. Yet he was also a former soldier who had grown dissatisfied with the USSR and left voluntarily. Other parts of Oswald's behavior threw suspicion on the entire assassination investigation. For example, he appeared to have been as much an anticommunist as a pro-Castroite; he served in the marines, where he was a marksman; and his brief stay in Russia led many to argue that he was in fact a CIA double agent.

The newly sworn-in President Lyndon Johnson knew that an inquiry had to quell fears among citizens that the Soviets or Cubans had assassinated the president, which led to the creation of the Warren Commission, headed by Chief Justice Earl Warren and including bipartisan officials from both houses of Congress and other parts of the government, including the former head of the CIA. But Johnson gave the Warren Commission two tasks, which might prove mutually exclusive. First, it had to determine who had actually killed Kennedy. Did Oswald act alone? Was there a conspiracy? Were other killers still at large? Second, the commission was charged with reassuring the American public. How could it do the latter if the answers to the former implicated the KGB, Castro, or other sinister elements beyond a "lone gunman"?

In addition, Johnson pressured the members to turn out a report quickly, a requirement that worked against a thorough investigation. Dozens of critical witnesses were never called to testify. The commission never addressed the discrepancies between the condition of Kennedy's body in Dallas and its condition in Bethesda, Maryland, at the official autopsy. It never called Jack Ruby to Washington to testify, although he had indicated that he would have much more to say there than in a Dallas jail. The commission's failure to investigate thoroughly opened the doors widely to a variety of conspiracy theorists. More than a few of them have turned up important evidence that the official story left something to be desired. Although several loose threads in the Warren Commission story remain, the essential evidence supports the conclusion that Oswald acted alone. The most challenged aspect of the evidence, the so-called magic bullet, was resolved by Gerald Posner, who used digitally enhanced versions of the film of the assassination made by Abraham Zapruder to show conclusively that there indeed had been a magic bullet that accounted for the multiple wounds.[45] "Conclusively" is a subjective term, however, in that dozens, if not hundreds, of "researchers" have created a cottage industry churning out the latest "evidence" that "proves" JFK was killed by a conspiracy of some type. No evidence will satisfy the dissenters, no matter what its nature.

Lyndon Johnson, Champion Logroller

Taking the oath of office while Air Force One remained on the tarmac at Love Field in Dallas, Lyndon Baines Johnson brought to the presidency vastly different strengths and weaknesses than had Kennedy. He never understood the Kennedy mystique.[46] Although he taught school briefly, for the better part of his life LBJ had been a politician and had never run any kind of for-profit enterprise. He was the third consecutive president to have entered the Oval Office without business experience, although Eisenhower's military service had come close in terms of organizational demands and resource allocation.[47] Like Kennedy, Johnson had fought in World War II, and he was the first congressman to enlist in the armed services, serving in the navy as a lieutenant commander. After the war, in 1949, he won a Senate seat. A tireless campaigner, Johnson knew when to get into the dirt, and he had his share of scandals in Texas. His most serious and potentially damaging relationship involved his onetime secretary Bobby Baker, who in 1963 was charged with influence peddling to obtain defense contracts for his own company. The connections to Johnson appeared pernicious enough that Kennedy sought to jettison the Texan before the reelection campaign of 1964, but he thought better of it when the electoral college map was laid before him. Kennedy needed Johnson to carry Texas and parts of the South. Democratic senators closed ranks around Johnson, JFK's media machine insulated him, and when Baker went to jail, the scandal did not touch Johnson.

As Senate majority leader, Johnson had no equal. His anticipation of potential pitfalls for legislation combined with his ability to jawbone friends and opponents alike made him the most effective politician in either house of Congress. His early election victories had come under a cloud of ballot-stuffing charges (he first won his Senate seat by only 87 votes), which did not seem to affect his ability to steer legislation through the process. Johnson liked to be around people—he and his wife, Lady Bird, entertained more than two hundred thousand dinner guests over a five-year period at the White House—and when LBJ had his choice, he preferred to be around women.[48]

Johnson had as many sexual escapades as Kennedy, including a long-running affair with Madeline Brown of Dallas. Like Bill Clinton twenty years later, LBJ would have sex in the Oval Office, and like Hillary Clinton, Lady Bird Johnson excused Lyndon's behavior by pointing out that he "loved people" and "half the people in the world are women."[49] Johnson's close ties to FBI director J. Edgar Hoover helped keep his liaisons secret: he had made a calculated choice to retain Hoover as director with the memorable phrase, "Better to have him inside the tent pissing out, than outside pissing in."

Having emerged from poverty and having seen firsthand as a teacher its impact on human life, Johnson used his legislative skills to mount the largest federal programs in history aimed at eliminating poverty. He enjoyed using government to help others, and America's affluence made it possible to do so. Announcing his proposals in a May 1964 speech at the University of Michigan, he promised to lead America "upward to the Great Society."

The campaign of 1964 was, for Johnson, merely a speed bump on the highway to that Great Society. The Texan dispatched his conservative Republican challenger, Barry Goldwater, with a mix of often irresponsible scare tactics and equally irresponsible promises of government largesse. Goldwater, the most ideologically "pure" candidate since William Jennings Bryan, ran as an unabashed conservative. He championed smaller government, states' rights (which, unfortunately, put him squarely on the wrong side of the Civil Rights Act of 1964), and a stronger front against communism than Johnson. His book, *Conscience of a Conservative* (1960), provided a list of Goldwater's policy positions, including abolition of the income tax and privatization of the Social Security system.[50] These were hardly radical positions, and even after the New Deal, a large segment of the public still thought "big government" programs to be a foreign concept. Known for his supposedly inflammatory comment (penned by Karl Hess and borrowed from Roman senator Cicero) that "extremism in the defense of liberty is no vice," Goldwater provided fodder for outlandish liberal cartoonists, who depicted him throwing nuclear bombs.

Goldwater, although a nonpracticing Episcopalian, had one set of Jewish grandparents, making him (and not Joe Lieberman in 2000) the first American of Jewish ancestry to run for either of the highest two offices in the land. His anticommunist and free-market credentials were impeccable. A World War II veteran and general officer in the air force reserve, he viewed combat in Vietnam as a clear-cut prospect: if the United States committed troops to Vietnam, it should do so intending to win and using any force necessary, including nuclear weapons. Johnson's crew demonized Goldwater, running what are widely acknowledged as some of the dirtiest ads in political history, one showing a little girl picking flowers just before an atomic blast goes off, convincing many Americans that Goldwater was a Dr. Strangelove.

Meanwhile, Johnson, who had never been considered a part of the Kennedy team, nevertheless walked under the bloom of Camelot. He smashed the Arizonan, winning by more than 430 electoral votes and garnering 16 million more popular votes. For Republicans, whose national political apparatus appeared in complete disarray, there were two silver linings to this storm. An important conservative youth movement, the Young Americans for Freedom (YAF), sprang up. This organization produced the young turks who would come into the Senate and House in the 1980s Reagan revolution. Another major benefit from that election for the conservatives was that a former Democrat, actor Ronald Reagan, made an impressive speech on behalf of Goldwater, alerting party brass to a new GOP star.

No one could deny the extent of Johnson's victory, though. Armed with his impressive electoral mandate, Johnson unleashed a flood of new federal spending. Sensing the wave of public sympathy and the unwillingness to oppose anything that Kennedy would have wanted, he moved quickly to push through Congress construction legislation, education bills, expansion of urban mass transit, and many other pork-barrel measures in addition to the needed and important

Civil Rights Act of 1964. All of this legislation sailed through, usually with Republicans providing the key margins. The Civil Rights Act in particular needed Republican support to get around Southern Democrats who vowed to filibuster the act to death.

Race, Rights, and the War on Poverty

Kennedy had scarcely addressed racial issues in his campaign or his two years in office. By 1963, however, a number of elements had coalesced to push civil rights onto the front pages of every newspaper. In February 1960, four black freshmen from North Carolina Agricultural and Technical College sat down at Woolworth's lunch counter in Greensboro and demanded service.[51] Segregation laws of the day meant that they had staged a supreme act of rebellion, and although the management refused to serve them, their numbers grew as other students and citizens joined them. After five days the owners shut down the store, unsure how to proceed. This began the sit-in movement. Blacks insisted on access to public places and the same market rights that whites enjoyed, and to accomplish this they staged sit-ins to disrupt normal business. If black people could not eat and drink at a lunch counter, no one could.[52] Students formed a new group, the Student Nonviolent Coordinating Committee (SNCC), to work with the Southern Christian Leadership Conference (SCLC).

Almost instantly other sit-ins occurred across the South, with some white supporters joining blacks. They received an intimidating reception. Some were arrested for trespassing, others beaten by mobs, . . . but sometimes they were served. Within a year of the Greensboro sit-in, more than 3,500 protesters had been jailed. Steadily, demonstrations against Jim Crow laws mounted, and other types of protests joined the sit-in. In 1961, to challenge segregated interstate bus terminals, the Congress of Racial Equality (CORE) instituted "freedom rides" carrying black and white passengers. Birmingham's city leadership was brought to heel in part by the losses to business caused by segregation.[53] A similar development was documented when Averett College, a small Baptist segregated school in Virginia, opened its doors to blacks not under government edict but under financial pressure.[54] This indicated that, given enough time, the market could produce change. Market processes, however, often work slowly.

Robert Kennedy, the attorney general, instead of acting in support of federal laws, called for a cooling-off period, until an incident at the University of Mississippi again placed a president in the position of having to enforce federal laws against the will of a state.[55] In 1962, James Meredith, the first black student to enroll at the university, was blocked by the efforts of Governor Ross Barnett, who defied federal marshals who had arrived to enforce desegregation laws. Robert Kennedy then sent troops in to preserve order. Meredith was admitted, and by then JFK had proposed civil rights legislation to Congress, but the issues had been ignored too long, and the laws had come too late to defray black impatience with second-class status.

White racists' reaction to black demands for rights rapidly spun out of control. In June 1962, Medgar Evers, an official of the Mississippi NAACP, was assassinated. Martin Luther King Jr. continued to instruct demonstrators to abstain from violence. King's strategy was to bring the attention of the white nonracist and nonsegregationist majority to bear upon the minority racists and to use righteous indignation as the weapon. This approach required a sharp awareness of the power of the media, which King had. King also appreciated that the power of the pen had been surpassed by the emotional, virtually real-time appeal offered by the television camera. To tap into America's sense of justice and morality, King perceived that black people not only had to force their adversaries into public acts of brutality, but also had to do so under the eyes of the omnipresent television cameras. He possessed this essential insight: that the power of mass demonstrations would not just sway policy makers from the sites of the demonstrations, but also public opinion across the country. This insight, of course, relied on the fact that the majority of the population was moral and just and that change was possible in a democracy.

The clearest test of King's strategy came on August 3, 1963, when King's nonviolent campaign climaxed in a march on Washington, D.C., of two hundred thousand blacks and whites. There, in front of the Lincoln Memorial, King delivered his immortal "I Have a Dream" speech. Telling the massive crowd that "we have come here today to dramatize an appalling condition. In a sense we have come . . . to cash a check," he cited the "magnificent words of the Constitution and the Declaration of Independence," a "promissory note to which every American was to fall heir."[56] King concluded his speech with words almost as famous as those of the Declaration to which he had referred, saying:

> I have a dream that one day on the red hills of Georgia the sons of former slaves and the sons of former slave owners will be able to sit together at the table of brotherhood. I have a dream that one day, even the state of Mississippi, a state sweltering with the heat of injustice . . . will be transformed into an oasis of freedom. . . . I have a dream that one day, down in Alabama, with its vicious racists . . . little black boys and little black girls will be able to join hands with little white boys and white girls as sisters and brothers. I have a dream today![57]

The moment became etched in the American memory as the multitude cheered and sang "We Shall Overcome," but unfortunately, the violence had just begun. Several weeks later a bomb detonated in a black Birmingham Baptist church and killed four children. Civil rights demonstrators were greeted by fire hoses, police dogs, and, when attackers thought they were anonymous, deadly force.

During a series of protests in Birmingham, Alabama, during May 1963, the police commissioner, Eugene "Bull" Connor, ordered his men to use dogs, tear gas, electric cattle prods, and clubs on nonviolent demonstrators—all under the lights of the television cameras. King was jailed by Connor, whereupon he wrote "Letter from Birmingham Jail," a defense of nonviolence rooted in Judeo-Christian and Enlightenment thought and Revolutionary principles, and quoting both Jefferson and Lincoln. "We will reach the goal of America in freedom," King wrote, "because the sacred heritage of our nation and the eternal will of God are embodied in our echoing demands."[58] Yet if King changed America, Connor changed King, who now decided that melting the hearts of Southerners might cost too many lives. After Birmingham, King shifted his strategy to persuading non-Southern Americans, outraged at what they had seen, to force the federal government into action.

The civil rights movement's legitimate goals did not protect it from infiltration by communist elements, which sought to radicalize it. That, in turn, only confirmed in the minds of some, such as FBI Director J. Edgar Hoover, that the communists were behind the protests.[59] They had almost nothing to do with the civil rights leadership, but that did not prevent Hoover from calling King "the most dangerous Negro . . . in this nation."[60] Although King's marital infidelities convinced Hoover that he needed watching, the murders of black leaders and bombing of black churches apparently did not warrant the resources of Hoover's FBI.[61]

There were, in fact, some "dangerous Negroes" in the land, most of them King's black opponents who thought his program too pacific and servile. One faction, the rapidly growing Black Muslim movement of Elijah Muhammad, saw King as a tool of "the white man." Muhammad, departing from traditional Islam, claimed to be the true Messiah. Muhammad hated America and embraced her enemies, and with a new acolyte, Malcolm X, he recruited thousands of members.[62] Advocating violence and black separatism, Muhammad and Malcolm ridiculed King and the civil rights movement, comparing the march on Washington to getting "coffee that's too black which means it's too strong. . . . You integrate it with cream, you make it weak."[63] Hoover's ever-vigilant FBI also kept constant files and wiretaps on Muhammad and Malcolm, but in this case there indeed was a threat to the public order afoot. After Malcolm X was assassinated in 1965, apparently at Muhammad's instructions, the movement (now prominently featuring a newcomer named Louis Farrakhan) turned increasingly violent and anti-Semitic. Between 1960 and 1970, Muhammad's power and health waned, but the rhetoric grew more aggressive, especially against the Jews, whom the Muslims blamed for every malady.

Faced with King's nonviolent movement on the one hand and the more radical racist initiatives on the other, on July 3, 1964, Congress passed the Civil Rights Act.[64] The gist of the act was unmistakable in that no one could ever again legally deny black citizens access to the institutions of the United States without being liable to criminal and civil prosecution. Segregation in public accommodations, such as restaurants, hotels, theaters, and transportation, was prohibited. Also outlawed was discrimination based on race in employment, and to enforce this section, the Equal Employment Opportunity Commission (EEOC) was formed. Passage of these laws coincided with another King-led movement to register black voters in Southern states, which culminated in a march from Selma to Montgomery to demand the right to vote. At the bridge over the Alabama River, state troopers mounted on horses intercepted the marchers and plunged into them with clubs, as television cameras followed the action. Within a year, Congress had passed the Voting Rights Act, with a higher percentage of Republicans than Democrats voting for the bill. Among those voting against it were prominent Democratic senators Albert Gore Sr. of Tennessee and a former member of the Klan, Robert Byrd of West Virginia. These two civil rights laws in fact only ensured enforcement of the Fourteenth and Fifteenth Amendments of a century earlier, and they worked: within a year black voter registration had leaped by 28 percent, and black majorities in many districts soon began to send representatives to Congress.[65]

Yet less than two weeks after the first of the civil rights acts had passed, the first large-scale race riots occurred, in Harlem. Further rioting followed in Rochester, Paterson, Philadelphia, and Chicago, with one of the worst episodes of violence occurring in August 1965 in Watts, California. There, following a police arrest (area black leaders had long complained that the Los Angeles Police Department was exceptionally racist and violent), the neighborhood broke up into a wave of burning, looting, and destruction, requiring National Guard troops and martial law to end the violence. Black activists, such as Stokely Carmichael and H. Rap Brown, blamed whites, and urged blacks to join the new Black Panther organization, whose unofficial motto was "Kill whitey."

White liberals responded to the wave of looting by producing reports. A National Advisory Commission on Civil Disorders in 1968 flatly misrepresented the problem, claiming that the riots were directed at "white-owned businesses characterized in the Negro community as unfair."[66] Then, as in later riots, *all* businesses were targets, and since the majority were black-owned, the damage was overwhelmingly detrimental to blacks. Legitimate protest, guided and directed, reminded its participants that they were in for the long term and that change would take time, no matter what the cause. The inner-city riots, on the other hand, lacked any organization or direction, appealing to the impulse to get back at someone or get quick restitution through theft. Typically, liberal historians claimed the problem was not enough cash—"programs like Model Cities had never been given enough money to work."[67] In fact, welfare and other assistance between 1965 and 1970 represented the largest voluntary transfer of wealth in human history, with no appreciable effect—indeed, with horrible consequences. Radical black leaders, such as Malcolm X, predictably blamed "white oppression" and "white middlemen" for the conditions of the local economy, but after the riots the local consumers did not "evince any great interest in promoting black capitalism or in 'buying black.' "[68]

Violence placed black leaders like King in a precarious position: having to fend off the radicals while turning up the heat on Washington. (King was booed when he appeared in Watts after the riots.)[69] Separatists led by Stokely

Carmichael demanded "Black Power!" and urged blacks to start their own businesses, schools, and militias. The Black Panthers protested a May 1967 gun-control law understanding that if only the police had guns, blacks would be helpless—and they organized community patrols to protect people from muggers as well as from mistreatment by police. Panther leaders fell far short of King, however, when it came to having either character or courage: Huey Newton went to prison for killing a police officer; Eldridge Cleaver left the country; and evidence surfaced revealing that other Panthers had executed their own members suspected of being informants. King might have been able to step into the chasm separating the radicals and the moderates if he had lived. But an assassin took King out of the picture in Memphis on April 4, 1968, where he had delivered his own eulogy: "I've been on the mountaintop."[70] A new storm of rioting ensued, including unrest in Washington, D.C. Predictably, the Johnson administration reacted by creating one of the largest bureaucracies since the New Deal and producing the first truly dependent class in American history.

Origins of Welfare Dependency

Lost in the violence, rioting, and assassinations was the simple fact that the Civil Rights Act had, in terms of the law, ended the last legal remnants of slavery and reconstruction. Yet Johnson immediately proposed a "legislative blitzkreig" that, in the process of the next two decades, would reenslave many poor and minorities into a web of government dependency.[71] Relying on questionable statistics from best sellers, such as Michael Harrington's *The Other America*, which maintained that millions of Americans languished in poverty, Johnson simplistically treated poverty as an enemy to be defeated. In his 1964 State of the Union message, he announced, "This administration today . . . declares unconditional war on poverty," and he declared that only "total victory" would suffice.[72] The United States, already a "rich society," Johnson observed, had the opportunity to move "upward to the Great Society."[73]

Johnson constructed a massive framework of new federal programs under the supervision of the Office of Economic Opportunity and the Department of Health, Education, and Welfare. Many of the programs seemed innocuous: the Job Corps presumably taught high school dropouts job skills; VISTA (Volunteers in Service to America) was little more than a domestic Peace Corps for impoverished areas; Head Start sought to prepare low-income children for schools by offering meals and other programs.

Without doubt, the most destructive of all the Great Society policies, however, involved a change in a New Deal program called Aid to Families with Dependent Children (AFDC). The original AFDC had been tightly restricted to widows, with the intention of giving taxpayer subsidies to once-married women who had lost the chief breadwinner in the family. In the 1960s, however, Johnson and Congress quietly changed AFDC qualifications to include any household where there was no male family head present, a shift that now made virtually any divorced or single mother of low income eligible for taxpayer money. The incentives of the program made it financially more lucrative *not* to be married than to be married. The message from Uncle Sam was, "If you are now married and poor, think about a divorce. If you're not married now, don't even think about getting married."

Seen in the numbers, the changes from the previous decade were shocking. In 1950, 88 percent of white families and 78 percent of black families consisted of a husband and wife in a traditional marriage.[74] These numbers had not changed since the Great Depression, but something happened after Great Society legislation: white percentages remained unchanged, but black families began to break up, beginning in 1967; then the percentage of intact black families began a steep slide. Within twelve years, the proportion was down to 59 percent, compared to about 85 percent of whites. During this fifteen- to twenty-year period, the percentage of black poor who lived in a single-female household shot up from under 30 percent to nearly 70 percent. White poor in single-female-household families increased by about half, but black poor in single-female households rose more than 200 percent, a fact that demonstrated the horrible incentives inserted into the war on poverty. Put another way, the war on poverty managed to destroy black marriages and family formation at a faster rate than the most brutal slaveholder had ever dreamed![75]

Only a government bureaucrat could fail to see the simple logic of what had occurred. A couple living together, but not married, with the male employed, stood to make slightly more than twice as much than if they were married. Since the courts had ruled that the presence of a man in the house could not be used as a reason to deny a woman "benefits" (a term we shall qualify for now, given the long-term harms done by these programs), then it *seemed* to make economic sense for a man and a woman to refrain from marriage and, instead, live together and combine their incomes. Social changes accounted for most of the fact that divorces rose 30 percent from 1950 to 1970, then went off the charts, nearly doubling again by 1975, but one cannot discount the economic incentives against marriage.[76]

This was nothing less than a prescription for the utter destruction of traditional black families, and had it been proposed by the Imperial Wizard of the KKK eighty years earlier, such a program would have met with a quick and well-deserved fate. But embraced by liberal intellectuals and politicians, the war on poverty and AFDC, especially after the man-in-the-house rule was struck down in 1968, was the policy equivalent of smallpox on inner-city black families in the 1970s. The AFDC caseload rose 125 percent in just five years, from 1965 to 1970, then another 29 percent during the following five years, producing a wave of illegitimate children.

Why were blacks disproportionately affected by the Great Society policies? Minority communities—especially black—were disproportionately concentrated in urban areas, especially inner cities.[77] Thus, federal welfare workers could much more easily identify needy blacks and enroll them in welfare programs than they could find, or enlist, rural whites in similar circumstances. It wasn't that there weren't poor whites, but rather that the whites were more diffused and thus difficult to reach. Policies designed for all poor overwhelmingly affected, or, more appropriately, infected, the black community.

Having unleashed a whirlwind of marriage destruction and illegitimacy, AFDC produced two other destructive side effects. First, because the single highest correlating factor in wealth accumulation is marriage, AFDC inadvertently attacked the most important institution that could assist people in getting out of poverty. A debate still rages about how this dynamic works, but there appear to be important social, sexual, and psychological reasons why men need to play a key role in the economic life of a family. But there is little reason to debate the data showing that married couples are more than the sum of their parts: they generate more wealth (if not income) than single people living together and obviously more than a single parent trying to raise a family.[78] Divorced families have less than half the median income of intact families, and even more to the point, have less than half the income of stepfamilies.[79]

A second malignant result of AFDC's no-father policy was that it left inner-city black boys with no male role models.[80] After a few years at places like Cabrini Green, one of "the projects"—massive public housing facilities for low-income renters that had degenerated into pits of drugs and crime—a young man could literally look in any direction and not see an intact black family.[81] Stepping up as role models, the gang leaders from Portland to Syracuse, from Kansas City to Palmdale, inducted thousands of impressionable young males into drug running, gun battles, and often death.[82] No amount of jobs programs would fill the void produced by the Great Society's perverted incentives that presumed as unnecessary the role of the father.[83]

Nor did the war on poverty have even the slightest long-run impact on reducing the number of poor. Indeed, prior to 1965, when Johnson had declared war on want, poverty rates nationally had consistently fallen, and sharply dropped after JFK's tax cut took effect in 1963. After the Great Society programs were fully in place—1968 to 1969—progress against poverty ground to a halt, and the number of poor started to grow again. No matter which standards are used, one thing seems clear: by the mid-1970s, the Great Society antipoverty programs had not had any measurable impact on the percentage of poor in America as compared to the trends before the programs were enacted. It would not be the last "war" the Johnson administration would lose.

"We're Not Going North and Drop Bombs"

Lyndon Johnson inherited not only the slain president's dangerous policy programs but also his poor cabinet choices and advisers. On the one hand, LBJ did not want to see Vietnam detract in any way from his ambitious social programs. On the other hand, he knew he had a conflict to manage (he carefully avoided the reality of the phrase "a war to fight"), and at the urging of his (really Kennedy's) advisers, he tried to deal with Vietnam quietly. This led to the most disastrous of wartime strategies.

Johnson first had to grapple with the unpleasant fact that he had inherited JFK's cabinet, the "best and the brightest," as David Halberstam would cynically call them. Both the circumstances of Kennedy's death and the general low esteem in which many of the Kennedy inner circle held of LBJ personally made his task of eliciting loyalty from the staff all the more difficult. He appeared to get on well with Kennedy's secretary of defense McNamara, whose facility—some would say alchemy—with numbers seemed to put him in a fog when it came to seeing the big picture. For such a man, throwing himself fully into the destruction of a communist system in North Vietnam would be difficult, if not impossible. McNamara's mind-set—that numbers alone determine the outcome of undertakings, from making cars to conquering enemies—helps explain why neither he nor most of Johnson's other advisers ever made a clear case to the American public as to why the United States needed to resist the expansionist North. They did not see much of a difference between the communists and the government in the South. Villagers' heads impaled on stakes, courtesy of the Viet Cong, simply did not register with the bean counters.

When it came to actual military strategy in Vietnam, McNamara was equally obtuse. He said of the military situation early in the war, "The greatest contribution Vietnam is making . . . is that it is developing an ability in the United States to fight a limited war, to go to war without necessity of arousing the public ire."[84] This admission was nothing short of astonishing. By conceding that the administration did not even want the public to view the North Vietnamese and Viet Cong—who were killing American sons—as the enemy, McNamara ceded the entire propaganda campaign to the communists and their allies. For the first time in American history, the government expressed no spirited animosity toward its enemy, provided U.S. citizens with no examples of North Vietnamese or Viet Cong atrocities (even though plenty existed), and refrained from speaking ill of Ho Chi Minh (let alone demonizing him). It was 180 degrees from the yellow-press positions a half century earlier. At no time did the administration launch even the most basic education campaign to explain the communists' objectives to the American people. Nor did any administration prior to Nixon even remotely suggest that the warlords in the North, particularly Ho Chi Minh, should personally face retaliation in response to their policies in the way Tojo, Mussolini, and Hitler had been singled out as individuals for their actions. Quite the contrary, Johnson deliberately avoided any air strikes that could conceivably have injured or killed Ho. Years later, in 1995, Colonel Bui Tin of the North Vietnamese Army was asked if the United States could have done anything to prevent a communist victory. He answered, "Cut the Ho Chi Minh Trail. If Johnson had granted General Westmoreland's request to enter Laos and block the Ho Chi Minh Trail, Hanoi could not have won the war."[85] The entire approach to the war literally stood the principles of victory on their head.[86]

Moreover, by 1966, if the question of complete victory was in doubt, then it was right to again ask if Vietnam was the line in the sand for resisting communism wholeheartedly. A poorly conceived and inadequately undertaken military action only compounded the larger point: why Vietnam? As the war dragged on, the only answer increasingly seemed to be, "Because we are there." In retrospect, a stronger response to either Berlin or Cuba may have proven more effective at stopping communism. When Ronald Reagan later referred to the "great lesson" the United States had learned in Vietnam, that "we sent men to fight a war the government wouldn't let them win," he reiterated the central fact that military action must be both purposeful and pragmatic. If Vietnam was ever the former—a point that still remains in doubt—it was never the latter.

In part, this end product stemmed from both Kennedy's and Johnson's reluctance to pursue the war in the first place. In part, it reflected the failure to grasp the fact that this was not, as critics later claimed, a civil war but a thoroughgoing invasion of the South by the North. General Vo Bam of the North Vietnamese Army let slip that in 1959 he had been instructed to lead the "liberation" of the South. But the failures also illustrated the radical left's complete dominance of the dialogue involving the war. Those sent to fight had virtually no voice at home: "A few photographs of Vietnamese villagers who had been disemboweled or had their heads impaled on posts [by the communists] would have destroyed all the leftist arguments and demonstrations from the beginning."[87]

Johnson, rejecting the advice of the Joint Chiefs of Staff (JCS) not to engage in a limited bombing of the North, or to use any sort of gradual escalation, chose to do just that. Like Kennedy, he hoped at first to get by with mere U.S. "support" of the ARVN. In July 1964, Johnson had boosted U.S. strength there to 21,000 men, up 30 percent from Kennedy's levels; then, in August, an incident occurred that sealed the involvement of the United States in Vietnam. On August second, the U.S. destroyer *Maddox*, operating in the Gulf of Tonkin off North Vietnam, reported that it was under attack from North Vietnamese PT boats. Questions later arose as to whether the *Maddox* had been attacked at all. Two days later a second attack supposedly occurred on the *Maddox* and a second destroyer, the *Turner Joy*, and this time the ships called for air support. Commander James Stockdale, one of the first aviators on the scene, performed a thorough reconnaissance and concluded in his official report that there were no North Vietnamese vessels in the area, and that the *Maddox* and *Turner Joy* had probably fired on each other in the haze.[88]

With only a cursory amount of information—and certainly no clear proof of attacks against the United States—Johnson went on television to announce that he had ordered air responses to the attacks. At the same time, he sent a resolution to Congress, which he wanted adopted retroactively, that was the "functional equivalent" of a formal declaration of war.[89] The August seventh Gulf of Tonkin Resolution said, "Congress approves and supports the determination of the President . . . to take all necessary measures to repel any armed attack against the forces of the United States and to prevent further aggression."[90] Johnson received all the support he needed. Only two senator (both Democrats) voted against the measure. Voting in favor were soon-to-be antiwar activists George McGovern, Eugene McCarthy of Minnesota, and William Fulbright of Arkansas (all Democrats).

Bobby Kennedy, still LBJ's attorney general, but future senator from New York, supported the 1964 war wholeheartedly.

Johnson, although vastly underestimating the undertaking to which he had committed the nation, did not lack an awareness of the implications of fighting a war on the Asian mainland, saying, "We're not going north and drop bombs at this stage. . . . I want to think about the consequences of getting American boys into a war with 700 million Chinese."[91] But the Viet Cong would not cooperate in letting the United States play a peripheral role. On Christmas Eve, 1964, Viet Cong bombed a Saigon hotel that quartered American junior officers, killing 2 and wounding 38. Then, on February 7, 1965, a mortar attack on the American air base at Pleiku resulted in more casualties. Hundreds of aircraft moved in, but Johnson refused to order a bombing campaign. The Viet Cong had already achieved a victory of sorts. More soldiers were needed to keep the aircraft safe; and as the security area around the bases was expanded, the ground troops needed more air power to keep them safe. It was a nonstrategy, a quicksand, with no hope of producing a victorious outcome.

Finally, in March 1965, more attacks led Johnson to approve a bombing campaign known as Rolling Thunder, and as the name implies, Johnson did not intend for this to be a knockout blow or an overwhelming use of power to intimidate the enemy into surrender, but an incremental gradualist strategy.[92] He denied outright the military's request to strike oil-storage facilities.[93] Quite the contrary, McNamara and Johnson picked the targets themselves, placing sharp restrictions on what was fair game, claiming the purpose of the operation was to present a "credible threat of *future* destruction [emphasis ours]."[94] In essence, McNamara had staged a giant demonstration, with live antiaircraft fire directed at U.S. airmen. It was immoral and wasteful, and it was guaranteed to produce a more determined enemy while at the same time doing nothing to limit the North's ability to fight. North Vietnam responded by erecting 31 acquisition radars, adding 70 MiG fighters, and installing deadly SA-2 surface-to-air missiles (SAMs). By 1967, Hanoi possessed some 7,000 to 10,000 antiaircraft guns and 200 SAM sites, and could claim credit for downing 80 U.S. aircraft.[95] Even then, American aircraft fighting over the North were instructed that they were "not, repeat, not authorized to attack North Vietnamese air bases from which attacking aircraft may be operating."[96] Nor did Johnson and McNamara permit American pilots to eliminate the SAM sites: "The rules of engagement throughout Rolling Thunder stipulated that American aircraft could only attack SAM sites that were *actually firing at them* [emphasis added]."[97] Limited war of this sort had been addressed by no less an expert than William Tecumseh Sherman a hundred years earlier: "War is cruelty," he said, "and you cannot refine it."

Meanwhile, on the ground, the United States had grown disenchanted with ARVN operations. By late 1965, U.S. troop numbers (including all personnel— naval, air, and other) had reached 200,000, a number well below what the JCS had categorically stated more than a year earlier would be needed to win. Based on the balance of forces alone, the war should have ended long before 1965. One of the problems involved the complete lack of strategy. General William West-moreland, named the new army commander in Vietnam in March 1965, was impatient with the South Vietnamese operations against the Viet Cong and had introduced search-and-destroy missions by American forces. Whereas U.S. artillery, air, and armor (to the extent it could be used) had previously supported the ARVNs, the new strategy called on the ARVN units to guard cities and strongholds—exactly what the South Vietnamese warlords wanted in order to preserve their troops from combat. Worse, it placed American troops in a position to absorb the bulk of the casualties.

Aimed at finding the communists in the countryside, eliminating them and their supply bases, and gradually expanding the safe area of operations, the search-and-destroy missions, as with all McNamara ideas, depended heavily on numbers and tallying, specifically of body counts. How many Viet Cong did an operation kill? The calculation turned into a giant con game. Forces in the field well knew that the VC tended to drag bodies off so as *not* to let their enemy know the casualty numbers, and that tactic, consequently, led to estimates. Before long the estimates were wildly inflated, and, grotesquely, the policy rewarded the production of any body, whether a genuine VC or not. Loyal or neutral Vietnamese caught in firefights were added to the body-count totals.

The policy had no grounding in common sense whatsoever: no democracy would willingly fight a long war of attrition. It goes against the grain of democratic republics to measure success purely in numbers killed, especially when the enemy, in this case, made clear that it welcomed such a tradeoff in human carnage. Ho Chi Minh had explained this exchange flatly to the French in the 1940s, saying, "You can kill ten of my men for every one I kill of yours, but even at those odds, you will lose and I will win."[98] Ho's statement reflected an awareness that the communists had no qualms about sacrificing one third to one half of their population to gain a strategic victory. Human life had little meaning to those running the war in Hanoi.

McNamara took his technical solutions to an absurd level when he proposed building a giant electrified reinforced fence across the North-South border to stop the flow of supplies. Quick fixes—technology substituted for a sound war-fighting doctrine—was what Clark Clifford, McNamara's replacement as secretary of defense, found when he arrived on the job in 1968. "It was startling," Clifford said, "to find out we have no military plan to end the war."[99] By that time, U.S. troop strength neared 470,000, and casualties mounted.

One massive problem that Johnson tried to ignore was that the allied forces (reinforced by Australian, Philippine, and New Zealand units) were not just fighting Viet Cong rebels in black pajamas, but also a large and well-equipped People's Army of Viet Nam (PAVN), or North Vietnam's Army. These troops received their supplies from no less than the Soviet Union itself, and they delivered them to the South along the infamous Ho Chi Minh Trail, a more than 350-mile pathway through the jungles of Laos, which terminated at strike points opposite Da Nang air base, and the Pleiku and Ankhe firebases.

For all these substantial (and, in most cases, debilitating) weaknesses, the United States still had to snatch defeat from the jaws of victory. The watershed event came with the so-called Tet Offensive on January 31, 1968, when the Viet Cong assaulted multiple targets throughout the South. VC troops even reached the U.S. embassy in Saigon, where they (contrary to popular movie renditions) were killed to a man. They stormed the old capital of Hue and surrounded the U.S. base at Khe Sanh. They made spectacular gains, but at great cost: for every American soldier or marine killed at Khe Sanh, 50 North Vietnamese died, a ratio "approaching the horrendous slaughter . . . between the Spaniards and Aztecs in Mexico or British and Zulus in southern Africa."[100] At Hue the surprised and outnumbered U.S. Marines evicted 10,000 Viet Cong and Vietnamese regulars from a fortified city in less than three weeks and at a loss of only 150 dead.

From that point on, any pretense that Vietnam was a civil war was over. The only hope the communists had to win had to come from direct, and heavy, infusions of troops and supplies from Hanoi, Moscow, and Peking. At Khe Sanh, nearly 25,000 air sorties subjected the seasoned North Vietnamese attackers to a merciless bombardment, killing 10,000 communists compared to 205 Americans.[101] One senior American general called Khe Sanh the first major ground battle won almost entirely by air power.[102] A U.S. military historian, Robert Leckie, referred to Tet as "the most appalling defeat in the history of the war" for Hanoi—an "unmitigated military disaster."[103] Even General Tran Van Tra, a top-ranking communist, agreed, "We suffered large sacrifices and losses with regard to manpower and material, especially cadres at the various echelons, which clearly weakened us."[104]

Yet the very failure of the communists' Tet Offensive illustrated the flawed nature of U.S. strategy. Here, in a single battle, Americans had achieved a fifty-to-one kill ratio, and yet the media reported this as a communist victory. EMBASSY IN SAIGON CAPTURED! read one erroneous headline. Television repeatedly showed a photograph of South Vietnamese police chief Nguyen Ngoc Loan shooting a man in the head, claiming the man was a "Vietcong suspect." In fact, the man was a Viet Cong colonel in civilian clothes—a man Loan knew personally—and, by the rules of war, a spy. Andrew Jackson had done almost exactly the same thing to British agents more than 120 years earlier. But Jackson did not have to deal with the power of television or the impact of the camera. Scenes were cut and spliced in the studios into thirty-second clips of marines and body bags, with an accompanying text, "American troops mauled."

After Tet, the "most trusted man in America," CBS news anchor Walter Cronkite, told his viewers the war was unwinnable, at which point Johnson reportedly said that if he had lost Walter Cronkite, he'd lost the American people. Even *Newsweek*—hardly an objective, patriotic source—admitted that for the first time in history the American press was more friendly to its country's enemies than to the United States. Ironically, the polls showed Johnson consistently drew higher support when he turned up the pressure and when he restarted the bombing of the North. Before the 1968 election, polls showed that no more than 20 percent supported withdrawal, and some of that 20 percent represented hawks who were dissatisfied with the apparent lack of conviction in the strategy.[105]

Coming Apart

No American war has ever enjoyed the full and unwavering support of the entire U.S. population. Federalists threatened secession in 1812 in protest of "Mr. Madison's War"; Henry David Thoreau was jailed over his opposition to the Mexican War (a conflict that even Lincoln challenged); and the Civil War produced protests against the draft that required the use of Gatling guns to disperse rioters. World War II came as close as any war to unanimous support, and even then there were dissenters. Vietnam differed sharply because without a declaration of war, the administration lost a tremendous psychological patriotic edge. People debated a policy decision as opposed to an act of national security. Moreover, inept handling of the press and failure to propagandize the conflict in the manner that a life and death struggle demands only invited rebellion and criticism at home. In short, Vietnam, in almost every respect, was a textbook example on how not to conduct a war. The media's proclivities toward an open society increasingly demanded that Americans consider the communists' point of view and questioned whether U.S. leadership had an interest in the outcome. This, in turn, meant that acts of defiance against the government were magnified, exaggerated, and highlighted.

Real dissent certainly existed. Selective service, better known as the draft, had been reinstituted during the Korean War and had been renewed regularly by Congress. But a host of exemptions, including those for marriage and education, allowed all married men plus upper- and upper-middle-class men to elude induction. This is not to say Vietnam was a poor man's war. Rifle companies suffered high numbers of casualties—mostly draftees—but proportionately the worst hit were flyers, virtually all of whom were volunteers, officers, and college graduates. It would have been irrelevant if the draft had produced genuine inequities: Radicals still would have claimed such injustice existed. A march for peace took place in Washington in late 1965, and a month earlier the first publicized case of a draft-card burning had occurred.

Pollsters swept into action, measuring support for the war. Unfortunately, polling, by the nature of its yes or no answers to questions, tends to put people into one of two camps, eliminating options. Consequently, depending on the wording of a particular poll, one could prove that the "majority" of Americans either approved of, or disapproved of, the Johnson administration's handling of the war at any given time. One segment of the population—which grew steadily, but which peaked at about one third—was referred to as doves. The doves themselves were split. One group criticized the Vietnam War primarily on moral grounds, namely, that the United States, as a "capitalist imperial" power, represented the embodiment of evil in the world; whereas communist states, no matter what their "excesses," nevertheless were forces for progress toward a utopian society. Most of those in this echelon of the dove wing consisted of die-hard communists, dropouts, social outcasts, militant anti-American revolutionaries, or disaffected youths who, whatever their education, were ignorant of the most basic elements of foreign policy.

Another dove wing, the liberal Democrats, generally embraced John Kennedy's original vision of "paying any price, bearing any burden" to advance democracy, but they nonetheless saw Vietnam as the wrong war in the wrong place. To this pragmatic wing, the general strategy remained sound, but Southeast Asia already looked like a quagmire the liberals wanted to avoid because it also threatened to suck funds from Great Society social programs. Many journalists, such as David Halberstam and Neil Sheehan, fell into this category.

The opposite segment of public opinion, labeled the hawks, represented the conservative anticommunists in the Republican and Democratic parties. Hawks viewed it as a critical signal to the Soviets to hold the line in Vietnam as a continuation of containment that had proved moderately successful in Korea, Iran, and—its greatest success—NATO and Western Europe. For the hawks, withdrawal was not an option because it would put into play the domino theory and topple the other states in Southeast Asia, threatening the entire southern fence holding in the Soviet empire. Among the hawk wing of the Democratic Party, the labor unions provided consistent support for the war. After Nixon's election, the so-called hard hats, who represented construction and line workers, frequently clashed with the student radicals and the hippies at protest marches.

Three Streams Converge

Vietnam was unique in rallying a large core of opponents—perhaps ultimately as large a share as the Tory population opposed to Washington's armies in the American Revolution. What made the Vietnam protests somewhat different was three forces that combined in the mid-1960s to produce the student mass demonstrations that disrupted American college campuses and ultimately spilled over into the cities.

The first stream to flow into the radicalism of the decade occurred when the baby boomers knocked on the doors of the universities. Boomers numbered some 79 million people born between 1943 and 1960. Coming of college age by 1959 (at the earliest), they ushered in a tidal wave of students into American universities, tripling the percentage of bachelor's degrees awarded to twenty-three-year-olds between 1950 and 1970.[106] The student population—already 2.5 percent in America—further expanded. This demographic quake alone would have sent shock waves through the system, despite the fact that two thirds of the boomers never went to college.

Something else relating to education was at work, however, namely the deprivatization of education in the United States. In the 1960s, the percentage of students attending public rather than private institutions rose from 59 percent to

73 percent, and the image of a college graduate as an elite member of society disappeared when millions of veterans took advantage of the G.I. Bill. Public universities reflected this transfer from private to public, especially in California, which opened three new campuses in 1964 and 1965.

By their very size, "whatever age bracket Boomers have occupied has been the cultural and spiritual focal point for American society as a whole."[107] More bluntly, it was always about *them,* and most of the cultural and spiritual trends were troubling: the boomer generation's death rates from suicide, drunk driving, illegitimate births, and crime set records, relatively and absolutely. The incidence of serious crime rose twice as fast for the boomer generation as for the population as a whole.[108] Meanwhile, families in which boomers were raised as well as their own marriages fell apart with growing frequency, with the ratio of divorces to marriages going from one in six in 1940 to one in three by 1970.

It is from this background of abundance, self-centeredness, and permissiveness, combined with instability and lack of direction, that the boomer students arrived on university campuses in the early to mid-1960s.[109] Because of lower standards, American university enrollment rose from 3.6 million students in 1960 to 9.4 million by 1975, when baby-boom enrollments began to flag. More than a thousand new colleges or universities—not counting hundreds of community colleges and technical and trade schools—opened during the expansion. In 1950, the United States had 1,859 public and private institutions of higher education, a number that had risen to 3,055 by 1975.[110]

Most of these were public universities (1,454, in 1975), reflecting the national sense that a college education was desirable and that a means to guarantee a college education needed to come from tax dollars. As a precursor to these attitudes, several studies purported to show that from 1947 to 1958 the "knowledge industry" had accounted for more than 28 percent of the nation's income, growing twice as fast as the GNP.[111] Other scholars argued that it had increased the nation's wealth by more than half, and Clark Kerr likened the university's transforming effect on the economy to that of the railroads.[112] By the end of the 1960s, nearly half of all young men were going to college, while at the same time a striking grade inflation had started, which was more pronounced for the boomer generation than any other in history. The average collegiate grade rose from C+ to B between 1969 and 1971, overlapping a historical SAT slide of at least 24 points for some schools and up to 50 points for others.[113] Never was getting a good grade so easy for so many people, yet never had it represented so little.

Some of the incentive for obtaining a higher education came from the oft-cited income statistics showing there existed a direct correlation between years of schooling and salary. In 1949, when the boomers' parents began to contemplate the future, the after-tax lifetime income for a person completing sixteen years of school was almost double that of a person with an eighth-grade education, a precursor to the late twentieth century, when real wages for those with less than a high school diploma fell, compared to college graduates, whose income rose at a strong rate.[114] Between 1956 and 1972, the lifetime income of men with college educations had increased to almost twice that of male high school graduates.

In the process of appreciating the genuine benefits of education, however, Americans deified the college degree, endowing it with magical powers of transformation that it never possessed. This nearly religious faith in education spending accounted for a second major factor that helped foster student riots in the 1960s: money, especially federal dollars. It began in 1958, when the National Defense Education Act not only expanded the federal education budget, but also marked the key shift by making Uncle Sam "the financial dynamic of education."[115] During the Great Society, Washington earmarked still more money for education, particularly for less affluent students. The flood of money was, as usual, well intended. Congress had originally sought to buttress math, science, and engineering programs at colleges and universities. In fact, the money merely filtered through the math and science programs in true academic egalitarian fashion on its way to liberal arts and social science programs.

This development by itself might not have produced such a disaster in other eras. In the 1960s, however, a third element combined with the explosion in student numbers and the rising tide of funding, namely, the leftward tilt of the faculty on campus. The academy always tended toward liberalism, but liberal inclinations were kept in check by religion, government, and society to render a relative degree of political balance for more than a century. In the 1930s, the artistic and intellectual elites rejected capitalism, many going so far as to endorse Stalinism. One study, at Bennington College from 1935 to 1939, showed that students' attitudes swayed dramatically as they matriculated through the university. Some 62 percent entered Bennington as Republicans, but by the time they graduated only 15 percent still considered themselves Republicans. On the other hand, the number of those who considered themselves socialist or communist *tripled* during the same period.[116]

With the end of McCarthyism, many universities found that not only could they not discriminate against communists, but they no longer had any right to question radical scholarship either. After all, the thinking went, "Who's to say what's right or wrong?" Such views did not go far in science, business, or engineering, but the requirements at most universities in general education fields meant that the extremely activist and liberal faculty elements were concentrated into required classes in history, English, philosophy, and social sciences—in other words, where they would reach the most students.

At the same time, students were inadequately grounded in the basic principles of capitalism or communism. By the end of 1962, the New York *Times* noted a discernible national trend against teaching about communism in schools.[117] The anti-McCarthy reaction at the university level led to a dramatic shift in the other direction. Conservatives were ostracized, viewed as no longer cutting-edge. Tenure committees increasingly had more Marxists on them, and those leftist scholars wielded the tenure knives as freely as the McCarthyites had on communists.[118] In part, this, too, represented a generational revolt against established existing faculty in colleges by young professors seeking to flex their muscles against groups (including many World War II vets) that they thought had given inordinate support to McCarthy's movement.[119] Consequently, just when students cognitively reached an age where they could understand the deeper issues of capitalism and communism, they arrived at universities ill prepared to challenge the increasingly radical university faculty they were likely to encounter in required classes.

Yet it would be inaccurate to portray the student protest movement as directed by the professors. Although faculty advisers may have provided ammunition for the cause, it was radical students who led the attack. Many of the agitators' leaders were "red-diaper babies" whose parents were Communist Party members or socialists. Some were not even students at the time, such as Tom Hayden of the University of Michigan, a journalist who worked as a field secretary for the Students for a Democratic Society (SDS). Hayden, later known for his famous marriage to actress Jane Fonda, cofounded the Students for a Democratic Society in 1960 with Al Haber, a local Michigan radical. Haber received support from the socialist Student League for Industrial Democracy. Though publicly anti-Soviet, they had no intention of opposing communism in word or in principle. Steeped in Marxism, both Haber and Hayden hated American capitalism and the middle-class society it produced. The committed Hayden—praised as "the next Lenin"—organized a meeting of activists in Port Huron, Michigan, in 1962 that produced the manifesto of the movement, called the Port Huron Statement.[120] The Port Huron Statement enjoined students to seize control of the educational system from the administrators and government, that is, from the taxpayers. Hoping to distance themselves from the Stalinist atrocities of the 1930s, the SDS and other radical organizations called themselves the New Left. One of the key tenets of the Port Huron philosophy was that the United States was the source of conflict and injustice in the world. Equally important, though, was the notion that "students were ideally suited to lead," and that the university was the ideal location, if not the only one, from which to launch the new radicalism.[121]

Consequently, at the very time that waves of new baby-boomer students were swarming into institutions of higher learning, they were greeted with a torrent of money and a liberal—if not radical—faculty that challenged traditional norms of patriotism, religion, and family. Reinforcing the message of the student radicals, the faculty provided social and intellectual cover for the disruptions that soon occurred, justifying the mayhem as necessary for education and social reform. Under such circumstances, the surprise was not that violent campus revolutions ensued, but that they took so long, especially in light of the Vietnam War, which provided a focal point for anti-American hostility and revolutionary rhetoric.

Red-Diaper Babies

At least some of the unrest emanated from Moscow, which trained and supported an extensive network of radical leaders for the purposes of disrupting American society and alienating youth from bourgeois ideas. Sit-in protests and mass demonstrations at California campuses appeared as early as 1958, usually directed at a specific incident or university policies. After 1964, however, at the University of California at Berkeley, the demonstrations grew increasingly violent under the Free Speech movement. According to the history of the American communist movement, "Communists and other varieties of Marxists and Marxist-Leninists were among the organizers and leaders" of the Free Speech movement.[122] SDS leaders, such as Carl Davidson, David Horowitz, Country Joe MacDonald, and other red-diaper babies, proudly proclaimed their Marxist-Leninist sympathies. Bernardine Dohrn, leader of the SDS in 1968, asked if she was a socialist, answered, "I consider myself a revolutionary Communist."[123]

Although some in the peace movement discouraged a communist presence, the Left did not need to be taken over in the conventional sense—a takeover from below had occurred in the form of an infiltration by many thoroughgoing communists and fellow travelers. In an absurd scene of supreme irony, suburban radicals such as Tom Bell of Cornell faced harassment and taunting from the audience at the 1968 SDS convention when members of the Progressive Labor wing howled curses at him for being too anticommunist. Here was a revolutionary who wanted to destroy or, at the very least, fundamentally eviscerate the foundations of American democracy and capitalism being called a "red baiter."[124] Consequently, just as the SDS had established itself on 350 to 400 campuses across the country, claiming perhaps a hundred thousand members, communist elements within the organization tore it apart, achieving the goal of the more militant communists of pushing the radical movement toward street violence, yielding its position of influence to the militant Weathermen.[125]

Thus, campus violence was not a case of emotions getting out of hand, as is sometimes portrayed. Nor was it a case of frustrated student radicals who "lacked the patience and discipline for nonviolent protest."[126] Rather, it represented a predictable evolution of events when a radical minority steeped in revolutionary tactics and filled with an ideology of terror attempted to impose its worldview on the majority by shutting down facilities. But as early as 1964, "spontaneous" protests for "student rights" were revealed to be organized, deliberate disruptions designed to choke off all educational activities.

It is important to establish clearly, in their own words, the goals and objectives of the radicals and to note that traditional means of social control, especially arrest and imprisonment for purposes of rehabilitation, had little meaning to people who viewed arrest as a status symbol. Jerry Rubin, one of the leaders of the New Left Yippie movement, expressed his contempt for the system within which most of the activists operated. Violating the law had no negative connotation for the Yippies, and few feared genuine reprisals from the "repressive establishment" they denigrated daily.[127] Destroying property, insulting police and city officials, polluting, and breaking the law in any way possible were jokes to some; to others, arrest only signified their commitment or validated their ideology. Rubin, called into court, laughed, "Those who got subpoenas became heroes. Those who didn't had subpoenas envy. It was almost sexual. 'Whose is bigger?' 'I want one, too.' "[128] The adrenaline rush of activism completely distorted reality. Susan Stern, a member of the violent Weathermen gang that blew up a University of Wisconsin lab, killing a student, had participated in the Chicago riots. Charged with aggravated assault and battery, and assault with a deadly weapon for attacking police (which carried a maximum penalty of forty years in prison), she recalled being "enthralled by the adventure and excitement of my first bust," oblivious to the prospect that she might spend most of her life behind bars.[129]

Radicals like Rubin noted that the essence of the movement was twofold: repel and alienate mainstream American society, setting the radicals up as anti-establishment heroes who would have a natural appeal to teens and college students seeking to break away from their parents; and refuse rational negotiation in order to polarize and radicalize campuses (and, they hoped, the rest of the United States). Rubin "repelled" and "alienated" quite well. As he once put it, "We were dirty, smelly, grimy, foul, loud, dope-crazed, hell-bent and leather-jacketed." The hippies took pride in the fact that they "were a public display of filth and shabbiness, living-in-the-flesh rejects of middle-class standards [who] pissed and s**t and f***ed in public." Far from hiding their drug use, Rubin noted: "We were constantly stoned and tripping on every drug known to man . . . [and were] outlaw forces of America displaying ourselves flagrantly on the world stage."[130]

For mainstream America, which often received skewed news reports of the ostensible causes of the disruption, it appeared that students only wanted to challenge unreasonable dress codes, or have a say in curriculum, or protest unpopular college policies. These causes for protest masked their true tactics, which were to use any initial demand as a starting point for closing the university, then destroying the rest of society. As radical leaders themselves later admitted, they practiced a strategy of constantly escalating demands so that no compromise could ever be reached with them. Rubin, who drafted many of these early tactics, explained: "Satisfy our demands and we go twelve more. . . . All we want from these meetings are demands *that the Establishment can never satisfy. . . .* Demonstrators are never '*reasonable*' [emphasis ours]." When the demands reached the point that no rational university administrator or public official could possibly comply with them, Rubin noted, "Then we scream, righteously angry. . . . Goals are irrelevant. The tactics, the actions are critical."[131] Yet Rubin was not being entirely candid: *Short-term goals* were irrelevant, but the destabilization of society as a long-term objective was quite relevant to the activists.

Over time, the movement not only grew more radical but also more blatantly anti-American. Peter Collier, on the staff of *Ramparts* magazine, recalled: "We had a weekly ritual of sitting in front of the television set and cheering as Walter Cronkite announced the ever-rising body count on CBS."[132] Actress Jane Fonda visited Hanoi in 1972 with her then-husband, activist Tom Hayden. In a famous photo, she posed sitting in the gunner's seat of a North Vietnamese antiaircraft gun—exactly the type used to shoot down the American pilots who were held nearby in the Hanoi Hilton prison, being tortured and starved—then spoke on Radio Hanoi as American POWs were forced to listen.[133]

Sex, Drugs, and Rock and Roll

Enhancing the freedom from responsibility and the associated notion that normal activities such as holding jobs and raising families were somehow meaningless, the new drug culture spread through the underculture like wildfire. Timothy Leary's famous call to tune in, turn on, and drop out reached innocent ears like a siren song, and many youth, already convinced their parents had lied to them about rock and roll, sex, and Vietnam, listened attentively. LSD (lysergic acid diethylamide) was the subject of extensive tests by the CIA in the 1950s. One CIA researcher recalled the lab staff using it themselves, saying, "There was an extensive amount of self-experimentation . . . [because] we felt that a firsthand knowledge of the subjective effects of these drugs [was] important."[134] LSD spread throughout the subculture and by the 1960s, dropping acid was equated with a religious exerience by Beat poet Allen Ginsburg.[135]

Increasingly, intellectuals in the 1960s advocated chemical use purely for pleasure and mind expansion. And not just LSD, but mescaline, heroin, amphetamines, Ditran, and other mysterious substances, all, of course, undergirded by the all-purpose and ubiquitous marijuana. Writer Ken Kesey credited his LSD trip for his insight in *One Flew Over the Cuckoo's Nest;* leaders of the Berkeley Free Speech movement saw drugs as a natural element in their attack on conformity; and indeed drug use was, in their view, "an important political catalyst . . . [that enabled] questioning of the official mythology of the governing class."[136] Or, as a veteran of the Free Speech movement bragged, "When a young person took his first puff of psychoactive smoke, . . . [he] became a youth criminal against the State."[137] It was all so much empty rhetoric, but when draped in the language of academia, it took on a certain respectability.

Sexual freedom without consequence was glamorized and pushed by Hollywood and the music industry. Censorship laws, which had eroded since the U.S. Supreme Court's *Roth* decision (1957), established that obscenity had to appeal to "prurient interests" and run contrary to "contemporary community standards." Justice William Brennan further eliminated barriers to imposing any limits by ruling that the public could not ban a work unless it was "utterly" without "redeeming social value."[138] This, of course, meant that no town, ever, could prohibit any book or movie, since someone could always find "redeeming social value" somewhere in the work.

The free love movement, supported by the hippies, also reinforced the attack on constraints. Two strains of free love arguments appeared. One held that any breaking of sexual taboos and any attack on censorship represented an advance against the male-dominated power structure. Thus, some supported the women's movement not because it allowed women to seek self-fulfillment outside the home, but because it undercut capitalism and traditionalism. A second, more radical, wave of sexual politics involved the quest for polymorphous perversity—a call to try everything, do everything, and ignore all restraints against homosexuality, pedophilia, and bestiality—and the destruction of all distinctions between men and women. Any type of affection that affirmed life, these advocates argued, was desirable. Marriage and heterosexuality inhibited such life affirmation and therefore were wrong.

No doubt some Americans held these views in all previous eras, but the physiology of conception placed severe constraints on "If it feels good, do it." Pregnancy out of wedlock was received with such social ostracism that it curtailed experimentation, even if social mores seemingly punished females more than the often unnamed male partners. The Pill changed that to the extent that the 1999 millennial issue of *The Economist* called it the greatest scientific and technological advance of the twentieth century.[139] Without question, the Pill also triggered a boom in women's education similar to what men had experienced: in medicine, first-year women students tripled within ten years of the spread of the Pill, and female MBA students nearly quadrupled. Whatever its beneficial effects, the Pill exacerbated the erotic impulses already spinning out of control.

Rock music reaffirmed the sexual and drug revolutions at every turn. By 1970, although still exceptionally popular, neither the Beatles nor their bad-boy counterparts, the Rolling Stones, had the aura of hipness, having ceded that to rising new and more radical groups whose music carried deeper drug overtones. Jimi Hendrix sang of flying on giant dragonflies and Jim Morrison of the Doors saw himself as the "lizard king." Pink Floyd, Jefferson Airplane, and Iron Butterfly unashamedly wrote music for drug trips.

By this time even clothing embodied antiestablishment traits. Blue jeans, the antifashion, completely dominated the youth culture, constituting what one author called the "Jeaning of America."[140] The entire genre emphasized sex and free love, pointing to the Woodstock music festival of August 15–17, 1969, as evidence of what a hippie republic would look like. "Peace, love, and rock 'n' roll," read the logos on commercial products celebrating the event. "Gonna join in a rock 'n' roll band . . . and set my soul free," wailed Stephen Stills, of Crosby, Stills & Nash (CSN), in the anthem of the three-day concert. CSN popularized the event with a top-forty song called "Woodstock," and the group starred in a full-length movie that followed. Woodstock was "touted as a new stage in the psychic evolution of the world, a mass celebration of what the 1960s was all about," an assertion defying reality.[141] When up to half a million hippies—the counterculture rock fans (including more than a few chronic drug users)—showed up at Max Yasgur's farm to hear a cornucopia of headline rock bands, the result was predictable: it had little to do with love or peace and quite a bit to do with money.

As one participant recalled, "There was a lot made of how peaceful the event was. But what else would half a million kids on grass, acid, and hog tranquilizers be? Woodstock, if anything, was the point at which psychedelics [drugs] ceased being tools for experience . . . and became a means of *crowd control*."[142] Said Grateful Dead guitarist (and drug addict) Jerry Garcia, "You could feel the presence of the invisible time travelers from the future," but Garcia apparently didn't see the "kids freaking out from megadoses of acid or almost audibly buzzing from battery-acid crank like flies trapped in a soda can."[143] Having celebrated drug use, within a few years Garcia, Sly Stone, David Crosby, Keith Moon, Janis Joplin, and Jimi Hendrix, among other participants at Woodstock, either died of overdoses or otherwise destroyed their careers or bodies. Other Woodstock veterans met similar distasteful ends. Felix Pappalardi of Mountain survived one drug overdose only to be shot by his wife in 1983.

Hendrix, already a guitar legend, wrapped up Woodstock with a "truly apocalyptic" vision of a "battlefield, [with] zombies crawling over a field littered with paper cups, plastic wrappers, and half-eaten food, gnawing on corn husks, slobbering over ketchup- and mustard-smeared half-eaten hot dog rolls sprinkled with ants. . . ."[144] The event generated the single largest pile of garbage of any event in human history, and when the perpetrators departed, they left the mess for someone else to clean up.

Less than a week before Woodstock, on August 9, 1969, the cult followers of Charles Manson broke into the house of director Roman Polanski in Bel Air, California. Polanski was away, but his beautiful pregnant wife, Sharon Tate, and four of her friends were home. Manson's gang—though not Manson himself—stabbed and butchered the houseguests, smearing slogans on the walls in the victims' blood. Reflecting the depravity of the counterculture, the underground paper *Tuesday's Child* named Manson its man of the year. Yippie leader Jerry Rubin said he fell in love with Manson's "cherub face and sparkling eyes," and Bernardine Dohrn, leader of the Weathermen, exclaimed, "Dig it! First they killed those pigs, then they ate dinner in the same room with them, then they even shoved a fork into [Sharon Tate's] stomach! Wild!"[145] If anything, the Manson murders hurled icy water on the sixties myth that drugs made people holy, nonviolent, or pure.

At any rate, the drug culture and the so-called hippie movement never amounted to more than a well-publicized fringe. It certainly did not outnumber the body of apathetic or apolitical youth, and, even though it enjoyed better publicity, the hippie movement may have had fewer adherents than a growing conservative student movement that had taken root two years before the Port Huron Statement. The media did not view conservative youth groups, such as the Young Americans for Freedom, as newsworthy, and thus they never received the attention or coverage of the radicals, but they were influential nonetheless. Traditionalists and conservatives, those that Richard Nixon would call the Silent Majority, all faded into relative nonexistence from the media's perspective. It was much more interesting to cover a firebombing or a riot.

Protests, Mobs, and the Media

Given the radicals' dominance of the antiwar movement, it should not be surprising that "the demonstrations at the time of the Democratic convention in August 1968, and the moratorium events of October 1969 were orchestrated by organizations with changing names but with essentially the same cast of leaders."[146] On March 31, 1968, Lyndon Johnson shocked the country with an unexpected announcement that he would not again seek the Democratic nomination for president. Polls had indicated that he probably would lose, especially with a challenge from the dovish side of the Democratic Party. Equally shocking to some was that one of the emerging "doves," Robert Kennedy, had abruptly repudiated his brother's war. Suddenly many who still yearned for the presidency of John Kennedy—and the magic of Camelot—found him available again in the person of Robert. But just two months after Martin Luther King's assassination, Bobby Kennedy, giving a speech in Los Angeles, was killed by Sirhan Sirhan. The motive given for the assassination—Sirhan was an Arab nationalist—remains puzzling to this day: Kennedy did not have a reputation as a strong friend of Israel, although he did come from New York, which had a strong Jewish lobby. Kennedy's assassination left a void among the antiwar Left in the Democratic Party, whose dove leadership now devolved to the rather bland Eugene McCarthy. Certainly, though, the antiwar Left would not unite behind Vice President Hubert H. Humphrey of Minnesota.

A tireless legislator and principal author of the affirmative action laws, Humphrey lacked the commanding presence of a national leader and could only have won by sidestepping the turmoil that the antiwar elements promised to bring to the Democrats' convention. Those groups sought to nominate McCarthy, a sincere-looking, soft-spoken senator from Minnesota who reminded people of a wise uncle. His appearance enhanced his antiwar positions, which were in many respects dangerous. Between 10,000 and 20,000 protesters moved into Chicago, with some of the most radical elements threatening to pour LSD into the city's water or throw acid into the eyes of policemen. Others promised to lead a 150,000-person march on the Amphitheater. Democratic mayor Richard Daley, having just regained control of the city from race riots, had no intention of allowing a new group to disrupt the Windy City when he authorized police to "shoot to kill" any suspected looters.

Daley placed the nearly 12,000-strong Chicago police on twelve-hour shifts, augmented by 7,500 army troops airlifted in from Texas, Oklahoma, and Colorado. He dispatched police to guard Chicago's water supply and assembled "Daley dozers," jeeps specially outfitted with rolls of barbed wire on the front to clear streets of demonstrators. More important, he had already infiltrated the radical groups, sabotaging their schemes to acquire buses, and giving out false information at phone banks.[147] After weeks of denying the protesters march permits, Daley relented. The first riot broke out on August 25, 1968, when the police charged Lincoln Park, driving the peaceniks out. One policeman told a reporter, "The word is out to get newsmen," and Daley himself implied that journalists would not be protected.[148]

A symbiotic relationship, which developed between the Chicago protesters and the news media, accelerated. But the journalists also failed to see the adroit manipulation by the demonstrators. Witnesses reported an absence of violence until the mobs saw television cameras, at which point they began their act. A later study by the national Commission on the Causes and Prevention of Violence reported that demonstrators stepped up their activities when reporters and photographers appeared, and, worse, camera crews "on at least two occasions *did stage violence and fake injuries* (emphasis ours)."[149] The city of Chicago issued a report on the riots charging that the news media was guilty of "surprising naïveté," but in reality the television cameras especially had encouraged and facilitated the rioters, and the images shifted all the blame to the police, who had their share of malignant club-wielding patrolmen. Advocates for maintaining public order were few and far between: NBC *Today Show* host Hugh Downs asked his viewers if the label "pigs" didn't apply to the Chicago police. Chet Huntley of NBC complained that "the news profession . . . is now under assault by the Chicago police," and Walter Cronkite said on the air that the "Battle of Michigan Avenue" made him want to "pack my bags and get out of this city."[150] Such rhetoric quickly faded as the media quietly reaffirmed its support of the Democratic Party in the general election.

The 1968 race pitted the inevitable winner, Humphrey, against the suddenly revived Richard Nixon, who had made one of the most amazing political comebacks of all time to capture the Republican nomination. Just six years earlier, when he lost the governor's race in California, Nixon had told reporters, "You won't have Dick Nixon to kick around anymore." Nixon resurrected himself largely because of the rampant lawlessness in the country and his insight that Americans longed for "law and order." He also understood that, if elected, he had to get the United States out of the war, one way or another, and he therefore claimed to have a "secret plan" to get America out of Vietnam. His anticommunist record suggested that whatever it was, it would not be concession to Hanoi. Claiming there was a "Silent Majority" of Americans who did not protest and did not demonstrate, but worked at their jobs, paid their taxes, and raised their families, Nixon appealed to the many who held the country together, kept the roads and Social Security funded, and raised kids who never broke any laws, yet who constantly found themselves portrayed by the media as boring, unimaginative, unhip, uncool, and generally not with it. In selecting Spiro T. Agnew, the governor of Maryland, as his running mate, Nixon further alienated the media and the elites, handing them a human lighting rod to absorb their attacks. During the first incarnation of the Republican "southern strategy," Nixon told southern convention delegates that he would not "ram anything down your throats" and that he disliked federal intervention. Many took Nixon's comments as code words for a lackadaisical approach to desegregation—which they may well have been—but he had also acknowledged that states did have legitimate constitutional protections against federal interference. At any rate, the southern strategy effectively nullified a strong third-party candidacy by former Alabama governor George Wallace, a segregationist and strong hawk.[151]

Although the margin of victory was somewhat distorted by Wallace, Richard Nixon won convincingly in the electoral college, 302 to 191. Wallace received nearly 10 million popular votes, along with 46 electoral votes in five southern states that almost certainly would have gone to Nixon in a two-way race. This meant that Nixon received only 43 percent of the popular vote, or about the same as in other three-way races, for example, Wilson in 1912 or Bill Clinton in 1992. He failed to carry a single large city, yet racked up California, Illinois, Ohio, and virtually all of the West except Texas.[152] Viewing the Nixon and Wallace states together spotlighted a strong rejection of LBJ and his policies. Of course, the press was unhappy with this result. Reporter David Broder warned that the "men and the movement that broke Lyndon Johnson's authority in 1968 are out to break Richard Nixon . . . [and it is] easier to accomplish the second time round."[153] Nixon saw the press as the enemy, telling his staff "nobody in the press is a friend."[154]

In fact, he was right. Virtually unnoticed, the media in America had undergone a fundamental and radical shift in the sixties. This began with journalists' utter failure to cover the Kennedy administration fairly and, subsequently, to cover the assassination either objectively or thoroughly. Seeking to recover lost ground and their journalistic virginity, members of the press had accelerated their attack on LBJ throughout the Vietnam War; then, when "their" candidate— Eugene McCarthy—scarcely made a dent in the Democratic nominating process, they opened up all their guns on Nixon. Most members of the press did not like Nixon, either personally or ideologically, and his "illegitimate" election allowed them to attack mercilessly.

"We Are All Keynesians Now"

Nixon came into office hoping to restore the pomp and circumstance of the White House, outfitting the marine guards with European-style ostentatious uniforms. Patriotic, convinced of the rightness of his position, Nixon unfortunately lacked the charisma that Kennedy, Jackson, or the Roosevelts had exhibited. His taste never seemed quite right: the new uniforms he had ordered for the White House guards only led to complaints that he was trying to create an "imperial" presidency. Having struggled through a poor childhood, Nixon never adapted to the modest wealth and trappings associated with the presidency. He never looked comfortable in anything less than a coat and tie. Yet he was a remarkable man.

Raised as a Quaker, he had played piano in church and was a high school debater. He entered the navy in World War II after putting himself through Whittier College and Duke University Law School. Elected to Congress from California in 1946, he was largely associated with anticommunism, especially the investigation of Alger Hiss. Criticized for failing to support desegregation issues, Nixon took states' rights seriously. The notion that he was a racist in any way is preposterous: since 1950, when it was definitely not fashionable, he had been a member of the NAACP, and he had received the praise of Eleanor Roosevelt for his nondiscrimination policies as chairman of the Committee on Government Contracts.

Politically, Nixon's election promises of respecting Main Street and upholding "law and order" had touched a desire among Americans to control the decade that had spun out of control.[155] Billed as the "the most reactionary and unscrupulous politician to reach the White House in the postwar era," Nixon was neither.[156] Both Kennedy and Johnson had exceeded Nixon in their ability to deceive and lie, and if one considers Nixon's economics, he was arguably was less conservative than Truman.

Far from retreating from liberalism, Nixon fully embraced the basics of New Deal economics and, at least in practice, continued to treat social programs as though they were indeed effective and justifiable public policies. "We are all Keynesians now," he stated, indicating a faith in Keynesian economics, or the proposition that the government, through fiscal and monetary policy, could heat up or cool off the business climate. With the remnants of Great Society congressional delegations entrenched, and with the Democrats controlling both houses of Congress, the giant welfare state of the Great Society promised to grow, and grow rapidly, without a chief executive holding it in check. Meanwhile, the bill for LBJ's programs started to come due under Nixon, and social spending rose dramatically during his administration, especially the budget for AFDC. Per-person costs to "lift" someone out of poverty went from $2,000 in 1965 to $167,000 by 1977.[157]

Even without the prodding of the Democrats, Nixon expanded government's scope and activities. Under his watch, the Environmental Protection Agency (EPA) came into being, with its tendency to acquire vast and unchecked powers over private property in the name of the environment. The agency had a $2.5 billion budget and had employed seven thousand people in less than two years.[158] Its Endangered Species Act of 1973 stopped construction of a $116 million dam in Tennessee because it might affect a fish called a snail darter, but that was only a taste of the runaway power the environmental agencies would later wield. By 1998, some 1,100 different endangered species were protected by the government to the extent that merely shining a light on a kangaroo rat at night—even if by accident—constituted a federal violation!

Farmers watched in horror as EPA agents, often dressed in black with firearms, sealed off their land or seized their equipment for threatening "wildlife preserves," otherwise known as rancid ponds. Restrictions on killing predators in the West grew so oppressive that ranchers engaged in the shoot-and-shovel approach, where they simply killed coyotes or wolves and buried the bodies. By the 1990s, a Florida man was sent to prison for two years after placing clean sand on his own lot; a Michigan man was jailed for dumping dirt on his property (because his wife had asthma); and an Oregon school district was taken to court for dumping sand on a baseball field. Land that was dry 350 of 365 days a year could be designated by the EPA as a "wetland"! The government claimed *private* land as small as 20 feet by 20 feet as a sanctuary for passing birds—or, as one wag called them, glancing geese. These and numerous other excessive and outrageous practices by the EPA and related land and environmental agencies went far beyond Teddy Roosevelt's goal of conserving wildlife and nature and bordered on elevating animals to human status.[159]

Such an approach was not surprising. A linchpin of the modern environmental movement, made popular in a 1968 book by biologist Paul Ehrlich, *The Population Bomb*, was the notion that people were reproducing far too rapidly and would soon create such environmental and population problems that the seas would dry up and "millions" would starve when the agricultural sector could not keep up.[160] "The battle to feed all of humanity is over," he intoned: "In the 1970s and 1980s *hundreds of millions of people* will starve to death in spite of any crash programs embarked upon now."[161] Malthus eventually repented of such preposterous views after he had written them. Almost two hundred years later, events proved Ehrlich's theories as wrong as flat-earth theories.[162] The United States—and the world, for that matter—continued to increase food production per capita, both on average and on every continent. Indeed, with very few exceptions, almost every twentieth-century famine was politically induced.[163] At the time Ehrlich predicted the deaths of "hundreds of millions," an Iowan named Norman Borlaug, who had grown up in the Depression-era Dust Bowl, concluded from observing dry midwestern fields that the problem was the lack of technology, not the application of it.[164] Borlaug engineered new strains of wheat, which expanded food production in sub-Saharan Africa, one of the slowest food-growing regions of the world. Not only did Borlaug's efforts produce more food overall, but his techniques increased production per acre.

Of more immediate impact on the Nixon-era economy was the environmental movement's attack on the automobile. Seeking to drastically cut back auto emissions, the EPA planned widespread new controls to "rein in" Detroit. Exhaust particles in the atmosphere, by then called smog, which included less visible but possibly more dangerous elements, had become an obvious problem in many cities, especially Los Angeles. The problem arose from the "tragedy of the commons," wherein it was in the individual interest of people to pollute, but in no one's individual interest to spend money for expensive pollution equipment on a car. Rather than provide tax incentives or other indirect methods to encourage people to move, on their own, to less polluting vehicles, the government used brute force. Even for those convinced that the government needed to act, the emphasis should have been on having the government set a standard—as it does with the department of weights and measures—and allowing Detroit to meet it by whichever means it found most effective or profitable. Instead, the EPA quickly drifted into determining which technologies cars "should" use. Without doubt, the air was cleaned up within twenty years, but other aspects of American life suffered dramatically as Americans saw taxes for the growing bureaucracy increase while their choices shrank, and there is no evidence that the same results could not have been achieved through market-oriented methods.

Similar measures passed by the 1968–74 congresses included the Occupational Health and Safety Act (administered by OSHA, the Occupational and Safety Health Administration), the Toxic Substances Control Act, and a series of clean air and pure food and drug acts. By 1976, businesses estimated that it cost $63 billion per year to comply with this legislation—money that ultimately did not come from the "evil corporations," but from (often low-income) consumers who paid higher and higher prices. At the same time, productivity fell. The Coal Mine Health and Safety Act reduced coal production by 32 percent. "Good," shouted the environmentalists, but it made America more dependent on foreign fuels. Worse, unemployment soared in states where federal pollution mandates forced vast new expenditures on scrubbers and other pollution-control devices.

Not only did Nixon fail to resist any of these measures, he embraced them, accelerating the growth of government on his own, even when legislation was not foisted on him. The White House staff, which before Kennedy consisted of 23, rose to 1,664 by the time of his assassination, then leaped to 5,395 by 1971.[165] Expanding government across a wide range of activities by maintaining the Great Society social programs and the space race, and adding the requirements of Vietnam and the cold war on top of all the new costs of the EPA and other legislation, had made Washington's debts such a drag on the economy that it had to slow down, if not collapse. The first sign that something was seriously wrong was inflation and its related effect, the declining value of the dollar abroad. Europeans, especially, did not want to hold dollars that had steadily lost their value. If the U.S. government could not control its appetites, then the international banking system—headed by American banks—could and did.

The postwar financial structure, created under the Bretton Woods agreement of 1944, called for foreign currencies to be pegged to the dollar—the international medium of exchange—and for the dollar to be held relatively constant to gold (at about $35 per ounce). A stable dollar was achieved through balanced budgets and fiscal restraint in the United States. Once the Great Society programs had kicked in, however, balancing the budget—especially under Nixon's Keynesian structure—was nearly impossible. Every new deficit seemed to call for new taxes, which, in turn, forced productivity and employment downward, generating more deficits. Eventually, Nixon severed the link to gold, and although many conservative economists howled, he had actually unwittingly foisted the dollar into an arena of international competition that imposed discipline on the U.S. Congress that it could never achieve itself. Within a decade, as electronic money transfers became common, the free-floating currency markets reacted swiftly and viciously against any government that spent money too freely. Nixon's paradoxical legacy was that he helped kill Keynesian economics in the United States for good.

The End of Vietnamization

"Peace with honor" had characterized Nixon's approach to getting the United States out of Vietnam. Along with his national security adviser, Harvard professor Henry Kissinger, Nixon had sought to combine a carrot-and-stick approach to dealing with Hanoi. The "carrot" negotiations involved continuing talks in Paris to get the North Vietnamese out of the South. After Tet, with the elimination of most of the VC armies, this would have amounted to a victory for the South. But Hanoi did not want any genuine negotiations and had stalled, hoping to run out the clock on the patience of the American public. Kissinger's "stick" included an accelerated bombing of the North combined with an immense resupply of the Vietnamese army, known as Vietnamization.

In reality, Vietnamization returned to the original Kennedy policy of supporting Vietnamese troops in the field, and by 1969 the Saigon government seemed much more enthusiastic about demanding that its own generals actually fight. As it turned out, as long as they had American air support and supply, the Vietnamese troops proved capable, holding their own against the communists. Nixon, whose name is strongly associated with the Vietnam War because of the protests, withdrew Americans at a faster rate than John Kennedy had put them in.

In May 1969, Nixon announced a new eight-point plan for withdrawing all foreign troops from Vietnam and holding internationally supervised elections. Under the new plan, the United States agreed to talk directly to the National Liberation Front (NLF), but behind the scenes it sent Kissinger to work the Soviet Union to pressure the North. That June, Nixon also withdrew the first large number of troops from Vietnam, some 25,000. Another 85,000 men would be brought home before the end of the year. This, obviously, was the corollary of Vietnamization—the withdrawal of American forces, which, after hitting a peak of 540,000 troops when Nixon came into office, steadily declined to only about 50,000 at the time of his resignation.

Another element of the stick strategy, though, was a renewed commitment to bombing North Vietnam. Here the United States missed yet another opportunity to take control of the conflict. Unlike Johnson, who had made the strategic bombing of the North ineffectual by selecting targets and instituting pauses and peace offensives, Nixon appreciated the necessity for pressure applied consistently and focused particularly on Hanoi. Still, North Vietnamese casualties were light, with only 1,500 civilians killed during the entire war compared to nearly 100,000 dead in the bombing of Tokyo in World War II. Such facts did not dissuade antiwar Senator George McGovern from telling NBC that the United States had conducted "the most murderous aerial bombardment in the history of the world," had engaged in "the most immoral action that this nation has ever committed," and had carried out a "policy of mass murder."[166] In fact, a real "mass murder" had occurred, although it had taken place nearly a year before, while Johnson was still in office.

In the fall of 1969 the Pentagon revealed that during the Tet offensive, American soldiers had entered a village at My Lai and massacred the inhabitants, including women and children. First Lieutenant William Calley, who had led the assault, was court-martialed and sentenced to life imprisonment for the murder of twenty-two unarmed civilians. A psychiatric team who examined the men concluded they were sane, and had known what they were doing at the time. Naturally, this incident fanned the flames of the antiwar movement, which derided soldiers as "baby killers." Calley's statement justifying his conduct indicated that he had not differentiated at all between Vietnamese civilians and Viet Cong or North Vietnamese soldiers. "It was no big deal," Calley said. "That was my enemy out there."[167]

It was not My Lai, but another action, this time by Nixon, that set off the protesters like never before. Nixon did not intend to let the communists attack allied bases from Cambodia with impunity, and beginning in March 1969, the president sent American aircraft on secret bombing missions over Cambodia, exposing North Vietnamese troops there to fire. A year later, on April 30, 1970, U.S. troops entered Cambodia to clear out the North Vietnamese sanctuaries. It was a move that should have occurred in 1965, and would have occurred in any declared war almost instantly. But this merely temporarily protected Americans already in the South. It did little to affect the attitudes of the North.

Instead, the bombing sparked new protests, with fatal results. At Kent State University, a bucolic, nonviolent Ohio campus prior to May 1970, a tragic shooting occurred when protesters had become so destructive that the National Guard was called out.[168] Students first torched the ROTC building, then attacked firemen who struggled to put out the fires, slashing their hoses. During subsequent protests, the guardsmen unexpectedly fired into the crowd, killing four. In May, at the all-black campus of Jackson State, rioting unrelated to the war resulted in the police killing two students. Both events solidified in the public mind the violent nature of the antiwar/"student" movements. From January 1959 to April 1970, more than 4,300 bombings racked universities, government buildings, and other facilities, at a rate of nine a day, most by the radical Weathermen.

Protest took on a form different from demonstrating or bombing: releasing secure or classified documents that could damage America's war efforts. In 1971, a former Defense Department official, Daniel Ellsberg, provided secret documents to the New York *Times*, which published the classified Pentagon study called *The History of the U.S. Decision Making Process in Vietnam*. These excerpts revealed that in many cases the Johnson administration had lied about U.S. involvement. Even though the documents only covered events until 1965, the nature of the analysis and the sources of some of the data would have exposed U.S. intelligence-gathering methods and threatened national security. For that reason, Nixon rightly fought their release in court, losing a Supreme Court decision that allowed their publication. The New York *Times* knew that all the significant information contained in the so-called Pentagon Papers had already been made public. The affair had nothing to do with informing the public and everything to do with further embarrassing the government, especially Nixon, who was tarred with Johnson's actions. Like the protests, publication of the Pentagon Papers only added to Hanoi's resolve, convincing the communists that America would soon crack. Nixon, on the other hand, thought that it was Hanoi that was close to surrender.

His one serious attempt at bringing the North to the bargaining table through bombing involved the April to August 1972 Linebacker offensive. Linebacker proved extremely successful: more than 70 percent of enemy tanks were destroyed or damaged by tactical aircraft and gunships, and by August, allied air power had virtually eliminated any armored capability in the North.[169] Linebacker II, unleashed in December after Hanoi had grown intransigent, consisted of an eleven-day bombing. According to one analyst of air power, "the effect of the . . . campaign on Hanoi's ability to resist was crushing. In what now stands as another preview of the functional effects achieved by allied air power two decades later in Desert Storm, the rail system around Hanoi was attacked with such persistence and intensity that poststrike reconnaissance showed that repair crews were making no effort to restore even token rail traffic."[170] Another source concluded that North Vietnam was "laid open for terminal destruction."[171] POWs in Hanoi confirmed that the North Vietnamese were nearly on the verge of collapse during the bombing, a view supported by the British and other foreign ambassadors there.

Even with the bombing pauses, Ho and the communist warlords in the North realized that they could not take much more punishment, and certainly they could not sustain any more "victories" like Tet. Until that time, there is considerable evidence that the North was counting on the antiwar protesters to coerce America into withdrawal, but Nixon had gone over the media's heads in November 1969 in a speech to the "great, silent majority," which was followed by a January 1970 Gallup Poll showing a 65 percent approval rating on his handling of the war. The protesters and their allies in the media had lost decisively and embarrassingly.

Developments in Vietnam always had to be kept in the context of the larger cold war strategy. Neither Kennedy nor Johnson had any long-term plan for dealing with the USSR or China. Nixon was convinced he could make inroads to each, possibly opening up a discussion that could ultimately reduce nuclear weapons and even, he thought, bring pressure to bear on Hanoi. In February 1969, Nixon circulated a memorandum outlining his plans for China, whose relations with the USSR had grown strained. Nixon perceived that the split was an opportunity to play one against the other, and he even cautioned Soviet leaders that the United States would not countenance an invasion of China.[172] Internally, Nixon and Kissinger referred to leverage against Russia as "playing the China card," starting matters off with "ping-pong diplomacy," in which the Chinese entertained the American table tennis team in April 1971. Nixon then shocked the world when, in 1972, he flew to Peking (later, under the new Anglo respelling of the Chinese alphabet, "Beijing"), where foreign minister Zhou Enlai greeted him and a military band struck up "The Star-Spangled Banner."[173]

It was a stunning and important meeting, leading to the phrase "It takes

Nixon to go to China" (meaning that only a conservative anticommunist would have the credentials to deflect attacks that he was selling out). Nixon's visit sent a message in all directions: to America's ally, Taiwan, it was a reality bath. Taiwan realistically had no claim to the hundreds of millions of people on the mainland, but Nixon also made clear he would not abandon the island to the communists. To the USSR, the China card meant that Soviet posturing toward Western Europe was complicated by the necessity of keeping a constant eye toward the East, where massive Chinese armies could overwhelm local defenses. But the entire diplomatic offensive was dropped by Nixon's successors, Gerald Ford and Jimmy Carter, and by the time Ronald Reagan came into office in 1981, time and the death of key players had eroded many of Nixon's gains.

Aside from Vietnam, Nixon had to continue to fight the cold war on a strategic level. That required a commitment to keeping the Soviets' nuclear arsenal safely locked up while offsetting their vastly superior land and tactical air power in the European/NATO theater. The problem here was that the United States had allowed much of its nuclear arsenal to grow outdated, a point Nixon hoped to correct. In 1969, the navy embarked on a study of its submarine force, leading to the funding and construction of state-of-the-art Trident ballistic missile submarines.[174] Independently, the navy, air force, and army had contributed toward developing new low-flying, air-breathing cruise missiles. Independent of those efforts, the United States had researched and started to deploy an antiballistic missile (ABM) defense network around the ICBM bases and Washington, D.C. All of these weapons were hugely expensive, reflecting a half decade's worth of neglect by McNamara and Johnson, and their funding added to the Nixon-era inflation.

When it came to matching weapons with the Soviets, the United States had a significant advantage in its capitalist agricultural system. The USSR was chronically short of food, which made it possible (when combined with the China card) for Nixon to follow up his China visit with a historic trip to the Soviet Union. Ushering in a new détente, or easing of tensions, between the two superpowers, Nixon met with Soviet Premier Leonid Brezhnev, promising the sale of $1 billion worth of grain. In return, Brezhnev quietly scaled down Soviet support for some terrorist activities. More important, though, the two countries hammered out an arms control treaty called SALT I (Strategic Arms Limitations Talks), signed in May 1972. Lacking the sophistication of American technology, Soviet military planners counted on sheer force and overwhelming numbers. Any launch of a nuclear attack against the United States had to be massive in order to destroy all U.S. bombers on the ground and knock out as many submarines as possible. But the development of ABM technology threatened to erase the Soviets' lead in pure numbers. Defensive weapons, which were far cheaper than the heavy nuclear missiles they would target, could offset many times their actual number because the launchers were reusable and the antimissile missiles plentiful.

Here was an area where the United States had a decisive technological and moral lead, but the SALT I treaty gave it away, getting little in return. No limits were placed on Soviet launcher numbers, or on sub-launched ballistic missiles, or bombers. The military, already seeing the USSR rapidly catching up in quality, and having watched the president bargain away a critical technological advantage, found itself preparing to defend the country with increasingly obsolete weapons. Nevertheless, Nixon had done what Truman, Eisenhower, Kennedy, and Johnson had not: he had negotiated deals with America's two archenemies and managed, at some level, to control further proliferation of nuclear weapons. For that, and many other reasons, Nixon was poised to coast to a reelection against a pitifully weak opponent. And at that moment, his insecurities triumphed.

America's Second Constitutional Crisis

Realizing they could not beat the United States as long as Nixon remained in the presidency, the North Vietnamese boldly sought to influence the November elections by convincing Americans of the hopelessness of their cause. On March 20, 1972, after Nixon had gone on television to lay out the history of months of secret—but so far, fruitless—negotiations with the communists, more than 120,000 North Vietnamese troops poured across the demilitarized zone into South Vietnam in a last-ditch desperate invasion. Supported by Soviet-made armor and artillery, the communists encountered the new ARVNs. Despite the initial surprise of the offensive, the troops from the South shocked Ho's forces by their cohesion, courage, and tenacity. Facing heavy use of enemy armor for the first time, the ARVNs held their ground, losing control of only one provincial capital. Nixon unleashed U.S. air power to shatter shipping and to resupply, and the offensive sputtered. Accurate numbers are hard to come by, but the communists lost between one fourth and one half of their entire invading force—staggering losses, again, for such a tiny country.

But the attack failed to achieve the communists' goals in the election. The Democratic front-runner, South Dakota senator George McGovern, promised a unilateral withdrawal if elected. As the favorite of the media and easily the most liberal candidate in history to run for president from either of the two parties, McGovern supported the legalization of marijuana and promised every American family an income floor of $10,000 from Uncle Sam. He had no plan for extracting the prisoners of war from North Vietnam, other than to just "ask" for their return. He alienated the Democratic Party's southern base, the union hard hats, and the social conservatives, but he thrilled the eastern elites.

Nixon crushed McGovern in November, sweeping all but 17 electoral votes and winning nearly 61 percent of the popular vote (including 56 percent of the blue-collar ballots). The press was outraged. One editor said, "We've got to make sure nobody even thinks of doing anything like this again," referring to Nixon's overwhelming victory over a full-blown liberal.[175] Film critic of *The New Yorker* magazine, Pauline Kael, reflected the elitism that pervaded much of the media when she said, "I can't believe it! I don't know a single person who voted for him!"[176] Nixon's affirmation by the public ended North Vietnam's hopes of using American public opinion to force an end to the conflict on the communists' terms.

Out of options, consequently, on January 23, 1973, Le Duc Tho of North Vietnam signed an agreement with U.S. Secretary of State William Rogers ending the war. Nixon made clear his intention of keeping U.S. warships in Southeast Asia and of using American air power stationed in Thailand or the Philippines to maintain the peace. The North promised to return all American POWs. Like any such agreement, it largely hinged on Nixon's willingness and ability to enforce it. For all intents and purposes, America's longest war was over, having cost 46,572 battle deaths and another 300,000 wounded, as well as consuming $165 billion.

Having won every major military encounter in the war, American armed forces withdrew and Vietnamized the war, as had been the intention since Kennedy. Vietnamization, however, worked only as long as the U.S. Congress and the American president remained committed to supporting South Vietnam with aid. In the wake of Nixon's resignation, however, Vietnam could no longer count on the president, and shortly thereafter Congress pulled the plug on further assistance, dooming the free government in the South. In the immediate term, Nixon had fulfilled his promise of withdrawing the American forces from Vietnam, but the media (and most historians) portrayed the war—which, up to that point, was a victory—as a loss.

There was little time for Nixon to enjoy this substantial achievement. Ever since the release of the Pentagon Papers, the Nixon White House had been obsessed with leaks and internal security. "Paranoid" might even describe the state of mind at 1600 Pennsylvania Avenue. Having special staff to dig up dirt on enemies and pester opponents was nothing new to the presidency. Franklin Roosevelt had had an "intelligence unit" supported by a State Department slush fund; Kennedy's questionable (if not illegal) contacts with the Mafia are well documented. Phone tapping had increased under both the Kennedy and Johnson administrations, as had bugging of suspects' hotel rooms and offices. Martin Luther King Jr. was one of the targets of the FBI's extensive bugging campaigns. Lyndon Johnson bugged Goldwater's campaign offices in 1964, and nothing was done about it. The press laughed it off.

There was a widespread (and realistic) view within the administration that the press was out to get Nixon. Nixon genuinely believed, though, that the security of the United States was at risk; thus he had approved the creation before the 1972 campaign of a "special investigations" unit (also known as the dirty tricks group or the plumbers [plumbers fix leaks]). Whatever delusions Nixon operated under, he nevertheless had convinced himself that attacks on his administration threatened the Constitution.

The plumbers broke into the Watergate building in Washington, D.C., in May 1972 and again on June 17. Even today it is unclear what their objective was. They were led by G. Gordon Liddy, a former attorney, prosecutor, and military officer, but there remains a controversy over who in fact issued the orders to the plumbers. At the time, most reporters took it on faith that the purpose of the break-in was to smear McGovern in some way. However, subsequent evidence has suggested—and a trial involving Liddy has confirmed—that the mastermind behind the break-in was Nixon's White House counsel, John Dean.[177] Authors Len Colodny and Robert Gettlin contend that the name of Dean's then-girl-friend, Maureen, was connected to a call-girl ring and that Dean dispatched the plumbers with cameras to photograph the key address book that would, or would not, prove her involvement. Several subsequent trials involving Liddy have sustained these allegations.[178]

At any rate, a security guard suspected a problem and called the police. Several burglars were arrested, including several Cubans hired by Liddy for the operation. A grand jury later indicted Liddy, E. Howard Hunt (Liddy's contact man in the break-in), and some other minor players, including some of the Cubans. Liddy, coming before an anti-Nixon judge, "Maximum" John Sirica, refused to talk, and was given the maximum: five years in prison and a massive fine for a first-time breaking and entering, all to intimidate the other defendants and the White House.

The Democratic congress, smelling Nixon's blood in the water, started investigations. A special prosecutor, Archibald Cox, of Harvard Law School, was appointed with immense powers to investigate the president, acquire evidence, and subpoena witnesses. With a staff of two hundred, and the full support of the anti-Nixon media (which could plant selective stories and generate rumors), the special prosecutor became a tool of the Democrats. In fact, the Constitution intended no such role for a special prosecutor, and expected partisan give and take. Indeed, the entire process of impeachment was *designed* as a form of political combat.

Dean informed Nixon about the break-in after the fact, misled him about its purposes, and convinced him that the plumbers' efforts had national security implications, thereby persuading Nixon to obstruct justice. Ordering the CIA to instruct the FBI, investigating the crime at the time, to abandon the case, Nixon broke the very laws he had sworn to uphold, and all over a break-in of which he had had no prior knowledge. He then compounded his guilt in the matter by not demanding that Dean resign immediately, by failing to open his files to the FBI, and by refusing to genuinely cooperate with the investigation. Instead, Nixon attempted a tactic that would twenty years later serve Bill Clinton quite well, telling his aides regarding the congressional investigations: "Give 'em an *hors d'oeuvre* and maybe they won't come back for the main course."[179] This worked for Clinton because he had the media on his side, but Nixon faced a bitterly hostile press. Accepting the resignations of Bob Haldeman, John Erlichman (another of those with knowledge of the dirty tricks), and Richard Kleindienst, and firing Dean in April 1973, scarcely did anything to quell the inquiries.

Congressional testimony, on July 13, 1973, revealed that all of the working conversations in the Oval Office were tape recorded. If there was a smoking gun implicating Nixon, lawmakers might be able find it. Paradoxically, Nixon had ordered the original taping system, which Johnson had installed, taken out, only to have replaced it later when he grew concerned that his Vietnam policies might be misrepresented.

A massive battle over the tapes and/or transcriptions of the tapes ensued, with Nixon claiming executive privilege and the Congress demanding access. The courts sided with Congress after a prolonged battle. On October 30, 1973, rather than surrender the tapes, Nixon fired the special prosecutor, Archibald Cox. He had first ordered the attorney general, Elliot Richardson, to sack Cox, but Richardson refused and then resigned. Then the deputy attorney general, William Ruckelshaus, refused to fire Cox, and also resigned. This Saturday Night Massacre produced outrage in Congress and glee in the media, which now had Nixon on the ropes. A grand jury indicted Nixon's close associates Chuck Colson, Haldeman, Erlichman, and the physically ailing former attorney general John Mitchell in hopes of obtaining evidence on Nixon himself, none of which was forthcoming.

Aware that he had no support in Congress or the media, Nixon tried one last appeal—to the American people. In a televised speech Nixon looked into the camera and said, "I am not a crook," but the public abandoned him.[180] An ABC poll conducted within days of the speech found that almost 60 percent of Americans did not believe "much of what the president says these days."[181]

The House of Representatives then voted overwhelmingly to conduct an impeachment investigation. The Judiciary Committee, which would handle the case against Nixon, was dominated by Democrats (21 to 17). But possibly the most dangerous foe was a man on the committee staff named John Doar, a liberal Republican, who despised Nixon and planned to "deluge the committee in a blizzard of documentation [while working] with a few select members of the team . . . to make sure that they reached the only acceptable objective, the removal of Richard Nixon from the White House."[182] Doar empowered a young lawyer, Hillary Rodham, to explore the history of impeachment, specifically to find a loophole around the "high crimes and misdemeanors" phrase so that the committee could impeach Nixon over the bombing of Cambodia. She soon fed Doar a stream of position papers, arguing against limiting the investigation to criminal offenses as contrary to the will of the framers of the Constitution—a stunning recommendation, given that twenty years later, her husband and his advocates would be arguing just the *opposite,* that *only* "criminal" offenses could be grounds for impeachment.[183]

Hillary Rodham's zealotry was unnecessary. Doing the math, Nixon knew that 18 of the Democrats would vote for articles of impeachment no matter what the evidence. All 21 did. Article II charged him with illegally using the powers of the executive, using the Internal Revenue Service to harass citizens, using the FBI to violate the constitutional rights of opponents, and knowing about—but taking no steps to prevent—obstruction of justice by his subordinates.[184] Unlike Bill Clinton, twenty years later, who had a Senate disinclined to depose him, Nixon lacked a block of Senate support. To make matters worse, Nixon's vice president, Spiro Agnew, had resigned in October 1973 after being indicted for bribery (while governor of Maryland) and after copping a plea to one charge of tax evasion.[185] To replace Agnew, Nixon had appointed Michigan Congressman Gerald Ford, a moderate of the Rockefeller wing of the GOP and a person sure to draw little criticism from Democrats.

With the Middle East in turmoil, oil prices rose sharply in 1973. Inflation soared, and the economy—Nixon's one hope of holding out against Congress—went into the tank. The House, preparing to vote on articles impeaching Nixon, was invested under the Constitution with the *sole* duty of establishing whether or not the actions constituted "high crimes" and whether they, in fact, violated the Constitution. If the House voted in favor of the articles (as it clearly would, in Nixon's case), the Senate would conduct a trial (requiring a two-thirds vote to convict) supposedly based *solely* on guilt or innocence of the charges, not on the seriousness of the charge. Key Senate Republicans, including Barry Goldwater and Howard Baker, told Nixon that many Republican senators were going to cross the aisle to vote against a Republican president.[186] Out of options, Nixon resigned on August 9, 1974, and Gerald Ford immediately became president. One month later, Ford issued a full and complete pardon for Richard Nixon. By then, Nixon had reached the apex as the liberals' most hated target in America.

Richard Milhous Nixon made one last comeback. Over the years his reputation abroad and his firmness and flexibility in dealing with the Soviets and Chinese had made him a valuable resource for world leaders. He wrote books, gaining a reputation that might leave some to think that the Richard Nixon of August 9, 1974, and the Nixon of April 22, 1994, the day he died and drew praise from a throng of world leaders and past presidents, were two different people.

More than a few Washington analysts have suggested that the honor given Nixon at his funeral stuck in the craw of others who had held the highest office, including Jimmy Carter and Bill Clinton, both of whom had expended considerable effort on their own legacies. After a monstrously failed presidency, Carter became a regular on the international peace circuit, finally winning the Nobel Peace Prize in 2002. Clinton, both during and after his presidency, deliberately shaped his policies and even specific actions with an eye toward how history would remember him. It was high irony indeed that by the time of his death, Richard Nixon had achieved broad-based respect that he had never enjoyed in life—and that he had lived long enough to make sure that five living American presidents attended his funeral and, even if unwillingly, paid homage to him.

CHAPTER TWENTY

Retreat and Resurrection, 1974–88

Malaise and Recovery

Having endured one of the most socially destructive decades in the nation's history, having lost a war for the first time, followed by the humiliation of a president's resignation, the United States arguably was at its lowest ebb ever in 1974. Births out of wedlock increased at epidemic levels, the economy stood on a precipice, and leadership was nowhere to be found—politically, morally, or culturally. Other civilizations had fallen from a golden age into the depths of tyranny and decline in a few years. Would the United States of America?

The constitutional crisis the United States had just weathered would have extracted a painful toll without any other new pressures. But war, hatred, and conflict never take a vacation. As world leader, the United States found itself continually involved in hot spots around the globe. Not only did the communist bloc sense America's weakness, but so did a wide range of minor foreign enemies, including small states that saw opportunities for mischief they otherwise would not have considered. As always—at least since the 1920s—the single person upon whom much of the world looked for a sign of American resolve and strength was the president of the United States.

Time Line

1973–75: OPEC raises oil prices; oil crisis

1974: Gerald Ford becomes president after Richard Nixon resigns; War Powers Act passed by Congress; busing battles begin in Boston

1975: Vietnam overrun by North Vietnamese; Communist Pol Pot regime overruns Cambodia; BASIC computer language invented by Bill Gates

1976: Jimmy Carter elected president; Steve Jobs and Steve Wozniak market first personal computers

1979: Camp David Accords; Iranians storm U.S. embassy in Tehran, take American hostages

1980: Soviets invade Afghanistan; U.S. Olympic ice hockey team wins the gold medal; Ronald Reagan elected president

1981: Reagan fires air traffic controllers; Reagan shot, nearly killed by John Hinckley; Congress passes Reaganomics tax cuts; Iranian hostages freed

1983: Economic recovery begins; "Star Wars" speech; marine barracks in Lebanon blown up; Soviets put short-range missiles in western USSR aimed at Europe

1985: Geneva conference with Reagan and Gorbachev

1986: Reagan and British prime minister Margaret Thatcher announce plan to install short-range missiles in Europe in response to Soviet SS-20s; "freeze movement" gains momentum

1986–87: Iran-contra affair

1987: Intermediate Nuclear Forces Treaty signed

Gerald Ford, Caretaker

Not many people wanted the job Gerald Ford inherited when Richard Nixon climbed aboard the official helicopter that took him into political exile on August 9, 1974. Ford immediately and seamlessly, under the terms of constitutional succession, moved into the Oval Office, as had Lyndon Johnson just over a decade earlier.

Nixon selected Gerald Ford in the wake of the Agnew scandal precisely because of Ford's milquetoast personality. A former star football player at the University of Michigan, Ford displayed little of the ferocity or tenacity in politics that was demanded on the gridiron. A lieutenant commander in the navy, Ford had returned to civilian life to win a seat in the U.S. Congress, which he held for more than twenty years. His congressional career featured service on the controversial Warren Commission that had blamed the JFK assassination on Lee Harvey Oswald.[1] He advanced to the position of minority leader, but he surrendered ground willingly and posed no obstacle to the Democratic majority. Ford struck many people as possessing only mediocre intelligence—Johnson said he was "so dumb he can't fart and chew gum at the same time"—and he was notoriously clumsy because of an inner ear condition.[2] This malady made him a target for every comedian on television, most notably Chevy Chase, whose *Saturday Night Live* skits featured the president stumbling and smacking people with golf balls.

Nevertheless, Ford had several attractive qualities, not the least of which was his personal honesty, a trait virtually no one doubted. After the lies of the previous fourteen years, the nation, like Diogenes, was seeking an honest man. And after a decade of turmoil, Ford's bland personality provided much-needed relief from the intensity of a Nixon or the egomania of a Johnson. Once in the presidency, Ford's unconfrontational nature ironically left him with few allies. Some conservatives abandoned the GOP, leaving the amiable Ford as alone politically in the White

House as his predecessor. He also offended those out for Nixon's scalp by pardoning Nixon for "any and all crimes" on September 8, 1974. Since Nixon had not been indicted for any crimes, not only did this prevent the attack dogs in Congress from continuing their harassment of the former president in private life, but it also took Nixon off the front pages of the newspapers. Most of all, it denied the media a chance to gloat over what journalists saw as "their" victory over Nixon.

Later, when commenting candidly about the Nixon pardon, Ford explained that he was stunned at the amount of legal work that he, the new president, would have had to participate in if any cases against Nixon went forward. The subpoenas for documentation alone, he noted, would have absorbed all of his staff's time, and he could not spend 99 percent of *his* time on the affairs of one man. Critics, of course, claimed that Nixon had brought Ford in as a quid pro quo, that knowing his own resignation was imminent, Nixon protected himself with a pardon deal. Such a scenario fits neither Ford's personality nor Nixon's own perceptions of the state of things when he had chosen the vice president.

None of Nixon's associates received pardons. By 1975, almost forty administration officials had been named in criminal indictments, including John Mitchell, John Erlichman, H. R. Haldeman, and G. Gordon Liddy. Charges included violations normally associated with the mob: fraud, extortion, illegal wiretapping, destruction of evidence, and obstruction of justice.[3] It was a record for corruption and criminality that exceeded everything in the past, with the exception, perhaps, of Grant's administration. Ford and Congress slowly uncovered violations of practice and law by both the FBI and the CIA, with the latter organization coming under new restrictions in 1974 that would subsequently prove short-sighted and, indeed, deadly. Meanwhile, public confidence in the office of the presidency had plummeted: a poll of that year revealed that more than 40 percent had "hardly any" confidence in the executive branch of government.[4]

North Vietnam immediately sensed a vacuum in American leadership. Already Congress had chipped away at the powers aggrandized by Kennedy, Johnson, then Nixon, and indeed all three presidents had overstepped their constitutional bounds. Congress placed several limitations on the executive, including the Jackson-Vanik and Stevenson Amendments of 1973–74, the Arms Export Control Act of 1975, and most important, the War Powers Act of 1974. The latter required a president to notify Congress within forty-eight hours if troops were dispatched overseas, and it allowed a window of only sixty days for those troops to continue operations without congressional ratification. These restrictions rightly attempted to redress the imbalance that had accumulated during fourteen years, but in many cases the laws hamstrung legitimate actions by presidents to deal with incidents long before they became major conflicts.

Congress also sought to seal its victory over the presidency through the budget process. Staff numbers exploded, and the House International Relations Committee staff tripled between 1971 and 1977. Overall, the ratio of unelected officials in Washington to elected representatives reached a stunning 5,400:1.

Worse, it put Congress in the driver's seat over Vietnam policy. Congress had already slashed military aid to South Vietnam. Once the North realized that Ford either could not or would not revive a bombing campaign, the South was ripe for a new invasion, which occurred in January 1975. ARVN forces evacuated northern provinces and within a matter of weeks, the communists surrounded Saigon. News footage showed American helicopters lifting off with U.S. citizens as helpless Vietnamese were kept off the choppers at gunpoint. Those images did not move Congress, where lawmakers repeatedly denied or ignored Ford's urgent requests to act. More than a hundred thousand Vietnamese "boat people," desperate to escape communism, took to the seas and suffered at the hands of pirates and the elements. Eventually, thousands of these Vietnamese immigrated to such far-flung locations as Los Angeles and Galveston, where they reestablished themselves to dominate the artificial fingernail businesses in the former (more than 50 percent of all nail salons were Vietnamese owned) and the fishing trade in the latter. They were fortunate. Of those who remained behind, more than a million were killed by the communist invaders during "reeducation" programs.

Dwight Eisenhower, lampooned by critics for espousing the domino theory, suddenly seemed sagacious. No sooner had the last Americans left Vietnam than a new communist offensive was under way in Cambodia. After the communist Khmer Rouge organization under Pol Pot conquered the country in April 1975, it embarked on a social reconstruction of the country unmatched even by Mao Tse-tung's indoctrination camps. More than 3.5 million people were forced out of cities into the countryside while communists rampaged through towns throwing every book they could find into the Mekong River. Sexual relations were forbidden, and married people could not talk to each other for extended periods of time. In mass public executions, entire families died together in the city squares. Although the western media ignored the developments, statistics eventually found their way into print. Almost 1.2 million Cambodians, or one fifth of the total population, were slaughtered in the "killing fields."[5]

Laos, it should be noted, had already fallen. By the end of the 1970s, the only domino left was Thailand, and it certainly would have collapsed next if Soviet support of the North Vietnamese had not suddenly dried up. But in 1979, North Vietnam broke with the Cambodian communist government, reinvaded Cambodia, and united it with the North Vietnamese dictatorship.

Middle East Instability, Economic Crisis

On top of the collapse of Vietnam, the erosion of American credibility internationally also harmed the nation's ability to maintain order in other Middle Eastern countries, with severe consequences for the economy. Understanding the events in the Middle East requires a review of the creation of the state of Israel in 1947. Following the revelations of the Holocaust, the European Jewish community revived demands for a Jewish state located in Palestine. In the Balfour Declaration, the British (who had governed the region after World War I through a mandate from the League of Nations after the partition of the Ottoman Empire) promised the World Zionist Organization a Jewish home in the traditional lands established in the Bible. Unfortunately, the British had also secretly guaranteed the Arabs the same land in return for an Arab uprising against the Turks. During the interwar period, the British curtailed Jewish migration to the region, which remained under the local control of Arab mufti.

For centuries, Jews in Europe had attempted to blend in, adopting local customs and languages and participating in the economic and political life of the European nations. Despite frequent and consistent anti-Jewish purges in almost every European country, the Jews remained optimistic they would be protected by democratic governments. Hitler changed all that. Jews concluded that no nation would ever protect them, and that their only hope of survival was through an independent Jewish state. Some European leaders agreed, and after the evidence of the Holocaust surfaced, Britain especially loosened immigration restrictions into Palestine.[6]

In America, a large, successful Jewish community had come into its own in the twentieth century. Roosevelt was the first to tap into the Jewish vote, which could swing such states as Illinois and New York.[7] Chaim Weizmann of the World Zionist Organization, after encouraging words from British (and Jewish) leader David Ben-Gurion, appreciated the political pressure 5 million Jewish voters could bring, directly targeting American Jewish support after 1942.

Harry Truman played a key role in the formation of Israel. Roosevelt's State Department opposed the plan, but Truman distrusted the "striped-pants boys" as he called them. Thus, when the newly formed United Nations General Assembly voted for the formation of a Jewish and an Arab state in territory formerly under the British mandate, it marked one of the rare times in the entire history of the United Nations that its membership substantially agreed with the American position. It is inconceivable that the tiny nation could have appeared at any other moment. Certainly, after 1947 the Soviets never would have permitted it, nor, of course, would the Arabs. Britain backed the plan only to the extent that it relieved the empire of her "Jewish problem." Except for Truman, American leaders opposed the formation of Israel. Secretary of the Navy James Forrestal complained that Jews exercised an undue influence over American policy. When Israel declared its independence on May 14, 1948, Truman quickly accorded her diplomatic recognition over the protests of the State Department and the Pentagon.

Israel's formation proved a watershed event for American goals, such as they were, in the Middle East, and it tied the two countries together for the remainder of the twentieth century. It permanently placed the United States in the unenviable position of having to referee two implacable foes. As soon as the UN partition scheme was pushed through, war broke out, mainly led by Egypt, but with elements of the Syrian, Jordanian, Iraqi, Lebanese, and Palestinian armies outnumbering the 20,000-man Israeli defense forces. Against all expectations, it was the Arab forces that suffered a humiliating defeat, and Israel secured her existence for a time. Although the United States had done little aside from recognizing the state of Israel, suddenly Truman (and soon, his successors) had to balance support for the only genuine democracy in the entire Middle East, Israel, against the abundant Arab oil supplies discovered in the region.

The United States had followed Britain into the Middle Eastern oil fields in 1924, with the American share of oil pumped from the desert growing steadily from one sixth of the total in 1936 to more than half by the end of World War II. Most of the crude came from Saudi Arabia, but there was oil everywhere, leading the head of the U.S. Petroleum Commission to refer to the Middle East as the "center of gravity of world oil production."[8] America's dependence on foreign oil or, better phrased, *Detroit's* dependence, became more acute during the next round of Arab-Jewish conflicts in 1956 with the Suez Crisis. As with the two wars that followed it, this struggle only marked a continuation of the unresolved hostilities lingering from the 1947–48 Arab-Israeli war.

In May 1967, Egypt and her Arab allies were ready to try again to evict Israel. After ejecting the UN peacekeepers, Egyptian President Abdel Gamal Nasser stated on Cairo Radio that the offensive was to be a "mortal blow of annihilation," and it was his intention to "wipe Israel off the map."[9] Again, Israel did not wait to be overwhelmed by the forces concentrating on her borders, but, as in 1956, launched air strikes that decimated Arab air power, thus exposing invading tank columns to merciless bombardment from the skies. The war lasted only six days, allowing Israel to capture the Golan Heights near Galilee, the Sinai, and the West Bank—all parts of the biblical boundaries promised the Jews. Yet even after smashing Arab military forces and unifying Jerusalem under Jewish control for the first time since A.D. 70, the Israeli victory did not produce a lasting peace.

Nasser's successor, Anwar Sadat, quickly rebuilt the Egyptian military and organized yet another invasion in 1973. Striking on Yom Kippur, the holiest of Jewish religious observance days, Sadat's well-coordinated attack this time attained success. Supplied by the Soviets, the Arab armies offset the Israeli advantages in the skies, knocking out 20 percent of Israel's planes in four days. Tel Aviv was in panic. Israeli (and American-born) Prime Minister Golda Meir persuaded Nixon to provide an emergency airlift of arms, which provided the logistics for a Jewish counterattack after days of absorbing blows. America's airlift was reminiscent of the Berlin effort, covering 6,400 miles per day and delivering thousands of tons of supplies. In his darkest hour Nixon, alone, virtually saved Israel.

Within a short period the Israeli counterattack routed the Arab armies. The Soviets, responding to Sadat's request for aid, threatened to enter the conflict. By that time, Nixon was spending virtually all his time combating the Watergate investigators and editing tapes. He deployed Kissinger to respond to the Soviet threat; and in an unprecedented occurrence, Kissinger, not Nixon, issued the orders for American military units to go on full-scale, worldwide alert—the first time since JFK had issued similar orders in 1962. Watergate had by then engulfed and distracted the president to the point where he could not conduct international negotiations.

The combatants brokered another truce, but this time the United States paid a heavy price for its involvement. In October 1973 the Organization of Petroleum

Exporting Countries (OPEC), which represented virtually all of the Muslim oil-producing nations, cut production of oil and boosted prices 70 percent. Two months later OPEC jacked up prices another 128 percent. Gasoline and home heating oil prices in the United States soared, to which Nixon, the born-again Keynesian, responded by imposing a price ceiling on oil. This made gasoline artificially cheap. Americans knew what gas was really worth, but the government had just encouraged them to act as though it cost a fraction of what it really did. Demand shot up; supply remained low, but prices were fixed. Available stores of oil disappeared as fast as people could pump the cheap gas into their cars. An incredible spectacle ensued of car lines at gas stations—sometimes reaching completely around city blocks—to purchase the scarce, yet still cheap, fuel. State governments instituted an array of gimmicks to limit consumption, including setting up an even-odd license-plate-number purchase system. None of it worked. The wealthiest nation in the world slowed to a crawl because the government had artificially lowered fuel prices.

The high cost of energy, in turn, sent price shocks throughout industry and commerce. Sugar, which cost 13 cents in 1970, had risen to 33 cents by 1974. Flour, at 11 cents per pound in 1970, had nearly doubled to 20 cents four years later. Steaks that had cost $1.54 per pound rose to $2.12 per pound in 1974. Stereos priced at $119 in 1970 rose to more than $154 in 1974, and a man's shirt rose more than 30 percent in price.[10] All consumers, not just drivers, were hurt by the government's flawed policies.

That did not stop Congress from getting into the act and setting the speed limit on federal highways at 55 miles per hour, a pace that was unrealistic for the vastness of places like Texas or Nevada, and one that often caused auto engines to operate at less than peak efficiency (thus burning more gas!). At the same time, Congress also established fuel-efficiency standards for all new cars, known as the CAFE regulations, which conflicted directly with the environmental pollution restrictions that lawmakers had earlier placed on automakers. Auto manufacturers responded by adopting lighter materials, such as aluminum and fiberglass, which proved less safe in the event of accidents. Gas mileage went up, but so did highway fatalities, even at slower speeds.

The blizzard of rules and regulations only displayed the utter incapability of the government to manage market-related issues. For example, to make cars safer, in 1966 the government implemented the National Traffic Motor Vehicle Safety Act—partly in response to Ralph Nader's *Unsafe at Any Speed*—requiring automakers to install as standard equipment seat belts, impact-absorbing steering columns, and padded dashboards.[11] These additions all drove up weight, which reduced gas mileage! Rather than trust consumers at the showroom to determine which "values" or characteristics were most important to them (good fuel economy, safety, or environment-friendly features), the government had created battling bureaus, each with its own budget justifications, lobbying against each other for funding.

In 1970 the Environmental Protection Agency decreed that auto companies had to reduce emissions to 10 percent of existing levels by 1976. Language contained in this bill, however, only affected autos made after 1970, by which time emissions in new cars had already been reduced from 70 to 80 percent. Thus, the new law required the existing autos to *further reduce* emissions (on the remaining 20 to 30 percent) by 90 percent, to a total emissions percentage of 3 percent! Achieving the last few percent of performance of anything is nearly impossible, and the man who coined the term "smog" referred to the EPA air quality standards as "absurd."[12]

Detroit had no choice but to comply. GM introduced the catalytic converter, which only worked with unleaded gasoline (the tetraethyl lead had been removed). This, in turn, entailed a sizable drop-off in power, but made for longer-lasting engines. To compensate for the power drop-off, automakers looked to professional racing for ideas, souping up engines with overhead camshafts, turbochargers, fuel injection, and a host of other high-performance equipment that soon became standard on passenger cars. But the entire process of regulating, then powering up, was the equivalent of adding a small anchor to a boat, then installing the extra engines to overcome the drag!

Fuel efficiency, of course, is desirable *if* the market determines that it is a more important use of scarce resources than, say, cost or safety. When the United States had limitless forests, colonists burned trees at record levels because they were cheap. Whale oil was only replaced as interior illumination when it got more expensive than John D. Rockefeller's kerosene. Thus, when it came to the "oil crisis," without the government interference, one fact is undeniable: in 1973 and 1974, American gasoline prices would have risen dramatically, and that, in turn, would have forced down auto use and/or caused consumers themselves to demand more fuel-efficient cars. Based on the evidence of history, these changes would have occurred sooner without Nixon's actions.

Honey, I Shrank the Economy!

Even though prices were controlled at the pump, Americans felt the oil price hikes ripple through the entire economy, via the industrial sector which had no government protection. This drove up the cost of production, forcing layoffs, pushing the United States into a steep recession. Unemployment rose to 8.5 percent in 1975—a postwar high—and the gross domestic product (GDP) fell in both 1974 and 1975. The oil-related recession cost the United States as much as 5 percent of its prehike gross national product (GNP), or a level *five times greater* than the cumulative impact of the Navigation Acts that had "started" the American Revolution.

Great Society spending and layers of federal regulations made matters worse. Some states and cities suffered even more than the nation as a whole. New York's liberal spending policies swung the city into bankruptcy, and the mayor asked for a federal bailout. New Yorkers had voted themselves into their problems, then looked to taxpayers from Colorado and Rhode Island to dig them out. President Ford, however, courageously promised to veto any federal bailout of the Big Apple.

A local newspaper, with typical New York attitude, ran the headline, FORD TO NEW YORK: DROP DEAD![13] In fact, Ford's decision not to reward the city for financial malfeasance was exactly the appropriate constitutional response. Left to their own devices, New Yorkers worked their city back into the black.

In almost every area of American life, the federal government had already done quite enough. Whether through the EPA, OSHA, the Consumer Products Safety Commission, or myriad other new agencies, government at all levels had started to heap voluminous oppressive regulations on business. In 1975 alone, 177 proposed "new rules appeared, as did 2,865 proposed amendments, for a total of 10,656 new and proposed rules and amendments, most of which applied to nearly all firms."[14] According to one study, environmental regulations enacted prior to 1990 by themselves—not including the 1970 Clean Air Act, the single largest antipollution law—reduced the GNP by 2.5 percent.[15] Activists such as Ralph Nader and the environmentalists expected the "evil" corporations to simply absorb the costs (never expressing concern about the average people who had invested in such businesses to provide funds for a new home or a college education for the children).

Companies, of course, did not just passively accept the new costly regulations. Instead, American business battled the government on three fronts, increasing spending for lobbyists in Congress, fighting the new rules in the judicial system and in the court of public opinion, and passing along the costs of the regulations to the consumers. Not surprisingly, the pages in the Federal Register, which contained these rules, ballooned from 10,286 in 1950 to 61,000 in 1978, and at the same time, the numbers of attorneys in the United States rose by 52 percent in a ten-year period. More important, district court cases grew 131 percent and U.S. appeals court civil cases, where product liability cases more likely occurred, exploded by 398 percent.[16] Predictably, corporations spent more on their legal divisions, while spending on research and development—the lifeblood of new products—consistently fell. There simply was not enough money to fund both lawyers and scientists.[17] Every dollar spent to influence a lawmaker or run consumer-friendly ads was a dollar not spent on developing better and safer products or reducing the costs of existing goods. By 1980, America had four times as many attorneys, per capita, as Germany and twenty times more per capita than Japan, both of which had surged ahead of the United States in productivity, the key indicator of real economic growth.[18]

Meanwhile, big business was working against itself by avoiding change and innovation the way dogs resist baths. Significantly, not one of the top fifty technological changes in twentieth-century America came from established leaders in the field.[19] IBM did not create the personal computer, nor did the calculator giant of IBM's day, the slide-rule company Keuffel, create the punch-card computer. Airplanes sprang from the minds of bicycle mechanics and word-processing programs from the scribblings of college dropouts. Cellular phones were not developed by AT&T or even the famous Bell Labs.[20]

Stability had served industry well when the United States passed some of the other fading economic powers, then easily perpetuated growth during the post-war decade when there was little competition. But then complacency set in. Once the Japanese and Germans reentered world markets, U.S. companies lacked the competitive edge that had served them well half a century earlier. Afraid of rapid change, corporations introduced only marginal improvements. Automakers for almost two decades thought that merely by tweaking a body style or introducing minor interior comforts they could compete with dramatic changes in actual auto design from Japan. Japanese carmakers had struggled for ten years to adapt their vehicles to American roads and to larger American physiques, so when oil prices suddenly placed greater value on smaller front-wheel-drive, fuel-efficient cars, Honda, Nissan, and Toyota were more than ready. To their discredit, American auto executives continued to denigrate foreign innovations. It took a bankrupt Chrysler Corporation, under Lee Iacocca—the brains behind the Ford Mustang—to shock Detroit out of its doldrums. "We were wrong," he courageously announced in one of his televised ads for Chrysler.[21]

New industrial evangelists like Iacocca, even had they been in the majority, constituted only half the equation for turning American business around. Labor, led by the hardscrabble union bosses who had achieved great gains at tremendous cost in the 1950s and 1960s, still acted as though it spoke for a majority of working Americans. By the 1970s, however, the unions were losing members at precipitous rates. Trade unions had formed a critical part of the Democratic Party's New Deal coalition, and the most important organizations—the AFL-CIO and the Teamsters—were able to demand exceptionally high wages for their members in the automobile, steel, and trucking industries. By 1970, a typical line worker in Detroit commanded $22 an hour, owned two cars, a boat, and a vacation home on a lake, or the equivalent of the earnings of a midlevel attorney in 2002. Miners and truckers, as well as those working in manufacturing jobs, had substantially higher incomes than many professionals and received better benefits than people in almost any income category.[22] Unionized employees routinely made between $10,000 and $12,000 per year with overtime. New homes sold for about $23,000, meaning that a worker dedicating 30 percent of his income to a mortgage could own a house in six or seven years, which compared quite closely to a 1990s professional earning a $70,000 salary and supporting a $150,000 mortgage.[23] Equally as valuable as cash, during the salad days of steadily increasing auto sales, auto and steel unions negotiated generous benefit and pension packages, adding to the real value of their contracts. Leaders such as George Meany of the AFL-CIO and Jimmy Hoffa of the Teamsters wielded tremendous influence, not only over the Democratic Party, but also over the nation's economy.

"Big Steel" and the auto companies, of course, did not just absorb these expenses, but passed them on to consumers, which added to inflation. American manufactured products, especially textiles, steel, autos, and electronics, rose in price relative to foreign competition. In steel alone, the cost of labor was six times that of foreign competitors.[24] Sometime in the early 1970s, prices exceeded the threshold that most consumers were willing to pay in order to remain loyal to

American-made products, and buyers began to switch to foreign goods. Recapturing formerly loyal customers is twice as difficult as holding them. Japanese and European manufacturers, who were turning out lower-priced quality goods, gained millions of new American customers in the 1970s. For the first time, "Made in Japan" was not viewed as a sign of cheap, shoddy goods, but as a mark of quality. Foreign competitors increased their steel production by some 700 million net tons, and builders scrambled to replace expensive American steel with fiberglass, aluminum, plastics, ceramics, and concrete.

American steel companies took the biggest hit of all. The industry had seen its international market share fall 20 percent since the Korean War, when U.S. steelmakers claimed 60 percent of the world's sales. Worse, only one new steel plant—a Bethlehem facility in Indiana—was constructed between 1950 and 1970. At the same time, Japan gave birth to fifty-three new integrated steel companies, most of them with brand-new efficient mills, and Japanese assets in steel plants rose 23 percent between 1966 and 1972, compared to an investment in American plants of only 4 percent. The overall output of U.S.-made steel barely changed between 1948 and 1982, leading many steel executives to try to diversify their companies. Layoffs began with the expectation that they would be temporary. Then weeks stretched into months and into years. By 1980, it was clear that after years of sounding unheeded warnings, the wolf had finally come, and the industry would never return to its 1960s peak.[25]

This was the last gasp of organized union power in manufacturing America. From 35 percent of the American workforce in 1960, union membership entered a downward spiral, to 27 percent of the workforce in 1990. That did not tell the whole story, however, because the hard-core industrial unions had plunged even more sharply than the total, which was kept afloat only by the two largest unions in America, the National Education Association (NEA) and the American Federation of State, County, and Municipal Employees (AFSCME). By 1980, AFSCME had twice the membership of the United Steel Workers.[26] Thus, it became eminently clear why organized labor had a commitment to a permanently large and growing government and to public schools: those employees—operating outside the free market—now represented unions' only hope of long-term survival.

The ensuing recession shattered the underlying premises of Keynesian economics once and for all. According to the prevailing Phillips Curve theory, an economy could not have both high unemployment and high inflation at the same time. This stemmed from the notion that inflation resulted from government spending for new jobs. It was all poppycock. The government could not create wealth in the 1970s any more than it could in the 1930s. More accurately, a bizarre expectations game occurred—"taxflation"—wherein businesses sensed that when new government programs were announced, their taxes would go up, and they responded by hiking prices merely in anticipation of the new taxes.

Gerald Ford possessed none of the qualities needed to deal with any aspect of the sinking economy. As a progressive (so called moderate) Republican, he sympathized with much of the Great Society spending. As a caretaker president, he did not possess the public support to force OPEC to increase production or lower prices. And, as a Nixon appointee, he faced a hostile and rogue Congress out to destroy all vestiges of the modern Republican Party much the way the Radical Republicans in Reconstruction had hoped to kill the Democratic Party. All Ford had in his favor was honesty, but his lack of imagination left him helpless in the face of further business declines. Having no desire for tax cuts that might revive the economy—and blocked by a spendthrift Congress that would not enact tax cuts anyway—Ford launched a campaign that was almost comedic in design. He sought to mobilize public support to hold down prices by introducing WIN (Whip Inflation Now) buttons.

The damage done to the American economy by almost a decade of exorbitant social spending, increasing environmental and workplace regulations, and Keynesian policies from the Johnson-Nixon administrations cannot be overstated. Yet just as government almost never gets the credit when economic growth occurs, so too its overall impact on the nation's business health must be tempered with the appreciation for the poor planning and lack of innovation in the corporate sector. All that, combined with the impact of greedy union demands in heavy industry, made any foolish policies of government relatively insignificant. Perhaps worst of all, inflation had eroded earnings, creating new financial pressures for women to work.

Sex, the Church, and the Collapse of Marriage

By the mid-1970s, women's entry into the workforce was being championed by the twentieth-century feminist movement. Armed with the Pill, feminists targeted the seeming lack of fairness in the job market, which punished women for dropping out of the market for several years to have children. But where their rhetoric failed to change corporations, the Pill changed women. By delaying childbirth, the Pill allowed women to enter professional schools in rapidly growing numbers.[27]

Paradoxically, the Pill placed more pressure on women to protect themselves during sex. And rather than liberating women for a career in place of a family, feminism heaped a career *on top of a family.* Women's workloads only grew, and the moral burden on women to resist the advances of males expanded geometrically. Equally ironic, as women entered the workforce in greater numbers, increasing the expectation that young married women would work, the "expectations index" for couples soared. Newlyweds saw larger houses with bigger mortgages and more upscale cars as the norm because, after all, they had two incomes. This created a feedback loop that forced women to remain in the labor force after childbearing, and in many cases, after they wished to leave their jobs outside the home.

With all biological consequences removed from engaging in pre- or extramarital sex, the only barrier remaining was religion. But the church had seen much of its moral authority shattered in the 1960s, when on the one hand, large numbers of white Christians had remained mute during the civil rights struggles, and on the other, liberal-leftist elements in the church had associated themselves with communist dictators. In either case, the church (as many saw it) had allied itself with oppression against liberty.

When it came to sex, traditional Christianity had appeared hypocritical. Wives who dutifully served their families had to deal with alcoholic husbands and domestic abuse. (It is crucial to understand that perception is reality, and while the vast majority of husbands loved and served their wives, the fact that *any* domestic abuse occurred without comment from the local pulpit or a visit from the pastor or priest was unacceptable.) The more traditional and fundamentalist churches that preached against divorce and railed against premarital sex, said little to nothing about spouse or child abuse in their own congregations. At the other extreme, churches attempting to reach out to women and portray themselves as modern opened their pulpits to female ministers but ignored the moral necessity of demanding chastity and commitment from Christians in sexual matters. The former group preached piety and practiced unacceptable toleration of sin, while the latter celebrated its toleration, but ignored holiness.

For all their failures to stand up for women's and civil rights, the hard-line fundamentalist churches nevertheless continued to grow throughout the 1960s and early 1970s, if for no other reason than it was clear they stood for clear and unwavering principles. Liberal Protestant denominations, on the other hand, shrank at shocking rates, despite their new inclusion policies. American Baptists, Disciples of Christ, Episcopalians, Lutherans, Methodists, Presbyterians, and United Church of Christ all lost members from 1960 to 1975. Although people claimed that they stayed home on Sunday because they thought churches were behind the times, those churches most behind the times seemed to thrive.[28] Southern Baptists nearly doubled in numbers of churches between 1958 and 1971. Even more astounding, televangelist Oral Roberts, a charismatic faith healer, reached 2.3 million viewers in a single broadcast, a number that nearly equaled the entire estimated Sunday attendance of *all* the Methodist churches in the nation! When one combined the audiences of the top eight televised ministries during a single broadcast—virtually all of them outside the mainstream—they matched that of the estimated church attendance of the top six denominations combined.[29] Indeed, one scholar, looking at these viewing trends, concluded that the numbers "reveal a previously unmapped dimension of religion in America, a basic fundamentalist orientation that cuts across denominational lines."[30]

Transcending denominational differences went so far as to see Protestants and Catholics beginning to share similar worship experiences. The Roman Catholic Church had modernized with its Vatican II (1962–65) Council, making such changes as having the priest face the congregation for mass (which now was said in English, not Latin). Nevertheless, the Catholic Church at midcentury witnessed a stunning decline, not only in members, but in clergy. American nuns decreased in number by 14,000 in the last half of the sixties, and by 1976,

45,000 priests and nuns had abandoned the cloth. (Among the vanguard order, the Jesuits, recruitment numbers plummeted by 80 percent in the 1990s.) Although American Catholicism revived in the latter part of the twentieth century because of immigration, it still had difficulty attracting young men to its seminaries and women to its convents. A subculture of homosexuality began to permeate the orders, driving out heterosexual men who vowed to remain celibate, creating what was called the "gaying and graying" of the Church. (In 2002, this exploded as a full-scale scandal when several lawsuits were brought against many priests for sexual abuse and pedophilia, threatening to bankrupt the Boston Catholic Church. But the Church claimed to be unaware of these offenses.) One subgroup within the Catholic Church, however, the Catholic Charismatic movement, nevertheless showed strong gains. It did so because it intersected with the Protestant "faith movement" with spiritual expressions such as speaking in tongues, healing, and other supernatural outpourings.

Clearly a major split had occurred in the American church from 1960 to 1975, and it did so rather rapidly. In 1962, for example, some 31 percent of those polled said that religion was losing its influence, almost twice as many as had answered the question affirmatively five years earlier.[31] At nearly the same time, the Federal Communications Commission had begun allowing television and radio stations to use paid programming to fulfill their public service broadcasting requirements. This silenced the mainstream liberal churches, which suddenly found that despite a decade's worth of monopoly over the airwaves, they could no longer generate enough funds to purchase airtime.[32] Instead, the so-called fundamentalist and Pentecostal denominations "dominated the airwaves, having 'honed their skills at the fringes of the industry.' "[33] Indeed, Pentecostal denominations—and even nondenominational congregations led by individual charismatic (in all senses of the word!) leaders—soared in membership. Oral Roberts, the best known of the "faith" ministers, built an entire university and hospital in Tulsa, Oklahoma, and some of his students, such as Kenneth Copeland, or contemporaries, such as Kenneth Hagin, developed powerful healing and "prosperity" ministries.

Traditional churches, of course, despised the charismatics, whose main identifying practice was that of speaking in tongues under the influence of the Holy Spirit. These charismatic churches featured several characteristics that antagonized the mainstream churches: they were racially integrated, they crossed all economic lines, and women had prominent positions of power in the organizations. Faith healer Katherine Kuhlmann, for example, had been the first female with a regular religious show on television. Discrimination still existed, and many of the Pentecostal denominations still frowned on interracial marriage. But compared to the mainstream church, the underground Pentecostal movement was remarkably free of racism, classism, and gender bias.

Instead of moving in the direction of their flocks, mainstream churches sought to be inclusive, leading them to reinterpret church practices in a number of areas. Most of the mainstream churches, for example, started to ordain women by the 1970s. These female ministers in liberal Protestant churches "tended to side with radical feminists on the most volatile issues of the day," especially abortion.[34] Scarcely had the ink dried on the key sexual reproduction case of the century, *Roe v. Wade* (1973), than the Methodists, Presbyterians, American Baptists, United Church of Christ, Disciples of Christ, and Episcopal Church all adopted proabortion positions.[35]

In 1973 the U.S. Supreme Court, hearing a pair of cases (generally referred to by the first case's name, *Roe v. Wade*), concluded that Texas antiabortion laws violated a constitutional "right to privacy."[36] Of course, no such phrase can be found in the Constitution. That, however, did not stop the Court from establishing—with no law's ever being passed and no constitutional amendment's ever being ratified—the premise that a woman had a constitutional right to an abortion during the first trimester of pregnancy. Later, sympathetic doctors would expand the context of health risk to the mother so broadly as to permit abortions almost on demand. Instantly the feminist movement leaped into action, portraying unborn babies as first, fetuses, then as "blobs of tissue." A battle with prolife forces led to an odd media acceptance of each side's own terminology of itself: the labels that the media used were "prochoice" (not "proabortion") and "prolife" not "antichoice." What was not so odd was the stunning explosion of abortions in the United States, which totaled at least 35 million over the first twenty-five years after *Roe*. Claims that without safe and legal abortions, women would die in abortion mills seemed to pale beside the stack of fetal bodies that resulted from the change in abortion laws.

For those who had championed the Pill as liberating women from the natural results of sex—babies—this proved nettlesome. More than 82 percent of the women who chose abortion in 1990 were unmarried. Had not the Pill protected them? Had it not liberated them to have sex without consequences? The bitter fact was that with the restraints of the church removed, the Pill and feminism had only exposed women to higher risks of pregnancy and, thus, "eligibility" for an abortion. It also exempted men almost totally from their role as fathers, leaving them the easy escape of pointing out to the female that abortion was an alternative to having an illegitimate child.

Fatherhood, and the role of men, was already under assault by feminist groups. By the 1970s, fathers had become a central target for the media, especially entertainment. Fathers were increasingly portrayed as buffoons, even as evil, on prime-time television. Comedies, according to one study of thirty years of network television, presented blue-collar or middle-class fathers as foolish, although less so than the portrayals of upper-class fathers.[37]

Feminists had unwittingly given men a remarkable gift, pushing as they had for no-fault divorce. Divorce laws began changing at the state level in the early 1970s, at which time a full court hearing and proof of cause was no longer required. Instead, if both parties agreed that they had irreconcilable differences, they simply obtained an inexpensive no-fault divorce. This proved a boon for men because it turned the social world into an "arena of sexual competition [making] men and women view each other as prey and their own sex as competitors to a degree that corrodes civility."[38] Divorce rates skyrocketed, with more than 1.1 million divorces occurring in 1979, and the number of children under the age of eighteen who lived in one-parent families rising during the decade of the 1970s from 11 percent to 19 percent. Although it took about twenty years for sociologists to study the phenomena, scholars almost universally agreed by the 1990s that children of one-parent families suffered from more pathologies, more criminal behavior, worse grades, and lower self-esteem than kids from traditional families.[39]

A husband, able to easily escape from matrimony because it no longer proved fulfilling (or more likely, he desired a younger woman), now only had to show that he could not get along with his current wife—not that she had done anything wrong or been unfaithful. In turn, the process called the "one-to-a-customer" rule by George Gilder in his controversial *Men and Marriage* was instantly killed.[40] In its place, wealthy older men could almost always attract younger women, but older women (*regardless* of their personal wealth) usually could not attract men their age, who instead snapped up younger "hard bodies" (as these physically fit women were called). Whereas in previous eras these younger women would have married middle- or lower-class men of roughly their own age and started families, they now became prey for the middle-aged wealthy men with "Jennifer Fever." The new Jennifer herself only lasted temporarily until she, too, was discarded.[41] Pools of available middle-aged women, often with money, and younger men may have seemed to sociologists to be a logical match, but in fact the two groups were biologically and culturally incompatible. Instead, young men with looks and vitality battled against older males with money and status for the affections of an increasingly smaller group of twenty- to thirty-year-old females, while an army of middle-aged female divorcées struggled to raise children from one or more marriages.

Feminism's sexual freedom thus placed older women into a no-win competition with the young, and in either group, the losers of the game had limited options. The process slowly created an entirely new class of females who lacked male financial support and who had to turn to the state as a surrogate husband, producing one of the most misunderstood political phenomena of the late twentieth century, the so-called gender gap. In reality, as most political analysts admit, this was a marriage gap. Married women voted Republican in about the same numbers as men did; it was only the single mothers, as casualties of the sexual free-fire zone the feminists had dropped them into, who saw government as a savior instead of a threat.

Meanwhile thanks to the women's movement, a new option opened to women in the 1970s that had not existed to the same degree in earlier decades: a career. Women applied to law and medical schools, moved into the universities, and even gradually made inroads into engineering and the hard sciences.

Inflation had actually smoothed the way for women to enter professional fields. As families struggled and a second income was needed, men usually preferred their wives to have the highest paying job possible. Personnel directors and

736 A PATRIOT'S HISTORY OF THE UNITED STATES

company presidents—usually men—could not help but appreciate the fact that many of their own wives had started to interview for jobs too. Over time, this realization helped override any macho chauvinism they may have possessed.

The working female brought a new set of economic realities. First, large numbers of women entering the workforce tended to distort the statistics. There is no question that more overall activity occurred in the economy as women now spent more on housekeepers, gas, fast food, and child care. But there were also hidden economic indicators of social pathology: suicides were up, as was drug use, alcoholism, clinical depression, and, of course, divorce. What went almost unnoticed was that productivity—the key measure of all wealth growth—*fell steadily* throughout the 1970s, despite a tidal wave of women entering the job markets.

As more people moved into the workforce, there were increased family pressures for child care. Once touted as the salvation of the working family, child care has been shown to be undesirable at best and extremely damaging at worst.[42] Moreover, with both parents coming home around six in the evening, families tended to eat out more, send out laundry more often, and pay for yard or other domestic work as well as additional taxes, all of which chewed up most of the extra cash brought in by the wife's job. Although by 1978 the median family income had risen to $17,640, up from $9,867 in 1970, that increase had occurred by having two adults, rather than one, in the workplace. Children increasingly were viewed as impediments to a more prosperous lifestyle and, accordingly, the number of live births fell sharply from what it had been in 1960.

All of these indicators told Americans what they already had known for years: the great prosperity of the 1950s had slowed, if not stopped altogether. Social upheaval, which was excused in the 1960s as an expression of legitimate grievances, took on a darker tone as illegitimacy yielded gangs of young boys in the inner cities, and in suburban homes both parents worked forty hours a week to stay afloat. It would provide the Democratic challenger to the presidency with a powerful issue in November 1976, even if no other reasons to oust Ford existed. But events abroad would prove disastrous for Gerald Ford.

Foreign Policy Adrift

Domestic issues may have absorbed Americans' attention more after Vietnam, but foreign threats had hardly diminished. Making matters worse, Ford was weak in dealing with foreign leaders. Soviet dictators, always probing for soft spots, found one at Vladivostok in 1974, when Ford met with Soviet Premier Leonid Brezhnev. A hard-line communist, Brezhnev nevertheless was vulnerable. He had suffered a series of strokes that had left him a semi-invalid, attended constantly by a KGB nurse who "fed him a daily stream of pills without consulting his doctors."[43] His entourage was followed everywhere by a resuscitation vehicle. When it came to bargaining with the "main adversary," as he viewed the United States,

Brezhnev differed little from Stalin. He was searching for a strategic advantage that could offset several new U.S. military technologies.[44]

Of most concern to the Soviets was the antiballistic missile (ABM) system allowed under SALT I. If deployed across the nation, even at low levels of effectiveness, antimissile missiles could effectively combat nuclear warheads aimed at the United States. The ABM system represented a tremendous bargaining chip against the Soviets, since their heavy land-based missiles represented their only guaranteed threat against the United States whereas American deterrent forces were evenly divided within the triad of submarine-launched ballistic missiles (SLBMs), long-range bombers, and ICBMs. Another concern for the USSR was the new MIRV capability of U.S. missiles. MIRV, or multiple independent reentry vehicles, meant that a single American ICBM could hit multiple targets. Its "bus" vehicle carrying up to ten MIRVs could deliver nuclear payloads to as many as ten different locations within a broad target area. Therefore, any advantage the Soviets had in sheer numbers of missiles was offset by the ability to convert existing U.S. ICBMs to MIRVs.

Political will, however, proved more important than advanced technology. As long as Nixon remained in office, he could with some degree of certainty keep together a pro-Pentagon coalition of Republicans and hawk Democrats (such as Richard Russell of Georgia and Henry "Scoop" Jackson of Washington). Ford, in contrast, was out of his element. He and his advisers failed to distinguish between warheads and launchers. The Russians enthusiastically agreed to a new SALT treaty (SALT II) that placed limits on launchers, leaving the United States at a permanent disadvantage, which could only be counterbalanced by introducing newer and more survivable submarines, bombers, and ICBM systems. To obtain a treaty that had so clearly put the United States at a disadvantage, Ford and Congress had assured the Joint Chiefs of Staff—without whose approval the treaty would never have passed—that programs such as the B-1 bomber, MX missile, ABM system, and Trident submarine would continue to be funded. Like the support of Vietnam, all these promises rested solely on the will and character of the president and Congress who stood behind them.

"I'll Never Lie to You"

Had Gerald Ford not had social decay and economic disruption to deal with, he still would have been hard pressed to defeat Georgia Governor James Earl "Jimmy" Carter in 1976. Carter was one of a line of presidential candidates to "run against Washington." Born in Plains, Georgia—the first president born in a hospital—Carter was raised in a religious household. He was a professed born-again Christian and a practicing Baptist. He graduated from the United States Naval Academy, entering the submarine service under the "father of the nuclear navy," Admiral Hyman Rickover. After his service ended, Carter ran his family's substantial peanut farm and seed enterprise, making him the first president since Truman to have any significant experience in private business. He entered Georgia politics, winning the governorship in 1970, which gave him all the qualifications—

except for foreign policy experience—to hold the highest office. He had improved the efficiency of his state government bureaucracy and ran it on budget, a point that allowed him to criticize Washington's deficit spending. A southerner and a Southern Baptist, Carter appealed to both white conservatives and the religious faithful who perceived that morality was slipping from public service. His military service suggested that he would not abandon the military, and his commitment to racial justice showed that he would not abandon blacks.

Carter also benefited from the self-destruction of the last Kennedy rival. Senator Edward "Ted" Kennedy, the youngest and last of Joe Kennedy's boys (and easily the least talented politically), had cultivated hopes of attaining the presidency that his brother Robert, in the eyes of many, had been denied by an assassin's bullet. Certainly the Democratic Party would have enthusiastically welcomed a Kennedy heading a ticket. But in July 1969, Kennedy drove his Oldsmobile off a bridge at Chappaquiddick Island, drowning his passenger, staffer Mary Jo Kopechne. The implications of cavorting with his young campaign worker were damaging, and probably contributed to Kennedy's decision to leave the scene of the accident. He did not even report the incident to police and made no effort to save the trapped woman as she drowned. The Kennedy spin machine immediately flew into high gear, containing the press coverage, inquest, and grand jury probe. Still, few scholars looking at the evidence have concluded anything other than the fact that Ted Kennedy was culpable in the death of Kopechne.[45] After lying low in 1972, Kennedy took the nation's political pulse in 1976, and found that tremendous resentment accompanied the unanswered questions about the incident. He quietly ceded the field to the Georgia governor.

Having begun a long preparation in 1974, Carter sealed the nomination and then led Gerald Ford by some thirty points in the polls. Selecting Walter Mondale of Minnesota as his vice presidential running mate, Carter nailed down his liberal base, then veered back to the center with pithy but pointed remarks. "I'll never lie to you," he told the public, then proved it by giving *Playboy* magazine an interview, the first presidential candidate to do so, in which he admitted that he had "lusted in his heart" after women. Such poor judgment undercut his image as a religious man and helped erode much of the lead he had built up. Ford proved little better. Having barely held off challenger Ronald Reagan in the Republican primary, Ford blundered by stating in a television debate that Eastern Europe was not under Soviet domination. Americans concluded that Ford was dense or uninformed. His running mate, moderate Kansas Senator Bob Dole, a disabled war veteran, was designated the attack dog, endowing him with a reputation for conservatism he did not deserve.

Ultimately, the campaign turned on the economy rather than either candidate's competence. Carter's aides concocted a "misery index" comprised of the unemployment rate added to the inflation rate, which, depending on the source, was 10 percent in 1975 (but had dropped back to about 6 percent at election time). Carter asked a simple question of the voters: "Are you better off today than you were four years ago?" Most people answered in the negative, giving Carter a

51 to 48 percent popular vote margin (but a much narrower electoral victory, 297 to 240). A swing of one large state, such as Ohio or Pennsylvania, would have made Ford president. Any Democratic strategist looking at the map would have been concerned. Carter had lost the entire West except for Texas, most of New England, and the key midwestern states of Illinois, Michigan, and Indiana. The party's success came almost entirely from the South, where only Virginia voted for Ford.

Attempting to enhance the outsider image, Carter walked rather than rode in his inaugural parade. He sold the White House yacht and adopted an informal atmosphere, even wearing a sweater instead of a suit during a televised "fireside chat." Like Ford's WIN button, though, the cardigan sweater gained a negative connotation, reflecting the president's inability to do anything about the ongoing energy crisis. Invoking a preacher's style of moral calling to the public, Carter encouraged Americans to turn down their thermostats and conserve. Labeling the energy crisis the "moral equivalent of war," Carter only stirred up memories of the last two wars the nation had entered, and lost—Vietnam and the war on poverty.

Adopting a comprehensive energy policy, Carter and Congress rolled out multimillion-dollar subsidies for solar and wind power, biomass, and other alternative fuels, virtually none of which could come online soon enough to affect the nation's immediate energy problems. Wind farms of massive and unsightly windmills only generated a fraction of the kilowatts of a soundly run coal-fired or hydroelectric plant. (Later, environmentalists would shut down the windmill farms in the San Francisco area because the windmill blades were killing birds.) Solar power, which worked well in places like Arizona and Florida, was dangerous to install and, at best, unreliable. In colder climates it was completely impractical.

The nation desperately needed new sources of energy, and the cheapest and safest was nuclear power. But already the antinuclear movement had demonized atomic energy, even though the nations with the longest history of nuclear power use—France and Japan—had never had a serious accident. Nuclear power in America had a similar spotless record until March 1979, when an accident at the Three Mile Island nuclear plant in Pennsylvania necessitated the release of radioactive gases. Not a single person was killed or injured, but the media and activists ensured that nuclear plant construction would be dramatically curtailed, if not stopped.

Leverage over foreign powers proved even more difficult for Carter than Ford because the new president imposed a requirement that countries observe basic human rights. Longtime allies in Asia, Latin America, and the Middle East suddenly became the objects of criticism. Although Carter did point out Soviet treatment of dissidents, he avoided any broad and energetic condemnation of either the Soviet or Chinese systems, both of which were inherently hostile to human rights. The entire policy, designed to reverse the realpolitik of Henry Kissinger, was fraught with danger. No nation—including the United States, with its history of slavery and its treatment of Native Americans and Japanese Americans during World War II—had hands that were entirely clean. On a practical level, spying demanded that one work with people of questionable character: murderers, terrorists, and people willing to sell out their own countrymen. From where else would the information come? And when it came to strategic issues, the time-tested rule was "My enemy's enemy is my friend."

Implementing the most idealistic foreign policy since Woodrow Wilson was Wall Street lawyer Cyrus Vance (secretary of state) and Columbia University professor Zbigniew Brzezinski (national security adviser), a Polish-born liberal wrongly portrayed as a cold war hawk. Carter also appointed Andrew Young, a veteran of the civil rights movement with no foreign experience, as the ambassador to the United Nations. Their inexperience compounded the impracticality of human rights emphasis in foreign policy.

Carter angered conservatives by winning Senate ratification of the treaty returning the Panama Canal Zone to the nation of Panama and announcing support of black majority rule in several African states. He denounced pro-U.S. Latin American dictators, which encouraged the Cuban-backed communist Sandinista guerrillas to overthrow the Somoza government in Nicaragua. In each instance, Carter traded the substance of strategic control and genuine working alliances for a shadowy world of public opinion and goodwill.

Carter finally appeared to have found his stride in foreign relations when he played a broker's role in negotiating a remarkable Middle East peace. Faced with prospects of another Arab-Israeli war, Carter invited leaders of Egypt and Israel to the Camp David retreat. Egypt was represented by its president, Anwar el-Sadat, who had allied with the Nazis in World War II. Israel sent its prime minister, Menachem Begin, who had engaged in terrorist activities against Palestinians as a member of Israeli Irgun commando units. These were fighters—men who knew war and had no illusions about the cost, but who were also fatigued and desperate for a compromise. Meeting in February 1979, with Carter smoothing over hard points and even jawboning the pair to keep them from walking out, Begin and Sadat signed the Camp David Accords, normalizing relations between Egypt and Israel and paving the way for Israel to withdraw from the Sinai Peninsula. The final agreement, however, was accomplished only when Carter bribed the signatories with "the largest-ever American foreign-aid package . . . a total of [$5 billion] over a three-year period."[46] Israeli withdrawal, in particular, came when Carter promised that the United States would construct two military airfields for Israel in the Negev. Money talked, at least temporarily. Arab states quickly denounced the agreement, and the fundamentalist wing of Islam threatened to boil over. Begin and Sadat won the Nobel Peace Prize in 1978, for which Sadat paid with his life in October 1981, when Islamic extremists in his own army assassinated him.

In fact, Egypt obtained everything it wanted but the Israelis were left to deal with the central canker sore of the region, the Palestinian issue. Israel had begun to sell land in the occupied territories (the West Bank, which is within Israel's biblical borders) to its own settlers in 1979, and Camp David did nothing to address the problem in favor of either side.

The apparent triumph of Camp David masked Carter's more significant weakness in dealing with the USSR. He canceled the planned B-1 bomber (which had been promised to the air force for its support of SALT II) and delayed the deployment of the MX missile (which had been guaranteed to the Joint Chiefs of Staff in return for the military's support of Salt II). Carter also ended all serious consideration of reviving the ABM, another promise related to SALT II that went down the drain.

If there was one thing the Soviets could smell, it was weakness in a leader. In short order, the number of worldwide terrorist incidents started to rise, with most of the funding coming from Moscow.

A far more dangerous development accompanied the Soviets' assessment that Carter was weak: the "window of vulnerability" opened. In the mid-1970s the Soviets developed two new ICBMs, the SS-18 and SS-19, which reflected a completely different nuclear strategy in that each carried a single huge warhead (as opposed to multiple warheads). The new missiles had one purpose: to burrow into American ICBM silos in a surprise attack and destroy U.S. missiles on the ground. Any astute observer would immediately ask if U.S. missiles would not be airborne the instant a Soviet launch was detected on radar, but this was a question of political will, not technology. Not only did the new heavy missiles of the Soviet missile forces indicate that there was serious consideration of a first-strike surprise attack, but publications by Soviet strategists themselves openly discussed their military doctrine. These publications increasingly were dominated by phrases such as "the first strike," the "offensive," and "surprise," which indicated that planning for a nuclear war—or, more precisely, to *fight and win* a nuclear war—had intensified since Nixon left office.

Cancellation of numerous new high-tech weapons by the Carter administration convinced many Soviet leaders that the president would not respond in the event of a surgical attack aimed "only" at American missile fields. Under such a scenario, the Soviets would destroy the U.S. ICBM fields, killing relatively few people, and the president would hesitate, or negotiate, while the Soviets reloaded their missile silos (a feature ours did not have), threatening a second all-out attack against a disarmed America's major cities. (For a number of reasons, bombers and SLBMs were not capable of taking out Soviet missile silos.)

This concept was poorly understood by the American media, which seemed capable only of parroting lines such as "We have enough warheads to blow up the world several times over." In fact, the proper illustration was two gunfighters: one draws first and shoots the gun out of the other's hand. Despite the fact that the other has a belt full of bullets, he is made helpless by the fact that the weapon needed to fire the bullets is disabled. Leverage came from available launchers, not warheads. Security came from will, not technology. Ford's and Carter's aura of weakness opened this window of vulnerability, which reached its widest level around 1979, when the United States came the closest to nuclear war than at any time in its history, including the Cuban crisis.

Carter had none of Franklin Roosevelt's luck. No sooner had he helped negotiate the Camp David Accords than a revolution in Iran, in January 1979, overthrew the pro-American shah with an Islamic fundamentalist, Ayatollah Ruhollah Khomeini. Carter made overtures to the new Islamic government, which rebuffed him, calling the United States the Great Satan before shutting off all oil exports to America. Failing to see the dangers posed by a new government that hated the United States, Carter did not withdraw the American embassy personnel. He antagonized the Iranian mullahs when, several months later, he admitted deposed Shah Mohammad Reza Pahlavi into the United States for medical treatment. Iranian mobs, fanned by the ayatollahs, erupted and stormed the U.S. embassy, taking hostage sixty-six Americans inside. Khomeini warned that any attempt to rescue them would result in their execution (although he later released all women, blacks, and one ill white male). Television pictures transmitted to North America revealed to a stunned public the raw hatred of the mobs. Carter seemed helpless to do anything about the situation. Lacking the impetuosity of a Teddy Roosevelt, who would have sent a military force to punish the Iranians, or the stoicism of a Coolidge to ride it out, or the deviousness of Nixon to strike through covert measures, Carter adopted halfway measures and always employed them too late.

Television made matters worse. News networks kept a daily tracking of the fiasco, leading each newscast with banners reading AMERICA HELD HOSTAGE. America, of course, was only held hostage if it allowed a foreign country to use the fifty remaining captives as leverage. The public, unable to do anything substantial, engaged in symbolic gestures like tying yellow ribbons around trees and flagpoles. Carter compounded the error by elevating the safe return of the hostages to his administration's top priority. American helplessness in Iran exposed the Camp David agreements as of minimal value, since Carter refrained from military action, in part because of fear that the Arab world would support the Iranians. Days turned into weeks, then into months.

Perceiving that Carter was distracted, the USSR staged a full-scale invasion of Afghanistan in December 1980 and installed a puppet government in Kabul. Carter belatedly ordered a defense buildup and sent warships to the Persian Gulf, but Afghanistan was already in Soviet hands.

With such futility in the Oval Office, it is not surprising that the brightest moment for Americans scarcely involved government. It came at the Winter Olympic Games held at Lake Placid, New York, when the U.S. ice hockey team, substantial underdogs to the professional Soviet skaters, played one of the most heroic games in Olympic history. The U.S. team grabbed the lead and, as the clock ticked down, the pro-American crowd waved American flags and chanted "U-S-A, U-S-A." In the final seconds, broadcaster Al Michaels delivered one of the most memorable lines in all sports history as the amateur American team beat the Soviets: "Do you believe in miracles? Yeeeesssss!" If only symbolically, the American Olympic ice hockey team had done what Carter could not.

Whipsawed between Afghanistan and Iran, in April 1980, Carter, having lost all initiative and the element of surprise, finally approved a risky scheme to rescue the Iranian hostages. The complex plan called for a hazardous nighttime desert rendezvous, with numerous aircraft, and operated on what military people call zero margin—no room for error. En route mechanical difficulties aborted the mission, but the choppers still had to refuel, and one, in the process of taking off during a windstorm, clipped a fuel plane with its rotor, causing a massive fireball. International news later broadcast video of Iranians waving the mutilated body parts of charred American troops. It is safe to say that even including the burning of Washington, D.C., in the War of 1812, the United States had never sunk to a lower, more humiliating point internationally.

Treating his inability to govern as a virtual crisis, Carter retreated to Camp David, emerging to deliver his famous "malaise" speech, although he never used the word specifically, blaming the American public for a national "crisis of confidence."[47] Andrew Young had already resigned in controversy, and Cyrus Vance quit in a disagreement over the Iranian rescue. Carter's solid personal character had been overwhelmed by his insistence on micromanaging the administration.

Absorbed with Afghanistan, Iran, and the Middle East, Carter failed to comprehend the significance of one of the most important and sweeping movements of the twentieth century, when a powerful resistance movement to communism arose in Poland and other parts of Eastern Europe. Cardinal Karol Wojtyla of Poland, John Paul II, had been elected pope in October 1978, the first non-Italian to be so honored since 1522, and quickly became the most popular pontiff in history. John Paul II energized anticommunism from the outside, while Polish shipyard worker Lech Walesa led a resistance from the inside in the form of strikes.

Ironically, Carter was not the only one distracted by Afghanistan: the Soviets seemed paralyzed by the growing independence of the trade unions in Poland and, in any event, could not financially continue to support the rotting carcass of the Eastern European communist states. The sword cut both ways. Where Stalin would have moved in to crush Walesa's Solidarity Union, so too a Truman or a Teddy Roosevelt would have moved to support such a movement. Instead, both Brezhnev and Carter floundered in the Iranian deserts and Afghan mountains.

"Well, There You Go Again!"
On every front, the United States seemed in decline. Economically, socially, and in international relations, by 1980 America was in retreat. Yet at this point of weakness, the nation stood on the edge of its greatest resurgence since the months following Doolittle's bombing of Tokyo. The turnaround began with an upheaval within the Republican Party.

Since the defeat of Goldwater in 1964, the American conservative movement had steadily given ground. Nixon and Ford, at best, were moderates on most hot-button conservative issues, and other potential Republican alternatives to Jimmy Carter—Nelson Rockefeller, for example—represented the blue-hair wing of the country-club GOP, which offered no significant change in philosophy from the Georgian's. Then onto the scene came a sixty-nine-year-old former actor, Goldwaterite, and governor of California, Ronald Wilson Reagan. At one time a New Deal Democrat who had voted four times for FDR, Reagan was fond of saying that he "didn't leave the Democratic Party; it left me." Reagan contended that the liberals of the 1970s had abandoned the principles that had made up the Democratic Party of John Kennedy and Harry Truman, and that those principles—anticommunism, a growing economy for middle-class Americans, and the rule of law—were more in line with the post-Nixon Republican Party.

Born in Illinois (and the first president ever to have lived in Chicago), Reagan created an alter ego for himself with his portrayal of Notre Dame football player George Gipp in *Knute Rockne, All American* (1940), in which he immortalized the line spoken by the dying Gipp to the Fighting Irish football team, "Go out there and win one for the Gipper." Later in public life, Reagan enjoyed being referred to as the Gipper. His most critically acclaimed role, however, had come in *King's Row* (1942). At Eureka College, he led a successful student strike aimed at restoring faculty members whom the school had fired, which later gave him the distinction of having been the only U.S. president to have led a student protest march. He headed the Screen Actors Guild in 1947, the Hollywood labor union for motion picture artists, energetically working to excise communists from its ranks, while at the same time endeavoring to clear the names of noncommunists who had been unfairly targeted by the FBI or HUAC. Just as the student strike had made him unique, the union experience marked him as the only twentieth-century American president to have served in a union position.

Never as overtly religious as Coolidge before him or George W. Bush after him, Reagan's moral sense was acute. When he learned that the Los Angeles Lakeside Country Club, to which he belonged, did not admit Jews, he resigned. At a World War II celebration of United America Days, where he honored a Nisei sergeant, Kazuo Masuda, who had died in the war, Reagan reminded the audience, "The blood that has soaked into the sands of the beaches is all one color. America stands unique in the world—a country not founded on race, but on . . . an ideal."[48] Only after his death in 2004 was Reagan's Christian faith more completely examined and publicized.

During the 1960s he began to explore a political career, first working for Goldwater, then running for governor of California. Reagan won the 1966 gubernatorial election, then reelection. He reformed welfare in one of the nation's most free-spending states, vetoed more than nine hundred bills (of which only one passed over his veto), and imposed a rule of common sense.[49]

Branded by his opponents as an extremist and an anticommunist zealot, Reagan in fact practiced the art of compromise, comparing success in politics to a batting average. He warned conservatives that the game required give and take, working with Democrats in California to shed seventy-five thousand from the state's welfare rolls while increasing benefits for the poorest. Bolstered by a winning smile, an indefatigable charm, and the ability to shrug off criticism with a wink and a grin, he drove his opponents into even greater froths. The most gifted presidential orator of the twentieth century, Reagan was ridiculed for reading from index cards, a habit he had picked up from his years on the rubber-chicken circuit giving speeches before chambers of commerce and community groups as official spokesman for the General Electric Corporation. Ridiculed for his acting background and characterized as a dim bulb, Reagan, in fact, wrote extensively, on almost every subject, with deep understanding.[50] The Gipper also put things in everyday language. Speaking of the dismal economy, he said, "A recession is when your neighbor loses his job. A depression is when you lose yours. A recovery is when Jimmy Carter loses his."

In the general election campaign, Reagan ran on three simple promises: he would revive the economy through tax cuts and deregulation, cutting the size of government; he would wage the cold war with renewed vigor; and he would address the nation's energy problems by seeking market solutions. He mollified moderates by naming George H. W. Bush of Texas, former CIA director, as his running mate, but the race belonged to Reagan. Turning Carter's own once-winning question around on the Georgian, the Gipper asked, "Are you better off today than you were four years ago?"[51] He also dusted off the misery index, which had risen sharply under Carter. Short-term interest rates, which had stood at 5.35 percent when Carter took office, had more than doubled to 12.29 percent in 1980, which Reagan did not hesitate to point out. The price of gold, traditionally a barometer of inflation, had gone off the charts during the Carter years, reaching its record high of $875 an ounce. At the same time (1980), Japan passed the United States as the world's largest auto producer, and one third of all Americans drove a Japanese car. Even if Carter been a competent president and candidate, those numbers would have done him in.

Though not trailing significantly in the polls, Carter knew he was in trouble. Democratic strategists had placed much of their hopes of keeping the White House on the presidential debates, where it was thought the younger, Washington-toughened Carter might expose Reagan as a doddering inexperienced political newbie. Yet whenever Carter distorted Reagan's record or tried to portray him as an extremist, the Gipper smiled, cocked his head, and quipped, "Well, there you go again," five words that Reagan credited with winning him the election. The debates made the incumbent look like a sincere but naive child arguing with his wise uncle. On election eve, despite surveys showing Reagan trailing, the Californian came back so strongly that Carter appalled Democrat strategists by conceding the campaign while the polls were still open in California. Reagan carried the electoral college 489 to 49, the most stunning and overwhelming loss for an incumbent since the ill-fated Hoover had gone down in

1932. The Republicans also gained thirteen seats in the Senate to win a majority there for the first time in nearly thirty years, and they picked up thirty-three House seats. But the desire for change in the nation was far deeper than that. Among the Democrats who had won election, some thirty to forty "boll weevils" from conservative districts supported stronger defense and tax cuts, and they voted for the Reagan proposals consistently. Many of them eventually switched parties.

Reaganophobia

Liberal textbook writers have endeavored to distort and taint Reagan's record more than they have any other subject except the Great Depression. They began by attempting to minimize the extent of Reagan's massive and shocking victory by pointing to low turnout, which had in fact been exacerbated by massive drives by liberals to register voters who in fact had no intention of ever voting.[52]

Another strategy to discredit Reagan was to attack his acting career, pointing to the absence of many critically acclaimed roles. This allowed them to label him a B actor. Yet this argument contradicted another line of attack on the Gipper, claiming that he had no genuine political instincts or serious policy ideas, and that he was merely a master of the camera. For example, a photo caption in *American Journey*, after acknowledging Reagan's communication skills, dutifully noted that "critics questioned his grasp of complex issues."[53] Reagan "was no intellectual," announced the popular textbook *The American Pageant*.[54]

Both the Democrats and the media continually underestimated Reagan, mistakenly thinking that his acting background and camera presence had supplied his margin of victory. Neither group took seriously his ideas—or the fact that those ideas were consistent and appealed to large majorities of Americans. Refusing to engage in combative dialogue with his media enemies Reagan repeatedly used them to his advantage, and kept his eyes on the prize. Reagan was in fact widely read and perceptive too: in 1981, he had latched on to a pathbreaking book by George Gilder, *Wealth & Poverty*, which to the lament of mainstream academics, turned the economic world upside down with its supply-side doctrine and stunning insights.[55]

Symbolically, although Carter had negotiated an end to the hostage crisis, the ayatollah did not release the prisoners until January 20, 1981, the day of Reagan's inauguration. (It was characteristic of Reagan, in his diary, to note how sorry he had felt for the departing Carter, who did not have the fortune of seeing the hostages released.) Symbolism aside, the Reagan Revolution shocked the FDR coalition to its roots. Even unions started to splinter over supporting some of Reagan's proposals, and although publicly the Democrats downplayed the extent of the damage, privately Democratic Party strategist Al From was so shaken that he initiated a study to determine if Reagan was a fluke or if a broad transformation of the electorate had started to occur.[56] He did not like the answers. Going in, Reagan knew that fixing more than a decade's worth of mismanagement in energy, monetary policy, national security, and other areas of neglect would be a long-term prospect. It required a policy style that did not veer from crisis to crisis, but which held firm to conservative principles, even when it meant disregarding short-term pain. Equally important, it meant that Reagan personally had to ditch the Carter "malaise" that hung over the nation like a blanket and replace it with the old-fashioned can-do optimism that was inherently Reaganesque.

The Gipper accomplished this by refusing to engage in Beltway battles with reporters or even Democrats on a personal basis. He completely ignored the press, especially when it was critical. Laughing and joking with Democrats, he kept their ideology, which he strenuously opposed, separate from the people themselves. These characteristics made it intensely difficult even for Washington reporters and die-hard Democrats to dislike him, although Carter resented the election loss for more than a decade. Reagan frustrated reporters and intellectuals with a maddening simplicity, asking why we needed the Federal Reserve at all and why, if the ozone layer was being destroyed, we couldn't replace it. He possessed a sense of humor and self-deprecation not seen since Truman. Having acted in his share of bad movies, Reagan provided plenty of ammunition to critics. When one reporter brought him a studio picture from a movie he had made with a chimpanzee, *Bedtime for Bonzo*, the Gipper good-naturedly signed it and wrote, "I'm the one with the watch."[57] Just two months after his inauguration, Reagan was the victim of an assassination attempt by John Hinckley. With a bullet still lodged in his chest, Reagan, taken into surgery, quipped to the doctors, "I hope you're all Republicans!"[58] In his 1982 State of the Union address, the Gipper quoted George Washington. Then, lampooning his own age, he added: "For our friends in the press, who place a high premium on accuracy, let me say I did not actually hear George Washington say that, but it is a matter of historic record." Aware the nation needed to revive the spirit of achievement, Reagan introduced everyday "American heroes" in his State of the Union messages.

When celebrating triumphs—whether over inflation, interest rates, unemployment, or communism—Reagan used "we" or "together." When calling on fellow citizens for support, he expressed his points in clear examples and heartwarming stories. An example, he said, was always better than a sermon. No matter what he or government did, to Reagan it was always the people of the nation who made the country grow and prosper. Most important, he did not hesitate to speak what he thought was the truth, calling the Soviet Union the "evil empire," a term that immediately struck a note with millions of *Star Wars* fans and conjuring up the image of a decrepit Soviet leader as the "emperor" bent on destroying the Galactic Republic (America). Once, preparing to make a statement about the Soviet Union, Reagan did not realize a microphone was left on, and he joked to a friend, "The bombing begins in five minutes." Horrified reporters scurried about in panic, certain that this gunslinger-cowboy president was serious.

But Reagan relied on more than language to accomplish his goals. Criticized as a hands-off president, he in fact was a master delegator, using a troika of Edwin Meese, James Baker, and Donald Regan (who held various advisory positions, with Meese and Regan actually trading jobs in 1985) to supervise every important issue. That left Reagan free to do the strategic thinking and to galvanize public opinion. Indeed, Reagan flustered his opponents, who thought him intellectually weak, precisely because he did not micromanage and thus devoted himself to the truly important issues, often catching his adversaries completely unaware. His grasp of the details of government, clear in his autobiography, *An American Life*, shows that in one-on-one meetings over details of tax cuts, defense, and other issues, Reagan had mastered the important specifics. However, he also believed in getting the best people and letting them speak their mind, even when he had made up his. He repeatedly left hotly charged meetings, telling the participants, "I'll let you know my decision," rather than embarrass the losing side in front of the winners.

Tax Cuts Revive the Nation

To say that Reagan had a single most important issue would be difficult, for he saw rebuilding America's economy and resisting Soviet communism as two sides to the same coin. Nevertheless, the key to the second came from success with the first: reviving the economy had to occur before the nation could commit to any major military expansion to resist the USSR. According to the traditional explanations, since the mid-1970s Reagan had steadily gravitated toward supply-side economics, touted by economists Arthur Laffer and Jude Wanniski. The supply-siders emphasized tax cuts to stimulate investment by making it more lucrative to build plants and start businesses instead of stimulating consumer demand, as Keynes and the Democrats had practiced for years. Cuts on the margin made a tremendous difference in purchasing and investing, the supply-siders argued, and the Laffer curve proved that tax cuts could actually increase revenues.[59] Reagan's vice president and opponent for the nomination, George H. W. Bush, had called supply-side cuts "voodoo economics," but it was common sense, representing a revival of Mellon's and Kennedy's tax policies, both of which proved extremely successful. In Reagan's hands, it became "Reaganomics."

   With the economy in such disrepair, Reagan easily persuaded Congress to back the concept, but he asked for an immediate 30 percent across-the-board cut (meaning that the wealthy would get tax relief too). Instead, Congress, afraid of appearing to favor the rich, strung the cut out for three years in 5, 10, and 10 percent increments through the Economic Recovery Act, passed in August 1981. In addition to lowering the top rates from 70 percent to 50 percent, and then still further, it lowered the all-important capital gains tax from 28 percent to 20 percent. Spreading out the cuts minimized the stimulus impact Reagan had sought. The economy recovered, slowly at first, then after the last segment of the cut was in place, rapidly. Lower capital gains rates caused investors to pump money into the economy as never before: their reported taxable income soared sevenfold and the amount of taxes paid by the investor classes rose fivefold.

   But in the interim, from 1981 to 1982 the economy dipped even deeper into recession, with unemployment reaching 10 percent in 1982. Federal Reserve chairman Paul Volcker, with encouragement from Reagan, contributed to some of the downturn by restricting the money supply as a means to squeeze the skyrocketing inflation out of the system. Volcker succeeded: in one quarter, the inflation rate dipped to zero. It had dropped overall from 12 percent just a few years earlier to 4 percent. It was a monumental accomplishment, but largely missed by the media, which focused, instead, on unemployment in the "Reagan recession" as journalists dubbed it.[60]

Reagan knew in his soul the tax cuts would work, but as his diary revealed, the dark days of late 1981 and early 1982 brought nothing but bad news:

Christmas [1981] The recession has worsened, throwing our earlier figures off. Now my team is pushing for a tax increase to help hold down the deficits. . . . I intend to wait and see some results.

Jan. 11 [1982] Republican House leaders came down to the W. H. Except for Jack Kemp they are h--l bent on new taxes and cutting the defense budget. Looks like a heavy year ahead.

Jan. 20 First anniversary of inauguration. The day was a tough one. A budget meeting and pressure from everyone to give in to increases in excise taxes . . . I finally gave in but my heart wasn't in it.

Feb. 22 Lunch on issues. I'm convinced of the need to address the people on our budget and the economy. The press has done a job on us and the polls show its effect. The people are confused about [the] economic program. They've been told it has failed and it's just started.

April 26 . . . at 10:15 addressed 2000 delegates of the U.S. Chamber of Commerce convention. What a shot in the arm. They interrupted me a dozen times or more. . . . The Dems are playing games—they want me to rescind the third year of the tax cuts—not in a million years![61]

And so on. By November the nation had started to pull out of the recession, and within a year it was rocketing ahead at a pace never before seen.

Determined to slash government regulation, Reagan benefited greatly from momentum already begun under Carter, for which, surprisingly, Carter took little credit during the campaign. Beginning in the mid-1970s, consumer groups had joined conservatives in working to deregulate the airline industry. Economist Alfred Kahn, who had joined the government's Civil Aeronautics Board in 1977, knew that a stranglehold on routes had kept airline prices high and the number of carriers low.[62] The government first allowed airlines to discount nonpeak hours, then, gradually, to discount all fares. At the same time, new competitors entered the market, forcing prices down further, until, by the 1980s, air travel was virtually deregulated. Lower prices put people on airplanes at astounding rates: in 1977, passenger boardings stood at 225 million, but by 1992 they had nearly doubled to 432 million. At the same time (contrary to critics' claims), eight of the ten major airlines had boosted their per-share earnings, all while lowering the number of fatalities per air mile traveled.[63]

In parcel delivery and overnight mail, United Parcel Service (UPS) and new-comer Federal Express also fought the postal service's monopoly and drove down rates by using jet aircraft to deliver mail.[64] Across the board, though, the percent-age of share of freight regulated by the federal government plunged in the 1980s in both rail and truck transportation.[65] Despite Reagan's affinity for chopping gov-ernment bureaus, he was able to eliminate only a few minor agencies during his term, a fact that reflected as much the previous success of deregulation of truck-ing and the air travel industry as it did his failures in cutting still more. He later referred to his inability to affect the scope of government as his greatest single failure in office. Ultimately, Reagan concluded that it was a task for another time and, perhaps, for another man or woman.

The tax cuts started to have their effect. Production, employment, job creation, and entrepreneurship all surged, soon achieving near-record levels. And, true to the supply-side promise, government revenues soared, increasing by more than one third during Reagan's eight years. Yet despite oceans of new money and Rea-gan's constant foot on the brake, government continued to spend more than it took in, increasing outlays by nearly 40 percent in the same period. To restrain spending, Reagan cut a deal with Congress in which the Democrats agreed to hold spending down in return for closing tax loopholes (which really involved raising taxes again, but only in specific industries, such as yachts and pleasure boats). No sooner had Congress closed the deal than it passed new higher spend-ing, generating sizable, but not record, deficits.

One of the most oft-repeated mantras of the 1980s—that Reagan's military buildup accounted for the extra expenditures—was utterly false.[66] Military bud-gets did grow, but barely. Defense spending never much exceeded $200 billion per year, whereas social spending under the Democrats consistently remained slightly higher. After Reagan left office, domestic nondefense spending was nearly double that of the Pentagon's budget.[67]

None of this seemed to faze average Americans, who could see by their wallets that the economy was growing by leaps and bounds. At the end of eight years of Reaganomics, America's revived industrial might had produced 14 million net new jobs. This was nothing short of stupendous, given that since 1970, all the European nations combined had *not generated a single net new job!*[68]

Most of these "gloomsters," as one economist called them, were stuck in the manufacturing mind-set, but even manufacturing had not declined as they claimed. Production as a share of U.S. gross domestic product dipped in the

1970s, but rose throughout the 1980s, reaching 36.1 percent in 1989, the highest level in American history![69]

Without question, however, America's traditional heavy industry had been taking it on the chin since 1970, and job losses in steel, textiles, and automobile industries particularly underscored the trauma. Entire cities dried up when manufacturing moved out, leading to the coining of a new term, the Rust Belt. But other, high-tech cities blossomed, and not just with services, but with new manufacturing industries.

While the industrial policy critics, mostly from the Democratic side, complained about the loss of blue-collar manufacturing jobs, a whole new computer industry had grown up under their noses. American computer manufacturers in the 1980s snapped up 70 percent of the world's software market and 80 percent of the world's hard-drive business, all while a fellow named Bill Gates came to completely dominate the human-to-machine interface known as computer "language." Nothing spoke to the lack of value in chip production more loudly than the plummeting prices of computer chips by the 1990s, when individual chips literally cost of a hundredth of a cent.

Silicon Valley replaced Detroit as the most important economic hub in the nation. Behind its laid-back style, Silicon Valley concealed a fiercely competitive collection of computer entrepreneurs whose synergy led to breakthrough after breakthrough. Eventually, the region would become so efficient and productive that in the late 1990s it had a severe recession. But at the beginning of the boom, Japan had nothing to match Silicon Valley.

By the end of the 1980s it took only half as much labor to purchase a gallon of milk as it had in 1950, the peak of heavy-industry America; and the cost in labor of a gallon of gasoline had fallen by two thirds. Some critics pointed to declining average wage growth as evidence that the U.S. economy, without heavy industry, would stagnate. In fact, wage growth was better when total compensation (such as medical benefits, retirement, and so on) was included, although the rate of increase had slowed some.

The result of the tax cuts, therefore, was not only revival of the economy but also restoration of confidence in American productivity and purpose. In addition, Reagan had mounted a strong counterattack on liberalism's dependency mentality, cracking it with the assistance of "blue-dog" Democrats who supported his tax relief. If he had not entirely rolled back government, Reagan had at least destroyed liberal assumptions that only a steadily growing government sector could produce economic stability and prosperity.[70] Yet tax cuts and the resurgence of the American economy only constituted part of Reagan's success.

Reagan dealt with foreign terrorists and usurpers quickly and decisively. Warned of a possible Cuban takeover of the little Caribbean nation of Grenada in 1983, he ordered in troops to thwart Castro's invasion. When a terrorist bombing in

1986 of a West German disco frequented by American GIs was linked to the radical Islamic state Libya and its unpredictable dictator Muammar al Qaddafi, Reagan authorized the bombing of the terrorist camps. American aircraft also struck Qaddafi's home, but the colonel was not home when the bombs fell. Nevertheless, he got the message, and Libya dropped off the international terrorist radar screen for the remainder of the decade. World terrorism fell sharply alongside the declining power of the Soviet Union, to the point where the number of reported incidents by 1987 was about half that of 1970.[71]

Only in one foreign policy situation—removal of the communist government in Nicaragua—was Reagan unable to make the progress he had hoped for. The communist regime in Nicaragua under Daniel Ortega, funded and equipped by Castro, not only gave the Soviets a foothold on the Central American mainland, but it also provided a staging area for terrorist activities against neighbors, such as El Salvador and Honduras. Reagan was committed to evicting Ortega's regime by supporting the pro-American rebels in his country, the contras. Congressional Democrats had continually thwarted any assistance to the contras, raising fears again and again of another Vietnam. Despite Reagan's concerns that Nicaragua could become a second Cuba, the Democrats turned back several aid packages. Frustration over this festering problem mounted within the administration.

Reagan also made a serious error by inserting peacekeeping troops in Lebanon. This was an expensive mistake, which he quickly repented. In 1983 he had dispatched American marines to Beirut to separate warring militias there. A suicide bomber drove a truck full of explosives through sentry checkpoints and blew up the marine barracks at the Beirut airport, killing 241 marines and wounding more than 100. Lebanon caused the president to rethink the key requirements for any future U.S. action. Military forces, he determined, should be committed only under the following conditions: (1) if the cause is "vital to our national interest," (2) if the commitment is made with "clear intent and support needed to win the conflict," (3) if there is "reasonable assurance" that the cause "will have the support of the American people and Congress," and (4) as a last resort, when no other choices remain.[72] Between 1988 and 2002, three U.S. presidents committed American forces (only two sent ground troops) to three major engagements— the Gulf War, the Bosnia/Kosovo conflict, and the war on terror in Afghanistan. In two of the three, Reagan's conditions were met, and both engagements proved militarily successful, receiving full backing of the public and Congress. However, in the third (Bosnia/Kosovo), where only U.S. air units were involved, the record was mixed: there was no vital interest, other options were not exhausted, and the public was far from united.

Later, in his dealings with the USSR, Reagan added yet one more strategic objective, known as the Reagan doctrine. Rather than contain the Soviet Union, the United States should actively attempt to roll it back. Freedom, he observed, "is not the sole prerogative of a lucky few, but the inalienable and universal right of all human beings. . . ." He predicted that "Marxism-Leninism would be tossed on the ash heap of history like all other forms of tyranny that preceded it."[73]

Microprocessors and Missiles

It was at that point that the new computer/information sector converged with Reagan's steadfast goal of defeating Soviet communism to produce one of the most amazing wonder weapons of all time. Perhaps the most amazing thing about it—the weapon was a space-based defense shield called Star Wars—was that it was not built and still has not been deployed (although parts of the technology are in use). Understanding the phenomenal impact of the computer on national security in the cold war, however, requires a cursory review of America's computer industry.

The rise of computers dates from Charles Babbage's nineteenth-century punch cards to the ENIAC computer of World War II. A key breakthrough occurred in 1952, when Texas Instruments researchers discovered that silicon, which could sustain temperatures of 1,200 degrees Celsius, was the perfect sealant for a transistor. In 1971 another company, Intel, managed to put an entire computer on a single chip called a microprocessor.

Virtually every other machine in human history had gotten more powerful by getting larger. This fact was epitomized by the internal combustion engines in use in Detroit's "muscle cars" at the very time the personal computer (PC) was invented. Obversely, computers promised to become more powerful the *smaller* they got, and to work faster the hotter they became. Chips, whose central element was silicon (available from ordinary sand), thus portended to offer a limitless resource, overthrowing the tyranny of physical materiality to a great extent. Finally, computers reinforced the pattern in American history that the most significant technological breakthroughs never come from leaders in the field but from total unknowns—many of them completely outside the field of their great success.

Within five years of the microprocessor's invention, Steve Jobs and Steve Wozniak, two California college dropouts, founded the personal computer industry with Apple Computers, Inc., in the Jobs family garage. Selling each Apple for $666, Jobs and Wozniak gained reputations as geniuses, and their company joined the Fortune 500 in less time than any company in history.[74] Apple was quickly eclipsed by other computer companies, but Jobs and Wozniak had "taken a technology of government and big business . . . and humanized it, putting power in the hands of the people in the most immediate sense of the term."[75] Starting from a time of essentially no computers in homes, the U.S. computer "population" had swelled to one computer for every 2.6 people by 1990. This amounted to the most rapid proliferation of a product in human history: the PC took only sixteen years to reach one fourth of all Americans compared to radio's twenty-two years, electricity's forty-six years, and television's twenty-six years.[76]

Computer technology alone did not ensure the success of the PC, however. An equally important breakthrough came from a Seattle-born Harvard dropout named Bill Gates, who, along with partner Paul Allen, cracked the language problem of programming computers, introducing BASIC in 1975, and founded Microsoft. Gates eventually developed the DOS system, used by virtually all computers by the 1990s. Solving the language problem was the equivalent of putting all of the trains of the 1850s on the same gauge rails. Gates reached his apex with the introduction of Windows, which used a point-and-click "mouse" controller to give the computer commands. In the process, he became the richest American in history, with a personal wealth exceeding that of Carnegie or Rockefeller in dollar equivalents.[77] Jobs, Gates, and the "boys of Silicon Valley" had not only transformed the information industry, but had touched off a revolution as profound as the industrial revolution, redefining every activity in terms of measurement, improvement, or facilitation through the application of computers. More important, as they did so, the prices of computers (especially microprocessors) plummeted, making them almost literally dirt cheap.[78] All that remained was to find a way for computers to "talk" to each other or, to stay with the railroad metaphor, to hook all the train tracks together.

In 1969, under a Pentagon contract, four universities connected their computers, and three years later e-mail was developed. By 1980, some online news and discussion groups had appeared. Although the World Wide Web was not formally inaugurated until 1991, and the early Internet was still complex and highly limited to select users, it was nevertheless hurtling full speed toward the business and civilian sectors. Government was involved in the original Pentagon hookups, but true intercomputer communication did not occur until the free market found ways to exploit its commercial potential.

This promise was seen in the burst of patent activity. (The total number of patents in the United States actually fell until the Reagan tax cuts.) High-temperature superconductors appeared early in the decade, which set in motion a torrent of patents—just under 150,000 by 1998, or triple what the number had been in 1980. This was the most rapid patent expansion in American history, eclipsing the period 1945–75, which had seen the introduction of the transistor, the polio vaccine, and the microprocessor.[79]

Computer technologies played a critical role in ending the cold war but only when they were placed in the policy "hands" of a leader who had the insight to use them to the fullest advantage. That leader was Ronald Reagan. In his first press conference, the president announced his opposition to the SALT II treaty, which the Senate had not passed in the wake of the Soviet invasion of Afghanistan. Announcing his intention to rectify the imbalance in forces between the United States and the USSR, Reagan signaled to the communist leadership that he would never allow the Soviet Union to attain military superiority. It was a message that terrified the entrenched Soviet leadership. In one of Yuri Andropov's final decrees before stepping down from his fifteen-year term as chairman of the KGB, he stated that the most pressing objective of all Soviet spies, whatever their rank or specialty, was to ensure that Reagan was not reelected.[80] Soviet resistance only convinced Reagan all the more. In short order, Reagan had authorized the construction of one hundred B-1 bombers, continued funding of the controversial B-2 Stealth bomber, commissioned a speedy review of the MX missile to determine the most survivable deployment disposition, and ordered the armed forces to deploy cruise missiles (some of them with nuclear warheads) on all available platforms. At the same time that he ditched SALT II, Reagan offered genuine reductions under the new Strategic Arms Reduction Talks (START), but movement from the Soviet side occurred only after the Reagan buildup. Moreover, the powerful Trident submarines went on station concurrent with Reagan's inauguration, and so, in a heartbeat of time, the window of vulnerability slammed shut.[81]

To anyone capable of evaluating the strength of the U.S. and Soviet economies, Reagan's defense budget illustrated another reality: he intended to spend the Soviets into the ground. The United States could continue to grow its defense sector severalfold without severe economic disruption. Soviet leaders knew that, and they knew they could not. Perhaps even more obvious, there was an innovation gap between the communist and capitalist systems that translated into nonmarket sectors like the military. A top-down structure like Soviet Russia adopted new technologies reluctantly and eyed with suspicion anything that threatened to overturn the existing military hierarchy.[82] The vise had been set. On March 8, 1983, Reagan gave it another twist.

Speaking to the American Association of Evangelicals, Reagan told the assembled clergy that "appeasement . . . is folly," for they could not ignore the "aggressive impulses of an evil empire."[83] Intellectuals and the media were angered and dumbfounded by the speech, which was received quite differently behind the Iron Curtain. Two former Soviet historians later reminded westerners, "The Soviet Union finds life-giving energy only in expansionism and an aggressive foreign policy."[84]

The "evil empire" speech paved the way for one of the most momentous events of the post–World War II era. On March 23, 1983, in a television address, after revealing previously classified photographs of new Soviet weapons and installations in Cuba, Nicaragua, and Grenada, and reviewing the Soviet advantage in heavy missiles, Reagan surprised even many of his supporters by calling for a massive national commitment to build a defense against ballistic missiles. He urged scientists and engineers to use any and all new technologies, including (but not limited to) laser-beam weapons in space.

A hostile press immediately disparaged the program, calling it Star Wars after the 1977 George Lucas film, but unwittingly the media and critics had only underscored the moral superiority of the system. In the film *Star Wars* everyone knew that Luke was the good guy and the evil emperor was a decrepit and corrupt dictator, much like the Soviet tyrants. Reagan's concept baffled reporters and Washington liberal elites who secretly viewed it as lacking sufficient intellectual weight. Stu Spencer, a political strategist, explained why Reagan was at once so popular with the public and so despised by the chattering classes: "Reagan's solutions to problems were always the same as the guy in the bar."[85]

The Gipper had always viewed MAD as an insane policy. He told Lou Cannon, "It's like you and me sitting here in a discussion where we are each pointing a loaded gun at each other, and if you say anything wrong or I say anything wrong, we're going to pull the trigger."[86] As early as 1967 he had been asking scientists and engineers about the technology of defeating ICBMs with antimissiles. He found support from Admiral James Watkins, the chief of naval operations, a devout Catholic who hated MAD and who was outraged by a pastoral letter from the U.S. Catholic bishops condemning the nuclear arms race without ever implicating the USSR as its cause. Watkins and army general John Vessey were encouraged to get beyond the narrow MAD thinking that had shackled the United States for twenty years.

Kremlin insiders were terrified about the proposed program, largely because they knew it would work. Since the early 1970s, Soviet scientists and engineers had conducted a dedicated program of testing for ruby quartz lasers and charged-particle beam weapons. When confronted by the massive cost of such weapons, however, especially when having to acquire technology commonplace in the United States, the Soviet Union gave up on lasers in favor of blunt instruments like the single warhead silo-buster missiles.

Several realities of Star Wars were irrelevant. It would not be ready for years. It might violate existing arms control treaties (but not the proposed START). Even when deployed, it could not be 100 percent effective against incoming warheads. And there were other complaints about Reagan's proposal. America's allies, except for the staunch supporter Margaret Thatcher, prime minister of England, were ill at ease with anything that would give either side a distinct edge, a stance that had evolved from the fear of provoking the Soviets into an invasion the Europeans could not withstand. The Soviets railed against it. But all of these criticisms of the Strategic Defense Initiative (SDI), as the program was formally called, were completely irrelevant to its intended result: to render obsolete, once and for all, much of the USSR's advantage in nuclear missiles.[87]

Reagan had been briefed on the concept in 1982. He and his national security adviser, Robert S. McFarlane, both despised the MAD strategy, believing it was both immoral and destabilizing. It locked the country into a position of barely staying even with the Soviets instead of permitting opportunities to seek superiority. Once he and McFarlane agreed on SDI, it took only a year to flesh out and propose in a national policy initiative. Star Wars "was an example of Reagan's ability to grasp a big new idea, simplify it, and sell it to the American people with consummate skill."[88] He wanted reductions, not limitations, but he knew that the Soviets would never negotiate while they held all the cards. Star Wars changed all that, literally in the space of an hour.

The Soviets had spent the better part of two decades and hundreds of billions of dollars constructing a specific class of weapons that, now, literally could be rendered useless in a matter of years. Clearly the Soviets knew SDI would work, and fully expected the United States to build and deploy it. That assumption left the Kremlin with two options, neither of them good. First, the Soviets could try to counteract SDI through technical modifications to their missiles—hardening the shells, spinning the rockets in flight, and using decoys. None of these were pursued because every one involved adding weight or cost to the missiles, and the USSR was already spending approximately 25 percent of its GNP on the military.

A second alternative was to defeat Star Wars through advanced computer applications, finding ways to outguess the SDI satellites. Reagan, however, had already thwarted that by banning advanced technology sales to the Soviet Union. The Soviets' hysteria over SDI, which became even more apparent later, belies the idea still promoted by some liberals that it had little effect in the downfall of the USSR. As Vladimir Lukhim, former Soviet ambassador to the United States, later said, "It's clear SDI accelerated our catastrophe by at least five years."[89]

Communism's Last Gasp

After Leonid Brezhnev died in 1982, and his successor, Yuri Andropov, died two years later, the leadership of the Communist Party of the Soviet Union fell to another ailing leader, Konstantin Chernenko. In 1985 he, too, died, at which time Mikhail Gorbachev, the "young" (fifty-four-year-old) new general secretary took control of the Kremlin. Gorbachev was immediately celebrated in the western media as a new type of communist who, journalists contended, understood incentives.

Lauded as a sophisticated and sensible reformer, Gorbachev differed little from any of his three dead predecessors, except that they were dead communists and he was still breathing. He did admit that the Soviet Union was in trouble. A dedicated Marxist-Leninist, married to a teacher of Marxism-Leninism, Gorbachev had no intention of abandoning the dream of victory over the West. As Arkady Shevchenko, a Soviet diplomat, pointed out, "Men do not reach the pinnacle of Communist power without . . . an abiding commitment to the rightness of the Soviet system."[90] As late as 1987, Gorbachev still thought "the works of Lenin and his ideals of socialism . . . an inexhaustible source of . . . creative thought, theoretical wealth, and moral sagacity."[91]

Indeed, Gorbachev saw the Stalin era and the Brezhnev period as simply a perversion of communist ideology, not its failure. In speeches before foreign audiences, he routinely portrayed the Soviet economy as "fundamentally sound and merely fatigued."[92] But his practical nature told him that the USSR was taking a beating in Afghanistan and was hopelessly outclassed by the U.S. economy, and that Reagan's Star Wars proposal had theoretically eliminated the only significant advantage the USSR still held over America—its ICBMs.[93]

Gorbachev also found himself bound by Andropov's policy of installing mobile, short-range SS-20 nuclear missiles west of the Ural Mountains. Although a smaller and potentially less destructive class of missiles, the SS-20s were in fact extremely destabilizing weapons. Their mobility made them impossible to verify in treaty negotiations: How many were there? Where were they? Also, unlike every previous class of nuclear weapon employed by the Soviet Union, these missiles were not aimed at the United States, but at European capitals (Bonn, Brussels, Paris, London). Their purpose was crystal clear. They existed to frighten Europeans into breaching the NATO pact, "delinking" Europe from the U.S. nuclear umbrella. Once that had been accomplished, the Soviets could again regain the offensive through intimidation and, if necessary, well-placed force.

Jimmy Carter had committed, in principle, to offsetting these weapons with Pershing and ground-based cruise missiles. Whether he ever would have deployed them was a question left unanswered by his defeat at the polls, but Reagan certainly had no hesitation in meeting the Soviet response. Working closely with Margaret Thatcher, Reagan persuaded NATO heads to accept the U.S. missiles on European soil. On November 14, 1983, after the Kremlin refused to withdraw its SS-20s, American cruise missiles and Pershings arrived in England and West Germany. When Gorbachev ascended to power, he intuitively concluded that the last hope of Soviet communism lay in the "Euromissiles," and Soviet propagandists mounted a massive campaign to intimidate the Europeans into demanding the removal of the NATO weapons. Soviet spy Vasili Mitrokhin reported that the KGB was confident it "possessed a nerve-hold on Western public opinion when it came to European attitudes toward the United States and NATO."[94]

Still attempting to shape American public opinion, the Soviets supported and funded the nuclear freeze movement, which sought to freeze all new construction or deployment of nuclear weapons, leaving the Soviets with a huge strategic advantage. This included a "status quo ante," that would return Europe to its condition before the missiles were installed. Virtually the entire European Left mobilized, using massive parades and demonstrations to intimidate the NATO governments.

By the time Gorbachev had become general secretary—and inherited both Afghanistan and the Euromissile crisis—he knew that he could not defeat the West. Gorbachev never considered a non-Communist Soviet Union. As dissident Vladimir Bukovsky has said, "He wants to save it, together with his skin."[95] But the general secretary could read, and his senior economist at the Soviet Institute of U.S. and Canadian Studies and economic adviser, Alexander Zaichenko, warned him that if he tried to rebuild the Soviet economic glass house, "it would shatter."[96] Zaichenko pointed out to Gorbachev that the USSR was spending 20 percent of its GNP on weapons and research, whereas the United States was spending only 3 to 4 percent.

Reagan appreciated Gorbachev's position, and he sensed in him a Russian leader who could actually be approached on a personal level. In 1985, at a Geneva meeting, Reagan managed to spirit Gorbachev away from his advisers—just the two men and their interpreters in a small cabin with a fire—and he spoke plainly, face-to-face with the communist premier. By the time the hour-and-a-half meeting ended, Reagan had told Gorbachev bluntly, "You can't win" an arms race, then he offered the olive branch by inviting the Russian to visit the United States. Gorbachev accepted, then insisted Reagan come to Moscow. Meeting privately, the leaders of the two superpowers had accomplished far more than their advisers ever thought possible.[97]

It did not hurt Reagan's leverage that the Soviets found themselves bogged down in Afghanistan fighting against the Muslim rebels. At first, Gorbachev had planned to sharply escalate their attacks on the rebels, but in March 1985, Reagan and his advisers developed a plan to arm the Afghans with a powerful Stinger antiaircraft missile. New evidence shows that although the CIA had tried to keep the Pentagon from providing support to the rebels (because it would interfere with low-level programs the CIA had), Reagan and a group of CIA officers nevertheless managed to get Stinger missiles into the hands of the anticommunist forces.[98] The missiles gave the Afghan warriors (including a young radical named Osama bin Laden) the capability of shooting down Soviet helicopters and even low-level fighters. Soviet losses mounted.

Following the failure of the nuclear-freeze propaganda campaign, Gorbachev gave up on the Euromissles. He agreed to remove the SS-20s, and opened up a dialogue with Reagan leading to the Intermediate Nuclear Forces (INF) Treaty (1987). The INF Treaty was the first of its kind. Both sides agreed to withdraw their weapons and to destroy the SS-20s and the Pershings. From there it appeared that Reagan's START Treaty would have clear sailing. In fact, however, it would not be needed: the Soviet Union would collapse before further treaties were required. When Reagan left office, he had greatly helped to cut down the rotting tree of Soviet communism. All that was needed for it to topple was a push from his successor.

Morning in America

Not since 1972 had a starker contrast been put before the American electorate than in the election of 1984. Reagan's conservatism had ridden a wave of triumph since 1980: the tax cuts had produced a tremendous boom, the stock market had taken off, and the armed forces were resupplied and rearmed. More important, the nation had shaken off much of the self-doubt that had lingered since Vietnam and deepened under Carter. At the GOP convention renominating Reagan and Bush, the theme was "It's morning in America." Reagan's natural optimism merged with the rapidly improving state of the Union to make him almost unbeatable.

Democrats ran former Minnesota senator and former vice president Walter Mondale, who was a New Deal liberal to the left of Carter. Mondale chose a woman, Geraldine Ferraro, as his running mate, but the gimmick backfired because she brought to the campaign a tremendous amount of baggage in the form of charges of corruption in her husband's business and in her own campaign funding. Mondale, with little in the Reagan record to criticize, focused on the budget deficits and hoped to make an issue of the Gipper's age. But to address the deficits, Mondale promised to raise taxes, claiming he was only being honest, and most Americans were wary of returning to the bad old days of high taxes and high unemployment. When a moderator raised the question of Reagan's age in a debate, the president, off the cuff, responded, "I won't hold my opponent's youth and inexperience against him." Even Mondale laughed at that clever turnaround, which left the age issue in the dust.

Mondale was crushed, losing every state but his home state of Minnesota (which he nearly lost as well), whereas Reagan had rolled up 59 percent of the popular vote, exceeding the victory margins of every other twentieth-century candidate except Roosevelt in 1936. His optimism remained undaunted: "America is back," he said. "It's morning again." For those who wanted to see the United States as the fount of evil in the world, this was distressing indeed.

Of course, to many others—especially those still trapped behind barbed wire and towers—his reelection was a sign of hope. Ten women in a Soviet forced-labor camp managed to smuggle out an unusual message on a tiny piece of tissue paper, which Reagan could barely read with a magnifying glass. It said, "Mr. President: We, women political prisoners of the Soviet Union, congratulate you on your reelection. . . . We look with hope to your country, which is on the road of *freedom* and respect for *human rights*."[99]

Despite his massive victory, Reagan soon faced a hostile Congress. In 1986 control of the Senate had shifted back to the Democrats. This was partly because of poor timing for Republicans, who had a number of key retirements. In part it also reflected the unwillingness of many Republicans to sign on to Reagan's values, distancing themselves from supply-side economics and the tax cuts. In 1986, Congress, browbeaten by the media over the deficits, tinkered with the tax code again, eliminating many deductions. This had no effect on the deficits, but it slightly reduced the rate of growth of the economy.

Even so, the phenomenal expansion put in place by the tax cuts in 1981 had produced astonishing growth. Contrary to Reagan's critics, who claim the "rich got rich and the poor got poorer," the blessings reached across the entire racial and class strata of American life. From 1982 to 1988, per capita income for whites rose 14 percent, and for blacks, 18 percent (compared to the Carter years of 2.4 percent for whites and 1 percent for blacks). Black unemployment was cut in half under Reagan, with 2.6 million African Americans joining the labor force, and the number of black families in the highest income bracket ($50,000 and over) rose by 86 percent.[100]

Reagan broke ground in other ways. In 1981 he had named the first woman to the Supreme Court when he appointed the moderate Arizonan Sandra Day O'Connor, and in 1986, when Chief Justice Warren Burger retired, Reagan moved conservative William Rehnquist into Burger's top slot. Rehnquist's seat was filled by another Reagan appointee, the brilliant Antonin Scalia, who would often be alone in his dissents until the appointment of his future soulmate, Clarence Thomas, by George H. W. Bush. But in 1988, Reagan's team failed him when, without properly solidifying support first, they sent to the Senate the name of another legal genius, Robert Bork, a federal appeals court judge and former U.S. solicitor general. The Democrats lay in wait for Bork. Caught completely unawares, the president saw his nominee fail to win Senate approval, giving rise to a new term: "to be borked."

The new-look court (with Anthony Kennedy eventually winning Bork's slot) reversed some two decades of legal liberalism and criminals'-rights decisions. States gradually won back some of their constitutionally granted powers, and the Court curtailed the easy filing of discrimination suits that had clogged the judiciary with thousands of questionable claims. Reagan's goal of "protecting the law-abiding citizens" was realized, and the public approval numbers reflected its appreciation.

A more serious reverse for the Reagan agenda came in November 1986 when news surfaced that administration officials had been involved in an effort to negotiate an arms-for-hostage deal with the Iranians. The United States had a long-standing set policy of refusing to negotiate with terrorists, but Reagan, who was personally troubled by the suffering of three Americans being held by radical Muslim groups in the Middle East, approved a deal that sent Iran weapons for use in Iran's war against Iraq. Even more troubling was the revelation that administration officials, apparently without Reagan's approval, had funneled money from that arms trade to the contra rebels fighting in Nicaragua against the communist government there. Marine Colonel Oliver North, who became the focal point of the congressional inquiry that followed, was given immunity and proceeded to take all the blame himself, insulating Reagan. Democrats on the committee were outraged. Having given North immunity to, in their view, implicate the president, all they had was a low-level colonel who had admitted to everything!

Critics of Reagan's administration cite the Iran-contra affair as the central reason why the Gipper's last four years were not as productive as his first term. Much more damaging, however, was the shift in control of the Senate, combined with a host of cabinet-level resignations, defections, and even a death (Commerce Secretary Malcolm Baldrige in a rodeo accident). Many of Reagan's key insiders left to take advantage of their temporary fame and marketability. Ultimately, however, Reagan realized that he had only enough time and energy left to see to fruition a couple of his most important agenda items, and at the top of the list was the demise of the Soviet Union.

By 1986, rumblings within the Soviet empire were a concern to the Kremlin. Dissidents had appeared with increasing frequency in Poland, Hungary, Lithuania, Estonia, Latvia, and other corners of the USSR. Meanwhile, more than 100,000 Soviet troops continued to be pinned down in Afghanistan, and air losses there to the Stinger missiles (supplied by the Reagan administration) had accelerated. This prompted Gorbachev to issue an order that marked the first significant fissure in the Soviet empire's wall: he ordered the withdrawal of 8,000 troops from

Afghanistan. It was the first time during the cold war that the Soviets had been stopped by a native population.

Reagan kept the pressure on. Visiting the Berlin Wall in 1987 in one of history's most memorable moments, he demanded, "Mr. Gorbachev, tear down this wall!" Ironically, a brief setback in market capitalism helped to tear down that wall. The Dow Jones dropped 508 points on October 19, 1987, in the worst decline since Black Tuesday in 1929. Much of the drop had to do with market perceptions that foreign loans, especially to communist countries, would not be repaid. Major banks turned off the credit spigots, and money flowing into Eastern Europe dried up. Anger over the false promises of communism boiled over in May 1988, when Hungary removed its single-party government and began to roll up its section of the Iron Curtain. Gorbachev, stung by Afghanistan, did not react. Poland followed.

On election day in the United States, November 4, 1988—when Reagan's successor, George H. W. Bush was winning his own landslide—a million people marched in East Berlin. Five days later, the crowds took picks and axes to the Berlin Wall, destroying it and signaling the beginning of the end of the cold war. "It's morning in America," Reagan's 1984 reelection campaign theme had proclaimed, and when the Gipper turned over the reins of power to Bush in January 1989, it was morning throughout much of the world. Ronald Reagan was in no small degree responsible for that dawn.

CHAPTER TWENTY-ONE

The Moral Crossroads, 1989–2000

Win One for the Gipper

When the Soviet Union abruptly fell apart in 1991, the nemesis that had opposed the United States in the cold war for almost fifty years vanished overnight. Communism's demise stunned observers across the ideological spectrum, instantly changing the focus of American domestic politics. Republicans, who had championed a strong, well-funded military, suddenly found themselves without a major issue, and Democrats, who had complained that the military-industrial complex siphoned off resources from needed social programs, no longer had an excuse for failing to solve domestic problems. Moreover, Republicans found that some of their voting base—engineers and defense-sector workers—had suffered an economic recession caused by the very success of Reagan's policies. Without the issue of Soviet communism to sharpen political choices, a move to the middle by both parties was natural, although not necessarily beneficial.

Standing before the exuberant GOP convention in 1988, Reagan urged the delegates to support his successor, Vice President George H. W. Bush, the party's nominee. "Go out there and win one for the Gipper," Reagan enjoined the Republican faithful. And although he would not officially leave office until January 1989, Reagan cordially and politely stepped off the stage he had held for eight years in order to turn the limelight on Bush. Five years later, in a poignant letter to the nation, Reagan announced he had Alzheimer's disease. His quick wit faded, as did his health, until his death in 2004.

Time Line

1988: George H. W. Bush elected president; Hungary begins rolling up Iron Curtain

1989: Berlin Wall falls

1990: Bush violates "read my lips" pledge on taxes; Iraq invades Kuwait; Bush announces Operation Desert Shield

1991: Operation Desert Storm evicts Iraq from Kuwait; Soviet Union collapses, replaced by Russia and independent states

1992: Bill Clinton elected president; Rodney King beating

1993: Travelgate; health care bill defeated; Branch Davidian compound at Waco destroyed by FBI and ATF agents; World Trade Center bombed by Al Qaeda; U.S. Rangers killed in Somali raids

1994: Republicans win House of Representatives for the first time in forty years, passes nine tenths of Contract with America; Special prosecutor appointed to investigate Clinton's Whitewater scandal

1995: Oklahoma City bombing

1996: Clinton reelected

1998: Lewinsky scandal breaks; Al Qaeda bombings of U.S. embassies in Africa; Clinton impeached; air war against Serbia

1999: Senate acquits Clinton

2000: Economy begins to slow; Y2K scare proves groundless

George Herbert Walker Bush came from a political family that many associated with privilege, even though his own money had come from hard work in the oil business. His father, Prescott Bush, had been a U.S. senator, and although the younger Bush had not held as many elective offices as a Walter Mondale or a Richard Nixon, he had been in and around Washington for long periods in his life. A fighter pilot who had seen combat in World War II, he returned to civilian life to make a fortune in petroleum, so he knew how the free market worked. He had served as ambassador, congressman, and, after the Nixon debacles, CIA director, restoring some of the confidence in that agency.

Bush suffered from lingering distrust by conservatives because of his 1980 primary campaign against the clearly more conservative Reagan, during which the Texan had called Reagan's supply-side theories "voodoo economics."[1] He was the last of the Teddy Roosevelt Progressive Republicans, although he lacked their righteous fervor. In contrast to the Democrats, however, Bush refused to abandon foreign affairs to serendipity. Unfortunately, he saw the economy in static terms, disdaining the benefits of tax cuts. Still, after eight years of defending Reagan's successful policies and seeing their benefits, he had no choice in 1988 but to run on the Reagan record. This proved to be his great mistake: by lashing himself to a mast that he had no real faith in, his convention pledge—"Read My Lips! No New Taxes"—would come back to haunt him. But that was 1990, and in 1988 Bush convinced enough Republicans that he was, indeed, a conservative. To further solidify their support, he chose young Indiana senator Dan Quayle as his running mate. Quayle had a strong promilitary record in the Senate (even though during the campaign questions arose about his serving in the National Guard instead of in the regular army in Vietnam), and he had impeccable bona fides with the Reaganites. Unfortunately, he was painted by the media as a dim bulb, and he contributed to the image with uninspiring and mistake-prone speeches.

Ironically, the real story of the 1988 election was not about what had happened on the winning Republican side, but about the troubling changes that had taken place inside the losing camp and their long-range implications. Democratic nominee Michael Dukakis, the liberal governor of Massachusetts, had continued the left-wing tilt of the party. A new rival wing of the party, the Democratic Leadership Council (DLC), had originated from strategist Al From's study of the 1984 election disaster, which argued that the party had lost the middle-class vote and needed to move toward the center. Although such a strategy might seem like common sense, it reflected the problems of the Great Society party that had become little more than a collection of special interests—minorities (especially blacks, Hispanics, homosexuals, and feminists), labor unions, and environmentalists. Internal polling by the DLC, however, showed that the Democratic Party "was losing elections because it embraced a public philosophy that repelled the working-class and middle-class voters."[2]

The DLC leadership took some very un-Democratic stands on certain issues, such as favoring free trade and a willingness to examine minor welfare reform. Members like Tennessee senator Al Gore and Arkansas governor Bill Clinton claimed to embrace the new high-tech economy. Michael Dukakis also seemed enthusiastic about the high-tech economy, running on the much-ballyhooed "Massachusetts miracle," his state's rebirth of jobs in the computer industry. When From and other DLC founders designed the centrist strategy, they envisioned it as providing a vehicle to the presidency for one man—Al Gore.

The strategy ran into trouble when the self-appointed civil rights spokesman Jesse Jackson announced plans to run as an unabashed liberal, forming the Rainbow Coalition, special interest groups that mainly had victimhood in common. Jackson had two personas. One was when he appeared in the inner cities, instructing kids to stay off drugs and to avoid having illegitimate children. The other Jesse whom most Americans saw was the man who ranted about insufficient government funding for social programs and cavorted with third-world terrorists. Jackson beat Gore in the South, but could not attract the moderate base elsewhere. Jackson's candidacy unintentionally handed the nomination to Michael Dukakis, who by all measures was nearly as liberal as Jackson.

In the general election, Dukakis actually ran well ahead of Bush early in the campaign, stressing competence over ideology. Then Bush's strategist, Lee Atwater, zeroed in on Dukakis's liberal policies in Massachusetts, including a prison furlough program. Contrary to the anti-Bush legends that have since appeared, it was Democratic Senator Gary Hart, in the primaries, who premiered the television ads featuring Willie Horton, an African American criminal who took advantage of his Massachusetts prison furlough to commit a rape. Atwater borrowed

Hart's concept and created a campaign ad featuring Massachusetts as a revolving door for criminals. Despite the fact that all the faces in the ad were white, Democrats complained that the ad was racist. It proved deadly to the Dukakis campaign. The coup de grâce was administered by the diminutive governor himself when, seeking to bolster his image as promilitary, he rode in a tank with only his small helmeted head sticking out of the massive armored vehicle. From then on, Dukakis could not escape editorial cartoons likening him to the cartoon soldier Beetle Bailey. Bush surged into the lead and on election day crushed the Massachusetts governor, grabbing 426 electoral votes, forty states, and more than 53 percent of the vote.

Communism Collapses in Europe

George Bush had differences with his predecessor over economic issues, but when it came to the cold war, he saw things much the same way as Reagan. Bush continued Reagan's hard-line policies, and no sooner had he taken office than massive anticommunist labor strikes occurred in Poland under the Solidarity movement led by Lech Walesa. At the same time, Hungary announced it would roll up its portion of the Iron Curtain. Having just pulled troops out of Afghanistan, Soviet strongman Mikhail Gorbachev had no appetite for sending tanks into Poland. The USSR looked on as the Poles demanded, and won, an agreement to hold free elections in 1990. Czechoslovakia and Romania soon followed; then travel restrictions to West Germany from East Germany were lifted. Berliners responded, in 1989, by smashing the most visible sign of oppression in the world—the Berlin Wall.

At that point, the Soviet Union itself was starting to unravel. Patriots in Estonia, Lithuania, and Latvia—the Baltic Republics brutally seized by Joseph Stalin in 1939—broke ties with the Soviet Union, again, with no retribution. Gorbachev, believing his western press clippings, assumed that Soviet citizens would view him the way American and European journalists saw him—as a "man of peace" and "reason" who had come to save the world. Instead, Soviet citizens, given a chance, in December 1991, to vote for the first time since the communists took power in 1917, turned the communists out in consecutive elections once and for all. Subsequently, Boris Yeltsin, the chairman of the Russian parliament, emerged as leader of the anticommunist movement, and shortly thereafter the once-independent republics, like Ukraine, peeled themselves off. Yeltsin presided over the creation of eleven separate republics, joined under the new Commonwealth of Independent States (CIS), which had none of the power, communist ideology, or malicious intent of its predecessor. The U.S. Congress authorized nearly half a billion dollars to assist the republics in becoming stable democracies, but much of the cash disappeared into a cesspool of bribery and Mafia-like operations. Lacking a tradition of either private property or rule of law, Russia would find that a peaceful transition to American-style capitalism would not come instantly.

Ironically, communism almost fell "too fast": American leaders for decades had supported prodemocracy forces in the Soviet Union, but at the moment of communism's collapse, Bush and his advisers appeared cautious, almost reticent, to acknowledge that the Soviet dictatorship was gone. They hesitated to recognize many of the newly independent republics.[3] The fact is that like most western anticommunists, Bush had not anticipated that the USSR would simply fall apart. He and Reagan had expected change, but the history of failed rebellions in Hungary, Czechoslovakia, and other parts of the communist bloc had convinced them that change would be evolutionary, and slow. For all of Reagan's insight (much of which had rubbed off on Bush), he did not see the moral abdication of the Soviet leadership coming. Soviet officials had ceased believing in the efficacy of Marxism/Leninism for years, a development characterized by Valery Boldin, Gorbachev's chief of staff, as the "internal capitulation" of Soviet leadership. The surrender by Soviet elites revealed what Polish dissident Adam Michnik called the "intimate bond [that] exists between force and deception. . . . Deception becomes a method of self-defense."[4] Boldin described the resulting western triumph as "a total rout of the . . . USSR and the moral devastation of a once powerful adversary."[5]

One author noted, "Just before the breakup of the USSR, the view of that country as a model of the most stable and durable regime in the world had gained wide acceptance among Western Sovietologists . . . there was not one American political scientist who predicted the collapse of the USSR."[6] Richard Pipes, a Harvard Sovietologist, had done so, but he was nearly alone. Most western intellectuals thought the Soviet government was indestructible, and liberals and conservatives alike had almost universally overrated the Soviet GNP and underrated its arms production.

There is a certain truth to the notion that freedom itself constituted a potent weapon in the demise of Soviet communism. Freedom's steady buffeting of the communist system was most visible in Berlin, when, during a concert in the mid-1980s by rock star Bruce Springsteen at the Berlin Wall, a scene took place that at one time would have seemed impossible to the party bosses. Springsteen naturally attracted thousands of free West Berliners, but hundreds of communist youths showed up on the other side of the wall to listen. When Springsteen sang "Born in the USA," there were thousands of ostensibly good socialists singing along, "Born . . . in the USA, I was . . . born in the USA." Soviet spy Vasili Mitrokhin's smuggled notes revealed that popular music and radio broadcasts from the West produced "unhealthy signs of interest in . . . pop stars" and led to an "almost surreal . . . musical subversion" in some cities.[7] The KGB estimated that 80 percent of its youth listened to western rock music broadcasts, which "gave young people [in the eyes of the KGB] a distorted idea of Soviet reality, and led to incidents of a treasonable nature."[8] Spy memos warned that rock and roll "has a negative influence on the interest of society, inflames vain ambitions and unjustified demands, and can encourage the emergence of informal . . . groups with a treasonable tendency."[9] Just as Ike had fought the Soviets of the 1950s with Louis Armstrong, Reagan and Bush ironically benefited from the influences of Madonna and Kiss!

The American public, although pleased with the apparent end of the cold war, remained skeptical and puzzled, unsure if the new system in Russia could last. A decade after the fall of communism, there has not yet been a single national celebration over the success, nor a monument to the victory. Communism went out with a whimper, not a bang, hobbling the victory dance.

Even before the cold war embers had stopped smoking, Bush and the Democrats in Congress started spending the "peace dividend" they anticipated would result from the reduction of military forces. The demobilization that ensued, although smaller in scale than the reduction in force associated with any previous war, nevertheless produced economic and social turmoil. In a period of only a few years, aerospace and shipbuilding giants were nearly out of business; thousands of engineers, especially in California, received pink slips. Companies scrambled to get out of defense contracting. Soldiers, airmen, and sailors were laid off, or "riffed," an acronym for "reduction in force." Bush foresaw a new world order arising out of the ashes of communism's defeat. His unfortunate phrase set off the paranoid at both political extremes, who for years had prophesied that a secret international United Nations–directed body would dominate the world's affairs. Right-wing conspiracy theorists fretted about Bush's involvement in the Trilateral Commission and the Council on Foreign Relations, whereas left-wing paranoids saw the new world order as the final triumph of a greedy oil cartel. Bush lacked the political imagination for such global nonsense. What the verbally challenged president meant was that the world agreed communism was doomed, and the developed nations (including Russia) had to think in terms of cooperation instead of conflict. To that end, he sought to bring many former East-bloc countries into NATO, and in 1991 Congress provided $400 million to help Ukraine and other fragments of the Soviet empire dismantle their nuclear weapons.

Saddam Hussein, Megalomaniac

Military leaders, having learned their lessons in Vietnam, had already sensed that the next war would not resemble the massive armored frontal battle in European forests or a Southeast Asian jungle planned for by strategists of the cold war. In all likelihood, new conflicts would involve a confrontation with a third-world power. The generals correctly anticipated the style of the threat, but they failed to anticipate the setting.

Communism had barely begun its collapse when Iraqi tanks rolled into neighboring Kuwait on August 2, 1990. Claiming that Kuwait was rightfully part of Iraq and illegally separated by international fiat, Iraqi dictator Saddam Hussein threatened all of the Persian Gulf with his large well-trained army. Hussein, who wore an army uniform, held the title of president, but he stood in a long line of third-world dictators like Idi Amin and Muammar al Qaddafi. Despite repeated warnings from American and Kuwaiti oil producers (who had witnessed the military buildup) and from the U.S. ambassador to Iraq, the Bush administration, preoccupied with Russia, was unprepared for the Iraqi invasion.

By invading another Arab state—rather than Israel—Hussein had the potential to capture and control large parts of oil production in the Middle East, creating a direct hazard to the free flow of oil at market prices. This danger, in turn, posed a clear risk to American national security. Hussein had the largest and best-equipped army and air force (aside from Israel's) in the Middle East.

Bush saw the peril of Hussein's control of the lion's share of Mideast oil: if Hussein succeeded in Kuwait, Saudi Arabia would be next. Uncharacteristically, Bush acted swiftly. Despite stiff resistance from Democrats in Congress, Bush mobilized an international response in the diplomatic arena: the United Nations imposed economic sanctions and prepared for military actions. He allowed a reasonable time for the economic pressure to work, at the same time instituting a buildup of troops in Saudi Arabia. Persuading the Muslim Saudis to permit large contingents of foreign (largely Christian and Jewish) troops in their nation was a foreign relations coup for the American president. Under operation Desert Shield, the United States sent 230,000 troops to ensure that the Iraqis did not invade Saudi Arabia, a force General Norman Schwartzkopf referred to as a "tripwire."

Democrats opposed plans to liberate Kuwait, raising the specter of another Vietnam. Senator Ted Kennedy and Congressman Richard Gephardt (Democrat of Missouri) warned of "80,000 body bags" returning U.S. dead from the Persian Gulf if a war broke out—a number greater than the entire toll of dead in the ten-year Vietnam conflict. But some isolationist conservatives, such as Nixon and Reagan speechwriter and presidential candidate Patrick Buchanan, also bitterly condemned Bush's actions as unchecked internationalism. A small antiwar movement organized, brandishing signs saying NO BLOOD FOR OIL and BURY YOUR CAR.[10]

The administration, however, had no intention of being sucked into another protracted conflict, and in fact intended to apply the lessons of Vietnam, which strategists and military theoreticians had studied for years. Moreover, Bush followed Reagan's rules for engagement. Bush and his strategic leadership team of Joint Chiefs chairman Colin Powell (the highest-ranking African American soldier ever) and Secretary of Defense Richard Cheney ensured from the outset that three critical differences would separate the war against Iraq from the failed Vietnam experience. First, Bush mobilized an international alliance such as the world had never seen. After securing authorization from the United Nations to repel Iraqi aggression, Bush persuaded (among others) Saudi Arabia, Egypt, Bahrain, the United Arab Emirates, Jordan, and most of the NATO countries to send military forces totaling 200,000. More impressive, he gained assurances from Israel that if the Iraqis launched missile or air attacks on the Jewish state, Israel would refrain from counterattacks, which could have caused all the other Muslim members of the alliance to quit.

Working with Russian leaders, Bush also obtained promises that Russia would not sell weapons to Iraq or offer other military assistance. This was remarkable in itself: it was the first time since the cold war had begun that the two superpowers were aligned on the same side of a fight. Finally, although Japan's pacifist post–World War II constitution prohibited it from sending ground troops, Bush gained a commitment for substantial Japanese funding of the effort. Since Japan had to import 100 percent of its oil, the Persian Gulf conflict clearly affected Japan's national security. All in all, Bush had accomplished a stunning diplomatic coup by aligning virtually the entire world against Hussein, even to the point of neutralizing the Israeli-Arab antagonisms.

Second, Bush's team was committed to not repeating the incrementalism that had characterized American involvement in Southeast Asia. Instead, in the Persian Gulf the United States followed the Reagan rules of identifying a clear objective, then deploying overwhelming force and sufficient matériel to accomplish the task. Whereas it took years to build up American forces in Vietnam to the 565,000 level, allied forces in the Gulf numbered 430,000 after only a few months. Moreover, the allies did not act until they had massed sufficient forces.

Finally, Bush established a clear exit strategy: liberate Kuwait (and force the removal of all Iraqi troops) and significantly diminish Iraq's ability to threaten her neighbors again. Although critics complained about the word "significantly," the objectives given to Allied Commander General Norman Schwartzkopf set specific reduction levels in tanks that would leave Iraq with no more than a "foot-soldier" army. As Powell had told his staff early on, "I won't be happy until I see those tanks destroyed. . . . I want to finish it; to destroy Iraq's army on the ground."[11]

"Cut Off the Head and Kill the Body"

Air power as a decisive (strategic) factor in war had been hotly debated since World War II's "strategic bombing survey." After Vietnam, criticism of air effectiveness escalated, to the point where the air force, army, and navy each undertook internal studies of the use of air power and engaged in planning for joint operations in which units of the different services would work together on the battlefield.[12]

Hussein's invasion of Kuwait offered a battlefield test of air power and its new doctrines. Here was a modernized enemy force, complete with top-level Soviet fighter planes, thick air defense around a major city, and troops who were dug in and (according to the prevailing views of strategic bombing in World War II) relatively safe from attacks from the air. Yet allied air strikes so effectively eliminated enemy opposition that the United States suffered fewer ground troops killed than in any major conflict in history, and the majority of those who perished were killed in either incidents of friendly fire or from a single long-range Scud missile attack on a barracks. Actual combat losses to the Iraqis were minuscule: 148 killed in the actual course of fighting.[13]

Using antiradar missiles, the coalition forces, in a matter of hours, eradicated all of Iraq's ability to "see" allied aircraft.[14] Without enemy radar to contend with, coalition aircraft losses dropped to one aircraft per 1,800 sorties, a rate fourteen times lower than during Vietnam's Linebacker II.[15] And nowhere was that total control more evident than in the air war against armor and men. Even the hunkered-down, dug-in Iraqi armor was helpless against the air campaign. One crew of an F-111 bomber summed matters up in a nutshell: "If armies dig in, they die. If they come out of their holes, they die sooner." Another likened the Iraqi army to a "tethered goat."[16] Using synthetic aperture radar (SAR) and other radar systems, virtually every vehicle that moved could be identified and tracked. "It was mind-boggling," one coalition radar operator marveled: "Sometimes there were so many [vehicles] you couldn't even count them all. . . . Then all of a sudden you don't see any more traffic. . . . [and they] left the road or stopped. Then you use your SAR and shazam! All of a sudden, we've got the exact number of vehicles, where they would be parked and we would relay that information to fighters and the Army. . . ."[17]

Mind-boggling was a good term for the carnage of Iraqi armored vehicles that followed. Over the course of the war, to February 14, 1991, the radar-supported bombers decimated the Iraqis, "plinking" 1,300 out of 6,100 tanks, and even increasing that rate, taking out 500 per day at the peak of operations! Using the advanced radar systems, high-altitude aircraft would simply "paint" an armored vehicle or tank with a laser, and attack craft would launch fire-and-forget laser-guided weapons that would lock onto the targets while the plane looked for another menace. Powell's prophecy—that he would "cut off the head and kill the body" of the Iraqi army—had been fulfilled.[18]

Schwarzkopf's daring February twenty-third offensive, which he called the Hail Mary, called for a feint into Kuwait where the Iraqi defenses were thickest, followed by a second fake by amphibious troops at the coast. Then he would use the cover of night to conduct a massive and unprecedented shift of tanks, troops, helicopters, and, most important, fuel and supply vehicles, far to the Iraqi flank in the desert. The war was over before it began: the Iraqis lost 76 percent of their tanks, 55 percent of their armored personnel carriers (APCs), and 90 percent of their dreaded artillery in approximately one hundred *hours*.[19] Iraqi soldiers, starving and mercilessly pounded by air strikes, surrendered to CNN newsmen, armed only with microphones, and deserted at rates of 25 to 30 percent.[20] Sensing they would be slaughtered if they remained anywhere near their vehicles, Iraqi drivers and gunners abandoned thousands of trucks, tanks, APCs, and scout cars on the famous Highway of Death leading out of Kuwait City. Estimates of Iraqi troop losses, although not entirely reliable, put the enemy death toll at 100,000, and the wounded at an equal number. Air power had proved so thoroughly destructive that the army only had to fire 2 percent of the 220,000 rounds of ammunition it had ordered for the theater.[21] The allied effort was a classic example of what Victor Davis Hansen called the western way of war, "all part of a cultural tradition to end hostilities quickly, decisively, and utterly."[22]

On February twenty-eighth, Hussein agreed to allied terms. Unfortunately, at no time did the United Nations resolution or American objectives include taking Baghdad or overthrowing Hussein, leaving him as a malignancy in the region for another decade. At the time, however, Bush's advisers feared such an action would have deployed American troops as "peacekeepers" in the middle of violent factions fighting for control of a Saddam-less Iraq. The experience in the Reagan administration when the marines were killed by a suicide truck bomber in Lebanon remained fresh in the president's mind. Meanwhile, Democrats at home used every opportunity to warn of a quagmire or another Vietnam. Coalition partners, especially Islamic states like Egypt, Turkey, and Saudi Arabia, feared that a fundamentalist Shiite regime might arise out of a Hussein-less Iraq. In short, from the perspective of 1992, there were compelling reasons to quit. These were reasons that—even with the hindsight of the later attacks of 2001—one must conclude seemed sound at the time.[23]

"A Kinder, Gentler America"

Successful prosecution of the Gulf War propelled Bush to unparalleled levels of popular support—but only briefly. The public quickly forgot his overseas accomplishments when a brief recession ended the decade-long Reagan boom. In 1991 and much of 1992 the economy slowed. Historically, it was a mild recession, but the media and the Democratic contenders for president in 1992 made it out to be the worst economy in the last fifty years, a phrase Bill Clinton used repeatedly in his campaign.

Bush had himself to blame. From the moment he took office, he believed the media "gloomsters" and Texas millionaire Ross Perot, who warned that the federal budget deficits had reached intolerable levels. When considered in real constant dollars, the deficits were slightly higher than in past decades, but hardly dangerous. Quite the contrary, the nation's GNP had grown faster than the deficits, reducing the real level of deficits-to-GNP throughout the Reagan/Bush years. But Bush had surrounded himself with Keynesian advisers who saw tax increases as the only solution to rising deficits.

What followed was one of the most incredible political meltdowns in history. In 1990, pressure built on Bush to compromise with Democrats in Congress to raise taxes, ostensibly to reduce the deficit. Yet Democratic congresses for thirty years had been comfortable with constant deficits, most of them proportionally higher than those existing in 1990. Only when it became a political weapon did they suddenly exhibit concern about the nation's finances, and then only in terms of raising taxes, not in terms of cutting massive federal expenditures. Bush agreed to cut spending in return for a $133 billion in new taxes—the largest tax increase in the nation's history. The agreement slammed the top rate back up to 31 percent from 27 percent; imposed so-called sin taxes on tobacco and alcohol, which penalized the poor; and eliminated exemptions. Most important, it put Bush in the position of reneging on his "read my lips, no new taxes" convention pledge.

Bush sorely underestimated the public resentment of a bald-faced lie, especially the reaction of conservatives. Worse, he overestimated the veracity of the

Democrats in Congress, where no substantive spending cuts took place. In the hinterlands, however, the Republican base was outraged, especially since Bush had marketed himself in 1988 as Reagan's successor specifically on supply-side principles. READ MY LIPS: I LIED, blared the New York *Post*'s front page.[24] Many abandoned the GOP in disgust.

Bush had put himself in a hole: having sided with the Democrats and their tax increases, Bush could not tout tax cuts as a means to end the economy's slide. In addition, he seemed out of touch with the lives of ordinary Americans and unwilling to embrace Reagan's legacy. Whereas Reagan had come into office eager to abolish the Department of Energy and the Department of Education (and had failed to do so), Bush had no such prejudices against big government. His campaign theme of a "kinder, gentler America" seemed to agree with Democratic criticisms that Reagan's America had been mean and harsh. Bush celebrated a "thousand points of light," a phrase that referred to the good deeds of millions of individual Americans who could privately shoulder some responsibilities carried by Uncle Sam. But he lacked a clear vision and obviously did not have Reagan's communication skills to enable him to go over the heads of the Washington/New York media elites, straight to American citizens.

Even when Bush took positions that were far to the left of his conservative base, such as pushing through the Americans with Disabilities Act (ADA) and stricter environmental laws, he won no praise from the media, but instead was criticized for not doing enough. When Thurgood Marshall, the only African American on the U.S. Supreme Court, retired, Bush nominated Clarence Thomas, a black conservative federal judge with an impeccable record. Instead of praising Bush's racial sensitivity, Thomas was nearly "borked" at the Senate hearings when a University of Oklahoma law professor, Anita Hill, claimed Thomas had sexually harassed her. After a high-profile Senate hearing Thomas was confirmed and became an outstanding and consistent justice.

Thomas was representative of a new class of African Americans who had become successful and prosperous with minimal, if any, aid from government. As such, he represented a significant threat to the civil rights establishment, whose central objective remained lobbying for government action on behalf of those it claimed to represent. Men and women like John Johnson, Michael Jordan, Herman Cain, and Oprah Winfrey illustrated by their success within the market system that political favors played almost no part in economic achievement for blacks. At the same time, a new class of conservative black intellectuals arose—Thomas himself and men like Shelby Steele, Walter Williams, Glenn Loury, and Thomas Sowell—that was at odds with the entrenched civil rights leadership, yet were deliberately ignored and trivialized by the media.

Episodes of racial injustice—no matter how unusual or atypical—turned into opportunities to once again mobilize black political support around civil rights themes. One such event occurred in April 1992, when four white Los Angeles police officers attempted to stop a black motorist who had run from them at speeds of more than a hundred miles per hour. The driver, Rodney King, repeatedly resisted the officers, and the police suspected he was high on a narcotic, possibly PCP (psychoactive drug phencyclidine), which diminishes pain receptors. When King did not respond to oral commands, the police beat him with their clubs and hit him with a Taser stun gun. A witness taped the entire episode with a video camera, and King sued the Los Angeles Police Department for violations of his civil rights. Tried in Simi Valley, a northern Los Angeles suburb, the officers were acquitted by an all-white jury, some of whom stated that when viewed in context, the tapes showed that King had appeared dangerous as he continued to resist.

When the verdict was announced, South-Central Los Angeles broke out in Watts-like riots and looting, protesting the appearance that the white officers got off the hook. It took troops three days to restore order, by which time fifty-four people had died and thousands of buildings had been damaged or destroyed. The Bush Department of Justice quickly hauled the officers up on federal civil rights charges, and on April 17, 1992, two of them were found guilty of violating King's civil rights and sentenced to thirty months in prison. It would not be the first racially charged case in Los Angeles to make news during the decade.

"I Didn't Inhale"

Bush's weakness on the economy opened the door for a serious challenge to the sitting president from the Democrats, but it was still one he should have weathered. Instead, Bush found himself besieged not by one, but by two political opponents.

Americans had become frustrated with the national debt and the annual deficits, but were unwilling to elect individual legislators who would resist the siren song of spending. A dynamic developed in which, to get elected, politicians of both parties would tout their ability to bring in dollars locally while opposing national spending programs in other districts.

Moreover, structural impediments to change had afflicted the House of Representatives, where, by law, spending bills originated. Having held the majority for almost forty years, the Democrats dominated committees, and they did so in such a way that there was little debate or discussion about many legislative items. Democrats controlled the rules committee, and simply prohibited extensive analysis of spending bills. Indeed, proposals to cut taxes, to restrain spending, and to force various caps onto the budgetary process never made it to the floor of the House for a vote. Democrat leaders killed the proposals in committee, quietly, and away from public roll calls. This process shielded Democrats from charges from opponents of being big spenders by keeping the votes secret: a politician could simply deny that he supported a particular measure and that was the end of it.

Politicians had also started to become permanent Washington fixtures. Far from the Jeffersonian ideal of citizen legislators, many of the people who ran the nation had never lived or worked outside of Washington; most of the members of Congress were lawyers who had gone straight from law school to government work. Few had ever run a business or had had to show a profit or meet a payroll.

In contrast, as legislators, when government ran short of money, they either ran a deficit or hiked taxes. There was never any talk of actually cutting back, or belt tightening. Gradually, popular resentment built up against "politics as usual."

It took the right person to tap into this well of anti-Washington sentiment. In 1992, H. Ross Perot, a Texas billionaire, burst onto the political scene. He had founded Electronic Data Systems (EDS) in 1962, turning it into a cash machine.[25] In 1979 he funded a successful effort to pluck several EDS employees out of revolutionary Iran, which author Ken Follett later turned into a best-selling novel, *On the Wings of Eagles*. After selling EDS to General Motors, he started Perot Systems. By the time he began to appear in public forums, Perot possessed a certain amount of credibility. He initially appealed to many as homey, sensible, and practical, but at the same time, he turned off elites like those swarming around the Clinton staff. (Clinton communications director George Stephanopoulos called Perot a "weird little man who was a ventriloquist's dummy for voter anger," a comment that itself showed how detached insiders like Stephanopoulos were).[26] Perot's business background attracted many who were outraged by out-of-control deficit spending, and his simple-sounding solutions on the surface had appeal. He played to his role as an outsider, claiming he owed nothing to either of the established parties. Denouncing campaign spending, Perot refused federal money and financed himself in 1992. He carefully avoided any abortion position that would have alienated the sea of moderates, and he stayed away from any specifics in his policy recommendations for as long as possible. Adept with charts and graphs, Perot was the master of the political infomercial, but he faltered badly when confronted by a forceful critic.

Unlike Reagan's, Perot's simple-sounding solutions were often contradictory and poorly grounded in political realities. After a brief infatuation with Perot, the media turned hostile in early summer, leading the Texan to withdraw from the race in July. The withdrawal, however, was another Perot ploy to avoid close inspection. He reentered the race in October, when the press had to pay more attention to the established candidates, and although the two-month hiatus may have cost him a few votes, Perot gained much more by avoiding the media scrutiny during the summer. He hoped to gain a plurality of the vote in enough states to snatch the presidency from Bush or Clinton.

The Democrats, in the wake of the 1988 Dukakis debacle, had listened to calls to move to the center. That year, Al From decided that Bill Clinton had to be made the chairman of the DLC, and he began to organize a structure that would facilitate a White House run by the DLC chairman. It was nothing less than a breathtaking transformation of American campaign finance practices. In 1990, Clinton accepted the position with the promise that he could use the resources of the DLC as a fund-raising apparatus. Indeed, from the outset, Clinton's primary purpose at the organization was raising money.

Bolstered by a series of New Democrat studies, Clinton supported several moderate positions, especially free trade through the North American Free Trade Agreement (NAFTA) and welfare reform rather than welfare expansion. Along with other New Democrats, Clinton touted law-and-order issues and railed against deficits. Above all, he sought to repackage old, dilapidated liberal ideas with new language, calling government spending "investment" and referring to taxes as "contributions."[27]

At the convention, Clinton chose as his running mate Al Gore of Tennessee, whom the DLC had originally intended as its model candidate back in 1988. Awash in money and wielding a series of policy proposals designed to win back the middle class, Clinton should have been a formidable candidate. As it was, he stumbled.

For one thing, he had dodged the draft during the Vietnam war. Reporters who had known the story all along and had failed to address it finally began to home in on his flight to England as a Rhodes Scholar (where he participated in antiwar protests) and on his manipulation of his college ROTC classification. There were equally damaging allegations of marital infidelity. Gennifer Flowers, a former lover, produced a tape-recorded conversation of Clinton telling her to lie about their relationship. Once again, the press had known about that relationship and effectively buried it until it could no longer be contained. Appearing with his wife, Hillary, on a *60 Minutes* television interview, Clinton evaded the Flowers allegations but admitted there had been "pain in their marriage," and the pair continued on as the happy (and ever politic) couple.[28]

As the first major candidate from the boomer generation, Clinton portrayed himself as young and hip, appearing on a nighttime television show in sunglasses to play the saxophone with the band, and answering questions about the type of underwear he wore on MTV. He admitted to smoking marijuana—but he "didn't inhale." (His brother, Roger, had been jailed for possession of cocaine.) When it came to women, Clinton had used state troopers in Arkansas to "introduce" him to various girls and then employed the bodyguards to transport the females to and from their assignations. Most of his former sex partners remained silent. The few who did speak up came under withering fire from Clinton allies, who vilified them as "nuts and sluts." (A female Clinton staffer was hired to specifically deal with "bimbo eruptions," claims by other women that they had had affairs with the candidate.)

Clinton's flagrant disregard of traditional morals outraged large segments of the public, who were already concerned about high crime rates, rising illegitimacy, soaring divorce numbers, and public schools that suffered from a plague of violence. Although George Bush confidently believed that his character would stand in stark relief to that of Clinton's, he himself had brazenly lied about the tax hikes.

On election day, Clinton effectively secured 43 percent of the vote. Bush netted only 37 percent, and the spoiler Perot siphoned off 19 percent. Perot's total was significant, equaling the amount won by Teddy Roosevelt in 1912, when he had essentially denied the presidency to William Howard Taft. It would be inaccurate, however, to claim that Perot stole the election from Bush: exit polls show that he took votes equally from both established candidates. Perot did damage Bush, however, by muddying the waters on Clinton's character, and by portraying both parties as equally guilty of deficits, insulating Clinton from tax-and-spend criticisms.

Given Clinton's anemic popular vote, historians, who, for the most part are liberals, have distorted the 1992 election to portray it as victory for liberalism. Emphasizing the turnout, it was claimed the election "reversed 32 years of steady decline in participation."[29] Yet the additional turnout was not for liberalism or Clinton, but for *Perot,* and constituted a protest vote of disgust against both major parties. The election proved little. Bush had run away from his conservative base and alienated the low-tax crowd, while Clinton, portraying himself as a New Democrat, had adopted many of the Republican positions. Perot had offered no specifics whatsoever. Yet Clinton, who ran as a "moderate," no sooner took office than he made a hard left turn.

The Clinton Presidency

Understanding the Clinton presidency requires an appreciation for the symbiotic relationship between Bill Clinton and his aggressive wife, Hillary. Mrs. Clinton, a Yale Law School grad and staffer in the Nixon impeachment, had harbored political ambitions for herself since her undergraduate days at Wellesley. Her personal demeanor, however, was abrasive and irritating and doused any hopes she had of winning a political seat on her own early in her life. When she met Clinton at Yale, he seemed a perfect fit. He was gregarious, smart, and charismatic, but not particularly deep. A sponge for detail, Clinton lacked a consistent ideology upon which to hang his facts. This was the yin to Hillary Rodham's yang: the driven ideologue Hillary ran her husband's campaigns, directed and organized the staff, and controlled his appearances. Since her political future was entirely in his hands, she willingly assumed the role of governor's wife after Clinton won his first election. When Clinton gained the presidency in 1992, Hillary was fully in her element.

Clearly an understanding had been struck long before the election: Hillary Clinton would play the loyal wife in order to gain power, and once in office, Bill would reward her through policy appointments that did not require Senate confirmation. The couple even joked to one reporter that if the voters elected Clinton, they would get "two for the price of one." Consummating the deal, the president immediately named Hillary to head a task force to review and fix the nation's health-care "crisis." The only real crisis was the lack of congressional will to cut costs or raise revenue for the costly and inefficient Medicare and Medicaid programs. Instead, Hillary Clinton and the Democratic National Committee diverted the debate to one of uninsurability, implying that any Americans who lacked insurance had no access to medical treatment. In fact, it meant nothing of the sort. Millions of Americans in sole proprietorships or other small businesses found it cheaper to pay cash for medical care, and there was always emergency medical care available to anyone, insured or not.

Mrs. Clinton had her opening to policy direction. Meeting with dozens of Democratic allies and experts in secret sessions—in clear violation of federal sunshine laws, as a subsequent court ruling later made plain—Hillary, with the help of Ira Magaziner, finally unveiled a health care plan so massive in scope that even other advisers were aghast. It was a political blunder of enormous magnitude. One of the administration's own economists had argued that "one of the first messages from the new Democratic administration should not be to put 1/7th of the American economy under the command and control of the federal government."[30] The plan dictated, among other things, the specialties medical students should pursue, where doctors could practice, and which physicians individual Americans would be allowed to see. More stunning, the proposal threatened to punish by fines *and jail* doctors who accepted cash for providing a service and patients who paid cash for health care! In addition, "employer mandates" for even the smallest of businesses to ensure employees would have been the death knell of millions of small businesses. When word of "Hillarycare" started to leak out, it produced a firestorm of opposition.

Radio talk show host Rush Limbaugh, who had a national weekly audience of nearly 20 million, led the assault by reading on-air critiques of the health care plan by Democratic consumer writer Elizabeth McCaughey. Needless to say, few legislators, and even fewer average citizens, had read the massive 1,342-page document, but McCaughey had, and Limbaugh exposed the details on a daily basis. Legislators of both parties ran for the hills away from Hillarycare, and it went down to ignominious defeat when the majority Democrats in the House refused to bring Hillarycare up for a vote. Arguably, it was the first time in history that a single radio (or television) personality had exercised so much influence in defeating unpopular legislation. In no way was the bill the "victim of . . . intense partisan wrangling" or "the determination of Republican leaders to deny the president any kind of victory on this potent issue," as liberal historians argued.[31]

Yet Clinton had not needed his wife's assistance to stumble out of the gate. One of his first initiatives involved removing the military's ban against homosexuals in active service. When military and profamily groups got wind of the plan, it generated such reaction that Clinton retreated to a compromise position of "Don't ask, don't tell."

Nor did his budget measures fare well: the first Clinton budget, a deficit-reduction plan, hiked taxes (including a Social Security tax on the elderly) and required a tie-breaking vote from his vice president. Early on, Clinton's war room of strategists had convinced him that he had to attack the deficits, and that such action would give him credibility in other (more liberal) initiatives. Treasury secretary Lloyd Bentsen impressed in unusually blunt language the significance of soothing Wall Street with his budget. "You mean to tell me," Clinton asked his advisers, "that the success of the program and my reelection hinges on . . . a bunch of f**king bond traders?" Nods from around the table greeted him.[32] To further portray himself as a moderate, Clinton instructed his vice president, Al Gore, to head a project called the Reinvention of Government. It was heralded as Clinton's response to conservative calls that the growth of government needed to be checked, and Gore soon dutifully reported that his group had lopped 305,000 off government job rolls. A closer look, however, revealed an ominous trend: 286,000 of those job cuts came from the Department of Defense.[33] It marked the beginning of a simultaneous slashing of military capability on the one hand and unparalleled military commitments abroad on the other. Within three years, Clinton had increased overseas deployments and, at the same time, reduced the total active-duty force from 2.1 million to 1.6 million, reduced the army from eighteen full-strength divisions to twelve (the Gulf War alone had taken ten), cut the navy's fleet from 546 ships to 380, and decreased the number of air force squadrons by one third.

Before long, even Clinton's most loyal staff became befuddled by his apparent lack of deeply held principles. After securing Clinton's election, James Carville, one of his political advisers, still did not know what he valued. Carville once took out a piece of paper, drew a small square, and tapped it with his pen: "Where is the hallowed ground?" he asked. "Where does he stand? What does he stand for?"[34] That his own confidants had no idea what principles Clinton would fight for was a troubling aspect of Clinton's character. Most serious, however, was another hangover from the campaign, a savings and loan investment called Whitewater that had involved the Clintons. The issues were serious enough that the Clinton-controlled Justice Department appointed a special prosecutor—an investigative holdover from the Nixon Watergate days—charged with looking into the land speculations.

Clinton had announced his intention to appoint a "cabinet that looked like America" by including plenty of women, blacks, and Hispanics. Yet within a few years his critics would joke that his cabinet in fact looked more like *America's Most Wanted*. More than a dozen special prosecutors had opened investigations into the administration's appointees. Clinton had invoked quotas on nearly every cabinet position, regardless of competence. Above all, party loyalists and fundraisers were to be rewarded. Ron Brown, chairman of the Democratic National Committee, was placed in the powerful cabinet post of secretary of commerce. This later facilitated the sales of high-tech weaponry to the communist Chinese government when authority was transferred early from the State Department, which had opposed such sales, to the pliant Commerce Department under Brown. Other cabinet officials ranged from barely competent to utterly incompetent. Clinton's surgeon general, Jocelyn Elders, committed one gaffe after another, testifying before a congressional hearing on gun control that "what we need are safer bullets" and calling for lessons in public schools on masturbation. Ultimately, the Clinton administration could not survive her inanities and dismissed her.

Where Elders was merely incompetent, many other appointees surpassed

Grant's or Harding's cabinet in their corruption or outright criminal behavior. Housing and Urban Development (HUD) Secretary Henry Cisneros was forced to resign after a sexual harassment suit; associate attorney general Webster Hubbell was indicted in the Whitewater investigation; Secretary of Agriculture Mike Espy was investigated for illicit connections to Arkansas-based Tyson Foods; and an independent prosecutor examined Interior Secretary Bruce Babbitt for illegal dealings with Indian tribes. Virtually all the investigations in some respect dealt with money, graft, and bribery, making a mockery of the Clinton campaign promise to appoint the "most ethical administration in history." It was an ironic turn, given Clinton's repeated claims that the Reagan era was a "decade of greed." Only the investment banker Robert Rubin, who handled Treasury, seemed remotely suited to the task.

At first, Clinton's choices for these departments seemed to reflect only his lack of executive experience, but events soon unfolded that made the placement of key individuals look suspiciously like Nixon-esque attempts to stack the system at critical positions with people who would either bend or break the law on the Clintons' behalf. Webster Hubbell and Vincent Foster, for example, who were law partners with Hillary at the Rose Law Firm in Arkansas, were brought into the Justice Department, where they could effectively block or derail investigations into the administration. Attorney General Janet Reno had to defer to Associate Attorney General Hubble on many occasions. In a shocking break with tradition, Clinton, immediately upon taking office, fired all 93 U.S. attorneys throughout the country, thereby nipping any federal investigations of him in the bud.

FBI background checks on White House personnel were also curtailed, apparently for what they might reveal about the appointees. All this only reinforced the suspicion that a number of individuals of questionable character worked in the administration, but it also proved dangerous, facilitating the attendance at White House functions of criminals such as drug-runner Jorge Cabrera. Among the other guests at Clinton functions was Wang Jun, an arms dealer who supplied Los Angeles street gangs with automatic weapons; international fugitive Marc Rich; and a steady stream of foreigners whose visits were arranged by John Huang, an indicted Arkansas restaurateur. According to the foreign visitors, they were explicitly told that they could influence the government of the United States by Huang, who himself visited the White House more often than members of Clinton's cabinet—always, he later testified, to arrange fund-raising with foreign nationals.

Clinton's disapproval numbers in public polls rose sharply, and surveys showed that people were increasingly convinced the government itself was getting out of hand. For the first time since before the New Deal, Americans started to become concerned about the dark side of programs deemed beneficial by the federal government.

Sex, Lies, and Monicagate

Whatever dissatisfaction the public had with government in general, nothing could hide the continued revelations about unethical and illegal activities by Clinton, his wife, or members of the cabinet. In particular, the Clintons' involvement in the bankrupt Whitewater Development Company in Arkansas and its domino effect in bankrupting the Madison Guaranty Savings & Loan forced a three-judge panel in 1994 to name an independent prosecutor, Robert Fiske, to investigate the Clintons' actions. No sooner had Fiske been appointed than the Clinton spin machine (the administration's media managers) initiated a campaign that would typify the Clintons' response to any charges. In 1994, a strategy of demonizing the messenger, which was first used on Fiske, would be finely honed for subsequent, and more effective, attacks on Fiske's successor, Judge Kenneth Starr. Starr had an impeccable reputation, but he soon found himself under daily attack by Clinton associate James Carville, who announced he would start his own investigation of Starr!

The special prosecutor's job was to investigate conflict of interest charges against the Clintons related to the Whitewater Development Company in Arkansas and promoter James McDougal. McDougal also ran the Madison Guaranty Savings & Loan, which had failed in 1989, but by 1993 evidence had surfaced that Madison funds had gone into Whitewater. Further evidence revealed that the Clintons received preferential treatment in the form of waived fees and had had their share of the down payment in the investments put up by McDougal or others. Billing records with Hillary's name on them surfaced, indicating that she had done substantial work on Whitewater while at the Rose Law Firm, and thus knew exactly where the money had gone, even though she later told a Senate committee that while she had signed the sheets, she had not done the actual work.

Yet the more one pulled on the Whitewater string, the more the fabric seemed to unravel. First there was "Travelgate," in which Hillary dismissed the employees of the White House travel office (a nonpartisan group) in order to replace them with the travel firm of her friends (and high-powered Hollywood producers) Harry and Susan Thomason. Still, there had been no illegality. What turned a presidential preference into an ethical and legal violation was that Mrs. Clinton, to provide a public relations cover for firing so many loyal employees in such a callous fashion, ordered an FBI investigation of Billy Dale, head of the travel office. A midlevel civil servant who had done nothing but hold a job that Hillary had coveted for her friends, suddenly found himself having to secure lawyers to defend against charges of corruption. Dale was acquitted of all charges, but he was nearly bankrupted.

There were too many improprieties in Travelgate to ignore, and the same three-judge panel that had appointed Starr empowered him to expand his probe into the travel office events. Then, in 1993, Vince Foster, a Rose Law Firm friend of Hillary's who had worked with her at the White House, was found dead at Fort Marcy Park, an apparent suicide. Again, there were enough irregularities in the U.S. Park Police investigation (such as possible movement of the body) that the three-judge panel ordered Starr to add that to his list. By then, as Clinton adviser George Stephanopoulos noted, "We had a team of lawyers, nicknamed the Masters of Disaster, whose sole job was to handle Whitewater and related inquiries."[35]

Despite the origins of this added tasking of Starr into separate, and apparently unrelated, cases by the three-judge panel, contemporary history textbooks continue to claim, "Starr moved aggressively to expand his inquiry . . . and seemed intent on securing an indictment against at least one of the Clintons."[36] Another textbook claimed, "Starr had been investigating the Whitewater matter for nearly four years without significant results," somehow ignoring indictments and convictions against Webster Hubbell, Susan McDougal, and James McDougal.[37] Starr was three for three before a young woman from Arkansas reacted to a story about Clinton that had appeared in *The American Spectator* magazine, one in which she was named as having been "procured" for Clinton by Arkansas state troopers. This forced the three-judge panel to put yet another investigation on Starr's plate. While that scenario unfolded, however, dissatisfaction with Clinton's policies—as opposed to allegations of corruption—led to another surprising change.

The Contract with America

Drawing upon the widespread unease with—and in some cases, outright fear about—the growing power and insulation of the federal government from the people who paid the taxes, the Republican Party under the leadership of Representative Newt Gingrich of Georgia devised a radical strategy. For essentially sixty years (allowing for two brief interludes in 1946 to 1948 and 1954 to 1956), the Democrats had held the House of Representatives, employing Tip O'Neil's maxim, "All politics is local." Because of Democratic dominance of the House, bills introduced by Republicans to lower taxes, impose term limits, or enact a line-item veto were not even brought up for a vote. This tactic allowed House Democrats to stay off record, and to bring home the pork while decrying national budget deficits, or to claim to favor measures on which they never had to vote. Gingrich, sensing that the public was frustrated with the inability to change things in Washington, created a ten-point Contract with America, which promised to bring to the House floor for a vote the following ten measures: (1) a balanced-budget law and a line-item veto to enforce it, (2) an anticrime package, (3) a welfare reform bill, (4) a family reinforcement act designed to increase adoptions and enforce child support laws, (5) an increased Pentagon budget and a prohibition on U.S. troops serving under United Nations control, (6) a product liability/legal reform bill and an end to unfunded federal mandates, (7) an increase in the senior-citizen Social Security tax limits, (8) a repeal of the "marriage tax" and a child tax credit, (9) a cut in capital gains taxes, and (10) a term limits bill. Overlaying all of these was an eleventh promise—reorganization of the House to ensure greater congressional accountability, which included opening committee meetings to the public, requiring that all laws that apply to the country also apply to Congress, cutting the number of committees and staff by one third, and requiring a three-fifths vote to pass any tax increase. The power of the Contract, however, was that Gingrich had managed to obtain the support of three hundred hopeful Republicans either in Congress or running for the House, demonstrating a virtual unanimity of purpose.

By persuading so many Republicans to stand together on these ten issues, Gingrich effectively "nationalized" the local House races and made the 1994 election a national referendum on Bill Clinton's presidency.[38] When the votes were counted in October, the results stunned virtually all political pundits, especially the big-name analysts in the media. For the first time in forty years, the Republicans had captured both the House and Senate. Wresting the House from the Democrats, Republicans had defeated thirty-five incumbents, including Tom Foley, the Speaker of the House, befuddling newscasters trying to explain the political shift they had denied would happen. ABC anchor Peter Jennings likened the vote to a "temper tantrum" by the voters.

For a temper tantrum, the voter response was surprisingly consistent and one-sided. In addition to the House and Senate gains, Republicans picked up eleven governorships. Although the media attempted to portray the election as a "reaction against incumbents," it was telling that every single Republican incumbent—House, Senate, or statehouse—won reelection. Only Democrats were thrown out. In the wake of the debacle, still other Democrats in the House and at the local level switched parties in droves, with some five hundred joining the Republican Party nationally, the most prominent of whom was the newly elected U.S. senator from Colorado, Ben Nighthorse Campbell, the first Native American senator.

Clinton, already in political hot water, brought in one of his old political advisers, Dick Morris, to craft a new plan to keep his floundering presidency afloat. Morris concocted a strategy called triangulation.[39] He reasoned that Clinton could portray the Republicans *and* his own party in Congress as obstructionists and claim to serve the greater good. This required a perceived move to the center. Morris urged Clinton to portray both Republicans and Democrats as squabbling children, who need his fatherly presence to serve the public. Consequently, in his first speech before the Republican-controlled Congress, Clinton said, "The era of big government is over" to wildly enthusiastic applause. But far from admitting defeat for his modernized New Deal-like programs, Clinton merely began a long series of deceptions designed to slow the Republican Revolution as much as possible, hoping Democrats would recapture the House and Senate in 1996.

House Republicans moved with unusual rapidity. They made good on their contract, bringing up for a vote on the House floor nine of the ten items (only term limits failed to get to the floor, and even that was debated in committee—

which had never happened before). Even more surprising, the House passed all nine, and the Senate brought to a floor vote six of them. The Supreme Court struck down term limits as unconstitutional before the Senate could act on it, and the line-item veto was ruled unconstitutional after Clinton had signed it into law.

Among the legislation that passed both houses, a welfare reform bill dramatically curtailed Aid to Families with Dependent Children (AFDC) programs, to the howls of protest from liberal groups, who prophesied that millions would be put on the streets. In fact, by the mid-1990s, welfare benefits at the state levels in New England had a generosity that rivaled that of socialist Sweden. Massachusetts, New York, New Jersey, Connecticut, Washington, D.C., and Rhode Island all had an after-tax value of welfare benefits (including food stamps, AFDC, public housing, Medicaid, and other subsidized services) that exceeded a $12-per-hour job. New York City's rates had reached the astronomical level of $30,700 per year, or more than the starting salary of a computer scientist or secretary. Clinton promptly vetoed the bill, whereupon the House passed it a second time. Clinton vetoed it a second time, before Morris's polling information told him that in fact the bill was quite popular. Finally, after at last signing welfare reform, Clinton claimed credit for it.

In the end, Clinton signed three of the contract items—welfare reform, unfunded federal mandates, and a line-item veto—and Congress overrode his veto of the stockholder bill of rights. For the business-as-usual crowd in Washington, it was a stunning display of promises kept: 40 percent of the items that the GOP had promised only to *bring to the floor for discussion* actually became law.[40] Clinton's own polling and focus group data from Morris and Clinton's pollster had confirmed he had to sign these pieces of legislation to maintain his triangulation.[41]

House conservatives mistook their stunning, but narrow, election as an overwhelming mandate for change. Instead of taking small steps, then returning to the voters to ask their validation, Republicans advanced on a number of fronts, including launching investigations of Whitewater and conducting an emotional hearing on the Waco, Texas, disaster in April 1993. At Waco, a sect of the Seventh-Day Adventists church, the Branch Davidians under David Koresh, had holed up in a compound after agents of the Bureau of Alcohol, Tobacco, and Firearms (BATF) botched a raid based on scanty evidence and unsubstantiated claims of child abuse. Ignoring several opportunities to arrest Koresh outside the compound and avoid a firefight, the agents, bolstered by the Texas Rangers and National Guard troops, attacked, firing gas grenades inside the buildings. Fires broke out instantly, killing eighty-two men, women, and children. Questions as to how the fires started implicated both the Davidians and the government.

Clinton claimed to have no knowledge of the operation, passing the buck to his attorney general, Janet Reno, who in turn did not take action against any of the FBI agents involved in improper and possibly illegal acts. Civil rights activists were outraged, and the GOP Congress, already concerned about the growing abuse of power by the IRS, BATF, and FBI, listened to witnesses from inside the compound describe attacks by a government tank that had smashed down the compound's walls and sharpshooters who had peppered the Davidian complex. Democrats, desperate to protect Clinton and Reno from any political fallout, muddied the waters sufficiently so that no government agents were charged. But in 1997 an independent filmmaker produced *Waco: The Rules of Engagement,* which casts doubt on government explanations that the Davidians had set the fires.[42]

Much of the support for congressional Republicans emanated from their curbing of federal power, especially in the law enforcement agencies. The 1992 shooting of Randy Weaver's wife by FBI sharpshooters at Ruby Ridge, Idaho, combined with Waco and alarming reports of brutal behavior by agents of the EPA, led to a sense that the federal government was out of control and that individual agents had started to act, in the words of Democratic congressman John Conyers, like "jack-booted thugs." Clinton was put on the defensive, and despite triangulation his poll numbers continued to fall. Then an explosion in Oklahoma City halted the congressional momentum while at the same time presenting Clinton with a golden opportunity to generate sympathy for the federal government.

A disaffected and mentally unstable Gulf War veteran, Timothy McVeigh, and at least one accomplice, Terry Nichols, planned, positioned, and detonated a massive bomb outside the Alfred P. Murrah Federal Building in Oklahoma City on April 19, 1995. The blast killed 169 men, women, and children—there was a day-care facility in the building—and constituted the worst terrorist attack up to that point in American history.

President Clinton traveled to Oklahoma City and, according to one of his worst journalistic enemies, "handled the ceremony with consummate skill."[43] He also took the opportunity, in a national address, to blame conservative "talk radio" (meaning Limbaugh) for an "atmosphere of hate" that had produced, in his view, Tim McVeigh. The president used the disaster to shift public attention from the abusive actions of government to the crazed behavior of the bomber and the American militia movement, which had steadily gained members prior to April 1995. McVeigh later admitted responsibility for the bombing and placed himself fully in the antigovernment movement, claiming that he was seeking retribution for the devastation at Waco two years earlier.[44] He had even attempted to time the explosion to coincide with the anniversary of the assault on the Branch Davidians. However, disturbing questions remain about the possibility of Middle Eastern terrorists in the bombing. Several sources, most recently Jayna Davis, have found links between the "third terrorist" ("John Doe #2"), Iraq, and possibly Al Qaeda.[45]

In the wake of Oklahoma City, Clinton's ratings rose from an anemic 42 percent to 51 percent, and he never really saw his popularity diminish again. But in his haste to lay the blame on antigovernment extremists, Clinton and the entire U.S. intelligence community missed several troubling clues that perhaps

McVeigh and Nichols had not acted alone. Nichols, for example, was in the same part of the Philippines—and at the same time—as Al Qadea bomb maker Ramzi Yousef. Moreover, numerous witnesses testified that McVeigh and Nichols lacked sufficient bomb-making skills, but that their bomb was a near-perfect replica of the 1993 World Trade Center bomb devised by Yousef. Certainly their actions, in light of the 1993 World Trade Center bombing and events overseas, were evidence that the United States was no longer safe from terrorism from any group inside our borders. McVeigh was sentenced to death in 1997. Four years later, when his appeals had run out, networks provided a grotesque minute-by-minute coverage of his final hours, further sensationalizing the most widely followed American execution since that of the Rosenbergs, and turning McVeigh's lethal injection into a public spectacle.[46]

Neither Waco nor the Oklahoma City bombings seemed to affect the recovering economy or the booming stock market. Clinton owed much of his renewed approval ratings to the 1990s boom. But could he claim credit for it?

Riding Reagan's Coattails: The Roaring Nineties

Having run against "the worst economy in the last fifty years" and having ridden into office by reminding themselves and George Bush, "It's the economy, stupid," the Clinton team knew that in fact the industrial and technological growth that had occurred since 1993 was in no small way the result of the Reagan policies they publicly derided. Despite tax hikes under Bush and Clinton, the incentives created in the Reagan years continued to generate jobs and growth. Clinton had one progrowth policy: the North American Free Trade Agreement (NAFTA), which would lower tariffs between the United States and its two major continental trading partners, Canada and Mexico. But it ran into stiff opposition from Clinton's own party in Congress. Environmentalists, labor unions, and protectionists all lobbied against the bill, and "Citizen Perot" led the anti-NAFTA crusade to television, where he faced Vice President Gore on CNN in a debate over the plan. (Gore won, hands down, leaving the flummoxed Perot to constantly ask the host, Larry King, "Are you going to let me talk? Can I talk now?") In Congress, however, the bill was saved only when a large percentage of Republicans in the House voted for it, whereas the Democrats voted in large numbers against it. NAFTA proceeded over the next several years to add large numbers of jobs to the U.S. economy, contrary to the dire predictions of its opponents.

More important to the financial markets, after the Republicans gained control of Congress, the message was that, indeed, the era of big government *was* over. Or so it seemed. At any rate, the financial markets reacted. Although Wall Street had crept upward from 1992 to 1994, the Dow Jones flew into the stratosphere, climbing further and faster than the market had at any time since the Great Depression. Individual Retirement Accounts (IRAs) swelled in value as yuppies, or young urban professionals, entered the stock market in growing numbers through their retirement plans. More Americans than ever held securities and paid attention to the markets—not as speculators, but as investors in their retirements and college tuition for their children.

Already on the defensive after the Oklahoma City bombing, Republicans nevertheless thought they could rebound by refocusing on the 1995 budget. Gingrich hoped to impose an austere but reasonable spending plan on Clinton, unaware that the president had already determined to use the budget impasse to close all nonessential government services and blame it on the Republicans. Documents later leaked out showing that in the summer, several months before the shutdown occurred, Clinton administration officials had met with leaders of the federal employee unions to ensure that they would side with the White House. When the GOP submitted its plan, Clinton refused to sign the bills and allowed all nonessential government services—parks, libraries, citizen assistance bureaus, museums, and all noncritical offices—to shut down. The media cooperated fully, characterizing Gingrich as Dr. Seuss's Grinch with the headline THE GINGRICH WHO STOLE CHRISTMAS, and despite the fact that Defense, the IRS, and other essential federal offices continued to work, portrayed the shutdown as a disaster. Television talk shows featured laid-off park rangers or private-sector entrepreneurs who supplied the government with goods—all of whom suddenly had no income. At the end of a few weeks, the media had convinced the public that the Republicans were to blame.[47]

The shell-shocked congressional Republicans did not recover their confidence for years. Portrayals of the Republican House members set new low marks for distortion, deception, and fear mongering in American politics. But it was effective. After 1995, many Republicans drifted to a more moderate position to avoid incurring the wrath of the Washington press corps.[48]

Still, Clinton's own polling told him the issue of fiscal responsibility that the GOP had advocated was warmly received in the heartland, and he could not ignore it. Clinton spoke with greater frequency about balancing the budget—a phrase uttered only by Republicans in the previous sixty years. He admitted that the robust economy had generated such tax revenues that with a modicum of fiscal restraint, the United States could balance the budget in ten years, or in seven years, or even sooner. Such talk only further accelerated the markets. By the time Clinton left office, the Dow had broken the 11,000 mark; and although it was already in retreat in Clinton's last six months, it produced consistent federal budget surpluses. Yet it would not be completely accurate to ascribe the exceptional economic growth of the 1990s entirely to the tax cuts of the 1980s, to the elections of 1994, or to Clinton's support of NAFTA. Powerful economic forces coalesced to contribute to the creation of such fantastic wealth.

Computer chip prices had plummeted at an annual rate of 68 percent since the 1980s, to the extent that by the year 2000 "the price of a bit is . . . close to a millionth of a cent as the billion transistor device—the gigachip—is introduced."[49] A single production line could fabricate 1.6 *trillion* transistors in twenty-four hours, and in 1999 alone, 50,000 trillion transistors were produced, providing such a surplus that Americans used them to play solitaire or to keep the interior temperature of Cadillacs at 65 degrees. Equally impressive, in 1999, Internet traffic and bandwidth doubled every three months, traveling over fiber cable that carried 8.6 petabits per second per fiber sheath, or a number equal to the entire Internet traffic per month carried in 1995. Indeed, the computer had spread more rapidly to one quarter of the population than any other technology in American history, except the cellular phone (sixteen years compared to thirteen).[50] That remarkable democratization of technology would quickly be eclipsed by yet another computer-related product, the Internet, which spread to a quarter of the population in merely seven years.[51]

Naturally, such stunning increases in productivity caused the value of tech companies to soar. Qualcomm, a company few people had even heard of prior to 1999, saw its shares rise in value by *2,619 percent* in less than two years! Brokerage and finance firms grew so fast they defied traditional accounting and measurement tools: employment only doubled in the brokerage business between 1973 to 1987, yet the number of shares traded daily exploded, from 5.7 million to 63.8 million. Although the Bureau of Labor Statistics recorded a 50 percent drop in productivity costs of computers from 1992 to 1994, in fact the costs had fallen at a rate closer to 40 percent per year, and those price declines only accelerated.

Astonishingly, Clinton actually sought to interfere with this growth. In 1993, the Clinton Justice Department initiated a campaign against the nation's largest operating systems company, Bill Gates's Microsoft, for allegedly bundling its Internet browser with its Windows operating system. In May 1998, the department's Antitrust Division filed suit against Microsoft. Nineteen states, seeing a new gravy train alongside tobacco litigation, joined the suit. The Justice Department contended that the bundling required consumers to buy both products and gave Microsoft an unfair advantage over Netscape and other rival companies. Yet Netscape was the industry *leader,* and there was no evidence that Microsoft met any of the traditional criteria that defined "restraint of trade." For example, Microsoft's prices on its products were falling, and its service was good. There were no barriers to entry into the browser market—indeed, Netscape dominated that market. But Americans seldom get worked up when the wealthy are targeted by government, and although consumer surveys showed that upward of 90 percent of Microsoft customers applauded the company, competitors were visceral in their anger toward Gates, who many claimed had stolen others' ideas.

Whereas monopoly theory posits that competitors should benefit from litigation against a monopolist, exactly the opposite happened with Microsoft. Every time the government advanced in the case, the stocks of virtually all of the computer companies—especially Microsoft's main competitors—fell.[52] Each time Microsoft gained ground, the share values of all Microsoft's competitors rose. Thus, while the federal and state governments engaged in an attack on a major American business in the name of promoting competition, in reality the market judged that the Microsoft suit was damaging the entire computer industry. An ominous reaction occurred in the wake of the Microsoft antitrust announcement when markets slowed, then as the case drew to a conclusion, turned downward.

By that time, some analysts had lumped these businesses into a catch-all phrase called the new economy, which included medical, optics, fiber, aviation, computers, software, telecommunications, and any other field that they could fit into the digital revolution. Computers produced remarkable increases in virtually all related fields and started to pull away from the otherwise impressive gains made in low-tech industries, at least until the year 2000.

A second contributing factor to the business boom of the nineties was the opening of markets in the former Soviet bloc. As Eastern European countries for the first time since 1939 engaged in free trade with the West, the resulting flow of goods and services eastward resembled the American entrance into western Europe at the end of World War II. U.S. entrepreneurs, oil experts, bankers, computer geeks, and academic consultants poured into Hungary, Romania, Poland, Ukraine, Russia, and the Baltic Republics. American overseas trade to those areas grew accordingly.

Still another part of the economic equation—low energy prices—played a role in sustaining the boom. The Gulf War had secured Middle Eastern oil at low prices, and although American oil companies, drillers, and refiners operated on thin profit margins, the cheap energy costs spilled over into almost every sector of the economy. Any products made with petroleum became cheaper to make; everything that was shipped by rail, truck, or aircraft was cheaper to transport, and the portion of manufacturing cost dedicated to energy plummeted. Even if goods did not seem cheaper on the rack or at the store, corporations reallocated resources within their firms toward research and development, turning out new products and adding value.

That did not guarantee that the rich got richer, especially when it came to businesses, where only thirty-four of the top one hundred firms in the *Wall Street Journal* in 1990 were still on the list in 1999. This trend was confirmed in the international arena (where, again, American companies were heavily represented): there was a 25 percent turnover among the top one hundred multinational firms from 1990 to 1997.[53] At the same time, the share of total corporate assets held by the top five hundred industrial firms fell by 20 percent, and the employment by those same firms fell 29 percent.[54] The share of gross domestic product generated by those firms plummeted 39 percent in thirteen years. With the economy growing, the expansion showed two clear trends. First, the growth came from small companies and new entrepreneurs; and second, there was tremendous turnover at the top, indicating extremely high levels of competition. Both trends were highly favorable for a vibrant economy.

Throughout the Bush and Clinton presidencies, Alan Greenspan, a disciple of free-market economist Friedrich Hayek and an avid reader of Ayn Rand, had served as chairman of the Federal Reserve Board. Greenspan had lived through the Ford/Carter inflationary years and had watched with concern the rise of federal deficits in the 1980s. Early in Clinton's term, while interest rates remained low, the president took an action that dictated the behavior of the Fed and its chairman for the entire decade. In order to show rapid progress against the "Reagan/Bush deficits," Clinton refinanced large chunks of the national debt at the lowest rates possible, regardless of the length of maturity. Much of this consisted of short-term bonds; but it had the effect of reducing the interest paid by the government on the debt, thus giving the appearance of reducing the deficits. By doing so, Clinton refused to refinance the debt in much longer term securities at a slightly higher rate. As long as inflation, and therefore, interest rates, stayed low, it was a good deal for the country. But the slightest uptick in inflation would add billions to the national debt and raised the specter of a massive refinancing of the debt at much higher prices.

Clinton's action in essence locked the Fed into a permanent antiinflation mode. Any good news in the economy—rising industrial production, higher employment figures, better trade numbers—might cause prices to go up, which would appear on Greenspan's radar detector as a threat. The chairman found himself raising the prime rate repeatedly, trying to slow down the stock market. It was a perverse situation, to say the least: the most powerful banker in America constantly slapping the nation's wage-earners and entrepreneurs for their *success*. Worse, Greenspan's actions resulted in a constant underfunding of business, a steady deflation affecting long-term investment. Although few spotted it (George Gilder and Jude Wanniski were two exceptions), the nation suffered from a slow-acting capital anemia.

Home prices continued to rise, though not at levels seen in the 1970s. As Americans invested in both homes and the stock market, wealth levels grew as never before. The 1990s saw more millionaires made than at any other time in American history, and at the same time, the "wealth gap" between the top 20 percent and the bottom 20 percent grew. Some of this was to be expected: in any growing, thriving economy, that gap should expand as rapid leaps of innovation and invention make entrepreneurs rich overnight. There was some disconcerting evidence, however, that the 1990s, much more so than the 1980s, was a decade of greed. For example, American family debt levels soared faster than ever, and the ratio of debt to equity in family homes rose steadily. A robust economy also provided Clinton with one of his main selling points—a claim to have provided budget surpluses resulting from his economic policies.[55] In fact, Clinton and Congress could enjoy (and spend) the fruits of a roaring economy provided by Reagan's policies and numerous other factors over which they had no control at all. Indeed, no genuine "surpluses" existed if one included the Medicare and Social Security trust funds that had long ago been folded into general revenues. But the balanced budgets helped insulate Clinton from attacks on his ethics and character, providing him with the critical flak jacket he needed late in the decade.

Prosperity, undergirded by liberty, continued to act as a magnet to draw people from all over the world to America's shores. Increasingly, Asian and Indian engineers populated the engineering departments of major American universities; West Indian and Jamaican immigrants carved out thriving restaurant and grocery businesses in Atlantic seaboard cities; and former "boat people" from Vietnam populated the fishing fleet on the Gulf Coast. The success of immigrants changed the look of America, and in the 2000 census individual Americans for the first time could mark their descent from more than one race, creating some fifty-seven new categories of ethnicities.[56] As early as 1990, the fastest-growing racial category on a census form was "other," in part representing a genuine feeling that people saw themselves as multiethnic, but also reflecting the position that one's race was only one of many determinants of self-identity. Already, multiracial groups composed 8 percent of Hawaii's population and 10 percent of Oklahoma's. Although traditionalists worried that such distinctions would open a Pandora's box of mixed-race claims, in fact it portended the genuine "end of racism" as author Dinesh D'Souza had prophesied almost a decade earlier.[57]

Whether racism and ethnic distrust had increased or decreased in the 1990s depended on which surveys one consulted. More Americans than ever before encountered people of all races, ethnic identities, and faiths in their daily routine. Affirmative action had placed, in many cases, disproportionate numbers of blacks and Hispanics in a wide variety of occupations, government service, and in higher education, although the same laws tended to exclude Asians and Jews.

Thus, as the year 2000 neared, racial harmony remained the dream Martin Luther King had had some twenty years before, but at the same time, the realization of that dream in practical terms was closer than ever because millions of black families had entered the middle class, become stockholders and business owners, professionals and labor leaders, executives and stars. Although the O. J. Simpson murder case in the early 1990s threatened to divide black and white America, even anger over that soon subsided. Despite its shortcomings, race relations at the end of the 1990s remained better than anywhere else in the world, as horrible race riots in England and Muslim gang attacks on native French citizens there would later attest.

Social Pathologies, Spiritual Renewal

Unlike the 1960s, when street crime led to surging gun ownership, in the 1990s it was renewed distrust of government that had sparked a rise in gun sales and concealed-carry laws. In the wake of the McVeigh bombing, gun control groups pressed for the Brady Bill, legislation named after President Reagan's press secretary Jim Brady, who had been wounded in the 1983 assassination attempt, and which had been advocated by his wife, Sarah. The Brady Bill required registration by gun purchasers and a waiting period before acquiring a gun, ostensibly to reduce gun crimes. Gun owners feared this was the first step in a national confiscation, as had occurred in the Weimar Republic in the 1920s, leaving the public defenseless against a tyrannical government.

There was one small detail that gun control groups ignored: gun crimes, according to both federal and state authorities, peaked in Bush's term, roughly two years before the Brady Bill kicked in. Under Reagan and Bush, prosecutions of federal gun violations had risen from 2,500 to about 9,500 in 1992.[58] This was remarkable because the call for new gun laws came on the heels of two years of *nonprosecution* of *existing* gun laws by the Clinton administration. It allowed Clinton to set up a self-fulfilling cycle: there were more gun crimes; therefore, the nation needed more gun laws. The Brady Act was passed in February 1994, followed by the Clinton-Gore semiautomatic ban later that year, yet gun prosecutions at the federal level continued to fall sharply, back to where the number had stood when Bush took office. It allowed Clinton, in the wake of several highly publicized gun crimes (including the Columbine High School shooting in April 1999), to paint gun owners as irresponsible at a time when his administration failed to enforce the existing gun laws. In fact, momentum swung toward less gun regulation: several states began to pass concealed-carry laws that tended to further reduce crime. Through a crime crackdown under Republican mayor Rudolph Giuliani, New York City homicides per hundred thousand were lower than in the 1800s.[59] Issues of gun ownership reached a key point in 2001 when the *Emerson* case in Texas came before a federal district court. It represented the first time since the Great Depression's original gun control laws had taken effect that the meaning of the Second Amendment was actually addressed in a higher court. The judges ruled that in fact the "right to bear arms" was an individual right, not a militia right, and therefore meant exactly what proponents of the amendment for years had said it did. Although the justices attempted to include language that might still allow state and local gun regulation, the critical issue of whether the "militia" referred to the National Guard units or to armed individuals was settled in favor of individuals.

Issues of gun control divided the public almost as sharply as the abortion issue. Each, in turn, was closely associated with particular religious viewpoints. A growing number of Americans seemed concerned about family values and social maladies including abortion, drugs, illegitimacy, and street crime, which were broadly linked to a decline in the spiritual side of American life.

The nation had slowly but steadily moved toward attitudes more favorable to religion, and generally—though not universally—expressed at the polls concerns against normalizing what were once considered objectionable or even deviant lifestyles. In early 2001, the Pew Charitable Trusts concluded a broad study of the role of religion in public life and found, "Americans strongly equate religion with personal ethics and behavior, considering it an antidote to the moral decline they perceive in our nation today."[60] This was accompanied by an "equally strong respect for religious diversity . . . [and] tolerance of other people's beliefs." Nearly 70 percent disagreed with the statement that the nation would "do well even if many Americans were to abandon their religious faith," and a similar percentage wanted religion's influence on American society to grow, whereas only 6 percent wanted it to weaken. Nearly 80 percent supported either a moment of silence or a specific prayer in public schools; and at a ratio of two-to-one the respondents agreed that prayer taught children that religion and God were important. Two thirds of the respondents were not threatened by more religious leaders becoming involved in politics. Majorities of Americans sensed a bias among journalists against Christians and 68 percent agreed that there was "a lot of prejudice [in the media] toward Evangelical Christians."

The spiritual renewal had started perhaps as early as the 1980s, when a Gallup survey found that 80 percent of Americans believed in a final judgment before God; 90 percent claimed to pray; and 84 percent said, "Jesus was God or the Son of God."[61] Most of the growth that had occurred in American Christianity came from one of two sources. First, Hispanic immigrants, who tended to be Catholics, brought renewed energy to the Roman Catholic Church, which, with 60 million members, was the largest denomination in the United States. Second, independent/nondenominational churches grew at astronomical rates. The largest churches in America—that is, a group of similarly minded believers at a single location—included Willow Creek (20,000 members) in Chicago, Crenshaw Christian Center (22,000 members) in Los Angeles, and Southeast Christian Church in Louisville (17,000 members). Focused on "soul winning" through modern methods—contemporary music, abundant church athletic and musical activities, large youth programs—these churches kept two groups who had abandoned the mainstream churches years earlier—males and young people.

A sure sign of a church in decline is the absence of men and a preponderance of elderly women. The newer churches had tapped into the call for men to be family heads, and, assisted by such independent programs as Promise Keepers, they emphasized strong traditional families with a male family leader. At the same time, the use of contemporary music, innovative teaching methods, and teen-oriented Bible messages brought millions of American youths to Christianity. By 1991, a survey showed that 86 percent of teens said they believed "Jesus Christ is God or the Son of God, and 73 percent considered regular church attendance an important aspect of American citizenship." An even more surprising, perhaps, statistic showed that nearly one third accepted the Bible as the literal word of God.[62]

Ever attuned to image and style, Clinton early in his presidency had suddenly begun attending church regularly. But Clinton best employed religion during the impeachment scandal, when he brought in several spiritual advisers, such as the Reverend Jesse Jackson (who at the time was secretly conducting his own extramarital affair) to help him deal with his "mistakes." In fact, the spiritual renewal that had begun percolating through the United States had not quite come to a boil by 1996, when Clinton campaigned for reelection, or even by 1998, when he was impeached, but the general sense of moral unease with the president's actions certainly came into focus after 1999.

"I Did Not Have Sex with That Woman"

The buoyant economy was a tremendous fire wall for Clinton against any Republican challenger in 1996. It was ironic that, having come into office criticizing the

Reagan policies, Clinton now claimed credit for them and fortified his reelection bid with them. Perhaps aware that any candidate would be a sacrificial lamb—the "Mondale of 1996"—the Republicans nominated warhorse Robert Dole of Kansas, who had walked point for Gerald Ford in 1976. Dole had paid his dues, and minor challenges from other candidates had failed to gain traction. Already the question before the electorate was clear: would any candidate running on "character issues" be sufficient to unseat a president in a booming economy in peacetime?

Ross Perot returned with another independent campaign as the nominee of the Reform Party. However, in 1996, the issues differed dramatically from those of 1992: budget deficits were gone or disappearing; unemployment had plummeted; and free trade no longer seemed a threat. Perot severely hurt himself by failing to attack Clinton's credibility and character problems, leaving Dole as the only real alternative to Clinton.

Dole lacked Reagan's charm and grace, and, though not without humor (Dole later appeared in clever Pepsi, Visa, and Viagra commercials), the GOP standard-bearer seemed too old (he was younger than Reagan, at 73, but seemed to lack energy). His vice-presidential nominee, tax-cutting advocate (and former Buffalo Bills quarterback) Jack Kemp, lacked the aggressiveness to attack weaknesses in the Democratic platform. Above all, Dole and Kemp still operated out of fear that lingered from the 1995 government shutdown, when the Democrats had successfully demonized Republicans as opposing children and the elderly.

Clinton's vulnerability lay in the serious character weaknesses—the lies about extramarital affairs had already become well-documented. Equally important, the Democratic National Committee had developed a strategy for burying the Republicans under a tidal wave of cash, from any source. Clinton rode the crest of that wave. Slowly at first, then with greater frequency, reports of Clinton's unethical and often illegal fund-raising activities began to appear in the press. Concern about money from the communist People's Republic of China, funneled through John Huang into the Clinton/Gore coffers, percolated through newsrooms, but the media never closed the loop of equating the cash with policy payoffs by the administration. Huang's cash payments were the most serious breach of government ethics since Teapot Dome and, more important, were grounds for a special prosecutor, but the Clinton Justice Department was certainly not about to conduct such an investigation.

With the Clinton media team in full spin mode, each new revelation was carefully managed by several loyalists who received talking points by fax machines each morning. They were immediately dispatched to the television talk shows to claim that (1) everybody does it, (2) there was really nothing illegal about the transactions, and (3) the allegations were merely Republican efforts to smear Clinton. Without a tenacious—or, more appropriate, vicious—press to look skeptically at every administration defense (and defender), as it had in the

Watergate era, Clinton successfully swept aside the most damaging issues of the campaign.

When the votes were tallied in November, Clinton still had not cracked the 50 percent mark, netting 49 percent, whereas Dole received 41 percent and Perot snatched 8 percent. Clinton increased his electoral margin over 1992 by 9 electoral votes, indicating the damage done to him by the ongoing scandals.

Even after his reelection, the character issue haunted Clinton in the form of an ongoing thorn in his side named Paula Corbin Jones. Named in *The American Spectator* "troopergate" story as having had an affair with then-governor Clinton, Jones set out to prove that something quite different had happened. In 1994, Jones filed a civil lawsuit against President Bill Clinton for sexual harassment during a political event at a Little Rock hotel while Clinton was governor of Arkansas. While working a meeting at the Excelsior Hotel in 1991, Clinton sent troopers to ask her to come up to a hotel room to meet the governor, and Jones claimed that once she had entered the room, and realized that only she and Clinton were there, Governor Clinton exposed himself and asked her to perform oral sex on him. Jones refused, left the room, then alleged that she had suffered "various job detriments" for refusing his advances.[63] The lawsuit proved historic because in 1997 the U.S. Supreme Court ruled against Clinton's legal claim that a citizen could not sue a president. Quite the contrary, the Supreme Court unanimously concluded "like every other citizen who properly invokes [the District Court's] jurisdiction . . . [she] has a right to an orderly disposition of her claims."[64] Or, stated another way, no citizen is above the law.

Jones's legal team began the discovery process, during which it gathered evidence and took depositions. Understandably, one of the questions the Jones legal team asked Clinton in his deposition required him to identify all the women with whom he had had sexual relations since 1986. (He was married the entire time.) Clinton answered, under oath, "none." Already Gennifer Flowers and former Miss Arkansas Sally Perdue had claimed to have had an affair with Clinton (Flowers's affair occurred during the time in question), but the Jones team found several others. One of them was Juanita Broaddrick, who contended that in April 1978, Clinton had raped her while he was attorney general of Arkansas, and while she had told a coworker at the time, she had not pressed charges.

In fact, one relationship was still going on at the time of Jones's suit—regular sexual liaisons at the White House between Clinton and a young intern, Monica Lewinsky. Most Clinton biographers disagree over whether Hillary knew about the ongoing liaisons or whether she was kept in the dark.[65] (She would have protected her husband to prevent their loss of power.) The fact that a president of the United States would boldly lie about his relationship with Lewinsky to representatives of a federal court would have gone unreported except for the work of an Internet sleuth, Matt Drudge. Drudge, who styled himself after Walter Winchell, the journalist who virtually invented the gossip column, ran a Web site in which he posted the latest rumblings from newsrooms around the country. He learned that *Newsweek* magazine had found out about the Lewinsky affair, but had determined to spike the story. Drudge ran with it, forcing the major media outlets to cover it and, in the process, establishing himself as the vanguard of a new wave of Internet reporters.[66]

The Clinton-Lewinsky case, therefore, became as significant for the change it heralded in journalism as it had done for the actual facts of the case. Already Rush Limbaugh had exposed the details of the Clinton health-care plan on AM radio. Now an unknown Internet reporter had broken a case that the major partisan press refused to uncover. Talk radio and the Internet joined a couple of conservative papers and the Fox News Network to provide, for the first time in fifty years, a genuine opposition press in America. The dominant liberal media would no longer control the spin of public events.

Meanwhile, a wave of indignation spread about the president's involvement with a young intern. Clinton concluded that he could not tell the public the truth because it would destroy him politically. In a televised appearance he blatantly lied to the nation, "I did not have sex with that woman, Ms. Lewinsky!" It harked back to Nixon's famous statement to the American people that their president was "not a crook."

Clinton's team revived the successful "nuts and sluts" strategy that had worked well in the early 1990s with Gennifer Flowers: painting Lewinsky, Jones, and Perdue as crazy or promiscuous. Yet no sooner had the first blast of public scorn receded when another woman, a supporter of the president's named Kathleen Willey, appeared on a national television news show to claim that Clinton had harassed her too, pinning her against a wall while he groped her in the White House.

Starr's investigation now had to shift gears. Independent counsels are charged with the task of investigating *all* episodes of obstruction of justice, including any new charges that arise during the original investigation. That, after all, was exactly what had sunk Nixon: investigations of subsequent infractions, not the burglary. The new allegations required Starr to investigate the Jones claims as well, and he was ordered to do so by the three-judge panel that had handed him the Foster and Travelgate cases. Starr's investigation was no more about sex than Al Capone's arrest had been about income tax evasion. Rather, it was about Clinton's lying to a grand jury—lying under oath. In fact, had Starr chosen, he could have packaged the Lewinsky/Travelgate/Whitewater/Foster/and John Huang finance abuses into a giant RICO case (racketeering charges that did not require a single criminal behavior but which covered a wide pattern of abuse).

Public opinion polls still reflected high job approval for Clinton, but his personal approval ratings started to sink. The public seemed willing to ignore the president's behavior as long as no obvious evidence of lying to investigators surfaced. However, Lewinsky's infamous blue dress, containing Clinton's DNA, surfaced, ensuring the public that neither Congress nor Clinton could get off without making difficult choices. Lewinsky, in one of her encounters with the president, had saved the dress she wore that night. Once again, the major media knew about the evidence and buried the story, and once again Matt Drudge pried it out of the pressrooms.

Drudge's revelations showed that the president was on record as having lied in front of a federal grand jury—a felony, and certainly grounds for removal. On August 17, 1998, he made a public apology to the nation. Having just weeks earlier flatly lied, he now admitted that "while my answers [to the grand jury] were legally accurate, I did not volunteer information. Indeed, I did have a relationship with Ms. Lewinsky that was not appropriate. In fact, it was wrong."[67] Even the apology, though, which included numerous explanations and rationalizations, was itself a political deflection to take the edge off the evidence that Starr was about to deliver.

In order to make abundantly clear the nature of Clinton's lies, Starr's report had to provide highly specific sexual details. The same critics who complained about lack of specificity in previous allegations suddenly wailed about Starr's evidence being *too* specific and personal.

Clinton counted on the House members, including many Republicans, to refuse to examine the Starr Report when it was finally submitted in September 1998. To his surprise, almost all Republicans and many Democrats examined the evidence. What they found was shocking. Not included in the public Starr Report that had hit newsstands shortly after it was delivered to Congress was confidential material relating to the rape allegations by Juanita Broaddrick. When combined with Kathleen Willey's testimony about Clinton's thuggish behavior toward her, it painted a portrait of a multiple offender and, possibly, a rapist. One House member said that what he had read nauseated him. There was bipartisan support to begin impeachment proceedings, with the House voting 258 to 176 for the inquiry. Even after the November elections shaved a handful of votes from the Republican ranks, the actual floor vote to impeach saw five Democrats join the House Republicans to vote for two articles of impeachment: obstruction of justice and lying to a federal grand jury. (It could easily have been three counts: later, Judge Susan Webber Wright would state that Clinton had submitted a false affidavit in her hearing as well, but she did not make this fact known until after the impeachment process. Wright was a Clinton appointee, and a former student of his when he had taught at the University of Arkansas.)

At that point, the media failed in its job of presenting facts and educating the public. Constitutionally, the purpose of the House investigation is to determine whether laws have been broken that pose a threat to the integrity of the legal system or whether the offense rises to the constitutional level called high crimes and misdemeanors. Simply engaging in behavior detrimental to the office of the presidency can be interpreted by the House as a "high crime"—different from a statutory crime. Whether or not an act is an impeachable offense is *strictly* within the jurisdiction of the House, according to the Constitution. Once the House has turned out articles of impeachment, the trial takes place in the Senate, whose *sole* constitutional duty is to determine the guilt or innocence of the accused—not to render judgment on the seriousness of the crimes. Clinton and the Senate Democrats counted on flawed public understanding of the Constitution, combined with the willing alliance of the media, to cloud the procedures. When the Senate trial began in early 1999, the House sent thirteen "managers" to present the case, pleading with the senators to examine the confidential material. The House managers, led by Henry Hyde of Illinois and counsel David Schippers, a Democrat, were convinced that an objective person reading the Broaddrick and Willey accounts would conclude that Clinton had lied and had done so repeatedly and deliberately, and that he posed an ongoing threat to other women in the White House. But Schippers was stunned to hear one senator state flatly that most of them had no intention of even looking at the evidence, and that even if there was a dead body in the Oval Office, "You wouldn't get 67 votes to convict."[68]

Republican senators, cowed by the polls, made it clear before the proceedings started that they would not call witnesses, introduce new evidence into the record, or in any way ask any questions that might embarrass the president. The trial was over before it had begun, and Clinton was acquitted by a vote of 56 to 44. Although four Republicans voted for acquittal, not a single Democrat voted for conviction.

Clinton and the Democrats crowed about the November elections in which the Republicans lost seats in the House (but still maintained a majority) as evidence that impeachment was misguided. Clinton tried to claim vindication by the vote. In fact, however, a cynical disgust had set in. Just as the Republicans had overestimated the strength of their 1994 victory, Clinton misread both the verdict of impeachment and the results of the two national elections in which he had failed to receive 50 percent of the vote in either. By 1999, surveys increasingly showed that people would not go into business with the president, or even allow him to babysit for their kids. The public tolerated him, but certainly did not trust him. Late-night comedians made Clinton a regular part of their routines, and *Saturday Night Live* mercilessly ridiculed him. By the time impeachment was over, Hubbell and the McDougals had been jailed; Vince Foster was dead; Elders and Espy had resigned in disgrace; and Dick Morris, Clinton's adviser, had quit in the midst of his own scandal with a prostitute. Later, on the basis of his fraudulent statement to Judge Wright, Clinton was disbarred in Arkansas.

Once cleared of the charges, Clinton embarked on a quest for legacy building, attempting to erase the state of the Lewinsky saga from his presidency. Much of his effort involved intervention abroad, although some of those initiatives had started long before any articles of impeachment were drawn up. Unfortunately, some of them were shaped and directed while Clinton's mind was on his impeachment battle, among other things.

Missions Undefined

Having avoided the military draft during the Vietnam era, President Clinton committed more troops to combat situations than any peacetime president in American history. Supporting a humanitarian food-delivery mission in Somalia in 1992, George Bush had dispatched 25,000 troops with the understanding that the United Nations would take over the job of food distribution. But in June 1993, after Pakistani peacekeepers were killed by local warlords, Clinton expanded the mission to hunt down the leading troublemaker, General Mohammed Adid.

Using seize-and-arrest missions, carried out by the Rangers and Delta Force, mostly in Mogadishu, American troops sought Adid without success, although they captured many of his lieutenants. The raids usually went off without a hitch, but one attempt to grab Adid turned into a disaster. When the plan went awry, American helicopters were shot down and 18 Rangers, pilots, and special forces troops were killed. One Ranger's dead body was dragged through the streets of Mogadishu.[69] Clinton pulled the American forces out, leading anti-American terrorists like Osama bin Laden and Saddam Hussein to coin a "Mogadishu strategy": killing enough American soldiers that a president would lose popular support for the mission.

Unlike Somalia, which the world soon forgot or ignored, a more troublesome sore spot was the Balkans, in which Croatia declared independence from Yugoslavia in 1991. Yugoslavia had been kept together in the communist era by Marshall Tito's delicate use of brute force and political balance. Once communism fell, each ethnic group again sought its own national status. Notions that these groups lived peacefully side by side under communism seriously underestimated the skill and oppressive force that Tito had used to keep the fractured nation together.

When Croatia withdrew from Yugoslavia, the major substate, Serbia, under President Slobodan Milosevic, sent troops to aid the local Serb sympathizers in putting down the Croatian rebellion. Croatia managed to stave off the Serbs, but Bosnia, which had declared independence in 1992, had mixed ethnic groups and multiple nationalities, presenting a more difficult task in resisting the Serbs. A new Balkan war started to erupt as the Serbs engaged in "ethnic cleansing," a process of outright killing of non-Serbs or, at the very least, driving them out of areas controlled by Milosevic's forces. Serb policies starkly resembled Hitler's campaign to eradicate the Jews, and Milosevic was personally so unappealing that he was easily demonized in the press. Although Clinton promised support to NATO, most Americans viewed the Balkans as a European problem. Moreover, with Russia's continued support of its old ally, Serbia, the old NATO-versus-Warsaw Pact antagonisms threatened to reignite.

NATO air power supported Croatian and Bosnian forces in driving back the Serbs. In 1995 the warring parties agreed to a meeting in Dayton, Ohio, where they signed the Dayton Accords, creating a unified but partitioned Bosnia with Muslims and Croats in one area and Bosnian Serbs in another. This agreement required the presence of 60,000 NATO peacekeepers, including 20,000 U.S. troops, which testified to the weakness of the settlement. United Nations investigators found mass graves containing 3,000 Muslims, leading to the indictments of several Serb leaders as war criminals.

Milosevic refused to go away, instead focusing on a new target, the region of Kosovo, controlled by a Serbian minority and populated by numerous Muslim Albanians. The Kosovo Liberation Army, a Muslim-armed terrorist organization, began a series of attacks on Serb targets in 1998, whereupon Milosevic dispatched more Serb troops. Western press reports of widespread atrocities—most of which were later shown to be unverifiable—once again prompted Clinton to commit American forces through NATO. Desperate to draw attention away from his White House scandals, yet aware that he did not dare repeat the Vietnam ground scenario in the Balkans, Clinton ordered the Pentagon to carefully conduct the campaign from 15,000 feet to avoid U.S. casualties. According to the U.S. Air Force chief of staff, Clinton made a "major blunder" in ruling out the use of ground troops from the beginning.[70] Despite steady bombardment, the Serbs suffered only minor military damage: the worst destruction involved a mistaken American attack on the Chinese embassy. The Serbs had fooled NATO, skillfully employing clever decoys in large numbers. Like the Gulf War, the Kosovo campaign featured a coalition of NATO aircraft, but unlike Desert Storm, it lacked any clear mission except to make Kosovo safe for the Kosovars. Once Milosevic had forced all the Kosovars out—which had been his objective—he agreed to negotiations. Less than a decade later, NATO commanders would admit they could not "keep peace" there any longer.

Another ongoing source of foreign policy trouble was the Middle East, especially the Arab-Israeli conflict. Since the administration of Jimmy Carter, American policy makers have expended countless hours and vast treasure on obtaining a peace in the region, specifically a lasting agreement between Israel and her Muslim neighbors.

Handshake agreements with photo opportunities, such as the Wye Plantation "nonagreement" between the Israelis and the Palestinians, played perfectly to Clinton's own inclinations for quick fixes abroad. Two interrelated challenges revealed the deadly weakness of this view of international affairs. The first was the revival of Saddam Hussein. During the Gulf War, George Bush and his advisers had chosen not to overthrow Hussein because it would, in all likelihood, have resulted in a bloody civil war among Sunni and Shiite Muslims, as well as the minority Kurds, and it risked escalation to a broader war involving Iran or Turkey. An inevitable American/NATO/allied occupation of Baghdad would have placed U.S. peacekeepers in constant danger from all parties. Thus, allied war aims in 1991 did not include removing Hussein; he was only to be rendered incapable of offensive military action. Many analysts in Europe and the Middle East thought internal opposition would force Hussein out anyway without additional pressure. That did not happen, and Hussein carried a grudge from his battlefield humiliation.

Where Clinton underestimated Hussein was in the Iraqi's ability and willingness to use terrorist weapons against western powers. In 1981 the Israeli Air Force had bombed the Iraqi Osirak nuclear power facility, claiming that Hussein intended it for the production of nuclear weapons. Iraq then took its nuclear program underground, employing as many as seven thousand in an attempt to manufacture a nuclear bomb or missile.[71] Hussein cleverly hid his main biological and chemical weapons facilities in defiance of United Nations resolutions. Throughout the Clinton administration, in speech after speech by Clinton, Al Gore, and other top Democrats, the point was reaffirmed that Saddam Hussein had chemical and biological weapons, and was likely getting nukes.

Another figure, whom the Clinton administration totally ignored, actually posed a more immediate threat. Osama bin Laden, a wealthy Saudi-born fundamentalist Muslim who had been exiled from his homeland and taken up residence in Afghanistan, directly attacked United States soil. On February 26, 1993, bin Laden's agents (using Iraqi passports) had set off a massive car bomb under the structure of the World Trade Center (WTC), killing seven people and wounding some seven hundred. They had intended to bring the WTC down but failed. Four Muslims were captured and tried, including Sheik Omar Abdel Rahman. In 1994 a New York City jury found all four guilty of murder. Ramzi Yousef, the mastermind behind the plan, was captured two years later and also convicted.

From the safety of Sudan, then Afghanistan, bin Laden planned his next strike against the United States. A plan to hijack several airliners over the Pacific was foiled. Then, in August 1998, powerful bombs ripped apart the American embassies in Nairobi, Kenya, and Tanzania, leaving 184 dead (including 12 Americans) and thousands wounded.[72] Clinton ordered retaliatory strikes, including the bombing of alleged terrorist camps in Sudan and bin Laden's headquarters in Afghanistan, but only an aspirin factory was hit. Clinton succeeded in proving to bin Laden that he wanted a bloodless victory from afar.

The entire Clinton approach to bin Laden (and all terrorists) was to treat terrorism as a law enforcement problem and not a national security/military issue. This policy had far-reaching (and negative) effects because when a terrorist like Ramzi Yousef is indicted, all evidence is sealed and cannot be used by the FBI or CIA to thwart other attacks. It was not a program designed to deal with the evil bin Laden. Bin Laden's forces staged other attacks: on the Khobar Towers in Dharan, Saudi Arabia; on the USS *Cole*; and a foiled assault on the USS *The Sullivans*—all without any serious retaliation by the United States under Clinton.

Only after 9/11 did evidence surface that Clinton had turned down not one but three offers from foreign governments to seize bin Laden, one by Sudan in 1996 and one by a Pakistani official working with an "unnamed Gulf State" in July 2000, and a third undated offer from the Saudi secret police, who had traced the luggage of bin Laden's mother when she visited him.[73] Having hurled expensive Tomahawks at unoccupied tents in a public show of force, Clinton thereafter, according to his advisers, demonstrated a consistent lack of interest in, or commitment to, the fight against terrorism. He consistently downgraded funding requests for the Central Intelligence Agency's human intelligence capabilities and rejected any attempts to watch terror suspects within U.S. borders, unless they were somehow tied to white militia groups.[74]

Yet as Clinton escaped conviction and coasted to the end of his second term, the threat of Osama bin Laden seemed remote, if not insignificant. Saddam Hussein posed what was thought to be a regional threat, but lacked (it was thought) the ability to launch direct attacks on the United States. Damaged but still determined, Clinton continued to rely on the economy to advance his proposals, though they became increasingly smaller in focus. Evidence had already begun to surface, however, that the economy was not in the great shape Clinton—and the country—thought. Worse, the terrorist threat he had all but ignored resurfaced in a tragic and horrific way.

CHAPTER TWENTY-TWO

America, World Leader, 2000 and Beyond

A Generation Challenged

During the 1990s, Americans were repeatedly reminded of "the greatest generation"—those who had come out of the Great Depression and swept away the Axis powers in World War II.[1] Implied in the term was the assumption that the United States had reached its apex of honor, courage, and determination in 1945, and had been on a downward slope ever since. The Clinton presidency seemed to underscore this assumption. The first boomer president, Clinton seemed to personify everything the GIs had not: a self-absorbed man who had avoided national military service and never delayed gratification.

Many Americans were beginning to doubt their own purpose, and America's position, in the world. Yet just when some thought that the horrors endured by the GIs could not be topped, nor their courage matched, and just as the nation's moral compass fluttered wildly, everything changed in a nanosecond. A bitterly contested election put an unlikely figure in the White House, but a bloodthirsty attack drew Americans together, at least temporarily, with direction and patriotism. An old enemy surfaced to remind the United States of its primacy in the world and of the relative irrelevance of international action.

Time Line

2000: Election of George W. Bush disputed by Al Gore; case goes to United States Supreme Court in December; Court rules that Gore's challenge is unconstitutional; Bush elected president by electoral college; Republicans win Senate and House for first time since the 1950s

2001: Muslim terrorists attack World Trade Center and Pentagon (9/11); Bush declares war on terror; United States invades Afghanistan and overthrows Taliban government friendly to Al Qaeda terrorists; Al Qaeda evicted from Afghanistan, assets frozen

2002: Al Qaeda bases in Afghanistan destroyed; "Axis of Evil" speech; D.C. Snipers; GOP wins historic election

2003: Operation Iraqi Freedom; Baghdad captured

2004: Saddam Hussein captured; Iraqi interim government assumes control of Iraq

Clintonism Collapses

After the 1996 election—and before the impeachment process had gained momentum—Bill Clinton stood atop the political world. His approval ratings held in the low 60 percent range; he successfully claimed credit for reforming welfare and for getting the North American Free Trade Agreement (NAFTA) passed; and he had mastered the new political art of triangulation. Pockets of hard-core liberalism remained—on the West Coast and in New England especially—but Clinton thrived largely by taking credit for conservative legislation, such as welfare reform, passed by the Republicans. Most of all, he pointed to the apparently healthy economy.

All of these benefits fell on the obvious Democratic nominee, incumbent Vice President Albert Gore Jr., who had easily won the Democratic nomination in Los Angeles.

Seldom in American history had sitting vice presidents lost during times of peace and prosperity (Richard Nixon, in 1960, is one of the few who did). The advantages of incumbency, combined with unease about changing horses, creates a powerful disadvantage for the challenger. Al Gore, however, could not boast too much about the economy without associating himself with his boss. Consequently, during his acceptance speech (where he introduced his mantra "I am my own man") and throughout his campaign, he shied away from the Clinton record, even to the extent that he did not tout the booming economy. A darker fact may also have influenced Gore's unwillingness to run on prosperity: storm warnings were appearing on the horizon by mid-2000, but subsequent review of Commerce Department statistics suggests the government had put the best possible spin on the nation's economic health, possibly even misstating the actual growth numbers.[2] Either way, Gore could see that he had no choice but to distance himself from the president.

As for Republicans, the race for the White House actually started with Bob Dole's defeat in November 1996. Many GOP analysts concluded that the party needed a "charisma injection," and that it could not afford to run any more "tired old men" merely out of obligation. Some Republicans yearned for a "GOP Clinton"—someone who could soften the ideological edges to appeal to the soccer moms and the independents who had deserted Dole in 1996.[3] However, any candidate had to represent strong conservative positions against gun control, abortion, and taxes.

In late 1999, just such a new star appeared on the GOP horizon when popular Texas Governor George W. Bush, the son of the former president, threw his hat in the ring. Bush, or Dubya, as he was called to differentiate him from his father, had gone from Midland, Texas, to Andover and Yale, where he admittedly achieved mediocrity. A typical frat boy, Bush graduated and served as a lieutenant in the air national guard, where he flew F-104 fighter planes. He received an MBA from Harvard (the first president ever to do so), where he began to take his education more seriously.[4] Returning to Midland, he attempted to make a career in the oil business, but it went badly. Bush and other investors had started a small company just as oil prices plunged worldwide. When his father ran for president in 1988, Dubya worked on his campaign as a speechwriter and made enough contacts to put together a partnership to purchase the Texas Rangers professional baseball team in 1989. Running the team as managing general partner, Bush later joked that his only noteworthy accomplishment had been trading home run star Sammy Sosa to the Chicago Cubs. In fact, he did an excellent job restoring the team to competitiveness on the field and solvency on the books.

After a wild youth in which he gained a reputation as a regular partygoer, Bush experienced a religious conversion in 1988, later becoming the first modern presidential candidate to specifically name Jesus Christ as the chief influence on his life. During the debates with Democratic presidential candidate Al Gore, Bush handled the pressure by fingering a tiny cross in his pocket. Time and again, whether in the postelection recount turmoil, or the horrific days following 9/11, Bush's religious faith was front and center. He had become, easily, the most publicly religious president since Lincoln.

In 1994, Bush ran for governor of Texas against a popular Democratic incumbent, Ann Richards, a silver-haired flamethrower who had lambasted the elder Bush at the 1992 Democratic campaign with the line, "Poor George! He was born with a silver foot in his mouth!" But two years later, "poor George's" son exacted political revenge. Richards badly underestimated Bush, mocking him as an intellectual lightweight, but he won with 53 percent of the vote. Clinging to the Right on matters of economics and taxes, Bush gained a reputation for working with political opponents to advance important legislation. Equally surprising, he made sharp inroads into the traditionally Democratic Hispanic vote. In 1998, he ran for reelection,winning in a landslide.

Bush had learned one lesson quite well from Clinton: money overcomes myriad political sins. He committed himself to raising more money, from more small donors, than any other candidate in history. This allowed him to turn down federal campaign funds, thereby freeing him from federal election spending limits. Breaking new ground by soliciting funds through the Internet, Bush hauled in thousands in $50 increments, and within three months of his announcement, had raised an astonishing $36 million. He would later prove to be the greatest political fund-raiser in American history, dwarfing the-then record levels of cash pulled in by Bill Clinton.

Understanding the reality that defeating an incumbent party during a peacetime good economy was a Herculean task, Bush quietly worked to gain the support of the more than thirty Republican governors, including his brother, Jeb Bush of Florida, whose state support he would need in November 2000 if he got that far. Bush's team also controlled the convention in Philadelphia, where the party was determined to shatter the image that it was for rich white men once and for all, with dozens of black, Hispanic, Asian, disabled, and women speakers. The only surprise was the selection of former Secretary of Defense Richard Cheney as the vice presidential nominee.

Gore looked forward to the televised debates, where his advisers were convinced their man's experience would easily carry the day. To their horror, Bush not only held his own, but he won all three. Worse for Gore, the Green Party fielded a candidate in the election, Ralph Nader, who was certainly guaranteed to take votes from the Democrat. Unable to run far enough to the left to capture Nader's supporters, Gore's chances slipped away. With Bush clinging to a narrow lead in the polls, on the last weekend of the election, a Democratic operative in New Hampshire discovered an old arrest record of Bush from his college days for driving under the influence. Pollsters found the race tightening up rapidly in the forty-eight hours before the election, and what had appeared at one point to be a Bush electoral landslide became the tightest race in American history.

The night began poorly for Bush when Gore "won" a shocker in Florida. The networks called that key state before the polls had closed in its western part, by all accounts causing numerous Bush supporters en route to abandon their intention to vote. After all, Gore had won the state. Or had he? After a few hours, the networks backtracked, saying Florida was too close to call.[5] In fact, Bush led in every tallied count in the state at the time, although he watched a large lead of more than 10,000 votes shrink to 537 in the final minutes of counting. By that time, every other state had been called (except Alaska and Hawaii, each of whose three electoral votes canceled the other out). With Florida's 25 electoral votes, Bush had 271, or one more electoral vote than necessary to win the election. Without them, Gore, who had narrowly won the popular vote (50.15 million to Bush's 49.82 million), would also take the electoral college.

At three o'clock in the morning, after the final votes in Florida had certified Bush the winner by 950 votes, Gore telephoned Bush with his concession. Under Florida's laws, however, the closeness of the vote triggered an automatic recount, so Gore, sensing he still had a chance, called Bush back an hour later to retract the concession. The recount cost Bush a few votes, but he still emerged with a 327-vote lead. Meanwhile, in Palm Beach County some residents claimed that they had been confused by the county's ballots.[6] Gore's advisers saw an opportunity to selectively use a hand recount in only Democratic strongholds where they could "find" the necessary votes to overcome Bush's slim lead.[7]

Like their Reconstruction Republican counterparts, the modern Democrats thought they had an edge because they controlled the voting machines in the local districts that would ultimately be involved in any recount, so naturally Bush petitioned a federal court to block *selected* hand recounts. By then, Bush had assembled a top-flight legal team, directed on the ground by former secretary of state and Reagan adviser James Baker. Bush, meanwhile, stayed behind the scenes at his ranch in Crawford, Texas. Gore assembled his own "dream team" of liberal lawyers, including Laurence Tribe and the protagonist in the Microsoft lawsuit, David Boies. Their strategy was simple: "Do everything you can to put numbers on the board. Whether they're erased or chiseled in granite, get them on the board."[8] To counter that, the Bush team emphasized the equal protection clause of the Constitution. Counting (or recounting) some votes and not others violated the principle of one man, one vote.

For days, panels of election officials stared blankly at ballots, trying to determine if a ballot had been punched or not. Determining intent in such circumstances was impossible. This painstaking process took time, but Florida law required that the secretary of state, Katherine Harris, certify the final results from all counties on the seventh day following the general election. Although the Florida Supreme Court prohibited Harris from certifying the results, giving the recount process still more time, overseas ballots had pushed Bush's lead to 930. Secretary of State Harris followed the Florida constitution and certified the election on November twenty-sixth, whereupon she declared Bush the winner. With the ballots counted three times, and the result each time in his favor, Bush made a national television appearance to claim victory.

Gore realized that he had seriously miscalculated the public relations fallout caused by calling for only a partial recount, and that the Constitution had put in place a ticking electoral college clock.[9] He then shifted gears, calling for a statewide recount. A key ruling by Florida Circuit Judge N. Sander Sauls rejected the request for a hand recount of selected (disputed) counties, and at the same time, the Republican-controlled Florida legislature prepared to appoint its own slate of federal electors if the dispute was not settled by the December twelfth constitutional deadline. By then, Gore realized he had shot himself in the foot by demanding selected initial recounts from three precincts in the state of Florida, which chewed a valuable amount of time off the clock, which might have permitted a statewide recount later. He appealed to the U.S. Supreme Court to extend Florida deadlines and to allow hand recounts. That same day, the U.S. Supreme Court vacated (set aside) the November twenty-first Florida Supreme Court ruling; in essence, ruling that the Florida Supreme Court had delivered a purely partisan decision. Yet the state justices responded by ordering a statewide recount of *all ballots* where no vote was detectable—some 43,000 ballots—essentially claiming that no choice was not an acceptable choice, and that all ballots, in essence, must have chosen a presidential candidate. When Leon County Judge Terry Lewis ordered the local boards to determine what constituted a vote, the Bush team told Gore lead attorney David Boies, "We just won this case."[10] Any variance by any local board in accepting votes after the fact constituted a violation of due process for all those who had already voted in all the other counties and whose votes were not going to be reinterpreted. Bush's victory may have been apparent to the Bush lawyers, though not to Gore's team, when on Tuesday, December twelfth—the federal deadline for the submission of all presidential electors' names—the United States Supreme Court reversed the Florida Supreme Court decision by a 5–4 vote. But the actual decision on key points was not that close. The key Supreme Court ruling was 7–2 that the hand-counting process violated federal equal protection clauses because of the absence of objective standards on the dimpled chads and other ballots. Five justices also stated that there was not enough time to count the votes (with the results due that day according to the Constituton). Gore conceded. Polls showed that people thought the Supreme Court had reached its decision on the merits of the case, not out of partisan leanings toward Bush.[11] Numerous media-sponsored recounts occurred in the wake of the election, well into May 2001. Most concluded that Bush would have won under almost any standard. A *USA Today/Miami Herald* survey of 61,000 ballots, followed by a broader review of 111,000 overvotes (where voters marked more than one candidate's name, and thus were disallowed), found that if Gore had received the manual recounts he had requested in four counties, Bush would have gained yet another 152 votes; and if the Supreme Court had not stopped the hand counting of the undervotes (ballots where a hole had not been punched cleanly through), Bush would have won under three of four standards for determining voter intent.[12]

More ominous overtones emerged from the election, which revealed a division in America identified by the colors of a countrywide county map. The counties Bush carried were colored red and Gore's blue. Gore carried only 677 counties in the United States, whereas Bush won 2,434, encompassing more than 2.4 million square miles to the blue states' 580,000 square miles. Most striking, with few exceptions, from New York to California, the entire map is red: Gore won some border areas, the coasts, and a thin line stretching from Minnesota down the Mississippi River. The visual representation of the election was stunning, with virtually all of the interior United States (or what elites often derisively refer to as "flyover country") voting for Bush. Symbolically, it appeared that the Democrats had been isolated into a few urban coastal cities, increasingly divorced from middle America.

Grand Corruption and Petty Larceny

Had Clinton chosen to view it in such a manner, Gore's defeat would not have meant a rebuke for his own presidency. After all, it could be reasoned, Gore had won a majority of the popular vote. But Clinton took the election as a plebiscite on his two terms and fumed that Gore had bungled a gift-wrapped package. But America had not seen the last of the Clintons.

In 1999, Hillary had already decided to run for the U.S. Senate seat held by the retiring Patrick Moynihan of New York. Along with Massachusetts and, perhaps, California, New York is one of the safest Democratic states in the United States. Having never lived in the state, and with little understanding of issues important to New Yorkers, Hillary donned a New York Yankees cap and purchased a mansion in Chappaqua, a posh New York City suburb that would permit her to claim residency. She faced a tough campaign against New York City Mayor Rudolph "Rudy" Giuliani, but he developed prostate cancer and, at the same time, his failing marriage was being splashed across tabloid pages. He handed over the nomination to Congressman Rick Lazio, who lost to Hillary heavily (53 percent to 45 percent).

With Hillary's November 2000 victory, the Clintons had a house. To furnish it, Hillary—who had just signed a massive, controversial $8 million book deal for her memoirs—registered with major stores in New York and Washington, almost as a newlywed couple would. Friends were asked by party loyalists to furnish the house as an appreciation of the eight years of service.[13]

An avalanche of gifts rolled in from the Clintons' registries (many, it was noted, from individuals or companies that still stood to gain from Senator Clinton's access to power): Glen Eden Carpets in Georgia gave two $6,000 carpets; Lynn Forester of New York City gave Hillary a $1,300 cashmere sweater; Arthur Athis in Los Angeles provided $2,400 in dining chairs; Walter Kaye of New York City donated more than $9,000 in gifts; and the Georgetown alumni, class of 1968, gave a designer $38,000 basket set.[14] Other presidents, especially the Reagans, had refurbished the presidential mansion and received gifts for redecorating, but all the gifts stayed at the White House, becoming gifts to the nation. Not with the Clintons. In January 2001, Hillary Clinton began shipping furniture from the White House to her New York home. These items had all been donated as part of the $396,000 redecoration undertaken by the Clintons in 1993 and were not private, but public, property. Under intense criticism, the Clintons returned four items clearly marked "National Park Service," and in another return, sent back a "truckload of couches, lamps and other furnishings."[15]

That was fairly insignificant next to some of the other actions by the departing president, most notably an orgy of pardons and commutations. Every president has an unlimited pardon power: there is no review, and it is absolute. On his last day alone, Clinton issued 140 pardons and 36 sentence commutations. One television commentator said, "Not since the opening of the gates of the Bastille have so many criminals been liberated on a single day."[16] Among those pardoned was a group of Puerto Rican terrorists responsible for 130 bombing attacks in Chicago, New York, and other locations. Perhaps more offensive was the pardon of Marc Rich, an international arms runner indicted in the United States for tax evasion and counts of fraud. Rich had fled to Europe, where he peddled (illegal) Libyan oil past embargoes and paid for the oil with grain (again illegal because it was embargoed).[17]

When he boarded the marine helicopter for the last time on January 20, 2001, to leave for his new life, Bill Clinton was departing as only the second president to be impeached; the first ever to have been charged with lying to a grand jury; the first ever to be disbarred; the first judged guilty of perjury against a federal court and forced to pay a fine; and the first sued in a civil suit for sexual harassment. His failure to earn the respect of the military could be seen in a small detail when the marine guards who stood by the presidential helicopter failed to execute a right face to stand facing the president's back as he walked away from the chopper. Yet these marine guards managed to relearn the maneuver after George W. Bush took office on January 20.

Clinton's legacy to his party was no less destructive than his imprint on the presidency. When he came to the office in 1992, the Democrats held both the House and the Senate and the governorship of New York as well as the mayoralities of New York City and Los Angeles. Within a decade, the Republicans held the House, the Senate, and the presidency, and conservative ideals were held by a slim majority of the United States Supreme Court justices. In states with a "pure" two-party legislature after 2002, there were twenty-five Republican chambers, twenty-two Democratic chambers, and two that were tied. Despite the perception that he was good for the party, most of the candidates Clinton personally campaigned for had lost, and few Democrats (except in the absolutely safest seats) could afford to be seen with him.

Team Bush

Although the transition was delayed by the Gore election challenge, Bush had his cabinet lined up even before the election. Colin Powell, former chairman of the Joint Chiefs of Staff, was secretary of state, and a former secretary of defense in the Ford administration. Donald Rumsfeld was tapped to be the secretary of defense. Not only did Bush appoint the highest-ranking African American in American history in the person of Powell, but he also named black Stanford professor Condoleezza Rice as his national security adviser, making her the highest-ranking black woman in the United States and the first woman or black named to the national security post. Rod Paige, Bush's secretary of education, became the first African American in that post. By the time Bush finished his appointments, he had more African Americans, women, and minorities in positions of power than any other administration.

Bush knew he would need some Democratic support. In the House, Republicans had lost a few seats in 2000, but they still held a slim majority. A number of incumbent Republican senators had lost close races, leaving the Republicans only the tie-breaking vote of Vice President Cheney (as Senate president) to retain their majority. This portended difficulty for Bush's program, which included a tax cut, partial privatization of Social Security, education reform, and deployment of the Strategic Defense Initiative. Pressing ahead with his agenda, Bush advanced a broad tax-cut plan to revive the economy, which had begun to turn down even before the election. The tax cuts involved a popular tax rebate for every American as well as longer-term tax reductions. With support from several Senate Democrats, the package passed. An education reform bill also emerged from Congress, emphasizing teacher accountability and test scores.

But then a surprise defection handed the Senate back to the Democrats. Vermont senator Jim Jeffords, a long-time liberal Republican, in May 2001 suddenly caucused with the Democrats, making South Dakota Senator Tom Daschle the majority leader. Jeffords's defection essentially blocked all further legislation for the rest of the year. The Democrats stalled Bush's judicial nominations, effectively blocked any discussion of Social Security privatization, and nipped at the edges of the tax cut (without publicly favoring a tax increase). American politics seemed bogged in a morass of obstructionism and delay, with Bush's popularity hovering in the low 50 percent range and the public nearly evenly split on policy prescriptions. No American had a clue that the world was about to change as surely as it had on December 7, 1941, at Pearl Harbor.

9/11

On the morning of September 10, 2001, the Washington *Times* carried the latest criticism by the National Academy of Sciences on the Bush administration's directives for controversial stem-cell research, and the New York *Post* carried the latest news about California Congressman Gary Condit, who was under investigation in the disappearance of a Washington intern, Chandra Levy, with whom he had a sexual relationship. CBS reported that pressure was mounting on Bush to do something about the deepening economic gloom. The Republicans in Congress had delayed immigration reform legislation until the White House plan to fix the Immigration and Naturalization Service had been submitted. Concerned groups had been warning that immigration policies were too liberal and immigrants too poorly screened. New doubts had surfaced about a controversial study of early American gun ownership (a thinly disguised attack on the National Rifle Association), leading to an investigation of the scholar who had produced it, and jury selection was proceeding in the murder case of Andrea Yates, who was accused of drowning her five children. All in all, September tenth seemed like just another day in America. Everything would change in less than twenty-four hours.

On September 11, 2001, President Bush was in Florida for an event in which he would read to a group of elementary school children to push his No Child Left Behind education proposal. As White House staffers left for the school at 8:42 A.M., their pagers and cell phones went wild. An aircraft had hit the North Tower of the World Trade Center (WTC). Early reports indicated that it had been a small twin-engine plane, and the only explanation was, as the president later recalled, that the pilot "must have had a heart attack."[18] Air traffic controllers in Newark, New Jersey, knew differently. Just across the Hudson River from Manhattan, they had followed the radar screens tracing American Airlines Flight 11, a Boeing 767 en route from Boston to Los Angeles. Then through the windows to the outside, they had watched as the aircraft descended, its transponder off. Controller Rick Tepper said, "One of the towers, one of the trade towers, is on fire."[19]

In fact, only minutes earlier, a radio signal from Flight 11 was heard in the Boston regional air traffic control center—an ominous voice saying, "We have some planes." Expecting a hostage situation from the first aircraft, FAA officials treated it according to protocol, not realizing that the hijackers had something far more deadly in mind than landing in Cuba. Hijacked Flight 11, with eighty-one passengers and eleven crew members, flew a straight path into the World Trade Center's North Tower, erupting into an inferno sending temperatures soaring to 1,800 degrees and engulfing the 110-story building in a ball of flame and smoke above the hundredth floor. As the emergency rescue teams raced to the site of the crash, most people still thought they were dealing with pilot error or a massive accident, not a deliberate act of terror. Glass, steel, and charred human remains rained down on the police and fire personnel who had rushed into the building, even as masses of frantic people streamed out. Many, trapped on the floors above the explosion, quickly realized they had no hope. Some jumped more than a hundred floors to their deaths. Others chose to remain, overcome by smoke inhalation or seared by the flames. Those on lower floors evacuated, efficiently and quickly, but surprisingly few doubted what had happened. "I knew it was a terrorist attack the moment I looked up and saw the smoke," said one survivor. "I saw the face of evil."[20]

By that time, the attention of news cameras and crowds was focused on the North Tower when a second jumbo jet, United Flight 175 from Boston to Los Angeles with fifty-six passengers and nine crew members, hurtled through the skyline, performing a sharp turn and crashing into the South Tower, generating a second massive fireball. In Florida, President Bush had just begun to read to second-graders when his chief of staff, Andrew Card, entered the classroom and whispered in his ear, "A second plane has hit the second tower. America is under attack."[21] Bush later remembered thinking, "They had declared war on us, and I made up my mind at that moment we were going to war."[22] CIA director George Tenet received the news in Washington. "This has bin Laden all over it," referring to the renegade terrorist Osama bin Laden.[23] He immediately recalled that the FBI had detained Zacarias Massoui in August after suspicions had been raised when he sought training at a Minnesota flight school. Tenet speculated that he might have a connection to the attack.

A shaken Bush appeared on television before the twin towers collapsed, informing the American public of "an apparent terrorist attack," promising (in "oddly informal" language) to chase down "those folks who committed this act."[24] Already, he was being urged to stay away from Washington and to board Air Force One as soon as possible. The FAA knew that more than 4,200 planes still filled the skies—thousands of potential bombs in the hands of terrorists—and officials had already decided to ground any remaining airborne planes when, at 9:03, they saw United Flight 175 fly into the South Tower. A conference call to other air traffic controllers confirmed what they dreaded. A third plane was in the hands of hijackers—American Flight 77, bound for Los Angeles from Washington with 58 passengers and 8 crew members. Shortly after Bush delivered his terse address to the nation at 9:41, Flight 77 reappeared over Washington, D.C., and crashed into the Pentagon, killing all aboard and 125 people inside the building.

By that time, the FAA had commanded all aircraft to land as soon as possible, anywhere. Word spread overseas, and international flights to the United States were grounded—just in time, as it turned out, since other hijackers were prepared to take control of still other airplanes targeted for Big Ben and Parliament in England.

Meawhile, fire and rescue teams at the World Trade Center struggled to get survivors out, hamstrung by communications glitches among police, fire, and the New York Port Authority, who had jurisdiction over the towers. "There's a lot of bodies," said one fireman, as he reached the forty-fifth floor of the South Tower.[25] Only sixteen people survived from the South Tower above the ninetieth floor, where the plane hit; none survived above the seventy-eighth floor crash line in the North Tower.

Although the buildings had been built to sustain accidental impacts of aircraft, no one dreamed that fully fueled jetliners would be deliberately aimed at the center of the structures. Even so, the towers stood for far longer than most structural analysts thought they could. Initial estimates that upward of ten thousand might have been killed were revised downward every minute the buildings stood—until 9:50 A.M. At that moment the South Tower collapsed and crumbled to the ground in a torrent of debris, dust, and thousands of human body parts, burying, among others, hundreds of firemen and rescue teams who had set up headquarters close to the building. Less than half an hour later, the other tower, with its massive antenna spike plunging straight into the middle of the disintegrating mass, imploded, with floors crashing straight down like pancakes. Hundreds of firefighters, trapped in the building, were crushed. News anchor Jon Scott, who provided a somber commentary on the morning's events, went silent for many moments as the towers disintegrated. "America, offer a prayer," he concluded.[26] One structural engineer marveled that the towers stood as long as they did, noting that the worst worse-case scenarios could not have envisioned such an attack: "You may as well be talking about giant objects from space."[27] New York's mayor Giuliani was a blur of energy, ordering certain areas evacuated, consoling firefighters and workers on the line, and supervising the environmental checks for poisonous gases and biological or other airborne threats.

At the time, one more plane was unaccounted for: United Airlines Flight 93 bound for San Francisco with forty-five people aboard had started an unauthorized climb at 9:35 A.M., raising concerns that it, too, had been hijacked. It had flown by Cleveland, made a U-turn, and then accelerated past Pittsburgh. Somewhere hear Shanksville, Pennsylvania, the plane wobbled out of control and plunged into a field, exploding in a fireball. Evidence soon surfaced that several courageous men and women led by Todd Beamer, who had heard of the WTC attack from other phone calls, realized their own aircraft was a suicide bomb headed for a target. The passengers had to overpower at least three men at the front of the plane or in the cockpit, one of them with bombs supposedly strapped to his body. Convinced the aircraft was turning for its final approach, Beamer said to the others, "Let's roll." Whether they succeeded in storming the cockpit, something forced the hijackers to crash the plane before reaching the intended target (which subsequent evidence indicates was the Capitol).[28]

Government offices in Washington had been evacuated, and President Bush was warned away by the Secret Service and the military. Air Force One was thought to be a prime target, since intercepts had showed that the terrorists knew Air Force One's code sign for that day. Bush maintained phone communication with Vice President Cheney, National Security Adviser Rice, and the Joint Chiefs of Staff, immediately ordering a massive manhunt for those responsible. "We're going to find out who did this. They're not going to like me as president," he said.[29] Bush was more blunt to Cheney: "We're going to find out who did this and we're going to kick their asses."[30]

Bush declared a DefCon 3, the highest level of military readiness in twenty-eight years. That evening the president went on television to address the nation. "These acts of mass murder," he said, "were intended to frighten our nation into chaos and retreat. But they have failed. . . . Terrorist attacks can shake the foundations of our biggest buildings, but they cannot touch the foundation of America."[31]

Within hours the CIA and FBI had conclusively determined that the hijackings were the result of Osama bin Laden's Al Qaeda terrorist network based in Afghanistan. For many years after 1993, when the first attack on the WTC by bin Laden's operatives failed, most Americans had dismissed him as a crackpot and a minor annoyance. Indeed, The first WTC bombing attempt killed only six people, and a bombing in Yemen, which he had also sponsored, did not kill a single American, frustrating bin Laden even more.

An elaborate rationale quickly sprang up among the blame-America-first crowd that bin Laden had only become obsessed with the United States after the Gulf War, when the presence of Americans on "holy" Islamic soil threatened to pollute bin Laden's homeland. But according to Gerald Posner, bin Laden was already committed to guerrilla war and terrorism by 1989. One member of Islamic Jihad had told Egyptian police that bin Laden wanted to launch a holy war throughout the world.[32] Other researchers agree that bin Laden's die was already cast, if perhaps accelerated by the Gulf War. One thing is certain: the CIA never paid bin Laden for his role in the anti-Soviet struggle in Afghanistan, nor was he ever pro-American prior to the Gulf War. Now, however, he was gleeful: "Its greatest buildings were destroyed," bin Laden exclaimed. "America! Full of fear. . . . Thank God for that."[33]

Six months after the attacks, FBI agents, diplomats, and reporters produced shards of evidence that the United States had had warning about 9/11. Yet a memo here and a report of suspicious activity there, dropped into the massive pile of more than three *million* pieces of intelligence information accumulated per day by the CIA and National Security Agency alone, constituted no warning at all. If anything, Congress learned that much of the information that intelligence agencies had accumulated had crashed into bureaucratic walls. The separation of the CIA and FBI prompted by Democrats in the wake of Watergate and exacerbated by a directive in the Clinton administration (referred to as the wall memo) now returned to plague the U.S. intelligence services. Over the next several months, the Bush administration studied the breakdown in intelligence, proposing the most massive reorganization of the government since the New Deal, highlighted by the creation of a Department of Homeland Security, which would facilitate information flow between the FBI, the CIA, and the NSA. It also split the Immigration and Naturalization Service (INS) into two parts, one focused on security, and one focused on facilitating the admission of new immigrants.

Immediately after the attacks, however, the administration's economic team swung into action, using free-market principles—not government power— whenever possible. Treasury Secretary Paul O'Neill jawboned bank executives to maintain the flow of credit to the airlines, which had come under massive financial pressure in the days after 9/11 when air ridership plummeted. The New York Stock Exchange (NYSE) and the other exchanges were shut down to prevent a panic. Once they reopened, the Dow still fell almost five hundred points in the first hours of trading but then stabilized.[34] The attacks hit the U.S. economy hard: one study put 9/11-related losses at almost $2 trillion.[35]

Very soon thousands of volunteers streamed into New York to help search for survivors or excavate the site. Thousands more lined up to give blood, and entertainers held massive telethons to generate millions of dollars in relief for the victims' families. Amid the rubble, workers unearthed a remarkable piece of steel: two girders, molded by the flames into a cross, which the workers raised up. One of the most memorable photos of the event—three firemen hoisting the American flag above the trade site soon emerged as the singular symbolic picture of defiance. It reflected the resolve that had surfaced in just a matter of days, surging past the grief as the nation set its jaw. Indeed, New York City immediately entertained designs to rebuild the massive WTC and began soliciting designs. (The winning design technically would be taller than either of the previous towers.)

The collapse of the buildings, symbolic though they were, remained insignificant next to the loss of the 2,749 people who died at the World Trade Center, the forty-five passengers and crew who died in Shanksville, Pennsylvania, and those who died in the crash at the Pentagon. The initial estimates suggesting that ten thousand might have died in New York alone had been thankfully proved wrong. In less than a year after the attack the Pentagon was rebuilt. Ironically, work crews had broken ground to build the massive Pentagon in 1941—on September eleventh.

Immediately after 9/11, the president still had to rally the nation, displaying the proper balance of defiance, sympathy, compassion, and resolution. Arguably his best speech, and one of the most moving presidential speeches since Reagan's ode to the *Challenger* crew in 1986, it was delivered on September fourteenth, designated by Bush as a national day of prayer and remembrance. (One of the first things the president did was to request that all Americans pray, and pray often, not only for the victims and their families, but also for the nation.) At the National Cathedral, Bush ascended the steps in the mammoth nave in total isolation. His words touched the nation:

On Tuesday, our country was attacked with deliberate and massive cruelty. We have seen the images of fire and ashes, and bent steel. Now come the names, the list of casualties we are only beginning to read. . . . They are the names of people who faced death, and in their last moments called home to say, "Be brave, and I love you." . . . War has been waged against us by stealth and deceit and murder. . . . This conflict was begun on the timing and terms of others. It will end in a way, and at an hour, of our choosing.[36]

After Bush's speech—to a room bursting with emotion—he flew to Ground Zero. After changing into a plain yellow windbreaker, Bush walked amid the firefighters and rescue workers who had been digging and excavating, some of them for three days straight. Mounting a twisted pile of steel and bricks and standing next to a retired fireman who had, by his own words, "scammed" his way in to help in the relief effort, Bush took the only public address system available—a bullhorn—and began to address the crowd of burly men. The bullhorn cut out during the president's prepared remarks, and someone shouted, "We can't hear you." Bush tried again, and again the shout came, "We can't hear you," at which point the president reacted on instinct, responding, "I can hear *you*. The rest of the world hears you, and . . ."—pointing to the spot where the buildings had stood, he shouted—"and the people who knocked these buildings down will hear *all* of us soon!"[37]

In two remarkable settings, the National Cathedral and the WTC site, and in two speeches—one formal, one impromptu—Bush had brought the nation together and set it on the task of finding and eliminating the perpetrators. Jonathan Alter, a journalist and bitter Bush foe, nevertheless sensed that a defining point had been reached: "This is a turning point in history," he told Bush press secretary Ari Fleischer. Or, as Bush put it just a few days later in a defiant message to a joint session of Congress, "Either you are with us, or you are with the terrorists." This quickly became known as the Bush Doctrine.

"It Starts Today"

On September 17, 2001, Bush met with his war cabinet, presenting the members with an unequivocal task. "It starts today," he said. "The purpose of this meeting is to assign tasks for the first wave of the war against terrorism."[38] Bush had already solicited advice: "I want the CIA to be the first on the ground" in Afghanistan, he instructed; "We'll attack with missiles, bombers and boots on the ground," he concluded.[39] As for bin Laden, Bush told the press he wanted the terrorist "dead or alive."

On October 7, 2001, a massive series of air strikes in Afghanistan smashed mainline Taliban forces, allowing the special forces and regular military, who had been airlifted in, to join forces with the Northern Alliance of anti-Taliban fighters. Code-named Operation Enduring Freedom, this was Bush's "new kind of war," lacking long, clear battle lines and instead using selected air power, highly trained commando and special forces units, and above all, electronic and human intelligence to identify and destroy Al Qaeda and Taliban strongholds. The UK *Telegraph* reported that a handful of U.S. Green Beret teams, directing air power before finishing the job on the ground, had killed more than 1,300 Taliban and Al Qaeda fighters. "You bomb one side of a hill and push them in one direction," observed a Green Beret spotter, "then bomb the next hill over and push guys the other way. Then, when they're all bunched up, you . . . drop right on them."[40]

Nevertheless, it took the press only a few weeks to flip from patriotic to harsh, with journalists invoking the shopworn "Vietnam" and "quagmire" lines less than a month into combat. *Newsweek's* Evan Thomas prophesied that the United States would need 250,000 troops on the ground (the real total was under 20,000). Terry Moran, the White House correspondent for ABC, dourly asserted, "I think the bad guys are winning."[41] ABC's Cokie Roberts grilled Rumsfeld, claiming, "There have been stories . . . that give the perception . . . that this war, after three weeks, is not going very well."[42] In fact, the journalists missed the evidence in front of their faces. Once the war on terror had been engaged, it played out along the same lines as most other western versus nonwestern conflicts. American air power utterly dominated the battlefield, and as in the Gulf War, the "combination of the information revolution and precision munitions . . . produced a quantum leap in lethality."[43] Small units of special operations troops on the ground, guiding the bombing with laser targeting, provided pinpoint targeting to enable the smart weapons to shatter Taliban forces on the ground. War analyst Victor Hanson summed up the combat situation: "Glad we are not fighting us."

Unlike the Soviet infantry and armor doctrines that had failed in Afghanistan just twenty years earlier, the U.S. military employed dynamic, not static, tactics. An armored division might be used for one purpose, a smart bomb for another; Green Berets and Delta Force for certain tasks; air power for yet others. Bush told correspondent Bill Sammon, "We fought the first cavalry charge of the twenty-first century—special forces and CIA agents on wooden saddles with some of the most sophisticated technology developed by mankind."[44]

In many ways, Operation Enduring Freedom was even more successful than Desert Storm, routing the Taliban and Al Qaeda and searching them out in the Tora Bora mountains, where bin Laden was thought to have holed up. A massive bombing of the mountains in December either drove bin Laden farther underground or seriously wounded him. Within a few months, the Taliban were evicted, and special forces had hunted down and killed hundreds of Al Qaeda terrorists and arrested thousands of others for interrogation. By 2003, bin Laden had not made a single verifiable public appeerence that could be time-stamped or dated, despite several tape recordings he released. In fact, he was becoming irrelevant as more subtle American financial attacks were shutting down much of the worldwide financial network supporting Al Qaeda and establishing a civilian functioning government in Afghanistan. One year after the attacks, it was thought that close to half of Al Qaeda's leaders were dead or in custody.

Another casualty of Operation Enduring Freedom was "gloomster" journalism. A Gallup Poll conducted in November 2001 found that 54 percent of the public disapproved of the news media, although Bush's ratings remained in the high 80 percent range. Indeed, the news media was the only major American organization to see its approval numbers decline (and the numbers declined precipitously). On the other hand, for the first time, polls asked people what they thought of cabinet members, and again, the results stunned the hostile media. Defense Secretary Rumsfeld had an 80 percent approval rating, Vice President Cheney had a 75 percent rating, and Secretary of State Powell topped the list with an 87 percent favorable rating. Bush's instincts for choosing competent people, far from insulating him from decision making, had proven prescient.[45]

Terrorists still had the potential for devastating attacks, and several were intercepted before completing their missions. Richard Reid (Muslim name Riady), an Al Qaeda-connected shoe bomber, attempted to smuggle explosives through his shoes into a passenger jet. Al Qaeda operatives blew up a Christian church in Pakistan, assassinated the newly named vice president in Afghanistan, and continued to make assassination attempts on U.S. soldiers overseas. A French freighter was bombed by Al Qaeda operatives; then, in October 2002, the island vacation area on Bali was rocked by a bomb explosion at a resort, killing 181 (mostly Australian) vacationers and employees. Adding to the terror—although not directly linked to the terrorist network—a team of snipers rained death on Virginia and Maryland citizens for almost a month. In March 2004, terrorists thought to be linked to Al Qaeda unleashed multiple bombs on Spanish trains, killing and wounding hundreds.

Bush had promised to carry the war not only to the terrorists but also to "those who harbor them," a clear threat to such Muslim states as Iran, Iraq, Sudan, and Yemen. Bush had made matters even plainer in his January 2002 State of the Union speech in which he referred to Iraq, Iran, and North Korea and other "states like these" as an "axis of evil" that had allied themselves with terrorists. It was abundantly clear which rogue states were next on the 9/11 hit list. Evidence that Saddam Hussein had links to the Al Qaeda terrorists, combined with continued reports that Iraq had violated United Nations resolutions requiring the nation to allow in weapons inspectors, made Hussein the next obvious target in the terror war.[46] Soon, other nations were reminded that 9/11 was an attack on all nations that embraced freedom and democracy.

The results of the first year and a half of the war on terror were impressive but difficult to fully evaluate, given the secretive nature of many of the important accomplishments. At minimum:

- Several hundred Al Qaeda members and suspected members were detained at Guantánamo Bay, Cuba, for incarceration and interrogation as prisoners of war.
- Approximately two dozen of bin Laden's top Al Qaeda leaders were dead or in custody.
- The Taliban were eradicated as the governing force in Afghanistan, and a new democratic government was installed. Schools previously closed to women were opened, and a spirit of liberty spread through a land that had known little.
- The FBI, the CIA, and allied intelligence agencies had successfully prevented another attack. Riady and José Padilla (the dirty bomber) had both been arrested before perpetrating any terrorist acts; several Al Qaeda cells (in Buffalo, Detroit, and the Pacific Northwest) were captured. In addition, British, Spanish, Moroccan, German, and other foreign intelligence networks had bagged several dozen Al Qaeda suspects.
- Millions of dollars in assets tied to Al Qaeda worldwide were frozen in U.S. and friendly banks.
- Khalid Shaikh Mohammed, Ramzi Yousef's uncle and the tactical mastermind behind the 9/11 plot, was captured.
- In 2004, a raid in Pakistan captured one of Al Qaeda's top computer nerds—Muhammad Khan—whose treasure trove of information threw the doors open to capturing dozens of cell members and breaking up a planned attack on the United States.

Many analysts suggested that the Bali bombing, the multiple attacks in Africa on Israeli embassies in late 2002, the Spanish train bombings in 2004, and bombings in Turkey and Saudi Arabia in 2004 indicated that Al Qaeda could no longer get through U.S. security and was therefore forced to strike softer targets. Of course, no one in the Bush administration or in the security agencies of America's allies believed the war on terror was over, but important inroads had been made into enemy geographical and financial strongholds.

In what some termed "the new normal," post-9/11 America seemed shaken from more than a decade's worth of doldrums into purpose and conviction. Perhaps it was fitting that in the 2001 World Series, played only a month after the towers fell, one of the teams was the New York Yankees. Then, at the quintessential American event, pro football's Super Bowl contest, this time between St. Louis and New England, the championship was won by . . . the Patriots.

Midterm Mayhem

Going into the summer of 2002, the Democratic Senate, thanks to its one-vote margin provided by the defection of Jim Jeffords, had elevated South Dakota's Senator Tom Daschle to the majority leader position. With his slim margin, Daschle successfully blocked Bush's judicial nominees, held up drilling for oil in the Arctic National Wildlife Refuge (ANWR), and stifled any attempt to cut taxes or otherwise stimulate the economy.

Lacking a majority in the Senate, in the early part of 2002, Bush and his political adviser Karl Rove embarked on a brilliant campaign strategy for the 2002 midterm elections to try to reclaim control of the Senate. Whereas by historical standards, the GOP should have lost nearly two dozen House seats and two Senate seats, the Republicans actually gained seats in both houses of Congress and increased their state legislature gains by some 200 seats. The result was an unprecedented midterm election.[47] The feat was even more impressive historically: because of the timing of the open Senate seats, the Republicans had to defend twenty, but the Democrats only had to defend fourteen. Realizing that mobilization for an Iraq war would take some time—especially since Al Qaeda was not entirely eliminated—Bush, Powell, Rumsfeld, and Rice made several policy speeches throughout the summer of 2002 emphasizing the threat posed by Iraq and its weapons of mass destruction. Democrats jumped at the bait, attacking the president for wanting to go it alone without the support of our allies or the United Nations. In fact, Bush intended all along to solicit support from important allies and to involve the UN, but he allowed the Democrats to stretch out their apparent opposition to the Iraq policy all summer, negating their advantage on some other election issues. In the fall, Bush brought a war resolution to Congress, forcing the Democrats—including Bush's future opponent in the November general election, Senator John Kerry of Massachusetts—to put themselves on record as supporting it. Bush then took his case to the UN in a powerful speech in which he offered not one shred of new evidence against Saddam Hussein; quite the contrary, he outlined eleven years of Iraqi violations of the UN's own resolutions. It was a masterful performance to the extent that it forced the UN to either act against Iraq or admit impotence and become completely irrelevant. The UN gave the administration a new resolution, and even Syria voted yes.

When the dust cleared on Election Day, the GOP had won a two-vote margin in the Senate and added to their majority in the House. The Republicans had made history. In virtually all of the victorious Republican senatorial campaigns, national security, in the form of the debate over the homeland security bill, provided much of the cushion. But other surprising signs of change were seen in the exit-polling data: candidates advocating privatization of Social Security won, and the prolife vote proved critical in many states. There was also evidence that Bush was eroding the New Deal coalition by siphoning off Hispanic and Jewish votes—not in overwhelming numbers, but enough to seriously damage the Democrats.[48]

Unlike Reagan, Bush used his majority to push big government programs such as a prescription drug bill and education reform, signing the single biggest entitlement since the Great Society (the Medicaid prescription drug bill). He also rolled back some traditionally liberal bastions, such as in the area of abortion, where his executive orders actually restricted abortions on federal property and with federal funds. In 2003 he signed into law a ban on partial birth abortions, in which an abortionist partially delivers a late-term baby before killing it.[49]

The "Axis of Evil"

Bush, in his 2002 State of the Union message, listed Iraq, Iran, and North Korea as an "axis of evil" and as indirect allies of Al Qaeda and as state supporters of terrorism.

Since 9/11, the administration had received information tying Saddam Hussein's Iraq to Osama bin Laden's terror network. Salman Pak, a training facility in Iraq, featured 737 jetliner fuselages that served little purpose except to give terrorists practice at taking over aircraft. The Iraqi foreign minister paid a visit to Czechoslovakia prior to 9/11, where, according to Czech sources, he met with hijacker Mohammad Atta. There were numerous other connections. Bush and his team decided that it was too dangerous to allow Al Qaeda to obtain chemical or biological weapons that virtually all nations had conceded were in Iraq. Clinton and Gore both had warned of the dangers of WMDs (weapons of mass destruction). A group of Democratic senators, including John Kerry, Carl Levin, and Ted Kennedy, urged Clinton to take action on Iraq's WMD. Iraqi dictator Saddam Hussein, however, refused to allow United Nations inspection teams to search his facilities, and he defied fourteen UN resolutions. Bush gave him one last chance.

After the "Axis of Evil" speech, Bush began a relatively long preparation period to ready the nation for war with Iraq if Hussein did not comply. Following the State of the Union, Bush, Secretary of State Powell, and Secretary of Defense Rumsfeld, along with British Prime Minister Tony Blair (who had received the same briefings) initiated a steady diplomatic assault on Iraq, painting for the U.S. and British public, and for the world community, a picture of a dictator who had weapons of mass destruction in his hands. These WMDs posed a particularly dangerous threat to American security because they could be easily brought into the United States by terrorists. Had one of the planes that hit the World Trade Center, for example, been carrying a small nuclear device or vials of VX gas, the death toll would have soared exponentially.

In September 2002, in his address to the United Nations, Bush detailed dozens of violations by Iraq. Bush and Powell succeeded in obtaining a unanimous resolution from the UN Security Council (Resolution 1441) that required new vigorous inspections of Iraq and a full disclosure by Hussein of all of his WMD programs. Bush expected that the Iraqis would either not comply or feign compliance. Either way, the president planned to have a military option available if, within a reasonable time, Saddam did not demonstrate total transparency. More important, the administration used each roadblock Saddam threw up as another piece of evidence that the regime itself could not be trusted and had to be dispatched. UN weapons inspectors, meanwhile, reported violation after violation, yet desperately sought to avoid labeling Iraq's noncompliance as such.

Behind the scenes, France, Germany, and Russia—all with powerful economic stakes in maintaining Saddam in power—sought to derail American and British attempts to establish a final enforcement date of Resolution 1441. Building a larger alliance of nations than his father had in 1991—Bush termed it "the coalition of the willing"—on March 17, 2003, Bush gave Saddam and his sons forty-eight hours to leave Iraq or face war. Exactly three days later, the United States, having convinced the Iraqis that any new conflict would look much like the Gulf War (with a long, protracted bombing campaign called shock and awe), instead launched a single intensive air strike against a location where informants had said Saddam and his sons were. Saddam was not killed but instantly the Iraqi army began to behave as though it had lost all command and control.

Coalition forces tore through Iraqi resistance even as pundits and military commentators ("embedded generals," as Rumsfeld called them) complained that American forces were too light and lacked sufficient boots on the ground.[50] Never have so many prognosticators and journalists been so wrong about so much: the "elite" Republican Guard, which supposedly would fight for every inch of Baghdad, collapsed without a fight.[51] On April ninth, in just over two weeks of fighting, mostly against irregular troops, American armor swept through the desert and into the center of Baghdad.[52] Once the local residents realized Saddam was indeed gone, large celebrations began, with Iraqis throwing flowers and cheering American soldiers with "Bush, Bush, Bush," and "We love America!" That day, in what was sure to be one of the most memorable scenes of the new century, Iraqi civilians, aided by American trucks, tore down a massive statue of Saddam in the center of Baghdad, then proceeded to drag the head around town as people beat it with their shoes and spat on it.

Nothing less than a complete transformation of war had been witnessed by the world, which saw twentieth-century mass tactics with the ancillary large casualties replaced by a technowar of unparalleled proportions. Merging MacArthur's island-hopping concepts with the air superiority gained in the Gulf War, the United States and allied militaries added a new element of unprecedented levels of special forces operating inside Iraq, often within the cities themselves. Those special ops forces used laser targeting devices to focus precision bombs so finely that there was virtually no collateral damage to civilian buildings or noncombatants. Yet the precise targeting was so perfect that tanks hiding underneath bridges were blown up without damaging the bridge over them, and Saddam's main command and control buildings were obliterated while shops next door remained open for business.

Iraq was a demonstration of the "western way of war" at its pinnacle—or what one Middle Eastern commentator glumly labeled an example of "Mesopotamian show and tell." The message was not lost on other regimes in the region or around the world. Libyan dictator Muammar al Qaddafi soon announced he was giving up his arsenal of WMD. It went unstated that he did not want the United

States to have a Libyan version of show and tell. On June 28, an interim free Iraqi government took official control of the nation and Hussein entered pleas before a judge within a week. Within a period of two years, Bush had effectively cleaned out two major terrorist harbors, neutralized a third, and prompted internal democratic change in Saudi Arabia.

Still, antiwar forces and many Democrats jumped at the chance to claim that the war on terror had failed, that Osama bin Laden was not in custody, and that the job in Afghanistan was unfinished. Terrorists flocked to Iraq after the invasion, and sporadic fighting continued well into 2004. But critics overlooked the fact that a free and democratic Iraq and Afghanistan had become the first true Arab democracies in the Middle East, and that Al Qaeda now was being sucked into combat there, rather than on American soil.

Although research teams failed to find the chemical and biological weapons that had resulted in the UN sanctions, many experts and Iraqi informants maintained that Saddam had transported the weapons of mass destruction out of the country just prior to hostilities. Many small amounts of biological and chemical weapons were nevertheless discovered in several locations, usually in artillery shells, indicating they had existed at one time. But whether the weapons were moved or were a massive deception by Saddam for some perverted pleasure of fooling the United States, one thing is clear: after 2003 he would never threaten any of his neighbors, or America, again. Equally important, Iraq would no longer be a training ground for hijackers.

By late 2004, Iraq was still far from a stable society; bin Laden had not been captured or killed; and with every new arrest of a terror suspect came an awareness of new vulnerabilities. But many terrorism experts thought that if the corner had not been turned, it was, at least, in sight. Even so, it is unlikely Americans will soon return to a 9/10 mentality.

CONCLUSION

If the immediate horror of 9/11 has dissipated, the attack nevertheless served as a profound reminder that buildings, however symbolic they might be, are nothing more than concrete and steel. The precious human lives they contained testified, by their loss, that what remains are ideas. Intending to shatter the "materialism" of the United States, Osama bin Laden's terrorists merely reminded the world of the supremacy of the intangible over the physical, of the spiritual over the temporal. Focusing Americans' thoughts once again on freedom—and its enemies—terrorists united a nation seriously divided by an election and elevated a president under fire to a position of historical greatness.

The fatal flaw of bin Laden—like Hitler, Stalin, and even the nearsighted Spaniards of five hundred years ago—was that they fixed their gaze on the physical manifestations of the wealth of the West, failing to understand that wealth is a mere by-product of other, more important qualities: initiative, inventiveness, hope, optimism, and above all, faith. The people who had set foot in Virginia and Massachusetts almost three centuries ago often arrived poor, usually alone, and certainly without lofty titles or royal honors. After they plowed the fields and founded their enterprises, it was not the farms alone that made Benjamin Franklin's Philadelphia flourish, nor trade alone that breathed life into the Boston of John Adams. Mere plantations did not produce George Washington and Thomas Jefferson, nor did a legal system spawn Alexander Hamilton and Abraham Lincoln. American determination and drive, vision and commitment came not from acquisition of material things—though the freedom to acquire things was a prerequisite. Rather, greatness came from an all-consuming sense that this was, after all, the "city on a hill," the "last, best hope for mankind." The United States was, and is, a fountain of hope, and a beacon of liberty.

American democracy flowed from the pursuit of opportunity, governed by respect for the law. American industry burst forth from the brains of Carnegie and Weyerhaeuser, Vanderbilt and Gates, most often coming from those owning the least in material goods. And American strength came from the self-assurance—

lacking in every other nation in the world by the twenty-first century (or what Bush called liberty's century)—that this nation uniquely had a charge to keep, a standard to uphold, and a mission to fulfill. In the end, the rest of the world will probably both grimly acknowledge and grudgingly admit that, to paraphrase the song, God has "shed His grace on thee." Knowing perfection is unattainable, Americans have not ceased in its pursuit. Realizing that war is unavoidable, Americans have never relented in their quest for peace and justice. But understanding that faith was indispensable, Americans have, more than any other place on earth, placed it at the center of the Republic. The American character, and the American dream, could never be disentangled, and ultimately the latter would go only as far as the former would take it.

NOTES

Introduction

1. David McCullough, *John Adams* (New York: Simon & Schuster, 2001), 469.

Chapter 1. The City on the Hill, 1492–1707

1. J. E. Olson and E. G. Bourne, eds., *The Northmen, Columbus, and Cabot, 985–1503* (New York: Charles Scribner's, 1906).
2. Joel Mokyr, *The Lever of Riches: Technological Creativity and Economic Progress* (New York: Oxford, 1990); Robert L. Jones, *The European Miracle* (Cambridge: Cambridge University Press, 1981).
3. James Burke, *Connections* (Boston: Little, Brown, 1978), 122–23; Carlo Cipolla, *Guns, Sails and Empires: Technological Innovations and the Early Phases of European Expansion, 1400–1700* (New York: Pantheon Books, 1965).
4. Esmond Wright, *The Search for Liberty: From Origins to Independence* (Oxford: Blackwell, 1995), 5.
5. Fernand Braudel, *Civilization & Capitalism, 15th–18th Century: The Wheels of Commerce*, vol. 2 (New York: Harper & Row, 1986), 211.
6. Wright, *Search for Liberty*, 15.
7. Oliver Perry Chitwood, *A History of Colonial America*, 3rd ed. (New York: Harper & Row, 1961 [1931]), 24.
8. Christopher Columbus, *The Diario of Christopher Columbus's First Voyage to America, 1492–1493*, abstracted by Fray Bartolomé de Las Casas, trans. Oliver Dunn and James E. Kelley Jr. (Norman, OK: University of Oklahoma Press, 1989), 57–69, entry for October 11, 1492.
9. Chitwood, *A History of Colonial America*, 27.
10. Columbus, *Diario*, 57–69.
11. Howard Zinn, *A People's History of the United States* (New York: Harper & Row, 1980), 7–11.
12. Christopher Columbus, *The Journal of Christopher Columbus*, trans. Cecil Jane (New York: Clarkson N. Potter, 1960), 191–201.
13. Samuel Eliot Morison, *Admiral of the Ocean Sea: A Life of Christopher Columbus* (Boston: Little, Brown, 1942), 5.
14. Inga Clendinnen, *Aztecs: An Interpretation* (New York: Cambridge University Press, 1991), 37–38 and passim.
15. Victor Davis Hansen, *Carnage and Culture: Landmark Battles in the Rise of Western Power* (New York: Doubleday, 2001), 195.
16. Geoffrey Parker, ed., *The Cambridge Illustrated History of Warfare* (Cambridge: Cambridge University Press, 1995).
17. Stuart Flexner and Doris Flexner, *The Pessimist's Guide to History*, updated ed. (New York: Perennial, 2000), 63.

18. Hansen, *Carnage and Culture*, 228.
19. Bernal Diaz, *The Conquest of New Spain*, trans. J. M. Cohen (Middlesex, UK: Penguin Books, 1974 [originally published circa 1576]).
20. Gilberto Freyre, quoted in Wright, *Search for Liberty*, 160. On the population of North America at this time and the impact of diseases, see Michael R. Haines and Richard H. Steckel, *A Population History of North America* (Cambridge: Cambridge University Press, 2000).
21. Hansen, *Carnage and Culture*, 4.
22. Robert C. Puth, *American Economic History*, 3rd ed. (Fort Worth: Dryden Press, 1993), 39.
23. James Axtell, "The Invasion Within: The Contest of Cultures in Colonial North America," in his *The European and the Indian: Essays in the Ethnohistory of Colonial North America* (New York: Oxford University Press, 1981), 41.
24. Las Casas, quoted in John Boyd Thacher, *Christopher Columbus: His Life, His Work, His Remains* (New York: Harper & Brothers, 1843), 63–64.
25. For a review of the literature on piracy, see B. R. Burg and Larry Schweikart, "Stand by to Repel Historians: Piracy and Modern Historical Scholarship," *The Historian*, March 1984, 219–34; for specific examples of pirate horrors, see Alexander O. Exquemelin, *The Buccaneers of America*, trans. Alexis Brown (Baltimore: Penguin, 1969 [1678 Dutch]).
26. Winston Churchill, *The Great Republic: A History of America* (New York: Random House, 1999), 14.
27. Stuart Flexner and Doris Flexner, *Pessimist's Guide to History: From the Big Bang to the New Millennium* (New York: Quill, 2000), 77–88.
28. Thomas Sowell, *Race and Culture: A World View* (New York: Basic Books, 1994), 26; William H. McNeill, *The Rise of the West: A History of the Human Community* (Chicago: University of Chicago Press, 1991), 667.
29. Jaime Vicens Vives, "The Decline of Spain in the Seventeenth Century," in *The Economic Decline of Empires*, ed. Carlo Cipolla (London: Methuen, 1970), 127.
30. Allan Greer, *The People of New France* (Toronto: University of Toronto Press, 1997).
31. Ibid., 5.
32. Ibid., 13–14.
33. Chitwood, *History of Colonial America*, 41.
34. Richard Hakluyt, *Principal Navigations, Voyages, Traffigues, and Discoveries of the English Nation* (London: J. M. Deut, 1926–31).
35. William H. McNeill, *The Pursuit of Power* (Chicago: University of Chicago Press, 1982).
36. Jack A. Goldstone, "Cultural Orthodoxy, Risk, and Innovation: The Divergence of East and West in the Early Modern World," *Sociological Theory*, Fall 1987, 119–135 (quotation on 119).
37. David S. Landes, *The Unbound Prometheus: Technical Change and Industrial Development in Western Europe from 1750 to the Present* (Cambridge: Cambridge University Press, 1969); Nathan Rosenberg and L. E. Birdsell Jr., *How the West Grew Rich: The Economist Transformation of the Industrial World* (New York: Basic Books, 1986); and Larry Schweikart, *The Entrepreneurial Adventure: A History of Business in the United States* (Fort Worth: Harcourt, 2000).
38. Philip F. Gura, *A Glimpse of Sion's Glory: Puritan Radicalism in New England, 1620–1600* (Middletown, CT: Wesleyan University Press, 1984).
39. The charter is found at http://www.mu.cc.va.us/home/nusageh/Hist121/Port1/VACom Charter.htm
40. Quoted in Wright, *Search for Liberty*, 119.
41. Shepard Kretch III, *The Ecological Indian: Myth and History* (New York: W. W. Norton, 1999), 79.
42. Philip L. Barbour, ed., *The Complete Works of Captain John Smith* (Chapel Hill: University of North Carolina Press, 1986); and Lyon Gardiner Tyler, ed., *Narratives of Early Virginia: 1606–1625* (New York: Charles Scribner's, 1907).
43. Interestingly, the Walt Disney Pictures film *Pocahontas* reversed this historical truth, having the Indian princess converting John Rolfe to animism.
44. James H. Merrell, *The Indians' New World: Catawbas and Their Neighbors from European Contact Through the Era of Removal* (New York: W. W. Norton, 1989), 36–37.
45. Edmund S. Morgan, *American Slavery, American Freedom* (New York: Norton, 1975); Abbot Emerson Smith, *Colonists in Bondage: White Servitude and Convict Labor in America, 1607–1776* (Chapel Hill: University of North Carolina Press, 1971).
46. See the entire issues of the *William and Mary Quarterly* for April 1999 and for January 1997,

but some of the relevant articles are James H. Sweet, "The Iberian Roots of American Racist Thought," (January 1997, 143–66); Robin Blackburn, "The Old World Background to European Colonial Slavery," (January 1997, 65–102); David Brion Davis, "Constructing Race: A Reflection," (January 1997, 7–21); David Waldstreicher, "Reading the Runaways: Self-Fashioning, Print Culture, and the Confidence in Slavery in the Eighteenth-Century Mid-Atlantic," (April 1999, 243–72); and Christopher L. Brown, "Empire Without Slaves: British Concepts of Emancipation in the Age of the American Revolution," (April 1999, 273–306). Also see Shane White, *Somewhat More Independent: The End of Slavery in New York City, 1770–1810* (Athens, GA: University of Georgia Press, 1994), for a discussion of the process of manumission in New York City.

47. Douglas M. MacDowell, *The Law in Classical Athens* (London: Thames and Hudson, 1978); Carl Bridenbaugh, *Jamestown, 1544–1699* (New York: Oxford University Press, 1980).

48. Chitwood, *History of Colonial America*, 65.

49. Merrell, *Indians' New World*, 244.

50. Quoted in Virginius Dabney, *Virginia: The New Dominion* (Charlottesville: University Press of Virginia, 1971), 62–63; Warren M. Billings, *The Old Dominion in the Seventeenth Century: A Documentary History of Virginia, 1607–1689* (Chapel Hill: University of North Carolina Press, 1975).

51. Chitwood, *History of Colonial America*, 81.

52. Ibid.

53. The Toleration Act is found in Woodrow Wilson, *A History of the American People*, vol. 1 (New York: Harper & Bros., 1902), 130a.

54. Ibid.

55. Leslie H. Fishel Jr. and Benjamin Quarles, *The Black American: A Documentary History* (Glenview, IL: Scott, Foresman, 1976), 20–21.

56. Ibid., 21–22.

57. Paul Johnson, "God and the Americans," *Commentary*, January 1995, 24–45.

58. Richard White, *The Middle Ground: Indians, Empires, and Republics in the Great Lakes Region, 1650–1815* (New York: Cambridge, 1991), x.

59. Virginia DeJohn Anderson, *New England's Generation: The Great Migration and the Formation of Society and Culture in the Seventeenth Century* (Cambridge: Cambridge University Press, 1991).

60. Found at http://www.yale.edu/lawweb/avalon/amerdoc/mayflower.htm.

61. William Bradford, *Bradford's History "Of Plymouth Plantation"* (Boston: Wright & Potter Printing, 1898), 114–16.

62. The best short biography of John Winthrop is Edmund S. Morgan's *The Puritan Dilemma: The Story of John Winthrop* (Boston: Little, Brown, 1958).

63. Clifford K. Shipton, "A Plea for Puritanism," *American Historical Review*, April 1935, 467.

64. Kretch, *The Ecological Indian*, 73.

65. Chitwood, *History of Colonial America*, 111.

66. Gura, *A Glimpse of Sion's Glory*, 7.

67. Robert G. Pope, *The Half-Way Covenant: Church Membership in Puritan New England* (Princeton: Princeton University Press, 1969).

68. Anderson, *New England's Generation*, 196.

69. Darren Staloff, *The Making of an American Thinking Class: Intellectuals and Intelligentsia in Puritan Massachusetts* (New York: Oxford University Press, 1998).

70. Gura, *A Glimpse of Sion's Glory*, 213.

71. A Maryland Anglican minister, in 1775, quoted in Daniel Boorstin, *The Americans: The Colonial Experience* (New York: Vintage, 1964), 351.

72. Patrick M. Malone, *The Skulking Way of War: Technology and Tactics Among the New England Indians* (Lanham, MD: Madison Books, 1991).

73. Johnson, "God and the Americans," 27.

74. John Courtney Murray, "The Problem of Pluralism in America," *Thought*, 65, September 1990, 323–28, quotation on 343.

75. Johnson, "God and the Americans," 28; Timothy L. Hall, *Separating Church and State: Roger Williams and Religious Liberty* (Urbana, IL: University of Illinois Press, 1998).

76. Perry Miller, "Errand into the Wilderness," *William and Mary Quarterly*, January 1953, 7–18, quoted in Wright, *Search for Liberty*, 213.

77. Jonathan R. T. Hughes, *The Vital Few: The Entrepreneur and American Economic Progress*, exp. ed. (New York: Oxford University Press, 1986), 65.

78. Murray, "Problem of Religious Pluralism," 345.
79. William Cronon, *Changes in the Land: Indians, Colonists, and the Ecology of New England* (New York: Hill and Wang, 1983), supports this point, further arguing that although the Europeans indeed changed the land through property ownership, Indians had their own ecological impact.

Chapter 2. Colonial Adolescence, 1707–63

1. Alexis de Tocqueville, *Democracy in America*, abridged, ed. Richard D. Heffner (New York: New American Library, 1956), 170.
2. Francis L. Broderick, "Pulpit, Physics, and Politics: The Curriculum of the College of New Jersey, 1746–1794," *William and Mary Quarterly*, 6, 1949, 42–68.
3. Benjamin Franklin, *Autobiography and Other Writings*, ed. Russell B. Nye (Boston: Houghton-Mifflin, 1958), passim.
4. Franklin, *Autobiography*, 38–40, 94–105.
5. Krech, *Ecological Indian*, passim.
6. Patrick M. Malone, *The Skulking Way of War: Technology and Tactics Among the New England Indians* (Baltimore: Johns Hopkins University Press, 1993).
7. Thomas C. Leonard, *News for All* (New York: Oxford University Press, 1995); Richard D. Brown, *Knowledge Is Power: The Diffusion of Information in Early America, 1700–1865* (New York: Oxford, 1989); Charles E. Clark, *The Public Prints: The Newspaper in Anglo-American Culture, 1665–1740* (New York: Oxford, 1994); and Michael Warner, *The Letters of the Republic: Publication and the Public Sphere in Eighteenth-Century America* (Cambridge, MA: Harvard, 1990).
8. Daniel Boorstin, *The Americans: The Colonial Experience* (New York: Vintage Books, 1964), 191–202.
9. Ibid., 209–39.
10. Clifton E. Olmstead, *History of Religion in the United States* (Englewood Cliffs, NJ: Prentice-Hall, 1960).
11. Edwin S. Gaustad, *The Great Awakening in New England* (Chicago: Quadrangle, 1968 [1957]); Jon Butler, *Awash in a Sea of Faith: Christianizing the American People* (Cambridge: Harvard University Press, 1990).
12. Ola E. Winslow, ed., *Basic Writings of Jonathan Edwards* (New York: New American Library, 1966), 115, 128–29; Perry Miller, *Jonathan Edwards* (Cleveland: World, 1959).
13. Quoted in John Morton Blum, et al., *The National Experience: A History of the United States*, 3rd ed. (New York: Harcourt Brace Jovanovich, 1973), 65.
14. Edmund S. Morgan, *American Slavery, American Freedom* (New York: W. W. Norton, 1975), passim.
15. Robert C. Davis, *Christian Slaves, Muslim Masters* (London: Palgrowe, 2002).
16. Frederick K. C. Price, *Race, Religion, and Racism*. 3 vols. (Los Angeles: Faith One Publishing, 2000–2002). Noah, not God, cursed Ham; there was no indication in the Bible that this curse was skin color. Noah, even if his curse was legitimate, could only affect Ham's son because Ham was blessed by God. There is no evidence of racial prejudice by Jesus or the disciples, and indeed one and perhaps two of the disciples were black. Of the family tree of Jesus, there are only a handful of women mentioned, and the evidence suggests that in each case the women were black or dark skinned, based on descent from the Hittites through Bathsheba.
17. Winthrop Jordan, *White over Black: American Attitudes Toward the Negro, 1550–1812* (Chapel Hill: University of North Carolina Press, 1968), passim.
18. Peter Kolchin, *Unfree Labor: American Slavery and Russian Serfdom* (Cambridge: Belknap, 1987).
19. Jack P. Greene, *Imperatives, Behaviors, and Identities: Essays in Early American Cultural History* (Charlottesville: University of Virginia Press, 1992).
20. Jordan, *White over Black*, 104–39.
21. Jeremy Atack and Peter W. Passell, *A New Economic View of American History*, 2nd ed. (New York: W. W. Norton, 1994).
22. Jordan, *White over Black*, 325–31, 356–57.
23. Scholars continue to debate the direction and intent of the Founders on the issue of slavery. William H. Freehling has argued that both the Northwest Ordinance and the abolition of the

slave trade constituted important victories on the road to abolition ("The Founding Fathers and Slavery," *American Historical Review*, February 1972, 81–93). William Cohen contends that Thomas Jefferson was committed publicly to ending slavery through at least 1784, when he supported the Ordinance of 1784 ("Thomas Jefferson and the Problem of Slavery," *Journal of American History*, December 1969, 503–26); also see Paul Finkleman *Slavery and the Founders: Race and Liberty in the Age of Jefferson* (Armonk, NY: M. E. Sharpe, 1996).

24. William W. Freehling, "The Founding Fathers: Conditional Anti-Slavery and the Nationalists of the American Revolution," in *The Reintegration of American History: Slavery and the Civil War*, William W. Freehling, ed. (New York: Oxford, 1994), 12–33.

25. On the transition of power from the governors to the legislatures, see Robert J. Dinkin, *Voting in Provincial America: A Study of Elections in the Thirteen Colonies, 1689–1776* (Westport, CT: Greenwood Press, 1977); Robert E. Brown, *Middle-Class Democracy and the Revolution in Massachusetts, 1691–1780* (Ithaca: Cornell University Press, 1955); J. R. Pole, "Representation and Authority in Virginia from the Revolution to Reform," *Journal of Southern History*, February 1958, 16–50; Jack P. Green, "The Role of the Lower Houses of Assembly in 18th Century Politics," *Journal of Southern History*, November 1961, 451–74.

26. Esmond Wright, *The Search for Liberty: From Origins to Independence* (Oxford: Blackwell, 1995), 327; Bernard Bailyn and Philip D. Morgan, eds., *Strangers Within the Realm* (Williamsburg, VA: Institute of Early American History and Culture, 1991); Bernard Bailyn, *The Peopling of British North America* (New York: Knopf, 1986).

27. David S. Landes, *The Unbound Prometheus: Technical Change and Industrial Development in Western Europe from 1750 to the Present* (Cambridge: Cambridge University Press, 1969); Joel Mokyr, *The Lever of Riches* (New York: Oxford, 1990).

28. Lawrence Harper, "Mercantilism and the American Revolution," *Canadian Historical Review*, 23 (1942), 1–15; Robert P. Thomas, "A Quantitative Approach to the Study of the Effects of British Imperial Policy on Colonial Welfare," *Journal of Economic History*, 25 (1965), 615–38.

29. Paul Johnson, *A History of the American People* (New York: HarperCollins, 1997), 91.

30. R. J. Brugger, *Maryland: A Middle Temperament, 1634–1980* (Baltimore: Johns Hopkins University Press, 1988), 87.

31. Thomas Doerflinger, *A Vigorous Spirit of Enterprise: Merchants and Economic Development in Revolutionary Philadelphia* (New York: W. W. Norton, 1986), 351.

32. John J. McCusker and Russel B. Menard, *The Economy of British America, 1607–1789* (Chapel Hill: Institute of Early American History and Culture and the University of North Carolina Press, 1985).

33. Schweikart, *Entrepreneurial Adventure*, 43; Alice Hanson Jones, *Wealth of a Nation to Be: The American Colonies on the Eve of Revolution* (New York: Columbia University Press, 1980).

34. Bernard Bailyn, et al, *The Great Republic: A History of the American People*, 3rd ed., (Lexington, MA: D. C. Heath, 1985), 89–90.

35. Marjorie Marion Spector, *The American Department of the British Government, 1768–82* (New York: Octagon Books, 1976 [1940]).

36. H. H. Peckham, *The Colonial Wars, 1689–1762* (Chicago: University of Chicago Press, 1964); Max Savelle, *Empires to Nations: Expansion in North America* (Minneapolis: University of Minnesota Press, 1974); D. E. Leach, *Roots of Conflict: British Armed Forces and Colonial Americans, 1677–1763* (Chapel Hill: University of North Carolina Press, 1986).

37. James T. Flexner, *George Washington: The Forge of Experience, 1732–75* (Boston: Little, Brown, 1965).

38. Douglas Southall Freeman, *George Washington: A Biography*, vol. 3. (New York: Charles Scribner's, 1948–1957), 89.

39. France's victory at Fort William Henry and its shameful role in the massacre that the Indians soon perpetrated was immortalized in James Fenimore Cooper's classic novel, *The Last of the Mohicans: A Narrative of 1757* (New York: State University of New York Press, 1983).

40. Francis Parkman and C. Vann Woodward, *Montcalm and Wolfe* (Cambridge, MA: DaCapo Press, 2001).

41. Fred Anderson, *Crucible of War: The Seven Years' War and the Fate of Empire in British North America, 1754–1766* (New York: Vintage, 2001).

42. Gordon S. Wood, *The Radicalism of the American Revolution* (New York: Knopf, 1992).

43. Lawrence Gipson, *The Coming of the American Revolution, 1763–1775* (New York: Harper, 1954); Richard Johnson, *Adjustment to Empire: The New England Colonies, 1675–1715* (New Brunswick, NJ: Rutgers University Press, 1981).

Chapter 3. Colonies No More, 1763–83

1. Barbara Graymont, *The Iroquois in the American Revolution* (Syracuse: Syracuse University Press, 1972); Francis Jennins, *The Ambiguous Iroquois Empire* (New York: W. W. Norton, 1984); Richard Aquila, *The Iroquois Restoration: Iroquois Diplomacy on the Colonial Frontier, 1701–1754* (Lincoln, NE: University of Nebraska Press, 1997).
2. Gregory E. Dowd, *A Spirited Resistance: The North American Indian Struggle for Unity, 1745–1815* (Baltimore: Johns Hopkins University Press, 1992); Howard Peckham, *Pontiac and the Indian Uprising* (New York: Russell and Russell, 1970).
3. Jack Sosin, *Whitehall and the Wilderness: The Middle West in British Colonial Policy, 1760–1775* (Lincoln, NE: University of Nebraska Press, 1961).
4. Dale Van Every, *Forth to the Wilderness: The First American Frontier, 1754–1774* (New York: Morrow, 1961).
5. Richard White, *The Middle Ground: Indians, Empires, and Republics in the Great Lakes Region, 1650–1815* (New York: Cambridge University Press, 1991).
6. Jack M. Sosin, *The Revolutionary Frontier, 1763–1783* (New York: Holt, Rinehart and Winston, 1967); John W. Shy, *Toward Lexington: The Role of the British Army in the Coming of the American Revolution* (Princeton: Princeton University Press, 1065).
7. Lawrence H. Gipson, *The British Empire Before the American Revolution* (New York: Knopf, 1954); Bernard Donoughue, *British Politics and the American Revolution: The Path to War* (London: Macmillan, 1964).
8. Lawrence Harper, "Mercantilism and the American Revolution," *Canadian Historical Review*, 23 (1942), 1–15; Peter McClelland, "The Cost to America of British Imperial Policy," *American Economic Review*, 59 (1969), 370–81.
9. Bernard Bailyn, *New England Merchants in the Seventeenth Century* (Cambridge, MA: Harvard University Press, 1955). Compare his assessment with the class-struggle model (rejected here) of Gary B. Nash, *The Urban Crucible: The Northern Seaports and the Origins of the American Revolution* (Cambridge, MA: Harvard University Press, abridged, 1986).
10. Pauline Maier, *The Old Revolutionaries: Political Lives in the Age of Samuel Adams* (New York: Knopf, 1980); and A. J. Langguth, *Patriots: The Men who Started the American Revolution* (New York: Simon & Schuster, 1988).
11. William B. Willcox, ed., *The Papers of Benjamin Franklin* (New Haven: Yale University Press, 1974), 18:102.
12. Winston Churchill, *The Great Republic: A History of America* (New York: Random House, 1999), 57.
13. George III quoted in Churchill, *Great Republic*, 58.
14. Chitwood, *History of Colonial America*, 517; Alan Brinkley, *American History: A Survey*, 9th ed., Vol. I (New York: McGraw-Hill, 1995), 104.
15. Oliver M. Dickerson, *The Navigation Acts and the American Revolution* (Philadelphia: University of Pennsylvania Press, 1951).
16. Paul Johnson, *A History of the American People* (New York: HarperCollins, 1997), 133; Esmund Wright, *Franklin of Philadelphia* (Cambridge: Belknap/Harvard, 1986).
17. Peter D. G. Thomas, *The Townshend Duties Crisis: The Second Phase of the American Revolution, 1767–1773* (Oxford: Clarendon Press, 1987); and his *Tea Party to Independence: The Third Phase of the American Revolution, 1773–1776* (Oxford: Clarendon Press, 1991).
18. Jerrilyn Marston, *King and Congress: The Transfer of Political Legitamacy, 1774–1776* (Princeton: Princeton University Press, 1987).
19. Schweikart, *Entrepreneurial Adventure*, chap. 1.
20. Charles Royster, *A Revolutionary People at War: The Continental Army and American Character, 1775–1783* (Chapel Hill, North Carolina: Institute of Early American History and Culture and University of North Carolina Press, 1979), 6.
21. Johnson, *History of the American People*, 133; Edmund S. Morgan and Helen M. Morgan, *The Stamp Act Crisis* (New York: Collier, 1962).
22. Adams quoted in Marvin Olasky, *Telling the Truth: How to Revitalize Christian Journalism* (Wheaton, IL: Crossway Books, 1996), 116.

23. Peter D. G. Thomas, *British Politics and the Stamp Act Crisis: The First Phase of the American Revolution, 1763–1767* (Oxford: Clarendon Press, 1975).
24. Schweikart, *Entrepreneurial Adventure,* "The Economics of Business," 54.
25. Chitwood, *History of Colonial America,* 522.
26. Ibid., 523.
27. Bernard Bailyn and J. B. Hench, eds., *The Press and the American Revolution* (Worcester, MA: American Antequarian Society, 1980); Thomas C. Leonard, *The Power of the Press: The Birth of American Political Reporting* (New York: Oxford, 1996); and Charles E. Clark, *The Public Prints: The Newspaper in Anglo-American Culture* (New York: Oxford University Press, 1994).
28. Wright, *The Search for Liberty,* 437.
29. L. H. Butterfield, ed., *The Adams Papers: The Diary and Autobiography of John Adams* (Cambridge, MA.: Harvard University Press, 1961), entry of August 14, 1769.
30. David Hackett Fischer, *Paul Revere's Ride* (New York: Oxford, 1994), appendix D.
31. Johnson, *History of the American People,* 142.
32. T. H. Breen, *The Tobacco Culture: The Mentality of the Great Tidewater Planters on the Eve of the Revolution* (Princeton: Princeton University Press, 1985).
33. Thomas Miller, ed., *The Selected Writings of John Witherspoon* (Carbondale, IL: Southern Illinois University Press, 1990), 140–41.
34. James H. Hutson, *Religion and the Founding of the American Republic* (Washington, DC: The Library of Congress, 1998).
35. M. Stanton Evans, *The Theme Is Freedom: Religion, Politics, and the American Tradition* (Washington: Regnery, 1994), 99.
36. Woodrow Wilson, *A History of the American People,* vol. 2 (New York: Harper & Bros, 1902), 215.
37. Fischer, *Paul Revere's Ride,* 64.
38. Thomas Hobbes, *The Leviathan* (Oxford: Clarendon Press, 1967 [1651]).
39. John Locke, *Two Treatises of Government,* Peter Laslett, ed., (New York: Mentor, 1965 [1690]); *The Works of John Locke,* 10 vols., (London: n.p. 1823).
40. Charles Montesquieu, *The Spirit of the Laws,* trans. Anne Cohler, et al. (Cambridge: Cambridge University Press, 1989).
41. Bernard Bailyn, *The Ideological Origins of the American Revolution* (Cambridge, MA: Harvard University Press, 1967).
42. Mark A. Beliles and Stephen K. McDowell, *America's Providential History* (Charlottesville, VA: Providence Foundation, 1989), 146.
43. Peter Marshall and David Manuel, *The Light and the Glory* (Old Tappan, NJ: Fleming H. Revell Co., 1977), 309.
44. Roger Finke and Rodney Stark, *The Churching of America, 1776–1990: Winners and Losers in Our Religious Economy* (New Brunswick, NJ: Rutgers University Press, 1992), 15–16.
45. Finke and Stark, *Churching of America,* 65.
46. Fischer, *Paul Revere's Ride,* 152.
47. Ibid., 153.
48. Michael Bellesiles, "The Origins of Gun Culture in the United States, 1760–1865," *Journal of American History,* September 1996, and his *Arming America: The Origins of a National Gun Culture* (New York: Knopf, 2000).
49. Clayton E. Cramer, "Gun Scarcity in the Early Republic?" unpublished paper available at www.ggnra.org/cramer, and his *Concealed Weapon Laws of the Early Republic* (Westport, CT: Praeger, 1999). Also see John Shy, *A People Numerous and Armed: Reflections on the Military Struggle for American Independence* (New York: Oxford, 1976).
50. Fischer, *Paul Revere's Ride,* 150–55.
51. Jim R. McClellan, *Changing Interpretations of America's Past: The Pre-Colonial Period Through the Civil War,* 2nd ed., vol. 1 (Guilford, CT: Dushkin-McGraw-Hill, 2000), 135.
52. John P. Galvin, *The Minutemen: The First Fight: Myths and Realities of the American Revolution* (Washington, D.C.: Brassey's, 1989).
53. Ralph Waldo Emerson, "The Minuteman," in Mayo W. Hazeltine, ed., *Masterpieces of Eloquence: Famous Orations of Great World Leaders from Early Greece to the Present Times* (New York: P. F. Collier & Son, 1905), 6001–2.
54. Benjamin Franklin to David Hartley, May 8, 1775, in William B. Willcox, ed., *The Papers of Benjamin Franklin,* vol. 22 (New Haven: Yale University Press, 1982), 34.

55. Fischer, *Paul Revere's Ride*, 155.
56. George Bancroft, *History of the United States*, vol. 4 (Boston: Little, Brown, 1855), 12.
57. Douglas Southall Freeman, *George Washington: A Biography*, 7 vols. (New York: Charles Scribner's, 1948–1957), 3:454.
58. Freeman, *George Washington*, 3:453; George Washington to Joseph Reed, November 28, 1775, in *The Writings of George Washington*, ed. John C. Fitzpatrick, from the Original Manuscript Sources . . . , Prepared Under the Direction of the United States George Washington Bicentennial Commission, 39 vols., (Washington, D.C.: Government Printing Office, 1931–1944), IV: 124.
59. Charles Royster, *A Revolutionary People at War: The Continental Army and American Character, 1775–1783* (Chapel Hill: University of North Carolina Press and Institute of Early American History and Culture, 1979), 29.
60. Quoted in Royster, *A Revolutionary People at War*, 29.
61. Franklin to Charles Lee, February 11, 1776, *Papers of Benjamin Franklin*, vol. 22, 343.
62. Chitwood, *History of Colonial America*, 546.
63. Victor Davis Hamson, *Courage and Culture: Landmark Battles in the Rise of Western Power* (New York: Anchor / Doubleday, 2002).
64. Royster, *A Revolutionary People at War*, 281.
65. George Washington to the President of Congress, December 27, 1776, in Fitzpatrick, *Writings of George Washington*, vol. 6, 444.
66. George Washington to John Cadwalader, December 27, 1776, in Fitzpatrick, *Writings of George Washington*, 6:446.
67. Thomas Paine, *Common Sense and the Crisis* (Garden City, NY: Anchor Books, 1973), 69.
68. Constantine G. Guzman, "Old Dominion, New Republic: Making Virginia Republican, 1776–1840," Ph.D. diss., University of Virginia, 1999.
69. Page Smith, *John Adams, 1735–1784*, vol. 1 (Garden City, NY: Doubleday, 1962), 270.
70. Larry Schweikart, ed., *Readings in Western Civilization*, 2nd ed. (Boston: Pearson Custom, 2000), 9–14.
71. Pauline Meier, *American Scripture: Making the Declaration of Independence* (New York: Knopf, 1997), 134.
72. Scot A. French and Edward L. Ayers, "The Strange Career of Thomas Jefferson: Race and Slavery in American Memory, 1943–1993," in Peter S. Onuf, ed., *Jeffersonian Legacies* (Charlottesville: University Press of Virginia, 1993), 418–56.
73. George Washington to the president of the Congress, December 23, 1777, *Writings of George Washington*, 10:194–95.
74. Chitwood, *History of Colonial America*, 572.
75. Russell Weigley, *The American Way of War: A History of United States Military History and Policy* (Bloomington, IN: Indiana University Press, 1973).
76. Franklin and Mary Wickwire, *Cornwallis: The American Adventure* (Boston: Houghton Mifflin, 1970), 386.
77. Wright, *The Search for Liberty*, 482.
78. Richard Morris, *The Peacemakers: The Great Powers and American Independence* (New York: Harper & Row, 1965).
79. James T. Hutson, *John Adams and the Diplomacy of the American Revolution* (Lexington, KY: University Press of Kentucky, 1980); Jonathan Dull, *A Diplomatic History of the American Revolution* (New Haven: Yale University Press, 1985); Ronald Hoffman and Peter J. Albert, eds., *The Treaty of Paris (1783)* in *A Changing States System* (Maryland Universities Press of America for the Woodrow Wilson International Center for Scholars, 1985); and Samuel Flagg Bemis, *The Diplomacy of the American Revolution* (Bloomington, IN: University of Indiana Press, 1957).
80. Sylvia R. Frey, *Water from the Rock: Black Resistance in a Revolutionary Age* (Princeton: Princeton University Press, 1991); Woody Holton, *Forced Founders: Indians, Debtors, Slaves and the Making of the American Revolution* (Chapel Hill: University of North Carolina Press, 1999).

Chapter 4. A Nation of Law, 1776–89

1. Gary Wills, *Inventing America: Jefferson's Declaration of Independence* (Garden City, NY: Doubleday, 1978).
2. Adams quoted in Winthrop Jordan and Leon Litwack, *The United States*, combined ed., 7th ed. (Englewood Cliffs, NJ: Prentice-Hall, 1991), 131.

3. Joseph J. Ellis, *Founding Brothers: The Revolutionary Generation* (New York: Vintage, 2002), 130.
4. Ibid., 121.
5. Gordon S. Wood, *Creation of the American Republic, 1776–1787* (New York: W. W. Norton, 1972) and Forrest McDonald, *E Pluribus Unum: The Formation of the American Republic, 1776–1790* (Boston: Houghton Mifflin, 1965).
6. Ellis, *Founding Brothers*, 8.
7. Bernard Bailyn, et al., *The Great Republic* (Lexington, MA: D. C. Heath, 1985), 132.
8. Ibid.
9. Paul Johnson, *A History of the American People* (New York: HarperCollins, 1997), 179.
10. Ibid.
11. Jackson Turner Main, *The Anti-Federalists: Critics of the Constitution, 1781–1788* (New York: Norton, 1961), 9.
12. Merrill Jensen, *The Articles of Confederation: An Interpretation of the Social-Constitutional History of the American Revolution, 1774–1781* (Madison, WI: University of Wisconsin Press, 1959); and *The New Nation: A History of the United States During the Confederation, 1781–1789* (New York: Knopf, 1950).
13. Jensen, *New Nation*, xiii.
14. Ibid., vii–xv.
15. Wood, *Creation of the American Republic*, 125–255.
16. Johnson, *A History of the American People*, 117.
17. Ibid., 116; Paul Johnson, "God and the Americans," *Commentary*, January 1995, 25–45.
18. Alexis de Tocqueville, *Democracy in America*, vol. 1 (New York: Vintage, 1935), 319.
19. Ibid., 316.
20. Edward L. Queen II, Stephen R. Prothero, and Gardiner H. Shattuck Jr., *The Encyclopedia of American Religious History* (New York: Facts on File and Proseworks, 1996), 682–86.
21. Thomas Buckley, "After Disestablishment: Thomas Jefferson's Wall of Separation in Antebellum Virginia," *Journal of Southern History* 61 (1995), 445–800, quotation on 479–80.
22. Michael Allen, *Western Rivermen, 1763–1861: Ohio and Mississippi Boatmen and the Myth of the Alligator Horse* (Baton Rouge: Louisiana State University Press, 1990), 58–87.
23. Reuben Gold Thwaites, *Daniel Boone* (New York: D. Appleton, 1902).
24. George Dangerfield, *The Era of Good Feelings* (New York: Harcourt, Brace, 1952), 116, 105–21.
25. Reginald Horsman, *The Frontier in the Formative Years, 1783–1815* (New York: Holt, Rinehart, and Winston, 1970), 32–36.
26. Ibid., 37, 84–87, 102–3; Francis S. Philbrick, *The Rise of the West, 1763–1830* (New York: Harper and Row, 1965), 104–33.
27. Michael Allen, *Congress and the West, 1783–1787* (New York: Edwin Miller Press), chap. 2; Hernando DeSoto, *The Mystery of Capital: Why Capitalism Triumphs in the West and Fails Everywhere Else* (New York: Basic Books, 2000).
28. Richard B. Morris, *The Forging of the Union, 1781–1789* (New York, 1987), 228.
29. For land and Indian policy, see see Michael Allen, "The Federalists and the West, 1783–1803," *Western Pennsylvania Historical Magazine*, 61, October 1978, 315–32 and "Justice for the Indians: The Federalist Quest, 1786–1792," *Essex Institute Historical Collections*, 122, April 1986, 124–41.
30. Jacob Piatt Dunn, "Slavery Petitions and Papers," *Indiana State Historical Society Publications*, 2, 1894, 443–529.
31. Peter S. Onuf, "From Constitution to Higher Law: The Reinterpretation of the Northwest Ordinance," *Ohio History*, 94, Winter/Spring 1985, 5–33.
32. Paul Finkleman, "States' Rights North and South in Antebellum America," in Kermit L. Hall and James W. Ely Jr., *An Uncertain Tradition: Constitutionalism and the History of the South* (Athens, GA: University of Georgia Press, 1989), 125–58.
33. Herbert James Henderson, *Party Politics in the Continental Congress* (New York: McGraw-Hill, 1975), 1–3.
34. Gilman M. Ostrander, *Republic of Letters: The American Intellectual Community, 1775–1865* (Madison, WI: Madison House, 1999).
35. Main, *Anti-Federalists*, viii–ix; Edmund S. Morgan, *Inventing the People: The Rise of Popular Sovereignty in England and America* (New York: W. W. Norton, 1988).

36. Jensen, *New Nation*, 125–28.

37. Hamilton quoted in Winston S. Churchill, *The Great Republic: A History of America* (New York: Random House, 1999), 97.

38. Edwin J. Perkins, *American Public Finance and Financial Services, 1700–1815* (Columbus: Ohio State University Press, 1994); E. James Ferguson, *The Power of the Purse: A History of American Public Finance, 1776–1790* (Chapel Hill: University of North Carolina Press, 1961); Bray Hammond, *Banks and Politics in America from the Revolution to the Civil War* (Princeton: Princeton University Press, 1957).

39. Charles T. Ritchenseon, *Aftermath of Revolution: British Policy Towards the United States, 1783–1795* (Dallas: Southern Methodist University Press, 1969).

40. Arthur P. Whitaker, *The Spanish-American Frontier, 1783–1795* (Boston: Houghton-Mifflin, 1927); Richard W. Van Alstyne, *The Rising American Empire* (New York: Oxford, 1960).

41. Van Beck Hall, *Politics Without Parties: Massachusetts, 1780–1791* (Pittsburgh: University of Pittsburgh Press, 1972); Ronald Hoffman and Peter Albert, eds., *Sovereign States in an Age of Uncertainty* (Charlottesville: University Press of Virginia, 1981); Peter S. Onuf, *The Origins of the Federal Republic: Jurisdictional Controversies in the United States* (Philadelphia: University of Pennsylvania Press, 1983).

42. Catherine Drinker Bowen, *Miracle at Philadelphia* (Boston: Little, Brown, 1966), 18.

43. Oscar Handlin and Lilian Handlin, *A Restless People: America in Rebellion, 1770–1787* (Garden City, NY: Anchor Books, 1982).

44. Rock Brynner, "Fire Beneath Our Feet: Shays' Rebellion and Its Constitutional Impact," Ph.D. diss., Columbia University, 1993; Daniel P. Szatmary, *Shays' Rebellion: The Making of an Agrarian Insurrection* (Amherst: University of Massachusetts Press, 1980); Robert A. Freer, *Shays' Rebellion* (New York: Garland, 1988); Bowen, *Miracle at Philadelphia*, 31.

45. Bowen, *Miracle at Philadelphia*, 31.

46. Charles Beard, *The Economic Interpretation of the Constitution* (New York: Macmillan, 1913), passim.

47. Wood, *Creation of the American Republic*, 469–564.

48. Bowen, *Miracle at Philadelphia*, 13.

49. Christopher M. Duncan, *The Anti-Federalists and Early American Political Thought* (DeKalb, IL: Northern Illinois University Press, 1995); and Main, *The Anti-Federalists*, passim.

50. Johnson, *History of the American People*, 187.

51. Melvin I. Urofsky, *A March of Liberty: A Constitutional History of the United States*, 2 vols. (New York: Knopf, 1988), I:91–92.

52. Johnson, *History of the American People*, 186.

53. Bailyn, *Great Republic*, 234.

54. Roger H. Brown, *Redeeming the Republic: Federalists, Taxation, and the Origins of the Constitution* (Baltimore: Johns Hopkins University Press, 1993).

55. Tocqueville, *Democracy in America*, I:213.

56. Howard A. Ohline, "Republicanism and Slavery: Origins of the Three-Fifths Clause in the United States Constitution," *William & Mary Quarterly*, 28, 1971, 563–84.

57. Max Farrand, ed., *The Records of the Federal Convention of 1787*, rev. ed., (New Haven: Yale University Press, 1937), I:193.

58. Donald L. Robinson, *Slavery and the Structure of American Politics, 1765–1820* (New York: Harcourt Brace Jovanovich, 1971), 180.

59. William H. Freehling, "The Founding Fathers and Slavery," *American Historical Review*, February 1972, 81–93 (quotation on 84).

60. Ellis, *Founding Brothers*, 89–90.

61. Ibid., 113.

62. Ibid., 158; Fritz Hirschfeld, *George Washington and Slavery: A Documentary Portrayal* (Columbia: University of Missouri Press, 1997); Robert E. Dalzell Jr. and Lee Baldwin Dalzell, *George Washington's Mount Vernon: At Home in Revolutionary America* (New York: Oxford, 1998), 112, 211–19.

63. William M. Wiecek, *The Sources of Antislavery Constitutionalism in America, 1760–1848* (Ithaca: Cornell University Press, 1977), 67.

64. Ibid.

65. Finkleman, "States' Rights North and South," passim.

66. William W. Freehling, "The Founding Fathers: Conditional Antislavery and the Nonradicaliza-
tion of the American Revolution," in Freehling, ed., *The Reintegration of American History:
Slavery and the Civil War* (New York: Oxford, 1994), 12–31.

67. Ellis, *Founding Brothers*, 93.

68. Johnson, *History of the American People*, 188.

69. Urofsky, *March of Liberty*, I:95–96; Wood, *Creation of the American Republic*, 533–35.

70. Main, *Anti-Federalists*, viii–x.

71. Wood, *Creation of the American Republic*, 533–35.

72. Beard, *Economic Interpretation of the Constitution*, passim.

73. Forrest McDonald, *We the People: The Economic Origins of the Constitution* (Chicago: University of Chicago Press, 1958); Robert McGuire and Robert L. Ohsfeldt, "An Economic Model
of Voting Behavior Over Specific Issues at the Constitutional Convention of 1787," *Journal of
Economic History*, 46, March 1986, 79–111; and their earlier article "Economic Interests and
the American Constitution: A Quantitative Rehabilitation of Charles A. Beard," ibid., 44, 1984,
509–20. See also Richard B. Morris, "The Confederation Period and the American Historian,"
William and Mary Quarterly, 3rd series, 13, 1956, 139–56.

74. Schweikart, *Entrepreneurial Adventure*, chap. 2, discusses these issues at length.

75. M. Stanton Evans, *The Theme Is Freedom: Religion, Politics, and the American Tradition* (Washington, D.C.: Regnery, 1994), 101.

76. George Bancroft, *History of the United States of America*, vol. 6 (New York: D. Appleton, 1912),
44–59.

77. Wood, *Creation of the American Republic*, 522.

78. Ibid., 537.

79. "Centinel" quoted in Michael Allen, "Anti-Federalism and Libertarianism," Reason Papers, 7,
Spring 1981, 85.

80. Jonathan Elliot, *The Debates of the Several State Conventions on the Adoption of the Federal
Constitution*, vol. 1 (Philadelphia: J. B. Lippincott, 1859), 44–46.

81. Clinton Rossiter, ed., *The Federalist Papers* (New York: Signet, 1961).

82. Paul Goodman, "The First American Party System," in William Nisbet Chambers and Walter
Dean Burnham, eds., *The American Party Systems* (New York: Oxford University Press, 1967),
56–89.

83. Charles Calomiris, "Alexander Hamilton," in Larry Schweikart, ed., *Encyclopedia of American
Business and Economic History: Banking and Finance to 1913* (New York: Facts on File, 1990),
239–48.

84. Bancroft, *History of the United States*, 6:380.

85. Main, *The Anti-Federalists*, 187–249.

86. R. Kent Newmeyer, "John Marshall and the Southern Constitutional Tradition," in Kermit L.
Hall and James W. Ely Jr., eds., *An Uncertain Tradition: Constitutionalism and the History of the
South* (Athens, GA: University of Georgia Press, 1989), 105–24 (quotation on 115).

87. Allen, "Antifederalism and Libertarianism," 86–87.

88. Wood, *Creation of the American Republic*, 542–43.

89. Robert A. Rutland, ed., *The Papers of James Madison* (Chicago: University of Chicago Press,
1962), 10:208; W. Cleon Skousen, *The Making of America* (Washington, D.C.: The National
Center for Constitutional Studies, 1985), 5.

90. Sol Bloom, *The Story of the Constitution* (Washington, D.C.: U.S. Sesquicentennial Commission, 1937), 43.

91. Stephen P. Halbrook, *That Every Man Be Armed: The Evolution of a Constitutional Right* (Albuquerque: University of New Mexico Press, 1984).

92. *Urofsky*, March of Liberty, I:108–10.

93. Ellis, *Founding Brothers*, 216.

Chapter 5. Small Republic, Big Shoulders, 1789–1815

1. Ralph Ketcham, *Presidents Above Party: The First American Presidency* (Chapel Hill: University
of North Carolina Press, 1984); Glenn A. Phelps, *George Washington and American Constitutionalism* (Lawrence, KS: University Press of Kansas, 1993); Stanley Elkins and Eric McKitrick,
The Age of Federalism (New York: Oxford, 1993); and John C. Miller, *The Federalist Era,
1789–1801* (New York: Harper, 1960).

2. Goldfield, et al., *American Journey*, 226.
3. See http://etc.princeton.edu/CampusWWW/Companion/freneau_philip.html for a brief biography of Freneau and Philip M. Marsh, *Philip Freneau, Poet and Journalist* (Minneapolis: Dillon Press, 1967).
4. Joseph J. Ellis, *Founding Brothers: The Revolutionary Generation* (New York: Vintage, 2002), 126.
5. Ibid., 121, 126.
6. Ibid., 121.
7. Douglas Southall Freeman, *George Washington, a Biography* (New York: Charles Scribner's, 1948–1957).
8. Leonard C. White, *The Federalists: A Study in Administrative History* (New York: Macmillan, 1948); Marcus Cunliffe, *George Washington* (Boston: Little, Brown, 1958).
9. John E. Ferling, *John Adams, A Life* (New York: Henry Holt, 1996); Gilbert Chinard, *Honest John Adams* (Boston: Little, Brown, 1933); Joseph J. Ellis, *Passionate Sage: The Character and Legacy of John Adams* (New York: W. W. Norton, 2001).
10. L. H. Butterfield, ed., *John Adams, Diary and Autobiography* (Cambridge: Belknap, 1961) allows Adams to speak for himself.
11. Adrienne Koch, *Jefferson and Madison: The Great Collaboration* (London: Oxford, 1964); Irving Brant, *James Madison* (Indianapolis: Bobbs-Merrill, 1941).
12. Paul Johnson, *A History of the American People* (New York: HarperCollins, 1997), 211.
13. Dumas Malone, *Jefferson and His Time*, 5 vols. (Boston: Little, Brown, 1948–1981); Noble Cunningham Jr., *In Pursuit of Reason: The Life of Thomas Jefferson* (Baton Rouge: Louisiana State University Press, 1987); Merrill Peterson, *Thomas Jefferson and the New Nation: A Biography* (New York: Oxford, 1970). A good overview of recent scholarship on Jefferson appears in Peter S. Onuf, "The Scholars' Jefferson," *William and Mary Quarterly*, 3d series, 50, October 1993, 671–99.
14. Thomas Jefferson, *Notes on the State of Virginia* (Boston: Wells and Lilly, 1829).
15. Larry Schweikart, *The Entrepreneurial Adventure: A History of Business in the United States* (Fort Worth: Harcourt, 2000), 64–67.
16. The Sally Hemings controversy, which erupted again in the 1990s when DNA tests showed that descendants had the DNA of the Jefferson family, remains clouded, and even the new tests do not establish Jefferson's paternity. Among the different views in the recent disputes, see Douglas L. Wilson, "Thomas Jefferson and the Character Issue," *Atlantic Monthly*, November 1992, 57–74; Scot A. French and Edward L. Ayers, "The Strange Career of Thomas Jefferson: Race and Slavery in American Memory, 1943–1993," in Peter S. Onuf, ed., *Jeffersonian Legacies* (Charlottesville: University Press of Virginia, 1993), 418–56; Lucia Stanton, "Those Who Labor for my Happiness: Thomas Jefferson and His Slaves," ibid., 147–80; and Paul Finkleman, "Jefferson and Slavery: Treason Against the Hopes of the World," ibid., 181–221.
17. Broadus Mitchell, *Alexander Hamilton: A Concise Biography* (New York: Oxford University Press, 1976); Forrest McDonald, *Alexander Hamilton: A Biography* (New York: Norton, 1979).
18. Cecilia Kenyon, "Alexander Hamilton: Rousseau of the Right," *Political Science Quarterly*, 73, June 1958, 161–78.
19. Joyce Appleby, *Capitalism and a New Social Order: The Republican Vision of the 1790s* (New York: New York University Press, 1984); Richard Buel Jr., *Securing the Revolution: Ideology in American Politics* (Ithaca: Cornell University Press, 1974); Lance Banning, *The Jeffersonian Persuasion: Evolution of a Party Ideology* (Ithaca: Cornell University Press, 1978); Semour Lipset, *The First New Nation: The United States in Historical and Comparative Perspective* (Garden City, NY: Doubleday, 1967 [1963]).
20. Charles Calomiris, "Alexander Hamilton," in Larry Schweikart, ed., *The Encyclopedia of American Business History and Biography: Banking and Finance to 1913* (New York: Facts on File, 1990), 239–48.
21. Johnson, *A History of the American People* (New York: HarperCollins, 1997), 212; W. G. Anderson, *The Price of Liberty: The Public Debt of the Revolution* (Charlottesville: University of Virginia Press, 1983).
22. Schweikart, *The Entrepreneurial Adventure*, 60–64.
23. Kenyon, "Alexander Hamilton," reprinted in Sidney Fine and Gerald S. Brown, *The American*

Past: Conflicting Interpretations of the Great Issues (New York: Macmillan, 1965), 251–65 (quotation on 257).

24. John Steele Gordon, *Hamilton's Blessing: The Extraordinary Life and Times of Our National Debt* (New York: Penguin, 1998).

25. Herbert Sloan, "The Earth Belongs in Usufruct to the Living," in Peter S. Onuf, ed., *Jeffersonian Legacies* (Charlottesville: University Press of Virginia, 1993), 281–315.

26. Naomi Lamoreaux, *Insider Lending: Banks, Personal Connections, and Economic Development in Industrial New England* (Cambridge, MA: Cambridge University Press, 1994); Larry Schwiekart, *Banking in the American South from the Age of Jackson to Reconstruction* (Baton Rouge: Louisiana State University Press, 1987); Lynne Pierson Doti and Larry Schweikart, *Banking in the American West from the Gold Rush to Deregulation* (Norman, OK: University of Oklahoma Press, 1991).

27. See Gerald Stourzh, *Alexander Hamilton and the Idea of Republican Government* (Stanford: Stanford University Press, 1970).

28. Curtis P. Nettles, *The Emergence of a National Economy, 1775–1815* (New York: Holt, Rinehart and Winston, 1962).

29. Johnson, *History of the American People*, 212.

30. Alexander Hamilton, "Report on Manufactures," in George Billias, ed., *The Federalists: Realists or Ideologues?* (Lexington, MA: D. C. Heath, 1970), 25.

31. Ellis, *Founding Brothers*, 74.

32. Thomas P. Slaughter, *The Whiskey Rebellion: Frontier Epilogue to the American Revolution* (New York: Oxford, 1986).

33. John Dos Passos, *The Men Who Made the Nation* (New York: Doubleday, 1957), 186.

34. Leland D. Baldwin, *Whiskey Rebels: The Story of a Frontier Uprising* (Pittsburgh: University of Pittsburgh Press, 1939).

35. *Annals of Congress*, May 1796, 92. Also see 1308–22.

36. Richard H. Kohn, *Eagle and Sword: The Federalists and the Creation of the Military Establishment in America* (New York: Free Press, 1975).

37. William Fowler, *Jack Tars and Commodores: The American Navy* (Boston: Houghton Mifflin, 1984).

38. Lewis Condict, "Journal of a Trip to Kentucky in 1795," New Jersey Historical Society Proceedings, new series, 4, 1919, 114.

39. Richard C. Knopf, ed., *Anthony Wayne, A Name in Arms: Soldier, Diplomat, Defender of Expansion Westward of a Nation* (Pittsburgh: University of Pittsburgh Press, 1959).

40. Reginald Horsman, *The Frontier in the Formative Years, 1783–1815* (New York: Holt, Rinehart and Winston, 1970).

41. Alexander De Conde, *Entangling Alliance: Politics and Diplomacy Under George Washington* (Durham: Duke University Press, 1958).

42. Page Smith, *John Adams*, vol. II, 1784–1826 (Garden City, NY: Doubleday, 1962), 831.

43. Louis M. Sears, *George Washington and the French Revolution* (Detroit: Wayne State University Press, 1960).

44. Alexander DeConde, *The Quasi-War: The Politics and Diplomacy of the Undeclared War with France, 1797–1801* (New York: Scribner, 1966).

45. Melvin I. Urofsky, *March of Liberty: A Constitutional History of the United States*, 2 vols. (New York: Knopf, 1988), I:125.

46. Smith, *John Adams*, 833.

47. Ibid., 909.

48. Ibid., 909.

49. Ibid., 833.

50. Ibid., 841.

51. Greville Bathe, *Citizen Genet, Diplomat and Inventor* (Philadelphia: Press of Allen, Lane and Scott, 1946); Gilbert Chinard, *George Washington as the French Knew Him* (Princeton: Princeton University Press, 1940).

52. Jerald A. Combs, *The Jay Treaty: Political Battleground for the Founding Fathers* (Berkeley: University of California Press, 1970).

53. Jordan, et al., *United States*, 7, 162.

54. Miller, *Federalist Era*, 168.

55. Ibid., 168.
56. John F. Hoadley, *Origins of American Political Parties, 1789–1803* (Lexington, KY: University of Kentucky Press, 1986).
57. John Lauritz Larson, "Jefferson's Union and the Problem of Internal Improvements," in Onuf, *Jeffersonian Legacies*, 340–69, quotation on 342.
58. Smith, *John Adams*, 842.
59. Paul Goodman, "The First American Party System," in William N. Chambers and Walter Dean Burnham, eds., *The American Party System: Stages of Political Development* (Cambridge: Oxford University Press, 1967), 56–89.
60. Miller, *Federalist Era*, 198 note.
61. Smith, *John Adams*, 846.
62. Ellis, *Founding Brothers*, 135.
63. Ibid.
64. Victor Hugo Paltsits, *Washington's Farewell Address* (New York: New York Public Library, 1935); Edmund S. Morgan, *The Genius of George Washington* (New York: Norton, 1981).
65. Morton Borden, *Parties and Politics in the Early Republic, 1789–1815* (Arlington Heights, IL: AHM Publishing Corporation, 1967), 8.
66. Ibid., 9.
67. Ellis, *Founding Brothers*, 190.
68. Ibid.
69. William C. Stinchcombe, *The XYZ Affair* (Westport, CT: Greenwood Press, 1980).
70. Theodore Roscoe and Fred Freeman, *Picture History of the U. S. Navy* (New York: Bonanza Books, 1956), 125 (fig. 257); Russell Weigley, *The American Way of War: A History of United States Military Strategy and Policy* (New York: Macmillan, 1973), 42–45.
71. Tindall and Shi, *America: A Narrative History*, 5th ed., 2 vols. (New York: W. W. Norton, 1999), 1:362.
72. Bailyn, et al., *The Great Republic*, 48.
73. Stephen G. Kurtz, *The Presidency of John Adams: The Collapse of Federalism, 1795–1800* (Philadelphia: University of Pennsylvania Press, 1957); Roger Sharp, *American Politics in the Early Republic: The New Nation in Crisis* (New Haven: Yale University Press, 1993).
74. Johnson, *History of the American People*, 234; James Sterling Young, *The Washington Community, 1800–1828* (New York: Harcourt Brace & World, 1966).
75. Smith, *John Adams*, 846.
76. Manning Dauer, *The Adams Federalists* (Baltimore: Johns Hopkins University Press, 1968).
77. Urofsky, *March of Liberty*, 177.
78. William A. Gouge, *A Short History of Paper Money and Banking in the United States* (New York: Greenwood Press, 1968 [1833]); John Taylor, *An Inquiry into the Principles and Policy of the United States* (Fredericksburg: Green & Cady, 1814).
79. Shane White, *Somewhat More Independent: The End of Slavery in New York, 1770–1810* (Athens, GA: University of Georgia Press, 1991), 26.
80. James E. Davis, *Frontier America, 1800–1840: A Comparative Demographic Analysis of the Settlement Process* (Glendale, California: A. H. Clark, 1977).
81. Constance McLaughlin Green, *Eli Whitney and the Birth of American Technology* (Boston: Little, Brown, 1956).
82. Alfred Conrad and John Meyer, "The Economics of Slavery in the Antebellum South," *Journal of Political Economy*, April 1958, 95–130.
83. Grady McWhiney, *Cracker Culture: Celtic Ways in the Old South* (Tuscaloosa: University of Alabama Press, 1988); Terry G. Jordan and Matti Kaups, *The American Backwoods Frontier: An Ethnic and Ecological Interpretation* (Baltimore: Johns Hopkins University Press, 1989).
84. George Dangerfield, *The Era of Good Feelings* (New York: Harcourt, Brace, 1952), 120.
85. In addition to the sources listed in note 16, see Fawn M. Brodie, *Thomas Jefferson: An Intimate History* (New York: Norton, 1974); Peter S. Onum and Jan E. Lewis, eds., *Sally Hemings and Thomas Jefferson: History, Memory, and Civil Culture* (Charlottesville: University Press of Virginia, 1999); Joseph J. Ellis, *American Sphinx: The Character of Thomas Jefferson* (New York: Knopf, 1997); Dumas Malone and Steven Hochman, "A Note on Evidence: The Personal History of Madison Hemings," *Journal of Southern History*, 61, November 1975, 523–28; Joseph J. Ellis, "Jefferson Post-DNA," *William & Mary Quarterly*, 126, January 2000, 125–38; material from the Monticello commission, available online at http://www.mindspring.com/~tjshcommission.

86. Malcolm J. Rohrbough, *The Land Office Business: The Settlement and Administration of American Public Land, 1789–1837* (New York: Oxford University Press, 1968).
87. Joseph H. Harrison Jr., "*Sic et non*: Thomas Jefferson and Internal Improvement," *Journal of the Early Republic*, 7, 1987, 335–49.
88. Larson, "Jefferson's Union," passim.
89. Ibid., 361.
90. Ibid.
91. Calhoun quoted in the *Annals of Congress*, 14th Congress, 2nd session, February 4, 1817; John Lauritz Larson, "Bind the Republic Together: The National Union and the Struggle for a System of Internal Improvements," *Journal of American History*, 74, 1987, 363–87.
92. Albert Gallatin, "Reports on Roads and Canals," document No. 250, 10th Congress, 1st session, reprinted in *New American State Papers—Transportation*, vol. 1 (Wilmington, DE: Scholarly Resources, 1972).
93. Carter Goodrich, *Government Promotion of American Canals and Railroads, 1800–1890* (Westport, CT: Greenwood, 1974 [1960]).
94. *Historical Statistics of the United States, Colonial Times to 1970* (White Plains: Kraus International Publications [U. S. Department of Commerce, Bureau of the Census], 1989), 1114–15.
95. Larson, "Jefferson's Union," 362.
96. John R. Nelson Jr., *Liberty and Property: Political Economy and Policymaking in the New Nation, 1789–1812* (Baltimore: Johns Hopkins University Press, 1987), 115–33; Drew R. McCoy, *The Last of the Fathers: James Madison and the Republican Legacy* (New York: Cambridge, 1989).
97. Burton W. Folsom Jr., *The Myth of the Robber Barons* (Herndon, VA: Young America's Foundation, 1991), chap. 1.
98. James Willard Hurst, *Law and the Conditions of Freedom in the Nineteenth Century United States* (Madison, WI: University of Wisconsin Press, 1964).
99. Morton Horowitz, *The Transformation of American Law* (Cambridge, MA: Harvard University Press, 1979).
100. Eric Monkkonen, "Bank of Augusta v. Earle: Corporate Growth vs. States' Rights," *Alabama Historical Quarterly*, Summer 1972, 113–30.
101. Schweikart, *Entrepreneurial Adventure*, 114.
102. Malcolm J. Rohrbough, *The Trans-Appalachian Frontier: People, Societies, and Institutions, 1775–1850* (New York: Oxford University Press, 1978).
103. "Louisiana Purchase," in Howard R. Lamar, ed., *The New Encyclopedia of the American West* (New Haven: Yale University Press, 1998), 657–58; Alexander DeConde, *This Affair of Louisiana* (New York: Charles Scribner's, 1976).
104. James Eugene Smith, *One Hundred Years of Hartford's Courant* (New York: Anchor Books, 1949), 82.
105. Seth Ames, ed., *Life and Works of Fisher Ames*, 2 vols. (Boston: Little, Brown & Co. , 1854), I:323–24.
106. Stephen E. Ambrose, *Undaunted Courage: Meriwether Lewis, Thomas Jefferson and the Opening of the American West* (New York: Simon & Schuster, 1996).
107. David Lavender, *The Way to the Western Sea: Lewis and Clark Across the Continent* (New York: Harper & Row, 1988).
108. William H. Goetzmann, *Army Exploration in the American West, 1803–1863* (New Haven: Yale University Press, 1959), and his *New Lands, New Men: America and the Second Great Age of Discovery* (New York: Viking, 1986).
109. Marshall Smelser, *The Democratic Republic, 1801–1815* (New York: Harper & Row, 1968), 111.
110. Ellis, *Founding Brothers*, 42.
111. Milton Lomask, *Aaron Burr: The Years from Princeton to Vice-President, 1756–1805* (New Haven: Yale University Press, 1979), and his *Aaron Burr: The Conspiracy and the Years of Exile, 1805–1836* (New Haven: Yale University Press, 1982).
112. William Ray, *Horrors of Slavery, or, The American Tars in Tripoli* (Troy, New York: Oliver Lyon, 1808); Cyrus Brady, *Stephen Decatur* (Boston: Small, Maynard, 1900).
113. Bailyn, *The Great Republic*, 276.
114. Richard B. Morris, ed., *Encyclopedia of American History, Bicentennial Edition* (New York: Harper & Row, 1976), 168.
115. Churchill, *Great Republic*, 112.

116. Harry L. Coles, *The War of 1812* (Chicago: University of Chicago Press, 1965), 86.
117. Ibid., 81.
118. Ibid., 71–106.
119. Ibid., 129.
120. Reginald Horsman, *The War of 1812* (New York: Knopf, 1969).
121. Bailyn, *The Great Republic*, 279.
122. Larson, "Jefferson's Union," passim.

Chapter 6. The First Era of Big Central Government, 1815–36

1. Stuart Flexner and Doris Flexner, *The Pessimist's Guide to History*, updated ed. (New York: Quill, 2000), 110.
2. Jeffrey Rogers Hummel, "Second Bank of the United States and Independent Treasury," in Larry Schweikart, ed., *Encyclopedia of American Business History and Biography: Banking and Finance to 1913*, 415–20.
3. Paul Johnson, *A History of the American People* (New York: HarperCollins, 1997), 288.
4. William N. Gouge, *A Short History of Paper-Money and Banking in the United States . . .* , 2 vols. (Philadelphia: T. W. Ustik, 1833), II:109.
5. Ralph C. H. Catterall, *The Second Bank of the United States* (Chicago: University of Chicago Press, 1903); Bray Hammond, *Banks and Politics in America: From the Revolution to the Civil War* (Princeton, NJ: Princeton University Press, 1957); Richard H. Timberlake Jr., *The Origins of Central Banking in the United States* (Cambridge: Harvard University Press, 1978); Larry Schweikart, "Jacksonian Ideology, Currency Control, and Central Banking: A Reappraisal," *Historian*, 51, November 1988, 78–102; Peter Temin, *The Jacksonian Economy* (New York: W. W. Norton, 1969); Murray N. Rothbard, *The Panic of 1819: Reactions and Policies* (New York: Columbia University Press, 1962).
6. Jordan and Litwack, *The United States*, 196.
7. Larry Schweikart, *The Entrepreneurial Adventure: A History of Business in the United States* (Fort Worth, TX: Harcourt, 2000), 101–2, 112–15.
8. D. E. Engdahl, "John Marshall's 'Jeffersonian Concept' of Judicial Review," *Duke Law Journal*, 42 (1992), 279–339; E. S. Crowin, *John Marshall and the Constitution* (New Haven: Yale University Press, 1919); H. J. Pious and G. Baker, "*McCulloch v. Maryland*: Right Principle, Wrong Case," *Stanford Law Review*, 9 (1957), 710–30; G. Edward White, *The Marshall Court and Cultural Change, 1815–1835* (New York: Oxford, 1991); Lawrence Friedman, *A History of American Law* (New York: Simon & Schuster, 1973). Taylor quoted in Johnson, *History of the American People*, 239.
9. "Rush-Bagot Agreement," in Richard B. Morris, ed. *The Encyclopedia of American History: Bicentennial Edition* (New York: Harper and Row, 1976), 186.
10. Alexis de Tocqueville, *Democracy in America*, II:144.
11. Schweikart, *Entrepreneurial Adventure*, 128; Joseph J. Fucini and and Suzy Fucini, *Entrepreneurs: The Men and Women Behind Famous Brand Names and How They Made It* (Boston: G. K. Hall, 1985), 13–16.
12. *Cincinnati Enquirer* quoted in William Strauss and Neil Howe, *Generations: The History of America's Future, 1584 to 2069* (New York: Morrow), 212.
13. William C. Davis, *Three Roads to the Alamo: The Lives and Fortunes of David Crockett, James Bowie, and William Barret Travis* (New York: Harper Perennial, 1999), 99.
14. Johnson, *History of the American People*, 361.
15. Ibid.
16. Schweikart, *Entrepreneurial Adventure*, chap. 3, passim.
17. Merrit Roe Smith, *Harpers Ferry Armory and the New Technology* (Ithaca, New York: Cornell University Press, 1977); David Hounshell, *From the American System to Mass Production* (Baltimore: Johns Hopkins University Press, 1984); David F. Noble, "Command Performance: A Perspective on the Social and Economic Consequences of Military Enterprise," in Merrit Roe Smith, ed., *Military Enterprise and Technological Change: Perspectives on the American Experience* (Cambridge: MIT Press, 1985); Donald Hoke, *Ingenious Yankees: The Rise of the American System of Manufactures in the Private Sector* (New York: Columbia University Press, 1989) and his "Product Design and Cost Considerations: Clock, Watch, and Typewriter Manufacturing in the 19th Century," *Business and Economic History*, 2nd series, 18 (1989), 119–28.
18. Barbara M. Tucker, "Forms of Ownership and Management," in Henry C. Dethloff and

C. Joseph Pusateri, eds., *American Business History: Case Studies* (Arlington Heights, IL: Harlan-Davidson, 1987), 60. Also see Barbara M. Tucker, *Samuel Slater and the Origins of the American Textile Industry, 1790–1860* (Ithaca, NY: Cornell University Press, 1984).

19. Schweikart, *Entrepreneurial Adventure*, 79.

20. Ibid., 102; Atack and Passell, *New Economic View of American History*, 150; Carter Goodrich, *Government Promotion of American Canals and Railroads, 1800–1890* (New York: Columbia University Press, 1960) and his *Canals and American Economic Development* (New York: Columbia University Press, 1961), and his *The Government and the Economy, 1783–1861* (Indianapolis: Bobbs-Merrill, 1967); Robert Shaw, *Erie Water West: A History of the Erie Canal, 1792–1854* (Lexington: University of Kentucky Press, 1968); Ronald W. Filante, "A Note on the Economic Viability of the Erie Canal, 1825–60," *Business History Review*, 48, Spring 1974, 95–102;

21. B. R. Burg, "DeWitt Clinton," in Schweikart, ed., *Encyclopedia of American Business History and Biography: Banking and Finance to 1913*, 123–30.

22. Atack and Passell, *New American View of American History*, 155–56; Roger Ransom, "Social Returns from Public Transport Investment: A Case Study of the Ohio Canal," *Journal of Political Economy*, 78, September/October 1970, 1041–64, and his "Interregional Canals and Economic Specialization in the Antebellum United States," *Explorations in Economic History*, 5, Fall 1967, 12–35.

23. James Mak and Gary M. Walton, "Steamboats and the Great Productivity Surge in River Transportation," *Journal of Economic History*, 32, 1972, 619–40, and their *Western River Transportation: The Era of Early Internal Development, 1810–1860* (Baltimore: Johns Hopkins University Press, 1975); Jeremy Atack, et al., "The Profitability of Steamboating on Western Rivers: 1850," *Business History Review*, 49, Autumn 1975, 350–54; Erik Haites and James Mak, "Ohio and Mississippi River Transportation, 1810–1860," *Explorations in Economic History*, 8, 1970, 153–80.

24. Wheaton J. Lane, *Commodore Vanderbilt: An Epic of the Steam Age* (New York: Alfred A. Knopf, 1942), 148; John G. B. Hutchins, *The American Maritime Industries and Public Policy, 1789–1914* (Cambridge, MA: Harvard University Press, 1941). See also Royal Meeker, *History of the Shipping Subsidies* (New York: Macmillan, 1905), 5–11, and Walter T. Dunmore, *Ship Subsidies: An Economic Study of the Policy of Subsidizing Merchant Marines* (Boston: Houghton-Mifflin, 1907), 92–103.

25. Schweikart, *Entrepreneurial Adventure*, 107–9.

26. John Steele Gordon, *The Scarlet Woman of Wall Street* (New York: Weidenfeld & Nicholson, 1988), 101.

27. John Majewski, "Who Financed the Transportation Revolution? Regional Divergence and Internal Improvements in Antebellum Pennsylvania and Virginia," *Journal of Economic History*, 56, December 1996, 763–88; John F. Stover, *American Railroads* (Chicago: University of Chicago Press, 1961) and his *Iron Road to the West* (New York: Columbia University Press, 1978).

28. Richard R. John, *Spreading the News: The American Postal System from Franklin to Morse* (Cambridge, MA: Harvard University Press, 1995) and his "Private Mail Delivery in the United States During the Nineteenth Century—a Sketch," in William J. Hauseman, ed., *Business and Economic History*, 2nd series, 15, 1986, 131–43.

29. George Dangerfield, *The Era of Good Feelings* (New York: Harcourt, Brace, and Co., 1952), 126.

30. Ray Allen Billington and Martin Ridge, *Westward Expansion: A History of the American West*, 6th ed. (Albuquerque: University of New Mexico Press, 2001), 104.

31. Norman A. Graebner, *Ideas and Diplomacy: Reading in the Intellectual Tradition of the American Foreign Policy* (New York: Oxford University Press, 2000, 214).

32. Metternich quoted in the *Washington National Intelligencer*, December 8, 1823; *L'Etoile* quoted in Dexter Perkins, *The Monroe Doctrine, 1823–1826* (Cambridge: Harvard University Press, 1927), 30.

33. Perkins, *Monroe Doctrine*, 30–31.

34. William M. Wiecek, "Old Times There Are Not Forgotten: The Distinctiveness of the Southern Constitutional Experience," in Kermit L. Hall and James W. Ely, eds., *An Uncertain Tradition: Constitutionalism and the History of the South* (Athens, GA: University of Georgia Press, 1989), 159–97, quotation on 164.

35. Robert P. Forbes, "Slavery and the Meaning of America, 1819–1833," Ph.D. Diss., Yale University, 1994.

36. Richard P. McCormick, "New Perspectives on Jacksonian Politics," *American Historical Review*, 65, October 1959–July 1960, 288–301, quotation on 289.

37. Richard P. McCormick, "Political Development and the Second Party System," in William Nisbet Chambers and Walter Dean Burnham, eds., *The American Party Systems: Stages of Political Development* (London: Oxford University Press, 1967), 90–116, quotation on 107, n. 14. See also his "New Perspectives on Jacksonian Politics," *American Historical Review*, 65, 1960, 288–301 and his *The Second American Party System: Party Formation in the Jacksonian Era* (New York: W. W. Norton, 1966).

38. McCormick, *Second American Party System*, 351.

39. Robert V. Remini, *The Jacksonian Era* (Arlington Heights, IL: Harlan Davidson, 1989), 12.

40. Robert V. Remini, *Martin Van Buren and the Making of the Democratic Party* (New York: Columbia University Press, 1959), 12–23.

41. Richard H. Brown, "Missouri Crisis: Slavery, and the Politics of Jacksonianism," in Stanley N. Katz and Stanley I. Kutler, *New Perspectives on the American Past, vol. 1, 1607–1877*, 241–56, quotation on 242.

42. Quoted in Remini, *Martin Van Buren and the Making of the Democratic Party*, 131.

43. Remini, *Martin Van Buren and the Making of the Democratic Party*, 132.

44. Brown, "Missouri Crisis," 248.

45. Ibid., 244–45.

46. James Stanton Chase, "Jacksonian Democracy and the Rise of the Nominating Convention," *Mid-America*, 45, 1963, 229–49, quotation on 232.

47. Robert V. Remini, *The Election of Andrew Jackson* (Philadelphia: J. B. Lippincott, 1963), 16.

48. Ibid.

49. Larry Schweikart, "Focus of Power: Henry Clay as Speaker of the House," *Alabama Historian*, 2, Spring 1981, 88–126.

50. Johnson, *History of the American People*, 323; Glyndon G. van Deusen, *Life of Henry Clay* (Boston: Little Brown & Co., 1937); Robert Remini, *Henry Clay: Statesman for the Union* (New York: W. W. Norton, 1991).

51. Johnson, *History of the American People*, 329.

52. Remini, *Election of Andrew Jackson*, 25.

53. Ibid., 28.

54. Ibid., 37.

55. Lynn Marshall, "The Strange Stillbirth of the Whig Party," *American Historical Review*, 72, January 1967, 445–69, quotation on 457; Joel H. Silbey, " 'To One or Another of These Parties Every Man Belongs': The American Political Experience from Andrew Jackson to the Civil War," in Byron E. Shafer and Anthony J. Bager, eds. *Contesting Democracy: Substance and Structure in American Political History* (Lawrence, KS: University Press of Kansas, 2001), 65–92, quotation on 76.

56. Daniel Webster, *The Private Correspondence of Daniel Webster*, Fletcher Webster, ed., 2 vols. (Boston: Little, Brown, 1875), I:473; Clay quoted in Johnson, *History of the American People*, 339.

57. Johnson, *History of the American People*, 342.

58. Edward Pessen, *Jacksonian America: Society, Personality, and Politics*, rev. ed. (Homewood, IL: Dorsey Press, 1978); Sean Wilenz, *Chants Democratic: New York City and the Rise of the American Working Class* (New York: Oxford University Press, 1984); Harry L. Watson, *Liberty and Power: The Politics of Jacksonian America* (New York: Hill and Wang, 1990).

59. Alexander Saxton, *The Rise and Fall of the White Republic* (New York: Verso, 1990).

60. Robert V. Remini, *Andrew Jackson and the Course of American Freedom, 1822–1832* (New York: Harper & Row, 1981), 261.

61. Ibid.

62. Ibid., 263.

63. Alfred A. Cowe, "Abuse of Power: Andrew Jackson and the Indian Removal Act of 1830," *Historian*, 65 (Winter 2003), 1330–53.

64. Michael P. Rogin, *Fathers and Children: Andrew Jackson and the Subjugation of the American Indian* (New York: Knopf, 1975).

65. "Proclamation of General Scott, May 10, 1838," in Glen Fleischmann, *The Cherokee Removal, 1838* (New York: Franklin Watts, 1971), 49–50.

66. Gary E. Moulton, ed., *The Papers of Chief John Ross*, vol. 1 (Norman, OK: University of Oklahoma Press, 1985), 636.

67. "A Native of Maine Traveling in the Western Country," New York *Observer*, December 1838, quoted in Grant Foreman, *Indian Removal: The Emigration of the Five Civilized Tribes of Indians* (Norman, OK: University of Oklahoma Press, 1966), 306–307; Francis Paul Prucha, William T. Hagan, and Alvin M. Josephy Jr., *American Indian Policy* (Indianapolis: Indiana Historical Society, 1971).

68. Fleischmann, *Cherokee Removal*, 73.

69. Theda Purdue and Michael Green, *The Cherokee Removal: A Brief History with Documents* (Boston: St. Martin's Press, 1995), 174–75.

70. Angie Debo, *And Still the Waters Run: Betrayal of the Five Civilized Tribes* (Princeton: Princeton University Press, 1973); Anthony F. Wallace, *The Long, Bitter Trail: Andrew Jackson and the Indians* (New York: Hill and Wang, 1993); Robert V. Remini, *Andrew Jackson and the Course of American Empire, 1767–1821* (New York: Harper & Row, 1977).

71. Joseph A. Durrenberger, *Turnpikes: A Study of the Toll Road Movement in the Middle Atlantic States and Maryland* (Valdosta, GA: Southern Stationery and Printing Company, 1931); Robert F. Hunter, "The Turnpike Movement in Virginia, 1816–1860," Ph.D. Diss., Columbia University, 1957; Daniel B. Klein, "The Voluntary Provision of Public Goods? The Turnpike Companies of Early America," *Economic Inquiry*, 28, October 1990, 788–812; David Beito, "From Privies to Boulevards: The Private Supply of Infrastructure in the United States During the Nineteenth Century," in Jerry Jenkins and David E. Sisk, eds., *Development by Consent: The Voluntary Supply of Public Goods and Services* (San Francisco: Institute for Contemporary Studies, 1993), 23–49.

72. Jordan and Litwack, *United States*, 266.

73. William H. Freehling, *Prelude to Civil War: The Nullification Controversy in South Carolina, 1816–1836* (New York: Harper & Row, 1966).

74. James L. Huston, "Property Rights in Slaves and the Coming of the Civil War," *Journal of Southern History*, 79, May 1999, 248–86, quotation on 261.

75. Jordan and Litwack, *United States*, 228.

76. Ibid., 229.

77. Gillon and Matson, *American Experiment*, 383.

78. Tindall and Shi, *America*, 1:458.

79. Ibid., 1:460.

80. Remini, *Andrew Jackson and the Course of American Freedom*, 360.

81. The view that Jackson disliked on principle central banks in general or the BUS in particular is found in a wide range of scholarship of all political stripes. See Hammond, *Banks and Politics in America from the Revolution to the Civil War*; Peter Temin, *The Jacksonian Economy* (New York: W. W. Norton, 1969); Arthur Schlesinger Jr., *The Age of Jackson* (Boston: Little, Brown, 1945); John McFaul, *The Politics of Jacksonian Finance* (Ithaca, NY: Cornell University Press, 1962); James R. Sharpe, *The Jacksonians vs. The Banks* (New York: Columbia, 1970).

82. See Schweikart, "Jacksonian Ideology, Currency Control and Central Banking," 78–102.

83. "Plan for a National Bank," in Amos Kendall to Andrew Jackson, November 20, 1829, Box 1, File 6, Andrew Jackson Papers, Tennessee Library and Archives, Nashville, Tennessee.

84. Richard Timberlake Jr., *The Origins of Central Banking in the United States* (Cambridge, MA: Harvard University Press, 1978), who is perceptive to centralization, still misses this point.

85. James A. Hamilton, *Reminiscences of James A. Hamilton* (New York: Charles Scribner, 1869), 167–68.

86. David Martin's three articles are critical in determining the Jacksonians' intentions: "Metallism, Small Notes, and Jackson's War with the B. U. S.," *Explorations in Economic History*, 11, Spring 1974, 297–47; "Bimetallism in the United States Before 1850," *Journal of Political Economy*, 76, May/June 1968, 428–42; "1853: The End of Bimetallism in the United States," *Journal of Economic History*, 33, December 1973, 825–44; J. Van Fenstermaker and John E. Filer, "Impact of the First and Second Bank of the United States and the Suffolk System on New England Money, 1791–1837," *Journal of Money, Credit and Banking*, 18, February 1986, 28–40;

Fenstermaker, *The Development of American Commercial Banking* (Kent, OH: Kent State University Press, 1965); Fritz Redlich, *The Molding of American Banking, Men and Ideas*, 2 vols. (New York: Johnson Reprint Co., 1968 [1947]); Larry Schweikart, "U.S. Commercial Banking: A Historiographical Survey," *Business History Review*, 65, Autumn 1991, 606–61.

87. Richard Timberlake, "The Significance of Unaccounted Currencies," *Journal of Economic History*, 41, December 1981, 853–66.

88. Edwin J. Perkins, "Lost Opportunities for Compromise in the Bank War: A Reassessment of Jackson's Veto Message," *Business History Review*, 61, Winter 1987, 531–50.

89. Tindall and Shi, *America*, 1:467.

90. The liberal spin on Jackson's presidency as champion of the common man is near universal. David M. Kennedy, *The American Pageant*, 12th ed. (New York: Houghton-Mifflin, 2002), 271, calls Jackson the "idol of the masses" who "easily defeated the big-money Kentuckian." Gillon and Matson (*American Experiment*) echo the theme by claiming, "It was clear to most obesrvers that the Democrats swept up the support of the northeastern working men, western farmers, rising entrepreneurs, shopkeepers, and ambitious professionals who favored Jacksonian attacks against privilege. . . ." (385). David Goldfield, et al., in *The American Journey: A History of the United States*, combined edition (Upper Saddle River, NJ: Prentice-Hall, 1998) portray Jackson as the champion of these who "felt threatened by outside centers of power beyond their control" (293) and who alienated "the business community and eastern elites" (301). The National Republican/Whig agenda allows John Murrin, et al. (*Liberty, Equality, Power*) to claim that the "Jacksonians were opposed by those who favored an activist central government" (441), when Jackson had expanded the power and scope of the central government more than Jefferson, Madison, Monroe, and Adams combined. *Liberty, Equality, Power* concludes, of the Bank War, that "a majority of the voters shared Jackson's attachment to a society of virtuous, independent producers . . . they also agreed that the republic was in danger of subversion by parasites who grew rich by manipulating credit, prices, paper money and government-bestowed privileges" (442). Of course, it isn't mentioned that the Jacksonians virtually invented "government-bestowed privileges," and that if one eliminates the "northeastern working men, western farmers, rising entrepreneurs, shopkeepers, and ambitious professionals," there would have been no one left to vote for Clay, yet the Kentuckian managed 530,000 popular votes to Jackson's 688,000. In short, either the nation was comprised of big-money aristocracies, or vast numbers of common people rejected Jackson—not a majority, but nowhere near the tidal wave of votes that many of the mainstream histories would suggest.

91. See Temin, *Jacksonian Economy*, passim.

92. Peter Rousseau, "Jacksonian Monetary Policy, Specie Flows, and the Panic of 1837," *Journal of Economic History*, June 2002, 457–88.

93. *Historical Statistics of the United States, Colonial Times to 1970* (White Plains: Kraus International Publications, 1989), I:211, 1114–15. Special thanks to Tiarr Martin, whose unpublished paper, "The Growth of Government During the 'Age of Jefferson and Jackson,' " was prepared for one of Schweikart's classes and is in his possession.

Chapter 7. Red Foxes and Bear Flags, 1836–48

1. Tindall and Shi, *America*, 1:474.

2. Richard Hofstadter, "Marx of the Master Class," in Sidney Fine and Gerald S. Brown, eds., *The American Past*, 3rd ed., vol. 1 (London: Macmillan, 1970), 460–80.

3. Maurice Baxter, *Henry Clay and the American System* (Lexington, KY: University of Kentucky Press, 1995).

4. Ronald Walters, *American Reformers, 1815–1860* (New York: Hill and Wang, 1978); Alice Felt Tyler, *Freedom's Ferment: Phases of American Social History from the Colonial Period to the Outbreak of the Civil War* (New York: Harper and Row, 1944).

5. Walters, *American Reformers*, passim.

6. The official history of the Seventh-Day Adventists appears at http://www. adventist.org/history.

7. Larry Schweikart, *The Entrepreneurial Adventure: A History of Business in the United States* (Fort Worth, TX: Harcourt, 2000), 210–11.

8. Robert Peel, *Christian Science: Its Encounter with American Culture* (New York: Holt, 1958).

9. Johnson, *History of the American People*, 297.

10. Walters, *American Reformers*, 27.

11. Quoted at http://xroads.virginia.edu/~HYPER/DETOC/religion/finney.html, from Finney's memoirs.

12. Tyler, *Freedom's Ferment*, 41; Walters, *Jacksonian Reformers*, 35–36.

13. Ray Allen Billington and Martin Ridge, *Westward Expansion*, 5th ed. (New York: Macmillan, 1982), 476–78.

14. Leonard Arrington, *Great Basin Kingdom: An Economic History of the Latter-Day Saints* (Lincoln: University of Nebraska Press, 1966 [1958]); B. H. Roberts, *A Comprehensive History of the Church of Jesus Christ of Latter-Day Saints* (Salt Lake City: Deseret News Press, 1930).

15. Frances S. Trollope, *The Domestic Manners of the Americans*, Donald Smalley, ed. (Gloucester, MA: Peter Smith Publisher Inc., 1974).

16. Johnson, *History of the American People*, 304.

17. Ronald G. Walters, *Antislavery Appeal: American Abolitionism After 1830* (New York: W. W. Norton, 1984), 9.

18. Walters, *Antislavery Appeal*, 62.

19. Walters, *American Reformers*, 50–55.

20. Johnson, *History of the American People*, 301.

21. Tyler, *Freedom's Ferment*, 110.

22. Walters, *American Reformers*, 50–55; Nathaniel Hawthorne, *The Blithedale Romance* (repr., New York: Oxford University Press, 1991).

23. Walters, *Antislavery Appeal*, 94.

24. Louis Menand, *The Metaphysical Club* (New York: Farrar, Straus and Giroux, 2001), 20.

25. Robert J. Loewenberg, "Emerson's Platonism and 'the terrific Jewish Idea,'" *Mosaic: A Journal for the Interdisciplinary Study of Literature*, XV, 1982, 93–108; Loewenberg, *An American Idol: Emerson and the "Jewish Idea"* (Washington, D.C.: University Press of America, 1984), and his "Emerson and the Genius of American Liberalism," *Center Journal*, Summer 1983, 107–28.

26. Arthur Bestor, *Backwoods Utopias: The Sectarian Origins and the Owenite Phase of Communitarian Socialism in America* (Philadelphia: University of Pennsylvania Press, 1970 [1950]), 103.

27. Ibid., passim; Tyler, *Freedom's Ferment*, 166–224.

28. Tyler, *Freedom's Ferment*, 485–486.

29. Ibid., 485.

30. Walters, *American Reformers*, 81.

31. Van Wyck Brooks, *The Flowering of New England, 1815–1865* (New York: E. P. Dutton, 1937); F. O. Mathiesson, *American Renaissance* (New York: Oxford University Press, 1941).

32. Michael Allen, "Who Was David Crockett?" in Calvin Dickinson and Larry Whiteaker, eds., *Tennessee: State of the Nation* (New York: American Heritage, 1995), 47–53.

33. William C. Davis, *Three Roads to the Alamo: The Lives and Fortunes of David Crockett, James Bowie, and William Barret Travis* (New York: HarperPerennial, 1999), 86.

34. Even objective biographers, such as Davis, admit that he probably killed more than 50 bears in the season he referred to—an astounding accomplishment if for no other reason than the sheer danger posed by the animals.

35. Davis, *Three Roads to the Alamo*, 313–37.

36. Allen, "Who Was David Crockett?," passim.

37. David Waldstreicher, "The Nationalization and Radicalization of American Politics, 1790–1840," in Byron E. Shafer and Anthony J. Badger, eds., *Contesting Democracy: Substance and Structure in American Political History, 1775–2000* (Lawrence, KS: University Press of Kansas, 2001), 37–64, quotation on 55.

38. Tindall and Shi, *America*, 1:477.

39. Larry Schweikart, *Banking in the American South from the Age of Jackson to Reconstruction* (Baton Rouge: Louisiana State University Press, 1987).

40. Jeffrey Rogers Hummel, "Martin Van Buren: The Greatest American President," *Independent Review*, 4, Fall 1999, 255–81, quotation on 261–62.

41. Freeman Cleaves, *Old Tippecanoe: William Henry Harrison and His Times* (Port Washington, NY: Kennikat Press, 1939), 284.

42. Michael F. Holt, *Rise and Fall of the American Whig Party: Jacksonian Politics and the Onset of the Civil War* (New York: Oxford University Press, 1999), 95; William J. Cooper Jr., *Liberty and Slavery: Southern Politics to 1860* (Columbia, SC: University of South Carolina Press, 2000).

43. Holt, *Rise and Fall of the American Whig Party*, 95.

44. Paul S. Boyer, et al., *The Enduring Vision: A History of the American People* (Lexington, KY: D. C. Heath, 1993), 279.

45. Norma Lois Peterson, *The Presidencies of William Henry Harrison & John Tyler* (Lawrence, KS: University Press of Kansas, 1989), 32.

46. Ibid., 45.

47. Edwin S. Corwin, *The President: Office and Powers, 1787–1957* (New York: New York University Press, 1957).

48. Dan Monroe, *The Republican Vision of John Tyler* (College Station, TX: Texas A & M University Press, 2002).

49. Bernard Bailyn, et al., *The Great Republic: A History of the American People* (New York: D. C. Heath, 1985), 398.

50. Frederick Merk, *Manifest Destiny and Mission in American History* (New York: Vintage, 1963), 46.

51. James D. Richardson, *A Compiliation of the Messages and Papers of the Presidents*, vol. 3 (New York: Bureau of National Literature, 1897), 2225.

52. Paul K. Davis, *100 Decisive Battles from Ancient Times to the Present* (New York: Oxford, 1999), 309; James Pohl, *The Battle of San Jacinto* (Austin: Texas State Historical Association, 1989).

53. Ray Allen Billington and Martin Ridge, *Westward Expansion: A History of the American Frontier*, 6th ed. (Albuquerque, NM: University of New Mexico Press, 2001), 143.

54. Carol Berkin, et al. *Making America*, 2nd ed. (Boston: Houghton-Mifflin, 1999), 383.

55. Tindall and Shi, *America*, 1:607.

56. John Quincy Adams, *The Diary of John Quincy Adams, 1794–1845*, Allan Nevins, ed. (New York: Longmans, Green, 1928), 573–74, February 27 and 28, 1845.

57. Billington and Ridge, *Westward Expansion*, 232; Richard R. Stenberg, "The Failure of Polk's Mexican War Intrigue of 1845," *Pacific Historical Review*, 1, 1935, 39–68; Ramon Ruiz, *The Mexican War: Was it Manifest Destiny?* (Hinsdale, IL: Dryden Press, 1963), 68–69; Justin H. Smith, *The War With Mexico*, 2 vols. (New York: Macmillan, 1919); Samuel Flagg Bemis, *A Diplomatic History of the United States* (New York: Holt, Rinehart and Winston, 1955).

58. Horace Greeley, New York *Tribune*, May 12, 1846.

59. Jim R. McClellan, *Historical Moments* (Guilford, CT: McGraw-Hill, 2000), I:23.

60. James K. Polk, *Polk: The Diary of a President, 1843–1849*, Milo Milton Quaife, ed. (Chicago: A. C. Clung, 1910), 437–38.

61. Robert W. Leckie, *Wars of America*, 334.

62. Robert P. Ludlum, "The Antislavery 'Gag-Rule': History and Argument," *Journal of Negro History*, 26, 1941, 203–43.

63. Ibid., 229.

64. David M. Potter, *The Impending Crisis*, completed and edited by Don E. Fehrenbacher (New York: Harper Torchbooks, 1976), 20.

65. Leckie, *Wars of America*, 341.

66. Ibid.

67. Ibid.

68. Henry W. Halleck, *Elements of Military Art and Science* (New York: Appleton, 1862), 414.

69. Potter, *Impending Crisis*, 3.

70. Leckie, *Wars of America*, 358; Winfield Scott, *Memoirs of Lieut. Gen. Scott, LLD, Written by Himself*, 2 vols. (New York: Sheldon, 1864), II:425.

71. New York *Sun*, May 15, 1846.

72. Brooklyn *Eagle*, June 29, 1846.

73. Potter, *Impending Crisis*, 6.

74. Robert J. Loewenberg, *Equality on the Oregon Frontier: Jason Lee and the Methodist Mission* (Seattle: University of Washington Press, 1976).

Chapter 8. The House Dividing, 1848–60

1. Wire service report from Alexandria *Gazette* and Virginia *Advertiser*, October 18, 1859.

2. Chicago *Press and Tribune*, October 21, 1859, in Richard Warch and Jonathon Fanton, eds., *John Brown* (Englewood Cliffs, NJ: Spectrum Books, 1973), 119–20.

3. New York *Tribune*, December 3, 1859.

4. C. Vann Woodward, *The Burden of Southern History* (New York: Mentor Books, 1968), 43–44.

5. Stephen B. Oates, *To Purge This Land with Blood: A Biography of John Brown* (New York: Harper & Row, 1970), 331–33.
6. Garrison writing in *The Liberator*, December 16, 1859.
7. Wendell Phillips, speech of November 1, 1859, in Louis Filler, ed., *Wendell Phillips on Civil Rights and Freedom* (New York: Hill and Wang, 1963), 101–2.
8. Alexander B. Callow Jr., *The Tweed Ring* (New York: Oxford University Press, 1965), 52.
9. Ibid., 54.
10. Charles Loring Brace, *The Dangerous Classes and Twenty Years' Work Among Them* (New York: Wynkoop and Hallenbeck, 1872).
11. Callow, *Tweed Ring*, 54.
12. Gustav Lening, *The Dark Side of New York, Life and Its Criminal Classes: From Fifth Avenue Down to the Five Points; a Complete Narrative of the Mysteries of New York* (New York: Frederick Gerhardt, 1873), 348; Edward Asbury, *The Gangs of New York: An Informal History of the Underworld* (New York: Alfred A. Knopf, 1927), 177.
13. Rudyard Kipling, "Across a Continent," quoted in Johnson, *History of the American People*, 511.
14. Carol Berkin, et al., *Making America: A History of the United States*, 2nd ed. (Boston: Houghton Mifflin, 1999), 315, map 11.1.
15. Shirley Blumenthal and Jerome S. Ozer, *Coming to America: Immigrants from the British Isles* (New York: Dell, 1980), 89.
16. Thomas Sowell, *Ethnic America: A History* (New York: Basic Books, 1981), 22.
17. Carl Wittke, *The Irish in America* (New York: Russell and Russell, 1970), 23–24.
18. Callow, *Tweed Ring*, 65–66.
19. Blumenthal and Ozer, *Coming to America*, 90.
20. Stephan Thernstrom, *Poverty and Progress: Social Mobility in a Nineteenth Century City* (Cambridge, MA: Harvard University Press, 1964), 184–85.
21. Lawrence J. McCaffrey, *The Irish Diaspora in America* (Bloomington: Indiana University Press, 1976), 93.
22. Nathan Glazer and Daniel Patrick Moynihan, *Beyond the Melting Pot* (Cambridge, MA: MIT Press, 1963), 224.
23. Ibid.
24. M. A. Jones, *American Immigration* (Chicago: University of Chicago Press, 1960), 155; Wittke, *Irish in America*, 154.
25. Virginia Brainard Kunz, *The Germans in America* (Minneapolis: Lerner Publications, 1966); Theodore Heubner, *The Germans in America* (Radnor, PA: Chilton, 1962).
26. Katherine Neils Conzen, *Immigrant Milwaukee, 1836–1860* (Cambridge, MA: Harvard University Press, 1976); "German Immigration," in Stanley Feldstein and Lawrence Costello, eds. *The Ordeal of Assimilation: A Documentary History of the White Working Class* (New York: Anchor Books, 1974).
27. Avery Craven, *The Coming of the Civil War* (Chicago: University of Chicago Press, 1942), 113.
28. Larry Schweikart, *Banking in the American South from the Age of Jackson to Reconstruction* (Baton Rouge, LA: Louisiana State University Press), 87; Ted Worley, "Arkansas and the Money Crisis of 1836–1837," *Journal of Southern History*, May 1949, 178–91 and "The Control of the Real Estate Bank of the State of Arkansas, 1836–1855," *Mississippi Valley Historical Review*, December 1950, 403–26.
29. Sowell, *Ethnic America*, 76–77; Frances Butwin, *The Jews in America* (Minneapolis: Lerner Publications, 1969). .
30. Irving Howe, *World of Our Fathers* (New York: Harcourt Brace Jovanovich, 1976), 82.
31. Ervin L. Jordan Jr., *Black Confederates and Afro-Yankees in Civil War Virginia* (Charlottesville: University Press of Virginia, 1995), 8.
32. Jeremy Atack, and Peter Passell, *A New Economic View of American History*, 2nd ed. (New York: W. W. Norton, 1994), 305; Michael Tadaman, *Speculators and Slaves: Masters, Traders and Slaves in the Old South* (Madison, WI: University of Wisconsin Press, 1989).
33. James L. Huston, "Property Rights in Slavery and the Coming of the Civil War," *Journal of Southern History*, 65, May 1999, 248–86.
34. Ibid., 262.
35. Ibid., 279.
36. Robert C. Puth, *American Economic History* (Chicago: Dryden Press, 1982), 192.

37. Atack and Passell, *A New Economic View of American History*, 315. For the economics of slavery, see Alfred Conrad and John Meyer, "The Economics of Slavery in the Antebellum South," *Journal of Political Economy*, 66, 1958, 95–130; Robert Fogel, *Without Consent or Contract: The Rise and Fall of American Slavery*, 4 vols. (New York: W. W. Norton, 1989–1992); Eugene Genovese, *Roll, Jordan, Roll: The World the Slaves Made* (New York: Pantheon, 1974); David Weiman, "Farmers and the Market in Antebellum America: A View from the Georgia Upcountry," *Journal of Economic History*, 47, 1987, 627–48; Paul David, "Explaining the Relative Efficiency of Slave Agriculture in the Antebellum South: Comment," *American Economic Review*, 69, 1979, 213–16; Robert W. Fogel and Stanley Engerman, *Time on the Cross* (Boston: Little, Brown, 1974).

38. Eric Foner, *Free Soil, Free Labor, Free Men: The Ideology of the Republican Party Before the Civil War* (New York: Oxford, 1995), 63.

39. Ibid., 62.

40. Gavin Wright, *Old South, New South: Revolutions in the Southern Economy Since the Civil War* (New York: Basic Books, 1986), table 2.4 on 27.

41. Ulrich Bonnell Phillips, *American Negro Slavery* (New York: D. Appleton Company, 1918), and his "The Economic Cost of Slave Holding in the Cotton Belt," *Political Science Quarterly*, 20, 1905, 257–75; Charles Sydnor, *Slavery in Mississippi* (New York: Appleton-Century, 1933).

42. Fred Bateman and Thomas Weiss, *A Deplorable Scarcity: The Failure of Industrialization in the Slave Economy* (Chapel Hill: University of North Carolina Press, 1981).

43. Jeffrey Rogers Hummel, *Emancipating Slaves, Enslaving Free Men: A History of the American Civil War* (Chicago: Open Court, 1996), 42.

44. John H. Moore, "Simon Gray, Riverman: A Slave Who Was Almost Free," *Mississippi Valley Historical Review*, 49, December 1962, 472–84.

45. Atack and Passell, *A New Economic View*, 337–39.

46. Leon Litwack, *Been in the Storm So Long: The Aftermath of Slavery* (New York: Vintage, 1979), 8.

47. Atack and Passell, *A New Economic View*, 341–45; Robert A. Margo and Richard H. Steckel, "The Heights of American Slaves: New Evidence on Slave Nutrition and Health," *Social Science History*, 6, 1982, 516–38.

48. Herbert Guttman, *The Black Family in Slavery and Freedom* (New York: Pantheon Books, 1976).

49. Kenneth Stampp, *The Peculiar Institution* (New York: Knopf, 1956); Gavin Wright, *The Political Economy of the Cotton South* (New York: W. W. Norton, 1978); Robert Evans Jr., "The Economics of American Negro Slavery," in *National Bureau for Economic Research, Aspects of Labor Economics* (Princeton: Princeton University Press, 1962); Yasukichi Yasuba, "The Profitability and Viability of Plantation Slavery in the United States," in Robert Fogel and Stanley Engerman, *The Reinterpretation of American Economic History* (New York: Harper & Row, 1971), 362–68.

50. Fred Bateman, James Foust, and Thomas Weiss, "Profitability in Southern Manufacturing: Estimates for 1860," *Explorations in Economic History*, 12, 1975, 211–31.

51. Mark Thornton, "Slavery, Profitability, and the Market Process," *Review of Austrian Economics*, 7 (1994), 21–27, quotation on 23.

52. Thomas D. Morris, *Southern Slavery and the Law, 1619–1860* (Chapel Hill: University of North Carolina Press, 1996); Andrew Fede, *People Without Rights: An Interpretation of the Law of Slavery in the U.S. South* (New York: Garland, 1992).

53. Schweikart, *Entrepreneurial Adventure*, 170–72.

54. James G. Ramsdell, "The Natural Limits of Slavery Expansion," *Mississippi Valley Historical Review*, 16, 1929, 151–71.

55. Claudia Goldin, *Urban Slavery in the Antebellum South* (Chicago: University of Chicago Press, 1976); Richard C. Wade, *Slavery in the Cities: The South, 1820–1860* (New York: Oxford University Press, 1964); Robert S. Starobin, *Industrial Slavery in the Old South* (New York: Oxford University Press, 1970).

56. Hummel, *Emancipating Slaves*, 23.

57. George Fitzhugh, *Cannibals All! Or, Slaves Without Masters* (Cambridge, MA: Harvard/Belknap, 1960).

58. Harrison Berry, *Slavery and Abolitionism, as Viewed by a Georgia Slave* (Atlanta: M. Lynch, 1861), 7, 24–25, 28, 32–35, 37–46.

59. George Fitzhugh, *Sociology for the South: Or the Failure of Free Society* (Richmond: A Morris, 1854), 245.

60. Ibid., 30, 170, 179.
61. Robert J. Loewenberg, *Freedom's Despots: The Critique of Abolition* (Durham: Carolina Academic Press, 1986).
62. Larry Schweikart, "Brothers in Chains: Emerson and Fitzhugh on Economic and Political Liberty," *Reason Papers*, 13, Spring 1988, 19–34.
63. Forrest G. Wood, *The Arrogance of Faith: Christianity and Race in America from the Colonial Era to the Twentieth Century* (New York: Alfred A. Knopf, 1990), 125.
64. Ibid.
65. Craven, *Coming of the Civil War*, 120.
66. Michael P. Johnson, "Denmark Vesey and His Co-Conspirators," *William and Mary Quarterly*, 58, October 2001, 915–76, and responses, ibid., January 2002; Eugene D. Genovese, *From Rebellion to Revolution: Afro-American Slave Revolts in the Making of the New World* (Baton Rouge, LA: Louisiana State University Press, 1979); George M. Frederickson and Christopher Lasch, "Resistance to Slavery," in Allen Weinstein and Frank Otto Gatell, eds., *American Negro Slavery: A Modern Reader*, 3rd ed. (New York: Oxford University Press, 1973).
67. Nat Turner, *The Confessions of Nat Turner, Leader of the Negro Insurrection in Southampton County, Virginia, Made to Thomas L. Gray* (Baltimore: Thomas R. Gray, 1831), 3–8.
68. Ibid.
69. City Ordinance of Washington, D.C., October 19, 1831, published in the Alexandria *Gazette*, October 26, 1831.
70. Ordinance published in the Maryland *Gazette*, October 20, 1831.
71. David Grimsted, *American Mobbing, 1828–1861* (New York: Oxford, 1998); Christopher Waldrep, *Roots of Disorder: Race and Criminal Justice in the American South, 1817–1880* (Urbana, IL: University of Illinois Press, 1998).
72. David Waldstreicher, "The Nationalization and Racialization of American Politics, 1790–1840," in Byron E. Shafer and Anthony J. Badger, *Contesting Democracy: Substance and Structure in American Political History, 1775–2000* (Lawrence, KS: University Press of Kansas, 2001), 37–64, quotation on 54.
73. Daniel Dorchester, *Christianity in the United States* (New York: Hunt & Eaton, 1895), 454.
74. Craven, *Coming of the Civil War*, 137.
75. Ibid., 137–138.
76. Michael F. Holt, *Rise and Fall of the American Whig Party: Jacksonian Politics and the Onset of the Civil War* (New York: Oxford University Press, 1999), 269.
77. Ibid., 272.
78. Ibid.
79. Glyndon G. Van Deusen, *William Henry Seward* (New York: Oxford, 1967), 122–28.
80. Elbert B. Smith, *The Presidencies of Zachary Taylor & Millard Fillmore* (Lawrence, KS: University Press of Kansas, 1988).
81. Hummel, *Emancipating Slaves*, 93.
82. Samuel J. May, *The Fugitive Slave Law and Its Victims*, rev. ed. (New York: American Anti-Slavery Society, 1861), 15; Stanley W. Campbell, *The Slave Catchers: Enforcement of the Fugitive Slave Law* (Chapel Hill: University of North Carolina Press, 1970).
83. David M. Potter, *The Impending Crisis, 1848–1861*. Completed and edited by Don E. Fehrenbacher (New York: Harper Torch Books, 1976), 132.
84. Craven, *Coming of the Civil War*, 323; Potter, *Impending Crisis*, 132–33.
85. Craven, *Coming of the Civil War*, 323.
86. C. Vann Woodward, "The Antislavery Myth," *American Scholar*, 31, 1962, 312–18; Charles L. Blockson, *The Underground Railroad* (New York: Berkeley, 1987).
87. Frank Luther Mott, *Golden Multitudes, The Story of Best Sellers in the United States* (New York: MacMillan, 1947); Edmund Wilson, *Patriotic Gore: Studies in the Literature of the American Civil War* (New York: Oxford, 1962); Charles Edward Stowe, *Life of Harriet Beecher Stowe* (Boston: Houghton Mifflin, 1889).
88. Potter, *Impending Crisis*, 140.
89. Hummel, *Emancipating Slaves*, 95.
90. Herbert Mitgang, ed., *Abraham Lincoln; a Press Portrait: His Life and Times from the Original Newspaper Documents of the Union, the Confederacy and Europe* (Chicago: Quadrangle Books, 1971), 373.
91. Holt, *Rise and Fall of the American Whig Party*, 572.

92. Roy F. Nichols, *The Democratic Machine, 1850–1854* (New York: Columbia University Press, 1932).

93. Johnson, *History of the American People,* 425–26.

94. Hummel, *Emancipating Slaves,* 96; William C. Davis, *Jefferson Davis: The Man and His Hour* (New York: HarperCollins, 1991), 251.

95. Hummel, *Emancipating Slaves,* 96.

96. See Stanley C. Urban, see the articles "The Ideology of Southern Imperialism: New Orleans and the Caribbean, 1845–1860," *Louisiana Historical Quarterly,* 39, 1956, 48–73; "The Africanization of Cuba Scare, 1853–1855," *Hispanic American Historical Review,* 37, 1957, 29–45.

97. Basil Rauch, *American Interest in Cuba,* 1848–1855 (New York: Columbia University Press, 1848); Charles H. Brown, *Agents of Manifest Destiny: The Lives and Times of the Filibusters* (Chapel Hill: University of North Carolina Press, 1980); Joseph Allen Stout Jr., *The Liberators: Filibustering Expeditions into Mexico, 1848–1862* (Los Angeles: Westernlore Press, 1973).

98. Nelson H. Loomis, "Asa Whitney, Father of Pacific Railroads," *Mississippi Valley Historical Association Proceedings,* 6, 1912, 166–75, and Margaret L. Brown, "Asa Whitney and His Pacific Railroad Publicity Campaign," Mississippi Valley Historical Review, 22, 1933–1934, 209–24.

99. James C. Malin, "The Proslavery Background of the Kansas Struggle," *Mississippi Valley Historical Review,* 10, 1923, 285–305 and his "The Motives of Stephen A. Douglas in the Organization of Nebraska Territory: A Letter Dated December 17, 1853," *Kansas Historical Quarterly,* 19, 1951, 31–52; Frank H. Hodder, "The Railroad Background of the Kansas-Nebraska Act," *Mississippi Valley Historical Review,* 12, 1925, 3–22; Robert S. Cotterill, "Early Agitation for a Pacific Railroad, 1845–1850," *Mississippi Valley Historical Review,* 5, 1919, 396–414; and Roy F. Nichols, "The Kansas-Nebraska Act: A Century of Historiography," *Mississippi Valley Historical Review,* 43, 1956, 187–212, provides a good overview of historians' assessments of the Kansas-Nebraska Act.

100. Malin, "Motive of Stephen A. Douglas," passim.

101. Robert W. Johannsen, *Stephen A. Douglas* (New York: Oxford, 1973).

102. William E. Parrish, *David Rice Atchison of Missouri: Border Politician* (Columbia, Missouri: University of Missouri Press, 1961), 161.

103. Potter, *Impending Crisis,* 203.

104. Allan Nevins, *The Emergence of Lincoln: Douglas, Buchanan, and Party Chaos, 1857–1859,* 2 vols. (New York: Charles Scribner's Sons, 1950), 1:164–65.

105. Potter, *Impending Crisis,* 222.

106. Allan Nevins, *Ordeal of the Union,* 2 vols. (New York: Charles Scribner's, 1947), 2:329–31.

107. Potter, *Impending Crisis,* 252.

108. Ibid., 262.

109. John Bassett Moore, ed., *The Works of James Buchanan: Comprising His Speeches, State Papers, and Private Correspondence* (Philadelphia: J. B. Lippincott, 1908–1911), 10:88.

110. William M. Wiecek, " 'Old Times There Are Not Forgotten': The Distinctiveness of the Southern Constitutional Experience," in Kermit L. Hall and James W. Ely Jr., eds., *An Uncertain Tradition: Constitutionalism and the History of the South* (Athens, GA: University of Georgia Press, 1989), 159–97, quotation on 170.

111. James L. Huston, *The Panic of 1857 and the Coming of the Civil War* (Baton Rouge: Louisiana State University Press, 1987).

112. Charles Calomiris and Larry Schweikart, "The Panic of 1857: Origins, Transmission, and Containment," *Journal of Economic History,* 51, December 1991, 807–34.

113. Johnson, *History of the American People,* 434.

114. From Abraham Lincoln's "House Divided" speech, June 16, 1858, in Roy P. Basler, ed., *Collected Works of Abraham Lincoln,* 8 vols. (New Brunswick, NJ: Princeton University Press, 1953), 2:465–66.

115. Nevins, *Emergence of Lincoln,* 174.

116. Potter, *Impending Crisis,* 299.

117. Stephen Douglas, speech at Milwaukee, October 14, 1860, in the Chicago *Times and Herald,* October 17, 1860.

118. Nevins, *Emergence of Lincoln,* 239.

119. New Orleans *Picayune* of April 29, 1860.

120. Robert A. Johannsen, "Stephen A. Douglas, Popular Sovereignty, and the Territories," *Historian*, 22, 1960, 378–95.
121. Johnson, *History of the American People*, 436.
122. Reinard H. Luthin, "Abraham Lincoln and the Tariff," *American Historical Review*, 49, July 1944, 609–29, quotation on 610.
123. Johnson, *History of the American People*, 438.
124. David Donald, *Lincoln Reconsidered* (New York: Vintage, 1961), 37–56.
125. Stephen B. Oates, *With Malice Toward None: The Life of Abraham Lincoln* (New York: Mentor, 1977), 72.
126. Ibid.
127. Ibid., 71.
128. Richard N. Current, *The Lincoln Nobody Knows* (New York: Hill and Wang, 1958), 59.
129. Current, *Lincoln Nobody Knows*, 59.
130. Ibid., 59–60.
131. Ibid., 63.
132. Quoted in Current, *Lincoln Nobody Knows*, 65.
133. Ibid.
134. Louis A. Warren, *Lincoln's Youth: Indiana Years, Seven to Twenty-One* (Indianapolis: Indiana Historical Society, 1959), 68–69, 233.
135. Henry B. Rankin, *Personal Recollections of Abraham Lincoln* (New York: G. P. Putnam's Sons, 1916), 323.
136. Noah Brooks, *Scribner's Monthly*, letter to the Reverend J. A. Reed, July 1893.
137. William J. Johnson, *Abraham Lincoln the Christian* (New York: Eaton & Mains, 1913), 172. Johnson quotes a "Lincoln Memorial Album" kept by O. H. Oldroyd, 1883, 336. Also see G. Frederick Owen, *Abraham Lincoln: The Man and His Faith* (Wheaton, IL: Tyndale House Publishers, 1981), 86–91. Elton Trueblood *Abraham Lincoln: A Spiritual Biography, Theologian of American Anguish* (New York: Walker and Company, 1986), 130.
138. Current, *Lincoln Nobody Knows*, 73.
139. Ronald C. White Jr., "Lincoln's Sermon on the Mount," in Randall M. Miller, Harry S. Stout, and Charles Reagan Wilson, eds., *Religion and the American Civil War* (New York: Oxford, 1998), 208–28; Philip Shaw Paludan, *A People's Contest: The Union and Civil War, 1861–1865* (New York: Harper & Row, 1988); David Hein, "Lincoln's Theology and Political Ethics," in Kenneth Thompson, ed., *Essays on Lincoln's Faith and Politics* (Lathan, MD: University Press of America), 105–56; Reinhold Niebuhr, "The Religion of Abraham Lincoln," in Allan Nevins, ed., *Lincoln and the Gettysburg Address* (Urbana, IL: University of Illinois Press, 1964).
140. Potter, *Impending Crisis*, 333.
141. Abraham Lincoln, "Speech Delivered at Springfield, Illinois, at the Close of the Republican State Convention by which Mr. Lincoln had been Named as their Candidate for United States Senator, June 16, 1858," in T. Harry Williams, ed., *Selected Writings and Speeches of Abraham Lincoln* (New York: Hendricks House, 1943), 53.
142. New York *Times*, June 23, 1857.
143. Potter, *Impending Crisis*, 337.
144. Roy F. Nichols, *The Disruption of American Democracy* (New York: Free Press, 1948), 221.
145. Harry V. Jaffa, *Crisis of the House Divided: An Interpretation of the Issues in the Lincoln-Douglas Debates* (Chicago: University of Chicago Press, 1982).
146. Potter, *Impending Crisis*, 342.
147. Basler, *Works of Lincoln*, vol. 3, 312–15.
148. Abraham Lincoln, "Mr. Lincoln's Opening Speech in the Sixth Joint Debate, at Quincy, October 13, 1858," in Williams, *Selected Writings and Speeches*, 74.
149. Basler, *Works of Lincoln*, 3:16 and 2:520.
150. Abraham Lincoln, "Address Before the Young Men's Lyceum of Springfield, Illinois, January 27, 1838," in *Williams, Selected Writings and Speeches*, 8.
151. Ibid.
152. Philip Paludan, *The Presidency of Abraham Lincoln* (Lawrence, KS: University Press of Kansas, 1994).
153. Potter, *Impending Crisis*, 389.

154. John G. Van Deusen, *The Ante-Bellum Southern Commercial Conventions* (Durham, NC: Duke University Press, 1926), 56–69, 75–79; Herbert Wender, *Southern Commercial Conventions, 1837–1859* (Baltimore: Johns Hopkins Press, 1930), 177–81, 211–35, and *De Bow's Review*, vols. 22–27, 1857–1859.

155. William L. Yancey's speech in *De Bow's Review*, 24, 1858, 473–91, 597–605.

156. *North American Review*, November 1886, "A Slave Trader's Notebook"; Nevins, *Ordeal of the Union*, 435–437.

Chapter 9. The Crisis of the Union, 1860–65

1. John Witherspoon Du Bose, *The Life and Times of William Lowndes Yancey*, 2 vols. (Birmingham, Alabama: Roberts and Son, 1892), 2: 457–60.

2. David M. Potter, *The Impending Crisis: 1848–1861.* Completed and edited by Don E. Fehrenbacher (New York: Harper Torch Books, 1976), 422.

3. Reinard H. Luthin, "Abraham Lincoln and the Tariff," *American Historical Review*, 49, July 1944, 609–29.

4. Allan Nevins, *The Emergence of Lincoln: Douglas, Buchanan, and Party Chaos, 1857–1859*, 2 vols. (New York: Charles Scribner's, 1950), 2:316.

5. Jeffrey Rogers Hummell, *Emancipating Slaves: Enslaving Free Men: A History of the American Civil War* (Chicago: Open Court, 1996), 131.

6. Horace Greeley, *The American Conflict*, 2 vols. (Hartford: O. D. Case, 1864), 1:380.

7. Nevins, *Emergence of Lincoln*, 328.

8. Potter, *Impending Crisis*, 496.

9. Nevins, *Emergence of Lincoln*, 2:321.

10. Johnson, *History of the American People*, 458.

11. William C. Davis, *Jefferson Davis* (New York: HarperCollins, 1991), 258.

12. Richard Bensel, *Yankee Leviathan: The Origins of Central Authority in America, 1859–1877* (New York: Cambridge, 1990), 133.

13. Ibid.

14. Nevins, *Emergence of Lincoln*, 330.

15. E. L. Harvin, "Arkansas and the Crisis of 1860–61," manuscript at the University of Texas.

16. Weicek, " 'Old Times There Are Not Forgotten,' " 173.

17. Roger W. Shugg, *Origins of Class Struggle in Louisiana: A Social History of White Farmers and Laborers During Slavery and After, 1840–1875* (Baton Rouge: Louisiana State University Press, 1939), 167.

18. Broadside, Jefferson Davis Papers, University Library, Washington and Lee University, Lexington, VA.

19. Ibid. See also Charles H. Wesley, "The Employment of Negroes as Soldiers in the Confederate Army," *Journal of Negro History*, 4, July 1919, 239–53.

20. William J. Davis, *Jefferson Davis: The Man and His Hour* (New York: HarperCollins, 1991), 495.

21. Marie Hochmuth Nichols, "Lincoln's First Inaugural Address," in J. Jeffery Auer, ed., *Antislavery and Disunion, 1858–1861: Studies in the Rhetoric of Compromise and Conflict* (New York: Harper & Row, 1963), 392–414.

22. Davis, *Jefferson Davis*, 325; Richard N. Current, *Lincoln and the First Shot* (Philadelphia: J. B. Lippincott, 1963). For interpretations of the Civil War, see Thomas J. Pressly, *Americans Interpret Their Civil War* (New York: Free Press, 1962 [1954]); Kenneth M. Stampp, "Lincoln and the Strategy of Defense in the Crisis of 1861," *Journal of Southern History*, 11, 1945, 297–323; James G. Randall, *Lincoln the President*, 4 vols. (New York: Dodd Mead, 1945–1955); Eba Anderson Lawton, *Major Robert Anderson and Fort Sumter* (New York: Knickerbocker Press, 1911).

23. Allan Nevins, *The War for the Union: The Improvised War, 1861–1862* (New York: Charles Scribner's Sons, 1959), 87.

24. Richard N. Current, *Lincoln's Loyalists: Union Soldiers from the Confederacy* (Boston: Northeastern University Press, 1992).

25. Virgil A. Lewis, *How West Virginia Was Made* (Charleston, West Virginia: News-Mail Company, 1909).

26. Nevins, *War for the Union*, 146–47; Daniel W. Crofts, *Reluctant Confederates: Upper South Unionists in the Secession Crisis* (Chapel Hill, NC: University of North Carolina, 1989).

27. Current, *Lincoln's Loyalists*, 4.
28. Mark Twain, "The Private History of a Campaign That Failed," in Justin Kaplan, ed., *Great Short Works of Mark Twain* (New York: Harper & Row, 1967), 145.
29. Johnson, *History of the American People*, 458–59.
30. Boyer, et al, *The Enduring Vision*, 408.
31. Twain, "Private History," 147–51.
32. James G. Randall, *The Civil War and Reconstruction* (Boston: D. C. Heath, 1937), 265.
33. Ibid.
34. Official Records of the War of the Rebellion (henceforth called OR), 70 vols. (Washington, D.C. : Government Printing Office, 1880–1891), 3:i and 303.
35. Nevins, *War for the Union*, 108–9.
36. *Harper's Magazine*, September 1855, 552–55.
37. Richard G. Beringer, et al, eds., *Why the South Lost the Civil War* (Athens, GA: University of Georgia Press, 1986); Richard N. Current, *Why the North Won the Civil War* (New York: Colier, 1962); David Donald, ed., *Why the North Won the Civil War* (Westport, CT: PaperBook Press, 1993).
38. Grady McWhiney and Perry D. Jamieson, *Attack and Die: Civil War Military Tactics and the Southern Heritage* (University, AL: University of Alabama Press, 1982).
39. Forrest McDonald and Grady McWhiney, "The Antebellum Southern Herdsman: A Reinterpretation," *Journal of Southern History*, 41, 1975, 147–66.
40. McWhiney and Jamieson, *Attack and Die*, 6.
41. Bernard DeVoto, *The Year of Decision, 1846* (Boston: Little, Brown, 1943), 203, 284.
42. McWhiney and Jamieson, *Attack and Die*, 7.
43. Davis, *100 Decisive Battles*, 318.
44. T. Harry Williams, *Lincoln and His Generals* (New York: Vintage Books, 1952), 7.
45. Ibid.
46. Nevins, *War for the Union*, 179.
47. Stanley Lebergott, "Why the South Lost: Commercial Purpose in the Confederacy, 1861–1865," *Journal of American History*, 70, June 1983, 58–74, and his "Through the Blockade: The Profitability and Extent of Cotton Smuggling, 1861–1865," *Journal of Economic History*, 41, December 1981, 867–88.
48. James MacPherson, *Ordeal by Fire: The Civil War and Reconstruction*, 3rd ed. (New York: McGraw-Hill, 2001), 272–76.
49. Shelby Foote, *The Civil War* (Public Broadcasting System) VHS, 9 vols. (Alexandria, VA: Florentine Films, 1989), vol. 1.
50. MacPherson, *Ordeal by Fire*, 228.
51. Ibid.
52. Randall, *Civil War and Reconstruction*, 275–76.
53. William H. Russell, *My Diary, North and South* (Boston: T.O.H.P. Burnham, 1863), 451.
54. Randall, *Civil War and Reconstruction*, 276.
55. Douglas Southall Freeman, *Lee's Lieutenants: A Study in Command* (New York: Charles Scribner's, 1946), 1:81–82.
56. Robert Underwood Johnson and Clarence C. Buel, eds., *Battles and Leaders of the Civil War*, 4 vols. (New York: Century Company, 1884–1887), 1:252.
57. Captain J. R. Hawley to his wife, September 25, 1861, Hawley Papers, Library of Congress.
58. Nevins, *War for the Union*, 238; Allen C. Guelzo, *The Crisis of the American Republic: A History of the Civil War and Reconstruction* (New York: St. Martin's, 1995).
59. William L. Barney, *Battleground for the Union: The Era of the Civil War and Reconstruction, 1848–1877* (Englewood Cliffs, NJ: Prentice-Hall, 1990), 158.
60. Williams, *Lincoln and His Generals*, 25.
61. Johnson, *History of the American People*, 475.
62. Stephen W. Sears, "Lincoln and McClellan," in Gabor S. Borrit, ed., *Lincoln's Generals* (New York: Oxford University Press, 1994), 1–50, quotation on 13–14.
63. Jeffrey Rogers Hummel, *Emancipating Slaves, Enslaving Free Men: A History of the American Civil War* (Chicago: Open Court, 1996), 163.
64. Gordon Warren, *Fountain of Discontent: The Trent Affair and Freedom of the Seas* (Boston: Northeastern University Press, 1981).
65. Randall, *Civil War and Reconstruction*, 577.

66. Ulysses S. Grant, *Personal Memoirs of U. S. Grant* (New York: Charles L. Webster, 1886), 1:311.
67. John H. Brinton, *The Personal Memoirs of John H. Brinton, Major and Surgeon, U.S.V., 1861–1865* (New York: Neale, 1914), 239.
68. Gillon and Matson, *American Experiment*, 574; New York *Times,* February 17, 1862.
69. Gillon and Matson, *American Experiment*, 575.
70. Randall, *Civil War and Reconstruction*, 529.
71. Gillon and Matson, *American Experiment*, 593.
72. Williams, *Lincoln and His Generals*, 272.
73. Frederick Blue, *Salmon P. Chase: A Life in Politics* (Kent, OH: Kent State University Press, 1987).
74. Roberta Sue Alexander, "Salmon P. Chase," in Larry Schweikart, ed., *Encyclopedia of American Business History and Biography: Banking and Finance to 1913* (New York: Facts on File, 1990), 88–105); David H. Donald, ed., *Inside Lincoln's Cabinet: The War Diaries of Salmon P. Chase* (New York: Longmans, Green, 1954).
75. Joseph Rishel, "Jay Cooke," in Schweikart, ed., *Encyclopedia of American Business History and Biography*, 135–43; Henrietta M. Larson, *Jay Cooke: Private Banker* (Cambridge, Massachusetts: Harvard University Press, 1936); Ellis Paxon Oberholtzer, *Jay Cooke: Financier of the Civil War*, 2 vols. (Philadelphia: Jacobs, 1907).
76. Jeffrey Rogers Hummel, "Confederate Finance," in Schweikart, ed., *Encyclopedia of American Business History and Biography*, 132–35; Richard Cecil Todd, *Confederate Finance* (Athens, GA: University of Georgia Press, 1954); John Christopher Schwab, *The Confederate States of America, 1861–1865: A Financial and Industrial History of the South During the Civil War* (New York: Charles Scribner's, 1901); James F. Morgan, *Graybacks and Gold: Confederate Monetary Policy* (Pensacola, Florida: Perdido Bay Press, 1985).
77. Douglas B. Ball, *Financial Failure and Confederate Defeat* (Urbana, IL: University of Illinois Press, 1991).
78. Although Judith Fenner Gentry labeled this a success, the Erlanger loan merely exposed the stark inadequacies of the Southern economy compared to the North's. See Gentry, "A Confederate Success in Europe: The Erlanger Loan," *Journal of Southern History*, 36, 1970, 157–88.
79. Larry Schweikart, *Banking in the American South from the Age of Jackson to Reconstruction* (Baton Rouge: Louisiana State University Press, 1987), chap. 7, passim.
80. Hummell, *Emancipating Slaves*, 236–37.
81. James T. Leach, "Proceedings of the Second Confederate Congress, Second Session in Part," 27 January 1865, Southern Historical Society Papers, 52, 1959, 242.
82. John H. Hagan to his wife, July 23, 1863, in Bell Irvin Wiley, ed., "The Confederate Letters of John W. Hagan," *Georgia Historical Quarterly*, 38, June 1954, 196.
83. Contrast this with David Donald's view that the South "Died of Democracy." See Donald, "Died of Democracy," in *Why the North Won the Civil War*, 77–90.
84. Bensel, *Yankee Leviathan*, passim.
85. Davis, *100 Decisive Battles*, 318.
86. John Cannan, *The Antietam Campaign* (New York: Wieser & Wieser, 1990); Jay Luvaas and Harold W. Nelson, eds., *The U.S. Army War College Guide to the Battle of Antietam* (New York: HarperCollins, 1988); James Murfin, *The Gleam of Bayonets* (New York: T. Yoseloff, 1965); Stephen Sears, *Landscape Turned Red* (New Haven: Tiknor & Fields, 1983).
87. Oates, *With Malice Toward None*, 334.
88. Ibid.
89. Ibid., 334–35.
90. Quoted in Oates, *With Malice Toward None*, 337.
91. Ibid., 339.
92. Ibid., 340.
93. Again, much of this material comes from Oates, *With Malice Toward None*, 346–47.
94. Leon Litwack, *Been in the Storm So Long: The Aftermath of Slavery* (New York: Vintage, 1980), 27.
95. Contra Howard Zinn, *A People's History of the United States, 1492–Present* (New York: HarperPerennial, 1995), 187–88.
96. Ira Berlin, Joseph P. Reidy, and Leslie S. Rowland, *Freedom's Soldiers: The Black Military Experience in the Civil War* (Cambridge: Cambridge University Press, 1998), 10.

97. Jay David and Elaine Crane, *The Black Soldier: From the American Revolution to Vietnam* (New York: William Morrow, 1971).

98. Williams, *Lincoln and His Generals*, 180.

99. Ibid., 242.

100. Duane Schultz, *The Most Glorious Fourth* (New York: W. W. Norton, 2002), 5.

101. Michael Shaara, *The Killer Angels* (New York: Ballantine, 1974); Mark Nesbitt, *Saber and Scapegoat: J.E.B. Stuart and the Gettysburg Controversy* (Mechanicsburg, PA: Stackpole Books, 1994); Emory M. Thomas, "Eggs, Aldie, Shepherdstown, and J.E.B. Stuart," in Gabor S. Boritt, ed., *The Gettysburg Nobody Knows* (New York: Oxford, 1997), 101–21; Edwin B. Coddington, *The Gettysburg Campaign: A Study in Command* (New York: Charles Scribner's, 1968); Emory M. Thomas, *Bold Dragoon: The Life of J.E.B. Stuart* (New York: Harper and Row, 1986).

102. Glenn LaFantasie, "Joshua Chamberlain and the American Dream," in Boritt, *Lincoln's Generals*, 31–55.

103. LaFantasie, "Joshua Chamberlain and the American Dream," 34.

104. Earl J. Hess, *Pickett's Charge: The Last Attack at Gettysburg* (Chapel Hill: University of North Carolina Press, 2001), passim.

105. James M. McPherson, *Battle Cry of Freedom* (New York: Oxford University Press, 1988), 661.

106. Allan Nevins, *The War for the Union,* vol. 3: *The Organized War, 1863–1864* (New York: Charles Scribner's, 1971), 110–11.

107. Gabor S. Boritt, "Unfinished Work: Lincoln, Meade, and Gettysburg," in Borit, *Lincoln's Generals*, 81–120, quotation on 83.

108. Michael Fellman, "Lincoln and Sherman," in Boritt, *Lincoln's Generals*, 121–59.

109. Ibid., 127.

110. http://ngeorgia.com/people/shermanwt.html.

111. John Y. Simon, "Grant, Lincoln, and Unconditional Surrender," in Boritt, ed., *Lincoln's Generals*, 163–98, quotation on 195.

112. Randall, *Civil War and Reconstruction*, 541, 543; George Cary Eggleston, "Notes on Cold Harbor," in Johnson and Buel, *Battles and Leaders*, 4:230–31.

113. Hummel, *Emancipating Slaves*, 274.

114. Berkin, *Making America*, 455.

115. Ibid., 456.

116. Randall, *Civil War and Reconstruction*, 550.

117. James G. Blaine, *Twenty Years of Congress: From Lincoln to Garfield*, 2 vols. (Norwich, CT: Henry Bill Publishing, 1884–1886), 1:444.

118. Orville H. Browning, *The Diary of Orville Hickman Browning*, ed., T. C. Pease and J. G. Randall, 2 vols. (Springfield, IL: Trustees of the Illinois State Historical Library, 1933), 1:600–601.

119. John Ellis, *The Social History of the Machine Gun* (New York: Pantheon, 1975); Paul Wahl and Donald R. Toppel, *The Gatling Gun* (New York: Arco, 1965).

120. Berkin, *Making America*, 458.

121. Ibid.

122. William Tecumseh Sherman, *Memoirs of General William T. Sherman*, 2 vols. (New York: Da Capo, 1984), 2:249.

123. Philip Shaw Paludan, "Religion and the American Civil War," in Randall M. Miller, Harry S. Stout, and Charles Reagan Wilson, eds., *Religion and the American Civil War* (New York: Oxford, 1998), 21–42, quotation on 25.

124. Victor Davis Hanson, *The Soul of Battle* (New York: Free Press, 1999), 173.

125. Ibid., 231.

126. Fellman, "Lincoln and Sherman," 142.

127. Ibid., 147.

128. Simon, "Grant, Lincoln, and Unconditional Surrender," 168.

129. Ervin L. Jordan, *Black Confederates and Afro-Yankees in the Civil War Virginia* (Charlottesville: University Press of Virginia, 1995), 51.

130. Ibid., 62.

131. Confederate States of America Congress, Minority Report [on the recruitment of black troops] (Richmond: Confederate States of America, 1865). See also Charles Wesley, "The Employment of Negroes as Soldiers in the Confederate Army," *Journal of Negro History*, July 1919, 239–53.

132. Jackson *News*, March 10, 1865, reprinted in John Bettersworth, *Mississippi in the Confederacy*, 2 vols. (Jackson: Mississippi Department of Archives and History, 1961), 1:246.
133. Jordan, *Black Confederates*, 72.
134. Thomas J. Wertenbaker, *Norfolk: Historic Southern Port*, 2nd ed. (Durham, North Carolina: Duke University Press, 1962), 220–21.
135. Berkin, *Making America*, 459.
136. http://www.ibiscom.com/appomatx.htm.
137. Jay Winik, *April 1865: The Month That Saved the Union* (New York: HarperCollins, 2001); Daniel Sutherland, "Guerrilla Warfare, Democracy, and the Fate of the Confederacy," *Journal of Southern History*, 68, May 2002, 259–92, quotation on 292.
138. Hummel, *Emancipating Slaves*, 291.
139. Second Inaugural Speech of Abraham Lincoln, March 4, 1865, in Williams, ed., *Selected Writings and Speeches of Abraham Lincoln*, 259–60.
140. Johnson, *History of the American People*, 495.
141. Washington *Evening Star*, April 15, 1865, and *National Intelligencer*, April 15, 1865.
142. http://members.aol.com/RVSNorton/Lincoln.html.
143. Louis Untermeyer, ed., *A Treasury of Great Poems English and American* (New York: Simon & Schuster, 1955), 904–5.
144. Gary Gallagher and Alan T. Nolan, eds., *The Myth of the Lost Cause and Civil War History* (Bloomington, IN: Indiana University Press, 2000).
145. James M. McPherson, *Ordeal by Fire* (New York: Alfred A. Knopf, 1982), 476.
146. Schweikart, *Banking in the American South*, 267–313.
147. Alan T. Nolan, "The Anatomy of the Myth," in Gallagher and Nolan, eds., *Myth of the Lost Cause*, 11–34, quotation on 20.
148. Frank Moore, *Rebellion Record: A Diary of American Events with Documents, Narratives, Illustrative Incidents, Poetry, Etc.*, 11 vols. (New York: D. Van Nostrand, 1861–1888), 1:844–46.
149. Allen Nevins, *The Emergence of Lincoln*, 2 vols. (New York: Charles Scribner's, 1950), 2:468.
150. Davis, *Jefferson Davis*, 514.
151. See, in addition to Hummel (who is the most articulate), Allen Buchanan, *Secession: The Morality of Political Divorce from Fort Sumter to Lithuania and Quebec* (Boulder, CO: Westview Press, 1991); Harry Beran, "A Liberal Theory of Secession," *Political Studies*, 32, December 1984, 21–31; Anthony H. Birch, "Another Liberal Theory of Secession," *Political Studies*, 32, December 1984, 596–602; Robert W. McGee, "Secession Reconsidered," *Journal of Libertarian Studies*, 11, Fall 1984, 11–33; Murray Rothbard, "War, Peace and the State, in Murray Rothbard, ed., *Egalitarianism as a Revolt Against Nature: and Other Essays* (Washington: Libertarian Review Press, 1974); Bruce D. Porter, "Parkinson's Law Revisited: War and the Growth of Government," *The Public Interest*, 60, Summer 1980, 50–68, and his *War and the Rise of the State: The Military Foundations of Modern Politics* (New York: Free Press, 1994); Robert Higgs, *Crisis and Leviathan: Critical Episodes in the Growth of American Government* (New York: Oxford University Press, 1987).
152. Zinn, *People's History*, 193.

Chapter 10. Ideals and Realities of Reconstruction, 1865–76

1. S. R. Mallory, Diary, Southern Historical Collection, University of North Carolina Library, cited in Allan Nevins, *The War for the Union: The Organized War to Victory, 1864–1865* (New York: Charles Scribner's, 1971), 295.
2. Otto Eisenschiml, ed., *Vermont General: The Unusual War Experiences of Edward Hasting Ripley, 1862–1865* (New York: Devin-Adair, 1960), 296–306.
3. New York *Tribune*, April 10, 1865.
4. Noah Brooks, *Washington in Lincoln's Time* (New York: Century Company, 1895), 219.
5. Marquis de Chambrun, "Personal Recollections of Mr. Lincoln," (New York: Charles Scribner's, January 1893), 13, 36.
6. Rembert Wallace Patrick, *The Reconstruction of the Nation* (New York: Oxford University Press, 1967), 53.
7. David Donald, *Lincoln* (New York: Simon & Schuster, 1995), 582–83.
8. Julian W. George, *Political Recollections* (Chicago: Jansen, McClurg, 1884), 260–61.
9. Claudia Goldin and Frank Lewis, "The Economic Cost of the American Civil War: Estimates and Implications," *Journal of Economic History*, 35, 1975, 294–396.

10. Hummel, *Emancipating Slaves*, 294.

11. Nevins, *War for the Union*, 374–75.

12. Robert Gallman, "Commodity Output 1839–99," in *National Bureau of Economic Research, Trends in the American Economy in the 19th Century*, vol. 24, Series on Income and Wealth (Princeton: Princeton University Press, 1960); Charles and Mary Beard, *The Rise of American Civilization* (New York: Macmillan, 1927); Stanley Engerman, "The Economic Impact of the Civil War," *Explorations in Economic History*, 3, 1966, 176–99; Jeffrey Williamson, "Watersheds and Turning Points: Conjectures on the Long Term Impact of Civil War Financing," *Journal of Economic History*, 34, 1974, 631–61.

13. Carl Schurz, *The Reminiscences of Carl Schurz*, 3 vols. (New York: The McClure Company, 1907–8), 3:167.

14. Ibid.

15. James G. Randall, *The Civil War and Reconstruction*, 693.

16. Ibid., 694.

17. Tindall and Shi, *America*, 1:792.

18. Ibid., 1:793.

19. Ibid., 1:792.

20. Richard Easterlin, "Regional Income Trends, 1840–1950," in Robert W. Fogel and Stanley I. Engerman, eds., *The Reinterpretation of American Economic History* (New York: Harper & Row, 1971), Table 1.

21. Atack and Passel, *A New Economic View of American History*, 379.

22. Berkin, et al., *Making America*, 476.

23. Hummel, *Emancipating Slaves*, 296.

24. Joseph Reid, "Sharecropping as an Understandable Market Response: The Postbellum South," *Journal of Economic History*, 33, 1973, 106–30; Robert Higgs, *Competition and Coercion: Blacks in the American Economy, 1865–1914* (New York: Cambridge University Press, 1977); and Stephen J. Decanio, "Productivity and Income Distribution in the Postbellum South," *Journal of Economic History*, 34, 1974, 422–46.

25. Roger Ransom and Richard Sutch, *One Kind of Freedom: The Economic Consequences of Emancipation* (Cambridge: Cambridge University Press, 1977); and their articles, "The Impact of the Civil War and of Emancipation on Southern Agriculture," *Explorations in Economic History*, 12, 1975, 1–28; "The Ex-Slave in the Postbellum South: A Study of the Impact of Racism in a Market Environment," *Journal of Economic History*, 33, 1973, 131–48; and "Debt Peonage in the Cotton South after the Civil War," *Journal of Economic History*, 32, 1972, 641–679.

26. Robert A. Margo, "Accumulation of Property by Southern Blacks Before World War I: Comment and Further Evidence," *American Economic Review*, 74, 1984, 768–76.

27. Robert C. Kenzer, *Black Economic Success in North Carolina, 1865–1995* (Charlottesville: University Press of Virginia, 1989), 18, table 5.

28. Theodore Rosengarten, *All God's Dangers: The Life of Nate Shaw* (New York: Alfred A. Knopf, 1974).

29. "Andrew Jackson Beard," in *A Salute to Black Scientists and Inventors*, vol. 2 (Chicago: Empak Enterprises and Richard L. Green, n.d.), 6.

30. Robert C. Kenzer, "The Black Business Community in Post Civil War Virginia," *Southern Studies*, new series, 4, Fall 1993, 229–52.

31. Kenzer, "Black Business," passim.

32. Leon Litwack, *Been in the Storm So Long: The Aftermath of Slavery* (New York: Vintage, 1980), 8.

33. Ibid., 18.

34. Ibid., 298.

35. Louis R. Harlan, *Booker T. Washington: The Making of a Black Leader, 1865–1901* (New York: Oxford, 1972), and his *Booker T. Washington: The Wizard of Tuskegee, 1901–1915* (New York: Oxford, 1983).

36. Walter I. Fleming, *Documentary History of Reconstruction: Political, Military, Social, Religious, Educational and Industrial, 1865 to the Present Time* vol. 1 (Cleveland, Ohio: Arthur H. Clark, 1905), 231–33.

37. Rembert W. Patrick, *The Reconstruction of the Nation* (New York: Oxford, 1967), 42.

38. David E. Bernstein, *Only One Place of Redress: African-Americans, Labor Relations and the Courts from Reconstruction to the New Deal* (Durham: Duke University Press, 2001).

39. Hummel, *Emancipating Slaves*, 317.

40. William S. McFeely, *Yankee Stepfather: O. O. Howard and the Freedmen's Bureau* (New York: Norton, 1968), 22.
41. Ibid., 33, 85.
42. Ibid., 89. See also Timothy L. Smith, *Revivalism and Social Reform in Mid-Century America* (New York: Harper & Row, 1957).
43. McFeely, *Yankee Stepfather*, 105.
44. Litwack, *Been in the Storm So Long*, 376.
45. Ibid., 386.
46. McFeely, *Yankee Stepfather*, 92.
47. Kenneth M. Stampp, *The Era of Reconstruction, 1865–1877* (New York: Vintage, 1963), 102.
48. Ibid., 102.
49. Ibid., 104–5.
50. Randall, *Civil War and Reconstruction*, 723.
51. Hummel, *Emancipating Slaves*, 299.
52. Patrick, *Reconstruction of the Nation*, 71.
53. Hummel, *Emancipating Slaves*, 299.
54. U.S. Statutes at Large, 14 (April 9, 1866), 27.
55. James E. Sefton, *Andrew Johnson and the Uses of Constitutional Power* (Boston: Little, Brown, 1980), 132.
56. Kenneth E. Mann, "Blanche Kelso Bruce: United States Senator Without a Constituency," *Journal of Mississippi History*, 3, May 1976, 183–98; William C. Harris, "Blanche K. Bruce of Mississippi: Conservative Assimilationist," in Howard N. Rabinowitz, ed., *Southern Black Leaders of the Reconstruction Era* (Urbana, IL: University of Illinois Press, 1982), 3–38; Samuel L. Shapiro, "A Black Senator from Mississippi: Blanche K. Bruce (1841–1898)," *Review of Politics*, 44, January 1982, 83–109.
57. Stampp, *Era of Reconstruction*, 174.
58. Ibid., 175.
59. Ibid.
60. Michael Perman, *The Road to Redemption: Southern Politics, 1869–1879* (Chapel Hill: University of North Carolina Press, 1984), 74–75.
61. John Hope Franklin, *Reconstruction After the Civil War* (Chicago: University of Chicago Press, 1961), 76.
62. Ibid.
63. Ibid., 77.
64. Frank P. Blair to Samuel J. Tilden, July 15, 1868, in John Bigelow, ed., *Letters and Literary Memorials of Samuel J. Tilden*, vol. 1 (New York: Harper & Brothers, 1908), 241.
65. David Montgomery, *Beyond Equality: Labor and the Radical Republican, 1862–1872* (New York: Alfred A. Knopf, 1967), 353.
66. Allan Nevins, *Hamilton Fish: The Inner History of the Grant Administration* (New York: Dodd Mead, 1936), 131–36.
67. Ulysses S. Grant, *Personal Memoirs of U. S. Grant* (New York: Smithmark, 1994).
68. Geoffrey Perret, *Ulysses S. Grant: Soldier and President* (New York: Random House, 1997).
69. James K. Medbury, *Men and Mysteries of Wall Street* (New York: Fields, Osgood, 1870), 264–65; Kenneth D. Acerman, *The Gold Ring: Jim Fisk, Jay Gould and Black Friday, 1869* (New York: Harper Business, 1988).
70. Burton Folsom Jr., *Myth of the Robber Barons: A New Look at the Rise of Big Business in America* (Herndon, VA: Young America's Foundation, 1991), 18.
71. Ibid.
72. Ibid.
73. Stephen E. Ambrose, *Nothing Like It in the World: The Men Who Built the Transcontinental Railroad, 1863–1869* (New York: Simon & Schuster, 2000).
74. Robert W. Fogel, *The Union Pacific Railroad: A Case of Premature Enterprise* (Baltimore: Johns Hopkins University Press, 1960); Jay Boyd Crawford, *The Credit Mobilier of America: Its Origins and History, Its Work of Constructing the Union Pacific Railroad and the Relation of Members of Congress Therewith* (New York: Greenwood Press, 1969).
75. Mark W. Summers, *The Era of Good Stealings* (New York: Oxford, 1993).
76. Perman, *Road to Redemption*, 135.

77. Ibid., 191.
78. Ibid., 217.
79. Ibid., 277.
80. Jennifer Roback, "The Political Economy of Segregation: The Case of Segregated Streetcars," *Journal of Political Economy*, 46, December 1986, 893–917.
81. Gillon and Matson, *American Experiment*, 635.
82. Ibid., 636.
83. Ari Hoogenboom, *Rutherford B. Hayes: Warrior and President* (Lawrence, KS: University Press of Kansas, 1995), 187.
84. Hayes quoted in Hoogenboom, *Rutherford B. Hayes*, 199.
85. Hoogenboom, *Rutherford B. Hayes*, 260.
86. Ibid., 278.

Chapter 11. Lighting Out for the Territories, 1861–90

1. Mark Twain, *Roughing It* (New York: Signet, 1962 [1872]), 29–30.
2. Howard R. Lamar, ed., *The New Encyclopedia of the American West* (New Haven: Yale University Press, 1998); Clyde A. Milner II, Carol A. O'Connor, Martha A. Sandweiss, eds., *The Oxford History of the American West* (New York: Oxford, 1994).
3. Frederick Jackson Turner, "The Significance of the Frontier in American History," presented at the American Historical Association, Chicago, 1893, and his *The Frontier in American History* (New York: Holt, 1935). Biographical works on Turner include Allan G. Bogue, *Frederick Jackson Turner* (Norman, OK: University of Oklahoma Press, 1998); Ray A. Billington, *Frederick Jackson Turner: Historian, Teacher, and Scholar* (New York: Oxford, 1973).
4. George Rogers Taylor, *The Transportation Revolution, 1815–1860* (New York: Holt Rinehart, 1962); Guy S. Callender, "The Early Transportation and Banking Enterprises of the States in Relation to the Growth of the Corporation," *Quarterly Journal of Economics*, 17 (1902), 111–62; and Albert Fishlow, "Internal Transportation," in Lance Davis, et al., eds., *American Economic Growth* (New York: Harper & Row, 1972), 468–547; Carlos Schwantes, *Long Day's Journey: The Steamboat and Stagecoach Era in the Northern West* (Seattle: University of Washington Press, 1999).
5. Daniel B. Klein, "The Voluntary Provision of Public Goods? The Turnpike Companies of Early America," *Economic Inquiry*, October 1990, 788–812; David Beito, "From Privies to Boulevards: The Private Supply of Infrastructure in the United States During the Nineteenth Century," in Jerry Jenkins and David E. Sisk, eds., *The Voluntary Supply of Public Goods and Services* (San Francisco: Institute for Contemporary Studies, 1993), 23–49; Christopher T. Baer, Daniel B. Klein, and John Majewski, "From Trunk to Branch Toll Roads in New York, 1800–1860," in Edwin Perkins, ed., *Essays in Economic and Business History*, 11 (1992), 191–209.
6. John D. Unruh, *The Plains Across: The Overland Emigrants and the Trans-Mississippi West, 1840–60* (Urbana, IL: University of Illinois Press, 1993) documented only 350 deaths from Indian attacks between 1840 and 1860.
7. Don Rickey Jr., *$10 Horse, $40 Saddle* (Lincoln, NB: University of Nebraska Press, 1976).
8. Edward Hungerford, *Wells Fargo, Advancing the American Frontier* (New York: Random House, 1949); Noel L. Loomis, *Wells Fargo* (New York: Bramhall House, 1968).
9. Louis C. Hunter, *Steamboats on the Western Rivers: An Economic and Technological History* (Cambridge: Harvard University Press, 1949).
10. Douglas J. Puffert, "The Standardization of Track Gauge on North American Railways, 1830–1890," *Journal of Economic History*, 60, December 2000, 933–60.
11. Carlos Schwantes, *The Pacific Northwest*, 2nd. ed. (Lincoln: University of Nebraska Press, 1996), 193–99.
12. William L. Lang, "Using and Abusing Abundance: The Western Resource Economy and the Environment," in Michael P. Malone, ed., *Historians and the American West* (Lincoln: University of Nebraska Press, 1983); Donald Worster, *Under Western Skies: Nature and History in the American West* (New York: Oxford University Press, 1992); John Opie, "The Environment and the Frontier," in Roger L. Nichols, ed., *American Frontier and Western Issues: A Historiographical Review* (Westport, CT: Greenwood Press, 1986); Terry L. Anderson and Donald R. Leal, "Free Market Versus Political Environmentalism," in Michael E. Zimmerman, ed., *Environ-*

mental Philosophy: From Animal Rights to Radical Ecology (Upper Saddle River, NJ: Prentice-Hall, 1998), 364–74.

13. Vernon Carstensen, *The Public Lands: Studies in the History of the Public Domain* (Madison: University of Wisconsin Press, 1962); Paul Wallace Gates, *History of Public Land Law Development* (Washington, DC: U.S. Government Printing Office, 1968).

14. Richard White, "It's Your Misfortune and None of My Own": *A History of the American West* (Norman, OK: University of Oklahoma Press, 1991); Patricia Limerick, *The Legacy of Conquest: The Unbroken Past of the American West* (New York: Norton, 1987); Douglass C. North, *Growth and Welfare in the American Past* (Englewood Cliffs, NJ: Prentice-Hall, 1966); Ronald Coase, "The Problem of Social Cost," *Journal of Law and Economics*, 3 (1960), 1–44.

15. John D. Haegar, "Business Strategy and Practice in the Early Republic: John Jacob Astor and the American Fur Trade," *Western Historical Quarterly*, May 1988, 183–202; Hiram M. Chittenden, *The American Fur Trade of the Far West*, 3 vols. (New York: Francis M. Harper, 1902); Michael F. Konig, "John Jacob Astor," in Larry Schweikart, ed., *Encyclopedia of American Business History and Biography: Banking and Finance to 1913* (New York: Facts on File, 1990), 13–25; Kenneth W. Porter, *John Jacob Astor, Business Man*, 2 vols. (Cambridge: Harvard University Press, 1931). On banking, see Lynne Pierson Doti and Larry Schweikart, *Banking in the American West from the Gold Rush to Deregulation* (Norman, OK: University of Oklahoma Press, 1991), passim.

16. Terry L. Anderson and Donald R. Leal, "Fishing for Property Rights to Fish," in Roger E. Meiners and Bruce Yandle, eds., *Taking the Environment Seriously* (Lanham, MD: Rowman & Littlefield, 1993), 161–84.

17. Robert Sobel and David B. Sicilia, *The Entrepreneurs: An American Adventure* (Boston: Houghton Mifflin, 1986), and Schweikart, *The Entrepreneurial Adventure*, 200–2.

18. Stephen J. Pyne, *Fire in America: A Cultural History of Wildland and Rural Fire* (Princeton: Princeton University Press, 1982), 11.

19. W. E. Haskell, *The International Paper Company: 1898–1924: Its Origins and Growth in a Quarter of a Century with a Brief Description of the Manufacture of Paper from Harvesting Pulpwood to the Finished Roll* (New York: International Paper, 1924).

20. Clinton Woods, *Ideas that Became Big Business* (Baltimore: Founders, Inc., 1959), 110.

21. Thomas R. Cox, *Mills and Markets: A History of the Pacific Coast Lumber Industry to 1900* (Seattle: University of Washington Press, 1974); Thomas R. Cox, et al., *This Well-Wooded Land: Americans and Their Forests from Colonial Times to the Present* (Lincoln, NB: University of Nebraska Press, 1985); Michael Williams, *Americans and Their Forests: A Historical Geography* (Cambridge: Cambridge University Press, 1989).

22. Don Worcester, *The Texas Longhorn: Relic of the Past, Asset for the Future* (College Station, Texas: Texas A&M University Press, 1987).

23. Jimmy M. Skaggs, *The Cattle Trailing Industry: Between Supply and Demand* (Lawrence, KS: University of Kansas Press, 1973).

24. Richard White, "Animals and Enterprise," in Milner, et al., eds, *Oxford History of the American West*, 237–73; Maruice Frink, et al., *When Grass was King: Contribution to the Western Range Cattle Industry Study* (Boulder: University of Colorado Press, 1956).

25. Robert M. Dykstra, *The Cattle Towns* (New York: Knopf, 1968).

26. Jimmy M. Skaggs, *Prime Cut: Livestock Raising and Meat-packing in the United States* (College Station: Texas A&M University Press, 1986); Ernest S. Osgood, *The Day of the Cattleman* (Minneapolis: University of Minnesota Press, 1929).

27. J. Marvin Hunter, *The Trail Drivers of Texas* (New York: Argosy-Antiquarian, 1963).

28. Richard Maxwell Brown, "Western Violence: Structure, Values, Myth," *Western Historical Quarterly*, February 1993, 5–10; and his *No Duty to Retreat: Violence and Values in American History and Society* (New York: Oxford, 1991).

29. Roger McGrath, *Gunfighters, Highwaymen & Vigilantes: Violence on the Frontier* (Berkeley: University of California Press, 1984).

30. Dykstra, *The Cattle Towns*, passim.

31. Paul Wallace Gates, *Free Homesteads for all Americans: The Homestead Act of 1862* (Washington, Civil War Centennial Commission, 1962); David M. Ellis et al., *The Frontier in American Developments: Essays in Honor of Paul Wallace Gates* (Ithaca: Cornell University Press, 1969); David B. Danbom, *Born in the Country: A History of Rural America* (Baltimore: Johns Hopkins

University Press, 1995); Morton Rothstein, ed., *Quantitative Studies in Agrarian History* (Ames Iowa: Iowa State University Press, 1993).

32. Wayne Broehl Jr., *John Deere's Company: A History of Deere and Company and Its Times* (New York: Doubleday, 1984); Oliver E. Allen, "Bet-A-Million," *Audacity*, Fall 1996, 18–31; Schweikart, *Entrepreneurial Adventure*, 63–65.

33. John T. Schlebecker, *Whereby We Thrive: A History of American Farming, 1607–1972* (Ames: Iowa State University Press, 1975).

34. Gerald McFarland, *A Scattered People: An American Family Moves West* (New York: Pantheon, 1985).

35. Johnson, *A History of the American People*, 515.

36. Larry Schweikart, "John Warne Gates," in Paul Pascoff, ed., *Encyclopedia of American Business History and Biography: Iron and Steel in the 19th Century* (New York: Facts on File, 1989), 146–47.

37. Andrew C. Isenberg, *The Destruction of the Bison* (Cambridge: Cambridge University Press, 2000).

38. Isenberg, *Destruction of the Bison*, 23; Shepard Kretch III, *The Ecological Indian: Myth and History* (New York: W. W. Norton, 1999), 106.

39. Kretch, *Ecological Indian*, 213.

40. Isenberg, *Destruction of the Bison*, passim.

41. Frank Gilbert Roe, *The North American Buffalo: A Critical Study of the Species in Its Wild State* (Toronto: University of Toronto Press, 1951), 609.

42. Edwin Thompson Denig, *Five Indian Tribes of the Upper Missouri: Sioux, Arikaras, Assiniboines, Crees, Crows*, ed. John C. Dwers (Norman, OK: University of Oklahoma Press, 1961), 79.

43. Kretch, *Ecological Indian*, 128.

44. Isenberg, *Destruction of the Bison*, 84.

45. Alfred W. Crosby, *Ecological Imperialism: The Biological Expansion of Europe, 900–1900* (New York: Cambridge University Press, 1986); William Cronon, *Changes in the Land: Indians, Colonists, and the Ecology of New England* (New York: Hill and Wang, 1983).

46. The million-dollar figure includes all related expenses. Bernard Bailyn et al., *The Great Republic: A History of the American People* (Lexington, MA: D. C. Heath, 1985), 522.

47. Helen Hunt Jackson, *A Century of Dishonor: A Sketch of the United States Government's Dealings with Some of the Indian Tribes* (Boston: Little, Brown, 1903 [1885]).

48. Richard White, "The Winning of the West: The Expansion of the Western Sioux in the 18th and 19th Centuries," *Journal of American History*, September 1978, 319–43.

49. Paul A. Hutton, *Phil Sheridan and His Army* (Lincoln, NB: University of Nebraska Press, 1985).

50. Evan S. Connell, *Son of the Morning Star: Custer and the Little Bighorn* (San Francisco: North Point Press, 1984), 127.

51. Robert G. Athern, *William Tecumseh Sherman and the Settlement of the West* (Norman, OK: University of Oklahoma Press, 1956).

52. Connell, *Son of the Morning Star*, 127.

53. Robert A. Trennert, *Alternative to Extinction: Federal Indian Policy and the Beginnings of the Reservation System* (Philadelphia: Temple University Press, 1975); Francis Paul Prucha, *The Great Father* (Lincoln, NB: University of Nebraska Press, 1984); Bernard W. Sheehan, *Seeds of Extinction: Jeffersonian Philanthropy and the American Indian* (Chapel Hill: University of North Carolina Press, 1973).

54. Schwantes, *Pacific Northwest*, 568.

55. Robert M. Utley, *Frontier Regulars: The United States Army and the Indian, 1866–1891* (New York: Macmillan, 1973).

56. Connell, *Son of the Morning Star*, 126.

57. Clyde Milner, "National Initiatives" in Clyde A. Milner II, Carol A O'Connor, and Martha Sandweiss, eds., *The Oxford History of the American West* (New York: Oxford University Press, 1994), 174.

58. Ray Allen Billington, *Westward Expansion* (New York: McMillan, 1974), 570.

59. J. W. Vaughn, *Indian Fights: New Facts on Seven Encounters* (Norman, OK: University of Oklahoma Press, 1966).

60. Alexander B. Adams, *Sitting Bull: An Epic of the Plains* (New York: Putnam, 1973); Joseph Mazione, *I Am Looking to the North for My Life: Sitting Bull, 1876–1881* (Salt Lake City: University of Utah Press, 1991).

61. John W. Bailey, *Pacifying the Plains: General Alfred Terry and the Decline of the Sioux, 1866–1890* (Westport, CT: Greenwood Press, 1979).

62. Doane Robinson, ed., "Crazy Horse's Story of the Custer Battle," *South Dakota Historical Collections*, vol. 6 (1912); Edgar I. Stewart, "Which Indian Killed Custer?" *Montana: The Magazine of Western History*, vol. 8 (1958).

63. Robert M. Utley, *The Lance and the Shield: The Life and Times of Sitting Bull* (New York: Holt, 1993).

64. Robert Utley, *The Last Days of the Sioux Nation* (New Haven: Yale, 1963); James Mooney, *The Ghost Dance: Religion and the Sioux Outbreak of 1890* (Chicago: University of Chicago Press, 1965).

65. Alyn Brodsky, *Grover Cleveland: A Study in Character* (New York: Truman Talley, 2000), 139.

66. Brodsky, *Grover Cleveland*, 139.

67. Peter Micelmore, "Uprising in Indian Country," *Reader's Digest*, reprint, November 1984; Andrew E. Serwer, "American Indians Discover Money Is Power," *Fortune*, reprint from Choctaw tribe, April 19, 1993.

68. Schweikart, *Entrepreneurial Adventure*, 575–76.

69. Kent D. Richards, *Isaac Ingalls Stevens: Young Man in a Hurry* (Provo, UT: Brigham Young University Press, 1979), passim.

70. Leonard J. Arrington, *The Mormon Experience: A History of the Latter-Day Saints* (New York: Vintage, 1979), and his *Great Basin Kingdom* (Cambridge: Harvard University Press, 1958).

71. Ken Verdoia and Richard Firmage, *Utah: The Struggle for Statehood* (Salt Lake City: University of Utah Press, 1996).

72. Howard R. Lamar, *The Far Southwest, 1846–1912* (New Haven: Yale University Press, 1966).

73. Victoria Wyatt, "Alaska and Hawaii," in Milner, ed., *Oxford History of the American West*, 565–601.

74. Noel J. Kent, *Hawaii: Islands Under the Influence* (New York: Monthly Review Press, 1983).

75. Harry N. Scheiber, "The Road to Munn," in Bernard Bailyn and Donald Fleming, *Perspectives in American History: Law in American History* (Boston: Little, Brown, 1971); Robert C. McMath Jr., *American Populism: A Social History* (New York: Hill and Wang, 1993).

76. Jeremy Atack and Fred Bateman, "How Long was the Workday in 1880?" *Journal of Economic History*, March 1992, 129–60; Robert Whaples, "The Great Decline in the Length of the Workweek," working paper, University of Wisconsin-Milwaukee, 1988; Albert Rees, *Real Wages in Manufacturing, 1890–1914* (Princeton: Princeton University Press, 1961); Clarence D. Long, *Wages and Earnings in the United States, 1860–1890* (Princeton: Princeton University Press, 1960).

77. Milton Friedman and Anna J. Schwartz, *A Monetary History of the United States, 1863–1960* (Princeton: Princeton University Press, 1963).

78. Schweikart, *Entrepreneurial Adventure*, chap. 5; Jac C. Heckelman and John Joseph Wallis, "Railroads and Property Taxes," *Explorations in Economic History*, 34 (1997), 77–99; Albro Martin, "The Troubled Subject of Railroad Regulation in the Gilded Age—a Reappraisal," *Journal of American History*, September 1974, 339–71; George H. Miller, *Railroads and the Granger Laws* (Madison: University of Wisconsin Press, 1971); Jack Blicksilver, *The Defenders and Defense of Big Business in the United States, 1880–1900* (New York: Garland, 1985).

79. George B. Tindall, "Populism: A Semantic Identity Crisis," *Virginia Quarterly Review*, 48, 1972, 501–18.

80. William Jennings Bryan, "Cross of Gold," July 9, 1896, in A. Craig Baird, *American Public Address* (New York: McGraw-Hill, 1956), 194–200.

81. Richard Hofstadter, *The Age of Reform, From Bryan to F.D.R.* (New York: Knopf, 1955).

Chapter 12. Sinews of Democracy, 1876–96

1. H. Wayne Morgan, *From Hayes to McKinley: National Party Politics, 1877–1896* (Syracuse: Syracuse University Press, 1969), 15–16.

2. Morgan, *From Hayes to McKinley*, 31.

3. Gillon and Matson, *American Experiment*, 774.

4. Morgan, *From Hayes to McKinley*, 39.

5. Ari Hoogenboom, *Rutherford B. Hayes: Warrior and President* (Lawrence, KS: University Press of Kansas, 1995), 366.

6. Morgan, *From Hayes to McKinley*, 33.

7. Ibid., 56.

8. Ibid., 117.

9. Justus D. Doenecke, *The Presidencies of James A. Garfield and Chester A. Arthur* (Lawrence, KS: University of Kansas Press, 1981).

10. See the Lincoln family website, http://home. att. net/~rjnorton/Lincoln66.html.

11. James C. Clark, *The Murder of James A. Garfield: The President's Last Days and the Trial and Execution of His Assassin* (Jefferson, North Carolina: McFarland & Company, 1993).

12. John G. Sproat, *The Best Men: Liberal Reformers in the Gilded Age* (New York: Oxford, 1968).

13. Harry Elmer Barnes, *Society in Transition: Problems of a Changing Age* (New York: Prentice-Hall, 1939), 448.

14. Barnes, *Society in Transition*, 449.

15. Ibid.

16. William P. Mason, *Water-Supply* (New York: Wiley and Sons, 1897), 466.

17. Earle Lytton Waterman, *Elements of Water Supply Engineering* (New York: Wiley and Sons, 1934), 6; Martin V. Melosi, *The Sanitary City: Urban Infrastructure in America from Colonial Times to the Present* (Baltimore: Johns Hopkins University Press, 2000).

18. Robin Einhorn, *Property Rules: Political Economy in Chicago, 1833–1872* (Chicago: University of Chicago Press, 1991), 16–19.

19. Paul Robert Lyons, *Fire in America!* (Boston: National Fire Protection Association, 1976), 52–54.

20. Stephen J. Pyne, *Fire in America: A Cultural History of Wildland and Rural Fire* (Seattle: University of Washington Press, 1982), 92.

21. Martin Gilbert, *A History of the Twentieth Century, 1900–1933*, vol. 1 (New York: Avon, 1997), 182.

22. Joseph Wall, *Andrew Carnegie* (New York: Oxford University Press, 1970); Andrew Carnegie, *Autobiography of Andrew Carnegie* (Boston: Houghton Mifflin, 1920); Stuart Leslie, "Andrew Carnegie," in Pascoff, ed., *Encyclopedia of American Business History and Biography: Iron and Steel in the 19th Century*, 47–41.

23. Schweikart, *Entrepreneurial Adventure*, 202–8.

24. Johnson, *History of the American People*, 554.

25. Allan Nevins, *A Study in Power: John D. Rockefeller*, 2 vols. (New York: Charles Scribner's, 1953), 1:328.

26. Leslie, "Andrew Carnegie," 69.

27. Johnson, *A History of the American People*, 552.

28. Schweikart, *Entrepreneurial Adventure*, 207.

29. Joseph Dorfman, *The Economic Mind in American Civilization*, 5 vols. (New York: Augustus M. Kelly, 1969), 3:117; Ida M. Tarbell, *The History of Standard Oil Company*, abridged, David M. Chalmers, ed. (New York: Norton, 1969), 27.

30. Schweikart, *Entrepreneurial Adventure*, 250.

31. D. T. Armentano, *The Myths of Antitrust: Economic Theory and Legal Cases* (New Rochelle, New York: Arlington House, 1972), 77.

32. Nevins, *Study in Power*, 2:76; 1:277–79.

33. John S. McGee, "Predatory Price-cutting: The Standard Oil (N.J.) Case," *Journal of Law and Economics*, October 1958, 137–69, quotation on 138.

34. Alfred D. Chandler Jr., *Visible Hand: The Managerial Revolution in American Business* (Cambridge: Harvard, 1977).

35. Ray Ginger, *Age of Excess: The United States from 1877 to 1914*, 2nd ed. (Prospect Heights, IL: Waveland Press, 1989), 34–35.

36. Joseph J. Fuchini and Suzy Fuchini, *Entrepreneurs: The Men and Women Behind Famous Brand Names and How They Made It* (Boston: G. K. Hall, 1985), 102–5; Lewis F. Smith and Arthur Van Vlissington, *The Yankee of the Yards* (New York: A. W. Shaw, 1928); Mary Yeager Kujovich, "The Refrigerator Car and the Growth of the American Dressed Beef Industry," *Business History Review*, 44, 1970, 460–82; "Armour & Company, 1867–1938," in N.S.B. Gras and Henrietta Larson, *Case Book in American Business History* (New York: F. S. Crofts, 1939), 623–43.

37. Alfried Leif, *"It Floats," The Story of Procter and Gamble* (New York: Holt, Rinehart and Winston, 1958); Alecia Swasy, *Soap Opera: The Inside Story of Procter and Gamble* (New York: Times Books, 1993).

38. Scott Derks, *Working Americans, 1880–1999*, vol. 1 (Lakeville, CT: Grey House Publishers, 2000), 12.

39. Derks, *Working Americans, 1880–1999*, I:26–27.

40. Dorothy and Thomas Hoobler, *The Irish American Family Album* (New York: Oxford University Press, 1995); James P. Mitchell, *How American Buying Habits Change* (Washington, DC: U.S. Department of Labor, 1959); James Michael Russell, *Atlanta, 1847–1890* (Baton Rouge: Louisiana State University Press, 1988); Derks, *Working Americans, 1880–1999*, I:17–25.

41. Matthew Josephson, *The Robber Barons: The Great American Capitalist 1861–1901* (New York: Harcourt Brace, 1934), 338 and chap. 14, passim.

42. Atack and Passell, *New Economic View of American History*, 414; James Stock, "Real Estate Mortgages, Foreclosures and Midwestern Agrarian Unrest, 1865–1920," *Journal of Economic History*, 44, 1984, 89–105; David B. Danbom, *Born in the Country* (Baltimore: Johns Hopkins University Press, 1995).

43. Schweikart, *Entrepreneurial Adventure*, 231; Stanley Lebergott, *Manpower in Economic Growth: The American Record Since 1800* (New York: McGraw-Hill, 1964), 524.

44. Clarence D. Long, *Wages and Earnings in the United States, 1860–1890* (Princeton: Princeton University Press, 1960); Paul Douglas, *Real Wages in the United States, 1890–1926* (Boston: Houghton-Mifflin, 1930).

45. Kenneth L. Sokoloff and Georgia C. Villafor, "The Market for Manufacturing Workers During Early Industrialization: The American Northeast, 1820–1860," in *Strategic Factors in Nineteenth Century American Economic History: A Volume to Honor Robert W. Fogel* (Chicago: University of Chicago Press, 1992), 36.

46. Burton Folsom Jr., "Like Fathers, Unlike Sons: The Fall of the Business Elite in Scranton, Pennsylvania, 1880–1920," *Pennsylvania History*, 46, October 1980, 291–309.

47. Daniel Aaron, *Men of Good Hope* (New York: Oxford, 1961).

48. Mark Alan Hewitt, *The Architect and the American Country House* (New Haven: Yale University Press, 1990), 133; David M. Potter, *People of Plenty: Economic Abundance and the American Character* (Chicago: University of Chicago Press, 1954).

49. Johnson, *History of the American People*, 567.

50. McClellan, *Changing Interpretations of America's Past*, 2:92.

51. Harold C. Livesay, *Samuel Gompers and Organized Labor in America* (Boston: Little, Brown, 1978), 8–9.

52. Ibid., 21.

53. Tindall and Shi, *America*, 2:918; Samuel Gompers, *Seventy Years of Life and Labor*, 2 vols. (New York: E. P. Dutton, 1925).

54. Livesay, *Samuel Gompers*, 50.

55. 1873 WL 8416 (Ill.), otherwise known as *Munn v. Illinois* when it reached the United States Supreme Court.

56. William Michael Treanor, "The Original Understanding of the Takings Clause and the Political Process," *Columbia Law Review*, May 1995, available online at http://www.law.georgetown.edu/gelpi/papers/treanor. htm; Anthony Saul Alperin, "The 'Takings' Clause: When Does Regulation 'Go Too Far'?" *Southwestern University Law Review*, 2002, 169–235.

57. Lease quoted in A. James Reichley, *The Life of the Parties: A History of American Political Parties* (Lanham, MD: Rowman & Littlefield, 1992), 135.

58. Schweikart, *Entrepreneurial Adventure*, 120–25; Gregory J. Millman, *The Vandals' Crown: How Rebel Currency Traders Overthrew the World's Central Banks* (New York: Free Press, 1995); Jonathan Lurie, *The Chicago Board of Trade, 1859–1905* (Urbana, IL: University of Illinois Press, 1979).

59. William "Coin" Harvey, *Coin's Financial School* (Chicago: Coin Publishing Company, 1894).

60. Sarah E. V. Emery, *Seven Financial Conspiracies That Have Enslaved the American People* (Westport, CT: Hyperion Press, 1975 [1887]); Mary Elizabeth Lease, *The Problem of Civilization Solved* (Chicago: Laird and Lee, 1895).

61. Richard Hofstadter, *The Age of Reform: Bryan to FDR* (Cambridge: Harvard University Press, 1955); Walter T. K. Nugent, *The Tolerant Populists: Kansas Populism and Nativism* (Chicago: University of Chicago Press, 1963).

62. Gillon and Matson, *American Experiment*, 761.

63. Ibid.

64. Alexander B. Callow Jr., *The Tweed Ring* (New York: Oxford, 1966), 145.

65. Mabel Dodge Luhan, *Edge of Taos Desert* (New York: Harcourt, Brace, 1937), 216–19.
66. Christopher Lasch, *The New Radicalism in America, 1889–1963* (New York: Knopf, 1966), 9.
67. Lasch, *New Radicalism*, 17; Jane Addams, *Twenty Years at Hull-house, With Autobiographical Notes* (New York: Macmillan Co., 1910).
68. Lasch, *New Radicalism*, 260.
69. Phillip Shaw Paludan, "Religion and the American Civil War," in Randall M. Miller, Harry S. Stout, and Charles Reagan Wilson, eds., *Religion and the American Civil War* (New York: Oxford, 1998), 24–40, quotations on 35.
70. The "Forgotten Man" is available at http://www.blupete.com/Literature/Essays/Best/Sumner Forgotten.htm.
71. http://www.blupete.com/Literature/Essays/Best/SumnerForgotten.htm.
72. Richard Hofstadter, *Social Darwinism in American Thought, 1860–1915* (Philadelphia: University of Pennsylvania Press, 1944).
73. See Staughton Lynd, "Jane Addams and the Radical Impulse," *Commentary*, 32, July 1961, 54–59.
74. John P. Burke, *The Institutional Presidency* (Baltimore: Johns Hopkins University Press, 1992).
75. Alyn Brodsky, *Grover Cleveland: A Study in Character* (New York: Truman Talley Books, 2000), 92.
76. Robert W. Cherny, *American Politics in the Gilded Age, 1868–1900* (Wheeling, Illinois: Harlan-Davidson, 1997), 1.
77. Mary R. Dearing, *Veterans in Politics: The Story of G.A.R.* (Westport, CT: Greenwood Press, 1974).
78. Brodsky, *Grover Cleveland*, 181–82.
79. Ibid., 182.
80. Paul Kleppner, *The Cross of Culture: A Social Analysis of Midwestern Politics, 1850–1900* (New York: Free Press, 1970).
81. Homer E. Socolofsky and Allan B. Spetter, *The Presidency of Benjamin Harrison* (Lawrence, KS: University Press of Kansas, 1987), 33.
82. In the past twenty years, a number of studies have appeared that question both the efficiency and the legal basis for antitrust legislation. See James Langefeld and David Scheffman, "Evolution or Revolution: What Is the Future of Antitrust?" *Antitrust Bulletin*, 31, Summer 1986, 287–99; Robert H. Bork, *The Antitrust Paradox: A Policy at War with Itself* (New York: Basic Books, 1978); Harold Demsetz, "Barriers to Entry," *American Economic Review*, 72, March 1982, 47–57; Yale Brozen, "Concentration and Profits: Does Concentration Matter?" *Antitrust Bulletin*, 19, 1974, 381–99; Franklin M. Fisher and John L. McGowan, "On the Misuse of Accounting Rates of Return to Infer Monopoly Profits," *American Economic Review*, 73, March 1983, 82–97; Dominick T. Armentano, *Antitrust and Monopoly* (New York: Holmes & Meier, 1982).
83. Stuart Bruchey, *The Wealth of the Nation: An Economic History of the United States* (New York: Harper & Row, 1988), 124.
84. Chandler, *Visible Hand*, 110–18.
85. Schweikart, *Entrepreneurial Adventure*, 195–97.
86. Naomi Lamoreaux, *The Great Merger Movement in American Business, 1895–1904* (Cambridge: Cambridge University Press, 1985); Louis Galambos and Joseph C. Pratt, *The Rise of the Corporate Commonwealth: U.S. Business and Public Policy in the Twentieth Century* (New York: Basic Books, 1988).
87. Brodsky, *Grover Cleveland*, 356.
88. Ibid., 363.
89. Ibid., 387.
90. Ibid., 422.

Chapter 13. "Building Best, Building Greatly," 1896–1912

1. "The Average American," *Current Literature*, 31, 1901, 421; George E. Mowry, *The Era of Theodore Roosevelt and the Birth of Modern America, 1900–1912* (New York: Harper Torchbooks, 1958), 2–3.
2. Scott Derks, *The Value of a Dollar: Prices and Incomes in the United States, 1860–1999* (Lakeville, CT: Grey House Publishing, 1999), 74.
3. Ibid., 73.

4. Derks, *Working Americans*, 57.
5. Ibid., 62.
6. Leon Trotsky, *My Life: An Attempt at an Autobiography* (New York: Charles Scribner's, 1930), 274.
7. Seymour Martin Lipset and Gary Marks, *It Didn't Happen Here: Why Socialism Failed in the United States* (New York: W. W. Norton, 2000), 16–17.
8. Ibid., 82.
9. Mowry, *Era of Theodore Roosevelt*, 5.
10. Louis Menand, *The Metaphysical Club* (New York: Farrar, Straus and Giroux, 2001), 353.
11. Linda Simon, *Genuine Reality: A Life of William James* (New York: Harcourt, 1998), xvi–xvii.
12. Ibid., xvii.
13. Ibid., 191.
14. Ibid., 232.
15. Ibid., 234.
16. A good summary of James's views is found at "William James and Pragmatism," http://expert.cc.purdue.edu/-miller91/
17. See Philip Jenkins, *Mystics and Messiahs: Cults and New Religions in American History* (New York: Oxford, 2000), 46–69.
18. Thomas Kinkade, *The Spirit of America* (Nashville: Thomas Nelson, 1998), 32.
19. Rhonda Thomas Tripp, compilers, *The International Thesaurus of Quotations* (New York: Thomas Y. Crowll, 1970), 1041.
20. Kinkade, *Spirit of America*, 109.
21. John. F. Kennedy, from Tripp, *Thesaurus*, 20.
22. H. Wayne Morgan, *William McKinley and His America* (Syracuse: Syracuse University Press, 1963), 23.
23. Quoted in Morgan, *William McKinley*, 185.
24. Ibid., 269.
25. Lewis L. Gould, *The Presidency of William McKinley* (Lawrence, KS: Regents Press of Kansas, 1980).
26. Ibid., 49.
27. Morgan, *William McKinley*, 295.
28. Denis Brian, *Pulitzer: A Life* (New York: John Wiley, 2001).
29. Morgan, *William McKinley*, 330.
30. Ibid., 356.
31. Ibid.
32. Frank Friedel, *The Splendid Little War* (New York: Bramhall House, 1959).
33. Leckie, *Wars of America*, 351.
34. Friedel, *Splendid Little War*, 22.
35. Leckie, *Wars of America*, 349.
36. Ibid., 556.
37. Pershing quoted on the San Juan Hill website, http://www.homeofheroes.com/wallofhonor/spanish_am/11_crowdedhour. html.
38. Leckie, *Wars of America*, 561.
39. Leon Wolff, *Little Brown Brother* (London: Longmans, 1961), 231.
40. Tindall and Shi, *America*, 2:1053.
41. Ibid., 2:1052.
42. Morris, *Rise of Theodore Roosevelt*, 719.
43. Morgan, *William McKinley*, 508.
44. Ibid., 521.
45. Brian Thornton, "When a Newspaper Was Accused of Killing a President," *Journalism History*, 26, Autumn 2000, 108–16, quotation on 108.
46. Edmund Morris, *The Rise of Theodore Roosevelt* (New York: Ballantine, 1979), 21.
47. Ibid., 22.
48. Ibid., 20.
49. Ibid., 314.
50. Ibid., 227.
51. Patrick F. Palermo, *Lincoln Steffens* (New York: Twayne, 1978), 15.
52. Johnson, *History of the American People*, 617; Theodore Rooseevelt, *Works* (New York: Charles

Scribner's, 1923–1926); H. C. Lodge and Theodore Roosevelt, eds., *Selections from the Correspondence of Theodore Roosevelt*, 2 vols. (New York: Da Capo Press, 1925).

53. Theodore Roosevelt, "Citizenship in a Republic," Speech at the Sorbonne, Paris, April 23, 1910, quoted online at http://www.theodoreroosevelt.org/life/quotes. htm.

54. Mowry, *Era of Theodore Roosevelt*, 113.

55. Ibid.

56. Schweikart, *Entrepreneurial Adventure*, 257.

57. George Bittlingmayer, "Antitrust and Business Activity: The First Quarter Century," *Business History Review*, Autumn 1996, available online at http://www._business._ku._edu/home/gbittlingmayer/research/Antitrustbusiness. pdf.

58. Tindall and Shi, *America*, 2:1086.

59. Ibid., 830.

60. Tindall and Shi, *America*, 2:1086.

61. Boyer, et al., *Enduring Vision*, 639.

62. Mowry, *Era of Theodore Roosevelt*, 132.

63. Ibid., 167.

64. Ibid., 205.

65. Roderick Nash, *The Wilderness in the American Mind* (New Haven: Yale University Press, 1967).

66. Shepard Kretch III, *The Ecological Indian: Myth and History* (New York: Norton, 1999), 21.

67. Andrew C. Isenberg, *Destruction of the Bison*, 189; Edmund Contoski, *Makers and Takers: How Wealth and Progress are Made and How They Are Taken Away or Prevented* (Minneapolis: American Liberty Publishers, 1997).

68. John Shelton Lawrence and Robert Jewett, *The Myth of the American Superhero* (Grand Rapids, MI: William B. Eerdmans Publishing, 2002), 58.

69. Tindall and Shi, *America*, 2:1065; Boyer, et al., *Enduring Vision*, 614.

70. *The Outlook*, editorial, 74, 1903, 961.

71. New York *Times*, March 25, 1911.

72. Quoted online at http://www.smplanet.com/imperialism/joining. html

73. Quoted at http://www. rose_hulman. edu/~delacova/canal/canal_history. htm.

74. Mowry, *Era of Theodore Roosevelt*, 159.

75. Judy Mohraz, *The Separate Problem: Case Studies of Black Education in the North, 1900–1930* (Westport, CT: Greenwood Press, 1979).

76. Quoted online at http://www.bowdoin.edu/~sbodurt2/court/cases/plessy. html

77. Robert L. Zangrando, *The NAACP Crusade Against Lynching, 1909–1950* (Philadelphia: Temple University Press, 1980); Stewart E. Tolnay and E. M. Beck, *Festival of Violence: An Analysis of Southern Lynchings, 1882–1930* (Urbana, IL: University of Illinois Press, 1995).

78. Gilbert Osofsky, *Harlem: The Making of a Ghetto* (New York: Harper Torchbooks, 1966), 4.

79. Ibid., 14.

80. Johnson, *History of the American People*, 665.

81. Alexander B. Callow Jr., *American Urban History: An Interpretive Reader with Commentaries* (New York: Oxford, 1969); James W. Johnson, *Black Manhattan* (New York: Alfred A. Knopf, 1930); Roi Ottley and William J. Weatherby, eds., *The Negro in New York: An Informal Social History, 1626–1940* (New York: Praeger, 1969).

82. Gilbert Osofsky, "Harlem Tragedy: An Emerging Slum," in Callow, *American Urban History*, 240–62.

83. Kathy Russell, Midge Wilson, Ronald Hall, *Color Complex: The Politics of Skin Color Among African Americans* (New York: Harcourt Brace Jovanovich, 1992).

84. Mowry, *Era of Theodore Roosevelt*, 220.

85. Ibid., 227.

86. Ibid., 239.

87. Ibid., 244–45.

88. Ibid., 230.

89. Ibid., 259.

90. Michael L. Bromley, *William Howard Taft and the First Motoring Presidency, 1909–1913* (Jefferson, North Carolina: McFarland & Company, 2003).

Chapter 14. War, Wilson, and Internationalism, 1912–20

1. Gilbert, *History of the Twentieth Century*, 185; Norman Angell, *The Great Illusion: A Study of the Relation of Military Power in Nations to Their Economic and Social Advantage*, 3rd ed. (New York: G. P. Putnam, 1911).
2. Ibid., 279.
3. Ibid., 51.
4. Ivan S. Bloch, *The Future of War in Its Technical, Economic, and Political Relations: Is War Now Impossible?* (New York: Doubleday & McClure, 1899).
5. Larry Schweikart, *The Entrepreneurial Adventure: A History of Business in the United States* (Fort Worth: Harcourt, 2000), 304–8; Folsom, *The Empire Builders: How Michigan Entrepreneurs Helped Make America Great*, passim; Henry Ford, in Jonathan R. T. Hughes, *The Vital Few: The Entrepreneurs and American Economic Progress*, exp. ed. (New York: Oxford University Press, 1986), 274–356; Allan Nevins and F. E. Hill, *Ford: The Times, the Man, the Company* (New York: Scribner's, 1954); Allan Nevins, *Ford: Expansion and Challenge, 1915–1933* (New York: Scribner's, 1957) and his *Ford: Decline and Rebirth, 1933–1962* (New York: Scribner's, 1963); Keith Sward, *The Legend of Henry Ford* (New York: Rinehart, 1948).
6. Folsom, *Empire Builders*, 142 and 171.
7. Schweikart, *Entrepreneurial Adventure*, 306.
8. Hughes, *Vital Few*, 292.
9. Schweikart, *Entrepreneurial Adventure*, 306.
10. Hughes, *Vital Few*, 306–23; Harold Livesay, *American Made: Men Who Shaped the American Economy* (Boston: Little, Brown, 1979), 159–72; David E. Kyvig and Myron A. Marty, *Nearby History: Exploring the Past Around You* (Nashville: American Association for State and Local History, 1982), 1–2; W. A. Simonds, *Henry Ford* (Los Angeles: F. Clymer, 1946).
11. Tom D. Crouch, *The Bishop's Boys: A Life of Wilbur and Orville Wright* (New York: W. W. Norton, 1989), 268.
12. Ibid., 368.
13. Robert R. Owens, *Speak to the Rock: The Azusa Street Revival: Its Roots and Its Message* (Lanham, MD: University Press of America, 1998), 53.
14. Rauedenbusch, *Christianity and the Social Crisis* (New York: Macmillan, 1907) and his *Christianity and the Social Order* (New York: Macmillan, 1915).
15. Goldfield, et al., *American Journey*, 673.
16. George Kibbe Turner, "The City of Chicago: A Study in Great Immoralities," *McClure's Magazine*, 30, April 1907, 575–92; Vice Commission of Chicago, *The Social Evil in Chicago* (Chicago: Vice Commission of Chicago, 1912).
17. Jane Addams, *A New Conscience and an Ancient Evil* (New York: Macmillan, 1912) and her *Twenty Years at Hull-House: With Autobiographical Notes* (New York: Macmillan, 1910) and *Peace and Bread in Time of War* (New York: Macmillan, 1922); John C. Farell, *Beloved Lady: A History of Jane Addams' Ideas on Reform and Peace* (Baltimore: Johns Hopkins University Press, 1967); James W. Linn, *Jane Addams: A Biography* (New York: Appleton-Century, 1935).
18. Alan Brinkley, *American History: A Survey Since 1865*, 2 vols. (New York: McGraw-Hill, 1999), 2:723.
19. Edmund Morris, *Theodore Rex* (New York: Random House, 2001).
20. John Morton Blum, *Woodrow Wilson and the Politics of Morality* (Boston: Little, Brown, 1956); Arthur S. Link, *Woodrow Wilson: A Brief Biography* (Cleveland: World Publishing, 1963); Edwin A. Weinstein, *Woodrow Wilson: A Medical and Psychological Biography* (Princeton: Princeton University Press, 1981).
21. George Grant, *Killer Angel* (Nashville: Cumberland House, 2001), 38.
22. Woodrow Wilson, *The State* (Boston: D. C. Heath, 1889), 638–40, 651–52, 656–61.
23. Johnson, *History of the American People*, 640.
24. Fred Greenbaum, "William Gibbs McAdoo: Business Promoter as Politician" in *Men Against Myths: The Progressive Response* (Westport, CT: Praeger, 2000), 131–52; John J. Broesamle, *William Gibbs McAdoo: A Passion for Change, 1863–1917* (Port Washington, NY: Kennikat Press, 1973).
25. Schweikart, *Entrepreneurial Adventure*, 279–82 and his Introduction in Larry Schweikart, ed., *Encyclopedia of American Business History and Biography: Banking and Finance in 1913*, xi–xxxi; Lynne Doti and Larry Schweikart, *Banking in the American West from Gold Rush to Deregula-*

tion; Larry Schweikart, "U.S. Commercial Banking: A Historiographical Survey," *Business History Review*, Autumn 1991, 606–61.

26. Charles W. Calomiris and Carolos D. Ramirez, "The Role of Financial Relationships in the History of American Corporate Finance," *Journal of Applied Corporate Finance*, 9, Summer 1996, 32–72.

27. Eugene N. White, *Regulation and Reform of the American Banking System, 1900–1929* (Princeton: Princeton University Press 1983); James Livingston, *Origins of the Federal Reserve System* (Ithaca, NY: Cornell University Press, 1986); Richard H. Timberlake, *The Origins of Central Banking in the United States* (Cambridge: Harvard University Press, 1978).

28. W. Elliot Brownlee, *Federal Taxation in America: A Short History* (Cambridge: Cambridge University Press and the Woodrow Wilson Center Press, 1996), and W. Elliot Brownlee, ed., *Funding the Modern American State, 1941–1945: The Rise and Fall of the Era of Easy Finance* (Cambridge: Cambridge University Press and the Woodrow Wilson Center, 1996).

29. Stanley Lebergott, *The Americans: An Economic Record* (New York: W. W. Norton, 1984), 407.

30. Gerald Eggert, "Richard Olney and the Income Tax," *Mississippi Valley Historical Review*, June 1961, 24–25.

31. Schweikart, *Entrepreneurial Adventure*, 277.

32. Robert Stanley, *Dimensions of Law in the Service of Order: Origins of the Federal Income Tax, 1861–1913* (New York: Oxford University Press, 1993).

33. Robert Higgs, *Crisis and Leviathan: Critical Episodes in the Growth of American Government* (New York: Oxford University Press, 1987).

34. George Bittlingmayer, "Antitrust and Business Activity: The First Quarter Century," *Business History Review*, 70, Autumn 1996, 363–401.

35. James Langefeld and David Scheffman, "Evolution or Revolution: What Is the Future of Antitrust?" *Antitrust Bulletin*, 31, Summer 1986, 287–99; Harold Demsetz, "Barriers to Entry," *American Economic Review*, 72, March 1982, 47–57; Yale Brozen, "Concentration and Profits: Does Concentration Matter?" *Antitrust Bulletin*, 19, 1974, 351–99; George Bittlingmayer and Thomas Hazlett, "DOS Kapital: Has Antitrust Action against Microsoft Created Value in the Computer Industry?" *Journal of Financial Economics*, March 2000, 329–59.

36. Brinkley, *American History*, 769.

37. McClellan, *Historical Moments*, 2:201–2.

38. Gilbert, *History of the Twentieth Century*, I:419.

39. Ibid., I:422.

40. Faragher, *Out of Many*, 652.

41. Murrin, *Liberty, Equality, Power*, 788.

42. Leckie, *Wars of America*, 631.

43. Thomas Kincade, *The Spirit of America* (Nashville: Thomas Nelson, 1998), 107.

44. Max Boas and Steve Chain, *Big Mac: The Unauthorized Story of McDonald's* (New York: New American Library, 1976), 3.

45. Leckie, *Wars of America*, 633.

46. Gilbert, *History of the Twentieth Century*, I:500.

47. Ibid., I:498.

48. Ibid., I:503.

49. Ibid., I:507.

50. Murrin, *Liberty, Equality, Power*, 794.

51. Gilbert, *History of the Twentieth Century*, I:531.

52. Paul Hollander, *Political Will and Personal Belief: The Decline and Fall of Soviet Communism* (New Haven: Yale University Press, 1999), 29.

53. T. Arthur Herman, *Joseph McCarthy: Reexamining the Life and Legacy of America's Most Hated Senator* (New York: Free Press, 2000), 69.

54. Ibid., 64.

55. Brinkley, *American History*, 792.

56. Johnson, *History of the American People*, 648.

57. Dick Morris, *Power Plays: Win or Lose—How History's Great Political Leaders Play the Game* (New York: ReganBooks, 2002), 68.

58. Davidson, et al., *Nation of Nations*, 760.

59. Frederick Allen, *Secret Formula* (New York: Harper Business, 1994), 28–66.

60. Jack High and Clayton A. Coppin, "Wiley and the Whiskey Industry: Strategic Behavior in the Passage of the Pure Food Act," *Business History Review*, 62, Summer 1988, 286–309.

61. James H. Timberlake, *Prohibition and the Progressive Movement, 1900–1920* (Cambridge, MA: Harvard University Press, 1963); Norman H. Clark, *The Dry Years: Prohibition and Social Change in Washington* (Seattle: University of Washington Press, 1965); John C. Burnham, "New Perspectives on the Prohibition Experiment of the 1920s," *Journal of Social History*, 2, 1968, 51–68, quotation on 51.

62. Johnson, *History of the American People*, 679.

63. Prince A. Morrow, "Report of the Committee of Seven on the Prophylaxis of Venereal Disease in New York City," *Medical News*, 79, December 21, 1901, 961–70, quotation on 967.

64. J. C. Burnham, "The Progressive Era Revolution in American Attitudes Toward Sex," *Journal of American History*, 59, March 1973, 885–908.

65. Allan M. Brandt, *No Magic Bullet: A Social History of Venereal Disease in the United States Since 1880*, exp. ed. (New York: Oxford University Press, 1987), 38–39.

66. Jonathan Zimmerman, *Distilling Democracy: Alcohol Education in America's Public Schools, 1880–1925* (Lawrence, KS: University Press of Kansas, 1999).

67. Gillon and Matson, *American Experiment*, 822.

68. Davidson, et al., *Nation of Nations*, II:795; Gillon and Matson, *American Experiment*, 820; Brinkley, *American History*, II:827.

69. Norman H. Clark, *Deliver Us from Evil: An Interpretation of Prohibition* (New York: Norton, 1976), 10, 83.

70. Mencken quoted in Johnson, *History of the American People*, 681.

71. Clark, *Deliver Us from Evil*, 9.

72. Johnson, *History of the American People*, 680.

73. Harry Elmer Barnes, *Society in Transition: Problems of a Changing Age* (New York: Prentice-Hall, 1939), 455.

74. Daniel J. Kelves, *In the Name of Eugenics: Genetics and the Use of Human Heredity* (New York: Knopf, 1985).

75. H. C. Sharp, "The Indiana Plan," in Proceedings of the National Prison Association (Pittsburgh: National Prison Association, 1909).

76. Clark, *Deliver Us from Evil*, 65; David Pivar, *Purity Crusade: Sexual Morality and Social Control, 1868–1900* (Westport, CT: Greenwood Press, 1973).

77. Berkin, et al., *Making America*, 606.

78. John R. Lott and Larry Kenny, "How Dramatically Did Women's Suffrage Change the Size and Scope of Government?" University of Chicago, John M. Olin Law and Economics Working Paper No. 60, 2nd series; John E. Filer, Lawrence W. Kenny, and Rebecca B. Morton, "Redistribution, Income, and Voting," *American Journal of Political Science*, 37, February 1993, 63–87; Charles Colson and Nancy Pearcy, "Why Women Like Big Government," *Christianity Today*, November 11, 1996; Joel H. Goldstein, *The Effects of the Adoption of Woman Suffrage: Sex Differences in Voting Behavior—Illinois, 1914–1921* (New York: Praeger Special Studies, 1984); Jody Newman, "The Gender Gap: Do Women Vote for Women?" *The Public Perspective*, 7, February/March 1996.

79. Grant, *Killer Angel*, 38.

80. Ibid.

81. Albert Gringer, *The Sanger Corpus: A Study in Militancy* (Lakeland, AL: Lakeland Christian College, 1974), 473–88; Grant, *Killer Angel*, 63.

82. Margaret Sanger, *The Pivot of Civilization* (New York: Brentanos, 1922).

83. Ibid., 108.

84. Ibid., 123.

85. Stephen Mosher, "The Repackaging of Margaret Sanger," *Wall Street Journal*, May 5, 1997.

86. Ibid.

Chapter 15. The Roaring Twenties and the Great Crash, 1920–32

1. David Burner, et al., *An American Portrait* (New York: Charles Scribner's, 1985); John Kenneth Galbraith, *The Great Crash of 1929*, 3rd ed., (Boston: Houghton Mifflin, 1972 [1955]); David Goldfield, et al., *The American Journey*, combined ed. (Upper Saddle River, NJ: Prentice Hall, 1998); John Mack Faragher, et al., *Out of Many: A History of the American People*, combined ed., 3rd ed. (Upper Saddle River, NJ: Prentice Hall, 1999). Typical statements are as follows:

"Business had done all too well. Corporations had boosted their profits . . . by keeping the cost of labor low. . . . People made up the difference between earnings and purchases by borrowing. . . . 1 percent of the population owned 36 percent of all personal wealth. . . . The wealthy saved too much . . . huge corporations ruled the economy . . . flooding the stock market with call money; manipulating stocks and bonds; and failing to distribute enough in wages to sustain consumer purchasing power." (James West Davidson, et al., *Nation of Nations: A Narrative History of the American Republic*, vol. 2: since 1865, 3rd edition [Boston: McGraw-Hill, 1998], 873–74); "In the twenties, the uneven distribution of income should have suggested that the nation was risking economic disaster. The slowly rising real wages of industrial workers were outdistanced by the salaries, savings, and profits of those higher on the economic ladder. . . . Forty percent of all families had incomes under $1,500. . . . Those who were getting rich, meanwhile, found their savings piled up out of all proportion to need [and] they turned to speculation in real estate and securities, both blown up into a bubble sure to burst. . . . Tax policies favored the rich, making even more unequal the distribution of income." (Winthrop Jordan and Leon F. Litwack, *The United States*, combined ed., 7th ed. [Englewood Cliffs, NJ: Prentice Hall, 1991], 664–65); "The most important weakness in the economy was the extremely unequal distribution of income and wealth. . . . the top 0.1 percent of American families . . . had an agregate income equal to that of the bottom 42 percent. . . . (Faragher, *Out of Many*, 719); "In 1929, nearly a third of the country's income was going to a twentieth of the population. . . . [overproduction of consumer goods] not only preceded the stock market crash: [17] helped cause it. . . . Speculation in stock prices had begun on the solid basis of profits. . . . But in time it turned to sheer gambling. . . ." (David Burner, Elizabeth Genovese, Eugene D. Genovese, Forrest McDonald, *An American Portrait: A History of the United States* combined ed., 2nd ed. [New York: Charles Scribner's, 1985], 614–15). John D. Hicks, in his textbook of the age, *Republican Ascendancy, 1921–1933* (New York: Harper Torchbooks, 1960), contended that "money had flowed in from all over the world to support the wild American speculation," and noted the observation, later used by Paul Johnson, that "many stocks that had never paid a dividend brought fantastic figures, and soared ever upward," *History of the American People* [New York: HarperCollins, 1997], 277).

2. Robert Sobel, *The Great Bull Market: Wall Street in the 1920s* (New York: W. W. Norton, 1968). For the debate over stock valuations, see Eugene N. White, "The Stock Market Boom and the Crash of 1929 Revisited," *Journal of Economic History*, 4 (Spring 1990), 67–83; and his "When the Ticker Ran Late: The Stock Market Boom and the Crash of 1929," in Eugene N. White, ed., *Crashes and Panics* (Homewood, IL: Dow Jones/Irwin, 1990); Gary Santoni and Gerald Dwyer, "Bubbles vs. Fundamentals: New Evidence from the Great Bull Markets," in ibid., 188–210; J. Bradford De Long and Andre Shleifer, "The Stock Market Bubble of 1929: Evidence from Closed-end Mutual Funds," *Journal of Economic History*, 51 (September 1991), 675–700; Peter Rappaport and Eugene N. White, "Was the Crash of 1929 Expected?" *American Economic Review*, 84 (March 1994), 271–81; Gene Smiley and Richard H. Keehn, "Margin Purchases, Brokers' Loans, and the Bull Market of the Twenties," *Business and Economic History*, 17 (1988), 129–42.

3. Edwin J. Perkins, "Charles E. Merrill," in Larry Schweikart, ed., *Encyclopedia of American Business and Economic History: Banking and Finance, 1913–1989* (New York: Facts on File, 1990), 283–90.

4. John A. Morello, *Selling the President, 1920: Albert D. Lasker, Advertising, and the Election of Warren G. Harding* (Westport, CT: Praeger, 2001).

5. Burt Noggle, "The Origins of the Teapot Dome Investigation," *Mississippi Valley Historical Review*, 44 (June 1957–March 1958), 237–66.

6. Robert James Maddox, "Keeping Cool with Coolidge," *Journal of American History*, 53 (June 1966–March 1967), 772–80, quotation on 779.

7. Burner, et al., *An American Portrait*, II:607; Gene Smith, *The Shattered Dream: Herbert Hoover and the Great Depression* (New York: William Morrow & Company, 1970), 47.

8. Donald R. McCoy, *Calvin Coolidge: The Quiet President* (New York: Macmillan, 1967).

9. Randall G. Holcombe, "The Growth of the Federal Government in the 1920s," *Cato Journal*, 16, Fall 1996, http://www.cato.org/pubs/journal/cj16n2_2.html, table 1.

10. Geoffrey C. Ward and Ken Burns, *Baseball: An Illustrated History* (New York: Borzoi, 1994), 209–10.

11. Jordan and Litwack, *The United States*, 645.

12. David Robinson, *From Peep Show to Palace: The Birth of American Film* (New York: Columbia University Press, 1996); Jack C. Ellis, *A History of Film*, 2nd ed. (Englewood Cliffs, NJ: Prentice-Hall, 1985), chap. 8; Tino Valio, "Grand Design," vol. 5, in Charles Harpole, ed., *History of the American Cinema* (Berkeley, California: University of California Press, 1995).

13. Robert W. Garnet, *The Telephone Enterprise: The Evolution of the Bell System's Horizontal Structure, 1876–1909* (Baltimore: Johns Hopkins University Press, 1985); John Brooks, *Telephone* (New York: Harper & Row, 1975).

14. Charles Merz, *The Dry Decade* (Seattle: University of Washington Press, 1969); The Prohibition Amendment: Hearings Before the Committee of the Judiciary, Seventy-fifth Congress, Second Session (Washington, D.C.: Government Printing Office, 1931); Herbert Asbury, *The Great Illusion: An Informal History of Prohibition* (New York: Greenwood Press, 1950); Mark Moore and Dean Gerstein, eds., *Alcohol and Public Policy: Beyond the Shadow of Prohibition* (Washington, D.C.: National Academy Press, 1981); W. J. Rorabaugh, *The Alcoholic Republic: An American Tradition* (New York: Oxford, 1979).

15. John C. Burnham, "New Perspectives on the Prohibition 'Experiment' of the 1920s," *Journal of Social History* 2, 1968, 51–68, quotation on 66.

16. Ibid.; John C. Burnham, "The New Psychology: From Narcissism to Social Control," in John Braeman, Robert Bremmer, and David Brody, eds., *Change and Continuity in Twentieth-Century America* (Columbus: Ohio State University Press, 1968), 351–97, quotation on 375.

17. Norman H. Clark, *Deliver Us from Evil: An Interpretation of Prohibition* (New York: W. W. Norton, 1976), 146.

18. Burnham, "New Perspectives on the Prohibition 'Experiment,'" passim; "The Progressive Era Revolution in American Attitudes Toward Sex," *Journal of American History*, 8, 1973, 885–908; and "The New Psychology: From Narcissism to Social Control," in John Braeman, Robert H. Bremer, and David Brody, eds., *Change and Continuity in Twentieth-Century America: The 1920's* (Columbus, Ohio: Ohio State University Press, 1965).

19. Clark, *Deliver Us from Evil*, 146–47. Also see Martha Bensley Bruere, *Does Prohibition Work? A Study of the Operation of the Eighteenth Amendment Made by the National Federation of Settlements, Assisted by Social Workers in Different Parts of the United States* (New York: Harper and Brothers, 1927).

20. Holcombe, "Growth of the Federal Government in the 1920s," table 4.

21. Mark Mazower, *Dark Continent: Europe's Twentieth Century* (New York: Alfred A. Knopf, 1999), 109.

22. Ibid.

23. Robert Sklar, ed., *The Plastic Age, 1917–1930* (New York: George Braziller, 1970), 93.

24. Thomas B. Silver, *Coolidge and the Historians* (Durham, NC: Carolina Academic Press, 1982), 20; Howard H. Quint and Robert H. Ferrell, eds., *The Talkative President: The Off-the-Record Press Conferences of Calvin Coolidge* (Amherst, MA: University of Massachusetts Press, 1964).

25. Silver, *Coolidge*, 26.

26. Stephen A. Schuker, "Charles G. Dawes," in Schweikart, *Encyclopedia of American Business History and Biography: Banking and Finance, 1913–1989*, 68–77, quotation on 72.

27. Ibid., 74.

28. Stephen A. Schuker, *The End of French Predominance in Europe: The Financial Crisis of 1924 and the Adoption of the Dawes Plan* (Chapel Hill, NC: University of North Carolina Press, 1986).

29. Davidson, *Nation of Nations*, 863.

30. McCoy, *Calvin Coolidge*, 367.

31. Johnson, *History of the American People*, 721.

32. McCoy, *Calvin Coolidge*, 384.

33. Joan Hoff Wilson, *Herbert Hoover: Forgotten Progressive* (Boston: Little, Brown, 1975).

34. David Burner, *Herbert Hoover* (New York: Afred A. Knopf, 1979), 234, 237.

35. Letter from Franklin D. Roosevelt to Hugh Gibson, in the Hoover Papers, Hoover Library, Stanford University, quoted in Martin L. Fausold, *The Presidency of Herbert C. Hoover* (Lawrence, KS: University of Kansas Press, 1985), 13.

36. William Allen White, *A Puritan in Babylon, the Story of Calvin Coolidge* (New York: Macmillan, 1938), 400.

37. Ibid. recorded the reaction in the White House to Hoover's nomination as "dismay . . . sadness, disappointment, regrets" (402).

38. Burner, *Herbert Hoover*, 180.

39. Fausold, *Presidency of Herbert C. Hoover*, 18.

40. Herbert Hoover, *American Individualism* (West Branch, Iowa: Herbert Hoover Presidential Library Association, 1971 [1922]).

41. Fausold, *Presidency of Herbert C. Hoover*, 24; Johnson, *History of the American People*, 737–39.

42. James Bovard, *The Farm Fiasco* (San Francisco, California: Institute for Contemporary Studies Press, 1989), 16.

43. Joseph S. David, *On Agricultural Policy* (Palo Alto, California: Stanford University, 1938), 435.

44. Johnson, *A History of the American People*, 733.

45. Larry Schweikart, "U.S. Commercial Banking: A Historiographical Survey," *Business History Review*, 65, Autumn 1991, 606–61; Gene Smiley, *The American Economy in the Twentieth Century* (Cincinnati, Ohio: South-Western Publishing Co., 1994), chap. 6; Peter Temin, *Did Monetary Forces Cause the Great Depression?* (New York: W. W. Norton, 1976) and his *Lessons from the Great Depression* (Cambridge, MA: Harvard University Press, 1989); Richard H. Keehn and Gene Smiley, "U.S. Bank Failures, 1932–1933: A Provisional Analysis," Essays in Economic History: Selected Papers from the Business and Economic Historical Society Meetings, 1987, 6 (1988), 136–56.

46. Jude Wanniski, *The Way the World Works: How Economics Fail—and Succeed* (New York: Basic Books, 1978).

47. Robert B. Archibald and David H. Feldman, "Investment During the Great Depression: Uncertainty and the Role of the Smoot-Hawley Tariff," *Southern Economic Journal*, 64 (1998):4, 857–79.

48. Douglas A. Irwin, "The Smoot-Hawley Tariff: A Quantitative Assessment," *Review of Economics and Statistics*, 80 (May 1998), 326–34; "Changes in U.S. Tariffs: The Role of Import Prices and Commercial Policies," *American Economic Review*, 88 (September 1998), 1015–26; and "From Smoot-Hawley to Reciprocal Trade Agreements: Changing the Course of U.S. Trade Policy in the 1930s," in Michael D. Bordo, Claudia Goldin, and Eugene N. White, *The Defining Moment: The Great Depression and the American Economy in the Twentieth Century* (Chicago: University of Chicago Press, 1998), 325–52. See also Barry Eichengreen, "The Political Economy of the Smoot-Hawley Tariff," in Roger L. Ransom, ed., *Research in Economic History*, vol. 12 (Greenwich, CT: JAI Press, 1989), 1–43.

49. Mario J. Crucini and James Kahn, "Tariffs and Aggregate Economic Activity: Lessons from the Great Depression," *Journal of Monetary Economics*, 38 (1996), 427–67, quotation on 458; Mario J. Crucini, "Sources of Variation in Real Tariff Rates: The United States, 1900–1940," *American Economic Review*, 84 (June 1994), 732–43.

50. Milton Friedman and Anna Jacobson Schwartz, *Monetary History of the United States, 1867–1960* (Princeton, NJ: Princeton University Press, 1963), versus Paul Kubic, "Federal Reserve Policy During the Great Depression: the Impact of Interwar Attitudes Regarding Consumption and Consumer Credit," *Journal of Economic Issues*, 30 (September 1996), 829–42.

51. William D. Lastrapes and George Selgin, "The Check Tax: Fiscal Folly and the Great Monetary Contraction," *Journal of Economic History*, 57, December 1997, 859–78.

52. Fausold, *Presidency of Herbert Hoover*, 160–61.

53. W. Elliot Brownlee, *Dynamics of Ascent: A History of the American Economy*, 2nd ed. (New York: Alfred A. Knopf, 1979), 409.

54. Ted Morgan, *FDR: A Biography* (New York: Simon and Schuster, 1985), 39. See also John T. Flynn, *The Roosevelt Myth* (New York: Devin-Adair Company, 1956).

55. Marvin Olasky, *The American Leadership Tradition: Moral Vision from Washington to Clinton* (New York: Free Press, 1999), 210.

56. Ibid., 215.

57. Dick Morris, *Power Plays: Win or Lose—How History's Great Political Leaders Play the Game* (New York: ReganBooks, 2002), 260.

58. Ibid.

59. Olasky, *American Leadership Tradition*, 222.

60. Roosevelt's speech in Sioux City, Iowa, September 1932, quoted in William E. Leuchtenburg, *Franklin D. Roosevelt and the New Deal* (New York: Harper and Row, 1963), 11.

61. Johnson, *History of the American People*, 741.

Chapter 16. Enlarging the Public Sector, 1932–40

1. The "two New Deals" theory includes Faragher, et al., *Out of Many*, 451–52; Johnson, *History of the American People*, 760.

2. Rexford Tugwell, "The Superpolitical," *Journal of Social Philosophy*, October 1939–July 1940, 107, quoted in Bernard Sternsher, *Rexford Tugwell and the New Deal* (New Brunswick, NJ: Rutgers University Press, 1964), 13.

3. Johnson, *History of the American People*, 756.

4. Henry Morgenthau Jr., "The Morgenthau Diaries, II, The Struggle for a Program," *Colliers*, October 4, 1947, 20–21, 45–47, quotation on 21.

5. Arthur M. Schlesinger Jr., *The Politics of Upheaval* (Boston: Houghton Mifflin, 1960), 379.

6. Raymond Moley's "Journal, 1936–1940," 3, in Box 1, Raymond Moley Collection, Hoover Institution Archives, Stanford, California.

7. Ibid., 5.

8. Ibid., 7.

9. Leuchtenberg, *Franklin D. Roosevelt*, 33.

10. Rexford Tugwell, *The Democratic Roosevelt* (Garden City, New York: Doubleday, 1957), 220–21.

11. James R. McGovern, *And a Time for Hope: Americans in the Great Depression* (Westport, CT: Praeger, 2000), xi.

12. Raymond Moley, *After Seven Years* (New York: Harper, 1939), 155.

13. Davidson et al., *Nation of Nations*, 929; Faragher et al., *Out of Many*, 451–52; Burner et al., *American Portrait*, 629–30.

14. Samuel Rosenman, ed., *The Public Papers and Addresses of Franklin D. Roosevelt* (New York: Random House, 1938–50), 5:19–21.

15. Willson Whitman, *Bread and Circuses: A Study of Federal Theater* (New York: Oxford, 1937); Grant Code, "Dance Theater of the WPA: A Record of National Accomplishment," *Dance Observer*, November 1939, 280–81, 290; "Footlights, Federal Style," *Harper's*, 123 (1936), 626; Mabel Ulrich, "Salvaging Culture for the WPA," *Harper's*, 78 (1939); "Work of the Federal Writers' Project of the WPA," *Publishers Weekly*, 135 (1939), 1130–35; *Time*, 31 (January 3, 1938), 55–56; Robert Binkley, "The Cultural Program of the W.P.A.," *Harvard Educational Review*, 9 (March 1939), 156–74; Willard Hogan, "The WPA Research and Records Program," *Harvard Educational Review*, 13 (1943), 52–62.

16. John T. Flynn, *The Roosevelt Myth* (New York: Devin-Adair Company, 1956), 46.

17. Harvey Klehr and Earl Haynes, *The American Communist Movement: Storming Heaven Itself* (New York: Twayne, 1992).

18. Goldfield, *American Journey*, 830.

19. Marc Weiss, *Rise of the Community Builders: The American Real Estate Industry and Urban Land Planning* (New York: Columbia, 1987).

20. Michael J. Webber, *New Deal Fat Cats: Business, Labor, and Campaign Finance in the 1936 Presidential Election* (New York: Fordham University Press, 2000), 15.

21. Leuchtenberg, *Franklin D. Roosevelt*, 152.

22. Eugene Gerhart, *America's Advocate: Robert H. Jackson* (Indianapolis: Bobbs-Merrill, 1958), 125–27; Ickes, *Diary*, 2:282–83.

23. New York *Times*, October 24, 1935.

24. Leuchtenberg, *Franklin D. Roosevelt*, 273; Robert and Helen Lynd, *Middletown in Transition* (New York: Harcourt, 1937), 489.

25. J. E. Kaufmann and W. H. Kaufmann, *The Sleeping Giant: American Armed Forces Between the Wars* (Westport, CT: Praeger Press, 1996), 12.

26. Paul Johnson, *Modern Times: A History of the World from the Twenties to the Nineties*, rev. ed. (New York: HarperCollins, 1991), 97.

27. Arthur D. Morse, *While Six Million Died: A Chronicle of American Apathy* (New York: Ace, 1968), 38.

28. Ibid.

29. Mark Mazower, *Dark Continent: Europe's Twentieth* Century (New York: Knopf, 1999), 27.

30. Harold Ickes, *The Secret Diary of Harold Ickes*, 3 vols. (New York: Simon & Schuster, 1954), 2:274.

31. Julius W. Pratt, *The American Secretaries of State and Their Diplomacy*, vol. XII, Cordell Hull, 1933–44, vol. I (New York: Cooper Square Publishers, 1964), 311.

32. Guenther Lewy, *The Cause That Failed: Communism in American Political Life* (New York: Oxford University Press, 1990), 179.

33. Joseph E. Davies, "What We Didn't Know About Russia," *Reader's Digest*, 40 (March 1942), 45–50, which was taken from his *Mission to Moscow* (New York: Simon and Schuster, 1941) and is quoted in Filene, *American Views of Soviet Russia*, 145.

34. Davies, "What We Didn't Know," 145.

35. Henry Morgenthau Jr., "The Morgenthau Diaries, IV: The Story of Lend Lease," *Colliers*, October 18, 1947, 16–17, 71–74.

36. New York *Times*, April 29, 1939; Norman Baynes, *The Speeches of Adolf Hitler*, 2 vols. (London: Oxford, 1942), 2:1605–56.

37. Johnson, *Modern Times*, 370–71.

38. James F. Dunnigan and Albert A. Nofi, *Dirty Little Secrets of World War II: Military Information No One Told You About the Greatest, Most Terrible War in History* (New York: Quill/William Morrow, 1994), 46–47; John Ruggiero, *Neville Chamberlain and British Rearmament: Pride, Prejudice, and Politics* (Westport, CT: Greenwood Press, 1999).

39. FDR quoted in Morgenthau, "Morgenthau Diaries, IV," 72.

40. Wayne S. Cole, *Roosevelt and the Isolationists, 1932–45* (Lincoln, NB: University of Nebraska Press, 1983).

41. Tindall and Shi, America, 2:1311.

42. Thomas E. Mahl, *Desperate Deception: British Covert Operations in the United States* (Washington, D.C.: Brassey's, 1998), 44.

43. Ibid., 74.

44. Ibid., 77.

45. J. Garry Clifford, "Grenville Clark and the Origins of Selective Service," *Review of Politics* 35 (January 1973), 33.

46. Arthur Herman, *Joseph McCarthy: Reexamining the Life and Legacy of America's Most Hated Senator* (New York: Free Press, 2000), 73.

47. Vandenberg, quoted in Cole, *Roosevelt and the Isolationists*, 328.

48. Walter L. Hixson, *Charles Lindbergh: Lone Eagle* (New York: HarperCollins, 1996), 105.

49. Mazower, *Dark Continent*, 141.

50. Leuchtenberg, *Franklin D. Roosevelt*, 312.

Chapter 17. Democracy's Finest Hour, 1941–45

1. L. Mosely, *Hirohito: Emperor of Japan* (Englewood Cliffs, NJ: Prentice-Hall, 1966), 207; Nagano, speaking to Prime Minister Konoe Fumimaro, on September 27, 1940, quoted in Edwin T. Layton, with Roger Pineau and John Costello, *And I Was There: Pearl Harbor and Midway—Breaking the Secrets* (New York: Morrow, 1985), 72.

2. Mosely, *Hirohito*, 208.

3. Courtney Browne, *Tojo: The Last Banzai* (New York: Holt, Rinehart and Winston, 1967), 116.

4. Ibid., 110.

5. H. P. Willmott, with Tohmatsu Haruo and W. Spencer Johnson, *Pearl Harbor* (London: Cassell & Co., 2001), 47.

6. Ibid.

7. Ibid., 40.

8. Robert B. Stinnett, *Day of Deception: The Truth About FDR and Pearl Harbor* (New York: Free Press, 2000), 19.

9. James F. Dunnigan and Albert Nofi, *Dirty Little Secrets of World War II: Military Information No One Told You About the Greatest, Most Terrible War in History* (New York: Quill, 1994), 288.

10. John F. Bratzel and Leslie B. Rout Jr., "Pearl Harbor, Microdots, and J. Edgar Hoover," *American Historical Review*, December 1982, 1346–47.

11. Gordon Prange, with Donald M. Goldstein and Katherine V. Dillon, *Pearl Harbor: The Verdict of History* (New York: McGraw-Hill, 1986), 308.

12. Gerhard Weinberg, *Germany, Hitler, and World War II* (Cambridge: Cambridge University Press, 1955).

13. Patrick J. Buchanan, *A Republic, Not an Empire* (Washington: Regnery, 1999).

14. Paul Johnson, *Modern Times: A History of the World, from the Twenties to the Nineties* (New York: HarperCollins, 1991), 410.

15. J. E.Kaufmann and W. H. Kaufmann, *The Sleeping Giant: American Armed Forces Between the Wars* (Westport, CT: Praeger Press, 1996), 174.
16. Hanson, *Carnage and Culture*, 366.
17. Frank Matthias, *The GI Generation: A Memoir* (Lexington: University of Kentucky Press, 2000).
18. Dunnigan and Nofi, *Dirty Little Secrets*, 26.
19. Mark Harrison, ed., *The Economics of World War II: Six Great Powers in International Comparison* (Cambridge: Cambridge University Press, 1998), fig. 1.6, 15–16.
20. David M. Glanz and Jonathan M. House, *The Battle of Kursk* (Lawrence, KS: University of Kansas Press, 1999), 39.
21. Ibid., 37.
22. Ibid., 37–38.
23. Dunnigan and Nofi, *Dirty Little Secrets*, 162–63.
24. Roper Poll done for *Fortune* magazine, 1941, cited in *The American Enterprise*, January/February 2003, 60.
25. Gallup Polls done in 1945, 1943, cited in *The American Enterprise*, 62.
26. Davidson, et al., *Nation of Nations*, 956.
27. Burton Folsom, "What's Wrong with the Progressive Income Tax?" *Viewpoint on the Public Issues*, May 3, 1999.
28. Davidson, et al., *Nation of Nations*, 958.
29. Larry Schweikart, *The Entrepreneurial Adventure: A History of Business in the United States* (Fort Worth, TX: Harcourt, 2000), 545.
30. Wayne S. Cole, *Roosevelt and the Isolationists, 1932–45* (Lincoln, NB: University of Nebraska Press, 1983), 14, 26, 99.
31. Johnson, *Modern Times*, 407–08.
32. Ronald W. Clark, *Einstein: The Life and Times* (New York: Avon, 1999), chap. 20, passim; Albert Einstein, *Out of My Later Years* (Secaucus, NJ: Citadel Press, 1956).
33. Clark, *Einstein*, 682–83.
34. Quoted in Johnson, *Modern Times*, 408.
35. See Michael Beschloss, *The Conquerors: Roosevelt, Truman and the Destruction of Hitler's Germany, 1941–1945* (New York: Simon & Schuster, 2002).
36. Ironically, as Ladislas Farago discovered, the Germans actually had obtained a Norden bombsight earlier through spies, but then forgot about it. See *The Game of the Foxes: The Untold Story of German Espionage in the United States and Great Britain During World War II* (New York: D. McKay, 1972 [1971]).
37. William Green, *Famous Bombers of the Second World War* (Garden City, NY: Hanover House, 1959), 24–36.
38. Mark Clodfelter, *The Limits of Air Power: The American Bombing of North Vietnam* (New York: Free Press, 1989), 9; Everest E. Riccioni, "Strategic Bombing: Always a Myth," U.S Naval Institute Proceedings, November 1996, 49–53; Melden E. Smith Jr., "The Strategic Bombing Debate: The Second World War and Vietnam," *Journal of Contemporary History*, 12 (1977), 175–91.
39. Cornelius Ryan, *The Longest Day* (New York: Simon & Schuster, 1959).
40. Dunnigan and Nofi, *Dirty Little Secrets*, 284.
41. Roger Daniels, *Concentration Camps, USA: Japanese Americans and World War II* (Malabar, Florida: Kruger Publishing Co., 1981).
42. Jordan and Litwack, *United States*, 708.
43. Ibid.
44. Ted Lawson, *Thirty Seconds over Tokyo*, ed. Robert Considine (New York: Random House, 1943).
45. Tindall and Shi, *America*, 2:1347.
46. Leckie, *Wars of America*, 797.
47. Tindall and Shi, *America*, 2:1349.
48. Ibid., 2:1350; Stephen E. Ambrose, *D-Day, June 6, 1944: The Climactic Battle of World War II* (New York: Simon & Schuster,1994).
49. Ambrose, *D-Day*, 190.
50. Ibid., 583.
51. Leckie, *Wars of America*, 804.
52. Stephen E. Ambrose, *Band of Brothers* (New York: Pocketbooks, 1992), 233.

53. Robert E. Sherwood, *Roosevelt and Hopkins: An Intimate History*, 2 vols. (New York: Putnam's, 1950), I:387–423; Johnson, *History of the American People*, 790.
54. Terry Anderson, *The United States, Great Britain, and the Cold War, 1944–1947* (Columbia, MO: University of Missouri Press, 1981), 4.
55. Andrew, *Sword and the Shield*, 133.
56. Victor Davis Hanson, *The Soul of Battle: From Ancient Times to Present Day, How Three Great Liberators Vanquished Tyranny* (New York: Free Press, 1999), 275.
57. Johnson, *Modern Times*, 414.
58. Ron Rosenbaum, *Explaining Hitler: The Search for the Origins of His Evil* (New York: Random House, 1998), 211.
59. Roger Manvell and Heinrich Fraenkel, *Heinrich Himmler* (New York: Putnam, 1965), 118–19.
60. Arthur D. Morse, *While Six Million Died: A Chronicle of Apathy* (New York: Ace, 1968), 14.
61. Ibid., 25.
62. Johnson, *Modern Times*, 420.
63. David S. Wyman, *The Abandonment of the Jews: America and the Holocaust, 1941–1945* (New York: Pantheon, 1984) and his *Paper Walls: America and the Refugee Crisis, 1938–1941* (Amherst, MA: University of Massachusetts Press, 1968).
64. Morse, *While Six Million Died*, 48.
65. Wyman, *Abandonment of the Jews*, x.
66. Ibid., xi.
67. Alfred Steinberg, *The Man from Missouri: The Life and Times of Harry S. Truman* (New York: Putnam, 1952), 301.
68. James Forrestal, *The Forrestal Diaries*, ed. Walter Millis with the collaboration of E. S. Duffield (New York: Viking, 1951), 344, 346, 348.
69. Richard B. Frank, *Downfall: The End of the Imperial Japanese Empire* (New York: Penguin Books, 1999), 131.
70. Frank, *Downfall*, 132.
71. Akira Iriye, *Power and Culture: The Japanese-American War, 1941–1945* (Cambridge, MA: Harvard University Press, 1981).
72. Robert Leckie, *Strong Men Armed: The United States Marines Against Japan* (New York: Random House, 1962), 189.
73. Alan Axelrod, *America's Wars* (New York: John Wiley, 2002), 411.
74. Leckie, *Wars of America*, 775.
75. Victor Davis Hanson, *Ripples of Battle: How Wars of the Past Still Determine How We Fight, How We Live, and How We Think* (New York: Doubleday, 2003), 19–60.
76. Sadao Asada, "The Shock of the Atomic Bomb and Japan's Decision to Surrender—a Reconsideration," *Pacific Historical Review*, 67 (November 1998), 477–512.
77. Ibid., 511.
78. Frank, *Downfall*, 161.
79. Ibid., 261.
80. Jordan and Litwack, *United States*, 724.
81. John Toland, *The Rising Sun: The Decline and Fall of the Japanese Empire* (New York: Bantam, 1970), 862fn.
82. Ambrose, *Band of Brothers*, 387.
83. Robert A. Pape, "Why Japan Surrendered," *International Security*, Fall 1993, 154–201.
84. Barton J. Bernstein, "A Postwar Myth: 500,000 U.S. Lives Saved," *Bulletin of Atomic Scientists*, 42, June/July 1986, 38–40, referring to JWPC 369/1 "Details of the Campaign against Japan," June 15, 1945, ABC File 384, RG 319, National Archives.
85. Robert James Maddox, "The 'Postwar Creation' Myth," *Continuity*, 24 (Fall 2000), 11–29.
86. Edward J. Dreas, *MacArthur's Ultra: Codebreaking and the War Against Japan* (Lawrence, KS: University of Kansas Press, 1992), 222.
87. Frank, *Downfall*, 29.
88. Asada, "The Shock of the Atomic Bomb," passim.
89. John Toland, *The Rising Sun* (New York: Bantam, 1970), 894–95.
90. Johnson, *Modern Times*, 426.
91. Frank, *Downfall*, 296.
92. William Verity, interview with the author, quoted for inclusion in *Marriage of Steel: The Life and Times of William and Peggy Verity* (Indianapolis, IN: Pearson Custom Publishing, 2000).

93. Paul Boyer, *By the Bomb's Early Light: American Thought and Culture at the Dawn of the Atomic Age* (New York: Pantheon, 1985), 23.

94. Merle Miller, *Plain Speaking: An Oral Biography of Harry S. Truman* (New York: Berkeley, 1974), 248; Peter Goodchild, *J. Robert Oppenheimer, Shatterer of Worlds* (Boston: Houghton Mifflin, 1981), 180.

95. Boyer, *By the Bomb's Early Light*, 193.

96. Edward F. L. Russell, *The Knights of Bushido: The Shocking History of Japanese War Atrocities* (New York: Berkeley, 1959 [1958]).

Chapter 18. America's "Happy Days," 1946–59

1. Arthur Herman, *Joseph McCarthy: Reexamining the Life and Legacy of America's Most Hated Senator* (New York: Free Press, 1990), 39.

2. *U.S. News & World Report*, November 15, 1946, 34.

3. Christopher Andrew and Vasili Mitrokhin, *Sword and the Shield: The Mitrokhin Archive and the Secret History of the KGB* (New York: Basic Books, 1999), 111.

4. Joseph W. Martin, *My First Fifty Years in Politics*, as told to Robert J. Donovan (New York: McGraw-Hill, 1960), 190.

5. Salvador de Madriaga, *The Anatomy of the Cold War* (Belfast, Ireland: M. Boyd, 1955); Gunter Lewy, *The Cause That Failed: Communism in American Political Life* (New York: Oxford, 1990).

6. Richard J. Walton, *Henry Wallace, Harry Truman, and the Cold War* (New York: Viking, 1976), 63–64.

7. Ibid; Robert James Maddox, *From War to Cold War* (Boulder, CO: Westview Press, 1989).

8. Andrew and Mitrokhin, *Sword and the Shield*, 114.

9. Robert Higgs, analysis online at http://www. independent. org/tii/content/pubs/review/TIR14higgs. html.

10. Harry R. Borowski, *A Hollow Threat: Strategic Air Power and Containment Before Korea* (Westport, CT: Greenwood Press, 1982).

11. Timothy Botti, *Ace in the Hole: Why the United States Did Not Use Nuclear Weapons in the Cold War, 1945–1965* (Westport, CT: Greenwood Press, 1996).

12. Leckie, *Wars of America*, 837; Samuel Eliot Morison, *The Two-Ocean War* (Boston: Little, Brown, 1963), 1046.

13. Johnson, *Modern Times*, 434.

14. Ibid., 438.

15. Daniel Yergin, *The Shattered Peace: The Origins of the Cold War and the National Security State* (Boston: Houghton Mifflin, 1978), 247.

16. Johnson, *History of the American People*, 797.

17. Yergin, *Shattered Peace*, 188.

18. Allen Weinstein and Alexander Vassiliev, *The Haunted Wood: Soviet Espionage in America, the Stalin Era* (New York: Random House, 1999); Harvey Klehr and John Earl Haynes, *The American Communist Movement: Storming Heaven Itself* (New York: Twayne, 1992).

19. John C. Culver and John Hyde, *American Dreamer: A Life of Henry A. Wallace* (Boston: W. W. Norton, 2000).

20. Yergin, *Shattered Peace*, 245.

21. Ibid., 246.

22. John Morton Blum, *The Price of Vision: The Diary of Henry A. Wallace* (Boston: Houghton-Mifflin, 1973), 589–601; Yergin, *Shattered Peace*, 253–54.

23. Herman, *Joseph McCarthy*, 80.

24. Andrew and Mitrokhin, *Sword and the Shield*, 106–9.

25. Martin Weil, *A Pretty Good Club: The Founding Fathers of the U.S. Foreign Service* (New York: Norton, 1978), 171.

26. George F. Kennan ("Mr. X"), "Sources of Soviet Conduct," *Foreign Affairs*, July 1947, 566–82.

27. Yergin, *Shattered Peace*, 323.

28. Divine, et al., *America: Past and Present*, 877.

29. Jeffrey Hart, *When the Going Was Good! American Life in the Fifties* (New York: Crown, 1982), 63.

30. Johnson, *History of the American People*, 817.

31. Divine, *America: Past and Present*, 881.

32. Paul K. Davis, *100 Decisive Battles from Ancient Times to the Present* (New York: Oxford, 1999), 420–24.

33. Michael Langley, *Inchon Landing* (New York: Times Books, 1979); Max Hastings, *The Korean War* (New York: Simon & Schuster, 1987).

34. Johnson, *History of the American People*, 823.

35. Ibid., 824.

36. Leckie, *Wars of America*, 909.

37. Gregg Herken, *Brotherhood of the Bomb: The Tangled Lives and Loyalties of Robert Oppenheimer, Ernest Lawrence, and Edward Teller* (New York: Henry Holt, 2002).

38. Weinstein and Vassiliev, *Haunted Wood*, 343; Robbie Lieberman, *The Strangest Dream. Anticommunism and the U.S. Peace Movement, 1945–1963* (Syracuse: Syracuse University Press, 2000).

39. Richard Rovere, *Senator Joe McCarthy* (New York: Harcourt, 1959).

40. Herman, *Joseph McCarthy*, 3–4; Ellen Schrecker, *The Age of McCarthyism: A Brief History with Documents* (Boston: Bedford Books, 1994).

41. Andrew and Mitrokhin, *Sword and the Shield*, 106 and passim.

42. Anthony Summers, *Official and Confidential: The Secret Life of J. Edgar Hoover* (New York: G. P. Putnam's Sons, 1993), 191.

43. Guenter Lewy, *The Cause That Failed: Communism in American Political Life* (New York: Oxford University Press, 1990), 101.

44. Klehr and Haynes, *American Communist Movement*, 181.

45. Robbie Lieberman, *Strangest Dream*, xv.

46. Ibid., 2.

47. As Rebecca West explained, "Everyone knew there were Communists, but very few people really believed it" (Rebecca West, *The New Meaning of Treason* [New York: Viking, 1964], 236–37), and as Leslie Fiedler put it, liberals seemed to think that Communists "were, despite their shrillness and bad manners, fundamentally on the side of justice" (Leslie Fiedler, "Hiss, Chambers, and the Age of Innocence," *Commentary*, August 1951, 119).

48. Michael Beschloss, "How Well Read Should a President Be?" *New York Times*, June 11, 2000.

49. Stephen E. Ambrose, *Eisenhower: Soldier General of the Army President Elect, 1890–1952* (New York: Simon & Schuster, 1983), I:178.

50. Johnson, *History of the American People*, 829; George F. Kennan, *Memoirs, 1925–50* (Boston: Little, Brown, 1967), 196, quoted in Johnson, *History of the American People*, 829; Robert R. Bowie and Richard H. Immerman, *Waging Peace: How Eisenhower Shaped an Enduring Cold War Strategy* (New York: Oxford University Press, 1998).

51. Hart, *When the Going Was Good!*, 67–68.

52. Ibid., 68.

53. Campbell Craig, *Destroying the Village: Eisenhower and Thermonuclear War* (New York: Columbia University Press, 1998), 22.

54. Fred Kaplan, *The Wizards of Armageddon* (New York: Simon & Schuster, 1983).

55. Craig, *Destroying the Village*, 51.

56. Robert Russo, *Bourque News Watch* (Canada), October 20, 1999.

57. Jack M. Holl, Roger M. Anders, and Alice L. Buck, *United States Civilian Nuclear Power Policy, 1954–1984: A Summary History* (Washington, D.C.: U.S. Department of Energy, 1986).

58. Tindall and Shi, *America*, 2:1487.

59. George Lardner Jr. and Walter Pincus, "Military had Plan to Blame Cuba if Glenn's Space Mission Failed," *Washington Post*, November 19, 1997.

60. William Strauss and Neil Howe, *Generations: The History of America's Future, 1584–2069* (New York: William Morrow, 1991), 261.

61. "America's Mood Today," *Look*, June 29, 1965.

62. William Strauss and Neil Howe, *The Fourth Turning: A Prophecy* (New York: Broadway Books, 1997), 166.

63. Ibid., 167.

64. Kenneth T. Jackson, *Crabgrass Frontier: The Suburbanization of the United States* (New York: Oxford, 1985).

65. Nicholas Dagen Bloom, *Suburban Alchemy: 1960s New Towns and the Transformation of the American Dream* (Columbus: Ohio State University Press, 2001).

66. Larry Schweikart, *The Entrepreneurial Adventure: A History of Business in the United States* (Fort Worth, TX: Harcourt, 2000), 375.

67. Scott Derks, *The Value of a Dollar: Prices and Incomes in the United States, 1860–1999* (Lakeville, CT: Grey House Publishing, 1999), 299–300.

68. See the official Rockwell Museum Web site, http://www. nrm. org/norman/.

69. Laura Claridge, *Norman Rockwell: A Life* (New York: Random House, 2001).

70. Mark Tooley, "Madness in Their Methodism: The Religious Left Has a Summit," *Heterodoxy*, May 1995, 6.

71. John A. Jakle and Keith A. Sculle, *Fast Food: Roadside Restaurants in the Automobile Age* (Baltimore: Johns Hopkins University Press, 1999); John A. Jakle, Keith A. Sculle and Jefferson S. Rogers, *The Motel in America* (Baltimore: Johns Hopkins University Press, 1996); John A. Jakle and Keith A. Sculle, *The Gas Station in America* (Baltimore: Johns Hopkins University Press, 1994).

72. Ray Kroc and Robert Anderson, *Grinding It Out: The Making of McDonald's* (Chicago: Contemporary Books, 1977).

73. Richard Kluger, *Simple Justice: The History of Brown v. Board of Education and Black America's Struggle for Equality* (New York: Norton, 1990).

74. Tindall and Shi, *America*, 2:1495.

75. Goldfield, et al., *American Journey*, 931.

76. Taylor Branch, *Parting the Waters: America in the King Years, 1954–63* (New York: Simon & Schuster, 1988); Robert Weisbrot, *Freedom Bound: A History of America's Civil Rights Movement* (New York: Norton, 1990).

77. Aldon D. Morris, *The Origins of the Civil Rights Movement: Black Communities Organizing for Change* (New York: Free Press, 1984); David Chappell, *Inside Agitators: White Southerners in the Civil Rights Movement* (Baltimore: Johns Hopkins University Press, 1994).

Chapter 19. The Age of Upheaval, 1960–74

1. Howard Brick, *Age of Contradiction: American Thought and Culture in the 1960s* (New York: Twayne, 1998).

2. John A. Andrew III, *The Other Side of the Sixties: The Young Americans for Freedom and the Rise of Conservative Politics* (New Brunswick, NJ: Rutgers University Press, 1997).

3. Christopher Matthews, *Kennedy and Nixon: The Rivalry That Shaped Postwar America* (New York: Simon & Schuster, 1996).

4. Brian J. Gaines, "Popular Myths About Popular Vote-Electoral College Splits," *PS: Political Science and Politics*, March 2001, 71–75.

5. Jeffrey Hart, *When the Going Was Good!: American Life in the Fifties* (New York: Crown, 1982), 156.

6. Thomas C. Reeves, *A Question of Character: A Life of John F. Kennedy* (New York: Free Press, 1991), chap. 3, passim.

7. Reeves, *Question of Character, Forum*, paperback ed. (Rocklin, CA: Forum, 1997), 68.

8. Herbert S. Parmet, *Jack* (New York: Dial Press, 1980), 320–33.

9. Reeves, *Question of Character*, 256.

10. Arthur Schlesinger, *Robert Kennedy and His Times* (Boston: Houghton Mifflin, 1978), 517–37; Reeves, *Question of Character*, 261.

11. Mark J. White, ed., *The Kennedys and Cuba: The Declassified Documentary History* (Chicago: Ivan R. Dee, 1999), quotation on 26, and "Notes on a White House Meeting, April 6, 1961."

12. Reeves, *Question of Character*, 262.

13. Ibid., 261.

14. John H. Davis, *The Kennedys: Dynasty and Disaster* (New York: SPI, 1992 [1984]), 247.

15. Paul Johnson, *Modern Times: A History of the World from the Twenties to the Nineties*, rev. ed. (New York: HarperCollins, 1991), 624.

16. Johnson, *Modern Times*, 624.

17. White, *The Kennedys and Cuba*, 220–25.

18. Ibid., 226–29.

19. Hugh Sidey, *John F. Kennedy: Portrait of a President* (Harmondsworth, England: Penguin Books, 1965 [1964]).

20. Fred Weir, "USSR 'Kept Secret the Deaths of First Cosmonauts,'" *The Independent* (London), April 14, 2001.

21. Scott W. Palmer, "Soviet Air-Mindedness as an Ideology of Dominance," *Technology & Culture*, 41, January 2000, 1–26.
22. Andrew Chaikin, "White House Tapes Shed Light on JFK Space Race Legend," www. space. com, August 22, 2001.
23. Ibid.
24. Walter A. McDougall, *The Heavens and the Earth: A Political History of the Space Age* (New York: Basic Books, 1985).
25. Dennis R. Jenkins, *Space Shuttle: The History of the National Space Transportation System, the First 100 Missions* (Cape Canaveral: Dennis Jenkins, 1992–2001).
26. Roger D. Launius, "NASA and the Decision to Build the Space Shuttle, 1969–1972," *The Historian*, Autumn 1994, 17–34; Richard P. Hallion, *The Hypersonic Revolution*, vols. 1–3 (Washington, D.C.: U.S. Air Force History Office, 1987, 1998); Larry Schweikart, "Hypersonic Hopes: Planning for NASP, 1982–1990," *Air Power History*, Spring 1994, 36–48.
27. Orley Ashenfelter, "Estimating the Effects of Training Programs on Earning," *Review of Economics and Statistics*, February 1978, 47–57.
28. Warren Brookes, *The Economy in Mind* (New York: Universe Books, 1982), 56; *New York Commerce and Finance Chronicle*, December 20, 1962.
29. Brookes, *Economy in Mind*, 58.
30. John Mueller, *The Classical Economic Case for Cutting Marginal Income Tax Rates*, House Republican Conference, Washington, D.C., February 1981. See Kennedy's speech to the New York Economic Club, December 14, 1962.
31. Johnson, *Modern Times*, 631.
32. William J. Duiker, *Ho Chi Minh* (New York: Hyperion, 2000).
33. Mark Haefele, "John F. Kennedy, USIA and World Opinion," *Diplomatic History*, 25, Winter 2001.
34. *Reporting Vietnam, Part One: American Journalism, 1959–1969* (New York: Library of America, 1998), 56.
35. John P. Roche, "The Demise of Liberal Internationalism," *National Review*, May 3, 1985, 26–44.
36. Ibid., 40.
37. John Newman, *JFK and Vietnam* (New York: Warner Books, 1992); David Kaiser, *American Tragedy: Kennedy, Johnson and the Origins of the Vietnam War* (Cambridge, MA: Belknap, 2000).
38. Lawrence S. Wittner, *Cold War America from Hiroshima to Watergate* (New York: Praeger, 1974), 226–227.
39. Kennedy quoted in Wittner, *Cold War America*, 229.
40. Ellen J. Hammer, *A Death in November* (New York: Oxford, 1987), 197.
41. Stanley Karnow, "The Fall of the House of Ngo Dinh," *Reporting Vietnam*, 94.
42. William Colby with James McCargor, *Lost Victory: A Firsthand Account of America's Sixteen-Year Involvement in Vietnam* (Chicago: Contemporary Books, 1989), 158.
43. See Henry Trewhitt, *McNamara* (New York: Harper & Row, 1971); Robert McNamara, *The Essence of Security* (New York: Prager, 1968); William W. Kaufman, *The McNamara Strategy* (New York: Harper & Row, 1964); Larry Schweikart, "Robert McNamara," in Larry Schweikart, ed., *The Encyclopedia of American Business History and Biography: Banking and Finance Since 1913* (New York: Facts on File, 1990), 251–67.
44. H. R. McMaster, *Dereliction of Duty: Johnson, McNamara, the Joint Chiefs of Staff, and the Lies That Led to Vietnam* (New York: HarperPerennial Library, 1998 [1997]).
45. Gerald Posner, *Case Closed: Lee Harvey Oswald and the Assassination of JFK* (New York: Random House, 1993). The literature on the Kennedy assassination is vast. For only a small sample, see Josiah Thompson, *Six Seconds in Dallas: A Micro-Study of the Kennedy Assassination* (New York: Bernard Greis, 1967); Sylvia Meagher, *Accessories After the Fact: The Warren Commission, the Authorities, and the Report* (New York: Vintage, 1976); Mark Lane, *Rush to Judgment* (New York: Holt, Rinehart 1966); Edward Jay Epstein, *Inquest: The Warren Commission and the Establishment of Truth* (New York: Viking, 1966); Harold Weisberg, *Whitewash*, 4 vols. (Hyattstown-Frederick, Maryland: H. Weisberg, 1965–1975); Robert G. Blakey and Richard N. Billings, *Fatal Hour: The Assassination of President Kennedy by Organized Crime* (New York: Berkeley, 1992); John H. Davis, *Mafia Kingfish: Carlos Marcello and the Assassination of John F. Kennedy*, 2d ed. (New York: Signet, 1989); Jim Garrison, *On the Trail of the Assassins: My Investigation and Prosecution of the Murder of President Kennedy* (New York: Sheridan Square Press, 1988); Robert J. Groden and Harrison Edward Livingstone, *High Treason: The Assassination of*

President John F. Kennedy, What Really Happened (Baltimore: Conservatory, 1989); Bonar Menninger, *Mortal Error: The Shot That Killed JFK* (New York: St. Martin's, 1992); David Lifton, *Best Evidence: Disguise and Deception in the Assassination of John F. Kennedy* (New York: Carroll & Graf, 1992). The first historian to examine the evidence was Michael L. Kurtz, *Crime of the Century: The Kennedy Assassination from a Historian's Perspective*, 2d ed. (Knoxville, TN: University of Tennessee Press, 1993).

46. Doris Kearns Goodwin, *Lyndon Johnson and the American Dream* (New York: Harper & Row, 1976), 177–78.

47. Tindall and Shi, *America*, 2:1520; Robert Caro, *The Years of Lyndon Johnson: The Path to Power* (New York: Knopf, 1982) and his *The Years of Lyndon Johnson: Means of Ascent* (New York: Knopf, 1990 [1989]); Paul Conkin, *Big Daddy from the Pedernales: Lyndon Baines Johnson* (Boston: Twayne, 1986); Joseph Califano Jr., *The Triumph and Tragedy of Lyndon Johnson: The White House Years* (College Station: Texas A&M University Press, 2000).

48. Paul F. Boller Jr., *Presidential Wives* (New York: Oxford, 1988), 387.

49. Johnson, *History of the American People*, 872.

50. Rick Perlstein, *Before the Storm: Barry Goldwater and the Unmaking of American Consensus* (New York: Hill and Wang, 2000).

51. See the reprints of news clippings from Greensboro papers in "A Sit-Down Becomes a Stand-off," in McClellan, *Historical Moments*, 2:394–99.

52. Dick Cluster, ed., *They Should Have Served That Cup of Coffee: Seven Radicals Remember the '60s* (Boston: South End Press, 1979).

53. Diane McWhorter, *Carry Me Home: Birmingham, Alabama: The Climactic Battle of the Civil Rights Revolution* (New York: Simon and Schuster, 2001); Robert Weems, *Desegregating the Dollar: African-American Consumerism in the Twentieth Century* (New York: New York University Press, 1998).

54. Lee S. Duemer, "Balancing the Books: Economic Incentives for Integration in the 1960s," *Southern Studies*, New Series, 7, Summer/Fall 1996, 79–90.

55. Goldfield, et al., *American Journey*, 932.

56. Martin Luther King Jr., "I Have a Dream," August 18, 1963, in McClellan, *Changing Interpretations*, 399–402.

57. Ibid.

58. Martin Luther King Jr., "Letter from Birmingham Jail," available online at http://almaz.com/nobel/peace/MLKjail. html.

59. Despite the fact that King was probably the only prominent American to be under surveillance by the KGB and the FBI simultaneously, Soviet records produced no evidence of communist influence on him. See Andrew and Mitrokhin, *Sword and the Shield*, 290.

60. Tindall and Shi, *America*, 2:1513.

61. D. L. Lewis, *King: A Critical Biography* (New York: Praeger, 1970); Michael W. Miles, *The Radical Probe: The Logic of Student Rebellion* (New York: Atheneum, 1971).

62. Daniel Pipes, "How Elijah Muhammad Won," online at http://www.danielpipes.org/article/341.

63. Jordan and Litwack, *United States*, 724.

64. Hugh Davis Graham, *The Civil Rights Era: Origins and Development of National Policy* (New York: Oxford University Press, 1990).

65. Stephen F. Lawson, *Running for Freedom: Civil Rights and Black Politics in America Since 1941* (New York: McGraw-Hill, 191).

66. Goldfield, *American Journey*, 951.

67. Ibid., 961.

68. Jonathan J. Bean, " 'Burn, Baby, Burn': Small Business in the Urban Riots of the 1960s," *Independent Review*, 5, Fall 2000, 165–88.

69. Spencer Crump, *Black Riot in Los Angeles: The Story of the Watts Tragedy* (Los Angeles: Trans-Anglo Books, 1966), 21.

70. Martin Luther King, *Strength to Love* (New York: Harper and Row, 1963); the "Mountaintop" sermon appears in *American Sermons: The Pilgrims to Martin Luther King Jr.* (New York: Library of America, 1999).

71. Charles Murray, *Losing Ground: American Social Policy, 1950–1980* (New York: Basic Books, 1984), 24.

72. Wittner, *Cold War America*, 239.

73. Ibid.

74. Murray, *Losing Ground*, 129.
75. See Murray's figures 9.2 and 9.3, *Losing Ground*, 130–31.
76. Patrick F. Fagan and Robert Rector, "The Effects of Divorce on America," Heritage Foundation Backgrounder, #1373, June 5, 2000, chart 3, "Divorces per 100 Marriages," 3; George Gilder, *Sexual Suicide* (New York: Quadrangle, 1973).
77. Murray, *Losing Ground*, passim.
78. Irwin Garfinkle and Robert Haveman, with the assistance of David Betson, U.S. Department of Health, Education and Welfare, "Earnings Capacity, Poverty, and Inequality," Institute for Research on Poverty Monograph Series (New York: Academic Press, 1977); George Gilder, *Wealth and Poverty* (New York: Basic Books, 1981).
79. Mary E. Corcoran and Ajay Chaudry, "The Dynamics of Childhood Poverty," *The Future of Children*, 7, no. 2, 1997, 40–54; Fagan and Rector, "Effects of Divorce," chart 9, "Median Income of Families with Children by Family Structure," 11.
80. Alan C. Acock and K. Hill Kiecolt, "Is It Family Structure or Socioeconomic Status? Family Structure During Adolescence and Adult Adjustment," *Social Forces*, 68, 1989, 553–71.
81. Judith Wallerstein, "The Long-Term Effects of Divorce on Children: A Review," *Journal of the American Academy of Child Adolescent Psychiatry*, 30, 1991, 349–60; Michael Workman and John Beer, "Aggression, Alcohol Dependency, and Self-Consciousness Among High School Students of Divorced and Non-Divorced Parents," *Psychological Reports*, 71, 1992, 279–86; David Popenoe, *Life Without Father* (New York: Martin Kessler Books, 1995).
82. John P. Hoffman and Robert A. Johnson, "A National Portrait of Family Structure and Adolescent Drug Use," *Journal of Marriage and the Family*, 60, 1998, 633–45; Robert L. Flewing and K. E. Baumann, "Family Structure as a Predictor of Initial Substance Use and Sexual Intercourse in Early Adolescence," ibid., 52, 1990, 171–81.
83. David Blankenhorn, *Fatherless America: Confronting Our Most Urgent Social Problem* (New York: HarperPerennial, 1996).
84. Norman Podhoretz, *Why We Were in Vietnam* (New York: Simon & Schuster, 1982), 80.
85. Richard H. Shultz Jr, *The Secret War Against Hanoi* (New York: HarperCollins, 1999), 205.
86. A. L. Gropman, "The Air War in Vietnam, 1961–73," in R. A. Mason, ed., *War in the Third Dimension* (London: Brassey's, 1986), 33–58, quotation on 34.
87. Kocher, "John Kennedy, Playing in the Sandbox," in his zolatimes Web article, "Viet Nam."
88. James and Sybil Stockdale, *In Love and War: The Story of a Family's Ordeal and Sacrifice During the Vietnam Years* (Annapolis: Naval Institute Press, 1990), see the appendix.
89. Jordan and Litwack, *United States*, 812.
90. "Gulf of Tonkin Resolution," in McClellan, *Historical Moments*, 2:434.
91. Jordan and Litwack, *United States*, 812.
92. Benjamin S. Lambeth, *The Transformation of American Air Power* (Ithaca, NY: Cornell University Press, 2000).
93. Robert Leckie, *The Wars of America*, rev. ed. (New York: Harper & Row, 1981 [1968]), 987.
94. Lambeth, *Transformation*, 17.
95. Ibid.
96. U.S. Air Force, *Air War—Vietnam* (New York: Bobbs-Merrill, 1978), 214.
97. Lambeth, *Transformation*, 18.
98. Ho quoted in Tindall and Shi, *America*, 2:1540.
99. Tindall and Shi, *America*, 2:1539.
100. Hanson, *Carnage and Culture*, 400.
101. Phillip B. Davidson, *Vietnam at War: The History, 1946–1975* (New York: Oxford University Press, 1988), 552.
102. Lambeth, *Transformation*, 23.
103. Leckie, *Wars of America*, 1006–7.
104. R. F. Ford, *Tet 1968: Understanding the Surprise* (Essex, England: Cass, 1990), 139, quoted in Hanson, *Carnage and Culture*, 404.
105. William Lunch and Peter Sperlich, "American Public Opinion and the War in Vietnam," *Western Political Quarterly*, March 1979, 21–24; John Mueller, *War, Presidents and Public Opinion* (New York: John Wiley, 1973); Leslie H. Gelb and Richard K. Betts, *The Irony of Vietnam: The System Worked* (Washington, D.C.: Brookings, 1979).
106. Richard J. Herrnstein and Charles Murray, *The Bell Curve: Intelligence and Class Structure in American Life* (New York: Free Press, 1994), 32.

107. William Strauss and Neil Howe, *Generations: The History of America's Future, 1584–2069* (New York: William Morrow and Company, 1991), 199–316.
108. Ibid., 305.
109. Lewis B. Mayhew, ed., *Higher Education in the Revolutionary Decades* (Berkeley, CA: McCutchan Publishing, 1967).
110. Chester E. Finn Jr., *Scholars, Dollars, and Bureaucrats* (Washington, D.C.: Brookings Institution, 1978), 21.
111. Fritz Machlup, *The Production and Distribution of Knowledge in the United States* (Princeton, NJ: Princeton University Press, 1962), 374.
112. Edward F. Denison, *Sources of Economic Growth and the Alternatives Before Us* (New York: Committee for Economic Development, 1962); C. P. Snow, *The Two Cultures and the Scientific Revolution* (New York: Cambridge University Press, 1959); and Clark Kerr, *The Uses of the University*, 3rd ed. (Cambridge, MA: Harvard University Press, 1982), 88.
113. Rex Jackson, Appendix to *On Further Examination*, "Comparison of SAT Score Trends in Selected Schools Judged to Have Traditional or Experimental Orientations" (Princeton, NJ: College Entrance Examination Board, 1977).
114. Elchanan Cohn, *The Economics of Education*, rev. ed. (Cambridge, MA: Ballinger, 1979), 49, tables 3–4; Herrnstein and Murray, *Bell Curve*, 95; L. F. Katz and K. M. Murphy, *Changes in Relative Wages, 1963–198* (Cambridge, MA: National Bureau of Economic Research, 1990), table 1.
115. Johnson, *Modern Times*, 641.
116. David Krech, Robert S. Crutchfield, and Edgerton L. Bellachey, *Individual in Society: A Textbook of Social Psychology* (New York: McGraw-Hill, 1962).
117. Richard Gid Powers, *Not Without Honor: The History of American Anticommunism* (New York: Free Press, 1995), 306.
118. Roger Kimball, *Tenured Radicals: How Politics Has Corrupted Our Higher Education* (New York: Harper & Row, 1990).
119. Ellen Schrecker, *No Ivory Tower: McCarthyism and the Universities* (New York: Oxford, 1986).
120. Tindall and Shi, *America* 2:1551.
121. David Steigerwald, *The Sixties and the End of Modern America* (New York: St. Martin's, 1995), 127–28, quotation on 127.
122. Harvey Klehr and John Earl Haynes, *The American Communist Movement: Storming Heaven Itself* (New York: Twayne, 1992), 151.
123. Klehr and Haynes, *American Communist Movement*, 159; Dohrn quoted in Peter Collier and David Horowitz, *Destructive Generation* (New York: Summit, 1989), 74; Thomas S. Powers, *The War at Home: Vietnam and the American People, 1964–1968* (New York: Grossman, 1973), 75–76.
124. Kirkpatrick Sale, *SDS* (New York: Random House, 1973), 466.
125. Guenter Lewy, *The Cause That Failed: Communism in American Political Life* (New York: Oxford University Press, 1990), 250–76.
126. Bruce J. Schulman, "Out of the Streets and into the Classroom? The New Left and the Counterculture in United States History Textbooks," *Journal of American History*, 85 (March 1999), 1527–34, quotation on 1529. See also Allan Matusow, *The Unraveling of America: A History of Liberalism in the 1960s* (New York: Harper & Row, 1984); William O'Neill, *Coming Apart: An Informal History of America in the 1960s* (Chicago: Quadrangle, 1971).
127. Paul Hollander, *Political Pilgrims: Travels of Western Intellectuals to the Soviet Union, China, and Cuba, 1928–1978* (New York: Oxford University Press, 1981), 181.
128. Jerry Rubin, *Do It: Scenarios of the Revolution* (New York: Simon and Schuster, 1970), 57.
129. Susan Stern, *With the Weathermen: The Personal Journal of a Revolutionary Woman* (New York: Doubleday, 1975), 142–45, 201.
130. Rubin, *Do It*, 169.
131. Ibid., 125.
132. Collier and Horowitz, *Destructive Generation: Second Thoughts About the Sixties*, 264.
133. Christopher P. Anderson, *Citizen Jane: The Turbulent Life of Jane Fonda* (New York: Holt, 1990).
134. Martin Lee and Bruce Shlain, *Acid Dreams* (New York: Grove Press, 1992 [1985]), 29.
135. Ginsburg quoted in Lee and Shlain, *Acid Dreams*, 111.
136. Lee and Shlain, *Acid Dreams*, 129.

137. Ibid.
138. Steigerwald, *The Sixties*, 169.
139. Claudia Goldin and Lawrence F. Katz, "On the Pill: Changing the Course of Women's Education," *Milken Institute Review*, Second Quarter, 2001, 12–21.
140. Beverly Gordon, "American Denim: Blue Jeans and Their Multiple Layers of Meaning," in George O. Carney, ed., *Fast Food, Stock Cars, and Rock 'n' Roll: Place and Space in American Pop Culture* (Lanham, MD: Rowman and Littlefield, 1995), 77–117.
141. David Dalton, "Finally, the Shocking Truth about Woodstock Can Be Told, or Kill It Before It Clones Itself," *The Gadfly*, August 1999, taken from *The Gadfly* online, http://gadfly.org/ 1999–08/toc. asp. Other comments and quotations are from the author's conversations with Dalton.
142. Dalton, "Finally, the Shocking Truth," author's conversations with Dalton.
143. Ibid.
144. Ibid.
145. Rubin and Dorn quoted in Lee and Schlain, *Acid Dreams*, 257.
146. Lewy, *The Cause That Failed*, 270.
147. Adam Cohen and Elizabeth Taylor, *American Pharaoh: Mayor Richard Daley: His Battle for Chicago and the Nation* (Boston: Little, Brown 2000), 462–63.
148. Ibid., 473.
149. The commission's report is quoted in Joseph C. Keeley, *The Left-Leaning Antenna: Political Bias in Television* (New Rochelle, NY: Arlington House, 1971), 109.
150. Cohen and Taylor, *American Pharaoh*, 474, 478.
151. Jordan and Litwack, *United States*, 816.
152. Wittner, *Cold War America*, 300–301.
153. William Safire, *Before the Fall: An Insider's View of the Pre-Watergate House* (Garden City, NY: Doubleday, 1975), 171.
154. Ibid., 70, 75.
155. Kevin Phillips, *The Emerging Republican Majority* (New York: Arlington House, 1969).
156. Wittner, *Cold War America*, 338.
157. Brookes, *Economy in Mind*, 150, and table 1.3.
158. Thomas C. Reeves, *Twentieth-Century America: A Brief History* (New York: Oxford, 2000), 215.
159. James Bovard, *Lost Rights: The Destruction of American Liberty* (New York: St. Martin's, 1994), 33–43 passim.
160. Paul Ehrlich, *The Population Bomb* (New York: Ballantine, 1968).
161. Ehrlich's 1971 edition of *The Population Bomb*, xi, quoted by Brian Carnell, "Paul Ehrlich," at www. overpopulation.com/faq/People/paulehrlich. html.
162. Thomas Malthus, *An Essay on the Principle of Population* (London: Reeves and Turner, 1878).
163. Julian Simon and Herman Kahn, *The Resourceful Earth: A Response to Global 2000* (Oxford: Blackwell, 1984).
164. Greg Easterbrook, "The Forgotten Benefactor of Humanity," reprinted in Larry Schweikart, ed., *Readings in Western Civilization*, 2nd ed. (Boston: Pearson Custom Publishing, 2000), 23–30.
165. "The Development of the White House Staff," *Congressional Record*, June 20, 1972; Arthur Schlesinger Jr, *The Imperial Presidency* (Boston: Houghton Mifflin, 1973).
166. Podhoretz, *Why We Were in Vietnam*, 156; Martin F. Herz, *The Prestige Press and the Christmas Bombing*, 1972 (Washington, DC: Ethics and Public Policy Center, 1980).
167. Leckie, *Wars of America*, 1018.
168. New York *Times*, May 5, 1970, and June 21, 1970.
169. Major A.J.C. Lavalle, ed., *Air Power and the 1972 Spring Invasion* (Washington, D.C.: USAF Southeast Asia Monograph Series, 1985), 57.
170. Lambeth, *Transformation*, 29.
171. Colonel Alan Gropman, USAF, "The Air War in Vietnam, 1961–73," in Air Vice Marshal R. A. Mason, RAF, ed., *War in the Third Dimension: Essays in Contemporary Air Power* (London: Brassey's, 1986), 57.
172. Wittner, *Cold War America*, 283.
173. John Mack Faragher, et al, *Out of Many: A History of the American People*, combined ed., brief 2nd ed. (Upper Saddle River, NJ: Prentice-Hall, 1999), 567.
174. Douglas Dalgleish and Larry Schweikart, *Trident* (Carbondale, IL: Southern Illinois University Press, 1984).

175. Johnson, *Modern Times*, 649.
176. Bernard Goldberg, *Bias: A CBS Insider Exposes How the Media Distort the News* (Washington, D.C.: Regnery Publishing, 2002), 24.
177. Len Colodny and Robert Getlin, *Silent Coup: The Removal of a President* (New York: St. Martin's, 1991); Joan Hoff, *Nixon Reconsidered* (New York: Basic Books, 1994).
178. "Liddy Gains Mistrial in Defame Suit," New York *Post*, February 2, 2001.
179. Wittner, *Cold War America*, 380.
180. Jordan and Litwack, *United States*, 844.
181. David Frum, *How We Got Here: The 70's: The Decade That Brought You Modern Life (for Better or Worse)* (New York: Basic Books, 2000), 26.
182. Barbara Olson, *Hell to Pay: The Unfolding Story of Hillary Rodham Clinton* (Washington: Regnery, 1999), 122.
183. Ibid., 124.
184. "Articles of Impeachment of Richard M. Nixon," August 20, 1974.
185. Stanley J. Kutler, *The Wars of Watergate: The Last Crisis of Richard Nixon* (New York: Knopf, 1990); Maurice Stans, *The Terrors of Justice: The Untold Side of Watergate* (New York: Everest House, 1978); H. R. Haldeman, *The Ends of Power* (New York: Times Books, 1978); Charles W. Colson, *Born Again* (Old Tappan, NJ: Chosen Books, 1976); John Dean, *Blind Ambition: The White House Years* (New York: Simon & Schuster, 1976).
186. Stephen E. Ambrose, *Nixon: Ruin and Recovery* (New York: Simon & Schuster, 1991).

Chapter 20. Retreat and Resurrection, 1974–88

1. Richard Reeves, *A Ford, Not a Lincoln* (New York: Harcourt Brace, 1975); Edward L. Schapsmeier and Frederick H. Schapsmeier, *Gerald R. Ford's Date with Destiny: A Political Biography* (New York: P. Lang, 1989); Gerald Ford, *A Time to Heal: The Autobiography of Gerald R. Ford* (New York: Reader's Digest, 1979).
2. Johnson, *History of the American People*, 906.
3. Anthony Lukas, *Nightmare: The Underside of the Nixon Years* (New York: Viking, 1976).
4. Tindall and Shi, *America*, 2:1593.
5. John Barron and Anthony Paul, *Peace with Horror* (London: Hodder and Stoughton, 1977), 136–49.
6. Yehuda Bauer, *From Diplomacy to Resistance: A History of Jewish Palestine, 1939–1945* (Philadelphia: Jewish Publication Society of America, 1970); Nicholas Bethell, *The Palestine Triangle: The Struggle Between the British, the Jews and the Arabs* (London: Andre Deutsch, 1979).
7. Joseph Schechtman, *The United States and the Jewish State Movement* (New York: Herzl Press, 1966).
8. *Oil Weekly*, March 6, 1944.
9. Paul Johnson, *Modern Times: A History of the World from the Twenties to the Nineties* (New York: HarperCollins, 1991), 666.
10. Scott Derks, *The Value of a Dollar: Prices and Incomes in the United States, 1860–1899* (Lakeville, CT: Grey House, 1999), 381.
11. Ralph Nader, *Unsafe at Any Speed* (New York: Grossman, 1965).
12. B. Bruce Briggs, *The War Against the Automobile* (New York: E. P. Dutton, 1977), 83.
13. Tindall and Shi, *America*, 2:1594.
14. Gene Smiley, *The American Economy in the Twentieth Century* (Cincinnati, OH: College Division, South-Western Publishing Company, 1994), 381.
15. Robert Crandall, *Why Is the Cost of Environmental Regulation So High?* (St. Louis: Center for the Study of American Business, Washington University, February 1992), 3.
16. Brookes, *Economy in Mind*, 111.
17. Schweikart, *Entrepreneurial Adventure*, chap. 11.
18. Ibid., 415.
19. Burton H. Klein, *Dynamic Economics* (Cambridge, MA: Harvard University Press, 1977).
20. Schweikart, *Entrepreneurial Adventure*, passim.
21. Paul Ingrassia and Joseph B. White, *Comeback: The Fall and Rise of the American Automobile Industry* (New York: Simon & Schuster, 1994); Lee Iaccoca with William Novak, *Iaccoca: A Biography* (New York: Bantam, 1984).
22. Derks, *Working Class Americans,* passim.

23. Derks, ed., *The Value of a Dollar, 1860–1899*, passim.
24. Kenneth Warren, *Big Steel: The First Century of the United States Steel Corporation, 1901–2001* (Pittsburgh: University of Pittsburgh Press, 2001).
25. John P. Hoerr, *And the Wolf Finally Came: The Decline of the American Steel Industry* (Pittsburgh: University of Pittsburgh Press, 1988); Hans G. Mueller, "The Steel Industry," in J. Michael Finger and Thomas D. Willett, eds., *The Internationalization of the American Economy, the Annals of the American Academy of Political and Social Science*, 460, March 1982, 73–82.
26. Goldfield et al., *American Journey*, 987.
27. Claudia Goldin and Lawrence F. Katz, "On the Pill: Changing the Course of Women's Education," *Milken Institute Review*, Spring Quarter 2001, 12–21.
28. Thomas C. Reeves, *Twentieth-Century America: A Brief History* (New York: Oxford University Press, 2000), 193.
29. Stephen W. Tweedie, "Viewing the Bible Belt," *Journal of Popular Culture*, 11, 1978, 865–76.
30. Ibid., 875–76.
31. Thomas C. Reeves, *The Empty Church: The Suicide of Liberal Christianity* (New York: Free Press, 1996), 126.
32. Laurence R. Innaccone, Roger Finke, and Rodney Stark, "Deregulating Religion: The Economics of Church and State," *Economic Inquiry*, 35, April 1997, 350–64.
33. Ibid., 361.
34. Reeves, *Empty Church*, 146.
35. "Ecumenical War over Abortion," *Time*, January 29, 1979, 62–63.
36. David Garrow, *Liberty and Sexuality: The Right to Privacy and the Making of Roe v. Wade* (New York: Macmillan, 1994).
37. Erica Scharrer, "From Wise to Foolish: The Portrayal of the Sitcom Father, 1950s–1990s," *Journal of Broadcasting and Electronic Media*, 45, Winter 2001, 23–40.
38. Robert Locke, "Why No-Fault Divorce Is the Key to Abortion," *Front Page Magazine*, March 26, 2001, at frontpagemag.com/archives/feminism/locke03–26–01p.htm.
39. Barbara DaFoe Whitehead, "Dan Qualye Was Right," *The Atlantic*, April 1993, and more broadly explained in her book *The Divorce Culture* (New York: Random House, 1996).
40. George Gilder, *Men and Marriage* (Gretna, LA: Pelican Publishing, 1986).
41. Barbara Gordon, *Jennifer Fever: Older Men/Younger Women* (New York: Harper & Row, 1988).
42. "Day Care Linked to Aggression in Kids," CBS News, April 19, 2001, citing a large study (1,300 children) by Martha Cox of the University of North Carolina.
43. Andrew and Mitrokhin, *Sword and the Shield*, 204.
44. Ibid., 206.
45. Richard L. Tedrow and Thomas Tedrow, *Death at Chappaquiddick* (Ottawa: Green Hill Publishers, 1976), is typical of most of the books looking at the incident.
46. Martin Gilbert, *A History of the Twentieth Century: 1952–1999* vol. 3 (New York: William Morrow, 1999), 3:544.
47. Cited in Garry Wills, *The Kennedy Imprisonment: A Meditation on Power* (Boston: Little, Brown 1982), 195.
48. Edmund Morris, *Dutch: A Memoir of Ronald Reagan* (New York: HarperCollins, 1999), 228.
49. Matthew Dallek, *The Right Moment: Ronald Reagan's First Victory and the Decisive Turning Point in American Politics* (New York: Free Press, 2000).
50. Kiron K. Skinner, Martin Anderson, and Annelise Anderson, eds. *Reagan, In His Own Hand: The Writings of Ronald Reagan That Reveal His Revolutionary Vision for America* (New York: Free Press, 2001).
51. Derks, *Value of a Dollar*, 405–11.
52. Tindall and Shi, *America*, 2:1610.
53. Goldfield, et al., *American Journey*, 1011, photo.
54. Thomas A. Bailey, et al., *The American Pageant*, 11th ed. (Boston: Houghton Mifflin, 1998), 2:993.
55. George Gilder, *Wealth and Poverty* (New York: Basic Books, 1981).
56. Kenneth S. Baer, *Reinventing Democrats: The Politics of Liberalism from Reagan to Clinton* (Lawrence, KS: University Press of Kansas, 2000), passim.
57. Johnson, *History of the American People*, 921.
58. Ronald Reagan, *An American Life* (New York: Pocket Books, 1990), 259–63.
59. Schweikart, *Entrepreneurial Adventure*, 338–40, 542–46.

60. Warren Brookes, "The Silent Boom," *The American Spectator*, August 1988, 16–19, and his "The Media vs. the Economy," in the *Detroit News*, December 29, 1988.

61. Reagan, *An American Life*, 315–17.

62. Thomas K. McCraw, *Prophets of Regulation: Charles Francis Adams, Louis D. Brandeis, James M. Landis, Alfred E. Kahn* (Cambridge: Belknap Press, 1984).

63. Ibid., 268; David Field, "Big Airlines Pack in Passengers, Profit," *USA Today*, April 1, 1997; Larry Schweikart interview with Tonya Wagner, Federal Aviation Administration, July 5, 1995.

64. Schweikart, *Entrepreneurial Adventure*, 439–40.

65. Paul Teske, Samuel Best, and Michael Mintrom, *Deregulating Freight Transportation: Delivering the Goods* (Washington, DC: AEI Press, 1995); James Bovard, "The Great Truck Robbery," *Wall Street Journal*, November 3, 1993; Glenn Yago, "The Regulatory Reign of Terror," *Wall Street Journal*, March 4, 1992.

66. Typical of this approach is Tindall and Shi, *America*, 2:1612: "Reaganomics departed from the Coolidge record mainly in the mounting deficits of the 1980s and in their major cause— growing expenditures for the armed forces." There is simply no evidence that the military budget grew in total dollars relative to the expenditures on "social spending" that accounted for the deficit.

67. Peter Sperry, "The Real Reagan Economic Record: Responsible and Successful Fiscal Policy," Heritage Foundation Backgrounder, #1414, March 1, 2001, chart 1, "Federal Revenues and Expenditures, 1980–1993," 3.

68. Gilder, *Wealth and Poverty*, passim, and his *Recapturing the Spirit of Enterprise* (San Francisco: ICS Press, 1992); W. Michael Cox and Richard Alm, *Myths of Rich & Poor: Why We're Better Off Than We Think* (New York: Basic Books, 1999).

69. Bruce Bartlett, "Tariffs and Alloy of Errors," *Washington Times*, April 1, 2002.

70. Steven F. Hayward, *The Age of Reagan: The Fall of the Old Liberal Order* (Boseville, CA: Prima Publishing, 2001).

71. Bernard Schafer, "The US Air Raid on Libya in April 1986: A Confidential Soviet Account from the Stasi Archives," Woodrow Wilson International Center for Scholars, Cold War International History Project, 2001.

72. Reagan, *An American Life*, 466.

73. Ibid., 556.

74. Michael Moritz, *The Little Kingdom: The Private Story of Apple Computer* (New York: William Morrow and Co., 1984).

75. Schweikart, *Entrepreneurial Adventure*, 435.

76. Joel Kotkin and Ross C. DeVol, "Knowledge-Value Cities in the Digital Age," research paper from the Milken Institute, February 13, 2001, 2, available at http://www.milkeninst.org.

77. William T. Youngs, "Bill Gates and Microsoft," in Youngs, ed., *American Realities: Historical Episodes, From Reconstruction to the Present*, vol. 2, 3d ed. (New York: HarperCollins, 1993); James Wallace and Jim Erickson, *Hard Drive: Bill Gates and the Making of the Microsoft Empire* (New York: Wiley, 1992).

78. See Adam D. Thierer, "How Free Computers are Filling the Digital Divide," Heritage Foundation Backgrounder, #1361, April 20, 2000.

79. Stephen Moore and Julian L. Simon, "The Greatest Century that Ever Was: 25 Miraculous Trends of the Past 100 Years," CATO Institute Policy Analysis, #364, December 15, 1999, Fig. 21, "Patents Granted by the United States," 23.

80. Andrew and Mitrokhin, *Sword and the Shield*, 243.

81. Jacques Gansler, *Affording Defense* (Cambridge: MIT Press, 1989); Fens Osler Hampson, *Unguided Missiles: How America Buys Its Weapons* (New York: W. W. Norton, 1989); Thomas McNaugher, *New Weapons, Old Politics: America's Military Procurement Muddle* (Washington, DC: Brookings Institution, 1989); Michael E. Brown, *Flying Blind* (Ithaca, NY: Cornell University Press, 1992); Jacob Goodwin, *Brotherhood of Arms: Geneva Dynamics and the Business of Defending America* (New York: Times Books, 1985).

82. Matthew Evangelista, *Innovation and the Arms Race* (Ithaca: Cornell University Press, 1988), 27–28; Peter J. Katzenstein, "International Relations and Domestic Structures: Foreign Economic Policies of Advanced Industrial States," *International Organization*, 30, Winter 1976, 1–45.

83. Gilbert, *History of the Twentieth Century*, 596, but the entire "evil empire" speech appears in *An American Life*, 369–70.

84. Paul Hollander, *Political Will and Personal Belief: The Decline and Fall of Soviet Communism* (New Haven: Yale University Press, 1999), 11.
85. Lou Cannon, "Reagan's Big Idea—How the Gipper Conceived Star Wars," *National Review*, February 22, 1999, 40–42, quotation on 40.
86. Ibid.
87. For typical college-level textbook assessments of Star Wars, see Bailey, et al., *American Pageant*, 998 ("Those who did not dismiss it as ludicrous feared that [it] might be ruinously costly, ultimately unworkable, and fatally destabilizing. . . ."); Brinkley, et al., *American History*, II:966, which emphasizes the Soviet reaction ("The Soviet Union reacted with anger and alarm and insisted the new program would elevate the arms race to new and more dangerous levels."); Goldfield, et al., *American Journey*, 1017, which questioned the feasibility of the technology, while still stressing the "destabilization" aspects ("All of the technologies were untested [which was completely untrue—they had almost all been tested for years, both in the U.S. and the USSR, and tested successfully]; some existed only in the imagination. Few scientists thought that SDI could work.") Other texts had similar comments. Davidson, et al., *Nation of Nations*, 1177, said, "Most scientists contended that the project was as fantastic as the movie [*Star Wars*]." Faragher, et al., *Out of Many*, 953, stated Reagan "claimed, though few scientists agreed, that satellites and lasers could create an impregnable shield—" (in fact, Reagan claimed no such thing). Surprisingly, one of the most otherwise liberal texts, Jordan and Litwack's *United States*, is fairly objective in its treatment—less than twenty words for the most important weapons proposal, arguably, in American history. What is astounding is how the technological questions and the destabilization questions, even when contained in the same paragraph, never raised the most obvious question by any of the authors: if the technology for Star Wars could not work, how could it possibly be destabilizing?
88. Johnson, *History of the American People*, 927.
89. Cannon, "Reagan's Big Idea," 40–42.
90. Hollander, *Personal Will*, 5.
91. Ibid., 100.
92. Ibid., 98.
93. Seweryn Bailer, "The Soviet Union and the West: Security and Foreign Policy," in Seweryn Bailer, et al., eds., *Gorbachev's Russia and American Foreign Policy* (Boulder, CO: Westview Press, 1988), 457–91, especially 458.
94. Andrew and Mitrokhin, *Sword and the Shield*, 484.
95. Ibid., 220; Barbara von der Heydt, *Candles Behind the Wall: Heroes of the Peaceful Revolution That Shattered Communism* (Grand Rapids, MI: William B. Eerdmans Publishing Co., 1993), 124.
96. Von der Heydt, *Candles Behind the Wall*, 124.
97. Reagan, *An American Life*, 11–15.
98. "Study Reveals 'Politicization' of Intelligence," *Washington Times*, October 9, 2000.
99. Reagan, *An American Life*, 606.
100. Ibid., 402.

Chapter 21. The Moral Crossroads, 1989–2000

1. John Robert Greene, *The Presidency of George Bush* (Lawrence, KS: University of Kansas Press, 2000); George Bush, *All the Best: My Life in Letters and Other Writings* (New York: Scribner, 1999); George Bush and Brent Scowcroft, *A World Transformed* (New York: Knopf, 1998).
2. Kenneth S. Baer, *Reinventing Democrats: The Politics of Liberalism from Clinton to Reagan* (Lawrence, KS: University of Kansas Press, 2000), 12.
3. Steven M. Gillon and Cathy D. Matson, *The American Experiment*, 1265.
4. Paul Hollander, *Political Will and Personal Belief: The Decline and Fall of Soviet Communism* (New Haven: Yale University Press, 1999), 22.
5. Ibid., 3.
6. Ibid., 7.
7. Andrew and Mitrokhin, *Sword and the Shield*, 548.
8. Ibid.
9. Ibid.
10. Curtis Peebles, *Dark Eagles* (Novato, CA: Presidio Press, 1995), 183.

11. Williamson Murray, *Air War in the Persian Gulf* (Baltimore: Nautical and Aviation Publishing Company of America, 1995), 26.

12. Rick Atkinson, *Crusade: The Untold Story of the Persian Gulf War* (Boston: Houghton Mifflin, 1993); Michael Gordon and Bernard Trainor, *The General's War* (Boston: Little, Brown, 1995); Tom Clancy and Chuck Horner, *Every Man a Tiger* (New York: G. P. Putnam's Sons, 1999); Frank N. Schubert and Theresa L. Kraus, eds., *The Whirlwind War: The United States Army in Operations Desert Shield and Desert Storm* (Washington, DC: Center of Military History, U.S. Army, 1994).

13. Tom Keaney and Eliot Cohen, *Revolution in Warfare?* (Annapolis, MD: Naval Institute Press, 1995); Richard Reynolds, *Heart of the Storm: The Genesis of the Air Power in the Persian Gulf Air Campaign Against Iraq* (Maxwell Air Force Base, AL: Air University Press, 1995).

14. Benjamin S. Lambeth, *The Transformation of American Air Power* (Ithaca, NY: Cornell University Press, 2000), 112.; Jeffrey Record, *Hollow Victory* (Washington, D.C.: Brassey's, 1993).

15. Peebles, *Dark Eagles*, 188.

16. Majors Michael J. Bodner and William W. Bruner III, "Tank Plinking," *Air Force Magazine*, October 1993, 31; Lambeth, *Transformation*, 123.

17. Tony Cappacio, "Air Force's Eyes in the Sky Alerted Marines at Khafji, Targeted Convoys," *Defense Week*, March 18, 1991, 7.

18. Barry D. Watts, letter to the editor, *Foreign Affairs*, November/December 1997, 180.

19. Keaney and Cohen, *Revolution in Warfare?*, 91–92.

20. Lambeth, *Transformation*, 128.

21. Atkinson, *Crusade*, 342.

22. Victor Davis Hanson, *Carnage and Culture: Landmark Battles in the Rise of Western Power*, (New York: Doubleday, 2001), 364–65.

23. Jonathan Rauch, "Why Bush (Senior) Didn't Blow It in the Gulf War," *Jewish World Review* (online edition), November 5, 2001.

24. Gillon and Matson, *American Experience*, 1270.

25. Gerald Posner, *Citizen Perot: His Life and Times* (New York: Random House, 1996).

26. George Stephanopoulos, *All Too Human: A Political Education* (Boston: Little, Brown, 1999), 82.

27. Rhodes Cook, "Arkansan Travels Well Nationally as Campaign Heads for Test," *Congressional Quarterly Weekly Report*, January 11, 1992.

28. David Maraniss, *First in His Class: A Biography of Bill Clinton* (New York: Simon & Schuster, 1995).

29. Murrin, et al., *Liberty, Equality, Power*, 1103.

30. Woodward, *The Agenda* (New York: Pocket Books, 1995), 122.

31. Gillon and Matson, *American Experience*, 1275; Brinkley, *Unfinished Nation*, 1014. The phrase used most by textbook authors is that the plan "pleased . . . virtually no one" (Murrin, et al., *Liberty, Equality, Power*, 1104). A similar phrase appears in Goldfield et al., *American Journey*, 1001, "something for everyone to dislike." This implied that it was a solid concept so cutting-edge that it would offend because of its revolutionary nature. None of these sources come close to delineating the vast aggrandizement of power in the federal government that the plan represented, or the intrusion into personal liberties as basic as choosing one's own doctor and pursuing the profession of one's choice. They are not even considered as possible sources of the widespread opposition.

32. Woodward, *The Agenda*, 24.

33. Robert "Buzz" Patterson, *Dereliction of Duty* (Washington, DC: Regnery, 2003), 5.

34. Woodward, *The Agenda*, 125.

35. Stephanopoulos, *All Too Human*, 416.

36. Murrin, et al., *Liberty, Equality, and Power*, 1105.

37. Brinkley, *Unfinished Nation*, 1019.

38. Once again, typical college textbooks seek to downplay the impact of the Contract or mischaracterize it entirely. Alan Brinkley, in *The Unfinished Nation*, claimed "Opinion polls suggested that few voters in 1994 were aware of the 'Contract' at the time they voted" (1015). Gillon and Matson, predictably, refer to the Contract as "a political wish list polished by consultants and tested in focus groups" (*American Experiment*, 1276), and Goldfield's *American Journey* portrayed the campaign's success as emanating from "personal animosity" (1001). Thomas Bailey et al. characterized the Contract as an "all-out assault on budget deficits and radical reductions

in welfare programs," and succeeded because Democrats' arguments were "drowned in the right-wing tornado that roared across the land. . . ." (*American Pageant*, 1002). Instead, at the time, many analysts on both the left and right viewed this as a watershed election about serious issues. See Michael Tomasky, "Why They Won: The Left Lost Touch," *Village Voice*, November 22, 1994; Al From, "Can Clinton Recover? Or Will GOP Prevail?" *USA Today*, November 10, 1994; Gary C. Jacobson, "The 1994 House Elections in Perspective," in Philip A. Klinkner, ed., *The Elections of 1994 in Context* (Boulder: Westview Press, 1996); and Franco Mattei, "Eight More in '94: The Republican Takeover of the Senate," in Philip A. Klinkner, ed., *Midterm* (Boulder, CO: Westview Press, 1996). Although Clinton's approval rating in the Northeast was 51 percent—hardly stellar for a liberal—in the rest of the country it averaged 45 percent.

39. Dick Morris, *Behind the Oval Office: Winning the Presidency in the Nineties* (New York: Random House, 1997), 100; Elizabeth Drew, *Showdown: The Struggle Between the Gingrich Congress and the Clinton White House* (New York: Simon & Schuster, 1996), 63.

40. See the PBS "Scorecard" on "Contract with America" items, available online at http://www.pbs.org/newshour/bb/congress/scorecard.html.

41. Morris, *Behind the Oval Office*, passim.

42. See Dick J. Reavis, *The Ashes of Waco: An Investigation* (Syracuse, NY: Syracuse University Press, 1998); "Waco—Rules of Engagement," Fifth Estate Productions, Director William Gazecki, 1997.

43. Ambrose Evans-Pritchard, *The Secret Life of Bill Clinton: The Unreported Stories* (Washington, DC: Regnery, 1997), 5.

44. Brandon Stickney, *All-American Monster: The Unauthorized Biography of Timothy McVeigh* (Amherst, NY: Prometheus Books, 1996).

45. Jayna Davis, *The Third Terrorist: The Middle East Connection to the Oklahoma City Bombing* (Nashville, TN: WND Books, 2004); Peter Lance, *1000 Years for Revenge: International Terrorism and the FBI* (New York: Regan Books, 2003). Lance is unconvinced of a connection, but admits there are numerous suspicious links between McVeigh, Nichols, Ramzi Yousef, Iraq, and Al Qaeda. He relies extensively on the word of Yousef's lawyer that there was no direct Al Qaeda support (308–18).

46. Lou Michel and Dan Herbeck, *American Terrorist* (New York: Regan Books, 2001).

47. Drew, *Showdown*, passim.

48. Evan Thomas, et al., *Back from the Dead: How Clinton Survived the Republican Revolution* (New York: Atlantic Monthly Press, 1997).

49. George Gilder, *Telecosm: How Infinite Bandwidth Will Revolutionize Our World* (New York: Free Press, 2000), 7.

50. Joel Kotkin and Ross C. DeVol, "Knowledge-Value Cities in the Digital Age," Milken Institute Study, February 13, 2001, 2.

51. Ibid.

52. George Bittlingmayer and Thomas W. Hazlett, "DOS Kapital: Has Antitrust Action Against Microsoft Created Value in the Computer Industry?" *Journal of Financial Economics*, 55 (2000), 329–359; Donald J. Boudreaux and Burton W. Folsom, "Microsoft and Standard Oil: Radical Lessons for Antitrust Action," *The Antitrust Bulletin*, Fall 1999, 555–76. Also see Bittlingmayer's "Antitrust and Business Activity: The First Quarter Century," *Business History Review*, Autumn 1996, 363–401.

53. Gary Quinlivan, "Multinational Corporations: Myths and Facts," *Religion and Liberty*, November/December 2000, 8–10.

54. James Rolph Edwards, "The Myth of Corporate Domination," *Liberty*, January 2001, 41–42.

55. Jeffrey A. Frankel and Peter R. Orszag, eds., *American Economic Policy in the 1990s* (Cambridge: MIT Press, 2002).

56. Solomon Moore, "Census' Multiracial Option Overturns Traditional Views," *Los Angeles Times*, March 5, 2001.

57. Dinesh D'Souza, *The End of Racism* (New York: Free Press, 1995).

58. "BATF Referrals for Prosecution Peak in 1992," *The American Guardian*, January 2000, 7.

59. FBI uniform crime rate data at www.guncite.com.

60. The Pew results appear online at http://www.publicagenda.org/specials/religion/religion.htm.

61. Thomas C. Reeves, *The Empty Church: The Suicide of Liberal Christianity* (New York: Free Press, 1996), 51–52.

62. Gallup cited in Reeves, *Empty Church*, 52.

63. *The Starr Report: The Official Report of the Independent Counsel's Investigation of the President* (Rocklin, CA: FORUM, 1998), n.3, 50.
64. *Jones v. Clinton*, 117 S. Ct. 1636, 1652 (1997).
65. Roger Morris, *Partners in Power: The Clintons and Their America* (New York: Regnery, 1999); Barbara Olson, *Hell to Pay: The Unfolding Story of Hillary Rodham Clinton* (New York: Regnery, 1999).
66. Matt Drudge, *The Drudge Manifesto* (New York: New American Library, 2000).
67. Steven M. Gillon, *The American Paradox: A History of the United States Since 1945* (Boston: Hougton-Mifflin, 2003), 444.
68. David Schippers, *Sell Out: The Inside Story of Clinton's Impeachment* (Washington: Regnery, 2000).
69. Mark Bowden, *Black Hawk Down: A Story of Modern War* (New York: Signet, 2000).
70. General Merrill A. McPeak, "The Kosovo Result: The Facts Speak for Themselves," *Armed Forces Journal International*, September 1999, 64.
71. Khidr Hamzah and Jeff Stein, *Saddam's Bomb Maker: The Terrifying Inside Story of the Iraqi Nuclear and Biological Weapons Agenda* (New York: Scribner, 2000).
72. Martin Gilbert, *History of the Twentieth Century*, 866.
73. "US missed three chances to seize Bin Laden," *Sunday Times* (UK), January 6, 2002.
74. An extensive review of the failures of the Clinton administration to pursue bin Laden appears in Richard Minitier, *Losing Bin Laden: How Bill Clinton's Failures Unleashed Global Terror* (Washington, DC: Regnery, 2003); Gerald Posner, *Why America Slept: The Failure to Prevent 9/11* (New York: Random House, 2003); Bill Gertz, *Breakdown: How America's Intelligence Failures Led to September 11* (Washington, DC: Regnery, 2002).

Chapter 22. America, World Leader, 2000 and Beyond

1. Tom Brokaw, *The Greatest Generation* (New York: Random House, 1998).
2. Department of Commerce report in August 2002, discussed in Robert Novak, "Clinton-Cooked Books?" www.cnn.com/insidepolitics, August 9, 2002.
3. Bob Woodward, *The Agenda: Inside the Clinton White House* (New York: Pocket Books, 1995).
4. J. H. Hatfield and Mark Crispin Miller, *Fortunate Son: George W. Bush and the Making of an American President* (New York: St. Martin's, 1999); George W. Bush and Karen Hughes, *A Charge to Keep* (New York: William Morrow and Co., 1999); Bill Minutaglio, *First Son: George W. Bush and the Bush Family Dynasty* (New York: Times, 1999); Frank Bruni, *Ambling into History: The Unlikely Odyssey of George W. Bush* (New York: HarperCollins, 2002). On the first two and a half years of the Bush presidency, see David Frum, *The Right Man* (New York: Random House, 2003).
5. "Five Weeks of History," *USA Today*, December 14, 2000.
6. Bill Sammon, *At Any Cost: How Al Gore Tried to Steal the Election* (Washington, DC: Regnery, 2001), 78.
7. Howard Kurtz, "Feeding the Media Beast: Leaks, Rats, and Black Berrys," *Washington Post*, December 17, 2000; George Bennett, "LePore: Ballot 'Probably Not the Wisest Thing,'" *Palm Beach Post*, December 16, 2000.
8. James V. Grimaldi and Soberto Suro, "Risky Bush Strategy Paid Off," Washington *Post*, December 17, 2000.
9. Sammon, *At Any Cost*, 181–200.
10. Grimaldi and Suro, "Risky Bush Strategy Paid Off."
11. *USA Today*, "Five Weeks of History."
12. "Florida Voter Errors Cost Gore the Election," *USA Today*, May 11–13, 2001.
13. Maureen Dowd, "Hillary's Stocking Stuffer," New York *Times*, February 21, 2001.
14. Barbara Olson, *The Final Days* (Washington, DC: Regnery Publishing, 2001).
15. See George Lardner Jr., "Clinton Shipped Furniture a Year Ago," Washington *Post*, February 10, 2001; "Hey, Wait a Minute," *The Hotline* (Washington), February 12, 2001.
16. John McLaughlin, *John McLaughlin's One on One*, January 26, 2001.
17. Olson, *Final Days*, chap. 10 details the Rich saga.
18. Dan Balz and Bob Woodward, "America's Chaotic Road to War," www.washingtonpost.com, January 27, 2002.
19. Alan Levin, Marilyn Adams, and Blake Morrison, "Amid Terror, a Drastic Decision: Clear the Skies," *USA Today*, August 12, 2002.

20. Interview with Charles Calomiris, September 18, 2001.

21. Balz and Woodward, "America's Chaotic Road to War."

22. Ibid.

23. Ibid.

24. Ibid.

25. Owen Moritz, "Chilling Tapes of Bravest in WTC," New York *Daily News*, November 16, 2002.

26. Bill Sammon, *Fighting Back* (Washington, DC: Regnery, 2002), 106.

27. Benjamin Kline, "No One Could Have Planned for This," Dayton *Daily News*, September 12, 2000.

28. Lisa Beamer, *Let's Roll! Ordinary People, Extraordinary Courage* (Wheaton, IL: Tyndale House, 2002).

29. Quoted in Nancy Gibbs, "Special Report: The Day of the Attack," *Time*, September 12, 2001, located at http://www.time.com/time/world/article/0,8599,174655–1,00.html.

30. Balz and Woodward, "America's Chaotic Road to War."

31. Quoted in Sammon, *Fighting Back*, 131.

32. Posner, *Why America Slept*, 30; Minitier, *Losing bin Laden*, 6–15.

33. Sammon, *Fighting Back*, 138.

34. Glenn Kessler, "Riding to the Economy's Rescue," Washington *Post*, September 25, 2001.

35. Peter Navarro and Aron Spencer, "September 11, 2001: Assessing the Costs of Terrorism," *Milken Institute Review*, Fourth Quarter, 2001, 17–31; Steven Brill, *After* (New York: Simon & Schuster, 2003).

36. Sammon, *Fighting Back*, 163–65. See also Larry Schweikart, "The Weight of the World and the Responsibility of a Generation," http://ashbrook.org/publicat/guest/01/schweikart/weightofworld.html.

37. Ibid., 189.

38. Bob Woodward and Dan Balz, "Combating Terrorism: It Starts Today," Washington *Post*, February 1, 2002.

39. Ibid.

40. Ben Fenton, "1,300 Enemy Men Killed by Handful of Green Berets," London (UK) *Telegraph*, January 9, 2002.

41. Sammon, *Fighting Back*, 263.

42. Ibid., 262.

43. Fareed Zakaria, "Face the Facts: Bombing Works," *Newsweek*, November 26, 2001, online edition quoted, http://www.msnbc.com/news/662668. asp.

44. Sammon, *Fighting Back*, 308.

45. Ibid., 274.

46. Martin, "9/11 Bombshell: New Evidence of Iraq-Al Qaeda Ties?"

47. Howard Fineman, "How Bush Did It," www.msnbc.com/news/832464.asp.

48. James Carney and John F. Dickerson, "W. and the 'Boy Genius,'" *Time* magazine, online edition, www. time.com/time/nation/article/0,8599,388904,00html.

49. David S. Broder, "Radical Conservatism," Washington *Post*, September 25, 2002.

50. Evan Thomas and Martha Brant, "The Secret War," *Newsweek*, April 14, 2003, at http://www.msnbc.com/news/899657.asp?0sl=-32.

51. Chris Matthews, writing in the San Francisco *Chronicle*, said the "invasion of Iraq . . . will join the Bay of Pigs, Vietnam . . . and Somalia in the history of military catastrophe." ("To Iraq and Ruin," August 25, 2002). R. W. Apple of the New York *Times*, even as American forces were annihilating enemy resistance, warned, "With every passing day, it is more evident that the allies made two gross military misjudgments in concluding that coalition forces could safely bypass Basra and Nasiriya." ("Bush Peril: Shifting Sand and Fickle Opinion," March 30, 2003). Former CNN correspondent Peter Arnett, in a widely publicized interview on Iraqi TV the same day said, "The first war plan has failed because of Iraqi resistance"—this about a war plan that had moved farther, faster, and more decisively (with fewer casualties) than any military campaign in human history. Maureen Dowd complained that the ground troops were left "exposed and insufficiently briefed on the fedayeen [Saddam's suicide squads]." ("Back Off, Syria and Iran," New York *Times*, March 30, 2003). Barry McCaffrey, a retired general, was one of many former military types whose assessment of the operations was completely adrift from reality. Said McCaffrey on the BBC, the United States "could take, bluntly, a couple to 3,000 casualties" (Reuters, March 24, 2003). As of 2004, with coalition forces still supporting the Iraqi in-

terim government, U.S. deaths in the campaign surpassed 1,000—a fraction of what it cost to take a single small island called Iwo Jima from Japan in World War II. For a summary of these and other egregiously wrong predictions, see "Hall of Shame," National Review Online, April 10, 2003.

52. David Zucchino, *Thunder Run: The Armored Strike to Capture Baghdad* (New York: Atlantic Monthly Press, 2004); Colonel Gregory Fontenot, et al., *On Point: The United States Army in Operation Iraqi Freedom* (Fort Leavenworth, KA: Combat Studies Institute Press, 2003); Bing West and Ray L. Smith, *The March Up: Taking Baghdad with the 1st Marine Division* (New York: Bantam Books, 2003); Williamson Murray and Robert H. Scales Jr., *The Iraq War: A Military History* (Cambridge, MA: Belknap Press, 2003); Rick Atkinson, *In the Company of Soldiers: A Chronicle of Combat* (New York: Henry Holt, 2004); Karl Zinsmeister, *Boots on the Ground: A Month with the 82nd Airborne in the Battle for Iraq* (New York: Truman Talley Books, 2003).

SELECTED READING

Below is only a partial listing of the sources cited most often in the endnotes.

Andrew, Christopher M. and Vasili Mitrokhin. *The Sword and the Shield: Mitrokhin Archive and the Secret History of the KGB*. New York: Basic Books, 1999.

Atack, Jeremy and Peter Passell. *A New Economic View of American History*, 2nd ed. New York: W. W. Norton, 1994.

Bailey, Thomas A. et al. *The American Pageant*, vol. 2, 11th ed. Boston: Houghton Mifflin, 1998).

Beliles, Mark A. and Stephen K. McDowell. *America's Providential History*. Charlottesville, VA: Providence Foundation, 1991.

Berkin, Carol et al. *Making America: A History of the United States*, 2nd ed. Boston: Houghton Mifflin, 1999.

Boyer, Paul S. et al. *The Enduring Vision: A History of the American People*. Lexington, MA: D. C. Heath, 1993.

Brinkley, Alan. *American History: A Survey*, 9th ed., 2 vols. New York: McGraw-Hill, 1999.

———. *The Unfinished Nation: A Concise History of the American People*, 3rd ed. Boston: McGraw-Hill, 2000.

Burner, David, Robert Marcus, and Emily S. Rosenberg. *An American Portrait*, 2nd ed., 2 vols. New York: Charles Scribner's, 1985.

Davidson, James West et al. *Nation of Nations: A Narrative History of the American Republic*, 2 vols., 3rd ed. Boston: McGraw-Hill, 2001.

Davis, Paul K. *100 Decisive Battles: From Ancient Times to the Present*. Oxford: Oxford University Press, 1999.

Derks, Scott. *Working Americans, 1880–1999: Volume I: The Working Class*. Lakeville, CT: Grey House Publishers, 2000.

Divine, Robert A. et al. *America, Past and Present*, 5th ed. New York: Longman, 1999.

Faragher, John Mack et al. *Out of Many: A History of the American People*, combined ed., 3rd ed. Upper Saddle River, NJ: Prentice-Hall, 2000.

Gilbert, Martin. *History of the Twentieth Century, Volume One: 1900–1933*. New York: Avon, 1977.

———. *History of the Twentieth Century, Volume Three: 1959–1999*. New York: William Morrow, 1999.

Gillon, Steven M. and Cathy D. Matson. *The American Experiment: A History of the United States*. Boston: Houghton Mifflin, 2002.

Goldfield, David et al. *The American Journey: A History of the United States*, combined ed. Upper Saddle River, NJ: Prentice-Hall, 1998.

Hanson, Victor Davis. *Carnage and Culture: Landmark Battles in the Rise of Western Civilization*. New York: Doubleday, 2001.

Johnson, Paul. *A History of the American People*. New York: HarperCollins, 1997.

Jordan, Winthrop and Leon Litwack. *The United States*, 7th ed., combined ed. Englewood Cliffs, NJ: Prentice-Hall, 1991.

Kennedy, David, Lizabeth Cohen, and Thomas A. Bailey. *The American Pageant*, 12th ed. Boston: Houghton Mifflin, 2002.

Leckie, Robert. *The Wars of America: A Comprehensive Narrative from Champlain's First Campaign Against the Iroquois Through the End of the Vietnam War*, revised and updated ed. New York: Harper and Row, 1981.

McClellan, Jim R. *Historical Moments: Changing Interpretations of America's Past*, 2nd ed., 2 vols., *Volume 1: The Pre-Colonial Period Through the Civil War* and *Volume 2: The Civil War Through the Twentieth Century.* Guilford, CT: McGraw-Hill, 2000.

Murrin, John M. et al. *Liberty, Equality, Power: A History of the American People*, 3rd ed. Fort Worth, TX: Harcourt Brace, 2002.

Randall, James G. *The Civil War and Reconstruction.* Boston: D. C. Heath and Company, 1937.

Schweikart, Larry. *The Entrepreneurial Adventure: A History of Business in the United States.* Fort Worth, TX: Harcourt Brace, 2000.

Tindall, George Brown and David Shi. *America: A Narrative History*, 5th ed., 2 vols. New York: W. W. Norton, 1999.

INDEX